COMPANION TO
HISTORIOGRAPHY

COMPANION TO HISTORIOGRAPHY

EDITED BY

MICHAEL BENTLEY

Professor of Modern History
University of St Andrews

London and New York

First published 1997
by Routledge
11 New Fetter Lane, London EC4PY 4EE
29 West 35th Street, New York, NY 10001

© 1997 Routledge

Typeset in Ehrhardt by
Mathematical Composition Setters Ltd, Salisbury, UK

Printed and bound in Great Britain by
TJ International Ltd, Padstow, Cornwall

British Library Cataloguing in Publication Data

A catalogue record for this book is available from the British Library

Library of Congress Cataloging in Publication Data

A catalog record is available on request

ISBN 0-415-03084-6

CONTENTS

Editorial Board   viii
Contributors   ix
General Introduction: The Project of Historiography
Michael Bentley   xi

PART I: BEGINNINGS – EAST AND WEST
   Introduction
   Paul Cartledge   3
1   The Evolution of Two Asian Historiographical Traditions
   David Morgan   11
2   Historiography and Ancient Greek Self-definition
   Paul Cartledge   23
3   Re-reading the Roman Historians
   Michael Comber   43
4   The Religion of Rome from Monarchy to Principate
   J. A. North   57
5   Late Antiquity and the Early Medieval West
   Peter Heather   69
6   Modernizing the Historiography of Rural Labour: An Unwritten Agenda
   Jairus Banaji   88

PART II: THE MEDIEVAL WORLD
   Introduction: Regarding Medievalists: Contexts and Approaches
   Julia M. H. Smith   105
7   The Historiography of the Medieval State
   Susan Reynolds   117
8   Saladin and the Third Crusade: A Case Study in Historiography and the
   Historical Novel
   Robert Irwin   139

9 Family, Gender and Sexuality in the Middle Ages
   Janet L. Nelson   153
10 The Medieval Nobility in Twentieth-Century Historiography
   Timothy Reuter   177
11 Medieval Military Historiography
   Bernard S. Bachrach   203
12 Popular Religion in the Central and Later Middle Ages
   Peter Biller   221

PART III: EARLY MODERN HISTORIOGRAPHY
   Introductory Survey: From the Renaissance to the Eighteenth Century
   G. E. Aylmer   249
13 The Idea of Early Modern History
   Wolfgang Reinhard   281
14 The Scientific Revolution
   Stephen Pumfrey   293
15 The Writing of Early Modern European Intellectual History, 1945–1995
   D. R. Woolf   307
16 The English Reformation, 1945–1995
   Patrick Collinson   336
17 Popular Culture in the Early Modern West
   James Sharpe   361
18 Revisionism in Britain
   Ronald Hutton   377

PART IV: REFLECTING ON THE MODERN AGE
   Introduction: Approaches to Modernity: Western Historiography since
   the Enlightenment
   Michael Bentley   395

IV.1 Revolution and Ideology
19 The Historiography of the French Revolution
   Jacques Solé   509
20 The Soviet Revolution
   Catherine Merridale   526
21 The Historiography of National Socialism
   Jane Caplan   545
22 Modern Italy – Changing Historical Perspectives since 1945
   John A. Davis   591
23 The Critique of Orientalism
   Ulrike Freitag   620

IV.2 Area Studies
24 The Historiography of Modern China
   Pamela Kyle Crossley   641

25 The English-Language Historiography of Modern Japan
    Alan Smith   659
26 Modern Indian Historiography
    C. A. Bayly   677
27 History in Africa
    David Birmingham   692
28 Modern American Historiography
    Carl N. Degler   709
29 Latin America
    Alan Knight   728

PART V: CONTEXTS FOR THE WRITING OF HISTORY

V.1 Hinterlands
30 Philosophy and Historiography
    William Dray   763
31 History and Anthropology
    Jordan Goodman   783
32 Archaeology and Historiography
    Guy Halsall   805
33 The History of Western Art History
    Nigel Llewellyn   828

V.2 Approaches
34 The Historical Narrative
    Peter Munz   851
35 The *Annales* Experiment
    George Huppert   873
36 Marxist Historiography
    S. H. Rigby   889
37 Women, Gender and the *Fin de Siècle*
    Olwen Hufton   929
38 World History
    R. I. Moore   941
39 Archives, the Historian and the Future
    Michael Moss   960

Index   974

EDITORIAL BOARD

CONTRIBUTORS

GENERAL EDITOR

Michael Bentley, *University of St Andrews*

EDITORIAL CONSULTANTS

Gerald Aylmer, *St Peter's College, University of Oxford*
David Morgan, *School of Oriental and African Studies, University of London*

CONTRIBUTORS

Bernard S. Bachrach, *University of Minnesota*
Jairus Banaji, *formerly St John's College, University of Oxford*
C. A. Bayly, *St Catharine's College, University of Cambridge*
Peter Biller, *University of York*
David Birmingham, *University of Kent*
Jane Caplan, *Bryn Mawr College, USA*
Paul Cartledge, *Clare College, University of Cambridge*
Patrick Collinson, *University of Cambridge*
Michael Comber, *St John's College, University of Oxford*
Pamela Kyle Crossley, *Dartmouth College, USA*
John A. Davis, *University of Connecticut*
Carl N. Degler, *Stanford University*
William Dray, *University of Ottawa, Canada*
Ulrike Freitag, *School of Oriental and African Studies, University of London*
Jordan Goodman, *UMIST*
Guy Halsall, *Birkbeck College, University of London*
Peter Heather, *University College, University of London*

Olwen Hufton, *European University Institute, Florence*
George Huppert, *University of Illinois at Chicago*
Ronald Hutton, *University of Bristol*
Robert Irwin, *London*
Alan Knight, *St Antony's College, University of Oxford*
Nigel Llewellyn, *University of Sussex*
Catherine Merridale, *University of Bristol*
R. I. Moore, *University of Newcastle-upon-Tyne*
Michael Moss, *University of Glasgow*
Peter Munz, *Victoria University of Wellington, New Zealand*
Janet L. Nelson, *King's College, University of London*
J. A. North, *University College, University of London*
Stephen Pumfrey, *University of Lancaster*
Wolfgang Reinhard, *University of Freiburg, Germany*
Timothy Reuter, *University of Southampton*
Susan Reynolds, *University of Oxford; Birkbeck and University Colleges, University of London*
S. H. Rigby, *University of Manchester*
James Sharpe, *University of York*
Alan Smith, *University of Glasgow*
Julia M. H. Smith, *University of St Andrews*
Jacques Solé, *University of Grenoble, France*
D. R. Woolf, *Dalhousie University, Nova Scotia, Canada*

GENERAL INTRODUCTION

The Project of Historiography

Michael Bentley

Fifteen years ago, when I first considered mounting undergraduate courses in 'historiography', most students and not a few colleagues possessed barely more than a blurred notion of what the word *meant*. Secretaries pronounced it 'history-graphy'. Professors, some of them major figures in their fields, advised that one could not teach the subject at all, either because it was too difficult and would 'confuse' the students, or, more radically, because the subject had no existence outside the particular historical problem one might be considering. It made sense, they said, to talk about the historiography of the French revolution or the historiography of feudalism; but there was no category, 'historiography', that one could discuss or teach. They were not aware, perhaps, that a sequence of ideas that had gained some currency in the 1970s and 1980s had already undermined these certainties in interesting ways.

A first subversion dwelt on the startling insight that students might understand more and develop faster if someone set about 'confusing' them with some serious thoughts about what they assumed the study of the past involved – assumptions which were and are often painfully innocent of all forms of criticism and lacking context for the historical writing that students regularly encounter. The second took into account important changes in how 'historiography' had modified as an idea both in its nature and its status. It had lost its character as a form of sophisticated description and moved in the direction of an explanatory discussion that demanded answers to hard questions about why historians write what they do and why past historians did it differently. The need for a book like this one echoes these perceptions even when many of its contributors would not wish to be associated with some of the styles of thought reflected in contemporary approaches to history or social science.

In its older form, historiography (or, as it was usually called, 'the history of historiography') reminded readers that historical writing has fashions in its method and approaches and attempted to provide as comprehensive an account as possible of the writings of previous historians. Some saw the task as a philosophical one and battled against the tightening grip of 'scientific' models – none more resolutely than the Italian Idealist thinker, Benedetto Croce.[1] But most writers went in the direction of 'empirical' study. This could be done with a Germanic commitment to systematic treatment, as in the pioneering account of Eduard Fueter at the turn of the century.[2] It could become an unconcealed mode of holier-than-thou liberalism in the hands of George Peabody Gooch.[3] It could become a concealed mode of Christian apologetic, as it did for Britain's most self-conscious historiographer, Herbert Butterfield.[4] It could turn into an annotated bibliography determined to list anyone who ever wrote anything: the besetting difficulty of a highly-scholarly compendium by the American historian Harry Elmer Barnes.[5] Each of these examples had its own point of view and distinctive tone; but joining them all together (and linking them with many other studies from the same period) were a series of characteristics which no longer go unchallenged. For what they all assumed was that the task of the historiographer should be seen as biographical, expository and corrective. Their books took shape from the lives and writings of the 'great historians' they wanted to bring to the reader's attention. Typically, they presented arguments about a single individual who had, by acclamation, become part of the historical canon from Thucydides to Gibbon and then onwards into the congested list of major professional historians working in

1   Noteworthy in Croce's astonishing output from this point of view are *Storia della storiografia italiana nel secolo decimonono* (2 vols, Bari, 1921); *Filosofia e storiografia* (Bari, 1949); *La dialetta hegeliana e la storia della storiografia* (Bari, 1952).

2   Eduard Fueter, *Geschichte der neuren Historiographie* (Munich and Berlin, 1911).

3   G. P. Gooch, *History and Historians in the Nineteenth Century* (1913) 'Happy in the treasures of his monastic library, the pious chronicler did not stop to investigate their value ...' (p. 1). 'Gibbon constructed a bridge from the old world to the new which is still the highway of nations, and stands erect after every other structure of the time has fallen into ruins' (p. 7). His judgement of Michelet's *French Revolution* is a memorable paradigm of this sort of criticism:

'... though the book possesses unique merits [it is 'a contribution to knowledge as well as to interpretation'], his judgement of the Revolution is unacceptable ... [H]e is too tender to the masses, he is too harsh to the Church. He regards the Revolution as a struggle between two conceptions of life, the life of rationalist democracy against Christian monarchy ... The execution of the work is not less faulty than its general conception. Some events are described with infinite detail, others no less important are scarcely noticed. The book swarms with errors, and suffers from exaggeration and effervescence'

(pp. 183–4).

Nobody ever accused Gooch of effervescence.

4   Herbert Butterfield's *oeuvre* concentrated, most atypically for his generation, on historiography rather than substantive historical writing. As G. R. Elton commented with not untypical sweetness, Butterfield rarely troubled the editors of learned journals. See in particular *The Whig Interpretation of History* (1931); *Christianity and History* (1949); *Man on his Past* (1955); *George III and the Historians* (1957).

5   Harry Elmer Barnes, *A History of Historical Writing* (1937, revised edn, NY, 1962). The index to this formidable work of scholarship is over thirty pages long and contains between 1,500 and 2,000 names.

the shadow of the magisterial figure of Leopold von Ranke. Their investigations gave rise to a text which abbreviated and epitomized what those historians had said – reducing the sixty volumes of Ranke to a few pages of pith, expanding the terse passages of Marx or Burckhardt to give the reader more idea of what the author intended to convey. Once beyond this expository role, they then turned to criticism; but the critique had a particular flavour. It showed where the authors under review had in some sense *gone wrong*. The point of the exercise lay in showing the 'modern' reader how historians of past ages, unblessed by the clinical judgement of the critic's own epoch and usually cursed by 'bias', had mangled the 'truth' through incompetence, wilful manipulation or – the ultimate patronage – through no fault of their own. Fingers were wagged at religious zeal, ears tweaked for thin or purblind research, heads patted for insight in advance of their time. The historiographer gave his contemporaries some reassurance that history advances towards truth by avoiding the mistakes committed by wanton predecessors. He (for there were no female historiographers of note in this period) told the fellow members of a professionalizing discipline what they wanted to hear and reinforced the claim of history to stand beside science as a means of appropriating reliable and permanent knowledge.

Thus historiography became, like theology, the study of error. And the result of that self-image has proved ruinous for the subject. If modern writers are correct and past writers are wrong, what is the point of bothering with what Condorcet or Theodore Mommsen or Bishop Stubbs happened to believe? They have, after all, been 'superseded'. If one does bother with them out of a respect for civilized values and the importance of having an educated mind – every sound Englishman should read Macaulay, every true Frenchman Michelet, and so on – then what can be done with those texts beyond paraphrasing them or telling the young to read them on the same grounds that one might tell them to read Shakespeare or Molière? The difficulty has proved intractable for generations of teachers, especially those who graduated in the West before about 1960. Approaching the subject with this baggage, they presented courses in 'historiography' that supposedly represented the leading edge of historical thought only to find that students deemed them pointless and campaigned for their removal to make way for something more 'relevant'. Many readers of this Companion will remember seminars in 'historiography' whose leaders had read the 'text' of the week while lacking any clear notion of what to do with it. Indeed the sad and brutal facts are these: historiography cannot be effectively taught or learned without a prior interest in epistemology; and no one is likely to take the trouble with challenging philosophical problems of that kind until he or she has come to appreciate that history is a theoretical subject.

At some point between 1960 and 1975, in most countries of the West, history took a turn towards theory. Why it did so raises difficult issues that we shall examine later in this volume. The point to be pressed here is that the arrival of theoretical models of one sort or another brought upon professional history an embarrassing sense of self-consciousness. Historians quite deliberately made models and drew graphs, spoke in -isms and -ologies, with a 'sixties contempt for those who did not. They began a journey (still continuing) away from telling the 'truth' about 'the' past towards a view that there are infinitely many sorts of past to talk about and towards a deep scepticism about the possibility of discerning the truth about most of them. For some, it has been a frustrating, even appalling transition and the period certainly provided more than one instance of *chic*, superficial fashion overriding patient research. Others, however, have found in it a new plausibility for the subject and a liberation for the individual attempting its study. Both points of view will appear in this book but, regardless of the point of view one may hold about the shifts in method and approach over the past thirty years, what seems clear is that a revolution in the understanding of historiography has proved one of its central consequences. Not only has historical writing itself received an irresistible impetus, that is to say, but the idea of historiography found itself swept along on the tide. The question, how and why did previous generations see their past(s) in ways different from those current now, became a serious issue for those trying to evaluate present perceptions rather than an optional visit to the National Portrait Gallery. The problem of how historical work *ought* to be done in a changed intellectual and political climate threw light backwards on how other generations and cultures had gone about it. The patronizing of past historians for having got the story wrong (or for having written stories at all) turned into a genuine curiosity about *why* their pictures and models look so strange to us and *why* they seemed persuasive to the particular audience for whom they had been intended. Historiography began to look like a first-rank subject in which, it was increasingly thought, serious historians needed encouragement and training – a training that would stimulate students to go beyond their immediate period or topic and examine the broader development of historical writing by relating it to various other forms of intellectual expression.

Acknowledging the challenge does not take one very far without a literature to which students and interested historians at all levels may be sent. And here there are profound problems. It is not that no literature exists: historiography is a subject whose bibliography has undergone enormous extension in the past two decades. But the material is frequently highly technical (especially in its more philosophical reaches) and its scope often turns out either too narrow to offer general guidance or so wide as to give the reader little more than a superficial impression. Perhaps this awkwardness lies so close to the heart of the subject that neither teachers nor books can change it. Whatever help secondary sources may provide, after all, it remains the case that the only way to understand historians is to read what they wrote; and any form of abbreviation or characterization will lose something. Many readers cannot spend weeks coping with a single author's historical works, on the other hand: they need urgent help in making sense of voluminous and elusive writers and of the schools and tendencies to which they may have contributed. Teachers no less urgently wish to have around them some basic texts to which they can direct pupils for initial orientation before writing that essay on Hitler or the coming project on the medieval family. For the general reader, intrigued by Marx as a historian or the Soviet

Revolution as a drama, some sense of context for such writers and events becomes the desideratum – a field-guide to the territory, as it were. These needs ought not to be beyond the capacities of a communicative and prolific profession. They have in some degree guided the modest ambitions of this *Companion to Historiography*.

Good books make good companions and the intention here has been to produce a volume that can be *read* rather than pulled from the shelf sporadically like an encyclopedia or compilation of historical 'facts'. Indeed, this collection of essays is as far from a mere work of reference as we could make it. If anyone needs a column of print on Lord Acton or a column and a half on Ranke, he or she will find little difficulty in tracking it down in these days of historical 'dictionaries'. Harder to find is an overview of developments within English or German historical practice within which the writing of these two writers might be located. So the starting point here has been that coverage of so vast an area as that bounded by historiography over the two and a half thousand years of its (Western) existence would prove less valuable (and less feasible in a single volume) than a series of studies whose analysis would remain relevant for subjects beyond the specific ones treated here. The emphasis would be placed, in other words, on approach and method as much as on content. By not including everything, conversely, it has become possible to insert important material about parts of the world – China, Japan, India, Africa – that frequently disappear in systematic treatments of European developments and which in no way replicate those experiences. Scaling down the space on the familiar canon of great historians has also allowed a greater concentration on changes since the Second World War. For young people trying to make sense of their own historiographical context, these years are the crucial ones because they made the perceptions of their parents and teachers and supplied the material against which many of the young stand in unconscious, or sometimes highly purposive, resistance. Balancing the competing claims of the general and the particular, of completeness and concentration, has proved no easier for this editor than it seemed to Ranke, who at least had talent on his side. But I have done my best within the parameters of the exercise and amid the often-acknowledged exasperations of a collaborative venture.

In the main body of the text we provide an understanding of development over time and a recognition of the spatial issues involved. The four sections dealing with ancient, medieval, early-modern and modern styles of historical writing operate in similar ways. Each has either an interpretative gloss on the essays that follow or, in the case of the later sections, a more extended introduction to historiographical changes within the period under discussion. In this way readers new to the period will find enough context to make intelligible the more detailed treatments of contemporary historiography reflected in the essays. Those essays offer a meditation by an expert on some aspect of the period's more recent historiography – usually one that has attracted interest or debate in the last thirty years or so. It goes without saying that the choosing of issues to include has turned on a compromise between the general purposes of the volume and the particular interest of the author. Another editor and other authors could identify precisely the same purposes and yet choose an entirely different range of topics to illustrate them. My own prejudice has been to concentrate on finding interesting and engaged authors rather than lurch towards the boring out of Calvinist relish. This procedure, compounded as any would have been by the defaulting of authors, leaves manifest gaps in the account but it also has enabled me to include some writing of extremely high significance and quality. Time having been satisfied, space receives its own treatment in a series of case-studies whose purpose is comparative as well as illustrative. No one should walk away from this volume thinking that the history of non-Western cultures is trivial or without its own special character. We then move on to think about more general contexts for the writing of history by situating the activity, first, against some other disciplines which have become especially important for how historians have seen their problems in the last few decades and, second, by examining some of the major new approaches to the subject that have often resulted from various forms of fertilization from beyond the acknowledged boundaries of the subject. The journey offered here is not the only one possible but I hope that readers with interests in any historical period or territory will find in it some of the stimulation I have received in watching it take shape.

The task of bringing forty essayists, each with a distinctive vision, topic and temperament, into a common framework would give pause to anyone familiar with the problems that beset the structuring of historical argument. To do so when the framework itself has frequently changed to accommodate a failure to commission a particular subject satisfactorily or, far more unsettling, to deal with someone else's failure to produce an essay when contracted to do so, has given editor and contributors alike a lesson in patience and persistence. But the overwhelming sense from the editorial end is one of gratitude. Many of these contributors provided their essays longer ago than either of us wish to remember. Not a single one has complained about the delays and disappointments that, almost inevitably, dog the progress of a large-scale undertaking of this kind. I am immensely conscious of their tolerance and encouragement. Of those who came into the project very late in the day – often to fill the place of those who had promised to arrive by mid-afternoon – I cannot speak too highly for their professionalism and unselfishness. It is a pleasure to record help at early stages of the book's preparation from Professor James Campbell and Dr Nicholas Purcell and throughout the enterprise from Dr Gerald Aylmer and Dr David Morgan whose expertise in, respectively, early-modern and Asian history has greatly enhanced the scope and content of what follows. I am also extremely grateful to Dr Paul Cartledge and Dr Julia Smith for supplying contextual glosses for the ancient and medieval sections and to a roll-call of friendly helpers at Routledge, most recently Samantha Parkinson, during the years of preparation. Finally but emphatically, I have to thank Jonathan Price. His was the original instinct out of which this volume arose and, during the period that I worked with him, he struck me as a figure rarely met with in academic publishing: a commissioning editor who is driven by the intellectual credentials of a project rather than its market-value or the demands of publishing as a streamlined, competitive branch of commerce. When others thought that this book might never happen,

Jonathan never wavered. When others lowered their sights, Jonathan always raised them again. When all around him were keeping their heads, Jonathan resolutely lost his – to the immense benefit of the book he inspired.

Michael Bentley
University of St Andrews
October 1996

I BEGINNINGS – EAST AND WEST

INTRODUCTION

Paul Cartledge

THE ANXIETY OF AMBIGUITY

History, the word, has a Greek etymology, being derived ultimately from a root meaning eyewitness, judgement and enquiry.[1] But only in our 'natural history' is that etymological connection at all closely maintained, and 'history' itself — whether the past, or the study of it, or of some of it — is and must remain a radically ambiguous term. Whence the coinage of 'historiography', struck in order to distinguish the study of and writing about some past facts from the facts themselves. But, since the distinction of facts from the writing about or of them is actually not at all clearcut — indeed is eminently contestable — a further meaning has been accorded to historiography, as meta-history or the study, from various standpoints, of the writing of history by others than the historiographer.[2] Both these senses are in play in Peter Heather's chapter (5), on the historiographical invention of 'Late Antiquity' as a concept.

Ancient historians, however, that is historians of Antiquity, tend as a breed not to concern themselves primarily with such higher-order semantic or (still less) philosophical issues. For most of them most of the time, history is history is history, as it were, and at least until quite recently Antiquity has unproblematically meant Greece and Rome, that is the world or worlds of Greek- and Latin-speakers divided off chronologically from the more or less text-free universe of the archaeological prehistorians at the upper end, and at the lower end from the far less easily defined post-Roman 'medieval' universe: in round figures, from *c.*1000 BC (or — see below — BCE) to *c.* AD/CE 500. Introspection and doubts, however, are steadily creeping into even this fairly hermetically sealed scholarly domain. For example, the difficulty of a specification of 'ancient' that excludes China, source of the oldest

---

1   References in Chapter 2, n. 3.
2   Classic is White 1973. But see the rejoinder by Momigliano 1981b. See also below, n. 8.

historiographical tradition in the world, is manifest: hence in part the decision to print David Morgan's chapter (1) first below, as a small gesture towards historiographical rectification and recuperation. Another sign of altering perspectives is the increasing use by ancient historians of the non-Christian BCE/CE (Before/Common Era) chronographic notation, in belated recognition of the need to problematize and avoid a form of chauvinistic or ethnocentric cultural determinism and, conversely, of the desirability of fostering a non-teleological cultural pluralism.

However, respect for the primacy of texts, and texts written in at least two 'dead' languages requiring a lengthy period of linguistic and cultural immersion before they can be 'read' at even the most straightforward level, has tended to inhibit any Gadarene rush towards modernity, let alone postmodernity, of local or global interpretation in this field of historiography. Ancient historians have even been relatively slow to deploy systematically the 'ancillary' disciplines of archaeology, epigraphy and numismatics to eke out or contextualize their preferred literary sources, let alone indulge in the consensual interdisciplinarity and comparativism rightly desiderated below by Jairus Banaji (Chapter 6), across the whole range of thematic and material issues confronting them in their potentially highly heterogeneous area and period. As for theory – or Theory – that, despite (or because of) its Aristotelian pedigree, has typically always been at a discount among them, more so than among their literary Classicist colleagues.

Yet, as ever, there have been exceptions, and some of the exceptional ancient historians have made contributions within ancient history and historiography, the impact and import of which have been felt and acknowledged quite widely beyond conventional disciplinary boundaries (themselves in process of dissolution). Three such historians writing in English (but not only in English) deserve special mention here, all born – not coincidentally – within four years of each other (1908–12): the Piedmontese Italian-Jewish intellectual historian Arnaldo Momigliano (a refugee to England from fascist persecution, d. 1987); the concept-driven sociological historian Moses Finley (American-Jewish by birth, but British by adoption following McCarthyite witchhunting, d. 1986); and, still alive and writing, the Marxist Geoffrey de Ste. Croix (of Huguenot descent, born to Christian missionaries in Macao).[3] Not for the first time one notices the impact of exile and transpatriation on ancient historiography, a trend set by Herodotus and Thucydides at its very outset. Only Momigliano, moreover, experienced fully the conventional, if dubiously beneficial, philological training of the typical classical historian.

NEW VARIETIES OF HISTORY: PROGRESS OR CHANGE?

To the ancient Greeks and Romans what was old, traditional, and ancestral was in principle good, what was new, the reverse: hence, Greek *neoterismos*

---

3 Momigliano: see Chapter 2, n. 5; cf. Finley 1986a. Finley: 1985; cf. 1981. Ste. Croix: 1975; 1981; cf. Cartledge and Harvey 1985.

('innovationism') or *neotera pragmata* ('newer transactions') meant revolution in an unwelcome negative sense, and precisely the same went for the Romans' *res novae* ('new things') (Finley 1986b). Of course, the Greeks and Romans did actually and inevitably innovate almost all the time, not least in historiography, which had after all to be invented and was so – for the Greeks – by Herodotus (*fl. c.*450 BCE), and – for the Romans some two and a half centuries later – by Fabius Pictor (though he wrote in Greek, the then culturally fashionable literary language). But Thucydides' reception of Herodotus set the dominant tone and mode: one might legitimately hope to improve on the manner of one's predecessor or predecessors, but not usually his or their matter. The prescribed limit of wholly acceptable novelty was to find a subject not treated historically hitherto, namely the major event or events of one's own lifetime, and it was then sometimes – but not always – thought to be an advantage for the historian to have been an eventmaker rather than a mere observer. 'New' historiography in the sense of radically innovatory kinds of writing about the past was almost by definition considered bad or worse historiography.[4]

To us, in the sharpest possible contrast, new is cool, the newer is the better. That in itself is a revolution (in a positive sense). Since the 1960s wave upon wave of supposedly new histories have beaten against the supposedly hidebound bastions of traditional historiography – the traditions attacked having typically been invented in the later Victorian era of positivism and scientism, intellectually speaking, and of macho drum-and-trumpet activism, pragmatically speaking. There is, though, an element of caricatural rhetoric in the representation of both sides of this opposition: the post-Victorian traditions were not quite as one-dimensional as they have been painted, the new traditions (though that word was of course avoided like the plague) not quite as unprecedented as their proponents and exponents have liked to pretend. Yet there is also an element of truth, in the sense of correspondence to the facts, in the claims of the New. After about 1960 History did seriously and irrevocably begin to decompose into a plethora of smaller histories (social, economic, religious, intellectual, cultural, women's and so forth), narrative history of events (meaning typically large-scale public events of politics, diplomacy and war) did cede pole position to analytical accounts of deep structures and spatio-temporal conjunctures, and new -isms (especially feminism, comparativism and constructionism) have joined the older empiricist and Marxist tendencies. (Rabb and Rotberg 1982; Hunt 1989; Burke 1991; see also n. 5).

Indeed, the pace of change has been such that the fashion for social and economic history (e.g. history from the bottom up, attempting to restore a voice to the voiceless, whether they be earth-coloured rustics or other literally as well as metaphorically enslaved and silenced majorities) was quite quickly succeeded by a still apparent rage for cultural and intellectual history, and innovative modes such as

---

4   Excellent bibliographies on the ancient historians, and the modern study thereof, in Momigliano 1980: 150–3; 1981a: 182–4; 1982; 1990. On the Greek historians see also Canfora 1985, further references in Chapter 2, n. 2. On the Roman historians, see further Chapter 3.

the women's history of the 1960s and 1970s have been fairly rapidly subsumed or superseded by even newer ones such as the gender/sexuality studies of the 1980s and 1990s (Scott 1988; Abelove *et al.* 1994). Worse still, from the point of view of conservatives, self-styled 'progressive' historiography, most noticeably in its postmodernist or New Historicist forms, not only has abandoned even the weakest versions of the nineteenth-century positivist claim that history was a science, no more and no less, but has even questioned the sacred notion of historical truth, in the name either of a rhetoric of discourse or of an ethical and/or cultural relativism.[5]

Of all this ferment the ancient world's accredited historians were blissfully innocent and ignorant. After Herodotus, the father not only of history for the Greeks but also of what some moderns might approve as having a more than passing resemblance to *Annales*-style total history, political history – sometimes enlarged by consideration of social, economic, intellectual and cultural factors, but more usually not – ruled the ancient roost more or less unchallenged. A moral point of view was not to be hidden behind the mask of faceless objectivity but rather, at least in the Roman case, proclaimed as the historian's ultimate task. Rhetoric, so far from being shunned as a shameful distortion or disguise, was praised and pursued as the necessary adornment of an essentially literary genre. Above all, history was regularly touted as useful, not merely diverting, and centrally important, a proper study for the ancient world's movers and shakers to whom it was mostly directed.[6]

THE NEW ANCIENT HISTORY AND THE OLD

Modern historians of antiquity find themselves for the most part in a very different situation, addressing small, socially unrepresentative readerships whose hands are far removed from the levers of power. Classics, once thought just the thing for aspiring nineteenth-century imperial administrators, now must not only run the gauntlet of non-academic debunkers without but also face the friendly fire of canon-debunkers within. Orientalists in the old and supposedly harmless descriptive sense now find themselves accused of orientalism in its new, unambiguously charmless signification. In response, some defenders of the old faith rather petulantly ask why we should study the Greeks and the Romans in particular if not as our admirable and imitable cultural ancestors and models. But others more open-mindedly and more boldly take the attacks on the chin, investigating historiographically how and why it was that such phrases as the Glory that Was Greece and the Grandeur that was Rome could ever have attained such general currency. The relativists and anthropologizers among them, moreover, rather than merely knocking the Greeks and Romans off their factitious paradigmatic pinnacle, seek to account for their undoubtedly inspired as well as inspirational cultural achievements through the

---

5 Appleby *et al.* 1994; Appleby *et al.* 1996; Veeser 1989; Veeser 1994. Broadly under the sign of the new historicism is Hartog 1988. Ankersmit and Kellner 1995 in fact reviews various such 'philosophies'.
6 De Romilly 1958, with discussion on pp. 67–81. Audiences of historians in antiquity: Momigliano 1978.

medium of a more inclusive historiography than the ancients themselves could have countenanced.[7]

It is precisely in this context that the ancient historians themselves have come under renewed critical scrutiny. Fathers of history and truth – or Fathers of lies, fiction, and rhetoric? Such has been the emphasis on what for want of a better word might be called the ancient historians' inventiveness that one leading student of Greece has recently felt obliged to mount a 'defence of the Greek historians'; it is a fair index of the nature and success of the attack that the burden of his defence is that they 'were not so unlike modern historians that we cannot read them as historians at all'.[8] It would be harder, as Michael Comber's chapter (3) shows, though not perhaps quite impossible, to construct such a defence of the Roman historians, since they were quite up front about the desirability, indeed necessity, for authorial pleading. Not even the rhetoric of impersonal objectivity (cf. Novick 1988) was deployed. Tacitus's famous prefatory *sine ira et studio* ('without anger and partisanship'), for example, had the strictly limited self-referential meaning that he himself personally had no cause to feel resentment or take sides in the subject-matter he had chosen to narrate – not that he did not feel indignation about the past or attempt vigorously, and often most subtly, to sway the reader towards one interpretation of it rather than another.

But if the manner of the ancient historians is controversial, their relative narrowness of scope is not. The sorts of agenda that a historian of antiquity influenced by recent turns in historiography more generally might wish to espouse simply could not begin to be addressed, if the ancient historians were all we had left to go on.[9] Consider, for example, religious history, the subject of Chapter 4. The ancients differed considerably in the amount of interest they took in and importance they allowed to religious phenomena, Thucydides occupying one end of the spectrum, that of almost complete denial, Livy the other. But not even Livy gives us nearly enough to begin to write a decent history of, say, religious change in the Late Republic and early Empire, roughly the last couple of centuries BCE and the first two CE. For that we must turn to archaeology, epigraphy and non-historical literary sources, complemented or informed by liberal applications of modern theory derived from comparative sociology and social anthropology.

THE BLACK ATHENA DEBATE: IS EAST EAST AND WEST WEST?

The liveliest current debate within ancient historiography, which is also the most embittered, and – worryingly – the one with the most potential practical relevance,

---

7 A subtextual reading of Herodotus, Thucydides and Xenophon is offered in Cartledge 1993.
8 Useful perspectives in Woodman 1988; Gill and Wiseman 1993; cf. Cartledge 1995. Quotation from Rhodes 1994: 169.
9 Compare and contrast Davies 1975 (recommending thirteen themes, area studies and approaches, none of which could be studied or taught chiefly let alone exclusively from the ancient literary historians) with the rejoinder by Brunt 1976.

concerns Martin Bernal's 'Black Athena' project.[10] Briefly, Bernal is a professor of Chinese government studies and not a specialist historian, let alone a historian of classical antiquity. He has nevertheless devoted two major tomes (so far) and a number of ancillary studies to charging the dominant tendency within ancient Greek historiography since the mid-eighteenth century (Roman history and historiography are largely spared) with what he regards as a lethal combination of anti-black racism and anti-semitism. As a result, credit has not been given where the credit is in Bernal's opinion due for the original creation of the Western tradition of culture and civilization: namely, in the first place to Africa, and more particularly to Egypt (the relevant Egyptians were for him in some useful sense 'black', if not necessarily negroid), and secondarily to Phoenicia (the Phoenicians were a Semitic people). And this despite the classical Greeks' own willingness to acknowledge that it was from those countries and peoples that they had taken over many of their most basic cultural tools and ideas lock, stock and barrel.

The contemporary political immediacy of this debate stems from the circumstance that Bernal's general thesis, both as an exercise in intellectual-social historiography and as a positive reconstruction of how it supposedly was, has been adopted as ammunition, in very simplified and often distorted forms, by promoters of various versions of Afrocentrism on and off American campuses. (Jews have been noticeably less keen to embrace Bernal's supposed recuperation of Phoenician influence on Greece.) Scholars, including prominent classicists, have taken reasoned and reasonable issue with Bernal, on points of both method and fact. One of the most prominent, Mary Lefkowitz, has gone to the lengths of publishing a book defiantly entitled *Not Out of Africa* directed not only or primarily at Bernal but at the more detectably outrageous variants of a recognizably Bernalian line on the ultimate ancestry of Western civilization (Lefkowitz 1995; Lefkowitz and Rogers 1996; cf. Levine 1989).

As in the recent German *Historikerstreit* over the responsibility of Germany or Germans for Nazism and more especially the Holocaust, we have here another sadly spectacular illustration of Benedetto Croce's dictum that all histor(iograph)y is present histor(iograph)y. Inevitably, as Julia Smith has put it below, 'in one way or another, *all* history is always ideological, relative and *zeitbedingt*'. Sometimes, indeed, as I have myself attempted to show here, conscious or subconscious definition of the group addressed in ideological terms can be an important or even the major goal of historiography. Such public and heated debates as that concerning 'Black Athena' are not perhaps entirely deleterious to the historical profession, in so far as they may foster a necessary self-reflexivity and send us back chastened to re-examine our intellectual and methodological roots and conceptual presuppositions. But they do little, on the other hand, to enhance History's positive reception and perception by wider society, and they do nothing to support claims that 'progress' in historiography is a measurably attainable goal.[11]

---

10 Bernal 1987–91. Further references and discussion Cartledge 1997.
11 Note the inverted commas of Finley 1977, of which the first chapter of Finley 1985 is a slightly revised extract.

REFERENCES

Abelove, H. *et al.* (eds) (1994) *The Lesbian and Gay Studies Reader*, New York and London.

Ankersmit, F. and Kellner, H. (eds) (1995) *A New Philosophy of History*, London.

Appleby, J., Hunt, L. and Jacob, M. (1994) *Telling the Truth about History*, New York.

—— *et al.* (eds) (1996) *Knowledge and Postmodernism in Historical Perspective. A Reader from 1700 to the Present*, London and New York.

Bernal, M. (1987–91) *Black Athena. The Afroasiatic Roots of Classical Civilization*, 2 vols (to date), London and New Brunswick, NJ.

Brunt, P. A. (1976) 'What is ancient history about?', *Didaskalos* 5.2: 236–49.

Burke, P. (ed.) (1991) *New Perspectives on Historical Writing*, Cambridge.

Canfora, L. (1985) 'Gli storici greci', in L. Firpo (ed.) *Storie delle idee politiche e sociali. I. L'antichità classica*, Turin.

Cartledge, P. (1993) *The Greeks. A Portrait of Self and Others*, Oxford.

—— (1995) 'Vindicating Gibbon's good faith', *Hermathena* 158: 133–47.

—— (1997) 'Classics: from discipline in crisis to (multi)cultural capital', in Y. L. Too and N. Livingstone (eds), *Pedagogy and Power: Rhetorics of Ancient Learning*, Cambridge.

—— and Harvey, D. (eds) (1985) *CRUX. Essays in Greek History Presented to G. E. M. de Ste. Croix on his 75th Birthday*, Exeter and London.

Davies, J. K. (1975) 'New ways of teaching ancient history', *Didaskalos* 5.1: 75–89.

Finley, M. I. (1977) '"Progress" in historiography', *Daedalus* 106: 125–42.

—— (1981) *Economy and Society in Ancient Greece*, ed. B. Shaw and R. Saller, London.

—— (1985) *Ancient History: Evidence and Models*, London.

—— (1986a) 'The historical tradition: the *Contributi* of Arnaldo Momigliano', in *The Use and Abuse of History*, 2nd edn, London.

—— (1986b) 'Revolution in antiquity', in Porter, R. and Teich, M. (eds), *Revolution in History*, Cambridge.

Gill, C. and Wiseman, T. P. (eds) (1993) *Lies and Fiction in the Ancient World*, Exeter.

Hartog, F. (1988) *The Mirror of Herodotus. The Representation of the Other in the Writing of History*, Berkeley.

Hunt, L. (ed.) (1989) *The New Cultural History*, Berkeley.

Lefkowitz, M. R. (1995) *Not Out of Africa: How Afrocentrism became an Excuse to Teach Myth as History*, New York.

—— and Rogers, G. M. (eds) (1996) *Black Athena Revisited*, Durham, NC.

Levine, M. M. (ed.) (1989) *The Challenge of 'Black Athena'* (*Arethusa* special issue).

Momigliano, A. D. (1978) 'The historians of the classical world and their audiences', *Annali della Scuola Normale Superiore di Pisa*, 3rd ser., 8: 59–75.

—— (1980) 'Ancient historiography in modern historiography', in W. Den Boer (ed.) *Les Études classiques aux XIXe et XXe siècles: leur place dans l'histoire des idées* (Entretiens Hardt 26), Vandoeuvres-Geneva.

—— (1981a) 'History and biography', in M. I. Finley (ed.) *The Legacy of Greece: A New Appraisal*, Oxford.

—— (1981b) 'The rhetoric of history and the history of rhetoric: on Hayden White's tropes', in E. S. Shaffer (ed.) *Comparative Criticism: A Yearbook* vol. 3, Cambridge.

—— (1982) 'The origins of universal history', *Annali della Scuola Normale Superiore di Pisa*, 3rd ser., 12: 556–60.

—— (1990) *The Classical Foundations of Modern Historiography*, Berkeley.

Novick, P. (1988) *That Noble Dream, The 'Objectivity Question' and the American Historical Profession*, Cambridge.

Rabb, T. and Rotberg, T. (eds) (1982) *The New History: The 1980s and Beyond. Studies in Interdisciplinary History*, Princeton.

Rhodes, P. J. (1994) 'In defence of the Greek historians', *Greece & Rome* 41.2 (October): 156–71.

Romilly, J. de (1958) 'L'utilité de l'histoire selon Thucydide', in O. Reverdin (ed.) *Histoire et historiens dans l'antiquité* (Entretiens Hardt 4), Vandoeuvres-Geneva.

Ste Croix, G. de (1975) 'Karl Marx and the history of classical antiquity', *Arethusa* 8: 7–41.

—— (1981; corr. impr. 1983) *The Class Struggle in Ancient Greece*, London.

Scott, J. W. (1988) *Gender in History*, New York.

Veeser, H. A. (ed.) (1989) *The New Historicism*, London and New York.

—— (ed.) (1994) *The New Historicism Reader*, London and New York.

White, H. (1973) *Metahistory: The Historical Imagination in Nineteenth-century Europe*, Baltimore.

Woodman, A. (1988) *Rhetoric in Classical Historiography*, London and New York.

1

THE EVOLUTION OF TWO ASIAN HISTORIOGRAPHICAL TRADITIONS

David Morgan

Historical writing, even 'historical-mindedness', has not been equally central in all parts of the Asian continent. The most conspicuous case of a society which seems to have lacked much of an interest in history, at least as it is conceived in the West, is India prior to the beginnings of Muslim conquest in the central Middle Ages. 'Historical writing', a modern Indian historian has suggested,

> was one of the least developed areas of ancient Indian culture. The mythological texts, the Puranas, did however include dynastic lists which contained rudimentary material for political history. A few Sanskrit texts from the Hindu 'middle ages' also record the achievements of individual monarchs or the history of regional dynasties . . . . Systematic chronicles of political events, especially wars, conquests, succession of dynasties and the like, really begin with the Muslim chroniclers.
>
> (Raychaudhuri 1988: 205)

Two quite independent traditions dominate historical writing in Asia during the pre-modern period: the Islamic and the Chinese. This chapter will be concerned with them. The Chinese tradition is much the older of the two. By definition, Islamic historiography (though it has older roots) began no earlier than the rise of Islam in the seventh century AD; whereas Chinese historical writing has a continuous history of its own from at least the time of Confucius (*c*.551–479 BC). As we shall see, although the two traditions differ fundamentally in all kinds of ways, they do have something in common so far as their beginnings are concerned. Confucius was concerned to preserve the memory and the legacy of a time in, for him, the fairly recent past, when Chinese society had existed in what he considered to have been the ideal form – the principal object of recording these details being to facilitate the recreation of that ideal society. The beginnings of Islamic historical writing, too, were associated with what, in time, came to be seen as the ideal society: the Islamic community in the days of the Prophet Muhammad and his immediate successors. This, too, was a Golden Age which many Muslims have always felt it incumbent on them to try to recover. However unlikely we may feel it

11

to be that Golden Ages did in fact once exist, this is a perception of the past towards which human beings seem to have a well-nigh universal tendency; and if it provided a stimulus to the writing of history, perhaps we should be grateful.

Granted that Muhammad was the last and the greatest of the Prophets sent by God to guide mankind in the right way, and that his life was a model which the good Muslim should try to emulate, how was the Muslim community to preserve the necessary knowledge of the details? This was evidently important. There was, of course, the Qur'an, the Holy Book which, so far from containing the words of Muhammad, was, so most Muslims came to believe, the literal word of God, co-eternal with God Himself. But specifically historical information is rather scant in the Qur'an. While Islam, like its relatives Judaism and Christianity, is certainly a historical religion, rooted in events believed actually to have happened in time and space, the Qur'an's main concerns are not historical, and it contains much less material of that type than the Old or New Testaments. Indeed, many of its historical references can only be understood in the light of other, probably later sources.

It was not until the ninth century AD that coherent historical narratives were first written. For the life of Muhammad they drew principally on *hadith*, that is to say on stories that the Prophet, in a particular circumstance, did or said such-and-such. These stories (or traditions, as they are often termed) seem at first to have circulated orally, there being some hostility to the notion of their being written down (though it has been argued that some material was in fact written down earlier than is generally thought). Whatever claims may be made for the faithfulness with which materials can be preserved by oral tradition, the situation had an inbuilt potentiality for the massive fabrication of *hadith* to suit particular points of view which were in need of support, or to deal apparently authoritatively with some new problem, perhaps a legal question which had arisen, and for the resolution of which the Qur'an seemed to provide no explicit guidance. Muslims were very well aware of this danger, and developed an elaborate science of *hadith*-criticism. This centred on the *isnad*, the chain of authorities: A heard from B, who heard from C, who heard from D that he heard the Prophet say that ... The kinds of questions to be asked were: were B and C contemporaries? Did they live anywhere near each other? From what was known of them, were they likely to be reliable witnesses? – and so on. By these methods vast numbers of traditions were rejected as spurious. The system, however, was by no means foolproof: obviously enough, a *hadith*-fabricator who wished to succeed would do very careful research so as to ensure that his *isnad* would stand up to investigation. The biographical dictionary, a very prominent Arabic and Persian literary genre which has provided historians with much valuable information, owed its origin to the necessity for establishing reliably the details of the lives of transmitters of *hadith*.

The question of the dating and reliability of the corpus of *hadith* is still a matter of very lively debate among scholars in Islamic studies. The spectrum of opinion ranges from conservative (that the traditions are by and large authentic and the transmitters by and large those who purport to be them) to very radical (little if anything actually dates from earlier than two hundred years after the time of Muhammad – a position not usually espoused by Muslim scholars). The orthodoxy among Western scholars is probably, at present, the position of Joseph Schacht (especially in Schacht 1950), who held that none of the legal traditions dated from much before AH 100 or so (the first half of the eighth century AD). This implies that all stories ascribed to the Prophet himself are likely to be spurious: but it should be said that a large (though not notably conservative) question-mark has been attached to Schacht's methods of dating (Cook 1992).

None of this, of course, concerned the first generations of Islamic historians. For them, the methods of *hadith*-criticism which the community's scholars had developed were adequate for the exposure of bogus traditions, and in due course collections of *hadith* were formed (the two most celebrated being those of Bukhari and Muslim), which thereafter were regarded as reliable and authoritative. From the collection and study of *hadith*, the next step was *sira*, lives of the Prophet based largely on the traditions. A number of these have survived, of which the best known is that of Ibn Ishaq (d. 768), in a ninth-century recension by Ibn Hisham (tr. Guillaume 1955).

The ninth and tenth centuries also saw the first connected histories of the Islamic conquests and the later development of the Muslim community: these too were heavily influenced by what one might call the *hadith* mentality. It should perhaps be remarked that while the time of the Prophet and the first four caliphs may have been regarded as a Golden Age, this is by no means the impression the early Arabic sources give us of the succeeding Umayyad caliphate (661–750), whose rulers are castigated for a variety of misdeeds, and especially for attempting to turn the Muslim caliphate into a form of secular kingship. What this tells us is not necessarily much about the quality, or morality, of the Umayyad caliphs, but rather that the surviving historical writing all dates from after 750, when the Umayyads were overthrown, vilified and as far as possible massacred by the new 'Abbasid caliphs. The most notable of all the historians of this period was Tabari (839–923), a Persian who, like all Persian scholars at this time, wrote in Arabic, and whose *Ta'rikh al -rusul wa'l-muluk* ('History of the Prophets and the Kings') ranks as the most important source for the first three centuries of Islam. This is a vast history, beginning with the creation of the world: its standard Arabic edition was published in thirteen volumes (7,787 pages of Arabic text), and the new English translation (Albany, NY, 1985–   ) is projected to run to thirty-eight volumes.

The special value of Tabari's history lies in what it preserves. Most of the earliest accounts of Islamic history are lost, but Tabari reproduces extracts from many of them. These are quoted *in extenso*, complete with chains of authorities in the manner of *hadith*. Tabari was the author of a commentary on the Qur'an, even longer than his History and even more esteemed: he was thoroughly familiar with the standard methods of *hadith*-criticism. He made no attempt to iron out contradictions or other difficulties, and does not interpose his own personality or judgement to any very significant extent. While it would be over-optimistic to say that he provides us with far earlier source material precisely as it was originally written, we are a great deal nearer to knowing what such sources contained than would have been the case had Tabari never written. It has been said that 'in effect his work presents a wide cross-section of the historical consensus of Islam as it had evolved during its first three centuries' (Hawting 1988: 401).

Tabari's history, though what we now have may well be much shorter than the original version, is a very long book indeed. It gave rise to an important though far briefer work: the first history in New Persian, the literary Persian which re-emerged in Iran after the Arab conquest, written in a slightly adapted form of the Arabic script and containing a great deal of Arabic vocabulary. This is what is known as the *Tarjama-i Ta'rikh-i Tabari* ('Translation of Tabari's History') by Bal'ami. The author was a minister of the Samanid ruler of Transoxania (roughly modern Uzbekistan), who was commissioned in 963 to prepare a Persian version of Tabari. Perhaps because of its unfortunate title, the *Tarjama* has received less than its deserts: far from being a mere abridged translation it is in reality an independent historical work, albeit one based on Tabari to a considerable extent. But this was standard practice: Islamic historians regularly tended to copy out or abridge their distinguished predecessors as far as possible, before going on to supplement them from their own knowledge and research. Bal'ami leaves out both the chains of authorities and the alternative versions of events, settling for just one, and adds much material of his own, particularly about events in Iran. While firmly positioned in the evolving tradition of Islamic historiography, Bal'ami had also produced something of a landmark work.

Meanwhile, history was emerging from the *hadith* environment and taking its place in a wider cultural world, that of *adab* (usually if not entirely satisfactorily translated as 'belles-lettres'). Ya'qubi (d. *c.*897), for example, was the author of the first Arabic attempt at a world history: this could not be attempted within the *hadith* framework, since the requisite chains of authorities, in the nature of the case, did not exist for history outside the Judaeo-Islamic tradition. More remarkable was the tenth-century historian Mas'udi, a prolific author of whose works two survive, the best known being the *Muruj al-Dhahab* ('Meadows of Gold'). Although Mas'udi, in broad outline, followed Ya'qubi's pattern of organization, with an account of biblical history, the pre-Islamic Arabs, other ancient nations (Persians, Greeks, Indians), the Prophet and the subsequent history of the Caliphs, his interests were far from conventional. One scholar has ascribed his undoubted 'originality and independence of mind' to 'his not having passed through a rigorous and prolonged academic training' (Dunlop 1971: 103). Be that as it may, he made claims for history as a discipline which even Sir Geoffrey Elton might have deemed more than sufficient:

The superiority of history over all other sciences is obvious. The loftiness of its status is recognized by any person of intelligence. None can master it nor gain certainty as to what it includes nor receive and transmit it except one who has devoted his life to knowledge, grasped its true meaning, tasted its fruits, felt its dignity and experienced the pleasure it bestows.

(quoted by Khalidi 1994: 133)

14

Mas'udi's works are an extraordinary combination of history and natural history, full of recondite information on the wide range of subjects that interested him. To take one example, those who suppose 'Istanbul' to be the Turkish name for Constantinople might notice Mas'udi's remarks, dating from the year 947, centuries before the Ottomans had been heard of. He tells us that the Greeks (i.e. the Byzantines of the tenth century) call it 'the City' (*bulin* in the Arabic script, which lacks the letter 'p': so Greek *polin*); 'and when they wish to express that it is the capital of the Empire because of its greatness they say Istan Bulin. They do not call it Constantinople. It is only the Arabs who so designate it' (Dunlop 1971: 106–7).

As time passed, history in the Islamic lands diversified into many other channels. Local histories, of a city or a region, appeared in great quantities, especially in Iran. With the dissolution of the effective power of the Caliphate in Baghdad and the rise of independent dynasties in various parts of the Islamic world, histories of individual dynasties were written, frequently in response to a commission from the current ruler or in hope of his favour. Likewise, panegyrical biographies of rulers became common: both Saladin (d. 1193) and Baybars, the later Mamluk ruler of Egypt and Syria (d. 1277) were the subject of several of these. Older patterns continued to be followed too. One of the most notable exponents of these was Ibn al-Athir (1160–1233), whose greatest work, the *al-Kamil* (twelve volumes of Arabic text) was an attempt to write a history of the entire period from the creation of the world to shortly before his own death. But Ibn al-Athir also wrote a dynastic history, of the family of Zengi, the ruler of Mosul whose descendants had lost their patrimony in Egypt and Syria to the usurper Saladin (to whom Ibn al-Athir, whose patron was a later Zengid of Mosul, was unremittingly hostile).

Until the Seljuk period (eleventh–twelfth centuries) the bulk of historical writing in the Islamic Middle East was written in Arabic. This applied even to the history of Iran, though important historians had already followed Bal'ami's example in writing in Persian. One of the most notable of these was Bayhaqi, who wrote a *Ta'rikh-i Mas'udi*. *Mas'ud* (d. 1041) was the Ghaznavid ruler of much of eastern Iran, Afghanistan and northern India whose empire was largely superseded by that of the Seljuks. Most of Bayhaqi's work has not survived, but what remains, written in a beautifully clear and elegant Persian, is an extraordinarily vivid and detailed account of the workings of the Ghaznavid government.

With the arrival of the Mongols in the Islamic world in 1219, much changed; and historical writing, too, felt the impact of the invasion and the incorporation of most of the Middle East into an empire which ultimately stretched uninterruptedly from Korea to Hungary. In Iran the invasion, catastrophic as it may have been in many respects, nevertheless inaugurated what is usually regarded as the best period of Persian historical writing. And it was largely in Persian: Arabic – a language in which the new non-Islamic masters of the world had little interest – now took second place, except in writings on Islamic law and theology. The range of interests shown by the Persian historians of the Mongol period is far wider than the previous evolution of historical writing would have led one to expect: the result is that some of those historians are among the most important available sources for the history of the Mongol Empire in general, not merely its Persian or Islamic sections.

Two of these historians may be singled out for mention: Juwayni and Rashid al-Din. Both were Persian bureaucrats who served the new Mongol government in Iran in high office. Juwayni (1226–83) was governor of Baghdad, and wrote a history of Genghis Khan, his conquests and the later history of the Mongol expansion. He travelled to Mongolia in search of information, and tells us much about the whole vast Mongol world, in an elaborate Persian style which was much admired and emulated. Rashid al-Din (1247–1318) was more remarkable. Ghazan, the newly converted Muslim Mongol ruler of Iran (d. 1304) commissioned him to write a history of the Mongols, the *Jami' al-tawarikh* ('Collection of Histories'), which survives almost *in toto* and is the most important single source on Mongol history of the period. Rashid al-Din later went on, however, to write a further history of all the peoples with whom the Mongols had come into contact – Indians, Chinese, Turks, Jews, even the Franks, the peoples of Europe whose backwardness and obscurity in the Middle Ages were usually rewarded with total indifference by Muslim writers. Rashid al-Din has been called, with some justice, 'the first world historian'.

The Mongol conquests inaugurated a period of Persian cultural hegemony, though Arabic chronicles of great importance continued to be written in Egypt and Syria, which escaped incorporation into the Mongol Empire. It could be argued that the last great medieval Muslim chronicle was produced in Egypt as late as the end of the eighteenth century: Jabarti's history of Napoleon's invasion. But elsewhere Persian was dominant: even, for long, in the Ottoman Empire. In northern India, where Muslim rule came to be established in the thirteenth century, historical writing was in Persian and followed Persian norms; indeed, the history of the pre-Mughal Delhi Sultanate is one of the few historiographical areas where the writing of the medieval chronicle might be said to remain alive and well to this day.

Something should be said about the North African Ibn Khaldun (1332–1406), perhaps the only Islamic historian (and proto-sociologist) of whom a Western historian may be expected to have heard. There is justice in this: he was certainly the most original historical thinker to have appeared in the medieval Islamic world. His fame derives not so much from the universal history he wrote, the *Kitab al-'ibar*, as from the introduction to it, the *Muqaddima*. In this he explored the causes of change in human societies, considering the influence of the physical environment, state formation, the power of tribal society with its *'asabiyya* ('natural solidarity' or 'group feeling'), religion, the corrosive effects of civilization and prosperity, with consequent decline, and so on. Ibn Khaldun had little influence in his own time, though he had an eventful life (for example, he met the conqueror Tamerlane at Damascus, and left an account of their conversation). But his ideas were much discussed by Ottoman thinkers in the seventeenth century, and they continue to exercise a considerable influence, by no means exclusively in the Islamic lands.

'China', it has been said, 'produced an historical literature, peculiar both in its merits and its limitations, but unique in the volume of its output and the length and continuity of its record' (Beasley and Pulleyblank 1961: 1). The continuous history of Chinese historical writing goes back at least to the time of Confucius, and in its traditional form it survived for as long as the Chinese Empire, that is, until the early twentieth century. It has received little attention from Western students of historiography. This is no doubt partly because of the sheer difficulty of getting at it. Chinese is not an easy language, and no one is likely to learn it simply in order to sample the nature and quality of its historiographical tradition. Nor has very much been translated into European languages. Much of even what has been translated makes little sense to anyone who does not already have a fairly considerable knowledge of Chinese history and culture. And in any case, Chinese historical writing is arguably 'culture-bound' to a greater extent than the world's other two great historiographical traditions, the Western and the Islamic. It seems not to have been influenced by them; nor did it itself influence them to any significant extent. It did have an influence, but this was mainly confined to East Asia: the historiographical traditions of Korea, Japan and Vietnam are, like so much else in the culture of those countries, to a considerable extent a colony of Chinese civilization.

There is nothing very 'religious' about Chinese historiography. The stories it tells are not concerned with prophets, the supernatural, magic or miracles. It is, however, intimately bound up with Confucianism, the ideology rather than the religion of the officials, the scholar-bureaucrats: it was they who both wrote and read history. Being concerned as it was with traditional rites, with family continuity and so forth, Confucianism was, inevitably, deeply interested in the past and in the precedents it provided. It has been suggested that for a Confucian, history in some sense took the place of the sacred writings which are so central in other cultures. The origins of historiography go back beyond Confucius. Ancestor-worship predated the great sage, and that required at least the preservation of genealogies, notably those of royal houses. Various of the states into which China was divided before unification by the First Emperor in 221 BC kept chronicles.

It was one of these chronicles, that of the state of Lu, known as the *Spring and Autumn Annals*, which conventionally marks the beginning of the continuous historiographical tradition. This is not so much because of the significance of the state itself or the information the chronicle contains as because it was believed to have been edited by Confucius himself, and thus to have provided a model which could never be ignored. It covered the years 722–481 BC, and is essentially a fairly arid record of major events, notably those of ritual significance. What was really important was that Confucius, in the process of editing, was thought to have introduced, by careful use of wording and terminology, a substantial measure of praise and blame. Not everyone, even in China, has found this easy to detect, and there is an ancient belief that what Confucius in fact did was to use the *Annals* as a class textbook: that is, that Confucius' commentary was an oral one, not to be found in the text itself. Be that as it may, one legacy of this belief about Confucius's

17

activity as a historian was the notion that the distribution of praise and blame ranked high among the historian's duties – even if many historians in practice hesitated thus to place themselves on a level with Confucius.

It was no doubt the difficulty of working out quite what Confucius' message in the *Spring and Autumn Annals* really was that gave rise to a number of commentaries on it. These appear to date from several centuries after Confucius' time, during the Han period (206 BC–AD 220). Rather different from these is what is known as the *Tso-chuan*, the 'Tradition of Tso'. This is much fuller than the *Annals*, and covers a slightly longer period. It has much less moralizing than the other commentaries, being composed mainly of narrative, and narrative frequently of a very lively kind. It is regarded as the first great masterpiece of Chinese literary prose, though it is not entirely clear whether it should be classified simply as history: a good deal of it may well have been based on fictional or semi-fictional stories about the great figures of the (by then fairly remote) past.

The great historiographical breakthrough came with the work of Ssu-ma Ch'ien (*c*.145–85 BC) and his father, Ssu-ma T'an, whose work he continued and completed. The two successively held the hereditary office of Grand Scribe or Grand Historian (*T'ai-shih*) in the unified China of the Han Dynasty. Their plan was to combine into a single work the existing materials and traditions on Chinese history from the earliest times to their own day. In so doing they set the basic pattern which, with modifications, was followed for the writing of official history in China until the end of the empire in 1911. This was a 'scissors-and-paste' approach. Materials from sources were collected together and reproduced unaltered except by abridgement, and the historian's personal views, if any, were kept completely distinct and separate. The historian's judgement, of course, came into play in the selection of appropriate excerpts, so it would be too simplistic to suggest that such a book can be treated as primary source material; though it may be nearer to it than a work wholly in the historian's own words might be. There is perhaps here a partial parallel to Tabari's approach. For more remote times, some of the material used might perhaps have been of doubtful authenticity or reliability, though for recent history, official government archives could be and were drawn upon, with all the advantages and difficulties which that implies.

The other respect in which the Ssu-mas established a pattern is in their organization of material according to topics. The *Shih-chi* ('Records of the Historian') was divided into five principal sections. First came the 'Basic Annals' (*pen-chi*), which recount the main events of the lives and reigns of the emperors. 'Tables' (*piao*) came next: these included, as well as appointments to noble titles under the Han, chronologies of the various independent dynasties of the pre-Han period. 'Monographs' (*shu*) followed: these dealt with aspects of government such as the calendar, rites and music. The next section, 'Hereditary Houses' (*shih-chia*) recounted the history of the separate pre-Han states: this was a category which the Ssu-mas' successors did not find necessary when writing the history of a united China. The longest section, 'Biographies' (*lieh-chuan* – literally 'assembled traditions') was a catch-all category which, though consisting largely of biographies of notable persons, also included anything for which an appropriate place had not been found elsewhere, such as relations with foreign countries. Biographies came to form an increasingly large proportion of the later official histories; but these were not biographies in anything like the modern Western sense. Their subjects were celebrated not for their individuality so much as for their representation as members of a group or class that was important to the proper functioning of the Chinese state.

All this may give the impression of a mechanical dryness; and indeed in some later histories this was precisely what was achieved. But as a reading, for example, of Raymond Dawson's (1994) translation of substantial parts of the material relating to the First Emperor shows very clearly, this is by no means the case so far as Ssu-ma Ch'ien's own work is concerned. It makes for extraordinarily vivid and interesting reading.

Pan Ku (AD 32–92) was responsible for the next stage in the evolution of Chinese official historiography. His history began as a private enterprise, and although it was later given official status and support, it is important to remember that, despite the dominance of the official histories, private works of history continued to be written throughout China's past. In his work Pan Ku dealt with 'The History of the Former Han Dynasty' (*Han shu*): in this respect, that of dealing exclusively with a single dynasty, he diverged from the pattern established by Ssu-ma Ch'ien; and it was Pan Ku's example which was followed thereafter. Chinese historians inevitably tended, therefore, to see their country's history in a dynastic framework (in which they have largely been followed by Western scholars).

After the Han the next major dynasty to rule the whole of China was the T'ang (AD 618–907). The government at this time set up a History Office, charged with the task of assembling and preparing materials for T'ang history. At intervals (effectively at the end of each reign) these were cast into chronicles known as 'Veritable Records' (*Shih-lu*). The Veritable Records were designed as much as anything to serve as a body of reference material for the use of officials in search of precedents. Like turn-of-the-century Cambridge, traditional China was convinced that nothing should ever be done for the first time (Cornford 1908: 15). Ultimately the pattern came to be that a newly installed dynasty would mark its accession by commissioning the writing of the official history of its predecessor: this would be compiled from the Veritable Records. For some centuries the official histories are what now survive: the Veritable Records have disappeared. But for the last two dynasties, Ming (1368–1644) and Ch'ing (1644–1911), both are still extant, so it is possible to see how the officials of the History Office dealt with the Veritable Records in using them as the basis of the official history.

Such a system of official historiography was unique in providing a continuous, detailed record of the past. However, it was not, by its very nature, very conducive to individuality or to the development of historical research and writing as a discipline. Many Chinese thinkers were indeed dissatisfied with the official pattern. Some wrote about its defects and what might replace or supplement it; others attempted themselves to do something about it. The most notable example of the latter phenomenon occurred during the Sung Dynasty (960–1279). Ssu-ma Kuang completed his *Tzu-chih t'ung-chien* ('Comprehensive Mirror for Aid in Government') in 1085. It covered the entire period from the end of the *Spring and Autumn Annals* to the accessions of the Sung, i.e. 403 BC–AD 959. The author was a leading statesman, so his book could hardly be said to have originated entirely from outside the official bureaucratic tradition. Indeed, he had official support for it. But what was unusual was not so much the form and organization of the work as the length of time dealt with and the fact that there was a single directing intelligence behind it: something which had long ceased to be the case so far as the official dynastic histories were concerned. And Ssu-ma Kuang was by no means reluctant to commit his own views to print, while nevertheless insisting on including details of events because they had occurred, even though they may have been less than morally improving. A later historian, Chu Hsi, produced an abridgement of Ssu-ma Kuang's work, the *Kang-mu*, which, containing as it did a much larger element of 'praise and blame', was more in accordance with Confucian notions of political morality: unfortunately it was this rather than the original which was widely read and came to be regarded as authoritative.

The scholar who is regarded as going farthest in parting company with the traditional conception of writing history lived under the Ch'ing Dynasty. Chang Hsüeh-ch'eng (1738–1801) argued that Chinese historiography was far too much concerned with minutiae, and that this made it difficult to see the wood for the trees. He wished to take a much broader view of the nature and purpose of history. He has been likened to Giambattista Vico, and might perhaps also be compared with Lord Acton as a profound historical thinker who, despite the best of intentions, failed to put his ideas into practice. Chang made little impact in his own day, and was speedily forgotten: he did manage to have one book published, but it does not appear among the 2,136 historical works to be found in the imperial library in 1782. His ideas were revived only in fairly recent times, as Chinese thinkers searched their scholarly tradition for foreshadowings of modern thought.

Most of what follows in this *Companion* is concerned with the immense richness and variety of Western historiography: modern historiography is in a real sense a manifesation of 'the triumph of the West'. Even in Part IV, where the modern historiographies of China, Japan, India and Africa are discussed – areas in which a very high proportion of the leading practitioners of historical writing are natives of the areas concerned, not Europeans or Americans – most are working to a greater or lesser extent within the parameters of Western historiography as it has developed since the Enlightenment. Of course there are differences: for example, some modern Muslim scholars approach Islam's sacred writings, as historical sources, from a perspective different from that of their non-Muslim colleagues; and some Chinese historians perhaps feel themselves obliged to accord their scholarly predecessors a degree of deference not always to be found in the sometimes fruitful, sometimes arid controversies which characterize much modern Western historical writing. But we should not forget, in our preoccupation with

Western historiography, that in the Islamic and Chinese traditional worlds there were two long-standing alternative historiographies which played an important – in the Chinese case a central – role in the intellectual development of those two great civilizations, and which are worthy of our attention and our respect.

REFERENCES

Beasley, W. G. and Pulleyblank, E. G. (eds) (1961) *Historians of China and Japan*, London.

Cook, M. A. (1992) 'Eschatology and the dating of traditions', *Princeton Papers in Near Eastern Studies* 1: 23–47.

Cornford, F. M. (1908) *Microcosmographia Academica*, Cambridge.

Dawson, R. (tr.) (1994) *Sima Qian: Historical Records*, Oxford.

Dunlop, D. M. (1971) *Arab Civilization to A.D. 1500*, London and Beirut.

Guillaume, A. (tr.) (1955) *Ibn Ishaq: The Life of Muhammad*, London.

Hawting, G. R. (1988) 'Tabari, Muhammad ibn Jarir', in J. Cannon *et al.* (eds) *The Blackwell Dictionary of Historians*, Oxford.

Khalidi, T. (1994) *Arabic Historical Thought in the Classical Period*, Cambridge.

Raychaudhuri, T. (1988) 'Indian historiography', in J. Cannon *et al.* (eds) *The Blackwell Dictionary of Historians*, Oxford.

Schacht, J. (1950) *The Origins of Muhamnedan Jurisprudence*, Oxford.

BIBLIOGRAPHICAL NOTE

The first point of reference should be a series of substantial volumes, 'Historical Writing on the Peoples of Asia', which arose from study conferences held at the School of Oriental and African Studies, University of London, in 1956–8. Of particular relevance to this essay are B. Lewis and P. M. Holt (eds) *Historians of the Middle East* (London, 1962) and W. G. Beasley and E. G. Pulleyblank (eds) *Historians of China and Japan* (London, 1961). The series also includes C. H. Philips (ed.), *Historians of India, Pakistan and Ceylon* (London, 1961) and D. G. E. Hall (ed.), *Historians of South East Asia* (London, 1961). Much of the material in these volumes is now inevitably out of date, but nothing has since been attempted on a remotely comparable scale.

A much shorter but slightly less out-of-date survey is D. Sinor (ed.), *Orientalism and History*, 2nd edn (Bloomington and London, 1970). This contains essays on Islam by B. Lewis and on China by E. G. Pulleyblank. It should be noted that the title of this book dates from before the time when the word 'Orientalism' regrettably acquired a pejorative sense. Useful short articles on both Islamic and Chinese historiography, by R. G. Irwin and T. H. Barrett respectively, may be found in J. Cannon, R. H. C. Davis, W. Doyle and J. P. Greene (eds), *The Blackwell Dictionary of Historians* (Oxford, 1988). Individual Chinese historians are conspicuous by their total absence from that work of reference; the Islamic world fares very slightly better, being represented by Tabari (G. R. Hawting), Ibn Khaldun and Rashid al-Din (D. O. Morgan).

On Islamic historiography, a well-established work of reference is F. Rosenthal, *A History of Muslim Historiography* (Leiden, 1952), but though massive this is much more limited in its scope than its title suggests. There is valuable material in C. Cahen, *Jean Sauvaget's Introduction to the History of the Muslim East* (Berkeley and Los Angeles, 1965), and in R. S. Humphreys, *Islamic History: a Framework for Inquiry*, revised edn. (Princeton and London, 1991). A learned discussion of the early period, from a conservative point of view, is A. A. Duri, *The Rise of Historical Writing among the Arabs* (Princeton, 1983). The most recent more general treatment, an interesting and lucid book containing many translated extracts, is T. Khalidi, *Arabic Historical Thought in the Classical Period* (Cambridge, 1994). He is also the author of *Islamic Historiography: The Histories of Mas'udi* (Albany, 1975); on the same historian see A. Shboul, *Al-Mas'udi and his World* (London, 1979). Ibn Khaldun has attracted a good deal of attention: one of the best studies is M. Mahdi, *Ibn Khaldun's Philosophy of History* (London, 1957). D. O. Morgan (ed.), *Medieval Historical Writing in the Christian and Islamic Worlds* (London, 1982), contains studies of, among others, Baybars' biographers (P. M. Holt), Ibn al-Athir (D. S. Richards) and some of the Persian historians of the Mongol period (D. O. Morgan). An outstanding study of another individual historian, from a later period, is C. L. Fleischer, *Bureaucrat and Intellectual in the Ottoman Empire: The Historian Mustafa Ali (1541–1600)* (Princeton, 1986). A short older survey which has been influential is H. A. R. Gibb, 'Tarikh', originally an article in the first edition of the *Encyclopaedia of Islam*, reprinted in his *Studies on the Civilization of Islam* (London, 1962), pp. 108–37. There is much of interest in D. M. Dunlop, *Arab Civilization to A.D. 1500* (London and Beirut, 1971), ch. 3, 'History and historians'.

For China, there is a detailed examination of official history in D. C. Twitchett, *The Writing of Official History under the Tang* (Cambridge, 1993). An older survey is C. S. Gardner, *Chinese Traditional Historiography* (1938; 2nd amended printing, Cambridge, MA, 1961). E. G. Pulleyblank, 'The historiographical tradition', in R. Dawson (ed.), *The Legacy of China* (Oxford, 1964), pp. 143–64, is very useful, as is an English version of an essay that appears in French in *Historians of China and Japan*: E. Balazs, 'History as a guide to bureaucratic practice', in his *Chinese Civilization and Bureaucracy*, ed A. F. Wright (New Haven and London, 1964), pp. 129–49. Of individual historians, Ssu-ma Ch'ien is the subject of B. Watson, *Ssu-ma Ch'ien: Grand Historian of China* (New York, 1958). Considerable parts of his work have been translated into English, notably by Watson; but for a flavour of it see the World's Classics selection, *Sima Qian* [Ssu-ma Ch'ien in Pinyin romanization], *Historical Records*, tr. R. Dawson (Oxford, 1994). For an example of the intractability to the non-specialist of much of the contents of the official dynastic histories, see H. F. Schurmann (tr.), *Economic Structure of the Yüan Dynasty* (Cambridge, MA, 1956).

2

HISTORIOGRAPHY AND ANCIENT GREEK SELF-DEFINITION[1]

Paul Cartledge

INVENTING HISTORY

The issue of the ancient Greeks' self-definition comprises a multivariate cluster of complex and highly unstable problems. One, central member of this cluster constitutes this chapter's topic – the ways in which the Greeks defined themselves as an ethno-cultural group through the medium of written historiography, from the time of Herodotus (fifth century BC/BCE) to that of Plutarch (first–second century AD/CE).[2] Our English word 'history', like French *histoire*, Italian *storia* and other such European equivalents, descends to us ultimately from the Greek *via* Latin, as does so much else of our cultural-intellectual baggage. But *en route* from Greece to Rome, and again, between the Renaissance and today, the word *historia* and its derivatives have changed crucially in their meaning – or rather meanings.

From its original senses of judgement and enquiry (which latter we preserve in 'natural history', a discipline whose antecedents may be traced back through Aristotle to the Hippocratic doctors of the fifth century and ultimately the Asiatic Greek 'philosophers of nature' in the sixth) ancient Greek *historia* came secondarily

---

1   An earlier version of the first four sections of this chapter appeared as Cartledge 1995. I am grateful to the editor of *BICS*, Professor Richard Sorabji, for allowing me to draw here upon that article, where some further bibliographical references may be found.

2   Recent work in ancient Greek historiography is usefully surveyed in Hornblower 1994 (note esp. the editor's introduction, 1–72, and the consolidated bibliography, 249–69); for a much longer perspective, going back to the sixteenth century, see Ampolo 1996. Add now Thompson 1996 , a wide-ranging and intelligent historiographical conspectus. The most recent monographic survey of ancient Greek history-writing known to me is Meister 1990; far more challenging is Desideri 1996. Both Ampolo and Desideri end with M. Bernal's *Black Athena* project, which since its inauguration in 1987 has acquired a formidable bibliographical tradition of its own. For this, and a more ample and nuanced collocation of ancient Greek with modern Western modes of historiography, see my Introduction on pp. 3–10.

to denote the results of such judgement and enquiry regarding human public political actions as related purely orally at first and then in written narrative prose.[3] That secondary usage is perhaps attested earliest in about 425 BCE, in the *Histories* of Herodotus (7.96), although for him the primary sense of enquiry remained paramount. His illustrious successor, and rival historiographer, Thucydides avoided the word altogether, surely deliberately, and preferred to describe his activity as 'writing up', using the impersonal language of documentary record. But Herodotus, too, firmly maintained the link between enquiry and record throughout his work, and, again like Thucydides, was preoccupied with explanation, from his preface onwards: 'This is an exposition of the research (*historia*) of Herodotus ... carried out ... especially to record the reason why they [the Greeks and the Persians] fought one another.'

However, by the time that *historia* had become domesticated at Rome as part of the cultural process whereby 'captive Greece' had in Horace's famous phrase 'captured her fierce conqueror', it had acquired a further, moralizing and justificatory, rather than documentary and explanatory, connotation. The chief function of history for the Romans, as Tacitus colourfully but conventionally claimed (*Annals* 3.65), was respectively to excoriate and to praise paradigmatic examples of human vice and virtue – the former usually, as in Tacitus' own case, far more assiduously than the latter.[4]

Of course, the polarity between Greek and Roman historiographical theory and practice should not be overdrawn. Even the fathers of Greek history – who were perhaps also the fathers of History as such – were as incapable as the rest of us are of avoiding the historian's engrained tendency to be the obedient servant of her or his own point of view.[5] Besides, the successors of Herodotus and Thucydides were mostly neither immune from nor averse to the dramatically moralizing or sensationalist uses of historical narrative.[6] The comparison, rather, raises the issue of the striking of a balance between objectivity of record and explanation, on the one hand, and conscious or unconscious ideology, on the other. In what follows I shall be exploring principally these two, ideological questions: how far, and in what ways, did the distinction and opposition of Greeks and non-Greek 'barbarians' influence or determine Greek historians' conceptions of their function? Second,

---

3 On the ancient meanings of *historia*, see Press 1982; Fornara 1983. On orality, see below, n. 7.

4 Tacitean historiography: Syme 1958 is classic; cf. Cook 1988: 73–96; longer perspectives are on offer in Woodman and Luce 1993; Cartledge 1989.

5 The (meta-)historiography of P. Geyl (e.g. *Debates with Historians* (1962 (1955)) and *Encounters in History* (1963 (1961))) and A. D. Momigliano (e.g. his multi-volume *Contributi alla storia degli studi classici e del mondo antico* or, selectively, *Studies in Historiography* (London, 1966), *Essays in Ancient and Modern Historiography* (Oxford, 1977) and *Studies on Modern Scholarship* (Berkeley, 1994)) is instinct with the injunction 'Study first the historian, not the history.' For other viewpoints on the 'objectivity question' compare and contrast Hartog 1988; and Novick 1988.

6 Post-classical so-called 'tragic' history is discussed in broad perspective, with special reference to Aristotle and Polybius, in Walbank 1985. C. W. Macleod's (1983) contention that Thucydides' history was already (in a different sense) tragic is provocative.

from the standpoint of their target audiences of Greek or Hellenized addressees, how far and in what ways did the Greek historians contribute to the formation of usable notions of 'Greekness'?

MYTH AND HISTORY

A deliberately challenging assertion by a historian of modern ideology provides a suitable starting-point: 'one of the uses of history has always been (in Western society at least) the creation of traditional mythologies attributing a historical sanctity to the present self-images of groups, classes and societies' (Stedman Jones 1972: 112). Herodotus and Thucydides, the latter especially, would have rejected that claim with contumely. Both were scornful of myth, which they consigned to the province of the poets, and our dichotomy of 'myth' and 'history' is in fact owed ultimately to them. But they reached that position by importantly different routes. Herodotus, crucially, drew the distinction between the timelessly distant rule of the sea by legendary King Minos of Crete and the certifiably authentic thalassocracy of Polycrates of Samos within living memory, on the grounds that only the latter belonged to 'the age of humankind as it is called' (3.122). And he declared himself obliged to relate, but free to disbelieve, the multiplicity of orally transmitted 'tales' he heard on his peregrinations round the Mediterranean and Black Seas (7.152). Thucydides went much further. He dismissed what he called 'the mythic' as no better than romance (1.21, 22), precisely because it was the product of unreliable and untested oral traditions. Whereas Herodotus was prepared to give credence to stories concerning events as much as two generations before his birth, Thucydides was from choice the contemporary historian *par excellence*. One of his chief reasons for choosing as his subject the great war between Athens and Sparta beginning in 431 was that it broke out in his own lifetime when he was already 'of an age to understand what was going on' (5.26) and could interrogate contemporaries, ideally event-making or eyewitness participants (1.22). His was a history written to be read and re-read.[7]

The Thucydidean model set the pattern for all subsequent Greek historiography, in this following respect at least: original history was contemporary history, picking up the narrative thread where one's predecessors had let it drop. For earlier periods than one's own the best one could normally hope for was to improve on the predecessors' manner, not their content. But in other respects Thucydides' successors differed as much from each other and from Thucydides as Thucydides had from Herodotus, whom he never once mentioned by name. Indeed, the only serious agreement Thucydides seems to have had with him was that a history should be about war.[8] But whereas Herodotus had chosen for his subject a Russian-style

---

7 Murray 1987, Thomas 1992; Steiner 1994. On contemporary Greek spectatorship and audiences, with special but by no means exclusive reference to the theatre, see Segal 1995; also very relevant to the performative aspect of early Greek historiography is Nagy 1996.
8 War in Greek historiography: Finley 1985: ch. 5 ('War and empire', 67–87).

'great patriotic war', Thucydides wrote up a war of Greek against Greek with minimal, indeed palpably inadequate, reference to the role of non-Greeks therein. Thucydides' war, however, would to Herodotus have seemed but a 'civil war among the Greek people', and such a war Herodotus deemed 'as much worse than like-minded war against a foreign enemy as war is worse than peace' (8.3). Not that Herodotus was simple-mindedly chauvinistic, by any means: to quote again from his preface, his self-appointed task was to celebrate 'the great deeds of both the Greeks *and* the non-Greeks', or, as they were by then collectively known, the 'barbarians'.

INVENTING THE BARBARIAN

In order for him to do that, of course, the barbarians had first to have been invented as a cultural category of Greek thought and discourse.[9] Indeed, it may very well have been to challenge and undermine the overwhelmingly negative construction of this cultural stereotype that Herodotus conceived and conducted his even-handed project of recuperative commemoration. Herodotus' ultimate literary model was Homer, and, seen from a post-Persian War perspective, the *Iliad* was among other things an epic of Graeco-barbarian military confrontation. Yet 'barbarian' was used just once in the *Iliad* and used descriptively, not pejoratively, to refer to the unintelligible non-Greek speech of the Carians of south-west Asia Minor. Throughout the poem, in fact, something like a parity of dignity and status was carefully maintained between the two sides, the non-Greek but Greek-style Trojans and the Achaeans – not yet the 'Hellenes', as the Greeks had agreed to call themselves by Herodotus' time, and still call themselves to this day. (Our term 'Greeks', to anticipate, is derived from the Romans' 'Graeci', a deliberately diminishing and ethnocentric term suitable for their conquered subjects.) Between Homer and Herodotus, in other words, a paradigm-shift of consciousness had occurred. So far from according parity to non-Greeks, the Greeks now primarily effected their self-identification through the polar opposition of themselves to the morally inferior barbarians – 'wogs', as it were, to borrow the language of a more recent colonialist discourse. Two factors, briefly, were chiefly responsible for this sea-change in attitude. First, there had been ongoing since about 750 a tidal wave of permanent emigration from the Greeks' Aegean and eastern Mediterranean heartlands, to sites almost all round the Mediterranean and Black Seas, so that Plato in the fourth century could speak amusingly of Greeks sitting 'like frogs or ants around a pond'. Differences between Greek settlers and indigenous 'natives' could hardly fail to be expressed, often militarily, and they were encoded in what has been called a 'colonial narrative' of Greek self-justification (Dougherty 1993; 1994). Conversely, cultural ties, and especially religious affinity, bound all Greek

---

9   Hartog 1988; Hall 1989; Georges 1994. Ascherson (1995) interestingly applies Hartog's and Hall's insights on a broader canvas, but he is demonstrably in error to claim that 'conveying information was the only purpose of all their [the historians'] arduous researching and writing' (78).

'colonists' both to their mother-cities and, through the Panhellenic shrines such as Olympia and Delphi, to each other and thereby served to foster a positive concept of 'Greekness'. Whether we define nations as imagined communities, or as objectively instituted entities, there existed by about 500 BC something that could be called a Greek 'nation'.[10] This was an unstable and inchoate compound of territoriality, ethnic homogeneity (common 'blood'), common culture and a sort of collective unconscious – almost all the factors widely understood as constituting nationality or ethnicity today (Glazer and Moynihan 1975; Smith 1986; Anderson 1991; Hobsbawm 1992; Miller 1995; see also n. 40 below).

What that inchoate nationhood signally lacked, however, was any strictly political component. To the contrary, a vital element in the earliest forms of Greek self-definition was a radically exclusive commitment to the individual and separate political community, often more on the scale of a town or even village than a city, of which one was a resident member. Greeks of another community were at first considered as much foreigners or strangers as were non-Greeks, and relations between Greek communities were as likely to be hostile as peaceful, let alone amicably co-operative. Indeed, identification with one's own community was strengthened by the peculiarly communal and civic form of infantry warfare that then predominated and gave political as well as military shape to the era (Hanson 1989; 1995).

It therefore required a major war of many Greeks against a non-Greek enemy on the scale of the Persian Wars written up by Herodotus to alter Greek politico-military self-definition decisively. Even the Persian Wars had only a limited effect, institutionally, since far more Greeks fought with than fought against the Persian-led invaders in 480 and 479, and what followed the loyalist Greeks' victory was more inter-Greek feuding and fighting rather than any broadly inclusive 'united nations' or 'united states' of Hellas. Nevertheless, that war of David against Goliath, and its geopolitical consequences, packed enough political punch to constitute decisively the other major factor determining the Greeks' overwhelmingly negative construction of 'barbarians'. Thereafter, being Greek comported a political as well as cultural component, in the form of civic republicanism as opposed to oriental despotism.(Steiner 1994; Thompson 1996; see also n. 13 below). That opposition, indeed, may have been the essential condition for the creation of Herodotus' history, if not of History itself (Momigliano 1979; Cartledge 1993a).

HELLENISM AFFIRMED: ETHNOGRAPHY AS HISTORY BY OTHER MEANS

Only the Spartans, in Herodotus's wide experience of the Greek world, preserved the old linguistic usage and refused to distinguish between Greek strangers (*xenoi*)

---

10   Walbank, 'The Problem of Greek nationality' (1951), repr. in Walbank 1985: 1–19; Finley, 'The ancient Greeks and their nation' (1954) repr. in Finley 1986: 120–33; cf. more broadly Saïd 1991.

and non-Greek 'barbarians', but then the literally xenophobic Spartans put their money where their mouths were and practised periodic expulsions of strangers, both Greek and non-Greek. The Spartans were odd Greeks in other ways too, so odd indeed that Herodotus reported some of their customs in his 'ethnographic' manner, almost as if he were describing those of non-Greeks (Cartledge 1993a). What is no less striking, though, is the relative disinterestedness with which he treated the customs of both Greeks and non-Greeks. Compare and contrast Herodotus' practice in this respect with, say, the triumphalist and ethnocentric annals of the pharaohs and the Assyrian monarchs, or with the Hebrew Bible's books of Samuel and Kings (Cook 1988: ch. 8). Herodotus was no mere sanctifying mythologer of an official Greek self-image (Momigliano 1966: 127–42). In this impartiality he had Homer's example to inspire him, but that by itself is unlikely to have been proof against the virulent new anti-barbarian prejudice. His own family background, with its close connections with non-Greek Carian families, may also have helped. But the primary explanation of his exceptional objectivity is to be sought rather in his acceptance of the revolutionary teachings of the itinerant Greek intellectuals known as the Sophists.

What was natural, what cultural or (merely) conventional in human social behaviour? To the ordinary Greek, as to most people in all societies, what was natural was right, and what their culture believed right or took for granted and habitually practised was natural. It required therefore an unusually powerful intellectual self-confidence to resist the everyday prejudice that Greek norms were natural and good, whereas those of barbarian culture were innately flawed. That antinomian confidence was possessed by the Sophist who blankly asserted that, since Greeks and non-Greeks had the same human bodies, the differences between them had to be (merely) conventional.[11] It was fully shared by Herodotus, who made the same point dramatically through the device of an emblematic (and *ben trovato*) anecdote set at the court of Persian Great King Darius and involving opposing Greek and Indian national burial customs. Every people, Herodotus taught by endorsing the praise-poet Pindar's adage 'custom is king of all' (3.38), regards its own customs as best, but whether they are in fact so is a different matter, one that has to be investigated empirically through a balanced cultural history of both Greeks and non-Greeks.[12]

Two illustrations will have to suffice, his treatment of women, and his discourse on despotic power. Respectable Greek women of citizen status were not supposed to be talked about, or even named, in public among unrelated men; it was an important part of a male Greek citizen's honour and self-esteem that he should be in a position to shield his womenfolk from such damaging talk (Cartledge 1993b).

---

11   The Sophist cited is Antiphon, possibly to be identified with the Athenian extreme oligarchic theoretician of 411: Gagarin and Woodruff 1995: 244–5 (fr. 7a 'On truth').

12   Sophistic relativism: de Romilly 1992. Herodotus' attitude to non-Greek religious customs: Gould 1994; Thompson 1996. R. Thomas has in preparation a monograph along the lines of 'Herodotus the Sophist'.

28

No such taboo constrained Herodotus (though it did the more conservative Thucydides), who indeed manipulated the usages of women in Greek and more especially barbarian societies as a means of indicating the proper, Greek way to treat them (Rosellini and Said 1978). Copulation in public, in the manner of beasts, placed a human society that tolerated such shameful (or shameless) behaviour at the furthest remove from the normative Greek end of the spectrum. Copulation in private but without benefit of legal matrimony ranked it only a little nearer. Those barbarian societies which, like Persia, practised polygamy were both naturally and culturally unGreek, but at least the Persians did recognize legal marriage and outlawed adultery. However, when a society combined polygamy with despotic power, as did Persia, then it entered Herodotus' alternative, political discourse of Greek self-definition.

The paradigm case for Herodotus' purposes was that of Great King Xerxes, son of Darius, whose invasion of Greece he represented as a war for the extinction of Greek liberty and imposition of slavery. It is no surprise to find Xerxes at the climax of the history involved back home in Susa in a sordid and ultimately gory plot to seduce a brother's wife, since one of oriental despotism's stigmata was precisely such gross mistreatment even (or especially) of close female relatives.[13] Another means employed by Herodotus to bring out the Greek–Persian polar dichotomy was to set against Xerxes ex-King Damaratus of Sparta, a political exile and formally a traitor to the loyalist Greek cause but nevertheless in Herodotus' book an unwavering spokesman for Greek civic values. Speaking of his fellow-countrymen with a properly Greek freedom of spirit and expression, Herodotus' Damaratus tells his incredulous Persian suzerain that, however greatly outnumbered, they will resist his horde to the death, since unlike his non-Greek subjects the Spartans acknowledge only one, non-human master – the law that they themselves have made and assented to as free citizens of a Greek community (7.104). That, *in nuce*, is Herodotus' deepest explanation of why the relatively few loyalist Greeks were able as well as willing to resist Xerxes' invasion, and to do so successfully.[14]

It was to Herodotus' great credit that he in no way disguised the Greeks' irreconcilable political divisions. Indeed, there is a tragic undertone to his despairing remark that 'in the three generations of Darius the son of Hystaspes, Xerxes son of Darius and Artaxerxes son of Xerxes more woes befell Greece than in the twenty generations preceding Darius' (6.98), since so many of those woes were self-inflicted. Following the Persian Wars the cause in chief was the rise of an Athenian Empire, many of whose more articulate Greek subjects felt – rightly or wrongly – that they had been delivered from an oriental despotism only to fall prey to a home-grown Greek tyranny (Tuplin 1985). Herodotus, however, who was

---

13   Hdt. 9.108–13, with Cartledge 1993a: 85–6. Add the mutilation of an anonymous sister-in-law of Xerxes, inflicted at the behest of Xerxes' wife Amestris, to the catalogue of despotic oriental mutilations in Steiner 1994: 154–5.

14   For a view of the *Histories* as a quasi-allegorizing tract for Herodotus' own times, see Moles 1996; cf. Thompson 1996.

himself for a time an imperial Athenian subject, did not scruple to state that in his view it was the Athenians who, on balance, had been the 'saviours of Greece' in the Wars, although he was careful to preface that contentious judgement by acknowledging that it would be 'resented by many' (7.139).

Moreover, it was to 'the Athenians' in an official response to their less than wholly resolute Spartan allies that Herodotus attributed a persuasive definition of Greekness which he clearly hoped would be found compellingly impressive far beyond its putative historical context of winter 480/79:

> Many very powerful considerations prevent us [from going over to the Persians]: first and foremost, the burning and destruction of our temples and the images of our gods; ... then, the fact of our being Greek – our common language, the altars and sacrifices we all share, our common mores and customs.
>
> (8.144)

Doubtless this was ideology, a conscious piece of retrospective mythologizing, but it was both symbolically apt and not without all purchase on fifth-century actuality, as Thucydides' very different history allusively testified.

HELLENISM UNDERMINED

Thucydides began his narrative where Herodotus had left off, in 478, but he normally avoided his predecessor's ethnographic manner and said remarkably little about non-Greeks, even though the war between Athens and Sparta had, he noted prefatorily, involved 'a part of the barbarian world' (1.1) and indeed had been eventually decided by the intervention of a barbarian, the Persian Cyrus the Younger, a great-grandson of Xerxes (2.65). The effect and no doubt the aim of this silence was to concentrate readers' attention on a Greek world 'convulsed' (3.82) by what we in Thucydides's honour refer to as the Peloponnesian War, that is, the war against Sparta and her allies seen from the Athenian side of the barricades. Thucydides was no less preoccupied than Herodotus with the image of Hellenism and Greek self-definition, but he opted for a negative approach and a portrayal imbued with sombrely tragic hues.[15]

In 431 the Hellenic world was at the height of its material prosperity and material preparedness. All the greater therefore was the ensuing catastrophe. The Spartans' announced war aim of liberating the Athenians' Greek subjects apparently appealed to many (2.8), or so it was maintained by Thucydides, himself no admirer of Athenian imperialism as it was conducted by hawkish democrats. With rare exceptions, however, the Spartans proved no more genuinely altruistic in their liberationist pretensions than their opponents. In the

---

15 The *Historical Commentary on Thucydides* in 5 vols by A. W. Gomme, as completed by A. Andrewes and K. J. Dover (Oxford, 1945–81), is standard; note also S. Hornblower's commentary in progress, of which two volumes (of 3) have so far appeared (Oxford, 1991–1996). Thucydides on Hellenism: Cartledge 1993a: 50–5.

course of an increasingly brutal and brutalizing war both sides cynically exploited liberation propaganda to intervene in the civil commotions that afflicted much of the Mediterranean Greek world. The destruction by mighty Athens of the little island-state of Melos in 416/15 was portrayed by Thucydides (5.84–116) as paradigmatic of the moral decline of Hellenism and the barbarization that had come to infect Greek self-perceptions and interrelations. The facts that Melos was oligarchically ruled and actively sympathetic to Sparta were not ignored but they were played down in his account.

In view of his minimal direct reference to barbarians, the one passage in which Thucydides does vent ethnocentric prejudice against them is all the more strikingly revelatory. In 413 a group of mercenaries from Thrace (roughly modern Bulgaria), whom the Athenians had hired but then found themselves unable to pay and dismissed, wreaked havoc and mayhem on a small village in central Greece as they returned home. They indiscriminately destroyed both sacred and secular property and slaughtered not only all the human beings they could lay their hands on, regardless of age and gender, but 'every living creature in sight' including farm animals and household pets. Thomas Hobbes, in the preface to his translation (the first to be done directly from the Greek), commented that Thucydides 'did never digress to read a lecture, moral or political upon his own text'. But this was not quite accurate. For in connection with the Thracian butchery Thucydides did explicitly opine that 'Like the most barbaric of the barbarian race, the Thracian people is most bloodthirstily murderous when its boldness is aroused', and of one particularly egregious act of slaughter involving all the boys in a school he remarked that 'This was a disaster for the whole community and second to no other disaster, being both unexpected and horrendous', indeed 'more deserving of lamentation for its magnitude than any other episode in the whole war' (7.29, 30).

Respect for Thracians generally will not have been enhanced by the fact that many were to be found among the permanent slave population at Athens – indeed, if Herodotus (5.6) is to be believed, poor Thracian parents actually sold their children to slave-traders. There is no doubt therefore that it was the barbarianness of the slaughter that particularly exercised Thucydides – the cowardly Thracians lacked the sort of true manly courage characteristic of Greeks that was required in a proper battle between adult men. However, there is reason to suspect that the specifically Thracian origin of these barbarian murderers may have contributed significantly to Thucydides' unusually explicit passion. His own father, Olorus, bore a Thracian name, thanks to a tie either of marriage or of ritualized friendship, and Thucydides himself retained hereditary property rights in the region (4.105).[16] It is not therefore unthinkable that by his condemnation of Thracians he was seeking to shore up his own compromised or challenged sense of personal Greek identity. This is very far from Herodotus' sadly unavailing project of buttressing through his historiography a parlous sense of Panhellenic solidarity.

---

16 Thucydides and Thrace: Herman 1990, at 349–50 (with alternative reconstructed *stemmata*).

PANHELLENIST FANTASIAS

As if in antiphonal response to Thucydides' threnody the first two decades of the fourth century resounded with speciously 'Panhellenist' speechifying and pamphleteering.[17] The Sicilian Sophist Gorgias and the Sicilian-Athenian speechwriter Lysias both delivered themselves of emollient pleas for Panhellenic unity at Olympia, one of the two major Panhellenic religious shrines (open to all and only Greeks for purposes of athletic competition). But their pleas went unheeded, as conquering Sparta and a resurgent Athens vied, all too successfully, for barbarian Persian financial support in their attempts to secure an Aegean hegemony. The upshot was a diplomatic victory for Great King Artaxerxes II that Xerxes would have envied. By the terms of the King's Peace (386) all the Greeks of Asia were once more consigned to Persian suzerainty, while the Greeks of Europe were implicated willy-nilly in a diplomatic settlement containing a barely veiled threat of renewed Persian military intervention, if only by proxy.

It was against that depressingly familiar background of inter-Hellenic strife that the Panhellenist refrain was taken up for their own reasons by two indefatigable Athenian publicists, the conservative, pro-Spartan *littérateur* Xenophon (*c.*427– 354) and the no less conservative, crypto-oligarchic pamphleteer Isocrates (436–338). Xenophon's first-hand knowledge of barbarians high and low was extensive, thanks to his service as a mercenary first under the Persian pretender Cyrus the Younger, then with a Thracian ruler, and finally under the Spartans in Asia led by his subsequent patron king Agesilaus II. Exiled from Athens as a traitor in the 390s, Xenophon spent most of the rest of his life in the Peloponnese, as a Spartan pensioner, thanks to Agesilaus. From his home base near Olympia he turned his hand to all the known genres of prose literature, including history, biography, memoirs and political theory. Indeed, he threw some of each into his every work, so that in the *Hellenica* ('Greek History'), for example, a covert pro-Spartanism keeps company with a powerful strain of rather banal philosophizing.[18]

Unlike Callisthenes (below), Xenophon was never quite a court historian, but a major theme of both the *Hellenica* and his posthumous encomium of Agesilaus was the conceit that, if only the mainland Greeks could be persuaded to unite under a strong leader to liberate their enslaved Asiatic brethren, the western Persian Empire was ripe for the plucking. In corroboration, he pointed to his own anti-Persian exploits with the 'Ten Thousand' Greek mercenaries under Cyrus but more especially to those of the 'Persian-hater' Agesilaus, whom he represented (or agreed to represent) as a second Agamemnon leading a new Trojan expedition. In fact, Agesilaus' hatred of Persia was not quite as consistent, let alone principled, as Xenophon sought to convey, but his supposed comment on the largest inter-Greek battle yet fought, 'Alas for for you, Hellas, those who are now dead were enough to

---

17 On Panhellenism generally see Perlman 1976.
18 Xenophon's historiography: Gray 1989; Cartledge 1993a: *passim*; Dillery 1995.

conquer all the barbarians had they lived' (*Agesilaus* 7.4), was typical of his or rather their Panhellenist big-talk.[19]

In his *Cyropaedia* ('Education of Cyrus'), however, a disguised monarchist tract cast in the form of a proto-romantic novel, Xenophon portrayed another face of the barbarian Other. Here the eponymous Cyrus the Great, founder of the Persian Empire, serves as the archetype of a positively regarded alien wisdom, a model for Greeks, or Greek rulers, especially those who foolishly harboured democratic aspirations, to copy rather than berate. This puts in their true perspective the sentimental nostrums of Panhellenism he expressed elsewhere.[20] Those pieties owed more to a dread of social revolution at home than to realistic hopes of military conquest and settlement in Asia, as transpires even more clearly through the voluminous works of Isocrates.[21]

Isocrates came from a wealthy slave-driven business background, but chose to make his living in and on the fringes of Athenian politics, first as a legal speech-writer, then as the successful founder of Greece's first institute for higher learning. He was a great fan of his own city's high culture, arguing that Hellenism, on which he placed a patriotic Athenian construction, was properly a matter of upbringing rather than of birth. This was an idea whose time was shortly to come in the post-Alexander 'Hellenistic' age. But he was no fan at all of his city's democratic constitution and feared that a recrudescence of Athenian democratic imperialism might jeopardize his enormous personal fortune. From his extended *Panegyricus* pamphlet of 380 onwards he contended unremittingly that Greeks should unite to subjugate and annex some large portion of the western Persian Empire, and drain off there a sufficiently large number of the hungry and rootless Greeks who might otherwise, he thought, covet and annex his estates. Disappointed in his initial addressees, the cities of Sparta and Athens, he turned thereafter to a string of kings or tyrants, until at last in Philip of Macedon (r. 359–336) he hit, by luck rather than judgement, upon a ruler who could deliver a Panhellenist agenda, if rather more aggressively than Isocrates would have wished.[22]

MACEDON AND GREECE

Two of Isocrates' pupils, reputedly, became historians, Ephorus of Cyme and Theopompus of Chios. Polybius (below) looked back to Ephorus as his only predecessor *qua* Greek 'universal' historian, but more immediately relevant is

---

19   Xenophon's Panhellenism is a major theme of Dillery 1995; cf. Cawkwell 1972; 1979.

20   The 'alien wisdom' of Xenophon's Cyrus: Momigliano 1975: 133–4; Hirsch 1985; Tatum 1989; Georges 1994.

21   Fuks, 'Isokrates and the social-economic situation in Greece' (1972), repr. Fuks 1984: 52–79. On Isocrates' politics generally see Baynes 1955; a more sympathetic picture in S. Usher, 'Isocrates: paideia, kingship, and the barbarians' in Khan (ed.) 1993: 131–45 (but see reply by Cartledge, ibid.: 146–53).

22   Isocrates and Philip: Perlman 1973; Markle 1976.

Theopompus' invention of a new historiographical mode – the construction of an era around the life and exploits of a single man. 'Never before', wrote Theopompus in the *Philippica* ('Philippic History'), 'had Europe borne such a man at all as Philip.'[23] The implied polarity of Europe and Asia goes back to Herodotus, but Theopompus' attitude to Macedon and indeed to Philip was by no means unambiguously complimentary. Like Agesilaus before him, Philip proclaimed his ultimate political goal to be a Hellenic war of revenge and conquest against Persia, but there were many Greeks, not only at Athens, who considered that as a Macedonian Philip's own Hellenism was not beyond cavil or challenge. Technically, he qualified as a Greek in that he and he alone of all the Macedonians was entitled, as king, to compete in the Olympics, but Demosthenes was exploiting a sympathetic vein when he sneered that in the old days you couldn't even get a decent slave from Macedon – the implication being that the Macedonians, being barbarians, were naturally slavish, but of poor quality even as slaves.[24] Yet it fell to Philip, paradoxically, to provide the closest semblance of a genuinely Panhellenic political union since the Persian Wars, indeed a more lasting and comprehensive such union in the form of what moderns call the League of Corinth founded in 338/7.[25]

The first agreed objective of this military-political alliance, which was founded after Philip's decisive overcoming of the last Greek resistance to Macedonian suzerainty of mainland Greece led by Athens and Thebes, was an invasion of Persia under Philip. However, although Philip laid the groundwork for, he was not himself destined to effect, the conquest of Asia, a process which would utterly transform among much else the issue of Greek self-definition both inside and outside the history-books. That was principally the achievement of his son Alexander the Great (r. 336–323). Yet, despite Alexander's best efforts to ensure that his official version of it was the universally accepted one, Alexander has ironically been rewarded with a near-total absence of extant contemporary literary commemoration.[26] In particular, we lack the contemporary histories of two northern Greeks: Callisthenes of Olynthus, younger relative of Alexander's old tutor Aristotle, whom Alexander appointed as his official court historian, and Hieronymus of Cardia, a high official who carved out something of a career on his own account in the bloody 'wars of succession' that followed Alexander's untimely death (Hornblower, J. 1981). Beginning with, and importantly through the medium of, their writings the cultural Hellenism of Isocrates, already something more universal and less political than that

---

23 Theopompus, *Philippic Histories*, Fragment 27 in Shrimpton 1991: 206 ('born' should be 'borne'); cf. Flower 1994.

24 Greek views of Macedon: Brunt 1976–83: I: xxxv–xxxviii; the negative view is already implicit in Herodotus, as persuasively interpreted by Badian 1994.

25 The so-called League of Corinth has been viewed rosy-tintedly as a proto-federal United States of Greece; for a soberly realistic appreciation, see rather Griffith in Hammond and Griffith 1979: 623–46.

26 The problem of Alexander-historiography is aptly summed up by its being compared to the search for the historical Jesus: failing reliable hard evidence, we all create an Alexander of our dreams. On the extant traditions see, e.g. Brunt 1976–83: I: xviii–xxxiv; II: 528–72.

of Herodotus, was revised and and redefined to suit its new 'Hellenistic' context, a world of Graeco-Macedonian territorial monarchies stretching from the Nile to the Oxus.[27]

Dispute continues, however, over the precise nature of the ensuing cultural mix (or mixes) of Hellenism (or Macedono-Hellenism) with the variety of subaltern oriental cultures the new rulers encountered.[28] At any rate, neither Alexander nor any of the so-called Successor kings should be seen as fundamentalist cultural crusaders, bent on exporting a militant Hellenism at any price. Alexander's callous execution of his official Greek historian Callisthenes in 327, for alleged treason in resisting the king's introduction of Persian court protocols, sufficiently shows that his own Hellenism was a supple instrument. But there is a sense in which Isocrates's non-genetic version of Hellenism provided the necessary lubricant to grease the moving parts of a massive and novel Greek political experiment in the bureaucratic control of many times more numerous 'barbarian' populations. At least it was now possible for some of these non-Greeks to become Greek by adoption, 'culture-Greeks', and to think, speak and behave in ways overtly identical to those of their political masters, with whom, in exceptional cases, they might also socialize.[29] For instance, so acculturated became the large community of diaspora Jews in Alexandria, Alexander's most potent eponymous foundation, that they had their sacred scriptures translated into the current *koine* ('common') dialect of Greek as early as the third century, since they no longer felt at home with classical Hebrew.

Against that relatively enlightened construction of Hellenistic Hellenism, however, there militated the long-standing negative stereotype of the barbarian, which had recently received its ultimate expression in the *Politics* of Aristotle. According to this, non-Greeks were often if not typically slavish by their very nature, and therefore unalterably so: it followed, by this perverse logic, that they ought also to be enslaved legally, for their own good. There is even a source alleging that Aristotle directly and explicitly advised his former pupil to treat all non-Greeks in this way on principle, but if so Alexander happily ignored the unhappy advice.[30] The tension between the two rival constructions of the barbarian – as irretrievably slavish or potentially Hellenizable – constituted a major and problematic ingredient in the historiographical heritage of Polybius.[31]

---

27 The liveliest if not necessarily always the most reliable recent overview of the Hellenistic world is Green 1993a. On Hellenistic politics see Will 1979–82. On society and economy, see Rostovtzeff 1941–53; with Momigliano 1994: 32–43. Hellenistic culture: Green 1993b.

28 See Cartledge's introduction to Cartledge *et al.* 1997.

29 'Culture-Greeks': Tarn 1952.

30 Alexander and Aristotle: Plut. *Moralia* 329b, with Hamilton 1973: 32–4 and 173 n. 10. Aristotle's 'natural slavery' doctrine: Cartledge 1993a: 120–6.

31 Classic is Walbank 1957–79; see also Walbank 1973; and on the historiography specifically, see further Derow 1994; Eckstein 1994; see also above, n. 6.

POLYBIUS BETWEEN GREECE AND ROME

Polybius (*c.*200–120) was a citizen of Arcadian Megalopolis, a comparatively new foundation of the 360s that stood as a testament of Sparta's definitive fall from the status of great power. Polybius's Megalopolis was Achaean, not merely in some nostalgic throwback to Homeric times, but as a member state of the Achaean federation instituted in 280. Such federations were both evidence of and an attempted compensation for the symbolic and actual debility of the individual city-state in the Hellenistic period foreshadowed in Philip's League of Corinth.[32] By the time of Polybius' birth, moreover, the centre of Mediterranean political gravity had shifted westwards, away from mainland Greece and its Macedonian overlords, away too from the other Successor kingdoms of Ptolemaic Egypt, Seleucid Asia and Attalid Pergamum, to the plain of Latium in Italy. As a leader of the Aetolian federation (Achaea's chief rival) had famously observed in 211, it was 'the clouds in the west' – i.e. Rome and her growing empire – that now loomed threateningly over Greek affairs.[33] Besides the threat Rome posed to the Greeks' political liberties, the western clouds jeopardized also their traditional self-identification by various forms of opposition to the barbarian.

By the end of the third century not only was Rome suzerain of Italy and Sicily, including the long-established Greek colonial settlements of the deep south (Magna Graecia or 'Great Greece' in Latin), but she had also twice defeated North African Carthage in major wars and was poised for further imperial advance on the eastern, Greek side of the Adriatic.[34] Polybius, looking back from the vantage point of the mid-second century, following Rome's definitive destruction of Carthage and conquest of all mainland Greece, saw Rome as the first power known to him to have established a truly universal dominion. He therefore considered the rise of Rome a fitting subject for his, the civilized world's first truly universal history, though he strove, as we shall see, to give his interpretation of that climax a peculiarly Greek spin.

Polybius was not, however, the first to write a history of Rome in Greek. He had been anticipated by the Roman senator Fabius Pictor, an active participant in the second Punic (Carthaginian) War of 218–202, Hannibal's war.[35] Polybius was not therefore the first to try to interpret the new superpower in Greek terms for a Greek-speaking readership, but he was the first Greek historian of Rome's imperial ascent, and his laboriously constructed forty-volume opus was written from deep inside what most of his Achaean and other Greek compatriots would have considered deeply alien, barbarian and indeed enemy territory. For in 167, as part of Rome's conquest of Greece, Polybius had been removed to Italy as one of the

---

32 Federal states: Walbank 'Were there Greek federal states?' (1976/7), repr. in Walbank 1985: 20–37.
33 'Clouds in the west': Polyb. 5.104.10, with Walbank 1957, ad loc.
34 Rise of Rome: Cornell 1995.
35 Fabius Pictor: Momigliano 1990: 80–108.

1,000 official Achaean hostages demanded by the Senate, and was not released until 150. Yet during his supposed house-arrest in and around Rome he had not languished abjectly but seized the main chance to ingratiate himself with a leading Roman, the younger Scipio, destroyer of Carthage in 146. He had also then conceived the project of writing a Thucydidean-style pragmatic history of Graeco-Roman relations, designed both to explain to the Greeks why they had been conquered and to recommend ways in which they might accommodate themselves to their new, subaltern status in an enlarged political universe.[36]

The latter became a necessity rather than a luxury after the Romans crushed a rebellion led by Polybius' own Achaean fellow-countrymen, and it was not simply for the sake of chronological tidiness that Polybius felt obliged to extend the compass of his history from his original terminal date of 168 to 146, the year in which Greece under the plangent title of 'Achaea' became a Roman protectorate. What made Polybius' historiographical task peculiarly delicate was that it required, in Herodotean terms, a defence of Greek enslavement by barbarians – ideologically, the world turned upside down. A further complication was that leading Romans had themselves willingly participated in the process of cultural Hellenization, to the extent indeed of having the calculated effrontery to appropriate the time-honoured Hellenic discourse of liberty and proclaim that they were ruling over Greeks in the name of their subjects' freedom! Moreover, these same Hellenized Romans were more than happy to manipulate the reverse side of that discourse, the Greeks' language and ideology of barbarism, for their own imperial ends. Polybius, nevertheless, made the very best of a rotten job, by in effect using Aristotle the political theorist to confute Aristotle the ethnocentric ideologue.[37]

Following a Greek tradition at least as old as Herodotus (5.78), Polybius found his most basic explanation of Rome's unprecedented and unparalleled military success in her domestic political arrangements, that is, in the workings of her constitution (*politeia*). This he analysed in neo-Aristotelian terms as a 'mixed' constitution, the mixture consisting in a balance rather than a blend of monarchy, aristocracy and democracy, in their good or best forms.[38] But whereas Aristotle in his desperate search for really existent examples of his ideal 'middling' constitution had even been prepared to accord barbarian Carthage honorary Greek status and treat it as an instance of the mixed polity, Polybius could not possibly follow his mentor here and more congenially, at least as far as his hosts were concerned, substituted for Carthage her Roman conqueror. In order, moreover, to get round the obstacle of Aristotle's barbarian-as-natural-slave doctrine, Polybius implicitly

---

36 Polybius between Greece and Rome: Momigliano 1975: 22–49; this chapter deals also with Posidonius, the first-century BCE Greek historian and philosopher from Syrian Apamea. On Roman–Greek mutual cultural reception see generally Gruen 1992.

37 Polybius' historiographical self-exculpation: 38.4.5-8, quoted by Derow 1994: 84–5. 'Freedom of the Greeks' propaganda: Badian 1970; Cartledge and Spawforth 1989: 74, 85.

38 Polybius on the *miktê* (mixed constitution): von Fritz 1954.

replaced the old Greek–barbarian polarity with a new tripartite classification of mankind into Greeks, barbarians and Romans.[39]

Ideology, however, was one thing, the facts – how it actually was – another. In the harsh world of *realpolitik* Rome ruled over a conquered Greece, albeit that the conquered managed to inject the conquerors' culture with a powerful dose of Hellenic serum. The many writings of Plutarch (*c*.45–120 CE), a Romanized Greek citizen of a small provincial town in old Greece, embody both the challenge to Greek identity posed by Roman political domination and one possible, creative response (Scardigli 1995, esp. Pelling 'Plutarch and Roman Politics', pp. 319–56; Swain 1996). Despite – or because of – Polybius and other willing adepts of the new order, Greeks of the early Roman imperial period were generally 'unable to determine whether the greatest military power in the Mediterranean world belonged to Us or to Them' (Browning 1989: 8). The eventual resolution of that crisis required the drastic step of the translation of the capital of the Roman Empire eastwards to Greek Byzantium, a new Rome, under Constantine in 330. Thereafter, and indeed down into the present era, Greeks have (sometimes) been content to call themselves 'Rhomaioi' ('Romans') as well as Hellenes.[40] But that solution of their crisis of identity was not available to Plutarch and his Greek contemporaries. Instead, Plutarch through the medium of historical biography set Greek and Roman culture, politics and morality in parallel, employing the device of individual comparisons and contrasts that favoured now one, now the other, while postulating or insinuating a fundamental homology between them.[41]

A no less imaginative reappropriation of the Hellenic past brings us back finally to our starting-point: the manipulation by Greeks of Plutarch's day and subsequently of their ancestors' heroic resistance to and/or conquest of Persia as a charter for their claim to 'favoured nation' status among Rome's many subjects. A particularly striking example of that claim may be descried, with an expert's eye, on the iconic monument of Hellenism *par excellence*, the Parthenon. There in 61/2 CE the Athenians, including prominently the (literally) new Roman citizen Tiberius Claudius Novus, had inscribed an honorific inscription for the emperor Nero that was conventional enough in its wording, but the setting of which gave it a far wider significance. By implying an honorific analogy between their city's past deeds and the contemporary exploits of Nero (or rather his army) in Armenia, the Athenians were seeking to do themselves as well as the emperor a favour.

---

39   The tripartition is first attested in the first century BCE (e.g. Cic. *De finibus* 2.49). On Diodorus Siculus, a Sicilian Greek universal historian contemporary with Cicero who incorporated Roman with Greek history, see Sacks 1990; 1994. A rather younger Greek contemporary, the antiquarian Dionysius from Herodotus' Halicarnassus, cunningly identified the Romans as Greek in origin: Gabba 1991; Hartog 1996: 183–200.

40   On modern Greek self-definition, see Herzfeld 1987; Just 1989; Peckham 1996.

41   The best account of Plutarch's parallelography known to me is Duff 1994.

The evidence suggests that the ploy was widely used in early Roman imperial Greece – and that it worked:

> If cherished cultural values meant that educated Greek provincials were predisposed to inject the memory of the Persian Wars with contemporary meaning, the incorporation of these wars into official [sc. imperial Roman] ideology is likely to have flattered the obsessive pride of subject-Greeks in their past.[42]

There, to conclude, is sanctifying mythology – with a vengeance.

REFERENCES

Ampolo, C. (1996) 'Per una storia delle storie greche', in S. Settis (ed.) *I Greci. I. Noi e i greci*, Turin.

Anderson, B. (1991) *Imagined Communities: Reflections on the Origin and Spread of Nationalism*, 2nd edn, London and New York.

Ascherson, N. (1995) *Black Sea*, London.

Badian, E. (1970) *Titus Quinctius Flamininus: Philhellenism and Realpolitik*, Cincinnati.

—— (1994) 'Herodotus on Alexander I of Macedon: a study in some subtle silences', in Hornblower 1994.

Baynes, N. H. (1955) 'Isocrates', in *Byzantine Studies and Other Essays*, London.

Browning, R. (1989) *History, Language and Literacy in the Byzantine World*, Northampton.

Brunt, P. A. (ed.) (1976–1983) *Arrian. History of Alexander*, 2 vols, Loeb Classical Library, Cambridge, MA.

Cartledge, P. (1989) 'The "Tacitism" of Edward Gibbon (two hundred years on)', *Mediterranean Historical Review* 4: 251–70.

—— (1990) 'Herodotus and "the Other": a meditation on empire', *Echos du Monde Classique/Classical Views*, n.s. 9: 27–40.

—— (1993a) *The Greeks: A Portrait of Self and Others*, Oxford.

—— (1993b) 'The silent women of Thucydides: 2.45.2 re-viewed', in R. M. Rosen and J. Farrell (eds) *NOMODEIKTES. Greek Studies in Honor of Martin Ostwald*, Ann Arbor.

—— (1995) '"We are all Greeks"? Ancient (especially Herodotean) and modern contestations of Hellenism', *Bulletin of the Institute of Classical Studies*, n.s. 2: 75–82.

—— and Spawforth, A. (1989) *Hellenistic and Roman Sparta: A Tale of Two Cities*, London and New York.

—— Garnsey, P. and Gruen, E. S. (eds) (1997) *Hellenistic Constructs: Culture, History and Historiography*, Berkeley.

Cawkwell, G. L. (ed.) (1972) *Xenophon. The Persian Expedition*, Harmondsworth.

—— (ed.) (1979) *Xenophon, A History of my Times*, Harmondsworth.

Cook, A. S. (1988) *History/Writing: The Theory and Practice of History in Antiquity and in Modern Times*, Cambridge.

Cornell, T. J. (1995) *The Beginnings of Rome: Italy and Rome from the Bronze Age to the Punic Wars (c. 1000–264 B.C.)*, London.

Derow, P. (1994) 'Historical explanation: Polybius and his predecessors', in Hornblower 1994.

Desideri, P. (1996) 'Scrivere gli eventi storici', in S. Settis (ed.) *I Greci. I. Noi e i Greci*, Turin.

Dillery, J. (1995) *Xenophon and the History of his Times*, London and New York.

---

42 Spawforth 1994: 246; the Parthenon inscription is *IG* ii².3277.

Dougherty, C. (1993) *The Poetics of Greek Colonisation: From City to Text in Archaic Greece*, New York.

—— (1994) 'Archaic Greek foundation poetry: questions of genre and occasion', *Journal of Hellenic Studies* 114: 35–46.

Duff, T. J. (1994) '"Signs of the soul". Moralism in Plutarch's *Lives*', unpublished Ph.D. thesis, Cambridge.

Eckstein, A. M. (1994) *Moral Vision in the Histories of Polybius*, Berkeley.

Finley, M. I. (1985) *Ancient History: Evidence and Models*, London.

—— (1986) *The Use and Abuse of History*, 2nd edn, London.

Flower, M. A. (1994) *Theopompus of Chios: History and Rhetoric in the Fourth Century B.C.*, Oxford.

Fornara, C. W. (1983) *The Nature of History in Greece and Rome*, Berkeley.

Fritz, K. von (1954) *Polybius and the Theory of the Mixed Constitution in Antiquity*, New York.

Fuks, A. (1984) *Social Conflict in Ancient Greece*, Jerusalem and Leiden.

Gabba, E. (1991) *Dionysius and the History of Archaic Rome*, Berkeley.

Gagarin, M. and Woodruff, P. (1995) *Early Greek Political Thought from Homer to the Sophists*, Cambridge.

Georges, P. (1994) *Barbarian Asia and the Greek Experience*, Baltimore and London.

Geyl, P. (1961) *Encounters in History*, London.

—— (1962) *Debates with Historians*, London.

Glazer, N. and Moynihan, D. P. (eds) (1975) *Ethnicity: Theory and Experience*, Cambridge, MA.

Gould, J. (1994) 'Herodotus and religion', in Hornblower 1994.

Gray, V. J. (1989) *The Character of Xenophon's Hellenica*, London.

Green, P. (1993a) *From Alexander to Actium: The Historic Evolution of the Hellenistic Age*, rev. edn, Berkeley.

—— (ed.) (1993b) *Hellenistic History and Culture*, Berkeley.

Gruen, E. S. (1992) *Culture and National Identity in Republican Rome*, Ithaca.

Hall, E. (1989) *Inventing the Barbarian: Greek Self-definition through Tragedy*, Oxford.

Hamilton, J. R. (1973) *Alexander the Great*, London.

Hammond, N. and Griffith, G. T. (1979) *A History of Macedonia*, II, Oxford.

Hanson, V. D. (1989) *The Western Way of War*, New York.

—— (1995) *The Other Greeks: The Family Farm and the Agrarian Roots of Western Civilization*, New York.

Hartog, F. (1988) *The Mirror of History. The Representation of the Other in the Writing of History*, Berkeley.

—— (1996) *Mémoire d'Ulisse. Récits sur la frontière en Grèce ancienne*. Paris.

Herman, G. (1990) 'Patterns of name diffusion within the Greek world and beyond', *Classical Quarterly* 40: 349–63.

Herzfeld, M. (1987) *Anthropology through the Looking-glass: Critical Ethnography in the Margins of Europe*, Cambridge.

Hirsch, S. W. (1985) *The Friendship of the Barbarians: Xenophon and the Persian Empire*, Hanover, NH.

Hobsbawm, E. J. (1992) *Nations and Nationalism since 1870: Programme, Myth, Reality*, 2nd edn, Cambridge.

Hornblower, J. (1981) *Hieronymus of Cardia*, Oxford.

Hornblower, S. (ed.) (1994) *Greek Historiography*, Oxford.

Just, R. (1989) 'The triumph of the ethnos', in E. Tonkin, M. McDonald and M. Chapman (eds) *History and Ethnicity*, London.

Khan, H. A. (ed.) (1993) *The Birth of the European Identity: The Europe–Asia Contrast in Greek Thought 490–322 B.C.*, Nottingham.

Macleod, C. W. (1983) 'Thucydides and tragedy', in id., *Collected Essays*, Oxford.

Markle III, M. M. (1976) 'Support of Athenian intellectuals for Philip: a study of Isocrates' *Philippus* and Speusippus' *Letter to Philip*', *Journal of Hellenic Studies* 96: 80–99.

Meister, K. (1990) *Die griechische Geschichtsschreibung*, Cologne.

Miller, D. (1995) *On Nationality*, Oxford.

Moles, J. L. (1996) 'Herodotus warns the Athenians', *Papers of the Leeds Latin Seminar* 9: 259–84.

Momigliano, A. D. (1966) *Studies in Historiography*, London.

—— (1975; repr. 1993) *Alien Wisdom: The Limits of Hellenization*, Cambridge.

—— (1977) *Essays in Ancient and Modern Historiography*, Oxford.

—— (1979) 'Persian Empire and Greek freedom', in A. Ryan (ed.) *The Idea of Freedom: Festschrift for Isaiah Berlin*, Oxford.

—— (1990) *The Classical Foundations of Modern Historiography*, Berkeley.

—— (1994) *Studies on Modern Scholarship*, Berkeley.

Murray, O. (1987) 'Herodotus and oral history', in H. Sancisi-Weerdenburg and A. Kuhrt (eds) *Achaemenid History* II. *The Greek Sources*, Leiden.

Nagy, G. (1996) *Poetry as Performance. Homer and Beyond*, Cambridge.

Peckham, R. Shannan (1996) 'Between East and West: the border writing of Yeoryios Vizyinos', *Ecumene* 3: 167–80.

Perlman, S. (1973) 'Isocrates' "Philippus" – a reinterpretation', in id. (ed.) *Philip and Athens*, Cambridge.

—— (1976) 'Panhellenism, the polis, and imperialism', *Historia* 25: 1–30.

Press, G. A. (1982) *The Development of the Idea of History in Antiquity*, Montreal.

Romilly, J. de (1992) *The Great Sophists in Periclean Athens*, Oxford.

Rosellini, M. and Saïd, S. (1978) 'Usages des femmes et autres *nomoi* chez les "sauvages" d'Hérodote', *Annuario della Scuola Normale Superiore di Pisa*, 3rd ser., 8: 945–1009.

Rostovtzeff, M. I. (1941–1953) *Social and Economic History of the Hellenistic World*, 3 vols, Oxford.

Sacks, K. S. (1990) *Diodorus and the First Century*, Princeton.

—— (1994) 'Diodorus and his sources: conformity and creativity', in Hornblower 1994.

Saïd, S. (ed.) (1991) *HELLENISMOS. Quelques jalons pour une histoire de l'identité grecque*, Paris.

Scardigli, B. (ed.) (1995) *Essays on Plutarch's Lives*, Oxford.

Segal, C. (1995) 'Spectator and listener', in J.-P. Vernant (ed.) *The Greeks*, Chicago.

Shrimpton, G. S. (1991) *Theopompus the Historian*, Montreal, London and Buffalo.

Smith, A. D. (1986) *The Ethnic Origins of Nations*, Oxford.

Spawforth, A. (1994) 'Symbol of unity? The Persian-Wars tradition in the Roman Empire', in Hornblower 1994.

Stedman, Jones, G. (1972) 'History: the poverty of empiricism', in R. Blackburn (ed.) *Ideology in Social Science: Readings in Critical Social Theory*, London.

Steiner, D. (1994) *The Tyrant's Writ: Myths and Images of Writing in Ancient Greece*, Princeton.

Swain, S. (1996) *Hellenism and Empire: Language, Classicism, and Power in the Greek World, AD 50–250*, Oxford.

Syme, R. (1958) *Tacitus*, 2 vols, Oxford.

Tarn, W. W. (and Griffith, G. T.) (1952) *Hellenistic Civilisation*, 3rd edn, London.

Tatum, J. (1989) *Xenophon's Imperial Fiction*, Princeton.

Thomas, R. (1992) *Literacy and Orality in Ancient Greece*, Cambridge.

Thompson, N. (1996) *Herodotus and the Origins of the Political Community. Arion's Leap*, New Haven, CT. and London.

Tuplin, C. J. (1985) 'Imperial tyranny: some reflections on a classical Greek political metaphor', in P. Cartledge and D. Harvey (eds) *CRUX. Essays in Greek History Presented to G. E. M. de Ste Croix*, Exeter and London.

Walbank, F. W. (1957–79) *Historical Commentary on Polybius*, 3 vols, Oxford.
—— (1973) *Polybius*, Berkeley.
—— (1985) *Selected Papers: Studies in Greek and Roman History and Historiography*, Cambridge.
Will, E. (1979–82) *Histoire politique du monde héllenistique*, 2 vols, 2nd edn, Nancy.
Woodman, A. J. and Luce, T. J. (eds) (1993) *Tacitus and the Tacitean Tradition*, Princeton.

3

RE-READING THE ROMAN HISTORIANS

Michael Comber

The combination of ethical and rhetorical preoccupations gives [antique historiography] a high degree of order, clarity, and dramatic impact. In the case of the Romans there is further a broad and comprehensive view of the extensive stage on which the political and military events occur. . . . The ethical and rhetorical approaches are incompatible with a conception in which reality is a development of forces. Antique historiography gives us neither social history nor economic history nor cultural history. These can only be inferred indirectly from the data presented.

(Auerbach, 1940)

Auerbach picks out ethical and rhetorical preoccupations as the two leading features of ancient historiography. Ancient historiography, in particular Roman historiography, was certainly ethical. And it was just as certainly rhetorical. But ethical historiography is not restricted to the ancient world.[1] Nor does anything prevent a work of history from combining incisive analysis with good writing. Indeed, good writing can facilitate analysis, be part of analysis (cf. Brunt 1980). Ancient historiography explored the truth as it saw it, and it explored it rhetorically. It demands also to be read rhetorically.

Ethical historiography was not an invention of the Romans. Already in Herodotus it is possible to trace an underlying pattern that might be called ethico-tragical – mutability of fortune, reciprocity of action (cf. Comber 1992) but it is not stridently assertive, not what the *History* was written to prove. It is assumed that the narrative of momentous events is sufficiently interesting in itself.

Thucydides similarly. There can still be detected an implied ethico-tragical subtext (cf. Macleod 1983), but it is even less pronounced than in Herodotus. It is

---

1   Cf. the final paragraph of Taylor 1965: 600. Recently, there even seems to have been a *fin-de-siècle* upsurge in the history of moral decline, e.g. Selbourne 1993. For a comparable 'end of *saeculum*' anxiety in the first century BC, cf. Weinstock 1971: 191ff.; Du Quesnay 1976.

true that Thucydides proclaims a more elevated purpose than his apparent target Herodotus:[2]

> And it may well be that my history will seem less easy to read because of the absence in it of a romantic element. It will be enough for me, however, if these words of mine are judged useful by those who want to understand clearly the events which happened in the past and which (human nature being what it is) will, at some time or other and in much the same ways, be repeated in the future. My work is not a piece of writing designed to meet the taste of an immediate public, but was done to last for ever.
>
> (i. 22.4)

But this may be seen as an example of literary *aemulatio* (rivalry) in a very combative form of writing.[3] And Thucydides' claim of didactic usefulness is very cautious and restrained. The assumption remains that the material is interesting in itself.

It is Polybius who stresses the didactic function of history. At the outset of his work, i. 1.2, Polybius states his twofold purpose: to provide useful training and experience for the practical politician; and to teach the reader how to bear the vicissitudes of fortune by describing those that have befallen others. There was also a further purpose; to explain, as a Greek, the Romans to the Greeks.[4] From now on Rome holds centre stage and the truly grand narrative enters historiography.[5] For Polybius, history meant universal history (iii. 32; also viii. 2.1–11, ix. 44). And universal history was Roman history (i. 3.4–5; also iii. 1.4, iv. 2.1ff.) since, owing to the workings of a seemingly purposive *Tyche* (Fortune), Rome had reached the position of world dominion.

Several of the key features of Roman historiography are already evident in Polybius: the sense of manifest destiny (cf. Williams 1968: 5–9); linked to which is the idea that Rome is the end of history;[6] together with its obverse, the idea that present-day Rome is the beginning of the end, the anxiety about the onset of decline from the summit of power.[7] This last is markedly different from the tragic notion of

---

2 Prompting Collingwood to take him to task for being a 'psychological' historian, a less 'pure' historian than Herodotus (Collingwood 1956 [1946]: 28–31).

3 Cf. e.g. Hecataeus' preface: 'Hecataeus of Miletus gives his account in the following way. I write up these matters as they seem to be true. For the accounts given by the Greeks are both many and ridiculous, so they seem to me.' See also Hesiod, *Theogony*, 27–8.

4 For Polybius' sources, see Walbank 1957–79: 26–35.

5 It is likely, however, that the Alexander historians introduced this. What is at issue here can be easily illustrated by a brief comparison of the *Odyssey* and the *Aeneid*. Odysseus' *nostos* (return) is that of a private individual; Aeneas' *nostos* is given world-historical significance. For the term 'grand narrative' see Lyotard 1984.

6 Cf. Gransden 1990: 48ff. For the present as the end of the history, see Hegel. There is, of course, a sense in which all history is the history of the present. But this is particularly so in the case of Roman history.

7 vi. 10.3, vi. 57.1–7, with Walbank ad loc., also Walbank 1957–79: I, 173.

divine *phthonos* (envy) and the dangers of great power that has fed into Herodotus and, arguably, into Thucydides too.[8]

The Romans were undoubtedly hospitable to a great deal of what they found in Greek and Hellenistic historical writing. But Roman historiography also had its own native traditions that distinctively reshaped this inheritance. And these were religious, sacral, monumental and nationalistic: the pontifical tradition of *annales* mentioned, for example, by Cicero:[9]

> History meant merely the compiling of annals. It was for this purpose, in other words, for the preservation of public records, that from the beginning of Rome right up to the pontificate of Publius Mucius (133 BC), the Pontifex Maximus used to commit to writing the complete history of each year. He made a fair copy, and put up the tablet in his residence so that it became public knowledge: even nowadays these are called the 'Great Annals'.

The convergence of the religious origins of the form with the moralizing tendency in Roman thought produces a compelling version of the trajectory of Roman history: the Romans' success depended upon respect for the gods and preservation of the ways of their forefathers.[10] This is clear in the work that may be credited with imposing a Roman stamp on historical epic, Ennius' *Annales*:[11]

> Moribus antiquis res stat Romana virisque[12]
> (The Roman state is built on ancient customs and on men)

Such an outlook persists both in poetry,[13] and, of course, in historical prose. One hundred and fifty years or so after Ennius,[14] the annalistic historian Livy, *Praefatio* 9, urges his readers to consider 'what kind of lives our ancestors lived, who were the

---

8   There is, of course, a deep vein of pessimism in ancient thought, e.g. the five races of men in Hesiod, *Works and Days*, 109–201. Edmunds 1975 likens the *stasis* chapters of Thucydides, iii. 82–3, to Hesiod's Iron Age. See also Macleod 1979. But the discourse of decline was given particular stress by the Roman historians. Cf. Williams 1968: ch. 9, Excursus, 'The Roman view of historical explanation', 619–33. See also Edwards 1993, esp. 1–33.

9   *De oratore* ii. 52. Cf. Frier 1979. We can get some idea of what these annals might have been like from, e.g. Livy ii. 21. But, on the question of the frequency, or the lack of it, with which the *Annales Maximi* were actually consulted, see Rawson 1971.

10   Their influence was omnipresent. From the walls of Roman houses, the wax masks of distinguished ancestors who had held curule office looked down. And whenever a member of the family was carried to his grave, these masks would be taken from the walls and displayed in the funeral procession, worn by actors dressed in the official garb and insignia of the deceased. Cf. Polybius vi. 53.4ff. with Walbank ad loc.; Livy xxxviii. 56.12–13; Diodorus xxxi. 25.2; Pliny, *NH* xxv. 4–14; Suetonius, *Vesp.* 19. See Price 1987, esp. 62–70.

11   For the title Annales, cf. Skutsch 1985: 6f.

12   *Annales* V.1 (Skutsch).

13   Cf. e.g. Horace, *Odes* iii. 6.5: dis te minorem quod geris, imperas (It is by holding yourself the servant of the gods that you rule). Cf. Brunt 1978.

14   For the date of Livy's first pentad, see Ogilvie 1965, at i. 19.2–3 and iv. 20.5–11; Luce 1965; on the preface, see Woodman 128–34; also Oppermann 1955: 87–8.

45

men, and what the means both in politics and war by which Rome's power was first acquired and subsequently expanded'.[15]

Praefatio 9 also invites the reader to consider how far things have declined:

> First, the sinking of the foundations of morality as the old teaching was allowed to lapse, then the rapidly increasing disintegration, then the final collapse of the whole edifice, and the dark dawning of our modern day when we can neither endure our vices nor face the remedies needed to cure them.

The terms in which Livy refers to decline recall his predecessor Sallust. *Avaritia* (avarice) and *luxuria* (luxury) make an appearance.[16] And at *Praefatio* 4, Livy writes of Rome 'now labouring under its own size' (*iam magnitudine laboret sua*) and of the present period when 'the might of an imperial people is beginning to work its own ruin' (*praevalentis populi vires se ipsae conficiunt*). The form of expression here prompts speculation. Similar phrases occur in two *Epodes* of Horace, 7.10:

> urbs haec periret dextera
> (This city might perish by its own right hand)

and, more closely, in 16.2:

> suis et ipsa Roma viribus ruit
> (And Rome through her own strength is tottering)

also in Propertius, iii. 13.60

> frangitur ipsa suis Roma superba bonis
> (Proud Rome is being destroyed by its own prosperity)

and Manilius, i. 912:

> imperium suis conflixit viribus ipsum
> (The empire itself is in conflict through its own strength)

It is tempting to suppose that all these writers had the same original analysis in mind, an analysis that is almost certainly to be traced back to the lost preface of Sallust's *Histories* (cf. Nisbet 1984; Woodman 1988: 131f.).

Sallust draws upon a different tradition from the annalistic one:[17] the tradition of the elder Cato. Cato, the man who brought Ennius to Rome,[18] did for historiography what Ennius did for epic: he added a Roman voice.[19] Cato rejected native Roman

---

15 Such an edifying exemplum is provided by the tale of Lucretia's *pudicitia* (chastity) with which Book i. 57–9 culminates. For the exemplary function of history as the apportioner of praise and blame, cf. also Tacitus, *Annals* iii. 65.1. But on this last, see Luce 1965.

16 *Praef.* 11. But not *ambitio* (ambition). Cf. Ogilvie 1965: 23f. and ad loc. For Livy, *ambitio* sets in as early as the regal period. Cf., e.g., i. 35.2, where Tarquinius Priscus is said to have been the first to have sought the kingship *ambitiose*.

17 Though the *Histories*, apparently, did not abandon the annalistic form.

18 Nepos, *Cato* 1.4.

19 Whether or not Cato was the first to attempt Roman history in the vernacular, what Mommsen says (*RG* i. 937) is basically correct: 'Prose offered him a more favourable basis [than poetry] and so he used all his unique versatility and energy to create a prose literature in his native language.'

annales as trivial, arid, uninterpreted.[20] He also rejected annalistic chronology, preferring to arrange his material by subject-matter, *capitulatim*.[21] His tone, however, was that of the *magni viri antiqui* (great men of old): rugged, Roman, censorious, archaizing.[22] And his significance for the subsequent development of historical prose was immense (cf. Badian 1966: 8ff.). After him, history was seen as the proper leisure-time activity of a man in public life;[23] and, furthermore, as an appropriate vehicle for polemic and *apologia* (Cato included his own political speeches, but, seemingly, no one else's). Finally, and most importantly, Cato wrote in Latin for his countrymen; the Greeks no longer counted politically: 'the history that mattered was now being written by Romans for Romans (Badian 1966: 10).

After Cato, therefore, there were two strands available to the practitioners of Roman history, *annales* and the *res gestae* of public figures. And, after Cato, those practitioners were predominantly men of affairs who viewed Roman history as an arena in which to carry on contemporary political struggles,[24] Roman history meant largely political and military history and was very much recent history, the history in which the authors themselves had often played a part. So, the stress was on the modernity of history and, in a particularly Roman twist, on the relevance of history to their own day, to contemporary politics. This is somewhat reminiscent of Polybius. But Polybius would not have countenanced the distortions made by Valerius Antias and Licinius Macer to enhance the history of their *gentes*.[25] And it is quite unlike Thucydides, who never claims that the historian can have any influence on the present. Both he and Herodotus are writing for future generations as much as for their own, and they stress this. That is a very uncommon note in Roman history. Roman historians seem to want to affect events now, in their own day.

---

20   iv. 1 (Chassignet); cf. Sempronius Aseillio 1–2 (Peter).

21   The Greek historian Ephorus had already done this, cf. Diodorus Siculus v. 1.4. Although Cato affected hostility to Hellenism, the very title of his work *Origines*, a translation of the Greek *Ktiseis*, bespeaks Hellenistic influence. Cf. von Albrecht 2: 'Cato is not only an opponent of the Greeks, but also their student.'

22   Norden i. 165, describes the style of the *Origines* as 'curt, rough, powerful'. Censorious, cf. e.g. vii. 9–10 (Chassignet) on the luxury of women; archaic, cf. e.g. the use of *ques* in i. 1 (Chassignet); curt, cf. the famous *rem tene, verba sequentur* 'stick to the point, the words will follow' (fr. 80.2 J).

23   Cf. i. 1–2 (Chassignet); also fr. 3 (Peter). This was quite different from Greece, as Cicero points out (*De oratore* 2.55). Thucydides was, of course, a man of affairs, as were Xenophon and Polybius, but generally speaking, Greek historians were not. Among Roman historians the proportions were reversed: Fabius Pictor, Cato, L. Calpurnius Piso, Licinius Macer, Sallust, Asinius Pollio and Tacitus were all political figures. But there is no sign of any political career for Cassius Hemina, Claudius Quadrigarius, Valerius Antias or Livy.

24   e.g. C. Gracchus, who wrote a propagandist biography of his brother; L. Calpurnius Piso (cos. 133), who wrote history from an aristocratic standpoint; C. Licinius Macer; C. Asinius Pollio; Sallust; and later, of course, Augustus. History in some ways, then, becomes assimilated to the memoir. Unlike Greek history, see n. 23 above. But, in recent times, cf. e.g. Winston Churchill, Harold Wilson, Barbara Castle, Tony Benn. Contemporary Conservative politicians appear to have found the form particularly congenial: Cecil Parkinson, Alan Clark, Kenneth Baker, Margaret Thatcher.

25   e.g. the *gens Valeria* with its thirty 'firsts', the prominence given to the Licinii. For Polybian bias, cf. Walbank 1957–79: 1. 11ff. Cicero (*Brutus*, 62) was alive to the dangers of the falsehoods put about in funeral laudations becoming historical currency.

Greek historians are more concerned with understanding and recording events for their own sakes or for future generations.[26]

Sallust fits into this pattern well. He came to writing history after retirement from a highly colourful if chequered political career,[27] and found in it ample opportunity for *apologia* (*BJ* 3.4.3f., 4.7f.; *BC* 3.3ff.) and social and moral usefulness.[28] And, like Cato, he abandoned the annalistic form. At least, he did so for his two monographs, *Catiline* and *Jugurtha*,[29] in which by concentrating upon a short span of history (a period of revolutionary unrest, a war) as wholly symptomatic of the state of the times,[30] he explores the nature and extent of Rome's moral decline. To some extent, Sallust moves away from the personal, individual causation of Cicero's letter to Lucceius.[31] In the *Catiline*, for example, he shows himself to be aware of economic and social factors: the impact of Sulla's veterans, the problem of debt (*BC* 11–13, 36–9). (But the prime cause is still socio-moral, the collapse of the *mos maiorum* (custom of our ancestors) (e.g. *Hist.* fr. 16 (Maur.)). For Sallust, the onset of decline coincided with the destruction of Carthage in 146 BC.[32] It was the cohesive force of the *metus hostilis* (enemy threat) that kept the moral fibres taut.[33] With the removal of

---

26 Though F. Nietzsche 1983: 57–123, says almost the exact opposite about the difference between the Greek and Roman approaches to history.

27 He was tribune in 52, expelled from the Senate in 50, praetor in 46, then governor of Africa, accused of extortion in 45, but acquitted after lavish bribery.

28 *BJ* 4.1f., 4.5f.; *BC* 3.1f. For the functionalism, history as the illustration of, and inspiration to, *virtus*, cf. Cicero, *Pro Arch.* 14. Note also the uneasy defensiveness in Sallust's attempt to justify the writing of history in Roman terms, the anxious stress on the greater benefit accruing to the state from his *otium* than from others' *negotium*. This is prompted by the Roman elevation of the active above the contemplative life, of *negotium* (work) above *otium* (leisure). The ideology is summed up by Cicero, *De off.* i. 70. Cf. the self-depreciation of Catullus, 51.13; and of Virgil, *Georg.* iv. 563f. See André 1966; Balsdon 1969.

29 Coelius Antipater is regularly said to have introduced the form of the historical monograph to Rome, e.g. by *RE* iv. 185ff. This is misleading. Coelius' work on the Hannibalic War was in seven books (*HRR* i. ccxv). What Coelius did was to break with the annalistic form by composing history *kata meros* and concentrating on a single war of brief compass. Indeed, *kata meros*, or *carptim* (*BC* 4.2), would be the closest approximation in the ancient world to the term 'monograph'. It is clear from Cicero's letter to Lucceius (*Ad fam.* v. 12) that the idea of the monograph was already current before Sallust (cf. Syme 1964: 57f.) But it seems to have been Sallust who was the first Roman exponent of what we would understand by the word. Such 'slenderness' has much in common with the aesthetic of the neoteric movement in Latin poetry.

30 This is one of the many signs of the influence of Thucydides upon Sallust, cf. Scanlon 1980. Cf. also Levene 1992.

31 In which Cicero urges Lucceius to indulge his friendship and enhance Cicero's role in quelling the Catilinarian conspiracy.

32 Other turning-points were chosen by other authors, Piso preferring 154 (Pliny, *NH* xvii. 244), Polybius 168 (xxxi. 25.3, vi. 575), and Livy's annalistic source 187 (xxxix. 6.7), when the army of L. Manlius Vulso returned from Asia after its victories over the Gauls, and brought foreign *luxuria* back with them. The source of this claim, at least in part, again appears to have been Piso. Pliny (*NH* xxxiv. 14) lists three items which according to Piso were first introduced to Roman society at Manlius's triumph, and these three items are among those found in Livy's list of things first brought over by Manlius's army. (I owe this reference to M. Pobjoy.)

33 The direct relationship between peace and decadence inverts Thucydides' view that war produces decline, expressed in iii. 82–3, a favourite passage of Sallust, cf. *BJ* 41–2.

Carthage, *virtus* (virtue)[34] is progressively assailed by *ambitio, avaritia* and *luxuria* in that order.[35] Society then falls into total decline, utterly at the mercy of *fortuna* (fortune).[36]

Much of this is influenced by rhetorical *convicium saeculi* (the lament over declining standards; literally, abuse of the times)[37] and it is easy to dismiss Sallust as hypocritical.[38] But, though over-schematic, Sallust's analysis is very far from being completely absurd or naive.[39] And it is very powerfully represented. The argument would have made considerably less impact if it had not been well expressed and well ordered. In other words, if it had not employed rhetoric.[40] Rhetoric, that is, not in its modern sense as a synonym for insincerity and bombast, but in its historical sense, the art of speaking well, the theory of effective communication in speech and writing, and the practice of it. In one classic formulation (Plato, Gorgias, 453a) rhetoric is defined as 'the manufacturer of persuasion'. This covers not only the way speeches are written, but also the way the whole presentation is persuasive, argues a particular case or interpretation and sets it out to be as cogent as possible: to put something across to the audience, deploying all the resources of *elocutio*, style, *dispositio*, arrangement, and *inventio*, the discovery of what needs to be said. And history, as Cicero points out (*Laws* 1.5) is an '*opus oratorium maxime*' (especially oratorical work). Tacitus had been one of the most foremost orators of his day. His *Annals*, then, will furnish an appropriate illustration.

ELOCUTIO

The period of the Early Empire was one that was grim, twisted, threatening. The smooth, flowing, periodic style of Cicero and Livy would have been unsuitably

---

34 For Sallust, a more comprehensive term than that espoused by the *nobiles*. He crucially shifts the emphasis towards the internal workings of the *ingenium* (natural ability) and *animus* (mind) and away from the external marks of birth and status. Thus virtue emerges as a broader concept, adapted to the meritocratic needs of the *novi homines* (in the widest sense, the first men of their family to hold curule office; in a special sense, the first to attain the consulship, something which, as far as we know, was achieved on only fifteen occasions between 366 and 63 BC. In Sallust, *novus homo* always involves a sense of opposition to the privilege of the *nobiles* as an exclusive social group). But *virtus* demands constant vigilance if it is not to be corrupted into *vitium* (vice), to which it is perilously close. Cf. *BC* 11.1). Sallust's approach, to focus on *virtus* in a time when, on his own theory of decline, there is none, is neatly inverted by Livy: the best examples of *virtus* are to be found by going much further back. Cf. Earl chs. 2 and 3. On the proems, see Büchner 1982: 93–130.

35 For luxury as an importation from abroad, see Griffin 1976.

36 Sallust combines the Thucydidean *gnome* (intelligence) and *tyche* with the topos of *arete* (virtue) and *tyche*. Cf. Edmunds 1975.

37 See Horace, *Odes*, ii. 15 with Nisbet and Hubbard ad loc.; Elder Seneca, *Controversiae* i. pr. 6ff. Cf. Bonner 1949: 61.

38 As Gibbon does most elegantly (*The Decline and Fall*, ch. 31): 'The historian Sallust, who usefully practised the vices which he has so eloquently censured.' Cf. Laistner 1947: 48.

39 Sallust's view, that a sudden and vast influx of wealth is corrosive of the *mos maiorum* and produces *anomie* bears a striking resemblance to that which Émile Durkheim puts forward in *Suicide*. Cf. Giddens 1985: 45: 'In circumstances of social disruption, the moral codes that customarily regulate individuals' social activities are placed under strain, and tend to lose their hold.'

40 On the whole topic, see Woodman 1988.

soothing. Tacitus chose a jagged, contorted, tense, anxious style, a style designed to keep the reader on edge, put the reader through it, a style like that of Sallust:[41] 'sentences cut short, unexpected halts, a dark conciseness'.[42] An important modification, however, is made by Syme (ii. 711–45; cf. Goodyear 1968). In *Annals* xiii–xvi, the Neronian books, Tacitus returns to a more 'normal' and more Ciceronian style. This carries meaning. The style simplifies as the autocracy becomes more overt, more straightforward. Style and historical analysis are interlocked.

DISPOSITIO

Tacitus may make a disingenuous complaint about the obstacles of the annalistic form (*Ann*. iv. 71.1) but his mode of narration is extremely adroit, juxtaposing and balancing different events, sequences, episodes, for connection, relief, contrast and implicit comment. Numerous examples are to hand, ranging from the large scale to the small scale. There are the parallels and contrasts between the Tiberian and Neronian books that reinforce the point made by the shift of style: the Neronian age is a cruder age than the Tiberian, its brutality is more naked.[43] Or the pointed ring-composition of *Annals* i.[44] Or the delaying of Sejanus's major entrance until *Annals*

---

41 Sallust might very well have viewed the florid, 'Asianist', and hence imported and unRoman, style of Cicero as itself a symptom of the all-pervasive decadence he sought to expose and berate.

42 Seneca, *Epistulae* 114.17. Cf. McDonald 1975. Tacitus was quite capable of writing in a Ciceronian style when appropriate, as the *Dialogus* shows.

43 The suspicions about Livia's role in Augustus' death (*Ann*. i. 5.1) ~ Agrippina's poisoning of Claudius (Ann. xii. 66ff.); *primum facinus novi principatus* (Agrippa Postumus, *Ann*. i. 6.1) ~ *prima novo principatu mors* (Junius Silanus, *Ann*. xii. 1.1); Livia ~ Agrippina; Germanicus ~ Corbulo; Sejanus ~ Tigellinus. Cf. Martin 1955; Syme 1958: i. 481ff.

44 *Ann*. i. 1.1: *Urbem Romam a principio reges habuere; libertatem et consulatum L. Brutus instituit* – *Ann*. i. 81.4: *quantoque maiore libertatis imagine tegebantur tanto eruptura ad infensius servitium.* Pace Auerbach, Tacitus in fact prompts the reader to infer a great deal about historical change. Auerbach's point, presumably, is that the idea of history as the product of forces is inimical to an ethical approach, in which crucial importance is placed upon individual moral choice. But is the opposition so clear-cut? 'Men', says Karl Marx, 'make their own history, but they do not make it under circumstances chosen by themselves, but under circumstances directly encountered, given and transmitted from the past.' And does Auerbach not underestimate the sensitivity of Tacitus, at least, to the role played in history by the complex interaction of character and circumstance? The principate was inevitable, and Tacitus recognized this (cf. *Hist*. i. 1.1; *Ann*. i. 9.5, iv. 33.2). He recognized, too, that it had its own internal dynamic. It imposed upon each successive emperor anew the same clear pattern, a pattern of ruthless dynastic murder (see n. 43 above), secrecy, hypocrisy and senatorial flattery. And yet it also allowed wide and dangerous scope for an emperor's character to express itself, and thus to affect and shape events in turn. It is the precise balance between the nature of the man and the nature of the principate itself that so exercises Tacitus in the Tiberian books of the *Annals*. *Dissimulatio* (dissimulation), for example, is a prominent feature both of the principate and of Tiberius. (For Tiberius' *dissimulatio* as an independently attested historical issue, see *Tabula Siarensis* Fragment II, Column b, 16 (Sherk 66.) A similarly kaleidoscopic combination of human and extra-human agency is evident in epic and tragedy. Cf. E. R. Dodds's notion of 'overdetermination', Dodds 1951: chs. 1 and 2. And the problem is one that we still wrestle with today. The agonizing over causation in the terrible Bulger case of 1993 attests to this: was such evil inherent in the child murderers or inherent in the society that produced them?

iv. 1 in order to underscore the year AD 23 as the turning-point of Tiberius' reign.[45] Or the way Capri emerges as an island haven, iv. 67, amid the grim realities of the amphitheatre disaster at Fidenae and the fire on the Caelian hill, iv. 62–5, and the Titius Sabinus affair, iv. 68ff. Or, finally, the predominance of the ablative absolute construction to express the consular year, a construction that cuts the consuls off from the rest of the sentence and, by extension, from the real business of government under the principate.[46]

Suggestive arrangement contributes significantly to the development of key themes such as the recurrent contrast with the Republic. This contrast is at once carried by the form itself. For *annales* are Republican in origin. Part of the point in Livy is to show the Republic going through its paces; part of the point in Tacitus is to show Rome going through a very different set of paces (Ginsburg 1981; and see n. 46). There are historiographical consequences, and Tacitus takes these up in *Ann.* iv. 32 and 33, where he discusses the difficulties and dangers of writing imperial history. This is immediately followed, *Ann.* iv. 34 and 35, by the fate of Cremutius Cordus, whose attempt to write history in the Republican manner landed him in court on a charge of *maiestas* (treason) for praising Brutus and Cassius.[47] The issue of freedom, and its demise, has already arisen earlier in the book, *Ann.* iv. 20–1, in the striking contrast between two different types of statesmen, Marcus Lepidus and Calpurnius Piso (cf. Wirszubski 1950: 166): the former prefiguring Agricola and Tacitus himself by collaborating with a bad emperor and attempting to ameliorate his behaviour, the latter prefiguring the more intransigent opposition against Nero. There then come in rapid succession several episodes illustrating the clash of freedom and servitude: first *Ann.* iv. 23–6, Tacfarinas leading all his Numidian savages '*cuncti quibus libertas servitio potior*' (all who preferred liberty to bondage);[48] next the slave-war started by Titus Curtisius, *Ann.* iv. 27; and finally, *Ann.* iv. 28, the degrading spectacle that marks the total lack of freedom at Rome, Vibius Serenus hauled back from exile, shaking his chains at his accuser, his own son. By *Ann.* iv. 74, with Tiberius on Capri, freedom has reached its nadir. And the book ends, *Ann.* iv. 75, with a dynastic marriage. Tacitus forbears to mention the offspring of this marriage: the emperor Nero.

---

45 Book iv opens with a unique mention of Tiberius' regnal year. Sejanus' appearances have been carefully rationed up to this point: i. 24.1; i. 69.5; iii. 16.1; iii. 29.4; iii. 35.2; iii. 66.3; iii. 72.3. There are further deferrals for the same purpose. It is clear from Dio LVII. 19.6 that the concentration of the praetorian guard into one camp mentioned by Tacitus in *Ann.* iv. 2.1 in fact took place in AD 20 and the 'state-of-the-nation' chapters, iv. 5 and 6, are held back from AD 14. Tacitus is unusual in fixing upon AD 23 as the turning-point. Both Suetonius and Dio preferred the death of Germanicus in AD 19.

46 Cf. Martin and Woodman 1989, at iv. 1.1.

47 This picks up *Ann.* iii. 76.2, the funeral of the grand Roman lady, Junia, niece of Cato, wife of Cassius, sister of Brutus.

48 *Ann.* iv. 24.1. Tacfarinas has already been compared to Spartacus, *Ann.* iii. 73.2. I owe these points to Dr C. B. R. Pelling.

INVENTIO

In an important chapter LIII. 19, Dio discusses the problems of writing imperial history. It deserves to be quoted in full:

> Thus the constitution was reformed at that time, as I have explained, for the better, and greater security was thereby achieved: it would indeed have been impossible for the people to have lived in safety under a republic. However, the events that followed that period cannot be told in the same way as those of earlier times. In the past all matters were brought before the Senate and the people, even if they took place at a distance from Rome: in consequence everybody learned of them and many people recorded them, and so the true version of events, even if considerably influenced by fear, or favour, or friendship, or enmity in the accounts given by certain authors, was still to a significant extent available in the writings of the others who reported the same happenings, and in the public records.
>
> But in later times most events began to be kept secret and were denied to common knowledge, and even though it may happen that some matters are made public, the reports are discredited because they cannot be investigated, and the suspicion grows that everything is said and done according to the wishes of the men in power at the time and their associates. In consequence much that never materializes becomes common talk, while much that has undoubtedly come to pass remains unknown, and in pretty well every instance the report which is spread abroad does not correspond to what actually happened. Besides this, the very size of the empire and the multitude of events which take place simultaneously make it very difficult to report them accurately. In Rome, for example, and in the subject territories events crowd upon one another, and in the countries of our enemies there is something happening all the time, indeed every day. Concerning these matters nobody other than those directly involved can easily obtain clear information, and many people never even hear in the first instance of what has occurred. So in my own account of later events, so far as these need be mentioned at all, everything I shall say will follow the version that has been made public, whether this is really the truth or otherwise. But in addition to these reports, I shall give my own opinion, as far as possible, on such occasions as I have been able – relying on the many details I have given from my reading or from hearsay, or from what I have seen – to form a judgement which tells us something more than the common report.

Much imperial history, then, took place behind closed doors and was shrouded in mystery. Hard facts were difficult to come by. There was, therefore, considerable scope for speculation and dramatic recreation. In other words, for *inventio*. A caveat, however, voiced by D. A. Russell:[49]

> [Inventio] is not 'invention' if by that we imply some degree of imaginative creation. It is simply the 'discovery' of what requires to be said in a given situation (*ta deonta heurein*), the implied theory being that it is somehow already 'there' though latent, and does not have to be made up as a mere figment of imagination. . . . The nature of ancient *inventio* and its difference from modern invention are of the first importance. Not only did the concept circumscribe the poet in ways we find surprising [in that he reproduced and expanded an inherited tradition, and rarely allowed himself to invent episodes or characters], but it actually liberated the historian, by giving him very much the same

---

49   1967: 135f. Cf. Wiseman 1981: 389.

range; this is why most ancient historians feel free to fill out the tradition with speeches, standardised accounts of embassies or battles, likely motivations, and other manifestations of *to eikos*. Both poet and historian operate within rules which were originally rhetorical.

Inventio is a vital part of Tacitus's attempt to explore the past rhetorically, an attempt that not only includes an extremely profound awareness of the problems of writing history itself but also allows space for other interpretations, for a range of possible points of view. For Tacitus' is a history in which the answers are neither easy nor final. Hence, the ubiquity of rumour. This is nothing so crude as a device for insinuation and innuendo.[50] Secrecy breeds rumour, as Dio (III. 19.4) points out, and Tacitus finds in it a means of demonstrating the elusiveness of truth,[51] and of dramatically reproducing the various reactions; tensions and fissures of the time.[52] One item both illustrates the investigative efficacy of this approach and possibly reveals how Tacitus might operate, the contrasting assessments of Augustus' reign, *Annals* i. 9–10. Behind this lies a summary of Augustus' reign in some identifiable but unknown first-century source BC that is also traceable in Dio.[53] Dio, however, has only the favourable picture. Even if Tacitus did get the idea of favourable and unfavourable comments from a source, it is highly likely that it was Tacitus himself who cast them in terms of conflicting reflections, and who worked up the hostile side, in particular, unmasking Augustus' hypocrisy with a devastating parody of the *Res Gestae*. But, as Syme says, in a response that does justice to Tacitus's method: 'Men must have said those things.[54] Tacitus employs a rhetorical fiction to expose an underlying truth.[55]

---

50 This standard allegation against Tacitus recalls Plutarch, *On the Malice of Herodotus* 8.

51 Cf. *Ann.* iii. 19.2, on the death of Germanicus; *Ann.* iv. 10–11, on the death of Drusus, especially iv. 11.3.

52 What people, ordinary people, took, however mistakenly, for the truth, is not only a significant part of the texture of events, but may also, on occasion, have a role in shaping those events. For example, the course the trial of Piso followed, *Ann.* iii. 10–19, would be unintelligible without a sense of the atmosphere surrounding it: the *idée fixe* that Piso had poisoned Germanicus under instructions from Tiberius. Cf. Shotter 1968. See Macaulay's account (Vol. 1, ch. 4, p. 442) of the rumours surrounding the death of Charles II. One of Macaulay's points here, that rumours tell us at least as much about the speakers and their audience as about their ostensible targets is amply brought out in Tacitus' usage.

53 LV. 135–41, Tiberius' encomium, and especially LVI. 43–5, Dio's own retrospect.

54 Syme 1958: i. 431. Cf. also i. 316. Cf. Byatt 1988: 499: 'All History is hard facts – and something else – passion and colour lent by men'.

55 Cf. Cicero, *Brutus*, 41: '*concessum est rhetoribus ementiri in historiis ut aliquid dicere possint argutius*' (Rhetors are allowed to tell lies in histories so that they can say something more clearly). Eisenstein might have advanced a similar argument in respect of the sequence of the Odessa Steps in *Battleship Potemkin*. Although this particular massacre did not in fact take place, the sequence powerfully focuses a historical truth. One is reminded of Jean Cocteau's famous remark 'History is an alliance of reality and lies. The reality of history becomes a lie. The unreality of the fable becomes the truth.' See also Wiseman, 1981; Gill and Wiseman 1983.

'Untrue is untrue'.[56] History is not that simple. It is, in Macaulay's words,

> a debatable land. It lies on the confines of two distinct territories. It is under the jurisdiction of two hostile powers; and like other districts similarly situated it is ill-defined, ill-cultivated and ill-regulated. Instead of being equally shared between its two rulers, the Reason and the Imagination, it falls alternately under the sole and absolute dominion of each. It is sometimes fiction, it is sometimes theory...[57]

This does not mean that we should scorn the boundary between fact and fiction, however tenuous that boundary may be, and however difficult it is to mark. History needs rhetoric (cf. White n.d.): facts have to be interpreted, material organized, details selected, events reconstructed, words matched to deeds.[58] But rhetoric can be an instrument for truth or an instrument for falsehood (cf. Brunt 1980). Not all rhetorics are equally valid. Some are more productive than others, explain more, liberate more possibilities. Judgements still have to be made (Plato, *Gorgias*, *passim*). In Tacitus, rhetoric is on the whole an instrument for truth, to probe, and to raise questions about, the past. Whether or not we agree with his conclusions or his ideological framework is beside the point. The contrast with the Republic, the decline of *libertas* (freedom), the servility of the Senate[59] are all weighty historical themes. This approach to truth may be one that is more associated with the historical novel.[60] But a reading of the Roman historians may prompt the salutary, if disconcerting, thought that perhaps that is what all history essentially is[61].

REFERENCES

Albrecht, M. von (1979) *Masters of Roman Prose*. (English translation 1989, Trowbridge, Wiltshire.)
André, J. M. (1966) *L'Otium dans la vie morale et intellectuelle romaine*, Paris.
Auerbach, E. (1946) *Mimesis*, Berne. (English translation Princeton 1953.)
Badian, E. (1966) 'The early historians', in T. A. Dorey (ed.) *Latin Historians*, London.

56 Leader in the *Guardian*, 29 January 1993, on the rumours surrounding John Major.

57 Cf. also Schama 1991.

58 Cf. Sallust, *BC* 3.2: '*facta dictis exaequanda sunt*' (the words must be equal to the deeds). Also, Gorgias, *peri phuseos* or *peri tou me ontos*, 3.84 DK.

59 Now amply confirmed by the *S C de Cn. Pisone Patre*. The amount of research Tacitus has done should not be underestimated, cf., e.g. *Ann.* iv. 11.4, iv. 53.3; Pliny, *Ep.* vi. 16, 20.

60 Cf. Woodman 5. See also, Lukács 1962. All ancient historians, of course, make their characters speak. It was, however, their practice to exclude verbatim speeches from their works, with the exception of brief quotations. All longer speeches, therefore, are composed by the authors themselves. This holds good even when the actual speech was publicly available, as was the case with Claudius's speech to the Senate in 48, substantial parts of which still survive on an inscription (*ILS* 212). Tacitus gives his version at *Ann.* xi. 24, and here, at least, he appears to have admirably reproduced the gist, the *xumpasa gnome*, as Thucydides would have it (i. 22.1), of what Claudius really said. Our problem is that we have no idea which speeches follow this pattern, and to what extent.

61 See P. Brendon on A. J. P. Taylor's view of history: 'History was simply an enjoyable form of story-telling', *New Statesman*, 21 January 1994.

I am grateful to Dr C. B. R. Pelling for allowing me to read his lecture-notes on the Roman historians. His work has been very influential on several of the ideas in this chapter.

Balsdon, J. V. P. D. (1969), *Life and Leisure in Ancient Rome*, London.
Bonner, S. F. (1949) *Roman Declamation*, Liverpool.
Brunt, P. A. (1978) '*Laus imperii*', in Garnsey and Whittaker (eds) *Imperialism in the Ancient World*, Cambridge.
—— (1980) 'Cicero and historiography', *Miscellanea Manni*: 311–40 (= *Studies in Greek History and Thought*, Cambridge, 1993: 181–209).
Büchner, K. (1982) *Sallust*, Heidelberg.
Byatt, A. (1988) *Possession*, London.
Comber, M. (1992) 'Herodotus' History', *Omnibus* 23: 8–10.
Dodds, E. R. (1951) *The Greeks and the Irrational*, Berkeley.
Du Quesnay, I. M. Le M. (1976) 'Virgil's fourth eclogue', *Proceedings of the Liverpool Latin Seminar* 2: 25–99.
Earl, D. C. (1961) *The Political Thought of Sallust*, Cambridge.
Edmunds, L. (1975a) *Chance and Intelligence in Thucydides*, Cambridge, MA.
—— (1975b) 'Thucydides ethics as reflected in the description of stasis (3.82–83)', *Harvard Studies in Classical Philology* 79: 73–92.
Edwards, C. (1993) *The Politics of Immorality in Ancient Rome*, Cambridge.
Frier, B. W. (1979) *Libri annales pontificorum maximorum*, Rome.
Giddens, A. (1985) *Durkheim*, Fontana Modern Masters, London.
Gill, C. and Wiseman, T. P. (eds) (1983) *Lies and Fiction in the Ancient World*, Exeter.
Ginsburg, J. (1981) *Tradition and Theme in the Annals of Tacitus*, New York.
Goodyear, F. R. D. (1968) *Journal of Roman Studies* 58: 22–31 (= *Papers on Latin Literature*, London, 1992: 125–37.)
—— (1972) *The Annals of Tacitus*, Cambridge.
Gransden, K. W. (1990) *Virgil: The Aeneid*, Cambridge.
Griffin, J. (1976) 'Augustan poetry and the life of luxury', *Journal of Roman Studies* 66: 87–105.
Hegel, G. W. F. (1858) *Lectures on the Philosophy of History*, tr. J. Sibree, London.
Laistner, M. L. W. (1947) *The Greater Roman Historians*, Berkeley.
Levene, D. S. (1992) 'Sallust's *Jugurtha*: an "historical fragment"', *Journal of Roman Studies* 82: 53–70.
Luce, T. J. (1965) 'The dating of Livy's first decade', *Transactions of the American Philological Association* 96: 209–40.
—— (1991) 'Tacitus on "history's highest function": *praecipuum munus annalium Aufstieg und Niedergang der römischen Welt*' ii. 33.4: 2904–27.
Lukács, G. (1962) *The Historical Novel*, Harmondsworth.
Lyotard, J.-F. (1984) *The Postmodern Condition*, Manchester.
Macaulay, T. B. (1849) *History of England from the Accession of James II* II, London.
McDonald, A. H. (1975) 'Theme and style in Roman historiography', *Journal of Roman Studies* 65: 1–10.
Macleod, C. W. (1979) 'Thucydides on faction', *Proceedings of the Cambridge Philological Society* 205 (n.s. 25): 52–68 (=Macleod 1983: 123–39).
—— (1983) 'Thucydides and tragedy', in *Collected Essays*, Oxford, pp. 140–58.
Martin, R. H. (1955) 'Tacitus and the death of Augustus', *Classical Quarterly* 5: 123–8.
—— and Woodman, A. J. (eds) (1989) *Tacitus: Annals IV*, Cambridge.
Nietzsche, F. (1983) 'On the uses and disadvantages of history for life', *Untimely Meditations*, tr. R. J. Hollingdale, Cambridge.
Nisbet, R. G. M. (1984) 'Horace's *Epodes* and history', in A. J. Woodman and D. West (eds) *Poetry and Politics in the Age of Augustus*, Cambridge.
Norden, E. (1923, reprint 1958) *Die antike Kunstprosa vom VI. Jahrhundert v. Chr. bis in die Zeit der Renaissance*, 4th edn, 2 vols, Leipzig.
Ogilvie, R. M. (1965) *A Historical Commentary on Livy Book 1–5*, Oxford.

Oppermann, H. (1955) 'Die Einleitung zum Geschichtsarerk des Livius' *Der altsprachliche Unterricht* 7: 87–98.

Price, S. (1987) 'The consecration of Roman emperors', in D. Cannadine and S. Price (eds) *Rituals of Royalty*, Cambridge.

Rawson, E. (1971) 'Royalty and power in traditional societies', *Classical Quarterly* 21: 158–69 (repr. in *Roman Culture and Society: Collected Papers*, Oxford, 1991).

Russell, D. A. (1967) 'Rhetoric and criticism', *Greece & Rome* 14: 130–44.

Scanlon, T. F. (1980) *The Influence of Thucydides upon Sallust*, Heidelberg.

Schama, S. (1991) *Dead Certainties (Unwarranted Speculations)*, London.

Selbourne, D. (1993) *The Spirit of the Age*, London.

Sherk, R. W. *The Roman Empire: Augustus to Hadrian*.

Shotter, D. C. A. (1968) 'Tacitus, Tiberius and Germanicus', *Historia* 17: 194–214.

Skutsch, O. (ed.) (1985) *The Annals of Quintus Ennius*, Oxford and New York.

Syme, R. (1958) *Tacitus*, 2 vols, Oxford.

—— (1964) *Sallust*, Berkeley and Cambridge.

Taylor, A. J. P. (1965) *English History 1914–1945*, Oxford.

Walbank, F. W. (1957–79) *A Historical Commentary on Polybius*, 3 vols, Oxford.

Weinstock, S. (1971) *Divus Julius*, Oxford.

White, H. (n.d.) 'History and theory', in H. White and F. E. Manuel (eds) *Theories of History: Papers Read at a Clark Library Seminar, March, 6, 1976*, Los Angeles.

Williams, G. W. (1968; repr. 1985) *Tradition and Originality in Roman Poetry*, Oxford.

Wirszubski, C. (1950) *Libertas as a Political Idea at Rome during the Late Republic and Early Principate*, Cambridge.

Wiseman, T. P. (1981) 'Practice and theory in Roman historiography', *History* LXVI 218 (October).

—— (1979) *Clio's Cosmetics: Three Studies in Greco-Roman Literature*, Leicester.

Woodman, A. J. (1988) *Rhetoric in Classical Historiography; Four Studies*, London.

—— (1982) 'Novel Histories', *Omnibus* 5.

4

THE RELIGION OF ROME FROM MONARCHY TO PRINCIPATE

J. A. North

INTRODUCTION

The first serious efforts to write a religious history of pagan Rome in the monarchic and republican periods were made about 200 years ago. They have continued fairly consistently ever since. The story of these efforts and of the influence they have had, or not had, on the understanding of Roman history is a series of paradoxes. In many ways, the subject has been persistently marginalized by the modern historical tradition of Roman history-writing. General histories and standard works have often relegated religion to a last separate chapter or even omitted it altogether. Meanwhile, books specifically devoted to it have remained the preserve of a minority of specialists, who have tended to be regarded as light relief on the fringes of serious issues such as the military, legal or administrative traditions of the republican elite.

This process of marginalization has, as will become clear, been in part justified by the theories the specialists have themselves propounded. The paradox is that the very theories – insecure ones as it now seems – that have marginalized the subject have simultaneously provided the established basis of a prominent and central theory about the rise of Christianity in the imperial period. It became at times little short of an article of belief that the weakness of the pagan tradition was a major cause of the appeal of external religious influences, and that the inherent absurdity of Graeco-Roman polytheism itself led to the so-called triumph of monotheism.

Another paradox is that students of the subject attained a most unusual degree of agreement for many years about the basic direction of the subject they were studying. The main lines of the tradition were set up in the early nineteenth century and it was well into the second half of the twentieth before any radical reconsideration began. Yet the theories themselves were highly speculative *a priori* constructions. The interest of the subject today lies not only in the continuing influence of these ideas, far from spent even now, but also in the rise and fall of a theory at once so flawed and yet so generally acceptable for so many decades.

The answer to these paradoxes lies in part in the nature of the source material on which our understanding has had to be based. There is a fundamental difference between our capacity to control theories about early Roman society and those about early Greek society: for Greece we have extant poetry in Hesiod and Homer, derived from oral tradition, that sets some limits to the possible interpretations; for Rome we have no such surviving texts. Indeed it is not much of an exaggeration to say that the written texts on which nineteenth-century historians relied for the understanding of monarchic Rome (traditionally *c*.800 BC–*c*.500 BC) came from the age of Augustus, 500 years after the monarchy's fall. It follows that all their theories of the development of Roman pagan religion were intellectual inventions of their own, depending as much on theoretical presuppositions as on any attempt to make sense of the actual source material preserved. We of today are only better placed in so far as archaeological material can be use to control and replace older views. This does not always lead to secure results, but it does effectively provide us with guidelines for interpretation.

THE ORIGINS OF THE SUBJECT

To say that the discipline as a discipline originated in the nineteenth century is not to deny that a great deal of study of its subject-matter had already taken place. The institutions of Rome had been the subject of attention and discussion since the Renaissance and religious institutions – priesthoods, sacrificial rituals, religious formulae and regulations – had had their share of attention amongst the rest. As in so many other areas, this very considerable body of learning and knowledge provided the material on which philosophical and historical thinkers began to work in the early nineteenth century. Here as in other areas, the results with the benefit of hindsight are more revealing about the nineteenth century than they are about ancient Rome.

The earliest books published specifically on the subject were J. A. Hartung's *Religion der Römer* (1836) and L. Krahner's historical survey, published in 1837. Krahner's very title shows how far the structuring principle of the history of Roman religion was established before any methodical study began: *Grundlinien zur Geschichte des Verfalls der römischen Staatsreligion bis auf die Zeit des Augustus* – the 'decline' of the state religion was to be the key theme of the subject for more than a century. Krahner's project was no more than to collect the key literary sources that, in his view, demonstrated the process of decline, already assumed to be historical fact.

Hartung, more interestingly, made the first attempt to locate the religion of Rome inside a wider comparativist perspective. Following the ideas of C. O. Müller (1825), and the debates that his work had started, Hartung argued that polytheism of the Roman type did not arise by way of deterioration from an original monotheism, but as the crystallization into the form of divine beings of what had originally been symbolic representations of natural forces. But his view too was that polytheism – not just Roman polytheism but any polytheism – faced inevitable decline as reason destroyed its indefensible assumptions. All the same, Hartung's effort stands out as an attempt to relate Roman religious institutions and the Roman form of polytheism to the wider debates about religious history of his time. Much of what was written later in the century, though technically far superior and progressively better informed, restricted itself to a Roman perspective and to an empirical approach. It was Krahner not Hartung who was to set the tone for the future.

THE DEVELOPMENT OF THE DISCIPLINE

Two elements of the nineteenth-century German historiography of Roman religion need to be emphasized. First, there was an extraordinary progressive improvement in the quality and complexity of the standard accounts of the subject. From Ambrosch (1840, 1843) through the handbook of Marquardt (1854) to Wissowa (2nd edn, 1912), there was a succession of analyses and handbooks, which collected and systematized the information available from literary and legal sources, integrated that with new information – steadily increasing at the time – from epigraphic sources, and began the process of opening the subject up to the flood of new data to be derived from the archaeology of Rome and Italy. A fair indication of the success of this sustained enterprise is that its culmination in the handbook of Wissowa (1912) is still today the standard source of basic information on Roman gods, rituals and priestly institutions.

The second element to be emphasized is in many ways the downside of the first one. It is very well illustrated by the views of the great historian Theodor Mommsen in his *Römische Geschichte* (1854). Mommsen was himself a major contributor to the interpretation of religious texts in many articles and in the publication of much epigraphic material, including the stone calendars of the Roman festivals, which provide the only core data for the early structure of the religion. Moreover, many of those who achieved most progress, including Wissowa himself, were pupils of Mommsen and owed much to his approach. But there can seldom have been a more negative evaluation of a religious system than Mommsen's on Rome. He thought the Romans had an unbelievably low level of understanding of the nature of their own gods and goddesses; that their religion was a matter of dry, everyday formulaic negotiation; that their gods provided no mythology, no art, no inspiration; that after the earliest period religion was reduced to an empty formalism quite devoid of any interior significance at all.

Whether because of Mommsen's extraordinary influence or for some other reason, this has been the dominant view ever since; its origins are, therefore, a matter of considerable importance. It has been argued with some plausibility (Scheid 1987) that, whether consciously or not, Mommsen is here following the views of G. W. F. Hegel. He too had taken the view that what characterized Rome above all was an unspiritual, practical, legalistic relationship with the gods in which the sole objective from the human side was short-term advantage in relation to everyday life (Hegel [1895] 1962: II, 298–323; Scheid 1987: 317–20). Whether or not it was really Hegelian influence that determined these views, it is certain that Hegel himself would have found very little in the views of a Mommsen or a Wissowa, had he been able to read them, that would have caused him to change his mind.

It would perhaps be better to put the point the other way round and say that this set of Hegelian views is a major factor in the construction of the historiographic tradition of which Mommsen is a spectacular example. The whole scholarly enterprise started from the assumption that the appropriate way to describe the religion of the Romans is by labelling and classifying, by the prioritizing of legalistic materials, by explaining all actions in terms of primarily pragmatic considerations. So Wissowa by the end of the century had provided a detailed, learned exegesis to a prescription that Hegel had written before the scholarly research had taken place at all.

In essence, what was offered by this stage was a stereotypical description of the behaviour of an elite Roman in the late republican period, modelled to a considerable extent on the extensive writings of Cicero. The Roman on this view was focused on practical considerations of city life. He accepted the existence of the gods and subscribed obediently to the ritual regulations handed down from the past, because they were hallowed by the tradition of the ancestors (the *mos maiorum*). But religion had no deeper meaning for him than this; he did not concern himself about the gods – unless he was writing a book on philosophy; and he did not speak or think about them – unless he was making a speech in the popular assembly. For him, religion was to all intents and purposes dead, killed by its own excessive ritualism, in a past about which he knew nothing. This view of elite religion was not to be challenged for many years; but in the meantime new issues began to draw the attention of the best scholars in the field.

THE STAGES OF THE PAST

It had always been part of the developing view that the religion of the Romans in the time of Cicero and his contemporaries was in a state of decline or degeneration compared to some unspecified point in the past. Around the turn of the century, this notion of finding stages of development or decline began to take on far more specific forms under the influence of contemporary anthropological theory. The first and in many ways the most impressive experiment in this direction was that of Herman Usener (1896), who argued that Roman gods started (stage one, *Sondergötter*) as expressions of highly specific activities after which they were called by directly intelligible words, then developed into more generalized occasional gods (stage two, *Augenblicksgötter*), and finally into fully-fledged gods with personalities and names that were no longer directly intelligible. These developed gods then appropriated the powers and identities of the more specialized ones and hence the system worked inescapably towards the eventual goal of monotheism.

A still more famous and influential theory, particularly in the English-speaking world, was that of W. Warde Fowler (1894; 1911), who exploited explicitly and directly the theories of Tylor (1891) and Frazer (1907–35), though he also knew and discussed the work of Mommsen and Wissowa (whose handbook he knew in the first edition of 1902). He started from the evolutionary theory that all religion originated in animism and that the earliest stage of Roman religion was the worship of *numina*, that is, of powers that were seen as residing in natural phenomena. Even though there was no ancient evidence of this very early phase, it proved possible to explain various features of the tradition along the lines of the theory. Thus the Romans had a tradition that, for much of the regal period of their history, they had no images of their gods. Some deities (e.g. Vesta) never did develop an anthropomorphic image and some (e.g. Terminus = the god 'Boundary-stone') were simply inherent in a physical object. So the religion of the *numina* came to represent what was called a 'pre-deistic' phase of Roman religious experience.

Warde Fowler took a more positive view of the subject than had his German predecessors and in this too he had a strong influence on what followed. He thought that the early stages he had reconstructed constituted the truly vigorous and truly Roman phase of the Roman people's religious experience. He thus gave far more substance to the idea, already implicit in earlier writing, that the religion of Cicero's day was a poor, pale shadow of what the experience of the Romans had once been. In the regal or pre-regal past that he had discovered, he thought he had found the true, genuinely felt, religious spirit of the people. Only later in the course of the republican period was this spirit destroyed, partly by foreign – that is, particularly Greek – influences, partly by priestly legalism and obsession with ritual, partly by the urbanization of Rome, which cut the people off from their roots in the country and left them out of sympathy with a calendar of rural festivals they no longer understood or needed (Warde Fowler 1911: 68–291). It is not hard to see, at a distance of eighty years, that the problems thus projected on to the Romans in fact had to do with the suspicion of the foreign, with the dislike of Catholic ritualism and with the distaste for the industrial revolution of an Anglican Oxford don with a well-developed passion for ornithology.

In many respects, however, the new approaches were a great improvement on the past. Anthropology created the possibility of new modes of perceiving pagan thought and practice and of re-evaluating the negative characterizations that had come to be relied on as if they were historical facts. Indeed, Usener and Warde Fowler were amongst the great pioneers in using the comparative approach, with notably fertile results at the time. The limitations, however, are also clear enough now: the framework within which their thoughts were formed was as dominated as ever by the assumption that Judaeo-Christian monotheism was the higher form of religion to which their stages of development would finally lead. It followed that polytheism was automatically doomed to failure; the only question was when and how it would fail.

The positive evaluation of polytheism had therefore to be placed back in the remote past, in the earliest periods of Roman history or even in their prehistory. This impulse of recognition of the divine in the Romans' early history was then crushed by the activities of the republican priestly colleges, especially the augurs and the pontiffs (*augures* and *pontifices*). We know that these colleges were powerful institutions in early Rome, that they kept written records from an early date and that they presided over subtle discriminations over points of religious law. In the late Republic, there is plenty of evidence that religious decisions were taken by the Senate, but only after elaborate consultations of the priestly colleges (on Roman priests, see Beard in Beard and North 1990; 19–48). The law of the augurs had in fact been the subject of one of the finest nineteenth-century studies by the Dutch scholar Valeton (1889–90; 1891a; 1891b; see Linderski 1986). Warde Fowler observed acidly (1911: 2) that for Mommsen religion held little interest, 'except in so far as it was connected with Roman law'. For him, however, the touch of the religious lawyers and ritualists was exactly what had destroyed the true religion of the Roman people, which could now be re-appreciated with the help of anthropology.

THE RISE AND FALL OF THE *NUMINA*

Warde Fowler had shown how a new and more creative approach could be taken to the understanding of paganism. The pity was that his picture became an established orthodoxy to be repeated and recycled in book after book through the middle decades of the century. Nor did this only happen in the specialist works dealing with Roman religion as such. The 'pre-deistic phase' became the most familiar known fact about the religion of Rome, and in many circles still is. Meanwhile, the death of pagan religion before the age of Cicero became an accepted truth for all Roman historians as well as for the historians of the rise of Christianity.

The historiography of Roman political history is particularly revealing in this regard. It became the accepted view that the elite of the middle and late Republic took so sceptical and rationalist a view about their own gods and goddesses that they regularly exploited the rules of the sacred law for short-term political advantages. So in the newly discovered science of prosopography starting from the seminal work of F. Münzer (1920) onwards, it became standard practice to calculate the decisions of the priestly colleges by listing the political affiliations of the members, on the assumption that they always voted for their political group's ticket, irrespective of the religious issue under discussion. This underlying assumption is never explicitly defended or justified, and indeed there is no evidence whatsoever that could be used for this purpose; but it is a useful assumption for political historians in so far as it legitimates ignoring the whole body of evidence concerned with religious factors in political life. The political-diplomatic narrative of Rome can be purified of such irrational factors and hence made acceptable to the modern sceptical eye. For those who take religious evidence seriously and think the Romans did so too, the whole modern discourse on Roman political life is thus fundamentally flawed, by making it conform to our patterns of rational behaviour.

Within the discipline of religious studies too, the effects of the orthodoxy were highly questionable. As Scheid (1987) pointed out, one weakness of the whole tradition of study, which Warde Fowler (1911) did nothing to overcome, is that polytheism as such was never properly analysed within it. The energy and interest were devoted to two issues: How did polytheism come to exist in the first place? And how did it crumble before the greater rationality of monotheism? In other words, the whole tradition of debate remained obdurately centred on an agenda dictated by Judaeo-Christian prejudices.

There was indeed much discussion of individual gods and goddesses, some of it of the very highest quality. In France, in particular, there has been a tradition that still continues today, of writing a *thèse* devoted to a single deity (Hercules, Apollo, Ceres, Mercury, etc.), and many of these works have become the standard reference books for their subject, with a finely rigorous tradition of the exegesis of the relevant texts. However, beneficial though these may have been as training for the individual researchers, the practice of abstracting one deity for special study has not encouraged any engagement with the phenomenon of polytheism or any radical reassessment of the overall consensus within which the subject had come to operate. Meanwhile, within the individual studies, the overall development postulated by the consensual view has tended to be rediscovered and reinforced, even though it was not always possible in individual cases to identify the stage at which the deity was still a '*numen*' or the moment of translation from '*numen*' into fully-fledged deity, which the consensus predicted must have happened.

The consistency and long duration of this consensus must be a cause for great puzzlement in retrospect. First, the whole theory of the pre-deistic phase of religious development derived from anthropological theories, which were themselves soon abandoned by the anthropologists; classical historians continued to believe in universal stages of human development long after everybody else had abandoned them. Secondly, even if the intellectual underpinning was still supposed to be sound and enduring, the theory itself was always a masterpiece of implausibility: according to the view of Warde Fowler, the real vitality of Roman paganism (the metaphor used is always biological) was draining away by the fifth century BC, leaving a spiritless remnant (1911: 270–1). The spiritless remnant then struggled on through the best part of 900 years, before being marginalized – though far from extinguished – by the emergence of new religious forms.

It would of course be an exaggeration to say that this whole edifice stood unchallenged into the 1950s and 1960s. There were partial challenges from many directions: Koch (1937, 1960) reassessed the role of mythology in relation to the Roman divine system and argued that early Roman religion showed far more creativity than the orthodox view allowed; Altheim (1930) argued that there was far earlier and profounder influence from the Greeks than the theory allowed; and some work started from altogether different assumptions, particularly that of Pettazzoni (1952) and those influenced by his methods, including Brelich (e.g. 1949; 1958; cf. Montanari 1988). But when Latte's new version of Wissowa's handbook appeared in 1960, he really reargued the old consensual position, despite his own subtlety and breadth of learning. Much was new and challenging in the book, but the intellectual framework – the pre-deistic phase, the priestly stranglehold, the long decline – was resumed from Warde Fowler. It was, however, in reaction to Latte's work that radical controversy, long simmering, began at last to surface.

One of the critical reviewers was Weinstock (1961), a learned exile from Nazi-controlled Europe, who worked in Oxford through the 1950s and 1960s. Weinstock was a cautious scholar, a passionate admirer of Mommsen and deeply reluctant to make claims that he could not substantiate. But he was responsible for dismantling considerable parts of the tradition, including the belief in early *numina*; meanwhile, his many years of patient work on the book that eventually appeared as *Divus Julius* (1971) had slowly convinced him that it made no sense to regard men such as Caesar, Pompey and Augustus, who devoted endless concern, time and money to their religious activities, as operating in a religious vacuum.

A major influence at this point (though not one Weinstock would have dreamed of recognizing) was Georges Dumézil, who had long been pursuing his own very independent path. Dumézil was an Indo-Europeanist, who believed that he could reconstruct by comparative methods the mythology and theology shared by all the groups deriving ultimately from the original Indo-European speakers. (For discussion: Littleton 1982; Momigliano 1987: 289–314; Belier 1991.) He claimed to have discovered a triple structure, which he initially took to have been the actual social structure of the Indo-European primitive tribesmen who spoke the language, but later regarded as a common inheritance of myths and divine systems shared by all their descendants – whether speakers of Sanskrit, Persian, Greek, Latin, Celtic, Germanic or any other members of the language group. The triple structure is: (1) Priests and Kings; (2) Warriors; (3) Farmers and Producers. He sought to show in the case of Rome that these structures were deeply embedded in the stories, rituals and divine groups we know of from early Rome (Dumézil 1941; 1966; 1968–73).

Reactions to Dumézil's work have varied from complete scepticism to complete conviction, but whatever the long-term judgement on his work may be, his impact on the discussion of Roman religion was at this point considerable. He was able to dispose conclusively of the supposed pre-deistic phase, which has not been seriously defended since, by showing that at least some degree of inheritance from the Indo-Europeans must be accepted. The names of some gods and the word *deus/dea* itself are shared with other Indo-European language groups. If so, the Roman gods are as old as the Romans themselves and cannot have evolved in Italy from the supposed *numina* (Dumézil 1966: 19–145; = 1970: 3–138). He also showed that in one form or another there was after all a Roman mythical inheritance for those who were prepared to look for it (Dumézil 1968–73). Finally, he established the possibility of analysing the Roman deities as a system rather than as individuals and thus created at least some prospect of progress in the understanding of the Roman version of polytheism. He also took a more positive view of the nature of later Roman religious life, partly because he denied the great break between pre-deistic and deistic Rome.

TOWARDS A NEW ORTHODOXY

It is a matter of considerable debate and anxiety whether Dumézil's project was not at root a racist interpretation of history (*contra* Scheid 1983). The issue turns on ambiguities in the process by which he himself thought that the inherited structures had been conveyed from generation to generation of Indo-European peoples. Was this a matter of linguistic and cultural continuity or rather one of genetic inheritance? There was, and is, no clear answer about his real understanding of this crucial issue. At least, he was not interested in the superiority of monotheism, and he had much imaginative sympathy for the nature of pagan experience; but he did not detach himself thoroughly from the assumptions of the old orthodoxy.

Another blow to the old consensus came from the discoveries of archaeologists working in the Rome area, or perhaps more accurately from a slow realization of the implications of their achievements. It has become progressively clearer and clearer that Roman society in the sixth century BC was being profoundly influenced, if not shaped, by many different foreign influences – not just that of the other Latins and the nearby Etruscans, but also that of Greeks and even Carthaginians. So far from living in cultural isolation and in strong continuity with their own past, the Romans of the later monarchy seem to have been a cosmopolitan society in touch with many other parts of the Mediterranean world (see now, Cornell 1995, esp. 151–72). These considerations alone would make many older theories untenable.

The next step was the recognition that much of what had passed for the history of Roman religion between 1836 and the 1960s was based on nothing more substantial than Christianizing misconceptions of what a proper religion ought to be like and a consequent failure to recognize the 'otherness' of pagan religious experience in terms of our own expectations. One example of this has already been touched on: it has often been argued that Roman religious rules were exploited by politicians for their own advantage and consequently that the whole religion was discredited by being mixed up in political action in an undesirable way. This judgement is in fact quite unsustainable in terms of republican Roman experience. There was no separation of religion from politics in the way we expect: all political action involved religion, took place in religious space and under religious rules. The priests arbitrated the action, but were themselves usually political actors or at least members of politically active families. The notion that involvement in politics would somehow discredit religion would simply have puzzled a Roman observer (Liebeschuetz 1979; North 1989: 582–90).

Another clear example is provided by the issue of foreign, especially Greek, influences: these have often been put forward as a corrosive factor, gradually isolating the Romans from their own traditions and showing the world that they could not rely on themselves in the religious sphere, but had lamely to adopt their neighbours' practices, a progressive public confession of their religious weakness. The facts are that the Romans consistently introduced cults from Italy, Greece and elsewhere at all periods we know about, including the periods of their most triumphant victories. There is no reason to think that they themselves or other peoples of the ancient world regarded this as a sign of weakness, as it no doubt would have been in a Judaeo-Christian context. The Romans recruited new gods just as they recruited new citizens, as their power and dominion expanded (North 1976).

The most critical arguments in this debate have concerned the nature of religious experience itself. The model we bring into play from our own society implies that true religious experience should be interior, personal, distinctively emotional and formed by sincere, shared beliefs. That such experience could not be discovered in the Roman sources for the late Republic and the early Empire used often to be taken as a sure sign that the society had lost contact with its own religious meanings. In retrospect that seems a clear case of judging pagan religiosity in terms of Judaeo-Christian expectations (Price 1984). These arguments and others dependent on the same shift of perspective have had considerable impact in the last ten years; it would be hard today to defend the consensus in its original form, though much work continues to use the old assumptions and to treat them as established historical facts (e.g. Scullard 1981).

CURRENT PROBLEMS

It could be said that the new orthodoxy has been more successful in achieving negative than positive positions. It is easier to discredit the misleading theories of the last century than to find a new way of expressing the significance and power of the religious institutions of republican Rome itself. On the other hand, where the interpretation of republican gods and religious institutions is concerned, much original and open-minded work has already appeared in several countries in the 1980s and 1990s (e.g. Scheid 1985; 1986; Montanari 1988; Beard 1989; Gordon 1990; Versnel 1993). In some respects, the loss of grand theories may be permanent, but desirable: it is for instance hard to see at the moment how a respectable historical theory of the early development of the religion of Rome can ever be rebuilt, when we have little or no secure ground on which to build it. If this is ever to be possible, it will have to be archaeological evidence from Rome and Latium that provides the new foundations.

Other problems can be, must be and are being reformulated in the light of the new positions. For instance, if it is true that religion and politics were always deeply intertwined in Roman political life, then the nature of the relationship needs to be redefined and a new way of describing their mutual evolution needs to be invented, if the distortion is to be redressed. We need to accept that the ancient sources have been read in the past in the light of our prejudices and that a new reading has to be established, closer to their own.

Again, if the idea is to be abandoned that Christianity drew strength from the failure of pagan religions, the whole interaction between the two needs to be reformulated. One question is whether the development of new religious forms in the Roman Empire was simply a matter of an invasion by outside agencies (i.e. Jews and Christians), or whether it should be seen as an evolution of the whole religious life of the Empire, including paganism. Another is how far paganism itself was transformed by becoming part of a religious confrontation between alternative religious possibilities, which in the world of republican Rome had been an inconceivable situation (North 1992).

Perhaps, however, the most important issue of all is to try to place republican religious experience in a framework that can explain its validity and power on its own terms. One attempt to do this was to argue that it should be seen as a public, not a private religion; if that was so, it was the modern attempt to impose our own expectations about private religious convictions that had misled generations of commentators. This may be seen as a somewhat over-simple distinction, concealing a more profound problem about the nature of pagan religious identity and personal religious experience. It may be that we should think, not that the private sphere was being starved at the expense of the public sphere, but that the personality of the citizen of an ancient city was far more wrapped up in the community than occurred in later forms of civic organization. Whether this is a more fertile expression of the situation, only future research will show; what is clear now is that the older models of interpreting the religious experience of the Romans were not sufficient and have to be completely replaced.

REFERENCES

Altheim, F. (1930) *Griechische Götter im alten Rom* (Religionsgeschichtliche Versuche und Vorarbeiten XXII, 1), Giessen.

Ambrosch, J. A. (1838) *Studien und Andeutungen im Gebiete des altrömischen Bodens und Kultus*, Breslau.

—— (1843) *Über die Religionsbücher der Römer*, Bonn.

Beard, M. (1989) 'Acca Larentia gains a son: myths and priesthood at Rome', *Images of authority* (Camb. Phil. Soc. Supp. 16) eds. M. M. Mackenzie and C. Roueché, 41–61, Cambridge

—— and North, J. (1990) *Pagan Priests: Religion and Power in the Ancient World*, London.

Belier, W. W. (1991) *Decayed Gods: The Origin and Development of Georges Dumézil's 'Idéologie tripartite'*, Leiden.

Brelich, A. (1949) *Die geheime Schutzgottheit von Rom*, Zurich

—— (1958) *Il politeismo*, Rome.

Cornell, T. J. (1995) *The Beginnings of Rome*, London and New York.

Dumézil, G. (1941) *Jupiter, Mars, Quirinus*, 3rd edn, Paris.

—— (1966) *La Religion romaine archaïque (avec un appendice sur la religion des Étrusques)* Paris (2nd edn, Paris, 1974; Eng. tr. by P. Krapp, Chicago, 1970).

—— (1968–73) *Mythe et épopée*, Paris.

Fowler, W. Warde (1894) *The Roman Festivals of the Period of the Republic*, London.

—— (1911) *The Religious Experience of the Roman People from the Earliest Times to the Period of Augustus* (Gifford Lectures, 1909–10), London.

Frazer, J. (1907–35) *The Golden Bough: A Study in Magic and Religion*, London.

Gordon, R. (1990), 'From Republic to Principate: priesthood, religion and ideology', in Beard and North 1990: 179–231.

Hartung, J. A. (1836) *Die Religion der Römer nach den Quellen dargestellt*, Erlangen.

Hegel, G. W. F. ([1895] 1962) *Lectures on the Philosophy of Religion*, trans. E. B. Spiers and J. Burdon Sanderson, New York.

Koch, C. (1937) *Der römische Jupiter* (Frankfurter Studien zur Religion und Kultur der Antike XIV), Frankfurt am Main.

—— (1960) *Religio: Studien zu Kult und Glaube der Römer* (Erlanger Beiträge zur Sprach- und Kulturwissenschaft. VII), Nuremburg.

Krahner, L. (1837) *Grundlinien zur Geschichte des Verfalls der römischen Staatsreligion bis auf die Zeit des Augustus*, Halle.

Latte, K. (1960) *Römische Religionsgeschichte* (Müller, I. von, Handbuch der klassischen Altertumswissenschaft V. 4), Munich.

Liebeschuetz, J. H. W. G. (1979) *Continuity and Change in Roman Religion*, Oxford.

Linderski, J. (1986) 'The Augural Law', *Aufstieg und Niedergang der römischen Welt* (ed. H. Temporini and W. Haase) II.16.2146–312, Berlin and New York.

Littleton, C. Scott (1982) *The New Comparative Mythology: An Anthropological Assessment of the Theories of Georges Dumézil* 3rd edn, Berkeley.

Marquardt, J. (1854) *Handbuch der römischen Altertümer*, vol. IV: *Römische Staatsverwaltung*, Leipzig.

Momigliano, A. D. (1987) *On Pagans, Jews and Christians*, Middletown, CT.

Mommsen, Th. (1854) *Römische Geschichte*, Berlin.

Montanari, E. (1988) *Identità culturale e conflitti religiosi nella Roma repubblicana*, Roma.

Müller, C. O. (1825) *Prolegomena zu einer wissenschaftlichen Mythologie*, Göttingen.

Münzer, F. (1920) *Römische Adelparteien und Adelsfamilien*, Stuttgart.

North, J. A. (1976) 'Conservatism and change in Roman Religion', *Papers of the British School at Rome* 44: 1–12.

—— (1989) 'Religion in Republican Rome', in *Cambridge Ancient History*, vol. VII.2, 573–624, Cambridge (to appear as part of M. Beard, J. A. North and S. R. F. Price, *Religions of Rome* (forthcoming)).

—— (1992) 'The development of religious pluralism', in J. Lieu, J. North and T. Rajak (eds) *The Jews among Pagans and Christians in the Roman Empire*, London and New York.

Pettazzoni, R. (1952) *Italia religiosa*, Bari.

Price, S. R. F. (1984) *Rituals and Power: The Roman Imperial Cult in Asia Minor*, Cambridge.

Scheid, J. (1983) 'G. Dumézil et la méthode expérimentale', *Opus* 2: 343–54.

—— (1985) *Religion et piété à Rome*, Paris.

—— (1986) 'Le flamine de Iuppiter, le général triomphant et les Vestales. Variations romaines sur la thème de la représentation des dieux', *La Temps de la Réflexion* 7: 213–30.

—— (1987) 'Polytheism impossible; or, the empty gods: reasons behind a void in the history of Roman religion', *History and Anthropology* 3: 303–25.

Scullard, H. H. (1981) *Festivals and Ceremonies of the Roman Republic*, London.

Tylor, E. B. (1891) *Primitive Culture: Researches into the Development of Mythology, Philosophy, Religion, Language, Art and Custom* 3rd edn, London.

Usener, H. (1896) *Götternamen: Versuch einer Lehre von der religiösen Begriffsbildung*, Bonn.

Valeton, I. M. J. (1889–90) 'De modis auspicandi Romanorum', *Mnemosyne* 17: 275–325; 418–52; 18: 208–63; 406–56.

—— (1891a) 'De iure obnuntiandi comitiis et conciliis', *Mnemosyne* 19: 75–113; 229–70.

—— (1891b) 'De inaugurationibus Romanis', *Mnemosyne* 19: 405–60.

Versnel, H. S. (1993) *Inconsistencies in Greek and Roman Religion*, vol. 2: *Tradition and Reversal in Myth and Ritual*, Leiden, New York and Cologne.

Weinstock, S. (1961) review of Latte 1960, *Journal of Roman Studies* 51: 206–15.

—— (1971) *Divus Julius*, Oxford.

Wissowa, G. (1912) *Religion und Kultus der Römer* (Müller, I. von, Handbuch der klassischen Altertumswissenschaft V.4), Munich.

5

LATE ANTIQUITY AND THE EARLY MEDIEVAL WEST

Peter Heather

The concept of Late Antiquity has, it seems to me, brought together in the last thirty to forty years studies in a number of related fields, which boundaries between the traditional scholarly disciplines had previously tended to keep apart. In historical terms, Late Antiquity bridges the traditional divide between the end of ancient history (the so-called 'Dominate'), and two subsections of medieval history: the Migration Period (the late fourth- and fifth-century invasions of the Roman Empire) and the Dark Ages (everything between these invasions and Charlemagne). It also extends into Byzantine Studies. More radically, Patristics – saints, scholars and the making of Christian doctrine – has now been thoroughly integrated into more 'mainstream' historical studies, without, of course, losing its particularities. Figures such as Jerome or Augustine continue to be studied for their contribution to Christian doctrine, but are now also seen as men of their times, making their way in particular historical contexts, and manipulating the cultural heritages available to them. Likewise, the evolution of particularly late-classical culture has in recent years been welded even more firmly to its broader historical context. Boundaries between the history and culture of the late and immediately post-Roman Mediterranean and Near Eastern languages and cultures – Syriac, Coptic, Armenian, Georgian and so on – have also been substantially eroded. The rise of Late Antiquity has re-emphasized that early phases in the development of these oriental linguistic cultures and the later evolutions of classical Graeco-Roman culture are both contemporary, and share a similar historical background. In similar vein, no serious scholar would now dispute that the end of the Graeco-Roman-dominated ancient world cannot even begin to be understood without some grasp of early Islamic, Arab history.

It would be nonsense to claim that there had never been any contact between these fields before, but it has certainly increased with the rise to prominence of Late Antiquity. One effect of all this has been to make Late Antiquity unstudyable. Few, if any, scholars have the philological competence to encompass the whole field, and it is hardly surprising that the study of Late Antiquity is increasingly marked by interdisciplinary projects. In the United Kingdom, for instance, the British Academy and the Leverhulme Trust are sponsoring a joint project on Late Antiquity and Early Islam organized in London by Averil Cameron, Lawrence Conrad and Geoffrey King. The title of this project speaks for itself, in terms of its basic aim of bringing together Islamic and non-Islamic specialists.[1] Simultaneously, the European Science Foundation is funding a five-year project on *The Transformation of the Roman World*. Here the focus is firmly European, but again late classical and medieval specialists in every discipline (archaeologists, art historians, historians, legal historians, etc.) are being brought together in a series of focused seminars and conferences.[2]

Rather than driving the reader to distraction by producing an exhaustive list of recent or current interdisciplinary initiatives, I shall instead indicate what to my mind represents more specific historiographical insights within the general gathering together of separate disciplines which has created Late Antiquity. For convenience, I shall subdivide what follows into two chronological periods: the later Roman Empire (*c.*AD 250–450), and the post-Roman West (*c.*450–700). The geographical focus will narrow somewhat over time, since it is artificial to divide the eastern and western halves of the Roman Empire in the fourth century, but I shall not attempt to cover developments in the eastern Mediterranean in the later section.

THE LATER ROMAN EMPIRE

There are many individual works that could and should be mentioned in any review of the historiography of the Later Roman Empire in the past thirty years. Texts have been edited or re-edited,[3] particular monographs have advanced understandings of particular authors or facets of period,[4] and papyrological evidence has been brought increasingly into the historical mainstream.[5] I would also consider the ever more frequent appearance of translations as a major advance, not least for the teaching of undergraduates. Now that classical languages in undiluted form play only a relatively minor role in school curricula, the future of the subject depends

---

1   Proceedings of the first two workshops have now been published as *The Byzantine and Early Islamic Near East* ed. A. M. Cameron *et al.*, vol. 1 (London, 1992); vol. 2 (London, 1994).

2   The project has five subgroups: *Imperium, Gentes et Regna, Settlement in Town and Countryside, Production, Distribution and Demand, Transformation of Beliefs and Culture, Power and Society.* Each group will eventually publish two volumes of papers, in addition to which there will be volumes of proceedings from the three plenary conferences. The first volumes should appear in 1997.

3   Important new editions of Late Roman texts have in particular appeared in the French Budé and Sources Chrétiennes series.

4   e.g. Cameron 1970; Sabbah 1978; Matthews 1989; Syme 1971; Dagron 1974; Hoffmann 1969; Demandt 1970. Note too, the important revisions of basic chronological matters in the works of T. D. Barnes such as *The New Empire of Diocletian and Constantine* (1982).

5   e.g. works such as Bagnall 1994 with refs. to the author's countless joint works with others such as K. A. Worp. See now also Rathbone 1991.

heavily on being able to spark the interest of students in the subject through sources in translation.[6] The few examples given in the footnotes will have to stand for all such worthy individual contributions, and the bulk of this chapter will be devoted to more general historiographical themes and issues.

Perhaps the most obvious revolution in the study of the Later Roman Empire over the last thirty years has been brought about by the publication of a significant and growing body of archaeological data. Just over thirty years ago, A. H. M. Jones published his monumental study of the Later Roman Empire. The book is essentially based on literary texts, although there is within it one stray footnote to Tchalenko's (1953) archaeological study of the villages of the Syrian limestone massif in the Late Roman period.[7] Jones's book remains indispensable, but no one would now dream of writing about Late Roman social and economic issues without having as firm a grasp of the archaeological as of the literary evidence.

There is no better place to begin than with Tchalenko's study itself (Tchalenko 1953). This recorded his exploration of a series of villages, datable by inscriptions to the third century AD and beyond, flourishing in the Syrian countryside in the late imperial period. He suggested that that the villages' evident prosperity was based on the commercial exploitation of olives, but the real impact of the book lay in its documentation of at least one area of solid rural prosperity under the Late Empire. Based on the texts – laws concerning fleeing peasants, for instance – Jones concluded that the Late Empire eventually taxed its rural economic base into general recession. Tchalenko's villages thus challenged the entire concept of Decline and Fall. If one rural area could flourish under the late Empire's tax structure, why not others? (Tchalenko 1953; cf. Jones 1964.) Full investigation of the archaeological evidence for rural prosperity across the whole of the Roman Empire (Hadrian's Wall to the Euphrates) is no mean undertaking, and it is hardly surprising that, despite much activity in the meantime, no full picture has emerged. It is already clear enough, however, that Tchalenko's villages are not an isolated example of rural prosperity, and that the overall picture is complicated. The currently available rural surveys would suggest, for instance, that the Italian countryside certainly saw considerable decline in the late imperial period. Rural dislocation is also visible in some areas of Britain in the fourth century, and the north-easternmost provinces of the Rhine frontier. On the other hand, rural prosperity in other areas peaked after c.AD 300 (North Africa, Syria and the Negev in modern Israel), and in others maintained itself at a, in imperial terms, historically high level (Spain, central and southern Gaul).[8] The traditional model of global rural economic decline has been thoroughly undermined.

---

6 There are too many relevant contributions to mention, but let me just note that volumes in the Budé and Sources Chrétiennes series all come with French translations, and that a series from Liverpool University Press, Translated Texts for Historians, is building up momentum rapidly, publishing a whole series of broadly Late Antique texts in translations from Greek, Latin and Syriac.

7 Jones 1964. Tchalenko's findings are mentioned in the last paragraph and footnote to chapter 20, 'The Land'. My thanks to Bryan Ward-Perkins for pointing this out to me.

8 The state of play at c.1990 is made conveniently accessible in Lewitt 1991, with refs.

Hand in hand with this has gone some reassessment of the modes of agricultural exploitation being employed. The traditional orthodoxy held that smaller landowners and free peasantry gave way increasingly in the late imperial period to large estates (*latifundia*). Here the evidence is much less clear cut and opinions vary greatly. The archaeological evidence does suggest, however, that, whatever their size, estates were not being worked by gangs of slaves. Rather, most land seems to have been parcelled up into smallholdings, being worked by tenant farmers, operating under a variety of tenurial conditions. This provides a plausible general context for the collapse of legal distinctions between free and unfree tenants (*coloni* and *servi*), which is a marked feature of fourth- to sixth-century imperial legislation.[9]

The archaeological revolution has also fed into understandings of urban transformation. Once again, an assumption of uniform decline (based largely on literary accounts of curials wanting to escape their towns) has given way to a much more variegated picture. Claude Lepelley (1979–81), for instance, using inscriptions and surviving monumental evidence, has documented the survival of traditional urban forms in North Africa on a hitherto unsuspected scale. Substantial urban excavations particularly at Antioch, Aphrodisias and Carthage have added to the picture. The imperial government continued to uphold traditions of monumental construction at Antioch into the middle of the sixth century, for instance, rebuilding the central areas of the city in a traditional manner even after the Persian sack of 540. Not, of course, that nothing changed. For one thing, the whole agenda of public building was certainly transformed by the Christianization of the Empire as the new religion powered a reorientation in the monumental geography of the ancient city. Not only did temples close and churches appear at the heart of cities, but Christianity (with its positive emphasis on the Holy Dead) also brought cemeteries inside town boundaries. Likewise, by the fourth century the imperial centre had confiscated control of most of the cities' traditional revenues, and it was increasingly imperial appointees rather than local men who decided what was going to be built, and where. One key to urban prosperity in the new conditions, well documented in the cases of Aphrodisias, Antioch and Carthage, seems to have been the acquisition of capital status – whether at provincial, diocesan or prefectorial level – within the imperial administrative hierarchy. Such cities became natural centres for rich men, and, it seems, continued to benefit from heavy spending.[10] For other cities, the situation is much less clear. The imperial government sometimes used the endowments of less important cities to the benefit of more

---

9   Again, there exists a very convenient introductory review: Wickham 1988: esp. 187–9 with refs. Jones had already emphasised the erosion of the distinction: Jones 1964: 792–803.

10   Particularly important for Antioch is Lassus 1986. Aphrodisias: Erim 1986; Rouché 1989. The British mission and University of Michigan team have published separate volumes of their findings. More generally, it now seems clear that Procopius is not far off the mark in portraying imperial governments of the sixth century as continuing to invest heavily in monumental urban building: Whitby 1987, and the same author's two papers in Freeman and Kennedy 1986.

favoured towns, and, in parts of the Empire beyond the Mediterranean, the city was anyway more of an artificial, cultural insertion than a naturally generated economic form. Thus relative urban decline was seemingly the fate of many smaller cities in Asia Minor, and some archaeologists of later Roman Britain consider that the provinces' *civitates* had already become centres of secular and religious administration rather than living economic and social centres by the year 400. Issues remain, but models based upon literary sources have been entirely superseded.[11]

The same is true for understandings of patterns of trade and exchange, both local and long-distance. From numerous excavations of late Roman urban and rural sites, and rural survey work, there has emerged a truly vast quantity of pottery evidence: sherds from amphorae (storage jars for a wide variety of products such as wine and olive oil), fine wares, coarse wares, lamps, etc. In many cases, provenances and closely dated typological sequences have been established, together with, in the case of some amphorae, a clear idea of what they originally contained. It is now possible, therefore, to map over time the changing distribution of certain wares (and hence, in the case of certain amphorae, of certain goods as well) from their particular places of origin across the Mediterranean world. Two points are already apparent. First, large amounts of both fine wares and oil and wine were being moved long distances around the Mediterranean in the fourth century. The products of North Africa predominated, but the Near East, particularly Syria, also exported substantial amounts of material. Second, throughout the Empire, more local pottery industries supplied the needs even of quite humble habitation sites.[12] Debate continues, however, on the broader significance of this evidence. An important Italian school, for instance, has argued that the long-distance movements represent genuine 'trade' in the goods concerned. Likewise, the more local industries raise the question of whether pottery manufacture and distribution can provide a model for the general level of sophistication in the economy. If so, one would envisage that even quite humble agriculturalists regularly sold or exchanged surpluses for the goods and services of specialists. Both lines of argument challenge strongly held traditional views of the ancient economy as consisting essentially of a series of self-sufficient landed estates with almost no room for the operation of market forces. But the jury is still out and intermediate positions have already been suggested.[13]

Apart from the archaeological revolution, assessments of the overall cultural context of the late imperial period have also been transformed, this time the

11 Useful introductory reviews, replete with references, are: Barnish 1989; Brooks 1986. On Asia Minor, see Mitchell 1993. Also very much to the point is Ward-Perkins 1984.
12 Hayes (1972), *Late Roman Pottery* is the basic guide to African Red Slip Ware (ARS); cf. Carandini *et al.* 1981 and a host of other studies. Ipswich and Oxford were centres of local pottery production, for instance, in later Roman Britain.
13 A good introductory review which also posits its own hypothesis is Wickham 1988: 190–3. The maximalist position has been adopted by Italian researchers, see Carandini *et al.* 1986. Others take the view that trade was not important, and that the late Roman economy, as other ancient economies, was overwhelmingly subsistence: e.g. Garnsey and Saller 1987 (following in the tradition of Finley 1985). A useful collection of papers is Garnsey *et al.* 1983.

reconsideration of old sources. In the anglophone world, the doyen of this movement has been Peter Brown. The mind goes immediately to his ground-breaking work on Augustine, but numerous essays and lecture series have given well-deserved attention to the likes of Paulinus of Nola, Ambrose of Milan and a host of others. Above all, it seems to me, as this kind of list suggests, that his work has brought a series of particularly Christian individuals and Christian writings (not, of course, by any means that Brown's work has been limited to Christian authors or topics) from the field of Patristics into that of general historical discussion. More particularly, he has explicitly and implicitly challenged the familiar refrain that the rise to prominence of miracle-working saints signalled both that superstition had replaced philosophy as the mood of the times, and led the population of the Empire to refuse to defend it in its hour of greatest need. Debate has moved on so far that it is hard to remember the impact of the famous article on the Holy Man, which argued that it was prosperity not poverty which drove Late Roman Syrians to consult holy problem-solvers. In every page of Brown's work, there is a refusal to subscribe to the tradition of Decline and Fall, and an emphasis on the excitement of the cultural dynamic let loose by the intrusion of mass Christianity into the late classical world. New value-structures, new subjects worth writing about, a whole new literary language: all have been noted and discussed with analytical and linguistic vigour.[14] The broader impact of his career can perhaps also be measured by the series of monographs from California University Press under his general editorship, and the overall title The Transformation of the Classical Heritage. The first volume in the series, drawing upon anthropological methods and lines of enquiry, undertook a general reconsideration of the role of public ceremonial in the fourth century and after. Currently numbering twenty-two, subsequent volumes have ranged from studies of pivotal figures and texts, to much broader manifestations of the transformations of the period.[15]

Not, of course, that Late Antiquity required Peter Brown to invent it. The range of source materials and subjects is much too interesting to have been left undisturbed for long. Indeed, the French might claim that they 'invented' it. In his obituary of Henri Marrou in Le Monde, André Mandouze commented, 'The name of Marrou will forever be attached to the discovery (or the rediscovery) of a huge field: that of this "antiquité tardif et chrétienne".' The French tradition has certainly proved particularly powerful with a range of scholars interested in a wide variety of subjects, and, in particular, the different admixtures of classical and Christian cultures which emerged at different points between the fourth and seventh centuries. Beyond Marrou who was interested amongst other things in St Augustine and, of course, the whole history of education in antiquity, the works of Jacques Fontaine are perhaps worth particular mention. Like Marrou, his writings again display a career-long

---

14 A few sample works: Brown 1967; 1972; 1981; 1992; 1971. For Brown's own view of his work in retrospect and a series of responses, see *Symbolae Ostoerus* 72, 1997.

15 First volume: MacCormack 1981. A full listing of titles can be found in the front of any book in the series; the most recent publication is McLynn 1994.

interest in the dynamism of late classical, particularly but not solely Latin, culture, and of the interaction of Christianity with established cultural modes. It is also indicative that French is the only language with an entire periodical – *L'Antiquité Tardif* (established as recently as 1993) – dedicated to Late Antiquity.[16]

Overall, a much stronger sense has emerged of the dynamism of the interaction between Christianity and the Graeco-Roman world. From the standpoint of the traditional value systems of the latter, the period is one of decline. One measure sometimes used is the declining number of volumes per century in the series of standard editions of classical texts as one reaches the third and fourth centuries. But many of the best-educated classicists of the fourth century (Augustine, Jerome, Rufinus, Basil, John Chrysostom; or, indeed, the mid- and later third: Origen, Eusebius of Caesarea) were attracted by their faith to turn their educations to a new purpose: Christianity. To make any real comparison, therefore, one would have also to include in the count volumes in such standard and comprehensive Christian series as the various Patrologia (Latina, Graeca, and perhaps also Orientalia).[17] And much recent work has indeed stressed the degree to which established techniques were applied by educated Christians to their new concerns. The general impact of Stoic and Platonic philosophy upon Christianity is well known and requires no belabouring here, but it is perhaps worth emphasizing the extent to which Christianity was still forming in the fourth century. The religious disputes of the period were traditionally characterized as curbing deviations from an established doctrinal norm: Orthodoxy. Much work of the last thirty years or so, particularly on the Arian dispute, has shown very clearly that much of what is now generally accepted as Orthodoxy was actually created in the course of these fourth-century debates. In these, a new Christian elite of classically-educated clerics, with (here and there, at least) a smattering of classical philosophy, used their intellectual armoury to attempt to make sense of their Christian source-texts.[18]

The degree to which fully-fledged Christianity was a product of dialogue with the Graeco-Roman world can be illustrated in less obvious but equally profound ways. The standard early medieval Christian mode of preaching from biblical texts – taking the audience through various layers of meaning from the literal/historical to the metaphorical/philosophical – deliberately echoed the approach of the secular classical grammarian to his canon of texts. Jerome, Augustine, Ambrose likewise were conscious literary stylists who made traditional kinds of choices between different modes of discourse, according to their perception of the audience for any particular piece of work (e.g. Young 1989; Oberhelman 1991, with refs.)

---

16 Posthumously, in the year of his death, Marrou published the significantly entitled volume *Décadence romain ou antiquité tardive* (1978). Fontaine's works include *Isidore de Seville et la culture classique dans l'Espagne wisigothique* 1959.

17 e.g. MacMullen 1988; ch. 1. An equally dismal estimate using different methods is Harris 1988.

18 There are significant differences over detail, but the broad picture emerges clearly. See generally Chadwick 1993; Young 1983. Or for more detailed argument, Lyman 1993; Williams 1987; McLynn 1994: 237ff.

The encounter between classical culture and Christianity thus sponsored a mutual transformation: arguably to the enrichment of both. At least, Christian ideologies authorized new subject matters and genres. Classical culture was elite in one way, or sets of ways defined by wealth, education and the privileging of certain forms of social action. And Christianity recognized new forms of elite behaviour: a man no longer had to be rich and well-educated if he was holy, and women could sometimes be more or less equally holy. Thus new social contexts, groups and classes are documented in saints' lives and miracle collections (not to mention sermons), opening up new worlds for the social historian. The need to spread the Gospel also provided an extra impetus for the creation of literatures. Particularly in the Near East, Syriac, Coptic, Armenian and other languages spawned exciting forms of literacy as the new religion made its impact.[19] Many scholars still mourn the passing of the old classical order, but, when applied to the cultural transformations of the late Roman period, the paradigm of decline and fall seems wildly insufficient.

Broadly the same judgement seems applicable to the political culture and institutions of the Later Roman Empire. There are, of course, too many relevant studies to mention. I would specifically draw the reader's attention to the legal historical work of A. M. Honoré, however, in bringing back to life the evolving legal framework of the later Empire. There is much to be learned from Jones, of course, but Jones's study has, I think, too strong a sense of timelessness. In his work, there is a tendency to see all late imperial legislation as illuminating the workings of a governmental machine set monolithically in place by Diocletian and his fellow Tetrarchs in c. AD 300. One of the many virtues of Honoré's work, however, has been to put personality and politics back into law-making (Honoré 1994; 1978). This has wide implications. Different political agendas and evolving political contexts between them created different kinds of law and even mutually contradictory rulings. In the same way, as a whole variety of studies have shown, institutions of government were not unchanging, but were transformed fundamentally over time as different interest groups took hold of them and adapted them to their own needs. Perhaps the classic illustration of this is the imperial bureaucracy. There is some evidence that it was originally designed to provide an alternative lever of power for emperors to use against the well-entrenched local landowning elites who governed the cities of the Empire. By the mid-fourth century, local elites had responded to this move (if move it was) by taking over the bureaucracy. Having learned Greek from the grammarian as usual, the progeny of the landowning classes of the eastern Mediterranean went on to learn Latin, shorthand or law; equipping themselves with the bureaucratic skills which were now the path to fame and fortune. Emperors complained and conducted periodic purges, but, in the end, they had largely to defer to local demands for access to central imperial office (a brief selection: Liebeschuetz 1972; Goffart 1974; Vogler 1979; Teitler 1985; Delmaire 1989; Heather 1994).

---

19 Alongside these successes, there were also shorter-lived failures, such as literary Gothic which was created to translate the Bible and died when Gothic Christianity lost its particularity.

One final shift in methodological emphasis is worth singling out. In 1971, the first volume of the *Prosopography of the Later Roman Empire* was published, covering the period AD 260–395. Since then, two subsequent volumes have appeared, taking the project down to the mid-seventh century. This project is concerned solely with secular and non-clerical figures, while the prosopography of the Christian Church is being handled, geographically subdivided, by teams of French scholars. So far, their progress has been less prompt, reflecting the wealth of information provided by Christian texts.[20] An example of what this kind of information can do is provided by the seminal work of John Matthews in his monograph on western aristocracies and a series of essays. Amongst other virtues, its powerful prosopographical emphasis (combining both Christian clerics and others) allows him to build up a new vision of the operation of politics and elite society in the late imperial period. Regime-building, individual ambition, political rivalry and connection emerge convincingly from his work as the real stuff of late Roman politics: the forces behind institutional transformation (Matthews 1976; cf. Matthews 1985). In my opinion, the prosopographical projects and Matthews's seminal study between them issue challenges which have yet to find a response. No answering study of the eastern Mediterranean in the fourth century has been attempted, for instance; nor have there been attempts to use the material gathered in the collections in a chronologically comparative manner. The prosopographies, it seems to me, should be more than convenient reference works.

THE EARLY MEDIEVAL WEST

Study of the early medieval West has been profoundly influenced by the historiographical revolution encapsulated in the rise to prominence of Late Antiquity. Indeed, Late Antiquity would certainly be taken by many to extend to at least AD 600. Thus, whereas the early medieval West has tended to be the preserve of Carolingianists going 'backward', as it were, recent years have seen an increase in the extent to which Merovingian Gaul and Visigothic Spain have become quarries for late-classicists and ancient historians. The full integration of Christian clerical sources and the more traditional secular ones has also become a standard feature of the historiography of this period too.

Likewise, archaeological investigation has had an increasing impact over the last thirty years. This can be seen nowhere more clearly than in current understandings of the largely Germanic groups who invaded the western Roman Empire in the fifth century, and around some of whom the successor kingdoms of the early medieval West formed. The old view, evolved at the turn of the century by the German

---

20 Secular: *The Prosopography of the Later Roman Empire*: vol. 1 (AD 260–395) ed. A. H. M. Jones, J. R. Martindale, J. Morris (Cambridge, 1971); vol. 2 (AD 395–527) ed. J. R. Martindale (Cambridge, 1980); vol. 3 (AD 527–641) ed. J. R. Martindale (Cambridge, 1992). Of the French project – *Prosopographie chrétienne du Bas Empire* – only 1 volume has appeared: A. Mandouze (ed.), *Prosopographie de L'Afrique chrétienne (303–533)* (Paris, 1982).

scholar Kossina and his school, was that each Germanic group mentioned in the literary sources had its own distinctive physical culture. This view prevailed pretty generally until the Second World War, and, in many places, as late as the 1960s. The mass of material excavated and studied since the war has made it clear, however, that there are many more named groups than distinctive cultural areas, and the idea that physical remains are a reliable guide to people's perceptions of their identity has been seriously challenged. The invading groups of the fifth century were not so clearly distinct from one another as older historiography supposed.[21]

More or less simultaneously, Reinhard Wenskus's revolutionary study of 1961 effectively made the same point from literary evidence. The history of known Germanic groups, he argued, suggests not solid boundaries and political continuity, but a very fluid situation where groups coalesced and fragmented with considerable ease. Wenskus argued that any ethnic group-identity in these social formations was really carried by a relatively limited part of their population – successful noble and royal clans – who gathered an otherwise fairly heterogeneous mass of population behind them. Wenskus's approach has been taken up and developed further by the so-called Vienna ethnogenesis school headed by Herwig Wolfram. Ethnicity has come to be seen as an ideology rather than a given biological fact, and this is a perspective with important implications for the histories of the successor states and, indeed, the Carolingian period. (Wenskus 1961; Wolfram 1988; Pohl 1988; Geary 1983.) Debate continues. It is now impossible to view the invading groups as simple, well-defined entities with long and continuous histories. Whether ethnicity was really the preserve of a very small proportion of their population or not is quite another matter. I have myself argued, for instance, that Gothic identity was shared by more of a caste, amounting to maybe as much as a fifth of the population, than a small group of noble clans. Others have reconsidered the archaeological evidence for the Anglo-Saxon invasions of Britain, and suggested, again contrary to currently-fashionable views, that substantial numbers of invaders were involved. Some have also argued, with slightly less success, that a strong ethnic divide continued to mark the history of the Frankish and Visigothic successor states, with Franks and Visigoths, rather than descendants of the areas' Roman populations, enjoying the majority of the spoils.[22]

In the early 1980s, Walter Goffart challenged traditional views of the end of the western Empire in two further ways. On one level, he mounted a very technical argument about the means by which the invading groups were integrated economically into their new, formerly Roman, territories. Rather than taking actual land, he suggested, a part of the normal tax revenue was simply reallocated to their

---

21 General methodological introduction: Shennan 1989; Germanic archaeology: Hachmann 1970; 1976.
22 Heather 1991; cf. Heather 1996; Harke 1990. Visigoths: Thompson 1969: ch. 9; Kampers 1979. Franks: Ebling 1974. General (and competing) visions of post-Migration Period ethnicity: Ebling et al. 1980; Geary 1986: ch. 4.

support, so that the invasions involved no large-scale expropriations of land from the Roman population. This perspective underwrote his second strand of argument which denied in more general terms the revolutionary nature of these events. The so-called invasions, he argued, were more a reshuffling of known quantities than the dismemberment by outsiders of a long-standing political entity. The invaders were small in number and had a long history of relations with the Roman state which had given them a positive reason to absorb its culture. There was also little violence involved in the process, and the eastern half of the Empire positively encouraged it, to weaken the western Empire and reduce the danger posed to itself by aggressive western leaders. In an already famous phrase, Goffart characterized the end of the Roman Empire as 'an imaginative experiment that got a little out at of hand' (Goffart 1980: 35; see also Goffart 1981, 1989).

The range of response to Goffart's work is a tribute to its vigour, coherence and importance. The more technical argument about the economic integration of the invaders has found both supporters and opponents (for continued debate: Barnish 1986; Wolfram and Schwarcz 1988). As regards the more general argument, I have to declare an interest. In my view, they demonstrably underestimate the degree of violence involved in the transition from Empire to successor states. I also think that numbers were much larger than he would allow, and that the eastern half of the Empire did a considerable amount to sustain the West. To my mind, therefore, conflict must remain a central and general feature of the transition from Empire to successor states, but others will disagree.[23]

Moving on to the historiography of the western successor states, measuring the degree of continuity from the Roman Empire has in many ways become the central issue of recent years. The issue has never been unimportant, but is closely related both to concepts of a cultural unity called Late Antiquity which endured Roman political collapse, and to the question, raised by Goffart, how we should envisage that collapse. Methodologically, prosopography has been as much of a growth industry for the successor states as for the Later Roman Empire. A series of German and Spanish researchers have between them compiled important prosopographical collections for the Merovingian Frankish and Visigothic Spanish kingdoms, and, as we have seen, the *Prosopography of the Later Roman Empire* now extends to AD 641 (Garcia Moreno 1974; Kampers 1979; Ebling *et al.* 1980).

One measure of continuity, making full use of this prosopographical interest, is the survival of old Roman landowning clans into the post-Roman period. Gaul, particularly southern Gaul where there is plenty of information, has seen much work on this. In so far as there is one, the consensus would seem to be that old Roman elites made central use of the Church as part of a strategy of survival, coming to dominate the episcopate of Frankish Gaul. From another perspective, the

---

23 Heather 1991: 309–30; 1995. There is also a substantial amount of archaeological as well as literary evidence that the long-term effect of Roman hegemony over the Germanic world was precisely to generate larger, more coherent entities, better able to resist Roman power: see Hedeager 1988: 129–43 with refs.

degree to which dominant groups among the invaders were quick to make an alliance with the Roman landowning class, sometimes to the detriment of relations with their poorer fellow-invaders, has also been underlined.[24]

Another plank in the broader argument for continuity has emerged from recent interest in the general phenomenon of literacy. Amongst other things, a stronger interest in language has led to greater emphasis on elite cultural continuity in both literary genres and styles of composition. Some very significant Merovingian Gallic writers – most prominently Gregory of Tours and Caesarius of Arles – formally distance themselves from the classical literary heritage. Closer inspection suggests, however, that such statements are deliberately misleading, and that these writers were educated in, and consciously used at least some aspects of, that heritage. Determinedly classicizing authors such as Venantius Fortunatus have come to look less odd, therefore, and there clearly existed in Merovingian Gaul a general audience for classicizing Latin composition. Similar points have been emphasized for Visigothic Spain, and even post-Roman Britain, where the education and literary skill of Gildas (the one surviving reflection of the age) have come in for reassessment. More generally, estimates of the bureaucratic quantity and quality of post-Roman government in western Europe have been revised significantly upwards.[25]

Many other manifestations of the phenomenon of continuity have also attracted interest: the survival, for instance, of Roman patterns of local dominance and patronage, of building or of the luxurious villa lifestyle. Some manifestations have even turned out to be rather surprising. A famous feature of the material culture of the successor states is the garnet-encrusted *cloisonné* jewellery of their elites. Recent investigations have shown that these badges of authority have their origin in Roman regalia. The main attraction of the garnet lay in the fact that its deep red colour made it the precious gem closest in colour to the imperial porphyry (Arrhenius 1985). Thus in many areas of western Europe, Roman social structures, Roman methods and Roman values can be seen to have survived Roman political collapse.

But the post-Roman West was at the same time a world of profound transformation. In some places, dramatic change is a much more obvious feature than continuity. Attempts have been made to trace Anglo-Saxon and Welsh estate structures back to Roman villas, but this now looks very doubtful, and in a host of other ways post-Roman Britain seems to have little to do with the Empire. Groups of non-literate, Germanic-speaking intruders forced their way into the Roman provinces, displaced its landed elite and created a new patchwork of polities amidst the almost total collapse of urban life and economic complexity. Some Roman values and methods survived in the west of the island, and more would be reintroduced

---

24   Roman elites: Heinzelmann 1975; cf. Van Dam 1985. Non-Roman elites: the general arguments of E. A. Thompson in papers such as Thompson 1963, reprinted in Thompson 1982.
25   See generally Wood 1994: chs 2, 7, 14; McKitterick 1990, esp. papers by Collins and Wood. Otherwise, George 1992; Klingshirn 1994; Lapidge and Dumville 1994.

from the continent, but the distinctively Roman features of Roman Britain seem to have little shaped its Anglo-Saxon successor states.[26]

Archaeological investigations have likewise demonstrated marked discontinuities in economic structures across the whole of former Roman western Europe. The whole region was to a considerable extent demonetarized by the end of the sixth century. Some gold coins were being issued, but these were of too high a value to play much of a role in everyday life, and minting of smaller denominations in silver and copper died out everywhere. Matching this, evidence for long-distance trading contacts virtually disappears in the course of the sixth century. There was some degree of continuity in the towns of some regions, but there is much evidence of general urban decline. Likewise, the available field surveys indicate a marked drop in rural settlement from the fifth century onwards. Further archaeological investigation will no doubt add to what remains a very preliminary overview; no doubt too, certain areas bucked the general trend. Already, for instance, excavations at several sites north and south of the Channel and North Sea (Hamwih, Dorestad, etc.) have revealed the growth in the later seventh century of northern trading networks of unexpected sophistication and extent, and alongside this the reintroduction of a lower-value, silver coinage: the so-called *sceattas*. None the less, it is hard to believe that the archaeological record will not continue to document a general and rather dramatic decline and simplification in economic structures in the immediately post-Roman West.[27]

In other areas, discontinuity was less abrupt and less immediately dramatic, but none the less profound. Even in literary culture, signs of change run deep. The Latin of some of the major literary figures of sixth-century Gaul as it survives in the *Epistolae Austrasiacae*, for instance, is non-classical in grammar and orthography. These men had evidently not received a full Latin education at the hands of a grammarian, a fact which in itself marks a fundamental shift in elite culture. In the late imperial period, correct language functioned as an elite caste-marker. While the classically inspired literary ambitions of these sixth-century writers is clear enough, that such members of the governing elite should not be masters of classical Latin demonstrates that language had ceased to define social status. It has even been argued with great vigour that the residual Latinity of written composition hides the fact that the real language of this post-Roman world was Romance and not Latin at all.[28]

It is also clear that this period saw a fundamental shift in patterns of political economy. All these states (except perhaps those of the Anglo-Saxons in Britain) inherited considerable powers of taxation from the Roman state: in particular, the

26 Some recent surveys: Davies 1983; Campbell 1991; Bassett 1989; cf., for a different angle, Blair 1991: ch. 1; Brooks 1986.

27 For introductions and refs., Wickham 1988; Lewitt 1991; Hodges and Whitehouse 1983; Astill 1985; Wood 1994: ch. 17.

28 Late Roman tradition: Kaster 1988. Post-Roman: (e.g.) Riche 1976; Wood 1994. On the evolution of Latin: Wright 1982; Banniard 1992.

right to levy a land tax on the agricultural sector of the economy, by far its largest component. As a whole host of studies have emphasized, these powers gradually dwindled, creating a different type of state in western Europe. Sometimes called (perhaps unhelpfully) 'proto-feudal', it was much less able to redistribute wealth within its bounds, operated via a governmental machine of much-reduced size and sophistication, and, in particular, no longer employed professional soldiers, but drew instead on local landowners and their dependents to form its armies. Indeed, elite militarization is a major feature of the period, representing a major transformation from the civilian bureaucratic elite lifestyles which characterized the Later Roman Empire. The main method of rewarding local supporters under these new conditions consisted seemingly of making grants of land from royal fiscs. Thus necessary processes of making friends and influencing people – among the groups who formed the basis of the royal army, for instance – tended to undermine the wealth of the central authority. It has been argued, indeed, that strong centralizing government was now only possible when sustained military expansion gave access to outside, renewable sources of wealth.[29]

The successor kingdoms were thus very different from the Later Roman Empire. There are some common elements, but also so many fundamental differences that the term continuity does not seem particularly helpful. Better, perhaps, is to envisage the Roman world as bequeathing some elements to a new social, economic and political order. Based on a series of royal courts, this new world was decidedly Christian and, for the most part, Latin. But an ideology of elite education and active composition had given way to passive literacy (the ability to read), and its social relations were to a considerable extent formed around the needs of raising armies (cf. esp. Wood 1994).

There has, of course, been much other work on the early medieval West. Traditional subjects such as the Papacy and monasticism have continued to be studied to great effect, although here too the heritage of the late Roman period has proved a fruitful avenue of study (Markus 1990). Likewise, the perennial process of editing, commenting upon and, as in the case of the later Roman Empire, translating the sources has occupied much well-placed scholarly attention. Again, these are not isolated endeavours. The old tradition of editing early medieval texts, for instance, always classicized their Latin. Recent understandings of linguistic change suggest that, prior to the Carolingian linguistic revival, such an approach is totally misplaced and that manuscript traditions should be allowed to speak for themselves.

More generally, there has, it seems to me, been a broadening of subject matter and methodology within the discipline. Here, I suspect, early medieval history is reflecting quite general trends in displaying a greater interest in social-historical topics, and incorporating insights derived from sociological and anthropological

---

29   The relevant bibliography is immense, but see, for instance, Wickham 1984; Garcia Moreno 1989; Brown 1984. On expansion, Collins 1983: chs 2, 4; Reuter 1985; 1991. For a different view, Durliat 1990.

studies. A prime example is Wallace-Hadrill's use of anthropologically observed African models in attempting to revise traditional notions of the Frankish feud (Wallace-Hadrill 1959, repr. in Wallace-Hadrill 1962: 25–48), and new methods have in general had a particularly marked influence upon how we might understand the very large corpus of early medieval legal texts. When they were first systematically studied in the nineteenth and early twentieth centuries, there was a natural tendency to view them as modern law codes, and to assume that what they said should happen, did. But the texts themselves are sometimes incoherent and self-contradictory, and it is unclear that either literacy or the competence of centrally organized legal systems was really sufficient in the early medieval West for written law codes really to have played a fundamental role in legal proceedings. Indeed, some of the legal texts clearly indicate that they were to be used alongside a body of oral custom. Likewise, recent studies using charters to focus on the practicalities of dispute settlement have made it clear that written law codes were rarely used, at least north of the Alps. But charters really only reveal the operations of what we would call civil not criminal law, and some scholars still take royal law-making as a very practical legal enterprise (Davies and Fouracre 1986; Wormald 1977; McKitterick 1989).

Interest in broader topics of social history has manifested itself elsewhere, too. The history of women has been a growth industry in the last ten to fifteen years, opening up interesting avenues into social organization. This is particularly true in the case of emerging insights into the various methods of arranging family finances to provide for marriage.[30] The spread of Christianity has likewise seen considerable work, with some shift of emphasis away from bishops towards, as it were, the foot soldiers: the laymen endeavouring to get to heaven, and the ordinary priest; trying to get them there. Local Church organization and missionary methods are just two of the topics currently attracting interest.[31] The socio-economic organization of the countryside – estate structure and rural settlement – is another subject of huge importance, where a few suggestive studies have appeared, but where much more work needs to be done.[32] The same is true of vertical and horizontal social bonds: topics clearly at least in part related to economic organization. A recent attempt to rewrite the history of feudalism merely whetted the appetite (Reynolds 1994).

Many more topics could and should be mentioned, but space is limited, and it is high time to bring this chapter to a close by reflecting briefly on how much difference the rise of the concept of Late Antiquity has made to the writing and indeed study of history. In terms of eroding traditional university departmental boundaries, the answer is relatively little. Even the formal division between Ancient and Medieval History, for instance, continues to exist in most places, and there are very few academic posts explicitly in Late Antique studies. In less formal terms,

---

30 Women: Baker 1977; Wemple 1981; Stafford 1983. Marriage: Goody 1983; 1977.
31 *Cristianizzazione* 1982; Blair and Sharpe 1992. The question of missionary methods has been raised amongst others by Flint 1991.
32 Contrast the very different views of slavery, for instance, in Giardina 1986 with Bonnassie 1991.

however, the differences seem dramatic. As I hope this chapter has shown, study of both the Later Roman Empire and the early medieval West will never be the same again. Graduate studies' programmes in Late Antiquity are also reasonably common, as are graduate seminars including historians of all kinds, patrists, classical humanists and oriental linguists. Whilst financial and other interests keep departmental barriers erect, it is a pleasure to be able to report on a subject area where intellectual barriers have been decisively lowered.

REFERENCES

Arrhenius, B. (1985) *Merovingian Garnet Jewellery: Emergence and Social Implications*, Stockholm.

Astill, G. (1985) 'Archaeology, economics, and early medieval Europe', *Oxford Journal of Archaeology* 4: 215–32.

Bagnall, R. S. (1994) *Egypt in Late Antiquity*, Princeton.

Baker, D. (ed.) (1977) *Medieval Women*, Oxford.

Banniard, M. (1992) *Viva Voce: Communication écrite et communication orale du IVe du IXe siècles en occident latin*, Paris.

Barnes, T. D. (1982) *The New Empire of Diocletian and Constantine*, Cambridge.

Barnish, S. J. B. (1986) 'Taxation, land and barbarian settlement in the western Empire', *Papers of the British School at Rome* 54: 170–95.

—— (1989) 'The transformation of classical studies and the Pirenne debate', *Journal of Roman Archaeology* 2: 385–400.

Bassett, S. (ed.) (1989) *The Origins of Anglo-Saxon Kingdoms*, Leicester.

Blair, J. (1991) *Early Medieval Surrey: Landholding, Church and Settlement before 1300*, Stroud.

—— and Sharpe, R. (eds) (1992) *Pastoral Care before the Parish*, Leicester.

Bonnassie, P. (1991) *From Slavery to Feudalism in South-western Europe*, trans. J. Birrell, Cambridge.

Brooks, D. A. (1986) 'A review of the evidence for continuity in British towns in the fifth and sixth centuries', *Oxford Journal of Archaeology* 5: 77–102.

Brown, P. (1967) *Augustine of Hippo: A Biography*, London.

—— (1971) 'The rise and function of the holy man in Late Antiquity', *Journal of Roman Studies* 61: 80–101; reprinted in id. *Society and the Holy in late Antiquity*, London, 1982.

—— (1972) *Religion and Society in the Age of St. Augustine*, London.

—— (1981) *The Cult of the Saints*, London.

—— (1992) *Power and Persuasion in Late Antiquity: Towards a Christian Empire*.

Brown, T. S. (1984) *Gentlemen and Officers: Imperial Administration and Aristocratic Power in Byzantine Italy A.D. 554–800*, Rome.

Cameron, A. D. E. (1970) *Claudian: Poetry and Propaganda at the Court of Honorius*, Oxford.

Campbell, J. (ed.) (1991) *The Anglo Saxons*, 2nd edn, London.

Carandini, A. *et al.* (1981) *Atlante delle forme ceramiche* I. *Enciclopedia dell'arte antica*.

Chadwick, H. (1993) *The Early Church*, rev. edn, London.

Collins, R. (1983) *Early Medieval Spain: Unity in Diversity 400–1000*, London.

Cristianizzazione ed organizzazione ecclesiastica delle campagne nell'alto medioevo (1982) Settimane di studi dell'centro italiano di studi sull'alto medioevo 28, Milan.

Dagron, G. (1974) *Naissance d'une capitale: Constantinople et ses institutions de 330 à 451*, Paris.

Davies, W. (1983) *Wales in the Early Middle Ages*, Leicester.

—— and Fouracre, P. (eds) (1986) *The Settlement of Disputes in Early Medieval Europe*, Cambridge.

Delmaire, R. (1989) *Largesses sacrées et res privata: l'aerarium impérial et son administration du IVe siècle*, Collection de l'École Française de Rome 121, Rome.

Demandt, A. (1970) 'Magistri militum', *RE* suppl. xii: 553–790.

Durliat, J. (1990) *Les Finances publiques de Dioclétien aux Carolingiens (284–889)*, Sigmaringen.

Ebling, H. (1974) *Prosopographie der Amtsträger des Merowingerreiches*, Beiheft der *Francia* 3, Munich.

—— Jarnut, J. and Kampers, G. (1980) '"*Nomen et gens*": Untersuchungen zu den Führungsschichten des Franken-, Langobarden- und Westgotenreiches im 6. und 7. Jahrhundert', *Francia* 8: 687–745.

Erim, T. K. (1989) *Aphrodisias*, London.

Finley, M. I. (1985) *The Ancient Economy*, 2nd edn, London.

Flint, V. (1991) *The Rise of Magic in Early Medieval Europe*, Oxford.

Fontaine, J. (1959) *Isidore de Seville et la culture classique dans l'Espagne wisigothique*, 2 vols, Paris.

Freeman, P. and Kennedy, D. (eds) (1986) *The Defence of the Roman and Byzantine East*, British Archaeological Reports 297, Oxford.

Garnsey, P. and Saller, R. (1987) *The Roman Empire: Economy, Society, and Culture*.

Garnsey P. *et al.* (1983) *Trade in the Ancient Economy*, London.

Geary, P. (1983) 'Ethnic identity as a situational construct in the early Middle Ages', *Mitteilungen der anthropologischen Gesellschaft in Wien* 112: 15–26.

—— (1986) *Aristocracy in Provence: The Rhone Basin at the Dawn of the Carolingian Age*, Philadelphia.

George, J. W. (1992) *Venantius Fortunatus: A Poet in Merovingian Gaul*, Oxford.

Giardina, A. (ed.) (1986) *Società romana e imperio tardoantica* III: *Le mercei. Gli insediamenti*, Rome and Bari.

Goffart, W. (1974) *'Caput' and Colonate: Towards a History of Late Roman Taxation*, Toronto.

—— (1980) *Barbarians and Romans A.D. 418–584: The Techniques of Accommodation*, Princeton.

—— (1981) 'Rome, Constantinople, and the barbarians', *American Historical Review* 76: 275–306.

—— (1989) 'The theme of "*The* Barbarian Invasions" in Late Antique and modern historiography', in E. K. Chrysos and A. Schwarcz (eds) *Das Reich und die Barbaren*, Vienna.

Goody, J. (1983) *The Development of Family and Marriage in Europe*, Cambridge.

Hachmann, R. (1970) *Die Goten und Skandinavien*, Berlin.

—— (1976) *The Germanic Peoples*, London.

Harke, H. (1990) '"Warrior graves"? The background of the Anglo-Saxon weapon burial site', *Past and Present* 126: 22–43.

Harris, W. V. (1988) *Ancient Literacy*, Cambridge.

Hayes, J. W. (1972) *Late Roman Pottery*, London.

Heather, P. J. (1991) *Goths and Romans 332–489*, Oxford.

—— (1994) 'New men for new Constantines? Creating an imperial elite in the eastern Mediterranean', in P. Magdalino (ed.) *New Constantines: The Rhythm of Imperial Renewal in Byzantium, 4th–13th Centuries*, London.

—— (1995) 'The Huns and the end of the Roman Empire in western Europe', *English Historical Review* 110: 4–41.

—— (1996) *The Goths*, Oxford.

Hedeager, L. (1988) 'The Evolution of Germanic society 1–400 AD', in R. A. F. Jones *et al.*

(eds) *First Millennium Papers: Western Europe in the First Millennium AD*, Oxford: 129–43.

Heinzelmann, M. (1975) *Bischofsherschaft in Gallien: Zur Kontinuität römischer Führungsschichten vom 4. bis zum 7. Jahrhundert: soziale, prosopographische und bildungsgeschichtliche Aspekte*, Munich.

Hodges, R. and Whitehouse, D. (1983) *Mohammed, Charlemagne and the Origins of Europe*, London.

Hoffmann, D. (1969) *Das spätrömische Bewegungsheer und die Notitia Dignitatum*, Düsseldorf.

Honoré, A. M. (1978) *Tribonian*, London.

—— (1994) *Emperors and Lawyers*, 2nd rev. edn, Oxford.

Jones, A. H. M. (1964) *The Later Roman Empire 284–602: A Social, Economic and Administrative Survey*, 3 vols, Oxford.

Kampers, G. (1979) *Personengeschichtliche Studien zum Westgotenreich in Spanien*, Münster.

Kaster, R. A. (1988) *Guardians of the Language: The Grammarians and Society in Late Antiquity*, Berkeley.

Klingshirn, W. (1994) *Caesarius of Arles: The Making of a Christian Community in Late Antique Gaul*, Cambridge.

Lapidge, M. and Dumville, D. (eds) (1994) *Gildas: New Approaches*, London.

Lassus, J. (ed.) (1986) *Les Portiques d'Antioche*, vol. 5 of *Antioch on the Orontes*, Princeton.

Lepelley, C. (1979–81) *Les Cités de l'Afrique romaine au Bas Empire*, 2 vols, Paris.

Lewitt, T. (1991) *Agricultural Production in the Roman Economy A.D. 200–400*, British Archaeological Reports 568, Oxford.

Liebeschuetz, J. H. W. G. (1972) *Antioch: City and Imperial Administration in the Later Roman Empire*, Oxford.

Lyman, J. R. (1993) *Christology and Cosmology: Models Of Divine Activity in Origen, Eusebius and Athanasius*, Oxford.

MacCormack, S. G. (1981; repr. 1990) *Art and Ceremony in Late Antiquity*, Berkeley and London.

McKitterick, R. (1989) *The Carolingians and the Written Word*, Cambridge.

—— (1990) *The Uses of Literacy in Early Medieval Europe*, Cambridge.

McLynn, N. B. (1994) *Ambrose of Milan*, Berkeley.

MacMullen, R. (1988) *Corruption and the Decline of Rome*, Yale.

Markus, R. (1990) *The End of Ancient Christianity*, Cambridge.

Marrou, H. (1978) *Décadence romain ou antiquité tardive*, Paris.

Il Matrimonio nella società altomedievale (1977), 2 vols, Settimane di Studio del Centro di Studi sul Alto Medioevo 24, Milan.

Matthews, J. F. (1975) *Western Aristocracies and Imperial Court A.D. 364–425*, Oxford.

—— (1985) *Political Life and Culture in Late Roman Society*, London.

—— (1989) *The Roman Empire of Ammianus*, London.

Mitchell, S. (1993) *Anatolia: Land, Men, and Gods in Asia Minor. II The Rise of the Church*, Oxford.

Moreno, L. A. Garcia (1974) *Prosopografia del Reino Visigoda de Toledo*, Salamanca.

—— (1989) *Historia de España visigoda*, Madrid.

Oberhelman, S. M. (1991) *Rhetoric and Homiletics in Fourth Century Christian Literature*, Atlanta.

Pohl, W. (1988) *Die Awaren*, Munich.

Rathbone, D. (1991) *Economic Rationalism and Rural Society in Third Century A.D. Egypt*, Cambridge.

Reuter, T. (1985) 'Plunder and tribute in the Carolingian Empire', *Transactions of the Royal Historical Society* 35: 75–94.

—— (1991) 'The end of Carolingian military expansion' in P. Godman and R. Collins (eds) *Charlemagne's Heir: New Perspectives on the Reign of Louis the Pious*, Oxford: 391–405.

Reynolds, S. (1994) *Fiefs and Vassals: The Medieval Evidence Reinterpreted*, Oxford.

Riché, P. (1976) *Education and Culture in the Barbarian West*, tr. J. J. Contreni, Columbia, SC.

Roueché, C. (1989) *Aphrodisias in Late Antiquity*, London.

Sabbah, G. (1978) *La Méthode d'Ammien Marcellin: Recherches sur la construction du discours historique dans les Res Gestae*, Paris.

Shennan, S. J. (ed.) (1989) *Archaeological Approaches to Cultural Identity*, London.

Stafford, P. (1983) *Queens, Dowagers and Concubines: The King's Wife in Early Medieval Society*, Georgia.

Syme, R. (1971) *Emperors and Biography: Studies in the Historia Augusta*, Oxford.

Tchalenko, G. (1953) *Villages antiques de la Syrie du nord*, Paris.

Teitler, H. C. (1985) *Notarii and Exceptores*, Amsterdam.

Thompson, E. A. (1963) 'The Visigoths from Fritigern to Euric', *Historia* 12: 105–26.

—— (1969) *The Goths in Spain*, Oxford.

—— (1982) *Romans and Barbarians: The Decline of the Western Empire*, Madison.

Van Dam, R. (1985) *Leadership and Community in Late Antique Gaul*, Berkeley.

Vogler, C. (1979) *Constance II et l'administration impériale*, Strasbourg.

Wallace-Hadrill, J. M. (1959) 'The blood-feud of the Franks', *Bulletin of the John Rylands Library, Manchester* 41(3): (reprinted in Wallace-Hadrill 1962: 25–48).

—— (1962) *The Long-haired Kings and Other Studies in Frankish History*, London.

Ward-Perkins, B. (1984) *From Classical Antiquity to the Middle Ages: Urban Public Buildings in Northern and Central Italy, A.D. 300–850*, Oxford.

Wenskus, R. (1961) *Stammesbildung und Verfassung: Das Werden der frühmittelalterlichen Gentes*, Cologne.

Whitby, L. M. (1987) 'Notes on some Justinianic constructions', *Byzantinische-neugriechische Jahrbücher* 23: 89–112.

Wickham, C. (1984) 'The other transition: from the ancient world to feudalism', *Past and Present* 103: 3–36.

—— (1988) 'Marx, Sherlock Holmes, and the late Roman commerce', *Journal of Roman Studies* 78: 183–93.

Williams, R. (1987) *Arius: Heresy and Tradition*, London.

Wolfram, H. (1988) *History of the Goths*, tr. T. J. Dunlap, Berkeley.

—— and Schwarcz, A. (eds) (1988) *Anerkennung und Integration: zu den wirtschaftlichen Grundlagen der Völkerwanderungszeit (400–600)* Denkschrift der österreichischen Akademie der Wissenschaften, phil.-hist. Kl. 193, Vienna.

Wood, I. N. (1994) *The Merovingian Kingdoms 450–751*, London.

Wormald, P. (1977) '*Lex scripta* and *verbum regis*: legislation and Germanic kingship from Buric to Cnut', in P. H. Sawyer and I. N. Wood (eds) *Early Medieval Kingship*, Leeds: 105–38.

Wright, R. (1982) *Late Latin and Early Romance in Spain and Carolingian France*, Liverpool.

Young, F. (1983) *From Nicaea to Chalcedon*, London.

—— (1989) 'The rhetorical schools and their influence on patristic exegesis', in R. Williams (ed.) *The Making of Orthodoxy: Essays in Honour of Henry Chadwick*, Cambridge: 182–99.

6

MODERNIZING THE HISTORIOGRAPHY OF RURAL LABOUR: AN UNWRITTEN AGENDA

Jairus Banaji

The last few years have seen some remarkable contributions to agrarian history. These include the powerful works by Helen Bradford (1987) and Tim Keegan (1987) on South African labour tenants,[1] Frank Snowden's (1986) chilling account of the domination of farm workers by *latifondisti* in the South of Italy, Sandro Carocci's (1988) huge and impressive monograph on late medieval Tivoli, Hans-Günther Mertens's (1983) excellent study of the wheat haciendas of Central Mexico, and, finally, Laird Bergad's (1990) brilliantly written history of the Matanzas sugar economy, which was based of course on slave labour. These are all fascinating contributions and they help enormously to expand the range of our understanding of rural relationships and of the extreme fluidity of agrarian forms. Some of this work, notably recent Latin American history, presupposes the revisionism of the 1960s, especially Charles Gibson's seminal rewriting of the history of debt-peonage to allow for a greater sense of autonomy and resistance in the *gañanes'* relations with their Spanish employers (Gibson 1964, with Taylor 1972 and Borah 1983: 177ff.). In particular, the idea that rural workers who had always been conceived simply as bonded labourers or slaves could actually exert significant bargaining power made it possible for other historians to insist on the distinction between more and less 'liberal' forms of peonage with diversified histories of recruitment (Knight 1986), and to open a space for new ways of thinking about 'traditional' institutions. There is a certain analogy here with the South African work on labour tenancy, since both Bradford and Keegan show how fiercely black labour tenants resisted their proletarianization, or how the institution of labour tenancy was itself, in an important sense, shaped by the resistance to proletarianiz-ation. Keegan in particular could also demonstrate the important differences in the relative positions of sharecroppers and labour tenants, while insisting that 'the

---

1   I owe these references to Gavin Williams.

"labour tenants" did not constitute a discrete group on the farms in contradistinc-
tion to the sharecroppers. Many families moved regularly from one form of tenancy
to another' (Keegan 1987: 253–4 n. 38). In the rather different world of late
medieval agriculture, Carocci reveals a similarly complex and fluid integration of
forms of tenancy and labour contract, which made the boundaries between tenants
and labourers and different sorts of rural workers immeasurably fluid (Carocci 1988:
452–3).

Students of the social and economic history of the ancient world have nothing
comparable to these works, with the exception, conceivably, of Dominic Rathbone's
recent study of the Appianus estate (Rathbone 1991), and few ancient historians
contemplating agrarian studies would seriously bother with comparativist
perspectives, except for the mystifying odd reference to English landed aristocrats
or Dutch rural capitalists. But the value of comparing *a* with *b*, *c*, *d* ... is that it
helps us to think more clearly about *a*, and it does this partly by expanding the field
of possible conceptualizations of *a*. The lack of interest in other periods of history
spawns a progressive conceptual atrophy, and it is this drying up of our sources of
conceptual understanding which is the biggest limitation on any progress in ancient
economic history – not (or not primarily) the alleged limitations of our sources.
Indeed, a prime symptom of conceptual atrophy is that the sources tell us much
more than we seem either able or willing to allow. They tell us repeatedly that paid
labour was used regularly and on a large scale, that the use of labour reflected
rational considerations, that the labour of tenants was frequently supervised[2] and so
on. Yet none of this has prevented scholars from believing that large owners were
fundamentally uninterested in the operation of their estates, and that this resulted
in the widespread leasing of land to 'small tenants'. At the root of this is the
common prejudice that ancient landowners lacked the economic rationalism that
God has bestowed on the modern world in an obvious desire to see capitalism
prosper. But the supposed lack of economic rationalism is simply a prejudice that
ignores the overwhelming evidence for perfectly 'rational' modes of organization
and methods of control, from the structuring of labour markets and widespread use
of paid labour to such basic features of Roman estate organization as the continuous
monitoring of labour costs,[3] careful attention to optimal gang size (Columella, *RR*
1.9.7ff.), use of sample checks to control the intensity of labour,[4] or formulation of

---

2 Owners *controlled* the labour of their tenants, see Columella, *RR* 1.7.1 ('avarius opus exigat quam
pensiones'), with Finley's remarks in the appendix to 'Private farm tenancy', in *Studies in Roman
Property*, ed., M. I. Finley (Cambridge University Press, 1976) p. 120 ('I see no choice,
therefore ... but to take *opus* here as simply "work"'), Pliny, *Ep.*, 9.37 ('operis exactores', for
sharecroppers), P.Oxy. 729.29–30 (137), P.Oxy. 3354.38–9 (257), P.Oxy. 1631.30 (280), where the
usual formula is *ton son epakolouthounton pasi tois ergois*, 'with your agents supervising all the jobs'.
3 Varro, *RR* 1.53 (gleaning), Columella, *RR* 2.2.12 (clearing stony ground), Pliny, *NH* 15.3.11
(harvesting olives, cf. Martinez-Alier 1971: 72, 'The main reason for choosing a method of harvesting is
the situation in the labour market'), 18.67.261, 18.7.38 (grain harvests).
4 Columella, *RR* 3.13.11–13 (trenching), 2.4.3 (ploughing), Palladius, *Opus agriculturae*, 2.3.2
(ploughing), 2.10.4 (hoeing).

performance standards to help owners define efficient manning ratios. Columella's reference (*RR* 3.13.12) to disputes between landowners and contractors over the quality of labour inputs implies a degree of self-interest that is scarcely any less impressive than Vincenzo Tanara's prescription of ploughing methods that would help Bologna landowners of the seventeenth century enforce a more efficient utilization of the labour of their *mezzadri*.[5] The treatment of slaves as fixed capital, the conception of hired labour as inherently alienated,[6] the pervasive use of contract workers, the emphasis on accountancy, the coexistence of negotiable and non-negotiable contracts, are all signs of a precocious modernism.

The agricultural writers approached issues with an intensely practical vision, as, no doubt, landowners did. From their work it is clear that owners could count on available supplies of free labour, notwithstanding the local shortages that characterize most labour markets.[7] In contrast, historians vastly underestimate the degree of landlessness in the ancient Mediterranean and the corresponding need for a considerable number of people to enter into wage employment for mere survival. But the arguments are not mainly empirical, and involve problems partly of economic understanding, partly of conceptualization. To take two rather different illustrations of this, Hopkins is particularly muddleheaded in the following passage where the extension of slavery to rural production is derived from the alleged absence of a labour market: 'In a society without a market in free labour, recruitment by force (i.e. slavery) was probably the only method of securing large numbers of full-time dependants with particular skills'. 'Slaves were the fuel of an agrarian revolution, a means of organising labour in an economy without a labour market.' Yet on the same page Hopkins refers to the 'extrusion of free peasants' creating 'a large pool of landless or underemployed citizens', and states, 'Cato ... assumed a *large pool of free labourers*' (Hopkins 1978: 111, 109; my italics). Since a 'large pool of free labourers' is precisely what most people mean by a labour market, one is left wondering whether Hopkins has some special definition of a 'market in free labour' and how all those free labourers eventually managed to survive. The second illustration involves a more persuasive sort of assertion, viz. A. H. M. Jones's view that 'Hired labourers seem very rarely to have been employed on a permanent basis' (Jones 1964: 2. 792–3). The problem here is partly a matter of closer attention to the detail of our evidence, but in part at least it stems from inadequate notions about what constitutes 'hired labour' or what we mean by a 'labour market'. More precisely, the issue is not whether estates retained permanent workers but whether such workers, who normally received rations from the estate, were really wage labourers of some kind.

There is considerable evidence for the use of permanent labourers, and at least one specific feature of this evidence also suggests that such workers were regarded

---

5   Tanara 1644, with basic discussion in Poni 1963.

6   An alienation of labour profoundly evident in Philo's description of agricultural hired labourers as motivated solely by pay, *Peri Georgias*, 4–5.

7   See Scheidel 1989 and the seminal article by Peter Brunt, 'Free labour and public works at Rome' (1980).

by their employers and managers as *hired* labourers. Thus in P. Amherst II 155 (fifth century, and of uncertain provenance), we have a wage account entitled *Log (os) sitou misthou ton georg (on) hemon syn th (e)o ιβ indik (tionos)*, that is, 'Account of the grain (paid as) wages to our *georgoi* for the 12th indiction', followed by a list of payments. These *georgoi* were clearly labourers retained by the estate on a permanent basis. Moreover, their allowances were seen by the estate administration as wages. Another important piece of evidence is P.Oxy. XLII 3048, dated 17–18 March 246. This includes a registration of grain stocks submitted by the landowner Calpurnia Heraclia for her holdings at five villages in the lower and eastern toparchies of the Oxyrhynchite nome (in Middle Egypt), and concludes with the statement, 'Out of the above-mentioned [stocks of grain], monthly allowances (*meniaiai syntaxeis*) are given to the chief managers and stewards and labourers and boys and monthly staff (*pragmateutais te kai phrontistai[s kai] georgois kai paidariois kai katameneiois*)'. Thus all these groups were part of the permanent labour force of Calpurnia's estate (all were entitled to monthly allowances). It is also interesting that field labourers were simply called '*georgoi*'. These documents show that the hiring of labour on a permanent basis was certainly more widespread than Jones seemed willing to allow.

This seems to me to have several implications. First, it restores a sense of realism to our accounts of the ancient world (more people depended on paid employment than scholars, even Marxist ones, are willing to accept) and begins to help us to move away from the abstractions in which so much of this historiography continues to revolve. Second, it allows us to appreciate the considerable sophistication displayed by owners in their use of labour and their structuring of labour supplies. For example, Rathbone's study of the deployment of labour on the Fayum estates of the Alexandrian landowner Appianus shows that permanent labourers of the kind mentioned above might be contractually differentiated into distinct groups distinguished by the length of their contracts with the estate. These groups comprised free labourers paid in both cash and kind, though the estate followed a system of wage payment and accounting vaguely similar to that used on Mexican haciendas until well into the twentieth century (Nickel 1991). In more general terms, the Appianus estate achieved a remarkable degree of flexibility in its use of labour. Apart from its contracts with the regular staff, it depended heavily on the employment of casual workers. Furthermore, at least some of this casual labour supply was secured through a system of labour tenancy with workers called *epoikiotai*.[8] The general impression is of an extremely sophisticated and flexible structuring of labour supplies, easily comparable to the situation on the Puebla wheat haciendas of the Maurer family, studied by Mertens.

A third implication concerns our notions of the 'colonate'. This, of course, has recently been the object of considerable iconoclasm but little real historical understanding. Certainly, much of the blame for this must lie with an earlier

---

8 Rathbone 1991: 146, 150, 182–3 for the *epoikiotai*, and ch. 3 on the permanent workers called *oiketai* and *metrematiaioi*.

generation of scholars who saw the colonate on an essentially feudal model, though as always with much uncertainty as to the actual organization of labour. The exaction of labour services manifestly did not occur in a characteristically feudal form, i.e. as labour dues imposed on a potentially independent peasantry, especially the heavier weekly services, despite sporadic evidence for seasonal works (the medievalist's 'boons'), such as imperial estates organizing part of the peak season supply by exacting services for ploughing, harrowing, harvesting, etc. (and this in the early Empire!).[9] However, a fiscal construction of the colonate encounters other difficulties. That fiscal considerations were indeed important is undeniable. That the repeated legal interventions to regulate the status of *coloni vis-à-vis* their masters were prompted solely or even largely by such considerations is much less obvious. Moreover, in the Codes, the fiscal requirements of the state are expressly contrasted with the rights of owners over their *coloni*, with the likely implication that the '*ius colonatus*' lay within the sphere of private law.[10] Lastly, a fiscal colonate would have no discernible implications for the organization of estates and the use of labour. All this has prompted scepticism. Thus a recent history of Egypt in the fourth century assures us that 'Recent scholarship has effectively demolished the view once prevalent that most independent farmers came under the domination of rich landlords in an arrangement usually referred to as the 'colonate' and seen as the precursor of medieval feudalism'.[11] Few would go as far as this but even among these scholars the colonate is now construed in terms of traditional types of tenancy, and the *colonus*, no longer a 'serf', is transformed into a free tenant, though with some ambiguity. Whereas Johnson and West were clearly not bothered by the considerable evidence for coercion and saw the *coloni* simply as free tenants who took land on lease (Johnson and West 1967: 31), Averil Cameron has recently tried to salvage some element of the traditional picture. Thus *coloni* were 'technically free tenants who were, in many areas, theoretically tied to their particular estates by imperial legislation, and *over whom the landlords had rights which can look very like the rights of owner over slave*' (Cameron 1993: 86; my italics). The compromise is evident and Cameron skirts the issue of the terms of tenancy. Arguing from the Apion archive, the French papyrologist Gascou believes that most 'tenants' took land from the Apions on the perpetual leases known as 'emphyteuseis', oblivious of the problem of where these 'tenants' would have found the resources to acquire and operate such leases (Gascou 1985: 9, 32). For Vera, too, the *colonus* is a '*fittavolo*', a free tenant, but for him the colonate signifies the dominance of rent tenancies. Throughout the late Empire peasants paid rents in kind.[12] Finally, in a recent monograph another Italian scholar, Marcone, defines the *colonus* as a 'small tenant

---

9 *CIL* VIII 25902 (Hr Mettich), 10570 (Suk el-Khmis), 14451 (Ain Zaga) and 14428 (Gasr Mezuar) all imply that even seasonal tasks were a source of grievance.

10 CJ XI.53.1 (371) is the clearest evidence of this, *Inserviant terris non tributario nexu, sed nomine et titulo colonorum.*

11 Bagnall 1993: 115, with a rather overstated interpretation of the work of Jean-Michel Carrié.

12 Vera, in Giardina 1986: 367ff., with an erroneous view of the Apion estates (on p. 412).

(*fittavolo*) who was nominally free but in practice reduced to bondage (*asservito di fatto*)' (Marcone 1988: 13), but makes no attempt to elucidate the kind of labour organization that embodied this factual subjection.

The whole of this nebulous new orthodoxy is based on the general presumption that large owners preferred to lease land to avoid the centralized operation or direct management of their estates. As Goffart says, 'late Roman landlords showed no particular desire to draw closer to their tenants, as fathers to a family. *Wealth allowed them absenteeism; there was no point in having tenants if they had to be closely supervised*' (Goffart 1974: 76) as if absenteeism precluded close supervision! The prejudice in favour of tenancy in this particular sense of a system minimizing the burden of direct management runs deep in the tradition of Roman historiography. Kaltenstadler (1984: 224), for example, despite the manifest uncertainties of the evidence of this particular treatise, affirms that Palladius in his *Opus Agriculturae* took the employment of tenants (*Pächtern*) for granted (it was 'self-evident' that owners used tenants), and that is why his work lacks any explicit reference to tenancy. The reasoning is obviously dubious, especially as others have seen the treatise as proof of persisting slavery,[13] but all it reflects ultimately is the Goffart-type prejudice that landowners, and in particular late antique landowners, abdicated managerial control over the operation of their estates.

Calculating that some 12 to 14 million Mediterranean inhabitants could have been living near the starvation level in the sixteenth century, Braudel noted, 'it is a possibility that cannot be ruled out. For we are never dealing with full-employment economies' (Braudel 1975: I, 454). It is certain that in large parts of the ancient Mediterranean, too, employers were usually able to find free workers as and when they needed them. Egypt is a particularly interesting case of this, for there the countryside had always comprised a large group of *demosioi georgoi*, who were quite distinct from the large and small landowners and may in fact be called 'the great mass of landless public peasants' (el Abbadi 1967: 219). Workers were available in plenty in the second century, when estates 'relied heavily on hired labour' (Bagnall 1974: 169). In the third century, Alexandria saw an influx of 'Egyptian' (that is, native or non-Greek-speaking) rural immigrants who were thought to be 'deserting their own villages to avoid agricultural labour'.[14] They, obviously, were landless labourers. Later in the century, large estates in the Fayum were drawing extensively on reserves of free labour.[15] Elsewhere in the Mediterranean, A. H. M. Jones has pointed to the 'large number of landless peasants' in a village register from Hypaepa, and to the 'exiguous size' of most holdings, concluding, 'These facts may help to explain where the labour came

---

13 Most recently, Morgenstern 1989, who is equally unconvincing.

14 P. Giss. 40, col. 2 = *Select Papyri* II 215 (vol. 2, p. 90f.) (AD 215), esp. 1.23ff., *hoitines pheugousi tas choras tas idias hina me er[gon] agroikon poiosi.*

15 Rathbone 1991: 152 calculates that even in quiet months 'hired outside labour still made up a third of the total labour input'.

from which worked the estates of the big landlords' (Jones 1974: 239–40). Finally, again in Egypt, a recent study of employment contracts notes that the number of such contracts (*Arbeitsverträge*) surviving from the Byzantine period (sixth to seventh centuries) far exceeds those of all earlier centuries put together (Jördens 1990: 148). Unless this is accidental, it must mean that wage employment had expanded significantly by the later period.

People entered paid employment in diverse forms characterized by widely differing degrees of coercion and bargaining strength, and by a great and impressive variety of contracts. To see this, however, we have to learn to think about labour markets in a new way and resist the common tendency to contrapose tenancy to wage labour, as if these were watertight and mutually impenetrable systems. It is a remarkable feature of the ancient evidence that through it we can proceed to such a reconstruction, so that ancient historians may eventually agree with students of other periods of agrarian history who have come to emphasize fluidity and flexibility as essential features of agrarian labour use. Both ancient and modern evidence shows that tenants might be degraded to the position of mere labourers – sharecroppers in Byzantine Egypt, Tuscan *mezzadri* in the late nineteenth century (Snowden 1989: 20–33); tenancy might provide the contractual form for a labour relationship, with a permanent tension between the aspirations of the tenant family and those of the employer; estates might recruit tenants who would be required to supply wage labour at lower cost; peasant families might move through a bewildering variety of contracts, for example, 'mixing sharecropping with labour tenancy, and possibly drifting in and out of sharecropping relations';[16] leaseholds, notably *mezzadria*, might operate more as labour contracts;[17] and finally, contracts themselves might be designed to allow for various forms of integration of tenancy and wage labour, such as the traditional *boaria* contract of Ferrara before the reduction of the *boaro* to a simple wage labourer (Roveri 1972: 25ff.; Giorgetti 1974: 321ff.), or the Oxyrhynchite wine leases where the lessees/employees were formally said to be 'leasing the tasks' but the agreement dealt at length with their work and remuneration,[18] or labour contracts where the employee might also engage in tenancy, as part of the same contract and on the side, so to speak.[19]

---

16 Keegan 1987: 74, and his statement, 'Indeed, many families experienced a bewildering succession of contracts of tenancy as they moved from farm to farm, some involving crop-sharing, some labour service, and others a combination of the two.'

17 See especially Jones 1968, with his reference to 'wage-type tenancy', and the general conclusion on p. 223 that the 'terms of Tuscan tenure confirm the nature of leaseholds, notably *mezzadria*, as labour contracts'; see also Carocci 1988: p. 446.

18 For example, P.Oxy. XLVII 3354 (257), which distinguishes no fewer than 33 separate tasks, or PSI XIII 1338 (299).

19 Cf. P.Vindob.Sal. 8 (323, BL 7.278), where the lease (of an orchard) is supplementary to a labour contract (for work in a vineyard). P.Grenf. I 58 (*c*.561), SB VI 9587 (6–7c.), SB VI 9293 (573, *BASP* XVI (1979): 233–4), and P.Vindob.Sal. 9 (509) have the formal appearance of leases but turn out, in substance, to be labour contracts.

Thus the recruitment of labour proceeded in more complex ways than our stultifying orthodoxies suggest. It is not true that tenancy automatically entailed a high degree of security.[20] On the contrary, a large if fluctuating percentage of Byzantine agricultural leases incorporate the so-called *eph'hoson chronon boulei* clause, which gave owners the flexibility of hiring and firing tenants at will. For this reason, as early as 1905, Waszyński concluded that the Byzantine tenant was simply a wage labourer (1905: 92, and esp. 157–8). This was especially true of the sharecroppers, who received their wages in the form of a share of the crop. Other historians have described specific groups or categories of sharecroppers as not vastly different in status from mere labourers (Brading 1978: 74; Firestone 1975: 7ff.; Giorgetti 1977: 225ff., esp. 231). In sixth/seventh century Egypt, they were usually easily evictable, semi-proletarianized and frequently subject to high rents.[21] On the other hand, they were employed chiefly by middling landowners and were not conspicuous on the large estates. (Alan Richards reports a similar pattern for the late nineteenth century.[22])

The evolution of those estates and their tendency to employ resident workers led to a progressive obliteration of the boundaries between terms like '*georgos*', '*oiketes*', and '*ergates*'. *Ergates* was the standard term for a casual worker, so the occasional extension of this word to cover resident workforces is indicative of their status as pure labourers. Similarly, the *georgoi* whom Libanius would rail against in the later fourth century were described indifferently as '*oiketai*', '*somata*', '*douloi*', '*ergatai*', and '*hoi ergazomenoi*'. As Finley noted, these terms should be taken as synonymous, 'all referring to Syrian peasants whose status is not definable by any single modern word, who were subject to a master (*despotes*) and yet were not chattel slaves (despite the appearance of the word *douloi* in the text)'.[23]

The labour relationships of the Byzantine large estates reflected the subjection of free labour in forms that gave large landowners well-nigh absolute power over their employees. The analogy of the power of masters over slaves was obvious and drawn repeatedly.[24] But even Hardy, who was inclined to see the resident workers as 'serfs', correctly emphasized the fluidity which characterized the recruitment of labour on the large estates, and noted, in particular, that 'the estate managers were apparently able to find workers as they needed them'.[25] Clearly, landowners like the Apions could count on a supply of labour from the neighbouring villages (*komai*)

---

20 Fenoaltea 1984: 663 claims, 'only a wage earner can be easily replaced, and therefore easily dismissed, at any time; rental agreements instead tend inevitably to be relatively long-term affairs. For a renter, therefore, the threat of dismissal is normally months or years away.'

21 Among fifth-, sixth- and seventh-century papyri there are about 24 share contracts where the share level is determinable; of these, 8 involve a $\frac{3}{4}$ share for the landlord.

22 Richards 1982: 67, 'Gali in 1889 spoke of sharecropping as being the most common mode of exploitation on medium properties.'

23 Finley 1980: 125–6, referring to Libanius's 47th oration.

24 In *Ep.* 24*.1 (*Œuvres* 46B, p. 384), Augustine asks whether landowners could, that is, had the legal right to, transform their *coloni* into slaves ('utrum liceat possessori servos facere colonos').

25 Hardy 1931: 122, 126 with his remark, 'The whole system was apparently quite fluid.'

and evolved a complex pattern of labour use which still needs reconstruction. Hardy himself leaves us with a strangely incongruous view of the Apion labour force, since the agricultural side is construed largely in terms of 'serfdom' and the industrial occupations in terms of a free labour market. It would make more economic sense to relate both groups of employees (permanent and temporary) to the pressures of the labour market, and to see the permanent workers as a type of wage labour force recruited on a long-term basis.

The general assumption in the imperial legislation is clearly that the *coloni adscripticii/georgoi enapographoi* were normally landless.[26] The closest one comes to an explicit definition of who the *coloni* were is a passage in Novel 162 of Justinian, where it is said that the *coloni* were in theory 'residents of estates and field labourers' (*oiketoras ton chorion kai ton agron ergatas*), with the further qualification that they were actually born on their employer's estate.[27] Similarly, in 570, North African landlords petitioned Justin II to prevent workers from deserting the estates where they were born.[28] Thus, if the *coloni* were free workers who were bound to estates by hereditary ties, it is easy to see why the employer's power over such workers was thought to be encapsulated in the threat of expulsion.[29] On the other hand, it is doubtful if the legislation seeking to reinforce the power of landlords over such workers ever completely succeeded in restricting their mobility, in the way early eighteenth-century Mexican *hacendados* wanted the Spanish authorities to do with the *indios gañanes*, invoking legal models that were ultimately late Roman.

The analogy with New Spain is significant in another way. In a classic essay on the 'Colonial origins of peonage in Mexico', first published in 1944, the historian Silvio Zavala drew a clear distinction between the institutions of the *encomienda* and the hacienda by defining the *hacendado* as essentially 'un patrón de asalariados', an employer of wage labour, and the *encomendero* as a 'protector señorial'. 'In the hacienda', wrote Zavala, 'the Indian is a free worker (*trabajador libre*) attracted by means of a voluntary contract. ... The *amo* has to pay a wage to the *gañan* in exchange for labour' (Zavala 1988: 56). It is unlikely that many scholars today would dispute this characterization. The proper economic category for this class of rural workers is not 'serfdom' but wage labour.

One implication of this is that the conditions of such workers would reflect the general evolution of the labour market. Jan Bazant (1977: 74ff.) has shown how on haciendas like Bocas in San Luis Potosí (in northern Mexico), the daily-rated permanent labourers faced a drastic alteration in conditions of employment in the

---

26 Nov.Just. 128.14 ('even if estate labourers should happen to have their own plot'), 162.2.1 ('unless they happen to be owners of some plot of their own').

27 Nov.Just. 162.2, with its reference to a previous constitution (*diataxis*) proposing the definition in question.

28 Nov.Just. II. 6 (570), where the workers' settlements are called *vici*.

29 CJ XI.48.21 (530), where resident employees (*adscripticii*) were said to be not distinctively different from slaves, given their total subjection to the employer's authority (*potestas*).

course of the 1870s when tenants and employees alike were subjected to a much tougher management regime and legal changes encouraged the introduction of a more flexible labour market. But the late nineteenth-century rural employers who began progressively to restructure rural labour relations by proletarianizing existing categories of labour were not shifting from a servile or serf-like labour force to wage labour, and it is misleading to describe the earlier patterns of control as 'non-capitalist labour practices' (Knight 1986: 49). Moreover, in other parts of the world the violent dispossession of land communities was still round the corner, and here the struggle of rural families to regain control over productive resources emerged in the form of sharecropping and labour tenancy. The South African material shows that 'Usually those without the resources to work the land themselves entered labour-tenancy agreements' (Keegan 1987: 77). Landless Boers complained that 'landowners much preferred black labourers, *who were given arable ground as pay*' (Keegan 1987: 33; my italics). On the settler plantations and estates in the Rift Valley Province of the White Highlands of Kenya,

> The term 'squatter' ... denoted an African permitted to reside on a European farmer's land, usually on condition he worked for the European owner for a specified period. In return for his services, the African was entitled to use some of the settler's land for the purposes of cultivation and grazing.
>
> (Kanogo 1987: 9)

By the terms of the 1918 Resident Native Labourers Ordinance, squatters were obliged to provide 'not less than 180 working days per year on a farm'.

> In return for this, the worker and his family were allowed to live on the farm and cultivate a part of the settler's land for [their] own use. *A minimal wage would be paid for the work done* .... The labourer was expected to feed and house himself and his family. More importantly, resident labourers would ensure the supply of sufficient and easily available labour to the farmers, for the squatters' *wives and children could be called upon at peak labour periods*, especially during the harvesting season.
>
> (*id.*: 37; my italics)

In Chile where *inquilinaje* 'remained the foundation of the rural labour system' into the 1930s, landowners demanded of their workers that

> Each family must provide the fundo one worker each day of the year at the rate of 50 centavos a day; the other individuals living in the house also have the obligation to work in the hacienda, earning whatever wage is paid to non-resident labourers, currently 80 centavos .... The women and children in each house are also obligated to work when called upon, except for the housewife. These will be paid 50 centavos respectively.[30]

The common feature of these accounts is the landowner's drive to control an expandable supply of labour (the labour of *families*) in exchange for payments that minimized cash flow and reduced wages below the ruling wage rate. From the standpoint of employers using large amounts of free labour, it was a perfectly

---

30 Loveman 1976: 30, citing a letter of the Sociedad Vinicola del Sur to the Labour Dept., dated 1914.

rational system which allowed both flexibility in the deployment of workers[31] and the chance of sustaining profitability by permanent control over labour costs. In the nineteenth century, one of the best-organized expressions of such a system was found precisely in Egypt, and evidence on the organization of Egyptian large estates in the late nineteenth and twentieth centuries may help us to understand the labour arrangements through which Byzantine large landowners could have drawn on the labour of their *georgoi*. Byzantine large estates used resident workers who were known either as *georgoi* (if they were ordinary field labourers) or by some description indicative of their skill (vinedressers, fruit workers and so on). On the Apion estates, the bulk of this labour force was concentrated in special settlements called *epoikia*. These were privately owned hamlets in which the full-time resident labourers (*georgoi*) were required to reside as part of their arrangement with the estate. But as to the nature of those arrangements and the contracts through which the *georgoi* (in this case, mostly landless peasants) attached themselves to large estates, the ancient evidence is, as usual, fragmentary and elusive, and its interpretation requires a model drawn from a wider range of historical experiences.

By the early 1870s, a third of the Egyptian rural population was landless. By 1917 this proportion was anywhere between 36 per cent (in the Delta) and 53 per cent (in Upper Egypt) (Owen 1969: 148, 240). Second, this whole period saw a rapid expansion of cotton exports, with much of this produced on large privately owned estates. In Lower Egypt, cotton acreage expanded from 856,000 feddans in 1884–5 to 1.4 million in 1912–13. These estates were largely business investments, like the Cuban sugar mills of the nineteenth century or the Gildemeister haciendas in Peru (see Taylor 1984), and thousands of other enterprises throughout the world. Their chief characteristic was a form of labour organization which concentrated resident labourers in settlements called *izbas* and extracted work from them under various systems of labour tenancy. Thus,

> Riaz Pasha preferred to farm his 530 feddan estate at Mahallat Ruh using the labour of a 100 families of service tenants (*tamaliyya*) each of whom received nearly a feddan of land at a much reduced rent in exchange for their services.
>
> (Owen 1981b: 230)

> J. F. Nahas describes a system by which each peasant family was required to supply an agreed number of workers at a daily wage to be determined in advance. Saleh Nour El-Din, on the other hand, gives details of an alternative system by which the labour-service was discharged on the proprietor's own land on a crop-sharing basis, with the workers taking one-fifth of the produce if the proprietor provided the animals, tools, and seed, and two-fifths if they did so themselves. Some wages might be paid, however, for extra work or for labor performed by wives.
>
> (Owen 1981a: 524)

Richards (1982: 65–6) notes that *izba* workers 'often owned their own hoe and sometimes a water-buffalo', and worked under supervision for the landlord. In fact,

---

31   By the very nature of the contract, which placed at the landlord's disposal the labour reserves of the *entire peasant family*, but also because landlords resisted regulation; for this see Rennie 1978: 88.

the system facilitated supervision by its physical concentration of workers and reduced the time required to reach the fields (so Lozach and Hug 1930; esp. 202). In both its social and topographical features, it was consciously designed to 'extract cheap labour from a well-disciplined peasant labour force' (Owen 1981b: 148). Of course, as in Latin America, in Egypt too, the Nationalists denounced the economic organization of these estates as 'feudal', but modern historians no longer accept this characterization. As Owen notes,

> far from having an obligation to provide the inhabitants of the ezba with land, as he would have had to under a classic type of feudal arrangement, [the proprietor] could always threaten them with the prospect of taking their small plot away from them, thereby reducing them to the state that all peasants were desperate to avoid – that of landless laborers dependent for their living on all the vagaries of seasonal employment.
>
> (Owen 1981a: 525)

Indeed, 'The old *pasha* class are better viewed as wealthy agrarian capitalists than as "feudalists" or "Ricardian parasites" ' (Richards 1993: 98).

The *izbas* provide a crucial link in the reasoning which may allow us to reconstruct the labour organization of Byzantine large estates. P.Oxy. XVIII 2197 (*c*.567?) shows that the estate was responsible for the condition/upkeep of the peasants' houses. Indeed, these were probably better constructed than the mud hovels nineteenth-century *tamaliyya* were housed in. The *epoikia* themselves were subject to intensive supervision, while P.Oxy. XIX 2239 (598) from the estate of the aristocrat Flavius John suggests that the *georgoi* (labourers) entirely lacked the power of decision-making, since labour was carefully supervised.[32] P.Princ.Univ. II 96 (566/7) implies that landowners had access to the labour of the tenant's family. At least two Apion documents suggest that labourers had individual accounts with the estate,[33] and finally, most interestingly, a recently published papyrus, P.Wash.Univ. II 102, which is certainly from the Oxyrhynchite, shows that individual *epoikia* were required to supply an agreed number of workers or labour days (*ergatai*) – in this case for sowing operations on the owner's *autourgia*.[34] All this suggests that late Roman estates made regular use of labour tenancy in one form or another, and that the inherently ambiguous position of the labour tenant as a type of free worker who had the attributes (if not also the consciousness) of a small peasant, but whose terms of employment allowed owners a wide margin of flexibility, including the power to dominate them and enforce slave-like conditions, accounts for the confused picture of such workers that we find both in the legal sources and in modern scholarship.

If the above interpretation of late antique labour relationships is at all plausible, it has at least three implications. First, it implies that there was widespread

---

32 Jeremias was recruited as a field boss (*epikeimenos*) and made to promise that he would inspire general enthusiasm among the workers.

33 P.Oxy. I. 137.19 (584), XVI 1988.25 (587), *en tois emois pittakiois*, cf. Preisigke, *Wörterbuch*, 1.311, s.v. 'pittakion', 1(e) 'Abrechnungsbuch, Kontobuch'. 669.

34 That is, the lands not used by the *epoikia* for their own subsistence.

landlessness with peasants seeking employment on large estates, as the Aztecs were forced to do from the later sixteenth century, when the hacienda emerged as the leading agricultural institution in New Spain. The second implication is that the function of the colonate was as much to do with landlord interests as with fiscal imperatives.[35] At least one late fourth-century constitution tells us in so many words that what the state saw itself doing was reinforcing the power of landlords over their labourers.[36] On the other hand, landlord pressure to restrict the mobility of tenants may simply have reflected a drive to reduce the bargaining power of workers.[37] Interpreted in these terms, the 'colonate' becomes an expression of the recalcitrance of labour rather than its ineluctable submission. Of course, a third and more general implication is that labour markets operate in more complex ways than ancient historians have been brought up to imagine.

REFERENCES

el-Abbadi, M. A. H. (1967) 'The edict of Tiberius Julius Alexander', *BIFAO* 65.

Bagnall, R. (1993) *Egypt in Late Antiquity*, Princeton.

Bagnall, W. S. (1974) 'The Archive of Laches: Prosperous Farmers of the Fayum in the Second Century', unpublished Ph.D. dissertation, Duke University.

Bazant, J. (1977) 'Landlord, labourer, and tenant in San Luis Potosí, northern Mexico, 1822–1910', in K. Duncan and I. Rutledge (eds) *Land and Labour in Latin America*, Cambridge.

Bergad, L. W. (1990) *Cuban Rural Society in the Nineteenth Century. The Social and Economic History of Monoculture in Matanzas*, Princeton.

Borah, W. (1983) *Justice by Insurance. The General Indian Court of Colonial Mexico and the Legal Aides of the Half-Real*. Berkeley.

Bradford, H. (1987) *A Taste of Freedom. The ICU in Rural South Africa 1924–1930*, New Haven and London.

Brading, D. A. (1978) *Haciendas and Ranchos in the Mexican Bajío. León 1700–1860*, Cambridge.

Braudel, F. (1975) *The Mediterranean and the Mediterranean World in the Age of Philip II*, 2 vols, London.

Brunt, P. (1980) 'Free labour and public works at Rome', *Journal of Roman Studies* 70: 81–101.

Cameron, A. (1993) *The Mediterranean World in Late Antiquity A.D. 395–600*, London.

Carocci, S. (1988) *Tivoli nel basso medioevo. Società cittadina ed economia agraria*, Rome.

Fenoalte, S. (1984) 'Slavery and supervision in comparative perspective: a model', *Journal of Economic History* 44: 635–68.

Finley, M. I. (1980) *Ancient Slavery and Modern Ideology*, London.

Firestone, Y. (1975) 'Crop-sharing economics in Mandatory Palestine – Part I', *Middle Eastern Studies* 11: 1ff.

Gascou, J. (1985) 'Les grandes domaines, la cité et l'état en Égypte byzantine', *Travaux et Mémoires* 9: 1–90.

---

35 The interaction between these sets of motives is nicely shown by Riley 1984.

36 CJ XI.52.1 (*c*.393), where Thracian landlords are legally empowered to control rural labourers 'et patroni sollicitudine et domini potestate'.

37 See Keegan 1987: 149: 'The capacity of the landlords to enforce their will on their tenants depended largely on their capacity to limit the latter's mobility ... tenants' bargaining power was proportionate to their ability to move off the farm and seek better terms elsewhere.'

Giardina, A. (ed.) (1986) *Società romana e impero tardoantico*, Rome and Bari.

Gibson, C. (1964) *The Aztecs under Spanish Rule. A History of the Indians of the Valley of Mexico 1519–1810*, Stanford.

Giorgetti, G. (1974) *Contadini e proprietari nell'Italia moderna*, Turin.

—— (1977) *Capitalismo e agricoltura in Italia*, Rome.

Goffart, W. (1974) *Caput and Colonate: Towards a History of Late Roman Taxation*, Toronto.

Hardy, E. R. (1931) *The Large Estates of Byzantine Egypt*, New York.

Hopkins, K. (1978) *Conquerors and Slaves*, Cambridge.

Johnson, A. C. and West, L. C. (1949; repr. 1967) *Byzantine Egypt: Economic Studies*.

Jones, A. H. M. (1964; repr. 1973) *The Later Roman Empire 284–602. A Social, Economic and Administrative Survey*, 2 vols, Oxford.

—— (1974) *The Roman Economy*, Oxford.

Jones, P. J. (1968) 'From manor to mezzadria. A Tuscan case study in the medieval origins of modern agrarian society', in N. Rubinstein (ed.) *Florentine Studies. Politics and Society in Renaissance Florence*, London.

Jördens, A. (1990) *Vertragliche Regelungen von Arbeiten im späten griechischsprachigen Ägypten*, Heidelberg.

Kaltenstadler, W. (1984) 'Arbeits- und Führungskräfte im *Opus Agriculturae* von Palladius', *Klio* 66: 223–9.

Kanogo, T. (1987) *Squatters and the Roots of Mau Mau 1905–63*, London.

Keegan, T. (1987) *Rural Transformations in Industrializing South Africa. The Southern Highveld to 1914*, London.

Knight, A. (1986) 'Mexican peonage: what was it and why was it?', *Journal of Latin American Studies* 18: 41–74.

Loveman, B. (1976) *Struggle in the Countryside. Politics and Rural Labor in Chile, 1919–1973*, Bloomington and London.

Lozach, J. and Hug, G. (1930) *L'Habitat rural en Égypte*, Cairo.

Marcone, A. (1988) *Il colonato tardoantico nella storiografia moderna*, Como.

Martinez-Alier, J. (1971) *Labourers and Landowners in Southern Spain*, London.

Mertens, H.-G. (1983) *Wirtschaftliche und soziale Strukturen zentralmexikanischer Weizenhaciendas aus dem Tal von Atlixco (1890–1912)*, Wiesbaden.

Morgenstern, F. (1989) 'Die Auswertung des *opus agriculturae* des Palladius zu einigen Fragen der spätantiken Wirtschaftsgeschichte', *Klio* 71: 179–92.

Nickel, H. J. (1991) *Schuldknechtschaft in mexikanischen Haciendas*, Stuttgart.

Owen, E. R. J. (1969) *Cotton and the Egyptian Economy 1820–1914*, Oxford.

—— (1981a) 'The development of agricultural production in nineteenth-century Egypt: capitalism of what type?', in A. L. Udovitch (ed.) *The Islamic Middle East, 700–1900*, Princeton.

—— (1981b) *The Middle East In the World Economy 1800–1914*, London and New York.

Poni, C. (1963) *Gli aratri e l'economia agraria nel Bolognese dal XVII al XIX secolo*, Bologna.

Rathbone, D. (1991) *Economic Rationalism and Rural Society in Third-century A.D. Egypt. The Heroninos Archive and the Appianus Estate*, Cambridge.

Rennie, J. R. (1978) 'White farmers, black tenants and landlord legislation: southern Rhodesia 1890–1930', *Journal of Southern African Studies* 5: 86–98.

Richards, A. (1982) *Egypt's Agricultural Development, 1800–1980*, Boulder, CO.

—— (1993) 'Land tenure', in G. M. Craig (ed.) *The Agriculture of Egypt*, Oxford.

Riley, J. D. (1984) 'Crown law and rural labor in New Spain: the status of *gañanes* during the eighteenth century', *Hispanic American Historical Review* 64: 259–85.

Roveri, A. (1972) *Dal sindacalismo rivoluzionario al fascismo. Capitalismo agrario e socialismo nel Ferrarese (1870–1920)*, Florence.

Scheidel, W. (1989) 'Zur Lohnarbeit bei Columella', *Tyche* 4: 139–46.

Snowden, F. M. (1986) *Violence and Great Estates in the South of Italy. Apulia 1900–1922*, Cambridge.

—— (1989) *The Fascist Revolution in Tuscany 1919–1922*, Cambridge.

Tanara, V. (1644) *L'economia del cittadino in villa*, Bologna.

Taylor, L. (1984) 'Cambios capitalistas en las haciendas Cajamarquinas del Peru, 1900–1935', *Estudios Rurales Latinoamericanos* 7: 93–129.

Taylor, W. B. (1972) *Landlord and Peasant in Colonial Oaxaca*, Stanford.

Waszyński, S. (1905) *Die Bodenpacht: agrargeschichtliche Papyrusstudien*, Leipzig.

Zavala, S. (1988) 'Orígenes coloniales del peonaje en México', in E. Trabulse (ed.) *Estudios acerca de la historia del trabajo en México*, Mexico City. (First published in *El Trimestre Económico* 10 (1944): 711ff.)

II THE MEDIEVAL WORLD

INTRODUCTION: REGARDING MEDIEVALISTS: CONTEXTS AND APPROACHES

Julia M. H. Smith

THE IDEA OF THE MIDDLE AGES

Historical periodization is often the bane of scholarship and the friend of administrative or bibliographical convenience.[1] But there is nothing at all new in the idea that the period between the ending of the Roman Empire and the onset of cultural, religious and political changes in the fifteenth–sixteenth centuries constitutes a distinct era in European history, sufficiently coherent to be amenable to study as a single period. The notion of a *medium aevum* first occurred to Renaissance humanists looking for a way to dissociate themselves from the immediate European past. For Petrarch,

> Long before my birth time smiled and may again,
> For once there was, and yet will be, more joyful days.
> But in this middle age time's dregs
> Sweep around us, and we bend beneath a heavy load of vice.
> (*Epistolae metricae* 3: 33, quoted in Kelley 1991: 220–1)

The generation of Renaissance scholars after Petrarch felt they had emerged out of the dregs and into a new dawn. They set aside the centuries that separated themselves from classical antiquity, and followed Petrarch in regarding the intervening era parenthetically as the 'Middle Age', thereby asserting their connectedness with the ancient world and its culture. But in so doing they created a periodization that is as problematic as it is useful. The chapters which follow amply demonstrate its usefulness, so a few words about its difficulties may help to introduce some of the issues under discussion.

---

1   This chapter owes much to the persistent questioning of the students who took History 300, 'Historiography' with me at Trinity College, Hartford between 1989 and 1995: I would like to thank them for sharing the adventure with me and for insisting that I clarify my thoughts.

Two difficulties immediately present themselves: when? and where? If the Middle Ages are that period in European history commencing in the post-Roman years, how does this periodization apply to those parts of Europe which had no Roman past, such as Ireland or Scandinavia? Irish historians are generally willing to accept a Middle Ages that began with the Anglo–Norman conquest in 1169 but lack unanimity about whether it is appropriate to follow common British, French or German parlance and speak of an 'early medieval' period in Irish history prior to the eleventh/twelfth century.[2] More pressing is the issue of extra-European cultures. Is it possible to speak of the Islamic Middle Ages, or Chinese or Japanese ones? To the extent that this has sometimes been done, it is one aspect of the European cultural imperialism to which Edward Said took such objection (Said 1978; cf. Chapters 1 and 23).

The Middle Ages as treated in the chapters which follow refer to a specifically European past. More precisely, their Europe 'is that part of the world which became a cultural unit thanks to the Germanic invasions of the Roman empire (Crone 1989: 149) together with its natural extension, the short-lived crusader colonies in Outremer (the medieval Near East), the subject of Robert Irwin's appraisal of Saladin and the Third Crusade (Chapter 8). Such a definition of Europe is of course highly tendentious – at the very least it omits the Balkans and the Slav lands of central Europe – but it is also the historiographical reality which informs these chapters. As Reynolds acknowledges explicitly, her discussion of the historiography of the medieval state only deals with France, Germany, Italy and the British Isles. Identical geographical constraints frame Timothy Reuter's discussion of the medieval nobility, Peter Biller's of popular religion, Janet Nelson's of family, gender and sexuality and Bernard S. Bachrach's of military historiography. Several reasons for this concentration on a 'core' region of western Europe are apparent. At one level, there is the straightforward matter of linguistic competence which hinders. many historians from moving beyond this core to work on areas which require specialization in unusual languages. At another, the emergence of history as an academic and professional discipline in the nineteenth century began in Germany, whence it spread to France and England and then to the United States. As the practice of history became established in universities, so there developed a common culture of method, purpose and personal or institutional affiliations (Gilbert 1965; cf. the remarks of Bentley, pp. 445–51). Lack of contacts can intensify linguistic barriers. Finally, as Biller eloquently demonstrates, until 1990 the historiography of Europe was riven for almost fifty years by the ideological cleft of the Iron Curtain (Chapters 12; cf. chapter 10). Although it is still too early to be able to assess the impact of the collapse of communism on the writing of history, readers should remember that most of the work discussed in these chapters was written during the Cold War. Ideological differences and restrictions on travel effectively excised the eastern part of the germanophone academic community.

---

2   Richter 1994: 3 n. 2; cf. the title of the most recent book on the subject, Dáibhí Ó Cróinín, *Early Medieval Ireland, 400–1200* (London, 1995).

If the idea of the 'Middle Ages' raises geographical concerns, it also raises temporal ones. When, chronologically speaking, is the period under discussion? Deciding when to start is a particularly acute problem. The issue here is what distinguishes the medieval world from its Roman predecessor. Debates about continuity or rupture have dominated the discourse in the two centuries since Gibbon posited a final death date of 1453 for the Roman Empire in his *Decline and Fall*. In the late nineteenth and early twentieth centuries, the poles of the discussion were underpinned by disagreement about how significant the Roman contribution was to the establishment of European identity. Discussions over the last two decades have shifted focus and instead have been dominated by a somewhat different paradigm, that of 'transformation', implying an evolutionary understanding of the simultaneity of both change and continuity. Reynolds, Bachrach, Reuter and Nelson are all alive to this debate and its implications for their theme. Despite the recent emergence of 'Late Antiquity' as a historical period with its own identity (journals, conferences, etc.; cf. Chapter 5) there remains no general consensus. A major reason for this is a complementary but distinct debate conducted by western European Marxist or Marxisant historians, a debate concerning the shift from the ancient, slave-based mode of production to the feudal (effectively medieval but pre-capitalist) one. This 'other transition', as Chris Wickham calls it to distinguish it from the more intensively studied shift to a capitalist economy, has been located as late as the year 1000 by Guy Bois (Wickham 1984; Bois 1992; see also Chapter 36). French medievalists are currently locked in animated debate about a 'feudal transformation' in the late tenth century, and the emergence after the millennium of a fundamentally different socio–political order.[3] Although this debate springs from work on sources from France south of the Loire, there has been a great tendency to generalize from it, by reading the part for the whole.

Conventional chronological markers which since at least the time of Jacob Burckhardt delimited the end of the Middle Ages have also been dissolved in recent years. Both Renaissance and Reformation are liable to be appropriated by medievalists; alternatively the idea of an 'Old Europe' persisting until the convulsions of the French Revolution and Napoleonic wars can enfold both medieval and early modern Europe into a single pre-modern, or pre-industrial period (see Van Engen 1994b: 407–9).

In neither geographical nor chronological terms is the notion of 'the Middle Ages' neutral, value-free and unproblematic. For all its faults, it remains in common usage, and will assuredly continue to do so. Part of its usefulness is simply its fuzziness, hallowed by five centuries of historical tradition.

WORDS, TEXTS AND MEANINGS

If it is hard to define medieval historians in terms of a shared period and region of study, what then does unite them? Two common threads run through the

---

3   The phrase 'feudal transformation' is the title of the English translation of one of the seminal French works in the debate. Poly and Bournazel 1991; cf. Bisson 1994 for feudal 'revolution'. For full references to this debate, see the bibliography provided by Reuter, Chapter 10, n. 17.

historiographical themes discussed in these six chapters, namely sources and language. Biller focuses his discussion of popular religion on the late Middle Ages in an explicit acknowledgement that his analysis is conditioned by the surviving source materials: there is simply not adequate evidence to pursue the questions that interest historians of lay religiosity before *c.*1200, and little enough for the thirteenth and fourteenth centuries. His frustration is a common one, to some extent reflected in all these chapters, most particularly with respect to the earlier Middle Ages. Modern scholarly access to medieval books and documents can be summarized as a series of intersecting narratives. One is the spread of literacy in the Middle Ages (a subject which has attracted much scholarly attention in the last decade); another is the story of the hazards of fire in a medieval castle, monastery or cathedral combined with the erratic ravages of Reformation, revolution and war; a third is the tale of the interests of medieval and humanist scholars themselves, who copied and circulated some texts but ignored others. Historians of the Middle Ages have to make do with a documentary base compiled by generally arbitrary and random circumstances. It is richer in some places than in others and some centuries than others, and although the seam of sources available to be mined generally thickens in the later Middle Ages, there are indeed places where it thins out.

Nevertheless, medieval historians' approach to these sources continues to develop ever greater sophistication. The mass of scholarship reviewed in these essays is the tiny tip of a huge iceberg, whose hidden bulk is the laborious work of textual scholarship. The disciplined study of sources – transcribing, dating, editing, calendaring, indexing, translating – has a continuous history since the publication of Jean Mabillon's *De Re Diplomatica* in 1681 (see Aris 1995; Alymer, *infra*: 267). A process begun in the seventeenth century by clerical scholars was forwarded in the nineteenth by the liberal-minded Germans who fostered a nascent German national identity by inaugurating the truly monumental *Monumenta Germaniae Historica* (MGH), whose first volume was published in 1826.[4] Still a vigorous publishing enterprise, the MGH itself offers a convenient index of changing editorial attitudes and practices across nearly two centuries, not only in matters such as the selection of texts, but also in the handling of complex manuscript traditions and editorial conventions.

None of the chapters here directly addresses these highly technical issues; instead, changing attitudes towards sources are accosted in rather different ways. Apropos Domesday Book, Nelson makes a point which is no less important for being so obvious, that different generations of historians bring different questions and interests to the same, well-known texts, for she points out that what was used for establishing aristocratic genealogies a century ago is now used for analysing gender difference in eleventh-century England (p. 164). Asking different questions of a familiar body of material is one of the ways in which the dialogue between

---

4   The classic account of the MGH is that of Knowles 1963: 63–97. There is also a brief discussion of the great legal historian Georg Waitz, who brought the standards and professionalism of the academic discipline of history to the MGH, by Benson and Weber 1995.

modern scholars and their medieval documents is repeatedly reframed. Reuter draws attention to a complementary development in the way historians handle their sources. He notes the way in which eleventh- and twelfth-century aristocratic genealogies were once used to establish the distant origins of those families but have more recently been deployed to evaluate the attitudes and assumptions of their compilers' own times (p. 190). Behind this changed approach lies the recognition, now very widespread, that medieval writers are usually a better guide to the mentalities of their own day than to the events of a distant past which they purport to describe.

Whatever subject they study, historians of the Middle Ages are never working on material in their own native language: the discipline requires a high level of linguistic and philological expertise whether in Latin, Greek and the medieval vernaculars or knowledge of modern foreign languages. Thus it is not surprising that one of the common hallmarks of these chapters is a sensitivity to language, and in particular to the subtleties of the meanings of words. Bachrach shows how changing meanings of the Latin word *milites* are central to debates about forms of soldiery, and in particular to the modern historiographical vogue for 'knighthood' (Chapter 11, esp. p. 211, also Chapter 10, at p. 191–2). Biller opens his chapter by unpicking the word 'religion' itself, whilst Reynolds worries about what modern terminology is most appropriate for describing medieval polities, and about the lack of correspondence between the terms used by historians writing in French, German and English.

But there is more at stake than simply individual words and their meanings. As historians are becoming increasingly aware, texts deploy rhetorical strategies which display some meanings and conceal others. That analysis of these can aid the study of medieval mentalities or of power relationships is implicit in both Reuter's discussion of the self-awareness (*Selbstverständnis*) of the medieval nobility, as well as in Nelson's discussion of recent work on gender and lordship. Biller also points to the growing interest in textuality and discourse by historians of popular heresy. For him, this is 'a grim weather forecast' (p. 239): it is certainly one that cannot be ignored. 'Textuality' and 'discourse' are terms adopted from literary theory and direct attention to the ways in which language constructs meaning, and to the problem of how, if at all, it is possible to break out of an eternally self-referential linguistic circle. Both medievalists' traditional philological and linguistic skills and recent emphasis on literary deconstruction 'focus a peculiar intensity upon the text as *text* ... prior to the meaning it produces' (Patterson 1994: 236). But the critical difference between the two approaches is the unavoidable epistemological problem of whether meaning exists independently of the texts. The traditional, positivist answer is affirmative, the deconstructionist one negative. Of these medieval chapters, Irwin's exploration of the relationship between historical and fictional accounts of the Third Crusade best illustrates the conditional and limited nature of historical meaning.

Discussion of rhetoric inevitably invites attention to audience. Except inasmuch as Biller refers to heretical groups as 'textual communities', that is, as groups whose members were defined by hearing or reading particular texts (p. 239), the medieval audience is not at issue here. Rather, the chapters of Bachrach, Nelson and Irwin raise important issues about who in the modern world are the 'consumers' of medieval history, the audience for whom historians write. In brief, the audience for the scholarship reviewed in these chapters does not consist only of other historians of the medieval world. Their audience may extend to other professional historians, and indeed to those outside the academic discipline altogether. Bachrach is aware that military historians, usually trained in much more recent history, are rarely *au courant* with the most recent medieval scholarship, and are thus liable to perpetuate outworn assumptions and interpretations. His is a subject in need of careful exposition to an audience wider than the circle of medievalists. The same holds true for the work on family, gender and sexuality surveyed by Nelson. These aspects of medieval society have been subjected to increasing scrutiny in the last couple of decades in response to the development of women's history and the history of sexuality as fields of study in their own right. The books and articles cited by Nelson are at least as likely to be read by specialists in the history of women, family and gender in other periods than the medieval as they are to be consumed by medieval historians. When debates are framed thematically not chronologically, it requires particular clarity of exposition to reach beyond the inner circle of medieval specialists to the wider historical audience.

By contrast, Irwin draws attention to an altogether different audience, the writers and readers of historical fiction. The career of Saladin and the events of the Third Crusade have had a particular appeal to a wide lay audience, in much the same way as have Joan of Arc, Robin Hood, the wives of Henry VIII or Martin Guerre. Irwin traces Saladin's posthumous reputation from the publication of Sir Walter Scott's novel *The Talisman* in 1825 through until the 1980s. He comments on the influence which academic historians of the last century have had on the work of novelists and popular historians (and vice versa). Although the establishment of a university-based historical profession introduced a distinction between professional and lay historians which did not exist in Scott's day, Irwin's message is that the divide remains permeable and malleable. As the academic study of the Middle Ages becomes ever more technical and specialized, Irwin invites historians to keep in mind the wider audience beyond their own professional circles.

Words and texts, meaning and interpretation are inextricably intertwined. Whilst this is a truism for any field of historical study, the long tradition of a discipline whose roots lay in seventeenth-century textual editing and nineteenth-century philology make the issues particularly clear in the study of medieval history. If there is a challenge ahead for medieval historians, it is to use the technical skills specific to their own discipline to negotiate the challenges thrown out by modern treatments of textuality (cf. Spiegel 1990; Kramer 1989).

HISTORIANS IN CONTEXT

It remains to make explicit a central implication of the preceding paragraphs. Put simply, not only medieval writers but *all* historians are affected by the mentalities,

110

assumptions and ideologies of their own day. The authors of these chapters and the scholars whose work they discuss are as context-bound as the twelfth-century compiler of an aristocratic genealogy, a ninth-century chronicler or a fourteenth-century preacher. What, then, is the context within which medieval history has been pursued within the last century? Three particular themes influence this scholarship: interaction with other academic disciplines, a historian's political climate, and his or her beliefs and ideologies.

Like any other branch of historical study, medieval history has been profoundly influenced by developments in other disciplines. Nelson and Biller both offer useful guides to important aspects of this. In the first place (in every sense), there is Marc Bloch and the tradition of '*annaliste*' history of which he was the co-founder in the 1920s (on the *Annales* school, see Chapter 35). From its very outset, the *Annales* movement set out to bring to bear upon the study of history the insights and methodologies of the burgeoning social science disciplines of the early twentieth century: sociology, economics and anthropology. Following Bloch's lead, successive generations of *annaliste* historians have devoted much attention to the Middle Ages, especially from the eleventh century onwards. Medievalists' debt to the sociology of religion is clear in Biller's chapter (p. 255–6) to anthropology in Nelson's (Chapter 9, *passim*). This influence has its own particular geography. The experimentation in method which characterizes so much *annaliste* writing has remained characteristically French; to the extent that it has been influential elsewhere, it has been most warmly received in the USA. A glance at the publication history of all the major *Annales* historians (medievalists and early modernists alike) shows that English translations were generally undertaken by and for Americans; until very recently, *annaliste* influence in Britain has been modest.

In the United States, recent medievalists have found it easy to marry the insights of French *annalistes* with the approaches of American cultural anthropologists, most notably Clifford Geertz. But Britain has its own, different tradition of social anthropology. This has also left its imprint, less trumpeted, but equally significant (for example, on much of the work of Nelson herself on rituals of royalty).[5] And Nelson's comments below point to specific aspects of this British strand of anthropologically informed approach to the Middle Ages. Attention to kinship structures and to marriage conventions offer a particularly good example of this.[6]

Not only cross-disciplinary fertilization shapes medievalists' scholarship. The political climate in which a historian writes is liable to leave its imprint. Irwin's chapter in this volume may stand as a case study of the effect of shifting political circumstances on historical interpretation of the Middle Ages, in this case Saladin

---

5 For a comment on the distinctions between US cultural anthropology and British social anthropology, see the introduction to Kuper 1992. As for the influence of social anthropology on British medievalists, Wallace-Hadrill 1959, with its explicit debt to his Manchester colleague Max Gluckmann, is an early and path-breaking example. Nelson's articles are collected together in Nelson 1986. On history and anthropology in general, see Chapter 31.
6 See Chapter 9, 162–3; 153 n. 4 below on the influence of Jack Goody.

and the Third Crusade. His chapter displays to the reader the early nineteenth-century Orient – exotic, different and even demonic; the character-forming and nation-moulding crusades of high Victorian imperialist writers replete with the chivalric values of the public-school ethos; two-party governance of the Kingdom of Jerusalem as conceived in New Deal America; Cold War reversal of the Victorian dialectic of conflict and victory that turned the Kingdom of Jerusalem into a case study in coexistence with the enemy, and, most splendidly of all, a Saladin of *c*.1950 vintage, the twelfth-century Winston Churchill in thin disguise, who 'raised Islam out of the rut of political demoralization … [and] … met the unforeseen challenge flung down to him by destiny.' (p. 145). Irwin demonstrates neatly how the work of novelists and scholars alike often (doubtless unconsciously) refracts images of the crusades through the prism of contemporary political preoccupations.

Reuter provides a convenient word for this: that historians' work is *zeitbedingt*, constrained by its period (p. 182). Examples are manifold, but a few to which chapters other than Irwin's draw attention need to be mentioned also. Biller points out that historians of the Middle Ages began to focus enquiry into popular, or lay, religion in the early 1960s, at exactly the time when the laity were rising to greater prominence in both Catholic and Protestant churches. The institution of a Department of the Laity by the World Council of Churches in 1954, and even more the Second Vatican Council of 1962–5, provide the immediate context for this shift in historiographical focus (p. 226). Similarly, it is no accident that the explosion of interest in women's and family history charted by Nelson rides on the back of the women's movement of the 1960s. (One might also add that, within the last very few years, the extension of the history of sexuality to investigate the history of same-sex relationships is effectively the historiographical 'outing' of gays.[7]) But Biller is quite right to note that the historiography of medieval women has followed no single direction, shifting focus from notable, exceptional abbesses and mystics to ordinary laywomen, even serving girls and that, at its best, the women's history of the 1990s avoids the 'crude presentist problematic' of the 1970s – the use of the history of medieval women's religion as a stick with which to beat contemporary clerics (Chapter 12, quotation on p. 234).

One of the strengths of Reynolds's chapter is to show how historians are not only *zeitbedingt* but also constrained by country. Her discussion of medieval polities and the ways in which modern historians have understood them distinguishes sharply the differing assumptions of French, German, English and Italian scholars. As modern states, both Germany and Italy were creations of the late nineteenth century, but as nations had a much older cultural identity. For this reason, she notes that German and Italian historians have readily taken it for granted that nation and state are different, whereas English historiography in particular is liable to equate the two in a single continuum stretching from the twentieth century right back into the tenth. If it is particularly hard to disentangle the historiography of medieval states or to make meaningful comparisons between medieval polities,

---

7 Most notably Boswell 1994; and for the rhetoric of homosexuality, cf. Leyser 1995.

Reynolds shows us that one of the reasons lies in the significantly different political environments within which the academic discipline of medieval history has developed in various European countries.

Beyond Europe, the study of medieval history has a quite different flavour again. On being questioned, North American and European scholars admit to perceiving advantages and disadvantages in the approaches of their transatlantic colleagues.[8] North Americans note that European historians rarely read outside their own national scholarly tradition; Europeans regard Americans' approach as 'global and eclectic ... if at times superficial and at other times liberating' (Geary 1994: 63). These distinctions emerge in choice of subject as well as of approach. Readers familiar with the field will observe that virtually none of the work on the medieval nobility cited by Reuter is by Americans and, conversely, that American contributions to the field surveyed by Nelson are enormous. Behind these transatlantic divergences lie distinctions deeper than simply ease of access to archives or choice of topic. As history became a professional, academic discipline in late nineteenth-century America, the Middle Ages attracted only modest attention. Not until after the First World War did that change significantly, and at no stage has medieval history enjoyed a sufficiently secure place in American university curricula for its practitioners to cease worrying lest they become dispensable.[9] Behind periodically recurrent fears about the health of medieval history (and medieval studies more generally) in the United States lies an ambivalence towards the European past which is deeply embedded in American culture. Monarchy, nobility and the interpenetration of church and state were all rejected in the eighteenth century, and the Middle Ages are readily construed as the antithesis of American values of modernity and progress.[10] Unsure whether 'to distance or to reappropriate' the European past, American attitudes towards the Middle Ages can be summed up as 'a continuing dialectic between connection and disjunction' (Van Engen 1994b: 414, 415). The Middle Ages play no positive role in constructing American national identity. In this respect, the difference between the United States and the United Kingdom could not be greater.

The third and last major influence contributing to the flavour of historians' work is that of the beliefs and ideologies which inform the subjects they choose, the questions they ask and the methods they pursue in answering them. Biller is particularly incisive here. He points out that much work on the medieval Church and religion remains confessional, even apologetic at times. Modern scholars have not ceased to play out the intellectual conflicts of the Reformation, and the backwash spills over into the late Middle Ages (Chapter 12, p. 223–4). He is equally clear that studies of medieval religion undertaken in communist Europe

---

8   These are explored by Geary 1994.
9   David 1935. The chapters in Van Engen 1994a contain the most recent soul-searching by North American medievalists.
10   A theme trenchantly explored recently by Patterson 1990. But T. F. Tout noted this as long ago as 1928 (1929: 9).

have their own agenda and interpretative framework, rarely intersecting with and often profoundly alien to those of Western historians.

Indeed, Marxism has been an issue in every field except that addressed by Irwin. Marxist analyses of 'feudalism' imply, as Reuter stresses, a wide-ranging set of interconnected ideas about political power and social relationships, which have generally been summarily dismissed by Western non-Marxist historians. In post-war Germany, debates proceeded along parallel tracks on either side of the Iron Curtain; the two have yet to be integrated (Chapter 10, p. 181–2). Outside Germany, medieval historians have often been able to ignore the segregated East German historians altogether. Reynolds exemplifies this, for her discussion of the historiography of the medieval German polity sidesteps the divide along the Berlin Wall entirely. She does, however, note the distinctive Marxist approach to assessing the difference between the ancient state and its early medieval successors, for this is a debate to which Western Marxist historians have contributed vigorously (Chapter 7). Indeed, historians have never needed to travel eastwards to encounter Marxist colleagues, for Marxist, or Marxist-inspired scholarship has its own indigenous tradition within Britain, France, Italy and Germany as well (Chapter 36). Bachrach points to one particular aspect of that, the economic determinism of the 'new archaeology' of the 1980s, where prejudices against aristocratic elites have left the archaeological study of castles and military fortifications neglected (p. 212–13; on 'new archaeology', see Chapter 32). Finally, it is also important to remember in this context that Marxist historians have generally not been concerned with the history of the family, or with the gendered construction of power relationships. As Nelson notes, the slave-using and peasant societies of the Middle Ages have certainly attracted their attention, but their gaze has not looked within peasant households (p. 158–9). The reasons for this go back to the way in which Marx and Engels themselves viewed the family and concentrated on production to the exclusion of reproduction (cf. Vann 1993).

Where does this leave the historian of the Middle Ages who neither subscribes to a church or sect, nor professes Marxism, feminism or any other -ism? At the very least, if a European s/he may well be bound within the tendency to 'teleological interpretation' which, in Reynolds's view, has dominated scholarship on the last 2,000 years of European history (p. 132). If English, such a person is particularly liable to the belief "'that strong, civilised government is a prerequisite of civilised life and human progress'" (p. 133, quoting R. R. Davies). If American and elderly, that person might conform to an ideology that is particularly hard to detect, most especially by those who subscribe to it. This is the pervasive – and only very superficially persuasive – view that objectivity, notably 'scientific objectivity', is the historian's achievable goal and that it is itself value-free. American Cold War ideology saw democracy and scientific empiricism as twin weapons in the fight against communism, and American medievalists were party to the consensus of historical opinion built around that belief.[11] But since the 1960s, the growing impact

---

11 Novick 1988. For an assessment of medieval history in Cold War America, see Johnson 1953.

of postmodernism has eroded all that. 'A fresh breeze for some, acid rain for others', postmodernism leads inevitably to the conclusion that, in one way or another, *all* history is always ideological, relative and *zeitbedingt*.[12]

Such a conclusion will disturb as many readers as it encourages. On the cusp of the new millennium, medieval history is becoming more lively and less consensual than ever before. Moreover, it is certainly fragmenting, as are so many other fields of historical study, into a cornucopia of sub-specialities of which no one can ever hope to master more than one or two. At its heart, though, there remains a shared commitment to the rigorous textual scholarship which forms the unseen foundations on which all these chapters rest. In the 500 years since Lorenzo Valla proved that the Donation of Constantine was a forgery, attention to the textual residue of the Middle Ages has been at the core of the discipline. There is no reason to think that it will be any different in the next 500.

REFERENCES

Aris, R. (1995) 'Jean Mabillon, (1632–1707), in Damico and Zavadil 1995.

Benson, R. L. and Weber, L. J. (1995) 'Geog Waitz (1813–1886)' in Damico and Zavadil 1995.

Bisson, T. (1994) 'The "feudal *revolution*"', *Past and Present* 142: 6–42.

Bois, G. (1992) *The Transformation of the Year 1000*, Manchester. (French original: *La Mutation de l'an mil*, 1989.)

Boswell, J. (1994) *The Marriage of Likeness: Same-Sex Unions in Pre-modern Europe*, New York.

Crone, P. (1989) *Pre-Industrial Societies*, Oxford.

Damico, H. and Zavadil, J. R. (eds) (1995) *Medieval Scholarship: Biographical Studies on the Formation of a Discipline*, New York.

David, D. C. (1935) 'American Historiography of the Middle Ages, 1884–1934', *Speculum* 10: 125–37.

Geary, P. J. (1994) 'Visions of medieval studies ln North America', in Van Engen 1994.

Gilbert, F. (1965) 'The professionalization of history in the nineteenth century', in J. Higham, L. Krieger and F. Gilbert, *History*, Englewood Cliffs.

Johnson, E. N. (1953) 'American medievalists and today', *Speculum* 28: 844–54.

Kelley, D. R. (1991) *Versions of History from Antiquity to the Enlightenment*, New Haven.

Knowles, D. (1963) *Great Historical Enterprises*, London.

Kramer, L. S. (1989) 'Literature, criticism and historical imagination: the literary challenge of Hayden White and Dominick LaCapra', in L. Hunt (ed.) *The New Cultural History*, Berkeley.

Kuper, A. (1992) *Conceptualising Society*, London.

Leyser, C. (1995) 'Cities of the plain: the rhetoric of sodomy in Peter Damian's "Book of Gomorrah"', *Romanic Review* 86: 191–211.

Nelson, J. L. (1986) *Politics and Ritual in Early Medieval Europe*, London.

Novick, P. (1988) *That Noble Dream: The 'Objectivity Question' and the American Historical Profession*, Chicago.

O'Cróinín, D. (1995) *Early Medieval Ireland 400–1200*, London.

---

12 Quotation from Novick 1988: 522. On postmodernism, see the remarks of Michael Bentley, pp. 490–4.

Patterson, L. (1990) 'On the margin: postmodernism, ironic history and medieval studies', *Speculum* 65: 87–100.

—— (1994) 'The return to philology', in Van Engen 1994a.

Poly, J.-P. and Bournazel, E. (1991) *The Feudal Transformation 900–1200*, New York. (French original: *La Mutation féodale, Xe–XII siècles*, Paris, 1980.)

Richter, M. (1994) *The Formation of the Medieval West: Studies in the Oral Culture of the Barbarians*, Dublin.

Said, E. (1978) *Orientalism*, London.

Spiegel, G. M. (1990) 'History, historicism and the social logic of the text in the Middle Ages', *Speculum* 65: 59–86.

Tout, T. F. (1929) 'History and historians in America', *Transactions of the Royal Historical Society* 4th ser., 12: 1–17.

Van Engen, J. (1994a) *The Past and Future of Medieval Studies*, Notre Dame, IL.

—— (1994b) 'An afterword on medieval studies, or the future of Abelard and Heloise', in Van Engen (1994a).

Vann, R. T. (1993) 'Marxism and Historians of the Family', in H. Kozicki (ed.) *Developments in Modern Historiography*, New York.

Wallace-Hadrill, J. M. (1959) 'The blood-feud of the Franks', *Bulletin of the John Rylands Library* 41: 459–87.

Wickham, C. (1984) 'The other transition: from the ancient world to feudalism', *Past and Present* 103: 3–36.

7

THE HISTORIOGRAPHY OF THE MEDIEVAL STATE

Susan Reynolds

It is not very easy to know what body of work to consider under the heading of the historiography of the medieval state.[1] On the one hand, a long tradition of empirical writing about the politics and administration of kingdoms and other polities, and of relations between them, is still vigorously alive, especially at regional or local level. If medieval kingdoms, principalities and lordships were states then this work must be part – and an important part – of the historiography of the state. On the other hand, a fair number of medieval historians, whether primarily concerned with political practice or with political ideas, maintain that the very use of the word 'state' is anachronistic and inappropriate for most, if not all, of the Middle Ages, since only in the later part of the period did the 'concept of the state' begin to emerge. This derives from a long tradition. In 1824 Leopold von Ranke described the polities that existed in Italy in 1494 as 'neither nations nor tribes; neither cities nor kingdoms; they were the first States in the world'.[2] At that time the origin of modern nations was traced back to barbarian tribes of the 'Age of Migrations',[3] but properly sovereign states were thought to have been impossible in medieval conditions: the sense of *res publica* had disappeared with the Roman Empire; feudal society relied on personal bonds rather than public institutions; and the universal claims of Pope and Emperor, together with the pyramidal and hierarchical structure of both Church and feudal society, inhibited the development of states.[4]

---

1   This chapter considers only part of western Europe (France, Germany, Italy and the British Isles).
2   'weder Völker, noch Stämme, weder Städte, noch Reiche, es sind die ersten Staaten der Welt': von Ranke 1874: 18. G. R. Dennis, in his translation (*History of the Latin and Teutonic Nations 1494–1514*, London, 1915; 38) translates *Stämme* as 'races'.
3   Some of the problems involved in the 'Age of Migrations' are discussed, e.g. by Wenskus 1974; Goffart 1981 and 1980: ch. 1; Reynolds 1983; James, 1982: 13–41.
4   Fédou 1971: 11–57 offers a recent version, giving *le système féodale* in its later stages a more constructive role. Cf. Reynolds 1994: 3–10, 17–34.

Nowadays historians quite often find the origin of the modern European state or nation-state in thirteenth-century 'national monarchies', of which France and England are their paradigmatic cases. Some see no problem in using the word state even earlier, though they do not always make clear the meaning they attach to it. Others remain reluctant to talk of states until after the Middle Ages, when forms of the word began to be used in its modern sense, on the ground that its use inevitably implies the ideology, constitution, technology and so on, associated with the modern state. It is not clear why this should be so. It certainly is not so when social anthropologists and ancient historians discuss states, stateless societies and the origin of states (e.g. Gluckman 1965; Fried 1967; Clastres 1974; Thapar 1984; Mann 1986). Historians of medieval Europe may in some ways have found their view of the state impeded by all the work that has been done recently on the origin of the modern state (e.g. Guénée 1971; Tilly 1975, 1990; Skalweit 1982: 123–54; Mann 1986; Genet 1990; Coulet and Genet 1990; Blockmans and Genet 1993). As in the nineteenth century, current definitions and discussions of the modern state may give the impression – however unintended – that only modern states are true states, or the only ones worth discussing.[5] It is easier to evaluate the differences between modern states and earlier polities,[6] and the way that historians write about them, if one starts from a definition of the state as such, rather than of the modern state.

In this chapter, while trying to indicate what I think the historians I mention have meant by 'the state', I shall myself use the word to refer to an organization of human society within a more or less fixed area in which the ruler or governing body more or less successfully controls the legitimate use of physical force. This definition is based on Max Weber's definition of a modern state, but is adapted to focus on the difference between societies in which the control of physical force is formally located and those in which it is not.[7] I differ from Weber in referring to 'control' rather than 'monopoly' and in the insertions of 'more or less'. Weber apparently thought that 'monopoly' made his definition specific to the modern state but some modern polities that are presumably reckoned to be states (like the United States) claim control rather than monopoly, and not all claim either very successfully. I also differ from English translations of Weber in referring to 'physical force' as opposed to 'violence', because 'violence' seems to me a tendentious translation of *physische Gewaltsamkeit*; and to 'area' rather than 'territory', because 'territory' in medieval contexts tends to get attached to a particular sort of polity called 'territorial principalities'. My definition, like Weber's, means that I do not regard the state as

---

5   Poggi 1990: 25, maintains that 'although one often speaks of "the modern state" … strictly speaking the adjective "modern" is pleonastic'.

6   I use the word polity to denote units of political organization in general, whether or not they are to be counted as states.

7   Weber 1958: 494: translated by Gerth and Wright Mills 1952: 78. The arguments of Ferguson and Mansbach 1988 and Abrams 1988, about the futility of the concept, and therefore of attempting definitions, are not concerned with the problems that confront social anthropologists and historians.

merely the ruler or governing body of a society (as Louis XIV allegedly maintained), nor as merely the body of citizens (as Walter Ullmann implied – Ullmann 1965: 17; 1977: 94, 118; though cf. Ullmann 1966: 87). It is the combination of both, expressing the relation between them. It is an organization or structure.

This working definition emphatically includes legitimacy: the government of a state has not merely coercive power, but a coercive authority that is generally – more or less, and however reluctantly – accepted by its subjects as legitimate. But the definition excludes any reference to ideology or the particular means of inculcating ideas of legitimacy. Respect for rulers makes their control of force less conspicuous but does not affect the fact that they control it or are supposed to do so. It also excludes any reference to law-making or other activities or functions of states apart from their control of legitimate force, which seems to me the function that distinguishes a state from other polities or lesser collectivities. Further, it does not refer to the size of the state, the taxes it raises, or its differentiated, bureaucratic or specialized institutions. All these are often included in definitions of the modern state but they are matters of degree which either make for untidy categories or require the ignoring of inconvenient evidence. Rulers who control the use of force generally receive dues and services of some kind. The difference between such dues and the regular taxes on which definitions of the modern state focus is often hard to draw in historical practice. Bureaucracy makes it easier to govern large areas, but the difference between states with some differentiated, record-keeping institutions and those without them seems less clear than the difference between both and stateless societies. 'Privatization' makes the institutions and functions of some contemporary states look less differentiated than they were until recently.

Lastly, my definition excludes any reference to sovereignty. That is deliberate, not because it enables me to squeeze medieval states, which are often said to have lacked it, into the category, but because sovereignty is so difficult to define in principle and locate in practice (Crick 1968; Ferguson and Mansbach 1988). The idea that medieval polities are supposed not to have been sovereign because of the universalist claims of pope and emperor seems to survive today chiefly in the minds of those who take their medieval history from old textbooks.[8] Though churches took the lead in literate and record-keeping administration, notably in the management of their lands; and though popes and some bishops came to rule particular areas in as statelike a way as did secular rulers, the authority of the pope over the whole Church was not statelike. It depended on moral authority and influence, not on coercive control.[9] As for imperial claims, they were discussed chiefly in the context of German or Italian politics. On occasion they provided an extra polemical force in disputes between emperors and other kings, but they clearly did nothing to diminish the autonomy of any other kingdom except those, like the

---

8   J. R. Strayer's definition of a state (Strayer 1970: 10) is criticized by Tilly 1975: 22–7, on the grounds, e.g. that it would include city-states, which Tilly considers too small, and polities ruled by bishops, which he thinks 'theocratic'; but cf. Waley 1961: 298; Canning 1991.
9   Marongiu 1977: 31–2 deals briskly with the superior authority of the Church.

Slav kingdoms on Germany's eastern borders, over which imperial claims rested on more specific grounds (Carlyle and Carlyle 1928: 149; Lewis 1954: 430; Pennington 1993: esp. 30–7; but cf. Matthew 1992). At first sight internal sovereignty poses a more serious problem. Medieval ideas of justice and custom limited the rights of rulers, just as the practicalities of communication made it difficult for them to enforce their rights over those to whom they delegated local authority. No medieval ruler therefore was sovereign in the way that later theorists of the sovereign state or sovereign nation-state would require. But then, as at least two medievalists have pointed out, layers of government, each with supposedly entrenched rights, were not peculiar to medieval states, nor was the idea that subjects should have rights against their governments (Tierney 1962–3; Pennington 1993).

Modern states are sometimes distinguished as being 'nation-states'. If the compound is not a tautology it presumably means that the territory of the state is occupied by people who are united by more than being under one state. What unites them and makes them a nation is generally taken to be some degree of common culture and belief in a common history. The difference between a nation and what is now often called an ethnic group may be that a nation is more often thought of as a group which has the right to political autonomy – ideally to be a state.[10] But not all groups thought of as nations attain that right. It is not clear that states that are considered to be more or less coextensive with nations are always more statelike than are those that are not. While it is necessary to understand nineteenth- and twentieth-century ideas about nations and their rights in order to understand the way historians have written about the states, nations and 'nation-states' of Europe, the statelike or unstatelike character of past polities is easier to discern if state and nation are disentangled.[11]

It is also useful to separate the phenomenon of the state from the concept of the state. Polities may have the characteristics I have suggested without anyone in them having any clear ideas about what distinguishes them from societies or polities without those characteristics. The absence in surviving literature or records of what looks to modern scholars like 'the concept of the state' or 'the modern concept of the state' is no argument against the existence of states in the European Middle Ages. Nor, of course, is the absence of approximations to the word 'state' in its modern sense (however defined) in any of the relevant languages used at the time. Medieval writers wrote about politics in a different way from their successors and used a different vocabulary. Whether this means that they had no concept of the state is doubtful: those who considered problems about limiting the power of rulers, or about their relation to law or to the Pope or each other, were concerned with something like what we might call problems of the state and its sovereignty.

---

10   The periodical *Nationes* has since 1978 published articles, mainly by German scholars, on the evidence of medieval national consciousness etc. On medieval solidarities and their relation to the idea of nationalism: Reynolds 1984: ch. 8, esp. pp. 250–6.
11   Stringer 1994. Strayer's stress on the affective feelings of a state's inhabitants (Strayer 1970: 5, 10, 45, 109) tends to confusion with a nation.

Besides, if it turns out that at least some people lived within states of some kind it seems likely that they had some idea of the kind of polity they lived in, even if their ideas were as vague and various as those that most modern people have about the state. This chapter, however, is about the historiography of the medieval state, as a phenomenon, whether historians think that it existed and how they write about it, not about the history of medieval ideas about polities or the words used to denote them.

Although some historians of the early Middle Ages still refer to 'tribes' (or even 'races') and to the bonds of vassalage in ways that suggest the survival of old ideas about national origins and the exclusively personal bonds of feudal society, most now seem relatively unworried about talking of the earliest medieval kingdoms as states. Perhaps Marxist (or Marx-inspired) discussions of the transition from the 'ancient state' to the 'feudal state' are responsible.[12] Though non-Marxist historians agree with the Marxists that the character of early medieval states changed fundamentally some time between the third and eighth centuries, many now seem to take a more optimistic view of government and of surviving elements of Roman administration than they used to do (e.g. Werner 1984: 317, 319–20; 1980: xiii, with refs.; Nelson 1992: 19–20; Wood 1994: 16, 60–70, 322–4). Kingdoms set up in Roman territory are generally called 'successor-states' (*Nachfolgestaaten*). Wolfram has described them as embodying 'a distinctive type of Latin statehood' which made them 'forerunners of the European type of state' (Wolfram 1970). Historians of Anglo-Saxon England would probably not agree with the contrast he drew with the early English kingdoms. Though the power of their kings was very unstable and literary sources make them look like little more than warlords, the tradition, current by 730, that in the time of King Edwin of Deira a woman could safely cross the whole island from sea to sea with a newborn child suggests that by then, if not earlier, people in northern England regarded kings as in some way responsible for enforcing law and order.[13] English society seems, moreover, to have already had quite complex governmental structures, some of which may have gone back to Roman times and would survive into the period when England was the most centralized and bureaucratic kingdom of western Europe (Campbell 1982: 58–61, 118, 240–1).

On the whole, however, recent historians of the early Middle Ages have been less interested in kingdoms than in what those who write in English call kingship. More attention has been focused on the rituals and symbols of government than on its structures or methods of administration (on symbols, e.g. Bak 1973; Nelson 1986). Relations of kings with their subjects are seen primarily in terms of interpersonal

---

12   For a recent interpretation and a survey of others: Wickham 1984.

13   Bede, *Historia Ecclesiastica*, ed. C. Plummer, Oxford, 1896, vol. i, p. 118 (II. 16). How exceptional Edwin's responsibility was depends on one's understanding of the 'bretwalda': Wormald 1983. A version of the topos occurs in *Two Saxon Chronicles Parallel*, ed C. Plummer and J. Earle, Oxford, 1892, vol. i p. 263 (1135). I do not know if it is found elsewhere.

relations between kings and followers, whether described as vassalage or *Gefolgschaft*, and of patronage through the grant of benefices or fiefs. This approach makes it easier to bypass the issue of statehood, using the word state on occasion but putting it safely within quotation marks.[14] An exception is J. L. Nelson who clearly has definitions of the state by non-medievalist students of comparative politics in mind when she draws attention to the emphasis, not only in Carolingian rhetoric but in royal policy, on the common duty of rulers and subjects to preserve the kingdom and maintain its law and order.[15] The characteristics she notes include the territorial definition of kingdoms, the assertion of royal control over coinage and fortifications, the sanctions threatened and sometimes imposed on rebellion and disobedience, royal supervision of the criminal jurisdiction exercised by landlords, and the obligations of all inhabitants of a kingdom to its defence.[16] Both rhetoric and practice drew on Roman survivals but a good deal was new. Since the 1970s archaeologists, numismatists and historians have drawn attention to the way that kings on both sides of the English Channel in the ninth century were beginning to exploit the resources of their kingdoms, and especially of their trade, more systematically.[17]

As studies of this sort remind us, the Carolingian empire did not cover as much of Europe as textbooks sometimes imply. Around its edges were societies with much less complex political organizations. What evidence there is suggests that governmental control within them was diffused, weak, and often unstable, though most had enough social differentiation to make them unlikely candidates for what social anthropologists call stateless societies – that is, societies that exist without any formally located control of coercive power. That did not prevent some from putting up long and stiff resistance to Carolingian expansion, which implies considerable internal solidarity. Some of this, like the fissions within the empire, can be explained in terms of differences which would once have been called tribal or racial and are now more often called ethnic. Ethnicity, however, seems relatively unimportant in, for instance, both Breton resistance and the degree of unity achieved in the duchy (Davies 1988: 201–13; Smith 1992: 3–4, 116–46). In England the differences between Britons and Anglo-Saxons look more problematical than they did to historians earlier in this century.[18]

All medieval historians would probably agree that the centuries after the fall of the Carolingian empire saw the political geography of Europe begin to take on a shape

---

14 e.g. Fossier 1991: 58–60; Keller 1989. Works on vassalage, benefices, etc. are cited in Reynolds 1994, esp. ch. 4. Goetz 1987 argues cogently for the impersonal and institutional qualities implied in Carolingian uses of the word but without defining his understanding of 'state'.

15 Professor Nelson tells me that she had in mind Weber's definition and discussions by social anthropologists, notably M. G. Smith.

16 Nelson 1988: 225–6. Génicot 1984: 147 also offers a definition. Cf. Ullmann 1969: pp. 110–21, though it is difficult to see how he deduces equality before the law from the idea of sovereignty (though not the state) that he sees in Carolingian government.

17 See works cited by Nelson 1992: 20.

18 Reynolds 1985 cites some of the relevant discussions.

that we can recognize today. Germany and France became separate and acquired their names, England became united, while polities emerged to the east of Germany that would, in one form or another, have a long life before them. It is easy to see why historians who reject the word state are tempted to think instead in terms of nations – the nations of their own day. The contribution of national consciousness or ethnicity to these units has often been noted: some historians pose the question whether ethnic units or nations predated states or vice versa (e.g. Graus 1965; Strayer 1966, 1970: 10–13, 45–9, 109; Ullmann 1977: 75, 118; Guénée 1971). Phrases like 'the rise of the national monarchies' or the use of 'national' as the corresponding adjective to the nouns state and kingdom suggest that others simply assume the connection.[19] For some the key stage in the emergence of states came with the moves towards more bureaucratic government at all levels, whether they place it in their area from the twelfth, thirteenth, or fourteenth century, or even later.[20] For others it came when the concept of the state was taken over from Aristotle or the texts of Roman law.[21] Whether or not they mean to imply that no polities could have the characteristics of states before academics had articulated the concept, readers may sometimes draw that inference.[22]

The most striking aspect of the way that medieval historians write about polities from the tenth century on – whether or not they call them states – is the degree to which it varies in the different traditions of historiography that have developed within the boundaries of modern states. Apart from a notable American tradition of comparing England and France, most historians of medieval Europe write chiefly about the past of what they see as their own nations.[23] Those who write about another country seem often to get absorbed into what Wickham has called its 'cultural solipsism'(Wickham 1992: 222–5 and n. 14). At the same time the long dominance of a model of feudal history derived from France has induced a tendency to generalize various phenomena, like the collapse or enfeeblement of the state in the tenth and eleventh centuries, to the whole of the former Carolingian Empire, if not to the whole of Europe. Areas where government did not apparently collapse thus seem more exceptional than they may have been. Because of the way that assumptions derived from the history of France have been incorporated into other national traditions I shall start there.

---

19 This usage may derive partly from the lack of adjectives corresponding to 'state' and 'kingdom' but it seems to reflect some genuine conflation or confusion of concepts. American medievalists may be additionally influenced by the use, going back to 1787, of 'nation' for the federal government of the United States to distinguish it from the separate states that joined to form the union: see Davis 1978: 79–84.

20 e.g. Strayer 1970; van Caenegem 1988; Canning 349–50. On the use of the word 'bureaucracy' for this period, see especially Clanchy 1993: 62–8, 85–7; Griffiths 1980. Cf. Werner 1980: x.

21 The most emphatic, frequent and influential exponent of this view was probably Walter Ullmann. See e.g. Ullmann 1966: 87; 1965: 17; 1968–9; 1977: 104, 119. Post 1964; Mager 1968.

22 e.g. works cited in previous note or Fossier 1982: II, 362. A comparison of the first sentences of chapter 10 in Duby 1987 and the translation by J. Vale (1991) suggests nuances in the connection between concept and phenomenon.

23 For some American works, below, n. 27. See also Campbell 1980b.

There seems to be overwhelming evidence that royal power in the western half of the Empire did indeed collapse so far in the tenth and eleventh centuries that the kingdom of the west Franks no longer formed anything that can be called a state. A series of regional studies following Duby's work on the Mâconnais has, however, mitigated the old view of the period as one of 'feudal anarchy' (surveyed in Balard 1991: 101–25). Few of them have focused primarily on what their authors would consider politics or political structures as such, for political history has been unfashionable in France. What they say about relations between nobles, and about noble rights over peasants, nevertheless suggests that most people lived for most of this period under a coercive control on which custom bestowed a fair degree of legitimacy – though less, presumably, when it was disputed between different lords. Looked at in a wider comparative context, this is less a stateless society than a society of unstable mini-states. Areas where counts or dukes maintained some control over lesser lords might count as larger, if still small and weak, states or near-states. Relations between lords who were themselves not under any effective coercive government, which are traditionally interpreted in terms of vassalage and fief-holding, were meanwhile rather like what we call 'international' (i.e. inter-state) relations. Peace was maintained, so far as it was, by alliances, sometimes cemented by kinship or marriage and again generally interpreted by historians in terms of vassalage; by negotiations and arbitrations in local assemblies; and through the associations to keep the peace that spread during the eleventh century. These last have been much studied.[24] The point here is that they were presumably important in direct proportion to the absence of pre-existing and effective coercive power. So far as they rested on ecclesiastical sanctions, they did not themselves provide anything like the settled coercive control implied by statehood.

Fighting between the effectively independent lords of this period is often called 'private war', but this is anachronistic.[25] It seems to be connected with the idea that the new lordships, in contrast to the counties and subdivisions of counties which had represented the 'public' power of the Carolingian state, were based on 'private property'. In Duby's words: 'Historians generally agree that feudalization represents a privatization of power' (Ariès and Duby 1988: 8). The analogy with late twentieth-century privatization of former governmental functions is attractive but, as modern privatization suggests, the Roman-law distinction between public (meaning – more or less – governmental), and private (covering relations between subjects) does not fit all societies.[26] The power exercised in medieval society by lords over people living in their inherited lordships, however conceptualized at the

---

24 Martindale 1992 cites earlier work and questions interpretations. My doubts about vassalage and fief-holding are explored in Reynolds 1994.
25 The expression seems to have been used less, even by late medieval academic lawyers, than by later historians: Keen 1965: 72–4, 78–81, 104, 108–9, 232; Cazelles 1960.
26 Moore 1972. The distinction is not, in any case, very consistently drawn in Roman-law practice: Walker 1980: 1013–14; cf. Marongiu 1977: 9–25. Cappellini 1986 has a bibliography. For the difficulty of applying it in early modern Italy: Chittolini 1994. Cf. Wormald 1980: 55, 57n.

time, was governmental ('public') in nature, and, however it originated, became legitimated by custom. In analysing medieval politics we need to notice that governmental power was indeed inherited and transferred in ways we associate with 'private property', but the categories 'public' and 'private' are too culture-bound and too slippery to use in analysis.

During the twelfth century more of France began to come under more effective and statelike control. At the same time the evidence of more literate and systematic government is clear – clearest on ecclesiastical estates but not only on them. Flanders and Normandy are the most often cited regions whose rulers controlled the legitimate use of force very effectively and used increasingly professional servants, keeping increasingly full records, to help them. That did not eliminate rebellion or disorder, especially when rulers died, but disobedience and rebellion were liable to fierce punishment. Reasonably intelligent and well-informed people in those areas must have known who was their lawful ruler. By the end of the century, if not before, the area under direct royal government had joined these statelike areas and during the thirteenth royal control spread and intensified. For R. H. Bautier, Philip II turned a feudal principality that had been dignified by its ruler's royal title into 'un État, la France' (Bautier 1982: 27; cf. Duby 1987: 345).

Royal jurisdiction in France remained much more restricted than it was in England, government in general was less centralized and its records have survived less well. All this, together with the recent distaste for political history, explains why French historians have not devoted a great deal of attention to thirteenth-century royal bureaucracy. They recognize nevertheless that it developed.[27] In J. R. Strayer's words, 'France was a mosaic state, made up of many pieces, and the bureaucracy was the cement which held all the pieces together (Strayer 1970: 53). The traditional emphasis on the fragmentation of sovereignty in a 'feudal hierarchy' may be excessive. Beaumanoir's use in the late thirteenth century of the word *souvrain* for holders of baronies has been more often noticed than his remark that, if he did not explain what he meant, his readers would think he meant the king, who was sovereign over all. Beaumanoir makes it clear that, although fighting between nobles was not prohibited, it was regulated, and regulated by royal authority.[28] Despite the arguments of Philip IV's reign about the relation of the king to the Pope and the Emperor, moreover, there had never been any real question of imperial authority in France since the Carolingian Empire broke up. Ecclesiastical jurisdiction, of course, was still formally independent and papal authority was formally accepted, but both Philip Augustus and St Louis had regulated, or threatened to regulate, the Church courts.

---

27 e.g. Duby 1987: 210–20; Balard 1991: 114; Paravicini 1980: 168–81, and works cited there. American historians, perhaps because of a tradition deriving from C. H. Haskins, have done a good deal of work on French government and administration, sometimes comparing it with England. See, e.g. the works of J. R. Strayer, J. W. Baldwin, E. A. R. Brown, R. W. Kaeuper, C. T. Wood.
28 Beaumanoir 1900, § 1043, 1667–89, 1702. Cf. Kaeuper 1988: 228–9, and problems of 'private war', pp. 185–99, 226–7, 231–60, and above, n. 25.

The wars and troubles of the fourteenth and earlier fifteenth centuries shook the French state hard (e.g. Cazelles 1982; Kaeuper 1988). The evidence of fifteenth-century reconstruction explains why historians who took their stand in the sixteenth century and telescoped the whole Middle Ages together as the time of feudalism, weak central government, and princely or seigniorial independence believed that state and nation were creations of the Renaissance. State power and national feeling in late medieval France have recently attracted a lot of attention, which has produced much new knowledge of that period, even if the old teleologies have not always been avoided. The statehood of the great principalities of Brittany and Burgundy has been noted but for French historians both state and nation primarily mean France (Guénée 1985: 79; Olland 1986; Balard 1991: 114–18; Jones 1990; Carbonell 1993). For the French, unlike the British, the two words seem in this context to mean much the same: the French state can, it seems, evoke much the same warm feelings as the French nation.[29]

German historians, whose traditions were formed against the background of Germany's political divisions before 1870 and of the eighteenth- and nineteenth-century linguistic nationalism that the divisions provoked, naturally find it easier to separate state and nation. That background explains the continuing interest of German medievalists ever since Gierke in the relation, or lack of relation, between *Herrschaft* (lordship, domination or rule) on the one hand and *Gefolgschaft* (following or retinue) or *Genossenschaft* (association or society) on the other. The English words suggested here are mere approximations. None has the resonance which the German words have acquired in a century and a half of historical use.[30] In the nineteenth century much attention was directed to different kinds of national identity or community which were perceived in the medieval Empire and the early medieval duchies. Since then it has shifted to the origin and development of the so-called territorial lordships or principalities of the later Middle Ages as prototypes of the modern state.

In 1939 Theodor Mayer argued that a decisive moment in German history came when the early medieval state, which had been held together by personal bonds between nobles and between them and the king (*der aristokratische Personenverbands-staat*) was superseded by what are called territorial principalities, whose rulers exercised authority over tracts of territory through more formal and impersonal institutions (*institutionelle Flächenstaaten*) (Mayer 1938–9: 46). He saw the feudal state (*Lehnsstaat*) as a secondary form of the *Personenverbandsstaat*. A further transitional form, the 'transpersonal' state, was later inserted in the typology (Beumann 1956). Also in 1939, however, Otto Brunner attacked the use of the word 'state' in any medieval context (Brunner 1939; 1956). Though not all historians have agreed that his preferred term, *Herrschaft*, is entirely free of its own anachronism, his views have had much influence. In 1990 the *Handwörterbuch zur*

---

29 Dyson 1980: vii, 4, 19–21, 162–81, *et passim* suggests the intellectual background for the difference.
30 Kroeschell, 1983; Graus 1986 and Kaminsky and Van Horn 1992 are helpful.

deutschen Rechtsgeschichte took the state to be a particular form of social organization that has developed chiefly, though not only, in Europe since the Middle Ages: late medieval structures might be considered statelike in so far as they endured to become the foundations of later states (Willoweit 1990; cf. Conze, *et al.* 1990; Moraw 1982; 1977: 60–4; Kroeschell 1978). The statehood or statelike character (*Staatlichkeit*) of German government before 1100 has, however, recently attracted renewed attention. (Keller 1989, 1991, 1993; on the earlier period: Goetz 1987).

Problems of definition have not prevented a great deal of work being done on the development of individual lordships from the twelfth century on (Arnold 1991, and works cited there), even if the terminology, the conceptual framework, and the rather narrow focus on Germany makes some of it difficult to use for comparative purposes. The teleological focus on what was to come may also have discouraged work on aspects of government that are now seen as irrelevant to later developments (Reuter 1993; Matthew 1992). A tendency to look for the origins of noble or princely independence and of later, highly legalized, forms of the noble right of feuding may explain the general assumption that kings of Germany kept the peace and controlled their nobles little better, if not worse, in the tenth and eleventh centuries than did the kings of France. This is surely improbable. If tenth- and eleventh-century Germany may, like France, be envisaged as a conglomeration of mini-states, they were nevertheless more comparable to states or provinces within a federal state (for royal legislation, see Krause 1965). However free a hand Otto I and his successors left to the dukes and counts to whom they necessarily delegated control of different parts of their large kingdom, they retained enough ultimate responsibility to punish fiercely the illegitimate use of physical force by dukes, counts, or anyone else when it seemed to threaten their own power and was brought to their attention.[31] In 1023 the bishop of Cambrai, which lay just within the border of the kingdom, seems to have thought that maintenance of the peace was a royal responsibility. When he was invited to join a peace association by other bishops of the province of Reims, whose dioceses lay over the border in the kingdom of France, he refused because it seemed to him unfitting to take on what he saw as a matter for the king.[32] His own exercise of authority over Cambrai presumably seemed to him legitimate since he held the county under a royal grant.[33] His acceptance of the delegated character of his coercive authority may have been exceptional. If not, then, so long as kings could on occasion dismiss dukes or counts, the kingdom looks more statelike than does France at the same time. It is, moreover, difficult to believe that a kingdom whose ruler wielded the power of the Saxon and Salian emperors was held together

---

31 This is argued, with some references, in Reynolds 1994: 406, 409–15.

32 Hoc enim non tam inpossibile quam incongruum videri respondit, si quod regalis iuris est, sibi vendicari presumerent: *Gesta episcoporum Cameracensium*, ed. L. C. Bethmann, in *Monumenta Germaniae Historica: Scriptores*, vol. 7, pp. 393–525, at p. 474.

33 *Diplomata Regum et Imperatorum Germaniae*, vol. 3: *Dip. Heinrici II* (Mon. Germ. Hist. 1900–3), no. 10.

merely by interpersonal bonds. Germany was certainly less centralized and less bureaucratically governed than the much smaller kingdom of England, though the absence of surviving records may exaggerate the difference. But not all states are equally bureaucratic and it is a narrow view of institutions which sees them only in administrative structures.

From the twelfth century both king and princes seem to have made use of the kind of literate servants whose skills should have made it easier to control the legitimate use of physical force over a wide area. German historians have tended to assume that professional or expert law did not impinge much on government before the fifteenth century, but records were being kept and law-cases argued with a new expertise well before then, both in royal and seigniorial courts (Reynolds 1994: 440–61). By 1300 civil wars had undermined royal authority so that the princes profited more from the new technologies of government than did the emperor. By the end of the Middle Ages the 'territorial principalities' look much more like states than does the kingdom (Moraw 1980; Patze 1980). If neither, then or earlier, fits the model of absolute, centralized sovereignty implied in some discussions of the modern state, nor do a good many modern states, especially those (like modern Germany) with federal constitutions.

Italian historians, for similar reasons to Germans, take the difference between nation and state for granted, but they have been less concerned with theoretical problems about medieval statehood.[34] When the characteristics of states (or modern states) are discussed by Italian medievalists there seems to be a fair measure of consensus. The standing armies and professional diplomacy that impressed nineteenth-century historians with the novelty of the 'Renaissance state' tend to be more emphasized than they are outside Italy, but now the growth of bureaucracy is also noted and so, thanks to long traditions of legal history, are legislative and jurisdictional capacity.[35] Discussion generally focuses on the later Middle Ages. Casual references may be made to small seigniorial states of the central Middle Ages; the Norman kingdom of Sicily may be described either as a feudal state or as moving towards statehood; and 'the papal state' is hallowed by tradition, but the first significant evidence of states after the Carolingians is often associated with the more or less independent cities of the 'age of the communes' (on the papal state, see nn. 8 and 37). The reasons are obvious: city government and jurisdiction, apart from fitting more obviously into the Roman-law category of public law, developed in ways that make them look more like modern states than do rural lordships. On the other hand, it has been pointed out that few communes were entirely independent *de facto*, let alone *de jure*, and that in thirteenth-century Florence, for instance, the control of physical coercion was

---

34 For comparisons with German ideas: Tabacco 1960; Schiera 1983; Fumagalli 1989. See also Galasso 1993.
35 e.g. Chittolini 1979: 14–15; cf. Chittolini 1988; Guarini 1978: 8–9; Pini 1981, esp. pp. 453–5, 489–90; Ryder 1976: vii, 368–71. Marongiu 1977 illustrates the close connection between legal history and what in English terms would be constitutional history.

formally divided just when bureaucracy was developing and autonomy seemed most complete.[36]

In the past twenty years the traditional view of the 'Renaissance state' as significantly new, modern and absolute has been much modified, though not universally abandoned. The enlarged 'regional states' (as Giorgio Chittolini has called them) of north and central Italy, like the kingdom of Naples and the papal state, are seen as neither despotically governed nor tidily centralized. Reacting against older concentration on the formal and bureaucratic institutions of central governments, Italian historians have noted the way that communes and local lords retained old functions or acquired new ones by delegation. They have also studied the networks of faction and patronage that make traditional distinctions between public and private look unreal.[37] The distinction between feudal government as old and weak on the one hand and bureaucracy as new and centralized on the other seems even more unreal if the academic and professional nature of the feudal law employed in Italian states is considered (Chittolini 1979: 36–100; Dean 1988; Reynolds 1994: 215–30, 249–56). The blurring of boundaries between old and new, public and private, state and society that appears in some of this work on late medieval and early modern Italy does not merely illuminate the working of government then and there. It also suggests the insights to be gained by abandoning teleologies based on models of the modern state which ignore the way that institutions work in practice.[38]

English historians have traditionally referred to England as a kingdom or a nation, but the word state has lately come into more frequent use – most notably, perhaps, as applied to the late Anglo-Saxon kingdom. The usage seems justified – although, in conformity with English traditions of empiricism, it is generally used without definition. The empirical tradition may itself have been fortified by the nature of the sources. Thanks to the unique survival of its vast records, more must have been written on the actual working of the central government of England than on that of any other medieval polity (recent surveys: Loyn 1984; Warren 1987; Brown 1989). By the late tenth century the power of the kings of England makes at least the part of their kingdom that lay south of the Humber fit my definition of a state. By the eleventh century they were raising taxes which, though not regular, were accepted as normal and legitimate, and a central bureaucracy was developing.[39] By the twelfth, although varying amounts of jurisdiction, especially over peasants

---

36   e.g. Chittolini 1979: xxx-xxxii, 15–16, 266; Tabacco 1989: 242, 273, 280, 284, though the translation of *statale* as 'statelike' introduces undue doubt. Pini 1981: 475–89, 505 (see esp. the analogy drawn by Ottokar with modern states cited on p. 489). Burke 1986 is a useful comparative discussion.
37   Jones 1978: 343–54; Hay and Law 1989: 75–7; Chittolini 1979; 1983; 1988; 1994; Guarini 1978 and forthcoming; Bertelli 1989. Opinions on the papal state differ: Caravale 1978; 128–9, 352–3; Prodi 1987: 38–40.
38   Cf. on a later period Barberis 1991.
39   Campbell 1975, esp. p. 51; 1980; 1982. Some reservations are expressed by Stafford 1989: v, 36, 81, 97–8, 135; Gillingham 1989; Frame 1990: 74–7. On later taxation and its effect on institutions: Harriss 1975.

and petty crime, were delegated to local lords, and although a good many towns were allowed a measure of autonomy, royal jurisdiction was supreme and pervasive. The implications of delegation were made clear during the thirteenth century by proceedings in the royal courts that summoned those with jurisdiction to produce evidence of their titles (Clanchy 1983: 143–61; Reynolds 1994: 361, 375–9). The standard view used to be that the central government became weaker in the later Middle Ages and ceased to develop. This offered what seemed the right background for a Tudor recovery based on a less centralized and bureaucratic system than that of sixteenth-century France, but the evidence for it has now been questioned. Despite civil wars and usurpations, the institutions of the central government apparently continued to function and become more elaborate, while lay professionals gradually took them over; the ways in which government relied on unpaid members of local elites changed but may not have meant much, if any, loss of supervision; and there is little evidence that law and order were significantly worse maintained than before (Gillingham 1987; Harriss 1993; Griffiths 1980).

Altogether it seems entirely reasonable to consider England a single state from at least the eleventh century, even if its boundaries were not yet those of the later Middle Ages and coercive control for long remained weak on its northern and western borders.[40] Papal authority in England, as in France and Germany, was moral, embarrassing rather than coercing kings. In Henry III's minority, after his father had formally subjected England and Ireland to Innocent III, papal legates exercised effective authority so long as they were in England, but even then the forces they could call on were local, not papal. Whether it is equally reasonable to think of the 'English state' as having enjoyed unique continuity since before the Norman Conquest is another matter. The implication that it still exists derives from a long tradition of seeing the history of the British Isles in terms of the inexorable progress of English rule to its manifest destiny of absorbing the 'Celtic fringe' without itself being significantly altered (Bentley 1993; Corrigan and Sayer 1985: 15–16). The 'continuous national history' of current British educational policy reflects this view: the characteristic conflation of state and nation is shown in the fact that 'national history' is supposed to concentrate on the history of government and politics (Samuel 1989). That the difference between the medieval kingdom of England and the modern British state is less than that between the medieval kingdom of France and the modern French state seems to be more often assumed than argued in terms of either geography or institutions – that is, the working of institutions rather than their names. The most obvious difference may lie in historiographical traditions.

Recently there has been an important change of focus: the British Isles are being studied as a whole, with comparisons across the board, while Wales, Scotland and Ireland are also looked at individually as more than archaic and anarchic fringes (W. Davies 1993; R. R. Davies 1990; Frame 1990; R. R. Davies 1988: 9–26; Gillingham

---

40 Though Harding 1993: 321 puts 'the making of the state' in the thirteenth. Cf. Kaeuper's references to 'the emerging state': Kaeuper 1988: 195–7.

1992, and earlier articles cited there). Their political traditions and structures were, it is clear, very different (though see Wormald 1986). Power in pre-conquest Wales was always fragmented and fluid. The extent to which early kings and later lords (including English marchers) exercised coercive power was variable: perhaps only the government of the thirteenth-century principality of Gwynedd constituted a state according to my definition (W. Davies 1990; R. R. Davies 1987: 59–76, 252–70, 363–70, 461–2). In the later Middle Ages Wales was ruled more like 'a collection of colonial annexes' than as part of the kingdom of England (R. R. Davies 1987: 462). Whether one counts it (like various parts of west and north France until 1558) as part of the English state depends not only on the varying degrees of control exercised but on whether one considers empires in general as single states or as some kind of hybrid (Thapar 1981).

Scotland, being a kingdom, was quite different. As in England, the king's control was not equally effective all over the kingdom, but here, even when coercive control became stronger and wider, government remained relatively unbureaucratic. Recent judgements that royal government in the later Middle Ages was fairly effective by the standards of the time may have been influenced by Scottish national feeling, just as earlier, more pessimistic views were by English national feeling, but they are also influenced by closer use of evidence. National solidarity, cemented by wars against England, perhaps made bureaucracy less necessary, but the difference between nationhood and statehood is exemplified by the position of the Highlands. In the fourteenth century John of Fordun maintained that, despite differences of language and way of life (which are now thought to have been increasing in his time) the Highlanders were part of the Scottish nation. Though hostile and cruel to the English-speakers of their own nation, they were faithful and obedient to king and kingdom, and could easily be made subject to law if they were ruled. It seems, however, that they were not very closely ruled. Perhaps the state (as distinct from both the kingdom and the nation) of Scotland could be envisaged as fading out towards the west and north, with the lordship of the Isles as a more or less independent state beyond. Comparisons with Brittany and Burgundy have been suggested, though the character of government in each was different (Smyth 1984: 175, 193, 229–38; Broun 1994; Barrow 1973, esp. 83–136; and 1980: 153–60; Grant 1984: 147–62 and 1988, citing and discussing Fordun).

Ireland was different again, with its early medieval layers of local kings, overkings and kings above overkings. Earlier sources suggest that none of them exercised coercive control of a statelike kind, but hints of development towards it have been found even before the English invasions of the twelfth century, chiefly, it seems, at the provincial (or overking) level (Wormald 1986 and works cited there, though cf. R. R. Davies 1988: 29 n. 56). From the early thirteenth century English rule in Ireland, in contrast to Wales, was intended to be centralized and bureaucratic on the English model. In practice, English institutions were little but 'a thinnish coating over a very unEnglish set of political facts'; the central government never controlled the area it claimed in anything like the way it did in England; and by the fifteenth century the supposedly controlled area was much reduced (Frame 1977: 5; cf.

Cosgrove 1987). Meanwhile, in independent Irish Ireland, the title of king was abandoned: 'the ceremonial and aristocratic king's court', in Katharine Simms's words, became 'the headquarters of a warlord, shorn of the trappings of royalty and using professionals to carry out the king's military and other functions (Simms 1987: 95). Those functions included some maintenance of law and order, but the control of physical force was probably too uncertain and divided to be considered statelike.

This essay has argued that, although not all historians who have written on the subject during the past twenty years or so would agree, their work nevertheless suggests that a good deal of western Europe was governed throughout the Middle Ages in polities that can reasonably be called states. The argument is not that statehood was universal or uniform in character. There were plenty of times and places where government was too weak and fluid, notably in border areas or in mountains or sea-marshes distant from those who claimed authority over them. There were also some areas over which no ruler claimed authority and in which a stable condition of apparent statelessness was maintained over long periods with perhaps no more – or even less – violence and disorder than in more statelike regions. Ireland is one possible candidate and Iceland is another (on Iceland: Miller 1990: 16–24 and 312 n. 16).

The history of Europe over the past two thousand years is an invitation to teleological interpretations. The way that bureaucracy, representative institutions and ideas of absolutism developed in the later Middle Ages all seem to point towards obvious features of early modern and modern states. But it may be less illuminating, even about the distinctiveness of modern states, to concentrate on what was to come than to look at both medieval and modern within their own contexts. Medieval states were, on the whole, smaller, weaker, less centralized, less bureaucratic and had less well-defined boundaries than modern states – or than the stereotype of the modern state. But the extent of their difference in all these respects varied in ways that cannot be studied if one starts by cutting polities before 1500, before 1300, or before any other date, out of the discussion. Concentration on those medieval states that lasted (however adapted) into modern times, whether as 'national monarchies' or as 'territorial states', may also be misleading in so far as it may imply that from the start they had greater staying-power, cohesion or efficiency than those that did not. Perhaps they had, but the case needs argument. States seem to have come and gone in European history and their forms have varied. Similarities and differences need to be studied both between periods and between polities within periods.

Within the Middle Ages, despite all the interesting and learned work that has been considered here and much that has not, there is room for more comparison. Nearly all medieval historians who are interested in forms and structures of government confine themselves to the state or states of what they regard as their own nation. Some proclaim the unique or exceptional character of medieval government in their own country, some seem to assume that the characteristics they identify in their own country and their own part of the period were determined by norms and conditions they consider typical of the Middle Ages in general. Neither line is convincing and neither is now justifiable. Enough work has been done to make possible some reasonably systematic comparison. That would mean not merely comparing whole polities as more advanced or backward, as more or less centralized or bureaucratic, as doomed to future success or future failure, but comparing different aspects of government in different polities – even polities in what are now thought of as different nation-states.

On the one hand, comparison might stimulate reconsideration of the relation between state structures and *histoire événementielle* – mere political events. Looking either at 'territorial lordships' or at royal government in eleventh- and twelfth-century France and Germany does not suggest that one was already foreordained to become a 'national monarchy' or 'nation-state' and the other to dissolve into a mass of more or less independent units. Perhaps the later division of Germany could be explained by, for instance, the early death of Henry VI rather than by fatal structural weaknesses. On the other hand, the relation between state structures and other, unpolitical aspects of history, which is beginning to attract more attention from non-Marxist historians, could do with more information about the European Middle Ages. Other European historians may share, if in a weaker form, the belief or assumption attributed to the English by R. R. Davies, namely 'that strong centralized government is a prerequisite of civilized life and human progress' (R. R. Davies 1979: 12). In view of all the changes going on in medieval Europe at the same time as new states were being formed and their government was developing, there may indeed be some connection between them. But what? More comparative work on states would illuminate one aspect of the problem.

REFERENCES

Abrams, P. (1988) 'Notes on the difficulty of studying the state', *Journal of Historical Sociology* 1: 58–88.
Ariès, P. and Duby, G. (ed.) (1988) *History of Private Life*, tr. A. Goldhammer, vol. 2, Cambridge, MA. (First published as: *Histoire de la vie privée*, Paris, 1985.)
Arnold, B (1991) *Princes and Territories in Medieval Germany*, Cambridge.
Bak, J. (1973) 'Medieval symbology of the state: Percy E. Schramm's contribution', *Viator* 4: 33–63.
Balard, M. (ed.) (1991) *L'Histoire médiévale en France: Bilan et perspectives*, Paris.
Barberis, W. (1991) 'Tradizione e modernità: il problema dello stato nella storia d'Italia', *Rivista Storica Italiana* 103: 243–67.
Barrow, G. W. S. (1973) *The Kingdom of the Scots*, London.
—— (1980) *The Anglo-Norman Era in Scottish History*, Oxford.
Bautier, R. H. (ed.) (1982) *La France de Philippe Auguste*, Paris.
Beaumanoir, Philippe de Remi, Sire de (1900) *Coutumes de Beauvaisis*, ed. A. Salmon, Paris.
Bentley, M. 'The British state and its historiography', in Blockmans and Genet 1993, 153–68.
Bertelli, S. (1989) 'Il Cinquecento', in de Rosa 1989, 2: 3–62.
Beumann, H. (1956) 'Zur Entwicklung transpersonaler Staatsvorstellungen', *Vorträge und Forschungen* 3: 185–224.

Blockmans, W. and Genet J. P. (eds) (1993) *Visions sur le développement des états européens*, Collection de l'école française de Rome 171, Rome.

Broun, D. (1994) 'The origin of Scottish identity', in C. Bjørn *et al.* (eds) *Nations, Nationalism and Patriotism in the European Past*, Copenhagen: 35–55.

Brown, A. L. (1989) *The Governance of Late Medieval England*, London.

Brunner, O. (1939; 4th rev. edn 1959) *Land und Herrschaft. Grundfragen der territorialen Verfassungsgeschichte Südostdeutschlands im Mittelalter*, Vienna. (Tr. H. Kaminsky and J. van Horn Melton as: *Land and Lordship*, Philadelphia, 1992.)

—— (1956) 'Bemerkungen zu den Begriffen "Herrschaft" und "Legitimität"', in id., *Neue Wege der Verfassungs- und Sozialgeschichte*, Göttingen: 64–79.

Burke, P. (1986) 'City-states', in J. A. Hall (ed.) *States in History*, Oxford.

Burns, J. H. (ed.) (1988) *The Cambridge History of Medieval Political Thought*, Cambridge.

Caenegem, R. C. van (1988) 'Government, law and society', in Burns 1988: 174–210.

Campbell, J. (1975) 'Observations on English Government from the Tenth to the Twelfth Century', *Transactions of the Royal Historical Society*, ser. 5, 25: 39–54.

—— (1980) 'The significance of the Anglo-Norman state in the administrative history of western Europe', in Paravicini and Werner 1980: 117–34.

—— (ed.) (1982) *The Anglo-Saxons*, Oxford.

Canning, J. (1988) 'Introduction [to the period 1150–1450]', in Burns 1988: 341–66.

—— (1991) 'A state like any other?', *Studies in Church History Subsidia* 9: 245–60.

Cappellini, P. (1986) 'Privato e pubblico (diritto intermedio)', in *Enciclopedia del diritto* 35, Milan: 660–87.

Caravale, M. (1978) 'Lo Stato pontificio da Martino V a Gregorio XIII', in G. Galasso (ed.), *Storia d'Italia*, vol. 9, pp. 1–371.

Carbonell, C. O. (1980) 'Les Origines de l'état moderne: les traditions historiographiques françaises', in Blockmans and Genet 1993.

Carlyle, R. W. and Carlyle, A. J. (1928) *A History of Mediaeval Political Theory in the West*, vol. 5, London.

Cazelles, R. (1960) 'La Réglementation royale de la guerre privée de saint Louis à Charles V', *Revue historique du droit français et étranger*, ser. 4, vol. 38: 530–48.

—— (1982) *Société politique, noblesse et couronne sous Jean le Bon et Charles V*, Geneva and Paris.

Chittolini, G. (1979) *La formazione dello stato regionale e le istituzioni del contado*, Turin.

—— (1983) 'Le "terre separate" nel ducato di Milano in età Sforzesca', *Milano nell'età di Ludovico il moro*, Milan.

—— (1988) 'Stati padani, "Stato del Rinascimento": problemi di ricerca', in G. Tocci (ed.), *Persistenzi feudali e autonomie comunitative in stati padani fra cinque e settecento*, Bologna: 9–29.

—— (1994) 'Il "privato", il "pubblico", lo stato', in G. Chittolini *et al.* (eds), *Origini dello stato. Processi di formazione statale in Italia fra medioevo ed età moderna*, Bologna: 553–89.

Clanchy, M. T. (1983) *England and its Rulers, 1066–1272*, London.

—— (1993) *From Memory to Written Record*, 2nd edn, London.

Clastres, P. (1974) *La Société contre l'état*, Paris. (Tr. by R. Hurley as: *Society against the State*, New York, 1977.)

Conze, W., Klippel, D. and Koselleck, R. (1990) 'Staat und Souveränität', in O. Brunner *et al.* (eds) *Geschichtliche Grundbegriffe* 6: 1–25, 98–128.

Corrigan, P. and Sayer, D. (1985) *The Great Arch: English State Formation as Cultural Revolution*, Oxford.

Cosgrove, A. (ed.) (1987) *A New History of Ireland*, II: *Medieval Ireland 1169–1534*, Oxford.

Coulet, N. and Genet, J. P. (ed.) (1990) *L'État moderne: le droit, l'espace et les formes de l'état*, Paris.

Crick, B. (1968) 'Sovereignty', in D. L. Sills (ed.) *International Encyclopedia of the Social Sciences*, vol. 15, New York.

Davies, R. R. (1979) *Historical Perceptions: Celts and Saxons*, Cardiff.

—— (1987) *Conquest, Co-existence and Change: Wales 1063–1415*, Oxford.

—— (ed.) (1988) *The British Isles 1100–1500*, Edinburgh.

—— (1990) *Domination and Conquest: The Experience of Ireland, Scotland and Wales 1100–1300*, Cambridge.

Davies, W. (1988) *Small Worlds*, London.

—— (1990) *Patterns of Power in Early Wales*, Oxford.

—— (1993) 'Celtic kingship in the early Middle Ages', in Duggan 1993: 101–24.

Davis, S. R. (1978) *The Federal Principle*, Berkeley, Los Angeles and London.

Dean, T. (1988) *Land and Power in Late Medieval Ferrara*, Cambridge.

Duby, G. (1987) *Le Moyen Âge de Hugues Capet à Jeanne d'Arc*, Paris. (Tr. by J. Vale as: *France in the Middle Ages*, Oxford, 1991.)

Duggan, A. J. (ed.) (1993) *Kings and Kingship in Medieval Europe*, London.

Dyson, K. (1980) *The State Tradition in Western Europe*, Oxford.

Fédou, R. (1971) *L'État au moyen âge*, Paris.

Ferguson, Y. H. and Mansbach, R. W. (1988) *The State, Conceptual Chaos and the Future of International Relations Theory*, Boulder, CO.

Fossier, R. (1982) *Le Moyen Âge*, Paris.

—— (1991) *La Société médiévale*, Paris.

Frame, R. (1977) 'Power and society in the Lordship of Ireland', *Past and Present* 76: 3–33.

—— (1990) *The Political Development of the British Isles, 1100–1400*, Oxford.

Fried, M. H. (1967) *The Evolution of Political Society*, New York.

Fumagalli, V. (1989) 'L'Alto medioevo', in de Rosa 1989: 1: 185–95.

Galasso, G. (1993) 'Stato e storiografia nella cultura del secolo XX', in Blockmans and Genet 1993.

Genet, J. P. (ed.) (1990) *L'État moderne: genèse*, Paris.

Génicot, L. (1984) 'Sur la survivance de la notion d'état dans l'Europe du nord au haut moyen âge', in L. Fenske, W. Rösener and T. Zotz (eds.) *Institutionen, Kultur, und Gesellschaft im Mittelalter: Festschrift für J. Fleckenstein*, Sigmaringen: 147–64.

Gerth, H. H. and Mills, C. W. (1952) *From Max Weber*, London and Boston.

Gillingham, J. (1987) 'Crisis or continuity? The structure of royal authority in England 1369–1422', *Vorträge und Forschungen* 32: 59–80.

—— (1989) 'The most precious jewel in the English crown', *English Historical Review* 104: 373–84.

—— (1992) 'The beginnings of English imperialism', *Journal of Historical Sociology* 5: 382–409.

Gluckman, M. (1965) *Politics, Law and Ritual in Tribal Society*, Oxford.

Goetz, H. W. (1987) 'Regnum: zum politischen Denken der Karolingerzeit', *Zeitschrift der Savigny-Stiftung für Rechtsgeschichte. Germ. Abteilung* 104: 110–89.

Goffart, W. (1980) *Barbarians and Romans*, Princeton.

—— (1981) 'Rome, Constantinople, and the barbarians', *American Historical Review* 86: 275–306.

Grant, A. (1984) *Independence and Nationhood*, London.

—— (1988) 'Scotland's "Celtic Fringe" in the Later Middle Ages', in R. R. Davies 1988: 118–41.

Graus, F. (1965) 'Die Entstehung der mittelalterlichen Staaten in Mitteleuropa', *Historica* 10: 5–65.

—— (1986) 'Verfassungsgeschichte des Mittelalters', *Historische Zeitschrift* 243: 529–89.

Griffiths, R. A. (1980) 'Public and private bureaucracies in England and Wales in the fifteenth century', *Transactions of the Royal Historical Society*, ser. 5, vol. 30: 109–30.

Guarini, E. F. (1978) *Potere e società negli stati regionali italiani fra '500 e '600*, Bologna.

—— (1994) 'Centro e periferia' in G. Chittolini *et al.* (eds), *Origini dello stato. Processi di formazione statale in Italia fra medioevo ed età moderna*, Bologna: 147–76.

Guénée, B. (1971) *L'Occident aux XIVe et XVe siècles: les états*, Paris. (Tr. J. Vale as: *States and Rulers in Later Medieval Europe*, London, 1985.)

Harding, A. (1993) *England in the Thirteenth Century*, Cambridge.

Harriss, G. L. (1975) *King, Parliament and Public Finance in Medieval England to 1369*, Oxford.

—— (1993) 'Political society and the growth of government in late medieval England', *Past and Present* 138: 28–57.

Hay, D. and Law, J. (1989) *Italy in the Age of the Renaissance*, London.

James, E. (1982) *The Origins of France*, London.

Jones, M. (1990) 'Le cas des états princiers: la Bretagne au moyen âge', in Coulet and Genet 1990.

Jones, P. J. (1978) 'La riscossa aristocratica', in R. Romano and C. Vivanti (eds) *Storia d'Italia: Annali*, Turin, 1: 337–72.

Kaeuper, R. W. (1988) *War, Justice and Public Order: England and France in the Later Middle Ages*, Oxford.

Kaminsky, H. and Van Horn, J. (1992) 'Translator's Introduction' to tr. of Brunner 1939.

Keen, M. H. (1965) *The Laws of War in the Later Middle Ages*, London.

Keller, H. (1989) 'Zum Charakter der "Staatlichkeit" zwischen karolingischer Reichsreform und Hochmittelalterlichem Herrschaftsausbau', *Frühmittelalterliche Studien* 23: 148–64.

—— (1991) 'Reichsorganisation, Herrschaftsformen und Gesellschaftsstrukturen im Regnum Teutonicum', *Settimane di Studio del Centro Italiano di Studi sull'Alto Medioevo* 38: 159–203.

—— (1993) 'Die Investitur', *Frühmittelalterliche Studien* 27: 51–86.

Krause, H. G. (1965) 'Königtum und Rechtsordnung in der Zeit der sächsischer und salier Herrscher', *Zeitschrift der Savigny-Stiftung für Rechtsgeschichte: Germanistische Abteilung* 82: 1–98.

Kroeschell, K. (1978) 'Herrschaft', in A. Erler and E. Kauffmann (eds) *Handwörterbuch zur deutschen Rechtsgeschichte*, vol. 2: 104–5, Berlin.

—— (1983) 'Verfassungsgeschichte und Rechtsgeschichte des Mittelalters', in A. Quaritsch (ed.) *Gegenstand und Begriffe der Verfassungsgeschichtsschreibungen*, Berlin: 47–77.

Lewis, E. (1954) *Medieval Political Ideas*, London.

Loyn, H. R. (1984) *The Governance of Anglo-Saxon England*, London.

Mager, W. (1968) *Zur Entstehung des modernen Staatsbegriff*, Mainz.

Mann, M. (1986) *The Sources of Social Power*, vol. 1, Cambridge.

Marongiu, A. (1977) *Storia del diritto italiano: ordinamento e istituto di governo*, Milan.

Martindale, J. (1992) 'Peace and war in eleventh-century Aquitaine', *Ideals and Practice of Medieval Knighthood*, ed. C. Harper-Bill and R. Harvey, vol. 4: 147–76.

Matthew, D. J. A. (1992) 'Reflections on the medieval Roman Empire', *History* 77: 363–90.

Mayer, T. (1938–9) 'Die Ausbildung der Grundlagen des modernen deutschen Staaten im hohen Mittelalter', *Historische Zeitschrift* 159: 457–87.

Miller, W. I. (1990) *Bloodtaking and Peacemaking*, Chicago.

Moore, S. F. (1972) 'Legal liability and evolutionary interpretation', in M. Gluckman (ed.) *The Allocation of Responsibility*, Manchester: 51–108.

Moraw, P. (1977) 'Fragen der deutschen Verfassungsgeschichte im späten Mittelalter', *Zeitschrift für Historische Forschung*, 4: 59–101.

—— (1980) 'Wesenszüge der "Regierung" und "Verwaltung" des deutschen Königs im Reich (ca. 1350–1450)', in Paravicini and Werner 1980.

—— (1982) 'Herrschaft im Mittelalter', in O. Brunner *et al.* (eds) *Geschichtliche Grundbegriffe*, III: 5–12.

Nelson, J. L. (1986) *Politics and Ritual in Early Medieval Europe*, London and Ronceverte, WV.

—— (1988) 'Kingship and empire', in Burns 1988: 211–51.

—— (1992) *Charles the Bald*, London.

Olland, H. (1986) 'La France de la fin du moyen âge: l'état et la nation', *Médiévales* 10: 81–102.

Paravicini, W. (1980) 'Administrateurs professionels et princes dilettantes', in Paravicini and Werner 1980: 168–81.

——and Werner, K. F. (eds) (1980) *Histoire comparée de l'administration (IVe–XVIIIe siècles)*, Munich.

Patze, H. (1980) 'Das Herrschaftspraxis der deutschen Landesherren während des späten Mittelalter' in Paravicini and Werner 1980: 363–91.

Pennington, K. (1993) *The Prince and the Law, 1200–1600: Sovereignty and Rights in the Western Legal Tradition*, Berkeley.

Pini, A. I. (1981) 'Dal comune città-stato al comune ente amministrativo', in G. Galasso (ed.) *Storia d'Italia*, vol. 4, Turin: 451–587.

Plummer, C. and Earle, J. (1892) *Two Anglo-Saxon Chronicles Parallel*, Oxford.

Poggi, G. (1990) *The State: Its Nature, Development and Prospects*, Cambridge.

Post, G. (1964) *Studies in Medieval Legal Thought*, Princeton.

Prodi, P. (1987) *The Papal Prince*, tr. S. Haskins, Cambridge. (First published as: *Il sovrano pontifice*, Bologna, 1982.)

Ranke, L. von (1874) *Geschichte der romanischen und germanischen Völker von 1494 bis 1514*, 2nd edn, Leipzig. (Tr. by G. R. Dennis: *History of the Latin and Teutonic Nations 1494–1514*, London, 1915.)

Reuter, T. (1993) 'The medieval German *Sonderweg*? The Empire and its rulers in the high Middle Ages', in Duggan 1993: 179–221.

Reynolds, S. (1983) 'Medieval *origines gentium* and the community of the realm', *History* 68: 375–90.

—— (1984) *Kingdoms and Communities*, Oxford.

—— (1985) 'What do we mean by Anglo-Saxon and Anglo-Saxons?', *Journal of British Studies* 24: 395–414.

—— (1994) *Fiefs and Vassals*, Oxford.

Rosa. L. de (ed.) (1989) *La storiografia italiana degli ultimi vent'anni*, Bari.

Ryder, A. (1976) *The Kingdom of Naples under Alfonso the Magnanimous: The Making of a Modern State*, Oxford.

Samuel, R. (1989) 'Continuous national history' in id. (ed.), *Patriotism*, London, 1: 9–17.

Schiera, G. N. (1983) 'A proposito della traduzione recente di una opera di Otto Brunner', *Annali dell'Istituto storico italo-germanico in Trento* 9: 391–410.

Simms, K. (1987) *From Kings to Warlords*, Woodbridge.

Skalweit, S. (1982) *Der Beginn der Neuzeit*, Darmstadt.

Smith, J. M. H. (1992) *Province and Empire*, Cambridge.

Smyth, A. P. (1984) *Warlords and Holy Men*, London.

Stafford, P. (1989) *Unification and Conquest*, London.

Strayer, J. R. (1966) 'The historical experience of nation-building in Europe', in K. W. Deutsch and W. J. Folz (eds) *Nation-Building*, New York.

—— (1970) *On the Medieval Origins of the Modern State*, Princeton.

Stringer, K. (1994) 'Social and political communities in European history', in C. Bjørn *et al.* (eds) *Nations, Nationalism and Patriotism in the European Past*, Copenhagen: 9–34.

Tabacco, G. (1960) 'La dissoluzione medievale dello stato nella recente storiografia', *Studi Medievali* 1: 397–445.

—— (1989) *The Struggle for Power in Medieval Italy*, Cambridge (tr. of *Egemonie sociali e strutture del potere nel medioevo italiano*, Turin, 1979, first published in Einaudi, *Storia d'Italia* ii(1), pp. 1–274).

Thapar, R. (1981) 'The state as empire' in H. J. M. Claessen and P. Skalnik (eds), *The Study of the State*, The Hague: 409–26.

—— (1984) *From Lineage to State*, Bombay.

Tierney, B. (1962) '"The prince is not bound by the laws". Accursius and the origins of the modern state', *Comparative Studies in Society and History* 5: 378–400.

Tilly, C. (ed.) (1975) *The Formation of National States in Western Europe*, Princeton.

—— (1990) *Coercion, Capital, and European States, AD 900–1992*, Oxford.

Ullmann, W. (1965) *History of Political Thought in the Middle Ages*, Harmondsworth.

—— (1966) *Principles of Government and Politics in the Middle Ages*, 2nd edn, London.

—— (1969) *The Carolingian Renaissance and the Idea of Kingship*, Cambridge.

—— (1977) *Medieval Foundations of Renaissance Humanism*, London.

Waley, D. (1961) *The Papal State in the Thirteenth Century*, London.

—— (1968–9) 'Juristic obstacles to the emergence of the concept of the state in the middle ages', *Annali di storia del diritto*, vol. 12–13: 43–64.

Walker, D. M. (1980) *Oxford Companion to Law*, Oxford.

Warren, W. L. (1987) *The Governance of Norman and Angevin England*, London.

Weber, M. (1958) *Gesammelte politische Schriften*, ed. J. Winckelmann, Tübingen.

Wenskus, R. (1974) 'Probleme der germanische-deutschen Verfassungs- und Sozialgeschichte im Lichte der Ethnosoziologie', in *Historische Forschungen für Walter Schlesinger*, Cologne and Vienna.

Werner, K. F. (1980) 'Introduction', in W. Paravicini and K. F. Werner (eds) *Histoire comparée de l'administration (IVe–XVIIIe siècles)*, Munich.

—— (1984) *Histoire de France: Les Origines (avant l'an mil)*, Paris.

Wickham, C. (1984) 'The other transition: from the ancient world to feudalism', *Past and Present* 103: 3–36.

—— (1992) 'Problems of comparing societies in early medieval Europe', *Transactions of the Royal Historical Society* ser. 6, vol. 2: 221–46.

Willoweit, D. (1990) 'Staat', in A. Erler and E. Kauffmann (eds), *Handwörterbuch zur deutschen Rechtsgeschichte*, Berlin, 4: 1794.

Wolfram, H. (1970) 'The shaping of the early medieval kingdom', *Viator* 1: 1–20.

Wood, I. (1994) *The Merovingian Kingdoms*, London.

Wormald, J. (1980) 'Bloodfeud, kindred and government in early modern Scotland', *Past and Present* 87: 54–97.

Wormald, P. (1983) 'Bede, *Bretwaldas* and the origins of the *gens Anglorum*', in P. Wormald et al. (eds) *Ideal and Reality in Anglo-Saxon Society*, Oxford.

—— (1986) 'Celtic and Anglo-Saxon kingship', in P. E. Szarmach (ed.) *Sources of Anglo-Saxon Culture (Studies in Medieval Culture* 20): 151–84.

8

SALADIN AND THE THIRD CRUSADE: A CASE STUDY IN HISTORIOGRAPHY AND THE HISTORICAL NOVEL

Robert Irwin

It seems unlikely that recent research by academics and publications such as the *English Historical Review* play much of a role in forming the contemporary British public's image of history. Rather, what Herbert Butterfield has termed ' "the picture gallery" of the past is a popular impression built up over the years from a general blurring of history, ballads, Biblical stories, local traditions, poetry and romance' (Butterfield 1924: 2). Here we are concerned with a specific form of romance, the historical novel, and its changing relationship with the advance of serious academic research. As for the historical novel, George Steiner has written in *Language and Silence* (1967)

> [T]his is a literary genre to which western civilization has given only cursory attention. It is difficult to get the range of historical fiction into proper focus. At times, its head is in the mythological stars, but more often the bulk of the thing is to be found in the good earth of commercial trash. The very notion brings to mind improbable gallants pursuing terrified yet rather lightly clad young ladies across flamboyant dust-wrappers.
>
> (Steiner 1967: 299)

In this genre, the past ceases to be merely a field for scientific enquiry. It becomes a source of entertainment, moral instruction, unexamined prejudice and historiographical cliché.

Some historical processes have attracted more novels than others. The Wars of the Roses (and especially the career of Richard of Gloucester) and the fortunes of the British navy during the Napoleonic Wars have each had so many novels written about them as to constitute subgenres within the genre of the historical novel. The same is true of the rise of Saladin, the downfall of the kingdom of Jerusalem in 1187 and the consequent Third Crusade. The popularity of such subject matter is understandable, for the story of the war between the Muslims and the Christians in the last decades of the twelfth century is rich in telling incidents and images of the sort which appeal to novelists: the youthful Saladin playing polo, the playmates of the young leper prince Baldwin sticking pins in his arm, the shocking promotion of handsome but foolish Guy de Lusignan to rule as king-consort in Jerusalem, the swashbuckling pirate raids of Reginald de Châtillon in the Red Sea, the nefarious and homicidical intrigues of the mysterious sect of the Assassins, the ill-fated encounter of the military orders with the Saracens at the Springs of Cresson, the heated strategic debates of the barons at Sephoria, the waterless slog of the Christian army towards their doom at Hattin, Guy's drink of sherbert and Saladin's beheading of Reginald of Châtillon, the angry clashes between Richard of England and Philip of France, the murder of Conrad of Montferrat in Tyre and, above all, the chivalrous exchanges between Richard and his noble antagonist Saladin.

Surely the historical novelist's task is made easier when the authors of the primary sources on which he ultimately depends also write like novelists? The twelfth-century chronicler Baha'al-Din ibn Shaddad's Life of Saladin is rich in telling detail and (perhaps invented) dialogue. More generally, as Gustave von Grunebaum has noted '[T]he Arab writer excels in observation of detail; he is unsurpassed in the telling of poignantly characteristic anecdotes' (von Grunebaum 1953: 278). As for the Christian side, M. R. Morgan (1973: 168) has observed how Ernoul's chronicle offers its readers a dual perspective, in which Saladin is presented as a historical villain, but an artistic hero, thereby creating a psychologically more satisfying narrative. Doubtless both Baha'al-Din and Ernoul, like modern novelists, were conscious of the need to attract as large an audience as possible for what they wrote. Hence their recourse to techniques which were later to be appropriated by novelists.

Since Sir Walter Scott (1771–1832) is widely regarded as the father of the historical novel, it is appropriate to begin an examination of how Saladin and his Christian antagonists have fared at the hands of the academics and the historical novelists with Scott's novel, *The Talisman* (1825). There is a large secondary literature on most of the historical novels on the Waverley series, among them *Ivanhoe*, *The Heart of Midlothian*, *The Antiquary*, *Rob Roy* and *Quentin Durward*. *The Talisman*, however, has received relatively little attention – indeed it is sometimes omitted altogether in critical discussions of Scott's work. Perhaps the preposterous plot has defeated the critics; it virtually defeats summary.

The action of *The Talisman* takes place during the Third Crusade. A Scottish knight, Sir Kenneth, after an inconclusive combat with an emir, strikes up a friendship with him. The emir, who is really Saladin under an alias, later turns up in the crusader camp disguised as a physician and heals the feverish Richard the Lionheart with a talisman. Sir Kenneth meanwhile has been given the task of guarding Richard's banner, but, after he has been lured away from the banner by what seems to be an appeal by the beautiful Edith, the banner is overthrown by unknown villains. Saladin begs for Kenneth's life. Later Kenneth returns to Richard's camp disguised as a Nubian slave and saves Richard's life. Then Kenneth's dog picks out Conrad of Montferrat as the villain who overthrew the banner. Kenneth fights and wounds Conrad. Kenneth then reveals that his real name is Prince David of Scotland. So he is of a rank to marry Edith Plantagenet without disparaging her.

The Talisman may not be a great work of literature, but it is still an interesting one. Scott was at some pains to get the details of the Western costumes, arms and armour right, relying here on the antiquarian researches of Joseph Strutt (1749–1802) and Samuel Meyrick (1783–1848).[1] He took less care with the Eastern elements in the story and *The Talisman*'s literary orientalism owes more to fictions by Lord Byron, Thomas Hope and James Morier than it does to serious research in oriental sources. Scott as a boy read 'the usual or rather ten times the usual quantity of fairy tales, eastern stories, romances, etc.' and in his single oriental novel, he owed a special debt to the *Arabian Nights*. The story's pervasive recourse to disguises may derive from Haroun al-Rashid's habit of wandering about disguised in the *Arabian Nights* stories. Certainly the legend over Saladin's tent 'Saladin King of Kings. Saladin Victor of Victors. Saladin must die!' has been lifted and adapted from 'The Sixth Voyage of Sinbad'.[2]

Despite the Tory romantic cast to his thought, Scott was no enthusiast for the crusades. Taking his lead from Gibbon and Hume (Tyerman 1988: 5–6), he regarded the crusades as a regrettable expression of religious fanaticism and human folly. Scott also tended to discount the role of religion and religious motivations in the history of the crusades. Chivalry was much more interesting to Scott. Much of the little that Scott knew about the history of the crusades was derived from Charles Mills's *The History of the Crusades* (2 vols, 1820). Mills (1788–1826) was a solicitor who turned to history writing and his history of the crusades was preceded by a *A History of Muhammedanism* (1817). Scott helped Mills, providing him with references from Scottish chronicles for the *History of the Crusades*. Mills's subsequent *History of Chivalry* (1825) was much influenced by Scott and his novels (Lee 1894: 444; Girouard 1981: 42–3). Nineteenth-century historians saw crusading and chivalry as intimately intertwined. (This view is no longer fashionable.)

Scott's vision of chivalry was influenced perhaps by the Gothic novel and certainly by Spenser and Malory. When in the opening of *The Talisman* Sir Kenneth rides across the desert towards the Dead Sea, he is re-enacting the ride of the Red-Cross Knight in the opening of Spenser's *Faerie Queene*:

> A Gentle Knight was pricking on the plaine,
> Y cladd in mightie armes and siluer shielde,

As for Scott's reading of Malory's *Morte d'Arthur*, this resurfaced in *The Talisman* in such elements as the strange vision of the ladies in the chapel, the dwarf and the samite arm. George Ellis's *Specimens of Early English Romances in Metre* (1805) fuelled Scott's medievalism. Folklore also played a part in the shaping of the novel and the central device of the talisman was inspired by legends attached to the Luck of the Lockharts of Lee.

---

1 On the antiquarian background to Scott's novels, see in particular Girouard 1981 and Strong 1978.
2 On oriental and pseudo-oriental stories for *The Talisman*, see Saffari 1972: 193–8; cf. Conant 1908: 253, 265; Caracciolo 1988: 11.

The language of chivalry in Scott's novels and those of his successors was high-flown and proud. Those who spoke this tongue spoke of honour, manliness and the service of women. In *The Talisman*, Richard the Lionheart's virtues and vices are part and parcel of the chivalric mode of behaviour Richard himself remarks '[T]hese Eastern people will profit by the Crusaders – they are learning the language of chivalry.' However, it is apparent in the novel that, although Saladin is one of the paynim, his courage, courtesy and generosity make him an exemplar of chivalry. He is indeed more chivalrous than his antagonists.

Scott's fictions were the subject of particularly searching scrutiny by the famous Hungarian Marxist literary critic, George Lukács, in his *The Historical Novel* (1937, Eng. tr. 1962). Notoriously, Lukács had little enthusiasm for the socialist realist and propagandist fictions churned out in Stalin's Russia. Instead he reverenced the romances of a Tory Scotsman. But for Lukács, Scott was 'the poet of the peasant, soldier and artisan' and his novels showed 'the complex and involved character of popular life itself'. Risking paradox, Lukács argued that Scott was anti-romantic for he avoided the Byronic hero and he chose to put ordinary folk at the centre of the picture. Scott's subject was social change and how people at all levels of society are affected by historical crises. So where does *The Talisman* with its aristocratic protagonists and exclusively chivalric preoccupations fit into Lukács's argument? It is not clear, for this novel is not mentioned at all in Lukács's book.

Orientalism (1978) is a polemical work by Edward Said, a Palestinian academic literary critic based in the United States. In *Orientalism*, certain academics (including H. A. R. Gibb and Bernard Lewis) and certain literary orientalists (including Flaubert and Mark Twain) are denounced for colluding with imperialism and racism by reifying Islam – pigeon-holing, stereotyping and travestying almost every aspect of Muslim history and culture. *The Talisman* is another incriminating document in Said's Black Museum. The critic fastens on the passage in which Sir Kenneth meets Saladin (in disguise). Kenneth praises Saladin as an individual, yet finds it curious that his race and religion boast descent from Iblis (the Devil). Said (1978: 101) remarks on the offensiveness of 'the airy condescension of damning a whole people "generally" while mitigating the offence with a cool "I don't mean you in particular"'. Said suggests that the accusation of descent from Iblis was something that Scott took from Beckford or perhaps Byron. In fact the descent of the Kurdish people from Iblis was part of medieval Arab folklore about the Kurds (and historically Saladin was of course a Kurd).[3] More generally, what is missing from Said's somewhat cursory and jaundiced reading of *The Talisman* is any appreciation of just how favourable Scott's portraits of Saladin and his Saracen physician are. Courageous, intelligent and magnanimous, they really come out better than Kenneth, Richard or any of the other protagonists in the story. While

---

3 On the popular belief that the Kurds descend from genies (who in turn descend from Iblis), see *Encyclopedia of Islam* (second edition) s.v. 'Kurds, Kurdistan.

one might wish that Sir Kenneth, not long in the Holy Land, would unequivocally express opinions such as that the Arabs are the equal if not the superior of Scotsmen, that Islam is a jolly good religion and the crusades are really just disguised imperialism, in the context of a novel set in the late twelfth century such remarks in the mouth of Sir Kenneth would strike most readers as anachronistic. Said's reading of Scott's novel is oddly naive (though hardly more so than his reading of George Eliot's *Daniel Deronda*).

While it is hardly possible to exaggerate Scott's influence on the nineteenth-century historical novel generally, the choice of Saladin and the crusades as topics was not followed by many novelists in that century. However, G. A. Henty (1832–1902) wrote a novel about the Third Crusade. Henty covered most periods. He was the author of yarns for boys with titles like *The Cornet of the Horse: A Tale of Malborough's Wars*, *With Kitchener in the Soudan* and *With Clive in India*. These and other rather formulaic novels by Henty made use of ripping adventures to teach past facts and present values. According to the Henty formula, the plucky lad leaves home, gets embroiled in great events, attracts a great man's attention and then, after distinguishing himself in some enterprise and gaining the great man's approval, he returns home.[4] *Winning his Spurs: A Tale of the Crusades* (1891) followed the winning formula.

Though the influence of Scott is evident in the novel, it is more that of *Ivanhoe* than of *The Talisman*. Early on in the book, Cuthbert, 'who art but a pert varlet' (Henty 1891: 38), asks Father Francis to give him a potted history of the crusades, at the end of which the thoughtful boy asks

> 'And think you, Father, that it will do good to England?' 'That do I my son, whether we gain the Holy Land or no. Methinks it will do good service to the nation that Saxon and Norman should fight together under the Holy Cross' (ibid. 42).

In Henty then, going on crusades is not merely character-forming, but nation-forming.

Henty presented Saladin as a brave warrior in the field who frequently exposed himself to danger. (There is no warrant for this in the original sources.) Taking a leaf from *The Talisman*, Henty has Cuthbert and Saladin converse in 'the lingua franca which was the medium of communication between people in those days'. Henty was notoriously an imperialist writer, but it is interesting to note that he has Saladin denounce both the imperialist crusades and Richard's massacre of Muslim hostages. Later on, a Muslim woman in Jerusalem picks up the anti-crusading argument and points out to Cuthbert that Jerusalem is a holy city for the Muslims too.

The historian A. J. P. Taylor, who remarked that '[T]rue history began with Sir Walter Scott; he felt himself back into time' (quoted in Humphrey 1986: 5), also confessed a youthful passion for Henty. Indeed, it was because of his reading of Henty that he felt confident enough to give tutorials on the Thirty Years War (Taylor 1983: 25).

---

4   On Henty's work in general, see Arnold 1980.

Henty's novel was written a few years before the first serious biography of Saladin appeared. This was by Stanley Lane-Poole, a member of a distinguished Scottish dynasty of scholars. His great-uncle Edward William Lane (1801–76) was the famous translator of *The Thousand and One Nights* and the compiler of the standard Arabic–English dictionary. Lane-Poole's *Saladin and the Fall of the Kingdom of Jerusalem* (1898) appeared, somewhat incongruously, in a series entitled 'Heroes of the Nations'. Saladin then took his place beside Garibaldi of Italy, William Tell of Switzerland and Gustavus Adolphus of Sweden. But it is hard to know which nation Saladin was a hero of – the Kurdish? the Turkish? the Egyptian? the Syrian? the Arab? or the Islamic nation?

Lane-Poole was an admirer of Scott and he contended that the latter's portrait of Saladin was drawn with 'insight and accuracy' (Lane-Poole 1898: 395–6). Although many of his details were wrong, Scott possessed the insight of genius into the fundamentals. In Lane-Poole's view, Saladin's 'chivalry to the crusaders was the good breeding of a gentleman' (ibid. 399). The Saladin created by Lane-Poole's pen was a very gentle gentleman, a rather quiet scholarly figure (not perhaps so very different from Lane-Poole himself). This quiet and unambitious man was drawn into great events against his will. Since Saladin was seen as primarily the leader of a *jihad* against the crusader states, well over half Lane-Poole's book is devoted to the years 1187–92 and everything in Saladin's earlier career is presented as preparing him for those momentous years.

Lane-Poole's interpretation of Saladin found its fictional echo in novels like Neville Meakins's *The Assassins. A Romance of the Crusades* (1902). In this novel, the Assassins of the title are fanatic scum recruited from the outcasts of the Near East. Hassan, half-Frankish, half-Arab, is raised and trained by the Assassins to kill Saladin. The story then is of Hassan's growing admiration for Saladin and his defection from the Assassins. Saladin is a hero of the Arab nation and an upholder of Muslim honour. Religion plays no significant part in the story.

Rider Haggard's *The Brethren* (1904) similarly presented a rather secular vision of religious conflict in the twelfth century. In Haggard's preposterous farrago, Saladin is the nonpareil of chivalrous values, rather than of Muslim ones. Indeed, all the Saracens are noble and chivalrous, somewhat on the pattern of the Zulus in Rider Haggard's other novels. A large part of chivalry is rescuing women from distress. Chivalry and the public-school ethos are hardly distinguishable. One applauds good play by either side and Christianity just happens to be the team that Haggard's plucky English lads are playing for. Haggard like Henty was a believer in British imperialism, but despite this he, like Henty, thought that the crusades were a bad thing and he used Saladin as his mouthpiece to denounce them.

It seems that Lane-Poole thought of Saladin as a sort of honorary hero of the Scottish nation. The same may also be true of Sir Hamilton Gibb (1895–1971). Gibb, who had attended Scott's old school, the Royal High School in Edinburgh, was soaked in the works of the novelist and later in life he used to recommend *The Talisman* to his students in Arabic as 'a work of art from which they could learn much about Islamic history'. Gibb, who was to have a distinguished career as an

Arabist and a historian of the Middle East, wrote not one biography of Saladin, but rather a series of studies which appeared in the 1950s and 1960s.[5]

Gibb offered an interpretation of Saladin which has influenced all subsequent readings of the man's life. According to Gibb, Saladin's predecessor Nur al-Din, the Turkish ruler of Aleppo and Damascus, 'operated from within the structure of politics of his age' – that is to say, dynastic politics, plots, revolts, ephemeral alliances, treacheries and so on. Saladin's moral qualities, however, made him a man out of his times, one who refused to play the political games of his age. Saladin was a man without guile, who rose above the intrigues of the factional interests around him. The prosecution of the *jihad* was a major aim, but not the primary goal. Although Gibb's interpretation of Saladin was broadly similar to Lane-Poole's, Gibb argued that the war against the crusaders was only one part of a much wider visionary programme to revivify and unite the Muslim community under the leadership of the Abbasid Caliphate in Baghdad. 'For a brief but decisive moment, by sheer goodness and firmness of character, he raised Islam out of the rut of political demoralization' (Gibb 1952: 105). Saladin created 'an impulse to unity' which 'sufficed to meet the unforeseen challenge flung down to him by destiny' (ibid. 106). He was the saviour of the Muslim community at an important stage during its long march through the centuries to salvation. Gibb's views found ample support in the propagandistic correspondence produced by Saladin's chancery. A scholar of distinction and a man of strong religious convictions, Gibb had produced a hero in his own image.

The appearance in 1936 of *Raymond III of Tripolis and the Fall of Jerusalem (1140–1187)* by Marshall Baldwin, an American historian, had a decisive influence on subsequent historical novels about Saladin and the Third Crusade. Hitherto the baronage of the Kingdom of Jerusalem had hardly featured in novels save as thinly drawn villains or as spear-carriers. Baldwin's book changed all that. Although it was a serious academic work of non-fiction, it clearly appealed to novelists. This was because Baldwin had presented the story of the loss of Jerusalem in human terms, as a story about the achievements and failures of individual men and women (rather than as the result of broad strategic and institutional developments). Baldwin's writing created a richly visualized image of Count Raymond as the intellectual, the statesman and the lost leader. He even put flesh on the man's bones, giving him a long nose and melancholy features.

Even more important, Baldwin discovered that the Kingdom of Jerusalem in the late twelfth century had a two-party system, like modern Britain and America, though, unlike Britain and America, there was only one chamber, the House of Lords. One party, the baronialist party, was headed by Raymond of Tripoli and included members of the Ibelin clan, Humphrey of Toron and William of Tyre. These were old hands in the Levant and they were in favour of statesmanlike coexistence and appeasement. The other party, the bad party, included men like

---

5   Gibb 1951; 1952; 1955. On Gibb's personality and achievement, see Hourani 1980.

Guy de Lusignan, Gerard de Ridefort and the Patriarch Heraclius. These were newcomers in the Near East, with little real understanding of the political realities of the region. They were greedy, fire-breathing, gung-ho aggressors. They were also not quite sixteen annas to the rupee. 'They were not the real, blooded nobility of the land, and in feudal days such things meant much' (Baldwin 1936: 62). In Baldwin's interpretation, the downfall of the Kingdom was due more to growing disunity among the baronage than to growing unity among the Muslims.

As we shall see, Baldwin's book influenced a whole series of novels about the downfall of the Kingdom of Jerusalem which took the baronial party's side. It also helped shape the relevant section of Sir Steven Runciman's three-volume *A History of the Crusades* (1951–4). It is not difficult to read Runciman's artfully structured and stylish historical trilogy as a novel. (In terms of style, it is interesting to note that Runciman has cited Beatrix Potter, the author of *Squirrel Nutkin* and *Peter Rabbit*, as a stylistic influence (Plante 1986), while Beatrix Potter herself cited Sir Walter Scott as her model: Carpenter and Prichard 1984: 420.) Runciman, a Hellenophile, is an enthusiast for Byzantine culture, but he has a more Gibbonian vision of the crusades as a story of Christian folly and fanaticism.

The story of the crusading principalities in the East is a prolonged dynastic saga, a story of royal and noble cousins, uncles, aunts, stepsisters and so on, with relatives throughout the Mediterranean world and indeed throughout Christendom. Runciman's presentation of noble intrigues in the Kingdom of Jerusalem in the late twelfth century may remind some readers of one or other of the novels of Dame Ivy Compton-Burnett. Runciman himself has remarked that 'You see historians are now terrified of telling a story, as though that were fiction, and not history. They forget that the word "history" means "story"' (Plante 1986).

In the second volume of his history, Runciman follows Baldwin's two-party interpretation of politics, in which baronial 'arties' face royalist 'hearties'. Runciman can see what his protagonists looked like and he helps his readers visualize them too. Raymond of Tripoli is described as 'a tall, thin man, dark haired and dark-skinned, his face dominated by a great nose, in character cold and self-controlled and a little ungenerous' (Runciman 1952: 405). Humphrey of Toron has 'a feminine beauty' (Runciman 1955: 30) and was 'gallant and cultured'. Reynald of Sidon is 'charming' (ibid.: 60). These are men who would not have been out of place in Bloomsbury circles. The gentle and melancholy Saladin would have been welcome too, for he was 'well-read' (iid.: 78). (There is in fact no evidence that he was even literate.) In Runciman's telling of the story, Saladin appears to lead the Muslim community in response to the Christian challenge. This challenge-and-response model may have owed something to Runciman's reading of Arnold Toynbee's *A Study of History* (1934–61).

Marshall Baldwin's two-party model of politics in Jerusalem was also taken up by historical novelists, almost all of whom polemicized valiantly though belatedly on behalf of the baronial party. Zofia Kossak's *The Leper King* (1945) attributes the fall of the Kingdom to the machinations of Reginald de Châtillon, ambitious women and the Templars (who are presented as secret adherents of some ancient pre-

Christian cult which meets under the Hill of Evil Council). The Arabs by contrast are all cultured and chivalrous.

In Evan John's *Ride Home Tomorrow* (1950), the hero thoughtfully remarks 'I have heard it said that there are two parties in the kingdom.' Evan John was a cultivated soldier who served with the British forces in the Middle East during the Second World War. His memoir *Time in the East* (1946) shows him already contemplating a novel about the crusaders and the settlers in the East – a novel which would lay bare their predicaments and failings, but which would also celebrate their heroism in the long-running struggle between Europe and Asia for control of the eastern Mediterranean. Although John evidently read Baldwin, he was unusual in the relatively favourable view he took of Reginald de Châtillon and his aggressive forward policy. (In this he anticipated the professional historian Joshua Prawer.) Moreover, though he was an admirer of Scott, John did not subscribe to Scott's (and Henty's and Haggard's) hostility to crusading. Rather he saw the crusades as an expression of a great Christian ideal.

Ronald Welch's novel for children, *Knight Crusader* (1954), came hot on the heels of the completion of the Runciman trilogy. Welch's novel is attractively written and it won the Carnegie Medal for children's literature. In *Knight Crusader*, the events of the 1180s are followed through the eyes of a young third-generation noble of the Outremer, Philip d'Aubigny of Blanchegarde. As so often in historical novels, great events serve as the backdrop to a young person's maturation. As the menace of Saladin looms larger, Philip learns to control his impetuousness, survive setbacks and become a leader of men. The book also offers its readership pleasant lessons on such matters as what the Kingdom must have looked and smelt like, and how the High Court and the *arrière ban* worked and who were the *pullani*. Philip is by birth a member of the baronial party and the appearance of Raymond of Tripoli's 'enormous nose' alerts us to the fact that Welch has read Baldwin. There are occasional errors in the story. Philip meets Saladin in combat on the battlefield, though historically Saladin was not one of those generals who led from the front and there is no record of him ever engaging in hand-to-hand combat. In common with so many historical novels set in the Middle Ages, religion and religious motives are marginalized, almost ignored. The Kingdom of Jerusalem is a secular kingdom and on the evidence of the text Philip d'Aubigny could be an atheist.

Graham Shelby's *Knights of Dark Renown* (1969) follows the Runciman storyline even more closely than does *Knight Crusader*. Although there is some invented material about the mutual love of Humphrey of Toron and Ernoul (the future historian), on the whole the story of the political defeat of the baronial party by reckless and choleric new men and the consequent downfall of the Kingdom is strong enough for the story to require only the lightest of fictional airbrushing by the author. Shelby, like Welch, argues the case for coexistence with the enemy. Not surprisingly, this is a theme which was popular with writers of the Cold War decades. Shelby's book is less well researched than Welch's. One knows that Shelby's Humphrey of Toron is cultured because he reads Ariosto (not just cultured, but prescient) and he writes 'letters, articles, criticisms' (for the *Jerusalem Post* perhaps) (Shelby 1969: 260).

Saladin is the yardstick of virtue by which the quarrelsome and reckless crusader barons are found wanting. Shelby's Saladin has a beard which stretched down to his chest. In this he is unusual. In most novels Saladin has a short beard. In *The Talisman* (ch. 2),

> His features were small, well-formed and delicate, though deeply embrowed by the Eastern sun and terminated by a flowing and curled, black beard which seemed trimmed with peculiar care. The nose was straight and regular, the eyes keen, deep-set, black and glowing and his teeth equalled in beauty the ivory of his deserts.

Historians, particularly popular historians who work mostly from secondary sources, are as keen as novelists to assist the reader to live in the minds of tempestuous lords and ladies and *see* how they actually looked. Thus from Runciman's *A History of the Crusades*, we learn that Saladin's face was 'melancholy in repose' (Runciman 1955: 78). Amin Maalouf's popular history, *The Crusades through Arab Eyes* (1983, tr. 1984) goes further than this: 'He was tall and frail with a short neat beard' and he had 'a passive and somewhat melancholy face which would suddenly light up with a comforting smile that would put anyone talking to him at their ease' (Maalouf 1984: 179). In Geoffrey Hindley's popular biography *Saladin* (1976) the eponymous hero is shortish, with a trim grizzled beard, though his hair was still black, and he sits on the saddle with the stylishness of a polo champion (Hindley 1976: 1). In P. H. Newby's *Saladin in his Time* (1983), the same man has a short dark beard rapidly turning grey and he is unnaturally spare from his constant campaigning (Newby 1983: 137). Geoffrey Regan's *Saladin and the Fall of Jerusalem* (1987) describes the great Muslim leader in early manhood as 'being of medium height, slender, with a dark complexion, dark eyes and a black beard, trimmed short in 'the Kurdish manner' (Regan 1987: 17). The knowing reference to 'the Kurdish manner' is a particularly nice touch, but as Lane-Poole pointed out so many years previously, in fact we do not know what Saladin looked like, except that late in life he had a beard – and we only know that because Baha'al-Din ibn Shaddad reports him tugging it at the Battle of Hattin (Lane-Poole 1898: 395). The intrinsically trivial instance of Saladin's beard should alert us to the fact that the boundary between historical fact and fiction is by no means as clear cut as one might have expected.

While popular and amateur historians embrace heroes readily enough, academics tend to be more chary. The American academic Andrew S. Ehrenkreutz's *Saladin* (1972) is a book which sets out aggressively to demolish the Saladin legend. Saladin is presented as a brutal warlord, a traitor to his Zengid masters, an unscrupulous propagandist, a man more interested in making war against his Muslim co-religionaries than in prosecuting the *jihad*, and the head of a greedy clan of kinsmen. While Lane-Poole's portrait of the hero of the nation was built up from material supplied by panegyrists in Saladin s entourage, Ehrenkreutz has tended to rely on more critical chroniclers, such as the Shia, Ibn Abi Tayyi and the pro-Zengid,

Mosuli Ibn al-Athir. Ehrenkreutz's study is to some extent an exercise in imagining what Saladin's career would have looked like then and now if Saladin had died in 1186, a year before his great victory at Hattin, for it is certainly true that only the last part of Saladin's career was mostly devoted to fighting the Christians.

As far as I know, Ehrenkreutz's debunking study of Saladin has won him no disciples among the historical novelists, even though it is easy to imagine that quite a good novel could be written about Saladin as a villain manipulating the vocabulary of Holy War in the interests of power politics. Ehrenkreutz's book was also severely criticized by some academics in the field and most extensively by Donald Richards in a review article in *The Islamic Quarterly* in 1973. Richards in summing up remarked:

> One approaches Ehrenkreutz's work with ready sympathy, hoping for a satisfactory re-examination of Saladin's career, because, seductive though it may be, Gibb's view seems just too good to be true. There are, however, such a number of inaccuracies, major and minor mistakes, slanted or unsupportable interpretations of texts, that one's sympathy evaporates and one begins to feel that perhaps Gibb's Saladin is a more acceptable figure after all.
>
> (Richards 1973: 158–9)

In *Saladin and the Politics of Holy War* (1982), Malcolm Lyons and D. E. P. Jackson consciously sought to present a more balanced picture of Saladin. Their study is carefully researched and sensitively written and has the additional merit of bringing new sources into play. Although it is perhaps regrettable that they chose to concentrate so much on the *jihad* and Saladin's later and more obviously virtuous years, still Lyons and Jackson have been at pains to present Saladin as a fairly conventional man, typical of his times and responding to the expectations of his contemporaries – not so much a hero who turned the tides of history. but rather a politician swimming along with those tides. In *Saladin und der dritte Kreuzzug* (1980), Hannes Mohring had taken a similar approach, stressing how Saladin in displaying generosity, forbearance and piety was conforming to the expectations of his followers.

An excessive focus on Saladin and his *jihad* has had a distorting effect on our understanding of what was going on in late twelfth-century Egypt and Syria. In order to assess Saladin's aims and assess the degree of freedom of action he possessed, we still badly need monographic studies of those around him, as well as more attention to be paid to Ayyubid society, economy and culture.

Currently the Christian side of the conflict is better covered. In the last few decades both the two-party model of Jerusalemite politics and the uncritical approval for the baronial party has been scrutinized, queried and finally demolished. Jonathan Riley-Smith (1973: 101–12) has drawn attention to material in the sources which suggested that Raymond of Tripoli was less than perfect as a lost leader. Joshua Prawer (1980) has re-evaluated the piratical activities of Reginald de Châtillon, suggesting that he was 'not a simple scheming robber lord', but that in seeking to sever or at least impede contacts between Egypt and Syria by control of the regions of Sinai and Transjordan, he was following a perfectly plausible grand strategy. Bernard Hamilton (1978) similarly has found much to admire in Reginald's career. Similarly, Benjamin Kedar (1982) has looked again at the life and works of the Patriarch Heraclius and queried the objectivity of William of Tyre's portrait of the man. R. C. Smail (1982) has queried the view that Guy de Lusignan was a weak and cowardly fool who blundered into catastrophe in 1187. Stephen Tibble (1989) has attacked the notion that the Kingdom fell prey to feuding factions of over-mighty barons, arguing that the baronage of the Kingdom of Jerusalem was if anything 'under-mighty'. Finally, Peter Edbury's 'Propaganda and faction in the Kingdom of Jerusalem: the background to Hattin' (1993), has demolished the theory that there ever were two groupings, a court party and a baronial party in consistent opposition to one another.

'All our ancient history, as one of our wits remarked, is no more than accepted fiction' (Voltaire 1785: 213). More recently Pierre Veyne has given more careful consideration to this *mot* of Voltaire and to the links between history and historical fiction. Veyne has concluded that the writing of history hardly differs from that of the novel, for 'it is anecdotal, it interests by recording as the novel does. It differs from the novel only in one essential point, history can afford to be boring without losing its value' (Veyne 1984: 11). Perhaps Veyne is right about this, yet at the end of my reading of histories and novels about Saladin and the Third Crusade I have to conclude not only that the novels show a close dependence on the histories, but also that the histories make use of the tricks of the novelist. (Popular historians make use of little else.) Most important of all (and this, of course, must be a subjective judgement), history, whether written by Lane-Poole, Gibb, Runciman or Prawer, has struck me as more interesting and better written than novels which covered the same ground. Clichés, stereotyping and moralizing are found in both fiction and historiography, but historical novelists tend to show a greater predilection for them. The historians, by contrast, strive for novelty, they often try to overturn older views and above all they seek for empathy with their subjects, trying thereby to place figures such as Saladin and Guy de Lusignan in the context of their times. But let the ex-historian and Semiticist John Wansbrough have the last word: 'every author creates not merely his own precursors, but the very record of their activity, and I should not like to see historians exempted from this responsibility' (Wansbrough 1987: 27).

REFERENCES

Arnold, G. (1980) *Held Fast for England*, London.
Baldwin, M. W. (1936) *Raymond III of Tripolis and the Fall of Jerusalem (1140–1187)*, Princeton.
Butterfield, H. (1924) *The Historical Novel*, London.
Caracciolo, P. (1988) 'Introduction', Caracciolo (ed.) *The Arabian Nights in English Literature: Studies in the Reception of* The Thousand and One Nights *into British Literature*, London.
Carpenter, H. and Prichard, M. (1984) *The Oxford Companion to Children's Literature*, Oxford.

Conant, M. P. (1908) *The Oriental Tale in England in the Eighteenth Century*, New York.
Edbury, P. (1993) 'Propaganda and faction in the Kingdom of Jerusalem: the background to Hattin', in M. Schatzmiller (ed.) *Crusaders and Muslims in Twelfth-century Syria*, Leiden.
Encylopedia of Islam
Gibb, H. A. R. (1951) 'The armies of Saladin', *Cahiers d'histoire égyptienne*, ser. 3, fasc. 4: 304–20.
—— (1952) 'The achievement of Saladin', *Bulletin of the John Rylands Library* 35: 44–60.
—— (1955) 'The rise of Saladin, 1169–1189', in M. W. Baldwin (ed.) *A History of the Crusades*, vol. 1, Pennsylvania.
Girouard, M. (1981) *The Return to Camelot: Chivalry and the English Gentleman*, New Haven and London.
Grunebaum, G. von (1953) *Medieval Islam*, 2nd edn, Chicago.
Hamilton, B. (1978) 'The Elephant of Christ: Reynald of Châtillon', *Studies in Church History* 15: 97–109.
Henty, G. A. (1891) *Winning his Spurs: A Tale of the Crusades*, London.
Hindley, G. (1976) *Saladin*, London.
Hourani, A. (1980) 'H. A. R. Gibb: the vocation of an orientalist', in Hourani, *Europe and the Middle East*, London.
Humphrey, R. (1986) *The Historical Novel as Philosophy of History*, London.
Kedar, B. Z. (1982) 'The Patriarch Heraclius', in B. Z. Kedar, H. E. Neyer and R. C. Smail (eds) *Outremer: Studies in the History of the Crusading Kingdom of Jerusalem*, Jerusalem: 177–204.
Lane-Poole, S. (1898) *Saladin and the Fall of the Kingdom of Jerusalem*, London.
Lee, S. (ed.) (1894) *Dictionary of National Biography*, vol. 37, London.
Maalouf, A. (1984) *The Crusades through Arab Eyes*, London.
Morgan, M. R. (1973) *The Chronicle of Ernoul and the Continuations of William of Tyre*, Oxford.
Newby, P. H. (1983) *Saladin and his Time*, London.
Plante, D. (1986) 'Profiles', *The New Yorker*, Nov.: 77.
Prawer, J. (1980) 'Crusader security and the Red Sea', in Prawer, *Crusader Institutions*, Oxford.
Regan, G. (1987) *Saladin and the Fall of Jerusalem*, Beckenham.
Richards, D. (1973) 'The early history of Saladin', *Islamic Ouarterly* 17: 158–9.
Riley-Smith, J. (1973) *The Feudal Nobility and the Kingdom of Jerusalem 1174–1277*, London.
Runciman, S. (1952) *A History of the Crusades*, II: *The Kingdom of Jerusalem and the Frankish East 1100–1187*, Cambridge.
—— (1955) *A History of the Crusades*, III: *The Kingdom of Acre and the Later Crusades*, Cambridge.
Saffari, K. (1972) *Les Légendes et contes persans dans la littérature anglaise des XVIIIe et XIXe siècles jusqu'en 1859*, Paris.
Said, E. (1978) *Orientalism*, London.
Scott, W. (1825) *The Talisman*, London.
Shelby, G. (1969) *Knights of Dark Renown*, London.
Smail, R. C. (1982) 'The predicaments of Guy of Lusignan, 1183–87', in B. Z. Kedar, H. E. Meyer and R. C. Smail (eds) *Outremer: Studies in the History of the Crusading Kingdom of Jerusalem*, Jerusalem.
Steiner, G. (1967) 'George Lukács and his devil's pact', in *Language and Silence*, London.
Strong, R. (1978) *And When Did You Last See Your Father? The Victorian Painter and British History*, London.
Taylor, A. J. P. (1983) *A Personal History*, London.
Tibble, S. (1989) *Monarchy and Lordships in the Latin Kingdom of Jerusalem 1099–1291*, Oxford.

Tyerman, C. (1988) *England and the Crusades 1095–1588*, Chicago and London.
Veyne, P. (1984) *Writing History*, Manchester.
Voltaire (1785) *Jeannot et Colin*, in *Œuvres complètes*, vol. 44, Paris.
Wansbrough, J. (1987) *Res Ipsa Loquitur: History and Mimesis*, Albert Einstein Memorial Lecture, Jerusalem.

9

FAMILY, GENDER AND SEXUALITY IN THE MIDDLE AGES[1]

Janet L. Nelson

Interest in the medieval family and the rights and roles of medieval women is not new. In the later nineteenth century, and in the earlier decades of the twentieth, in the wake of the suffrage movement, a flurry of works carried 'the woman question' back into the Middle Ages.[2] Since the early 1960s, medievalists' study of the history of family, gender and sexuality has flourished and diversified. These are trends in line with the developing interest in these fields within academic history as a whole, and well reflected in the foundation of new anglophone periodicals.[3] Various factors have contributed: the ongoing interest of social and political historians in noble families' role in consolidating and transmitting power over time (Chapter 10, this volume); the strengthened impact of social anthropology on

1   It is not possible to cover the whole of this vast field. The focus will be on central-western Europe (the former Carolingian Empire) and England, partly because these regions are most likely to be covered by historiography available in English, also because major debates have turned on evidence from there. Nevertheless, a few references to Byzantium, Scandinavia, the Celtic lands, Spain and central Europe, for all of which there are burgeoning historiographies, will enable interested readers to follow up relevant material. For the earlier Middle Ages, there is a fine annotated bibliography: Affeldt *et al.* 1990. I am very grateful to Paul Fouracre and especially Julia Smith for valuable criticisms, and to Michael Bentley for editorial *constantia*.

2   For the impact of this in the field of Anglo-Saxon historical scholarship, see Stafford 1995; for medieval Germany, see Braun 1901. See also A. L. Erickson's introduction to her new edition of Clark 1992, and Berg 1996.

3   *The Journal of Interdisciplinary History* (1970–); *Journal of Homosexuality* (1973–); *Social History* (1975–); *Signs* (1976–); *The Journal of Family History* (1976–); *History Workshop Journal* (1976–); *Gender and History* (1989–); *Journal of the History of Sexuality* (1990–); *Women's History Review* (1992–). It must be said, however, that the proportion of medieval contributions to these and other more marginally relevant journals has been quite low, and is barely rising.

4   The work of J. Goody has been exceptionally fruitful: see, among much else Goody 1976, 1983. See further pp. 162–3. See also Strathern 1972, 1980, 1987, and Moore 1988, with many suggestive lines of approach, and excellent bibliography.

social history;[4] the growth of historical demography, helped by the application of computing (Laslett and Wall 1972; Flandrin 1979; Wall 1983); the academic establishment of medieval archaeology distinct from its associated fields in Near Eastern and classical studies;[5] the emergence of medieval canon law as a major subdiscipline and resultant intensive study of the medieval Church's role in the development of legal theory and practice on marriage (Brundage 1975, 1977; Payer 1984b; Reynolds 1994); the flourishing of classical, Late Antique and Byzantine history and the willingness of Western medievalists to collaborate and engage with these (see Cameron and Kuhrt 1983; Archer *et al.* 1994; Laiou 1993); the bringing of 'fringe-areas' like the Celtic lands and Scandinavia into the European mainstream (see Davies 1983; Jenkins and Owen 1980; Sawyer 1989, 1990; Sawyer and Sawyer 1993: chs 8 and 9; Jochens 1980, 1986; Clover 1993); growing interest in the history of everyday life (Goetz 1993a; Haldon 1986), of private life (Ariès and Duby 1987–8), of childhood (Ariès 1962; and the contributions in *Studies in Church History* 31 (1993) on the theme of 'The Church and Childhood') and, above all, in the history of women – these last, especially, reflecting urgent concerns in the world beyond academe.[6] It has become clear that there was not just one family-form, but many, in the Middle Ages, hence that there are multiple histories of the family; and that these cannot be understood apart from the history of gender, nor private life understood as a separate sphere hermetically sealed from public life.[7] Medievalists have become more eclectic, and more critical, in their use of material, more anxious to check laws against other evidence: in the earlier period notably charters, or even archaeology (Wickham 1994; see also Halsall 1996), in the later period, massive documentation of legal practice through notarial records, wills, contracts (see Hughes 1975; 1978; Barron and Sutton 1994; cf. also Rosenthal 1990). For the most part, and despite brave attempts to recover oral traditions,[8] and to deploy archaeology, we are stuck with the written. But historians are becoming, wise to the changing significance of formulae, alert to rhetoric, and willing to learn from literary analysts.[9] The most important trend in the historiography of the family over the past thirty years or so has been the refusal of marginality, and the insistence on the intimate linkage of family/families to the

---

5 Cf. recent object lessons in James 1989; Hamerow 1994; and for illuminating syntheses of archaeological and historical approaches, Wickham 1994.

6 Cf. francophone historiography from Grimal 1966, 1977; Duby and Perrot 1991. Cf. anglophone historiography: Baker 1977; contributions to *Studies in Church History* 27 (1991), on the theme of 'Women in the Church', and 34 (1997), on 'The Church and Gender' Partner 1983, and Bennett 1994.

7 Cf. Elshtain 1981. The phrase 'domestic solicitude', from the ninth-century work *De Ordine Palatii*, was used repeatedly by D. Herlihy (see p. 160) to stress the 'private' aspects of women's property managements in the earlier Middle Ages but paradoxically in its original context related to the queen's role in palace administration: cf. for the difficulties of applying the public/private distinction in earlier-medieval contexts, Nelson 1989.

8 Geary 1994 does justice to the importance of the family and women in this context.

9 e.g. White 1993; Barthélemy 1993, esp. pp. 61–4. Historians of gender have been in the forefront: see Kay and Rubin 1994 and Stafford 1997.

most central themes of social, political economic and cultural history.[10] There is, further, an increasingly widespread (though still not widespread enough) perception that gender too belongs with family among the central themes, and that family and domesticity are not interchangeable terms.

THE MEDIEVAL FAMILY AND GENDER IN CONTEXT

For some early medieval historians, the history of the family has remained rooted in the study of the barbarian laws, which survive as codified in the fifth, sixth and seventh centuries. Ethnic specificity seems a given in this material, each set of laws being attached to a *gens* or 'people' (hence describable as 'gentile' law). Thus historians have compared 'the Frankish family' with 'the Lombard family', or 'the Visigothic family', and an ideal-type 'Germanic family' with 'the Roman family'. The Roman/German divide remains axiomatic.[11] The picture can be widened to compare and contrast the 'Germanic' family with the 'Irish' (or Celtic) family (Herlihy 1985: ch. 2). Laws cover marriage and the treatment of women: though the picture varies (in the Lombard laws, for instance, the husband is envisaged as administering his wife's property, whereas this is not stated in the laws of the Salian Franks; divorce was allowed for in Anglo-Saxon laws, but not in Frankish laws), common traits are more or less fierce penalties for abduction and rape, some provision for female inheritance, insistence on the widow's status and economic protection through dower (property given her by her husband at marriage), and reference to more or less extensive kinship arrangements. Much recent historiography on the family and women has continued on the assumption that gentile laws governed behaviour, and hence described statistical norms.

Some historians, however, have stressed the ideological function of law, in projecting an image of rulership on behalf of the lawmaker, and in expressing values – the values of the dominant class – which were typically conveyed by (among other things) statements of gender relations: women are weak and in need of male protection (see Wormald 1977; Wickham 1994: 123, 206, 212–14; Davies 1982: 79; cf. Scott 1986: 1067: 'Gender is a primary way of signifying relationships of power'). Laws thus read need to be offset against other evidence – historical narratives, documents, incidental references in saints' lives – to gain any sense of social practice. On that basis, the position of widows can be regarded as precarious (see Parisse 1993; Nelson 1995), and while a more extensive circle of kin might have been invoked in special circumstances, such as liturgical commemoration, for most purposes, most people's primary experience can be reconstructed as involving a small, 'nuclear',

---

10 Duby and Le Goff 1977 dealt largely with aristocratic families, and Italian ones especially. Mitterauer and Sieder 1982 and Berguière *et al.* 1996 were more broadly conceived. The political and social history of the earlier Middle Ages is illuminated by Le Jan 1995.

11 See King 1972; Drew 1988, and the same author's introductions to her translations of *The Burgundian Code* (Philadelphia, 1977), *The Lombard Laws* (Philadelphia, 1973) and *The Law of the Salian Franks* (Philadelphia, 1991); cf. also Wemple 1981; Ennen 1989.

family. A. C. Murray has argued that this was true even among 'Germanic' barbarians in the earliest documented period, i.e. the fifth and sixth centuries. Murray has cast serious doubt on the historic existence of the extended-family, the *Sippe*, hypothesized by modern (German) historians.[12] If Murray is right, the 'German'/'Roman' divide (in this respect, anyway) dwindles into insignificance. In a general comparative survey, David Herlihy suggested that the early medieval Irish preserved the kindred as the basis of 'archaic' household organization for much longer than the 'Germans' did, and so contrasted an original hypothetically strong Germanic *Sippe* with its subsequent 'weakening'. Usefully, if belatedly, Herlihy added differential status or class into his model, with important implications for gender too: the large household, Irish or German, was for the elite. At this level,

> resource polygyny resulted in widespread concubinage, the gathering of women in the households of the powerful, and a shortage of brides, especially on the lower levels of society ... The dearth of women assured them favourable marriage terms, but had as counterpart frequent abductions ... Considerable promiscuity, obscuring lines of descent through males, enhanced the importance of matrilineal ties ...
>
> (Herlihy 1985: 55)

This 'archaic' scenario, allegedly true of Ireland, has been depicted for Anglo-Saxon England, the Carolingian world and twelfth-century France.[13] The implication is that family and gender must be studied together.

Herlihy (1985: 52, 61) implies that elite practices resulted in shortage of women, in effect some kind of lordly rationing, lower down the scale. Can this be corroborated from work on peasant societies? A number of ninth-century estate surveys (polyptychs), including lists of peasant households, made by large-scale ecclesiastical landlords in the heartlands of the Carolingian Empire have been the focus of much recent work.[14] Great ingenuity is needed to derive from these snapshots something like three-dimensional images of households. Many commentators interpret the basic residence groups as nuclear families, one family per hearth and per *mansus* (land sufficient to maintain a household unit) (cf. Herlihy 1985: 68–71; cf. also Toubert 1996). The manse is agreed to have been a hereditary peasant holding, though the evidence leaves it unclear whether daughters inherited alongside, or only in place of, brothers. There was great variety in household

---

12 Murray 1983. Cf. on Anglo-Saxon families, Fell 1984; and cf. Davies 1988, drawing on extensive charter evidence for ninth-century Brittany.

13 Ross 1985; Rouché 1987, esp. pp. 471–9; Duby 1978: 94–5 depicts '[the] genetic vigor of the males ... the women who were enjoyed by men of great family along the way ... servant-girls and prostitutes who might briefly distract them. ... [Th]e partners whom they did acknowledge may have been ... the family's bastard daughters, who formed a kind of pleasure reserve within the household itself ... [with] bastards scattered far and wide.' Bouchard 1981, depicts aristocrats conscientiously avoiding consanguineous marriage.

14 For well-translated extracts, see Duby 1965. The collected studies of Devroey 1993 provide an excellent entrée. See also Ring 1979; Kuchenbuch 1978: 76–94, and his contributions to Affeldt and Kuhn 1986: 227–43; Zerner 1979; Goetz 1991; Herlihy 1985: 62–72. Power [1924] 1963: 18–38, is a powerful imaginative reconstruction of the life of a peasant household.

structures, however. Several hearths to 1 manse held by peasants with similar names have been interpreted as a reversion to an earlier multiple-family model (two-generation, with brothers coexisting) (Ring 1979; Bessmerny 1984). Opportunities for new household-formation occurred when manses were created from land reclaimed from waste. (Devroey 1993: ch. 9). Some households had 2 or even 3 manses, and included single adults, among them still unmarried sons and daughters. Some free-peasant households had slaves: on the estates of the monastery of Prüm in 892, 25 per cent of manses had one or more *mancipia* living with the free-peasant family, while at Lauterbach in Bavaria, two generations earlier, 47 free persons were distributed among 11 peasants holdings, but 10 slaves were distributed among only 3 of those holdings. Recorded numbers of children per couple ranged in a single village from 6 (1 family) to none (4 families), with 17 out of 29 families having between 2 and 4 children (Goetz 1993a: 124–5, 274). Quite large differentials of size and wealth thus existed between one peasant family and another in the same village. The imbalance in adult peasant sex ratios has suggested the likelihood of female infanticide among peasant households on the estates of the monastery of St-Germain near Paris.[15] Despite the difficulty of correlating this with poor households, the contemporary evidence of penitentials also suggests (what is likely on comparative grounds) that poor parents regularly found difficulty in feeding their families (Schmitz 1982; Payer 1984).

Changes in family fortunes over time did not only result from accidents of mortality. Coleman argued that there was evidence for peasant hypergamy on the estates of St-Germain: i.e. enterprising men of servile status married free women, or heiresses of free tenements.[16] But all the peasant families evidenced in the surveys existed within a lordship. The word *familia* at this period (and for long after) more often meant the dependants of the aristocratic lord and his household than it meant the modern idea of the biological family (Hammer 1983). The strategies pursued by peasants and lords, as discernible in the polyptychs, have been seen as converging to maintain an equilibrium between manses and households: it was in the lord's interest as well as the peasant family's to preserve the basic structure of manses (or part-manses) because dues and renders were calculated on that basis (Coleman 1977).

'A dynamic social model of rural society in the early Middle Ages' can thus show lords' interests helping to shape 'the origins of the western European family' (Hammer 1983). Carl Hammer's study of Lauterbach, Bavaria, an extremely rare example of a lay seigneury in the ninth century, showed a bipartite estate with the lord's directly farmed demesne surrounded by dependent tenements. There were also a large number of *mancipia*. Hammer interprets them as slaves. Fifty-seven tenants (including only 10 *mancipia*) farmed 11 dependent holdings, and 37

---

15   Coleman 1976. Against Coleman's argument, see Zerner 1979; Herlihy 1985: 64–7; Goetz 1993b: 45. For a wider perspective on the problem, see Halsall 1996: 15–16.
16   Coleman 1971/2; cf. Weinberger 1973, showing collective functional adaptation to changing circumstances. Zerner-Chardavoine 1981 stresses local variation.

mancipia were attached to the demesne farm ('manor house') itself. Twenty-three of those *mancipia* were women who, Hammer inferred, produced cloth in the manorial textile workshop (*gynaeceum*). Hammer was able to show the likelihood of a degree of endogamy on the estate and further suggested that the estate's population was maintained by the lord's arranging marriages of his *mancipia* with those of neighbouring lordships, periodic transfers of *mancipia* between one lordship and another reuniting servile families 'seigneurially', that is, in terms of the lord's ownership. Thus, in early medieval Bavaria can be found something resembling the 'western European family, characterized by relatively mature partners and simple household-structures, together with a high incidence of unmarried persons'.[17] Like Coleman, Hammer sees the interests of both lords *and* peasants being served by these arrangements. He argues that peasants gained security from their place in the seigneuries, while lords maximized the 'administrative efficiency' of their holdings. Hammer was clear about the preponderant weight of lordship, however, and regarded the persistent presence of slavery as a clinching factor. Free peasants coexisted with slaves within the *familia*. The lord's control of the slaves, even if numerically a minority, had implications for the free. Hammer has recently drawn attention to eighth-century evidence for a Thuringian lord's arranging of a marriage-ceremony between a servile widow on one of his holdings and a recently bought Bavarian captive (he was apparently a free peasant who had been kidnapped while travelling), with the explicit aim of encouraging the acquisition (who happened to be highly skilled) to feel more settled in his new lot (Hammer 1995). How far such findings can be generalized remains problematic. Pierre Bonnassie has reaffirmed the pervasiveness of slavery in Carolingian Gaul, and sees this as representing continuity from Late Antiquity. But any slavery in Carolingian Bavaria and Thuringia would need to be assigned different origins. In any case, as Hans-Werner Goetz has recently argued, the legal state of unfreedom in the Carolingian period is not the same thing as classical slavery: *socially*, both the free and the unfree were subjected to lordship, yet people in both categories could and did marry, and intermarry.[18]

How did lords negotiate with peasants? Gender has barely figured in debate over the terms of this negotiation (whether essentially oppositional, or mutually accommodating), despite clear evidence for lords wielding a degree of control over the marriages of their dependants (*servi* and *mancipia*).[19] If serfdom within seigneuries

17 Hammer 1983: 248, where and argument for long-term continuity is advanced: 'cultural patterns imposed by the aristocracy on its plantation slaves (*sic!*) for admin efficiency may have been so deeply implanted and pervasive that they survived the decline after the eleventh century of the institutional environment which had nurtured them'.

18 Bonnassie 1991; Goetz 1993; Wickham 1994: ch. 7 has challenged the generalizing of the bipartite seigneurial model, as well as the hypothesis of a significant amount of slavery, in the earlier medieval West. See also Davis 1996: an excellent overview.

19 Women scarcely featured in Marc Bloch's essays on social and economic history, and his generation of *annalistes* were scarcely concerned with the history of women, let alone gender. But see some qualifications, and explanations, in Davis 1992.

was well established already in the ninth century, how should we explain the persistence of slavery throughout the Middle Ages in the far northern, eastern and southern reaches of Europe? A gender dimension to the problem has recently been highlighted by Susan M. Stuard, who argues that slavery for women persisted, especially in the towns of Mediterranean Europe, partly because it was fed by the ready supply of Balkan slaves, but more specifically because it met the labour demands of great households, and the demands of masters generally for sexual and social power (Stuard 1995; cf. Klapisch-Zuber 1985). This evidence for slavery's *persistence* in southern Europe cannot serve to explain (*pace* the title of Stuard's article) the *decline* of slavery north of the Alps in the old Carolingian heartlands. Here, Stuard falls back on the work of Herlihy, who surmised the prevalence, through the ninth century, of textile workshops staffed by unfree women, at seigneurial estate-centres. He suggested that these women were in effect barrack-slaves, living together at their workshops, rather than in families (Herlihy 1990; cf. Stuard 1995). That lords, and others, sometimes took advantage of the sexual services of young female dependants is likely enough; but this need say nothing about the women's legal status.[20] The fact that 'women tended to congregate in the households of the powerful, even on monastic estates'[21] suggests that such a concentration of activity had an economic purpose. How widespread it was is debatable: there are very few references to locations west of the Rhine. Herlihy thought that thanks to urbanization and labour shortage, women's textile work was 'domesticated' in the central Middle Ages, shifting from the female-slave workshop of the Carolingian period into the free artisan family:[22] a view that fits with Herlihy's broader argument about the evolution of the family (see p. 161).

The debate over the origins and significance of merchet in medieval England represents something of a re-run of the Carolingianists' argument (Searle 1979). Merchet was a customary payment frequently paid by a villein (unfree peasant) father to the lord for permission for his daughter to marry. Eleanor Searle interpreted it as a tax on property being alienated as dowry and so a feature of rational lordly administration. 'Control [over marriage] was exerted by the lord over male and female alike' (ibid. 42). Searle's critics objected that this was a tax on 'persons', not property.[23] They widened the picture to include France, relating

---

20   The Capitulary *de Villis* c. 43, ed. A. Boretius, *Monumenta Germaniae Historica, Capitularia*, vol. I (Hanover, 1884), p. 87, gives no indication that the workers at *genitia* lived on site, though that may be implied by *de Villis*, c. 49, ibid., and by other texts cited by Herlihy 1990: 79. For the question of slavery, see p. 158.

21   Herlihy 1985: 67; 1990: 36–8, 84–5, Herlihy cites a mixed bag of evidence, much of it from other times and places, to suggest an association of earlier medieval *gynaecea* with 'slavery, imprisonment and illicit sex'.

22   Cf. some evident reservations of Stuard 1995: 15, noting the consequent loss of economies of scale, and reduction in the effectiveness of supervision, and her suggestion (ibid. 23–6) about a revival of household slavery associated with textile production in later medieval Italy. Cf. p. 160 for Herlihy's further suggestion that at least in Paris, women operated as 'independent artisans' outside the home.

23   Brand *et al.* 1983, clarifying that the issue is between 'opposed "world-views"'. Cf. also Razi 1979.

seigneurial dues on marriage to the wider question of changing marriage-rules in the period after the eleventh-century reform movement, and, most important, linking seigneurial licence to marry with vestiges of servitude. Gender, however, barely came into that debate either.[24]

Family and gender have been brought within a single perspective in recent historiography on the gendering of work in the relatively well-documented later medieval period. After noting the way labour shortage drove up men's wages after the Black Death, Herlihy asked: 'if working men benefited from their own falling numbers, what were the experiences of working women?' His answer is that women benefited only in the short term. Just as towns in the twelfth and thirteenth centuries had opened up opportunities for women to work outside the home as 'independent artisans', followed by male foreclosing of those opportunities in the early fourteenth century through various forms of restrictive practice, so, after the relatively favourable environment of the later fourteenth and early fifteenth centuries, women at the end of the Middle Ages were thrust back into their traditional marginal and highly dependent occupations, notably domestic service. The chronology varies, and Judith Bennett has mounted a forceful challenge to the medieval/early modern divide; but there seems to be general agreement that women evinced a gender-specific vulnerability to fluctuations in the wider economy, and especially to demographic change.[25]

CHANGE IN THE CENTRAL MIDDLE AGES?

In 1962, David Herlihy's 'Land, family and women' appeared in *Speculum*, the journal of the Medieval Academy of America. This article seemed to set the historiography of the medieval family on a new tack. Herlihy argued that women could be observed in the period between the eighth and twelfth centuries playing 'an extraordinary role in the management of family property'. Herlihy's thesis combined a whole cluster of social factors to explain women's 'prominence': the relative freedom allowed women in early medieval law, especially in rights to inherit, administer and alienate property; the allocation of gender roles in aristocratic families in ways that assigned 'domestic responsibility' including the economic management of landed resources, to women; ideas of chivalry which underscored that role-division; and, last but not least – explaining the particular importance of women in regard to land and family in the eleventh century – the consequences of the physical mobility of the male aristocracy, i.e. their absence at war, leaving their wives/widows in charge of family property.[26]

---

24 But Clarke 1987 shows some women paying merchets for themselves, and for daughters. Leyser 1995: 120–1 notes both that women with means to do so paid to secure the right to choose a husband, and that local custom varied a lot. Cf. another debate over the constitution of peasant households; Razi 1993 stresses structural change over time.

25 Herlihy 1990: 150. Compare now Goldberg 1992; and, for a gloomier but not essentially different view, Bennett 1988 and 1994; 50–64.

26 Recent work on the role of aristocratic women in family formation includes Riley-Smith 1992, 1997; Geary 1994: 48–80; Le Jan 1995: 52–7. Cf. also McNamara and Wemple 1988.

The ideological thrust of Herlihy's project was revealed in his hypothesizing one further factor: 'the influence of the Christian Church'. Herlihy's was essentially a functionalist and evolutionary account of the medieval family's emergence as a moral unit, egalitarian and distinctive: Western culture in a nutshell? Part and parcel of this model were the implied progressive (in both senses) influence of the Catholic Church, and a linear development in women's history.[27] Monogamy eventually triumphed, thanks to steady ecclesiastical pressure first in the Carolingian period, then again, more solidly institutionalized, from the eleventh century onwards.[28] A more or less stable institution emerged: the Western family. Thereafter, despite changes in the labour market, there was no going back. Women's position was legally secure, and ecclesiastically validated.

What gave Herlihy's conclusions their edge was the fact that they were based not on the soft, impressionistic evidence of prescriptive or literary texts but on hard data, a computerized analysis of 1,000 charters. This was impressive pioneering in the early 1960s. While Herlihy claimed that his findings were confirmed by other evidence, that women's 'position of prominence' was 'saluted ... in the charged sentiment of troubadour poetry' as well as in the charters' 'dry Latin', it was Herlihy's precocious mastery of computer technology that stamped his findings with special authenticity. The sharp new quantitative methods seemed to offer an escape from the hazy old qualitative ones. Moreover, the premise for Herlihy's findings had been supplied in an article published by him three years earlier in which he used the same evidence to chart, graphically (this was the first article ever published by *Speculum* to feature a graph[29]), the massive increase in Church property over the centuries from the eighth to the twelfth.

Herlihy's aggregative approach in his 1962 article has largely been superseded by soundings taken in specific archives, focusing on particular regions, families or family-types, in more limited time-frames (Barthélemy 1993; Aurell 1995; Le Jan 1995). Royal families, especially well documented, have been well to the fore in this historiography, sometimes treated as paradigmatic, for instance by Georges Duby

---

27 *Friedelehe*, allegedly a distinctively Germanic form of semi-marriage that did not involve dower, has been depicted as withering away during the Carolingian period: see Wemple 1981: 82–3; Le Jan 1995: 271–4, though Herlihy 1985: 51 saw it as equivalent to clandestine marriage which 'constituted a major problem for the Church over the entire Middle Ages'. *Friedelehe* is a modern historians' construct.

28 Herlihy's views are clearest in two articles, 'The making of the medieval family', and 'The family and religious ideologies in medieval Europe', first published in the *Journal of Family History* 8 (1983), pp. 116–30 and 12 (1987), pp. 3–17, now reprinted in the posthumous volume of Herlihy's collected essays, Herlihy 1995: 135–73.

29 Molho, 'Introduction' to Herlihy 1995: xv, à propos Herlihy 1985. Maybe this says less about historians' reluctance to use new technology than about the overwhelming preponderance of literary scholars amongst American medievalists: see Herlihy's computer-based analysis in his presidential address to the Medieval Academy of America in 1983, 'The American medievalist', in Herlihy 1995: 381–92, showing that only 28 per cent of the membership in 1982 were historians (and 52 per cent literary and linguistic scholars). Nowadays, it should be added, the literary scholars are at the forefront in humanities computing.

who offered the eleventh- and twelfth-century Capetians as evidence for a 'lay model of marriage',[30] but analysed with notable finesse by Pauline Stafford, who made the inspired choice of a woman's individual life-cycle as the frame for her study of medieval queens, thereby eschewing linear or teleological history. The historiography of medieval queens and queenship has in fact proved an especially good instance not only of its subject's centrality to the political and social history of the period in general but of the need for appropriate frameworks for studying royal women within the developmental cycles of royal families.[31] Medieval historians still have much to learn from anthropologists.

Herlihy's suggested link between women's property/property management and the Church's acquisition of vast landholdings has been much more directly and controversially proposed by Jack Goody, an anthropologist with strong interests in cross-cultural and historical comparisons (Goody 1983; cf. also Goody 1968: 'Introduction'; 1972; 1976). Goody's starting-point was not property but prohibited degrees of marriage which, he observed, became exceptionally extensive (compared with those of other cultures) in earlier medieval Latin Christendom, until by the eleventh century they were understood as banning marriage between sixth cousins. Goody went on to link these rules with other traits of ecclesiastical teaching: the insistence on *both* partners' active consent to marriage, the forbidding of divorce, and the strong discouragement of such 'strategies of [familial] continuity' as widow-remarriage and adoption. All this amounted to ecclesiastical interference in secular 'strategies of heirship'. The common consequences were the accumulation of property in female hands, ecclesiastical support for female disposition of such property, and increased landed endowment for the Church by women. The consequences were intended: Goody's avowedly 'materialist' explanation was that the Church made the rules to maximize its own material benefits.

Goody's thesis has generated much debate. Clearly the *extent* of the prohibited degrees remains problematic (Brooke 1991: 134–5) but extending prohibited degrees of marriage would not in fact have increased the likelihood of benefits to the Church (d'Avray 1992). Further, ecclesiastical interests were not opposed to lay interests: noble family-strategists and the churches they patronized were bound by the oblated sons who staffed medieval monasteries, each bringing a landed gift; and nobles were the great patrons of reform.[32] But there has been a fruitful interplay between Goody's ideas and Duby's hypothesis of fundamental change in the eleventh century. According to Duby, the patrilineal family replaced an earlier

---

30 Duby 1978, 1981. Cf. Brooke 1991: 126–57, stressing, pp. 142–3, the congruence of aristocratic and ecclesiastical interests. Herlihy too (Herlihy 1995: 161–2) pointed out the disparity between prescriptive (ecclesiastical) and descriptive (lay) models.

31 Parsons 1993 and 1995. See also Fradenberg 1991. Von Euw and Schreiner 1991, and Davids 1995 are thicker on description and thinner on theory. Cf. also Nelson 1977; and now Baker 1993, mostly on the central medieval period and especially Duggan 1997. For the notion of the domestic cycle, see Goody 1958.

32 Lynch 1976; Bouchard 1987; Boswell 1988; Nelson 1993. For the Carolingian period, see now De Jong 1996. For twelfth-century change, see Berend 1994.

bilateral system, and primogeniture replaced partible inheritance.[33] By a process of 'downward diffusion', the new model spread from magnate to castellan level, with hereditary surnames and coats of arms the signs of the new patrilineages. D. O. Hughes added a further important element to this model: she argued that the changes identified by Duby were accompanied by a further significant shift in the disposition of resources within the family: bridewealth, or dower, given by groom to bride at marriage, was replaced by dowry, vested by the bride's parents in the couple, in practice the groom.[34] Further changes have been linked with this: a demographic shift in overall sex ratios, meaning more, hence 'cheaper', women (L'Hermite-Leclercq 1991); the superseding of the wife's entirely free disposition over her property by the husband's control during his lifetime, and the wife's life-interest only after her husband's death; hence a marked diminution in the aristocratic woman's power over property and within the family (Duby 1983; Herlihy 1985: 82–111; Aurell 1995: 255; cf; Aurell 1985). In this model, family history is geared into wider eleventh-century histories: on the one hand, to that of a 'feudal mutation' which entailed, along with the imposition of seigneurial power over serfs in place of masters' ownership of slaves, a narrowing of family lines and the establishment of a power conceived of as essentially military and masculine (Barthélemy 1988); and on the other to the movement for Church reform (Moore 1985; Head and Landes 1992).

Various qualifications have been proposed for the Duby model of 'revolutionary' change. Goody pointed out that both dower *and* dowry direct property towards women, and that in both cases women's greater economic independence could result. He suggests, further, that 'the move to direct dowry ... might be one aspect of the Church's increasing interest in marriage and inheritance'.[35] Herlihy, basically accepting Duby's model, and surely influenced, too, by Goody, argued that the prerequisite to these changes in family-structure was 'the long-delayed success ... of the Church's protracted struggle to impose ... monogamy'. The 'principal cause', Herlihy thought, was ecclesiastical reform which 'required the recovery and stabilisation of the Church's landed endowment' and so forced the aristocracy to find ways of preserving their resources. The dynastic shedding of surplus sons, and the effective disinheritance of daughters, were the result (Herlihy 1985: 86–8; cf. also Wollasch 1980).

The Church's rules, as Herlihy himself pointed out, were not new. Eleventh-century changes can be located in a longer time-span. The fundamental importance of the couple was not new (Toubert 1977; Bouchard 1981; Le Jan 1995). Nor, on

---

33 Duby 1977, a collection of translated essays, originally published over the preceding decade or so, largely based on Duby's researches on the Cluny charters; Barthélemy 1988. Cf. also Gies and Gies 1989: ch. 6 ('the family revolution').

34 Hughes 1978: 276–85. Cf. Aurell 1995: 485, on 'dowry triumphant', in Catalonia *c*. 1160.

35 Goody 1983: Appendix 2, 'From brideprice to dowry?', pp. 255–61: this is the exact opposite of the trend diagnosed by Duby in the eleventh/twelfth centuries, towards diminishing endowment for the Church.

the other hand, had widows earlier necessarily had truly free disposition of their dower (Althoff 1993; Nelson 1995). Further, patrilineal ties never wholly displaced bilateral ones. Rather than seeing the power of women through the family waxing until the eleventh century and waning thereafter, the individual women's power might be seen changing through a lifetime, in keeping with the gendered rhythms of her life-cycle but also with the developmental cycle of the family itself.[36] Unique documentation in the form of the Domesday Book comes from eleventh-century England. What was used a century ago to produce the genealogical history of aristocratic families is now being used to document gender difference. Again the interests of lords, including and especially the king, in controlling women and claims through women lie behind much of the documentation (Stafford 1989). Such interventions of political power into the field of gender and family impose a rethinking of the distinction between public and private. Further examples are incest/sexual offences cited as grounds for confiscation of property; and the protection of widows cited as the motive for 'justice', whether by kings, nobles or later medieval town governments. In these cases, the construction and legitimation of (masculine) power depended on gender (Lees 1994; Hadley 1997; Gröbner 1995).

Finally, in addition to biological kin, a medieval person had spiritual kin, and these relationships were often very important to individuals. From the Carolingian period onwards, the Church increasingly stressed the bonds and responsibilities of godparenthood (Lynch 1986). Lay people responded, perhaps partly because godparenting continued some features of the already familiar institution of fosterage. Churchmen too, denied biological parenthood, became the spiritual fathers of those they baptized or confirmed. In the Carolingian period, spiritual ties formed through rituals of Christian initiation were shaped into instruments of political authority by popes, emperors and kings (Angenendt 1984; Smith 1992: 108–15). The paternal bond between a spiritual guide, or confessor, and the individuals he counselled had great social importance, both in Byzantium and, increasingly well documented from the thirteenth century, in the West too (Morris 1995, esp. ch. 4; Vauchez 1987; Coakley 1991).

NEW APPROACHES TO THE PERSON, THE BODY, GENDER AND SEXUALITY

If gendering the past is not to produce a 'history that stands still', then histories of gender, family and sexuality need to be integrated with histories of change. Though Foucault's interest in the history of sexuality barely extended to gender, and he, sadly, did not live to tackle the Middle Ages, nevertheless historians of Antiquity,

36   Stafford 1997, and Stafford in Duggan 1997; also Smith 1997. Cf. for rejection of male-centred periodizations, Kelly 1984.

and of Late Antiquity, with special interests in handling literary and archaeological evidence, have been at the forefront of attempts to rethink the family as a site of power. They have insisted on considering gender history as well as women's history; and thus on rewriting history at large (cf. Foxhall 1994; Archer *et al.* 1994). They have shown how Christianity meant rethinking of attitudes to the body, and how the virgin female body in particular became the apt symbol of purity (Clark 1983, 1986; Brown 1988; Cooper 1992; Cameron 1994).

Historians of the Middle Ages have been slower to appreciate the significance of such new approaches, despite a large historiography on early medieval female religious, and despite long-standing claims about the prominence of women in heresy and dissent in the central medieval period. But the scene has been changing rapidly in the past decade. In place of earlier reproductions of medieval hagiography, recent work has highlighted tension in representations of gender by the medieval hagiographers themselves (Smith 1995; Fouracre and Gerberding 1996; Lifshitz 1988). Complementing earlier studies on the importance of women in the commemoration of the dead is a recent emphasis on ambiguities here, women being associated with the marginal and the polluted (Leyser 1979: ch. 5; Geary 1994: ch. 2). The centrality of concern over priestly celibacy and the prominence of sexual language in the writings of the leading reformers have long been recognised. R. I. Moore has taken the lead in explaining why nicolaism was the prime object of the reformers' attack (cf. C. Leyset in Hadley 1997). This was not just for practical reasons linked with property. To define a spiritual elite and to construct its social power within the Western Christian tradition, the rhetoric of ritual purity was required. Its strongly gendered implications marched with 'a general marginalisation of female spirituality' (Elliott 1993: 103). To the choice increasingly emphasized by ecclesiastical reformers in the eleventh and twelfth centuries gender gave differential weight. Women manoeuvred within rules and strategies devised by men. At aristocratic level, this must account not only for the small numbers of nuns (or canonesses) as compared with monks throughout the Middle Ages, but for the specific problems of religious women in the period following the reforming Great Leap Forward of the eleventh century.

Yet analysis of the plentiful records of male and female religious experience has offered an entrée into intimate histories of individual lives. This has been a major growth area of the past decade or so, and also the site of important breakthroughs. Although so much of the medieval evidence of sexuality is prescriptive (Flandrin 1983; Brundage 1977), it has proved possible to recover something of the experiential.[37] Even for the earlier Middle Ages, when sanctity, male as well as female, must be seen overwhelmingly as a set of constructs that met the changing needs of male religious and secular elites, saints' lives can be re-read to reveal

---

37   Path-breaking here has been the work of C. Walker Bynum 1982, 1987, 1991, 1986. See also Bolton 1976, 1977. For earlier medieval material, see the contributions of C. Leyser and J. L. Nelson to Hadley 1997. For general orientation, see Salisbury 1990.

gender-specific 'real-life' particularity. Significantly, the 'familial environment' in which Smith finds early medieval female saints presented is that to which Bynum found later medieval female saints firmly attached (Bynum 1984; Smith 1995: 26–8). A similar trait could be noted, and a parallel drawn, in the 'private and mystical' style of female piety perhaps practised and certainly typified by female saints, as approved by the churchmen who controlled these representations in the earlier and in the later Middle Ages.[38] In the earlier and later Middle Ages alike, holy women concern themselves with food: providing for others gives their own self-denial special meaning (Bynum 1987; cf. also Bell 1985). The very gender-stereotyping of some historical writing tells much about audiences as well as authors,[39] while letters and poems can reveal something of inner lives; still more so can spiritual writings, which become much more plentiful from the twelfth century onwards.[40] On this basis, John Boswell has argued that the Church showed a degree of tolerance for homosexuality down to the twelfth century, but that hostile attitudes hardened thereafter (Boswell 1980; Moore 1987).

Recent work on medieval canon law and theology strengthens the idea of change in more than one direction. Medieval marriage doctrine took shape in the twelfth century, with the canonists' emphasis on consent reflecting, John Baldwin argues, 'the absolute symmetry of the theologians' doctrine of the marital debt' (that is, the obligation to engage in sexual relations) (Baldwin 1993; cf. Baldwin 1991). Yet the symmetry was surely incomplete. Moralists regarded women as less rational, weaker than men, yet abler with words: women were encouraged to put their powers of persuasion to moral uses, to be their husbands' guides to virtue (Farmer 1986). Physicians' two-seed theory, according to which both partners to intercourse needed to experience desire in order to emit seed, also imputed greater sexual appetite to women than to men: women, unlike men, experienced a twofold delight in intercourse: the emission of her own seed and the reception of the man's (Baldwin 1993; see further Laqueur 1990; Green 1990; Camille 1994; Karras 1996). Moreover, characteristic of the twelfth as well as the thirteenth century were literary representations of rape which stressed the difficulty of distinguishing it from adultery, and depicted male violence as the frustrated expression of love, while suggesting, at the same time, male anxieties over the fragility of social order and control.[41] Ambiguity seems ever-present once representations of gender are viewed in context across a broad front.

---

38 Smith 1995: 34–5; Bynum 1991: 160–219; Simons 1994. See further for the earlier medieval period, Wittern 1994; Corbet 1986; and for the later period, Atkinson 1983; Kieckhefer 1984; Dinzelbacher and Bauer 1988; Beer 1992.

39 For Liudprand of Cremona's depictions of powerfully sexual women, see Buc 1995; and the paper of R. Balzaretti in Hadwell 1997.

40 For a ninth-century example, see Neel 1991; for Heloise, Hildegard, and others, see Newman 1995. Cf. also Dronke 1984; Partner 1993.

41 Gravdal 1991. But it must be noted that the historical evidence cited at p. 164, n.35, for the contemporary practice of 'feudal law' is thin.

In the later Middle Ages, Baldwin suggests that assymetries became more evident, as in learned and in courtly discourses misogyny, often in crude and violent form, became acceptable.[42] R. Howard Bloch, attempting to historicize literary manifestations of late medieval woman-hating, has offered an explanation in terms of mistrust of writers and texts: like women, writers 'provoke contradiction', employ 'the ruses of rhetoric'.[43] Sarah Kay (like Baldwin) turns to philosophical, and specifically epistemological, change in the thirteenth and fourteenth centuries to supply the context for late medieval misogyny. Jean de Meun rejects the Thomist synthesis, rejects knowledge based on nature, that is, on sense-perception, and gendered feminine, in favour of a higher knowledge directly derived from God.[44] Yet such higher, mystic knowledge was accessible also to women; and recent scholarship has highlighted this very same later medieval period as one that saw the proliferation of Lives of virgin saints, of Marian devotion and of the widespread cult of St Anne, the grandmother of Christ.[45] Maternity was idealized: yet the sometimes problematic and painful reality of motherhood is revealed in accusations of maternal infanticide (Opitz 1990; cf. also Coleman 1976; Herlihy 1985: 64–7; Goetz 1993: 45; Halsall 1996: 15–16). A final example of later medieval ambiguity might be seen in the historiography of prostitution. Reviled by some moralists as the lowest of the low, yet accepted as 'necessary sewers' for men's filth, and otherwise treated as integral parts of their community, prostitutes were licensed and regulated by governments as an aspect of public order and sanitary control. and a source of modest profits (Rossiaud 1978, 1987; Trexler 1981; Otis 1985; Roper 1989; Karras 1996).

There has been enormous growth in the historiography. But these innovations have not fundamentally altered an underlying trait long predating the 1960s: in the England of the 1920s, though the editors of the medieval volume in the prestigious Legacy series found space for a breezy chapter on 'the position of women' by Eileen Power (Crump and Jacob 1926), the mainstream of medieval scholarship as typified in the old *Cambridge Medieval History* remained resolutely focused on political, military and constitutional history. The *New Cambridge Medieval History*, though much broader in scope, has envisaged no chapters on family, gender or sexuality: despite the vast output on those topics since the 1960s, the historiography has tended on the whole to be, in both senses, contained within older categories. The history of the family has not ignored sex, but there has been a reluctance to historicize sexuality, still less to regard this reluctance as problematic.

This tendency has not been radically diminished by one genuinely new environmental factor to have emerged over the past thirty years, the feminist

---

42   But for very crude misogyny well before this, see Ziolkowski 1989.
43   Bloch 1987: 19, and cf. ibid. 18: 'More than mere encumbering ambiguity, woman is defined, above all, as embodying the spirit of contradiction'. See now Bloch 1991.
44   Kay 1994. Cf. also Rubin 1994, with further references; and Rubin 1992.
45   Heffernan 1988; Cazelles 1991; Ashley and Sheingorn 1990. Warner 1976 brilliantly pioneered such a historicizing approach.

movement. This has produced an explosion of women's history which has necessarily amplified the historiography of the family too. Yet the concept of gender, with its theoretical load and its connotations of socially constructed difference, has failed to penetrate the vocabulary of most historians writing, even recently, on medieval families and/or women. In much of the historiography theory has been self-consciously eschewed, in favour of (often unavowed) functionalism. Women's history has seldom been integrated into wider socio-political history.[46] A recent brilliant account of the workings of social memory in the Middle Ages proceeds without highlighting women (Fentress and Wickham 1992). A fine book about medieval European expansion pays rather little attention to women's contribution (Bartlett 1993). The work of families has not really been considered, or critically assessed, in many works on medieval economies.[47] Conversely, historians of childhood and the family have not taken on board the implications of recent redatings of the decline of slavery. The history of sexuality has been ghettoized, though interesting work has been done for the Late Antique period and is beginning to surface in medieval historiography as well. It is worth noting also a marked lack of ideological conformism among women's historians and feminist historians working on the Middle Ages, and hence a welcome plurality of approaches and emphases.

Marxists have emphasized the link between family and property in a radically different way from the legal historians: male domination (patriarchy) is seen as built into the capitalism which developed from the later Middle Ages onwards, gender bias fundamentally disadvantaging women's participation in waged work.[48] The historians of the *Annales* school, which has included leading French medievalists from Marc Bloch onwards, aimed to produce a kind of historical anthropology. Kin-relations were a central feature of Bloch's 'feudal society',[49] and the ideology of knighthood was understood (though not named) as a construction of masculinity (cf. Barthélemy 1988; Lees 1994; Hadley 1997; Gröbner 1995). What still remains to be done, in many areas of medieval research, is not just the bringing of women's history into the mainstream (did women have a Renaissance?) but the gendering of history – that is, the discerning of difference and complementarity in women's and men's experience. Granted that the early Renaissance was a time of change, gender-specific rhythms need to be defined. The late Middle Ages may well have seen the imposition of more controls on women, their firm relegation to the home. But the tempi of change need to be closely monitored, and regional variation accounted for.

---

46 Rigby 1995 is an honourable and distinguished exception.
47 Though see Kroemer 1982; and for recent work, Hanawalt 1986; Uitz 1990 (mainly on Germany and the Baltic); Goldberg 1995. The picture is brighter in the very late medieval/early modern period: Howell 1986; Wiesner 1994.
48 Bennett 1994 exemplifies the fruitful combining of Marxist with feminist insights. Cf. Bennett 1991. See also Rigby 1995, esp pp. 243–83.
49 Bloch's *Feudal Society* was not translated into English until 1961, twenty years after it appeared in France.

Historians are currently debating the extent and durability of women's participation in later medieval urban market economies. Fifteenth-century York has produced rich evidence for women's work opportunities in domestic service, with concomitant late marriage, more financial input and so an enhanced role in the marital relationship foreshadowing what used to be claimed as an early modern type of companionate marriage.[50] Florence presents a quite different aspect, with female domestic slavery, large age-differentials between wives and husbands, and extended family arrangements even relatively far down the social scale, typifying a Mediterranean model.[51] Did the two distinct marriage models persist despite economic and demographic change affecting all later medieval societies? Did cultural difference therefore prove remarkably resistant to wider/higher-level changes? Have historians underestimated the differential significance of class, patrilineal family structures being restricted in practice to life at the top?[52] It was elite urban families which had certain characteristics of 'clans': even if not landowning groups, sprawling networks of kin had great political and social importance.[53] Recent studies have observed that widowhood, a gender-specific category, was a status of enhanced vulnerability as much as of relative 'liberation': economic status made a crucial difference.[54] The Church probably did not inhibit widow-remarriage (d'Avray 1992: 76 n. 20). It did provide some protection for widows wishing to remain chastely unmarried, in house-convents or as anchoresses (Leyser 1995: ch. 8; and Cabre I Pairet 1989). Nevertheless, poor widows living alone were at the bottom of every social heap: such abject and isolated powerlessness must counterbalance tendencies to generalize, and idealize, evidence for medieval women's empowerment through the family. In the end, despite vast gains in knowledge and insights, much of the historiography has been less radical in jettisoning old interpretative models than its rhetoric might suggest. There have been many hopeful new developments. But there is a great deal more to hope for from the new generation and the twenty-first century, if boundaries can be broken and ghettoes destroyed.

---

50 Goldberg 1992, modifying the chronology of change suggested by Stone 1979.

51 Klapisch-Zuber 1985; cf. Hajnal 1965; Smith 1983, 1992; cf. now Biller 1992, showing the effects of this Mediterranean–northern European divide on the advice given in penitential handbooks.

52 Hughes (1978) herself stressed this, noting that the relationship between artisan spouses in later medieval Genoa was likely to resemble the companionate marriage sometimes thought typical of the early modern period: artisan couples worked as a team and shared an economic stake. At this level dowry was relatively insignificant. Cf. Hughes 1975.

53 Heers 1977. See Herlihy 1995: 210–14 on the size of the Florentine Bardi family in different contexts: the 'clan' was not the property owner, yet 120 adult males of the *famiglia* swore peace in 1342 with their traditional rivals the Buondelmonti. Similar observations about the contexts within which kinship operated, and the resultant different sizes and contours of the family, could be made for the early Middle Ages: see Leyser 1968, reprinted in Leyser 1982: ch. 7; Althoff 1990: ch. 2.

54 See Parisse 1993 and Nelson 1995 for further references. See also Chabot 1988, and C. Opitz's qualified answer, in *Histoire des Femmes*, pp. 323–8, to the question: were widows free?

REFERENCES

Affeldt, W. and Kuhn, A. (eds) (1986) *Frauen in der Geschichte VII*, Düsseldorf.
Affeldt, W., Nolte, C., Reiter, S. and Vorwerk, U. (eds) (1990) *Frauen im Frühmittelalter*, Frankfurt.
Althofk, G. (1990) *Verwandte, Freunde und Getreue*, Darmstadt.
Angenendt, A. (1984) *Kaiserherrschaft und Königstaufe*, Berlin and New York.
Archer, L. Fischler, S. and Wyke, M. (eds) (1994) *Women in Ancient Societies. An Illusion of the Night*, London.
Ariès, P. (1962) *Centuries of Childhood*, New York.
—— and Duby, G. (eds) (1987–8) *A History of Private Life*, tr. A. Goldhammer, I: *From Pagan Rome to Byzantium*; II: *From Feudal Europe to the Renaissance*, Cambridge, MA. and London. (First published as: *Histoire de la vie privée*, 5 vols, Paris.)
Ashley, K. and Sheingorn, P. (eds) (1990) *Interpreting Cultural Symbols: Saint Anne in Late Medieval Society*, London.
Atkinson, C. (1983) '"Precious balsam in a fragile glass": the ideology of virginity in the later Middle Ages', *Journal of Family History* 8: 131–43.
Aurell, M. (1985) 'La détérioration du statut de la femme aristocratique en Provence (Xe–XIIIe siècles)', *Le Moyen Âge*: 5–32.
—— (1995) *Les Noces du comte. Mariage et pouvoir en Catalogne (785–1213)*, Paris.
Baker, D. (ed.) (1977) *Medieval Women*, Oxford.
—— (ed.) (1993) *Queens, Regents and Potentates*, Dallas.
Baldwin, J. (1993) 'Consent and marital debt', in Laiou 1993.
—— (1991) 'Five discourses on desire: sexuality and gender in northern France around 1200', *Speculum* 66: 797–819.
Barron, C. and Sutton, A. (eds) (1994) *Medieval London Widows*, London.
Barthélemy, D. (1988) 'Kinship', in Ariès and Duby 1987–8: II, 85–155.
—— (1993) *La Société dans le comté de Vendôme de l'an mil au XIVe siècle*, Paris.
Bartlett, R. J. (1993) *The Making of Europe: Conquest, Colonization and Cultural Change, 950–1350*, Harmondsworth and Princeton.
Beer, F. (1992) *Women and Mystical Experience in the Middle Ages*, Woodbridge.
Bell, R. (1985) *Holy Anorexia*, London.
Bennett, J. (1991) 'Misogyny, popular culture, and Women's work', *History Workshop Journal* 31: 166–88.
Bennett, J. M. (1988) '"History that stands still": women's work in the European past', *Feminist Studies* 14: 209–83.
—— (1994) 'Medieval women, modern women. Across the great divide', in A.-L. Shapiro (ed.) *Feminists Revision History*, New Brunswick: 47–72.
Berend, N. (1994) 'Une invisible subversion: la disparition de l'oblation irrévocable des enfants', *Médiévales* 26: 123–36.
Berg, M. (1996) *Eileen Power*, London.
Berguière, A., Klapisch-Zuber, C., Segalen, M. and Zonabend, F. (eds) (1986) *Histoire de la famille*, 2 vols, Paris (English translation 1996).
Bessmerny, J. (1984) 'Les structures de la famille paysanne dans les villages de la Francia au IXe siècle', *Le Moyen Âge* 90: 165–93.
Biller, P. (1992) 'Marriage patterns and women's lives: a sketch of a pastoral geography', in P. J. F. Goldberg (ed.) *'Woman is a Worthy Wight': Woman in English Society c.1200–1500*, Stroud: 60–107.
Bloch, M., (1961) *Feudal Society*, tr. L. A. Manyon, London.
Bloch, R. Howard (1987) 'Medieval misogyny. Woman as riot', *Representations* 20: 1–24.
—— (1991) *Medieval Misogyny and the Invention of Western Romantic Love*, Chicago.
—— (1976) 'Mulieres sanctae', in Stuard 1976.

Bolton, B. (1977) '*Vitae matrum*: a further aspect of the '*Frauenfrage*', in Baker 1977.
Bonnassie, P. (1991) *From Slavery to Feudalism*, Cambridge.
Boswell, J. E. (1980) *Social Tolerance and Homosexuality*, Chicago.
—— (1988) *The Kindness of Strangers. The Abandonment of Children in Western Europe*, Harmondsworth.
Bouchard, C. (1981) 'Consanguinity and noble marriages in the tenth and eleventh centuries', *Speculum* 56: 268–87.
—— (1987) *Sword, Miter and Cloister: Nobility and the Church in Burgundy (980–1198)*, Ithaca.
Brand, P., Hyams, P. and Faith, R. (eds) (1983) 'Seigneurial control of women's marriage', *Past and Present* 99: 123–48.
Braun, L. (1901) *Die Frauenfrage: Ihre geschichtliche Entwicklung*, Leipzig; repr. Berlin and Bonn, 1979.
Brooke, C. N. L. (1991) *The Medieval Idea of Marriage*, Oxford.
Brown, P. R. L. (1988) *The Body and Society. Men, Women and Sexual Renunciation in Early Christianity*, New York.
Brundage, J. (1975) 'Concubinage and marriage in medieval canon law', *Journal of Medieval History* 1: 1–17.
—— (1977) *Law, Sex and Christian Society in Medieval Europe*, Chicago.
Buc, P. (1995) 'Italian hussies and German matrons. Liutprand of Cremona on dynastic legitimacy', *Frühmittelalterliche Studien* 29: 207–26.
Bynum, C. Walker (1982) *Jesus as Mother: Studies in the Spirituality of the High Middle Ages*, Berkeley and Los Angeles.
—— (1984) 'Women's stories, women's sanctity', in R. Moore and S. Reynolds (eds) *Anthropology and the Study of Religion*, Chicago. (Reprinted in Bynum 1991: 27–51.)
—— (1987) *Holy Feast and Holy Fast: the Religious Significance of Food to Medieval Women*, Berkeley and Los Angeles.
—— (1991) *Fragmentation and Redemption*, New York.
—— Harrell, S. and Richman, P. (eds) (1986) *Gender and Religion: On the Complexity of Symbols*, Boston.
Cameron, A. (1994) 'Early Christianity and the discourse of female desire', in Archer *et al.* 1994.
—— and Kuhrt, A. (eds) (1983) *Images of Women in Antiquity*, London.
Camille, M. (1944) 'The image and the self: unwriting late medieval bodies', in Kay and Rubin 1994.
Cazelles, B. (1991) *The Lady as Saint: A Collection of French Hagiographic Romances*, Pennsylvania.
Chabot, I. (1988) 'Poverty and the widow in later medieval Florence', *Continuity and Change* 3: 291–311.
Clarke, A. (1992) *The Working Life of Women in Seventeenth-century England*, ed. A. L. Erickson, London.
Clarke, E. (1987) 'The decision to marry in thirteenth- and early fourteenth-century Norfolk', *Mediaeval Studies* 49: 496–516.
Clark, E. A. (1983) *Women in the Early Church*, Wilmington.
—— (1986) *Ascetic Piety and Women's Faith*, Wilmington.
Clover, C. J. (1993) 'Regardless of sex: women and power in early northern Europe', in N. Partner (ed.) *Studying Medieval Women, Sex, Gender, Feminism*, Cambridge, Mass.
Coakley, J. (1991) 'Gender and the authority of friars: the significance of holy women for thirteenth-century Franciscans and Dominicans', *Church History* 60: 445–60.
Coleman, E. (1971/2) 'Medieval marriage characteristics. A neglected factor in the history of medieval serfdom', *Journal of Interdisciplinary History* 2: 205–19.
—— (1976) 'Infanticide in the early Middle Ages', in Stuard 1976.

—— (1977) 'People and property: the structure of a medieval seigneury', *Journal of European Economic History* 6: 675–702.

Cooper, K. (1992) 'Insinuations of womanly influence: an aspect of the Christianisation of the Roman aristocracy', *Journal of Roman Studies* 82: 150–64.

Corbet, P. (1986) *Les Saints ottoniens*, Sigmaringen.

Crump, A. and Jacob, E. (1926) *The Legacy of the Middle Ages*, Oxford.

Davids, A. (ed.) (1995) *The Empress Theophano*, Cambridge.

—— (1982) *Wales in the Early Middle Ages*, Leicester.

Davies, W. (1983) 'Celtic women in the early Middle Ages', in Cameron and Kuhrt 1983.

—— (1988) *Small Worlds*, London.

—— (1996) 'On servile status in the early Middle Ages', in M. L. Bush (ed.), *Serfdom and Slavery. Studies in Legal Bondage*, London: 225–46.

Davis, N. Z. (1992) 'Women and the world of the *Annales*', *History Workshop Journal* 33: 121–37.

d'Avray, D. L. (1992) 'Peter Damian, consanguinity and church property', in L. Smith and B. Ward (eds) *Intellectual Life in the Middle Ages. Essays presented to Margaret Gibson*, London: 71–80.

De Jong, M. (1996) *In Samuel's Image. Child Oblation in the Early Middle Ages*, Amsterdam.

Devroey, J.-P. (1993) *Études sur le grand domaine carolingien*, London.

Dinzelbacher, P. and Bauer, D. R. (eds) (1988) *Religiöse Frauenbewegung und mystische Frömmigkeit im Mittelalter*, Cologne and Vienna.

Drew, K. F. (1988) *Law and Society in Early Medieval Europe*, London.

Dronke, P. (1984) *Medieval Women Writers*, Cambridge.

Duby, G. (1965) *Rural Economy and Country Life in the Early Medieval West*, London.

—— (1977) *The Chivalrous Society*, London.

—— (1978) *Medieval Marriage, Two Models from Twelfth-century France*, Baltimore.

—— (1983) *The Knight, the Lady and the Priest*, London.

Duby, G. and Le Goff, J. (1977) *Famille et parenté dans l'occident médiévale*, Rome.

Duby, G. and Perrot, M. (eds) (1991) *Histoire des femmes en occident*, 5 vols, Paris.

Duggan, A. (ed.) (1997) *Queens and Queenship in Medieval Europe*, Woodbridge.

Elliott, D. (1993) *Spiritual Marriage, Sexual Abstinence in Medieval Wedlock*, Princeton.

Elshtain, J. (1981) *Public Man, Private Woman: Women in Social and Political Thought*, Princeton.

Ennen, E. (1989) *Women in the Middle Ages*, Oxford.

Euw, A. von, and Schreiner, P. (eds) (1991) *Kaiserin Theophanu*, Cologne.

Farmer, S. (1986) 'Persuasive voices. Clerical images of medieval wives', *Speculum* 61: 517–43.

Fell, C. (1984) *Women in Anglo-Saxon England*, London.

Fentress, J. and Wickham, C. (1992) *Social Memory*, Oxford.

Flandrin, J. (1979) *Families in Former Times*, Cambridge.

—— (1983) *Un temps pour s'embrasser. Aux origines de la moralité sexuelle occidentale (VIe–Xe siècles)*, Paris.

Fouracre, P. and Gerberding, R. (1996) *Later in Merovingian France*, Manchester.

Foxhall, L. (1994) 'Pandora unbound. A feminist critique of Foucault's *History of Sexuality*', in A. Cornwall and N. Lindisfarne (eds) *Dislocating Masculinity: Comparative Ethnographies*, London.

Fradenberg, L. (ed.) (1991) *Women and Sovereignty*, Edinburgh.

Geary, P. (1994) *Phantoms of Remembrance. Memory and Oblivion at the End of the First Millennium*, Princeton.

Gies, F. and Gies, J. (1989) *Marriage and the Family in the Middle Ages*, London.

Goetz, H. W. (ed.) (1991) *Weibliche Lebensgestaltung im frühen Mittelalter*, Cologne and Vienna.

—— (1993a) *Life in the Middle Ages from the 7th to the 13th Century*, tr. A. Wimmer, Notre Dame, IL. (First published as: *Leben im Mittelalter vom 7. bis zum 13. Jhdt.*, Munich, 1986.)

—— (1993b) 'Serfdom and the beginnings of a "seigneurial system" in the Carolingian period', *Early Medieval Europe* 2: 20–51.

Goldberg, P. J. P. (1992) *Women, Work and Life-cycle in a Medieval Economy; Women in York and Yorkshire. c.1300–1520*, Oxford.

—— (1995) *Women in England c.1275–1525*, Manchester.

Goody, J. (ed.) (1958) *The Developmental Cycle in Domestic Groups*, Cambridge.

Goody, J. (1968) *Succession to High Office*, Cambridge.

—— (1972) 'The evolution of the family', in P. Laslett (ed.) *Household and Family in Past Time*, Cambridge.

—— (1976) 'Inheritance, property and women: some comparative considerations', in J. Goody, J. Thirsk and E. P. Thompson (eds) *Family and Inheritance. Rural Society in Western Europe 1200–1800*, Cambridge: 10–36.

—— (1983) *The Development of the Family and Marriage in Europe*, Cambridge.

Gravdal, K. (1991) *Ravishing Maidens. Writing Rape in Medieval French Literature and Law*, Philadelphia.

Green, M. (1990) 'Female sexuality in the Medieval West', *Trends in History* 4: 127–58.

Grimal, P. (ed.) (1966) *Histoire mondiale de la femme*, Paris.

Gröbner, V. (1995) 'Losing face, saving face: noses and honour in the late medieval town', *History Workshop Journal* 40: 1–15.

Hadley, D. (ed.) (1997) *Images of Masculinity in the Middle Ages*, London.

Hajnal, J. (1965) 'European marriage patterns in perspective', in D. V. Glass and D. E. C. Eversley (eds) *Population in History*, London: 101–46.

Haldon, J. (1986) 'Everyday life in Byzantium: some problems of approach', *Byzantine and Modern Greek Studies* 10: 51–72.

Halsall, G. (1996) 'Female status and power in early Merovingian central Austrasia: the burial evidence' *Early Medieval Europe* 5: 1–24.

Hamerow, H. (1994) 'The archaeology of rural settlement in early medieval Europe', *Early Medieval Europe* 3: 167–79.

Hammer, C. (1983) 'Family and *familia* in early medieval Bavaria', in R. Wall (ed.) *Family Forms in Historic Europe*, Cambridge.

—— (1995) 'A slave marriage ceremony from early medieval Germany', *Slavery and Abolition* 16: 243–9.

Hanawalt, B. (ed.) (1986) *Women and Work in Pre-industrial Europe*, Bloomington.

Head, T. and Landes, R. (eds) (1992) *The Peace of God. Social Violence and Religious Response in France around the Year 1000*, Ithaca.

Heers, J. (1977) *Family Clans in the Middle Ages. A Study of Political and Social Structures in Urban Areas*, New York.

Heffernan, T. (1988) *Sacred Biography*, Oxford.

Herlihy, D. (1985) *Medieval Households*, Cambridge, Mass. and London.

—— (1990) *Opera Mulieria: Women and Work in Medieval Europe*, New York.

—— (1995) *Women, Family and Society in Medieval Europe*, ed. A. Molho, Providence, RI, and Oxford.

Howell, M. C. (1986) *Women, Production and Patriarchy in Late Medieval Cities*, Chicago and London.

Hughes, D. O. (1975) 'Domestic ideals and social behaviour: evidence from medieval Genoa', in C. E. Rosenberg (ed.) *The Family in History*, Philadelphia.

—— (1978) 'From brideprice to dowry in Mediterranean Europe', *Journal of Family History* 3, 262–96.

James, E. (1989) 'Burial and status in the early medieval West', *Transactions of the Royal Historical Society* 39: 23–40.

Jenkins, D. and Owen, M. E. (eds) (1980) *The Welsh Law of Women*, Cardiff.

Jochens, J. (1930) 'The Church and sexuality in medieval Iceland', *Journal of Medieval History* 6: 377–92.

—— (1986) 'The medieval Icelandic heroine: fact or fiction?', *Viator* 17: 35–50.

Karras, R. M. (1996) *Commen Women. Prostitution and Sexuality in Medieval England*, Oxford.

Kay, S. (1994) 'Woman's body of knowledge: epistemology and misogyny in the Romance of the Rose', in Kay and Rubin 1994.

Kay, S. and Rubin, M. (eds) (1994) *Framing Medieval Bodies*, Manchester.

Kelly, J. (1984) 'Did women have a Renaissance?', in *Women, History and Theory*, Chicago.

Kieckhefer, R. (1984) *Unquiet Souls. Fourteenth-century Saints and their Religious Milieu*, Chicago.

King, P. D. (1972) *Law and Society in the Visigothic Kingdom*, Cambridge.

Klapisch-Zuber, C. (1996) *Women, Family and Ritual in Renaissance Italy*, Chicago.

Kroemer, B. (1982) 'Von Kauffrauen, Beamtinnen, Ärztinnen, Erwerbstätige Frauen in deutschen mittelalterlichen Städten', in A. Kühn (ed.) *Frauen in der Geschichte*, Düsseldorf.

Kuchenbuch, L. (1978) *Bäuerliche Gesellschaft und Klosterherrschaft im 9. Jhdt, Studien zur Sozialstruktur der* familia *der Abtei Prüm*, Wiesbaden.

Laiou, A. E. (ed.) (1993) *Consent and Coercion to Sex and Marriage in Ancient and Medieval Societies*, Washington.

Laqueur, T. (1990) *Making Sex: Body and Gender from the Greeks to Freud*, Cambridge, MA.

Laslett, P. and Wall, R. (eds) (1972) *Household and Family in Past Times*, Cambridge.

Lees, C. A. (1994) *Medieval Masculinities: Regarding Men in the Middle Ages*, Minneapolis.

Le Jan, R. (1995) *Famille et pouvoir dans le monde franc (VII–Xe siècle)*, Paris.

Leyser, K. J. (1968) 'The German aristocracy from the ninth to the early twelfth century', *Past and Present* 41: 25–53.

—— (1979) *Rule and Conflict in an Early Medieval Society*, London.

—— (1982) *Medieval Germany and its Neighbours 900–1250*, London.

Leyser, H. (1995) *Medieval Women, A Social History of Women in England 450–1500*, London.

L'Hermite-Leclercq, P. (1991) 'L'ordre féodale', in Duby and Perrot 1991: 217–60.

Lifshitz, F. (1988) 'Les femmes missionaires: l'exemple de la Gaule franque', *Revue d'Histoire Ecclésiastique* 83: 5–33.

Lynch, J. H. (1976) *Simoniacal Entry into Religious Life*, Columbus, OH.

—— (1986) *Godparents and Kinship in Early Medieval Europe*, Princeton.

McNamara, J. L. A. and Wemple, S. (1988) 'The power of women through the family in medieval Europe, 500–1100', in M. Erler and M. Kowaleski (eds) *Women and Power in the Middle Ages*, Athens, GA.

Mitterauer, M. and Sieder, R. (1982) *The European Family: Patriarchy to Partnership from the Middle Ages to the Present*, Chicago.

Moore, R. I. (1985) *The Origins of European Dissent*, Oxford.

—— (1987) *The Formation of a Persecuting Society*, Oxford.

Moore, H. L. (1988) *Feminism and Anthropology*, Oxford.

Morris, R. (1995) *Monks and Laymen in Byzantium, 843–1118*, Cambridge.

Murray, A. C. (1983) *Germanic Kinship Structure. Studies in Law and Society*, Toronto.

Neel, C. (tr.) (1991) *Handbook for William: A Carolingian Woman's Counsel for her Son, by Dhuoda*, London.

Nelson, J. L. (1977) 'Queens as Jezebels', in Baker 1977.

174

—— (1989) 'The problematic in the private', *Social History* 15: 355–64.

—— (1993) 'Parents, children and the Church in the earlier Middle Ages', *Studies in Church History* 32: 81–114.

—— (1995) 'The wary widow', in W. Davies and P. Fouracre (eds) *Property and Power in the Early Middle Ages*, Cambridge.

Newman, B. (1995) *From Virile Woman to Woman Christ. Studies in Medieval Religion and Literature*, Philadelphia.

Opitz, C. (1990) 'Von Kinderwunsch und Kindermord. Mütterschaft und Mütterlichkeit vom 13. bis zum 15. Jhdt.', in Opitz, *Evatöchter und Braute Christi. Weiblicher Lebenszusammenhang und Frauenkultur im Mittelalter*, Weinheim.

Otis, L. (1985) *Prostitution in Medieval Society. The History of an Urban Institution in Languedoc*, Chicago.

Pairet, M. Cabre I (1989) '*Deodicatae y Deovotae*. La regulaçion de la religiosidad femenina en los condados catalanes, siglos IX–XI', in A. Muñoz Fernández (ed.) *Las mujeres en el cristianismo medieval*, Madrid.

Parisse, M. (ed.) (1993) *Veuves et veuvage dans le haut moyen âge*, Paris.

Parsons, J. C. (ed.) (1993) *Medieval Queenship*, New York.

Parsons, J. C. (1995) *Eleanor of Castile*, New York.

Partner, N. (1993) 'No sex, no gender', in Partner (ed.) *Studying Medieval Women*, Cambridge MA: 117–41.

Payer, P. J. (1984a) 'The humanism of the penitentials', *Medieval Studies* 46: 340–54.

—— (1984b) *Sex and the Penitentials: The Development of a Sexual Code, 550–1150*, Toronto.

Power, E. (1963) *Medieval People*, London. (1st edn: London, 1924.)

Razi, Z. (1979) 'The Toronto School's reconstitution of medieval peasant society: a critical view', *Past and Present* 85: 141–57.

—— (1993) 'The myth of the immutable English family', *Past and Present* 140: 3–44.

Reuter, T. (1976) *The Medieval Nobility*, London and Amsterdam.

Reynolds, P. L. (1994) *Marriage in the Western Church: The Christianisation of Marriage during the Patristic and Medieval Periods*, Leiden, New York and Cologne.

Rigby, S. (1995) *English Society in the Later Middle Ages: Clans, Status and Gender*, Manchester.

Riley-Smith, J. (1992) 'Family traditions in the Second Crusade', in M. Gervers (ed.) *The Second Crusade and the Cistercians*, New York.

—— (1997) *Western Arms-bearers, their Families, and Crusading to Jerusalem*, Cambridge.

Ring, R. (1979) 'Early medieval peasant households in central Italy', *Journal of Family History* 2: 2–25.

Roper, L. (1989) *The Holy Household*, Oxford.

Rosenthal, J. (1990) *Medieval Women and the Sources for Medieval History*, Athens, Ga.

Ross, M. C. (1985) 'Concubinage in Anglo-Saxon England', *Past and Present* 108: 3–34.

Rossiaud, J. (1978) 'Prostitution, youth and society in the towns of south-eastern France in the fifteenth century', in R. Forster and O. Ranum (eds) *Deviants and the Abandoned in French Society*, Baltimore.

—— (1987) *La Prostitution médiévale*, Paris.

Rouche, M. (1987) 'The early Middle Ages in the West', in Ariès and Duby 1987–8: I.

Rubin, M. (1992) 'The culture of Europe in the later Middle Ages', *History Workshop Journal* 33: 162–75.

—— (1994) 'The person in the form', in Kay and Rubin 1994.

Salisbury, J. E. (1990) *Medieval Sexuality: a Research Guide*, New York and London.

Sawyer, B. (1989) 'Women as land-holders and alienators of property', in K. Glente and L. Winther-Jensen (eds) *Female Power in the Middle Ages*, Copenhagen.

—— (1990) 'Women as bridge-builders', in I. Wood and N. Lund (eds) *People and Places in Northern Europe, Essays in Honour of P. H. Sawyer*, Woodbridge.

—— and Sawyer, P. (1993) *Medieval Scandinavia*, Minneapolis and London.

Schmitz, G. (1982) 'Schuld und Strafe. Eine unbekannte Stellungnahme des Rathramnus von Corbie zur Kindestötung', *Deutsches Archiv* 38: 363–87.

Scott, J. (1988) *Gender and the Politics of History*, New York and London.

Searle, E. (1979) 'Seigneurial control of women's marriage: the antecedents and function of merchet in England', *Past and Present* 82: 3–43.

Simons, W. (1994) 'Reading a saint's body', in Kay and Rubin 1994.

Smith, J. M. H. (1992) *Province and Empire. Brittany and the Carolingians*, Cambridge.

—— (1995) 'The problem of female sanctity in Carolingian Europe *c.*750–920', *Past and Present* 146: 3–37.

—— (1997) 'Gender and ideology in the earlier Middle Ages', *Studies in Church History* 34.

Smith, R. (1983) 'Hypothèses sur la nuptualité en Angleterre aux XIIIe-XIVe siècles', *Annales ESC* 38: 107–36.

Stafford, P. (1977) 'Sons and mothers: family politics in the early Middle Ages', in Baker 1977.

—— (1989) 'Women in Domesday', in *Medieval Women in Southern England*, Reading Medieval Studies 15, Reading.

—— (1995) 'Women and the Norman Conquest', *Transactions of the Royal Historical Society* 6th ser., 4: 221–50.

—— (1997) '*La mutation familiale*: a suitable case for caution', in J. Hill and M. Swann (eds) *The Community, the Family and the Saint. Patterns of Power in Early Medieval Europe*, Leeds.

Stone, L. (1979) *The Family, Sex and Marriage in England, 1500–1800*, Cambridge.

Strathern, M. (1972) *Women in Between: Female roles in a Male World*, London.

Stuard, S. M. (1995) 'Ancillary evidence for the decline of medieval slavery', *Past and Present* 149: 3–28.

—— (ed.) (1976) *Women in Medieval Society*, Philadelphia.

Toubert, P. (1977) 'La théorie du mariage chez les moralistes carolingiens', in *Il matrimonio nella società altomedievale. Settimane di Spoleto* 14: 233–82.

Trexler, R. (1981) 'La prostitution florentine', *Annales ESC* 26: 983–1015.

Uitz, E. (1990) *Women in the Medieval Town*, London.

Vauchez, A. (1987) *Les Laïcs au moyen âge: pratiques et expériences réligieuses*, Paris.

Wall, R. (ed.) (1983) *Family Forms in Historic Europe*, Cambridge.

Warner, M. (1976) *Alone of all her Sex. The Myth and the Cult of the Virgin Mary*, London.

Weinberger, S. (1973) 'Peasant households in Provence *c.*800–1100', *Speculum* 48: 247–57.

Wemple, S. F. (1981) *Women in Frankish Society: Marriage and the Cloister. 500–900*, Philadelphia.

White, S. (1993) 'Stratégie rhétorique dans la *conventio* de Hugues de Lusignan', in *Mélanges offerts à G. Duby*, Aix-en-Provence.

Wickham, C. (1994) *Land and Power. Studies in Italian and European Social History, 400–1200*, London.

Wiesner, M. (1994) *Women and Gender in Early Modern Europe*, Cambridge.

Wittern, S. (1994) *Frauen, Heiligkeit und Macht*, Stuttgart.

Wormald, P. (1977) '*Lex scripta* and *verbum regis*: legislation and Germanic kingship from Euric to Cnut' in P. Sawyer and I. Wood (eds) *Early Medieval Kingship*, Leeds.

Wunder, H. (1987) 'Frauen in der Gesellschaft Mitteleuropas im späten Mittelalter und in der frühen Neuzeit (15.–18. Jhdt.)', in H. Valentinitsch (ed.) *Hexen und Zauberer. Die grosse Verfolgung: ein europäisches Phänomen in der Steiermark*, Graz and Vienna.

Ziolkowski, J. M. (1989) *Jezebel, A Norman Latin Poem of the Early Eleventh Century*, Los Angeles.

10

THE MEDIEVAL NOBILITY IN TWENTIETH-CENTURY HISTORIOGRAPHY[1]

Timothy Reuter

At the international congress of historical sciences held at Vienna in 1965, one of the Large Themes was the ruling classes (*classes dirigeantes*) from antiquity to modern times. For the Middle Ages, papers were given by Gerd Tellenbach and K. B. McFarlane.[2] It was characteristic of post-war medieval historians that the papers both summed up the state of play and made programmatic reference to the future. Similar surveys, accompanied either by criticisms of current orthodoxies or by an agenda for future investigations, were produced in the 1950s and 1960s by Georges Duby,[3] Léopold Genicot,[4] Karl Leyser (1968), Karl Schmid (1957; 1959), Giovanni Tabacco (1960; 1966; see also Tabacco 1973), among others. As so often, by the time scholars have begun to set out programmes for future

1 I should like to thank Chris Wickham for incisive and helpful comments on an earlier draft. In spite of the general title, attention will be concentrated on the core regions of Europe in the early and high Middle Ages, because the methodological and historiographical problems thrown up have been most intensively discussed for this region and period, especially by German historians, whose work will be cited extensively in what follows. The temporal and geographical peripheries will be sketched more lightly.

    The accompanying references offer an eclectic rather than an exhaustive bibliography. It includes in particular works important for the historiographical development, and survey articles, especially those in English. These can be turned to for more substantial bibliographies. Reference may be made at this point to a number of useful summary articles in encyclopaedic works: Scheyhing 1964; Kuhn *et al.* 1973; Conze *et al.* 1978 (covering the entire development from early antiquity to the twentieth century); Werner *et al.* 1977–80; Evergates 1987.

2 Tellenbach 1965a and 1965b, McFarlane, 1965. Three other participants withdrew at a late stage, according to Tellenbach (1965a: 317). For the flavour of contemporary debates it is also important to consult the interventions in *Actes*, vol. 5, Vienna, Verlag Ferdinand Berger & Söhne, 1968, pp. 155–66.

3 Duby 1962 conveniently available in English with other relevant essays of his from the 1960s and early 1970s as *The Chivalrous Society* (1977).

4 Genicot 1962a; 1962b. See more recently Genicot 1975.

research it is a fair bet that enough work has already been done for the topic's light and shade to be perceptible. This was certainly true here: what had once appeared to be an antiquarian sidetrack, whose subject matter represented a brake on more progressive features of medieval life, now seemed all-pervasive and highly significant. Even areas of life formerly perceived as set apart from or opposed to the nobility – monasticism, for example, or early urban elites – revealed their aristocratic streak.[5] The subject also seemed to offer a bridge between different approaches to history: the history of *mentalités* and that of political power. The realization that nobility is a matter of consciousness as well as of being has been one of the most valuable insights of recent scholarship: nobility is not just an objective state but a state of mind, of *Selbstverständnis* ('self-understanding', 'self-awareness'), a term which denotes the view held by a person or group of themselves (by contrast with the view of others or of the historian who perceives them).

Most of the surveys mentioned above dealt primarily with the period from the ninth to the mid-twelfth centuries, and this has certainly attracted the most attention and revealed the most uncertainties; but the nobilities of the time of the barbarian invasions or in the early Carolingian era have seemed almost equally in need of study. As will be seen, the nobilities of the later Middle Ages present rather different problems, and the following survey will concentrate largely on the period before 1250. It will be helpful to begin by examining the concepts and definitions of nobility available and the ways in which these fit into more general frameworks of interpretation, and then to look at some of the difficulties created by the sources, before surveying the historiography.

In virtually all societies visible to the medieval historian's naked eye there is a ruling group (*Oberschicht*, *ceti dirigenti*, *classe dirigeant*), distinguished from the rest of society by its greatly superior economic resources and its ability to translate these into political power. Concomitant with this are a different lifestyle, mentality and status.[6] 'Ruling group' or 'class' ought to be a sufficiently neutral term, but it evidently carries too many overtones of 'class struggle' for historians to feel comfortable with it, and it also says nothing about how the members of the group acquired their membership. Western European languages offer two other terms – nobility and aristocracy – which have been more generally

---

5   One of the ways in which the seeming contrast between an aristocratic and a monastic outlook was being reduced was through the more intensive study of significant works of medieval historiography, many of which were produced in a monastic environment (hence the phrase 'monkish chronicles' common in nineteenth-century historiography) but have turned out on renewed inspection to reflect their authors' social origins just as strongly: for a classic study along these lines see Beumann 1950.

6   The only evident exception is medieval Iceland, and here it is far from clear whether the low degree of social stratification suggested by the sagas is fact or fiction. Other acephalous societies like pre-Carolingian Saxony and (probably) the Elbe Slavs were by no means egalitarian because acephalous. See Wickham 1992: 238–41, for discussion and further references.

used.[7] The terms *ought* to be used to distinguish between two different things. A noble is, strictly speaking, a person whose (normally privileged) status is legally defined, which means that one can be a noble without exercising power. An aristocrat, by contrast, is someone who exercises power as a result of being well-born in a socially rather than legally defined sense: this implies the inheritance of wealth, power and social (but not legal) status, and it does not preclude some degree of social mobility. In practice the two terms have rarely been distinguished in this way; they have been felt to overlap sufficiently to be interchangeable, and when they are found close together this is all too often mere stylistic variation. In so far as a distinction *is* observed, it is more one between a nobility as a set of individuals whose status is legally defined and an aristocracy as that same set perceived as a sociologically defined group. In what follows the two terms will also be used as loosely interchangeable, but with the slight distinction just mentioned.

The reason for the terminological and definitional imprecision is simple: in practice, any distinction between a nobility and an aristocracy is hardly sustainable for the period before about 1250, nor is it present in the terminology used by the sources.[8] The position later was somewhat clearer: at least in principle a firm legal distinction evolved between the English peerage and everybody else,[9] while elsewhere also the nobility was legally defined as to both membership and status.[10] The ruling groups of the early and high Middle Ages were not. Some historians have wished to maintain the late medieval distinction and so to define early medieval elites as aristocracies rather than nobilities.[11] Others have turned the distinction on its head: once status is defined by law, then a nobility is no longer as noble as it was. Definitions, like sumptuary legislation or the 'creation' of nobles, are a sign that nobility is no longer self-evident; legislation must protect the truly noble against *de facto* usurpations of their rights and standing. This has been a particularly convenient line of argument for those who have wished to talk of a nobility for an era or region where legal texts mention no such thing. Thus the absence of any special *Wergeld* for 'crimes' against nobles in *Lex Salica*, it has been argued, shows

---

7   French: *noblesse, aristocratie*; German: *Adel, Aristokratie*; Italian: *nobilità, aristocrazia*; Spanish: *nobleza, aristocracia*. On the distinction see the articles cited above, n. 1; Keeler 1968, Powys 1984 are also conceptually helpful. For an example of the kind of imprecision which can all too easily arise see Nicholas 1992: 248: 'A nobility is a group of persons in which membership is transmitted by fixed criteria, most often descent, while an aristocracy is less rigidly defined. Early medieval Europe had both a nobility and an aristocracy. Since no biologically closed group can perpetuate itself, the nobility had to be replenished by intermarrying with aristocratic families.'
8   There is no precise equivalent of 'aristocracy' in the sources of the early and high Middle Ages; when these do not refer directly to *nobiles* they use terms like *primores, optimates, maiores natu, principes,* etc., best translated as 'leading men'.
9   McFarlane 1973, esp. pp. 122–5. See now the useful syntheses by Given-Wilson 1987, esp. pp. 62–6 and Crouch 1992, esp. pp. 104–5.
10   The classic text for Germany is Schulte 1922; cf. Scheyhing 1964–71: 48–50.
11   Bloch 1961: 283–92, 320–31, is the classic statement of this view.

not that there was no nobility in sixth-century Francia but rather that it was so powerful that it could refuse to admit a fixed tariff for offences against its members (Wenskus 1959). Late medieval legal definitions certainly often went hand in hand with the ruler's ability to create a noble, an ability whose very existence has been denied for the period 600–1100 (see Thegan, *Vita Hludowici imperatoris*, ed. Tremp 1995: 232; and n. 14 below).

The idea that a nobility can be said to have existed even when a legal definition for it was lacking can thus be defended, but this has not made the historian's task easier, for the undefinable still needs to be defined in some other way. Studies of words have turned out to be less helpful than might a priori have been expected. Etymology in particular is a poor historian: the roots of *Adel-/Edel*-words in the Germanic languages may suggest that the term was originally cognate with property, but that hardly shows much about the connotations of the words at the time when they were used in the sources we have to deal with, nor about their links with the words we find in Latin sources.[12] Synchronic surveys of usage have been more helpful: we are now reasonably well informed about the use of *nobilis* and its cognates in the Carolingian and post-Carolingian eras (Goetz 1983; see also Genicot 1962b). However, this information reveals a wide spectrum of meaning for the word and hence reinforces caution. It is of little help in the interpretation of critical passages, where the danger remains that historians will simply hear the echoes of their own voices. Two frequently cited passages from Carolingian texts illustrate this. The first is an answer given by Charlemagne (or in his name) to a royal official enquiring about the status of the children of a marriage between a free man and an unfree woman: it says simply 'there is nothing other than free or slave'. This has been taken to show Charlemagne's 'policy' (by implication, one of non-recognition) towards the nobility, even to prove that there was no such thing as a nobility in Carolingian Francia. Taken in context, however, it means simply that everyone must be either free or unfree – *tertium non datur* – and thus carries no implications about possible distinctions among the free.[13] The other passage is an accusation allegedly flung at Archbishop Ebo of Reims in 833: 'The emperor made you a free man, but not a noble, for that is impossible.' Ebo had risen from being an imperial serf to high ecclesiastical office, having been manumitted by Louis the Pious on the way, whom he had now betrayed (Thegan, *Vita Hludowici imperatoris*, c. 44, ed. Tremp 1995: 232). The charge can be – and has been – read in a number of different ways: as implying that the emperor could not, as a question of right and law, ennoble; as implying that the emperor could not ennoble at all, for much the same reason that he could not make black white; or as

---

12 Kuhn *et al.* 1973: 59–60; Scheyhing 1964: 71: cols 41–2; Green 1965. For the Anglo-Saxon terminology see Loyn 1992, summarizing his earlier articles on the topic (listed ibid. 392).
13 'non est amplius nisi liber aut servus', *Responsa misso cuidam data*, Monumenta Germaniae Historica, Capitularia regum Francorum, ed. Alfred Boretius and Viktor Krause, Hanover, 1893, vol. 1, no. 58, ch. 1, p. 158. For recent discussion see Müller-Mertens 1963: 60; Tellenbach 1988: 861 n. 10 [article first published 1966]; Fleckenstein 1981: 73.

implying that Ebo in particular was so ignoble in spirit that no one could have ennobled him.[14]

The link between birth, privilege and power given by nobility must be considered together with the paradigm of medieval politics inherited from nineteenth-century constitutional historians. Particularly important here was the nature of *royal* power. Even in recent writing the king has often been identified with the state; it might be conceded that his powers were ultimately rooted in those of the 'people', but this is conceived of as an amorphous proto-democratic group of property-owners rather than a small number of aristocrats, while the king's authority is seen as the source of all other legitimate 'public' power.[15] Nobles, found both exercising extensive 'public' power and in opposition to the king, were thus almost automatically illegitimated. They might be perceived either as 'feudal', hence opposed to modernization and progress, or as 'particularist', hence opposed to the king who was seen as the ancestor of the modern state (in Wilhelmine Germany indeed as something more than that) and so once more against modernization and progress because hindering the formation of the nation. Either way they were abusing power which was merely theirs in trust.[16]

The distinction between 'public' and 'private' power raises a much wider question, that of the concept of power with which medieval historians have operated and still operate. It is clear that medieval elites, however defined, exercised social, economic and political power over the rest of the population; but the relationship between these kinds of power and the power they held as members of the political community remains ill-defined, in spite of much discussion. It is by no means clear that power was a single currency, which merely came in different-sized banknotes. Marxist analyses of feudalism have conceived of it as a complete social nexus in which the possession of status and resources gave the ability to wield coercive power and hence turn political power into economic power (surplus extraction without

---

14 For the first two possibilities see Werner 1978: 180 with n. 85; Bullough 1970: 76 with n. 3. See now Airlie 1995. The third possible interpretation should be seen in the context of the medieval distinction between the nobility of the flesh and the true nobility of virtue, which has not yet received a comprehensive survey.

15 Böckenförde 1961; Keller 1986: 13–55, 510–11, has thoughtful further comments and rich bibliography. I know of no comparable study for French or English historiography, though for England there is a running fire of sarcastic comment in this direction to be found in Richardson and Sayles 1963 and 1966.

16 Critchley 1978, esp. pp. 159–91, is helpful on the notion of the aristocracy as 'feudal' and therefore 'unprogressive' and 'reactionary'. Kern 1954 (the edition of choice because of its rich annotation, though the text is unchanged from that of the first edition of 1914; there is an abridged English translation of the first edition under the rather misleading title *Kingship and Law in the Middle Ages*, by S. B. Chrimes, Oxford, Basil Blackwell, 1939) is not only a remarkable book in its own right but gives a valuable historiographical insight into 'two worlds, one dead, one struggling to be born'. In retrospect his use of the term 'right of resistance' has been misleading, since it was rarely claimed, let alone claimed successfully, as a legally enforceable right, and not at all before the thirteenth century; 'legitimacy of resistance' would have been better and would still have shown that many 'rebels' were not in their own eyes acting wrongly.

ownership of the means of production). This has been seen on this side of what used to be the Iron Curtain as thoroughly misleading. 'Feudalism', conceived of as a form of distribution of political, military and administrative power, has been sharply distinguished from private lordship over peasants or dependants ('seigneurialism') and it has generally been denied, often as a knee-jerk response, that there is any necessary link between the two, and more radically, that the former existed at all (Brown 1974; Reynolds 1994). Following the end of the Cold War, the issue appears to be being taken up again, this time with fewer preconceptions and ideological debts. The discussion could profitably be accompanied by a more explicit consideration of the notions of power with which historians work.[17]

The most articulate attacks on the view of noble 'public' power as essentially usurped and abused were made in German-speaking historiography in the first half of the century. These in effect reversed the traditional view, arguing that noble power was primary, innate, 'autochthonous' (inborn), hence prior to and so at least as legitimate as royal power.[18] Although these views were often couched in a form now termed *zeitbedingt* ('determined by its period', meaning suffused with Nazi or reactionary ideology and phraseology), the responses underlying the theories cannot have been merely *zeitbedingt* in this sense, for in French and English historiography there was also a move away from the traditional preconceptions of constitutional history – one need here only contrast some generational extremes: Marc Bloch with Charles Petit-Dutaillis, or K. B. McFarlane with Gaillard Lapsley.[19] It is hard to explain why intellectual climates as different and as separated as those of England, France and Germany in the period between the wars should have produced a willingness to rethink preconceptions, unless we invoke supranational trends beyond the intentions and circumstances of individual academics or academic communities.

The initial way out, however, the assumption of 'autochthonous' noble rights and powers, has turned out to be difficult to demonstrate conclusively, and it has also

---

17 For the links, or lack of them, between 'feudalism' and 'seigneurialism', and recent debates on the dating and nature of fundamental shifts in European society in the period between 900 and 1050 see Bois 1992 and the critical comments by Guerreau 1990, and by various authors (with a response by Bois) in 'L'An mil: rythmes et acteurs d'une croissance', *Médiévales*, 21 (1991): 3–114. See also Barthélemy, 1992 and Bisson 1994 (see also the critiques by Dominique Barthélemy, Stephen White, Timothy Reuter and Chris Wickham, and Bisson's response, *Past and Present*, forthcoming). A methodologically and conceptually very fruitful approach to historians' use of the term 'power' is offered by Davies 1990.

18 Some of the more important works in chronological order of publication: von Dungern 1908; Waas 1919; Schulte 1922; von Dungern 1927; Otto 1937; Gladiß 1938; Schlesinger 1941; Dannenbauer 1958: 121–78 [first published 1941]; Mayer 1950. The development of the argument is recollected, not wholly in tranquillity, in Mayer 1959, especially in his long introductory essay, pp. 463–503. The best guide in English to all these developments is the valuable historiographical introduction to Brunner 1992: xiii–lxi.

19 Besides Bloch 1961, see also Bloch 1936a and 1936b. See also the remarks of Kaminsky and van Horn Melton (Brunner 1992: xxvii). On McFarlane's historiographical context see the introduction by Gerald Harriss to McFarlane 1973: vii–xxxvii, Leyser 1976, and the remarks by Hicks 1991.

been found not all that helpful as a tool for analysing the politics of the early and high Middle Ages.[20] It is clear that throughout the period it was possible to view the public exercise of power as originating in its delegation to an official, who was hence rightfully subject to control and supervision from above. Widely known texts like the Bible and the literature of ancient Rome provided the concepts, the vocabulary and the rhetoric needed to do this, and so contemporary sources which made use of these might thus appear to support the modern view of legitimate power as derived from above. Yet it is equally clear that those who opposed rulers or treated the 'offices' they held as if they owned them often did so with a strong sense of right.[21] This was sustained, however, not so much by the myth or reality of the distant origins of 'autochthonous' noble power alone, which contemporary sources in any case do not describe in such terms, as by the whole aristocratic culture of which they were a part. There were thus (potentially) competing views on the origins and legitimacy of power rather than a single view. The functionalist style of argument as deployed by social scientists may help here: questions and indeed answers about the origins of a social practice ('how did this practice come about?') are irrelevant to a synchronic understanding of how it works in a given society at a given time ('what is its function, how does it work now?').

The approach which has been adopted in more recent work, often implicitly rather than explicitly, is to take noble power as given rather than to take a legitimist view as to who was on the right side. Such an approach, which may be termed historicist (in the sense that it treats a period in terms of its own preconceptions and attitudes) has been part of a more general paradigm shift. Although the new paradigm was not to be fully or widely articulated until long after the Second World War, and although there is no one author who can be said to have articulated it fully, it has today become an orthodoxy so established as itself perhaps to invite challenge. The principal working assumption on which it rests is a view of medieval kingdoms as governed by largely co-operative oligarchies. The success of rulers is not to be measured by the extent to which they could crush nobles or force them to do their will; rather, the normal forms of politics were co-operative and collective, and conflicts between rulers and nobles were exceptional rather than built into the system. Such trends have not been universal, and even in the 1990s there is no difficulty in finding historians who think and write in terms of Strong and Weak Kings (the Strong Kings being those who curb the power of the nobility).[22] But the majority of historians working on medieval politics would probably now feel instinctively that it was rather old-fashioned, even naive, to think and write in these terms. Only in those regions of Europe until recently dominated by a Marxist or

---

20 Mitterauer 1972. For an English-language survey of the related debate about whether there were any 'free' in the Frankish Empire other than nobles – with the *liberi* being declared to have been *liberi regis*, dependent military colonists whose 'freedom' they owed to the king – see Staab 1980.

21 As Kern 1954 demonstrated at length. For analyses of the consensual view of the Ottonian polity as it applied to rebellions see Althoff 1989a and Reuter 1991.

22 Sellar and Yeatman 1960 provide an invaluable guide to the terminology, on whose medieval origins see Leyser 1982b: 243–4. For typical survivals of this approach see, e.g. Williams 1990: 251, 253, 257.

vulgar materialist orthodoxy has the paradigm shift not been felt at all.[23] A number of explanations may be offered for this: the roots of Marx's own view of the world in nineteenth-century ideas of progress; the historical circumstances in which those states came into being between 1917 and 1950, largely in opposition to local nobilities; the official glorification of state power coupled with deep state insecurity. All this left little room for the luxury of questioning a simple equation of rulers' interests with the common weal. Even after the upheavals of 1989–90 the first signs are that the habits of mind which go with insecure nationalism and politicizing Catholicism will not make it easy to accept the paradigm.

The development of the paradigm has been made possible by the methodological assumption that a medieval polity should be defined not through its rules, whether written or unwritten, but in terms of its practices: the historian as constitutional lawyer has been replaced, though slowly and by no means completely, by the historian as sociologist or social anthropologist. While both approaches are in a sense concerned with practice, the constitutional historian sees some practices as 'legitimate' – meaning sanctioned by norms which are in principle accessible in written documents or implicit in certain privileged kinds of source, especially legal texts – others as existing merely in practice or even as illegitimate. The sociological approach, by contrast, derives the rules from the practice, and is prepared to live with contradictions and tensions without feeling obliged to resolve them along the scale between lawful and unlawful. Such developments have been visible not just in historians' attitudes to the relations between kings and nobles but also in their increased interest in such things as feud and dispute settlement or in rituals of all kinds, whether social or political.[24]

A detailed examination of the role played by the medieval nobility both in the past and in current historiography must begin with genealogy and prosopography, for these supply historians with their raw material: without knowing something about people's families, one cannot say much about whether they were new members of a ruling group or owed their membership of that group to birth. Genealogy, like heraldry, has its origins in noble families' own aspirations to possess (and if necessary invent) as impressive an ancestry as possible, and to legitimate, indeed to copyright, their claims to it; from the family myths of the early Middle Ages through the court genealogists of the dynastic epoch between 1300 and 1800 down to modern genealogists both academic and non-academic, truth and accuracy have been among the first casualties of these aspirations.[25] Modern academic practitioners of genealogy, even when not *parti pris* in the sense that the court genealogists of

---

23 The flavour can best be sampled from the various 'official' national histories produced between about 1955 and 1985, for example Herrmann 1982, Töpfer 1983, Gieysztor *et al.* 1968; Barta *et al.* 1971.

24 See Koziol 1992; Althoff 1990, for ritual and conflict; more generally on dispute settlement see e.g. Davies and Fouracre 1986.

25 For a useful survey of the history of genealogy see Beech 1992: 198–203; see also Lhotsky 1971 and Moeglin 1985. Further illustration, some of it richly comic, may be found in the vast literature dealing with the pseudo-science of heraldry.

earlier centuries were, have often identified emotionally with their subject matter and been seduced by the intellectual gymnastics involved in defending their hypotheses – the nature of the sources available means that certainty and established truth are hard to come by – against proponents of rival hypotheses.[26] Yet genealogy is still indispensable for a study of the nobility in any region or period, since it is impossible to discuss the links (or lack of them) between power, wealth and birth unless you have some knowledge of who was related to whom. Genealogy is also the one universal component of all national or regional historiographies – even in those regions untouched by the *nouvelles vagues* of more recent historiography, genealogists will have been at work.

Genealogy is inherently diachronic; its concern is the study of relationships between the members of a biologically defined group over time.[27] In the twentieth century its synchronic cousin, prosopography, has seemed more fruitful and more intellectually respectable. Between the end of the First World War and the 1960s there was a widespread belief among European historians that prosopography would yield the clue to many poorly understood phenomena, a belief by no means dead in the 1990s. It seemed particularly appealing in the 1950s and early 1960s, since it meshed neatly with the proto-Fukuyaman belief that ideology and/or history had come to an end. Prosopography seemed to fill the gap: tell me your origins and connections and I will predict what your behaviour must have been when I have no direct evidence for it, and explain it by them when I do. The historians of such disparate eras as Late Antiquity and sixteenth- or eighteenth-century England were seduced by its charm, and so also were medieval historians. For other periods and regions the use of prosopography met with some opposition of principle ('[taking] the mind out of history', to quote A. J. P. Taylor on Lewis Namier), but there was only a flicker of such opposition from medieval historians in the late 1930s and early 1940s, a reflection no doubt of medieval historians' general unwillingness to engage in debate on interpretation or methodology.[28] Ambitious projects, influenced

---

26 For a recent exemplary demonstration of this one may examine the embittered and largely unproductive debates about the identity of a count 'Kuno of Öhningen' and about the relationship, or lack of it, of Duke Hermann II of Suabia and Margrave Ekkehard I of Meißen to the Ottonian house and its significance for the German royal succession in 1002: cf. the most recent contribution, Wolf 1991, esp. p. 49 n. 11, a lengthy (but not exhaustive) bibliography of earlier works on the subject, and also Hlawitschka 1987; Althoff 1989b; Jackman 1990, which does not wholly fulfil the promise of its subtitle. Further instalments are, alas, forthcoming.

27 'Biological' is here of course a term of convenience; since even married humans are not necessarily monogamous, kinship is an ascribed or assumed status rather than a biological fact, even if the assumption is generally correct. One should also note the existence of artificial forms of kinship – spiritual and adoptive – though the latter played little role in medieval Europe before the revival of Roman law in the twelfth and thirteenth centuries, studied recently by Lynch 1986 and Jussen 1991.

28 The debate among German historians, notably Walter Schlesinger, Gerd Tellenbach and Martin Lintzel, in the early 1940s about the role of the aristocracy in the creation of an east Frankish or 'German' kingdom was fuelled in part by a dislike of the prosopographical methods practised by Tellenbach (1939); the controversy is most conveniently followed in Kämpf 1955, where the major contributions are reprinted with *addenda*, and in the summary – written *cum ira et studio* – in Brühl 1990: 367–76.

particularly by the prosopographies produced by ancient historians, were set up even before the advent of reliable, flexible and affordable forms of electronic data processing; some of these have did, others have borne some fruit, and there is even a journal to sample and market the wares.[29] There is of course no inherent reason why such techniques should be applied to the nobility alone, and indeed many prosopographical studies, especially those relating to later medieval topics, have concerned themselves with other definable groups: university graduates, inhabitants of towns, clerics and members of religious orders. Yet the surviving sources make elites, and hence inevitably nobilities, almost the only groups which can be satisfactorily prosopographized for much of the Middle Ages, just as they are in antiquity.

It has been peculiarly difficult to do either genealogy or prosopography for the period between the late fifth century and the late eleventh or early twelfth century, because of the name-giving habits then current. The multiple names used by the aristocracy of Roman antiquity, which identified both individuals and their membership of families, had dropped out of use even among the senatorial aristocracy of Gaul and their descendants by about 600. For the next half-millennium almost everyone in Europe whose name we know at all carried a single name drawn either from a small fixed stock of Roman and biblical names or from a much larger and variable stock of Germanic, Celtic and Slavic names and name-elements. This makes it difficult to take an isolated mention of, say, *Heinricus*, and relate it to a specific Henry, or to determine the relationship of this Henry to other individuals; the problems are rather like those faced by modern social historians practising nominal record linkage between different sets of sources,[30] but they present themselves in a peculiarly acute form. Only gradually, as a result of

---

29 On what has turned out to be the over-ambitious idea of a prosopography of the western European kingdoms up to 1200 pursued at the German Historical Institute in Paris in the 1960s and 1970s, see Werner 1977b. The project suffered not only from being card-index-based but also from more fundamental problems including those arising out of the practice of single naming (see below at nn. 31ff.). Beech 1992 gives details of several other projects and of the development of the subject as a whole; see also the works cited below, n. 54. The periodical *Medieval Prosopography*, Kalamazoo, University of Western Michigan Publications, 1980– , has a strong emphasis on later medieval topics and on England, but not so strong as to exclude other matter completely.

30 The problem is essentially that of deciding on what grounds a Jane or John Smith found, say, in an electoral register can be identified with another Jane or John Smith found, say, in a set of tax records, and with what degree of confidence; for an introduction to and bibliography on the issues involved and the way in which the difficulties can be overcome with the aid of computers see the editorial and articles by P. Adman, S. W. Baskerville and K. F. Beedham, H. Rhrodri Davies, S. King, J. E. Vetter, J. R. Gonzalez and Myron P. Gutmann in *History and Computing* 4/1, 1992, pp. iii–vii, 2–51. It may be that more attention should be paid by medievalists to these techniques, though it is unusual for medieval data-sets to be as homogeneous as those available from the period from 1600 and later, and still more unusual for there to be more than one such data-set from the same place and period. It is easier to show dependences between necrologies than to identify the individuals recorded in them; whereas the former technique has led to the successful reconstruction in substance of the lost necrology of Cluny, those historians who have studied *libri memoriales* are backing steadily away from the idea of identifying their contents. See n. 35, and also Wollasch *et al.* 1982.

processes still badly in need of further investigation,[31] did distinguishing elements emerge: the earliest forms are the repeated use of a specific set of names or name-elements by members of a kindred ('leading names'),[32] and, related to this, of names of prominent ancestors, but we later find supplementary patronymics, as in names like Harald Sigurdsson (Slav, Scandinavian and Celtic naming conventions were in any case rather different); double names, as in Raymond Berengar or *Petrus qui et Suevus*;[33] family names referring to important centres of lordship;[34] nicknames and surnames denoting geographical or social origin or occupation, though these were on the whole used for members of other social strata than those which concern us here.[35]

Faced with the sea of uncertainty presented by single naming, historians were long forced to depend on casual (often also untestable or unreliable) mentions of relationships in charters and narrative sources in order to establish genealogies. Not surprisingly, there have been attempts to overcome these drawbacks. From the eighth century onwards there survive several groups of sources containing huge numbers of names. Among these are significant collections of early medieval charters (using the term in a loose sense to refer to all written records of legal transactions), which generally list the names of between ten and fifty witnesses: the archives of Lucca, St Gallen and Cluny offer particularly rich collections. *Libri memoriales* — books kept by churches for the purpose of recording the names of the dead in commemorative prayer — and the necrologies which between the tenth and the twelfth centuries came to replace them, have also preserved enormous numbers of names from the late eighth century onwards.[36] *Libri memoriales* in particular contain many group entries, lists of names entered by a single hand. Many of these are ecclesiastical in origin and represent the membership of a monastery or nunnery

---

31 Now being undertaken by a community of scholars coordinated by Monique Bourin of Tours; see most recently Bourin and Chareille 1992, a collection devoted in particular to the naming practices applied to women and to clerics.

32 For a discussion of the significance of 'leading names' see Werner 1978: 149–53; Wenskus 1976: 41–65; Werner 1977; Mitterauer 1988. One must distinguish between leading-names proper, used intact from generation to generation, and so-called Germanic variation, in which the names of the next generation are formed by combining front and back elements drawn from the parents' or close relatives' names (e.g. a daughter of a Gauzbert and a Chlothilde might be called Gauzhilde).

33 Otto of Freising, *Gesta Friderici I. imperatoris* II 5, ed. Georg Waitz and Bernhard von Simson (Monumenta Germaniae Historica, Scriptores rerum Germanicarum in usum scholarum 46) Hanover, 1912, p. 105. The form 'X qui et Y' was often used for popes, who from the late tenth century onwards took a papal name on consecration, a practice which has received some attention from historians. To my knowledge the formula as applied to laymen has not been investigated.

34 For the literature on naming by 'family seats' see the account of the 'Schmid-Tellenbach thesis' at n. 47.

35 Notoriously, the most common modern surnames in western European countries are derived from common or prominent medieval occupations (smith, miller, tailor, shepherd, etc.), and the greatest number of modern surnames are derived from place names (but not from 'family seats'!).

36 For these sources and the development and criticism of the methodology used on them see Tellenbach 1957; Schmid 1957, 1959; Leyser 1982a: 168–70; Constable 1972; Schmid and Wollasch 1975; Hlawitschka 1982; Althoff 1992: 37–68.

in confraternity with the house keeping the *liber memorialis*. But the names included in other entries suggest that they consist of living and dead members of kin-groups and are thus exclusively or primarily lay in composition. Witness-lists in charters also frequently contain kin-groups, not always explicitly labelled as such, and a good collection of charters from the same area stretching over a period of time will thus provide much information on kindreds.

Both witness-lists and *libri memoriales* provide genealogical material of a kind which traditional genealogy finds hard to handle: people who are evidently related to one another but in an undefinable way. When traditional genealogy did exploit such material it often relied on unsubstantiated and unsubstantiatable guesswork in order to do so, and the results were often hardly more than fantasy. In the 1950s and 1960s this Gordian knot was cut. The construction of genealogies was still seen as legitimate where the information was available to do so – indeed, without *some* secure genealogies it would have been impossible to determine membership of kin-groups from bare names. But guesswork was disallowed: the premise was that one should have the courage to accept gaps. The masses of names were instead to be used to construct 'floating kindreds', of whose members it could be said only that they were in some way related to one another (cf. Schmid 1957; 1959). An implicit methodological assumption here was that in the single-name period names and name-elements did go some way to identify individuals as members of kindreds, at least within the Frankish Empire and its peripheries. If you were called Rorgo or Unruoch or Gauzbert then your contemporaries knew who you were and to whom you were related (an assumption more difficult to make for Anglo-Saxon England, however, where so many people appear to be called Æthel- or Ælf-something) (Werner 1978: 149–51). Coupled with information about landownership and office-holding, even isolated references to names can also be used to construct 'floating kindreds', the assumption being that two Gauzberts or two Ricdags holding land in the same place fifty or a hundred years apart were very probably related to one another.[37]

Such techniques need to be practised within a tight framework of command of all the sources pertaining to the history of a region. More intensive study of *libri memoriales* has shown that entries which look at first like kindreds may in fact be other kinds of group, such as networks of friendship and alliance,[38] while the use of names alone to construct kindreds has been somewhat discredited by indiscriminate application of the technique.[39] It has also been questioned on methodological grounds: though names were probably more uniquely identifying than they now seem to us, counter-examples have been adduced of the same name's turning up in

37 Werner 1978: 149–73; Sturm was probably the first explicit and systematic exploiter of the technique.
38 On these changes of perception see Althoff 1992: 37–68.
39 As by and large in Wenskus 1976, and quite unacceptably in Gewin 1964. Some idea of what the method used to excess can produce may be had from contemplating the 'somewhat simplified' genealogy of English kings in Sellar and Yeatman 1960: 35.

different kindreds or social classes, in other words in contexts where the various holders were almost certainly *not* related to one another.[40] On a quite different note, there is the question of what you can use a floating kindred *for*, once you have constructed it; the answers, once the methodological excitement has died down, have often been rather disappointing, though we shall see one use later (at n. 46). We certainly have enough information about the behaviour of members of known kindreds not to want to suppose that kindred-membership resembled membership of a modern political party (except inasmuch as members of modern parties often see other members of the same parties as their main political enemies).

Although some progress has thus been made in identifying nobles and relating them to one another, the nobility has remained hard to define, and in many regions and periods hard to identify with precision. Yet an understanding of its nature – and by implication of the nature of the power it exercised – has seemed crucial for those periods in medieval European history where substantial political and social changes are suggested either prima facie by the sources themselves or else by a powerful tradition of historical interpretation. Where a break in continuity has appeared to be comprehensive and self-evident the study of the nobility has perhaps seemed less attractive; but it has been commoner to find evidence pointing both to rupture and to continuity. At that point, whether the subject is the barbarian settlement of the Roman Europe,[41] the rise of the Carolingians (Ebling 1976; Werner 1982; Geary 1985), the emergence of new kingdoms and principalities after the break-up of the Carolingian Empire,[42] the seemingly widespread elimination of older noble families in much of Europe between 1050 and 1250,[43] or the numerous occasions on which contemporary moralists or modern historians or both have perceived the rise of a new elite ('men rising from the dust'),[44] close attention has been paid to elites and their composition in the hope of understanding the nature of contemporary political changes more closely and of deciding how far these in fact occurred.

The *locus classicus* for such a debate is that on the origins of the principalities in post-Carolingian Europe. Who were the new men of west and east Francia and of the old Lombard kingdom, and what was the nature and origin of their power? On the

---

40　Claimed by Holzfurtner 1982; countered by Goetz 1985 and 1987.

41　Stroheker 1948; Selle-Hosbach 1974; Gilliard 1979. On the Ostrogothic/Lombard kingdoms of Italy and the Visigothic kingdom of Spain see Claude 1971; García Moreno 1974; Kampers 1979; Jarnut 1972; Ebling *et al.* 1980.

42　On the survival of trans-regnal aristocracies in the tenth century see now the suggestive comments by Airlie 1993; for the problems of the accompanying political developments see Barraclough 1976 (oversimplified but still worth reading); Gieysztor 1968; Brühl 1990.

43　On the elimination of families see the discussion in Genicot 1975 (pp. 18–21 in Eng. tr in Reuter 1978). Note, however, that those families which inherited collaterally (or by force) from such extinct 'lines' tended to stress or invent continuity, and note also that only after a more strongly patrilineal conception of family developed was it easily possible for families to become 'extinct'. See McFarlane 1973: 142–76.

44　This has been extensively studied in connection with Anglo-Norman and Anglo-Angevin rulership: see for example Southern 1970. Green 1986: 133–93; Newman 1988; Turner 1988.

whole an older generation of historians took the view, summed up in a vividly impressionistic sketch by Marc Bloch which drew largely on west Frankish evidence, that the men who rose to the top in the late ninth and early tenth centuries were indeed new men.[45] Their descendants in the eleventh and twelfth centuries had evident difficulty in tracing their ancestry back beyond the late ninth century, often indeed beyond the millennium, as can be seen from historical and genealogical writings dedicated to or commissioned by them (and hence presumably meeting with their approval), which frequently stressed their ancestors' humble origins: descent from a crossbowman, a forester or whatever (see on this Martindale 1977; Bouchard 1981; Dunbabin 1992). The more recent revision of this view owed much to the methodological developments in genealogy. In many cases it could be shown that the 'new men' of the tenth and eleventh centuries were not as new as all that; they could be linked to Carolingian 'floating kindreds'.[46] The fact that their descendants in the twelfth century no longer perceived their own origins in this way was explained as the product of a change in family structure. This is the thesis of Gerd Tellenbach and Karl Schmid, developed primarily on the basis of Frankish and east Frankish material, which has exercised much influence on French historians such as Duby (1962) and English historians such as Holt (1982–5). Until the late tenth century nobles perceived their families laterally, with no special emphasis on direct ancestors in the male line as against collateral relatives who were still alive or only recently dead. Such a patrilineal emphasis only emerged in the late tenth and early eleventh centuries, with a crystallization of family consciousness around castles and specific landholdings, and later around 'surnames' derived from these 'family seats'; but the result was that nobles in the late eleventh and twelfth centuries who contemplated their ancestries lacked the material to go back beyond the great divide around 1000, much as we often do even with our superior archival resources.[47]

The revision is attractive, but has its own difficulties. For most of the societies of medieval Europe it is difficult to show that there was at any stage a general awareness of *all* extended kin: the terminology for distant cousins, for example, is lacking, and this is not wholly explicable by pointing to the use of Latin for much of the sources from which we derive our evidence.[48] Nor did awareness of distant kin

---

45 Bloch 1961: 283–92; Bloch was here much indebted to Guilhiermoz 1902.

46 For the west Frankish kingdom, the pioneer work was done by Karl-Ferdinand Werner (1958–60); references to more recent work may be found in Martindale 1977, Bouchard 1981 and Dunbabin 1992, and in a general survey in Bisson 1990. For similar problems in establishing family continuity in the east Frankish kingdom see Schimd 1957; 1959; 1964; Freed 1984; 1986.

47 Besides Schmid 1957 and 1959, see Schmid 1964. For English-language accounts see Freed 1984 and 1986.

48 The Latin terminology has been surprisingly little investigated; but see Thais 1976; Goody 1983. More could be done with the evidence from the Church's prohibition of incestuous marriages, on which see Brooke 1989, esp. pp. 133–41, and Schadt 1982. For the more explicit (though not necessarily more real) Anglo-Saxon and Celtic evidence see, respectively, Loyn 1974, though with a questionable analysis of the absence of extended Anglo-Saxon kinship terminology, and Charles-Edwards 1993, with very full bibliographical information.

disappear after the tenth century. In other words, we are not dealing with a single form of family consciousness, but with a bundle of family consciousnesses, which overlapped and, taken as a whole, probably changed more slowly than the idea of a Great Shift in family structure would allow.[49] After all, similar problems of continuity crop up in considering the rise of the Carolingians and their followings in the eighth century, or the origins and nature of the elites of the barbarian kingdoms in the sixth and seventh centuries, and these cannot so easily be attributed to shifts in family consciousness.[50]

There has thus been a tendency in more recent work to put aside the question of origins, and simply examine actions and attitudes. After all, even if the *principes* of post-Carolingian Francia were indeed all descended from Carolingian noble families, the political situation in which they operated was post-Carolingian; contrariwise, even if all the families of the new *principes* had in fact been descended from crossbowmen or pedlars and owed their rise to *virtus* rather than *nobilitas* (in modern terms meritocratic rather than aristocratic), the second generation would still have constituted a ruling elite within the same post-Carolingian framework. One thing apparent in the behaviour of all those who are or were said to have 'risen from the dust', or at least of those who having risen succeeded in staying risen, was their determination to shake the dust from their shoes, to behave in established ways rather than establish new ways of behaving. Questions of aristocratic origins have thus not completely lost their interest, but the explicit sources dealing with them are now examined more as interesting in themselves and for the period in which they were written than for their information about the period to which they refer, much as the works of the great medieval historians are now studied as much as records of their authors' minds as for their 'factual information'.[51]

The dominant concern in recent historiography on the nobility of the high Middle Ages (meaning the era after the shift in family consciousness, real or supposed, had occurred), has been with the socialization and 'civilization' of the class, in the sense developed by Norbert Elias (1969; 1979 see also Jaeger 1985; Scaglione 1991; Crouch 1992), and its concomitant extension to take in groups not previously included. A number of key points have emerged. First, historians have noted the clericalization of the warrior ethos. This is apparent not only from the development of ecclesiastical rituals for blessing arms and those who carry them, including a rite

---

49 See the debate between Leyser 1968; Bullough 1969; Leyser 1970. The point was well made by both sides.
50 For a vigorous assertion of continuity between the nobilities of the Merovingian and Carolingian eras see Werner 1978. For the question of the 'origins' of the Frankish nobility see the debate between Irsigler 1969 (English translation of chapter 3 in Reuter 1978: 105–36), and Grahn-Hoek 1976. There are valuable comments and insights on the issues involved in Geary 1985. There appears to be too little material to say much about what became of the early nobilities of the barbarian kingdoms in England, Spain and Italy.
51 See n. 5, and for further discussion of the issues raised here Reuter 1994b and 1994a.

for the making of what would slowly come to be called a knight (*miles, Ritter, chevalier*),[52] but also from the appearance of a tripartite scheme for the division of society into 'those who fight, those who plough and those who pray', which occurs sporadically from the late ninth century and more continuously from the early eleventh century. This cut across not only socially or legally defined class divisions, but also the traditional Christian division between clerical and lay; and it legitimized and at the same time sought to control and restrain fighting as an activity (Duby 1980; see, for a critical appraisal: Le Goff 1979; Oexle 1978, 1981, 1984; Moore 1984). Second, and closely linked with this, historians have noted the merging of the two groups, *nobiles* and *milites* (nobles and warriors). This took a number of different forms. From the late tenth century onwards nobles used or were given the title *miles* ('soldier', 'warrior'), which had previously applied to the fighting men of their followings, whether free or unfree.[53] As early as the ninth century there is evidence that entry into adult noble life was marked by a (secular) ceremony conferring arms, and with the development of more formal ecclesiastical rites of dubbing in the eleventh and twelfth centuries entry not only into what came to be the profession of knighthood but also into the ranks of the nobility was often marked by such a ceremony (Nelson 1989). This cut two ways, however: if the *nobiles* became *milites*, the *milites* equally became *nobiles*, for the ceremonies applied just as much to the sons of kings and established nobles and princes as they did to those who had genuinely risen socially. Much work has been devoted to delineating the considerable regional differences in this respect, but the general European tend, which with some time-lag extended even beyond the boundaries of the former Roman Empire, was towards a merger of the groups of *nobiles* and *milites*, complete in most of Europe by the later Middle Ages and in some parts of Europe considerably earlier.[54] The merger did not anywhere make a mere knight the equal of a prince or a king's son in all things,[55] but it did make the two at least for some purposes members of a group set apart from the rest of society, a group which came to have a common identity, interests and ethos. This merger of two previously separate groups also created tensions and status anxieties. Both the comparative fluidity of knighthood in its early phases and the possibility of assuming noble status by using economic resources to pursue a noble way of life led to reactions on the part of the now expanded noble class: entry into knighthood came to be more tightly controlled, and sumptuary legislation aimed at preventing

---

52 On these developments see Flori 1983 and also Erdmann 1935.

53 On the development of this terminology see Duby 1977; Johrendt 1971 (hectographed typed thesis), summarized conveniently in Flori 1976; van Luyn 1971.

54 Exactly when this process was complete is a matter of some debate, due in part to failure to distinguish between the adoption of the title *miles* by nobles, the adoption of dubbing ceremonies by nobles and *milites*, and the ascription of noble status to *milites* (or to dubbed *milites*). See for different regions of Europe Fleckenstein 1989a and 1989b [first published 1977 and 1974, respectively]; Bisson 1990; Barbero 1987; Flori 1988; Fleming 1990; Evergates 1995.

55 Cf. Bur 1977: 417: 'If thus all princes are knights, it is rare to find a knight who could claim a princely title', cited by Koziol 1992: 406 n. 72.

the tacit assumption of noble status, though no doubt it was often unsuccessful in doing so.[56]

The attention paid to these developments by historians is easily explained. Not only is the existence of a broad though internally subdivided class of nobles one of the fundamental features of the society of the *ancien régime* in Europe between the middle of the thirteenth century and the French Revolution; there are also obvious links here with the emergence not only of a courtly literature but also of a courtly way of life and a chivalric code of conduct.[57] The specific rite of passage which defined and controlled entry into the group conferred not only status but also obligations. The duties ascribed to 'those who fight' by ecclesiastics and writers of literature were those which before the emergence of knighthood had been ascribed to kings: the protection of the poor and the defenceless, meaning widows, orphans and the Church. Holy war against the enemies of Christianity, as practised above all in the crusades, was merely a logical extension of this.[58] Imitation of kingship was visible in other ways as well. Just as to be chivalrous you need a horse (*cheval*), so to live the courtly way of life you need a court, and the study of the court in the high and late Middle Ages, both as an institution and as a way of life, has received much attention from medieval historians in recent decades.[59] The palaces and residences established by rulers came to be imitated by princes and lesser men. Indeed, such visible symbols of power were perhaps more important for lesser nobles, for whereas kings and princes could derive their self-understanding from their kingdoms and principalities, lesser nobles from the eleventh century on, as we have seen, often defined it in terms of their 'family seat', a castle or aristocratic country house (to use a somewhat anachronistic term).

Though so far it may have seemed as if the trends within the historiography of medieval Europe have been Europe-wide, the intensity of interest has varied greatly. Outside the core area of Carolingian Europe – France, Germany, northern Italy – there has often been more silence than discourse. The kingdoms of England Sicily and Jerusalem in the high Middle Ages were kingdoms of conquest. The nobilities which established themselves there were indeed created *ex nihilo*, or so it seemed, and this was part of their own legitimatory myth: the *nobilitas* of the ruling elites was the product of their *virtus*, their inherent virtue, which they had shown by conquest.[60] For

---

56   See on these aspects of the later medieval nobility McFarlane 1973 and the more general survey by Rosenthal 1976.
57   Besides Elias 1969 and 1979; Jaeger 1985; Scaglione 1991; Crouch 1992, see in particular Keen 1984 and the various works of Joachim Bumke, esp. Bumke 1982.
58   The classic study is Erdmann 1935. For the extensive work done in the wake of Erdmann's pioneering study see Mayer 1988: 8–37, 292–3.
59   See (besides Elias 1969 and 1979; Jaeger 1985; Scaglione 1991; Crouch 1992, and the works cited in n. 57) Fleckenstein 1990. The allusion in the text is to Neil Denholm-Young's remark 'It is impossible to be chivalrous without a horse'.
60   Such a view plays on the contrast between true nobility which lies in noble actions or feelings and mere nobility of birth, *nobilitas carnis*. The topic needs further investigation; for an introductory orientation see the remarks in Jaeger 1985 and Scaglione 1991.

Sicily and Jerusalem this was a self-evident product of the cultural and religious caesura implied by conquest.[61] In England, by contrast, the idea that the Norman Conquest represented such a caesura has been denied as often as it has been posited. Nevertheless, there is evidently little reason to assume continuity of the political elite across the break of 1066 (or across the reign of William I, since it is now clear that the Anglo-Saxon elite was not eliminated at a stroke).[62] The comparative lack of interest shown until fairly recently in the nobility of the Anglo-Saxon era has a rather different explanation. It is due not so much to the fact that the Anglo-Saxon nobility had largely ceased to exist by the time of the Domesday survey as to the survival, indeed dominance, of an orthodoxy within Anglo-Saxon historical studies which retained a highly traditional conception of the relationship between ruler and people long after similar views had been abandoned or substantially modified for other periods and regions.[63] Moreover, the sources for Anglo-Saxon history from the mid-eighth to the mid-eleventh century appeared neither to force questions about the nature of the nobility on historians' attention nor to offer easy answers to those who did pose them. This has been true of other parts of the European periphery as well. To be able to perceive the political and social operation of a nobility in action, one must both be able to practise genealogy with some plausibility and at the same time have some evidence for the details of political interaction. Where the narrative sources lack the necessary juiciness, the study of the nobility becomes very difficult, even where normative sources such as law-codes might at first sight seem to make it perfectly possible.[64] This is true not only of most of Anglo-Saxon history after Bede's death, but also of Visigothic and Asturian Spain or of the Celtic, Scandinavian and Slav peripheries of Europe until the high Middle Ages – though for the Celtic and Scandinavian worlds something can be saved if the historian is willing to accept the internal coherence, if not the literal truth, of the picture presented by literary evidence such as sagas and poetry. The study of the nobility is also difficult in regions and periods where the socio-legal status of *individuals* below the level of royalty cannot easily be clarified (as again in most of the regions just mentioned). But see now Clarke (1994).

Only of the nobility in the social, political and cultural history of the later European Middle Ages can we say that the study of the subject has been truly

---

61   On the nobility in the kingdom of Jerusalem see Mayer 1988: 152–76; Prawer 1968; Riley-Smith 1973. For the legitimizing effects of conquest in Sicily see Loud 1981, esp. 111–14.

62   Fleming 1991 is both an important discussion and a valuable guide to the previous literature on this subject. For the ideology of conquest see also Garnett 1986.

63   The orthodoxy was established by Stenton in 1970 and defended with sometimes inquistorial vigour after his death by Dorothy Whitelock, Henry Loyn, R. Allen Brown and Doris Stenton: see for example the remarks in the 3rd edn, revised by Doris Stenton and Dorothy Whitelock, p. 723: 'Sir Frank Stenton was not convinced by the work on this period of [various other scholars], whose books and articles are therefore here omitted', or Loyn in 1992: 'Although modifications are now appearing ... in the main Stenton's picture still holds the centre of the stage for the modern student', a sentence retained unchanged from the first edition of 1962.

64   For Visigothic Spain, typical in this respect, see Claude 1971; García Moreno 1974; Kampers 1979; Ebling 1980.

Europe-wide. Here the exponential growth in the quantity and quality of evidence available from the twelfth century onwards in most regions of Europe has made a change of focus both possible and essential. A single princely family, even a single aristocrat, in the later Middle Ages can, often be studied in a depth simply inconceivable for earlier centuries. Even studies of lesser nobles often have to proceed by examining a selected group rather than a whole class.[65] The mass of material in the archives also means that there is still a great deal of positivist slogging to be done, of establishing who did what and to whom. Late medieval historiography is therefore still regionalistic, particularist and nominalist, and on the whole its practitioners address themselves to colleagues working within the same region rather than to a wider professional public.[66] The question of whether a nobility existed (and if so, what its nature was) is here not seriously at issue; hence the nobilities of later medieval Europe are simply part of the historiographical landscape. It is precisely this omnipresence of the subject (even when we allow for the emergence of an autonomous urban or bourgeois culture during the same period) that makes it virtually impossible to discuss it in historiographical rather than bibliographical terms.

Two issues have dominated. The first is the question of nobles' relation to their king or prince, in other words of the legitimacy of their political behaviour and aspirations, and here the discussion has proceeded along lines very similar to those we have already noted for the early and high Middle Ages.[67] The second, which has been posited in a number of different regional historiographies, as so often in medieval historiography without much interaction taking place, is the idea that there was a general late medieval 'crisis of the nobility'. This in turn is linked with the more general issue of how far there was a late medieval economic and social crisis, to use an overworked but perhaps necessary term.[68] Such a linkage also shows that the study of the nobilities of later medieval Europe has a different quality to that of its counterpart for the period before about 1250: the density and variety of evidence available makes possible a view of the society as a whole in a way found only for brief periods in restricted regions in the earlier era. The fruitful element of tension provided by the uncertainty about the status and nature of the nobility for so many different aspects of the historiography of the earlier Middle Ages is much less evident for that of the later Middle Ages: the nobility is, to change the metaphor, bread and butter rather than caviar. Attention to noble consciousness and noble being is no longer one of the few available means to avoid being forced to perceive the world medievalists study as one which consisted largely of kings and saints.

---

65   e.g. Saul 1986, a substantial and respectable monograph confined largely to three families in one county.

66   Though there are exceptions, notably Contamine 1976 (essentially on the later Middle Ages in spite of the title); Fleckenstein 1985; Jones 1986.

67   For England see for example the works discussed in the survey article Horrox 1992.

68   The literature on the real or alleged late medieval crisis can only be sketched here; for a general guide see the contributions in Aston 1985, and for two important works which relate the notion more specifically to our theme see Bois 1976 and Sablonier 1979.

REFERENCES

Airlie, S. (1993) 'After empire – recent work on the emergence of post-Carolingian kingdoms', *Early Medieval History* 2: 153–61.

—— (1995) 'The aristocracy', in R. McKitterick (ed.) *The New Cambridge Medieval History*, II: *c.700–c.900*, Cambridge: 431–50.

Althoff, G. (1989a) 'Königsherrschaft und Konfliktbewältigung im 10. und 11. Jahrhundert', *Frühmittelalterliche Studien* 23: 265–90.

—— (1989b) 'Die Thronbewerber von 1002 und ihre Verwandtschaft mit den Ottonen', *Zeitschrift für die Geschichte des Oberrheins* 137: 453–9.

—— (1990) *Verwandte, Freunde und Getreue. Zum politischen Stellenwert der Gruppenbindungen im früheren Mittelalter*, Darmstadt.

—— (1992) *Amicitiae und Pacta. Bündnis, Einung, Politik und Gebetsgedenken im beginnenden 10. Jahrhundert*, Hanover.

Aston, T. H. (ed.) (1985) *The Brenner Debate*, Cambridge.

Barbero, A. (1987) *L'aristocrazia nella società francese del medioevo. Analisi delle fonti letterarie (secoli X–XIII)*, Bologna.

Barraclough, G. (1976) *The Crucible of Europe*, London.

Barta, I. *et al.* (1971) *Die Geschichte Ungarns*, ed. E. Pamléni, Budapest.

Barthélemy, D. (1992) 'La mutation féodale a-t-elle eu lieu?', *Annales ESC* 47: 767–77.

Beech, G. (1992) 'Prosopography', in J. M. Powell (ed.) *Medieval Studies. An Introduction*, 2nd edn, Syracuse.

Beumann, H. (1950) *Widukind von Corvey*, Weimar.

Bisson, T. N. (1990) 'Nobility and family in France: a review essay', *French Historical Studies* 16: 597–613.

—— (1994) 'The "Feudal Revolution"', *Past and Present* 142: 6–42.

Bloch, M. (1936a) 'Les noblesses – reconnaissance générale du terrain', *Annales d'histoire économiques et sociales* 8: 238–42.

—— (1936b) 'Sur le passé de la noblesse française: quelques jalons de recherche', *Annales d'histoire économiques et sociales* 8: 366–78.

—— (1961) *Feudal Society*, tr. L. A. Manyon, London.

Bockenförde, E.-W. (1961) *Die deutsche verfassungsgeschichtliche Forschung im 19. Jahrhundert*, Berlin.

Bois, G. (1976) *Crise du féodalisme. Économie rurale et démographie en Normandie orientale du début du 14e siècle au milieu du 16e*, 2 vols, Paris.

—— (1992) *The Transformation of the Year 1000*, Manchester.

Bouchard, C. B. (1981) 'The origins of the French nobility: a reassessment', *American Historical Review* 86: 501–32.

Bourin, M. and Chareille, P. (eds) (1992) *Genèse médiévale de l'anthroponymie moderne*, II: *Persistances du nom unique*, Tours.

Brooke, C. (1989) *The Medieval Idea of Marriage*, Oxford.

Brown, E. A. R. (1974) 'The tyranny of a construct: feudalism and historians of medieval Europe', *American Historical Review* 79: 1063–88.

Brühl, C. (1990) *Deutschland —— Frankreich. Die Geburt zweier Nationen*, Cologne.

Brunner, O. (1992) *Land and Lordship. Structures of Governance in medieval Austria*, tr. H. Kaminsky and J. van Horn Melton, Philadelphia. (First published in German in 1939; tr. from the rev. edn of 1959.)

Bullough, D. A. (1969) 'Early medieval social groupings: the terminology of kinship', *Past and Present* 45: 3–18.

—— (1970) '*Europae pater*: Charlemagne and his achievement in the light of recent scholarship', *English Historical Review* 85: 59–105.

Bumke, J. (1982) *The Concept of Knighthood in the Middle Ages*, New York.

Bur, M. (1977) *La Formation du comté de Champagne. v.950-v. 1150*, Nancy.

Charles-Edwards, T. (1993) *Early Irish and Welsh Kinship*, Oxford.

Clarke, P. A. (1994) *The English Nobility Under Edward the Confessor*, Oxford.

Claude, D. (1971) *Adel, Kirche und Königtum im Westgotenreich*, Sigmaringen.

Constable, G. (1972) 'The *Liber Memorialis* of Remiremont', *Speculum* 47: 261–77.

Contamine, P. (ed.) (1976) *La Noblesse au moyen âge*, Paris.

Conze, W. *et al.* (1978) 'Adel, Aristokratie', in O. Brunner, W. Conze and R. Koselleck (eds) *Geschichtliche Grundbegriffe. Historisches Lexikon zur politisch-sozialen Sprache in Deutschland*, 1: *A–D* Stuttgart: 1–48.

Critchley, J. S. (1978) *Feudalism*, London.

Crouch, D. (1992) *The Image of Aristocracy in Britain, 1000–1300*, London.

Dannenbauer, H. (1958) 'Adel, Burg und Herrschaft bei den Germanen', in id., *Grundlagen der mittelalterlichen Welt*, Stuttgart. (First published in 1941.)

Davies, W. (1990) *Patterns of Power in Early Wales*, Oxford.

—— and Fouracre, P. (1986) *The Settlement of Disputes in Early Medieval Europe*, Cambridge.

Duby, G. (1962) 'Une enquête à poursuivre: la noblesse dans la France médiévale', *Revue Historique* 226: 1–22.

—— (1977) *The Chivalrous Society*, tr. C. Postan, Berkeley.

—— (1980) *The Three Orders: Feudal Society Imagined*, tr. A. Goldhammer, Chicago. (First published as: *Les Trois Ordres ou l'imaginaire du féodalisme*, Paris.)

Dunbabin, J. (1992) 'Discovering a past for the French aristocracy', in P. Magdalino (ed.) *The Perception of the Past in Twelfth-Century Europe*, London: 1–14.

Dungern, O. von (1908) *Der Herrenstand im Mittelalter*, Papiermühle.

—— (1927) *Adelsherrschaft im Mittelalter*, Munich.

Ebling, H. (1976) *Prosopographie der Amtsträger des Merowingerreiches von Clothar I. (613) bis Karl Martell (741)*, Munich.

—— Jarnut, J. and Kampers, G. (1980) '*Nomen et gens*. Untersuchungen zu den Führungsschichten des Franken-, Langobarden- und Westgotenreiches im 6. und 7. Jahrhundert', *Francia* 8: 687–745.

Elias, N. (1969) *Über den Prozess der Zivilisation: soziogenetische und psychogenetische Untersuchungen*, 2 vols, 2nd edn, Frankfurt am Main. (English translations under various titles.)

—— (1979) *Die höfische Gesellschaft: Untersuchungen zur Soziologie des Königtums und der höfischen Aristokratie*, 4th edn, Darmstadt. (Published in English as: *The Court Society*, tr. E. Jephcott, Oxford, 1983.)

Erdmann, C. (1977) *The Origins of the Idea of Crusade*, tr. M. W. Baldwin and W. Goffart, Philadelphia. (First published as: *Die Entstehung des Kreuzzugsgedankens*, Stuttgart, 1935.)

Evergates, T. (1987) 'Nobility and nobles', *Dictionary of the Middle Ages*, 9: *Mystery Religions – Poland*, New York: 147–52.

—— (1995) 'Nobles and knights in twelfth-century France', in T. N. Bisson (ed.) *Cultures of Power: Lordship, Status and Process in Twelfth-century Europe*, Philadelphia: 11–35.

Fleckenstein, J. (1981) 'Adel und Kriegertum und ihre Wandlung im Karolingerzeit', *Settimane di Studio* 27: 67–94.

—— (ed.) (1985) *Das ritterliche Turnier im Mittelalter*, Göttingen.

—— (1989a) 'Die Entstehung des niederen Adels und das Rittertum', in id. *Ordnungen und formende Kräfte des Mittelalters. Ausgewählte Beiträge*, Göttingen: 333–56. (First published in 1977.)

—— (1989b) 'Zum Problem der Abschliessung des Ritterstandes', in id. *Ordnungen und formende Kräfte des Mittelalters. Ausgewählte Beiträge*, Göttingen: 357–76. (First published in 1974.)

197

—— (ed.) (1990) *Curialitas*, Göttingen.

Fleming, R. F. (1990) 'Landholding by *milites* in Domesday Book: a revision', *Anglo-Norman Studies* 13: 83–98.

—— (1991) *Kings and Lords in Conquest England*, Cambridge.

Flori, J. (1976) 'Chevaliers et chevalerie au XI siècle en France et dans l'Empire germanique. A propos d'un livre récent', *Le Moyen Âge* 82: 125–36.

—— (1983) *L'Idéologie du glaive. Préhistoire de la chevalerie*, Geneva.

—— (1988) 'Chevalerie, noblesse et lutte de classes au moyen âge d'après un ouvrage récent', *Le Moyen Âge* 94: 257–74.

Freed, J. B. (1984) *The Counts of Falkenstein: Noble Self-consciousness in the Twelfth Century*, Philadelphia.

—— (1986) 'The German nobility in the High Middle Ages', *American Historical Review* 91: 553–75.

García Moreno, L. A. (1974) *Prosopografica del reino visigodo de Toledo*, Salamanca.

Garnett, G. (1986) 'Coronation and propaganda: some implications of the Norman claim to the throne of England in 1066', *Transactions of the Royal Historical Society* 5th ser., 36: 91–116.

Geary, P. (1985) *Aristocracy in Provence*, Philadelphia.

Genicot, L. (1962a) 'La Noblesse au moyen âge dans l'ancienne Francie', *Annales ESC* 17: 1–17.

—— (1962b) 'La Noblesse au Moyen Âge dans l'ancienne "Francie". Continuité, rupture ou évolution?', *Comparative Studies in Society and History* 5: 52–9. (Tr. into English as: 'The nobility in medieval Francia: continuity, break or evolution?', in F. L. Cheyette (ed.) *Lordship and Community in Medieval Europe: Selected Readings*, New York: 128–36.

—— (1975) 'Les Recherches relatives à la noblesse médiévale', *Bulletin de l'Académie Royale de Belgique*, Classe des Lettres, 5e série: 45–68. (Tr. into English as: 'Recent research on the medieval nobility', in T. Reuter (ed.) *The Medieval Nobility. Studies on the Ruling Classes of France and Germany from the Sixth to the Twelfth Century*, Amsterdam: 17–35.)

Gewin, J. P. J. (1964) *Die Verwandtschaften und politische Beziehungen zwischen den westeuropäischen Fürstenhäusern im Frühmittelalter*, The Hague.

Gieysztor, A. (ed.) *L'Europe aux 9e–11e siècles*, Warsaw.

—— *et al.* (1968) *A History of Poland*, Warsaw.

Gilliard, F. (1979) 'The senators of sixth-century Gaul', *Speculum* 54: 685–97.

Given-Wilson, C. (1987) *The English Nobility in the Later Middle Ages*, London.

Gladiß, D. von (1938) 'Adel und Freiheit im deutschen Staat des frühen Mittelalters', *Deutsches Archiv für Erforschung des Mittelalters* 2: 172–89.

Goetz, H.-W. (1983) '"Nobilis". Der Adel im Selbstverständnis der Karolingerzeit', *Vierteljahresschrift für Sozial- und Wirtschaftsgeschichte* 70: 153–91.

—— (1985) 'Zur Namengebung in der alamannischen Grunbesitzerschicht der Karolingerzeit. Ein Beitrag zur Familienforschung', *Zeitschrift für die Geschichte des Oberrheins* 133: 1–41.

—— (1987) 'Zur Namengebung bäuerlicher Schichten im Frühmittelalter. Untersuchungen und Berechnungen anhand des Polyptychons von Saint-Germain-des-Prés', *Francia* 15: 852–77.

Goody, J. (1983) *The Development of the Family and Marriage in Europe*, Cambridge.

Grahn-Hoek, H. (1976) *Die fränkische Oberschicht im 6. Jahrhundert*, Sigmaringen.

Green, D. H. (1965) *The Carolingian Lord*, Cambridge.

Green, J. A. (1986) *The Government of England under Henry I*, Cambridge.

Guerreau, A. (1990) 'Lournand au Xe siècle: histoire et fiction', *Le Moyen Âge* 96: 519–37.

Guilhiermoz, P. (1902) *Essai sur l'origine de la noblesse en France au moyen âge*, Paris.

Herrmann, J. (ed.) (1982) *Deutsche Geschichte in 12 Bänden, 1: von den Anfängen bis zur Ausbildung des Feudalismus Mitte des 11. Jahrhunderts*, Cologne.

Hicks, M. (1991) 'Bastard feudalism: society and politics in fifteenth-century England', in id., *Richard III and his Rivals: Magnates and their Motives in the Wars of the Roses*, London: 1–40.

Hlawitschka, E. (1982) 'Zur Erschliessung der Memorialüberlieferung aus dem Kloster Fulda', *Deutsches Archiv für Erforschung des Mittelalters* 38: 166–79.

—— (1987) *Untersuchungen zu den Thronwechseln der ersten Hälfte des 11. Jahrhunderts und zur Adelsgeschichte Süddeutschlands. Zugleich klärende Forschungen um 'Kuno von Öhningen'*, Vorträge und Forschungen, Sonderband 35, Sigmaringen.

—— (1990) 'Nochmals zu den Thronbewerbern des Jahres 1002', *Zeitschrift für die Geschichte des Oberrheins* 137; 460–7.

Holt, J. C. (1982–5) 'Feudal society and the family in early medieval England, I–IV', *Transactions of the Royal Historical Society*, 5th ser., 32 (1982): 193–212; 33 (1983): 193–220; 34 (1984): 1–25; 35 (1985): 1–28.

Holzfurtner, L. (1982) 'Untersuchungen zur Namensgebung im frühen Mittelalter nach den bayerischen Quellen des achten und neunten Jahrhunderts', *Zeitschrift für bayerische Landesgeschichte* 45: 3–21.

Horrox, R. (1992) 'Local and national politics in fifteenth-century England', *Journal of Medieval History* 18: 391–403.

Irsigler, F. (1969) *Untersuchungen zur Geschichte des frühfränkischen Adels*, Bonn.

Jackman, D. C. (1990) *The Konradiner. A Study in Genealogical Methodology*, Frankfurt am Main.

Jaeger, S. (1985) *The Origins of Courtliness: Civilizing Trends and the Formation of Courtly Ideals, 939–1210*, Philadelphia.

Jarnut, J. (1972) *Prosopographie und sozialgeschichtliche Studien zum Langobardenreich in Italien (568–774)*, Bonn.

Johrendt, J. (1971) *'Milites' und 'militia' im 11. Jahrhundert. Untersuchungen zur Frühgeschichte des Rittertums in Frankreich und Deutschland*, Erlangen.

Jones, M. (ed.) (1986) *Gentry and Lesser Nobility in Later Medieval Europe*, Gloucester.

Jussen, B. (1991) *Patenschaft und Adoption im frühen Mittelalter. Künstliche Verwandtschaft als soziale Praxis*, Göttingen.

Kampers, G. (1979) *Personengeschichtliche Studien zum Westgotenreich in Spanien*, Münster i. W.

Kämpf, H. (ed.) (1955) *Die Entstehung des deutschen Reiches*, Darmstadt.

Keeler, S. (1968) 'Elites', in D. L. Sills (ed.) *International Encyclopedia of the Social Sciences*, vol. 5, New York: 26–9.

Keen, M. (1984) *Chivalry*, New Haven.

Keller, H. (1986) *Zwischen regionaler Begrenzung und universalem Horizont, 1024–1250*, Berlin.

Kern, F. (1954) *Gottesgnadentum und Widerstandsrecht*, 2nd edn by R. Buchner, Darmstadt.

Koziol, G. (1992) *Begging Pardon and Favor. Ritual and Political Order in Early Medieval France*, Ithaca.

Kuhn, H., Wenskus, R. *et al.* (1973) 'Adel', in J. Hoops, *Reallexikon der germanischen Altertumskunde*, 1: *Aachen–Bajuwaren*, 2nd edn by H. Beck *et al.*, Berlin: 58–76.

Le Goff, J. (1979) 'Les Trois Fonctions indo-européennes. L'historien et l'Europe féodale', *Annales ESC* 34: 1187–1215.

Le Jan, R. (1995) *Famille et Pouvoir dans le Monde Franc (VIIe-Xe Siècle): Essai d'Anthropologie Sociale*, Paris.

Leyser, K. (1968) 'The German aristocracy from the ninth to the early twelfth century. A historical and cultural sketch', *Past and Present* 41: 25–53. (Reprinted with a few additions in Leyser 1982a.)

—— (1970) 'Maternal kin in early medieval Germany', *Past and Present* 49: 126–34.

—— (1976) 'K. B. McFarlane, 1902–66', *Proceedings of the British Academy* 62: 485–507.

—— (1982a) *Medieval Germany and its Neighbours, 900–1250*, London.

—— (1982b) 'Some reflections on twelfth-century kings and kingship', in Leyser 1982a.

Lhotsky, A. (1971) *'Apis Colonna*, Fabeln und Theorien über die Abkunft der Habsburger', in id., *Aufsätze und Vorträge*, 2: *Das Haus Habsburg*, ed. H. Wagner and H. Koller, Munich.

Loud, G. A. (1981) *'Gens Normannorum*: myth or reality', *Anglo-Norman Studies* 4: 104–16.

Loyn, H. (1974) 'Kinship in Anglo-Saxon England', *Anglo-Saxon England* 3: 197–209.

—— (1992a) *Anglo-Saxon England and the Norman Conquest. A Social and Economic History of England*, 2nd edn, London.

—— (1992b) 'Kings, gesiths and thegns', in *The Age of Sutton Hoo: The Seventh Century in North-western Europe*, Woodbridge: 75–81.

Luyn, P. van (1971) 'Les *milites* dans la France du XIe siècle. Examen des sources narratives', *Le Moyen Âge* 77: 5–51, 193–238.

Lynch, J. (1986) *Godparents and Kinship in Early Medieval Europe*, Princeton.

McFarlane, K. B. (1965) 'The English nobility in the later Middle Ages', in *XIIe Congrès international des sciences historiques*, 1: Rapports: grands thèmes, Vienna: 387–45.

—— (1973) *The Nobility of Later Medieval England*, Oxford.

Martindale, J. (1977) 'The French aristocracy in the early Middle Ages. A reappraisal', *Past and Present* 75: 5–45.

Mayer, H. E. (1988) *The Crusades*, tr. J. Gillingham, 2nd edn, Oxford.

Mayer, T. (1950) *Fürsten und Staat*, Weimar.

—— (1959) *Mittelalterliche Studien*, Sigmaringen.

Mitterauer, M. (1972) 'Formen adliger Herrschaftsbildung in hochmittelalterlichem Österreich. Zur Frage der autogenen Hoheitsrechte', *Mitteilungen des Instituts für österreichische Geschichtsforschung* 80: 265–338.

—— (1988) 'Zur Nachbenennung nach Lebenden und Toten in Fürstenhäusern des Frühmittelalters', in F. Seibt, (ed.) *Gesellschaftsgeschichte. Festschrift für Karl Bosl zum 80. Geburtstag*, Munich: 386–99.

Moeglin, J.-M. (1985) *Les Ancêtres du prince. Propaganda politique et naissance d'une histoire nationale en Bavière au moyen âge (1180–1500)*, Geneva.

Moore, R. I. (1984) 'Duby's eleventh century', *History* 69: 36–49.

Müller-Mertens, E. (1963) *Karl der Große, Ludwig der Fromme und die Freien*, Berlin.

Nelson, J. L. (1989) 'Ninth-century knighthood: the evidence of Nithard', in C. Harper-Bill, C. Holdsworth and J. L. Nelson (eds) *Studies in Medieval History presented to R. Allen Brown*, Woodbridge: 255–66.

Newman, C. E. (1988) *The Anglo-Norman Nobility in the Reign of Henry I. The Second Generation*, Philadelphia.

Nicholas, D. (1992) *The Evolution of the Medieval World. Society, Government and Thought in Europe*, 312–1500, London.

Oexle, O. G. (1978) 'Die funktionale Dreiteilung der Gesellschaft bei Adalbero von Laon', *Frühmittelalterliche Studien* 12: 1–54.

—— (1981) 'Die Wirklichkeit und das Wissen: ein Blick auf das sozialgeschtliche Œuvre von Georges Duby', *Historische Zeitschrift* 232: 61–91.

—— (1984) *'Tria genera hominum*: zur Geschichte eines Deutungsschemas der sozialen Wirklichkeit in Antike und Mittelalter', in L. Fenske, W. Rösener and T. Zotz (eds) *Institutionen, Kultur und Gesellschaft im Mittelalter: Festschrift für Josef Fleckenstein zu seinem 65. Geburtstag*, Sigmaringen.

Otto, E. F. (1937) *Adel und Freiheit im deutschen Staat des frühen Mittelalters*, Berlin.

Powys, J. K. (1984) *Aristocracy*, Oxford.

Prawer, J. (1968) 'The nobility and the feudal regime in the Latin kingdom of Jerusalem', in Cheyette 1968.

Reuter, T. (ed.) (1978) *The Medieval Nobility. Studies on the Ruling Classes of France and Germany from the Sixth to the Twelfth Century*, Amsterdam.

—— (1991) 'Unruhestiftung, Fehde, Rebellion, Widerstand: Gewalt und Frieden in der Politik der Salierzeit', in S. Weinfurter (ed.) *Die Salier und das Reich*, 3: *Gesellschaftlicher und ideengeschichtlicher Wandel im Reich der Salier*, Sigmaringen.

—— (1994a) 'Karl Leyser as a historian', in K. Leyser, *Communications and Power in Medieval Europe: The Gregorian Revolution and Beyond*, ed. T. Reuter, London.

—— (1994b) 'Pre-Gregorian mentalities', *Journal of Ecclesiastical History* 45: 465–74.

Reynolds, S. (1994) *Fiefs and Vassals. The Medieval Evidence Reinterpreted*, Oxford.

Richardson, H. G. and Sayles, G. O. (1963) *The Governance of Medieval England*, Edinburgh.

—— (1966) *Law and Legislation from Aethelberht to Magna Carta*, Edinburgh.

Riley-Smith, J. (1973) *The Feudal Nobility and the Kingdom of Jerusalem, 1174–1274*, London.

Rosenthal, J. T. (1976) *Nobles and the Noble Life, 1295–1500*, London.

Sablonier, R. (1979) *Adel im Wandel. Eine Untersuchung zur sozialen Situation des ostschweizerischen Adels um 1300*, Göttingen.

Saul, N. (1986) *Scenes from Provincial Life. Knightly Families in Sussex, 1280–1400*, Oxford.

Scaglione, A. (1991) *Knights at Court: Courtliness, Chivalry and Courtesy from Ottonian Germany to the Italian Renaissance*, Berkeley.

Schadt, H. (1982) *Die Darstellung der Arbores Consanguinitatis und der Arbores Affinitatis*, Tübingen.

Scheyhing, R. (1964) 'Adel', in A. Erler and E. Kaufmann (eds) *Handwörterbuch der deutschen Rechtsgeschichte*, 1: *Aachen–Haussuchung*, Berlin.

Schlesinger, W. (1941) *Die Entstehung der Landesherrschaft*, Dresden.

Schmid, K. (1957) 'Zur Problematik von Familie, Sippe und Geschlecht: Haus und Dynastie beim mittelalterlichen Adel', *Zeitschrift für die Geschichte des Oberrheins* 105: 1–62.

—— (1959) 'Über die Struktur des Adels im früheren Mittelalter', *Jahrbuch für fränkische Landesforschung* 19: 1–23. (Tr. into English as: 'On the structure of the nobility in the earlier Middle Ages', in Reuter 1978.)

—— (1964) 'Bemerkungen zur Frage einer Prosopographie des früheren Mittelalters', *Zeitschrift für württembergische Landesgeschichte* 23: 215–27.

—— and Wollasch, J. (1975) '*Societas et fraternitas*. Begründung eines kommentierten Quellenwerkes zur Erforschung der Personen und Personengruppen des Mittelalters', *Frühmittelalterliche Studien* 9: 1–48.

Schulte, A. (1922) *Der Adel und die deutsche Kirche im Mittelalter*, 2nd edn, Stuttgart.

Sellar, W. C. and Yeatman, R. J. (1960) *1066 and All That*, Harmondsworth.

Selle-Hosbach, K. (1974) 'Prosopographie merowingischer Amtsträger in der Zeit von 511–613', reprographically published dissertation, Bonn.

Southern, R. W. (1970) 'Ranulf Flambard' and 'The place of Henry I in English history', in *Medieval Humanism and Other Studies*, Oxford.

Staab, F. (1980) 'A reconsideration of the ancestry of modern political liberty: the problem of the so-called "king's freemen" (*Königsfreie*)', *Viator* 11: 51–70.

Stenton, F. (1943) *Anglo-Saxon England*, Oxford. (3rd edn, 1970.)

Stroheker, K. H. (1948) *Der senatorische Adel im spätantiken Gallien*, Tübingen.

Tabacco, G. (1960) 'La dissoluzione medievale dello stato nella recente storiografia', *Studi medievali*, terza ser., 1: 397–446.

—— (1966) *I liberi del re nell'Italia carolingia e postcarolingia*, Spoleto.

—— (1973) 'La connessione fra potere e possesso nel regno franco e nel regno longobardo', *I problemi dell'occidente nello secolo VIII*, Settimane di studi sull'alto medioevo 20: 120–68.

Tellenbach, G. (1939) *Königtum und Stämme im Werden des deutschen Reiches*, Weimar.

—— (ed.) (1957) *Studien und Vorarbeiten zur Geschichte des großfränkischen Adels*, Freiburg im Breisgau.

—— (1965a) 'Einleitung', in *XIIe Congrès international des sciences historiques*, 1: *Rapports: grand thèmes*, Vienna.

—— (1965b) 'Zur Erforschung des hochmittelalterlichen Adels (9.–12. Jahrhundert)', in *XIIe Congrès international des sciences historiques*, 1: *Rapports: grand thèmes*, Vienna.

Tellenbach, G. (1988) 'Rechtlicher Anspruch und soziale Geltung in der Geschichte des Adels im hohen Mittelalter', in id., *Ausgewählte Abhandlungen und Aufsätze* 3, Stuttgart.

Thais, L. (1976) 'Saints sans famille? Quelques remarques sur la famille dans le monde franc à travers les sources hagiographiques', *Revue Historique* 225: 3–20.

Topfer, Bernhard (ed.) (1983) *Deutsche Geschichte in 12 Bänden, 2: Die entfaltete Feudalgesellschaft von der Mitte des 11.bis zuden siebziger Jahren des 15. Jahrhunderts*, Cologne.

Turner, R. V. (1988) *Men Raised from the Dust. Administrative Service and Upward Mobility in Angevin England*, Philadelphia.

Waas, A. (1919) *Vogtei und Bede in der deutschen Kaiserzeit*, 2 vols, Berlin.

Weinskus, R. (1959) 'Amt und Adel in der frühen Merowingerzeit'. *Mitteilungen Universitätsbund Marburg* 1(2): 40–56.

—— (1976) *Sächsischer Stammesadel und fränkischer Reichsadel*, Göttingen.

Werner, K.-F. (1958–60) 'Untersuchungen zur Frühzeit des französischen Fürstentums, 9.–10. Jahrhundert', *Die Welt als Geschichte* 18 (1958); 256–89; 19 (1959): 146–93; 20 (1960): 87–119.

Werner, K.-F. (1977a) 'Liens de parenté' et noms de personne. Un problème historique et méthodologique', in J. Le Goff and G. Duby (eds) *Famille et parenté dans l'occident médiéval*, Collection de L'École Française de Rome 30, Rome.

—— (1977b) 'Problematik und erste Ergebnisse des Forschungsvorhabens "PROL" (Prosopographia Regnorum Orbis Latini). Zur Geschichte der west- und mitteleuropäischen Oberschichten bis zum 12. Jahrhundert', *Quellen und Forschungen aus italienischen Archiven und Bibliotheken* 57: 69–87.

—— (1978) 'Important noble families in the reign of Charlemagne', in Reuter 1978.

—— *et al.* (1977) 'Adel', *Lexikon des Mittelalters*, 1: *Aachen bis Bettelorden*, Munich.

Werner, M. (1982) *Adelskreise im Umfeld der frühen Karolinger*, Sigmaringen.

Wickham, C. (1992) 'Problems of comparing rural societies in early medieval western Europe', *Transactions of the Royal Historical Society*, 6th ser., 2: 221–46.

Williams, D. (1990) 'The Peverils and the Essebies 1066–1166: a study in early feudal relationships', in id. (ed.) *England in the Twelfth Century. Proceedings of the 1988 Harlaxton Symposium*, Woodbridge.

Wolf, A. (1991) 'Königkandidatur und Königsverwandtschaft. Hermann von Schwaben als Prüfstein für das "Prinzip der freien Wahl"', *Deutsches Archiv für Erforschung des Mittelalters* 47: 45–117.

Wollasch, J. *et al.* (1982) *Synopse der cluniacensischen Necrologien*, 2 vols, Munich.

11

MEDIEVAL MILITARY HISTORIOGRAPHY

Bernard S. Bachrach

INTRODUCTION

Beginning in the early twentieth century a scholarly consensus gradually formed concerning the configuration of medieval military history. This consensus was confirmed in three magisterial historical syntheses. The pioneering work was carried out by the German historian Hans Delbrück, whose monumental *Geschichte der Kriegskunst im Rahmen der politischen Geschichte* began appearing in 1900.[1] In England, Sir Charles Oman began his studies with a short undergraduate Oxford essay, *The Art of War*, published in 1885[2] and built this study over the next generation into a magisterial two volume work, *History of the Art of War in the Middle Ages*, which finally was completed in 1923 (Oman 1924). The French historian, Ferdinand Lot, although he was a generalist in medieval history, provided the third leg of this triad. Following the end of the Second World War and probably stimulated by it, he published his exceptionally important *L'Art militaire et les armées au moyen âge et dans la Proche-Orient* (1946).

For Delbrück, Oman, Lot and those who followed in their wake, battles were the essence of military history and not much else mattered.[3] With combat in the field as its focus, medieval military history was reduced to a rather simple formula. Prior to the Middle Ages battle in western Europe was dominated by the highly trained and well-organized infantry legions of the Roman Empire. Then, for several hundred

---

1 Hans Delbrück, *Geschichte der Kriegskunst im Rahmen der politischen Geschichte*, 6 volumes (Berlin, 1900–36) of which volumes 2 and 3 are relevant to the present study. These are now available in English translation by Walter J. Renfroe as *History of the Art of War within the Framework of Political History*, vols 2 and 3 (Westport, CT, 1975–82).
2 This study is best consulted in Oman, *The Art of War in the Middle Ages*, revised and edited by John H. Beeler (Ithaca, New York, 1953). Oman's essay, which won the Lothian Prize, was originally written in 1884.
3 Smail 1967: 14–17 provides an excellent exposé of this problem.

years, the barbarians who destroyed the Roman Empire and created the Dark Ages fought on foot according to the tribal customs which they had brought with them from the German forests. These barbarians, gathered into embarrassingly small armed groups (much imagination was expended to explain how they managed to conquer the Roman Empire), fought each other in an ongoing search for greater and greater amounts of plunder and the irrational pursuit of glory. War, as commonly understood in Western civilization, ceased to exist.

As Europe gradually emerged from the Dark Ages, a process for which many causes were postulated, feudalism came to characterize life in the West; the true Middle Ages had arrived. Thus, knights, who were feudal vassals serving their feudal lords for forty days in return for fiefs, dominated warfare by the use of mounted shock-combat tactics, i.e. feudal warfare. These tactics, it came widely to be believed, had been made possible by stirrups. Medievalists thus were encouraged to compare heavily armed knights to modern tanks which were presumed to roll over anything in their path.[4]

However, the chivalric warriors of feudal Europe also were seen as highly individualistic in their *mentalité* and ostensibly lacking in anything resembling military discipline. Thus, military historians were torn between images of the tank and of the aviation aces of the first World War in a continuing search for modern analogues to make the feudal Middle Ages comprehensible to military buffs. In this context, feudal generalship, as demonstrated through the adroit deployment by military historians of a careful selection of anecdotes illustrating gross stupidity, was considered an oxymoron.

Feudal castles were regarded as the home base for these heavily armoured feudal warriors, who were organized into such small groups that they hardly merited being called armies. The strongholds were thought to have begun as motte-and-bailey works of earth and wood. From these humble, almost barbarian beginnings, they gradually evolved into concentric stone fortifications of immense size and sophistication. From these feudal castles, mounted knights (a favoured synonym for heavily armoured feudal warriors) raided the humble farmsteads of defenceless serfs. These poor unfortunates belonged to neighbouring feudal lords and to their feudal vassals who also lived in feudal castles but rarely came out to defend their lowly dependants.

The mounted knight thus terrorized the countryside in an ongoing search for booty and sport. He practised for this warfare during tournaments in which jousts and mêlées abounded, wealth, fame and glory were attained, and few if any participants were killed or even injured. These games, the essence of chivalry, were the putative training ground on which mounted feudal knights – the only people who putatively counted in medieval warfare – learned how to fight one another. Should a real battle ever occur an enemy knight preferably was not to be killed but

---

4　This argument reached its high point of popularity with the publication of White 1962. White provides extensive bibliographical references.

just as in the tournaments he was to be unhorsed, captured, stripped of his gear and held for ransom. It was usual, however, even to avoid such sham battles.

When the feudal lord and his feudal knights were attacked by real armies (historians had great trouble accounting for these forces since feudal knights fighting on horseback with mounted shock combat tactics were not much in evidence and, in addition, it was difficult to see such armies as small forces) the flower of chivalry ran off and hid in their feudal castles. Feudal sieges, although recognized as important by scholars, were not seriously studied because they were not regarded as real battles. Real battle, i.e. battle in the field and more especially 'decisive battle', was the true subject of study for the proper military historian. From such battles the *cognoscenti* could draw lessons, and then articulate broad-gauged generalizations which would make a sociologist weep with joy.

According to this consensus, however, several centuries slipped by and the feudal mode of military life eventually broke down under the impact of the growing development of towns and the centralized state. Kings, who obtained substantial amounts of money garnered from taxing the rising middle classes in the newly emerging urban centres, were able to pay for small standing armies and hire mercenaries to help fight their wars. At the same time, merchants and guildsmen developed urban militias and also hired mercenaries to help them defend the walls of their cities and towns against feudal knights who were still searching for booty. The chivalric classes took an unconscionably long time to realize that they were anachronisms. Thus, in the final analysis, merchant gold replaced feudal honour as the nexus which undergirded military life.

The emerging bureaucratic monarchs and their cash-rich bourgeois allies, together with the development of the longbow, crossbow and gunpowder, gradually destroyed chivalry and with it the feudal Middle Ages. Now this lengthy end to medieval military history is being seen as a series of 'revolutions' which coveniently foreshadow Michael Roberts' 'military revolution' of the early modern era (see e.g. Roberts 1993). All of this change, whether revolutionary or not, was accomplished in preparation for the emergence of the national armies which, with great amounts of money and rapidly evolving technology, were to dominate the battlefields of Europe in the future.

A useful if only partial summary of this *status questionis* was provided by J. F. Verbruggen in 1954. As will be seen below, however, he introduced some important innovations which nevertheless have been very slow to be appreciated.[5] At present the most complete summary of the state of the question concerning the military in medieval Europe is to be found in *La Guerre au moyen âge* by Philippe Contamine. This work originally was published in 1980, and in the treatment of a select group

---

5   Verbruggen 1954 was not easily accessible to most readers. Indeed, this work ostensibly came to be appreciated as a result of the translation by Sumner Willard and S. C. M. Southern (*The Art of Warfare in Western Europe During the Middle Ages from the Eighth Century to 1340* (Amsterdam, 1977)). However, it is important to note that the extensive footnote apparatus of the original Dutch edition was omitted from the translation.

of topics Contamine also identifies various changes that have been made in the synthesis that had been crafted by Delbrück *et al.*[6]

TOWARDS A NEW CONSENSUS

The picture of medieval military history which is emerging today is very different from that just described. Continuity between the ancient and medieval periods is the dominant theme of contemporary research. The term 'Dark Ages', which served as a staple for the transition from the ancient to the medieval world, has been eliminated as a historiographical concept. Cities did not become deserted ruins, roads and bridges were maintained (indeed, the road system of western Europe in 600 was better than in 1600), learning did not disappear and the economy did not devolve into autarky.[7] The military organization of the so-called barbarian tribes, now more properly characterized as the Romano-German successor states of the Roman Empire, 'recalls *Romania* and not *Germania*' (see e.g. Bachrach 1972: 128).

The grand strategies or military policies that were developed by men such as Theodoric the Great and Clovis, who were responsible for military decision-making in the Romano-German kingdoms of early medieval Europe, generally showed no inclination to eliminate the vast physical infrastructure of fortified cities, fortresses, ports and roads that had been created by the Empire.[8] In addition, the decision-makers found that the corpus of ancient military science, available in books such as Vegetius's *De re militari*, which was known in the West from its edition made at Constantinople in 450, reinforced these tendencies towards continuity.[9] Further reinforcement of Late-Antique ideas came as a result of the substantial direct contact of Westerners with the Byzantine and later with the Muslim military which both were heirs of Rome's martial legacy. In a reciprocal manner, access to information concerning the past provided additional stimuli for military commanders in the West to take advantage of the physical legacy bequeathed to them by the Empire.

This continuity between the later Roman Empire and the Middle Ages, however, is not to be understood as sclerotic rigidity or stasis. Rather it should be seen as gradual and incremental change over many centuries within a system rooted firmly in the ancient world. Thus, for example, the works of Vegetius not only were copied but also epitomized, glossed and translated from Latin into the vernacular languages of western Europe during the Middle Ages (Shrader 1976). The fortifications of the great Roman walled cities were improved and expanded, efforts

---

6   This work in now in its fourth edition (Paris, 1994), but the major advance over previous editions is to be found in the new bibliographies. The first edition was published in English translation with an updating of the bibliography by Michael Jones as *War In the Middle Ages* (Oxford, 1984).

7   On various of these topics see Brühl 1975; Durliat 1990; Werner 1984; McKitterick 1989.

8   Johnson 1983 provides a useful introduction to this very important topic along with a considerable bibliography.

9   See, for example, Bachrach 1985c, with the literature cited there.

were made to maintain the Roman roads, bridges and ports. It was no accident, for example, that William the Conqueror's invasion force sailed for England in 1066 from the old Roman port of Saint-Valéry-sur-Somme. Nor was it happenstance that the Norman duke landed his army at the Roman port of Aderita (Pevensey) which had had facilities for disembarking mounted troops since the Roman period (Bachrach 1985b).

MILITARY ORGANIZATION

These massive indications of continuity on a broad front usurp the position of the undisciplined 'feudal knight' as the key figure of medieval military history. The story begins in the later Roman Empire with the militarization of the civilian population. The imperial army, especially in the West, gradually devolved into soldier-farmers and soldier-city dwellers. At the same time the civilian population, both rural and urban, within the Empire, was progressively militarized. City walls were defended by urban militias and rural defence forces served on the frontiers where great landowners built fortifications (see e.g. Bachrach 1993c).

The Germanic peoples, who came to settle within the empire, were drawn, in general, from populations that long had been in contact with Roman civilization and were thoroughly influenced by it. For example, the Goths, Vandals, Burgundians and Lombards, already were converted to Christianity when they were drawn across the imperial frontier. The Roman government provided for the armament and support of these so-called invaders or conquerors with tax revenues – this was the case even in Britain, as evidenced by the *hospitalitas* agreements made by Vortigern with Hengist and Horsa.[10]

Many Germanic and other peoples, e.g. Sarmatians and Alans, from beyond the frontiers, had served the imperial military in various capacities for several hundred years prior to the establishment of the Romano-Germanic kingdoms in the western half of the empire (see e.g. Bachrach 1973). Even the military organization, strategy and battle tactics of the Huns were fundamentally transformed by their sojourn on the frontiers of the Roman Empire and through service as auxiliaries in the imperial army (Lindner 1981; Bachrach 1994b).

Throughout the period of the later Roman Empire and of its successor states in the West, all able-bodied secular male adults, who lived in and around the great fortified urban centres, which for the most part had been given new walls at a great expenditure of human and material resources during the fourth century, were organized into a militia in order to defend the city. Also those men who lived in or near the many other fortifications which dotted the countryside of the West, were trained to defend the walls of these *castra*, *castella* or lesser strongholds. In the countryside, free farmers, dependent cultivators and in some places even slaves, whether 'Roman' natives or 'barbarian' newcomers, were provided with arms,

---

10 In general, see Goffart 1989, with the corrections and additions by Durliat 1988, and regarding England, see Bachrach 1988 and 1990. Both are reprinted in Bachrach 1993a.

trained and mobilized for the local defence, e.g. the 'great *fyrd*' in Anglo-Saxon England. By and large these defence obligations were limited to military operations undertaken within the *civitas*, i.e. the local administrative district of imperial orgin, in which the militiamen lived.[11] This tradition of the local militia used for the local defence remained a constant throughout the Middle Ages in areas that had once been a part of the Roman Empire and beyond its erstwhile frontiers as well. It was not an innovation of the later Middle Ages created by burghers and guildsmen to defend their new-found wealth from greedy feudal knights.[12]

Recent research has now made it clear that beginning with the Romano-German kingdoms of the early Middle Ages and in their successor states throughout the duration of the Middle Ages, civilians of sufficient means, regardless of their ethnic backgrounds, had military obligations that went well beyond participation in the local defence. These men, e.g. the 'select *fyrd*' in Anglo-Saxon England, were required to campaign beyond their home district, i.e. the *civitas*, *pagus* or county (the shire was a subdivision of the county headed by a *vicecomes* or sheriff). Thus, these select levies undertook offensive operations that might last several months.[13]

This obligation to participate in *expeditio* or *hostis* was dependent in large part upon the wealth of the person in question. Such campaigning was undertaken ostensibly at the expense of the individual militiaman and the only significant compensation he was likely to obtain was a share in the booty that a successful expedition might yield. Over time this practice is seen by some scholars to have had the effect of weakening the economic position of small landholders who were pressed into service too frequently and for too long a period of time.[14]

From a numerical perspective, the militarized civilian population throughout the Middle Ages provided the overwhelming majority of the armed forces for local defence and also the rank and file of the armies which carried out major offensive operations which were aimed at permanent conquest. However, these part-time soldiers were significantly strengthened both for local defence and while on *expeditio* by units of professional troops which were organized in a vast variety of ways. First and foremost among the professional soldiers were the armed followers (*clientela*) of the more important men in society including the king. Most of the members of such a *Gefolgschaft* served in the household of the man who supported them, other men were established with their families

---

11 Bachrach 1993c 58–9, and the literature cited there.
12 This subject is in need of a great deal more work. However, see, for example, the regional studies by Bachrach 1987 and 1993b; and Powers 1988.
13 The situation has been best elaborated with regard to England. See, for example, the now classic works Hollister 1962 and 1965. With regard to the continent see Bachrach 1972: levies, *passim*; and 1974. Both are reprinted in Bachrach 1993a.
14 Müller-Mertens 1963: 93–111 is compelled by his Marxist imperative to see this service as very burdensome, one might even say exploitative. Regarding booty as presented in the *Histories* of Gregory of Tours see Weidemann 1982: II, 279–81.

in military colonies, or as garrisons in local strongholds, and sometimes on lands of their own.[15]

Medieval historians have given a great deal of attention to these armed followings of powerful men. Yet, much of this effort has been thoroughly misplaced by its focus on so-called feudal armies and the feudal host. The armed followings of the great men, including emperors and kings, were very important during the later Roman Empire, e.g. the famous general Belisarius had a *Gefolgschaft* of 7,000 effectives, and this type of arrangement continued to be so throughout the history of the medieval West. Indeed, the liveried *servientes* of the magnates in the later Middle Ages are thought to characterize 'Bastard Feudalism' (see e.g. Dunham 1970).

The men who served in these followings were described in Latin, as well as in various vernacular languages, by a plethora of words. However, the English word 'vassal', from the Latin *vassallus* which is derived from the Celtic *gwas* meaning 'boy', has become the (somewhat misleading) commonplace pseudo-technical term to describe these soldiers. Many and varied technical and non-technical terms also were used during the millennium under discussion here to describe the remuneration provided to these men. However, the term 'fief', derived from the word *feo*, i.e. a gift from the treasury (*fiscus*) which would seem to have obliged the recipient to serve the giver in a military capacity, has prevailed in scholarly usage and this, too, is rather unhelpful.[16]

Remuneration for these men ranged on the lower end of the scale from room, board and armament, which were provided to a serf or poor freeman, to the possession and ultimately even the ownership of extensive lands which entailed access to rents and even to government tax revenues. These great assets generally were given to magnates who commanded substantial armed followings of their own. The frequent distinction made by scholars between private and public in these matters is rather confusing and much more research is required. In this context, for example, the breadth and nature of the resources accounted under the heading of fief is misleading. A payment from the royal treasury or the comital fisc would seem to make the vassal an employee of the government despite whatever oaths or ceremonies, e.g. homage, in which the vassal may have partaken (ibid.). In this context, it must be emphasized that Roman *milites* during the later Empire took an oath to the emperor.

Scholarly focus on the means by which the armed followers of a king, bishop, duke, count or abbot, not to mention the merely wealthy layman, were remunerated throughout the Middle Ages has also proved misleading in some respects. The model generally employed, but rather poorly understood both from a structural and a military perspective, is that derived from the systematic efforts that were

---

15 Reynolds 1994 has now provided a searching evaluation of the unwarranted assumptions scholars have been making about vassals and fiefs for the past century and more. This work will now form the basis for further discussion of 'feudalism'.

16 See the various positions illuminated by Reynolds 1994: chs 2 and 3.

employed by King William I following his conquest of England in 1066. It was William's aim to secure the availability on a regular basis of many of the soldiers (*milites*) who had participated in the conquest for expeditionary service during a period of perhaps forty days each year. Thus William granted on average a holding of 1.5 hides, i.e. about 50 per cent more wealth than was required by an ordinary family for its sustenance, to a great many of these soldiers (most recently, see Morillo 1994).

William's initiative, as ostensibly recorded in Domesday Book, amounted to a tenurial revolution because of its vast scale and organization. The grants made by William to these *milites* were, however, royal lands and thus these troops can hardly be construed as being anything other than agents of the government. The belief by some scholars that England belonged to William by right of conquest does not meaningfully alter this observation.

Whatever may have been the impact of William's actions on the history of landed property in England, his efforts to assure the readiness for war of a cadre of professional soldiers through the distribution of government lands ended, on the whole, in failure. Thus, by the reign of his successor, William Rufus (d. 1100), two major developments had begun to compensate significantly for William's faulty system. First, the English kings increasingly commuted the military service owed by these *milites* to a money payment (scutage) which then was used to purchase the service of professional soldiers who often are styled mercenaries in the sources (see e.g. Powicke 1962). The second development, the 'money fief', was a variation on the mercenary theme which aimed to avoid some of the stigma as well as the socio-political risks inherent in buying the services of soldiers. These types of risk, for example, became exceptionally obvious in the city states of Renaissance Italy where captains of mercenary bands took control of the government. Thus, a lord–vassal bond was created to 'soften' the impersonality of the cash nexus through the use of oaths that were strengthened by religious sanctions. The money fief, however, was ostensibly a contract for military service (Lyon 1957 remains basic).

By relying heavily on the use of money payments to secure elite forces, William the Conqueror's youngest son, Henry I, and more particularly his Angevin successors provided the Anglo-Norman and the Angevin Empires, respectively, with great flexibility in developing both grand strategy and campaign strategy. The use of scutage, and especially of the money fief, with frequent modification of detail to account for changing economic, social and political circumstances, continued throughout western Europe during the Middle Ages (Morillo 1994; Lyon 1957). The survival of written contracts, despite their time-conditioned nature, and the fixing of terminology by scribes have helped to create an illusion that the use of money to secure military service was a dramatic development of the high Middle Ages when, in fact, there was little new and certainly nothing revolutionary taking place.

The so-called 'feudal host', composed of knights serving their lords for a period of forty days in return for their fiefs, had little positive to contribute to medieval military organization. The very obvious limitations to the formulation of strategy and the difficulties imposed upon the prosecution of extended campaigns by a six-week term of service undermined, even under best-case conditions, whatever positive qualities William the Conqueror may have envisioned in such a 'feudal' system. Thus it is not surprising to find more references to the 'feudal host' in the works of modern writers, although less so among modern specialists in medieval military history, than in the medieval sources.

The growing recognition that feudalism, however defined, is of little importance to medieval history, in general, has gradually inspired the realization that feudalism is of no particular value to the study of medieval military history. Of course, views such as 'Cavalry was the essential feature of a medieval army, and the knights who formed it were the essential feature of medieval society' (Davis 1989: 11) die hard despite the facts. Thus, as revision takes place, it is important to emphasize that scholars have shown that throughout the history of medieval Europe, beginning with the Romano-German kingdoms of the early Middle Ages, policy decisions were taken at the highest levels of society in an effort to ensure that units of fighting men were equipped with horses. This emphasis on providing war horses for the army is a constant throughout the Middle Ages and has nothing in particular to do either with knights or with feudalism (Bachrach 1985a).

However, just as the term 'knight' prejudices the meaning of the term *miles*, so the use of the term 'cavalry' is misleading because it masks the tactical flexibility of medieval mounted troops. Warren Hollister made the point exceptionally well when he observed:

> In every important battle of the Anglo-Norman age, the bulk of the feudal cavalry dismounted to fight. At Tinchbrai in 1106. ... In 1119 ... at Bremule. ... At Bourg Theroulde (1124) ... at Northallerton (1138). ... [and] At Lincoln (1141) the ... knights ... dismounted and fought as infantry.
>
> (Hollister 1965: 131–2)

We may now safely ignore the terms 'feudal', 'cavalry' and 'knight' used by Hollister, which have the capacity seriously to compromise our understanding of medieval warfare. Nevertheless, we must recognize the fact that far more often than not mounted troops fighting in western Europe and while on the crusades in the Middle East dismounted in order to engage the enemy on foot (Morillo 1994; Bradbury 1992). Indeed, only among the mounted troops of nomad peoples such as the Huns and the Mongols, where each soldier had his own fire-power in the form of a compound bow, was cavalry institutionalized as the basic or dominant element of the army on the field of battle.

With feudalism and mounted shock-combat now on the wane as motifs, chivalry is the one remaining support for the misleading view of medieval war propagated by Oman, Delbrück and Lot. Hyperbolic accounts of combat in epic poems such as the *Song of Roland* as well as the ill-informed comments of monkish chroniclers have influenced generations of medievalists while at the same time providing a basis for explaining the social prominence of 'knights' as a class with a self-evident military mission that justified the importance of this *ordo*. The willingness of those in the

Middle Ages who saw themselves as members of the *ordo* of fighters to propagate the myth that they were 'the essential feature of a medieval army' is hardly surprising. These men liked to see themselves as heroes, however fantastic the situation might be. Indeed, Western civilization for several millennia has had an addiction to the heroic. In addition, the *ordo* of fighters sought to legitimize itself by informing society of the centrality of its military mission through the sponsorship of entertainment, e.g. troubadours and tournaments.[17] The relevance of this chivalric ideology to warfare remains to be demonstrated. As I have concluded elsewhere, 'medieval chivalry is to medieval warfare as courtly love is to medieval sex' (Bachrach 1988a).

The gradual decline of the 'man on horseback' as the focus of medieval military history has encouraged specialists to think about medieval warfare differently and this has hastened the fall of the feudal knight as a historiographical symbol. Ironically, it had long been recognized by Delbrück *et al.* that throughout the Middle Ages warfare was dominated by sieges. However, the doctrinaire insistence of specialists in military history that battles were the only proper subject for military historians to study ostensibly nullified this fact and gave solace to institutional historians working on feudalism and literary scholars who pursued the chivalric ideal.

Recently, however, some specialists have begun to abandon the focus on battle and have turned to the severely neglected subject of sieges. Thus, for example, in his new book on medieval siege warfare, Ray Bradbury correctly observes 'there was a direct continuity throughout our period [450–1565]' and regards as his 'most notable conclusion' the finding of 'how similar are the methods and conventions [of siege warfare] applied at the start, and still at the end'. Bradbury begins with the obvious insight, 'siege warfare was Roman rather than barbarian'. Indeed, towns and cities, most of which remained within their Roman-built defences for the greater part of the Middle Ages, were the usual objects of sieges. As more and more studies of siege warfare are being published a new and proper focus of medieval warfare is becoming evident.[18]

The dominance of siege warfare brings to the fore the matter of military architecture, technology and logistics. Much work has been done recently on fortifications by both archaeologists and historians of architecture. This work has resulted in the generation of a considerable amount of data regarding architectural styles and building technology with some meagre attention to material and social costs of construction.[19] However, these studies generally are of little direct value to the military historian in their present form (see e.g. Bachrach 1992). The connections between design, technology, costs and actual warfare have not been developed.[20] Indeed, the so-called 'new archaeology' exhibits a vigorous ideological

---

17   The basic work describing this ideology remains Keen 1984.

18   Bradbury 1992: 333, 2, respectively, for the quotations, and for a general examination of the state of the question see Bachrach 1994c.

19   Excellent bibliographies are to be found in Contamine.

20   See the pioneering effort by Bachrach 1984.

bias, often of an economic determinist cast, against both military history and the upper classes.[21]

While Marxist detritus distorts the role of fortifications in the Middle Ages, the romanticized 'old soldier syndrome' delays the discussion of both military technology and logistics that is vitally needed. Nevertheless, a few scholars, with the requisite background in physics, have considerably advanced our knowledge of various types of siege engines and other missile weapons.[22] The gap between our scientific knowledge of how various mechanical devices were constructed, how they operated and the role they played in particular combat situations remains to be bridged.[23]

A similar situation obtains regarding arms and armour. Much has been done with manuscript illustrations and surviving artefacts as well as with regard to metal-working.[24] However, study of design and manufacture have yet to be related either to the economy or to warfare in a meaningful manner on a consistent basis. For example, the work of Salin and Smith in the laboratory is more than a generation old but cost-models for the making of swords and armour in order to supply troops have not been developed nor have the costs of arrow-making been adequately explored. Indeed, the entire arms industry, with the exception of some specialized studies of the later Middle Ages, remains to have its history written.[25]

Current knowledge with regard to combat techniques, i.e. how weapons and allied technology were used, is also very mixed. For example, it has now been established that from the eighth century, when stirrups were introduced into the West, to the twelfth century at least three major combat techniques were developed to take advantage of this curious device in combat. The couched-lance technique, which is generally regarded as a fundamental prerequisite for mounted shock-combat as traditionally understood, was a product of the twelfth century and required significant concomitant developments in the design of the saddle before it could be used with any consistency.[26]

With regard to archery, crossbows, swords, axes and various types of pole weapons there is more imagination than factuality to be found in traditional scholarship. More specifically, anecdotes remain the basic evidence found in scholarly works, whether they are culled from medieval sources of dubious value or from uncontrolled modern experiments. Popularizations are usually even less critical.[27]

Naval warfare and all the prerequisites for its execution is one of the subjects traditionally seen as marginal by medieval military historians. A large and very

---

21 Fehring 1991 represents the tradition which prevails on the continent while Samson (ibid.: xiii of the translator's preface) would appear to lament this.

22 DeVries 1992: 95–110 provides a helpful treatment of this neglected topic.

23 See the recent efforts by Rogers 1992.

24 Nicolle 1988 is basic but one should also become familiar with Robinson 1975.

25 The relevant literature is available in Contamine 1994.

26 DeVries 1992: 95–110 reviews the problem in detail.

27 Bradbury 1985 does a better job than most.

valuable body of scholarly literature concerning the construction of ships and to a lesser extent regarding ports and other docking facilities has been developed. This is largely the result of intensive archaeological work done in northern Europe and of underwater archaeology in the Mediterranean. Model building has been of exceptional importance but this type of 'experimentation' often is not scientifically controlled and much work is done to justify a particular interpretation as with William the Conqueror's horse-transports. In addition, costs have not been adequately assessed. On the whole there is a great need to have this work integrated into the study of military history.[28]

The question of cost, whether for fortifications or weapons, brings into sharper focus the matter of logistics. The cliché that an army travels on its stomach was as true during the Middle Ages as in any other period of history. Indeed, the manufacture and distribution of equipment is as fundamental a part of making war as the supply of troops with food and shelter, the availability of transport, and the maintaining of fortifications, bridges, roads, wagons, beasts of burden, ports and ships.[29]

The recognition that medieval warfare was dominated by the siege of large urban centres has brought into question the notion that medieval armies were small. This fundamental and most influential characteristic of Delbrück's synthesis was first undermined for the later Roman Empire by the work of Theodor Mommsen. Now it is clear that the number of men under arms during the later Roman Empire was very large as compared, for example, with the period of Julius Caesar and Augustus. It is established that c. 425, the regular army for both the eastern and the western halves of the Empire probably reached a peak of around 645,000. In the reign of Justinian (d. 565) 645,000 men were considered necessary for the defence of the Empire despite its much truncated area.[30]

However, little attention has been paid by medievalists either to the later Roman evidence or to Delbrück's rule that 'it is impossible to feed large armies on a barter-economy basis' (Delbrück 1900–36). This rule was based on the erroneous assumption that autarky prevailed in Europe during the later Roman Empire and the Middle Ages (cf. Dopsch 1911–13). In 1968, however, Karl Ferdinand Werner vigorously chided medievalists for uncritically accepting the arguments for small numbers put forth by Delbrück and his followers and observed:

> in contrast to the extraordinary mistrust of critical efforts which accompany every effort to establish a greater troop strength, it must be emphasized that the effective scholar does not gain distinction simply because he estimated the smallest possible number for any army but because his methods bring him closer to the truth and, in addition, he can prove his point.
>
> (Werner 1968: 813–14)

28　Unger 1980 and Lewis and Runyan 1985 are good places to start.
29　See the pioneering survey by Bachrach 1993d.
30　See Mommsen 1889. Indeed, most recent scholars, as their work is summarized by Hoffmann 1969/70, see the armies of the later Roman Empire as very large.

Now the ability to muster large forces is gradually being established. It has recently been shown, for example, that Attila's forces at the battle of Châlons in 451 was in the neighbourhood of 40,000 to 50,000 effectives while the army of the imperial coalition led by Aetius was at least of the same order of magnitude and perhaps even 50 per cent larger (Bachrach 1994b). In 585, the Merovingian king, Guntram, set in motion both the standing army of his portion of the *regnum Francorum* as well as almost all his select militia for the purpose of crushing the usurper Gundovald. This force probably reached 20,000 effectives and ended the war with the successful siege of the old Roman fortified city of Convenae (Bachrach 1994a). Werner has shown that when most of western Europe was unified under Charlemagne, the Carolingians could muster from all the empire, excluding Italy, for simultaneous major campaigns in excess of 100,000 effectives, of whom at least 35,000 were heavily armed troops with horses. Individual armies of 35,000 to 40,000, though hardly common, were not unknown (Werner 1968, and accepted by Contamine 1994).

After Europe was divided by Charlemagne's grandsons, the armies mustered in the Carolingian successor states were smaller than those previously put into the field. Nevertheless, the city of Angers provided about 1,000 men for the select levy of the Angevin count during the mid-eleventh century, while the walls of this urban centre required some 1,500 local militiamen for its defence (Bachrach 1989). Across the Rhine, by the middle of the tenth century, the German kings commanded the service of some 15,000 heavily armed mounted troops, a force proportionally not inconsistent, in the light of economic and demographic growth, with the territory's capacity under Charlemagne. At the battle of the Lechfeld in 955, Otto the Great's army of 8,000 to 10,000 effectives constituted only a part of the campaign forces available to the ruler of the German kingdom: at the same time another major army raised largely in Saxony attacked the Slavs (Werner 1968, and accepted by Contamine 1994).

Under rather similar circumstances in England during the later ninth and tenth centuries, where foreign invasions and civil wars also took their toll upon the military, effectives were not lacking. Alfred the Great's burgs were garrisoned by 28,000 paid troops, while the five-hide system of military recruitment for the select levy provided a further 20,000 well-trained troops for campaigns. In addition to these forces, the Anglo-Saxon kings could draw upon their own personal armed followings and those of their magnates for offensive operations. At the battle of Hastings, King Harold mustered some 8,000 troops, mostly of the select levy, but this constituted only a small fragment of his campaign army.[31]

Unfortunately, this revisionist approach has not yet had an impact on the military demography of the crusades.[32] After the First Crusade, the armies of many individual Western states continued to increase in size and thus reflected the

---

31   Contamine 1994, in general, and for the battle of Hastings, in particular, Bachrach 1985b and 1986.
32   France 1994: 122–41 sticks with the old conservative views.

significant growth in Europe's population and wealth that was taking place. In England, for example, the Plantagenet monarchs in the twelfth century could raise some 20,000 mounted troops, while at the battle of Bouvines in 1214 the opposing armies may have reached a combined total of 40,000 men. Towards the end of the century, Edward I (d. 1307) mustered some 25,000 infantry and perhaps 5,000 horsemen on a recurring basis for his wars in Wales and Scotland; and French royal forces probably reached the same order of magnitude, with the south of the kingdom alone deemed able to provide Philip the Fair (d. 1314) with some 20,000 effectives. By contrast, the military forces available to the very populous Italian city states in the thirteenth and fourteenth centuries, both for defensive operations and for offensive efforts against nearby adversaries, seem immense. For example, Florence would appear to have mustered for offensive operations a force of 2,000 horsemen and 15,000 infantry.[33]

The great complexity of medieval warfare, which necessitated the defence of massive fortifications, the orchestration of extensive siege operations and the supply of large armies required considerable staff work and sophisticated leadership. Now, thanks in large part to the efforts of Verbruggen and Allen Brown, it is well understood that medieval military commanders were as good or a poor as any in history and that they were educated to their job properly.[34]

It is clear that military education in the Christian West, like that of the Byzantines and the Muslims, adhered to the principles articulated by the Greeks and practised by the Romans. One learned how to be a commander by reading military handbooks, studying history and through personal experience in subordinate positions. The copying, epitomizing and translating of Vegetius's *De re militari*, discussed above, gives ample evidence, as do translations of Julius Caesar's writings into the vernacular, that medieval military commanders knew that they could learn from books how better to master the art of war (in general, see Contamine 1994).

In-depth planning can be seen to obtain with regard to a series of early medieval building projects, which highlight grand strategic thought. Charlemagne's Rhine–Main–Danube canal was intended to connect the North Sea to the Black Sea and thereby provide the Carolingians with a logistic asset of immense importance. Offa's Dyke, which was twice the length of the combined Antonine and Hadrianic walls, the Danewirke and the *Limes Saxonicus* all illustrate sophisticated strategic thinking and also the institutional infrastructure to make it happen. Bede's belief that Britons in the fifth century, whom he generally found to be less than admirable, built both the Hadrianic and Antonine walls, though bad history, is a significant comment on his confidence in early medieval strategic thought and logistic capacity (see Bachrach 1993d).

---

33 Contamine 1994 provides a good summary of the growth in the size of armies.

34 Bradbury 1992: 80 summarizes the present situation with the angry observation: 'There are still historians who sneer at medieval commanders as if they were fools or idiots, but in all areas of war commanders, then as since, were quite capable of carefully weighing up the position and coming to sensible and practical decisions.'

The 'lessons' belatedly learned by the failure of the Maginot line have, in the eyes of some modern scholars, discredited early medieval strategic thought, which was, in part, based on wall building. For example, Offa's Dyke is seen as a strategic dinosaur that cost too much to build and by a process of circular argument is presumed never to have worked effectively. Some devotees of the new archaeology even doubt that it was built for military purposes. However, if we are to pay attention to judgements based on modern events, it is worth calling attention to the fact that modern experts tend to approve the defence-in-depth concept, e.g. NATO's strategy versus the Warsaw Pact. Thus, it must also be emphasized, if the presentists' game is to be played, that medieval strategists, like their later Roman predecessors, also employed the defence-in-depth concept. The great success of the systems which were built by Alfred the Great in Wessex and Fulk Nerra in Anjou eloquently testify to medieval strategic flexibility in defensive thinking.[35]

In terms of campaign strategy, modern research has made clear that from intelligence gathering to securing the final victory, whether with the disposition of captured fortifications or with the pursuit of the defeated enemy army, successful medieval commanders understood what was to be done and how to do it. On the offensive, manpower was mobilized in large numbers, equipment of all types was available, victualling was supplied and transport was arranged. Defensively, fortifications were prepared to withstand sieges, the countryside was stripped of supplies, mobile forces were put into the field to harass the enemy and deter the establishment of sieges.

Medieval tactics were no more or less sophisticated than those used in the ancient world or the early modern period. For example, the generalship of both William the Conqueror and Harold Godwinson, at all levels of responsibility and no less in the field at Hastings, have been shown to have been exemplary. Both commanders had the enemy thoroughly scouted. Harold's plan was to bottle up William's forces in the region of Hastings. To this end Harold advanced south and took the high ground on the road north from Hastings. Before leaving London, however, he sent the royal fleet with reinforcements to attack William from the sea and to destroy the Normans' ships. Harold's deployment at Hastings on the high ground was intended to undermine the effectiveness of William's attack and especially of his horsemen who would have to charge uphill. Harold's short-term problem was a lack of effectives and especially of highly-trained manpower due to the fact that less than three weeks earlier he had fought a major battle at Stamford Bridge and he had rushed south with only a fraction of his seasoned veterans. At Hastings, Harold had to depend, in large part, on *fyrd* troops and then he was only able to muster a very small fraction of the number of men eligible for military service.

Harold's manoeuvring forced William to choose between fighting quickly or retreating to Normandy. Both Harold and William knew that if the latter were to fight, his forces first would have to make a seven-mile march to the field that Harold

---

35 For Alfred see Abels 1988; and for Fulk Nerra, see Bachrach 1983.

had selected for the battle. Then the Norman duke would have to dislodge a marginally numerically inferior force from a very strong position. Thus, William demonstrated that he fully understood the importance of using firepower to 'soften up' by missile barrages a well-emplaced enemy before committing his foot and mounted forces to the attack. His archers and crossbowmen rained arrows and bolts on the Anglo-Saxon phalanx causing serious damage. Nevertheless, the combined efforts of William's foot and horse failed to break the Anglo-Saxon infantry formation through the morning and well into the afternoon. Finally, William deployed the 'feigned retreat' tactic which worked because Harold's phalanx was composed, by and large, of the least well-trained fighting men in the Anglo-Saxon army, i.e. the 'great *fyrd*' of the region, and they had little or no experience with this tactic. However, the extensive losses suffered, including Harold's two most able commanders, in the wake of two successful feigned retreats severely weakened the Anglo-Saxon formation. Thus, when Harold was felled by an arrow and the royal banner went down, the normal signal for retreat, the Anglo-Saxons began to retire from the field after some nine hours of bloody battle. William, nevertheless, ordered hot pursuit in order to inflict maximum casualties on the enemy (see Morillo 1994).

The view of warfare in the Middle Ages that was developed during the first half of the twentieth century is being taken to pieces during the second half of the century. The destruction of this synthesis has not proceeded evenly. This is true, in part, because studies of the very complex nature of medieval warfare, i.e. grand strategy (military policy), campaign strategy, battle tactics and combat techniques, are advancing at different rates. Thus, for example, the image that medieval warfare was dominated by the feudal knight riding over his enemies with mounted shock-combat tactics dies very slowly especially among those military historians who do not do research in this period, and even more so among the overwhelming majority of medievalists, who do not study military history at all. A new synthesis is at least a decade away.

REFERENCES

Abels, R. (1988) *Lordship and Military Organization in Anglo-Saxon England*, Berkeley.

Bachrach, B. S. (1972) *Merovingian Military Organization: 481–751*, Minneapolis.

—— (1973) *A History of the Alans in the West*, Minneapolis.

—— (1974) 'Military organization in Aquitaine under the early Carolingians', *Speculum* 49: 1–33.

—— (1983) 'The Angevin strategy of castle-building in the reign of Fulk Nerra', *American Historical Review* 88: 533–60.

—— (1984) 'The cost of castle-building: the case of the tower at Langeais, 992–994', in K. Reyerson and F. Powe (eds) *The Medieval Castle: Romance and Reality*, Dubuque, IA.

—— (1985a) 'Animals and warfare in early medieval Europe', *Settimane di Studio del Centro Italiano di Studi sull'alto Medioevo* 31, Spoleto (repr. in Bachrach 1993a).

—— (1985b) 'On the origins of William the Conqueror's horse transports', *Technology and Culture* 26: 505–31.

—— (1985c) 'The practical use of Vegetius' *De re militari* during the early Middle Ages', *The Historian* 47: 239–55.

—— (1986) 'Some observations on the military administration of the Norman Conquest', in R. A. Brown (ed.) *Anglo-Norman Studies VIII*, Woodbridge.

—— (1987) 'The northern origins of the peace movement at Le Puy in 975', *Historical Reflections*/Réflexions Historiques 14: 405–21.

—— (1988a) '*Caballus et caballus* in medieval warfare', in H. Chickering and T. Seiler (eds) *The Story of Chivalry*, Kalamazoo.

—— (1988b) 'Gildas, Vortigern and constitutionality in sub-Roman Britain', *Nottingham Medieval Studies* 32: 126–40.

—— (1989) 'Angevin campaign forces in the reign of Fulk Nerra, Count of the Angevins (987–1040)', *Francia* 16(1): 67–84.

—— (1990) 'The questions of King Arthur's existence and of Romano-British naval operations', *The Haskins Journal* 2: 13–28 (repr. in Bachrach 1993).

—— (1992) Review article of Pounds 1990 and Kenyon 1990, *Albion* 24: 301–4.

—— (1993a) *Armies and Politics in the Early Medieval West*, London.

—— (1993b) *Fulk Nerra, the Neo-Roman Consul, 987–1040. A Political Biography of the Angevin Count*, Berkeley and Los Angeles.

—— (1993c) 'Grand strategy in the Germanic kingdoms: recruitment of the rank and file', in F. Vallet and H. Kazanski (eds) *L'Armée romaine et les barbares du IIIe au VIIIe siècle*, Paris.

—— (1993d) 'Logistics in Pre-Crusade Europe', in J. A. Lynn (eds) *Feeding Mars: Logistics in Western Warfare from the Middle Ages to the Present*, Boulder, CO.

—— (1994a) *The Anatomy of a Little War: A Diplomatic and Military History of the Gundovald Affair: 568–586*, Boulder, CO.

—— (1994b) 'The Hun army at the battle of Chalons (451): an essay in military demography', in K. Brunner and B. Merta (eds) *Ethnogenese und Überlieferung: Angewandte Methoden der Frümittelalterforschung*, Vienna and Munich.

—— (1994c) 'Medieval siege warfare: a reconnaissance', *The Journal of Military History* 58: 119–33.

Bradbury, J. (1985) *The Medieval Archer*, New York.

—— (1992) *The Medieval Siege*, Woodbridge.

Brühl, C.-R. (1975) Palatium *und* Civitas: *Studien zur Profantopographie spätantiker* Civitates *vom 3. bis zum 13. Jahrhundert*, 1: *Gallien*, Cologne and Vienna.

Contamine, P. (1994) *La Guerre au moyen âge*, 4th edn, Paris. (English tr. of 1st edn: *War in the Middle Ages*, tr. N. Jones, Oxford, 1984.)

Davis, R. H. C. (1989) *The Medieval Warhorse, Origin. Development and Redevelopment*, London.

Delbrück, H. (1900–36) *Geschichte der Kriegskunst im Rahmen der politischen Geschichte*, 6 vols, Berlin.

DeVries, K. (1992) *Medieval Military Technology*, Peterborough, Can.

Dopsch, A. (1911–13) *Die Wirtschaftsentwicklung der Karolingerzeit vornehmlich in Deutschland*, 2 vols, Weimar (2nd edn, Weimar, 1922; repr. Weimar, 1962).

Dunham, W. H. (1970) *Lord Hastings' Indentured Retainers, 1461–1483; the Lawfulness of Livery and Retaining under the Yorkists and Tudors*, Hamden, CT.

Durliat, J. (1988) 'La salaire de la paiz sociale dans les royaumes barbares (Ve-VIe siècles)', in *Anerkennung und Integration*, Vienna.

—— (1990) *Les Finances publiques de Dioclétien aux Carolingiens (284–889)*, Sigmaringen.

Fehring, G. P. (1991) *The Archaeology of Medieval Germany, an Introduction*, tr. R. Samson, London and New York.

France, J. (1994) *Victory in the East: A Military History of the First Crusade*, Cambridge.

Goffart, W. (1989) *Romans and Barbarians: Techniques of Accommodation*, Princeton.

Hoffmann, D. (1969–70) *Das spätrömische Bewegungsheer und die* Notitia Dignitatum, Epigraphische Studien 7.1 and 7.2, Düsseldorf.

Hollister, C. W. (1962) *Anglo-Saxon Military Institutions on the Eve of the Norman Conquest*, Oxford.
—— (1965) *The Military Organization of Norman England*, Oxford.
Johnson, S. (1983) *Late Roman Fortifications*, Totowa, NJ.
Keen, M. (1984) *Chivalry*, New Haven, CT.
Kenyon, R. (1990) *Medieval Fortifications (The Archaeology of Medieval Britain)*, New York.
Lewis, A. R. and Runyan, T. J. (1985) *European Naval and Maritime History, 300–1500*, Bloomington, IN.
Lindner, R. P. (1981) 'Nomadism, horses and Huns', *Past and Present* 92: 3–19.
Lot, F. (1946) *L'Art militaire et les armées au moyen âge et dans la Proche-Orient*, 2 vols, Paris.
Lyon, B. D. (1957) *From Fief to Indenture*, Cambridge, MA.
McKitterick, R. (1989) *The Carolingians and the Written Word*, Cambridge.
Mommsen, T. (1989) 'Das römischen Militärwesen seit Diocletian', *Hermes* 24: 195–279.
Morillo, S. (1994) *Warfare under the Anglo-Norman Kings, 1066–1135*, Woodbridge.
Müller-Mertens, E. (1963) *Karl der Grosse, Ludwig der Fromme und die Freien*, Berlin.
Nicolle, D. C. (1988) *Arms and Armour of the Crusading Era: 1050–1350*, 2 vols, White Plains, NY.
Oman, C. W. C. (1924) *History of the Art of War in the Middle Ages*, 2nd edn, 2 vols, repr. New York, 1964.
—— (1953) *The Art of War in the Middle Ages*, rev. and ed. by J. H. Beeler, Ithaca, NY.
Pounds, N. J. G. (1990) *The Medieval Castle in England and Wales: A Social and Political History*, New York.
Powers, J. (1988) *A Society Organized for War. The Iberian Municipal Militias in the Central Middle Ages, 1000–1284*, Berkeley and Los Angeles.
Powicke, M. (1962) *Military Obligation in Medieval England*, Oxford.
Reynolds, S. (1994) *Fiefs and Vassals: The Medieval Evidence Reinterpreted*, Oxford.
Roberts, M. (1993) 'The military revolutions of the Hundred Years' War', *The Journal of Military History* 57: 241–78.
Robinson, R. H. (1975) *The Armour of Imperial Rome*, New York.
Rogers, R. (1992) *Latin Siege Warfare in the Twelfth Century*, Oxford.
Shrader, C. R. (1976) 'The ownership and distribution of manuscripts of Flavius Vegetius Renatus' *De re militari* before the year 1300', Ph.D. dissertation, University of Columbia.
Smail, R. C. (1967) *Crusading Warfare, 1097–1193*, Cambridge.
Unger, R. W. (1980) *The Ship in the Medieval Economy*, London.
Verbruggen, J. F. (1954) *De Krijgskunst in West-Europa in de Middeleeuwen, IXe tot begin XIV eeuw*, Brussels. (English tr.: *The Art of Warfare in Western Europe during the Middle Ages from the Eighth Century to 1340*, tr. S. Willard and S. C. M. Southern, Amsterdam.)
Weidemann, M. (1982) *Kulturgeschichte der Merowingerzeit nach den Werken Gregors von Tours*, 2 vols, Mainz.
Werner, K. F. (1968) 'Heeresorganisation und Kriegsführung im deutschen Königreich des 10. und 11. Jahrhunderts', *Settimane di Studio di Centro Italiano sull'alto Medioevo* 15, Spoleto.
—— (1984) *Les Origines (avant l'an mil): Histoire de France*, Paris.
White, L. T. (1962) *Medieval Technology and Social Change*, Oxford.

12

POPULAR RELIGION IN THE CENTRAL AND LATER MIDDLE AGES

Peter Biller

The meanings of the word 'religion' need first to be recalled. In the earlier and central Middle Ages 'religion' continued in its classical meaning of 'cult' and 'worship', with the added sense of 'monasticism' or 'monastic devotion'. Thus around 1000 such a phrase as 'the dominance of monasticism in religion' (in Latin) would have been a tautology. The phrase 'popular religion' would have been meant 'cult *or* a monastery (or monasteries) with a great following among the people'. A particular 'religion', meaning the *ensemble* of faith, cult and ecclesial body of a particular 'religion', such as 'the Christian religion' or 'the Jewish religion', was not possible, except through the approximate equivalents of 'law' or 'sect', as in 'the law (or sect) of the Jews, or Muslims, or (from the mid-thirteenth century) of the Mongols'. These early medieval semantic preferences – for using words which denoted *parts* of what we call 'religion', such as the 'faith' or 'cult' of a particular group, and for using the word 'religion' itself to denote devotion, cult or monasticism – do not only concern the lexicographer. They were deeply rooted in the way early medieval people saw things, and in the dominance of monasticism. Corresponding to later changes in awareness was the later infiltration, by around 1300, of 'the Christian (or other) religion', expressing an ensemble rather than just 'cult'. This sense only became really widespread in the early modern period.[1]

There is a general problem about the relation between modern historians defining and explaining phenomena within a category, 'popular religion', and those people in the past whose minds and actions may have been conditioned among other things by the lack of this phrase in this modern meaning. There is also an immediate practical problem of the definition to be used in a survey of modern historians, whose usage of 'religion' varies. The juxtaposition of one medieval and three modern definitions

---

1 On the history of the word 'religion', see Bossy 1982 and Biller 1985b. Mollat 1977 provides a useful discussion of key-words used in the study of medieval popular piety, and Boyle 1982 attacks the contrasting of 'popular' and 'learned' piety.

suggests cutting the Gordian knot at an angle. Medieval canon law divides Christians into two groups (clergy and lay) or three (clergy, religious and lay). In the standard mid-twelfth-century collection of canon law, Gratian's *Decretum*, a twofold division keeps the clergy and religious in one group (carrying out divine office, dedicated to prayer and contemplation).

> However the other kinds of Christians are the lay. For the Λαὸς is the people. These [the lay] are allowed to possess temporal things. ... They are permitted to marry, till the earth, judge between man and man, litigate, place offerings on altars, pay tithes, and they can be saved thus [leading this form of life] so long as they have done good and avoided vices.[2]

My purpose in citing this is not to trace how this 'constructs' subordination and passivity among the laity.[3] Rather, I want to benefit from several advantages in Gratian's text. One is the massive simplicity of the definition of the 'people', the 'lay', all who are not clergy or religious (or specially saintly). Another is the absence of the anachronist 'class' from the meaning of 'people'. Another is the way this definition overlaps with one of three *images* of 'popular religion' which André Vauchez listed in his concluding comments at a conference on medieval popular religion in 1976 (Vauchez 1976: 429–44 ('Conclusion')). The first of these *images* was folkloric 'religion', the second mass explosions of piety and 'religious' sentiment (such as crusading enthusiasm or flagellant movements), and the third consisted of the everyday 'religious' beliefs, devotions and practices of the laity in their parishes and confraternities. Gratian points to this third *image*. This third sense will be the principal meaning of 'popular religion' in this chapter, henceforth released from quotation marks. The recurrence of quotation marks will be a signal that 'religion' is being used more broadly.

The mid-1970s were rich in thought about what the study of medieval 'popular religion' should be. Some of the work had the programmatic excitement of enthusiastic historians who were writing their own methodologies. The historio-graphic past of 'popular religion' had a schematic clarity in their discussions, but to an ideologically more tepid surveyor – the author of this chapter – this past looks less clear and more miscellaneous and varied. Let me begin by imagining it as terrain which has been presented in a series of coloured maps, overlaid with cellophane transparencies which allow the viewer to see correlations between the physical geography and some short-term patterns of exchange: academic maps, but also geopolitical, ideological, religious, chronological.

An academic map shows at a distance medievalists in colleges and universities dotted round the world; they are most numerous in North America. A broader map encloses 'popular religion', and this is a map which shows the various forms of

---

2   C.12 q.1 c.7, in E. Friedberg, ed., *Corpus Iuris Canonici*, 2 vols, Leipzig, 1879, 1, col. 678: *Aliud vero est genus Christianorum. Λαὸς enim est populus. His licet temporalia possidere ... His concessum est uxorem ducere, terram colere, inter virum et virum iudicare, causas agere, oblationes super altaria ponere, decimas reddere, et ita salvari poterunt, si vicia tamen benefaciendo evitaverint.*

3   See comment on this by Le Bras 1959: 172–3.

'ecclesiastical' history, the history of the Church, the clergy, the religious orders, and Church institutions. It shows the institutional academic and publishing structure; the national academies; the series of record publications, supplying papal or episcopal registers. It also shows the Churches and religious orders, their publishers and journals, the interweaving with universities, for example the presence (often in theology faculties) in German universities of chairs of evangelical or Catholic Church history. Here there is traditional history of the Church and its clergy and institutions, whose basic features are almost as slow-changing as rock-formations.

The transparencies show some quite large things. One ideological cellophane has the Iron Curtain and the Wall, and in places like the Charles University in Prague or the Karl-Marx-University in Leipzig several decades of religion imprisoned behind the iron bars of the inexorable succession of socio-economic formations.[4] Orthodox 'religion' was accorded study as the ideology of the prevailing political and social order, and heretical 'religion' as, necessarily, the vocabulary of movements of dissent from or revolt against this order. Scriptural status had been given to comments on both these points made by Friedrich Engels in his *Peasant War in Germany* (1927: 51–5). Projection into the past was exemplified here in this form: a revolutionary tradition had its forerunners in medieval heresy or radical 'religious' movements. Leipzig historians such as Ernst Werner, Gottfried Koch, Martin Erbstösser[5] and Gerlinde Mothes (Mothes 1983; an account of Lollardy) kept up a flow of publications of this sort between the late 1950s and the early 1980s.[6] Easy to map: but we must remember also the reactions. For example, look with a magnifying glass at one dot on the western side of the Berlin Wall. It is a historian at the Kirchliche Hochschule, Kurt-Viktor Selge, writing on radical 'religious' movements around 1200. Writing as he does in the late 1960s, he is not only combining high traditions of German scientific and evangelical historical scholarship, but also looking over the Wall as he underlines the theme of preaching,[7] in his anxiety to whittle away the role played by poverty. 'Anxiety': because he is acutely aware of the grim dogmas just over the Wall which are inscribing 'poverty' on to any phenomena that were both 'religious' and radical. Another ideological transparency is confessional-religious: Catholic and Protestant. With apparently declining religions and the ecumenism of around 1960, it appears to get fainter. Perhaps only 'appears'. How *passionate* is Eammon Duffy's magnificent 1992 account of the vitality of late medieval religion – in his *The Stripping of the*

---

4 See Dorpalen 1985; for later decline, Iggers (1989) and 1991: 1–37.
5 The main works can be quickly traced through the entries in the indexes in two successive bibliographies, Grundmann 1967, and Berkhout and Russell 1981. A few more obscure eastern European works can be found in a bibliography from communist Hungary, Kulcsár 1964.
6 A good recent account is given in part 2 of Malecsek 1994.
7 The main work is Selge 1967. A sharp discussion of this point in Selge (without the ideological point at issue here) was given by Lambert 1977: Appendix C, pp. 353–5, and was not repeated in the revised 2nd edn of 1992. A brief account of Selge's career and works is given by Malecsek 1994: 77–9.

Altars: Traditional Religion in England 1400–1580. The transparency mapping the cradle-religions of historians shows that, despite veneers of modern academic jargon and what they call 'problematic', it is still necessary to ask basic and obvious questions about alignments between Protestantism and Catholicism and choice of subject and approach.

Riffling through the cellophanes we come across several marked 'France'. An early one has French Catholics, Gabriel Le Bras and two canons, F. Boulard and Etienne Delaruelle, with André Vauchez added later. Another one has places such as Fanjeaux and Toulouse in the south, and in the north Paris with its *Annales* and such figures as Jacques Le Goff, Emmanuel Le Roy Ladurie and Jean-Claude Schmitt. Let us dwell for a moment on this one, to glimpse the complexity which a monograph, called *'Annales' and Medieval Popular Religion*, would have to address. Lines go out from *Annales* towards those parts of eastern Europe where periods of liberalization (and the personal contacts of a Jacques Le Goff, married to a Pole) allowed in such an influence. And they go westward, especially to those historians who participated in Le Goff seminars. An American example is Lester K. Little, in his attempt to trace profound affinities and correlations between the socio-economic – the new prominence of money, towns and the merchant around 1200 – and the new prominence of absolute individual poverty in the spirituality of the same period (Little 1978; see also d'Avray 1985: part 4). This was in part inspired more distantly by the *Annales* saint and martyr, Marc Bloch, whose two feudal ages are updated, and more closely by Le Goff's papers and seminars on the friars and towns. This work stimulated more, perhaps, than Le Goff's famous demonstration of *La Naissance de purgatoire* (1981), which was transforming the afterlife from two (heaven and hell) to three (heaven, hell and purgatory) in the late twelfth century: a transition from binary to tertiary in 'religious' mental geography which had a structural correspondence with deep social transformations.[8] Le Goff presented friars almost as pastoral sociologists, concerned with size of population. Large numbers were needed to provide material support for friars living off many small donations, and towns contained more sins and therefore needed pastoral work more urgently. There is a touch of mid-twentieth-century French Catholic *sociologie regligieuse*. In England Alexander Murray's cartography of friars and Italian towns echoes this voice: friars are in the new 'housing-estates' (Murray 1972: 85–6). Elsewhere in England David d'Avray's literary analysis of similitudes used in friars' sermons – as much royal or chivalric or rural as mercantile and urban – allows him to refine Little's thesis about money and mendicant spirituality (d'Avray 1985: pt. 4), while his specialization in texts which concern communication lead him towards literary theory (d'Avray 1990 and 1994). Back in France, one generation down from Le Goff, there is Jean-Claude Schmitt, *annaliste* and at an early stage propounder of a two-culture approach which owes much to the early modern historian Carlo

---

8   Penetrating on Le Goff 1981 is Southern 1982. Le Goff's principal articles on friars and urbanization appeared in *Annales. Economies. Sociétés. Civilisations* 23 (1968), 335–52, and 25 (1970), 924–65.

Ginzburg. Carlo Ginzburg owed much to *Annales*, and also to Russia: Ginzburg's father and professor of Russian literature at Pisa, Leone Ginzburg, may have facilitated the influence of the two-culture theories of Bakhtin. *Annales* in general and Ginzburg and Bakhtin in particular have influenced the two-culture history of the Russian medievalist, Aaron Gurevich, and Ginzburg also features on another map, along with Jean Delumeau, Natalie Davis and John Bossy, which shows the influence of early modernists on medieval historians of popular religion. Lines criss-cross throughout.

From these various maps and transparencies I am selecting a few, and these I am necessarily simplifying. Their titles are: the rise of the laity; 1970s theorizing, two-cultures and reaction towards the centre-ground; women's history; popular heresy; the future.

THE RISE OF THE LAITY

Begin with the map of traditional ecclesiastical history, and two details seen through a magnifying glass. Oxford, around 1950: the medieval history tutor at Oriel, William Pantin (Knowles 1974), a pious lay Catholic who could be seen in his confrater's gown at mass at the Benedictine hall of St Benet's on a Sunday (ibid. 456; and personal observation), is writing his history of the Church in England in the fourteenth century. He sets this within an old confessional polemic about the state of the later medieval Church. His Church is seen positively, viewed forward from the great reforms of 1215, rather than negatively, an abuse-ridden institution viewed backwards from 1517. Supporting this positive view is a large section which describes the great series of manuals written to instruct parish priests on how to deal with and instruct their parishioners (Pantin 1955: 189–219). Another detail is one of his postgraduate research pupils, Leonard Boyle, a Dominican from Donegal, who is to take the concern with this sort of instruction of friars and parish priests much further, in a series of (still-continuing) brilliant and fundamental studies (see Boyle 1981). In both historians the laity may be only passive and only implied, as it were at the end of the line of what is being studied. Although the object of study is, for example, a 1320s manual written to advise parish priests on how to deal with and to instruct to parishioners, when he gets up in the pulpit on Sunday – to instruct in English forms of baptism for emergencies, or give advice on breast-feeding and child-care to mothers (Pantin 1955: 197, 199) – there is a faint but distinct shift in focus towards those who are in front of such a priest.

This foreshadowing of the rise of the laity is one among many. The rise itself is a minor historiographical result of a bit of mid-twentieth-century Church history. There was debate in the modern French Catholic Church about the impact of modern industrial society and 'dechristianization', and a consequent pastorally driven concern to use *sociologie religieuse* to investigate the patterns of religious practice of modern men and women. Ill-translated as 'sociology of religion' and better translated as 'religious sociology', this meant geography; rural opposed to urban; the observable externals of religious behaviour, such as attendance at mass and communion; and statistics of such things.[9] Energetically promoted by Canon F. Boulard, it resulted in 1947 in the publication by the *Cahiers du clergé rural* of the first-ever map of a nation's religious practice. Boulard himself wrote that this religious sociology went back to a questionnaire about religious statistics and history, written by Gabriel Le Bras and published in the *Revue d'Histoire de l'Église de France* in 1931 (Boulard [1955] 1960: xxv). Church and academia met in the figure of the Catholic Le Bras.[10] He was also deeply concerned with the state of Christianity in modern France and the use of sociology. He was a pioneer in exploiting medieval canon law as an avenue to the 'religious sociology' of the past. He had a strong view of the laity as an autonomous object of study,[11] and one meeting-point of medieval Church and laity, marriage, had elicited from him an astonishingly advanced study as far back as 1927. (Le Bras 1927).

Born of a pastoral concern about modern religious practice, *sociologie religieuse* also infiltrated the minds of those who looked at the religion of more remote periods, at the same time finding a natural ally in the strength of geography in *Annales*. Through these years the laity were also rising more broadly in the Catholic and Protestant Churches. Milestones were the World Council of Churches instituting its Department of the Laity at Evanston, Illinois, in 1954, and the Second Vatican Council (1962–5) issuing its Decree on the Apostolate of the Laity and adopting for the liturgy languages which could be understood by the laity. One book from this period is direct evidence on a classic historiographical theme, something which is new (or something old which has been refound) which is looking for (or refinding) a past. Published by the World Council of Christian Churches in 1963, its title was *The Layman in Christian History*.[12] The editors claimed the volume was the first-ever such general survey, and they professed themselves astonished at the information uncovered (Neill and Weber 1963: 11). Like historians of the masses or of women, they saw themselves as recovering what had been 'hidden from history'. A touch of anglophone insularity – ignoring earlier French work – slightly erodes the claims, but there is a broad truth. The laity now emerged into bright sunlight, blinking, autonomous. Ended were centuries of a historiographically passive and subordinate existence, of being tucked away in a little chapter at the end of a massive volume of Church history.[13] Ended their conceptually vague existence as 'medieval popular devotion', which usually meant

---

9   A convenient introduction is Boulard 1955.

10   On Le Bras, see Études d'Histoire du Droit Canonique dédiées à Gabriel Le Bras, 2 vols, Paris, 1965, 1, pp. v–vi (outline of career), ix (studies on Le Bras), ix–xxxiii (Le Bras's works, classified – e.g. section 6, 'Sociologie et Géographie Religieuse', pp. xix–xxiii).

11   See for example the brief canon-legal and classifying comments on the medieval laity in Le Bras 1959.

12   Neill and Weber 1963. Medieval chapters came from R. W. Southern, 'The Church of the Dark Ages, 600–1000', pp. 88–110, and C. N. L. Brooke, 'The Church of the Middle Ages, 1000–1500', pp. 111–134.

13   In the first volume I pull off the shelves, the thirteenth-century vol. 4 in Hauck 1887–1920, inside 1,015 pages of fine positivist Church history, lay piety receives treatment in pp. 901–5.

two things, generalizations about blurred boundaries of the natural and supernatural and a concentration on external practices appropriate to 'medieval' mentality (Vauchez 1975: xv). Ended a historiographic existence which was the counterpart of the passivity and subordination of Gratian's definition and other evidence produced by medieval clerics. The story after 1963 was of the laity's conquest and settlement, and it can be resumed in a succession of titles. *I laici nella 'societas christiana' dei secoli XI e XII* (1968): the papers of an international conference. *La Religion populaire au Moyen Age: Problèmes de méthode et d'histoire* (1975): methodology from Raoul Manselli. *La Religion populaire en Languedoc* (1976): articles displaying a wide range of approaches from the annual Fanjeaux colloquium on the religious history of medieval Languedoc. *Religion vécue du peuple chrétien* (1979): two volumes edited by Jean Delumeau, with much of the first again showing a wide range of approaches to medieval lay religion. (chs 7–12 in vol. 1 cover the Middle Ages). *Les Laïcs au Moyen Âge: Pratiques et expériences religieuses* (1987): a general account (though based on articles) from today's principal heir of Le Bras, André Vauchez.

1970s THEORIZING, TWO CULTURES AND REACTION TOWARDS THE CENTRE-GROUND

The mid-1970s were a fertile period for programmatic and theorizing work about popular religion among both medieval and early modern historians, work usually marked by the attempt to deepen the subject through reading in anthropology. Take the years 1974–6. The year 1974 saw an influential volume edited by C. Trinkaus and H. Oberman, *The Pursuit of Holiness in Late Medieval and Renaissance Religion*. Here are some of its contents, in ascending order. Thomas Tentler published a trailer for his monograph on late medieval confession, which, in pursuing to its death the theme of confession as an instrument of 'social control', illustrated the declining usefulness of this sort of import from sociology (Trinkhaus and Oberman 1974: 103–26). A. N. Galpern's account of late medieval religion in Champagne, on the other hand, was a sign of its decade (ibid. 141–76). A definition of religion was taken from an article by Robin Horton in the *Journal of the Royal Anthropological Society* 90 (1970): 'Religion can be looked upon as an extension of the field of people's social relationships beyond the confines of purely human society.' Thus Galpern juxtaposed the devolvement of a ruler's power, in a fragmented decade, with the power which 'God had devolved on the Virgin Mary – and on the saints, those independent power-brokers in an age of bastard feudalism' (ibid. 168). Galpern displayed rich sources and very real understanding of piety placed in the service of the dead and its meeting-point with solidarity in communities (saints as patrons of confraternities, parishes, towns, etc.). He used anthropology and his language was suggestive – for example, the cult of saints in terms of 'client-patron relations'. It was a potent brew, fermenting in the following decade. Finally, Natalie Davis surveyed 'Some tasks and themes in the study of popular religion' (ibid. 307–36). She passed in review, for criticism, approaches in which one norm was used as a bench-mark (e.g. an approach where a clerical version of Christianity was used as a bench-mark by which to judge other forms of Christianity); in which the relation of clergy to laity is seen in one direction only, guidance and creativity from the clergy; in which magic and religion are held apart (as by Keith Thomas) in a way which fragments what may have been experienced as a unity and perpetuates a later historian's penchant for weeding the rational from the irrational; finally, approaches in which religion is seen only as a projection of the social, rather than also as its shaper. Again, reading in anthropology leavened the text: held up as a model was Clifford Geertz's account of religion in Java.

Along with Manselli's general account of medieval popular religion (see Manselli 1975), 1975 also saw the most famous of the articles which the early modernist John Bossy was writing, as he prepared himself for his general history of later medieval and early modern Christianity. This was 'The social history of confession in the age of Reformation' – with much more that was medieval than the title indicates (Bossy 1975); to Bossy we return later. Alongside the *Cahiers de Fanjeaux* volume on popular religion, 1976 saw a large programmatic article on the study of medieval popular religion. Its starting point was an attack on one of the founding fathers, Canon Etienne Delaruelle.

A large part of the history of the rise of the laity could be traced through the works and career of Delaruelle.[14] Born in 1904 and ordained in 1934, he spent his middle years as Professor of Ecclesiastical History at the Institut Catholique of Toulouse. A closer account of him both as priest and historian of popular religion would trace the close links between the two,[15] establishing the pastoral and ecclesiological bases of his concern for the (lay) Christian people. Although he was commissioned to co-write the Schism volume in A. Fliche and V. Martin's *Histoire de L'Eglise*, the massive 1,200-page synthesis of faith in the Church in part 2 (part 1 was ecclesiastical-political) was in fact his work alone.[16] The new was marked here in two ways – the centrality itself, in the volume, of a 270-page section entitled 'The religious life of the Christian people', and the vast range of sources which he arrayed and analysed. Bossy's 1970 article on the religion of the people of Catholic Europe is partly a reflection on the data supplied by these pages as well as the Le Bras–Boulard tradition (Bossy 1970). Delaruelle's general survey of 1964 was preceded and succeeded by articles published over four decades (1929–73), whose thematic progression could be taken to mark his move from the second to the third of Vauchez's *images* of popular religion, from the crusade towards 'the religious culture of the laity'. One central article which was representative of Delaruelle's later work, deals with eleventh- and twelfth-century French laity and their *culture religieuse* (Delaruelle 1968). There is a *tour de force* of juxtaposition: a statistical

---

14 On Delaruelle see Guillemain 1972; Vauchez 1975: xiii–xix; Vicaire 1976. Bibliography: Delaruelle 1975: xxiii–xxviii.
15 See the comments on Delaruelle as priest, and further literature cited by Guillemain 1972: 354–5.
16 Delaruelle *et al.* 1962–4. Delaruelle's sole authorship of part 2 is not indicated in the text, Guillemain 1972: 359.

iconography of Romanesque frescoes, the rites of a most widely diffused liturgical book (the tenth-century Romano-Germanic Pontifical), vernacular manuscripts of parts of Scripture and scraps of evidence (especially miracle-collections) on preaching. The remark when discussing eleventh- to twelfth-century frescoes, that pre-eleventh-century images were still around, perhaps not in current taste but still there to affect eleventh-century onlookers, is the casual aside of a scholar steeped in the sources. All the things surveyed were 'means of formation of the laity', means at the disposal of an educating clergy.

Shortly after Delaruelle's death (1971) the approach epitomized here proved a vulnerable target for a young *annaliste* out to make his mark, Jean-Claude Schmitt, in a programmatic article on popular religion and folkloric culture. (Schmitt 1976b). Yes, together with Le Bras, Delaruelle had turned attention from the Church and its institutions to the religious life of the masses. But the theme ran in one direction, evangelization of the laity by the clergy (compare Davis). To the laity Delaruelle attributed emotionalism, childishness, ignorance, simplicity – pure doctrine was handed down, but filtered and distorted in reception. Moving on, Schmitt attacked the use of a bench-mark of pure Christianity to divide popular religion into various parts, religion and folklore ('Christian', 'pagan survivals', 'aberrations'), proposing the unitary study of all that was *lived* as 'religion', according to Schmitt's wide definition (compare again Davis). What was then proposed was an approach which seemed to have both Engels and Antonio Gramsci in the background. The Church and its clergy monopolized the book, and thus the interpretation of the world, and was the ideologist of the existing feudal social order (thus far Engels in updated language). Ruling ideology (Christianity) encounters what is opposed, folkloric culture, and there is a process of Christianity's assimilation (*récuperation*) of some elements of folkloric culture in order to render the ruling ideology more effective – in the terms of Antonio Gramsci (my addition), in its 'hegemonic role'. If socio-political opposition was found in heresy, as Engels had maintained, the geographi- cally and chronologically sporadic appearance of heresy might pose a problem. With such opposition transferred to folkloric culture – ubiquitous in time and place – the problem disappeared.

One element in a sermon, the *exemplum* (story), was the meeting-point of clerical and folkloric. The *exemplum* put over a point about Christian faith or morals, but often used elements of folklore to do so. Collections of *exempla*, especially of the thirteenth century, were relics of this process and prime evidence of it, and the best of them might go further than be examples of *récuperation*: they might even describe occasions of it. Schmitt published a trailer in the Fanjeaux volume on *religion populaire*, the analysis of an *exemplum* which showed clerical culture allied to the ruling generation (the aged) repressing a folkloric rite involving youth, dancing and wooden horses (Schmitt 1976a). In 1979 came the *magnum opus* (Schmitt 1979; Eng. tr. 1983). The Dominican Stephen of Bourbon's collection of *exempla* contained one which described a legend and cult across which Stephen had stumbled when preaching to peasants in a country area, the Dombes, a little to the north of Lyons. The legend was about a faithful dog who was unjustly killed, Saint

Guinefort. The cult consisted of peasants remembering and venerating Saint Guinefort as a martyr, and peasant women with ill children practising rites at the site of the dog's death, in order to obtain miraculous cures. Schmitt gave the 600-word text[17] a deep reading which fills a 200-page book. There is a setting of Stephen, of *exempla*, of the area; invocation of interdisciplinarity, especially between history and anthropology; 'structural' analysis of the legend; diagrams and maps; archaeology of the site of the cult. In his broader interpretation Schmitt accorded the women, practitioners of these rites, a central role in the ideological as well as biological reproduction of their community (ibid. 175), and he claimed long duration for the cult, finding evidence of its later existence in the seventeenth and early nineteenth centuries. An example of the usually hidden but profound and fundamental fact, the existence and opposition of clerical and folkloric cultures, was the continuity of this cult between the twelfth century (Schmitt's hypothesis for its origin) and the turn of the nineteenth century: the period of 'the structural permanence of an ideological system in which folklore played an essential albeit a secondary role' (ibid. 178).

Folklorizing was not new, and the 'thin veneer of Christianity' approach had been given new impetus and authority in Jean Delumeau's book on early modern Catholicism, which had suggested with deliberately crude provocativeness that seventeenth-century pastoral comments on Breton peasants (sunk in animist religion, worshipping spirits in trees, stones and springs) could be projected back and applied to the rest of medieval Europe.[18] Less noticed had been an important but unassuming article of 1973 by an American specialist on heresy and inquisition, Walter Wakefield, who pointed to the rich evidence of peasant materialist beliefs found in late thirteenth-century inquisitors' interrogations in Languedoc.[19] But Schmitt's bizarre story, the élan of the execution of this work by a young *annaliste* star who proclaimed indebtedness to the Jacques Le Goff; and the dazzle of the interdisciplinary techniques on display: all of these gave the book an immediate fame, and a diffusion which was then expanded by its quick translation into English (1983). The fame, of course, also had much to do with the vogue for culture-conflict in the 1970s and beyond. An earlier manifestation of the vogue had been Carlo Ginzburg's sixteenth-century study, *Cheese and Worms* (1976), which had also hypothesized long duration in the past of usually hidden orally transmitted peasant beliefs.[20] Later – that is to say, later in their appearance in Western languages – were the works of the Russian medievalist Aaron Gurevich. In 1964–5 Gurevich

---

17 Original and translation are given by Schmitt [1979] 1983: 2–6.

18 Delumeau [1971] 1978: 161–6 – inside a section (part 2, chapter 3) entitled 'The legend of the Christian Middle Ages'.

19 Wakefield 1973. Similar material is to be found in Jacques Fournier's register – see de Llobet 1976, esp. pt. 2, pp. 112–15 (where, however, they mingle with 'croyances traditionelles' and 'superstitions'). See also Biller 1991, particularly pp. 146–7.

20 Ginzburg 1976; Eng. tr., 1980. For the hints and hypotheses of the possibility of long subterranean duration, see Ginzburg 1980: 20–1 (and long note 143–4), 58, 86, 112, 117.

had bravely ground out a philosophico-historical reworking of Marxism,[21] in order to make room for his studies of popular culture/religion, which lie broadly in the same methodological field as those of Ginzburg and Schmitt.[22]

Through the 1970s and beyond there were other historians tilling the more conventional field of the religion of the laity, within the best French Catholic tradition of Delaruelle and his predecessors but going far beyond them. The giant has been Vauchez, first with the masterpiece of his *thèse d'état* on sanctity in the later Middle Ages (1981). This produced a statistical geography of canonizations and the cult of saints between 1198 and the mid-fifteenth century, which has vast implications for the regionalism of popular religion. Following this there has been much work: articles and books on medieval popular religion (Vauchez 1987), including historiographic reflections on medieval popular religion and its historians (e.g. Vauchez 1976: 429–44; 1975; 1981: 2–4; 1994; 1992) and the organization and running of conferences on the theme. Vauchez's output has been remarkable: large, open to the new, and sane. It is also characterized by its occupation of a centre-ground: mainly Christianity rather than folklore, and mainly orthodoxy rather than heresy, although neither folklore nor heresy are ignored.

There is profit in pursuing the themes of the previous sentence through a more extreme and very original historian, Bossy, who was writing through this period. Key dates are 1970 (his article on the religion of Catholic Europe), 1982 (a programmatic article on 'religion' and 'society') and 1985 (his general synthesis, *Christianity in the West 1400–1700* [note: '1400' is not to be taken too seriously, for Bossy's 'traditional Christianity' usually goes much earlier]. Like Davis, Schmitt and others, the Bossy of the 1970s was very receptive to anthropology. Advanced works jostle in the brief bibliography of *Christianity in the West*, including Schmitt's holy dog – though probably only because Bossy loves dogs. Fundamentally, however, Bossy's approach has been Catholic-conservative. For him as for Vauchez, the people's Christianity, not folklore, is central, and orthodoxy, not heresy – though he goes further than Vauchez in his sniffy comments on heretics.[23] His picture is a backcloth to later changes (coming with reform, post-reform, or as early as Jean Gerson and the fifteenth century). The theme of a later shift to interiorization is set against this: a medieval Church of very locally varying communities in which sacraments intertwine with kin and community. Medieval confession is more public than private. Greater medieval emphasis on the seven deadly sins is aligned with proportionately greater emphasis on

---

21 Articles published in *Voprosii istorii* 1964–5, and translated into English as Gurevich 1965 and 1966. Representative of later Gurevich: *Historical Anthropology of the Middle Ages* (1992).

22 Principal translations into English are Gurevich 1985 and 1988. What Gurevich had to offer that was rare (particularly his grasp of medieval Scandinavian sources), together with the popularity of two-culture history, the opening-out of relations with Russian historians, and the fame and moral reputation of a historian who had held out during difficult years – all this meant an open welcome for Gurevich in the West in the 1980s and early 1990s. An eventual bibliography of the traces this has left in translations and articles in Western journals and international conference proceedings will be large.

23 Bossy 1985: 81. His 'People of Catholic Europe' begins with comment on historians' excessive interest in dissent and insufficient interest in orthodoxy, pp. 51–2.

a person harming his neighbour (horizontal), as opposed to later greater emphasis on the Ten Commandments and proportionately greater emphasis on direct offense of God (vertical) (for the sharpest account of this see Bossy 1988). It is the strongest fresco of medieval popular Christianity that has ever been painted, even though individual medievalists carp at its bold schematicism and the mistakes inevitably made by Bossy in their specialist patches. The picture is a warm one – perhaps we can see this as a side-effect of 1960s liberal Catholicism's colder view of post-Tridentine Catholicism? No need for hesitant conjecture on another point. This is a polemic, launched by Bossy both in this book and in earlier articles, which appeared to have precision in the use of words as their object (Bossy 1982a, 1982b). As stated earlier, 'religion' had meant cult or worship, then monasticism; only in the sixteenth century particular religions; only with Durkheim the capital-lettered abstraction, 'Religion'. Similarly 'society' had meant relationship or company; only in the sixteenth century particular objective entities, communities; and only in modern times a capital-lettered abstraction which could be equated, as by Durkheim, with 'Religion'. The equation of 'Religion' and 'Society' is the object of Bossy's wrath. His plea is for much more than precision in the use of words: to see things in their own terms, to see religion in its own terms, not as something else, and certainly not as 'society'; to see past people, inside a 'religion', envisaging things and their actions in 'religious' terms, and in their 'religious' terms; and for historians to be willing to accept this. Ideologically very unlike his fellow-anthropology readers of the 1970s, this historian of popular religion has had this message about how it should be done. Put back in the centre traditional orthodox Christianity, lived by the people, he has said; see it in their terms; and begin your study with prayer and the sacraments.

What Schmitt brought to bear upon the Dominican Stephen of Bourbon's *exemplum* about a dog was himself, his brilliance and his own and *annaliste* baggage of the 1970s. What if one approaches Stephen of Bourbon as a Vauchez, or a Bossy? The holy dog would be sidelined, though not completely ignored, by historians who would note other *exempla* in Stephen. Consider themes and references in them: knowing that it is a feast-day in towns through the sound of bells, but in the country through the silence of the ploughs[24] (Stephen 1877: 273); a knight pondering the nativity (ibid. 84); a noblewoman having doubts about faith:[25] a man called John going off to a place which produced good pictures, Fontaine near Cambrai, to buy a picture of the Virgin Mary to take back to his house;[26] processions of marriage parties, with music, to the outside door of a church in Dijon in the year 1240.[27] *This* ordinary framework of the religious life of the laity is the quotidian picture, the picture of the ordinary: and the main part of the picture? Between Schmitt and a Bossy or Vauchez (hypothesized as reading Stephen of Bourbon), what is going up or down are the general proportions of the

---

24 Bossy's sharpest account of this is in Bossy 1988.

25 Ibid. 69. In Murray 1981 there is brilliant use of Thomas of Cantimpré's exempla to investigate varieties of belief, unbelief and doubt – see especially pp. 294–8.

26 Stephen 1877: 129 (see note on the problem of identifying which Fontaine he visited).

27 Stephen 1877: 365. One example of the use of *exempla* to investigate orthodox lay religious practice is in Biller 1991: 133–7.

ordinary and the bizarre in presentations of medieval popular religion. And *that* is a historiographical theme which is affected by other things in the observer's outlook, including the degree to which the observer essentializes the concept 'medieval' and fills it with deductions from modern connotations of the word 'medieval'.

WOMEN

Two periods of political movements had their counterparts in the writing of history (see Hanawalt 1987). The medieval historiography which was the correlative of the fight for women's rights in the years around 1900 had touched here and there on 'religion'. Lina Eckenstein, for example, had drawn attention to the role of pious women in the 'religious' charitable and hospital movement of the twelfth and thirteenth centuries (Eckenstein 1896), while Eileen Power had ventilated the themes of the relevance for women of the images of particular figures in religious culture (Eve, Mary Magdalen, Mary) and the opportunities, albeit for only a few, in nunneries: to avoid men, to be educated, to rule and administer, to reach heights spiritually.[28] Translation of the writings of mystics – for example, of both Mechtilds, whether of Hackeborn or Magdeburg (Anon. 1875 and Bevan 1896) had kept the existence of the latter alive for a Victorian reading public. The historiography which arose with the renewal of the fight against the oppression of women in the 1960s is ever-expanding and sometimes changing in direction – witness, for example, the deflection towards 'the social and cultural construction of gender', detectable by the mid-1970s. Only a few salient points in the tale of its interweaving with medieval 'religion' can be picked out here.

There has been a very rapid transition from little to big, and from some crudeness in early cartography to much greater sophistication. (I write as a feminist and as an enthusiast for the fact and wider diffusion of women's history.) In the earliest stage feminist presentism linked hands with what was easiest to find in the sources, and together these procured the predominance of nuns, mystics and heretics. In the prominence of nuns the older theme of 'opportunities' was writ larger.[29] Powerful early medieval abbesses could play a big role in a 'golden age' picture of an as yet not 'gendered' early medieval Europe. Mystics were original and powerful women whose 'voices' could perhaps still be heard, whose move towards direct union with God tended to bypass the intermediary of the ministrations of a male clerical hierarchy and Church. Heresies protested, perhaps, against the existing socio-political order – hence the prominence of 'religious' women preaching in them. All three sorts were women who renounced marriage and sex: renounced men. There was an irony here in the chronological overlapping of the appearance of the early monographs and syntheses – Koch (on heresy and women) (see n. 36 below), Shahar (1983: chs 3 (nuns), 8 (women as witches and heretics)),

---

28   See the brief sketch, Power 1926 (esp. at pp. 402–5, 413), and the very sober picture of Power 1922. On Power, see Smith 1986.
29   For this in earlier historiography see Hanawalt 1987: 9–10.

Ennen (1984: ch. 2, pt. 3 (religion – nuns, beguines and saints) – and the works of the historians of the Christian laity, Delaruelle and others. The latter had brought about the rise of the laity, the Common Man or Woman, at the expense of Church institutions, priests, monks and nuns, and (but only to some extent) the saint. But the former preserved and even heightened the attention paid to the elite, nuns, 'religious' women and female saints, at the expense of the Common Woman and her religion.[30] The general revolution in popular religion therefore met a strong contrary movement in this medieval women's history. An incidental consequence is my more frequent use in this section, so far, of 'religion' in its narrower early medieval sense.

The previous paragraph caricatures to make a point. The extraordinary strength of a distinctively women's 'religious' movement in the twelfth and thirteenth centuries, especially in the Low Countries and Rhineland Germany, was a matter of observation at the time. It is there in the records, and it had received remarkable description and (as far as possible) statistical treatment in 1935.[31] What medieval nuns and female visionaries now received from the 1960s onwards was also, in many cases, superlative scholarship, here exemplified from two wings. Representative of much good positivist research within traditional ecclesiastical history was Micheline de Fontette's magisterial treatment of the canon law of female 'religious' (1967). On another wing and leading among those interpretative historians whose work has been fertilized by encounters with modern anthropology has been Caroline Bynum.[32] She has demonstrated the significance of food and fasting to 'religious' women, and has analysed the work of contemplative women in order to establish a contrast between males (still bound by binary systems of gender when attributing femaleness to Christ) and females (freer of such polarism and unitary in their attribution of *humanity* to Christ). There is the suggestion that the patterns she discerns in her deep scrutiny of writings from and about a small group of intensely ascetic women should be extrapolated and applied to the religious outlook of the less-known multitudes of other medieval women. Clearly this last contention, if sound, would erode the significance of my distinction between 'religious' women (nuns, mystics, etc.) and the ordinary laywoman.

If one surveyed the study of women and medicine in the Middle Ages, it would be more appropriate to highlight the fine research scholarship and sophisticated methodology now being brought steadily to bear on the subject by Monica Green than the crude presentist problematic of earlier studies which have been so roundly criticized by Green (Green 1988–9 and 1994). Just so with medieval religion and women, where the main contemporary fact is the large volume and advanced

---

30   This point has been argued at greater length in Biller 1991. A notable early part-exception to the claim is Huyghebaert 1968: 390–5.
31   Grundmann 1935. This masterpiece is the starting-point for all work on the women's 'religious' movement of this period.
32   Bynum 1982; 1987; 1991. Much that is relevant to religion, women and the body is contained in Bynum 1995; I am grateful to Dr Simon Ditchfield for the loan of his copy.

methodology of work currently under way, in particular in the areas of distinctive patterns in the cult of the saints or in holy figures in some way held up as models or objects of veneration. Vauchez's cartography has been fundamental here, in its mapping of patterns of female canonization. (Vauchez 1981, esp. 402–10, 427–48; 1987: pt. 4). The detail of a Michael Goodich discussing Margaret of Città di Castello as patroness of serving-girls and the broad picture suggested by Jeremy Goldberg's selection of texts bearing on the piety of laywomen are two examples among many of the fruitful meeting-point of the best strands in the modern socio-demographic and religious studies of medieval women.[33]

Two surveyor's points need to be made. First, it is difficult to think of any other area in medieval popular religion which is receiving quite as much attention, any area in medieval popular religion which is therefore more likely to be changed and unrecognizable in ten years time. Second, there seems a gap between the multiplicity and illumination of many sharply focused studies and what a general synthesizing account of the religion of the ordinary woman might be. The slowness of emergence of such a general view may be rooted partly in an ideological problem. There is circumstantial but good evidence of a picture of thirteenth-century women which an historian, say, of nineteenth-century French Catholicism might find familiar: ordinary women as the props of the Church, more assiduous mass-attenders and communicants than their menfolk (Biller 1991: 139–41), more engaged in pious charitable work.[34] Such large facts would need to be at the centre of description and debate – but when so much early historiography is drenched with how abhorrent the Church and its theologians and clergy were, there may be reluctance to go down this path.

HERESY

I am turning to popular heresy as one example among many, a weathervane whose changing directions over several decades have registered the historiographical winds which blew.

What we have in the 1950s and much of the 1960s is the social in various shades of grey. Dark-shaded behind the Iron Curtain, as already noted, in Engels-based studies of heresies as movements of political and social protest directed against the ideologist of the existing order, the Church; spotted and speckled in such a representative journal of the new as *Past and Present* in its dabblings in examining eastern European works and using some of the vocabulary (Biller 1994); a very light shade of grey in the works of American historians belonging (only very loosely) to the Columbia group of heresy scholars, inspired by Austin Evans, who 'had the soul of a liberal Protestant, with mildly "capitalist" leanings'. Evans liked to establish 'profound social changes ... towns ... urban industries' as the backgrounds against

---

33 Goodich 1982: 156. See also the treatment of female saints, pp. 173–85. Goldberg 1996, chapter 10 section iv, pp. 279–90, deals with lay piety.
34 An example of a modern local study is Cullum 1992.

which to set the growth of heresy. And he had a penchant for thinking that 'merchants favoured non-orthodox ways of thought and religions' (ibid. 45).

The second half of the 1960s saw two publications signalling 'French academic dominance' (Vauchez 1994) A colloquium held in Royaumont in 1962 had brought together virtually all the world's specialists on medieval heresy. There were old squabbles about Eastern origins of dualism and squabbles between materialist and spiritualist interpretations, jostling with the themes of town heresy and country heresy. Most significant were the sheer numbers and variety of views represented (from England Margaret Aston and Gordon Leff), and the presence of the avant-garde of one sort of history of popular religion in the person of Delaruelle and *annaliste* avant-gardism in the person of Jacques Le Goff. The proceedings were published in 1968, edited by Jacques Le Goff under the title *Hérésies et sociétés dans l'Europe préindustrielle (11e–18e siècles)*. This volume remains for many later specialists the point of departure. After Royaumont there was the birth of Fanjeaux. Papers delivered at a colloquium held there in 1965 were published as the first volume of the series 'Cahiers de Fanjeaux' in 1966. Delaruelle was a founding father (Guillemain 1972: 359–60), and his Institut Catholique of Toulouse was, as it continues to be, one of the two sponsoring institutions. Each subsequent year has seen a colloquium on one or other theme in the 'histoire religieuse du Languedoc' in the central medieval period, followed a year later by publication. Fanjeaux has tended to unite powerful regional historians, main-line historians of popular religion such as Vauchez and Jacques Chiffoleau, and the occasional Parisian trendy. Heresy and inquisition recur, interspersed with years on such themes as popular religion (1976), assistance and charity (1978), pilgrimage (1980), liturgy and music (1982), women (1988), and the parish (1990). The resulting (and continuing) ensemble of studies provides the most varied, dense and historiographically advanced picture of the religious life of a medieval region – with heresy at its centre – that has ever been seen.

There was some sidelining of heresy, as evinced in the principal large work to appear on heresy from a historian associated with *Annales*, Le Roy Ladurie's *Montaillou*.[35] Ladurie, principally a historian of early modern and later Languedoc, moved chronologically when seeing and seizing the wonderful opportunities offered by an earlier document, the register of the inquisitor Jacques Fournier. But he carried with him the *annaliste* interest in folkloric religion. He underlined what he found that was folkloric in the very late Catharism he examined, ignoring the much less folklorized Catharism one finds earlier and in lowland and urban Languedoc, and he underplayed the practice of orthodox Catholicism, which is richly attested in the register he was using.

Elsewhere the vehicle of protest, outside Soviet satellite countries, was in general

---

35 *Montaillou, village occitan de 1294 à 1324*, Paris, 1975 – 642 denser pages reduced to 383 pages (of larger print) in the English tr., *Montaillou. Cathars and Catholics in a French village 1294–1324*, London, 1978; the latter also has the advantage of an index based on a table of Montaillou families. To the reviews listed in Berkhout and Russell 1981: 41 (no. 532), one should add Benad 1990.

decline. The years of *Past and Present*'s dabblings, for example, were 1952–74. However, one tiny part flourished. In 1962 Gottfried Koch had published a book which united women's oppression and Engels on medieval heresy.[36] Women's oppression was a part of general feudal oppression, against which popular heresy was directed: hence women's prominence in heresy. This influenced far more than those who directly read this fairly rare and German book. And it was an ancestor of a very recent book whose other ancestors include Occitan and romantic-historical cultivation of Catharism, *Les femmes Cathares*, written by the *directrice* of the Centre des Etudes Cathares at Carcassonne (formerly Centre National des Etudes Cathares at Villegly, near Carcassonne) (Brenon 1992). Despite the woman-hating element in Catharism, and the better claims of the Waldensians for feminist attention, Cathars are ever more prominent on this particular stage.

So far I have not defined my terms. 'Popular heresy' has been treated as self-evidently relevant to this chapter, as a sub species of 'popular religion'. Looked at more closely, however, such major and long-lasting movements as Catharism and Waldensianism are traduced by the phrase 'popular heresy', half of which comes from the vocabulary of the inquisitor or polemical theologian ('heresy', 'sect'), half from the generalizing category of a modern historian ('popular'). The earlier medieval sense of the word 'religion' applies to some elements in these movements. That is to say, those people among early Waldensians who renounced property and family and preached were, broadly speaking, like early Franciscans, 'religious', following (even if in a new interpretation) a 'religious' way of life, and on their way to becoming, if recognized, a 'religious' order (see Biller 1985a). Preachers among the Cathars, the perfects, followed a similar way of life, and in villages and small towns in Languedoc, in the early days before the crusade in 1209, these men and women, who had solemnly professed and prayed and fasted, lived openly and communally in 'religious' houses.[37] Vocabulary needs to be more ecclesiastical for the broader setting of the 'religious' in Catharism, which was, in Cathar terms, a Church, with diocesan organization and a hierarchy from bishops downwards.

Properly speaking, then, studies of these 'popular heresies' are not necessarily studies of popular religion in the sense used in most of this chapter. For example, a study of Catharism which focuses on Cathar bishops, organization and institutions, and their administration of ritual can be seen as old-fashioned 'ecclesiastical history, not Delaruelle-(or later-)style history of popular religion. The same point can be made about Waldensians, whose historiography traditionally focused on the Order of Brothers founded by Valdes – underplaying the Sisters, through Protestant embarrassment at a past which included nuns.

While earlier work surveyed in this section needs 'religion' in quotation marks, this ceases to be true in more recent years – in the case of the Waldensians, from 1984. Three books chart the rise and progress of the Waldensian 'laity', two from

---

36 Koch 1962. On Koch, see Malecsek 1994: 74–5 (uncritical of the thesis), and, on the theme, Biller 1997. Lollardy has attracted the best treatment of this theme: McSheffrey 1995.

37 The clearest account is still Guiraud 1907: vol. 1, ch. 5, esp. pp. cv–cxiv.

1984. One was the *thèse d'état* of Gabriel Audisio on Waldensians in the Luberon both before and after the Reformation (Audisio 1984). He gave precedence and greater attention to the Waldensian 'believers', first in a dense socio-economic cultural picture of them, then in an account of their principally orally held and transmitted beliefs and their practices. In second place only and treated more briefly was the clerical element: the *barbes*, their organization and their books. The latter were subtly interwoven, but always with an insistence, almost that of a French Catholic pastoral sociologist, on the pre-eminence of the everyday religious *actions* of the lay Waldensian (e.g. as shown in bequests in wills). A minor point in the book concerns the long tradition of polemicists accusing Waldensians of nocturnal incestuous sexual orgies and some instances of pressure, perhaps torture, inducing suspects to confess such actions. Audisio declares for the past objective reality of these actions, seen by him as the maintenance of ancestral peasant rites (ibid. 261–4; Cameron 1984). I am noting his brief discussion only for what it shows about the strength in France of the folklorizing approach to popular religion. The other book was based on an Oxford D.Phil. by Euan Cameron, who treated the related Vaudois of the Alps between the Dauphiné and Piedmont and over the same period.[38] The rise of the laity is even starker. Cameron excludes the 'clergy' of the medieval Waldensians and their books from his picture, focusing entirely on the beliefs and practices, the lived religion, of the followers. Cameron's picture has much in common with Audisio's, but he inserts it into two cultures. Waldensian lived religion is oral, proverbial, peasant, rural – virtually an expression of popular culture.

Only recently published is Pierette Paravy's *thèse d'état* on religion in the Dauphiné from the fourteenth to the sixteenth centuries (Paravy 1993). There had been a notable beginning in Audisio, and comparison of Waldensian and Catholic wills and hence of their religious acts. Paravy provides a frame with ecclesiastical history (the dioceses, bishops and pastoral visitations of the Dauphiné), and within this sets and juxtaposes Catholic and Waldensian Christianity and sorcery: all sorts of Church and popular religious history brought back into unity. Both Catholic and Waldensian laity had already risen, and now they are juxtaposed at length. Paravy's broad scope, systematic approach and massive research allow a reconstruction of breathtaking depth and power.

Nineteen-eighty-four and 1993 mislead here. A socio-popular cultural study of heresy in fourteenth-century Piedmont published in 1977 had already gone down this path. It was written by Grado Merlo, a historian acutely aware both of the historiography of Delaruelle and his fellow Italians Ginzburg and Giovanni Miccoli and also of the best modern positivist research from West Germany (Merlo 1977). Further, there is an elementary point about the evidence which erodes most attempts to date 'the rise of *heretical* laity'. There is little direct evidence on Catholic laity, but vast direct evidence on heretical laity. From the late 1230s there

---

38 Cameron 1984; there is a sane discussion of immorality charges, ibid. 108–11.

are the interrogations of heretics, and most of those interrogated were 'believers' (the laity), not heresiarchs ('clergy'). Consequently, regardless of historiographical trends, ever since such evidence began seriously to be used, its sheer pressure has meant *some* presence of heretical 'laity' and their religion in written history.

Concern with oral and written culture continued, with other contemporary concerns discernible in the background, more closely literary theory and textuality, more globally and intangibly the communications revolution of our age. Heresy's weathervane turned also with this wind. Most notably it turned with a book by Brian Stock, published in 1983, which saw the central medieval rise of heresies as the by-product of a seismic shift in the relations between oral and (increasingly present) literate cultures, and bequeathed to later heresiologists the phrase for heresies of 'textual communities' (Stock 1983). Most recently it has turned with a collaborative work on medieval heresy and literacy, in which oral and written modes of communication are investigated for the light they can throw on popular heresy (Biller and Hudson 1994). A grim weather forecast: there will be much to come, written in prose laden with abstract terms taken from literary theory, on heresy as text and discourse.

As this survey picks out lines of historiographical development in the modern study of medieval heresy, it distorts. Important scholars are omitted, simply because they do not neatly illustrate the pattern which is being suggested here. In Great Britain, for example, massive contributions have been coming from Anne Hudson, Bernard Hamilton and Malcolm Lambert.[39] Let us conclude with two of these, Hamilton and Moore, a pair united as opposites. Moore is a man of ideas, an intellectual's heresiologist who looks at heresy and repression in the central Middle Ages, while at the same time absorbing and responding to theory and the most innovative new work being done by historians in many fields. He then meditatively rethinks his subject – a magisterial recent example is his 'Heresy, repression and social change in the age of Gregorian reform' (Waugh and Diehl 1996). One outcrop of his concerns was his *Formation of a Persecuting Society. Power and Deviance in Western Society 950–1250* (Oxford, 1987), where he juxtaposed heretics, Jews, lepers and homosexuals and suggested some blurring of categories (for example, heretics seen as similar to lepers) and some similarity both of treatment and the timing of increase in persecution. The thesis based upon these observations, and expressed succinctly in the book's title, has had a powerful impact, setting the agenda for discussion among historians of all these groups. By contrast, Hamilton is a research-scholar's heresiologist, who looks at Cathars and their eastern connections, while mulling over such problems in the sources as, 'Is the document authentic which describes an eastern missionary at a late twelfth-century council of Cathars in Languedoc?' (Hamilton 1978). Forensic brilliance is displayed in Hamilton's solutions of these problems, as well as mastery of both western (Latin and Occitan) and eastern (Greek and old Slavonic) sources. The solutions in

---

39   These are surveyed in Biller 1994.

239

themselves rewrite parts of Cathar history. Asking how eastern texts came into western languages (Latin and Occitan) led Hamilton to look at all the jigsaw pieces in the puzzle of how Catharism came to the west. They fell into place – and what resulted, recently, is the first coherent account of this heresy's acquisition of western form (Hamilton 1994).

Moore's and Hamilton's brilliant achievements in debate or pure research are the obvious points being made in the conclusion to this survey, but not the only ones. Take a Sunday painter's view of Hamilton and Moore, ignoring the sophistication of these scholars and their arguments. Hamilton may say that he condemns inquisitors, but he tries to understand them on their own terms, in his *The Medieval Inquisition* (1981). His concentration on the eastern origins of the Cathars is in a long tradition, which goes back to medieval Catholic writers' attempts to provide heresies with pedigrees. Then consider Moore. As one turns his pages, what one encounters is an author who does not believe what medieval clerics write, who analyses their depictions of heresy as constructions and emphasizes the theme of repression. A more profound historiographical account than can be given here would investigate these hints of survivals of ancient confessional antipathies and sympathies. Moral: a survey of modern historiography distorts when only selecting for attention what is new.

THE FUTURE

The poverty of direct evidence will continue to shape study. The historian of the very late Middle Ages and later can turn to evidence which is itself evidence of past direct focus on the religious behaviour of the laity: lists of mass-attenders and communicants, records of episcopal visitations, pastors' comments, ultimately entries in parish priests' diaries.[40] Turn, however, to the thirteenth and fourteenth centuries, and what the historian finds in episcopal visitation records is, almost entirely, attention to churchy things: the fabric or debts of a church, the behaviour of a clergyman. The thinness of direct evidence of lay religious behaviour is a fact of life for any historian of popular religion in the thirteenth or fourteenth centuries, whatever his or her historiographical approach. Some historians sensibly prefer an abundance of sources and therefore a neighbouring theme: d'Avray works on sermons. Those who stay with the theme perform feats of acrobatics. Examples of ingenuity are Schmitt's with *exempla*, or Alexander Murray when using these and other sermon materials to investigate the religion of the poor, piety and unbelief, and confession (Murray 1974; 1972; 1981). Ingenuity of this sort has not yet been sufficiently applied to the interpretation of the registers of inquisitors, whose interrogations often reveal much of the reality of orthodox practice through question and answer about its opposite.

---

40 See the account of such sources in Delumeau [1971] 1978: 134–41. Toussaert 1963 was a pioneering work in the use of statistically treatable evidence about religious practice as it began to be available, in the later fifteenth century.

It is easy to project forward work which is already strongly in progress. Already noted is the probable further illumination of women and religion. To this should be added what is closely related, more important work on the theme of religion and the body from its recent principal exponent, Miri Rubin (1991; 1994). Medieval religion (in all its senses) and medicine have long been linked in study. Now, however, there is mushrooming growth in the study of medicine in all periods, which is being accelerated by drug companies' investment – in Great Britain, the Wellcome Trust's encouragement of the foundation of university posts in the history of medicine. Clearly there will be more work on relations with medieval medicine.[41] There will also be more synthesizing general work on medieval popular religion from the current *maestro di coloro che sanno*, Vauchez.

Here are two more speculative suggestions. The oral and written are not yet played out, as also the ancient theme of the mingling of the natural and supernatural. They could develop more in a direction suggested by Peter Brown (1975). Venturing into the alien territory of the Latin West in the central Middle Ages, Brown has used the history of the use of the ordeal to settle legal disputes, declining towards the end of this period (clerical participation was banned in 1215), to suggest a weakening of the general suffusion of things with the supernatural, accompanied by sharp refocusing and more defined location in some areas, for example in the sacraments. Something like this frames a book by Colin Morris which is about the Church – cultic in 1050, pastoral in 1250 (see Morris 1989: 'conclusions' esp. p. 580) – and something like it would seem to provide a useful general approach for a younger and central medieval Bossy. Consider two themes among many. In the earlier Middle Ages the Bible (or one of its parts) was usually a large book: magnificent, sacred. Around 1200 its books acquired chapter divisions, for easy reference, riffling the pages to find your text, and some copies were very small, for utility – to be carried by mendicant friars out to quote and comment: the Book to some degree desacralized. Dominant in tenth-century 'religion' (now in its monastic sense) were religious orders whose daily round was performance of the liturgy, dominant in what was new in thirteenth-century 'religion' were mendicant friars whose job it was to go around preaching, half of which was explaining and instilling doctrine. Tenth-century liturgies provide orders for a bewildering number and variety of daily things: still in the thirteenth?

Regionalism in Christianities is far from new. One of the few concrete contemporary points to press itself into the brief and mainly abstract texts of the new theology which began to develop in Laon and elsewhere in the early twelfth century was regional variations in Church customs and marriage. A sharp observer of the contemporary Church writing a confessor's manual around 1215, Thomas of Chobham, observes regional variation as a generality, as well as individual instances

---

41   From an immense bibliography I select first the recent general comments on various aspects of the relation between medicine and medieval Christianity by Nutton 1995: 73–9, 146–53, and second, one illustrative example of the sophistication of modern study of this theme, Ziegler 1995. The historiography of 'Medieval medicine and religion' would need a separate treatment.

of it.[42] Ecclesiastically Robert Brentano pointed the way in his extended comparison of the churches of England and Italy in the thirteenth century (Brentano 1968), and religiously Vauchez has done this on one theme, the cartography of later medieval canonization. An eventual picture of popular religious regionalisms into which one could set, for example, the northern European woman who invoked St Margaret when in labour while her southern sister invoked the Virgin Mary or Christ might be as revolutionary in its illumination of its subject as historical demographic studies have been revolutionary in their illumination of north-western and southern European marriage-systems. Would popular religious regionalism show some of the long duration which has been shown so clearly in demography?

REFERENCES

Anon. (tr.) (1875) *Select Revelations of S.Mechthild, Virgin, Taken from the Five Books of her Spiritual Grace, and Translated from the Latin by a Secular Priest*, London.

Audisio, G. (1984) *Les Vaudois du Luberon. Une minorité en Provence (1460–1560)*, Gap.

Benad, M. (1990) *Domus und religion im Montaillou*, Spätmittelalter und Reformetion new series 1, Tübingen.

Berkhout, C. T. and Russell, J. B. (1981) *Medieval Heresies. A Bibliography 1960–1979*, Toronto.

Bevan, F. (tr.) (1896) *Matilda and the Cloister of Hellfde. Extracts from the Book of Matilda of Magdeburg*, London.

Biller, P. (1985a) '*Multum ieiunantes et se castigantes*: medieval Waldensian asceticism', in W. J. Sheils (ed.) *Monks, Hermits and the Ascetic Tradition*, Studies in Church History 22, Oxford.

—— (1985b) 'Words and the medieval notion of "Religion"', *Journal of Ecclesiastical History* 36: 351–69.

—— (1991) 'The common woman in the western Church in the thirteenth and early fourteenth centuries', in W. J. Sheils and D. Wood (eds) *Women in the Church*, Oxford.

—— (1992) 'Marriage patterns and women's lives. A sketch of a pastoral geography', in Goldberg 1992.

—— (1994) 'La storiografica intorno all'eresia medievale negli Stati Uniti e in Gran Bretagna (1945–1992)', in Merlo 1994.

—— and Hudson, A. (eds) (1994) *Heresy and Literacy, 1000–1530*, Cambridge Studies in Medieval Literature 23, Cambridge.

Bossy, J. (1970) 'The Counter-Reformation and the People of Catholic Europe', *Past and Present* 47: 51–70.

Bossy, J. (1975) The social history of confession in the age of Reformation', *Transactions of the Royal Historical Society*, 5th ser., 25: 21–38.

—— (1982a) 'Some elementary forms of Durkheim', *Past and Present* 95: 3–18.

—— (1982b) 'Social England', *Encounter* September–October: 46–51.

—— (1985) *Christianity in the West 1400–1700*, Oxford.

—— (1988) 'Moral arithmetic: Seven Sins into Ten Commandments', in E. Leites (ed.) *Conscience and Casuistry in Early Modern Europe*, Cambridge and Paris.

Boulard, F. (1955) *Premiers itinéraires en sociologie religieuse*, with preface by G. Le Bras, Paris. (English tr.: *An Introduction to Religious Sociology Pioneer Work in France*, London, 1960.)

---

42 Boyle 1981: IV, pp. 93–4 n. 3. Pastoral and social regionalism is the theme of Biller 1992.

Boyle, L. E. (1981) *Pastoral Care, Clerical Education and Canon Law, 1200–1400*, London.
—— (1982) 'Popular piety in the middle ages: what is popular?', *Florilegium* 4: 184–93.
Brenon, A. (1992) *Les Femmes cathares*, Paris.
Brentano, R. (1968) *Two Churches. England and Italy in the Thirteenth Century*, Princeton.
Brown, P. (1975) 'Society and the supernatural: a medieval change', *Daedalus* 104: 133–51. (Repr. in Brown 1982: 302–32.)
—— (1982) *Society and the Holy in Late Antiquity*, London.
Bynum, C. (1982) *Jesus as Mother. Studies in the Spirituality of the High Middle Ages*, Berkeley, Los Angeles and London.
—— (1987) *Holy Feast and Holy Fast. The Religious Significance of Food to Medieval Women*, Berkeley, Los Angeles and London.
—— (1991) *Fragmentation and Redemption. Essays on Gender and the Human Body in Medieval Religion*, New York.
—— (1995) *The Resurrection of the Body in Western Christianity, 200–1336*, New York and Chichester.
Cameron, E. (1984) *The Reformation of the Heretics. The Waldenses of the Alps 1480–1580*, Oxford.
Cullum, P. H. (1992) '"And hir name was Charite": charitable giving by and for women in late medieval Yorkshire', in Goldberg 1992.
d'Avray, D. L. (1985) *The Preaching of the Friars. Sermons diffused from Paris before 1300*, Oxford.
—— (1990) 'The comparative study of memorial preaching', *Transactions of the Royal Historical Society*, 5th ser., 40: 25–42.
—— (1994) *Death and the Prince. Memorial Preaching before 1350*, Oxford.
Delaruelle, E. (1968) 'La culture religieuse des laïcs en France au XIe et XIIe Siècles', *I Laici* (1968). (Repr. in Delaruelle 1975).
Delaruelle, E. (1975) *La Piété populaire au moyen âge*, Turin.
Delaruelle, E., Labande, E.-R. and Ourliac, P. (1962) *L'Église au temps Grand Schisme et de la crise conciliaire (1378–1449)*, Paris.
Delumeau, J. (1971) *Le catholicisme entre Luther et Voltaire*, Paris. (Eng. tr.: *Catholicism between Luther and Voltaire: A New View of the Counter-Reformation*, intr. by J. Bossy, London and Philadelphia 1978.)
—— (ed.) (1979) *Religion vécue du peuple chrétien*, 2 vols, Toulouse.
Dorpalen, A. (1985) *German History in Marxist Perspective: The East German Approach*, London.
Duffy, E. (1992) *The Stripping of the Altars: Traditional Religion in England 1400–1580*, New Haven, CT.
Eckenstein, L. (1896) *Women under Monasticism*, Cambridge.
Engels, F. (1927) *The Peasant War in Germany*, London. (Original German ed. 1850).
Ennen, E. (1984) *Frauen im Mittelalter*, Munich. (English tr.: *Medieval Women*, Oxford, 1989.)
Fontette, M. de (1967) *Les Religieuses à l'âge classique du droit canon. Recherches sur les structures juridiques des branches féminines des ordres*, introduction by G. Le Bras, Paris.
Ginzburg, C. (1976) *Il formaggio e i vermi: Il cosmo di un mugnaio del '500*, Turin. (Eng. tr.: *The Cheese and the Worms. The Cosmos of a Sixteenth-century Miller*, London and Henley, 1980.)
Goldberg, P. J. P. (ed.) (1992) *Woman is a Worthy Wight. Women in English Society c.1200–1500*, Gloucester.
—— (ed.) (1996) *Women in England c.1275–1525*, Manchester.
Goodich, M. (1982) Vita Perfecta: *The Ideal of Sainthood in the Thirteenth Century*, Stuttgart.
Green, M. (1988–9) 'Women's medical practice and health care in medieval Europe', *Signs. Journal of Women in Culture and Society* 14: 434–73.

—— (1994) 'Documenting medieval women's medical practice', in L. García-Ballester, *et al.* (eds) *Practical Medicine from Salerno to the Black Death*, Cambridge.

Grundmann, H. (1935) *Religiöse Bewegungen im Mittelalter. Untersuchungen über die geschichtlichen Zusammenhänge zwischen der Ketzerei, den Bettelorden und der religiösen Frauenbewegung im 12. und 13. Jahrhundert und über die geschichtlichen Grundlagen der deutschen Mystik*, Historische Studien 267, 1st edn, Berlin; 2nd edn, Darmstadt, 1961. (Eng. tr.: *Religious Movements in the Middle Ages*, Notre Dame, 1996.)

—— (1967) *Bibliographie zur Ketzergeschichte des Mittelalters (1900–1966)*, Rome.

Guillemain, B. (1972) 'Le chanoine Etienne Delaruelle, historien de la vie religieuse au moyen âge (1904–1971)', *Annales du Midi* 84: 353–60.

Guiraud, J. (1907) *Cartulaire de Nôtre Dame de Prouille précédé d'une étude sur l'albigéisme languedocien aux XIIe et XIIIe siècles*, 2 vols, Paris.

Gurevich, A. (1965) 'Certain aspects of the study of social history (historical social psychology)', *Soviet Studies in History* 3: 17–64.

—— (1966) 'Universal law and special regularity in history', *Soviet Studies in History* 5: 3–17.

—— (1985) *Categories of Medieval Culture*, London.

—— (1988) *Medieval Popular Culture: Problems of Belief and Perception*, Cambridge.

—— (1992) *Historical Anthropology of the Middle Ages*, Chicago.

Hamilton, B. (1978) 'The Cathar council of St Félix reconsidered', *Archivum Fratrum Praedicatorum* 48: 23–53.

—— (1981) *The Medieval Inquisition*, London.

—— (1994) 'Wisdom from the East: the reception by the Cathars of eastern dualist texts', in Biller and Hudson 1994.

Hanawalt, B. A. (1987) 'Golden ages for the history of medieval English women', in S. M. Stuard (ed.) *Women in Medieval History and Historiography*, Philadelphia.

Hauck, A. (1887–1920) *Kirchengeschichte Deutschlands*, 5 vols in 6, Leipzig.

Huyghebaert, N. (1968) 'Les femmes laïques dans la vie religieuse des XIe et XIIe siècles dans la province ecclésiastique de Reims', in *I laici* 1968.

Iggers, G. G. (1989) 'New directions in historical studies in the German Democratic Republic', *History and Theory* 28: 59–77.

—— (ed.) (1991) *Marxist Historiography in Transformation. New Orientations in Recent East German History*, Providence and Oxford.

I laici nella 'societas christiani' dei secoli XI e XII (1968) Milan.

Knowles, M. D. (1974) 'William Abel Pantin, 1902–1973', *Proceedings of the British Academy* 60: 447–58.

Koch, G. (1962) *Frauenfrage und Ketzertum im Mittelalter: die Frauenbewegung im Rahmen des Katharismus und des Waldensertums und ihre sozialen Wurzeln (12.–14. Jahrhundert)*, Forschungen zur mittelalterlichen Geschichte 9, Berlin.

Kulcsár, Z. (1964) *Eretnekmozgalmak a XI–XIV. században*, A Budapesti Egyetemi Könyvtár Kiadványai 22, Budapest.

Lambert, M. D. (1977) *Medieval Heresy. Popular Movements from Bogomil to Hus*, London.

—— (1992) *Medieval Heresy. Popular Movements from the Gregorian Reform to the Reformation*, Oxford.

Le Bras, G. (1927) 'Mariage', *Dictionnaire de Théologie Catholique*, vol. 9, pt. 2, Paris: cols 2123–2317.

—— (1959) *Institutions ecclésiastiques de la Chrétienté médiévale*, Paris (= A. Fliche and V. Martin (ed.) *Histoire de l'Église* 12, Part 1).

Le Goff, J. (1981) *La Naissance de purgatoire*, Paris. (Eng. tr.: *The Birth of Purgatory*, Chicago, 1984).

Le Goff, J. (ed.) (1968) *Hérésie et société dans l'Europe préindustrielle (11–18e siècles)*, Paris and The Hague.

Le Roy Ladurie, E. (1975) *Montaillou, village occitan de 1294 à 1324*, Paris.

Little, L. K. (1978) *Religious Poverty and the Profit Economy in Medieval Europe*, London.

Llobet, G. de (1976) 'Varieté des croyances populaires au comté de Foix au début du XIVe siècle d'après les enquêtes de Jacques Fournier', in *Religion populaire en Languedoc*

McSheffrey, S. (1995) *Women and Men in Lollard Communities 1420–1530*, Philadelphia.

Malecsek, W. (1994) 'Le ricerche eresiologiche in area germanica', in Merlo 1994.

Manselli, R. (1975) *La Religion populaire au moyen âge: problèmes de méthode et d'histoire*, Montréal.

Merlo, G. G. (1977) *Eretici ed inquisitori nella società piemontese del trecento*, Turin.

—— (ed.) (1994) *Eretici ed eresie medievali nella storiografica contemporanea*, Bolletino della società di studi valdesi 174, Torre Pellice.

Mollat, M. (1977) 'Les formes populaires de la piété au moyen âge. Introduction au colloque sur la piété populaire', in *Études sur l'économie et la société de l'occident médiéval XIIe–XVe siècle*, London.

Morris, C. (1989) *The Papal Monarchy. The Western Church from 1050 to 1250*, Oxford.

Mothes G. (1983) *England in Umbruch. Volksbewegungen an des Wende vom Mittelalter zur Neuzeit*, Forschungen zur mittelalterlichen Geschichte 28, Weimar.

Murray, A. C. (1972) 'Piety and impiety in thirteenth-century Italy', in C. J. Cuming and D. Baker (ed.) *Popular Belief and Practice*, Studies in Church History 8, Cambridge.

—— (1974) 'Religion among the poor in thirteenth-century France. The testimony of Humbert de Romans', *Traditio* 30: 285–324.

—— (1981) 'Confession as a historical source in the thirteenth century', in R. H. C. Davis and J. M. Wallace-Hadrill (eds) *The Writing of History. Essays presented to Richard William Southern*, Oxford.

Neill, S. C. and Weber, H.-R. (eds) (1963) *The Layman in Christian History. A Project of the Department on the Laity of the World Council of Churches*, London.

Nutton, V. (1995) 'Medicine in Late Antiquity and the Early Middle Ages' and 'Medicine in Medieval Western Europe, 1000–1500', in L. I. Conrad *et al.* (eds) *The Western Medical Tradition. 800 BC to AD 800*, Cambridge.

Pantin, W. A. (1955) *The English Church in the Fourteenth Century. Based on the Birkbeck Lectures, 1948*, Cambridge.

Paravy, P. (1993) *De la chrétienté romaine à la réforme en Dauphiné. Evêques, fidèles et déviants (vers 1340–vers 1530)*, 2 vols, Collection de l'École Française de Rome 183, Rome.

Power, E. (1922) *Medieval English Nunneries c. 1275 to 1535*, Cambridge Studies in Medieval Life and Thought, Cambridge.

Power, E. (1926) 'The position of women', in G. C. Crump and E. F. Jacob (eds) *The Legacy of the Middle Ages*, Oxford.

La religion populaire en Languedoc (1976): *La religion populaire en Languedoc de XIIIe siècle à la moitié du XIVe siècle*, Cahiers de Fanjeaux 11, Toulouse.

Rubin, M. (1991) *Corpus Christi: The Eucharist in Late Medieval Culture*, Cambridge.

—— (1994) 'The person in form: medieval challenges to bodily order', in S. Kay and M. Rubin (eds) *Framing Medieval Bodies*, Manchester.

Schmitt, J.-C. (1976a) '"Jeunes" et danse des chevaux de bois. Le folklore méridional dans la littérature des "exempla" (XIIIe–XIVe siècles), in *La Religion populaire en Languedoc*.

—— (1976b) '"Religion Populaire" et culture folklorique', *Annales ESC* 31: 941–53.

—— (1979) *Le Saint Lévrier: Guinefort guérisseur des enfants depuis le XIIIe siècle*, Paris. (Eng. tr.: *The Holy Greyhound. Guinefort, Healer of Children since the Thirteenth Century*, Cambridge Studies in Oral and Literate Culture 6, Cambridge and Paris, 1983.)

Selge, K.-V. (1967) *Die ersten Waldenser*, Arbeiten zur Kirchengeschichte 37, Berlin.

Shahar, S. (1983) *The Fourth Estate. A History of Women in the Middle Ages*, London and New York.

Smith, R. (1986) 'Introduction' to E. Power, *Medieval People*, 9th edn, London.

Southern, R. W. (1982) 'Between Heaven and Hell', *Times Literary Supplement* June 18: 651–2.

Stephen of Bourbon (1877) *Tractatus de variis materiis praedicabilibus*, in A. Lecoy de la Marche (ed.) *Anecdotes historiques et apologues tirés du recueil inédit d'Etienne de Bourbon dominicain du XIIIe siècle*, Paris.

Stock, B. (1983) *The Implications of Literacy. Written Languages and Models of Interpretation In the Eleventh and Twelfth Centuries*, Princeton.

Toussaert, J. (1963) *Le Sentiment religieux en France à la fin du moyen âge*, Paris.

Trinkaus, C. and Oberman, H. (eds.) (1974) *The Pursuit of Holiness in Late Medieval and Renaissance Religion*, Leiden.

Vauchez, A. (1975) 'Etienne Delaruelle historien', in Delaruelle 1975.

—— (1976) 'Conclusion', in *La Religion populaire en Languedoc*, 1976 Cahiers de Fanjeaux 11, Toulouse.

—— (1981) *La Sainteté en Occident aux derniers siècles du moyen âge, d'après les procès de canonisation et les documents hagiographiques*, Bibliothèque des Ecoles Françaises d'Athènes et de Rome 241, Rome.

—— (1987) *Les Laïcs du moyen âge: Pratiques et expériences religieuses*, Paris.

—— (1992) 'Conclusion', *Fin du monde et signes des temps. Visionnaires et prophètes en France mériodionale (fin XIIIe–début XVe siècle)*, Toulouse.

—— (1994) 'Les recherches françaises sur les hérésies médiévales au cours des trente dernières années (1962–1992)', in Merlo 1994.

Vicaire, M.-H. (1976) 'L'apport d'Etienne Delaruelle aux études de spiritualité populaire médiévale', *La religion populaire en Languedoc*

Wakefield, W. L. (1973) 'Some unorthodox popular ideas of the thirteenth century', *Medievalia et Humanistica*, n.s. 4: 25–35.

Waugh, S. L. and Diehl, P. D. (eds) (1996) *Christendom and its Discontents. Exclusion Persecution, and Rebellion, 1000–1500*, Cambridge.

Ziegler, J. (1995) 'Medical similes in religious discourse. The case of Giovanni di San Gimignano OP (ca. 1260–ca. 1333)', *Science in Context* 8: 103–31.

III EARLY MODERN
HISTORIOGRAPHY

INTRODUCTORY SURVEY: FROM THE RENAISSANCE TO THE EIGHTEENTH CENTURY

G. E. Aylmer

In all ages and all human societies the history that has been written (or spoken) has been inseparable from the history through which the writers (and speakers) have lived. Few would wish to deny that what historians produce, like other forms of human thought and expression, is subject to change over time. Since the content of their thought and writing is itself concerned, in greater or lesser part, with changes over time, it would be strange – indeed paradoxical – if this were not so. There is, however, little agreement as to how and why history, in the sense of what historians think and say, changes as and when it does. It is easy to postulate two extreme views on this, though few people today would be content with either as a sufficient explanation. At one end of the scale, history can be thought of as an autonomous intellectual discipline, with its own methodology and conventions, which has changed because its practitioners have become dissatisfied with its descriptive and explanatory capacity, and have seen – or thought that they have seen – a better way of doing it. At the other end of the scale, we may think of history as having been wholly conditioned by changes in the society in which historians are living; such external influences may be scientific, technological, military, economic, demographic, social, political, religious, cultural, etc., but these are what bring about different ways of thinking about the past and different ways in which it is portrayed in the writings of historians; naturally these include different explanations of historical change and continuity. For just as the pace and impact of other changes in human life have not been uniform in all times and places, so likewise changes in the practice of historical study and expression have come about unevenly.

I

In the case of the Christian West from the fifteenth to the eighteenth centuries of our era, there is certainly no lack of developments, external to the craft and discipline of history itself, which might be invoked in order to explain such changes. As can be seen from other chapters in this book, some of these developments have themselves been called in question during recent years. None the less, we need to take note of each in turn before it can be discarded in favour of some other kind of explanation. Such possible influences must obviously include the cultural and educational movement known as Humanism; amongst others must be the Renaissance itself (if indeed so vast and amorphous a phenomenon can be identified at all), the advent of printing, the discoveries in the non-European world and the establishment of European colonial empires in parts of it, the increased knowledge and understanding of the natural world (whether or not we wish to speak of the 'Scientific Revolution'), the Reformation and the divisions and conflicts which followed within Western Christendom, the changes in the methods of warfare and in the fiscal and administrative structure of the state, the shift of wealth and power from southern and central Europe to the North Atlantic seaboard, and the eventual beginnings there of a recognizably 'modern', urban, commercial and partly bourgeois society, based on a more sophisticated capitalist economic system, although still relying on slave labour in the European empires overseas. No doubt this list could be lengthened and amended. Moreover, the reader will have noticed that one of the possible influences which have just been noted relates to the actual means of transmitting the written word. A generation ago 'the medium is the message' was a fashionable slogan; since then more solid and detailed historical analysis has been undertaken, to argue the case for the printed book having transformed the content of what was published.[1] Before we return to this hypothesis, we need to survey the kinds of history which were being written during what are often known as the late Middle Ages and the early modern period. One difficulty which is obvious at once is the impossibility of applying a uniform chronological structure across the whole of Europe. Most significantly for our purposes, Italy was far ahead of the northern countries in many essential respects. So it is natural to start there.

II

Petrarch, or Francesco Petrarca to give him his full Italian name (1304–74), is famous as a poet, letter-writer, essayist and scholar. He is not usually thought of as a historian at all. Yet he seems to have been the first person, at least in the Christian world, to express in writing the fundamental idea of linear, as opposed to cyclical movement or periodicity in history – something which has been taken for granted almost ever since. His admiration for the ancient world of Greece and Rome rested on his excellent command of classical Latin, since his Greek was rudimentary. He described the fifth to fourteenth centuries AD as the 'middle age', a period of

---

1 McLuhan 1962 is the most relevant work by this once intellectually fashionable author. See Eisenstein 1979 for a more detailed and sober assessment, which – unfortunately for our purposes – says little specifically about historical writing, except on the transmission of the Greek and Latin classics.

relative 'darkness' from which he believed the world was re-emerging in his own time. That he managed to express this idea without being accused of heresy or even impiety may seem remarkable, but he was not a theologian or a spokesman for ecclesiastical reform. His professions of orthodox belief were probably sincere, and he may not himself have quite grasped the potentially subversive force in his threefold division of history, which only came to full fruition as a means of explaining and interpreting what had happened since classical times three or four hundred years later.[2]

Among the salient features of humanist history the most obvious is stylistic. Leonardo Bruni (c.1370–1444) and his successors, first in Florence and then elsewhere in Italy, modelled both their Latin and the form of their histories on the surviving works of the Roman historians, in particular Livy and, perhaps more surprisingly, Sallust.[3] The distinction which they drew between 'annals' and 'histories', the latter being more concerned with causes and explanations, and not tied to a strict chronological sequence, owed more to the influence of Tacitus.[4] Bruni's *History of the Florentine People* runs from the semi-legendary foundation of the city to the year 1402. Exceptionally for Italians of his time, Bruni knew Greek and had read Thucydides.

Following the precedent of Petrarch, some humanist historians began to show an awareness of historical change. This, however, conflicted with another aspect of the classical heritage: the belief in history as a form of applied morality, as philosophy teaching by example. This was to assume that human behaviour was constant in all times and places, and that characters and situations recurred from age to age with little variation save names, dates and locations. Parallels did not need to be searched for, since they were self-evident for all to see. If this means only that human nature is imperfect, and that certain attributes are found in virtually all individuals at all times, then it may be no more than a harmless truism. But it fails utterly to explain why some principles and practices are found in one society and not in another. Whereas material changes are too obvious to be wholly denied, moral and psychological differences within humanity are reduced almost to vanishing point on such an assumption of uniformity. Curiously this view has revived in the later twentieth century with the reaction against the belief in progress which character-ized so much of Western thought from the eighteenth century at least until 1914 (and with less conviction until much more recently than that). If the idea of progress entails belief in the ascent of human nature to perfection, or even an

---

2   The bibliography is vast. See Cassirer *et al.* 1948; reprinted 1961 and later), Part I, translated H. Nachod, for a useful introduction and selection. There are pioneering articles on Petrarch's sense of periodicity by Ferguson 1939.

3   Cochrane 1981 is a truly encyclopedic work, the fullest and most up-to-date treatment known to me in English. See Bk I, ch. 1 for the Florentine origins, on which see also Fryde 1980, reprinted in Fryde 1984. I have also relied heavily upon Holmes 1969 and Martines 1979 for the cultural and political background.

4   Burke 1966. Burke 1969 remains the most stimulating and suggestive short survey.

assumption of continuous improvement, then indeed we may be tempted to reject it and agree instead with the humanists that situations and types of conduct do constantly recur, and that there can be regression as well as advance. Many of the greatest thinkers of the fifteenth and sixteenth centuries certainly believed that historical change is more cyclical than linear: forms of government change in a particular sequence; similar kinds of crisis arise and can only be resolved in identical ways. Thus the outbreak of the Peloponnesian War between Athens and Sparta in the 430s BC is directly comparable to the crises of 1914 and/or 1939. Alexander the Great, Tamerlane, and Napoleon I may all be treated as a single genus of would-be world conquerors; and so on. Why human life is valued more highly in some societies than in others, why the arts are cultivated more in some, mass entertainment more in others, why the pace of technological and economic change has varied so much: this view of human nature and of history helps little, if at all, with these and many other questions which have confronted human beings in all ages.

Bruni had several contemporaries, rivals and successors as historians, both in Florence and elsewhere in Italy. Some authorities would rank Flavio Biondo (1392–1463) even more highly. This may be left to specialists (see Cochrane 1981: 34–40). More important, humanist history can be distinguished in language and structure from the annalistic form of most medieval chronicles. Yet it might well have remained stuck in this excessively imitative mould but for another influence which also arose from the humanist movement. This was the desire not only to emulate the ancients in style and purpose, but wherever possible to establish what they had actually written. Great advances were made in this respect as a result of more early manuscripts being discovered, or rediscovered, within western Europe and of others being brought from Byzantium. Helped partly by refugee scholars fleeing from what was left of the Eastern Empire in the face of the Ottoman Turks, more of the educated elite, first in Italy and then more widely, were able to read and understand classical Greek. This process was hastened but not caused by the fall of Constantinople in 1453.[5] Once textual and philological scholarship was applied to the pagan literature of the ancient world, it was perhaps only a matter of time before the same criteria were used to examine the records of the Christian Church and even the sacred texts of Scripture. In the great majority of cases this was not in any way intentionally anti-religious; indeed in northern Europe the whole movement is sometimes known as Christian Humanism. But the rigorous study of texts and documents could, and sometimes did, have anti-clerical or anti-ecclesiastical implications, with damaging results. The most famous act of scholarly demolition was the demonstration by Lorenzo Valla (1407–57) that the so-called Donation of Constantine, the basis of some extravagant papal claims, had been forged at least 400 years after its purported date.[6] Much of the work undertaken by linguistic and

5   Bolgar 1954 and Highet 1949 both contain a wealth of information besides many helpful insights. Reynolds and Wilson 1991 is the clearest and most comprehensive brief account; it assumes a minimum knowledge of Latin. I am most grateful to Professor Andrew Watson for directing me to this work.
6   See Cochrane 1981: 148. There are several other accessible accounts.

textual scholars in the fifteenth and sixteenth centuries was of a more humdrum, unsensational nature than this. Several of the criteria which they established for the provenance of documents and the reliability of texts are still in use today, even if we normally take them for granted; and we do of course have some scientific methods of assessing the age and authenticity of both written and unwritten materials which were not available to them.

So much of modern historical study rests on this basis that the methods themselves deserve a brief review. The ways of testing the age and genuineness of manuscript sources which we have inherited from the humanist scholars of the Renaissance are customarily divided into internal and external, but this is unhelpfully schematic. It is best to start with the most basic questions: are the writing materials (papyrus, parchment, paper, etc. and the ink or other fluid) such as would have been available and in use at the purported date of authorship? Are the handwriting and the language those of the epoch in question, likewise the contents? To answer these questions might (and still may) involve philological questions of great complexity, and require a deep understanding of Hebrew, Aramaic, Greek, Latin and even the vernacular languages of earlier times. Assessment of content might entail minute scrutiny for factual errors, anachronisms or anticipations; it might also raise the more difficult issues of attitude, outlook and belief. One standard assumption in source criticism today, which we owe directly to German *Quellenkunde* developed in the late eighteenth and nineteenth centuries, is that the oldest surviving version of a text is not necessarily the most authentic in the sense of being the closest to the original; a version of a later date may have been based on an earlier, more authentic one which has not survived.[7] All this no doubt is boringly obvious to us, but it seems not to have been self-evident even to the greatest minds during Petrarch's 'dark centuries': Augustine, Bede, Aquinas and others. And we should therefore show a decent humility in such matters. In the days of manuscript copying, often no doubt in ill-lit and unheated premises, a single mistake, or a sequence of errors (e.g. a word or line left out or misplaced, as well as a mis-reading) could enter into what became the standard version, equivalent to uncorrected typing or printing mistakes today. There could, however, also be deliberate omissions, additions and alterations, arising from the prejudices, interests and beliefs of the scribal copyists. The citation of exact numbers is one usually obvious, and often harmless, type of anachronism. The population of cities, the size of armies, the fatal casualties in battles and massacres, and so on, must always be treated with extreme caution, even in the best surviving texts of otherwise reliable and truthful authors. The meaning of certain controversial, general terms is another such area where anachronism is all too easy: Plato and Aristotle are rightly

---

7 Langlois and Seignobos 1898. It is fashionable to sneer at this work and at similar manuals as dull and outmoded; but, apart from the new electronic dimension, and the use of computers, the need for such guides has by no means been superseded. Reynolds and Wilson 1991: ch. VI and Notes, pp. 288–94, is among the best and most up-to-date of these. For a valuable introduction to one major use of quantification, see Kenny 1982.

revered as the founders of Western political thought, yet for them 'democracy' stopped short of women, slaves and even resident aliens.

Some modern historians of the Renaissance may seem to suggest that these changes in the techniques of scholarship were an essential preliminary to all the other developments in historical thought and writing. And for those concerned with origins, with the beginnings of nations or churches, and the earliest reliable authorities for these foundations, such was indeed the case. Other concerns of historians during the fifteenth and sixteenth centuries arose at much the same time but more or less independently. One obvious case is that of explanation, historical causes and effects, in particular the role of divine intervention. Belief in God's providence as the first cause of everything can all too easily be a substitute for trying to explain anything. Alternatively, belief in a kind of cosmic first cause (which is not in itself specifically Christian, being Aristotelian or anyway Greek in origin) is also compatible with an intense and critical interest in secondary causes, that is, with particular explanations of whatever it may be. Only by invoking the miraculous or the occult does a historian risk confusing first and secondary causes. For example, if I wish to believe that it was a pigeon and not a rook which has just flown across the field in front of my window as I write this, a vague, generalized belief that what has happened is an infinitely small and trivial part of the way in which the universe is ordered, whether by God or Nature, is neither here nor there. Even if the bird had been a raven or an eagle, this might have been something to excite ornithologists, but would still have been well within the limits of the natural world. If, however, I were to start reading some prophetic meaning into the colour of the bird or (apart from the direction of the prevailing wind) into the direction of its flight, then I should be joining company with soothsayers and other readers of auguries such as palmists and astrologers.

This may seem a little remote from changes in historical scholarship since the fifteenth century. Invocation of the miraculous, as opposed to divine providence operating through normal, that is, natural processes of cause and effect, is unusual today, outside religious belief and what is still sometimes called sacred history. Christians are committed to belief in the miracles recorded in the New Testament, or at a very minimum in the greatest of these – the Incarnation and Virgin Birth, the Resurrection and the Ascension. The occurrence of miracles in subsequent Christian history, and how they should be authenticated, has been a subject of passionate controversy for many centuries. Not surprisingly this was much intensified by the confessional conflicts of the sixteenth and seventeenth centuries, although its origins go back earlier than that. The philological learning and textual criticism of scholars during the generations immediately preceding the Reformation created a new intellectual context, with partly different criteria, for the assessment of miracles, at least as to how and when they were first recorded, and so for their use in historical explanation. Thoroughgoing philosophical scepticism about the very possibility of miracles could not be expressed openly with safety before the eighteenth century. But this is by no means the same thing as scholars demonstrating the fraudulence of forged or garbled accounts of particular miracles, or of those recorded only in corrupt texts. Historians could likewise be persuaded by the new scholarship to reject particular national or ecclesiastical myths without in any way challenging the tenets of revealed religion. For example, the credibility of King Arthur, for whose existence no written evidence survives earlier than the twelfth century, was first called in question by the papal tax collector and historian, Polydore Vergil of Urbino, who spent many years in England. His 'History' was completed by 1513 and was first published (that is, printed) in 1521. In it he also demolished the alleged Trojan origins of the ancient Britons; a similar campaign was also under way in the case of the Franks, the ancestors of the French, whose 'Trojanness' was also first challenged by an Italian.[8] Somewhat by contrast with this, the French-educated philosopher and historian, John Mair or Major, an almost exact contemporary of Polydore, accepted the legends both of Brutus (the Trojan prince) and of Arthur; on the other hand, he too rejected the belief that Christianity had been introduced into Britain by Christ's follower, Joseph of Arimathea in the later first century AD, favouring instead a semi-legendary British king called Lucius in the mid-second century, who was said to have requested a mission from the then Pope, this story paying no regard to Roman imperial control and religious policy at that time.[9] Whatever its other limitations, Mair's *History* does show considerable skill in keeping English and Scottish developments in some kind of balance, more or less by the device of devoting alternative chapters to each country. As anyone who has tried to deal with two linked but distinct subjects in a single narrative will know, this is no mean achievement.[10]

III

The writings of some Renaissance historians can be related more directly to the new forms of scholarly learning and textual criticism than those of others. The two German humanist historians of the earlier sixteenth century, Johannus Aventinus of Bavaria and Beatus Rhenanus of Sélestat in Alsace, both came to analytical narrative via textual studies.[11] The most obvious exceptions to this, though by no means the only ones, are the two great Florentines of the high Renaissance: Nicolò Machiavelli (1469–1527) and Francesco Guicciardini (1483–1540).[12] Both composed histories

---

8   Hay 1952; for the text, *Camden Society*, old series, vols 29 and 36, ed. H. Ellis (1844 and 1846), and Royal Historical Society, *Camden Third Series*, vol. 74, ed. D. Hay (1950). For the Franks, see Cochrane 1981: index entry 'Paolo Emilio', esp. pp. 345–8.
9   McKisack 1971: 22 explains why this mattered more after England's break with Rome; it is discussed at greater length in other recent works.
10   Major 1892. Major or Mair is accorded more respectful treatment in histories of philosophy during this period, but that is not our concern here.
11   Strauss 1963; D'Amico 1988. I am extremely grateful to Professor Dr Wolfgang Reinhard (the author of Chapter 13 for having arranged a visit to the Bibliothèque Humaniste de Sélestat during a European Science Foundation Conference in Strasbourg.
12   The literature on Machiavelli is immense and that on Guicciardini considerable. For a comparative treatment of them as historians, Gilbert 1965, esp. Pt II, chs 5–7, remains the best introduction.

of their own city. Written during the earlier 1520s, when he was in opposition, having been driven from office, Machiavelli's narrative stretches from the origins of Florence to the death of Lorenzo Medici on the eve of the French invasion in 1494, the most recent sections thus being within his own adult lifetime and the beginnings of his career as an administrator; it was published a few years after his death as *The History of Florence and the Affairs of Italy*. He starts with the barbarian invasions of the fourth and fifth centuries AD and the fall of the Roman Empire in the West. Having been founded as a colony of neighbouring Fiesole, Florence – so he tells us – was destroyed by the Ostrogoths and later rebuilt by Charlemagne: all this was semi-legendary. Only from the thirteenth century is Machiavelli's account grounded on reliable evidence and freed from patriotic mythology. It is primarily a political and military narrative. Although he tells us that he will deal with the internal divisions and conflicts of the republic, Machiavelli does not in fact show much interest in the economic basis of Florentine power, nor in the social divisions which underlay the great plebeian revolt of 1378–81 (see Book III). In fact the *History's* main interest is the fact of its being by the author of *The Prince* and the *Discourses on Livy's History of Rome*. As to the latter work, there is no concern with the texts of Livy and the problems which these raise; the *Discourses* are essentially a commentary on the rise and decline of republican governments and considerations as to how a republic's greatness may be prolonged.

Fourteen years younger than Machiavelli and less controversial both politically and intellectually, Guicciardini wrote two histories of Florence, neither of which was published until long after his lifetime. The earlier of them, composed in 1508–10, covered the city's history from the late fourteenth century until recent times; the second version, written in the later 1520s, just after the death of his older friend, covered a longer span of time. Although each consulted – and admired – the other, neither had access to the other's manuscript when writing their respective histories. However, Guicciardini's fame rests on his *History of Italy*, written during the last years of his life, in 1538–40. It begins, in effect, where Machiavelli's *History of Florence* leaves off, with the French invasion of 1494 (when the author was a boy of ten or eleven), and reaches 1534. It is therefore very much a contemporary history, and was intended for publication, in order to recount and to explain the evils which had befallen his country during the writer's lifetime, although it did not actually appear in print until he had been dead for over twenty years. In spite of his religious orthodoxy as a believing Catholic never having been called in question, unlike the charges of irreligion levelled against Machiavelli, this did not prevent the posthumous condemnation of Guicciardini's work, and his *History* being placed on the papal Index of prohibited works. The likeliest reason for this was that he had not felt able to disguise his conviction that successive Popes and their advisers were at least in part to blame for Italy's misfortunes. Thus the greatest and most controversial political writer of his time wrote a history which ended twenty-five or thirty years before the date of its composition, whereas the more detached and scholarly historian's greatest work was truly contemporary, starting forty-six and ending only six years before it was written. Both of them wrote in the vernacular, with an educated, but not necessarily learned or academic readership in mind. Both saw Italian affairs from a Florentine perspective, Guicciardini less crudely so than Machiavelli. Neither is much concerned with events in the peninsula south of Rome, except where international diplomacy or major military operations are involved. Neither could be called sympathetic to their own city's great rival, the republic of Venice. Ironically it was that city which furnished the model for republican government among historians and political thinkers north of the Alps, not least in England; moreover the next truly great Italian historian was a Venetian.[13]

IV

Outside Italy it was the religious upheavals of the Reformation, the Counter-Reformation and the so-called Wars of Religion which did more than anything else to shape the writing of history during the sixteenth and earlier seventeenth centuries. There were Lutheran, Erasmian and Papal Catholic accounts of events in the fateful years 1517–21, and indeed earlier; and in England there were both Catholic and Protestant versions from and before 1529–33, and from a rather later date Calvinist historical writing too. As we shall see, one leading Calvinist author got into serious trouble with his own party because his history was not sufficiently partisan.[14] Not that the reverse is true; polemical history is not necessarily of poor quality. Some of the greatest works which have survived from the ancient world utterly disprove this: Thucydides, Tacitus and others. But it is often hard to see what the polemicists of the Reformation and Counter-Reformation added to the writing of history, qualitatively speaking, at least until we reach the later sixteenth century in France.[15]

Among contemporary historians of these conflicts, the Lutheran Johannes Philippson, better known as John Sleidan, has been the most highly praised by modern commentators. Certainly he did not tell deliberate untruths, invent facts or suppress inconvenient ones. For example, he did not conceal the disputes between Luther and Erasmus, Luther and Zwingli; he died before the split between the

---

13 This is to by-pass Carlo Sigonio (1523–84), originally from Mòdena, whose *De Regno Italiae* crowned a successful – and lucrative – career as professor at Bologna. Writing in Latin, he seems – even in his own time – to have been something of a historian's historian; for some periods and aspects between the seventh and thirteenth centuries his scholarship was highly original and of lasting value. See McCuaig 1989. His friend and later rival Francesco Robortello is credited with having produced 'the first handbook of textual criticism', in 1561 (see Kelley 1970: 113 and n. 61).

14 Probably the greatest of Calvinist historians is discussed below. The intellectual evolution of another can be followed in Trevor-Roper 1966 and McFarlane 1981: index entry 'Historiography'.

15 Not to burden the text with catalogues of names, the following are among the principal figures whose work would need to be discussed in order to weigh this judgement: besides Sleidan (for whom see below), note M. F. Illyricus, alias Vlačić, and the other so-called 'Magdeburg Centuriators' (written 1539–46), Lutheran; Cesare Baronio (1518–1607), Italian, papal Catholic. For a full modern commentary, see Dickens *et al.* 1985: chs 1–5.

Evangelical (Lutheran) and Reformed (Calvinist) churches had become irrevocable. Yet on some issues of fundamental interest he explains disappointingly little: why, for instance, the Lutheran movement led to a permanent breach in the unity of Western Christendom, whereas earlier heresies had been suppressed, if not annihilated by the Catholic Church. One, rather narrowly confessional, answer to this might be to say that Protestantism was not simply another heresy or even a schism, but a restoration, a return to the true Church, free of papal Roman accretions and corruptions. It can hardly have been because Luther was a more admirable individual than, for example, John Hus, or even necessarily because the Church was in a worse condition during the early 1500s than it had been a century and a half earlier. Indeed the ending of the papal schism (in 1415) and then the defeat of the conciliar movement in the course of the fifteenth century meant that in some respects the Church of Luther's day was actually stronger, more formidable, than it had been in the time of Wyclif or Hus. Returning to Sleidan, we should remember that, while a historian contemporary with the events which are being recounted has enormous advantages, there is a corresponding unavoidable loss of perspective. Writing in the 1540–50s he could not know whether the Protestant Reformation would either take over or destroy the Catholic Church, itself be defeated if not wiped out, or (as was in fact to happen) lead to a permanent split in the Western Church. By the time of the greatest historical writings which were stimulated by the religious conflicts, approximately from the 1580s to the 1610s, the probable outcome was clearer, although it was hardly beyond dispute until the second half of the seventeenth century, if not even later than that.[16]

There are of course those who would say that, if the historian attends to truth, accuracy and a sense of proportion, and tells a clear, coherent story, then the facts will speak for themselves. The interpretation which is most nearly correct will then become self-evident to the careful reader. This may sometimes be so, but far from always. Telling what happened by no means automatically explains how it happened, still less why. Naturally all historians are the product of their time, all have their prejudices and limitations. This does not amount to saying that the writing of history would somehow be better done if they abandoned all explanation and interpretation; an assumption of Olympian detachment, a pretence of complete objectivity can be more insidious than prejudice or even bias, so long as we remember the immortal dictum 'Comment is free, facts are sacred.' Nowhere is this truer than in dealing with the religious passions and the denominational conflicts of the sixteenth and seventeenth centuries.

The relations of Christian Europe with the non-European world provided a more or less concurrent but distinct stimulus to historical thought and writing. For

---

16 There is a helpful brief discussion in Dickens 1976: 202–6; see also Dickens *et al.* 1985: ch. 1. A minor curiosity in the second (1689) English version of Sleidan is that the publisher or the translator includes commendatory quotations by Gilbert Burnet, J.-A. de Thou, Jean Bodin and Paul of Sarpi: one of the earliest such 'puffs' known to me, with the worthy Whig bishop (as we shall see) being a little out of his intellectual class (Sleidan 1689: verso of title page).

example, where did the native inhabitants of America fit into the biblical account of the human story (or even into, say, the Herodotean scheme of things)? And if India could be worked in via the conquests of Alexander the Great, what about the civilizations of the Far East? The voyages of discovery and then the adventures and conquests of the Spaniards in Central and South America produced some vivid historical writing, much of it now easily accessible in modern English translations (e.g. Diaz 1963; de Zarate 1968). It might, none the less, be argued that contact with non-Europeans had a greater influence on political and moral thinking than on straightforward historical writing. This can be seen in *Utopia*, the most famous work by the humanist scholar, lawyer, Lord Chancellor and finally martyr, Sir (to Catholics Saint) Thomas More. Later in the sixteenth century the same theme appears in some of the *Essays*, especially 'Of Cannibals', by the French humanist and *politique*, Michel de Montaigne. In the case of the Ottoman Turks, however, as with the Mongols in the thirteenth to fourteenth centuries, Christian Europe was very much on the defensive for most of the fifteenth and sixteenth centuries and again, with the second siege of Vienna, as late as the 1680s. Historians of a speculative bent had a quite different problem there: what if anything was the connection between Turkish military superiority and the Muslim religion? (The words 'Islam' and 'Islamic' were very seldom used, at least in English.)

We have already seen something of how the wars between France and the Habsburgs affected the writing of history in Italy; and a mainly negative point has been suggested about the historiographical impact of the Reformation and Counter-Reformation. By contrast, it is instructive to compare two French historians of the epoch of the so-called Wars of Religion: Lancelot-Voisin de la Popelinière (1541–1608) and Jacques-Auguste de Thou, *alias* Thuanus (1553–1617). Both cover the years from the 1540s to the later 1570s, but de Thou goes on to the 1600s. De la Popelinière's book is entitled a 'History of France'; de Thou's a 'History of his own Time'; the latter actually cites the former as one of his authorities for part of the 1570s. The former summarizes sympathetically speeches which were made by the latter's father in his judicial capacity.[17] The facts that the one was a Huguenot and the other a Catholic seem to make little difference to them as historians. Both were essentially *politiques*, in the sense of putting national unity under a strong monarch, and internal peace, above denominational loyalty. And perhaps not surprisingly in view of this, both got into trouble with their own side: de la Popelinière with the synod of La Rochelle in the 1580s, which may well be why he never continued his history, and de Thou with the Holy Office in the 1600s, which partly explains the complicated publishing history of his work. The Huguenot historian's other work was a kind of compendium, called a 'History of Histories', published when he was eventually received back into favour in 1599. Both of his were written in French, whereas de Thou's was in Latin and published in sections

---

17   Christophe de Thou (1508–82) was First President of the Paris *parlement* in 1572; the historian was his third son (Lalanne 1977: 1713–14).

from the 1600s on; there was no complete edition until the 1730s (in Latin) and no French translation of even the greater part until the 1740s (curiously, part appeared in English a little before that). Their impartiality can be assessed where it is possible to make a direct comparison: on the beginnings of the troubles around 1560 and on the St Bartholomew massacre in 1572. Both blame the ambitions of aristocratic factions and (by implication) royal weakness more than religion as such; neither gives Calvin much prominence, or explains properly how the 'Reformed' (or Calvinist) churches differed from the Lutheran churches, or what the main theological and ecclesiological barriers were to Protestant–Catholic reunion. It would be a mistake to claim that either is an intellectual figure of the stature of their near contemporaries, Bodin and Montaigne. Maybe this is a useful reminder that someone can be a good historian without having a philosophical mind. They may both be contrasted with lesser and more partisan historians of the same and closely parallel events. Faminius Strada's *De Bello Gallico*, translated into English as *The History of the Low-Countries' Warres* in 1650, is much concerned with the causes of the Dutch revolt against Philip II of Spain. Among these Strada includes the growth of heresy, the presence in The Netherlands of Spanish soldiers, the King's more rigid enforcement of his father Charles V's edicts, the appointment of additional bishops, the excessive influence of Cardinal Granvelle, the disappointed hopes of the regional and local nobility, and the severe punishment of delinquents. None the less, he is convinced that there were two fundamental sources of the evils which followed: 'the causes ... which hitherto I have numbered up severally and shewed them to proceed from the Lords and Commons, did at last all meet in one point of concurrence in the Prince of Orange' (Book III, p. 43).

Besides this, Calvin had a more powerful and more damaging appeal to the laity than Luther had had, and the Calvinists were to blame for the outbreak of disorders ('tumults' as his translator calls them), in both France and the Low Countries (Book III, pp. 56, 61–2). E. C. Davila too, whose *History of the Civil Warres of France* was first translated into English in 1647 (perhaps itself a significant date), also leaves his readers in no doubt about the pernicious nature of Calvin's appeal (Book I, pp. 33–4, of the 1758 translation). Such crude stereotyping is quite absent from both the Catholic de Thou and the Protestant de la Popelinière.[18]

Still, impartiality is not all, and some would rate two other of their near-contemporaries above both of these French authors. William Camden (1551–1623), schoolmaster, herald and antiquary, is best known as one of the founders of chorography, that is, the history of localities and regions. Indeed his *Britannia* (original edition 1586, first English version 1610) is probably the most famous and

---

18 It is hard to understand the English Royalist Sir Philip Warwick's assertion (Warwick 1701: 240) that Davila's work was John Hampden's '*vade mecum*'. Apart from its only having been available in Italian until four years after the great Parliamentarian was dead, the main drift or bias of the work would scarcely have commended it to him; a parallel between England under Charles I and the French monarchy from 1559 to 1598 is difficult to sustain.

arguably the most remarkable achievement of its kind, if not the earliest.[19] This is far more ambitious in its scope than the works on individual cities and counties, though the very fact of their being narrower in focus makes the best of them easier reading. It is, however, his *Annales rerum anglicarum et hibernicarum regnante Elizabetha* (first edition, reaching 1588, published 1615, completed 1625, full translation 1635) which entitles Camden to be regarded as the founder of 'civil history' in England, and supports the claim that he was in fact the greatest historian of his age.[20] Perhaps it is an idle game to play at constructing any such kind of league table. Other present-day commentators might see either de Thou or the Venetian Paul of Sarpi (1562–1623) as *primus inter pares*.

Although it is not his only historical work, it is by the *Historie of the Councel of Trent* (published in London, in Italian 1619, in English 1620, under an assumed name) that Sarpi's reputation stands or falls. And it may be significant that he only started work on it after the bitter quarrel between the Venetian government and the papacy in the 1600s, while his own attempted assassination by agents of a rival religious order may also have made him more critical of the Counter-Reformation Church and its policies. The best modern work on Sarpi in English is committed to the thesis that he was a secret unbeliever, which is not directly to our purpose here.[21] Unlike the French historians discussed above, unlike Guicciardini and to a large extent Machiavelli, he was not a contemporary of the events about which he wrote. Having only been born in the year of the Council's final session, he had to collect all his own source materials, although the official publications of the Church provided a large body of these. Sarpi has often been accused of serious bias. While he seems to be trying to let the facts speak for themselves, his work is clearly dedicated to the proposition that the Catholic Church could and should have reached an accommodation with the Protestants, especially after the death of Martin Luther in 1547, which removed the need for a humiliating climbdown by either party. In the mid-seventeenth century a Jesuit historian, Sforza Pallavicino, was commissioned to write an alternative history of the Council, designed to rebut Sarpi. The great German historian of the nineteenth century, Leopold von Ranke (see Michael Bentley, 'Approaches to Modernity' pp. 395–506, below) concluded that Sarpi had got the worst of it in some respects; more recently, however, historians who have worked on the sixteenth-century Church have shown that he had access to documentary sources which were then lost, or anyway were not used

---

19 Southern 1973, esp. pp. 257–63, conveys a marvellous evocation of William Lambarde (*c*.1536–1601) together with his contemporaries and successors, and offers a fascinating parallel with the antiquaries of the early twelfth century. See also Levy 1967; McKisack 1971; Levine 1987, esp. ch. 3; and Woolf 1990.
20 Trevor-Roper 1972, reprinted in Trevor-Roper 1985. While I am reluctant to disagree with an author from whose writings on historians I have gained so much over many years, Trevor-Roper does seem slightly 'over the top' in his comparison of Camden with his greatest continental contemporaries.
21 Wootton 1983. For the composition and publication of the *Historie*, see Yates 1944, amended on a few points by Trevor-Roper and Wootton.

by Pallavicino, and which if known to Ranke would have led him to a different judgement (Ranke 1891: vol. III, App. II, pp. 103–38).

Historians of particular topics or themes seem to have been in fashion around the turn of the sixteenth–seventeenth century. There is a kind of parallel between Sarpi's less well-known (and actually *more* polemical) *History of Benefices*, written between 1606 and 1613 but not published for fifty years after his death, and the work which some claim as the greatest historical achievement by an Englishman in that epoch. John Selden (1584–1654) had already written a lot, especially considering his relative youth, and including his longest work, *Titles of Honour* (1614). This is an account of the origin and development of all the upper ranks of society, from kings down to gentlemen, since the earliest times. One famous passage in the first edition seemed to imply that kings were created by, and so answerable to, peoples, instead of vice versa; and this was to be silently amended in the second edition, after Selden had been in trouble both as a scholar and as a Member of Parliament. But it is his next major work, the *Historie of Tithes*, which prompts the parallel with Sarpi, and has led to his acclamation as the founder of 'problematic history', at least in Britain.[22] This book got him into serious difficulties both with the Jacobean Church hierarchy and with its royal head and governor. When called to answer for the alleged implications of his work, which proved that a compulsory tax of $\frac{1}{10}$ to support the clergy was not *jure divino*, i.e. could not be traced continuously from biblical times, Selden vigorously denied that he intended to undermine the clergy's right to this tax; and since a strongly Erastian belief in the supremacy of the civil over the ecclesiastical power was one of his most consistent political principles, he may well have been sincere in this. He would not have been against tithes as a tax authorized either by the Crown in Parliament or by the immemorial custom of the common law. The contrary view was taken by his fellow-antiquary, the slightly older Sir Henry Spelman (*c.*1564–1641), who has in turn been portrayed as the most original scholar of his time, through his work on the origins of English feudalism.[23] Spelman published much less in his own lifetime than Selden had, but in the longer run his work on the Norman origins of feudal tenures and on the monarchical creation of Parliament in the thirteenth century were to be decisive in shaping later historical thought and writing. Even he, however, was capable of gross anachronism in his eagerness to defend tithes against Selden, or rather against those who might misunderstand or deliberately misuse his friend's work (Woolf 1990: 29n., 79, 275–6, 223–4 n., 75, 319). Again it is probably a futile exercise to offer a kind of order of merit within the antiquarian movement of the time. Perhaps Spelman was the most penetrating investigator of particular concepts and institutions; Selden had a wider range, for example knowledge of languages, and was better at producing completed books. By any

---

22 See Fussner 1962, esp. ch.11, for this claim. Christianson 1984; Berkowitz 1988; Woolf 1990, esp. ch. 7, all provide more measured assessments.

23 Pocock 1957 (and Pocock 1987) is the best treatment of Spelman.

standards, these two, together with Camden and Sir Robert Bruce Cotton (1586–1631) (Sharpe 1979) were in their different ways among the pre-eminent.

Although they were opposed to each other on the freedom of the seas (including the issues of blockade and neutral rights, so important to maritime powers), a parallel can be drawn between Selden and the great Dutch jurist, Hugo Grotius (1583–1645). Best known as the virtual founder of modern international law, his achievement as a historian has been treated as of only secondary importance. From our point of view this is not so. He is said to have been influenced by the examples of Guicciardini and de Thou, as well as by the classical model of Tacitus. His longest and probably most important historical work, *De Rebus Belgicis*, in two parts, translated respectively as the *Annals* and the *History of the Low-Countrie-Warrs*, begins in the 1550s with a brief retrospect to Charles V and Luther. While Grotius paid full attention to religion and the divisions which it created, he definitely regarded political and social causes, in the form of resistance to Spanish tyranny, as the primary cause of the wars. Once or twice his analysis falters just where we would like it to be specific: thus he says that in the renewal of resistance and the first major successes of the revolt (in 1572–3), the Calvinists came out on top in the north, but unfortunately without explaining how or why. And he chronicles the Spanish recovery of control over the southern provinces during the years 1578–84, but – apart from strictly military factors – he only implies that a reaction against extreme religious fanaticism (in this case Protestant) may have been partly responsible, without explaining why this should have been a more powerful factor in the south than in the north. As he comes to his own lifetime, and particularly to the period of which he had first-hand memory, his treatment becomes more and more detailed, devoting a book (equivalent to a very long chapter) to every year from 1589 to 1609. He is particularly effective at portraying the growing war-weariness on both sides during the 1590s and 1600s, yet at the same time explaining how mutual rigidity and mistrust acted as barriers to the making of peace, and finally prevented the conclusion of more than a twelve years' truce. It is instructive to compare his account with the best works on The Netherlands Revolt and the war against Spain written in this century, and to see how far changes in emphasis and interpretation are due to new evidence having come to light, and how far to changes of approach on the part of historians.[24] This is well worthwhile since Grotius was undoubtedly one of the most intellectually distinguished writers of contemporary history in the whole of early modern Europe. Many would add that his humane, ecumenical, middle-of-the-road yet principled standpoint in the ideological conflicts of his time also makes him one of its most admirable figures.[25]

---

24   Hugo Grotius, *De Rebus Belgicis: Or, The Annals, and History of the Low-Countrey-Warrs* ... trs. T. Manley, London, 1665. Prelims. + 974 pp. + Table [i.e. Index]) is said to have been substantially complete by 1614 but to have been revised during the last years of his life. Knight 1925, though a little dated, is still the fullest straightforward biography in English. See also Haitsma 1985 (I am grateful to Michael Bentley for this reference.)
25   For recent assessments, see Trevor-Roper 1967; 1985; 1987; using the indexes; Tuck 1979: ch. 3; 1993, esp. ch. 5.

If modern Dutch historiography was born out of the long conflict with Spain, from the mid-sixteenth to the mid-seventeenth century, Spanish historical writing might perhaps be expected to reflect the celebration of Spain's rise to European hegemony and world empire, followed by puzzlement at the evidence of decline. Juan de Mariana (1535–1624) was, and remains, the best-known Spanish historian of his time. His *General History of Spain* (tr. 1699) runs from the earliest times to the death of King Ferdinand in 1515, with a supplement coming down to Philip III in 1621. His treatment of the sixteenth and early seventeenth centuries is summary and annalistic. Mariana's most important achievement was probably to establish a reliable chronology for the Iberian peninsula from Roman times on. His discussion of the different languages of Spain (Book I, ch. ii) encourages the reader to anticipate a balanced, comparative approach. In fact his judgements are rigidly nationalistic and confessional. The motives for the Portuguese discoveries and their establishment of an overseas empire are categorized as greed and ambition (Book XXV, ch. vi), whereas 'The most Honourable and Advantageous Enterprise that Spain ever undertook was the Discovery of the West Indies' (Book XXVI, ch. ii). Curiously there is no mention of Magellan's voyage and the completion of the first circumnavigation by his companions. On the religious divisions of the sixteenth century Mariana is more Catholic than the popes. Erasmus was 'a Person of great Learning but no good Reputation'; of Calvin and his successor Beza, he writes 'the former was wicked, the latter if possible worse'. William of Orange is, perhaps predictably, the main villain of the Dutch Revolt. The Spanish nation was punished by God for its sins (which are not spelled out) in the defeat of the Armada. Mariana approved of the Moriscoes' banishment in 1607: 'this wicked Race'. De Thou's *History* is roundly condemned: 'A false Catholic does more harm than an open heretic, as says St. Bernard.' On the other hand, when he reaches the respective deaths of the two great rulers, Ferdinand of Aragon and Philip II, he does attempt to strike some kind of balance by summarizing the vices as well as the virtues of each. Even so, it is a little hard to see why Mariana's reputation should stand so high; lack of home-grown competition may be part of the answer.

V

Parallel with these currents in historical scholarship and writing, another type or genre appeared, which owed much to Renaissance humanism, yet was definitely post-Renaissance in spirit. These were guides or compendia to different kinds of history, as distinct from works on the authenticity of sources. One of the earliest, and because of its author the best known, is Jean Bodin's *Methodus ad facilem historiarum cognitionem* (first published in 1566, first English translation 1945), Bodin's fame is greatest as a political theorist, for having helped to originate and then for having strenuously advocated the concept of absolute political sovereignty; and, like other intellectuals of this period, his religious orthodoxy has been called in question. Our concern here is with him as a writer about history and historians, and by modern standards the value of his work is bound to appear extraordinarily uneven. He goes into quite excessive detail refining and extending Aristotle's notion of climate and geography as determining influences on the character of different peoples, and hence on their various forms of government and political behaviour. He demolishes briskly and very effectively the idea of the five great temporal monarchies, the last being that of the present age and so the prologue to the Second Coming of Christ. He is fascinated, one might say obsessed, by the supposed historical and political significance of different numerals and of more complex numbers. He was, however, among the first post-humanist authors to put forward the argument, which later became commonplace, that the Moderns had surpassed the Ancients through the great inventions or innovations of their time: to the usual trio of printing, gunpowder and the magnetic compass (revolutionizing the media, warfare and transoceanic navigation) he added as a fourth advances in medicine, where he might be considered prematurely optimistic in spite of the great achievements of such figures as Vesalius and Paracelsus. His *Methodus* went through many editions, and he had many emulators, imitators and rivals in his own and other countries. Here too the Italians may have got in first, in the sense of anticipating his work though not in equalling its originality.[26] In this field de la Popelinière's second work, *L'Histoire des Histoires, avec l'Idée de l'Histoire accompli Plus le Dessein de l'Histoire nouvelle des François* (1599), is of particular interest. Certainly he had a less creative and wide-ranging mind than Bodin; on the other hand, he had already proved that he could write conventional history at a very high level of competence before he started to theorize about it; and, if he had fewer original ideas, he also had fewer silly ones. He disposed trenchantly, and one might think definitively, of the Franks' supposed Trojan origins (as we have seen, he was not the first here). He went on to offer a shrewd, strictly historical explanation for the beginnings and then the tenacity of this myth in post-Roman Europe. Among modern historians, he awarded the palm to Guicciardini: 'il a surpassé les Anciens et nouveaux en verité de la plus part de ses Narrez' (I, 407–13). But, whatever his faults, Thucydides remains 'le Prince de l'Histoire' (II, 17). Moreover, although this is harder to document from specific passages, de la Popelinière seems to have more awareness than Bodin of historical context and change, likewise of the historian's duty to offer opinions and judgements, but also to provide the evidence with which the reader can reach alternative conclusions (II, 292–318). His own and de Thou's respective handling of the 1572 massacres provide excellent examples of this practice. It would be foolish to exaggerate de la Popelinière's modernity, and in so doing to disregard his own warnings against anachronism, but he does seem to be

---

26   In England, Blundeville 1574, drawing on the work of two Italians, one published in 1560; see H. G. Dick's edn in *Huntington Library Quarterly* 3 (1939–40): 149–70. Passages categorizing different kinds of history are scattered in Francis Bacon's philosophical writings; some will think that his *The Historie of the Raigne of King Henry the Seventh* (1st edn, London, 1622) should have been discussed in this chapter, but it is no more original – in terms of historical writing – than numerous other works which have had to be omitted. For Germany see Keckermann 1610.

groping his way towards some of the ideas which were to be developed by Vico and others much later.[27]

Professional historians of the nineteenth and twentieth centuries have gained more from the advances in the actual techniques of scholarship which were made during the sixteenth and seventeenth centuries – *érudition* as the French called it – than from histories of particular countries, institutions and movements, or from books about history written during this period. In part this was simply a continuation and refinement of methods which had already emerged in Renaissance Italy and then in France.[28]

One feature of history as it is taught, particularly in schools, which has often been denounced for making it dull, is having too many dates. Whether or not this is a fair criticism, we certainly take for granted nowadays that there is an agreed chronological framework (apart from minor differences in the calendar) for all history since the beginning of the Christian era. And we calculate backwards from there, though with increasing caution and approximation the further that we go and the less that we have by way of reliable first-hand written sources. The establishment of an agreed chronology had preoccupied writers and thinkers long before the time of the Renaissance. The ancient Greeks counted years from the earliest known Olympiads, though they were very unsure of a date even so central to their own history (or their national mythology perhaps) as the siege of Troy and its literary embodiment in the Homeric poems. The Romans dated events yearly from the supposed foundation of their city, consistently if on shaky evidence. The Jews worked forward from the Creation, or more confidently from the Flood and the re-peopling of the world by Noah and his descendants. There were also astronomical records from the histories of non-Christian societies in both the Near and Far East. The greatest individual work of harmonizing these various traditions, while keeping all the rest ultimately subordinate to the Judaeo-Christian framework, was undertaken by Joseph Justus Scaliger (1540–1609), of Italian descent but resident mainly in France and a convert to Protestantism. His greatest work, the Latin title of which has been translated as *Emendations of Chronology*, was not definitive; nor was he alone and unchallenged in this field. But at least by the opening of the seventeenth century there was an agreed chronology from the later centuries BC until the modern era, though this did not solve the problem of gaps in the written

---

27 I am not aware of any modern critical edition of his or of de Thou's works, though there are many articles on both in French and other journals; see Kinser 1966. The English Jacobite historian, Thomas Carte, de Thou's eventual editor, himself deserves a full study. Butterfield (1955: Appendix I, 'La Popelinière's *Histoire des Histoires*,' pp. 205–6, and Butterfield 1981: 189–90) emphasizes the more conservative, backward-looking side of his thought, but does not mention the *Histoire de France*. Dickens *et al.* (1985: ch. 4, pp. 73, 84–5, 102) treat him more sympathetically than they do de Thou.

28 Again the bibliography is enormous. I have found Kelley 1970 the most helpful, but see too Huppert 1970: chs 2 and 8 for de la Popelinière, likewise almost entirely on his *Histoire des Histoires*; unlike Kelley, he stops short of de Thou. Among the most recent works, see Schiffman 1991, esp. ch. 2. I am grateful to Professor Daniel Woolf for drawing my attention to this work.

record, e.g. for pre-Roman and again for immediately post-Roman times in Britain and elsewhere.[29]

The greatest achievement of the two groups known as the Bollandists and the Maurists was, as members of Catholic religious orders in seventeenth-century France, to prove the compatibility of faith and learning. They were able to produce more accurate texts of saints' lives and of other sources for early and medieval Church history without arousing the same intense ecclesiastical hostility as other scholars had encountered since the Protestant Reformation. Besides their prolific editions of texts, one of the Maurists, Jean Mabillon (1632–1707), wrote what became, and for long remained, the classic guide to the correct interpretation of official documents, *De re diplomatica* (1681); this has provided the foundation for parts of the more modern manuals mentioned earlier in this chapter. Finally, in the earlier eighteenth century, the Italian L. A. Muratori (1672–1750) applied similar techniques to further areas of secular as well as Church history, notably in the study of early Italy; his work too was only to be surpassed by the great collaborative research and publishing ventures of the nineteenth century.[30]

The rapid spread of translations from Latin as well as Greek into the various vernacular languages of Europe was certainly made possible, and was perhaps only brought about, by the parallel growth of printing. It is not the case that works ceased to be transmitted in manuscript after the fifteenth century. Still less is it the case that Latin was suddenly displaced as the language of international scholarly discourse. None the less, the output of printed books and other kinds of publication grew at a portentous rate; at the same time, more and more books were either written in vernacular languages or quickly translated into them. As with most so-called 'counter-factual' arguments, we cannot prove how historical writing would have developed from the fifteenth to eighteenth centuries if the old method of manuscript copying had remained as the sole means of transmitting the written word; we cannot 're-run' the period without the printing press. To give just one example, the appearance in several vernaculars of Plutarch's *Lives of the Famous Greeks and Romans* helped to set a fashion for short biographies, some of more value than others to subsequent historians. And, at what might seem like another extreme, while Spelman was wrestling with the meaning and historical significance of a *feudum* and Selden with such titles as earl, count and knight, Sir Walter Ralegh (*c*.1552–1618) was writing his *History of the World* as a prisoner of state in the Tower of London. Feeling that he was in enough trouble already, Ralegh tells us that he is avoiding contemporary history; and the work, as published, begins with the Creation and ends with the Roman wars against Macedonia in the late second century BC. Although he was to become something of a cult-figure with the Puritan

---

29 See Grafton 1983); vol. II appeared too late for use in this chapter but is clearly definitive; see also Grafton 1991, esp. ch. 4 on Scaliger's chronology.
30 See Knowles 1963 on the Bollandists and the Maurists; for the growing awareness of non-literary evidence, Momigliano 1966, esp. ch. 1, 'Ancient History and the Antiquarian' (first published 1950); for Muratori, see Momigliano 1977: ch.16, 'Mabillon's Italian Disciples'.

imperialists of the next generation, Ralegh is not particularly forward-looking as a historian. He does indeed concentrate on secondary causes, taking for granted God's purpose as the first cause of all things; he had been accused of religious heterodoxy, if not of downright atheism, but his treatment of the pre-Christian era is still constrained by the need to fit (one is tempted to say, to cram) everything into a chronological framework of only 4,000 years or so, and in doing this to give the sacred books of the Old Testament priority over all other sources for the history of the earliest times.[31] This view of human origins with its accompanying chronology was not overthrown by any single dramatic secular victory over the Church, but through a whole series of developments over several generations. Among these was an increasing interest in non-literary evidence, from archaeology, and eventually from geology and fossil study too, together with the study of tombs, inscriptions, coins and other human artefacts. The origins and rise of Christianity itself and the story of the early Church were of course to be reserved and treated as 'sacred history' long after the literal truth of the Old Testament had been discarded in most educated circles (notwithstanding a revival of such belief among the crudely fundamentalist groups of our own time, if more so in the United States than in Europe). Even in the later eighteenth century Gibbon was to be savagely attacked in print for his allegedly irreverent handling of the early Church; but at least he was not charged with heresy or brought to trial for blasphemy. This, however, is to anticipate.

VI

Just as the religious conflicts of the sixteenth century had provided subject matter for many historians in different parts of Europe, so – not surprisingly – did the Civil Wars and related upheavals in seventeenth-century Britain. It is not of course that everyone wrote contemporary history and nothing else suddenly from 1640 on. The antiquarian movement continued at the same very high level of achievement, at least until the beginning of the eighteenth century, with particularly great advances being made in the study of Anglo-Saxon (now known as Old English). More in the tradition of Ralegh than of Camden, Spelman, Selden and their successors, John Milton's *History of Britain*, probably written during the Interregnum but not published until 1670, likewise (if for different reasons) avoids anything contemporary, except for one excursus drawing a parallel between the Britons when the Romans withdrew in the fifth century and the situation after the overthrow of the monarchy and the Anglican Church in the 1640s. Milton begins with the earliest times but has to admit that nothing certain is known of Britain before the coming of the Romans, and – in a slightly take-it-or-leave-it manner—he gives us a summary of what is in Geoffrey of Monmouth, including the fable of Brutus the Trojan; by

---

31 The remarkable comparative date lists, which form the Appendix to Ralegh's *History*, show that Scaliger had added 682 years to the age of the world by recalculating the length of a calendar year.

contrast with this, for the post-Roman, Christian period he shows more scepticism towards such embroideries. For example, he was doubtful about the existence of King Arthur. He finishes with the Norman Conquest, relating William's victory in 1066 to the moral and cultural decline which he discerned in the Anglo-Saxons during the preceding years. If this work was not by Milton, it would not be worth more than a passing mention.

Many of those who wrote about contemporary events did so in order to explain, or more often to justify their own part in these. In the case of women biographers on both sides, it was usually a matter of extolling the roles of their respective husbands.[32] Royalists who wrote after the defeat of the monarchy and before its restoration naturally had a very different perspective from those writing after 1660. For posterity it is both fortunate and confusing that the foremost Royalist author (and some would say the greatest English historian of the century), Edward Hyde, later Earl of Clarendon, wrote the earlier part of his *History of the Rebellion* during the later 1640s, very close in time to the events with which he was concerned, and then the latter part during his second exile (in the years 1668–70). In his last years he also wrote a self-justificatory autobiography, which he called a *History of his own Life* (presented rather artificially in the third person, calling himself 'he' throughout); in some versions this is partially combined with the text of the *Rebellion*, of which the first edition did not appear until nearly thirty years after his death, in the early 1700s.[33] Like many great works, it is a flawed masterpiece, often anthologized for its character sketches. Just as Sarpi was convinced that the Council of Trent should have healed the breach in Western Christendom, so Hyde believed that King and Parliament could and should have reached an agreement at some stage in 1640–2; despite criticizing the unwisdom of Charles I and some of his advisers, he seems at times to lay the entire blame for the rebellion and the war on the sinister machinations of what he calls 'the faction', the inner ring of radical leaders in the two Houses of Commons and Lords. At a more fundamental level, Hyde had three main problems to solve, for himself and for his readers: how and why the rebellion could take place at all; how and why the King was defeated (and later executed); how and why his eldest son was restored to the throne without further bloodshed after eleven years of republican rule. Predictably he invokes first causes, before proceeding to secondary causes, and the disasters of the 1640s give him more

---

32   The lives of Colonel John Hutchinson, by his widow, Lucy; of William Cavendish, first Duke of Newcastle, by his wife, Margaret; and of Sir Richard Fanshawe, by his widow, Ann, may be cited as examples. For other works by women authors, see Crawford 1985: App. 1. Apparent works of history by women authors are mostly on the borderline between court memoirs and fiction; I am most grateful to Dr Anne Laurence for guidance on this.

33   The original title of the book which he began writing in 1646 was 'A True Historicall narration of the Rebellion and civill warres in England begunne in the yeare 1641, with the precedent passages and Actions that contributed therunto'; as published it is shortened to *The History of the Rebellion and Civil Wars in England Begun in the year 1641*, ed. W. D. Macray (6 vols, Oxford, 1888; repr. 1988), which remains the least imperfect edition.

difficulty than the happy events of 1660. He begins by asserting that nothing 'less than a general combination and universal apostasy in the whole nation from their religion and allegiance' could account for what had happened (Book I, para. 1). But Hyde seems to see that, as with all invocations of first causes, this is to over-explain. And he then observes that, besides 'the immediate finger and wrath of God', the diligent observer

> will find all this bulk of misery to have proceeded, and to have been brought upon us, from the same natural causes and means which have usually attended kingdoms swollen with long plenty, pride and excess, towards some signal mortification and castigation of Heaven.
>
> (I, 2)

The notion of peoples and nations being surfeited with peace and plenty, and failing to appreciate that 'they had never had it so good', was something of a truism in seventeenth-century thought.[34] Finally, in his conclusion, Hyde can only record that 'in this wonderful manner, and with this miraculous expedition did God put an end in one month [i.e. May 1660] to a rebellion that had raged near twenty years' (XVI, 247). Apart from his portraits of individuals, Clarendon is at his best on the divisions and irresolutions within the Royalist ranks. He is correspondingly at his weakest in his apparent inability to grasp the motives of those on the other side; hence his resort to conspiracy theory with 'the faction' and their even more extreme allies and successors. Yet we have only to compare him with other historians of these same events, of whatever persuasion, to appreciate his achievement, and to regret that he never completed his 'True Historicall narration ....' as a work distinct from *His own Life*. He did, however, continue this political autobiography down to the date of his second exile, and it thus forms a valuable, if exceedingly prejudiced, first-hand source for the years 1660–7.

Like the Reformation and the English Civil War, other great contemporary conflicts stimulated the writing of recent history. Two such cases are the revolt of The Netherlands and the Thirty Years War. Grotius, who wrote in Latin and was later translated, has already been discussed. Whether the work of P. C. Hooft (1581–1647) would be ranked with that of Sarpi and de Thou if more of us could read Dutch with fluency must remain an open question; certainly he is regarded as one of the greatest figures in Dutch literature. Three other, more strictly contemporary historians of the revolt may be more valuable as first-hand witnesses, though – as we should all know – witnesses can be untruthful, biased or simply mistaken.

Seventeenth-century Germany produced philosophers and jurists of the first rank, but no historian of quite comparable distinction. Samuel Pufendorf (1632–94) wrote an officially commissioned history of the Swedish monarchs and

---

34 See Macgillivray 1974: Appendix, where medical metaphors of purges and bleedings are shown to have been more usual than scriptural citations of peace and plenty, etc.

their deeds and then, recalled to his homeland, one on the 'Great Elector' of Brandenburg-Prussia. More interestingly, he also wrote (uncommissioned so far as is known) one of the earliest general histories of Europe. His method here was to devote a chapter to each kingdom or other state. In every case he begins with a brief glance back to the origins of the nation or people in question, pre- or post-Roman as the case may be; he then proceeds to provide a fairly detailed chronological narrative, mainly political, diplomatic and military in content but with some ecclesiastical matters also included; this is rounded out with a kind of balance-sheet of the strengths and weaknesses, the virtues and failings of the state or people concerned, and concludes with a short survey of their relations with the other states of Europe. This treatment is applied first to the Roman Empire itself, then to eleven existing secular powers and to the papacy; Italy as such is excluded, while Poland and Muscovy are included, but Bohemia and Hungary only as provinces of the German Empire, which by this time was in effect the Austrian Habsburg Empire. Such a method leads to a great deal of repetition as well as to some strange omissions. None the less, it is a gallant effort; and, short of a radically different approach by topics or themes, this structure proved to have set a very long-lasting precedent. Pufendorf's more often cited *Compleat History of Sweden* is little more than an immense enlargement of the Swedish chapter in his *Introduction to the History of the Principal Kingdoms and States of Europe*, with 70 pages swelling to over 600. The structure is identical and the content adds disappointingly little except for a narrative laden with detail. Although he was far from being irreligious, Pufendorf's own confessional position seems of little consequence; perhaps one could guess that the author was not an extreme Papalist or Calvinist, but eighty or a hundred years earlier even those of a moderate persuasion wrote history with more intense religious commitment.

Contemporary correspondence and record sources are available in great quantities by the seventeenth century. So modern scholars are not dependent on historians of the time, unless like some of those who have been discussed they were participants in the events which they recount or explain and their work thus supplements other original sources. Others continued to present materials for much earlier periods of history. J. L. von Mosheim (*c*.1694–1755), like Pufendorf, was a German Lutheran, but unlike him was a historian of the ancient world whose work was drawn upon by other historians in the eighteenth century; and he therefore belongs more with the technical scholars discussed above. All in all, there is no simple formula to explain why in some ages and some societies the finest and most creative minds have devoted themselves to the writing of history, let alone to what kind of history.

VII

There was no slackening in the output of historical works during the later seventeenth and earlier eighteenth centuries, either in Britain or in most other European countries. Such books were increasingly written and published in the vernacular, and were often translated into other contemporary languages.[35] 'History' would therefore seem to have been a paying proposition, for printers and publishers, if not always for authors. Yet, apart from the striking progress in 'erudition', it is hard to identify any single work before the last quarter of the eighteenth century which compares with the greatest achievements of the previous two or three centuries. In Britain such eminent public figures as the diplomat Sir William Temple, the Tory statesman Henry St. John, Viscount Bolingbroke, the Whig churchman Bishop Gilbert Burnet, and – a little later – the great Scottish philosopher David Hume, besides many lesser writers, seem to have been more concerned with lucidity and elegance of expression than with close investigation of the evidence or the proper balance between research and exposition. A striking feature of the earlier eighteenth century is the emergence, principally but not exclusively in France, of what is sometimes called 'philosophic history'. This is not only because a good deal of it was written by men who were, and are, more famous as philosophers than as historians. Among the characteristics of such historical writing during what has become known as the 'Enlightenment' were the conviction that the Moderns were superior to the Ancients, that on balance there is progress in human civilization, but that human nature at its most basic level is a constant factor, although ease and affluence may corrupt humanity's natural goodness. Perhaps such views were the product of a more secular, in some sense a more materialistic age, though obviously not all the philosophers and historians of the time subscribed with equally strong conviction to all these tenets. The historical works of Voltaire (1694–1778) exhibit an extraordinary range and diversity. They include the most vivid of political and military narratives in *The History of Charles XII* (the warrior king of Sweden); the most ambitious attempt yet made to portray a whole society 'in the round', giving due weight to the economy, the arts and sciences, in *The Age of Louis XIV*; and the widest-ranging general and comparative reflections, in the *Essay on the Customs and Spirit of Nations* and in his article on 'History' for the great, multi-volume *Philosophical Dictionary*, edited by some of his contemporaries among the French *philosophes*. Arguably, however, the most profound work of historical analysis was by another French author, Montesquieu (1689–1755). The *Considérations sur les causes de la grandeur des Romains et de leur décadence*, first published in 1734 and revised in 1748, is in length no more than an extended essay.[36] It was not based on particularly deep research into original sources; but, as a study of historical causation, of the interaction between individuals, institutional structures and external pressures, it is an intellectual achievement of astonishing power, and this in spite of the author being much better known for his far longer, more elaborate work, *De L'esprit des lois* (1748).

---

35   For example Pietro Giannone, whose *Civil History of the Kingdom of Naples* appeared first in Italian (1723) and was banned almost immediately by the Church authorities; it was published in English, translated by an ex-Jacobite, a few years later (2 vols, folio, London, 1729–31). Gibbon is said to have been influenced by Giannone's work during his first visit to Lausanne.

36   The most accessible English version is ed. and transl. D. Lowenthal (Glencoe, IL., 1965).

Edward Gibbon (1737–94) is perhaps the greatest historian who has ever written in English. If history is regarded primarily as a branch of literature and only secondarily as a social science, his claims are hard to challenge. This does not mean that his masterpiece, *The History of the Decline and Fall of the Roman Empire* (first published in six volumes, 1776–88), is or should be beyond criticism. His learning was immensely impressive. Although Gibbon studied Greek (and we know that he read several of the greatest classic works in the original), his command of that language was never as fluent and perfect as it was of Latin. This is often alleged to have been a handicap in the latter part of his *History* where sources in Greek were sometimes his chief or even sole authority; in fact it seems more plausible to suggest that he felt a profound lack of sympathy, let alone affection, for the Byzantine (or later Eastern Roman) Empire. Many other charges have been brought against him: his sneering treatment of Christianity, or at least of the Church, his condescending attitude towards women, his 'Eurocentrism', his apparent indifference to the huge slave population whose labours underpinned so much of the economy of the ancient world of Greece and Rome, his complacent political and social conservatism. As against this, the conception, scope and sweep of his work are breathtakingly magnificent; besides his inimitable style, many of his judgements of individuals and of situations are shrewd and perceptive; finally, his general standard of accuracy is awesome.

It may be worth considering the structure of his great work, and to ask ourselves how this affected Gibbon's treatment of his subject. He had already decided, before he began to write, that the so-called 'Age of the Antonines', or to be precise the years AD 98–180, was the vantage point from which he would look both forward and back:

> If a man were called to fix the period in the history of the world during which the condition of the human race was most happy and prosperous, he would, without hesitation, name that which elapsed from the death of Domitian to the accession of Commodus. The vast extent of the Roman Empire was governed by absolute power, with the guidance of virtue and wisdom.
>
> (Gibbon 1896–1900: I, 78)

The reader will notice that, while this is by no means identical with Petrarch's threefold division of history, the similarity is obvious, except that (as is allowed to emerge in the course of the *Decline and Fall*) Gibbon regarded his own time and not the Renaissance as the age of recovery when the world of the Antonines had at last been equalled and in some important respects actually surpassed. Because of the assumptions which he made about the second century AD, he was able to deal retrospectively – and very summarily – with the collapse of the Roman Republic and its replacement by the principate and then the Empire. His praise for Julius Caesar is indeed less qualified than it is in the case of Augustus; he seems to have no regrets about Rome's Republican past, and to see Nerva, Trajan and Hadrian effectively taking up where Augustus had left off. His explanation of 'decline' (often wrongly identified with his famous phrase 'the triumph of barbarism and religion', which is actually more of a synonym than a cause) is thus conceptually as well as chronologically different from Montesquieu's 'decadence'. None the less, some comparison is possible between them. Gibbon seems to imply that the Roman Empire might have solved its problems, and perhaps have continued indefinitely, but for the internal solvent of Christianity and the external catalyst of the invasions, although the more specific factors of the politicization of the army and its constant interference with the succession, together with the foundation of a second imperial capital in the East, are accorded at least equal weight. Montesquieu, by contrast, lays much more emphasis on the sheer over-extension of Rome's Empire, even before the fall of the Republic, and on the unresolved internal conflicts; in his case extraneous forces, including the new religion, are discussed but given less weight. The references in Gibbon's notes to his French forerunner tend to be critical and patronizing; and he may have been unaware of his own intellectual indebtedness. Gibbon was normally generous and honest in acknowledging the help of other modern authorities; his reliance on the chronology of the earlier French scholar S. le Nain de Tillemont (1637–98) is expressed with open gratitude. Very occasionally he forgot, or failed to acknowledge, an intermediate authority; for example, he corrected Grotius's translation of the Greek author Procopius's *Military History* without reference to the French savant of the early eighteenth century, Jean Barbeyrac, who had already made the identical point.[37]

The proportions of his work have sometimes been criticized, the first three centuries having as much space as the last nine. This is not altogether fair. He followed the precedent of previous historians by inserting analytical, or survey-type chapters, to break and vary the flow of narrative, for example those on the Empire's northern and eastern neighbours, and in later volumes on the Arabs, the Turks and the nomadic peoples of central Asia. The most famous (or notorious) of these intermissions is chapter 15, on the reasons for the rise and eventual triumph of Christianity; many religious believers, then and now, cannot forgive him for setting divine providence aside and concentrating on the secondary causes of this most extraordinary of historical phenomena. Not for nothing was Gibbon a friend and admirer of the greatest of all religious sceptics, the philosopher (and historian) David Hume. Obviously there are aspects even of those centuries to which he devoted most detailed attention where Gibbon's work has been superseded or revised by more recent scholars. His achievement and its limitations should serve to remind us that the initial assumptions of all historians shape, if they do not wholly predetermine, their researches and writings. In this Gibbon is typical rather than unique, unsurpassed though he remains in so many other respects.

It would be absurd (and impertinent) to imply that the *Decline and Fall* was based on Montesquieu's *Considérations*. Yet, when he reached the end of the western Roman Empire (in the later fifth century AD), Gibbon's 'General

---

37 *Histoire des Anciens Traitez* ... (folio. Amsterdam and The Hague. 1739), Part II, arts 99, n. 4, 196, n. 7, 197, nn. 11–12 (pp. 81, 184, 187); compare *Decline and Fall*, ch. XLI, n. 1 (ed. Bury), IV, 271.

Observations' are strangely similar to the arguments of his predecessor, but shifted forward in time instead of being located at the downfall of the Republic:

> the decline of Rome was the natural and inevitable effect of immoderate greatness. Prosperity ripened the principle of decay; the causes of destruction multiplied with the extent of conquest; and, as soon as time or accident had removed the artificial supports, the stupendous fabric yielded to the pressure of its own weight. The story of its ruin is simple and obvious; and, instead of inquiring why the Roman Empire was destroyed, we should rather be surprised that it had subsisted so long.
>
> Gibbon 1896–1900: IV, 161, ch. 38

As to another of Gibbon's distinguishing features, if history 'is little more than a register of the crimes, follies and misfortunes of mankind' (ch. 3), why do some societies in some epochs appear to display a growth in power and wealth and an improvement in the quality of life, others their decline and deterioration? Gibbon is rightly renowned for his use of irony in making historical judgments, but the trouble with ironists is to know when they mean us to take them seriously. By contrast, it may be thought that Montesquieu is being praised too easily here: what passes in a long essay will not do in a multi-volume narrative. And we do know, from the *Esprit des Lois*, that he like Bodin before him was much influenced by the classical (post-Aristotelian) leaning towards geographical and climatological determinism in human affairs, likewise towards a cyclical view of political and social change, also inherited from the Ancients, in this case through the medium of Machiavelli's *Discourses on Livy's History* and other Renaissance works. Montesquieu's own most original prescription for preserving the political health of a society was a mixed or balanced constitution, including the separation of the powers (executive, legislative and judicial), the former of which he identified correctly and the latter mistakenly as being present in Hanoverian Britain. A further and in one case decisive variation or refinement of this was provided by Hume (1711–76), but in his *Essays*, not in his *History of England*. This was the possibility of establishing and maintaining republican government over an extensive territory and a large, diverse population, which virtually all previous political theorists and historians had assumed to be impossible. The substitution of political representation for direct participation, applied to the popular, potentially democratic element in government, together with the practice of separation and the federal principle, helped to bring about what may fairly be regarded as the greatest pragmatic success story of the eighteenth-century Enlightenment: the United States constitution of 1788. The 'Founding Fathers', as those responsible for this have become known, included several who were well read in the historiography and the philosophy both of the classical world and of post-Renaissance Europe. Flawed, not to say bedevilled, as it was, by the issues of race and ethnicity, the subsequent near-elimination of the native North Americans and their culture, and the continuing exploitation of black slaves, from Africa originally via the Caribbean, this constitution, on which the modern United States of America was founded, thus incorporated both positive and negative elements of the Western heritage, in the self-delineation of which historians had played their part, indeed had at times assumed a leading role.

275

At a distance of over 200 years we should be capable of a certain detachment. In Gibbon's work it has been said that erudition, elegance of presentation, and the temper of enlightened or philosophic history met and were triumphantly joined together. Yet his achievement was an end product, the culmination of post-Renaissance European historical writing. There still seems to have been little awareness of the economic element in historical change. The seventeenth-century English republican James Harrington had argued strenuously for the material basis of politics. He maintained that the distribution of landed property determined the the balance of political power; and, further, that the inevitable concentration of landownership in ever fewer hands, thus leading to an ever narrower political oligarchy, could only be checked, let alone reversed, by the passage and strict enforcement of an 'Agrarian', a law to limit the size of holdings. This was a conscious echo of the Gracchi's programme in republican Rome. It is true that Voltaire devoted considerable attention to the development of French commerce under Louis XIV; but, apart from the enlightened policies of Colbert and the damaging over-taxation due to the King's repeated wars, he shows little sense of the influences which might tend to accelerate or to retard economic growth. Not until the English agronomist, Arthur Young (1741–1820), writing in the very late eighteenth century, do we find the relative backwardness of most French compared to English farming practice being related to questions of land tenure and seigneurial jurisdiction. As to the relative technological and economic stagnation in the ancient world, there is just one passage in Montesquieu's *Considérations* where he fastens on the likely key:

> Les citoyens romains regardaient le commerce et les arts comme l'occupation d'esclaves; ils ne les exerçaient point. S'il y eut quelques exceptions, ce ne fut que de la part de quelques affranchis qui continuaient leur première industrie.
>
> (ch. X, final paragraph)

Full citizens, he tells us, could properly engage only in war and agriculture. But neither he, nor Voltaire, nor even Gibbon explored this theme in any detail. Curiously, in his *Introduction to the History of Europe*, Pufendorf had made a virtually identical point about the Spaniards, though not in relation to slavery.

VIII

Another way of looking at historical writing during these centuries would be by considering its readers. How far were the changes in its form and content due to changes in the kind of people for whom history was written? Printers and booksellers were after all business men (occasionally women), as well as being in some instances people of strong religious or political convictions. Apart from the obvious point, already emphasized, of the general, European-wide increase in vernacular, as opposed to Latin publications, can anything be said about the class or occupational character of the reading public for such works? There was certainly a market for history in Italy, France, England and probably Germany from the sixteenth century on. We can be sure of this from the sheer number of titles, many of mediocre quality and no particular interest, which are known to have appeared,. It is tempting to suggest that a predominantly aristocratic, courtly and clerical readership was replaced by one with a larger lay, middle-class element. It would be most unwise to suppose that courtiers, nobles and their families, or indeed priests and pastors were any less literate or any less interested in history by around 1700 than they had been in (say) 1500. But it does seem reasonable to suggest that the balance of the potential readership at which booksellers and authors were aiming had shifted somewhat; not perhaps towards the commercial and industrial classes as a whole, but at least towards non-clerical members of the professions, merchants and – especially on the seaboard of north-west Europe – those engaged in overseas trade, shipping and colonization. Because it is virtually impossible to put facts and figures on such a generalization as this, we should not be led to abandon the hypothesis altogether.

At the same time it is difficult to maintain that the greatest, or even the most representative examples of historical writing display more specifically 'bourgeois' characteristics by the end of the period than they already possessed at the beginning. We have only to think of the great Italians from the century or so 1430–1540 to become aware of this. Paradoxically, it might well be argued that Bruni, Machiavelli, Guicciardini and others were if not bourgeois at least distinctively 'civic' historians to a greater extent than could be said of (for example) Clarendon, Burnet, Hume and Gibbon. The market was a vital factor, especially at the 'Grub Street' end of the publishing trade and the authorial profession. More scholarly historians, writing for the educated minority, could not totally neglect market considerations unless they had a patron who was also a paymaster; and, like everybody else, they were themselves the products of the society in which they lived. Yet to what extent they consciously aimed at a particular readership remains problematic, and can easily be exaggerated. Truly popular history – in England of the chap-book variety – did aim at a mass, and therefore by definition at a little educated public; the serious history which appeared in massive folio or stout octavo volumes was equally obviously being bought by the better-off, latterly a more laicized, less Latinate readership. Only the copies which found their ways into such libraries as were open to the poor and unprivileged might have constituted a partial exception to the reading of serious history being effectively limited to the more affluent sections of society. Within the limits which have been suggested here, changes in what was being supplied by writers may have been more significant than changes in what was being demanded by their readers. It is surely beyond dispute that producer, distributor and consumer were in a situation of mutual dependence. Books were a market commodity; and there is no reason to suppose that historical writing was an exception to this rule.[38]

---

38 For books printed in the British Isles and in English printed elsewhere, see Pollard and Redgrave 1976–91; Wing 1972–88; *Subject-index* 1981; Robinson *et al.* 1981; *Eighteenth-century STC* (2 vols microfiche 1990). The creation on disc of a European short-title catalogue may be suggested as a worthy cultural objective for either the European Union or the European Science Foundation.

New intellectual tendencies, new ideological forces,.some already in existence but still hidden from general view, and of little consequence before the nineteenth century,[39] were to shift the Western tradition of historical thought and writing in fresh directions. They were to change it more fundamentally than anything had done since the humanist movement and the printing press back in the fifteenth century.

REFERENCES

Berkowitz, D. S. (1988) *John Selden's Formative Years. Politics and Society in Early 17th-Century England*, Washington, DC.

Berlin, I. (1976) *Vico and Herder. Two Studies in the History of Ideas*, London.

—— (1979) *Against the Current. Essays in the History of Ideas*, ed. H. Hardy, London.

Blundeville, T. (1574) *The True Order and Method of Writing and Reading Histories*, London.

Bodin, Jean (1566) *Methodus ad facilem historiarum cognitionem*. English translation, *Method for the Easy Comprehension of History*, trans. and ed. Beatrice Reynolds, New York, 1945.

Bolgar, R. R. (1954) *The Classical Heritage and its Beneficiaries from the Carolingian Age to the End of the Renaissance*, London.

Burke, P. (1966) 'A survey of the popularity of ancient historians, 1450–1700', *History and Theory* 5 pp. 135–52.

—— (1969) *The Renaissance Sense of the Past*, London.

Butterfield, H. (1955) *Man on his Past: The Study of the History of Historical Scholarship*, Cambridge.

—— (1981) *The Origins of History*, London.

Cassirer, E., Kristeller, P. O. and Randall, J. H. Jr. (eds) (1948) *The Renaissance Philosphy of Man*, Chicago.

Christianson, P. (1984) 'Young John Selden and the Ancient Constitution, 1610–1628', *Proceedings of the American Philosophical Society* 128(4): 271–315.

Cochrane, E. (1981) *Historians and Historiography in the Italian Renaissance*, Chicago and London.

Crawford, P. M. (1985) Ch. 7 in M. Prior (ed.) *Women in English Society 1500–1800*, London.

D'Amico, J. F. (1988) *Theory and Practice in Renaissance Textual Criticism. Beatus Rhenanus between Conjecture and History*, Berkeley, Los Angeles and London.

Diaz, B. (1963) *The Conquest of New Spain*, tr. J. M. Cohen, Penguin Classics, Harmondsworth.

Dickens, A. G. (1976) *The German Nation and Martin Luther*, London.

—— Tonkin, J. M. and Powell, K. (1985) *The Reformation in Historical Thought*, Cambridge, MA.

Eighteenth-Century Short Title Catalogue.

Eisenstein, E. L. (1979) *The Printing Press as an Agent of Change. Communications and Cultural Transformations in Early Modern Europe*, 2 vols, Cambridge.

Ferguson, W. K. (1939) *American Historical Review* 45: 1–28.

Fryde, E. B. (1980) 'The beginnings of Italian humanist historiography: the "New Cicero" of Leonardo Bruni', *English Historical Review* 95: 533–52.

---

39 Giambattista Vico, *Principi di Scienza Nuova* ... was first published in 1725, with the definitive third edition in 1744; but it was written in Neapolitan Italian and seems to have had little influence for several decades. Berlin 1976 provides exciting insights; see also three further studies by Berlin 1979, Introduction by R. Hausheer. The new advances in historical scholarship and the new trends of thought are discussed in the Introduction to Part IV, this volume.

—— (1984) *Humanist and Renaissance Historiography*, London.

Fussner, F. S. (1962) *The Historical Revolution. English Historical Writing and Thought 1580–1640*, London.

Giannone, P. [1723] (1729–31) *Civil History of the Kingdom of Naples*, 2 vols, London.

Gibbon, E. [1776–88] (1896–1900) *History of the Decline and Fall of the Roman Empire*, ed. J. B. Bury, 7 vols, London.

Gilbert, F. (1965) *Machiavelli and Guicciardini: Politics and History in 16th-Century Florence*, New York.

Grafton, A. (1983) *Joseph Scaliger: A Study in the History of Classical Scholarship*, vol. 1, Oxford.

—— (1991) *Defenders of the Text: The Traditions of Scholarship in an Age of Sciencee 1450–1800*, Cambridge, MA.

Haitsma Mulier, E. O. G. (1985) 'Grotius, Hooft and the writing of history', in A. C. Duke and C. A. Tamse (eds) *Clio's Mirror. Historiography in Britain and the Netherlands*, Britain and The Netherlands 8, Zutphen.

Hay, D. (1952) *Polydore Vergil: Renaissance Historian and Man of Letters*, Oxford.

Highet, G. (1949) *The Classical Tradition: Greek and Roman Influences on Western Literature*, Oxford.

Holmes, G. (1969) *The Florentine Enlightenment 1400–50*, London.

Huppert, G. (1970) *The Idea of Perfect History: Historical Erudition and Historical Philosophy in Renaissance France*, Urbana and Chicago.

Keckermann, B. (1610) *De natura et proprietatibus historiae, comentarius*, Hanover.

Kelley, D. R. (1970) *Foundations of Modern Historical Scholarship: Language, Law and History in the French Renaissance*, New York and London.

Kenny, A. (1982) *The Computation of Style: An Introduction to Statistics for Students of Literature and Humanities*, Oxford.

Kinser, S. (1966) *The Works of Jacques Auguste de Thou*, The Hague.

Knight, W. S. M. (1925) *The Life and Works of Hugo Grotius*, The Grotius Society Publications 4, London.

Knowles, D. (1963) *Great Historical Enterprises*, London.

Lalanne, L. (1977) *Dictionnaire historique de la France*, 2nd edn, Paris.

Langlois, C. V. and Seignobos, C. (1898) *Introduction to the Study of History*, first English edn, London.

Levine, J. M. (1987) *Humanism and History: Origins of Modern English Historiography*, Ithaca, NY.

Levy, F. J. (1967) *Tudor Historical Thought*, San Marino, CA.

McCuaig, W. (1989) *Carlo Sigonio: The Changing World of the Late Renaissance*, Princeton.

McFarlane, I. D. (1981) *Buchanan*, London.

Macgillivray, R. (1974) *Restoration Historians and the English Civil War*, The Hague.

McKisack, M. (1971) *Medieval History in the Tudor Age*, Oxford.

McLuhan, M. (1962) *The Gutenberg Galaxy: The Making of Typographic Man*, London and Toronto.

Major, J. (1892) *A History of Greater Britain*, ed. A. Constable, with a Life of the Author by J. G. A. Mackay, Scottish History Society, 1st ser., vol. 10.

Marina, R. F. F. John de (1699) *The General History of Spain*, with his own Continuation and the Supplement of two other authors, tr. Captain John Stevens, folio, London.

Martines, L. (1979) *Power and Imagination: City States in Renaissance Italy*, New York; London, 1980.

Momigliano, A. D. (1966) *Studies in Historiography*, New York; repr. London, 1969.

—— (1977) *Essays in Ancient and Modern Historiography*, Oxford.

Pocock, J. G. A. (1957) *The Ancient Constitution and the Feudal Law: A Study of English Historical Thought in the 17th Century*, Cambridge.

Pocock, J. G. A. (1987) *The Ancient Constitution and the Feudal Law: A Study of English Historical Thought in the 17th Century. A Reissue, with a Retrospect*, Cambridge.

Pollard, A. W. and Redgrave, G. R. (1976–91) *A Short-Title Catalogue ... 1475–1640*, rev. by W. A. Jackson, F. S. Ferguson and K. F. Panzer, 3 vols, London.

Ranke, L. von (1891) *History of the Popes*, 3 vols, London.

Reynolds, L. D. and Wilson, N. G. (1991) *Scribes and Scholars: A Guide to the Transmission of Greek and Latin Literature*, 3rd edn, Oxford.

Robinson, F. J. G *et al.* (eds) (1981) *Eighteenth-Century British Books: An Author Union Catalogue*, 5 vols, Folkestone.

Schiffman, Z. S. (1991) *On the Threshold of Modernity: Relativism in the French Renaissance*, Baltimore and London.

Sharpe, K. M. (1979) *Sir Robert Cotton, 1586–1631: History and Politics in Early Modern England*, Oxford.

Sleidan, J. (1689) *The General History of the Reformation of the Church ... from ... 1517 to ... 1556* tr. from the Latin by Edmund Bohun, Esq., large quarto or small folio, London.

Southern, R. W. (1973) 'Aspects of the European tradition of historical writing: 4. The sense of the past', *Transactions of the Royal Historical Society*, 5th ser., 23, pp. 243–63.

Strauss, G. (1963) *Historian in an Age of Crisis: The Life and Work of Johannes Aventinus 1477–1534*, Cambridge, MA.

Subject-index Accessing Early English Books 1641–1700: Index to Units 1–32 of the Microfilm Collection (1981), vol. 3, Ann Arbor.

Trevor-Roper, H. R. (1966) 'George Buchanan and the Ancient Scottish Constitution', *English Historical Review, Supplement 3*.

—— (1967) *Religion, the Reformation and Social Change*, London.

—— (1971) *Queen Elizabeth's First Historian: William Camden*, London. (Repr. in Trevor-Roper 1985.)

—— (1985) *Renaissance Essays*, London.

—— (1987) *Catholics, Anglicans and Puritans: 17th-Century Essays*, London.

Tuck, R. (1979) *Natural Rights Theories: Their Origin and Development*, Cambridge.

—— (1993) *Philosophy and Government 1572–1651*, Cambridge.

Warwick, Sir Philip (1701) *Memoires of the Reign of King Charles I*, London.

Wing, D. (1972–88) *Short-Title Catalogue ... 1641–1700*, rev. by J. J. Morrison *et al.*, 4 vols, New York.

Woolf, D. R. (1990) *The Idea of History in Early Stuart England*, Toronto.

Wootton, D. (1983) *Paolo Sarpi: Between Renaissance and Enlightenment*, Cambridge.

Yates, F. A. (1944) 'Paolo Sarpi's "Historie of the Counsel of Trent" ', *Journal of the Warburg and Courtauld Institutes* 7: 123–44.

Zarate, A. de (1968) *The Discovery and Conquest of Peru*, tr. J. M. Cohen, Penguin Classics, Harmondsworth.

13

THE IDEA OF EARLY MODERN HISTORY

Wolfgang Reinhard

German historians have an industry they call 'Periodisierung', and they take it very seriously. It is not unknown to English scholars but they, with typical Anglo–Saxon levity, treat it with less reverence, for they look upon it as a recreation rather than as a science, and when they engage in it they do not consider they are on oath. They are right: periodisation, this splitting up of Time into neatly balanced divisions is, after all, a very arbitrary proceeding and should not be looked upon as permanent. The utility of such dividing lines comes from their experimental and tentative nature, for if they are accepted as easily removable signposts along the road of Time periodisation itself becomes an agent of criticism by forcing historians to vindicate their own selections of dates, thereby providing a powerful stimulus to new ideas. The vitality of historical writing derives strength from constant revisions caused by the discoveries of research, and very often some suggestions inspired by periodisation provide a new approach.

(Williams 1967: 1)

C. H. Williams was certainly right with this statement. However, considering the unavoidable necessity of periodization for historians, it still needs a complement. If we define scholarship in the most elementary way as the production of verifiable statements, we include the obligation to reflect upon and to verify statements about historical periods, because almost every product of historical scholarship includes a statement on periodization, at least implicitly. Even the most pragmatic and rather arbitrary selection of two years to identify a portion of history could result in the smuggling of some theoretical concept into apparently factual statements. Quite often, perhaps, historians may not even notice what they are doing. The choice of 1485 and 1603 as limits of a book on English history may be an absolutely harmless conventional decision, but it could still further the controversial conception that such things as a special 'Tudor regime' or a particular kind of 'Tudor Parliament' or a genuine 'Tudor style' in building existed. And if this were not the case, at least the assumption is conveyed that crown and dynasty are the factors which really matter in history. Thus a simple concept of a period in history is always a reduced kind of theory of history. And it is very well known now that historical research and

281

historiography by necessity always include theory. A historian who claims to work without theoretical concepts simply introduces theory subconsciously or under cover, sometimes with rather dubious results.

On the other hand, periodization in the tradition of individualizing historiography has become superfluous as a result of history's turn to structuralism. The idea of a historical epoch such as 'The Early Modern Period of European History, 1494–1789' is no longer in full vogue. We no longer believe in periods with clear-cut temporal limits as totalities or historical individual phenomena of a higher order. From that point of view, the debate on periodization appears outdated. However, communication among scholars cannot do without some reasonable subdivision of history. And in addition, the organization of the art is based on such subdivisions. Journals specialize in our period (*Archiv für Reformationsgeschichte*, *Sixteenth Century Journal*, *Zeitschrift für Historische Forschung*, Journal of Early Modern History) and academic positions are defined accordingly (cf. *Newsletter: Historians of Early Modern Europe*). What has died intellectually is very much alive socially! Like most scientific concepts, a historical period such as the early modern one also has a remarkable social dimension. After all, the idea of early modern history is based upon the expansion and growing differentiation of the historical profession. Therefore, the application of 'Parkinson's Law' to the profession provokes the question, whether chairs of early modern history are established because of the existence of early modern history, or whether early modern history has to exist for the sake of the respective academic chairs.

Historical periodization is necessary, as has been demonstrated, but nevertheless historical periods should be considered as purely artificial constructs. This is not to say that they are creations of complete arbitrariness. Proposed periodizations will only be accepted by scholars and by the general educated public under certain conditions. First, they have to correspond to the state of the academic debate concerning the respective period. The revision of an established concept of periodization is only possible when a critical mass of new knowledge has been accumulated. This was demonstrated by experience, when Heinz Schilling and the author tried to introduce the concept of 'confessionalization' to revise the periodization of early modern German and European history (Schilling 1988; Reinhard 1989). Second, besides these strictly academic preconditions, acceptance of new concepts is based upon several other preconditions, much more than just the interest of a pressure group of historians.

One essential is that the proposed periodization conforms with the predominating ideology, especially with a consistent idea of national history. European or world history is still not written by Europeans, but by Englishmen, Frenchmen, Germans, etc. from their national points of view.[1] Probably, the respective national ideas of history provide an explanation of the different weight the problem of

---

1 Perhaps inter-European collaboration on the ESF project 'The origin of the modern state, 12th–18th c.' will change this.

periodization has in different countries. Apparently, historians from nations with a broken political tradition are more inclined to reflect upon periodization than others whose national identity has never been put to the test. Therefore, the most elaborate arguments in favour of a particular 'Early Modern History' have been produced by Germans, who almost lost their historical identity after 1945. This connection becomes evident from the parallel case of the 'Early Bourgeois Revolution' ('Frühbürgerliche Revolution'), a concept created by historians of the former German Democratic Republic for the period 1476–1535 in German history. It was meant as an instrument to replace a broken national tradition by a new and better one. Consequently, it disappeared silently when the German Democratic Republic broke down (cf. Steinmetz 1985). But this case is exceptional only because of its undisguised character. It is just an open manifestation of a latent general principle which is at work everywhere.

By a kind of silent general European agreement, also accepted by many historians from outside Europe, the coincidence of certain steps towards the modern national state in England, France and Spain with the culmination of the Renaissance in many European countries, with the great discoveries and with the Protestant Reformation in Germany is considered to be the beginning of a new period of history (Hauser 1963; Skalweit 1982). Sometimes this 'early modern Europe' is to include only the sixteenth and seventeenth centuries,[2] but as a rule its end in the French Revolution is held to be even more self-evident than its beginnings. Historians from all countries use this concept without much reflection. With some remarkable exceptions (Hassinger 1959) historiography has made no active contribution to the development of the concept of 'early modern history'. Debates, if there were any, occurred on a metahistorical level. Therefore, as examples have shown, a complete review of historiography would not be worth while for our purpose.

The terms 'early modern history', 'frühe Neuzeit', 'historia moderna', 'histoire moderne', 'storia moderna' almost never appear as entries in dictionaries and encyclopaedias. I think 'Frühneuzeit' was used for the first time explicitly in German, when the philosopher Wilhelm Kamlah in 1957 tried to establish an epoch of that name (Kamlah). His starting-point is the contemporary reflection about our age, which is characterized by anxiety because of the continuous and rapid change in the world. But if our age is the object of our anxiety, its existence cannot be denied, and the question as to whether historical periods exist at all has to be answered in the affirmative, at least for the 'modern period' ('Neuzeit') we live in. The ancient Greeks and Romans did not know that they lived in 'Antiquity'; 'Antiquity' as a historical period is the product of Renaissance humanism. Modern man, however, knows that he is living in 'modern times' ('neue Zeit'). But in a sense the same is true of medieval man too, who of course did not know that he

---

2   Cf. the original limitations and the progressive extension of the 'cohort' of historians covered by the HEME Newsletter.

lived in the Middle Ages according to modern periodization, but who knew very well that he lived in the middle period of grace between the first and the second coming of Christ. This is the time which is counted by our Christian chronology BC and AD up to the present day. Therefore, in our Western world there are at least two ages, constituted as historical periods by their knowledge of themselves: the Middle Ages and the modern period ('Neuzeit'). Traditionally, they are considered historical individualities, separated from each other by the Protestant Reformation. However, according to their salvational self-definition the Middle Ages would still have continued, had not the modern period ('Neuzeit') constituted itself as new in contrast to them.

But the Protestant Reformation as a dividing line between the ages appears questionable, because it never considered itself 'new' and its view of the future was very 'medieval', consisting of the expectation of 'dear doomsday' (Martin Luther) very soon. Innovation was always non-intentional in those days and disguised as a return to good old times. Modern self-consciousness began with Descartes in 1637, increased in the 'querelle des anciens et des modernes', and succeeded finally in the Enlightenment. Descartes's intentions went far beyond those of the humanists and of Martin Luther. He no longer wanted to renew anything, but desired instead to start from zero by laying the foundations of a new methodical science, which by technological and medical application would create a new age of welfare for humanity (Kamlah 1957: 325). The pathos of modernity is also the pathos of progress. This radical innovation went far beyond a new start in philosophy because of its coincidence with the rise of empirical science. Kepler, Galileo, Huygens and other scientists are at least as important as Descartes, because it was this alliance of philosophy and science that initiated that permanent change which became our fate up to the present day (ibid. 327). And the modernity of the 'modern period' consists in nothing else but the consistent acceptance of this change.[3]

In the beginning, however, acceptance was far from general, but rather exceptional. Galileo was condemned, and Descartes and Grotius were afraid of a similar fate. The new age became hidden behind the conservatism of that period, until the great breakthrough of the eighteenth century. But it was prepared and to a certain extent anticipated by humanism and the Renaissance, a fact which suggests the use of the term 'early modern period' ('Frühneuzeit') (Kamlah 1957: 327) In contrast to the Enlightenment the Renaissance founded its remarkable enthusiasm for innovation upon the idea of a return to antiquity, an antiquity which had been identified as such for the first time. With Descartes, however, innovation became autonomous and self-sufficient. But already in the Renaissance Leonardo da Vinci and Nicolò Machiavelli represented that will to power which became essential for modern self-consciousness, as modernity consists in the progressive overpowering of the world by science and technology (ibid. 330). Therefore, the 'early modern

---

3 Probably about the same time, during the English Revolution, political discourse dropped legitimation by precedent for the first time and referred to innovation according to reason instead, cf. Hill 1967: 178.

period' ('Frühneuzeit') is not an age in the same sense as the Middle Ages and the 'modern period' ('Neuzeit') itself, but rather a transitory phase, and a historical period of its own only as far as its own acceptance of innovation goes. Obviously, Kamlah thinks that Descartes marks the transition from the early modern to the modern period, but his own argument leads to the conclusion that an extension of the early modern period until the breakthrough of modern self-consciousness in the Enlightenment is more reasonable. A comparative analysis of periodizations has demonstrated that it is more useful to begin a new historical period when some characteristic innovation has become predominant, and not at the time of its first appearance (van der Pot 1951: 19–34) In 1969 Kamlah published a revised version of his essay, in which he dropped the term 'early modern period' ('Frühneuzeit') tacitly (Kamlah 1969). By this time, however, it had already become popular with German historians.

Some years later, Reinhart Koselleck produced similar results from a different point of view. His main interest was the change of German social and political consciousness in the late eighteenth century. For this purpose he developed the instrument of 'Begriffsgeschichte', whereby the use of important historical notions is analysed carefully from the synchronic and the diachronic perspective, e.g. the change in meaning of the German term 'Bürger' from the member of an urban corporation in about 1700 to the citizen of a state in about 1800 to the bourgeois non-proletarian in about 1900 (Koselleck 1979: 116) The notions of a new time ('neue Zeit') and modern history ('neuere Geschichte') made their way slowly but successfully from about 1500 to the eighteenth century. The abbreviation 'Neuzeit', however, did not appear before the nineteenth century. And, we should add, the term 'Frühneuzeit' not before the twentieth. But the eighteenth century knew that mankind had lived in a new time for three centuries (Koselleck 1977: 277), centuries which had been different from the Middle Ages and antiquity, which both had become the objects of a detached and critical historical approach (Koselleck 1979: 540). Nevertheless, the notion of 'new time' ('neue Zeit') as a rule still did not include the historical experience of continuous innovation and the expectation of permanent progress in the future (Koselleck 1977: 276).

Therefore, the new term 'contemporary period' ('neueste Zeit'), which appeared in the late Enlightenment and became popular during the French Revolution, was quickly accepted to express the experience of rapid historical change. In spite of his theoretical reserve against periodization Leopold von Ranke used to lecture, on 'contemporary history' ('Geschichte der neuesten Zeit' or 'neueste Geschichte'), beginning either with Frederick II of Prussia or with the American or French Revolution (ibid. 269, 278). Only then did the specific consciousness of modernity of the period ('Neuzeit') reach its culmination.[4] The creation of 'contemporary history' ('neueste Geschichte') should be considered the most mature stage of

---

4 The creation of a revolutionary calendar starting with a new era was certainly the most radical expression of this new consciousness of modernity.

'modern history' ('Neuzeit'), a maturity expressed in Koselleck's very German formula of 'temporalization of history' ('Verzeitlichung der Geschichte'). From now on, time is considered not only the pattern of history, but a driving force in it. Consequently, after 1780 it became possible to use the noun 'history' ('Geschichte') as a collective singular designating history in the abstract, whereas before that time 'history' had always been in need of an object or a subject. In detail, 'temporalization' means first of all 'acceleration' ('Beschleunigung') of history. From now on, new experiences follow each other in shorter and shorter intervals. Instead of producing a series of events of the same quality the future is no longer predictable. As a consequence, the present tends to become a time of permanent transition. The basic uniqueness of unpredictable events promotes sensitivity to the uncontemporaneity of the contemporaneous – the perspectivism of historicism is not far away (ibid., *passim*). All this becomes evident towards the end of the eighteenth century, but 'temporalization of history' developed during the three centuries of the 'so-called early modern period', leading to 'that particular kind of acceleration which is typical of our age' (Koselleck 1979: 19).

In 1990 Johannes Burkhardt used these suggestions to define the 'early modern period' and at the same time tried to fill this theoretical framework with real historical content (Burkhardt 1990). He is well aware of concepts which consider the period between 1500 and 1800 as a mere secondary subdivision of a much longer era. Nevertheless, he accepts the 'decisive turn to modernity' about 1800 as self-evident and believes that about 1500 another important step in the same direction occurred. But he introduces Elizabeth Eisenstein's argument in favour of the years around 1500. According to her, the well-known sudden success of printing all over Europe was of central importance for the further course of history, comparable only to the first invention of writing and the alphabet in its consequences for communication and the accumulation of knowledge. Martin Luther knew very well that the printing revolution was a necessary condition for the success of his Reformation. The spread of literacy for religious reasons meant better education of the people, but also facilitated the establishment and rule of bureaucratic government, with the creation of new kinds of sources for historians as a consequence.

The 'early modern period' is defined as a transitional age when the structures of the medieval way of life were still alive, whereas at the same time developments were on their way which would lead to the present state of things. However, old and new cannot be separated neatly. On the contrary, it is exactly their mutual interpenetration which characterizes the 'early modern period' ('Frühe Neuzeit') as that part of our modern age ('Neuzeit') which still disavowed its modernity (ibid. 365). Norms and legitimation were grounded on the idea of a stable world and therefore claimed permanent validity. Innovations were rarely accepted; to prove innovation meant to discredit a case. Special strategies had to be developed to master that change which had become unavoidable. They all resemble each other, because they always try to fit things into an immutable order.

In this sense humanism and Renaissance, in spite of their innovatory elements, were possible only as an imagined return to a classic age after a period of decadence.

Revolutionary movements always claimed to return to some old order which had become perverted by innovation. Certainly, the German peasants' war went beyond that point with its programme of 'divine law' ('göttliches Recht'), but this divine law was based on an evangelical movement which intended a return to the pure doctrine of original Christianity. The religious impulses of the sixteenth century had confessionalization as their consequence, activities with conservative intentions but far-reaching unintended consequences. With very similar instruments Lutherans, Calvinists and Catholics tried to 'Christianize' Europe, but from the viewpoint of their respective confessions. The great European witch craze of the sixteenth and seventeenth centuries fits well into this context as another transitory phenomenon. Once, one used to live with magic; later, after the Enlightenment, one did not take it seriously any longer. But now, under the pressure of thorough Christianization, one should get rid of it, but is still under its sway emotionally and therefore tends to panic. But the attractive plurality of Europe's cultural landscape is also a product of the plurality of 'confessionalizers'.

But the largest gains from confessionalization went to the modern state. As a rule, churches needed state help with their programme of Christianization. In return, states gained new powers, additional resources and ideological legitimation, all of which gave them a push towards their own institutionalization. A particularly important case is the institutionalization of war, when several forms of more or less legitimate use of violence were reduced to the state monopoly in that field, culminating in the creation of the 'miles perpetuus', the standing army, during the seventeenth century. In domestic politics the new tendency towards a general levelling down of the subjects, creating an equality not so much of rights as of their loss, was in conflict with the traditional hierarchical order of the society of estates. In England, Poland and other countries the outcome was an institutionalized participation of the higher estates in state power. Elsewhere, the minimum solution was a legal fixation of social hierarchies and a reinforcement of the predominant position of the nobility via their new cultural role in court society. Thus discipline imposed from above by church and state corresponded to self-imposed discipline from below when European elites were civilizing themselves (cf. Elias 1976), with the result that the gap between elite culture and popular culture widened.

The greater part of the European economy retained its feudal and agrarian character. Within this traditional framework, however, the new forces of a market economy were at work. Agrarian surplus production for the market initiated social change, with the dissolution of feudalism in England and the creation of a new serfdom east of the Elbe as the extreme cases. The growing rural population was employed in out-work, especially textiles, to such an extent that sometimes the countryside was changed by this trade in the sense of a 'proto-industrialization' (cf. Mendels 1972; Kriedte 1980: 96). Greater demand, last but not least from princes waging war, led to the growth of the mining and arms industries. An expansion of commerce was the consequence of this development and of the great discoveries. New forms of monetary transaction became necessary, once again with the states' demand for credit in the lead. In addition, states started a kind of economic policy to increase their revenue. But all these innovations remained under the sway of a static conception of the economy. The amount of resources available was considered a constant figure; the idea of economic growth did not yet exist.

Fundamental change only occurred in the eighteenth century, when according to Koselleck the 'temporalization of history' took place. Now the otherness of the past and the openness of the future were discovered. The present became a mere instant of a process of development, which was cheerfully accepted and used to legitimate further innovations.

Certainly this latest description of early modern Europe is largely correct. But does it really constitute a historical period of its own with exact temporal limitations? Apparently Burkhardt had to work under such an assumption, given by his editor. This special need to establish an independent early modern history, however, is not only the consequence of institutional development where early modern history has become an academic subject of equal rank with others. It may also have to do with the state of mind of leading German historians after the Second World War. The catastrophic end of the national power-state in Germany in 1945 produced a shift of attention to the historic world of the Old Empire, which despite or perhaps because of its political weakness allegedly had preserved peace and order for several centuries (e.g. Angermeier 1984; Dickmann 1959; 1971).

In other European countries the historiographical situation was completely different. 'Storia moderna' in Italy and 'Histoire moderne' in France by origin were defined as what was left over when medieval history had become a profession of its own and when in the late nineteenth century 'Storia contemporanea' and 'Histoire contemporaine' had originated, both as a result of political change, when national unity had been achieved in Italy,[5] and when the 'party' of the French Revolution had finally come to power in the French Third Republic.[6] The periodization of this almost residual (early) modern history was until recently characterized by a similar lack of imagination. In France and Britain, in Spain and Portugal it was subdivided mainly according to dynasties or even rulers, if they lived long enough.[7] Even if intended as an instrument of mechanical chronology this procedure showed a tendency to create periodological concepts. Perhaps the 'century of Louis XIV' introduced by Voltaire into historiography did really exist, perhaps it is reasonable to speak of the 'Spain of the Catholic kings'. But doubts are permitted concerning the France of Louis XV or the Spain of Philip IV.

---

5   Cf. Barbagallo 1988; Soldani 1978. I am obliged to Ilaria Porciani (Florence) and Pierangelo Schiera (Trento) for these references.

6   Furet 1988; Keylor 1975: 171–4, 219. Voss 1972: 88–100, 374. I am much obliged for excellent information on the French case to Robert Descimon (Paris).

7   e.g. Lavisse 1901–11; Clark 1934–81; Pidal 1976– . I received additional information from Gerald Aylmer (Oxford), and several students of my seminar on 'Die Frühneuzeit als Epoche' at Freiburg University in winter 1990/1.

The conventional subdivision of Portuguese history by the years of dynastic change (1385, 1580, 1640, 1816/20) was challenged as early as 1842. The state of society and the development of institutions was proposed as a criterion instead of dynastic events. In our day Vitorino Magalhaes Godinho drew upon Portugal's position in the world economy and accordingly established subdivisions in the middle of the fifteenth century, when the country reacted to overseas expansion, at the crisis of 1545–50, and at the recovery around 1670–80. The most recent general history of Portugal attempts a compromise using as key dates 1415, 1495, 1580, 1640, 1750 (Godinho 1968; Valerio 1988; Serrao 1977–).

To periodize Italian history before 1870 by rulers was simply not possible. In addition, humanism and the Renaissance allowed no break about 1500. They started to grow in the fourteenth century, flourished in the fifteenth and still included the sixteenth (Ferguson 1948; Hall et al. 1979). Nobody has ever tried to establish the beginning of the Italian wars in 1494 as an essential watershed in Italian history.

Obviously, different countries for very good reasons use different criteria of periodization. It was the mere coincidence of political progress in western Europe and the German Reformation which created the idea of a general threshold about 1500. But it is difficult to make Portugal fit into this framework, and in the case of Italy it is impossible. In addition, different areas of history, such as politics, religion, culture and the economy, have their own rhythm of development and therefore, as a rule, their own adequate temporal subdivisions. Consequently, historiography has not been able to prove that a consistent early modern period was beginning about 1500 everywhere in Europe.

On the contrary, structuralist historians have for long claimed that certain significant patterns of the so-called early modern period, such as an agrarian economy with static mentality, a hierarchy of estates, a political order based on personal relations, a predominance of Christianity, had been present long before 1500. Not only historians with a certain affinity to the Nazi view of history such as Otto Laufer (1936) or Otto Brunner (1958), but also the German émigré Dietrich Gerhard (1955–6; 1962) and a prominent member of the *Annales* group such as Jacques Le Goff (1983) spoke of 'Old Europe' or the 'Long Middle Ages'. Finally in 1974 the *Zeitschrift für Historische Forschung* was founded, designated to combine late medieval and early modern studies. Its editors distinguished three periods of post-ancient history, an 'Archaic Age' up to the eleventh or twelfth century, an 'Old European Age' from the twelfth to the early nineteenth century, an 'Industrial Age' from then to the present time (Kunisch et al. 1974). Others make different proposals, e.g. Dietrich Gerhard goes back to the eighth century (Gerhard 1981). Sometimes the debate seems to return to that Italian tradition where 'Storia moderna' included everything after the end of the Roman Empire.[8] In short, the replacement of 'early modern' by 'Old European' failed to produce a more distinguishable temporal borderline between historical periods!

---

8 Barbagallo 1988: 567. Somehow this tradition has been revived by the *Storia d'Italia* published by Einaudi (Turin), where vol. II (1974) is called *Dalla caduta dell'impero romano al secolo XVIII*.

But from the point of view of structural history this is unavoidable, because the beginning and the end of different structures almost never coincide in time. A historical period in the sense of structuralist history could be defined by the simultaneous presence of certain fundamental patterns, which begin and end at different times. Nevertheless, we do not know if an interconnection between parallel structures exists and how it works. Therefore, for a structuralist historian, the problem of the totality of a historical period, of an epoch being a historical individuality of a higher order, is either a premature, or perhaps even the wrong question. It corresponds too much to the ideology of historicism, but not at all to that of structuralism. (cf. Pomian 1978).

The irreversible change of structures should be called 'revolution', in contrast to structurally determined historical events or reversible cycles, such as demographic crises or trade cycles. An application of this strict definition of 'revolution' to the French Revolution, this allegedly self-evident end of everything which character-izes early modern history, leads to the dissolution of this borderline, too. A structural change occurred only in the fields of political, legal and perhaps intellectual history, whereas the economy and society remained very much the same. And even in culture and politics much continuity down to the nineteenth or even twentieth centuries has been identified by historical research inside and outside France.[9] Today, a strong minority of French historians is quite willing to extend their 'Histoire moderne' to 1830 or even later.[10] The change of consciousness identified by Koselleck is but a part of the picture. And it is closely connected with the self-interpretation of the French Revolution as a radical new start in history. Therefore, in accepting the French Revolution as a clear division of historical periods, historians follow the sources as they ought to, but in doing so they accept the propagandistic self-image of the revolutionaries.

This leads us back to Kamlah's argument. Innovative self-definition has been identified as the essential characteristic of modernity. Therefore, modernity culminates in the French Revolution, although this claim to modernity does not so much describe real historical change, but rather the mental process of creating a self-image based on the 'temporalization of history' and the consequent expectation of continuous progress in the future. Such self-definition of an age, and thinking of ages in general, however, are based on a monist concept of the totality of a historical period. In this sense, the 'temporalization of history' has been the necessary precondition of the creation of historical individualities of a higher order. But recent postmodern philosophy has demonstrated how obsolete modern unitary thinking has become in the meantime. From this point of view, the will to unitary solutions and notions appears as the characteristic intellectual habit of the 'modern period' ('Neuzeit'), but at the same time also as the typical illusion of this 'modern period'. Today this unitary approach is no longer possible and not even desirable (Welsch

---

9   Against 'la fausse clarté émise par la Révolution' (Hartog 1988: 82) cf. Reichardt and Schmitt.
10   I am obliged to Robert Descimon, Paris, for information on the relevant opinion poll among French historians.

1987; cf. also Blumenberg 1988). Therefore, the 'modern period' was the only age that ever existed, because it thought of itself and created itself as a historical period. And there will never be another age again, because thinking of ages has come to an end together with the modernity of the 'modern period'.

Under such circumstances our 'Idea of an early modern history' becomes a paradox, because it has been exposed as part of a disintegrating illusion at a time when 'early modern history' as a profession has reached the culmination of its expansion. Perhaps our argument is wrong, because what is so powerful simply cannot be illusory. But I should rather prefer a different solution. I should like to consider 'early modern history' ('Geschichte der frühen Neuzeit') merely as a pragmatic specialization of scholars inside the historical profession, based on certain traditions of the art on the one hand, and on the necessity to deal with specific sources, communication processes and institutions of that time on the other.

REFERENCES

Angermeier, H. (1984) *Die Reichsreform 1410–1555*, Munich.
Barbagallo, F. (1988) 'Le origini della storia contemporanea italiana tra metodo e politica', *Studi Storici* 29(4): 567–85.
Blumenberg, H. (1988) *Die Legitimität der Neuzeit*, 2nd edn, Frankfurt.
Brunner, O. (1958) 'Inneres Gefüge des Abendlandes', in *Historia Mundi*, vol. 6, Berne.
Burckhardt, J. (1990) 'Frühe Neuzeit', in R. van Dülmen (ed.) *Das Fischer Lexikon Geschichte*, Frankfurt.
Clark, G. (ed.) (1934–81) *The Oxford History of England*, 16 vols, Oxford.
Dickmann, F. (1959) *Der Westfälische Frieden*, Münster.
—— (1971) *Friedensrecht und Friedenssicherung*, Göttingen.
Elias, N. (1976) *Über den Prozeß der Zivilisation*, 2 vols, Frankfurt. (English translation, *The Civilizing Process*, 2 vols, Oxford, 1994.)
Ferguson, W. K. (1948) *The Renaissance in Historical Thought*, Cambridge, MA.
Furet, F. (1988) 'Histoire universitaire de la Révolution', in F. Furet and M. Ozouf (eds) *Dictionnaire critique de la Révolution française*, Paris.
Gerhard, D. (1955–6) 'Periodization in European history', *American Historical Review* 61(4): 900–13.
—— (1962) 'Zum Problem der Periodisierung der europäischen Geschichte', in *Alte und neue Welt in vergleichender Geschichtsbetrachtung*, Göttingen.
—— (1981) *Old Europe, A Study in Continuity. 1000–1800*, London.
Gondinho, V. Magalhaes (1968) 'Periodizaçãoa, in *Dicionario de Historia de Portugal*, vol. 3, Lisbon.
Hall, M. Boas *et al.* (1979) *Il rinascimento. Interpretazioni e problemi*, Bari.
Hartog, F. (1988) *Le XIXe siècle et l'histoire. Le cas de Fustel de Coulanges*, Paris.
Hassinger, E. (1959) *Das Werden des neuzeitlichen Europa 1300–1600*, Brunswick.
Hauser, H. (1963) *La Modernité du XVIe siècle*, 2nd edn, Paris.
Hill, C. (1967) *The Century of Revolution, 1603–1715*, London.
Kamlah, W. (1957) '"Zeitalter" überhaupt, "Neuzeit" und "Frühneuzeit"', *Saeculum* 8(4): 313–32.
—— (1969) 'Vom theologischen Selbstverständnis zum historischen Verständnis der Neuzeit als Zeitalter', in id., *Utopie, Eschatologie, Geschichtstheologie*, Mannheim, Vienna and Zurich.
Keylor, W. R. (1975) *Academy and Community. The Foundation of the French Historical Profession*, Cambridge, MA.

Koselleck, R. (1977) '"Neuzeit". Zur Semantik moderner Bewegungsbegriffe', in id., *Studien zum Beginn der modernen Welt*, Stuttgart.
—— (1979a) 'Begriffsgeschichte und Sozialgeschichte', in id., *Vergangene Zukunft. Zur Semantik geschichtlicher Zeiten*, Frankfurt.
—— (1979b) 'Vergangene Zukunft der frühen Neuzeit', in id., *Vergangene Zukunft. Zur Semantik geschichtlicher Zeiten*, Frankfurt.
—— (1990) 'Wie neu ist die Neuzeit?', *Historische Zeitschrift* 251(3): 539–52.
Kriedte, P. (1980) *Spätfeudalismus und Handelskapital*, Göttingen.
Kunisch, J. *et al.* (1974) 'Vorwort', *Zeitschrift für historische Forschung* 1(1): 1.
Lauffer, O. (1936) *Die Begriffe 'Mittelalter' und 'Neuzeit' im Verhältnis zur deutschen Altertumskunde*, Berlin.
Lavisse, E. (1901–11) *Histoire de la France*, 18 vols, Paris.
Le Goff, J. (1983) 'Pour un longue moyen âge', *Europe* 61(654): 19–24.
Mendels, F. F. (1972) 'Proto-Industrialization', *Journal of Economic History* 32(2): 241–62.
Pidal, R. Menendez (ed.) (1976–) *Historia de España*, 2nd edn, Madrid.
Pomian, K. (1978) 'Periodisation', in J. Le Goff (ed.) *La Nouvelle Histoire*, Paris.
Pot, H. J. H. van der (1951) *De periodisering der geschiedenis, Een overzicht der theorieen*, The Hague.
Reichardt, R. and Schmitt, E. (1980) 'Die französische Revolution – Umbruch oder Kontinuität?', *Zeitschrift für historische Forschung* 7(3): 257–320.
Reinhard, W. (1989) 'Reformation, Counter-Reformation, and the early modern state. A reassessment', *Catholic Historical Review* 75(3): 383–404.
Schilling, H. (1988) 'Die Konfessionalisierung im Reich. Religiöser und gesellschaftlicher Wandel in Deutschland zwischen 1555 und 1620', *Historische Zeitschrift* 246(1): 1–45.
Serrao, J. V. (ed.) (1977–) *História de Portugal*, Lisbon.
Skalweit, S. (1982) *Der Beginn der Neuzeit*, Darmstadt.
Soldani, S. (1978) 'Risorgimento', in *Il mondo contemporaneo*, vol. 1.3, Florence.
Steinmetz, M. (ed.) (1985) *Die frühbürgerliche Revolution in Deutschland*, Berlin.
Valerio, N. (1988) 'Sobre a divsão da historia de Portugal em periodos', in *Estudios e ensaios em homagem a Vitorino Magalhaes Godinho*, Lisbon.
Voss, J. (1972) *Das Mittelalter im historischen Denken Frankreichs*, Munich.
Welsch, W. (1987) *Unsere postmoderne Moderne*, Weinheim.
Williams, C. H. (ed.) (1967) *English Historical Documents 1485–1558*, London.

14

THE SCIENTIFIC REVOLUTION

Stephen Pumfrey

The Scientific Revolution is a periodization which has structured research in the subdiscipline of the history of science since A. R. Hall published a textbook with that title in 1954. It still holds a place on reading lists, alongside very recent *Reappraisals of the Scientific Revolution* or assessments of *The Scientific Revolution in National Context*, collections which question and modify but which none-the-less are structured around the concept (Lindberg and Westman 1990; Porter and Teich 1992; Cohen 1994). Other early modern historians routinely deploy it when they trespass warily into the field. It is such a commonplace that it can be mistaken for a merely descriptive term of the undoubtedly great changes in world-view commencing in the time of Nicholas Copernicus (d. 1543) and ending with Isaac Newton (d. 1727). In fact, it is a very interpretative category. It owes its coherence to historical and philosophical assumptions which the research it has encouraged has left in deep, even terminal crisis.

Every useful periodization depends upon historians' assumptions about why it makes sense. Unlike the contemporaneous movements of the Reformation, or even the Renaissance, the Scientific Revolution was proposed by twentieth-century historians using criteria to which the historical agents could not have assented. It structured the new approaches to the natural world manifested by such independent and different contemporaries as Francis Bacon and Johann Kepler into a coherent narrative of progress, from the first revolts against to the final overthrow of the medieval world picture, the limitations of which must be remembered.[1]

The idea of 'the Scientific Revolution' implies three claims of hindsight. First, there was revolutionary discontinuity. Second, the new order that emerged was (our modern) science. Third, the process was *the* once-and-for-all intellectual

---

[1] See the recent analysis by Feldhay 1994.

transformation. That even Isaac Newton effectively rebutted all three does not mean the historian is not the better judge, but that they must be foregrounded and tested. If there was a Scientific Revolution, then we have found something momentous in the history of human thought. As its early advocate Herbert Butterfield famously put it in his influential text:

> Since the Scientific Revolution overturned the authority in science not only of the middle ages but of the ancient world – since it ended not only in the eclipse of scholastic philosophy but in the destruction of Aristotelian physics – it outshines everything since the rise of Christianity and reduces the Renaissance and the Reformation to the rank of mere episodes . . . [I]t looms so large as the real origin of the modern world and of the modern mentality that our customary periodization of European history has become an anachronism and an encumbrance.
>
> (Butterfield 1949: viii)

Butterfield was, like Hall, a historian by training (the scourge, indeed, of Whig political history), and was not critical enough of science's claims to progress and objectivity. Most subsequent historians of the Scientific Revolution have received their primary training in science or science studies (notably its philosophy and sociology). Given the importance of science in late twentieth-century culture, they were initially more concerned with ahistorical understandings about the nature of science, and with debates about the putative moment of its birth, than with understanding the sixteenth and seventeenth centuries *per se*. This explains in part why other historians have often found the history of science to be peculiarly different.

Current belief in science has been well served by writing that chronicles and celebrates the establishment of modernity, and thoroughgoing histories have sometimes been as welcome as were the secular church histories of the Enlightenment to conservative divines. The symbiosis of science with its history accounts for several features of the historiography.

First, until the 1960s much professional history of science, and still many non-specialized and science-textbook accounts, were 'Whig histories of science' that used present beliefs about good science as a teleological filter in a search for historical origins. It assembled a cast of heroic anticipators (such as Vesalius for anatomy or Giordano Bruno for beliefs in an infinite universe), and looked for factors inhibiting the progress of reason, often identified as the lingering influence of university scholastics and dogmatic theologians). Roy Porter suggests that postwar concerns about totalitarian repression of free enquiry encouraged historians to romanticize early scientists into bold adventurers of the intellect. Popular, yet historiographically informed texts like Arthur Koestler's *The Sleepwalkers*, or even Bertolt Brecht's *The Life of Galileo*, were more literary expressions of the trend (Porter 1986: 295; Koestler 1964; Brecht 1975).

Second, the historiography has most clearly reflected trends, not in history, but in contemporary philosophical and sociological models of what it is to do science, for which the Scientific Revolution has been a testbed. Arguments, now regarded as misdirected, raged about whether Copernican astronomy was accepted because it was more rational or elegant, and whether or not Galileo *needed* to perform experiments with falling bodies in order to elaborate his new science of motion.[2]

Third, it is only in the last thirty years that academic specialization has produced an independent subdiscipline of the history of science (even of the Scientific Revolution itself) that looks more towards history and less over its shoulder at the philosophy of science. A major reason for independence is that recent research in the Scientific Revolution has actually undermined the periodization's *raison d'être* as the birth of modernity. Writers like Theodore Rabb and Robert Mandrou were the vanguard of a new generation of writers who comfortably integrated changes in science with social, political and religious developments (Rabb 1975; Mandrou 1973). All the same, much historiography of the Scientific Revolution betrays the reflexive nature of the genre: it seeks to produce reliable explanations about what, historically, have counted as reliable explanations. Its writing can, proudly, claim to be more critical than established fields of history about how it explains, and to be more explicit about methodology.

One of the most influential of recent works, Shapin and Schaffer's *Leviathan and the Air Pump*, examines how the very idea of a 'matter of fact' was *constructed* in Restoration England (Shapin and Schaffer 1985). The authors explain their use of concepts from anthropology, ethnomethodology, the sociology of knowledge and discourse theory as they argue that facts and authority depended upon ideological relations of power. The interdependence of science, religion, politics and social codes of behaviour controversially assumed by the authors (as it was in Hobbes's *Leviathan*) is diametrically opposed to the original conception of the Scientific Revolution, and will mark the terminus of our exploration here.

What has changed most noticeably in thirty years is not the *explanandum*, but the *explanans*. Iconoclasts have destroyed some of the myths, and provoked a more critical usage of the term 'revolution', which had come to include imperceptible evolutions from 1500 to 1750. Yet many historians will agree with Porter that, in the seventeenth century at least, there was conscious challenge, resistance, struggle and conquest (Porter 1992: 299). Aristotelian natural philosophy, entrenched in Europe's universities, churches and in the 'common-sense' world-view of most educated people, was replaced by concepts and practices more like those of modern science, established in new institutional locations such as learned societies. There is still considerable agreement about the more specific elements of the transition. The fundamental metaphor for 'nature' changed from a developing organism to an interlocking machine – Dijksterhuis's *Mechanization of the World Picture* (Dijksterhuis 1961). The metaphysical language for describing processes and analysing causes shifted from a scholastic elaboration of the 'qualities' of everyday experience to quantitative mathematics (Burtt 1932). In cosmology the shift was, to use the title of Alexandre Koyré's classic, *From the Closed World to the Infinite*

2 See Westman 1975, especially Imre Lakatos and Elie Zahar, 'Why did Copernicus' research program supersede Ptolemy's?' The Galileo arguments are assessed in Drake 1978.

Universe. Newton successfully synthesized Galileo's terrestrial mechanics with Kepler's of the solar system into universal physical laws that annihilated the Aristotelian distinction between a perfect heavens and a corrupt Earth. Newtonian matter theory, of atoms attracting and repelling each other across void spaces, despite its objections to Descartes's alleged materialism, effectively ended serious belief in the subtle spirit matter of Renaissance magicians, and consolidated a divorce of soul from 'mere' matter which Carolyn Merchant has called *The Death of Nature* (Merchant 1982). Changes in the 'natural history' of plants and animals were less spectacular, clustering around new, rational systems of classification. Underlying them was the rejection of the occultist doctrine of microcosm and macrocosm, with its implication that all objects (stars, stones, human organs and even words) bore magical resemblances to each other.[3]

To these intellectual transformations can be added a smaller number of agreed social transformations. Institutions like the Royal Society, founded in 1660, and an associated increase in publications, created a new, more public and less state-controlled community of investigators (McLellan 1985). Where Aristotelianism had sought to understand nature as a form of *vita contemplativa*, the new science embodied a rhetoric of progress over the ancients, especially regarding its utility and capacity to control natural processes for human benefit. Men from lower social groups with technical and practical skills were more easily able to contribute, especially as experimental methods of investigation replaced the philosophical analysis of classical texts. *Francis Bacon: Philosopher of Industrial Science*, as Benjamin Farrington's work described him, was the most influential propagandist of these new activities (Farrington 1951).

The interpretation of these changes as a revolutionary break has always been contested. Evidence that the agents themselves cited precursors is added historians' detection of continuities and influences. In his *Système du Monde*, Pierre Duhem set out to show the enduring legacy of Thomas Aquinas's and other scholastics' Christianized Aristotelianism, and in 1952 Alistair Crombie saw no rupture from *Augustine to Galileo* (Duhem 1913–59; Crombie 1952) Recently, William Wallace has painstakingly demonstrated Galileo's debt to Jesuit sources and teachers (Wallace 1984). Today many take the view of John Schuster who, in his useful survey, argues that continuist/discontinuist debates about the topic are sterile artefacts of historians' selective stresses (Schuster 1990). The division nevertheless encodes real disagreements about what happened.

The notion that science was the decisive break with ancient and medieval thought has always been an ideological one. It was first elaborated by secularizing Enlightenment historians like Condorcet (see Lindberg 1990). Such accounts encouraged a positivist view of science, building fact upon fact faster and faster upon Newton's firm foundations. Positivism was extended to the social sciences by Auguste Comte, and is evident in Leopold von Ranke's idea of history. Unlike 'break', however,

---

3　For an influential analysis of this shift in 'episteme' see Foucault 1970: chs 1, 5.

'revolution' implies that the process was effectively complete by 1700.[4] This conception emerged from twentieth-century critics of positivism. In 1924 Edwin Burtt applied to the history of science the neo–Kantian position that all knowledge is framed within prior mental categories. In the provocatively entitled *Metaphysical Foundations of Modern Science* (Burtt 1932) he argued that medieval categories (of form and substance for example) were overturned by a mathematical metaphysics of space, time and motion. After Galileo and Newton, we were just mopping up. Alexandre Koyré was further influenced by Lévy-Bruhl's anthropology, and enlarged the metaphysical framework to include '*idées transcientifiques*' of philosophy and religion. Descartes and Galileo, through the adoption of Platonism, were his key 'founders of modern science' who 'had to destroy one world and replace it by another'. These notions, of a completed epochal transformation of consciousness, acted as complex influences in Butterfield and Hall's idea of revolution, and have been resurrected by Hans Blumenberg (Blumenberg 1983 and 1987). But as historians put flesh on the metaphysical bones, they rediscovered that the science had been practised by real people in a past which was indeed another country.

Nevertheless, the conclusion that science was a world-view going beyond fact and reason to questions of religion, philosophy and aesthetics has endured and evolved. Harvard historians first used early modern case studies to counter a Cold War suspicion of technoscience, and to bridge C. P. Snow's *Two Cultures* of arts and science. In the 1970s such studies offered a way out of philosophers' failure to agree about an essence of science. A pivotal work was T. S. Kuhn's *The Copernican Revolution* where he influentially argued that the move to a heliocentre model of the cosmos was a transition between two world-views of different, rather than inferior and superior sets of values. He generalized his concept of scientific change as a paradigm shift in *The Structure of Scientific Revolutions*, surely the most influential history-of-science text. But this work inaugurated critiques of the Scientific Revolution which are still being worked through. Not only did it deny that there had been one basic shift, but it suggested that all paradigms were equally 'scientific' relative to their local or historical contexts (Kuhn 1957 and 1962).

This placed a bomb of a question under the resolutely idealist previous history of the Scientific Revolution. What had, in fact, persuaded seventeenth-century philosophers to adhere to new paradigms of knowledge, practice and communication? Kuhn suggested that the answers lay less in the philosophy than in the sociology of past scientific communities. That Kuhn's then radical suggestions now seem insufficiently socio-historical indicates the depth of the crisis in Scientific Revolution historiography.

Shapin and Schaffer are typical of a current generation that opposes idealist or 'internalist' history of systems of scientific ideas. It was previously opposed by 'externalism', mainly that of Marxist histories. These remain a useful corrective but

---

4   A survey of applications of the term in the history of science is Cohen 1985.

are now viewed (by neo-Marxians as well) as maintaining another sterile opposition – between the ineffective superstructures of early modern philosophies of nature and their base of rising capitalism. Following Boris Hessen's seminal reading of Newton's *Principia* as (in its productive parts) a response to new technical problems in mining, gunnery, etc., Edgar Zilsel articulated the still-fruitful hypothesis that a new scientific method emerged from the co-operation of systematic 'head knowledge' with practical 'hand knowledge' embodied in a growing entrepreneurial class.[5] This materialist and determinist history was equally 'Whiggish' in that it used its own criteria of good science to divide the past into progressive and merely speculative elements. Brian Easlea's recent, provocative and readable Marxist interpretation avoids these errors (Easlea 1980).

A number of related 'methodological turns' are now leading writers on the Scientific Revolution out of these various impasses, some of which are imports familiar to other historians. Most now insist on a thoroughgoing contextualism. Some, using a stronger historicism, maintain that early modern science must be explained in terms not of our but of the actors' own categories and boundaries of natural knowledge. This can in turn lead to a close linguistic attention to the discourses and rhetorics in which new approaches were couched and then interpreted by the audiences. These methods tend to prevent explanatory recourse to modern intellectual structures that allegedly lay behind (or above) revolutionary science. In short, they treat early modern science as part of historically evolving cultural contexts, amenable to the same kind of analysis as religious or political systems. In doing so, they clearly put into question the idea of a unique and uniquely Scientific Revolution. The most systematic justification for doing so comes from the new, post-Kuhnian sociologies of scientific knowledge.[6] But early, influential, and here more relevant, justification has come from Scientific Revolution historiography itself. Since, a priori, sixteenth- and seventeenth-century scientists had no access to our reasons for approving their work, many a posteriori case studies have accumulated which show that their reasons were indeed not our reasons. Nor were they those proposed by theorists of a Scientific Revolution.

This has left a paradox The dominant areas of research still cluster around the individuals, texts and practices made canonical by the old conception of the Scientific Revolution. There is more work on Newton than on his contemporary and rival Leibniz, on Kepler's *New Astronomy* than on the Jesuit Riccioli's *New Almagest*, on the trial of Galileo than on the incarceration of the magician Campanella, even though today's writers often deny that the former were more scientific than the latter. Despite these traces of Whiggism, much recent work has unravelled the threads of the old narrative.

For one thing, we now have images of 'revolutionary' natural philosophers considerably at odds with their expected character. In astronomy, Kuhn's depiction

---

5   Hessen 1971; Zilsel 1941. His more general thesis is reprinted in Kearney 1964; 86–99. A recent development is Bennett 1991.

6   A recent introduction is Collins and Pinch 1993.

of Copernicus as a conservative, who placed the sun at the centre of a largely unchanged cosmological framework, has been confirmed. If the revolution is deferred until the astronomical work of Johann Kepler, we find it moulded by his commitments to a Platonic 'harmony of the spheres' (see Field 1988). It has proved impossible to separate 'forward-' from 'backward-looking' components.

The complexity is reflected in excellent new biographies, such as Victor Thoren's of Tycho Brahe or Richard Westfall's of Isaac Newton. (Thoren 1990; Westfall 1980). The complexity is most evident in Newton. Rattansi and McGuire pioneered the recovery of Newton's belief that he was a privileged addition to an ancient 'Hermetic' tradition of secret knowers of cosmic mysteries. Dobbs has established that his immense alchemical labours were too informed by the traditional search for divine, occult natural powers to be called proto-chemistry (McGuire and Rattansi 1966; Dobbs 1991). These are further confirmations that Newton's religious interests, notably in biblical prophecy, were not peripheral to his natural philosophy. Indeed his physics of forces was but part of an attempt to demonstrate that God's providential agency worked throughout the world, in opposition to what he saw as the atheistic and materialistic philosophical tendencies of his age. These might be called Newton's '*idées transcientifiques*', but they were not a break with the past.

Writers have followed three responses to this attack on a clearly separable domain of emerging science. The first is to posit that an individual or group embodied two contradictory practices. A recent alternative to Marxian divisions is Brian Vickers's suggestion of distinct sign systems, or *Occult and Scientific Mentalities in the Renaissance*.[7] This saves the Scientific Revolution but, for some, with too much violence to the intellectual coherence of individuals and groups.

Vickers's defence specifically emerged in the face of a second response, of admitting the full range of influences and traditions that shaped the new science. After Koyré had opted for Platonism, the Renaissance scholar Frances Yates proposed Hermeticism. Closely allied to Renaissance Platonists, Hermetic *magi* like Giordano Bruno followed additional imperatives to discover and harness nature's magical sympathies. For Yates (1964) this evolved into experimentation (an aspect which Koyré had thought insignificant). The 'Yates thesis', which also claimed Hermetic precursors to Copernicanism, mechanism and mathematization, is now regarded as wildly over-extended, but it has focused attention on the real contributions of what Brian Copenhaver (1990) more soberly calls 'occultism'.

A more enduring claim was established at the same time by Walter Pagel and Allen Debus, for a 'tradition' loosely derived from the alchemical physician and religious radical Paracelsus. 'Paracelsians' rarely embraced their namesake's wider ideology – and the idea of a tradition is rather suspect. Nevertheless, these exponents of what Debus called *The Chemical Philosophy* sought to replace

7   Brian Vickers, 'Analogy versus identity: the rejection of occult symbolism, 1580–1680', in Brian Vickers (ed.), *Occult and Scientific Mentalities in the Renaissance*, Cambridge, Cambridge University Press, 1984, pp. 95–163. Other contributors take a different view.

scholasticism with an alchemical world-view which they frequently justified as that described in the Genesis account of Creation. Figures in this tradition such as J. B. van Helmont had considerable influence upon canonical 'chemists' like Robert Boyle (Pagel 1958; Debus 1972).

These and similar developments have diffused attention from a hard core of 'revolutionaries' to a much more problematic set of previously neglected yet widely read philosophers. Both Yates and Debus assumed the basic contours of the revolution narrative but, in recovering the importance of these groups, can now be see to have problematized it. The study of Paracelsianism in particular has led to a deeper awareness of simultaneous innovations in medicine, chemistry and even natural history. These innovations were ignored in older accounts of the Scientific Revolution because they did not fit the model of change derived from the exact, mathematical sciences. Historians have now adduced a confusing set of influences from stoicism to (perhaps more significantly) classical scepticism (Popkin 1964). In a similar vein, Charles Schmitt, Mordechai Feingold and others have re-examined science in the universities (Schmitt 1983; Feingold 1984). It remains true that they rarely fostered new science (although they trained most of the innovators), but neither were they the hidebound irrelevances they are presented as in the rhetoric of a Francis Bacon. Hard-to-classify hybrids abound, such as the atomist, even Copernican, Aristotelian Catholics studied by Beverley Southgate (1993). The picture of a clean break became so blurred that in 1982 Charles Webster showed how a surprisingly unchanged constellation of scientific, religious and political concerns, ranging from witchcraft to matter theory, existed *From Paracelsus to Newton* (Webster 1982).

Webster's approach represents a third response, which has been to take seriously the connections, categories, classifications and intellectual maps used by the actors themselves, even if continuing belief in witchcraft does not intuitively seem compatible with experimental science. His monumental *Great Instauration* documents the centrality of English radical movements in the development of Bacon's vision of a new science – and yet their purpose was to inaugurate the Millennium of religious and social justice (Webster 1975)! This kind of work reconnects intellectual with political and social history. Larry Stewart has recently situated the endgame of the revolution in England – the triumph of Newtonianism – in the context of the expansion of commercial culture (Stewart 1992). More narrowly, Robert Westman's study of the reception of Copernicus has revealed the importance of disciplinary divisions in Renaissance universities between astronomy and cosmology. Only where these did not function, primarily in princely courts, did it make sense to consider a sun-centred universe as a physical reality (Westman 1980).

A result of this third response is historians' general preference now to write, not of 'science', but of 'natural philosophy'. The word 'scientist' is, of course, a nineteenth-century creation. Barbara Shapiro is one historian who has developed the argument that the Renaissance equivalent of *scientia* (the ideal of certain knowledge) was in fact abandoned during the Scientific Revolution as a legacy of the schools' dogmatic over-confidence in their metaphysics (Shapiro 1983). To insist upon the category of natural philosophy is not a nicety. Natural philosophers of all kinds, and Newton considered himself one, purported to explain the entire universe and its relations with its creator. Whereas modern science (disingenuously perhaps) denies connections to political, social and religious systems of thought, natural philosophy embraced them.

This is a good point at which to consider changing views about the relation between religion and the new natural philosophy. Before Koyré, the sociologist Robert Merton, picking up on previous claims that Protestants led the new thinking, developed Max Weber's connection of capitalism with an ascetic Protestant ethic to include science. In England, he argued, certain norms encouraged Puritans to pursue practical science: it glorified the Creator, improved the human condition and distracted one from the sensual. (Merton 1978). The Merton thesis still informs debate, although, having been countered by evidence of the diversity of early modern religious belief, it now resembles other outdated attempts to hitch together supposedly modern developments into a single dynamic. John Morgan finds Puritans who deplored science. Mulligan and the Jacobs have found the Royal Society, a crucible of the new philosophy, to be dominated by Anglicans, although John Henry has recently argued for a more general Anglican influence.[8]

In the face of this body of writing, there is no longer much room for the old chestnut, expressed in A. D. White's title, of the *Warfare of Science with Theology* (White 1960). The notion that science, as free enquiry, had to be separated from personal or state religious commitments, founders upon the evidence that almost all the protagonists held sincere Christian beliefs, and that these were constitutive of their philosophy. They underwrote, for example, the very lawlikeness of Creation that was being sought. In his recent authoritative analysis, John Brooke prefers to write of the diversity of interactions between early modern science and religion, and specifically of differentiation rather than separation (Brooke 1991: 75–81).

Nevertheless, most historians would agree with Olaf Pedersen that Counter-Reformed authorities, with their power to enforce education in Thomistic Aristotelianism, impeded development and speeded the shift of centres of innovation to northern Europe (Pedersen 1981). That these included the Catholic France of Descartes and the Académie Royale des Sciences suggests that the reasons lay more in high Church and state politics than in some inimical Catholic mindset. Stimulating revisionist readings by Pietro Redondi and Mario Biagioli of the trial of Galileo for heresy in 1633 suggest that the Inquisition could have outmanoeuvred hard-line theological opposition to Copernicanism, but chose not to (Redondi 1987; Biagioli 1993). A further complication comes from recent demonstrations of the vitality of Jesuit science, which contributed significantly to new experimental

8   For references and a review of the debate see Brooke 1991: 109–14, 366; Henry 1992.

sciences, admittedly within the parameters of orthodox theology.[9] But in Protestant countries these parameters existed, if more unobtrusively. Newton's natural philosophy reflected his anti-Trinitarian beliefs which, perforce, he kept secret.[10] Our present position, then, is that religion remained as constitutive of the new natural philosophies as it had been of the old, and not in any simple or revolutionarily modern way.

Given the intimacy of religious and political ideology in early modern Europe, it is not surprising that recent work has also focused on the political context and meanings of the new science. Some of the most successful demonstrations are studies of individuals, where historians of science take account of the subordinate part that natural philosophy played in the life of men wrongly thought of as only 'scientists'. Furthermore, the view that the 'world natural' was ordered similarly to the 'world politick' was a widely held one. Hobbes, of course, is one writer whose political concerns clearly overshadowed his natural philosophical ones. But he and the colonial landowner Boyle could agree that how one guaranteed authoritative knowledge of nature had implications for how citizens would recognize the authority of a government (see Shapin and Schaffer 1985). Again, Francis Bacon was, first and foremost, a Stuart statesman and lawyer. Keeping this in mind, Julian Martin has shown that his plans for an organized community of applied science, far from being Farrington's liberal philosophy of industrial society, were inspired by his general strategy of bringing dangerous independence of mind under royal control (Martin 1992). Courts sponsored learning for good reasons. There is clear evidence that the more occult philosophers who flourished in central European courts troubled by religious and political divisions were pursuing a new 'pansophia' around which Christian Europe might unite. The importance of micropolitics has also been demonstrated. Exciting new work by Biagioli shows how Galileo's career and his science, which has been criticized as rashly cavalier, can be read as the appropriate kind of gift exchange between a princely patron and a court philosopher. Indeed, the general connection between the new science and the new social settings in courts is now a major growth point (Biagioli 1993; Moran 1991).

There is good evidence, then, that natural philosophies were constructed and assessed in relation to large- and small-scale interests which, while they have been the stuff of religious, political and social history, have only recently preoccupied the historian of the Scientific Revolution. Those who hold that early modern science was a social construction have, therefore, become less interested in finished textual products and more interested in the processes by which groups negotiated what was true in nature. The most systematic and controversial work of this kind, to date, is

---

9   See William B. Ashworth, Jr, 'Catholicism and Early Modern Science', in David C. Lindberg and Ronald L. Numbers (eds), *God and Nature: Historical Essays on the Encounter between Christianity and Science*, Berkeley, CA., University of California Press, 1986, pp. 136–66. There are other excellent essays in the collection. For Jesuit work in electricity and in general see the excellent Heilbron 1982: 93–106, 160–7; for magnetism see Pumfrey 1990.

10   See Brooke 1991: 45, 144–51; for an account based on psychohistory, see Manuel 1974.

Steven Shapin's *A Social History of Truth* (Shapin 1994). It is part of a trend concerned not with individuals but institutions, networks, classes and their appropriate codes of behaviour. These histories require access not just to the canonical texts, but to archives of unguarded papers and draft works, and records of debate and daily work. Hence the explosion of work based on correspondence circles, like that of Samuel Hartlib, whose extensive papers are now computerized (see Webster 1975; Greengrass *et al.* 1994). Societies and academies like the ever-popular Royal Society, the Jesuit Collegio Romano, and provincial groups such as one in Caen trace new scientific discourse to more general forms of communication and association in an emergent 'public sphere' (Lux 1989).

Women were, of course, generally excluded from such a public sphere of science as effectively as they had been from universities and learned academies. Gender history is now successfully displaying other ideological determinants of the new science. A ground-breaking and still controversial work was Carolyn Merchant's *The Death of Nature*. She posited a gendered relationship between the probing male philosopher and a female cosmos, and she argued that Renaissance conceptions of a quasi-animate 'Mother Nature' provided constraining norms upon the exploitation of natural resources. In her (and Easlea's) polemical readings, coldly rational mechanical philosophers recast nature as an entity passive enough for her commercial rape, and set the course for our environmental crisis (Merchant 1982; Easlea 1980). Feminist historians have related the gendered (even misogynist) discourse in which philosophers like Bacon conceptualized the process of discovery to the gender relations of contemporary society. Medical histories of the body have re-read anatomical developments in this light, and Londa Schiebinger has used them to explain women's intellectual exclusion. Others have argued, Patricia Phillips empirically and Sylvana Tomaselli more theoretically, that early modern women did contribute to scientific culture (see Laqueur 1990; Schiebinger 1989; Phillips 1990; Tomaselli 1985). While we have to conclude that the Scientific Revolution was the creation of white European males, feminist historiography has displayed it as part of its social matrix.

Where, then, is the historiography of the Scientific Revolution going? If it is measured by the column inches it fills in the annual bibliography of *Isis*, it is in decline. Its value has decreased as an origin myth for science studies, which now focus on the twentieth century. By the same token, it will be freer to cement links with other branches of history. These are pursuing similar sociological, and linguistic 'turns', turns that suppose cultural achievement to be more the product of transpersonal social or discursive systems than perceptions of reality by gifted subjects. New organizing narratives will be welcomed in some quarters and resisted by hard-core localists. One emerging approach integrates the critique, crisis and re-establishment of authoritative grounds for natural knowledge with the similar crises in early modern Europe about certainty in religion and politics. Barbara Shapiro has built around Popkin's notion of a sceptical crisis. The team who recently produced the valuable textbook *The Rise of Scientific Europe* emphasize urbanization when they compare the science of mainstream and marginal countries (see Schuster 1990;

Shapiro 1983; Goodman and Russell 1991). More typical is the discord in the studies of *The Scientific Revolution in National Context*, about what was revolutionized, why, or even when (Porter and Teich 1992). The future promises a chaotic, if sometimes constructive, pluralism. As the editors of *Reappraisals of the Scientific Revolution* remarked, 'historians of science are in greater disagreement today about how to conduct their craft than the ubiquitous metaphor of the Scientific Revolution suggests. In the end, the reader will have to decide (Lindberg and Westman 1990: xx). Readers and writers can at least look forward to a stimulating future.[11]

REFERENCES

Ashworth, W. B. (1986) 'Catholicism and early modern science', in D. C. Lindberg and R. L. Numbers (eds) *God and Nature: Historical Essays on the Encounter between Christianity and Science*, Berkeley.

Bennett, J. A. (1991) 'The challenge of practical mathematics', in S. Pumfrey, P. L. Rossi and M. Slawinski (eds) *Science, Culture and Popular Belief in Renaissance Europe*, Manchester.

Biagioli, M. (1993) *Galileo, Courtier: The Practice of Science in the Culture of Absolutism*, Chicago.

Blumenberg, H. (1983) *The Legitimacy of the Modern Age*, Cambridge, MA.

—— (1987) *The Genesis of the Copernican World*, Cambridge, MA.

Brecht, B. (1975) *Leben des Galilei*, Frankfurt.

Brooke, J. H. (1991) *Science and Religion: Some Historical Perspectives*, Cambridge.

Burtt, E. A. (1932) *The Metaphysical Foundations of Modern Science*, rev. edn, London.

Butterfield, H. (1949) *The Origins of Modern Science, 1300–1800*, London.

Cohen, H. F. (1994) *The Scientific Revolution. A Historiographical Enquiry*, Chicago.

Cohen, I. B. (1985) *Revolution in Science*, Cambridge, MA.

Collins, H. and Pinch, T. (1993) *The Golem: What Everyone Should Know about Science*, Cambridge.

Copenhaver, B. P. (1990) 'Natural magic, hermetism and occultism in early modern science', in Lindberg and Westman 1990.

Crombie, A. (1952) *Augustine to Galileo: The History of Science, A.D. 400–1650*, London.

Debus, A. G. (1972) *The Chemical Philosophy. Paracelsian Science and Medicine in the Sixteenth and Seventeenth Centuries*, 2 vols, London.

Dijksterhuis, E. J. (1961) *The Mechanization of the World Picture*, Oxford.

Dobbs, B. J. T. (1991) *The Janus Face of Genius: The Role of Alchemy in Newton's Thought*, Cambridge.

Drake, S. (1978) *Galileo at Work: His Scientific Biography*, Chicago.

Duhem, P. (1913–59) *Le Système du monde: Histoire des doctrines cosmologiques de Platon à Copernic*, 10 vols, Paris.

Easlea, B. (1980) *Witch-Hunting, Magic and the New Philosophy: An Introduction to Debates of the Scientific Revolution, 1450–1750*, Brighton.

Farrington, B. (1951) *Francis Bacon: Philosopher of Industrial Science*, London.

Feingold, M. (1984) *The Mathematicians' Apprenticeship: Science, Universities and Society in England*, Cambridge.

Feldhay, R. (1994) 'Narrative constraints on historical writing: the case of the Scientific Revolution', *Science in Context* 7: 7–24.

---

11 Since this essay was written, an important though conservative study has already appeared. See Cohen 1994.

Field, J. V. (1988) *Kepler's Geometrical Cosmology*, London.

Foucault, M. (1970) *The Order of Things: An Archaeology of the Human Sciences*, London.

Goodman, D. and Russell, C. A. (eds) (1991) *The Rise of Scientific Europe 1500–1800*, Sevenoaks.

Greengrass, M., Leslie, M. and Raylor, T. (1994) *Samuel Hartlib and Universal Reformation: Studies in Intellectual Communication*, Cambridge.

Hall, A. R. (1954) *The Scientific Revolution 1500–1800. The Formation of the Modern Scientific Attitude*, London.

Heilbron, J. L. (1982) *Elements of Early Modern Physics*, Berkeley.

Henry, J. (1992) 'The Scientific Revolution in England', in Porter and Teich 1992.

Hessen, B. (1971) *The Social and Economic Roots of Newton's* Principia, New York.

Kearney, H. F. (1964) *Origins of the Scientific Revolution*, London.

Koestler, A. (1964) *The Sleepwalkers: A History of Man's Changing Vision of the Universe*, Harmondsworth.

Kuhn, T. S. (1957) *The Copernican Revolution: Planetary Astronomy in the Development of Western Thought*, Cambridge, MA.

—— (1962) *The Structure of Scientific Revolutions*, Chicago.

Laqueur, T. (1990) *Making Sex: Body and Gender from the Greeks to Freud*, Cambridge, MA.

Lindberg, D. C. (1990) 'Conceptions of the Scientific Revolution from Bacon to Butterfield', in Lindberg and Westman 1990.

—— and Westman, R. S. (eds) (1990) *Reappraisals of the Scientific Revolution*, Cambridge.

Lux, D. S. (1989) *Patronage and Royal Science in Seventeenth Century France: The Académie du Physique in Caen*, Ithaca, NY.

McGuire, J. E. and Rattansi, P. M. (1966) 'Newton and the "Pipes of Pan"', *Notes and Records of the Royal Society* 21: 108–43.

McLellan, J. E. (1985) *Science Reorganised: Scientific Societies in the Eighteenth Century*, New York.

Mandrou, R. (1973) *Des Humanistes aux hommes de science (XVIe et XVIIe siècles)*, Paris.

Manuel, F. E. (1974) *The Religion of Isaac Newton*, Oxford.

Martin, J. (1992) *Francis Bacon, the State, and the Reform of Natural Philosophy*, Cambridge.

Merchant, C. (1982) *The Death of Nature: Women, Ecology and the Scientific Revolution*, London.

Merton, R. K. (1978) *Science, Technology and Society in Seventeenth Century England*, Brighton.

Moran, B. T. (1991) *Patronage and Institutions: Science, Technology and Medicine at the European Court, 1500–1750*, Woodbridge.

Pagel, W. (1958) *Paracelsus. An Introduction to Philosophical Medicine in the Era of the Renaissance*, Basle.

Pedersen, O. (1981) 'Science and the Reformation', in L. Grane (ed.) *University and Reformation*, Leiden.

Phillips, P. (1990) *The Scientific Lady: A Social History of Women's Scientific Interests, 1520–1918*, London.

Popkin, R. H. (1964) *The History of Scepticism from Erasmus to Descartes*, Asen.

Porter, R. (1986) 'The Scientific Revolution: a spoke in the wheel?', in R. Porter and M. Teich (eds) *Revolution in History*, Cambridge.

—— and Teich, M. (eds) (1992) *The Scientific Revolution in National Context*, Cambridge.

Pumfrey, S. (1990) 'Neo-Aristotelianism and the magnetic philosophy', in J. Henry and S. Hutton (eds) *New Perspectives on Renaissance Thought*, London.

Rabb, T. K. (1975) *The Struggle for Stability in Early Modern Europe*, New York.

Redondi, P. (1987) *Galileo: Heretic*, Princeton.

Schiebinger, L. (1989) *The Mind has no Sex? Women in the Origins of Modern Science*, Cambridge, MA.

Schmitt, C. B. (1983) *Aristotle and the Renaissance*, Cambridge, MA.

Schuster, J. A. (1990) 'The Scientific Revolution', in R. C. Olby, G. N. Cantor, J. R. R. Christie and M. J. S. Hodge (eds) *Companion to the History of Modern Science*, London.

Shapin, S. (1994) *A Social History of Truth: Civility and Science in Seventeenth-Century England*, Chicago.

—— and Schaffer, S. (1985) *Leviathan and the Air Pump. Hobbes, Boyle and the Experimental Life*, Princeton.

Shapiro, B. J. (1983) *Probability and Certainty in Seventeenth-Century England: A Study of the Relationship between Natural Science, Religion, History, Law and Literature*, Princeton.

Southgate, B. C. (1993) *Covetous of Truth: The Life and Work of Thomas White, 1593–1676*, Dordrecht.

Stewart, L. (1992) *The Rise of Public Science: Rhetoric, Technology and Natural Philosophy in Newtonian Britain, 1660–1750*, Cambridge.

Thoren, V. E. (1990) *The Lord of Uraniborg: A Biography of Tycho Brahe*, Cambridge.

Tomaselli, S. (1985) 'The Enlightenment debate on women', *History Workshop Journal* 20: 101–24.

Vickers, B. (1984) 'Analogy versus identity: the rejection of occult symbolism, 1580–1680', in B. Vickers (ed.) *Occult and Scientific Mentalities in the Renaissance*, Cambridge.

Wallace, W. A. (1984) *Galileo and his Sources: The Heritage of the Collegio Romano in Galileo's Science*, Princeton.

Webster, C. (1975) *The Great Instauration. Science, Medicine and Reform, 1626–1660*, London.

—— (1982) *From Paracelsus to Newton: Magic and the Making of Modern Science*, Cambridge.

Westfall, R. S. (1980) *Never at Rest: A Biography of Isaac Newton*, Cambridge.

Westman, R. (1975) *The Copernican Achievement*, Berkeley.

—— (1980) 'The astronomer's role in the sixteenth-century: a preliminary study', *History of Science* 18: 105–47.

White, A. D. [1896] (1960) *A History of the Warfare of Science with Theology in Christendom*, 2 vols, New York.

Yates, F. A. (1964) *Giordano Bruno and the Hermetic Tradition*, London.

Zilsel, E. (1941) 'The origins of William Gilbert's scientific method', *Journal of the History of Ideas* 2: 1–32.

15

THE WRITING OF EARLY MODERN EUROPEAN INTELLECTUAL HISTORY, 1945–1995[1]

D. R. Woolf

Intellectual history, which includes but is no longer synonymous with the 'history of ideas', has come a good distance since the Second World War. Although in some respects its basic terrain remains the same – the whole sphere of human thought – the approaches taken to mapping that terrain are now as diverse as the branches of history. This is in large measure because the single most significant thing that has happened to intellectual history in the past fifty years is its adoption of the vocabulary, techniques and even the agendas of other historical subdisciplines, of related humanities subjects such as philosophy and literary theory, and even of some more far-flung disciplines within the social sciences. This chapter will review the major changes, including the most recent developments, in early modern intellectual history-writing under the following broad categories: the history of science; history of political thought; history of communications (especially print); history of historiography and scholarship; and cultural history. It will focus on the specific contributions of a number of individuals or 'schools' whose works have had, in the phrase of one of them, the late T. S. Kuhn (for whose work see below, under the history of science), a 'paradigmatic' influence on their subdisciplines. Two qualifications are in order: since there is no space for a vast inventory of names and titles, I have opted to present what seem, to me at any rate, the major issues and contributions; and since the book in which this chapter appears is aimed predo-

1 I wish to acknowledge the financial support of the Research Development Fund of Dalhousie University, and also of the Social Sciences and Humanities Research Council of Canada. I am grateful to Gerald Aylmer, Jack Crowley and Kathryn Brammall for their comments on earlier versions of this chapter, to Donald R. Kelly and Fernando Cervantes for bibliographical suggestions, and for comments on early modern intellectual history generally to several successive sets of students in my advanced and graduate course on early modern thought and culture. This chapter is an attempt at a brief synthesis of a vast amount of historiographical literature in a number of subfields; it makes no pretence at comprehensiveness.

minantly at English-speaking readers, I have concentrated largely (though not exclusively) on Anglo-American material, and European material available, with some important exceptions, in translation.

Before we can map the travels of intellectual history in recent decades, it is necessary briefly to discuss where it stood in 1945. The standard approach to what is often called 'the history of ideas' popular in the early years of the twentieth century focused primarily on the acknowledged 'Great Texts' of Western culture, secondarily on the lives and lesser works of the authors of those texts, and even less on the external social and political context, or even on the parallel writings of more obscure authors roughly contemporary with the Greats. At its simplest, authors from Plato and Aristotle through St Augustine, St Thomas Aquinas, William of Ockham and Machiavelli, to Montesquieu, Hume, Kant and Marx could be treated as 'disembodied heads', magisterial minds whose thought systems were either so representative of their epochs as to make study of those epochs (even of the *Zeitgeist*, the so-called 'mind' or 'spirit' of an age) largely redundant, or, alternatively, so far 'ahead of their times' as to make study of those times irrelevant. The major weaknesses of this approach were threefold: (1) its bestowal of an unrealistic coherence on the thought system of individual thinkers (explaining away apparent and often glaring contradictions in order to relay the 'whole' picture); (2) its creation of imaginary lineages of thinkers (pedigrees of influence, for instance, which often could not be justified either textually or through external evidence); and (3) its promotion of specific texts, rather than ideas, as the central subject of investigation. With some exceptions, what one got in intellectual historiography up to, say the 1930s, was thinker-by-thinker histories of particular aspects of the history of thought, either within a particular era or across lengthier spans of time. The effects of this can best be observed in a number of surveys of the history of political thought – in classic works on particular eras or ideas such as those by J. W. Allen (1977) and John Neville Figgis (1914), for instance, as much as in the influential overview *A History of Political Theory* (1937) by George Holland Sabine, reprinted as recently as 1993; and in the history of science. The former field treated virtually all subsequent thinkers as what Alfred North Whitehead once termed a series of footnotes to Plato; the latter reduced its own subject to a long march of progress, complete with periodic surges forward behind the leadership of a few geniuses from Pythagoras, Euclid and Archimedes, through Copernicus, Kepler and Newton to Lamarck, Darwin and Einstein.[2]

Over and above the difficulties already cited, two problems stand out with this 'Greats' approach. First, it is reductionist in so far as it attributes most significant developments in the history of Western thought largely to the achievements of a few men and (much more rarely) women of acknowledged genius, ignoring or at best underplaying their historical context. It treats the forerunners and contemporaries of the Greats as footsoldiers in the wars of truth, able to take small, anticipatory

2   Cohen 1994; see also Michel Foucault's criticism of this approach and its emphasis on continuity and tradition, in Foucault 1976.

steps but lacking the knowledge or vision necessary to make major strategic gains. Second, this approach is inherently teleological, always assuming, in the spirit of nineteenth-century optimism, that knowledge must be going *somewhere*, along a particular path towards some sort of absolute, or at least superior, truth. The nature of that truth depends very much upon the values of the historian making the judgement. No one would now read Burckhardt's account of the Renaissance without taking into account the political and aesthetic presuppositions that motivated him to describe the state as a 'work of art'. Over half a century later, in similar fashion, Friedrich Meinecke's brilliant study of the rise of 'modern' (which in fact meant nineteenth-century German) historical consciousness, *Historism*, focused almost exclusively on those thinkers who in his view had made the national 'state' the architectural centre of their histories (Meinecke 1972).

Intellectual history really began to come into its own as a kind of 'elite' branch of the historical discipline as a whole after the First World War, as repugnance towards political history followed the collapse of the nineteenth-century empires, amid a general cynicism towards European leaders who had so recently led Europe into catastrophe. Many historians contributed to the promotion of intellectual history to a high rank at this time, among them the idealist philosophers Benedetto Croce and R. G. Collingwood (each of whom was significantly a practising historian as much as a philosopher) (Croce 1990; Collingwood 1993); the German Meinecke; the Americans Carl Becker (1991), Vernon Parrington (1987) and Perry Miller (1939); and the founding *Annales* historian Lucien Febvre in France. But the scholar most indelibly associated with intellectual history was Arthur O. Lovejoy, who established the important *Journal of the History of Ideas* in 1940, and who wrote several influential methodological essays and a magisterial book, *The Great Chain of Being* (Lovejoy 1936; Wilson 1980, 1982; Boas 1969). Lovejoy, whose influence over intellectual history would remain all-pervasive until the 1960s, is often lumped with the 'traditional' historians of ideas because, like them (and unlike more recent intellectual historians), he continued to focus on better-known authors, at the expense of the less well-known and of social, economic and political contexts; moreover, something of the same sort of teleology animates his writings. But Lovejoy did make two departures of significance for subsequent intellectual history-writing.

The first of these, best exemplified in *The Great Chain of Being*, was the reorganization of the history of thought away from a text-by-text approach to one that was idea-centred. Lovejoy promoted to centre stage what he referred to as the 'unit idea'. This was not a single, undifferentiated concept, passed like a baton from one age to the next, unchanged in all but name, but something rather more subtle. Lovejoy's unit idea might best be considered as a molecule with a variety of constituent atoms and changing numbers or configurations of electrons (this analogy is not frivolous, given the prominence of nuclear physics at the time at which he wrote). The nucleus of 'essential meaning' in an idea such as the separation of powers, or the 'noble savage', or the Great Chain of Being, would perennially remain the same. But the precise formulation of unit ideas, the media through which they would be expressed, and the social or political uses to which they might be put could change quite dramatically from period to period and genre to genre, making ideas, in the words of Kenneth Minogue, 'rather like randy chemical elements in an unstable soup' (1988: 186). This method in effect allowed Lovejoy to have his 'soup' and also eat it: to study a concept such as the Great Chain of Being over a very long span of time without having to assert the absurd proposition that the idea as understood in the Middle Ages was the same, or even close to the same, as that understood in the Enlightenment. His second departure, found in Lovejoy's methodological essays, was to claim an exceptionally wide range of subject matter for the intellectual historian, ranging far beyond the relatively limited topics available to previous generations; and while he could not possibly have anticipated the vast array of themes and materials of interest to intellectual historians today, his delineation of a variety of areas seems in retrospect a remarkably good start.

This overview of the subdiscipline as a whole has been necessary, because it is in early modern history – the period running from the Renaissance to the Enlightenment, including humanists at one end and *philosophes*, polymaths and physiocrats at the other – that many, though by no means all, of the most important changes in method and focus over the past three or four decades have occurred. But enough of the roots: it is high time we turned to the branches. While the subdisciplines can be studied separately, and will to some degree be so examined here, it is important to recognize that the conceptual innovations in one field frequently spill over into others. For this reason, it seems best to start with a subfield of intellectual history the changes within which have in part occasioned developments in other subfields. We begin, therefore, with the history of science.

HISTORY OF SCIENCE

The 'scientific revolution' of the sixteenth and seventeenth centuries – a term first coined as early as 1913 and turned into a full-scale historiographical concept by the historian Alexander Koyré in the 1930s – continues to exercise a fascination over both historians of science and those early modern scholars whose primary interests lie elsewhere. (See Pumfrey, above 293–306.) But there have been some quite 'revolutionary' changes in the ways in which such intellectual phenomena are studied. The teleology of intellectual history is perhaps nowhere more evident than in traditional accounts of the history of science, particularly (but by no means exclusively) when written by those who are scientists first and historians second: Jacob Bronowski's popular book and television series, *The Ascent of Man* (1974), is a good example, its Whiggishness betrayed by its very title. In its most naive version, this sort of scientific history, which descended from the British philosopher William Whewell (1794–1866), was given its familiar form early in this century by the influential medievalist Pierre Duhem (1861–1916). It tells the story of the triumph of modern reason and progress, unshackled from the chains of medieval and ancient thought systems by such forward-looking early visionaries as the medieval Parisian scholars, Jean Buridan and Nicole Oresme (to whom Duhem himself first drew attention), and fully realized in the Renaissance and seventeenth century by

Copernicus, Galileo and Kepler (in physics); Vesalius and Harvey (in anatomy); Bacon and Descartes (in the logic of scientific enquiry); and Newton in optics, mathematics and just about every other branch of science.[3] Such an account does more than merely leave out the numerous thinkers on whose ideas these men built, while making its heroes into either prophets or Promethean demigods; after all, were that the only problem, it could presumably be easily rectified merely by adding further detailed studies of secondary thinkers. The most serious flaw, from the point of view of many scholars, is that this history of science has been written to emphasize gradual, evolutionary change; even during such a central period of achievement as the Scientific Revolution, emphasis has been placed on the steady march of progress.

In the wake of early twentieth-century historians of science such as Pierre Duhem, Alexander Koyré, E. J. Dijksterhuis and the American philosopher E. A. Burtt, who had each contributed in different degrees to the establishment of History of Science as a field independent of both philosophy and history proper, the first post-war treatments of science in the early modern period tended to concentrate on the issue of the relative importance of medieval versus Renaissance contributions to scientific knowledge, highlighting such issues as the theory of inertia, to which medieval scholars such as Buridan and Oresme were seen, following Duhem, as early contributors through the idea of 'impetus' (Clagett 1959). But from the point of view of a reader outside these sometimes highly technical debates, and interested in how the history of science relates more generally to early modern intellectual history, the most significant developments occurred in the 1960s. A vociferous debate on the 'proper' way of writing the history of science, and, more broadly, on the construction of any sort of history of intellectual change, was ignited in 1962 with the publication of Thomas S. Kuhn's enormously influential book on *The Structure of Scientific Revolutions* (1970). Kuhn (1922–96), who himself had moved from a formal training in the physical sciences to an interest in their history, was influenced by the hypothesis of Koyré that the early modern period had marked a sharp break, rather than a continuity, with medieval science. Kuhn argued that traditional accounts of the history of scientific disciplines (Herbert Butterfield's *Origins of Modern Science* (1965)), long the most easily readable textbook on the subject, could serve as an example) had utterly missed an important point: that scientific change manifestly did *not* occur in a rational, slow-but-steady march of 'accretion'; rather, it occurred in large blips or 'paradigm shifts', often as much by accident as through the application of rational methods. Or, more correctly, while 'normal' science, practised from day to day by the scientific community, might often proceed quite slowly, steadily and methodically, it did so only because of the almost ruthless dominance over research of a set of beliefs, theories and hypotheses – even a set of agreed-upon questions – known as a paradigm.

---

3   This chapter had already been substantially drafted before H. F. Cohen 1994 appeared. I am, however, much indebted to that book for correcting several points of my interpretation. Other very helpful overviews of the subject may be found in I. B. Cohen 1985: ch. 26 and Lindberg 1990.

The paradigm of any discipline was self-reinforcing, to the extent that its theories, once taken as 'laws', set the agenda for further research, which in turn tended to fill in and reinforce the paradigm rather than, at least initially, to contradict it. The principal activity of normal, as opposed to revolutionary, science, was thus a type of puzzle-solving, not designed to test theories but to take them as given, thereby allowing the scientist to get on with the job of practical research.

Major changes of the sort witnessed in the sixteenth and seventeenth centuries occurred because of a superabundance of anomalies in existing paradigms. These anomalies were observable natural phenomena which apparently contradicted the paradigm unless one invented burdensome, untidy and complicated theories to cover them. Initially explained away or ignored, the anomalies would in due course strain the paradigm of any discipline to the point where it collapsed. The discipline would then experience a chaotic crisis stage, during which normal loyalty to the paradigm would be suspended and the rules constraining research in particular directions relaxed. During this period no particular theory or set of theories would hold the field. Only the eventual success of a new paradigm, its emergence from a number of contesting theories, would restore order, for the time being, and bring back 'normal science'.

Kuhn's point in this was not so much that periods of revolutionary science are episodes of intellectual anarchy. On the contrary, he emphasized that one paradigm would not be abandoned until another one was at hand, and that the shift from one to another would be very sharp and quick, not gradual (there is, as one critic has put it, no 'interregnum' between paradigms) (Lakatos and Musgrave 1970; Andersson 1994; Verronen 1986). He wished to demonstrate, from a sociological point of view, that the norm in science was not free-thinking, bold experimentation and vision, but quiet, empirical work in the trenches of academic and industrial laboratories. This theory put Kuhn in opposition not only to the Whig history of science, but also to the philosophy of science formulated by Sir Karl Popper in *The Logic of Scientific Discovery* (1959), the English translation of which appeared only three years before Kuhn's book. According to Popper, no scientific theory is really ultimately *verifiable*; the principal mark of a good theory over a bad one (and hence of good over bad science) is that it can potentially be proved false. Thus for Popper, unlike Kuhn, the principal task of science remained the testing of theories, albeit now freed from any quest for ultimate truth.

The Scientific Revolution of the early modern era would appear to offer a gift-wrapped example of Kuhn's theory of intellectual change, though Kuhn himself refrained from calling the Revolution *in itself* a paradigm shift:[4] the paradigms of ancient and medieval science, dominated by Aristotle, Galen, Ptolemy and others, and based largely on the study of authorities rather than upon observation and experimentation, gave way in the sixteenth century as persons interested in what was broadly called natural philosophy (there were, of course, not yet 'scientists' or a 'scientific community' in anything like a modern sense) detected, reported and tried to make

---

4   See H. F. Cohen 1994: 125ff. for some of the implications of this aspect of Kuhn's study.

sense of exceptions. In the realm of astronomy and physics, for instance, various explanations were put forward by Copernicus, Tycho, and others, for the observed irregularities in the orbits of the planets. Several theories, such as René Descartes's famous idea of a universe where motion and attraction were controlled by a plenum of interlocking cosmic vortices, would be advanced in turn to explain the coherence of matter and the nature of motion. Only the eventual success of Newton's mathematical model of gravitation succeeded in ending the reign of Aristotelianism and establishing a new paradigm; astronomical physics was thereby restored to a 'normal' phase till the advent of relativity in the early twentieth century, when subatomic physics and quantum theory caused a new crisis, and another paradigm shift.

Kuhn's model has been criticized from several perspectives: it has been pointed out that the notion of a paradigm is ill-defined; that some scientific disciplines have never experienced one dominant paradigm; and that his model does not apply nearly as well to modern scientific research, with its very rapid changes and near-instantaneous communication of results through monthly journals, the internet and even the popular media.[5] As a tool for the analysis of *historical* intellectual change (and not just that in the history of science), however, it has set off a series of debates among various learned communities both within and outside the history of science. Philosophers of the social sciences and political theorists have debated the usefulness of the paradigm. And historians, too, have long found Kuhn's model useful in explaining both the process of historical change and major historiographical shifts in their own fields, since the dominance of certain questions, issues, models, and even of particular journals, presses and monographs, appears to control the way in which historical discourse unfolds.[6]

Within the history of science, the discussion has gone far beyond Kuhn's original thesis and turned – rather like the issues in political thought which will be mentioned below – into a dialogue on the proper method of studying scientific change as a problem in intellectual history. The parties to this debate are sometimes known as 'internalists' and 'contextualists', and the issues they raise mirror concerns within intellectual history as a whole. Internalists, most notably (for the early modern era) scholars like A. C. Crombie (1952, 1963), A. R. Hall (a former pupil of Herbert Butterfield) (1983, 1993) and Hall and Hall (1988), maintain that the correct approach to understanding the science of past times remains the elucidation of texts, particularly those of the most significant authors: thus Copernicus's *De revolutionibus orbium coelestium*, or Newton's *Principia*, are intrinsically worth more attention than the works of more obscure Renaissance polymaths such as Johannes Trithemius or Girolamo Cardano, or of a conventional Aristotelian philosopher such as John Case, despite (or perhaps because of) Copernicus's or Newton's atypicality.

5 On Kuhn see the essays in Lakatos and Musgrave 1970, especially J. W. N. Watkins's dismissal of the concept of 'normal science', and Margaret Masterman's tabulation of at least twenty-one different uses of the word 'paradigm' in the first edition of *Structure*; see also, however, Kuhn's reply to his critics in this volume and in the postscript to the 1970 edition of his own book.
6 For applications, see the various essays in Gutting 1980, in particular articles by Sheldon S. Wolin and David Hollinger.

This approach has several merits. In the first place, it has produced some very good analyses of the work of the Greats, and it does 'explain', at one level, the process of scientific change as a transferral of ideas from person to person and era to era, providing hard evidence of such a tradition through careful and rigorous scholarship. It also provides a simplified narrative of how science got where it is today without complicating the story with wrong turns, backward steps and the distracting background noise supplied by external context. It must also be admitted that the internalist approach generally exhibits a level of scientific and mathematical sophistication which is often well beyond the capacity of the average history student to master, though easily understood by the scientifically inclined; hence it has had great appeal to practising scientists. What it manifestly does not do, however, is to take much note of social and political contexts; and it avoids outright the problems posed in the 'sociology of knowledge' developed by Max Weber and Karl Mannheim earlier this century, and applied to science (in their different ways) first by Robert K. Merton (1970), an American sociologist, and later by Kuhn and Popper.

The critics of the internalist approach are less a single school than a variety of scholars united in agreeing upon its inadequacy. Some, such as the late Charles Schmitt (1983), have shown that long-accepted axioms (the intellectual bankruptcy of Aristotelianism by 1550, for instance) are simply no longer tenable. The work of Schmitt (1972, 1984), Paul Grendler (1989) and many Italian scholars on Renaissance universities has shown that the authority of Aristotle as the dominant philosopher of nature remained secure well into the seventeenth century. Religious belief, whether Catholic, Protestant or sectarian, is no longer seen as an interfering, conservative ideology but as an impetus to investigation (though attempts to link experimental science with a 'puritan' mindset have not met with wide acceptance). Pietro Redondi's (1987) recent study of Galileo within the context of the seventeenth-century Roman Counter-Reformation (building on the work of pioneering scholars of early modern heresy such as Delio Cantimori (1992)) has suggested that mainstream Galileo experts have been too ready to exculpate their hero from the charge of heresy. Other research has demonstrated the importance of millenarian ideas in the writings of, among others, Kepler and Bacon. The early seventeenth-century Scottish inventor of logarithms, John Napier, developed that important tool to assist in his calculation of world chronology up to the appearance of the Antichrist. Frank E. Manuel (1963) forcefully reminded us three decades ago that the great Sir Isaac Newton passed his later years applying his mathematical knowledge to the elucidation of problems of alchemy and chronology, including the time of the reappearance of the Messiah, and further work is now in progress on Newton's alchemical and millenarian manuscripts, deposited at Cambridge and in Israel. Several historians have argued persuasively that the 'important' questions facing scientists from the seventeenth century on were not necessarily deemed important by their predecessors. Political and social upheavals have played their part in the reinterpretation of scientific history. In *The Great Instauration* (1975), a lengthy study of the 'Baconian' scientific investigations in revolutionary England of the 1650s, Charles Webster emphasized political and religious factors in explaining the emergence of the Royal

Society and the beginnings of British empirical science. These occurred because the Puritan, apocalyptic environment of revolutionary England created a climate favourable to carrying out the conquest of nature, and lured numerous educational and philosophical reformers such as Jan Amos Comenius and Samuel Hartlib to England, where they helped promote research. Webster's attention to the Royal Society's origins has been extended by Michael Hunter (1989; 1995) and most recently by Steven Shapin (1994), in a bold revaluation of the 'social history' of truth.

Elsewhere in Europe, the importance of institutions such as the French academies has been well established, and more recent scholarship has stressed the equal importance of private collections of natural 'curiosities' by *virtuosi*, educated laymen who communicated their findings through correspondence, books, learned societies and the earliest scientific journals, such as the French *Journal des Savants* and the English *Philosophical Transactions of the Royal Society* (see e.g. Findlen 1994). Magic, alchemy, Neoplatonism, Pythagoreanism and Paracelsianism, once banished to the footnotes as irrational 'wrong turns' on the road to modern truth, have now been reintegrated into mainstream history of science by scholars such as Richard Westfall, Allen G. Debus, Margaret and J. R. Jacob (who have also theorized a link between English science of the late seventeenth century and the Whig–Anglican settlement of Church and state in 1688), and the historian of scepticism, Richard H. Popkin.[7] The more esoteric aspects of this magical tradition, which dates back to Plato and Pythagoras, have been proved to have had considerable impact on early modern science by scholars such as Frances Yates (1991), Paolo Rossi (1968), Eugenio Garin (1978, 1983) and D. P. Walker (1958, 1972). Others have stressed the social and political context of scientific research: Michael Hunter (1989, 1995) and Roy Porter (1995) in their studies of the various branches of science and their place in Augustan England, and R. J. W. Evans (1984) in a brilliant landscape of the mental world of the Holy Roman Emperor Rudolf II (1576–1612), whose court boasted such luminaries as Tycho Brahe and Johannes Kepler. A feminist and environmentalist perspective on the Scientific Revolution has been introduced by Carolyn Merchant (1980), who has argued that it ushered a period in which science reoriented itself towards the conquest of nature, which in turn was gendered increasingly gendered as a female, awaiting dominance (Merchant 1980). The reader should take note of the formidable but immensely useful *Cambridge History of Renaissance Philosophy*, published in 1988, which is an excellent recent guide not only to early modern science but to virtually all aspects of the 'high' intellectual history of early modern Europe (Schmitt *et al.* 1988). Finally, the emergence of mathematically-based probability theory has been studied in detail by Lorraine Daston (1988).

---

7   Only a selection of these prolific authors' works are noted here: Westfall 1980; Webster 1982; Debus 1991; Jacob 1988; Popkin 1979. It must surely be added, though, that the link between magic and experimental science was an obvious one as early as the great multi-volume work, in the 1920s and 1930s, of Thorndike 1923–58.

HISTORY OF POLITICAL THOUGHT

In the history of political thought, even more than in the history of science, early modern European scholars have played a critical role. The principal change of the last thirty years has been a decisive shift away from the study of great texts as containers of coherent, complete thought systems (reading a text such as Hobbes's *Leviathan*, as one political philosopher put it, 'over and over' till the argument became clear) to the study of them as literary and linguistic constructions or 'speech-acts' deriving not just from the genius of a mind like Hobbes's, but from the context within which that author wrote, and from the purpose he had in writing. The issues here echo to a large degree those raised by Kuhn for the history of science, though the discussion has gone in different directions. A number of scholars, such as the political theorist John Dunn (1969) and the historian Peter Laslett (1960; a path-breaking study of Locke's *Two Treatises*) have contributed to a shift in focus that began in the late 1950s. But the influence of two scholars, each with strong attachments to both the disciplines of political science and history, stand out as most responsible for the reconstruction of the history of political thought along contextual lines.

J. G. A. Pocock (1924–), a New Zealander, was trained at Cambridge by Herbert Butterfield, but spent the greater part of his career in the United States prior to his recent retirement from the Johns Hopkins University. In a voluminous number of essays (on the meaning and political significance of terms like 'virtue' and 'credit') as well as in two very important books, *The Ancient Constitution and the Feudal Law* (1987) and *The Machiavellian Moment* (1975). Pocock drew attention to the *linguistic* (as opposed to the political or social) contexts within which thought about politics took place in the early modern era. In other words, he shifted attention away from classic *texts* (though these still merit attention in his works) to the competing *languages* in which they were written, and through which dialogue, debate and practical action took place. These languages assume something of the role played for Kuhn by paradigms, and indeed Pocock has explicitly adopted the latter term in his own writings. *The Ancient Constitution*, which predated Kuhn's *Structure* by five years, deals with the importance of conflicting legal systems, codified and customary, Roman and common-law, on the development of historical thought, and hence on political theory which at that time was rooted in argument from the past. Although Pocock had not yet formalized his method (this he would do in a number of essays during the 1960s), his depiction of the English 'common-law mind', unfamiliar with European philology and insulated from comparison with European legal systems, anticipates it in large measure.[8]

The Machiavellian Moment treated the central place in Western political thought of the language of 'civic humanism', the importance of which for Quattrocento Florence had already been emphasized by German émigré scholars such as Hans

---

8 For discussion of Pocock's method see Höpfl 1975; Hampsher-Monk 1984.

Baron for the early fifteenth century and Felix Gilbert for the early sixteenth.[9] Civic humanism, as discussed by Pocock, was a constellation of terms, concepts and categories – a language – derived from classical authors but reformulated in Renaissance Florence within the context of the early Renaissance city republics. Competing for dominance with rival languages (those of radical millenarianism, or of secular *imperium*, for example), from which it adopted certain elements, civic humanism achieved its most sophisticated treatment in the sixteenth century. This occurred just as most of the republics were giving way to the *de facto* monarchies of families such as the Medici; its clearest articulations are to be found in the works of Machiavelli and Guicciardini, and in some less well-known but important contemporaries such as Gasparo Contarini and Donato Gianotti, two authors concerned less with 'virtue', in Machiavelli's sense, than with establishing and maintaining the sort of stable commonwealth represented by another republic, Venice. The discourse of republicanism would subsequently be transmitted to the Atlantic world, and especially to British North America, via seventeenth-century English writers such as James Harrington, where it would remain influential, though much changed in meaning, up to the American Revolution. In each case, the transplanting of a language such as civic humanism from one socio-political habitat (Cinquecento Italy) to others (Puritan England or colonial Philadelphia) changed the character of the discourse and allowed for varied interpretations and uses of the works of writers such as Machiavelli which the original authors could not possibly have anticipated. This model allows Pocock to demonstrate lines of intellectual affiliation (always thoroughly documented by precise textual references) without positing spurious chains of influence or giving earlier writers a clairvoyant power of 'anticipation' of a future concept, après Lovejoy. The republicanism of the late eighteenth century could thus be shown to be *similar* but not *identical* to that developed by Machiavelli's contemporaries, which in turn differed in many ways from the formulation of earlier Italian rhetoricians such as the Florentine chancellor and historian of the Quattrocento, Leonardo Bruni. The obvious strengths of Pocock's approach to the history of political ideas, which is really a history of political *languages*, are twofold. In the first place, it grants due attention to context without necessarily *reducing* a text, in a mechanistic fashion, to that context, or making the claim that *all* texts are of equal significance: if Machiavelli were merely a writer of the commonplace, there would hardly be any point in studying his work in detail. Second, Pocock's approach to political thought allows for a relativist, non-teleological account of the process of intellectual change.

Written in a dense, complex style, Pocock's works have received relatively less attention from writers on intellectual history methodology in recent years than have the essays of Quentin Skinner 1940–), Professor of Political Science and most

---

9   Baron 1966; Gilbert 1965. What has become known as the 'Baron thesis' has been subjected to intense scrutiny and criticism by various scholars, in particular Baron's thesis of a sharp break between 1397 and 1402 in humanist consciousness, driven by the threat to Florence of the duke of Milan, Giangaleazzo Visconti. For some examples, see Hankins 1995.

recently Regius Professor of Modern History at Cambridge. Skinner is the author of, among other works, a short book on Machiavelli, a longer book on Hobbes, a number of edited collections, and a two-volume survey of early modern political thought which focuses on the changes in political vocabulary occasioned by the Renaissance and Reformation, and how these were affected by events. He remains most famous, however, for a number of essays which have inspired considerable debate among early modern scholars (Skinner 1978; 1981). In the best known of these, 'Meaning and understanding in the history of ideas', first published in 1969 in the journal *History and Theory* (Skinner 1969), Skinner denounced a variety of sins in the traditional history of political thought and, by extension, throughout the historiography of ideas. These included its focus on great ideas and great men; its Whiggish back-projection of modern values on to the past; its bestowal of philosophical coherence on authors who may in fact have changed their minds and certainly revised their arguments over time; and, finally, its confusion of an author's intention *in* writing a text (which can be ferreted out from the text itself) with the intention *to do* something, which may or may not have got done and is usually difficult to establish.

Though their approaches are in many respects similar, Skinner lays comparatively more stress than Pocock on the continuing importance of classic texts. Consequently, critical as he is of the 'timeless questions' approach of political philosophers, he is particularly vehement in criticizing two types of historian: on the one hand, he denounced Lovejoy's unit-idea approach for its reification of thought, and its virtual removal of ideas from the context of real political events; on the other, he was equally unsympathetic to the opposite viewpoint, best represented by the political determinism of L. B. Namier, that ideologies could simply be reduced to the cynicism of competing interests and political 'structures'. Borrowing from philosophers as diverse as Ludwig Wittgenstein, J. L. Austin and Wilhelm Dilthey, Skinner has urged historians of political thought neither to abandon intellectual history for events, nor to substitute it for events, but to study the ways in which texts are written within a set of political, social and literary conventions which they often challenge and ultimately subvert. The scholar must study not just what a past writer has said, but his purpose in saying it – what Austin called its illocutionary force. When, for instance, Machiavelli composed *The Prince*, he was doing so within a set of conventions which included both the genre (traditional 'advice to princes' literature) and the terms used, such as 'virtue' and 'fortune'. He wrote the book not to defend such conventions, or intentionally to challenge them, but instead to convey a particular set of messages in response to a particular situation (i.e. the need for a strong leader to rid Italy of the hated foreign armies). What Machiavelli, Hobbes, Locke, Montesquieu or Rousseau wrote in their own times had a particular significance for them, and may have been inspired by a variety of motives, some of which will more likely than not elude the historian, but others of which will be evident in their texts. A work as written was intended to evoke a certain range of responses at a particular time, not to speak to all times, and we must not confuse our own understanding of a given text with the author's original intentions.

Skinner's directives did not preclude the use of an author's work for radically different purposes than he intended; thus, in the two-volume *Foundations of Modern Political Thought* (1978) Skinner was able to demonstrate how the Huguenot resistance theorists during the French religious wars made use of arguments for resisting or deposing a bad monarch previously formulated by Catholic writers (their arch-enemies) such as the Jesuit Juan de Mariana. The primacy of events is paramount here: all the political texts studied by Skinner were written in response to events, and ideological change occurred as the pressure of those events caused individual writers to challenge or modify the conventions within which they wrote. This is how words, ideologies and concepts such as 'the state' come into being, and how existing words can radically change their meanings over time. Although Skinner differs from and is critical of his explanation of terminological change, the Marxist literary critic and philosopher Raymond Williams has, from a different perspective, pushed this point home in his influential work, *Keywords* (1976). This shows how widely words have shifted in resonance and meaning over time ('innovation' and 'democracy', now seen as desirable things, immediately spring to mind, since neither was much valued in the early modern era). Similar aims and methods may be found more recently in the current German philosophical endeavour known as *Begriffsgeschichte*, associated with the work of Rolf Reichardt, Joachim Ritter and especially Reinhart Koselleck, an ongoing multi-authored investigation of the evolution of political and philosophical concepts – a kind of 'conceptual' history that departs sharply from older traditions of German *Ideengeschichte* and *Geistesgeschichte*.[10]

For Skinner, as for Pocock, it is again not simply contexts but specifically the linguistic context – the range of possible terms and their meanings (literal and implied) – which constitutes the political thought of an age: treating a text as entirely attributable to political events and circumstance is in the end no more desirable than to treat it, or the thoughts it conveys, as a completely autonomous, timeless icon. The brilliant thinkers of the past were not prisoners of their categories, but they did work within them, often stretching, reshaping or distorting them to suit their own ends and audiences. Machiavelli did this with the classical and Christian concepts of virtue; Jean Bodin, the French polymath of the 1560s and 1570s, did so with the nascent vocabulary of 'the state'; the Flemish philosopher Justus Lipsius did so with ancient Stoicism, which he helped to adapt for a Counter-Reformation context; and the political thinkers of the seventeenth century, such as Grotius, Hobbes and Locke, borrowing many elements from all of these predecessors, again shifted discussion to natural rights, the relationship between the individual and the state, and the philosophical underpinnings of private property.

Much attention has been paid to evaluating the relative importance of text and context, and the proportions which each should occupy in the historian's account.

---

10   The leading Anglo-American exponent of *Begriffsgeschichte* is Melvin Richter, whose *The History of Political and Social Concepts: a Critical Introduction* (1995) had not yet appeared when this chapter went to press.

After numerous published essays concerned with criticizing and evaluating the importance of Skinner's contribution, the discussion of methods had, by the late 1980s, seemingly exhausted itself. Despite the undeniable importance of the work of Pocock, Skinner and their students and allies, little consensus exists on a 'correct' method of doing the history of political thought. There is, at least, more work being done on well known authors from Machiavelli to Montesquieu (Tuck 1993), as well as on previously little-known or 'second-rank' writers, or on those whose major achievements have traditionally been located in other disciplines, such as the historian Edward Gibbon and economic thinkers such as Adam Smith and the French physiocrats. There has also been a revolt, which in certain ways goes beyond the critiques of Pocock and Skinner, against a too narrowly conceived notion of what constitutes political thought: thus, Nannerl O. Keohane (1980), in a panoramic view of French social and political thought from the Renaissance to the eighteenth century, deals with relatively obscure literary and scholarly figures such as Etienne Pasquier as well as with the 'masters'. The Canadian political scientist J. A. W. Gunn (1969, 1983) has explored the role of concepts such as liberty, public interest and property as expressed in such disparate sources as parliamentary debates and pamphlet literature. From another vantage point, feminism has contributed much in recent years to re-readings of authors such as Machiavelli and Rousseau, as central political terms such as 'patriarchalism' (the subject of an impressive study by the American Gordon J. Schochet (1975)) are investigated not only for what they say about formal political power but also for their influence on household power structures and the relations between the sexes: Hanna F. Pitkin (1984), for instance, in a bold re-reading of Machiavelli, centres on the metaphor of Fortune as a woman, using it to draw conclusions about the nature of political power in the Renaissance, and thereby adding a further element, gender, to the determinants of political language.

COMMUNICATIONS HISTORY: ORALITY AND THE ROLE OF THE PRINTING PRESS

As the earlier account of changes in the historiography of the history of science indicates, some considerable attention has been paid by recent intellectual historians to the role of communications in early modern society. A central issue here is the role of the printing press and of books in the promotion and shaping of knowledge. Much scholarship since 1945 has tended to downplay the role of the press, to see it as essentially a technological innovation (albeit a very important one), and to stress the fact that much knowledge had already been, and continued to be, communicated by means of manuscript and word of mouth; and some recent writing has cautioned against placing too great an emphasis on the press in view of the remarkable resilience of manuscript culture, especially among elite patronage circles.

Early quantitative and theoretical investigations of the history of the book did not necessarily contradict this. Father Walter J. Ong's important 1958 study of the sixteenth-century French pedagogue Peter Ramus (Pierre de la Ramée) and the influence of his textbooks of logic on European thought showed that the ubiquity of Ramus's books (and those of other educational reformers) reflected a more wide-spread cultural change, away from an orally based society in which perception, communication and education took place primarily through dialogue (and secondarily through manuscript), towards a visually oriented culture, for which knowledge was contained spatially in a paper box, the book, rather than transmitted rhetorically. Ong did not praise this transformation; if anything, he regarded Ramus's simplification of knowledge as reductionist, and he echoed the view, which dates back to Plato, that writing (and a fortiori, print) made thought more superficial (Ong 1958). A somewhat similar argument has been recently advanced by Anthony Grafton and Lisa Jardine, who have traced the transition from 'humanism' to the 'humanities' as a change from deep understanding of texts to a more utilitarian study of them for practical purposes (Grafton and Jardine 1986). This would appear to be a perfect demonstration of the awesome power of the press, but Ong stopped short of ascribing this putative shift from oral to visual primarily to the advent of print, preferring to see it, and the textbooks it generated, as symptoms rather than causes.

More or less the same conclusions were reached by the French historians Lucien Febvre and Henri-Jean Martin, whose pioneering study of the 'coming of the book' helped to found a whole genre of *histoire du livre* (Febvre and Martin 1984). 'Book history' proceeds on the assumption that changes in knowledge, literacy and education, and indeed broader social and economic transformations such as class formation, can be assessed by analysing, for content form, and genre, large numbers of printed books on a variety of subjects. Many historians go far beyond the content of the books (which to some degree remains an author-based form of intellectual history, howsoever quantified), to measure, where records allow, the social background of their readership, the existence and accessibility of public libraries and personal lending networks, and even the place of the book as a gift to be displayed rather than read – the remote progenitor of our 'coffee-table book'. This methodology, with its frequent use of quantifiable data to supplement traditional textual analysis, has so far proved more useful towards the end of the early modern and into the modern era, when such records as those of public lending libraries become more common. For the earlier period, scholars are compelled to rely on the scattered evidence of printers' inventories, wills, private library lists, auction catalogues and readers' annotations of the books that they owned. Nevertheless, some outstanding studies have been done for France by Roger Chartier (whose recent *The Order of Books: Readers, Authors and Libraries in Europe between the Fourteenth and Eighteenth Centuries* (1994) offers a brief but illuminating survey of the topic), François Furet and Jacques Ozouf (1982), while Robert Darnton (1979) has examined the publishing history and reception of a major work in Enlighten-ment intellectual history, the *Encyclopédie*, and more recently the circulation of forbidden literature in pre-revolutionary France (1995).

Most of this scholarship concedes the vast importance of the printing press as a medium in the making of early modern culture, rather than as an explicit agent of intellectual and social change: the press is seen as having facilitated the communication of knowledge, rather than as having created knowledge. That view was explicitly challenged by Elizabeth Eisenstein in 1979. Her lengthy book *The Printing Press as an Agent of Change* argued that the press must be viewed not merely as an instrument of change but as its initiator. Citing a huge array of evidence ranging from the books themselves, through the technology of printing, to the organization of printers' shops, Eisenstein has contended that the press managed to create new types of knowledge, not merely ease the spread of old ones.[11] The influence of the press was far-reaching and ultimately ubiquitous, extending to social structure as well as to ideas; it allowed the emergence of, for instance, the class of individuals known as 'men of letters', distinct from and more heterogeneous than the limited intelligentsia which had developed within the medieval Church.

While not all historians would accept Eisenstein's formulation, her work has revived interest in printing history. Other scholars have pursued the subject further. Robert Scribner (1981), a student of popular culture, has demonstrated the importance of graphic propaganda (in the form of illustrative woodcuts) in the Lutheran Reformation. In a similar vein, Tessa Watt (1991) has recently published a prize-winning study of English *Cheap Print and Popular Piety* from the Reformation to the beginning of the English Civil War. Fine work has been done by Robert Mandrou (1964) and Roger Chartier (1987) on popular printed genres (pamphlets, ballads, chap-books and *canards*, while Margaret Spufford (1981) and Bernard Capp (1979) have respectively contributed interesting works on popular fiction and its readership in seventeenth–century England, and on the early modern almanac. Exceptionally thorough studies have been made of the print culture of particular places. Miriam Usher Chrisman (1982) has used the book as an index of social and religious change in sixteenth–century Strasbourg, focusing on the social as well as intellectual differences between Latin and vernacular cultures; comparable books have been written by Albert Labarre (on Amiens), Henri-Jean Martin (on Parisian printing) and Michel Marion (on Parisian private libraries). Because intellectual history as a whole has been moving in general to accord greater place to language and communications, print historians have started to pay renewed attention to earlier treatments of the issue of communications change, most notably the classic scholarly work of Lewis Mumford (1934) and the more popular studies by Marshall McLuhan (1962), which in some ways anticipated Eisenstein. The trend in this direction has been further reinforced by the growing significance of 'semiotics' – the study of communications as a system of signs and codes – so that not only the 'message', or content, of a book is considered but also the process whereby that message is transmitted and received. The activities of the relatively new but wide-reaching Society for the History of Authorship, Reading, and Publishing (SHARP) have further promoted early modern studies of books, their owners and readers, though most of its members work on the better-documented nineteenth and twentieth centuries.

---

11 Eisenstein 1979; this massive work is abridged, with illustrations, in Eisenstein 1983.

HISTORY OF SCHOLARSHIP AND HISTORIOGRAPHY

All disciplines are, not surprisingly, interested in their own origins. History is no exception, and changes in the way in which the history of history has been written reflect many of the developments already discussed. Up to the late 1950s, accounts of historical scholarship in early modern Europe tended to reduce the subject to a litany of names and titles, with most attention being lavished on a select company of major historians from Leonardo Bruni to Edward Gibbon. In the 1960s and early 1970s, in the wake of Pocock's work on *The Ancient Constitution and the Feudal Law* (discussed above under political thought), scholars such as Julian H. Franklin (1963), Donald R. Kelley (1970) and George Huppert (1970) turned away from the study of narrative historians to the non-narrative legal and philological studies of the Renaissance, especially in Quattrocento Italy and sixteenth-century France. According to these modern historians of history, the most important developments in the methodology of historical research, and in the formulation of working concepts such as 'feudalism', are to be found less in the elegant Latin of Bruni and Poggio, or the lively vernacular of Machiavelli and Guicciardini, than in the long, and often tedious, researches of bibliophiles, jurists, philologists and antiquaries from the Italians Lorenzo Valla and Flavio Biondo, through the French jurists François Baudouin, François Hotman and Jean Bodin, to the detailed methodological writings of late seventeenth-century figures such as Tillemont, Du Cange, Muratori, the Bollandists and Mabillon. The work of the érudits in absolutist France has been exhaustively analysed in Barret-Kriegel (1988).[12]

Individual historians, scholars and polymaths still attract researchers, in part because they make perfect topics for doctoral theses. Essays and books on such historical thinkers as Francesco Guicciardini (such as those by Vittorio de Caprariis (1950) and, more recently, Mark Phillips (1977)), and Pierre Bayle (by Elisabeth Labrousse (1963–4 remains authoritative for its subject)) continue to appear, and enormous attention has been paid to the work of perhaps the strangest of all the *érudits*, Giambattista Vico, whose often opaque masterpiece, the *New Science*, has become a kind of byword for the historiographical vision of nascent historicism. Vico has been taken generally as a transitional figure, whose historical thought, with its emphasis on stages of human development, mark him variously as either a late Renaissance *savant* or a very early philosopher of history – a bridge between humanism at one end of the period and Herder and Hegel at the other. It is fair to say that more has been written about Vico (who had been largely ignored till the nineteenth century) as linguist, historian, philosopher and early sociologist than about any other early modern historian or historical philosopher except perhaps

---

12 On the great erudite projects of the seventeenth century the classic account in English is still that of Knowles 1963, now modified by Barret-Kriegel (1988) with volumes on Mabillon (I) and on the Maurists and the 'Académies de l'histoire' (III). On the period as a whole, a very useful, though now somewhat dated, survey of early modern historical thought, focusing on issues such as the development of a sense of anachronism, can be found in Burke 1969.

Machiavelli or Gibbon.[13] Related to the research on Vico is other work on the 'discovery of time', the slow process whereby early modern people gradually lost confidence in the biblical account of the Creation as having taken place in seven days and moved from a chronology of five or six thousand years' duration (as calculated in the extremely erudite works of Renaissance scholars such as Joseph Scaliger, Denis Petau, James Ussher and even, as we have seen, Newton himself) to one of many millions of years. Thus Joseph M. Levine, Roy Porter, Don Cameron Allen, Paolo Rossi (1984), Stephen Toulmin and June Goodfield (1965) have demonstrated how the discovery of fossils gradually eroded confidence in the biblical account, forcing scholars and, eventually, a wider public to conceive of 'geological time' well before Charles Lyell's geological findings and Darwin's evolutionary theories solved the related problem of the descent of humanity; and the Renaissance literary 'discovery' of time has been explored by Ricardo Quiñones (1972), a scholar of comparative literature in the tradition of the Germans Erich Auerbach and Ernst Robert Curtius. Grafton (1993) is the most sophisticated analysis of Renaissance chronology.

Other historiographers have continued to emphasize changes in formal historical writing – what contemporaries called 'histories' or *res gestae*, from Louis Green's (1972) study of the transformation of the late medieval Italian chronicle into the humanist history, and Nancy S. Struever's (1970) subtle treatment of the influence of rhetoric on Florentine historical consciousness, to Orest A. Ranum's (1980) book on the French Historiographers Royal of the seventeenth century (Cochrane 1981). Operating within the same intellectual environment that has spawned the more ambitious project of *Begriffsgeschichte*, Arno Seifert (1976) and Joachim Knape (1984) have contributed informative works on the history of the word 'history' and its cognates in the early modern era; and Girolamo Cotroneo's (1971) study of the *trattatisti*, Renaissance and Counter-Reformation authors in the genre of *ars historica* ('art of history'), has now superseded earlier work in that area. Useful summaries of the Italian historical literature of the Renaissance are available in a lengthy book by Eric Cochrane on *Historians and Historiography in the Italian Renaissance* (1981), while more specialized works and essay collections have been contributed by Pompeo Giannantonio (1972) and Salvatore Camporeale (1972) on Lorenzo Valla, Eckhard Kessler (1978) on the historical thought of Petrarch, and Agostino Pertusi (1970), William J. Bouwsma (1968) and David Wootton (1983) on Venetian historiography. Many books in the field suffer from the same kind of teleology that marks other areas of intellectual history. F. Smith Fussner's argument, put in 1962, that a kind of 'historical revolution' analogous to the scientific one took place in early seventeenth-century England has found few supporters, but there remains a tendency, as with the history of science, to view changes in the history of scholarship as inherently progressive, marching towards the modern system of critical research and evaluation of evidence. In very recent

---

13 Vico 1948. The secondary literature on Vico is too vast even to begin to take note of here, but a valuable brief study is Burke 1985. A new translation of Vico by David Marsh is underway.

years, however, some students of the history of historical consciousness, influenced by the *Annales* school, by post-structuralist literary theory and by the boom in studies of popular culture, have begun to investigate history as a mode of discourse, as a cultural problem the explanation of which must include but go beyond texts, to study the social circulation of historical knowledge among and between classes, and its past sociological and anthropological importance. It remains unclear at the present time exactly what form such investigations will take, however; there is as yet no equivalent, for the early modern period, of Bernard Guenée's (1980) *Annales*-influenced research into medieval historical culture.

THE ARRIVAL OF CULTURAL HISTORY

The *Annales* 'school' would need little further attention here, were it not for the fact that some *Annales* historians have, in the past two decades, increasingly moved away from the sort of highly quantitative social history practised by the late Fernand Braudel and into intellectual history. To some degree such concerns were always part of the *Annales*' 'total history' approach, even in Braudel's economically orientated work. One of his teachers, Lucien Febvre (d. 1956) – the pre-eminent early modernist among the first generation of *Annales* historians – is now perhaps best known for an exciting, if contentious, investigation of the limiting power of vocabulary on the development of atheism in sixteenth-century France, through a close study of Rabelais and his mental environment (Febvre 1982). But it is in the last two decades that intellectual history, often reformulated by left-leaning historians as the less elitist-sounding 'Cultural History', has really begun to occupy the attention of historians within and just outside the *Annales* framework.

Much of this new cultural perspective has to do with re-reading old texts in new ways, to tease out not just what they say but what they assume or even leave unsaid about the events or beliefs they describe. *Montaillou*, Emmanuel Le Roy Ladurie's investigation of heresy and life in a thirteenth-century village, was an important influence – almost paradigmatic, one might say! – and many more of these 'micro-histories' have appeared in the past few years. Such works draw heavily on the language, though generally not the heavily quantitative methodology, of the social sciences. In particular, they have been inspired by the writings of such modern ethnographers as Claude Lévi-Strauss, Marshall Sahlins and E. E. Evans Pritchard, the anthropological essays of the historically minded Clifford Geertz and the analyses of ritual by Victor Turner, to name a few (Burke 1992). There has also been a resurgence of interest in the writings of some early twentieth-century sociological, psychological and anthropological theorists such as Arnold van Gennep (1960; on rites of passage), Maurice Halbwachs (1958 and 1976; on group psychology and collective memory), Emile Durkheim (1994; on primitive types of classification) and Marcel Mauss (1954; on gifts as a form of exchange). At the same time, the influence on intellectual history of older sociological models, both the individualism represented by Max Weber or the grand post-war macrohistorical schemes of Barrington Moore and Talcott Parsons, has steadily declined since the early 1970s.

Among the most notable 'micro-histories' to adopt the anthropological approach Carlo Ginzburg's *The Cheese and the Worms* (1980) stands out as a celebrated study of the colourfully heterodox cosmos of a late sixteenth-century Friulian miller named Menocchio; this book has shed new light on the relationship between educated and popular culture, and shown how the marginally literate could combine elements of oral and written culture into a distinctive world-view. David Warren Sabean's *Power in the Blood* (1984) is a set of complex essays on 'village discourse' in early modern Germany. In a similar vein one may also list Judith Brown's (1986) description of the mental and sexual life of an Italian lesbian nun at the beginning of the seventeenth century; Mark Phillips's (1987) account of the outlook of early Medici Florence in the context of a single minor merchant and his humanist and commercial activities; Steven Ozment's (1983) investigation of German familial relations and emotions through the letters of a Nuremberg couple; Paul Seaver's (1985) reconstruction from manuscript of the mentality of the atypically prolific Nehemiah Wallington, a seventeenth-century London artisan; and Natalie Zemon Davis's numerous essays on popular beliefs, attitudes, pardon tales and rituals in sixteenth-century France, including her retelling of *The Return of Martin Guerre* (1983), a famous incident of impersonation in a sixteenth-century French village. The word 'mentality' (or, as frequently, the French form *mentalité*) figures prominently in such studies, and though the term is extremely amorphous (Vovelle 1990), it may be said to include the conceptual and linguistic universe of early modern people: not so much what they thought as the ways in which they thought it – how they constructed thought and speech out of the language, ideas, material objects, games, rituals and social relations that surrounded them. Through all of this, there has been a clear tendency to devalue the Great Man and the Great Idea and to come instead to an understanding of the more commonplace and ordinary, of 'everyday' attitudes toward facts of life such as sex, recreation and illness – and, ultimately, even death itself, the subject of major studies by Philippe Ariès (1981), Pierre Chaunu (1978) and Michel Vovelle (1983).

Among the tools borrowed from anthropology by historians of mentality, the most important may be that which Clifford Geertz termed 'thick description', the intensive study of social rituals as a type of communication, in which the structure, as well as the content, of the ritual is decoded for its multiple levels of meaning. Here the question arises whether techniques used by an observant, physically present anthropologist (Geertz's much-cited dissection of a Balinese cock-fight, for instance) can be applied retroactively to documents or artefacts, the sole surviving traces of past events: in other words, does thick description lead the historian on to thin ice (Geertz, 1993; 1983; 1980)? Critics of anthropologically inspired histories such as those listed above point to their limited evidentiary foundation. They are invariably based on single incidents or cases, which, however interesting and entertaining, may be misleading as to the outlook of society as a whole, or even of particular segments of society. Often, though not always, they derive (as in the case of Ginzburg's work) from notes and records kept by contemporaries who were outside and above, and in some instances hostile to, the culture being described. Are inquisitorial records a reliable guide to the thought of the persecuted Menocchio?

How much weight can be placed on the reminiscenses, many years later, of a print-shop worker recalling a mid-eighteenth century 'massacre of cats', as described by Robert Darnton (1984; 1990)? More positivistically inclined socio-cultural historians, following the lead of Durkheim, point persistently to the question of typicality and to the need to quantify or 'measure' such incidents in a systematic and rigorous fashion. In response, the practitioners of what a recent volume of essays, edited by Lynn Hunt, has called *The New Cultural History* (1989), assert the necessity of moving away from the intellectual 'centre' of society towards the margins, in order to take account not only of the popular but also of the deviant and irrational. Astrology and popular prophecy, mesmerism, witchcraft, antinomian, heretical and millenarian religious beliefs, and, most recently, atheism have been among the most-studied topics of the past two decades – loud echoes from the history of science can be heard here. A very rich literature now exists for witchcraft in particular, which successfully combines social-psychological and anthropological explanations with the type of vigorous archival research in local archives most often associated with social history, and applies this to the study of the numerous books about witchcraft that appeared between 1480 and 1700. The result has been a colourful and multi-stranded tapestry depicting witchcraft variously as crime, sin, social relationship, as well as idea – a happy marriage of intellectual and social history. While witchcraft studies abound, the outstanding example of work which treats it as an intellectual as much as a social problem is Keith Thomas's magisterial book *Religion and the Decline of Magic* (1971), which looks at all types of early modern English popular supernatural belief, not only witchcraft. This has been revised in some important respects by such scholars as Christina Larner (1984; 1981), Carlo Ginzburg (1983) and John P. Demos (1982), the last a historian of colonial New England; and a growing body of literature on witchcraft beliefs and practices in Switzerland, Germany, Italy and France, by H. C. Erik Midelfort (1972) and E. William Monter (1976), among others, has filled out the picture further; an excellent survey of the subject and its historiography has been published by Brian P. Levack (1992; 1995).[14] Diabolism's implictions for the conquest of Spanish America has recently been investigated by Fernando Cervantes, while the general impact of European culture in the New World has been well handled in several wide-ranging studies (Brading 1991; Pagden 1982; MacCormack 1991).

Perhaps the most pressing question of the past decade or so has been the nature of the relationship between 'popular' and 'elite' culture. The earliest summaries of literature on popular culture, most notably those by Peter Burke (1994) and Robert Muchembled (1985), suggested that the early modern period is best understood as an era of growing separation between the culture of the educated and that of the illiterate, as the former tried to distance themselves from a culture they increasingly

---

14   Another survey is provided in Klaits 1985. There is also an extensive literature on the witch hunts from a feminist perspective, such as, most recently, Hester 1992; although the claims and assertions put forth in some of this literature are often extreme and ahistorical, the gender dimension of the witch hunts is an important one on which considerable research remains to be done.

327

found distasteful and 'vulgar' in the modern sense of that word. More recent interpretations have retained the importance of social and economic stratification as a controlling factor in intellectual and cultural history, but have jettisoned the notion of a sharp rift in cultures, opting rather for a more dynamic picture whereby multiple layers of culture, beliefs and ideas, originating within but not confined to the various orders of society, continued to interact. Roger Chartier (1987, esp. 71–109 and 240–64), for instance, has recently argued that the elites of France sought not simply to abandon or repudiate popular culture but to drag it into educated respectability, a task accomplished in part by subverting it with their own beliefs and values. These were often conveyed informally (in sermons, proclamations and public rituals), but could also be more deliberately transmitted in printed media such as the *Bibliothèque Bleue*, a series of cheap books published from the late seventeenth century for the 'benefit' of popular audiences which sanitized the ribald and heterodox tales and ballads in oral culture; the connection between the historiography of culture and that of communications, described above, has of necessity become a close one. This model is now being put to the test for other regions of Europe and served as a major theme of an international conference on the history of popular culture held at the University of Essex in April 1991 – an excitingly anarchic three-day meeting which was, the present author recalls, unable to produce any sort of consensus as to what precisely constituted 'popular' culture, let alone how best to study it![15]

Although Marxism has only had limited relevance to early modern European intellectual history, at least in the North Atlantic world, the writings of the pre-war Italian revisionist Marxist Antonio Gramsci are regaining stature; Gramsci conceived of intellectual change in a way which loosely anticipates Kuhn, as a process whereby one among a number of competing cultures achieves 'hegemony' over others which nevertheless may endure and strive toward its subversion.[16] Similarly, the long-neglected Russian critic Mikhail Bakhtin, author of a suggestive, if now widely criticized, study of popular culture in the writings of Rabelais (Bakhtin 1984), is reappearing in the footnotes of scholars studying forms of popular festivities (for instance, carnivals, processions and charivari, as explored by Emmanuel Le Roy Ladurie (1979) and Natalie Zemon Davis (1975) among others) and their relationship with early modern theatre.

There can be little doubt that as we move towards the twenty-first century, intellectual historians of early modern Europe will have to continue to take account of anthropology, sociology and social psychology. Even psychohistory (in the Freudian–Eriksonian sense of a psychoanalysis of the lives of past subjects through their writings and recorded actions) seems to be making a cautious comeback after decades of existence on the margins of political history, as a potential instrument for explaining intellectual change: recent psychobiographical works have examined the early lives of France's Louis XIII and Britain's Charles I for deeply buried explanations of their later careers (Marvick 1986; Carleton 1995). Historians will

---

15 For a recent anthology on popular culture, see Mukerji and Schudson 1991.
16 Two accessible recent anthologies of Gramsci's writing are Gramsci 1977.

also have to take note of literary theory, though here the long-standing disciplinary barriers, if often hurdled, remain very much in place. However much they may claim to be interested in literature, historians have since Ranke thought of themselves as students of fact. Old habits die hard, even among intellectual historians, who have always used texts relatively more than documents, and visited libraries with greater frequency than archives. Because literary theory is writing about writing, it seems to many to be yet one step further removed from 'reality'. That this is changing has much to do with historical circumstances within the Western intellectual community over the past few years – for instance with the fact that some of the most influential figures, such as Michel Foucault (1926–84), have been historians of sorts, albeit not of the kind that usually inhabits history departments. Foucault's work, which has been steadily gaining influence since his death, stressed ruptures and discontinuities in the history of knowledge rather than smooth evolution. He repudiated any sort of hunt for the origins of modern ideas in favour of an attempt to uncover various historical strata of knowledge, which could be best represented not as an unbroken story, but in a genealogy or 'archaeology' of knowledge. One of his first books, *The Order of Things*, explained early modern intellectual history as a succession of 'epistemes', controlling modes of representing knowledge (the Renaissance emphasis on analogy, for instance, versus the Enlightenment stress on listing and breaking down entities into their constituent parts). These epistemes bear some resemblance to Kuhn's scientific paradigms but the two ought not to be confused, since Foucault was more concerned to demonstrate homologies between disciplines than to account for the existence of any agenda-setting paradigm within a particular discipline.[17]

In the wake of Foucault's various works on the history of madness, sexuality and punishment (many of which have focused on what Foucault himself called the 'classical' period between the late Renaissance and the early nineteenth century), intellectual historians and literary scholars alike have turned their attention to discourse, to the nature of power relations both political and intellectual. For the literary scholars, such enquiries, often known as the 'New Historicism', take the form of an analysis of literary texts as artefacts, and, conversely, of artefacts, rituals and images as literary texts; this has further narrowed the gap between historical and literary studies (Veeser 1989, 1994; B. Thomas 1991).

Yet outside this immediate circle, it must be said that relatively little use, thus far, has been made of Foucault, and still less of various other forms of post-structuralism. Intellectual historians are increasingly employing fashionable terms like 'deconstruction', 'reader-response' and 'hermeneutics', but the number of early modern historians who have read (much less understood) Derrida, Gadamer, Goldmann, Lukács, Lacan, Lyotard, de Certeau and Barthes remains small; this is in striking contrast to the nearly godlike status these critics now enjoy among the

---

17 Foucault 1994; 1965; 1970; a selection is available in Foucault 1984. As with Vico, the quantity of material on Foucault is vast, and growing yearly; a good introduction to certain aspects is the collected volume Jones and Porter 1994.

intellectual historians of nineteenth- and twentieth-century Europe, for instance Dominick LaCapra (1985, 1983) and Hayden White (1973, 1987). It is to be expected, however, that just as early modernists have now adopted Geertz and Gramsci into their family, so post-structuralism of various sorts will continue to seep into books and periodicals. There is something of a trendy rush to be fashionably multidisciplinary here – it is no accident that major granting agencies, especially in North America, are increasingly willing to support historical investigations that draw on literary as well as social science techniques or sources – and much of what is now being done may not long stand the test of time. Intellectual history, may, in short, be at a crossroads, a period of paradigm 'crisis' such as that proposed by Kuhn, though it is unclear whether out of all this any single method is likely to command the support of a majority of historians. For all this apparent Babel, and perhaps because of it, it is a particularly exciting time to be an intellectual historian of early modern Europe.

REFERENCES

Albritton, C. C. (1980) *The Abyss of Time: Changing Conceptions of the Earth's Antiquity after the Sixteenth Century*, San Francisco.
Allen, D. C. (1964) *Doubt's Boundless Sea: Skepticism and Faith in the Renaissance*, Baltimore.
Allen, J. W. (1977) *A History of Political Thought in the Sixteenth Century*, London and Totowa, NJ.
Andersson, G. (1994) *Criticism and the History of Science: Kuhn's, Lakatos's, and Feyrabend's Criticisms of Critical Rationalism*, Leiden and New York.
Ariès, P. (1981) *The Hour of Our Death*, tr. H. Weaver, New York.
Bakhtin, M. (1984) *Rabelais and his World*, tr. H. Iswolsky, Bloomington.
Baron, H. (1966) *The Crisis of the Early Italian Renaissance: Civic Humanism and Republican Liberty in an Age of Classicism and Tyranny*, Princeton.
Barret-Kriegel, B. (1988) *Les historiens et la monarchie*, 4 vols., Paris.
Becker, C. (1991) *The Heavenly City of the Eighteenth-Century Philosophers*, New Haven, CT.
Boas, G. (1969) *The History of Ideas: an Introduction*, New York.
Bouwsma, W. (1968) *Venice and the Defense of Republican Liberty: Renaissance Values in the Age of the Counter-Reformation*, Berkeley.
Brading, D. A. (1991) *The First America*, Cambridge.
Bronowski, J. (1974) *The Ascent of Man*, Boston.
Brown, J. C. (1986) *Immodest Acts: The Life of a Lesbian Nun in Renaissance Italy*, New York.
Burke, P. (1969) *The Renaissance Sense of the Past*, London.
—— (1985) *Vico*, Oxford.
—— (1992) *History and Social Theory*, Cambridge.
—— (1994) *Popular Culture in Early Modern Europe*, rev. edn, Aldershot.
Butterfield, H. (1965) *The Origins of Modern Science, 1300–1800*, New York.
Camporeale, S. (ed.) (1972) *Lorenzo Valla. Umanesimo e teologia*, Florence.
Cantimori, D. (1992) *Eretici italiani del Cinquecento e altri scritti*, ed. A. Prosperi, Turin.
Capp, B. (1979) *English Almanacs, 1500–1800: Astrology and the Popular Press*, Ithaca, NY.
Carleton, C. (1995) *Charles I: The Personal Monarch*, 2nd edn, London and New York.
Cervantes, F. (1994) *The Devil in the New World*, New Haven, Conn.
Chartier, R. (1987) *The Cultural Uses of Print in Early Modern France*, tr. L. G. Cochrane, Princeton.
—— (1988) *Cultural History: Between Practices and Representations*, tr. L. G. Cochrane, Ithaca, NY.

—— (1994) *The Order of Books: Readers, Authors and Libraries in Europe between the Fourteenth and Eighteenth Centuries*, tr. L. G. Cochrane, Oxford.

Chrisman, M. U. (1982) *Lay Culture, Learned Culture, Books and Social Change in Strasbourg, 1480–1599*, New Haven, CT.

Clagett, M. (ed.) (1959) *Critical Problems in the History of Science*, Madison, WI.

Cochrane, E. (1981) *Historians and Historiography in the Italian Renaissance*, Chicago.

Cohen, H. F. (1994) *The Scientific Revolution: A Historiographical Inquiry*, Chicago.

Cohen, I. B. (1985) *Revolution in Science*, Cambridge, MA.

Collingwood, R. G. (1993) *The Idea of History*, ed. J. van der Dussen, Oxford.

Cotroneo, G. (1971) *I trattatisti dell'ars historica*, Naples.

Croce, B. (1990) *Benedetto Croce. Essays on Literature and Literary Criticism*, ed and tr. H. E. Moss, Albany, NY.

Crombie, A. (1952) *Augustine to Galileo: The History of Science, A.D. 400–1650*, London.

—— (1963) *Scientific Change: Historical Studies in the Intellectual, Social, and Technical Conditions for Scientific Discovery and Technical Invention*, New York.

Darnton, R. (1979) *The Business of Enlightenment: A Publishing History of the Encyclopédie, 1775–1800*, Cambridge, MA.

—— (1984) *The Great Cat Massacre and Other Episodes in French Cultural History*, New York.

—— (1990) *The Kiss of Lamourette: Reflections in Cultural History*, New York.

—— (1995) *The Forbidden Best-sellers of Pre-revolutionary France*, New York.

Daston, L. (1988) *Classical Probability in the Enlightenment*, Princeton.

Davis, N. Z. (1975) *Society and Culture in Early Modern France: Eight Essays*, Stanford.

—— (1983) *The Return of Martin Guerre*, Cambridge, MA.

Debus, A. G. (1991) *The French Paracelsians: The Chemical Challenge to Medical and Scientific Tradition in Early Modern France*, Cambridge.

De Caprariis, V. (1950) *Francesco Guicciardini: Dalla politica alla storia*, Bari.

Demos, J. P. (1982) *Entertaining Satan: Witchcraft and the Culture of Early New England*, New York.

Dunn, J. (1969) *The Political Thought of John Locke: An Historical Account of the Argument of the 'Two Treatises of Government'*, London.

Durkheim, E. (1994) *Durkheim on Religion*, ed. W. S. F. Pickering, Atlanta, GA.

—— (1995) *The Elementary Forms of Religious Life*, tr. and ed. K. E. Fields, New York.

Eisenstein, E. L. (1979) *The Printing Press as an Agent of Change: Communications and Cultural Transformations in Early Modern Europe*, 2 vols, Cambridge.

—— (1983) *The Printing Revolution in Early Modern Europe*, Cambridge.

Evans, R. J. W. (1984) *Rudolf II and his World: A Study in Intellectual History, 1576–1612*, 2nd edn, Oxford.

Febvre, L. (1982) *The Problem of Unbelief in the Sixteenth Century: The Religion of Rabelais*, tr. B. Gottlieb, Cambridge, MA.

—— and Martin, H.-J. (1984) *The Coming of the Book*, tr. D Gerard and ed. G. Nowell-Smith and D. Wootton, London.

Figgis, J. N. (1914) *The Divine Right of Kings*, 2nd edn, Cambridge.

Findlen, P. (1994) *Possessing Nature: Museums, Collecting, and Scientific Culture in Early Modern Italy*, Berkeley.

Foucault, M. (1965) *Madness and Civilization: A History of Insanity in the Age of Reason*, tr. R. Howard, New York.

—— (1970) *The Order of Things: An Archaeology of the Hunan Sciences*, New York and London.

—— (1976) *The Archaeology of Knowledge*, tr. A. M. Sheridan-Smith, New York.

—— (1984) *The Foucault Reader*, ed. P. Rabinow, New York.

—— (1994) *The Birth of the Clinic: An Archaeology of Medical Perception*, tr. A. M. Sheridan Smith, New York.

Franklin, J. H. (1963) *Jean Bodin and the Sixteenth-Century Revolution in the Methodology of Law and History*, New York.
Furet, F. and Ozouf, J. (1982) *Reading and Writing: Literacy in France from Calvin to Jules Ferry*, Cambridge.
Fussner, F. S. (1962) *The Historical Revolution*, New York.
Garin, E. (1978) *Science and Civic Life in the Italian Renaissance*, tr. P. Munz, Gloucester, MA.
—— (1983) *Astrology in the Renaissance: The Zodiac of Life*, tr. C Jackson and J. Allen, London.
Geertz, C. (1980) *Negara: The Theatre State in Nineteenth-Century Bali*, Princeton.
—— (1983) *Local Knowledge: Further Essays in Interpretive Anthropology*, New York.
—— (1993) *The Interpretation of Cultures: Selected Essays*, London.
Gennep, A. van (1960) *The Rites of Passage*, tr. M. B. Vizedom and G. L. Caffee, Chicago.
Giannantonio, P. (1972) *Lorenzo Valla, filologo e storiografo dell' umanesimo*, Naples.
Gilbert, F. (1965) *Machiavelli and Guicciardini: Politics and History in Sixteenth-Century Florence*, Princeton.
Ginzburg, C. (1980) *The Cheese and the Worms: The Cosmos of a Sixteenth-Century Miller*, tr. J. and A. Tedeschi, Baltimore.
—— (1983) *Night Battles: Witchcraft and Agrarian Cults in the Sixteenth and Seventeenth Centuries*, tr. J. and A. Tedeschi, Baltimore.
Grafton, A. (1993) *Joseph Scaliger*, vol 2. Oxford.
Grafton, A. and Jardine, L. (1986) *From Humanism to the Humanities: Education and the Liberal Arts in Fifteenth- and Sixteenth-Century Europe*, Cambridge, MA.
Gramsci, A. (1977) *Antonio Gramsci: Selections from the Political Writings, 1910–1920*, ed. Q. Hoare and tr. J. Mathews, London.
Green, L. (1972) *Chronicle into History: An Essay on the Interpretation of History in Florentine Fourteenth-Century Chronicles*, Cambridge.
Grendler, P. F. (1989) *Schooling in Renaissance Italy: Literacy and Learning, 1300–1600*, Baltimore.
Guenée, B. (1980) *Histoire et culture historique dans l'Occident médiéval*, Paris.
Gunn, J. A. W. (1969) *Politics and the Public Interest in the Seventeenth Century*, London.
—— (1983) *Beyond Liberty and Property: The Process of Self-recognition in Eighteenth-Century Political Thought*, Kingston.
Gutting, G. (ed.) (1980) *Paradigms and Revolutions: Applications and Appraisals of Thomas Kuhn's Philosophy of Science*, Notre Dame and London.
Halbwachs, M. (1958) *The Psychology of Social Class*, tr. C. Delavenay, London.
—— (1976) *Les Cadres sociaux de la mémoire*, Paris.
Hall, A. R. (1983) *The Revolution in Science, 1500–1750*, London.
—— (1993) *All was Light: An Introduction to Newton's Opticks*, Oxford.
—— and Hall, M. B. (1988) *A Brief History of Science*, Ames.
Hampsher-Monk, I. (1984) 'Review article. Political languages in time – the work of J. G. A. Pocock', *British Journal of Political Science* 14: 89–116.
Hankins, J. (1995) 'The "Baron Thesis" after forty years', *Journal of the History of Ideas* 56: 309–38.
Hester, M. (1992) *Lewd Women and Wicked Witches: A Study of the Dynamics of Male Domination*, London.
Höpfl, H. (1975) 'John Pocock's new history of political thought', *European Studies Review* 5: 193–206.
Hunt, L. (ed.) (1989) *The New Cultural History*, Berkeley.
Hunter, M. (1989) *Establishing the New Science: The Experience of the Early Royal Society*, Woodbridge.
—— (1995) *Science and the Shape of Orthodoxy: Intellectual Change in Late Seventeenth-Century Britain*, Woodbridge.

Huppert, G. (1970) *The Idea of Perfect History: Historical Erudition and Historical Philosophy in Renaissance France*, Urbana.

Jacob, M. C. (1988) *The Cultural Meaning of the Scientific Revolution*, Philadelphia.

Jones, C. and Porter, R. (ed.) (1994) *Reassessing Foucault: Power, Medicine, and the Body*, London and New York.

Kelley, D. R. (1970) *Foundations of Modern Historical Scholarship: Language, Law, and History in the French Renaissance*, New York.

—— (1990) *The History of Ideas: Canon and Variations*, Rochester, NY.

—— and Popkin, R. H. (eds) (1991) *The Shapes of Knowledge from the Renaissance to the Enlightenment*, Dordrecht and Boston.

Keohane, N. O. (1980) *Philosophy and the State in France: The Renaissance to the Enlightenment*, Princeton.

Kessler, E. (1978) *Petrarca und die Geschichte: Geschichtsschreibung, Rhetorik, Philosophie im übergang vom Mittelalter zur Neuzeit*, Munich.

Klaits, J. (1985) *Servants of Satan – The Age of the Witch Hunts*, Bloomington.

Knape, J. (1984) *Historie in Mittelalter und früher Neuzeit: Begriffs- und gattungsgeschichtliche Untersuchungen im interdisziplinären Kontext*, Baden-Baden.

Knowles, D. (1963) *Great Historical Enterprises*, London and New York.

Kuhn, T. S. (1970) *The Structure of Scientific Revolutions*, Chicago.

Labrousse, E. (1963–4) *Pierre Bayle*, 2 vols, The Hague.

LaCapra, D. (1983) *Rethinking Intellectual History: Texts, Contexts, Languages*, Ithaca, NY.

—— (1985) *History and Criticism*, Ithaca, NY.

Lakatos, I. and Musgrave, A. (eds) (1970) *Criticism and the Growth of Knowledge*, Cambridge.

Larner, C. (1981) *Enemies of God: The Witch-Hunt in Scotland*, London.

—— (1984) *Witchcraft and Religion: The Politics of Popular Belief*, ed. A. Macfarlane, Oxford.

Laslett, P. (ed.) (1960) *Locke, Two Treatises of Government*, Cambridge.

Le Roy Ladurie, E. (1979) *Carnival in Romans*, tr. M. Feeney, New York.

Levack, B. P. (ed.) (1992) *Articles on Witchcraft, Magic, and Demonology*, 12 vols, New York.

Levack, B. P. (1995) *The Witch-Hunt in Early Modern Europe*, 2nd edn, London.

Levine, J. M. (1977) *Dr Woodward's Shield: History, Science, and Satire in Augustan England*, Berkeley.

—— (1987) *Humanism and History*, Ithaca, NY.

Lindberg, D. C. (1990) 'Conceptions of the Scientific Revolution from Bacon to Butterfield: a preliminary sketch', in D. C. Lindberg and R. S. Westman (eds) *Reappraisals of the Scientific Revolution*, Cambridge.

Lovejoy, A. O. (1936) *The Great Chain of Being*, Cambridge, MA.

MacCormak, S. (1991) *Religion in the Andes*, Princeton.

McCuaig, W. (1989) *Carlo Sigonio: The Changing World of the Late Renaissance*, Princeton.

McLuhan, M. (1962) *The Gutenberg Galaxy: The Making of Typographic Man*, Toronto.

Mandrou, R. (1964) *De la culture populaire aux XVIIe et XVIIIe siècles: La Bibliothèque bleue de Troyes*, Paris.

Manuel, F. B. (1963) *Isaac Newton, Historian*, Cambridge.

Marvick, E. W. (1986) *Louis XIII: The Making of a King*, New Haven, CT.

Mauss, M. (1954) *The Gift: Forms and Functions of Exchange in Archaic Societies*, tr. I. Cunnison, Glencoe, IL.

Meinecke, F. (1972) *Historism*, tr. J. E. Anderson [tr. rev. by H. D. Schmitt], London.

Merchant, C. (1980) *The Death of Nature: Women, Ecology, and the Scientific Revolution*, San Francisco.

Merton, R. K. [1938] (1970) *Science, Technology and Society in Seventeenth-Century England*, New York.

Midelfort, H. C. E. (1972) *Witch Hunting in Southwestern Germany, 1562–1684*, Stanford.

Miller, P. (1939) *The New England Mind: The Seventeenth Century*, New York.

333

Minogue, K. (1988) 'Method in intellectual history: Quentin Skinner's *Foundations*', in J. Tully (ed.) *Meaning and Context: Quentin Skinner and his Critics*, Cambridge.

Monter, W. (1976) *Witchcraft in France and Switzerland: The Borderlands during the Reformation*, Ithaca, NY.

Muchembled, R. (1985) *Popular Culture and Elite Culture in France, 1400–1750*, tr. L. Cochrane, Baton Rouge.

Mukerji, C. and Schudson, M. (eds) (1991) *Rethinking Popular Culture*, Berkeley.

Mumford, L. (1934) *Technology and Civilization*, New York.

Ong, W. J. (1958) *Ramus, Method, and the Decay of Dialogue: from the Art of Discourse to the Art of Reason*, Cambridge, MA.

Ozment, S. E. (1983) *When Fathers Ruled: Family Life in Reformation Europe*, Cambridge, MA.

—— (1986) *Magdalena and Balthasar: An Intimate Portrait of Life in 16th-Century Europe*, New York.

—— (1990) *Three Behaim Boys: Growing up in Early Modern Germany*, New Haven, CT.

Pagden, A. (1982) *The Fall of Natural Man*, Cambridge.

—— (ed.) (1987) *The Languages of Political Theory in Early-Modern Europe*, Cambridge.

Parrington, V. L. (1987) *Main Currents in American Thought: An Interpretation of American Literature from the Beginnings to 1920*, 3 vols, Norman, OK.

Pertusi, A. (ed.) (1970) *La storiografia veneziana fino al secolo XVI. Aspetti e problemi*, Florence.

Phillips, M. (1977) *Francesco Guicciardini: The Historian's Craft*, Toronto.

—— (1987) *The Memoir of Marco Parenti: A Life in Medici Florence*, Princeton.

Pitkin, H. F. (1984) *Fortune is a Woman: Gender and Politics in the Thought of Niccolò Machiavelli*, Berkeley.

Pocock, J. G. A. (1975) *The Machiavellian Moment: Florentine Political Thought and the Atlantic Republican Tradition*, Princeton.

—— (1987) *The Ancient Constitution and the Feudal Law: A Study of English Historical Thought in the Seventeenth Century. A Reissue with a Retrospect*, Cambridge.

Popkin, R. H. (1979) *The History of Scepticism from Erasmus to Spinoza*, rev. edn, Berkeley.

Popper, K. (1959) *The Logic of Scientific Discovery*, New York.

Porter, R. (1977) *The Making of Geology: Earth Science in Britain, 1660–1815*, Cambridge and New York.

—— (1995) *Disease, Medicine and Society in England, 1550–1860*, 2nd edn, New York.

Quiñones, R. (1972) *The Renaissance Discovery of Time*, Cambridge, MA.

Ranum, O. A. (1980) *Artisans of Glory: Writers and Historical Thought in Seventeenth-Century France*, Chapel Hill, NC.

Redondi, P. (1987) *Galileo: Heretic*, tr. R. Rosenthal, Princeton.

Richter, M. (1995) *The History of Political and Social Concepts: A Critical Introduction*, New York.

Rossi, P. (1968) *Francis Bacon: From Magic to Science*, tr. S. Rabinovich, London.

—— (1984) *The Dark Abyss of Time: The History of the Earth and the History of Nations from Hooke to Vico*, tr. L. G. Cochrane, Chicago.

Sabean, D. (1984) *Power in the Blood: Popular Culture and Village Discourse in Early Modern Germany*, Cambridge.

Sabine, G. H. (1993) *A History of Political Theory*, 4th edn, rev. T. L. Thorson, Fort Worth, TX.

Schmitt, C. B. (1972) *The Faculty of Arts at Pisa at the Time of Galileo*, Florence.

—— (1983) *John Case and Aristotelianism in Renaissance England*, Kingston.

—— (1984) *The Aristotelian Tradition and Renaissance Universities*, London.

—— et al. (eds) (1988) *The Cambridge History of Renaissance Philosophy*, Cambridge.

Schochet, G. J. (1975) *Patriarchalism in Political Thought: The Authoritarian Family and Political Speculation and Attitudes Especially in Seventeenth Century England*, New York.

Scribner, R. (1981) *For the Sake of Simple Folk: Popular Propaganda for the German Reformation*, Cambridge.

Seaver, P. S. (1985) *Wallington's World: A Puritan Artisan in Seventeenth-Century London*, Stanford.

Seifert, A. (1976) Cognitio historica: *Die Geschichte als Namengeberin der frühneuzeitlichen Empirie*, Berlin.

Shapin, S. (1994) *The Social History of Truth*, Chicago.

—— (1996) *The Scientific Revolution*, Chicago.

Skinner, Q. (1969) 'Meaning and understanding in the history of ideas', *History and Theory* 8: 3–53.

—— (1978) *The Foundations of Modern Political Thought*, 2 vols, Cambridge.

—— (1981) *Machiavelli*, New York.

—— (1985) *The Return of Grand Theory in the Human Sciences*, Cambridge.

—— (1996) *Reason and Rhetoric in the Philosophy of Hobbes*, Cambridge.

Spufford, M. (1981) *Small Books and Pleasant Histories: Popular Fiction and its Readership in Seventeenth Century England*, London.

Struever, N. S. (1970) *The Language of History in the Renaissance: Rhetoric and Historical Consciousness in Florentine Humanism*, Princeton.

Thomas, B. (1991) *The New Historicism: and Other Old-Fashioned Topics*, Princeton.

Thomas, K. (1971) *Religion and the Decline of Magic*, New York.

Thorndike, L. (1923–58) *A History of Magic and Experimental Science*, 8 vols, New York.

Toulmin, S. E. and Goodfield, J. (1965) *The Discovery of Time*, New York.

Tuck, R. (1993) *Philosophy and Government, 1572–1651*, Cambridge.

Veeser, H. A. (ed.) (1989) *The New Historicism*, New York.

—— (1994) *The New Historicism Reader*, New York.

Verronen, V. (1986) *The Growth of Knowledge: An Inquiry into the Kuhnian Theory*, Jyvaskyla.

Vico, G. (1948) *The New Science of Giambattista Vico*, tr. T. G. Bergin and M. H. Fisch, Ithaca, NY.

Vovelle, M. (1983) *La Mort et l'occident. de 1300 à nos jours*, Paris.

—— (1990) *Ideologies and Mentalities*, tr. E. O'Flaherty, Cambridge.

Walker, D. P. (1958) *Spiritual and Demonic Magic from Ficino to Campanella*, London.

—— (1972) *The Ancient Theology: Studies in Christian Platonism from the Fifteenth to the Eighteenth Century*, London.

Watt, T. (1991) *Cheap Print and Popular Piety, 1550–1640*, Cambridge.

Webster, C. (1975) *The Great Instauration. Science, Medicine, and Reform, 1626–1660*, London.

—— (1982) *From Paracelsus to Newton: Magic and the Making of Modern Science*, Cambridge.

Westfall, R. S. (1980) *Never at Rest: A Biography of Isaac Newton*, Cambridge.

White, H. (1973) *Metahistory: The Historical Imagination in Nineteenth-Century Europe*, Baltimore.

—— (1987) *The Content of the Form*, Baltimore.

Williams, R. (1976) *Keywords: A Vocabulary of Culture and Society*, New York.

Wilson, D. J. (1980) *Arthur O. Lovejoy and the Quest for Intelligibility*, Chapel Hill.

—— (1982) *Arthur O. Lovejoy: An Annotated Bibliography*, New York.

Wootton, D. (1983) *Paolo Scarpi: Between Renaissance and Enlightenment*, Cambridge.

Yates, F. A. (1991) *Giordano Bruno and the Hermetic Tradition*, Chicago.

16

THE ENGLISH REFORMATION, 1945–1995

Patrick Collinson

I

The English Reformation was a drastic caesura, the greatest of all disjunctions in the history of a nation which has lived by a virtuous myth of continuity: greater than the revolution of the mid-seventeenth century, which was to such an extent reversed in the Restoration, or deferred and displaced into a process of more gradual political, constitutional and social change, that only Marxists and some pure Whigs are sure that those events are properly called the English Revolution. It is harder to pretend that the Reformation never happened, although, as we shall see, there are historians who would like to try; while, in the light of the latest scholarship it begins to look as if the condition of insisting that it did happen may be the admission that it was not such a drastic event or process after all.

The Reformation constituted the Church of England as self-sufficient, subject to the supremacy of the king, or the king-in-Parliament, rather than the Pope. Without the Reformation, it is likely that modern England would not have been so insular, that it would not have proved so difficult in the late twentieth century to decide on its relation to continental Europe. The Reformation in the circumstances of its enactment was no less creative for the English state, profoundly affecting the relations within the polity of crown, Parliament and law. Belief and its expression in public worship were so far transformed that in public perception 'the old religion' had been changed into something new, with cultural consequences so extensive as to differentiate two different forms of Christian civilization. One of the most Catholic of countries became, if not one of the most Protestant, virulently anti-Catholic, a xenophobic hatred of 'popery' becoming one of the defining features of its post-Reformation nationhood.

Beyond these aspects, which constitute the core of the subject, 'the Reformation' is a historical construct, an exercise in reification which lumps together a variety of things as if they constituted a coherent set of processes and circumstances. In so far as such a procedure is legitimate, the Reformation may be said to have redistributed landed property (following the dissolution of the monasteries and the secularization of other assets devoted to 'superstitious' purposes), modified the social structure which the land supported, redefined economic and social policy (including interest rates and social security), virtually invented (according to some) the modern family, and brought in its train developments in education, primary, secondary and tertiary, which had large implications for both literate and illiterate culture. Perhaps it had something to do with the Scientific Revolution. Certainly it affected profoundly perceptions of national identity and destiny, how the nation imagined itself in time and space. And these changes proved, with the passage of time, to have been irreversible, a burning of many of the boats which had brought the English people to where they were when the Tudor dynasty assumed power, at the turn of the fifteenth and sixteenth centuries.

So far as the historiography of the subject is concerned, the most important consequence of the Reformation was that it divided in religion a nation which, in its Catholicism, had been in principle and to a great extent in fact ideologically united. While Henry VIII and his immediate successors elevated religious unity to new heights of virtue and political correctness, their conflicting religious policies and settlements were ironically counter-productive, creating religious differences which have persisted ever since. Acts of Uniformity which required the entire population to participate in standardized acts of worship were defied or covertly evaded by significant numbers of both Catholic and Protestant dissenters. Religious dissent was to prove one of the most disruptive as well as creative forces in the making of modern English society. It also divided historians of the events themselves, so that the historiography of the English Reformation has always been in itself a contested, confessional thing.[1] It was so as early as the later sixteenth century, when the martyrologist John Foxe wrote his massive and tendentious history of the Church, *Acts and Monuments*, which his Catholic critics denounced as a pack of lies.[2]

Not only have there been, in every century since the Reformation, histories of the subject written in the interests of Roman Catholicism and of various kinds of Nonconformity, as well as from the standpoint of the Church of England. The established Church itself has contained more than one historiographical standpoint, reflecting tensions between Anglo-Catholic and Protestant (later 'evangelical') tendencies These became pronounced and institutionalized in the nineteenth century with the rise of the Oxford or 'Tractarian' Movement and the hostile responses to this Catholicizing trend of organized evangelical and liberal forces.

---

1   On this and other aspects of the pre-1945 historiography, see O'Day 1986. See also Dickens and Tonkin 1985.

2   On Foxe, see Mozley 1940; White 1963; Haller 1964; Olsen 1973; Bauckham 1978; Firth 1979; Collinson 1985, reprinted in Collinson 1994a: 151–77. The text of Foxe is widely available only in the highly unsatisfactory nineteenth-century eight-volume edition of S. R. Cattley and George Townsend (London, 1837–41). However, there is now a British Academy Research Project, directed by Professor David Loades, which is intended to produce a new and scholarly edition in both conventional and electronic forms.

Among the matters disputed between these parties (which included ritual, the nature of sacraments and ministry, and the fabric and decoration of churches), the Reformation itself became a bone of contention.[3] What difference had it made? Was the Church of England as redefined by the Reformation a Protestant Church, *tout court*? or was it as much Catholic as Reformed, essentially the same Church as the pre-Reformation Church and at one with other ancient churches which, like itself, retained the apostolic ministry and a Catholic liturgical and sacramental tradition, Rome included?

These questions were the legacy of the polemics of the age of the Reformation itself. Was Rome Babylon and the pope Antichrist? What was the spiritual destiny of ancestors who had perished before the Reformation? Where did the Church of England stand in relation to other, non-episcopal reformed churches, and how essential was episcopacy? If the Prayer Book was modelled on the traditional liturgies, was that something to be applauded or deplored? Was the Bible the only law for Christians, or were their consciences also bound either by the traditions of the Church or by the mandate of the Christian prince? While such questions patently separated Roman Catholics and Dissenters from the Church of England, in less explicit and more complicated ways they distracted the established Church itself.

In the court of history, these particular divisive issues have translated into the crude Sellar and Yeatman-type question: Was the English Reformation a good thing or a bad thing? And how big a thing was it? Was the Reformation no more than a politically and circumstantially motivated 'act of state', something to do with 'the King's Great Matter' (the divorce), bringing about beneficial but less than fundamental ecclesiastical reforms? Or was it a religious revolution, a total repudiation of the immediate past? In the late nineteenth and early twentieth centuries, a liberalized and influential Anglo-Catholicism was in the ascendant in both the Church and academic circles. That favoured the 'Catholic and Reformed' outlook and cut the Reformation down to size.[4]

II

We have now mapped out a historiographical minefield in which some of the mines were laid a very long time ago. However, for a couple of decades after the Second World War, it was a quiet minefield. Anglo-Catholic complacency and lack of interest aside, the reason for peace may have been a state of hostilities elsewhere, in the neighbouring seventeenth century. From the late 1940s to the mid-1960s, the bombardments exchanged across a terrain known as 'the Rise of the Gentry' (or 'The Crisis of the Aristocracy') drowned all music but its own. This historiographical

---

3 MacCulloch 1991. The 'myth', in part an Anglo-Catholic myth, is that there was no English Reformation to speak of.

4 A late example of Anglo-Catholic scholarship (according to its critics, flawed for that reason) was Dugmore 1958. For a modern, sophisticated version of 'Catholic and Reformed', see Milton 1995.

slogging match, which was to prove as inconclusive as any of the major conflicts of the twentieth century, was not a disinterested debate about changes in the distribution of wealth and in social status, however desirable such a discussion may have been. It had to with explaining the Civil War which, for some of the protagonists, was the English Revolution. That this debate (which was compared at the time in scale and substance to the debate about nature of the French Revolution, compressed into a couple of decades) engaged so much interest was due in part to the stature and rhetorical brilliance of the principal participants: R. H. Tawney, Hugh Trevor-Roper, Lawrence Stone, who directly debated the 'gentry' issue; and Christopher Hill, for whom it was a side-show and diversion from the serious Marxist agenda. These titans (mostly to be found in the University of Oxford) had no equivalent in the field of English Reformation Studies, a term not even in use in this period, for Reformation Studies hardly existed.

But it was not simply a matter of personality and talent. Underlying these engagements, which have continued more recently with different battle plans and under new generations of commanders, was the shared assumption that somewhere in the seventeenth century was to be found the fulcrum, or cusp, of modern English history. The peculiar importance of the century was the one thing not in dispute. While all this went on in Oxford, Tudor historians in London and Cambridge were reconstructing, on the basis of patient archival research, a process of state formation, the making of the polity and constitution which would tear itself apart under the Stuarts. While Sir John Neale's books on the Elizabethan parliaments (1949; 1953; 1957) were self-consciously about an institution with a manifest, seventeenth-century destiny, Sir Geoffrey Elton, whose work concentrated on the 1530s, 'The Age of Thomas Cromwell', made no connection between his 'Tudor Revolution in Government' (Elton 1953) and later revolutions, later denying that there was a 'High Road to Civil War' leading from the sixteenth to the seventeenth century (Elton 1974).

The Henrician phase of the Reformation was always close to the centre of Elton's interests. The great Reformation parliamentary statutes of which Cromwell was a prominent draftsman, and especially the 'Act in Restraint of Appeals', articulated national sovereignty and underwrote the indispensable role in the implementation and exercise of that sovereignty of a framework of law defined by Parliament.[5] For Elton, it was not in question that the Reformation happened, or what it consisted of: a series of effective public measures, fundamentally adjusting the relations of Church and state. But it was a question who was responsible, intellectually and managerially, 'King or Minister?', Henry VIII or Cromwell?[6]

---

5   See many of the articles and essays in *Studies in Tudor and Stuart Politics and Government* (1974, 1976) and the retrospective *Thomas Cromwell* (1991); as well as Elton's textbooks, *England Under the Tudors* (1955, rev. edn 1974), *Reform and Reformation, England 1509–1558* (1977).
6   Elton 1954, reprinted in Elton 1974–6: 1.173–88. The question of agency is further advanced, and complicated, in Nicholson 1977; Coleman and Starkey 1986; Fox and Guy 1986. A challenge to Elton's 'Cromwellianism' was already implicit in Scarisbrick 1968.

So, such active historical investigation of the subject as there was before the 1960s concentrated on the implementation of changes the nature and significance of which were not in doubt. Elton would declare in his second Tudor textbook, *Reform and Reformation* (1977: 371), that by the end of the reign of Edward VI (1553), England was nearer to being a Protestant country than to anything else. His sometime supervisor Neale had earlier written that by the time Elizabeth came to the throne in 1558, Protestantism was no longer a partisan but a national cause (Neale 1957: 24). The Roman jurisdiction had been abolished and the royal supremacy set up in its place. Much of the elaborate apparatus of late medieval devotion had been dismantled, together with the institutions which sustained it, monasteries and chantries. The state had endorsed and enforced modified doctrinal formulae, culminating in the undisguised Protestantism of the Edwardian Homilies and the Forty-two Articles of Religion. Archbishop Cranmer and his colleagues had incorporated protestant teaching in a deceptively traditional liturgical framework in the Book of Common Prayer. The priesthood was no longer celibate. Between 1553 and 1558, Queen Mary's attempt to put back the clock misfired, a miserable failure historically significant only in that it secured for the whole Protestant nation the paradoxical triumph of the individual martyr.

All these things were done with the instrument of legislation, whether in the form of parliamentary statute or of injunctions issued by virtue of the royal supremacy. The Prayer Book itself, technically speaking, was a mere appendix or schedule to the parliamentary acts of uniformity (1549, 1552, 1559). That Tudor historians should have fastened on this kind of documentation, made available to students in collections like Gee and Hardy's *Documents Illustrative of English Church History* (1896) Tanner's *Tudor Constitutional Documents* (1922) and Elton's *The Tudor Constitution* (1960), answered to the political-constitutional leanings of early twentieth-century English historiography, later denigrated by Professor A. G. Dickens as a form of myopia, notoriously in evidence when Maurice Powicke described the Reformation as a mere 'act of state', 'a parliamentary transaction' (Powicke 1941: 1 and *passim*).

In 1972 Elton took this politically inspired Reformation out into the country at large in the most substantial of all his books, *Policy and Police*. The subtitle is significant: *The Enforcement of the Reformation in the Age of Thomas Cromwell*. But Elton's principal source was Cromwell's government files. He looked out on England from behind Cromwell's desk, as it were, seeing and hearing what Cromwell was told, and perhaps participating in some of the optical and aural illusions which always afflict ministers.

But it would be a mistake to suppose that until very recently, sixteenth-century historians never stirred outside the Public Record Office in Chancery Lane. There was a distinct tradition of local antiquarian research only waiting to be tapped and synthesized into a new and more broadly based national history of the subject. Yet it is hardly an exaggeration to say that, until the 1960s, the dissolution of the monasteries was the only aspect of the Reformation to be thoroughly researched at every level, from the religious houses themselves in their local context, to the central business of the Court of Augmentations, and from almost every kind of relevant documentation. The topic had always enjoyed a high and confessionally charged profile (from Spelman 1698, through Cobbett 1824–7, to Gasquet 1888–9 and Baskerville 1937). It fitted comfortably within the tradition of English historiography with its respect for institutional archives. And the repercussions of the redistribution of monastic property, the subject of a considerable academic industry (see especially Habbakuk 1958), made a kind of anteroom to the seventeenth-century 'Rise of the Gentry' debate. Indeed, so much attention was paid to the dissolution that exhaustion later set in, so that the topic tends to be relatively neglected in the torrent of more recent Reformation scholarship. This suggests a failure of imagination on the part of historians, who seem to underestimate the impact of the dissolution on the imagination and memory of the sixteenth century itself (Aston 1973, repr. in Aston 1984: 313–47). However, out of the mid-twentieth century preoccupation with the last days of the English monasteries emerged one work of scholarship of enduring value: the third volume of Dom David Knowles's *The Religious Orders in England* (1959).[7]

During these relatively quiet years there appeared a history of the English Reformation written on the generous scale of nineteenth-century scholarship, a more generous treatment of the subject than most publishers would now tolerate. *The Reformation in England* (1950–4) by Philip Hughes was a three-decker affair which consequently avoided the constraints affecting all one volume accounts of the subject, which have impeded the recognition that it was only in the later sixteenth century that the Reformation really took hold. The historian who begins the story with a fast bowler's long run from behind 1500, as he must, will have written a book of acceptable length by the time he reaches 1559 and the Elizabethan Settlement, so called.[8] Hughes was a Roman Catholic priest, writing at a time as yet unaffected by the ecumenism emanating from the Second Vatican Council. His confessional bias was rarely obscured, his wide learning equally apparent, so that this ambitious study hardly deserves to live in the rain shadow obscuring books written a generation ago.

III

The year 1964 is the major landmark and even watershed in this story. It was in that year that A. G. Dickens published the first edition of a book proclaimed by its reviewers as nearly definitive of its subject, *The English Reformation*. It was after that publication, *propter* no less than *post hoc*, that there began what Dickens in his

---

7 See also Woodward 1966; Youings 1971. On the chantries, see Kreider 1979.

8 See, for example, Parker 1950. In the original, 1964, edition of *The English Reformation*, A. G. Dickens dealt with the Elizabethan Settlement of 1559 and its implications in what amounted to a postscript. In the revised edition of 1989, this was extended to three chapters, 'The Foundation of Elizabethan England', 'The Residual Problems' and 'An Epilogue', but still adding up to less than 60 pages out of a total of 396 pages of text.

preface to the revised edition of 1989 called 'an ever-growing Niagara of books and articles on the English Reformation'.[9]

Another significant shift may be detected from 1957, the year in which Patrick Collinson completed his London Ph.D. thesis, 'The Puritan classical movement in the reign of Elizabeth I'. There were to follow several decades of publications on and around the subject of Elizabethan Puritanism and the post-Elizabethan Church and religion, including *The Elizabethan Puritan Movement*, published in 1967. According to conventional taxonomies and periodization, Puritanism was another scene, a post-Reformation phenomenon operating on the periphery of the established Church and belonging to the future, the first chapter of the history of Nonconformity and Dissent. But Collinson found that he was writing the history of the Reformation itself, for the years when, for many practical purposes, it could be said to have really happened. As a series of studies of what, on the continent, is called Protestantization, this served as a corrective to Anglo-Catholic presumptions, for it located somewhere within the establishment itself the force of evangelical Protestantism. But in that it placed the effective Reformation some way into Elizabeth's reign it also pointed in a revisionist direction. Needless to say, there has been another Niagara, a veritable Victoria Falls, of publications on the Anglo-American subject of Puritanism, which even the wide-angle lens of this chapter cannot attempt to capture.[10]

To return to A. G. Dickens: in 1964 he had recently moved from the G. F. Grant chair of history at the (then) relatively obscure University of Hull (Philip Larkin was as yet little known) to the chair of history at King's College London. The change of air coincided with a development in publishing strategy which was to turn him into a national and even international figure in Reformation Studies, both insular and continental. It was the publisher B. T. Batsford who suggested that he should write a book of general scope and interest, the first of several (see especially Dickens 1966; 1968; 1974).

Hitherto, and over a period of some twenty-five years, Dickens had published a succession of closely researched and beautifully crafted articles and essays on the process of religious change in his native Yorkshire, beginning with the topic of Catholic 'survivalism' and recusancy in the later sixteenth century, but soon embracing almost every recorded aspect of sixteenth-century religion and culture

---

9   Dickens 1989: 9. The original edition (1964) was followed by a slightly revised, paperback edition (Fontana) in 1967. The first edition was dedicated to 'my colleagues in the Tudor seminar', S. T. Bindoff, C. W. Dugmore, Joel Hurstfield and Patrick Collinson. These were all appointed or recognized teachers of the University of London who were at the time participating in a Tudor Special Subject for history students.

10   Collinson 1967. Essays and studies earlier and later than 1967 are collected in Collinson 1983. See also Collinson 1979; 1982; 1988. See also the many important publications of Professor Peter Lake, and especially *Moderate Puritans and the Elizabethan Church* (1982) and *Anglicans and Puritans? Presbyterianism and English Conformist Thought from Whitgift to Hooker* (1988). There is an extensive bibliography for Puritanism in Collinson 1987. More recently, see Bremer 1993.

in that region.[11] His work had begun ahead of the post-Second World War opening up of local archives through county and diocesan record offices and owed a particular debt to a canon of York Minster, J. S. Purvis, a man who devoted his life to dusting down the records of the diocese and province of York and a good example of behind-the-scenes antiquarianism at work. The voluminous materials Purvis helped to conserve are now available to all in the Borthwick Institute of the University of York, two institutions undreamed of when Dickens began work in the mid-1930s[12].

In 1959, Dickens had published a collection of Yorkshire studies, *Lollards and Protestants in the Diocese of York*, the most notable and influential of which argues that the roots of religious change were as much endemic as exotic, to be found not only in the influence of the continental Lutheran and Zwinglian reformations but in the native Wycliffite tradition of 'Lollard' or heretical dissent. Readers of *Lollards and Protestants* were not slow to conclude that, if the Reformation had been to that extent precociously self-generating in remote and relatively backward Yorkshire (although Dickens had denied its backwardness), a fortiori in the more southerly and easterly counties where it was thought to have enjoyed its strongest support. Dickens himself extended the argument in his inaugural lecture from the King's College chair, 'Heresy and the origins of English Protestantism'.[13]

The advent of Dickens brought about both a major and a minor revolution in Reformation Studies. To begin with the minor: the spin-off from *Lollards and Protestants* revived interest in a subject long since put out to grass, the sixteenth-century vestiges of the Lollard tradition, richly documented but without conspicuous curiosity in a book by J. A. F. Thomson, *The Later Lollards 1414–1520*, which made its appearance in 1965. How coherent and significant was this tradition of native English dissent? Was it not perhaps one of those invented traditions, invented, that is, for their own polemical purposes by the first Protestant reformers themselves? – a suggestion made in 1964 by Margaret Aston (Aston 1964; repr. in Aston 1984: 219–42). Was Lollardy really the springboard for Protestantism as Dickens had suggested? Did Protestantism need and benefit from such a springboard (Knecht 1972)? Was Lollardy as readily absorbed into the wider and deeper Reformation tradition, a redundant movement which had served its function, as Dickens had assumed? Did it not rather persist, unassimilated, as a sectarianism

---

11   Many of these are collected in Dickens 1982 and 1994, which also contains the edited materials of the last days of the Suffolk religious house of Butley Priory.

12   There are many relevant pamphlets in the long-running Borthwick series, 'Borthwick Papers'. See also a number of documentary collections and calendars in the parallel series, 'Borthwick Texts and Calendars: Records of the Northern Province', and especially Smith 1973. As an example of Purvis's useful work, see his *Tudor Parish Documents of the Diocese of York* (1948).

13   Reprinted in Dickens 1982: 363–82. *Lollards and Protestants in the Diocese of York*, originally published by the Oxford University Press in 1959, is reprinted by the Hambledon Press in both hardback and paperback edns (1982).

more radical than mainstream Puritanism which would come into its own in the next century (Davis 1983; Martin 1989; Marsh 1994; Hill 1986; Spufford 1995)? More recently, our capacity to engage with such questions has been greatly assisted by the vast learning of Professor Anne Hudson, the ultimate authority on the relation of the Wycliffite textual tradition to what she has called 'the Premature Reformation';[14] and also by a number of microcosmic studies of the Lollard–Protestant–Radical interfaces conducted at grass-roots level (Davies 1991; Hope 1987; Plumb 1986; 1995).

These local studies are a small part of the rich harvest which has been gathered in since A. G. Dickens gave his lead in the exploitation of the resources of local record offices and regional archives. After 1964, Dickens himself played a reduced role in the direct prosecution of these studies,[15] but hoped to encourage and direct the work of a coming generation of local historians of the Reformation. Some of these initiatives were somewhat abortive, failing to produce monographs or even completed doctoral theses.[16] But the more general inspiration of Dickens and his writings was no doubt one of the factors favouring the post-1964 explosion of Reformation Studies, which would eventually give birth to such major achievements as Christopher Haigh's *Reformation and Resistance in Tudor Lancashire* (1975) and Susan Brigden's *London and the Reformation* (1990).[17] Haigh and Brigden were pupils, not of Dickens, but of G. R. Elton in Cambridge.

Meanwhile, the standing of ecclesiastical history in this country, including the history of the Church in the Reformation age, had been immeasurably strengthened by two great institutions, both in their inception the almost single-handed creation of C. W. Dugmore. In 1950, when he was Bishop Fraser Lecturer in Ecclesiastical History at the University of Manchester, Clifford Dugmore launched *The Journal of Ecclesiastical History*, original published by Faber and Faber and in more recent years a Cambridge University Press journal. So great has been its contribution to Reformation and Puritan Studies that it has required careful management of the '*JEH*' to preserve its wider scope and coverage of (in principle) all periods and

14 Hudson 1988. See also many of Professor Hudson's collected papers in *Lollards and their Books* (1985); and the documents published in *Selections from English Wycliffite Writings* (1978).

15 Professor Dickens lived in Essex in the 1960s and I believe had some intention to do for that county what he had earlier done for Yorkshire. Perhaps the coincidental appearance of a somewhat indifferent book on the Reformation in Essex (Oxley 1965) was a deterrent and helped to deflect his attention towards the German Reformation. But see, from a later date, his lecture on the Reformation in Northamptonshire: 'Early Protestantism and the Church in Northamptonshire' (1983–4).

16 Those who did not complete doctorates included K. G. Powell, whose valuable publications on the Reformation in Gloucestershire and Bristol included 'The Beginnings of Protestantism in Gloucestershire' (1971); Imogen Luxton, whose work was concentrated on Warwickshire, and who published 'The Reformation and Popular Culture' (1977); and Dorothy Carr, who worked on the southern counties, and collaborated with A. G. Dickens in a useful collection of documents for students, *The Reformation in England* (1967).

17 See also another regional study (of the Reformation in the West Country), coming out of the University of York and grafted on to a distinct school of south-western history at Exeter, Whiting 1989; and, more recently, Skeeters 1993.

aspects of Church history.[18] And then, in 1961, soon after taking up the chair of ecclesiastical history at King's College London (where he was the colleague of A. G. Dickens and the present writer), Dugmore founded the Ecclesiastical History Society, whose proceedings are annually published in the series *Studies in Church History*, now in its 32nd volume, plus sundry *Subsidia* volumes. Strange to say, '*SCH*' has not been notable for many studies of the English Reformation, as such.[19]

Yet another significant factor promoting the modern rush of Reformation Studies has been an initiative taken jointly by Felicity Heal (another Elton pupil) and by Rosemary O'Day (out of the King's College London stable) who from 1970 onwards convened a biennial Colloquium of Reformation (originally 'Local Reformation') Studies, regularly attended by as many as seventy, mostly younger, researchers, leading directly or indirectly to an irresistible tide of publications.[20] By now the author of *Ecclesiastes* might well have complained that of the making of many books, and even more articles, on the English Reformation, there was no end.

To rehearse the titles of all these studies would turn this chapter into a mere catalogue. Most of them are listed or otherwise noticed in the revised, 1989, edition of Dickens's *English Reformation* and in his article 'The early expansion of Protestantism in England 1520–1558'; in Christopher Haigh's 'The recent historiography of the English Reformation'; and in Rosemary O'Day's book *The Debate on the English Reformation*.[21]

But it has to be admitted that only now and again does the 'trickle-down' factor, research supervisors and their disciples, produce historical works with real staying power, which will be more than works of useful reference into the next century. The value of this 'Niagara' in sum may have been worth less than that of a single if very large book, the most imaginative and wide-ranging work of cultural and intellectual history written in twentieth-century England: Sir Keith Thomas's

---

18 Professor Dugmore's editorial successors were Peter Linehan and Brendan Bradshaw, Martin Brett and Diarmaid MacCulloch. Bradshaw and MacCulloch, like Dugmore, are sixteenth-century specialists. It goes without saying that an even more exhaustive survey than this would refer to many articles in the American journals *Church History* and the *Sixteenth Century Journal*.

19 However, vol. 3, ed. G. J. Cuming (Leiden, 1966), included Collinson 1967, Dickens 1967; vol. 9, *Schism, Heresy and Religious Protest*, ed. D. Baker (Cambridge, 1972), Bowker 1972; vol. 16, *The Church in Town and Countryside*, ed. D. Baker (Oxford, 1979), Cross 1979; vol. 18, *Religion and National Identity*, ed. Stuart Mews (Oxford, 1982), Hudson 1982a and 1982b; vol. 21, *Persecution and Toleration*, ed. W. J. Sheils (Oxford, 1984), Elton 1984; vol. 30, *Martyrs and Martyrologies*, ed. Diana Wood (Oxford, 1993), 'John Foxe and the Traitors: the Politics of the Marian Persecution'. *Subsidia* 2, *Reform and Reformation: England and the Continent c.1500–c.1750*, ed. D. Baker (Oxford, 1979) (a *Festschrift* for C. W. Dugmore) contained, among other papers on aspects of the Reformation, G. R. Elton 1979.

20 The proceedings of some of the earlier meetings were published in O'Day and Heal 1976; Heal and O'Day 1977; O'Day and Heal 1981. Since 1994 an annual Reformation Conference has been held in Cambridge.

21 Dickens's article originally published in *Archiv für Reformationsgeschichte* 78 (1987); reprinted in Dickens 133–49; summarized in *The English Reformation*, 1989 edn., pp. 325–34. Haigh's article originally published in *The Historical Journal* 25 (1982), 995–1007; and in revised form in Haigh 1987.

Religion and the Decline of Magic, which first appeared in 1971.[22] Thomas's book covers the extended period of what may be called the long Reformation, from the late fourteenth to the late seventeenth centuries, but its vision and its curiosity transcend more conventional Reformation Studies, suggesting that myopia is a relative affliction, and that not only old-fashioned political historians have been limited by a kind of tunnel vision. Thomas creates almost horizonless landscapes in which the features are witchcraft, astrology, divination, prophecy and dreams, creating at least the illusion[23] that this is an account not of what people were supposed to believe but of what they did believe (as well as of what many did not believe, or at least did not practise); and what is more, of the function of those beliefs. That Thomas's functionalism has been challenged as anthropological fashions have changed (Geertz 1975; Thomas 1971: 91–109), and would now be considered by Thomas himself to be somewhat dated, is no threat to the long life which this extraordinary book is sure to enjoy.

IV

In spite of so much almost frenzied activity, when Rosemary O'Day's *Debate* appeared in 1986 the modern debate had hardly begun, although the first shots had been fired two years earlier by Professor J. J. Scarisbrick in the published version of his Ford Lectures, *The Reformation and the English People* (1984). It was in 1987 that the current debate about the English Reformation began in earnest, and with a certain amount of heat with Christopher Haigh's publication of an edited collection of essays, mostly reprinted from learned journals, which he called *The English Reformation Revised*.[24] Haigh (1993: 335) has subsequently explained that the title intended a revision of the English Reformation, not of Dickens's *The English Reformation*. Nevertheless, the ambiguity was not lost on his readers. His initiative, and that of Scarisbrick, rapidly came, in the vulgar manner of much historical discourse, to be dubbed 'revisionism', a revisionism aimed overtly and aggressively at Dickens's account of the subject. Looking for a point at which the tide had turned, Haigh (1993: 28–9) singled out Margaret Bowker's 1981 study of the early Reformation in the diocese of Lincoln under Bishop John Longland. This vast diocese was to sixteenth-century England what 'middle America' is to the modern United States. If the Reformation was so late as to be almost non-existent, or at least non-observable, in the ten counties which stretched from the Humber to the Thames and from the north Midlands to the

---

22 A paperback edition appeared from Penguin Books in 1973.

23 The illusion may inhere in what Diarmaid MacCulloch has called the 'obstinately anecdotal' nature of Thomas's 'treasure trove' of evidence. 'Looking through the voluminous surviving archives of Tudor England, ... I am impressed by how little talk there is of witches and magic' (MacCulloch 1990: 169).

24 The only item in the collection not previously published was Ronald Hutton's analysis of churchwardens' accounts for evidence of the imposition and reception of the Reformation changes, 'The Local Impact of the Tudor Reformations', pp. 114–38.

Home Counties, how could one adhere to the doctrine of early and popular reformation?[25]

Even more crudely, Reformation revisionism has been equated with a Roman Catholic backlash against Dickens's supposed Protestant bias, thus reviving a confessional taking of sides which some might think out of place in the late twentieth century and certainly detrimental to true scholarship. Haigh (1993: vii–viii) has been at some pains to point out that he is not a believing and practising Roman Catholic. But Scarisbrick is, and so is Eamon Duffy, author of the most substantial, brilliant and influential of revisionist accounts of the subject, *The Stripping of the Altars: Traditional Religion in England c.1400–c.1580* (1992).[26] It appears that revisionism of the Scarisbrick–Duffy variety knows that the Reformation happened and deeply regrets it; while Haigh's formally value-free revisionism doubts the reality of 'the Reformation' as anything more than a convenient (or inconvenient?) historical construct, and addresses the history of a number of discrete 'reformations' which punctuated the sixteenth century; and not only the sixteenth century, there being no sound reason to elevate the Reformation, so called, above the Arminian–Laudian episode of the seventeenth century or the Methodist and evangelical revivals of the eighteenth and nineteenth (See Haigh 1993: Introduction, 'Interpretations and Evidence').

With the publication of *The Stripping of the Altars*, followed hard on its heels by Haigh's *English Reformations: Religion, Politics and Society Under the Tudors* (1993), Reformation revisionism, as a coalition of interests and insights, may be said to have come to full fruition, and even to have become the new orthodoxy, displacing Dickens's *English Reformation*, in such significant places as student essays and examination scripts, as the most plausible account of its subject. We may compare the current situation with the Dickensian orthodoxy of Professor Claire Cross's *Church and People: 1450–1660* (1976).[27]

What is at stake? Dickens wrote in 1964 to redress the balance of that 'political myopia' which, as we have seen, he diagnosed in the older historians. The Reformation arose, in underestimated measure, from 'Protestant convictions in English society', which in some regions were accentuated at an early date.[28] It was a movement and process as much social and authentically religious as political, and it involved what G. K. Chesterton once called 'the people of England that never have

---

25 Dickens's counter-argument is that it is a mistake to suppose that the historian has a commanding view of the entire religious scene on the basis of the evidence which happens, patchily, to survive. (Dickens 1983–4.) While this is formally correct, it is perhaps unlikely that religious dissent can have existed in strength (outside the Chiltern Hills of Buckinghamshire, where we know that it did) without leaving more traces in the judicial and administrative records of an episcopate such as Bishop Longland's.
26 Yale University Press sold an unusually large number of copies of the original, hard-cover edition, and the book appeared in paperback in 1994.
27 But note the cautious resistance to the new orthodoxy offered by Diarmaid MacCulloch in, amongst other places MacCulloch 1991; 1990; 1992.
28 Preface to the 1989 edn., p. 11.

spoken yet': a very Foxeian perception of what the Reformation was about. To that extent Dickens was interested in the Reformation as something pushed forward 'from below', as well as by the 'from above' world of high politics and Cromwellian bureaucracy.

Dickens was and is properly insistent that he had no intention of downplaying the political factors. Statutes, injunctions, prayer books and the like provide the essential coherence and structure of the subject. A history of the Reformation which left such things out would not be a history of the Reformation. It is, in any case, a legitimate question whether Dickens, whose original interests lay in the high culture of the Italian Renaissance, is a social historian at all or what sort of social historian he is. On the one hand, he is deeply read in the social record, especially of sixteenth-century Yorkshire. On the other, he is happily innocent of grand theory, a fierce opponent of Max Weber,[29] and not concerned to pursue the questions which interest his most illustrious pupil, the leading historian of the German Reformation as a social movement, Dr R. W. Scribner.[30] The approach is observational and empirical, owing nothing to anthropology, let alone to Bakhtin or Foucault or any other sources or springs of non-English thought. However, Dickens's essential contribution lay in the claim, which he believes to be empirically supportable, that in sixteenth-century England, even early sixteenth-century England, the Protestant Reformation was an idea whose time had come, carried on a generous social groundswell.

It is this contention with which revisionism takes issue, barring no holds in its counter-insistence that (in Scarisbrick's words), on the contrary, 'on the whole, English men and women did not want the Reformation, and most of them were slow to accept it when it came' (Scarisbrick 1984: 1). In his 'Recent Historiography' essay, which is more polemical than its bland title may suggest, Haigh makes the useful, procedural point that, in principle, the Reformation can be understood as a process working with some rapidity, early and fast Reformation, or as late and slow Reformation; and as a process initiated from above, or from below. Whereas Elton was credited with a theory of fast Reformation from above, the Cromwellian Reformation, Dickens was said to favour fast Reformation from below, a people's Refor-mation (Haigh 1988: 19–28). Revisionists are, of course, committed to slow Reformation from above, if not to no Reformation at all.

Dickens (1989: 11) has successfully defended himself against the unjustified charge of having 'the naive ambition' to write about the subject entirely and one-sidedly from below. No one has attempted such an absurd enterprise, it being universally understood that everything that happened in the sixteenth century was a complex

---

29   Dickens has often made clear his contempt for the arguments both of Weber's *The Protestant Ethic and the Spirit of Capitalism* and R. H. Tawney's *Religion and the Rise of Capitalism*, of which he has tended to make an unwarranted conflation. See, for example, Dickens 1966: 178: 'Nowadays no one has a kind word for Max Weber's thesis ... this specious theory, which was given a new lease of life – yet very little more bone and sinew – by R. H. Tawney's *Religion and the Rise of Capitalism*.' Needless to say, this seriously misrepresents the standing of 'the Weber thesis' in the 1960s, and for some time after that.

30   Scribner 1977. See also some of the essays collected in Scribner 1987.

matter of negotiation within and between the layers of society and government.[31] Only on the nature of the balance to be struck is there room for disagreement.

On the contrary, the slow–fast issue is genuinely contentious and divisive, with the episode of Mary's reign serving as a test case. Historians like Dickens still speak of the Marian 'reaction', believing that Mary's reactionary and repressive policies were bound to fail, and even insisting that her failure would have become ever more apparent if she had lived and reigned to a ripe old age (Dickens 1989: 309–15; 1994: 130–2). Nowhere is the transparent 'Whiggishness' of Dickens's version of the English Reformation more in evidence than at this critical point. Not only *soi-disant* revisionists find this hard to accept.[32] Historians of religion in the later sixteenth century, whether their interests primarily concern Catholics or Protestants and Puritans, are increasingly persuaded by their own grass-roots research and reinterpretation of the evidence that nothing was irrevocably decided before 1559, or even much before the 1580s. Historians of post-Reformation Catholicism no longer write, as Dickens once did, of a defeated but lingering 'survivalism'. Professor John Bossy's grand thesis about the death of the old Catholicism being the precondition for the birth of an essentially new, dissenting, 'English Catholic Community' has received much critical attention, from Haigh and others. We now acknowledge significant continuities between late Henrician and Marian Catholicism and the Catholic community which regrouped, outside and to some extent inside the established Church, in the decades after the Reformation, the victim of political extinction and exclusion but not of its own pathology.[33] Historians of so-called 'Puritanism' believe that the ministry of the godly Elizabethan and Jacobean preachers was the real Reformation, in a transformational and more than merely formal sense (Collinson 1984; see also p. 342, n. 10). An important and idiosyncratic work of art history, Margaret Aston's *The King's Bedpost*, underlines the fragility of the Protestant Settlement as late as 1570.[34]

There have been two particular points at issue, the one concerning so-called anticlericalism, the other the early dissemination of Protestantism; and a wider issue about the nature and vitality of what Eamon Duffy calls 'traditional religion' before and throughout the Reformation onslaught on it.

---

31 See some recent and sensitive treatments of the negotiation of religious change in Craig 1991; 1992; 1993a; 1993b.

32 But for the revisionist rehabilitation of the reign of Mary as a time of promising Catholic reconstruction, 'at one with the larger Counter-Reformation', see Duffy 1992: 524–64; and the rather cooler endorsement of Haigh 1993: 203–18: 'At the parish level English Catholicism recovered under Mary – not everywhere and in all respects ... but on the whole' (p. 215); 'the Marian Church was the Church of the 1520s writ later' (p. 217).

33 A long-running discussion can be traced through the following publications, in order of their appearance: Bossy 1962; 1975; Haigh 1981; Holmes 1982; Haigh 1984; McGrath 1984; Haigh 1985; Walsham 1993; Carrafiello 1994.

34 Aston 1993. This book relocates the famous allegorical painting known as 'Edward VI and the Pope' to a critical moment in the reign of Elizabeth I. See also Aston 1988. The importance of the reign of Elizabeth for the consolidation of Protestantism in one English county is emphasized by MacCulloch 1981 and 1986. See also MacCulloch 1990.

Anticlericalism is a term not at home in the sixteenth century, deriving as it does from the deeply fractured politics of late nineteenth-century France. In the perception of revisionists, it is doubtful whether the antipathy felt by some lay persons for some priests, personality clashes, quarrels over details of tithe payment rather than the principle of tithe itself, can be properly called anticlericalism. Even the notion of a more general conflict of interest between the laity, as such, and the clergy, *ecclesia Anglicana*, makes too much of the particular prejudices of lawyers and Londoners, especially London lawyers. It is more doubtful still (according to these critics) that anticlericalism can be regarded as a major cause of the Reformation. It is suggested that non-revisionists, desperate to discover sufficient causality outside politics, have had to invent anticlericalism.[35] The revisionist argument has been overstated, especially in Christopher Haigh's over-confident assertion, making much of the unpopularity of a new breed of clergy emerging from the Reformation: ' "Anticlericalism", in short, was not a cause of the Reformation; it was a result.'[36] The famous *cause célèbre* of the semi-heretical Londoner Richard Hunne and his quasi-judicial murder was not an invention (Ogle 1949; Wunderli 1981; Brigden 1990: 98–103). The vigorous heresy hunts conducted by the early Henrician bishops can only be accounted for in the words used by the French gentleman in the Paris zoo: 'This animal is wicked. When it is attacked, it defends itself.'

If the Reformation was a speedy success, we must believe not only that the old religion was dying on its feet but that the essentials of Protestantism were effectively disseminated and assimilated, Dickens and Elton would say, by the end of Edward's reign. Dickens believes that if we totalize all the findings of many local studies, adding a large prosopography of early Protestants compiled by Dr John Fines, we shall indeed find that by 1553 Protestantism had become 'a formidable and seemingly ineradicable phenomenon', at least in the more populous, wealthy and politically significant areas of the south and east, 'the heartland of the English Reformation'.[37] This is a technique of counting heads and of sticking pins into the

---

35 Haigh 1983. See also Brigden 1981. For evidence that the term anticlericalism is here to stay, in late medieval and Reformation studies, see a Europe-wide collection of studies, Dykema and Oberman 1993.

36 I recall a slightly less stark formulation when Dr Haigh read a version of this essay to a Local Reformation Studies Colloquium at York in 1978. Whereas in rural parishes, anticlericalism was more evidently a result than a cause of the Reformation, it may have worked as a causal factor in the towns, where there were certainly lay–clerical tensions which the sixteenth century tended to resolve (to the advantage of lay interests). A. G. Dickens responded to Haigh in 'The Shape of Anticlericalism and the English Reformation' (1987) and in an abbreviated form as 'Anticlericalism, Catholic and Protestant' in *The English Reformation*, 1989 edn, pp. 316–25. It is a fair question whether either Haigh or Dickens has been sufficiently sensitive to anticlericalism as a late medieval literary topos, part of the Satire of Estates. The whole question is placed on firmly empirical ground in Marshall 1994.

37 See n. 19 above. John Fines's *Biographical Register of Early English Protestants c.1525–1558* was published from A to C by the Sutton Courtenay Press (Appleford, 1981). The remainder was made available by the West Sussex Institute of Higher Education in 1986. Fines's census counts some 3,000 persons. Although it is an invaluable research tool it must be used with care, since the criterion for inclusion is (for the most part) a criminal (heretical) record, and it must neither be assumed that all those included were 'Protestants', nor that all early Protestants are included.

map, and to be sure by now the map fairly bristles with pins. But while this establishes in many places the presence of Protestant cells, these appear to have been minority groups. This approach cannot explain the process by which a form of Protestantism became the religion of the conforming majority.[38]

Nor, in spite of high hopes raised in the heady 1960s and 1970s, can evidence of spontaneous mass conversion be found in the religious statements ('soul bequests' and other pious bequests) included in the last wills and testaments made by the significant minority of Tudor men and women who made wills.[39] This is evidence, invaluable evidence, of many thousands of individual responses to officially inspired and legally enforced religious change rather than of an unprompted desire for change.[40] The same can be said of what the accounts of parish income and expenditure kept by churchwardens tell us about alterations to the fabric of parish churches and changes in public devotion. By and large these important sources (the favourite court of appeal of revisionists), which occur patchily, and very sparsely for the north of England, are evidence for the remarkable effectiveness of Tudor government, even in the enforcement of what revisionists are sure were very unpopular policies, rather than of the spontaneity of the Reformation in this form and sense.[41]

In the early 1990s it looked as if Eamon Duffy's *The Stripping of the Altars* had made a case for the health and vigour of traditional, pre-Reformation religion, and of a Church which Haigh has called 'a lively and relevant social institution', which in its essentials will not be overthrown. This was not 'superstition' (uttered in criticism of Sir Keith Thomas), unless all religion was (and is?) superstitious, for the superstition–religion distinction has always been arbitrary and even spurious. Nor are we talking about 'popular religion', an overworked and unfortunate term

---

38 This can be read out of the following local studies: Craig 1991 and 1993b, especially for the highly revisionist account contained in this thesis of the Reformation in the market town of Hadleigh, Suffolk, for long regarded, following Foxe, as a precocious hothouse and, as it were, open university of reform; Cross 1982; Litzenberger 1993 (and Powell 1971); Sheppard 1983. Above all this is what one learns from Brigden 1990. Studies more supportive of the Dickens perspective include Clark 1977 and G. J. Mayhew 1983. See also Mayhew 1987.

39 The use of wills for this purpose was pioneered by A. G. Dickens. See Dickens 1959: 171–2, 215–18, the 1964 edn of *The English Reformation*, pp. 191–2 and the 1989 edn, pp. 214–15. The progressive refinement of the method, and the growing recognition of its limitations, can be traced through Spufford 1971 and 1974; Zell 1977; Clark 1977: 58–9, 74–6; Cross 1984; Alsop 1989; MacCulloch 1990: 130–5; Marsh 1990.

40 Duffy 1992: 504–23. A new level of post-revisionist sophistication in the treatment of this subject, expert in its statistical methodology, is registered in Litzenberger 1993. See Craig and Litzenberger 1993.

41 Hutton 1994. Churchwardens' accounts are important sources through long stretches of Duffy 1992 and Haigh 1993. We begin to move beyond revisionism in Craig 1993a; and with Kümin 1992. Drs Craig and Kümin are collaborating in a major study of churchwardens in the Reformation period. See also Carlson 1995. This is the appropriate point to note a burgeoning interest in the late medieval and Reformation parish, as well as such collateral topics as the religious gild or fraternity. See, for example, Wright 1988. A survey of the institutional study of Church and clergy (including the episcopate) in the sixteenth century, since 1945, would require another chapter as long as this.

in so far as it indicates, not a socially cross-sectional religious consensus, but an invidious distinction between the beliefs and habits of the illiterate and ordinary masses and clerical and lay elites. As the poet Browning put it, ironically, a hundred years ago: everyone believed, in that dear Middle Age these noodles praise; everyone extending, for Duffy, from Henry VIII to the ploughman with his paternoster. Above all, this religious world we have lost did not die of natural causes. In Haigh's neat formulation, 'it was the break with Rome which was to cause the decline of Catholicism, not the decline of Catholicism which led to the break with Rome' (Haigh 1993: 28).

Whether we shall remain satisfied that the Reformation was simply imposed on an unwilling and unconvinced population, 'obedience rather than conversion',[42] is less certain. It is a question begged by Duffy, who does not seek to explain the motivation of the reformers, and it is handled somewhat prejudicially by Haigh, who works with a rather unreal notion of a Protestantism so exalted and exacting that it is hardly surprising that no one wanted to buy it. Further work is needed, and is indeed proceeding, to penetrate more of the innerness of the 'negotiation' or 'brokering' of the Reformation at local levels.[43] Even Haigh admits that by the end of the sixteenth century, England was fast becoming a Protestant nation, if not exactly a nation of Protestants,[44] a distinction not as contrived and sophistical as it may appear at first sight. Early seventeenth-century England in its public culture was manifestly an anti-Catholic nation, its new calendrical celebrations affirmative of Protestant nationhood and a Protestant dynasty (Cressy 1989). The failure of the dynasty to live up to these expectations was almost certainly the principal cause of political destabilization as the century progressed (Lake 1989; Clifton 1973; Walsham 1994; Scott 1990).

While further work on the complexities of the Protestantizing process continues, we may rest provisionally content with a hypothesis in the form of a simple syllogism. If the Protestant Reformation was as novel, alien and rebarbative as it has been represented by the revisionists, it could not have taken hold. But it did take hold. Ergo, it cannot have been all that novel, alien and rebarbative. The continuities of the age of the Reformation deserve emphasis no less than the discontinuities and from now on may receive it, this being the likely direction of a post-revisionist historiography of the subject.[45] The moral world of the early seventeenth century

---

42 Haigh 1993: 21. Obedience as a motif of the English Reformation is accentuated in Rex 1993.

43 See my remarks in Collinson 1994: 1–29. Some of the best insights into negotiation and 'brokerage' will be found in Craig 1991, 1992, 1993a, 1993b.

44 Haigh 1993: 280. In the context of a chapter called 'Evangelists in Action', Haigh modifies positions taken up earlier. However, he still writes (Haigh 1993: 282–3) of 'awesome and perhaps unachievable standards', 'too intellectual and demanding a religion, above the capacities of ordinary people'.

45 There is post-revisionist mileage in the following recent aspectual studies: Byford 1988; Watt 1991; Walsham 1995. There is an important argument running through Lake and Dowling and especially in Peter Lake's contribution, to the effect that Protestantism was not the most suitable ideology upon which to found a national Church. For the 'Anglican' enterprise of constructing a more 'broad-bottomed' base, see Lake 1988 and his further and forthcoming publications on the seventeenth century.

would not have been unrecognizable to a denizen of the early sixteenth century. Religious routines and habits die hard. Observing his flock as they came and went and said their prayers without, he thought, any apparent feeling, a Jacobean curate in Derby asked them, assuring them that he meant no harm: 'I can tell you what religion is fittest for you. Even that which we call the old religion.'[46]

Who made Protestant England? There was no English Luther, no Calvin. Three names can be mentioned, as it were in dispatches: the Bible translator, William Tyndale, who enabled God to speak in a more or less colloquial English, a fact which revisionism almost overlooks, but what a fact! (Hammond 1982; Daniell 1994.) Queen Elizabeth I, who almost held it all together, demanding no more than an outward conformity, resisting centrifugal and sectarian forces, guided more by a conservative instinct for inert survival than by any far-sighted vision;[47] and Archbishop Thomas Cranmer, whose Book of Common Prayer skilfully ameliorated and minimized the sense of drastic change, above all in his handling of those 'occasional offices', or 'rites of passage', which are the heart and soul of any religion: birth, marriage, death.[48]

That may seem to suggest that England became Protestant by a process of osmosis, in a fit of absence of mind: that this was a Reformation without tears, or blood and sweat. Nothing could be further from the truth. Mary's reign provided the blood and tears. The sweat was the underestimated sweat of all those 'godly' ministers for whom converting and consolidating sermons were the be-all and end-all of their vocation and function (Collinson 1989). And perhaps the most effective sweat was expended by ministers, schoolmasters and householders as they deployed that primary weapon of indoctrination, the catechism, for it was catechisms which probably effected the religious re-formation of the English people growing up in the three generations between the Elizabethan Religious Settlement and the Civil War. The many hundreds of separate catechisms which still survive, if only in one or two well-used copies (that is to say, hundreds of distinct titles), some running into scores of editions, may not be conclusive evidence of a success story, for they cannot tell us where they have been and what they have done. But they do suggest that in England that enhanced understanding of religious basics which all confessions in seventeenth-century Europe took seriously in hand was a Protestant understanding of (in the words of a once very familiar catechism) 'the chief end of man'.[49]

---

46   Quoted, Collinson 1994: 91. An important study (Boulton 1984) of turn-of-the-century Southwark establishes that 'everyone' took communion once a year, round about Easter, in that teeming suburb where Shakespeare was in lodgings at the time. What could be more a matter of routine than that?

47   The religion of Elizabeth I is variously assessed in Haigh 1988: 27–46, and in Collinson 1994a: 87–118.

48   MacCulloch 1996 supersedes all earlier studies of Cranmer. See also Ayris and Selwyn 1993; Brooks 1991; Collinson 1992.

49   Green 1995. For the Europe-wide campaign to internalize Christian 'basics', and especially knowledge of the Ten Commandments, and whether it was or was not equivalent to a process of primary Christianization, see the divergent views of Delumeau 1978 and Bossy 1985; and Bossy 1988. And see Strauss 1978. The 'chief end of man' was the subject of the first question in the Shorter Westminster Catechism.

APPENDIX

In all historical topics subject to revisionism and post-revisionism, there is the risk of a vicious spiral, twisting out of control into a narrowing scholasticism. How is one to teach a subject which finds itself in that condition? If Reformation Studies are to enjoy any continuing vitality, there must be more to them than the ever-closer scrutiny of the religious entrails and financial dealings of the weighty parishioners of Much-Binding-in-the-Marsh. Some of the more hopeful developments of the 1980s and 1990s have been transgressive, crossing disciplinary frontiers once fiercely defended. The work of Margaret Aston (1988; 1993) and John King (1989) from this period demonstrates the importance of iconography in the study of what was also a reformation of images. Patrick Collinson (1986; 1988) has explored the late sixteenth-century shift from an iconoclastic reform of images to an almost iconophobic rejection of pictures, even Sir Philip Sidney's 'speaking pictures', fictions. Tessa Watt (1991) and Alexandra Walsham (1994) have warned against the excesses of his too facile argument. Simultaneously, the so-called 'new historicism' currently fashionable in North American departments of English Literature has begun to explore with a new respect the literary texts of the age which C. S. Lewis once wrote off as 'drab', an episode coinciding with the first age of the Reformation and once thought to have impeded the full flowering of the English Renaissance. From the angle of the Reformation Studies reviewed in this chapter, the brilliant fireworks let off by the arch-new historicist, Stephen Greenblatt (1980; see Veeser 1989), may prove to have less enduring value than the more disciplined scholarship of John King, who has dismissed the notion of a drab age with his *English Reformation Literature* (1982; see also White 1993). But in directions such as these we are only just starting out.

REFERENCES

Alsop, J. D. (1989) 'Religious preambles in early modern wills as formulae', *Journal of Ecclesiastical History* 40: 19–27.

Aston, M. (1964) 'Lollardy and the Reformation: survival or revival', *History* 49: 149–70. (Repr. in Aston 1984.)

—— (1973) 'English ruins and English history; the Dissolution and the sense of the past', *Journal of the Warburg and Courtauld Institutes* 36: 231–55. (Repr. in Aston 1984.)

—— (1984) *Lollards and Reformers*, London.

—— (1988) *England's Iconoclasts*, 1: *Laws against Images*, Oxford.

—— (1993) *The King's Bedpost: Reformation and Iconography in a Tudor Group Portrait*, Cambridge.

Ayris, P. and Selwyn, D. (1993) *Thomas Cranmer: Churchman and Scholar*, Woodbridge.

Baker, D. (ed.) (1972) *Schism, Heresy and Religious Protest*, Studies in Church History 9, Cambridge.

—— (1979a) *The Church in Town and Countryside*, Studies in Church History 16, Oxford.

—— (1979b) *Reform and Reformation: England and the Continent c.1500–c.1750*, Subsidia 2, Oxford.

Baskerville, G. (1937) *English Monks and the Suppression of the Monasteries*, London.

354

Bauckham, R. (1978) *Tudor Apocalypse*, Appleford.

Bossy, J. (1962) 'The character of Elizabethan Catholicism', *Past and Present* 21: 39–59.

—— (1975) *The English Catholic Community 1570–1850*, London.

—— (1985) *Christianity in the West 1400–1700*, Oxford.

—— (1988) 'Moral arithmetic: Seven Sins and Ten Commandments', in E. Leiter (ed.) *Conscience and Casuistry in Early Modern Europe*, Cambridge.

Boulton, J. P. (1984) 'The limits of formal religion: the administration of Holy Communion in late Elizabethan and early Stuart London', *London Journal* 10: 135–54.

Bowker, M. (1972) 'Lincolnshire 1536: heresy, schism or religious discontent?', in D. Baker (ed.) *Schism, Heresy and Religious Protest*, Cambridge.

—— (1981) *The Henrician Reformation in the Diocese of Lincoln under John Longland, 1521–1547*, Cambridge.

Bremer, F. J. (ed.) (1993) *Puritanism: Transatlantic Perspectives on a Seventeenth-Century Anglo-American Faith*, Boston, MA.

Brigden, S. (1981) 'Tithe controversy in Reformation London', *Journal of Ecclesiastical History* 32: 285–301.

—— (1990) *London and the Reformation*, Oxford.

Brooks, P. N. (1991) *Thomas Cranmer's Doctrine of the Eucharist*, rev. edn, London.

Byford, M. S. (1988) 'The price of Protestantism: assessing the impact of religious change on Elizabethan Essex: the cases of Heydon and Colchester, 1558–1594', unpublished Oxford D.Phil. thesis.

Carlson, E. (1995) 'The origins, function and status of the office of churchwarden, with particular reference to the diocese of Ely', in Spufford 1995.

Carr, D. and Dickens, A. G. (1967) *The Reformation in England*, London.

Carrafiello, M. (1994) 'English Catholicism and the Jesuit mission of 1580–1581', *Historical Journal* 37: 761–74.

Clark, P. (1977) *English Provincial Society from the Reformation to the Revolution: Religion, Politics and Society in Kent 1500–1640*, Hassocks.

Clifton, R. (1973) 'Fear of Popery', in C. Russell (ed.) *The Origins of the English Civil War*, London.

Cobbett, W. (1824–7) *A History of the Protestant Reformation in England and Ireland*, London.

Coleman, C. and Starkey, D. (eds) (1986) *Revolution Reassessed: Revisions in the History of Tudor Government and Administration*, London.

Collinson, P. (1966) 'Episcopacy and reform in England in the later sixteenth century', in G. J. Cumins (ed.) *The Province of York*, Leiden.

—— (1967) *The Elizabethan Puritan Movement*, London.

—— (1979) *Archbishop Grindal 1519–1583: The Struggle for a Reformed Church*, London.

—— (1982) *The Religion of Protestants: The Church and English Society 1559–1625*, Oxford.

—— (1983) *Godly People: Essays on English Protestantism and Puritanism*, London.

—— (1984) 'The Elizabethan Church and the new religion', in Haigh 1984.

—— (1985) 'Truth and legend: the veracity of John Foxe's Book of Martyrs', in A. C. Duke and C. A. Tamse (eds) *Clio's Mirror: Historiography in Britain and the Netherlands*, Britain and the Netherlands 8, Zutphen. (Repr. in Collinson 1994.)

—— (1986) *From Iconoclasm to Iconophobia: The Cultural Impact of the Second English Reformation*, Reading.

—— (1987) *English Puritanism*, Historical Association Pamphlet, rev. edn.

—— (1988) *The Birthpangs of Protestant England: Religious and Cultural Change in the Sixteenth and Seventeenth Centuries*, Basingstoke.

—— (1989) 'Shepherds, sheepdogs, and hirelings: the pastoral ministry in post-Reformation England', in W. J. Sheils and D. Wood (eds) *The Ministry: Clerical and Lay*, Studies in Church History 29, Oxford.

—— (1992) 'Thomas Cranmer', in G. Rowell (ed.) *The English Religious Tradition and the Genius of Anglicanism*, Wantage.

—— (1994a) *Elizabethan Essays*, London and Rio Grande.

—— (1994b) 'England', in B. Scribner, R. Porter and M. Teich (eds) *The Reformation in National Context*, Cambridge.

—— and J. S. Craig (eds) (1997) *The Reformation in English Towns*, Basingstoke.

Craig, J. S. (1991) 'The Bury Stirs revisited: an analysis of the townsmen', *Proceedings of the Suffolk Institute of Archaeology and History* 37: 208–24.

—— (1992) 'The "godly" and the "froward": Protestant polemics in the town of Thetford, 1560–1590', *Norfolk Archaeology*: 279–93.

—— (1993a) 'Cooperation and initiatives: Elizabethan churchwardens and the parish accounts of Mildenhall', *Social History* 18: 357–80.

—— (1993b) 'Reformation, politics and polemics in sixteenth-century East Anglian market towns', unpublished Cambridge Ph.D. thesis.

—— and Litzenberger, C. J. (1993) 'Wills as religious propaganda: the testament of William Tracy', *Journal of Ecclesiastical History* 44: 415–31.

Cressy, D. (1989) *Bonfires and Bells: National Memory and the Protestant Calendar in Elizabethan and Stuart England*, London.

Cross, C. (1976) *Church and People: 1450–1660*, London.

—— (1982) 'The development of Protestantism in Leeds and Hull, 1520–1640: the evidence of wills', *Northern History* 18: 230–8.

—— (1984) 'Wills as evidence of popular piety in the Reformation period: Leeds and Hull 1520–1640', in D. Loades (ed.) *The End of Strife: Reconciliation and Repression in Christian Spirituality*, London.

Daniell, D. (1994) *William Tyndale: A Biography*, New Haven, CT. and London.

Davies, R. G. (1991) 'Lollardy and locality', *Transactions of the Royal Historical Society* 6th ser., 1.

Davis, J. F. (1983) *Heresy and Reformation in the South-East of England 1520–1559*, London.

Delumeau, J. (1978) *Catholicism between Luther and Voltaire*, London.

Dickens, A. G. (1959) *Lollards and Protestants in the Diocese of York*, Oxford. (Repr. London, 1982.)

—— (1966) *Reformation and Society in Sixteenth-Century Europe*, London.

—— (1967) 'Secular and religious motivation in the Pilgrimage of Grace', in G. J. Cuming (ed.) *The Province of York*, Leiden.

—— (1968) *The Counter-Reformation*, London.

—— (1974) *The German Nation and Martin Luther*, London.

—— (1982) *Reformation Studies*, London.

—— (1983–4) 'Early Protestantism and the Church in Northamptonshire', *Northamptonshire Past and Present* 8: 27–39. (Repr. in Dickens 1994.)

—— (1987) 'The shape of anticlericalism and the English Reformation', in E. I. Kouri and T. Scott (eds) *Politics and Society in Reformation Europe*, Basingstoke. (Repr. in Dickens 1994.)

—— (1989) *The English Reformation*, 2nd edn, London.

—— (1994) *Late Monasticism and the Reformation*, London and Rio Grande.

—— Tonkin, J. and Powell, K. (1985) *The Reformation in Historical Thought*, Oxford.

Duffy, E. (1992) *The Stripping of the Altars: Traditional Religion in England c.1400–c.1580*, New Haven, CT. and London.

Dugmore, C. W. (1958) *The Mass and the English Reformers*, London.

Dykema, P. A. and Oberman, H. (eds) (1993) *Anticlericalism in Late Medieval and Early Modern Europe*, Leiden.

Elton, G. R. (1953) *The Tudor Revolution in Government*, Cambridge.

—— (1954) 'King or minister? The man behind the Henrician Reformation', *History* 39: 216–32.

—— (1955; rev. edn 1974) *England under the Tudors*, London.

—— (1972) *Policy and Police: The Enforcement of the Reformation in the Age of Thomas Cromwell*, Cambridge.

—— (1974) 'A high road to Civil War?', in *Studies in Tudor and Stuart Politics and Government*, vol. 2, Cambridge.

—— (1974–6) *Studies in Tudor and Stuart Politics and Government*, 3 vols, Cambridge.

—— (1977) *Reform and Reformation. England 1509–1558*, London.

—— (1984) 'Persecution and toleration in the English Reformation', in Sheils 1984.

—— (1991) *Thomas Cromwell*, Headstart History Pamphlet.

Fines, J. (1981) *Biographical Register of Early English Protestants c.1525–1558*, Appleford.

Firth, K. R. (1979) *The Apocalyptic Tradition in Reformation Britain 1530–1645*, Oxford.

Fox, A. and Guy, J. (1986) *Reassessing the Henrician Age: Humanism, Politics and Reform 1500–1550*, Oxford.

Gasquet, F. A. (1888–9) *Henry VIII and the English Monasteries*, London.

Geertz, H. (1975) 'An anthropology of religion and magic, I', *Journal of Interdisciplinary History* 6: 71–89.

Green, I. (1995) *The Christian's ABC: Catechisms and Catechising in England c.1530–1740*, Oxford.

Greenblatt, S. (1980) *Renaissance Self-fashioning: From More to Shakespeare*, Chicago.

Habbakuk, H. J. (1958) 'The market for monastic property, 1539–1603', *Economic History Review*, 10: 362–80.

Haigh, C. (1975) *Reformation and Resistance in Tudor Lancashire*, Cambridge.

—— (1981a) 'The Continuity of Catholicism in the English Reformation', *Past and Present* 93: 37–69. (Repr. in Haigh 1987.)

—— (1981b) 'From monopoly to minority: Catholicism in early modern England', *Transactions of the Royal Historical Society*, 5th ser., 21: 129–47.

—— (1982) 'The recent historiography of the English Reformation', *The Historical Journal* 25: 995–1007. (Repr. with revisions in Haigh 1987.)

—— (1983) 'Anticlericalism and the English Reformation', *History* 68: 391–407. (Repr. in Haigh 1987.)

—— (ed.) (1984) *The Reign of Elizabeth I*, London.

—— (1985) 'Revisionism, the Reformation and the history of Elizabethan Catholicism', *Journal of Ecclesiastical History* 36: 394–406.

—— (ed.) (1987) *The English Reformation Revised*, Cambridge.

—— (1988) *Elizabeth I*, London.

—— (1993) *English Reformations: Religion, Politics and Society under the Tudors*, Oxford.

Haller, W. (1964) *Foxe's Book of Martyrs and the Elect Nation*, London.

Hammond, G. (1982) *The Making of the English Bible*, Manchester.

Heal, F. and O'Day, R. (eds) (1977) *Church and Society in England, Henry VIII to James I*, London.

Hill, C. (1986) 'From Lollards to Levellers', in *The Collected Essays of Christopher Hill*, 2: *Religion and Politics in 17th Century England*, Brighton.

Holmes, P. (1982) *Resistance and Compromise: The Political Thought of the English Catholics*, Cambridge.

Hope, A. (1987) 'Lollardy: the stone which the builders rejected', in P. Lake and M. Dowling (eds) *Protestantism and the National Church in Sixteenth-Century England*, London.

Hudson, A. (1978) *Selections from English Wycliffite Writings*, Cambridge.

—— (1985) *Lollards and their Books*, London and Ronceverte, WV.

—— (1988) *The Premature Reformation: Wycliffite Texts and Lollard History*, Oxford.

Hughes, P. (1950–4) *The Reformation in England*, 3 vols, London.

Hutton, R. (1987) 'The local impact of the Tudor Reformations', in Haigh (1987).
—— (1994) *The Rise and Fall of Merry England: The Ritual Year 1400–1700*, Oxford.
King, J. N. (1982) *English Reformation Literature: The Tudor Origins of the Protestant Tradition*, Princeton.
—— (1989) *Tudor Royal Iconography*, Princeton.
Knecht, R. J. (1972) 'The early Reformation in England and France', *History* 57: 1–16.
Knowles, D. (1959) *The Religious Orders in England*, 3: *The Tudor Age*, Cambridge.
Kreider, A. (1979) *English Chantries: The Road to Dissolution*, Cambridge, Mass.
Kümin, B. (1995) *The Shaping of a Community: The Rise and Reformation of the English Parish c.1400–1560*, Aldershot.
Lake, P. (1982) *Moderate Puritans and the Elizabethan Church*, Cambridge.
—— (1988) *Anglicans and Puritans? Presbyterianism and English Conformist Thought from Whitgift to Hooker*, London.
—— (1989) 'Antipopery: the structure of a prejudice', in R. Cust and A. Hughes (eds) *Conflict in Early Stuart England: Studies in Religion and Politics 1603–1642*, London.
Litzenberger, C. (1993) 'Responses of the laity to changes in official religious policy in Gloucestershire (1541–1580)', unpublished Cambridge Ph.D. thesis.
Luxton, I. (1977) 'The Reformation and popular culture', in Heal and O'Day 1977.
MacCulloch, D. (1981) 'Catholic and Puritan in Elizabethan Suffolk: A county community polarises', *Archiv für Reformationsgeschichte* 72: 232–89.
—— (1986) *Suffolk and the Tudors*, Oxford.
—— (1990) *The Later Reformation in England 1547–1603*, Basingstoke.
—— (1991) 'The myth of the English Reformation', *Journal of British Studies* 30: 1–19.
—— (1992) *Building a Godly Realm: The Establishment of English Protestantism 1558–1603*, Historical Association 'New Approaches in History' 27, London.
—— (1996) *Thomas Cranmer: A Life*, New Haven and London.
McGrath, P. (1984) 'Elizabethan Catholicism: a reconsideration', *Journal of Ecclesiastical History* 35: 414–28.
Marsh, C. (1990) 'In the name of God? Will-making and faith in early modern England', in G. H. Martin and P. Spufford (eds) *The Records of the Nation: The Public Record Office 1838–1938*, Woodbridge.
—— (1994) *The Family of Love in English Society, 1550–1630*, Cambridge.
Marshall, P. (1994) *The Catholic Priesthood and the English Reformation*, Oxford.
Martin, J. (1989) *Religious Radicals in Tudor England*, London and Ronceverte, WV.
Mayhew, G. J. (1983) 'The progress of the Reformation in East Sussex 1530–1559: the evidence from wills', *Southern History* 5: 38–67.
—— (1987) *Tudor Rye*, Falmer.
Mews, S. (ed.) (1982) *Religion and National Identity*, Studies in Church History 18, Oxford.
Milton, A. (1995) *Catholic and Reformed: The Roman and Protestant Churches in English Protestant Thought, 1600–1640*, Cambridge.
Mozley, J. F. (1940) *John Foxe and his Book*, London.
Neale, J. E. (1949) *The Elizabethan House of Commons*, London.
—— (1953) *Elizabeth I and her Parliaments, 1559–1581*, London.
—— (1957a) *Elizabeth I and her Parliaments, 1584–1601*, London.
—— (1957b) *Essays in Elizabethan History*, London.
Nicholson, G. D. (1977) 'The nature and functions of historical argument in the Henrician Reformation', unpublished Cambridge Ph.D. thesis.
O'Day, R. (1986) *The Debate on the English Reformation*, London and New York.
—— and Heal, F. (eds) (1976) *Continuity and Change: Personnel and Administration of the Church in England, 1500–1642*, Leicester.
—— (eds) (1981) *Princes and Paupers in the English Church*, Leicester.
Ogle, A. (1949) *The Tragedy of the Lollards' Tower*, Oxford.

Olsen, V. N. (1973) *John Foxe and the Elizabethan Church*, Berkeley, Los Angeles and London.
Oxley, J. E. (1965) *The Reformation in Essex to the Death of Mary*, Manchester.
Parker, T. M. (1950) *The English Reformation to 1558*, London.
Pettegree, A. (1996) *Marian Protestantism: Six Studies*, Aldershot.
Plumb, D. (1986) 'The social and economic spread of rural Lollardy: a reappraisal', in W. J. Sheils and D. Wood (eds) *Voluntary Religion*, Studies in Church History 23, Oxford.
—— (1995) 'A gathered Church? Lollards and their society', in Spufford 1995.
Powell, K. G. (1971) 'The beginnings of Protestantism in Gloucestershire', *Transactions of the Bristol and Gloucester Archaeological Society* 90: 141–57.
Powicke, M. (1941) *The Reformation in England*, London.
Purvis, (1948) *Tudor Parish Documents of the Diocese of York*, Cambridge.
Rex, R. (1993) *Henry VIII and the English Reformation*, Basingstoke.
Scarisbrick, J. J. (1968) *Henry VIII*, London.
—— (1984) *The Reformation and the English People*, Oxford.
Scott, J. (1990) 'England's troubles: exhuming the Popish Plot', in T. Harris, P. Seaward and M. Goldie (eds) *Religion in Restoration England*, Oxford.
Scribner, R. W. (1977) 'Is there a social history of the Reformation?', *Social History* 4: 483–505.
—— (1987) *Popular Culture and Popular Movements in Reformation Germany*, London and Ronceverte, WV.
Sheils, W. J. (ed.) (1984) *Persecution and Toleration*, Studies in Church History 21, Oxford.
Sheppard, E. (1983) 'The Reformation and the Citizens of Norwich', *Norfolk Archaeology* 38: 84–95.
Skeeters, M. C. (1993) *Community and Clergy: Bristol and the Reformation c.1530–c.1570*, Oxford.
Smith, D. M. (ed.) (1973) *A Guide to the Archive Collections in the Borthwick Institute of Historical Research*, Borthwick Texts and Calendars: Records of the Northern Province 1, York.
Spelman, H. (1698) *History and the Fate of Sacrilege*, London.
Spufford, M. (1971) 'The scribes of villagers' wills in the sixteenth and seventeenth centuries and their influence', *Local Population Studies* 7: 28–43.
—— (1974) *Contrasting Communities: English Villagers in the Sixteenth and seventeenth Centuries*, Oxford.
—— (ed.) (1995) *The World of Rural Dissenters, 1520–1725*, Cambridge.
Strauss, G. (1978) *Luther's House of Learning: Indoctrination of the Young in the German Reformation*, Baltimore and London.
Thomas, K. (1971) *Religion and the Decline of Magic*, London. (Paperback edn, Harmondsworth, 1973.)
—— (1975) 'An anthropology of religion and magic, II', *Journal of Interdisciplinary History* 6: 91–109.
Thompson, J. A. F. (1965) *The Later Lollards 1414–1520*, London.
Tyacke, N. (ed.) (1997) *The Long Reformation*, London.
Veeser, H. A. (ed.) (1989) *The New Historicism*, London.
Walsham, A. (1993) *Church Papists: Catholicism, Conformity and Confessional Polemics in Early Modern England*, Woodbridge.
—— (1994) ' "The Fatall Vesper": providentialism and anti-popery in late Jacobean London', *Past and Present* 144: 36–87.
—— (1995) 'Aspects of providentialism in early modern England', unpublished Cambridge Ph.D. thesis.
Watt, T. (1991) *Cheap Print and Popular Piety 1560–1640*, Cambridge.
White, H. (1963) *Tudor Books of Saints and Martyrs*, Madison.

White, P. (1993) *Theatre and Reformation: Protestants, Patronage and Playing in Tudor England*, Cambridge.

Whiting, R. (1989) *The Blind Devotion of the People: Popular Religion and the English Reformation*, Cambridge.

Wood, D. (ed.) (1993) *Martyrs and Martyrologies*, Studies in Church History 30, Oxford.

Woodward, G. W. C. (1966) *The Dissolution of the Monasteries*, London.

Wright, S. (ed.) (1988) *Parish, Church and People: Local Studies in Lay Religion 1350–1750*, Leicester.

Wunderli, R. M. (1981) *London Church Courts and Society on the Eve of the Reformation*, Cambridge, MA.

Youings, J. (1971) *The Dissolution of the Monasteries*, London.

Zell, M. (1977) 'The use of will preambles as a measure of religious belief in the sixteenth century', *Bulletin of the Institute of Historical Research* 1: 246–9.

17

POPULAR CULTURE IN THE EARLY MODERN WEST

James Sharpe

I

Over the last two decades popular culture in early modern Europe has been a major growth area in historical studies. This growth has been, in large measure, an aspect of that broadening of the historian's agenda which has opened up a number of aspects of past experience of that period to serious historical investigation (one thinks also of the family, community life, crime and popular disorder). Writing on this subject has been conducted by historians working from within different intellectual traditions and with different scholarly objectives.[1] As we shall see, these diversities of approach have ensured that there are still many unresolved problems in the field. Nevertheless, the body of work produced to date is impressive, and many features of the world of our lowly-born ancestors have been uncovered.

Despite this success, we must confront a fundamental problem before turning to a review of what has been written and what conceptual issues remain to be considered. This is that no wholly satisfactory definition of 'popular culture' has yet been formulated. 'Culture' in this context is probably best defined in an anthropological sense, as the whole social context within which the individual exists. Thus Bronislaw Malinowski defined culture as

> inherited artifacts, goods, technical processes, ideas, habits and values. Social organization cannot really be understood except as part of culture; and all special lines of inquiry referring to human activities, human groupings and human ideas and beliefs can meet and become cross fertilized in the contemporary study of cultures.
>
> (Malinowski 1937: 7)

---

1   Apart from Burke 1978 and Muchembled [1978] 1985, the history of popular culture in the early modern period is probably best approached through collections of essays: Beauroy *et al.* 1976; Davis 1975; Kaplan 1984; Reay 1985. For a recent work of synthesis, see Spierenburg 1991.

In this sense culture, as the sum total of learned behaviour, makes society possible by providing individuals with a common knowledge and a common sense of how they ought to interact with their fellow human beings. It is, essentially, the organized behaviour of mankind.

Defining 'popular' is a little more difficult. Most historians dealing with the subject seem to accept, usually implicitly, a residual definition: 'popular' culture is the culture of people who are not members of elites. This, at first sight, is a fairly straightforward definition, but one riven by a number of complications. First, it raises the problem of where to draw the line between 'elite' and 'popular', and might lead to assumptions that the two are hermetically sealed from each other. Second, the essentially non-homogeneous nature of 'non-elite' people makes discussing a monolithic 'popular' culture very difficult. There were substantial differences in economic stratification during the early modern period, for the 'non-elite' comprehended everybody from master-craftsmen and substantial peasant farmers to beggars and landless labourers. There were also separate occupational cultures, whilst regionality also created diversity: the culture of Scottish fishermen would probably have been very different from that of a Bavarian peasant, although both were undoubtedly members of the 'popular' classes. Gender also creates problems. Most aspects of popular culture studied by historians of the early modern era were male concerns, although it is now obvious that some aspects of popular culture were in large measure female concerns. And, to take a subject which has attracted some attention but which deserves further investigation, popular culture was also complicated by contemporary views of the age-hierarchy: at least some early modern societies accepted the presence of informal societies of youths and unmarried men. 'Popular culture' is one of those useful blanket terms which historians have to use, but whose essentially problematic nature should not be lost sight of.

II

In 1978 two books were published on early modern popular culture, both of them the products of scholars who have since become recognized as experts in the field. One, written by the English scholar Peter Burke, has received considerable attention. The other, written by the French scholar Robert Muchembled, and not translated into English until 1985, received less attention in the anglophone world, yet is important in demonstrating an approach to the subject.

Burke's project was to provide an initial chart of the potentialities for the study of popular culture. Obviously, in 1978 the chances of producing a full synthesis of early modern popular culture were limited (they are, indeed, not much more hopeful at present). Burke set out to make his readers aware of the problems and methodologies involved in the topic. The problem of the lack of evidence loomed large, and, given the unlikelihood of gaining direct access to the thoughts of peasants and craftsmen in the past, he suggested various 'oblique' approaches to such evidence as does survive. He at least recognized gender as an issue ('there is little to say about women, for lack of evidence. There is a 'problem of women' for historians of popular culture as there is for social anthropologists') without suggesting how it might be tackled (Burke 1978: 49). He also suggested a strategy for coping with regionality. He spoke of a

> stock or repertoire of the forms and conventions of popular culture. ... In any one region this stock or repertoire was fairly limited. Its riches and variety are apparent only when the inventory is extended to the whole of Europe; when this is done, the variety is so bewildering as almost to hide the recurrence of a few basic types of artifact.
>
> (ibid. 116)

Thoughtful, tentative, wide-ranging, Burke's book remains an essential introduction to the subject.

Perhaps the work's most striking feature, however, is the third part, on changes in popular culture. One chapter is devoted to the 'reform' of popular culture, what Burke terms the 'Triumph of Lent' (that is, over carnival). Here we see the agents of the state and, perhaps more directly, of the state Church (whether Protestant or Counter-Reformation Catholic) attacking popular culture. Burke argued that this process differed from earlier reform movements in that 'it encompassed a major shift in religious mentality or sensibility. The godly were out to destroy the traditional familiarity with the sacred, because they believed that familiarity breeds irreverence' (ibid. 212). The pressure brought to bear on popular culture was aided by other trends. The spread of literacy and of cheap printed works created changes in popular culture, although, as Burke was aware and as we shall see later, the exact nature of these changes remains problematic. Burke also claimed to have identified a 'withdrawal of the upper classes' from popular culture. Around 1500 all social groups shared a similar culture, or at least enjoyed social spheres which overlapped. By 1800 (and a good deal earlier in some areas) elites had separated themselves out of this pool of common, shared culture. They had their own cultural norms, and became distanced from those of the common people.

Muchembled's work differed from Burke's on a number of levels. The most obvious is that, whereas Burke offers a sketch map of European developments, Muchembled based his arguments squarely on the archives of what is now northern France. The most important is that whereas Burke received his historical training from Oxford tutorials, Muchembled gained his from the *Annales* tradition: that decisive strand in French historical writing which included such great names as Lucien Febvre, Marc Bloch and Fernand Braudel, and which owed much of its intellectual origins to the work of Emile Durkheim. One area of central concern to this school was *mentalité*: a term which defies direct translation into English, but which comprehends both the attitudes of people in the past and their deeper cognitive processes. Reading Burke, one always has a slight sense of accompanying an outsider looking in. Muchembled is anxious to get inside the peasant experience and the peasant mind. He devotes only a short section to sources and methods, and then plunges into the world of insecurity and fear experienced by the peasants of the Nord, the rural culture and popular customs of the region, and also its urban popular culture.

The world Muchembled portrays was not idyllic. 'This culture', he writes, 'was in reality a system of survival, and the world was full of dangers, both real and imaginary, which neither the Church nor the state could combat efficaciously' (Muchembled [1978] 1985: 4). The inhabitants of this world, experiencing fear, uncertainty, hunger, poverty and the threat of war, enjoyed, necessarily, a *mentalité* far different from that of the inhabitants of the modern West. The need for protection meant that such modern concerns as the primacy of privacy and individuality were largely lacking:

> we have to imagine every man not as an individual but as part of a collectivity … surrounded by multiple circles of kinship, friendship and solidarity that protected him, but the interests of which he also had to defend against other men equally wrapped in similar protective networks.

(ibid. 39)

Yet Muchembled, like Burke, is concerned not only with evoking early modern popular culture, but also with its repression. His portrayal of this rests on two main processes: the 'constraint of bodies and the submission of souls' which followed the 'acculturation' of the lower orders through being 'Christianized' by the Counter-Reformation; and the advent of what Muchembled terms a 'mass culture' of printed works which ultimately impressed the values of the centralizing power of the state on the masses, and hence destroyed the old oral popular culture.

III

As the analysis of these two works demonstrates, historians of popular culture in the early modern West are faced by conflicting approaches. One of these is to study the culture in terms of its more striking and better documented aspects: rituals, carnivals, riots, witchcraft trials, popular recreations. The other (and the two are far from mutually exclusive) is to try to look at the subject along lines suggested by Malinowski's definition of culture: to examine those thought-processes, that totality of mediated relationships, that shared discourse, which make society, community, or even the basic interaction of two individuals from the same culture, possible. This latter approach involves studying those apparently trivial matters which in fact mean so much in everyday life: the clothes people wear, the food they eat, the way they address each other, the way they maintain what might be described as 'front', the way in which they gesture or walk, their general comportment, what makes them laugh. And (seeing that the history of popular culture is *history*) now such matters changed over time, and how such changes were connected with other social developments.

All of this constitutes a demanding, if exciting, and potentially fascinating, agenda. Attempts to meet that agenda confront an enormous initial problem: evidence. We have very little direct evidence about the popular classes before the nineteenth century. Most of them (although far from all) were illiterate, living in an oral culture which has left few traces for the historian. Obviously, some artefacts remain, although even these are few before the eighteenth century. Hence Peter Burke, in an early essay on the subject, listed 'woodcuts and painted icons, spoons and jugs, chairs and tables, caskets and cradles, samplers and bed-spreads, ploughs and saddles ... there are even whole homes, preserved in open-air museums at Aarhus, Arnhem, Bucharest and elsewhere' (Burke 1976: 77) The limitations of what can be done with such sources are, however, clear: what the historian needs is direct access to the thoughts of ordinary people in the past, in much the same way as an anthropologist seems to have direct access to the thoughts of his or her informants while conducting fieldwork. A few lucky breaks aside, however, such evidence is rarely forthcoming.

Historians of early modern popular culture have, therefore, resigned themselves to the fact that such information as they use comes to them usually in a mediated form, and that the mediators were often elite people, frequently hostile to popular culture. There were a few early sympathetic observers of popular beliefs, one of the more remarkable being the seventeenth-century Englishman John Aubrey, but by that century most elite observers found many aspects of popular culture distant, if not repugnant. Indeed, a number of elite people, in their capacities as state or ecclesiastical officials, were active, as our examination of the work of Peter Burke and Robert Muchembled has demonstrated, in eradicating many aspects of popular culture. Yet it was this, paradoxically, which ensured the production of one of the main bodies of source material upon which historians of popular culture draw. Much of what we know about popular culture in the early modern period comes from the archives of courts before which practitioners of popular culture found themselves in trouble, At their best, these court records and cognate categories of official documentation can be vast in content and rich in detail. The archives of the administration of the Dukes of Württemberg, for example, allowed David Sabean (1984) to examine a number of aspects of popular culture: how magistrates in the 1580s attempted to enforce communion, and how this conflicted with popular views which saw communion in terms of enmity and friendship; a peasant prophet who emerged at the end of the Thirty Years War; a witchcraft case of 1683; the career of a paranoid pastor at the turn of the eighteenth century; the investigation of the murder of another pastor; and, at the end of the eighteenth century, an incident in which a village sacrificed a live bull in hopes of averting cattle plague. And, we should remind ourselves, that most celebrated study of medieval peasant *mentalité*, Emmanuel Le Roy Ladurie's work on Montaillou, was based on the records of an ecclesiastical inquisitor.[2] Further materials are provided by the popular press. From the late sixteenth century a number of European countries experienced the production of cheap and ephemeral literature aimed at the lower orders. The first major study of this type of material (setting aside the scholarly editions assembled in the nineteenth century) came in 1964 with Robert Mandrou's study of the *bibliothèque bleue* of Troyes. Subsequent studies included Bernard Capp's work on

---

2   Le Roy Ladurie 1978. For two other influential works based on Inquisition records, this time from early modern Friuli, see Ginzburg 1980 and 1983.

English almanacs, Margaret Spufford's work on English chap-books, and Joy Wiltenburg's comparative study of attitudes to women in the popular press of Germany and England, while Simon Schama made extensive use of this type of material in his cultural history of the seventeenth-century Dutch Republic.[3] Concentration on the printed word should not, of course, obscure the importance of visual images in popular culture: Bob Scribner's (1981) work on the use of pictorial propaganda in the Lutheran Reformation suggests the wider importance of this type of material.

The problem remains of assessing the significance of printed works in popular culture. For Muchembled, as we have seen, the main implication of the spread of cheap literature was that it eroded the old oral culture: 'it becomes difficult to believe', he wrote, 'that this literature could be anything other than a disorderly popularization of the principal themes of learned culture, mixed with bits and pieces of traditional popular culture' (Muchembled [1978] 1985: 288) There are a number of obvious questions: who produced this literature? why was it produced? who read it ? (and did they read it to their illiterate friends?) and how was it read? These issues deserve more space than can be afforded them here: there are, however, three points which can be made. First, this popular printed material remains one of the great unworked sources in European social history. Second, it was designed to sell, and hence was, arguably, more likely to reflect popular attitudes than to attempt to change them: this allows us to suggest that these ballads and chap-books do offer a way into popular mentality. And, third, the literature was conservative. It did not envisage a new social order, but at best suggested amendments, based on traditional morality, to an idealized version of the existing one. Moreover, many of the themes of this literature were becoming obsolete. The knightly romances that still figured in early eighteenth-century chap-books were no longer of interest to the elites of the period, although they had been so in the fifteenth century. The mass production of almanacs in post-Restoration England popularized notions of astrology just when such notions were becoming less fashionable among the educated.

What this literature does, if nothing else, is force historians to consider the interface between elite and popular culture. Here, too, the problems are massive. First, it is becoming obvious that it is not wholly profitable to think in terms of a simplistic elite/popular dichotomy. There are poles: what went on at Louis XIV's Versailles, it seems safe to assume, was rather different from doings in Robert Muchembled's peasant communities in the Nord. Yet there was shared ground which shifted over the centuries, not least in response to broader socio-economic trends. The model is not one of a simple downward diffusion of elite values, or of the repression of popular culture as these values were enforced, although both of these processes were present. As students of popular culture in late twentieth century industrialized states have pointed out, the people are not victims or

3 Capp 1979; Spufford 1981; Wiltenburg 1992; Schama 1987. For a further discussion of the popular press in the United Provinces, see van Deursen 1991: ch. 9.

uncritical consumers of what comes to them culturally from above, but rather users of it. Similarly, for Roger Chartier the type of process favouring state formation described by Muchembled had to 'compromise with tactics of consumption and utilization on the part of the men and women whom they had the task of shaping'.[4] And we return to the problem of the lack of homogeneity in the popular classes, and the fact that their composition changed over time. Over much of Europe the seventeenth century witnessed the emergence of an upper stratum of rich and increasingly literate peasants. While we should remain nervous of any simple notion of 'acculturation',[5] it is likely that these people would acquire many of the values of the church, the state and their social superiors. David Sabean's description of local office-holding in Württemberg shows how many villagers could be sucked into the lower reaches of the state administrative system (1984: 14–17).

Perhaps the most fruitful area for studying the interface between elite and popular culture, if only because of the wealth of relevant documentation, lies in religion. Muchembled, in attempting to explain the mental world of the late medieval peasant, stresses that, although it differed from elite Christianity, this world was 'marked by and permeated with Christian doctrine ... an entity that we could call either a folklorized popular Christianity or a Christianized popular culture' (Muchembled 1978). Working out the nature of this entity, and how it changed over time, has proved essential to historians of popular culture (the danger is, of course, that popular culture will simply be equated with popular religion and popular superstition). Many of the relevant issues have been discussed in an excellent recent book by David Gentilcore, a regional study of Otranto, a backward region in southern Italy.[6] Rather than seeing developments in terms of repression by 'elite' Christianity, Gentilcore stresses the mediation and negotiation in which the Catholic Church involved itself after the Council of Trent. He showed how there were shared values and fears at all levels of society, 'over which hovers the church, attempting to define, regulate and reform access to the sacred' (Gentilcore 1992: 17). And, in his discussion of local, 'popular', beliefs, Gentilcore emphasizes their rational and pragmatic nature: 'people chose from a myriad of remedies available the one (or ones) with the best track record for their particular malady or misfortune'. (ibid. 106). Once more, we find ourselves confronted with the problem of understanding practices which, however alien to us, were rational in the sight of our ancestors.

IV

If one accepts that much of what we know about popular culture in the early modern period comes through mediated sources, the problem of lack of evidence

---

4 Chartier 1988: 41. For some comments by a student of current popular culture, see Fiske 1989a: 4–7. Cf. Fiske 1989b.
5 The case against the usefulness of 'acculturation' in this context is argued by Wirth 1984.
6 Gentilcore 1992. For a discussion of similar problems in a Protestant context, see Luxton 1977.

seems less dismaying: as Robert Darnton (1985: 12) has put it, 'the archives from the old regime are exceptionally rich, and one can always put new questions to old material'. The next difficulty lies in interpreting such records as are at our disposal. 'It is not so much the documents that are lacking', J. C. Schmitt (1983: 171) has remarked, 'as the conceptual instruments necessary to understand them'. The material which we have has to be (to use a currently fashionable term) 'read' and decoded: as Burke pointed out, 'insiders are rarely conscious of their own cultural codes. They take for granted much of what historians most want to know' (Burke 1987: 15). But concern over how to 'read' these sources, to get at what the insiders took for granted, leads the historian very rapidly into the world of theory. Interestingly, historians of early modern popular culture have had little recourse to the richest theoretical perspective for social history, Marxism. Thus the distinguished French scholar Hichel Vovelle, while describing himself as 'a historian formed by Marxist methodologies who is far from denying them', has commented on

> a sort of unspoken agreement, which judging from their silence involved a number of Marxist historians, confining themselves to the sphere of the economy, and of social structure but within strict limits ... leaving to others more qualified than themselves the more complex territories of religious history, mentalities, and sensibilities.[7]

Some Marxist historians have attempted to grapple with the problem of popular culture, and to relate it to such established concerns as economic development, class formation, class consciousness and class struggle: some of Edward Thompson's work comes readily to mind here.[8] Yet it remains clear that those historians of early modern popular culture who have addressed social theory have tended to eschew Marxism.

Most use has been made of concepts borrowed from social anthropology. There are obvious attractions in a discipline whose traditional core has been the study of 'primitive' societies for students of 'pre-industrial' culture. A number of historians of early modern popular culture have made the connection. Robert Darnton, discussing the notion of an *histoire des mentalités*, has remarked that

> the genre has not yet received a name in English, but it might simply be called cultural history: for it treats our own civilization in the same way that anthropologists study alien cultures. It is history in the ethnographic grain.

(Darnton 1985: 11)

Similarly, a leading historian of medieval popular culture could claim to be studying 'an unexplored layer of medieval culture in terms that are perhaps closest to social anthropology' (Gurevich 1988: xviii). Peter Burke (1987), indeed, has written an 'historical anthropology of early modern Italy', in which he argues for a

---

7 Vovelle 1982: 3. Another relevant essay in this collection is Medick 1982.

8 Perhaps the best demonstration of this point is Thompson 1991. Two other works which relate aspects of popular culture to the more familiar concerns of social historians are Malcolmson 1973 and Bushaway 1982.

distinctive 'historical anthropology' which can be set against more mainstream social history. The basic thinking behind such claims is twofold. First, a number of the areas which social historians of the early modern period study (kinship, witchcraft, ritual, popular culture) are staples of anthropological scholarship. And, second, both disciplines involve a conceptual leap, in which the investigating scholars have to divest themselves of the assumptions of their own cultures and confront 'the other'. To cite Darnton again,

> one thing seems clear to everyone who returns from fieldwork: other people are other. They do not think the way we do. And if we want to understand their way of thinking, we should set out with the idea of capturing otherness.
>
> (1985: 12)

Anthropology has proved especially attractive to historians attempting to study ritual, a topic which has attracted considerable attention from anthropologists, and in which 'the other' can often be found operating at full power. We return to the problem of understanding what people in the past were doing with their 'mental tools', of decoding the structures of their thought, of analysing 'not merely what people thought but how they thought – how they construed the world, invested it with meaning, and infused it with emotion' (ibid. 11). Burke, in his description of 'historical anthropology', argues that one of its five distinctive features is an emphasis on the importance of ritual. Two others, directly cognate with that emphasis, are a concern with 'thick description' in the Clifford Geertz mould, rather than change over time, and the rejection of an intellectual 'Great Tradition' based on Marx and Weber for one derived from Emile Durkheim, Arnold van Gennep, Marcel Mauss (we return to the French intellectual model) and such more recent scholars as Geertz, Victor Turner and Pierre Bourdieu (Burke 1987: 3). Such an approach would accept that behind ritual there lurks a world of signs and symbols which, if read properly, leads to an understanding of underlying structures of thought. For the behaviour of individuals is always constrained by a 'collective mentality', however much free play it is given within those constraints.

The problem with this avowedly anthropological approach to early modern ritual, and to other aspects of the popular culture of the period, is that a concern about 'reading' can all too easily slide into over-interpretation. Despite the similarities between some of the objectives and areas of subject matter of social history and social anthropology, and despite the usefulness of anthropology to historians of popular culture and social historians more generally, it remains clear that there are sufficient differences between the aims and methodologies of the two disciplines to make too avid a borrowing of techniques from anthropology a risky enterprise. It is all too easy for historians borrowing the concepts of social anthropology to lose sight of what Edward Thompson (1972) has termed 'the discipline of historical context'. Peter Burke has also offered a caveat: 'to historians', he writes,

> it seems obvious that the meaning of a sign changes in the course of time, varies with the situation in which it is used, and may be manipulated by the individual using it – which is not to deny the possibility of the sign in some sense manipulating the user.
>
> (1987: 5)

369

But even when a suitable caution is exercised, historians still suffer from the disadvantage that they cannot, in any direct sense, do fieldwork in the anthropologist's fashion: this can easily lead them to read too much into the information they do have.[9] The labours of folklorists bring to our attention the instructive example of the Somerset singer Sidney Richards, who, asked the significance of a particular wassail custom by a song collector, shifted uncomfortably and replied hesitantly, 'Well, I reckon it were just an excuse for a good booze-up'.[10]

Even without the problems attendant on over-interpretation, working out what rituals, festivals and carnivals were about is a difficult business. The problems have been well discussed by the American scholar Michael D. Bristol. First, Bristol makes the important point that not everything that happens in carnival is simply symbolic:

> The violence of festive misrule is not always symbolic, and, whether symbolic or not, it is certainly not an incidental feature ... the transgressions connected with festive misrule are real and ... in the violence of festive misconduct real and sometimes irreparable damage will be done.
>
> (1985: 33)

This has serious implications for one of the standard interpretations of carnival, which sees it as a cathartic and reintegrative phenomenon. The 'festive misrule' acts as a safety valve, or the ceremonial forms or the transgressions committed are a sort of 'public rehearsal in which the desirability of social peace and economic co-operation are re-derived' (ibid. 34). He also suggests problems, of wider relevance to the history of popular culture, in accepting carnival as a 'conservative force', suggesting that 'it is necessary to ask who is conserving what and at whose expense'. We return to the idea that the forms of festive life, like other aspects of popular culture, are open to appropriation, and that the outcome of such appropriation by the lower orders might not always to be the benefit of dominant social strata (ibid. 39). As events at Romans in France in 1579–80 demonstrated, a festival which got out of hand could have severe repercussions for the social order.[11]

A further difficulty, of special relevance to advocates of the technique of thick description,[12] lies in the problem of typicality. In his discussion of historical anthropology, Burke stresses that it depends heavily on studies which 'are often deliberately microscopic and focus on small communities ... to achieve greater depth as well as more colour and life' (Burke 1987: 3). This is indeed true, and excellent studies have been produced along these lines. Yet we are sometimes at a loss to know how typical of wider tendencies the results found in a particular

---

9 For discussions illustrating this point, see Darnton 1985: ch. 4, 'Text, symbols and Frenchness: historical uses of symbolic anthropology'; and Clark 1983.

10 Sleeve notes to Shirley Collins, *Adieu to Old England*, Topic Records.

11 Le Roy Ladurie 1980. For a wider-ranging discussion of some of the issues relevant here, see Mullet 1987.

12 The classic discussion of this technique is Geertz 1973: part 1, 'Thick description: toward an interpretive theory of culture'.

micro-study are. John Bossy, for example, has commented on the tendency of English social historians to place so much emphasis on one settlement, Terling in Essex, 'which has had to bear a weight of socio-cultural model-building as groan-making as the demographic pit-machinery grinding night and day over Devon's poor Colyton'.[13]

A work in which the problems of typicality are of central importance is Carlo Ginzburg's *The Cheese and the Worms*, a description of the cosmos of a sixteenth-century Friulian miller, Domenico Scandella, also known as Menocchio. This study raises a number of conceptual issues. It plunges us into the problem of the relationship between elite and popular culture. Menocchio had studied a number of 'elite' texts (he was especially taken by one of the staples of those chivalrous tales which were just becoming unfashionable in elite circles, the *Travels* of Sir John de Mandeville). Yet he had not received them passively, but provides us with a good example of a phenomenon to which we have alluded, that of somebody from the 'popular' classes bringing his or her own culture to bear in his or her reading of an upper-class text. It shows how Inquisitorial records can form the basis of an exploration of popular culture. And it also raises the issue of how much we may conclude from the mental world of one individual. Ginzburg accepts that Menocchio was an unusual individual, pointing out that even his neighbours, on the strength of their evidence to the Inquisition, regarded him as a little odd. Yet he emphasizes the value of a detailed case study of this type as an alternative to studies of the masses based on quantification, and also makes another point which leads us straight back to the constraints of culture. Menocchio's distinctiveness, argues Ginzburg (1980:xx–xxi)

> had very definite limits. As with language, culture offers to the individual a horizon of latent possibilities – a cage in which he can exercise his own conditional liberty. With rare clarity and understanding, Menocchio articulated the language that history put at his disposal.

Thus even this 'exceptional' figure was ultimately locked in the same peasant culture as those who argued points of theology with him, or told him to hide his opinions lest he should get into trouble. And his case does show how these obscure villagers were willing to discuss points, that their mental world was not simply one of total restraint. Thus even the superficially 'atypical' case, if 'read' properly, can inform our view of the typical. And, of course, we have no way of knowing how many other Friulians, or their contemporaries in other regions, were located on the interface between literate and oral culture, and were making their own readings of and drawing their own conclusions from the printed works that came their way.

Another problem facing historians of popular culture, not least those who are attracted to anthropology or micro-studies, is that of assessing change over time, traditionally the primary concern of historians. Obviously, analysis, explication or 'reading' in a thick-descriptive manner are useful and instructive exercises. Yet at

---

13 Bossy 1982: 49. The village alluded to here is the subject of Wrightson and Levine 1979.

some point somebody has to take these more or less isolated pieces of information and attempt to fit them into a pattern which demonstrates chronological change. Virtually from the start some historians of popular culture rejected the notion of an immobile, 'traditional' pre-industrial world: things did change in the lives of the peasants and urban lower orders in the centuries before the nineteenth, albeit sometimes very slowly. Where such changes can be traced (often through studying ritual) interesting insights have been gained. Peter Burke's work on carnival in Venice, for example, shows how the commercialization of a festivity could produce homogenization (Burke 1987: ch. 13). Changes in civic ritual in England between the late Middle Ages and the end of the eighteenth century are symbolic of a shift from an organic view of the body politic to a class-based one (James 1983; Borsay 1984). Execution rituals in Elizabethan and Stuart England developed in line with processes of state formation, with the Reformation, and with changing attitudes to death (Sharpe 1985). In that same society, a ritual calendar based on affirming Englishness and Protestantism replaced the ritual calendar of the late medieval Church (Cressy 1989). It is this need to weave what can be discovered about popular culture into wider themes of historical change which provides the main safety rail preventing historians of popular culture from falling into the crevasses of antiquarianism.

Yet beneath our concern for studying change over time there lies a deeper, more fundamental problem: as we have argued, one of the main potential goals among students of early modern popular culture has been to determine what people in the past were like: to find in what ways they were 'other' from the people who write and read academic history in the late twentieth century. Some historians of popular culture, notably Robert Muchembled, have stressed the 'otherness' of peasants in the early modern period. Others, notably Alan Macfarlane, have stressed continuities.[14] Whichever view we take, addressing the issue does lead us back to confronting that most fundamental 'change over time', the why and how of the process by which the peasant of the sixteenth century was transformed into the citizen of the post-industrial Western state. An influential thinker here has been the German sociologist Norbert Elias, whose ideas have been particularly influential on Pieter Spierenburg (1991), the author of a recent synthesis on early modern popular culture (Spierenburg 1991). Elias has seen the main lines of cultural development since the late Middle Ages in terms of a 'civilizing process' which involved both the social structure and the psychic structure of individual personalities.[15] This is an ambitious project, no doubt, but thinking along these lines does offer immense possibilities. Spierenburg contends that 'it is a basic tenet of the history of mentalities that the entire personality structure of people in the past is different from what it is today' (1991: ix). If this contention is correct (and I think that few would be so definite on

---

14 Macfarlane strongly argues for continuities in English history in a number of works, notably *The Origins of English Individualism* (1978) and *The Culture of Capitalism* (1987).
15 *The Civilizing Process: the History of Manners*, (1978) is the part of Elias's œuvre which has most bearing on the current discussion.

the point as is Spierenburg), historians of popular culture would seem well placed to investigate an issue of fundamental historical importance.

V

Ending a chapter of this type with thoughts on future directions of study in the field under consideration is always an attractive option. Obviously, much work needs to be done on the history of popular culture in the early modern West, in terms both of creating more empirically based studies, and also of how to refine and sharpen the conceptual frameworks needed to understand empirical evidence more deeply. Even so, the achievement so far has been considerable. What might once have been simply written off by an older brand of scholarship as meaningless customs or empty peasant superstitions have now been subjected to serious historical investigation, and much has been done to reconstruct the culture and mental world of our early modern ancestors. We return to the point made at the beginning of this chapter, that the study of popular culture is just one facet of a desire to broaden the scope of history and to reconstruct aspects of the human past which might previously have been thought of as inaccessible or unworthy of study.

It should also be remembered that western Europeans, with whom this chapter has largely been concerned, were also having their own views of the world broadened over the early modern period as contacts with non-European cultures increased. Many Europeans now found themselves confronting 'the other' in colonial contexts, a development which offers interesting possibilities to the historian of popular culture. Let us take two examples. First, Britain's colonies in North America would seem to offer scope for investigation, not least because of the richness of their surviving archives. Although the situation probably changed as the zeal of the early settlers became diluted by more arrivals in the eighteenth century, it seems likely that study of popular religion will prove the most fruitful line of approach for the seventeenth. Certainly work by David D. Hall (1989) suggests this, although more recently Richard Godbeer (1992) has demonstrated the complexities of popular belief even in the seventeenth century. Second, Spain's colonies in South America experienced situations very different from those obtaining in New England. Here a more deliberate attempt to Christianize the Indians could, at its worst, result in an exercise in 'acculturation' in which the culture of the natives, and, indeed, most of the natives themselves, was obliterated (see e.g. Clendinne 1982). Where these processes were less total, a new cultural mix containing elements of the old culture and the colonial one could be achieved.[16] But the story of how European popular culture reacted in the New World remains largely unwritten.

So the difficulties of studying the popular culture of the early modern period remain: the lack of evidence, the problem of the relationship between popular and

---

16 Some interesting lines of enquiry are suggested in Cerventes 1991.

elite culture, the need to keep a balanced view of the subject's relationship to other social theory and conceptual frameworks and methodologies derived from other disciplines. Even so, as we have seen, the field has proved a lively one, and scholars working in it have achieved a great deal. Above all, in attempting to decode 'the other', historians of popular culture in the early modern West have repeatedly achieved one of the main objectives of history, that of confronting their readers with unfamiliar experiences and inviting them to understand them and, through that process, come to grips with the variety of ways in which human beings have been capable of organizing their social, economic, and mental worlds. As Robert Darnton (1985: 12) has put it, 'we continually need to be shaken out of a false sense of familiarity with the past, to be administered doses of culture shock'. Studying early modern popular culture is an excellent way of meeting this need.

REFERENCES

Beauroy, J., Bertrand, M. and Gargin, E. T. (eds) (1976) *The Wolf and the Lamb: Popular Culture in France from the Old Regime to the Twentieth Century*, Saratoga.

Borsay, P. (1984) ' "All the town's a stage': urban ritual and ceremony 1660–1800', in P. Clark (ed.) *The Transformation of English Provincial Towns 1600–1800*, London: 228–58.

Bossy, J. (1982) 'Out of the system', *Encounter*, September–October 59 (3–4): 46–51.

Bristol, M. D. (1985) *Carnival and Theatre: Plebeian Culture and the Structure of Authority in Renaissance England*, New York and London.

Burke, P. (1976) 'Oblique approaches to the history of popular culture', in C. W. E. Bigsby (ed.) *Approaches to Popular Culture*, London: 69–84.

—— (1978) *Popular Culture in Early Modern Europe*, London.

—— (1987) *The Historical Anthropology of Early Modern Italy*, Cambridge.

Bushaway, B. (1982) *By Rite: Custom, Ceremony and Community in England 1700–1800*, London.

Capp, B. (1979) *Astrology and the Popular Press: English Almanacs 1500–1800*, London.

Cerventes, F. (1991) 'The devils of Queretaro: scepticism and credulity in late seventeenth-century Mexico', *Past and Present* 130: 51–69.

Chartier, R. (1988) *Cultural History: Between Practices and Representations*, tr. L. G. Cochrane, Ithaca, NY.

Clark, S. (1983) 'French historians and early modern popular culture', *Past and Present* 100: 62–99.

Clendinne, I. (1982) 'Disciplining the Indian: Franciscan ideology and missionary violence in sixteenth-century Yucatan', *Past and Present* 94: 27–48.

Cressy, D. (1989) *Bonfires and Bells: National Memory and the Protestant Calendar in Elizabethan and Stuart England*, London.

Darnton, R. (1985) *The Great Cat Massacre and Other Episodes in French Cultural History*, Harmondsworth.

Davis, N. Z. (1975) *Society and Culture in Early Modern France: Eight Essays*, Stanford.

Deursen, A. Th. van (1991) *Plain Lives in a Golden Age: Popular Culture Religion and Society in Seventeenth-Century Holland*, Cambridge.

Elias, N. (1978) *The Civilizing Process: The History of Manners*, Oxford.

Fiske, J. (1989a) *Reading the Popular*, Boston.

—— (1989b) *Understanding Popular Culture*, Boston.

Geertz, C. (1973) *The Interpretation of Cultures*, New York.

Gentilcore, D. (1992) *From Bishop to Witch: The System of the Sacred in Early Modern Otranto*, Manchester.

Ginzburg, C. (1980) *The Cheese and the Worms: The Cosmos of a Sixteenth-Century Miller*, London and Henley.

—— (1983) *The Night Battles: Witchcraft and Agrarian Cults in the Sixteenth and Seventeenth Centuries*, London, Melbourne and Henley.

Godbeer, R. (1992) *The Devil's Dominion: Magic and Religion in Early New England*, Cambridge.

Gurevich, A. (1988) *Medieval Popular Culture: Problems of Belief and Perception*, Cambridge.

Hall, D. D. (1989) *Worlds of Wonder, Days of Judgement: Popular Religious Belief in Early New England*, New York.

James, M. E. (1983) 'Ritual, drama and social body in the late medieval English town', *Past and Present* 98: 3–29.

Kaplan, S. L. (ed.) (1984) *Understanding Popular Culture in Europe from the Middle Ages to the Nineteenth Century*, Berlin and New York.

Le Roy Ladurie, E. (1978) *Montaillou: Cathars and Catholics in a French Village 1294–1324*, London.

—— (1980) *Carnival at Romans*, London.

Luxton, I. (1977) 'The Reformation and popular culture', in F. Heal and R. O'Day (eds) *Church and Society in England: Henry VIII to James I*, London.

Macfarlane, A. (1978) *The Origins of English Individualism*, Oxford.

—— (1987) *The Culture of Capitalism*, Oxford.

Malcolmson, R. W. (1973) *Popular Recreations in English Society 1700–1850*, Cambridge.

Malinowski, B. (1937) 'Culture', E. R. A. Selgin and A. Johnson (eds) *The Encyclopedia of the Social Sciences*, New York.

Mandrou, R. (1964) *De la culture populaire aux XVIIe et XVIIIe siècles: La Bibliothèque bleue de Troyes*, Paris.

Medick, H. (1982) 'Plebeian Culture in the Transition to Capitalism', in R. Samuel and G. Stedman Jones (eds) *Culture, Ideology and Politics*, London.

Muchembled, R. (1978) *Culture populaire et culture des élites dans la France moderne (XVe–XVIIIe siècles)*, Paris. (Tr.: 1985 *Popular Culture and Elite Culture in France, 1400–1750*, Baton Rouge and London.)

Mullet, K. (1987) *Popular Culture and Popular Protest in Late Medieval and Early Modern Europe*, London.

Reay, B. (ed.) (1985) *Popular Culture in Seventeenth-Century England*, Beckenham.

Sabean, D. (1984) *Power in the Blood: Popular Culture and Village Discourse in Early Modern Germany*, Cambridge.

Schama, S. (1987) *The Embarrassment of Riches: An Interpretation of Dutch Culture in the Golden Age*, London.

Schmitt, J.-C. (1983) *The Holy Greyhound: Guinefort, Healer of Children since the Thirteenth Century*, Cambridge.

Scribner, R. W. (1981) *For the Sake of Simple Folk: Popular Propaganda for the German Reformation*, Cambridge.

Sharpe, J. A. (1985) '"Last dying speeches": religion, ideology and public execution in seventeenth-century England', *Past and Present* 107: 144–67.

Spierenburg, P. (1991) *The Broken Spell: A Cultural and Anthropological History of Preindustrial Europe*, New Brunswick.

Spufford, M. (1981) *Small Books and Pleasant Histories: Popular Fiction and its Readership in Seventeenth-Century England*, London.

Thompson, E. (1972) 'Anthropology and the discipline of historical context', *Midland History* 3(1): 41–56.

—— (1991) *Customs in Common*, London.

Vovelle, M. (1982) 'Ideologies and mentalities', in R. Samuel and G. Stedman Jones (eds) *Culture, Ideology and Politics*, London: 2–11.

Wiltenburg, J. (1992) *Disorderly Women and Female Power in the Street Literature of Early Modern England and Germany*, Charlottesville and London.

Wirth, J. (1984) 'Against the acculturation thesis', in K. von Greyerz (ed.), *Religion and Society in Early Modern Europe 1500–1800*, London.

Wrightson, K. and Levine, D. (1979) *Poverty and Piety in an English Village: Terling 1525–1700*, New York.

18

REVISIONISM IN BRITAIN

Ronald Hutton

'I frequented the schools of the philosophers and found nothing but preparation for the overthrow of doctrines.' So wrote the homilist whom theologians call Pseudo-Clement, recalling his experience as a student in third-century Rome. He had made the discovery, often equally shocking to newcomers, that scholarship almost invariably proceeds by amending previous assertions. In that sense the writing of history is usually in its essence revisionism. Nevertheless, the expression came to be applied to particular developments in historiography in British and North American universities during the 1970s. There was a widespread impression that these represented challenges to established views of a scale and force unusual by the normal standards of the historian's profession. It is the contention of this chapter that such an impression was correct, and that there were three principal reasons for this phenomenon.

The first was the expansion of higher education which took place in western Europe and North America during the 1950s and 1960s, resulting in a greater number of professional historians than ever before. Not only did this make more likely a multiplicity of differing viewpoints, but it reduced the hitherto marked influence of a small number of distinguished scholars over the disposal of posts, and thus arguably encouraged independence amongst their juniors. The contraction of posts which set in during the 1980s, especially in Britain, did not result in a reversion to the previous situation. Not only was the total number of historians still much greater than it had been in 1960 but the increased competition for employment or promotion encouraged debate and publication. The tone of disputation was probably more acrimonious in the smaller academic world of 1945–65, but the pace and range of argument was considerably greater in the following decades. During the 1970s more works of history were written than ever before, and by 1990 the total of new titles was still higher.

The second factor was what might be called the archival revolution in Britain, the opening of county record offices across the nation after 1950, and the transfer of documents from thousands of private or official collections to these and older repositories. As a result, historians suddenly had a much larger body of source material within easy access than ever before, inviting a reworking of existing ideas which had been based upon more limited evidence. The third reason for a rejection of accepted models was the least tangible, consisting of the general distrust of established values which developed in western Europe and America during the 1960s. The dissolution of the European colonial empires and the spread of militarism and Marxist revolution in their former possessions, the discovery of reliable contraception, the marked growth of secularism in formerly Christian cultures, the unprecedented increases in economic production and social affluence in industrialized nations, and the consequent threat to the world ecosystem, represented perhaps the principal reasons for this change of attitudes. It called into question most of the assumptions upon which societies and polities in the so-called West had been constructed during the previous century or longer. As traditional historiography had been so much bound up with these assumptions, some reaction against it was likely to occur.

The results of these factors, in unison, were certainly remarkable. Around 1970 it was still known for a high-ranking historian, criticized by a junior one in a different university, to write to the latter's head of department demanding that his critic be rebuked. In 1975, in Cambridge, I heard a tutor's first book praised by colleagues for having presented research which questioned existing interpretations in such a way as to conceal the destructive force of his discoveries. By the next decade, such attitudes had become almost unthinkable. During the 1970s in British academe, the favourite villain of conversation was still the 'young man in a hurry'. By 1990 it had become the middle-aged drone, who had written nothing to justify tenure of a university post. Somebody who came to be regarded as one of the greatest 'revisionists' of all described to me how, in about 1970, he realized that he could trust virtually nothing that he had been taught about early Stuart history: 'I decided that I could believe that James I and Charles I existed, but everything else I had to discover for myself.' It was not in fact chiefly upon his area of expertise that the impact of these changes was felt. Nothing in the province of historiography, for example, compared with the alterations in views of British prehistory. During the 1970s experts on the Neolithic completely jettisoned existing notions of its dates, its periodization, the nature of its supreme deity, the significance of its principal monuments and the existence of the race of people which was supposed to have brought it to an end. The national mythology which was most extensively reworked after 1960 was that of the Republic of Ireland, the most recently created state in the Western world and the one most obviously dependent upon a particular notion of history. Yet the concept of 'revisionism' emerged within universities in the United States, Canada and Britain, and was concerned primarily with British history between about 1500 and about 1800.

That this was so was partly because both British and North Americans regarded this period as crucial to the formation of their common political and religious traditions. It had also been served by able historians who had presented a detailed and long-lasting account of how those traditions were formed. The challenge was to be mounted not at the weakest points of this account but at the strongest, supplied by the person whom one of the participants in the subsequent controversy was to describe as 'Clio's darling'. This was the Englishman Samuel Rawson Gardiner, who between 1856 and 1901 had published successive volumes of a narrative history of the British Isles from 1603 to 1656, based upon an unprecedented amount of archival research. His aim was to discover the origins of three characteristics of his England, of which its inhabitants were fiercely proud: English hegemony over the archipelago, a monarchy limited by parliamentary democracy, and a national Church limited by freedom of worship for dissenters. He located them in an accelerating struggle between the first two Stuart monarchs and what he sometimes termed 'the spirit of the nation', embodied most effectively in Parliament. During the early twentieth century his portrait of events remained the standard one upon both sides of the Atlantic, although everybody lost interest in its Scottish and Irish dimensions when the independence of most of Ireland destroyed that aspect of the English achievement. Yet the results differed markedly on opposite sides of the Atlantic. In America from 1924 onwards Wallace Notestein reinforced Gardiner's picture of an increasingly powerful House of Commons, responding to popular wishes and pitting itself against royal claims. He founded a school which lasted into the 1970s, dedicated to the editing and publication of sources for the Parliaments of the period. In England during the 1950s, Sir John Neale did provide an account of the Parliaments of Elizabeth I, which detected the origins of the growth of the importance of the Commons described by Gardiner and Notestein. But after 1910 English historians of the early Stuart period were content to accept Gardiner's narrative and redirected their attentions to discovering presumed socio-economic causes for the political changes which that story portrayed. It was a quest which most obviously drew upon the ideas of Karl Marx. Around 1970 it was still in progress, represented most prominently in England by Christopher Hill and in America by the Englishman Lawrence Stone. Their works depended fundamentally upon the ideas that central politics had responded to social changes, and that the new importance of the Commons was associated with a relative decline in the strength of Crown and aristocracy and a rise in that of lesser landowners. By 1970, it had been proved that in the House of Commons itself, Civil War Royalists and Parliamentarians had been remarkably similar in social background and economic fortune. Some scholars had therefore turned to studying provincial society in search of a clearer picture of the war's origins, taking advantage of the large-scale foundation of county record offices.

Both thrusts of research, in America and England, came to instil doubts in some of those at work. The county studies revealed a society both fragmented and conservative, reacting to events at the political centre rather than imposing its will upon them, in which the Civil War partisans were small minorities struggling against confusion, apathy and local self-interest. Alan Everitt widely publicized this picture in the 1960s, and in 1976 John Morrill drew upon what was by then a fairly large body of local work to argue for a prevalent provincial mentality which was intensely localized and essentially passive in national affairs. He did not deny the importance of ideology to the few partisans, and left open the possibility that Parliament's cause might have had a greater appeal to commoners. But it was his characterization of the majority which made the most impact on his readers. Among them were scholars based in North American universities who had been continuing the Notestein tradition of a concentration upon Parliaments and begun in the process to fault the master's views. They had been encouraged in this by an essay published in 1965 by England's leading early Tudor historian, G. R. (later Sir Geoffrey) Elton. The latter put forward two arguments. One, aimed at those who sought a social origin for the Civil War, pointed out that as the nation had apparently been as united against Charles I in 1640 as it was divided by him in 1642, the war had to be the result of short-term political developments. This reflected also upon Notestein and Neale, whom Elton attacked directly with an assertion that Tudor Parliaments had been characterized chiefly by consensus and by skilful royal management, and that this had broken down subsequently because of the ineptitude of the Stuart kings, not because of any wish on the part of the Commons. Elton was opposed by some of Notestein's followers in America, but some of their colleagues came to be convinced that his criticisms had in fact been too cautious.

In 1975 and 1976 two of them, Paul Christianson and Conrad Russell, published essays calling for a new framework of early Stuart history. The former made Stone his main target, arguing that parliamentary sovereignty and a decline in power of the Crown and nobility were consequences of the Civil War instead of preconditions. He emphasized the vital importance of the peerage in the preceding four decades. Russell took issue most strongly with Notestein, inspired by the comparative work upon seventeenth-century regimes lately undertaken by historians of Europe as a whole. He claimed that English Parliaments of the age were typical of it, in being weak institutions with no common body of people or of beliefs opposed to the Crown. In December 1977 *The Journal of Modern History* (*JMH*) devoted a whole issue to five essays by different contributors from North American universities, one of them Christianson. Their collective import was to reinforce the assertions made in the previous year, especially those of the superior importance of the peerage and of the existence of a prevailing language of co-operation in the English political nation until the Civil War broke out. They also proved that the demands for a fundamental change of views first heard in 1976 were shared by a relatively large and determined body of academics. Countenance was given to them by John Morrill's work on the provinces and by Geoffrey Elton's contemporary addresses to the Royal Historical Society describing the spirit of political consensus prevalent in Tudor England. In 1978 the English equivalent to the *JMH* volume was published, in the shape of essays upon the same period from seven more writers, gathered by Kevin Sharpe into a book entitled *Faction and Parliament*. They were not directly encouraged by the previous seven pieces, representing instead parallel work which had reached broadly similar conclusions through more detailed case studies. They stressed that quarrels between Crown and Commons were often produced by divisions among royal councillors, that the peerage was important to the political process and that the seventeenth-century expressions 'Court' and 'Country' referred not to opposed groupings but to overlapping and complementary spheres. In the next year Russell brought out the book *Parliaments and English Politics, 1621–1629*, a careful narrative and analytical study of the subject which surpassed Gardiner's account and demonstrated all the assertions made in his pioneering essay. This work established that the call for a major reinterpretation amounted to more than a volley of polemics. It commanded respect not merely for the depth of its scholarship but for the courtesy of its tone: indeed, it was largely because of Russell's natural gentility that the controversy which he helped to provoke never achieved the bitterness of many others within academe. The book was followed by two others in 1981 which shared its qualities as well as its attitudes, Roger Lockyer's biography of Buckingham and Anthony Fletcher's study of the outbreak of the Civil War. Both emphasized the complexity of early Stuart politics and the importance of accident and of practical problems in them.

Three sorts of reaction to these publications soon became clear. One, very common among non-specialists, was expressed by a Tudor historian in 1980, who told me that the period 1603–42 now seemed so confusing that she no longer knew how to teach it to students. Another was trumpeted by Paul Christianson in 1981, that only the 'old and the obstinate' now failed to accept the new ideas about that period. The third was the category of people whom he chose thus to define. Between 1978 and 1982 a total of eight writers, six based in the United States, expressed reservations about the views concerned. All of them agreed that the model of Notestein and Gardiner had been found wanting, and some felt that its critics were closer to the truth. Stone, who had been the principal living target of the criticisms, never replied to them. Instead, over half the published pieces which took issue with the new ideas were the work of two men, colleagues at Washington University, St Louis. They were also the first to respond. The more entertaining was J. H. Hexter, the more substantial was Derek Hirst, who like Russell and Stone was an Englishman working in America. At first sight he was a curious person to find in the role. He had published a first book upon parliamentary elections which had undermined Notestein's picture of them, and contributed the essay upon the nature of Court and Country to *Faction and Parliament*. His belief was that the old and the new models were both wrong in important respects. He and Hexter demonstrated convincingly that the Lords, although important, were not the manipulators of the Commons and that ideological factors did play a consistent part in the problems experienced by the first Stuart kings in working with Parliaments. The two of them also employed the word 'revisionism' to characterize the views which they were contesting. They used it immediately, in 1978, and Hirst did so consistently thereafter: within two years it had become standard. In the early 1970s it had been commonly used by Marxists to describe those who adulterated and betrayed true doctrine, and did not therefore have very flattering connotations. Of those to whom it was applied in this debate, only Christianson, who came close to being their ideologue, adopted it readily in print. But it was not Hirst who first applied it to this context. In the winter of 1977–8, at a seminar in London, Russell himself had been asked for a term to define those who shared his approach, and settled upon 'revisionists' as the best which he could find. Before printing it, Hirst had applied to him and been given leave to use it.

During the 1980s the debate lost pace. Morrill and Sharpe, who had both contracted for large-scale works to accompany Russell's, grew cautious and postponed them in order to prepare the ground with excellent small-scale studies. Hexter ceased to write on the subject and Christianson concentrated upon a single individual, John Selden. It was left to Derek Hirst, in 1986, to produce a textbook upon the whole period 1603–58 which attempted, with much success, to rationalize the achievements of the controversy and to present a new narrative based upon them. Even so, the work was delivered years after its intended date, after repeated rewriting, so nervous had all the participants in the controversy become of each other. The book helped to establish which of the new arguments had become firmly accepted. The Civil War was now viewed clearly as the product of short-term political problems, but in a state afflicted by functional breakdown in the fiscal system and disagreements over the form of the Church, both issues with long-term antecedents. Parliaments were extremely important to the process of government, but were becoming neither stronger nor more innovatory. The monarchy was more of an innovator, responding to practical problems which needed to be viewed with more sympathy than before, although Charles I was still a disastrous ruler. But the details of this picture remained the matter for controversy, and during the 1980s another group of scholars proposed that major elements of the revisionist case had been faulty. They came from different generations and traditions. Johann Sommerville was a historian of political thought, Richard Cust and Thomas Cogswell interested in public reactions to royal policies. David Underdown, Stephen Roberts and Ann Hughes were all concerned with provincial society, and more impressed than previous workers in the genre with the lack of clearly defined county communities and distinctive local mentalities. They stressed instead the existence of ideological and cultural divisions in the localities and the importance of social factors as determinants of Civil War allegiance. All three were touched by a radical socialism which gave them an instinctual sympathy with commoners and a propensity to credit them with more than material or regional concerns: if they respected one of their predecessors more than others, it was Christopher Hill. In a set of monographs published during the decade these writers questioned many of the assumptions of those termed revisionists, and in 1989 Cust and Hughes edited a volume entitled *Conflict in Early Stuart England*. This they presented as a 'post-revisionist' collection, imitating the tactic of pooled contribution employed in the celebrated edition of the *JMH* and in *Faction and Parliament*. Including the editors there were again seven historians involved. One of them had given an essay (like Hirst) to Sharpe's collection, illustrating the difficulty of consigning individuals firmly to historiographical groupings. What they did prove between them was the importance of ideology and the existence of a complex series of religious, fiscal, political and constitutional disputes at all levels of a functionally defective early

Stuart system, some long-lasting and all inclined to simplify and polarize drastically at moments of crisis.

Nevertheless, the process of 'revisionism' was continuing even while these writers attempted to declare it out of date. G. R. Elton (latterly Sir Geoffrey) steadily developed his attack upon the Neale view of Elizabethan Parliaments, culminating in a book in 1986 which asserted that they exhibited all the features detected by those of Russell in those of 1603–29. Quarrels within them reflected divisions within the government, no organized opposition to the Crown existed in either House, and no shift of power occurred within the institution. This was underpinned in the same year by one of the contributors to the 'revisionist' issue of the *JMH*, Mark Kishlansky of Chicago University, who took a neat revenge upon Hirst by challenging him upon the ground of his original research, parliamentary elections. Kishlansky argued powerfully that before 1640 such events were expressions of conflict and co-operation within the landed elite, rarely motivated by ideology or subject to popular will. Finally Conrad Russell himself, having devoted a decade to disproving old explanations of the English Civil War, spent another in extensive research for the genuine causes. The result, in 1990–1, was a pair of large books which traced the long-term origins of the conflict to fiscal and religious issues, to factors of personality, and to the relationship between England, Scotland and Ireland. In doing so he became the first historian of the period since Gardiner to work with as many issues at once and upon all three kingdoms, although the vision which he produced was quite different from that of the great Victorian.

So what had, in fact, been achieved during these fifteen years? It had been demonstrated, conclusively, that the English Civil War was not an inevitable event; that the central conflict between kings and parliaments was the most important cause of its outbreak; and that historians of the early Stuart period had to study the court and House of Lords as well as the House of Commons, and the British Isles as a whole instead of concentrating upon England. Each of these new beliefs overthrew others which had been universally accepted for at least fifty years and some which had been standard for over a century. In the process the history of those years 1603–42 had become much better grounded in documentary evidence than ever before, and also considerably more complex and contentious. By 1990 two large issues in particular were still in debate. One was the extent to which the people of the time were aware of, or sought, long-term constitutional aims. The other was why they adhered to one or the other of the Civil War parties. There was a growing sense of the need to reconstruct, much better than before, the social, religious and political milieu from which Royalists and Parliamentarians arose.

Although the name 'revisionism' was first applied to work upon the early Stuarts, it was very swiftly appropriated by historians of neighbouring subjects. The first of these to be subjected to the process was the English Reformation, which had been regarded as the religious equivalent of the Civil War as a formative event for the ideas and institutions of the English-speaking world. From the sixteenth until the mid-twentieth century that world had been predominantly a Protestant Christian one, and the story of the Reformation was accordingly portrayed within it as both inevitable and triumphant. But whereas in 1970 the basic narrative of the early Stuart age was still Gardiner's, about 100 years old, that for the Reformation had been published only six years before. It was the textbook by A. G. Dickens, who summed up not only a great deal of his own research but centuries of English Protestant tradition. The latter depended upon assertions that the late medieval Church had been decayed and unpopular, that the reformed faith made proportionately rapid progress at all levels of society and that by the death of Edward VI, in 1553, England was predominantly a Protestant nation. Thus the reign of Catholic Mary was seen as a futile attempt to revive a dying religion, and her brutality believed to have reinforced the attachment of her subjects to the new one. As a result, the latter was swiftly and permanently re-established as soon as Elizabeth succeeded. Dickens was the finest scholar in the field, as well as a devout Protestant. Understandably, his portrait was copied by virtually all other textbooks on Tudor England until the end of the 1970s, including those of Elton which were the most widely read. But by that decade three factors were working against it. One was the flow of diocesan records into the new record offices, which told a much more complex tale. The second was the school of research students working on Tudor central politics which Elton had built up at Cambridge. They, and others, uncovered a succession of factional conflicts in which final choices of religious policy were determined largely by accidents of mortality and personality. The third was the general decline of Christianity in the English-speaking world. To agnostics and atheists the attraction of the Reformation was very hard to see, for it involved a mass destruction of tangible objects of beauty (carvings, stained glass, paintings and metalwork), and a substitution of printed words which had very little appeal to those not imbued with their faith.

A challenge to the accepted view developed out of the sort of detailed county studies which had already made such an impact upon the historiography of the Civil War. From 1965 a small but growing number were devoted to the Reformation, and most emphasized the slow and uneven nature of the process at a local level. The most significant was Christopher Haigh's monograph on Lancashire, published in 1975. Having commenced work on it to discover why that county remained more Catholic than any other, he completed it with the suspicion that for most of the Tudor period Lancashire had been more typical than exceptional in its very limited reception of religious change. Before the end of the decade Haigh had combined the import of the new studies of the provinces and of central politics to provide a comprehensive new view of the English Reformation. It portrayed a popular and flourishing late medieval Church, destroyed slowly by an alliance between a tiny number of local Protestants, concentrated in the south-east, and successive sets of court politicians, often opportunists. What secured an ultimate Protestant victory was only the early death of Mary without an heir and the exceptionally long life of Elizabeth. The reformed faith did not command the allegiance of most of the English until the middle of Elizabeth's reign, and never enjoyed the degree of popularity which had been accorded to the old Church, especially in rural areas. By arguing for all this, Haigh (himself an agnostic) gave obvious offence to Protestants.

But by suggesting, explicitly, that English Catholicism had lost the struggle partly because of its own tactical blunders, he gave only slightly less irritation to the adherents of Rome.

In 1979 Haigh was appointed to a fellowship at Oxford and there, in the heart of English academe, he was in a position to give the maximum publicity to his ideas. He aired them all to packed lecture halls and seminars and founded a notably iconoclastic postgraduate discussion group. The result was to display to a greater degree a phenomenon also very apparent in the debate on the early seventeenth century: that actual publications represented only the tip of an iceberg of verbal argument. In both cases the issues were discussed far more avidly in formal and informal academic gatherings than they were in print, and many more people expressed adherence or opposition to them in such situations than addressed them in their own writings. It was widely expected around 1980 that Haigh would soon publish his lectures in a textbook which would generate a set of replies. Instead, like most of the so-called Stuart revisionists, he proceeded far more cautiously, preferring to print his papers individually during the early 1980s. The books which supported his case were produced by others, a detailed study of the diocese of Lincoln by Margaret Bowker which came out in 1981 and a fiery set of lectures from J. J. Scarisbrick, published in 1984. Scarisbrick, the much-respected biographer of Henry VIII (and a devout Catholic) surveyed the whole period up till 1570 and thoroughly endorsed Haigh's opinions regarding the popularity of the old Church and the slow and reluctant acceptance of the new one. In the same year Robert Whiting deposited a doctoral thesis on Devon and Cornwall (published in 1989) which provided more evidence for the thriving condition of traditional English religion upon the eve of the Reformation. What was especially impressive about this work was not merely its quantity of documentation but the fact that Whiting himself was a confirmed evangelical Protestant.

In 1987 Haigh himself at last published a textbook, boldly entitled *The English Reformation Revised*, but adopted for it the format which had featured in the controversy over the early Stuart age, of a set of essays by different contributors. In this case, however, the pieces were not produced for the occasion. All but one had already been published, up to fifteen years before, and they represented between them the growth of the new view of the Reformation. Haigh's preface linked it to the simultaneous challenge made to the former orthodoxy concerning the early seventeenth century, cheerfully claiming for both the label of revisionism which most of the Stuart historians concerned had avoided. As a result, some hostile critics henceforth applied it to all the contributors to the volume, whether they identified with it or not. At the same time the term 'post-revisionist', which was appearing in Stuart studies, also surfaced in the context of the Reformation (used of himself by the young historian Glyn Redworth). In both areas of research it had the same rough connotation, of people who found the revisionists more persuasive than the traditional authorities, but both defective. Those most frequently assigned by others to this category, apart from Redworth, were Diarmaid MacCulloch, John Guy and that same Robert Whiting already mentioned above. Unlike their Stuart equivalents, however, they never once operated as a group, nor regarded themselves as one.

Their arguments collectively recognized that the pre-Reformation Church was both a dynamic and well-loved institution and the object of fierce criticism by lay and clerical writers: attachment to a religion did not preclude dissatisfaction with the way it was run. They stressed that government policy was formed by personal religious commitment, often providing a coherent programme, as well as by squalid manoeuvres for power. MacCulloch argued that pre-Reformation native heresy did have considerable influence upon the form of English Protestantism and that in some communities the latter made progress as rapidly as Dickens had thought. Whiting insisted that the collapse of the old religion was extremely fast once the Reformation began, and other research did at least support his assertion that certain aspects of it (pilgrimages, shrines, guilds, obits and cults of saints) went into swift and permanent decline once challenged. By 1991, even more than in early Stuart historiography, all the principals of the original debate were still active in it. They included Dickens himself. But much of the old orthodoxy is gone for ever. It was now almost universally accepted that the old Church had flourished until the moment that the Crown embraced reform, that the religious struggle was protracted and determined by royal whim and dynastic accident, and that England had become an unmistakably Protestant nation by the 1580s, rather than by the 1550s. The new consensus recognized that there was an immense variation of intensity and duration of reform between localities, that the government could compel external conformity with its wishes much faster than changes of personal belief, and that a long interval could exist between a loss of faith in Catholicism and an enthusiastic acceptance of Protestantism.

It was not until the mid-1980s that another, and much larger, sphere of interest was claimed for the label of revisionism, and this development was wholly the work of one individual, J. C. D. Clark. His early career at Cambridge had not been prosperous: despite obvious intelligence he did not secure a first-class degree and his research, upon mid-eighteenth-century party politics, did not lead to academic preferment. He left the profession for the business world. A less highly motivated person would simply have forgotten academe, while a political radical might have found reason for losing faith in the whole system of higher education. But Jonathan Clark was a political and religious reactionary, deeply in love with the past, and having secured a research fellowship at his old university he returned literally with a vengeance. His attack upon the existing historiography, presaged by an essay in 1980, really opened with a review article in 1984, followed by a pair of books during the next two years. Between them these suggested that the seventeenth and eighteenth centuries in England formed a continuous whole in which hierarchy, deference and authority were the key concepts of politics and religion the most emotive factor. This 'ancien régime' was said to have lasted until 1828–32, when it began to alter as a result of political circumstance. Clark denied that the period which he had defined ever underwent any class conflict or dramatic economic change, and claimed that Parliament remained for the whole of it a relatively weak and hesitant body in which parties had difficulty in preserving their identity if dynastic and religious conflicts were absent. Its most powerful and aggressive component remained the Crown, which was only challenged if the current monarch happened to be of a religion or a dynasty to which other members of the institution objected. Each of these proposals violated part of the existing notion of the age concerned, and would by themselves have generated considerable debate. But whereas the other so-called revisionists had tended to address issues rather than historians (at least in print), Clark's arguments were ferociously *ad hominem*. He believed that most scholars of his chosen epoch had distorted the truth about it, and so betrayed their duty and the people about whom they wrote, because of their own political prejudices. Thus, they had inflated the importance of any elements within it which could win the approval of modern liberals or socialists, and consistently disparaged or neglected what Clark took to be the dominant culture of monarchy, aristocracy and Church. Those whom he accused included a great many of the most prestigious figures in modern academe, including Hexter, Hill and the man whom many regarded as the leading figure in early eighteenth-century studies (and who certainly led them in Cambridge), Sir John Plumb. Clark applied to himself the name of 'revisionist', and claimed to be part of the same movement as those to whom this term had been applied in Stuart studies, sharing the same opponents.

The result was a furore. On the one hand, Clark became an instant celebrity, awarded a post at All Souls College, Oxford, and profiled in a national newspaper as 'The Don Who is Rewriting History'. On the other, he became probably the most hated living historian. A Stuart specialist, losing his temper loudly with a colleague at an academic gathering, could find no worse term of opprobrium for him than that he was even more obnoxious than Jonathan Clark. Professors who had grown up in an era in which it was considered disgraceful for a scholar to feature in a newspaper at all, now found the aforesaid Dr Clark denouncing them to the press. A letter defending Plumb against his attack was duly published in reply, signed by all the Cambridge history professors except Sir John himself and (significantly) Elton. Sir Geoffrey's abstention, and implied support for Clark, was typical of the rifts opened by the latter's assertions. Essays were rushed into print to refute or amend them. The journal *Parliamentary History* held a symposium on the issues raised. Clark's treatment of opponents received no public commendation but caused much private glee. His conception of English history was endorsed by nobody in its entirety, but by several writers in part. The early Stuart specialists whom he had claimed as allies all responded rather coolly to the suggestion, while recognizing that they had some ideas and opponents in common. Late Stuart historians were gratified by the interest which Clark drew to their relatively neglected period, and hostile to his assumption that its political changes were essentially minor. Georgian scholars often relished the excitement which he had provided in their field. A spectrum of 'post-revisionist' opinion materialized almost immediately, united by the belief that Clark had performed a valuable service in drawing attention to important features of eighteenth-century English society, particularly the religious element, which had hitherto been neglected. Yet it was also accepted by the same writers that he had exaggerated them in turn, at the expense of elements of radicalism, dissent, commercial culture and social change which had also been present.

These, then, were the developments in recent English historiography to which the term 'revisionism' has most commonly and consistently been applied. The account given above, bound within a strict word limit, has inevitably made crude simplifications of the ideas involved and omitted mention of some work relevant to the discussions concerned. It has also failed to include important scholarship to which some have applied the same label. Thus, from 1978 onwards the Cambridge historian Alan Macfarlane has published a series of major books concerning the development of English society which challenged all previous thought on the matter and Marxist thought in particular, holding that the English had always possessed much the same social structures and attitudes. He linked himself to the same mood which produced the Stuart revisionists, and shared some of their antagonists (such as Stone) and some of their defenders (such as Elton). But he was not directly associated with the debates described above, he was not part of a body of thinkers and the main emphasis of his argument lay upon the Middle Ages. He was certainly a part of the same tendency in academe which produced early modern revisionism, but better viewed in the context of all the changes sweeping away old concepts of the British past, from the New Stone Age to the present. Also excluded from this chapter have been dramatic new assertions regarding relatively small issues. The most celebrated of these would probably be J. C. Davis's attack on the Marxist historians of the Civil War, such as Christopher Hill, for their alleged misrepresentation of the so-called 'Ranters'.

Something that must be stressed now, which was only implicit before, is that the debates outlined above directly involved only some of the specialists at work in each field. It was perfectly possible for the others to produce important work which did not engage directly in these controversies. Admittedly it was less easy for them to avoid being assigned to either of the opposed camps and sometimes to both, successively or even simultaneously. At times this process was manifestly unjust, but it often reflected a complex reality, in which individuals could indeed be both for and against the presumed groupings. The most prominent case is that of Sir Geoffrey Elton. He was, as has been shown, the forefather or prophet of early Stuart revisionism and one of the few senior historians to show sympathy for J. C. D. Clark. But to revisionists in Reformation studies, he was associated with the old order. His position was further complicated when, in 1986, his own revision of Neale's theories appeared alongside a book edited by two of his former pupils and intended to re-evaluate Sir Geoffrey's own most famous work, *The Tudor Revolution in Government*. Many of the pieces openly challenged his findings. The title, *Revolution Reassessed*, resembled that of Haigh's textbook on the Reformation, the format of each was identical and the two were understandably often referred to together as exercises in 'revisionism'. Yet when one of the editors reviewed a book on Cardinal Wolsey in 1990, which explicitly declared itself to be a revisionist work and made Sir Geoffrey one of its main targets, he coldly disassociated himself from the term. Indeed, he recalled, quite correctly, that it had originated as a piece of Marxist jargon.

Similar difficulties surround the use of the opposed term 'Whig', which featured prominently in the debates. It originated, of course, in seventeenth-century Scotland as a name for Presbyterian rebels, and was applied as an insult to one of the two opposed political parties which appeared in England around 1680. It was soon adopted by that party and stuck to it for two centuries. Then in 1941 the Cambridge scholar Sir Herbert Butterfield applied it to historians who had overemphasized and glorified developments in the past which had created the institutions and attitudes of the modern age. It was thus, once again, an expression of opprobrium, and the more effective in that Butterfield himself never named the guilty parties. Instead it became a means to castigate individuals who were presumed to commit the fault concerned, selected according to the whim of the person employing it, and was cheerfully taken up by most of those called 'revisionists' in the 1970s and 1980s. They used it to characterize Gardiner, Notestein, Dickens, Plumb and other exponents of the old orthodoxies who could not be grouped under the label of Marxist. Of all the participants in the debates concerned, only Hexter was prepared to apply it to himself, and then only in the sense that he celebrated past developments which produced aspects of modernity of which most people were proud, without distorting the record to do so. Among everybody else it was a term of criticism, increasingly applied to writers who had themselves issued challenges to former ideas. It was, in fact, the equivalent of the term 'revisionist', as originally used among Marxists, the word of abuse for an opponent within the same broad ideological camp as oneself. Thus, Derek Hirst used it in 1978 to asperse the ideas associated with Gardiner and Notestein, Mark Kishlansky used it in 1986 to attack Derek Hirst, and Kishlansky himself received the label from a younger historian, J. S. A. Adamson, in 1991. In part this did reflect a genuine progression of ideas, in part the simple truth that nothing galls antagonists more than to employ their own favourite expression of disdain against them.

All this might be taken to indicate that the controversies engendered by so-called revisionism were highly artificial creations produced by accidents of personality among historians. Certainly specialists in the late Stuart period sometimes looked on in amazement at the fuss going on around them. After all, the years 1660–1714 had long been regarded as crucial to the development of the English Church and state and had been the preserve of the historians most clearly to be characterized as Whigs (and most literally, as they had belonged to that party). In the 1970s and 1980s research into them continued steadily, with differences of opinion but within a wider sense of community and co-operation. The same tranquillity was found in late medieval studies. Obviously, what distinguished these quieter areas of scholarship was that they had not attracted the attention of a figure like Gardiner, capable of fastening a structure of interpretation about them which was accepted and elaborated by generations of successors. The air of unreality which sometimes appeared to cling to the debates between revisionists and their opponents was reinforced by the nebulous nature of the groupings concerned. After all, despite the efforts of Christianson, Haigh and Clark to perceive unified aims, revisionism never achieved the status of a school of academic thought. It had no journal, no conferences and no keynote addresses. Those associated with it had little personal contact and often disagreed with each other.

And yet their efforts did produce an enormous, and enduring, shift in the historiography of early modern England. It ceased to be a eulogy of the characteristics of the realm of Victoria, and a quest for their origins. Protestantism, representative democracy and a powerful middle class were no longer seen as organic and irresistible growths from early modern English society. In the changed circumstances of the late twentieth century, these things had come to seem much more fragile creations, and (to some) much less worthy of respect. In a sense the view of the past thus produced came close to that of the greatest of all genuine Whig historians, Lord Macaulay, who had regarded his world as the product of human effort aided by providential good luck. But Macaulay and his kind had viewed the ultimate victors of early modern England as heroic progenitors, whereas in large part revisionism consisted of a novel sympathy with the vanquished. It could be suggested that Tudor Catholics, Stuart monarchs, Georgian aristocrats and American Indians were all beneficiaries of the same recoil of opinion which occurred in the Western world in the 1960s. As traditional institutions and values came to be questioned, it was easier to pity the victims of the processes which had created them.

But more was achieved than a mere reversal of sympathies or even a greater balance between them. The arguments created by revisionism set new standards of research, involving a more careful inspection of more documents. They established, apparently for ever, that the causes of the political events of early modern England were in the main political, and that chance and short-term planning by individuals could produce immense change. They proved the supreme importance of central politics in national affairs. In addition they created a new sense of the sheer complexity of the past and the great extent to which it differed from the present. It has ceased to provide easy answers to large questions. Instead the study of it now offers a much greater variety and richness of experience. More than before, it belongs to all of the dead, and all of the living.

REFERENCES

Adamson, J. S. A. (1991) 'Politics and the nobility in Civil War England', *Historical Journal.*
Cogswell, T. (1989) *The Blessed Revolution*, Cambridge.
Dickens, A. G. (1964) *The English Reformation*, London.
Elton, G. R. (1986) *The Parliament of England 1559–81*, Cambridge.
Fletcher, A. (1981) *The Outbreak of the English Civil War*, London.
Gardiner, S. R. (1856–85) *The History of England from the Accession of James I to the Outbreak of the Civil War*, 10 vols, London.
—— (1888–93) *The History of the Great Civil War*, 4 vols, London.
—— (1895–1901) *The History of the Commonwealth and Protectorate*, 4 vols, London.
Guy, J. (1988) *Tudor England*, Oxford.
Haigh, C. (1975) *Reformation and Resistance in Tudor Lancashire*, Cambridge.
Kishlansky, M. (1986) *Parliamentary Selection*, Cambridge.

Lockyer, R. (1981) *Buckingham*, London.

MacCulloch, D. (1990) *The Later Reformation in England*, Basingstoke.

Neale, J. E. (1953–7) *Elizabeth I and her Parliaments*, 2 vols, London.

Notestein, W. (1924) *The Winning of the Initiative by the House of Commons*, New Haven, CT.

Redworth, G. (1987) 'The Henrician reform of the Church: a post-revisionist view', *History Today*.

Roberts, S. K. (1985) *Recovery and Restoration in an English County*, Exeter.

Scarisbrick, J. J. (1984) *The Reformation and the English People*, Oxford.

Sommerville, J. P. (1986) *Politics and Ideology in England 1603–1640*, London.

Stone, L. (1972) *The Causes of the English Revolution*, London.

Underdown, D. (1985) *Revel, Riot and Rebellion*, Oxford.

Whiting, R. (1989) *The Blind Devotion of the People*, Cambridge.

IV REFLECTING ON
THE MODERN AGE

INTRODUCTION: APPROACHES TO MODERNITY: WESTERN HISTORIOGRAPHY SINCE THE ENLIGHTENMENT

Michael Bentley

'Modernity' carries a number of resonances and dangers as we review developments in historical thought and practice over two of its most critical centuries. Not least, it invites a collapse into precisely one of those developments – the nineteenth-century notion of a 'Whig' understanding of history – which would see the period as a process of constant 'advances' towards a sophisticated present from a primitive past, giving prizes along the way to those historians who sound precocious and patronizing those who do not. But it seems important to establish some base-lines to the enquiry and to give necessary shape to an account which, reduced to a list of great writers and random subjects, would become as long and boggling as the period itself. It was in this period that history discovered its identity as a discipline: a distinctive way of organising and representing knowledge. During these years its practitioners acquired the rationale, the techniques and the self-awareness that would lead to their displaying the characteristics that we think of as 'modern' attributes in historiography. They exhibited source-criticism at new forensic levels; they created texts of massive proportion and complex structure; they deployed ideas picked up from other kinds of enquiry; they talked and argued and quarrelled about how the job should be done in a vocabulary quite unavailable to Suetonius or Bede, Guiccardini or Bodin. The story cannot be read, however, as a single narrative. It is better seen as a series of overlapping (and often contradictory) moods and doctrines whose interaction we must heed and explain if the account is to go beyond a roll of honour or the flat description of forgotten books.

Standing back from any specific works of history, one can ask immediate questions about the character of eighteenth-century historiography before its character underwent a series of shifts in the intellectual revolution known as the Enlightenment. It was the product, plainly, of a distinctive environment which had felt the effects of an epoch of scientific advance in the generation of Sir Isaac

Newton (1642–1727). This new climate supplied a fresh sense of time itself, wrenching temporal understanding away from the relativistic models that had seemed natural to medieval authors and substituting a notion of absolute time that passed independently of the world whose changes it measured—a notion deeply embedded in all views of the past until the twentieth century offered a fundamental revision in the wake of a second revolution in science and philosophy.[1] More tangibly, the offensive mounted by science and the astringent philosophies of Descartes, Spinoza and Locke could not but exert pressure on divine explanations of the universe and, by extension, on its past. These ideas, plus the reverberations of a changing order in the growth of states and their mutual relationships, helped give rise to what Eric Voegelin called a dominant 'sense of epoch' in the new century:

> We do not find before 1700 a comprehensive interpretation of man in society and history that could take into account the constituent factors of the new situation, that is: the breakdown of the Church as the universal institution of Christian mankind, the plurality of sovereign states as ultimate political units, the discovery of the New World and the more intimate acquaintance with Asiatic civilizations, the idea of the non-Christian nature of man as the foundation for speculation on law and ethics, the demonism of the parochial, national communities and the idea of the passions as motivating forces of man. Only after 1700 does the cumulative effect of these various factors make itself felt in the acute consciousness that, in the aggregate, an epoch has come to an end and that the new situation requires a gigantic effort of interpretation in order to recover for the existence of man in society and history a meaning which could substitute for the lost meaning of Christian existence.[2]

This view has implications. It means that Bossuet's *Universal History* of 1681 had lost much of its contemporary relevance before the book reached its audience.[3] It means that one needs to be cautious before declaring eighteenth-century writing 'empirical', as modern writers often do,[4] partly because empiricism (in so far as it involves a lack of theoretical assumption) is impossible in practice and unthinkable in the abstract, partly because these authors responded to a series of stimuli which made their work look devoid of concepts since they were attempting to defy overarching explanations of the world familiar to their grandfathers. Certainly those who seriously addressed the status of knowledge as an issue began with the questions raised by 'empirical' science; but the thought applies little to those writing history who had their own priorities and starting-points. Dr Johnson's kicking against a stone in order to refute a philosophical enemy was more sophisticated

---

1 I simplify here part of the thrust of an interesting argument about modern conceptions of time: see Wilcox 1987. Cf. Whitrow 1988; Rotenstreich 1987.

2 Voegelin 1975: 5. For more details see Maner 1982.

3 Bossuet 1681 had been neither universal nor informed by the critical techniques of the French school associated with Jean Mabillon whose *De Re Diplomatica* was published in the same year. It perpetuated divine motivation as the guiding force in the world. A recent study is Meyer 1993.

4 e.g. Patrick Gardiner (1959: 5), who believes that 'a strong emphasis upon considerations of an empirical character remains its most striking feature'; cf. Haddock 1980: 73; Jann 1985: xvi–xix.

(because more pointed), after all, than its violence suggests; and historians, in kicking against their own forms of contemporary resistance, did not operate randomly or in innocence. So robust a thinker as Dr Johnson understood, for example, the distinction between 'a journal, which has regard only to time, and a history which ranges facts according to their dependence on each other, and postpones or anticipates according to the convenience of narration'.[5] His contemporaries also used the language of 'anachronism' as a form of criticism: there are examples of it in English from the mid-seventeenth century. Two terms escaped currency, however, until around 1780: the idea of a 'period' of history designating a stretch of time with an internal unity;[6] and, more important, the notion of a 'source' understood as comprising one of the elements out of which a historical text might flow just as a river originates in its source. William Robertson in his history of America seems to have been the first to use the word in that sense in 1777.[7] What was absent in historical thinking for the first three-quarters of the eighteenth century seems, from a modern perspective, quite as suggestive as what was present.

Another characteristic of that thinking makes one think hard again about the allegation of empiricism. For one of the most prevalent modes of representing the past lay in creating moral lessons with historical events as their illustrations. The view that history was fit only for 'philosophy teaching by example' did not originate in the eighteenth century: it occurs in classical writers and Renaissance writers rediscovered it (Culler 1985: 4). But Lord Bolingbroke's *Letters on the Study and Use of History* (1752) gave the concept a contemporary cachet and few authors of his day avoided giving a patina to their text that was intended to elevate the mind of the reader or bend it towards a particular conclusion. This operation was not carried out empirically; it required authors to come to their task with a sense of commitment, even if they would have had difficulty in defining the message that they intended to convey.

The early eighteenth century had sometimes gone beyond such expressions of doctrine, especially in Italy where it had done so at two levels. So far as historical practice went, the monumental work of collection and edition associated with Ludovico Muratori (1672–1750) – 'the grandfather of modern historiography'[8] – brought a distinguished tradition of Italian writing since the Renaissance to a

---

5 Samuel Johnson to Mr Cave, n.d. (*c.*1742), in James Boswell, *The Life of Samuel Johnson LL.D.* (2 vols, 1791), I, 155. By a 'journal' Johnson obviously has in mind what later historical thinkers refer to as 'chronicle'.

6 I do not mean to overlook earlier deployments of 'period' in the more limited sense of conveniently divided units of time such as 'ages' or 'centuries': we see those in various forms from the Renaissance onwards. For coverage of this wider period, see Hay 1977.

7 Robertson 1777. Robertson (1721–93), was Principal of Edinburgh University and Historiographer Royal. The study of America followed two volumes on the *History of Scotland* (1759) and three volumes on the reign of Charles V.

8 Hay 1977. Muratori was aware of the work of the Maurists and went on to prepare a vast collection of documents intended to throw light on the medieval period in Italy, the *Antiquitates Italicae Medii Aevi* (1738–42). He also wrote about theatre, ethics and religion.

conclusion in the twenty-eight volumes of *Rerum Italicarum Scriptores*, which began to appear in 1723 and was remarkable for its precocity seen against instances of the nationalistic search for origins that characterizes so much European historiography in the first half of the nineteenth century. At a second level of argument, however, Italian precocity ran still deeper. In his own lifetime Giambattista Vico (1668–1744) remained all but unknown, a struggling and impoverished professor of rhetoric at the University of Naples. When he died his ideas died with him. Only when the French historian Jules Michelet rediscovered and popularized his thinking did Vico's originality as a historical thinker begin to emerge. In the twentieth century, with its absorption in the nature of language and its relationship to what holders of a given vocabulary can think and what they cannot, he has become almost a guru, particularly since Vico meets most modern norms of intellectuality by having lived a thankless life marked by incessant adversity. His *New Science* (1725–44) is now often read as the first serious treatment of the issues raised in modern philosophy of history, marking the moment when historical thinking came of age.

We can say at once that much of this recent opinion verges on the absurd. In the first place, other scholars could match the range of ideas that we associate with Vico, none more powerfully than another Neapolitan historian, Pietro Giannone (1676–1748), who wrote a successful history of the kingdom of Naples.[9] Vico's own historical writing, dating from the early part of his life, remained completely traditional.[10] His Catholicism not only endured (unlike Giannone's) but formed an element in rationalizing his views about history, chopping off significant areas of human enquiry as raising questions answerable only by God. Chief among these was the natural world – since God made it, only he could comprehend it – but Vico held that man made something, too: he constructed, through the various epochs of his history, the civil society in which he lives. Because he had made it, moreover, he could, in principle, discover the truth about it. This idea, Vico's *verum factum* principle, formed the starting-point for much of his thought about why history mattered and why the vaunted new 'science' of the Newtonians would remain chimerical. Certainly the world needed a new science but it would not find one in mathematics or physics but rather by focusing on what man, with his restricted faculties, might competently investigate. This task, he sees at once, raises problems of its own and, since no one has addressed them,

> we must proceed as if there were no books in the world.
> But in this dense night of darkness which enshrouds earliest antiquity so distant from us, appears the eternal light, which never sets, of this truth which is beyond any possible doubt: that the civil world has itself been made by men, and that its principles therefore can, because they must, be rediscovered within the modifications of our own human

9 I am grateful for John Robertson's correction over this point. A prescient series of remarks about the strength of Giannone appears in Barnes 1962: 129–30.

10 *De antiquissima Italorum sapientia ex linguae Latinae originibus eruenda* (3 vols, Naples, 1710). But there had been a hint of things to come in his dissertation on methodology, *De nostri temporis studiorum ratione* (1708).

mind. And this must give anyone who reflects upon its cause to marvel how the philosophers have all earnestly endeavoured to attain knowledge of the natural world which, since he made it, God alone knows, and have neglected to meditate upon this world of nations, or civil world, knowledge of which, since men had made it, they could attain.

(Vico 1982: 198)

It was an arresting proposition but would remain no more than that unless Vico could suggest a better method of research than meditation.

This he did and hinted at its content in the word 'modifications'. Now some nineteenth-century writers (and particularly Vico's countryman, Benedetto Croce) fastened on the term in order to make Vico sound as though he had been born a follower of Hegel a century too soon (cf. Walsh 1976: 144). In fact, Vico had groped his way towards an idea of the greatest importance. He believed that societies changed non-randomly, that each phase of their changing needed to be seen as part of an entire series and that at each point in their development they exhibited characteristics – and only those characteristics – that were appropriate to their location in this process of transformation. As Isaiah Berlin expressed it,

> in the individual and society alike, phase follows phase not haphazardly (as the Epicureans thought) nor in a series of mechanical causes or effects (as the Stoics taught) but as stages in the pursuit of an intelligible purpose – man's effort to understand himself and his world, and to realise his capacities in it.

(Berlin 1976: 34–5)

The modifications in world-view that Vico writes about have to be seen in this light: they give a clue to the moments when history moves from one phase to another. And the clue to the modifications comes, as one might expect from a professor of rhetoric, in language. So long, therefore, as we can reconstruct the vocabulary of past civilizations, we can re-enter their thought world and understand their history.

What Vico said about the past, as opposed to how to study it, was far less impressive. In Book Four of the *Scienza Nuova*, he invents a series of rigid triads, 'the three sects of times which the nations profess in the course of the lives' (Vico 1982: 250). Rather 'the' than 'their' because the course is common: it takes the form of an endless cycle of advance and regression – *corsi e ricorsi* – as all societies proceed from an age of gods, through an age of heroes to an age of men; and then back to the beginning again. Each age produces distinctive configurations, so one has three kinds of nature, three of custom, three of natural law, three of civil statehood, and so on. None of this seems plausible but it hardly matters. What Marx and others were to take away from Vico was a sense of how historical change might be viewed and investigated. In the long term his ideas would help form one vital pole of argument about history that affected discussion until the First World War.[11] In the short term he was, like the rest of us, dead. His death in 1744 left the

---

11   His life and work have come under recent revaluation in Lilla 1993.

399

intellectual world untroubled, the content of historical writing unchanged and its centre of gravity not in Naples but in Paris.

THE ENLIGHTENMENT

Many of the characteristics attributed promiscuously to eighteenth-century historiography become more persuasive when directed at a special form of it: that inspired by the renaissance (primarily French) of ideas and cultural ambitions which modernity has come to call the 'Enlightenment'. This intellectual environment (at its most intense between, say, 1750 and 1790) gave rise to historical enquiry of a marked character and one by no means shared by other countries in other decades. It promoted a singular sense of the present as a moment of exceptional importance and weight in the history of the world. The *philosophes* of Paris seemed transparently pleased to be living in the eighteenth century and to have transcended the Greek and Roman cultures by which their contemporaries elsewhere still appeared obsessed. 'European elites had lived since the Renaissance with a culture borrowed from antiquity,' writes François Furet,

> a period whose artists and authors represented unsurpassable models and whose literary genres constituted the authoritative canons of beauty and truth. Now Europe was raising the question of its cultural autonomy: the academic quarrel between 'ancients' and 'moderns' in France at the end of Louis XIV's reign ultimately centred on the notion that classical culture was not a past but a present.
>
> (Furet 1984: 81)

Because the present had won a new pedigree at the expense of the past, only parts of the past interested the Enlightenment. Its prophets retained a veneration for the classical world; and they displayed a new enthusiasm for quite recent history which would show how their own superior culture evolved. In theory such a sense of evolution might produce a conception of the long-term transitions from ancient to modern times, as one of the Enlightenment's most suggestive exemplars, Condorcet, implies in the introduction to his best-known historical essay:

> All peoples whose history is recorded fall somewhere between our present degree of civilisation and that which we still see among savage tribes; if we survey in a single sweep the universal history of peoples we see them sometimes making fresh progress, sometimes plunging back into ignorance, sometimes surviving somewhere between these extremes or halted at a certain point, sometimes disappearing from the earth under the conqueror's heel, mixing with the victors or living on in slavery, or sometimes receiving knowledge from some enlightened people in order to transmit it in their turn to other nations, and so welding an uninterrupted chain between the beginning of historical time and the century in which we live.
>
> (Condorcet 1795: 8)

But pieties of this kind rarely transcended theory. In practice the Enlightenment amused itself with celebrated figures in modern history such as Charles XII or Louis XIV. One much-recalled text, Voltaire's *Essai sur les mœurs* of 1756, did, it is true, attempt a more ambitious survey of world history in order to frame an answer to

Bossuet's despised work of 1681, though even there the novelty appeared more in the territory covered geographically than in the periods Voltaire treated chronologically. For the most part, however, the Enlightenment omitted from its purview periods of history that it found distasteful and, since the whole of the Middle Ages was found coarse and untutored, this meant that medieval history had little presence in Paris.

Enlightened history discovered grounds for satisfaction in the present and to this extent it harboured philosophical pretensions. Indeed, one notices at once that its spokesmen – for they are mostly men – established reputations as philosophers, mathematicians, statesmen or *belle-lettristes* before taking to history. Once having taken to it, they displayed an undercurrent of opinion about the past which might be reduced to three central properties. First, they argued a position that shrieked secularism. The easiest prediction to make about any work inspired by the French Enlightenment is that it will attack organized religion and betray that sardonic anticlericalism found in most other statements by the *philosophes*. Second, they reflected a cynicism about the motivations and moral capacities of individuals while elevating *l'esprit humain* to new levels of moral authority, thus granting the impersonal force what they denied in its agents. Third and most significant, they constructed texts in which satire does not stop at the clerics but rather forms a crucial part of the tone for the entire enterprise. The story turns out well because it turns out in the present; and the telling of the story can therefore afford a certain buoyancy. Wit consequently does service for thought but often does it brilliantly. The result is the opposite of tragedy. Each author brings to the task a different collection of skills and moods, but the general point requiring stress is one made by Hayden White: that the Enlightenment bequeathes no tragic history just as (and for the same reason that) it leaves no tragic literature. Its satire functions not as a decorative motif in its texts but as a fundamental mode of representation (White 1973: 66).

If there seems less satire than elsewhere in Condorcet's posthumous *Esquisse* of 1795, then the circumstances of its writing more than explain the peculiarity. He had enjoyed a life in which talent and noble birth coalesced to make him secretary of the Académie des Sciences by the time he was 30. The Revolution proved his undoing. He had collaborated in it at first but opposed the new Jacobin constitution and found himself forced into hiding. After his detection and arrest he was thrown into prison where he died in 1794, possibly by his own hand. His essay reflecting on the history of humanity stems from these last, difficult years; and although the tone lacks the cockiness of Voltaire, the text offers perhaps the most rounded illustration of Enlightenment method and assumptions in their application to history. Montesquieu (1749) had been more profound in his better-known comparative study of law but Condorcet presents a more relevant model to those wishing to form a view of the French Enlightenment's tendencies in historiography.

Like Vico, Condorcet thinks in threes. Humanity's history falls into three stages. The first runs from the darkness of an unknowable primitivism up to the development of language; our views of it rest necessarily on conjecture and travellers' tales. A second phase, hardly more accessible to the present, moves from the coming of language to the introduction of alphabetic writing which Condorcet invests with signal importance. The third phase comprises, simply, everything else. Because he sees the second stage as having been completed by the time of the Greeks, this latter section of history runs from the classical period to the present. From this point forward in the narrative the historian does have access to the truth via the writings of contemporaries and the epoch offers a continuum,

> linked by an uninterrupted chain of facts and observations. ... Philosophy has nothing more to guess, no more hypothetical surmises to make; it is enough to assemble and order the facts and to show the useful truths that can be derived from their connections and from their totality.
>
> (Condorcet 1795: 9)

He then goes on to subdivide his three phases into a further triad of which the last is the most interesting. It begins with the revival of science and the development of printing; it proceeds to show how science later threw off the yoke of 'authority'; and that leaves the author with the present—a culture about which he can feel optimistic, despite his own misfortunes, because science will point the way to the future. His first book had been a study of integral calculus. In a real sense his last one was, too.

Perhaps the absorption with philosophy and science militated against the production of a great French historian in this generation. The French had to wait until the Revolution became the focus of modern experience and the stuff of a new history that Michelet would make his own fifty years later. The country which ought to have produced an enlightened historiography – America, the child of Parisian ideas – again did not do so in a significant form before 1800. Instead the extension of 'enlightened' thought into historical practice occurred elsewhere, most notably in Scotland and England.

That Scotland should have received the teaching of France will surprise no one familiar with the traditional affinity between the two societies. It is especially well reflected in the biography of David Hume (1712–76) whose *History of England* (1754–62) constitutes a *locus classicus* for those exploring the Enlightenment's sense of history. Still known to the British Library Catalogue as 'David Hume *the Historian*', he is better known (and with good reason) as a philosopher. Hume had spent many years alternating between Europe and Britain before accepting a post in 1752 as librarian to the Faculty of Advocates in Edinburgh where he had access to the sources that would allow him to write history. He intended from the start that his historical books would make some money to compensate for the abysmal sales of his philosophical works. And since the more recent periods of the English past attracted both him and his likely audience, and 'being frightened with the notion of continuing a narrative through a period of seventeen hundred years' (Hume 1754–62: I, xi), he began there and wrote the story backwards, in effect, over the next decade. The 'first' volume on the Stuarts caused him constant grief because of allegations that followed relating to its sympathy with Charles I and the Stuart cause; and those insinuations (that he was a Tory historian blind to the virtues of the Whig revolution of 1688) certainly diverted attention from the degree to which Hume reflected the presuppositions of the Enlightenment throughout the work.

Not that his philosophical sophistication interfered with the text: one of its surprises lies in the degree to which Hume forgot his own doctrines, over causation for example, the moment he turned to writing about past events. Indeed, he forgot about so much that it becomes tempting to see neither an enlightened nor an unenlightened historian in Hume so much as a bad one *tout court*. But the echoes of Parisian salons occur too frequently for that. He shared the loathing of Paris for barbarous epochs such as the Anglo-Saxon period and dismissed them as quickly as possible without any need for research:

> We can say little, but that they were in general a rude, uncultivated people, ignorant of letters, unskilled in the mechanical arts, untamed to submission under law and government, addicted to intemperance, riot and disorder. ... The conquest put the people in a situation of receiving slowly from abroad the rudiments of science and cultivation, and of correcting their rough and licentious manners.
>
> (ibid. I, 305–6)

Even in the Stuart volume, Hume's Parisian assumptions shine through the narrative, despite his fondness for romance in the pre-Civil War years, in his treatment of evidence and readiness to use the conjectural method when speaking of matters for which he has no evidence at all. Consider what he cannot possibly 'know', for example, in one of his most famous passages – that describing the execution of Charles I in 1649:

> It is impossible to describe the grief, indignation, and astonishment, which took place, not only among the spectators, who were overwhelmed with a flood of sorrow, but throughout the whole nation, as soon as the report of this fatal execution was conveyed to them. . . . On weaker minds, the effect of these complicated passions was prodigious. Women are said to have cast forth the untimely fruit of their womb: others fell into convulsions, or sank into such a melancholy as attended them to their grave: nay, some, unmindful of themselves, as though they could not, or would not, survive their beloved prince, it is reported, suddenly fell down dead. The very pulpits were bedewed with unsuborned tears.[12]

These methods are less grossly exposed in William Robertson of Edinburgh, whose histories of Scotland and America, beside his better-known study of Charles V, suggest a wider vision and a more historical mind.[13]

England's relations with the Continent notoriously had a different tone from the Scottish, but Edward Gibbon's travels had long since overcome any sense of distance. The death of his father in 1770 led him to settle in London; he had

---

12   Ibid. VIII, 137–8. For the significance of the 'conjectural' approach, see Peardon 1933; 10–11 and *passim*.

13   Robertson's books enjoyed a long life as well as extraordinary sales by eighteenth-century standards. Edward Freeman later recalled that 'the superficial Robertson' was an author still in use at Oxford when he was an undergraduate there in the 1840s. See Bentley 1993: 139.

lived before then mainly in Lausanne and had travelled considerably. The famous visit to Rome had occurred in 1764 and intention became reality from 1768 when he began the narrative of *The Decline and Fall of the Roman Empire* (1776–88), which by the end of the nineteenth century attained the status of Boswell on Johnson as a work of literature and which today remains the one historical study that most educated people would identify as an example of eighteenth-century historical writing. That he had a grasp greater than either Boswell or Johnson of the issues raised by a large-scale historical project had apparently eluded both of them in a three-way conversation of 1775 to which Boswell gives us an allusion:

> JOHNSON. 'We must consider how very little history there is; I mean real authentick history. That certain Kings reigned, and certain battles were fought, we can depend upon as true; but all the colouring, all the philosophy of history is conjecture.'
> BOSWELL. 'Then, Sir, you would reduce all history to no better than an almanack, a mere chronological series of remarkable events.'
> Mr. Gibbon, who must at that time have been employed upon his history of which he produced the first volume in the following year, was present; but did not step forth in defence of that species of writing. He probably did not like to *trust* himself with JOHNSON!
>
> (Boswell 1791: II, 365–6)

Unlike most of his contemporaries, Gibbon believed he could recreate a past entire by paying attention to the known sources and discovering new ones in artefacts and the eighteenth-century mania for inscriptions. This determination, his talent for evocation and a prose of unsurpassed pointedness almost displaced him, indeed, from the model of representation that we are characterizing as an Enlightenment approach.

What kept him there was his irony: a Tacitean manner as *dix-huitième* as a tricorn hat.[14] The account works, as Gay points out, on at least two levels simultaneously. The public level of intention offered by his actors has one tone, the private reality a different one; 'he compels the reader to become his accomplice and to draw the unpleasant, generally cynical, inference for himself' (Gay 1975: 47). His sources never matched his creativity. Neither did the criticism that he brought to the ones he had. But he invented a text containing both meaning and explanation. The Romans lost their way by following courses and suffering adversities which would undermine any society and Gibbon's account of the undermining is conceived as a general explanation, not a particular one. He thinks, in other words, nomothetically; he explains the events by identifying the laws which govern them. There are many of these – the effeminacy generated by a lack of war, the unforeseen effects of economic exploitation, the weakness attending the expansion of empires, and so on. But one of them is critical and forms the subtext of the book as a whole. This lies in the contention that freedom is the guarantor of civic health – 'the happy parent taste and science' (Gibbon [1776–88] 1909: I, 64) – and its denial the harbinger of

---

14   On Gibbon's debt to Tacitus, see Gay 1975, esp. 26. Cf. Burrow 1985; Porter 1988.

social sclerosis. Everything else follows. Not least, this means that government must avoid the pitfalls of crude democracy and remember that

> the firm edifice of Roman power was raised and preserved by the wisdom of ages. The obedient provinces of Trajan and the Antonines were united by laws and adorned by arts … [T]he general principle of government was wise, simple and beneficent.'
>
> (ibid. I, 31)

Yet of course Gibbon's starting-point is itself a derivative from that recent past on which enlightened opinion rested. His book celebrates implicitly the English constitutional settlement of 1689 and the freedom that it bestowed by chastizing the Romans for having won the same prize and having lost it.

Through these books and less accomplished instances of an Enlightenment sensibility, the new historical values found expression. The importance for any critical form of enquiry of intellectual self-confidence and a rejection of metaphysical authority needs little argument; and to that extent the climate generated in Europe after 1750 contributed unquestionably to the development of historical ideas. It is less obvious how much it limited them. In generalizing its perceptions of a particular present and ironing out kinks in the human condition, eighteenth-century thought lost contact with the specific and the particular about which historians ultimately want to know. In reducing the world to law, the Enlightenment's understanding of history truncated the past as a domain for enquiry. It also became out of date virtually the moment it was announced. For the revolution of 1789 shattered more than French society, just as Napoleon's armies brought about the destruction of more than life and property. Dislocations across Europe gave rise to questions about the nature of states and the origins of cultural identity, about the *differences* between histories rather than their commonality. For philosophers as much as for historians, the world after 1789 called for something higher than cynicism, more memorable than the tattle of the *salon*, more plausible than the publicizing of progress and the hidden hand of *l'esprit humain*.

THE COUNTER-ENLIGHTENMENT

All the glitter of Paris easily outshone a story of impending change east of the Rhine. Yet although that story lacked the gloss of the Enlightenment, it turned out to have more significance for the writing of history than what had taken place in France and Britain. The confused organism of principalities and potential states that would later coalesce as 'Germany' had begun to acquire its own voice by 1800. It was a timid voice at first. German intellectuals stood in awe of French achievement and culture. They copied British historiographical models drawn in particular from Hume, Robertson and Gibbon.[15] They shared a European fascination with Sir

---

15 See McClelland 1971: 13. For a recent magisterial survey of German intellectual currents, see Sheehan 1989, esp. chs 6 and 9.

Walter Scott.[16] In the last third of the eighteenth century the German-speaking world nevertheless gave rise to the most talented array of intellectuals, artists and poets that has been squeezed into one or two generations in modern times: Goethe, Kant, Herder, Schiller, Hegel, Beethoven, Heine, Schubert. Some of their achievement ran parallel with the Enlightenment and fed on what others had sown. But more was original and, so far as the central characteristics of Enlightenment thought went, counter-thematic. In sharing Sir Isaiah Berlin's category of a 'Counter-Enlightenment' we are therefore calling attention to an important distinction rather than a frontal opposition.[17] We shall dwell on it, nevertheless, because no other intellectual initiative has played so great a role in fashioning attitudes to modern historical thinking.

Institutions played a considerable part in establishing a new understanding of history in Germany.[18] Two foundations – the University of Göttingen in 1737 and the new University of Berlin in 1810 – engage with the relevant events at a number of points. Göttingen became a point of entry for external, and especially British, ideas; and because it established the first historical school in Germany, the way opened for widespread reception of historical models from abroad. It generated, however, distinctive ideas of its own. Law and philology gained a status and collegiality with history which has since become a hallmark of German historical education (Breisach 1983; McClelland 1971: 16). They won that status not least because of the distinction of those appointed to teach. Looking back from the eve of the First World War, the historian G. P. Gooch (himself a sort of enlightened liberal) saw in Göttingen in the last part of the eighteenth century an unequalled academic community:

> While the new era of classical research is connected with Berlin, the historical study of jurisprudence is identified with Göttingen. Though Gesner and Heyne made the Hanoverian foundation the centre of philological studies for half a century, the political and historical sciences had always been strongly represented. Pütter in German law, Martens in International law, Spittler, Schlözer, Gatterer in history, Achenwall in statistics, formed a galaxy or which no other seat of learning could boast.
>
> (Gooch 1913: 42)

August Ludwig von Schlözer (1735–1809) concerned himself with translating Russian sources into German: a precondition for advances in German projects. But he also recommended against the current taste for the history of violence and war (*Mordgeschichte*) and believed that 'greater revolutions have often resulted from the quiet musings of the genius and the gentle virtue of the man of wisdom than from the violence of all-powerful tyrants'.[19] Johann Christoph

---

16   For Scott, see Bann 1984. For Scott and Ranke, see Gilbert 1990: 37.

17   For explication of Berlin's views, see Gray 1995 and their polemical development in Gray's other recent writing.

18   I shall use the term 'Germany' as a convenient shorthand, despite the dangers of the term when referring to German history before 1871.

19   Quoted in Reill 1975: 45. I am greatly indebted to Professor Reill's account in this section. Cf. Winter 1961.

Gatterer (1727–99) considered the problems of method in history and in his work on diplomatic, numismatics and genealogy called attention to a variety of *Hilfswissenschaften*.[20]

In the case of Berlin, the circumstances of the university's foundation outweighed its intrinsic importance. The French Revolution had occasioned more alarm than admiration in Germany and the Napoleonic occupation had hardly lessened the concern. One result emerged in a new sense of Germanic nationalism, originally among the intelligentsia and later reflected in political and military elites. It comprised in effect the rejection of inferiority and asserted the claim to a history no less valuable than those of other cultures. Herder had argued in his *Reflections on the Philosophy of the History of Mankind* (1784–91) that the unit of analysis should be the *Volk*. The events around him persuaded him that it was time for the German people to see themselves as one of Europe's *Völker* and to look for their identity in the past. 'I do not believe,' he wrote in 1793, 'that the Germans have less feeling than other nations for the merits of their ancestors. I think I see a time coming when we shall return more seriously to their achievements and learn to value our old gold' (quoted in Gooch 1913: 54). It was in that spirit that national leaders such as vom Stein and intellectuals such as Humboldt put their weight behind the idea of a new university in Berlin: one that would act as a treasure house for the gold of the German past.

Certainly it would attract scholars in other areas too; one of Humboldt's first *coups* lay in enticing the gifted jurist Savigny to the new institution. But Stein's special interest explicitly comprised the German past and it was in this field that Berlin would prove particularly powerful. Stein had known the Danish bureaucrat Barthold Georg Niebuhr for some years. He brought Niebuhr to the University to develop his work in Roman history while acting as plenipotentiary for Prussia in discussions with Britain during the wars of liberation. Niebuhr's achievement in his *History of Rome* (1811–12) would dominate Roman scholarship, as we shall see, until the work of Theodor Mommsen later in the century. But Stein wanted to go further than the classical period. He pressed for research and teaching in German history. One crucial outcome took shape in 1821. Under the guidance of an extraordinary archivist, Carl August Friedrich Pertz, a vast project to be called the *Monumenta Germaniae Historica* would identify, edit, annotate and print the dispersed record of the German people: its folk-tales, its literature, its charters, its manuscripts. Over a century and a half later that project still continues.[21] A further outcome had equally momentous consequences. In March 1825 the University appointed Leopold von Ranke to its teaching complement on the strength of his

---

20 For Gatterer and others, see the symposium 'Enlightenment Historiography: Three German Studies', *History and Theory*, Beiheft 11 (1971): 1–86.

21 Perhaps one might note *en passant* that a French initiative in the wake of the *Monumenta* – the *Collections de documents inédits sur l'histoire de France* which began to appear from 1836 – owed its inspiration to Guizot and tried to achieve for France a similar objective to that reflected in Stein's project.

recently published history of early modern Europe from 1494 to 1535.[22] Over the next half-century he would introduce a revolution into the writing and teaching of history and give German history the self-confidence that Stein would have wished. Both in Ranke and more crudely in his pupils one can see a distinctive style of history running from the expulsion of Napoleon to the ascendancy of Kaiser Wilhelm:

> Out of the Wars of Liberation arose the myth of the Spirit of 1813 cultivated by Prussian-oriented historians from Droysen to Meinecke and central to the beliefs of the German historist[23] tradition. From this perspective the reformed Prussian monarchy marked a high point in the history of human freedom, a society in which the individual was fully free, but at the same time was integrated into a social whole. Here was the core of the 'German conception of freedom', of the ideas of 1813, which German historians contrasted sharply with the atomistic view of society supposedly inherent in the ideas of 1789.
>
> (Iggers 1983: 21)

This rejection of 'atomism' and the affirmation of 'historism' issued directly from the Counter-Enlightenment and they afford an instance of how one cannot explain the nineteenth-century German experience in institutional terms alone. An important intellectual shift had plainly taken place and the new context makes little sense until one first understands it.

We have seen that Enlightenment history had claimed a status for itself as 'philosophical' to the extent that historical enquiry had a moral function, that of teaching by example. The German connection with philosophy rested on a firmer base. It took seriously the claim of historical writing to represent a sector of epistemology, i.e. it constituted a series of truth-claims about the past which required testing and validation in the same way as any other assertion of knowledge. For that reason the philosophies of Immanuel Kant, Johann Gottfried von Herder and G. W. F. Hegel assumed special significance for two generations of German students and teachers and it barely overstates the case to see the tenor of German historiography down to 1914 as having taken its character from a sympathy with, or aversion to, the cluster of philosophical positions often described as 'Idealist'.[24] To dwell on a difficult philosophical position may strike the reader as unnecessary when reviewing what historians wrote, but the contentions here will be that the view of the past constructed as a by-product of Idealist thought operated as an alternative assumption to that presented by the Enlightenment and that an adequate conception of nineteenth-century historiography will elude anyone who has not grasped that the argument wound between two poles and not around one of them.

---

22 *Geschichten der romanischen und germanischen Völker von 1494 bis 1535* (1824), usually translated literally and dismally as the *Histories of the Latin and Teutonic Nations*.

23 The concept of 'historism' is discussed later in this essay.

24 I shall use the capitalized form of the word to denote this philosophical meaning as opposed to the ascription of an elevated ethical position in politics or social thought that is normally connoted by lower-case idealism.

Kant's spectacular achievement or disservice in *The Critique of Pure Reason* (1781) consisted in his separation of the real, existing world from the individual trying to make sense of it. For the divide envisaged by Kant between the 'knowing subject' (the observer) and his 'object' (the thing observed) was no trivial matter of distance or convenience or intelligence or disinformation. It derived from a fundamental and intractable truth. The 'knowing subject' gains his 'knowledge' of the world by processing internally the various kinds of sense-data available to him. But the data – the perfume of the flower, the taste of the sugar, the image of the landscape – can never be transcended to give him knowledge of the thing that lay behind the bouquet, the taste and the perception. His 'knowledge' will never be more than an awareness of reality's effects on him; he can never transcend his body's confinements in order to investigate the external object – the *Ding-an-sich* or thing-in-itself – in the thing's own terms rather than the ones necessarily limiting his understanding. In so far as he claims 'knowledge' of reality, he is merely making a claim on behalf of pictures and sensory impressions gained of an external world which certainly exists and stimulates the impressions but which he can never know as he knows himself and his own thought-world.

If these ideas have any validity in thinking about the present world-in-itself, they presumably have no less force in contemplating the past world. Indeed, their urgency will increase because the very pastness which interests historians builds its own barriers against our finding out about it with the facility that we sometimes can bring to bear in the present. Kant himself did nothing to help his audience see the implications of his Idealism for historical enquiry. He wrote only one short essay about history[25] and, as in the case of David Hume, he leaves his philosophy behind the moment he thinks about 'old, half-effaced information from archives' (quoted in Beck 1963: vii) and writes like a Voltairean schoolboy. Others did see those implications, however, and the idea that the past does not exist (by definition) and that we can never *re*-construct it but only *construct* in our present a picture or image or model of it – one whose truth we can test only by its internal coherence with evidence rather than through a one-to-one correspondence with the erstwhile *Ding-an-sich* – we owe ultimately to Kant. It has proved a powerful strain in Western historical thought from his own day to our own through the writing of Dilthey, Croce, Collingwood and Oakeshott in contesting scientific models of understanding in Europe and that of Becker and Beard in dissolving superficial views of historical 'objectivity' in the United States.[26]

---

25 The tenor of Kant's writing on history can be gleaned from his essay 'Idea for a Universal History from a Cosmopolitan Point of View', printed in Beck 1963. For philosophical treatments of his historical ideas, see Galston 1975 and Yovel 1980.

26 On the latter movement, see Novick 1988, esp. 250–78. We do not have a synthetic overview of Idealist historical thought, though much suggestive material can be found in Jacobitti 1981, Ermarth 1978 and Liebel 1963/4. R. G. Collingwood is best approached through the posthumous compilation, *The Idea of History* (1946) and glossed in Mink 1969. Michael Oakeshott's formidable essay *On History* (1983) can be complemented by Goldstein 1976.

The tight rationalism of Kant's thought finds no reflection in Herder's chaotic system of speculation, but like Vico, with whom he bears close comparison (see Berlin 1976), Herder seems in retrospect an author marking a watershed in his recommendations over how the past must be understood. He reversed the Enlightenment's readiness to belittle cultures unlike its own by seeing that change over time was a crucial feature of how the world worked, that each *Volk* bore within itself the seeds of its own transformation which demanded a language of analysis relevant to its epoch and that it was pointless to criticize the classical world, for example, as though it were an apprentice version of the modern one. 'The Romans were precisely what they were capable of becoming; everything perishable belonging to them perished, and what was susceptible of permanence remained' (quoted in White 1973: 76). He does not remove reality from the observer, as Kant does. Rather he announces the principle that reality should be seen not as a state or a fixed given, but as a happening, a process of becoming through time. Both of his leading notions were to become part of historical thinking over the next century. His disavowal of anachronism and the suggestion that historians must conceive the subject in terms of the epoch studied gave impetus, in the absence of a still-neglected Vicoan approach, to the style of history that Friedrich Meinecke called *Historismus* or 'historism'. '[T]he essence of historism', he explained, 'is the substitution of a process of *individualising* observation for a *generalising* view of human forces in history . . .'. The whole process depended on breaking down the rigid ways of thought attached to the concepts of Natural Law

> and its belief in the invariability of the highest human ideals and an unchanging human nature that was held to be constant for all ages. ... Only by a deeper understanding of the human soul could the old Natural Law and the new naturalism be transcended and a new sense of history achieved.[27]

This determination to study the past for its own sake and in its own terms, rather than as a vehicle for generalization and law-building, dominated German historiography in the nineteenth century. The second formative idea – that reality must be sought in transformation – lies at the heart of Hegel's philosophy of history which gave rise to a cult following in the first half of the century and affected historians across Europe during the second.

For Hegel, the separation of man from his world seemed as intolerable as Kant's logic seemed impeccable. His system bridged the chasm by organizing reality as an evolving happening to which both mind and world contributed because – the end point of his complex metaphysics – mind and the world were joined together in a dialectical relationship which would ultimately show them to be the same reality differentiated by the abstractions of understanding. History was the story of this

---

27 Meinecke 1972: IV, 3–4. It should be noted that 'historism' in Meinecke's sense is not only different from but contradictory to the predictive and determinist concept of 'historicism' developed by Karl Popper in his *The Poverty of Historicism* (1957). In this discussion 'historist' will relate to Meinecke's sense, 'historicist' to Popper's.

unfolding relationship and therefore had a special urgency for Hegel. He had no interest in empiricism, which would simply mislead because it lacked philosophical insight. History was centrally a philosophical activity which tracked the destiny of the world's mechanism which Reason had revealed. His students in the philosophy faculty of the University of Berlin found little to resemble the lectures of Niebuhr or the man who prided himself on his loathing for Hegel, Leopold von Ranke. Judging from their lecture-notes, from which the posthumous *Lectures on the Philosophy of History* were compiled, they found little intelligible at all. But the ascription to certain civilizations in the past of a functional role in the working out of an entire cosmology through the famous dialectic of thesis, antithesis, synthesis inspired those whose history had lost meaning under the logic-chopping of rationalism. Those, like Ranke, who hated it could not avoid it. Those who, like Nietzsche in the nineteenth or Spengler and Toynbee in the twentieth century, gravitated to a form of history which shaped the events of the past into a grand philosophical system worshipped implicitly at his shrine. Those who, like Marx, escaped the system by hijacking it and running it off in a new direction acquired a vehicle of enormous potential for transforming conceptions of how the past grew into the present.

Contrasting the Enlightenment mode of historical thinking in France and Britain with a Counter-Enlightenment persuasion in the German-speaking world has helped identify, then, twin poles of argument. Looking forward from 1800 it becomes possible now to discern clusters of historiography separated by those poles and the lines of force surrounding them. To the Enlightenment's influence we can readily trace the origins of a school, predominantly but not exhaustively French, that wished to see history as a social science. This is the world of Comte and Taine, of Fustel de Coulanges and Gabriel Monod, of Henry Thomas Buckle in England and a coterie of Americans. At the opposite end of the spectrum we shall discover a resistance to *Naturwissenschaft* as a key to historical method and the call for a distinctive *Geisteswissenschaft* which will acknowledge the autonomy of history as a human discipline, seeking forms of analysis and explanation quite foreign to the laboratory and the scientific journal. These will range from Macaulay and Carlyle on the British side, through Michelet on the French to several persuasions of writer by the end of the nineteenth century. And in the vacuum between these poles we shall discover Germany's greatest historian, owing allegiance to neither of their positions and transparently the victim of both.

ROMANTICISM

The competing persuasions available to historical thinkers and writers by the turn of the nineteenth century did not confine themselves to their own territories, insulated from world events. They co-mingled and drew both strength and opposition from events taking place 'on the ground'. Among the most significant determinants after 1815 was the defeat of revolutionary sentiment and its further repression in England; a period of intense rethinking of the recent past in France by a generation

411

needing to accommodate the enormities of the Revolution, the Directorate and Napoleon; and the birth of a new American sensibility, fresh from its second defeat of the British in 1814 and finding a historical version of itself that would reflect the uniqueness of the American venture. To make all these projects sound the same stretches credibility and does little justice to the singularities of each. Yet since we are searching for intellectual environments in which to locate the writing of history, there remains some point in grouping together forms of writing which their authors would never have grouped, using the retrospect which they manipulated with some distinction in their histories but which was denied to them when they tried to understand their own location just as we struggle to make sense of ours. Grouping invites categories and perhaps the idea of 'romanticism' does less violence to these histories than might some alternatives.

Romantic historiography took its focus and its audience in resistance to the cold and clinical perspectives associated with rationalism. Not that it abandoned evidence or wanted to see historical accounts reduced to hagiography: many of the Romantics held a sophisticated view of the relationship between evidence and text and criticized their Enlightenment predecessors for behaving in a cavalier spirit when faced with stubborn facts. None of them expressed that criticism more cuttingly than Thomas Babington Macaulay in his evisceration of Hume in 1828. It is true that Hume's 'Tory' credentials upset Macaulay's Whig ones but the ammunition used by the latter concerned the technical question of evidence and argument rather than Hume's political drift:

> Without positively asserting much more than he can prove, he gives prominence to all the circumstances which support his case; he glides lightly over those which are unfavourable to it; his own witnesses are applauded and encouraged; the statements which seem to throw discredit on them are controverted; the contradictions into which they fall are explained away; a clear and connected abstract of their evidence is given. Everything that is offered on the other side is scrutinised with the utmost severity; every suspicious circumstance is a ground for comment and invective; what cannot be denied is extenuated or passed by without notice; concessions even are sometimes made; but this insidious candour only increases the effect of the vast mass of sophistry.
>
> (Macaulay [1828] 1956: 81)

Rather than attempt to beat the Enlightenment at its own game, the Romantics sought to transcend the world of flat, nomological *reportage* and to produce a history that was creative and alive and the reverse of value-free. Some of them – a very few – had read Vico. More of them had come into contact with German literature and conceived an admiration for Goethe or Schiller. Most of them had discovered in Savigny and Niebuhr models of how to undertake rigorous enquiry. Where they went further was in their understanding of how a historical text should look and what a reader would gain from it. They addressed consciously what Gibbon had achieved on the run – the need to hold attention and keep a reader reading. They chose to make history learn from literature and to function in the same way. It would have the captivation produced by a Waverley novel and its illumination of reality would operate through broadly the same mechanisms that Scott employed.

Its truth would be poetic and not merely expository. Its method would embrace intuition as much as analysis; its explanations would turn on the particularities of persons, the unrepeatability of events.

All of this would work itself out against the background of revolution, liberty and repression. The events of 1789 and again of 1830 affected romantic historians in a central and inescapable way; and when those revolutions turned to counter-revolutions, history became the torch that liberals might carry in defiance. 'The liberal historians of the restoration [in France]', one scholar recently judged,

> rescued the pre-revolutionary past. What took place after 1830 amounted to a reordering, a recomposition of the national tradition. Michelet went beyond the views of Guizot, Mignet and Thierry and wrote what his contemporaries called symbolic history, an interpretative narrative in which events were related to the unfolding of a more general purpose. He felt he was lending his voice to the people, that he was speaking on behalf of the masses whom previous historians had condemned to silence. National history was related to the patterns of universal history. The Revolution was situated within the vaster continuity of world, even cosmic history.
>
> (Crossley 1993: 42–3)

A full understanding of these authors, most of whom had been born just after the French Revolution and who had grown up during the 1810s and 1820s, requires an acknowledgement of how conscious and contrived was this search for poetic expression through the medium of reviviscence and at what level the search took place. To see them as practitioners of no more than a 'florid rhetorical style' for 'readers who seek entertainment rather than instruction' misses their purpose and substitutes an inappropriate test for them to fail.[28] When Carlyle deemed it 'part of [his] creed that the only Poetry is History, could we tell it right' (quoted in Rosenberg 1985: 48), he voiced an aspiration fundamental to romantic historical thought and showed why an obsession with how to write history books figured so generally in this genre. The text had to carry the same ontological weight as a poem. If its language carried beyond the conversational, so did its message; and it is therefore less than intelligent to criticize Macaulay or Carlyle or Michelet for an over-rich style: one might as well seek to diminish Keats or Coleridge or Emerson or Thoreau for the same reason. Like poetry, moreover, romantic history was afflicted by structure and the question how best to arrange the writing to make its point tell. On this issue the studies taking their moment of origin in the period from 1830 to 1850 suggest a complete unanimity. The vehicle of romantic history was narrative; but it asked for imagination beyond the putting of events in chronological order along the lines that the eighteenth century had so frequently thought adequate. It began with the criticism that the Enlightenment and its disciples had 'miserably neglect[ed] the art of narration, the art of interesting the affections and presenting pictures to the imagination'. (Macaulay [1828] 1956: 83). Only a skilful narrative

---

28 Barnes 1963: 232, 190 alluding respectively to Carlyle and George Bancroft. Of the latter, Barnes writes engagingly that '[t]he damage done to sane perspective in American history by his works was almost incalculable, if not irreparable' (232).

would have the literary power to delineate truths about liberty and the congealing of peoples into new formations that this generation wanted to portray. Besides, narrative had an explanatory value in talking about processes, perhaps in talking about anything at all. 'Cut us off from Narrative', Carlyle intoned, 'how would the stream of conversation, even among the wisest, languish into detached handfuls, and among the foolish utterly evaporate!' (Carlyle [1830] 1956: 91).

Poetic truth and narrative method brought another impulse: the need to silhouette the guiding historical personality, the luminous moment of action. The purpose of the story lies in taking the reader to an ocean-floor of ultimate reality but on reaching it the reader rarely discovers large structures or geological formations. One is taught to think about collectivities as agglommerations of tiny individuals and as existing only in and through them. There exists a world of the social – indeed Michelet has some claim to have been the first to develop it – but we are never allowed to forget that history is 'the essence of innumerable biographies'. This environment is one where heroes and heroines flourish and have meaning which historians must identify and exhibit. The licence does not stop at writing lives of unpleasant tyrants, as Voltaire did; it encompasses the presentation of individuals in a positive light as bearers of the *Zeitgeist* or beacons of hope. They might be great leaders, as Carlyle made Cromwell or Frederick the Great. They might be faceless members of the crowd milling about the guillotine, a constant presence in Michelet's history of the French Revolution but, as Owen Chadwick cautions, never a social force or movement in the modern sense because writing that turns on individuals knows no movement, only the agents whose several efforts might be so labelled. 'Though he wrote of the crowd, the crowd was to him a collection of free individuals, each of whom he would describe if he could, (Chadwick 1975: 198). This thought serves all the Romantics. They each tried to describe every person, every thought, every action, every horse, every tree. The practicalities of text and source, nothing else, hindered them. For the work was inspired by the drive to evoke and make present by an effort of imagination and will.

Carlyle (1795–1881) and Macaulay (1800–59) sprang from the same generation as Michelet but the particularities of their Scottish and English backgrounds naturally franked their divergent careers and impact. Undoubtedly the Scotland of Annandale and Edinburgh marked Carlyle's imaging and expression, though in his case the importation of Schiller, whose life he wrote, and German philosophy had equal effect. Between them, these conflicting tensions produced an approximation to a prophet rather than a social commentator and a prose style that the twentieth century cannot tolerate for more than a couple of sentences. His two central works of history, if one disregards a poor edition of Cromwell's letters and speeches, were *The French Revolution* of 1833–42 and his life of *Frederick the Great* (1858). Both of them held a major place in British historiography in the nineteenth century until the urge towards a 'scientific' historiography began to redraw the priorities in the 1860s. The quality that most guaranteed their success lay in their pictorial character. Carlyle fills the mind with images which, once created, do not leave it. One of the most startling and permanent surrounded his account of the execution of

Robespierre, following the suicide attempt that had blasted his jaw, at the end of volume three of *The French Revolution* and it may stand for others in its theatrical sliding of tense, the familiarity of Christian-name terms with the actors, the repetition of adjective and noun to deepen atmosphere, the near-physical sense of presence so that the reader's own moment becomes the afternoon of 28 July 1794.

> At four in the afternoon, never before were the streets of Paris seen so crowded. From the Palais de Justice to the Place de la Révolution, for *thither* again go the Tumbrils this time, it is one dense stirring mass; all windows crammed; the very roofs and ridge-tiles budding forth human Curiosity, in strange gladness. The Death-tumbrils, with their motley Batch of Outlaws, some Twenty-three or so, from Maximilien [Robespierre], to Mayor Fleuriot and Simon the Cordwainer, roll on. All eyes are on Robespierre's Tumbril, where he, his jaw bound in dirty linen, with his half-dead Brother and half-dead Henriot, lie shattered. ... At the foot of the scaffold, they stretched him out on the ground till his turn came. Lifted aloft his eyes again opened; caught the bloody axe. Samson wrenched the coat off him; wrenched the dirty linen from his jaw: the jaw fell powerless, there burst from him a cry; – hideous to hear and see. Samson, thou canst not be too quick!
>
> Samson's work done, there bursts forth shout on shout of applause. Shout, which prolongs itself not only over Paris, but over France, but over Europe, and down to this generation.[29]

The *Führerprinzip* of his later years did nothing to help Carlyle's popularity, especially in his encomium on Frederick the Great who, for all his undoubted success, looked neither like an 1848 revolutionary nor an 1858 Palmerstonian.

> To many it appears certain there are to be no Kings of any sort, no Government more; less and less need of them henceforth, New Era having come. Which is a very wonderful notion; important if true; perhaps still more important, just at present, if untrue! My hopes of presenting, in this Last of the Kings, an exemplar to my contemporaries, I confess, are not high.[30]

Yet Carlyle's hold is all too easily minimized in modern recollection. One does well to recall a figure like James Anthony Froude who, though his own historical work went in very different directions, retained always his sense of overwhelming indebtedness to Carlyle's example. 'Carlyle to me spoke as never man spoke ... [I]n all that I thought or attempted, I allowed his judgement to guide me.'[31]

Despite his lionization in Cheyne Row in his later years, Carlyle never reached the inner core of Britain's governing classes. Macaulay was born in it. Having a father who had held a diplomatic post as governor of Sierra Leone gave one a certain start in life: and Zachary Macaulay's son in his turn had a professional career that looked like Gibbon's: Member of Parliament, cabinet office in Melbourne's

---

29 Thomas Carlyle, *The French Revolution* (3 vols, 1833–42), III, 242–3. For a full analysis of his method in this text, cf. Sorenson 1983.

30 *History of Friedrich II of Prussia, called Frederick the Great* (8 vols, 1858–65, 1897 edn, I, 16–17). Carlyle's shade would not have been amused when H. D. Traill forgave him in the Gladstonian edition of 1897 on the ground that he probably did not believe what he wrote (xiii–xiv).

31 Dunn 1961–3: I, 210–12. Recent studies of Carlyle and his impact include Le Quesne 1982 and Campbell 1993.

government.[32] But of course historians are more interested in his *History of England* (5 vols, 1849–61), which remained unfinished at his death and had, indeed, paid the price of all narrative by never getting further than the reign of William III, despite an original intention to come down to 1830.[33] Like Hume, he achieved a major *succès d'estime*. But he did much else like Hume, for all the waspish words of his essay on how to write history. He celebrated the Glorious Revolution backwards, when he wrote about the period before 1688, and forwards when he looked ahead of it. He needled the Church because it stood in the way of liberty; but then he attacked everything so defined. He wrote some of the greatest paragraphs ever composed about the history of England as well as some of the silliest and some (more tellingly) that Hume could have written himself. Note the supposed reception of General Monk's declaration for a free Parliament:

> As soon as his declaration was known, the whole nation was wild with delight. Wherever he appeared thousands thronged round him, shouting and blessing his name. The bells of all England rang joyously: the gutters ran with ale; and night after night, the sky five miles round London was reddened by innumerable bonfires.
>
> (Macaulay I, 128)

It hardly mattered. Macaulay turned history into a rival for the three-decker novel and quite overcame among the booksellers the careful scholarship of a Thomas Arnold or Henry Hart Milman. Perhaps these 'Liberal Anglicans' had the making of a new historical method (see Forbes 1952, *passim*), but it was Macaulay who reached the readers. The sales of the first two volumes, which came out in 1849, had been striking enough in Britain. In America they sold 200,000 sets in the first year.

Not that America lacked a historiography of its own: indeed in George Bancroft (1800–91) it had discovered possibly its first major historian and another witness to the Romantic persuasion. As a son of religious Dissent in Massachusetts he reflected the provincialism of Carlyle. In everything else he echoed Macaulay. Although he tried Harvard for a short period on his return from studying in Germany, he disliked the environment and did not succeed in it. Schoolteaching came no more easily. He found his *métier* through holding government positions and maintaining an active political life while writing his ten-volume *History of the United States*. Like Macaulay he was a Whig, though one understood in its American sense; he later became a Democrat. His dovetailing into the emerging American state went quite as far as Macaulay's into the British. He played a role in nominating Polk for the presidency.

---

32   Macaulay sat in the House of Commons for the Whig interest in 1830–4, 1839–47 and 1852–6. He held government office as secretary for war from 1839 to 1841 and paymaster-general in Russell's government in 1846–7.

33   'How far I shall bring the narrative down I have not determined. The death of George the Fourth would be the best halting place. The history would then be an entire view of all the transactions which took place between the revolution, which brought the crown into harmony with the parliament, and the revolution which brought the parliament into harmony with the nation' (Macaulay to Macvey Napier, 20 July 1838, quoted in Millgate 1973: 125). Had he continued at the density suggested by his account of the Restoration and Revolution, the project would have taken twenty volumes to complete.

He served as Polk's Secretary of the Navy in 1845–6, the year before Macaulay joined Russell's government. Then Polk made him ambassador to Britain, so he met Macaulay and Milman and Hallam and other celebrated figures in the British historical establishment. After the Civil War his affinities with Andrew Johnson led to his appointment at Berlin where his acquaintances ran from Bismarck and Moltke at one end of the spectrum to Ranke and Mommsen at the other.

But Bancroft's intellectual contacts turned out the more significant. Unusually for one of his generation, he studied at Göttingen after completing his first degree at Harvard and then moved around Berlin and elsewhere, attending courses by Hegel and Schleiermacher in Berlin, spending time with Goethe at Weimar. He thus felt the full weight of Counter-Enlightenment thought but carried it only as a form of Christian optimism and liberal triumphalism which marked his historical work throughout a long career of writing. Coupled with immersion in the state (the *fons et origo* of so much romantic thought), his uplift produced narratives of remarkable simplicity of view. He saw social history working itself out in the state-order and in the special order produced by Americans. Even a work from late in his life on the history of the constitution contains the plenitude of thankfulness that would irritate the generation of Beard and Elmer Barnes beyond description. Consider his very first paragraph:

> The order of time brings us to the most cheering act in the political history of mankind, when thirteen republics ... formed themselves into one federal commonwealth. There was no revolt against the past, but a persistent and healthy progress. The sublime achievement was the work of a people led by statesmen of earnestness, perseverance, and public spirit, instructed by the widest experience in the forms of representative government, and warmed by that mutual love which proceeds from ancient connection, harmonious effort in perils, and common aspirations.
>
> (Bancroft 1882: I, 3)

Six hundred and fifty pages later, as we come to the end of his story, the mood has not altered. '[A] new people had risen up without king, or princes, or nobles' and had written for themselves a constitution which they might almost have found dictated on Sinai.

> In the happy morning of their existence as one of the powers of the world, they had chosen justice for their guide; and while they proceeded on their way with a well-founded confidence and joy, all the friends of mankind invoked success for their endeavour as the only hope for renovating the life of the civilized world.
>
> (ibid. II, 367)

Though Bancroft had spent a little time in Paris it seems that Jules Michelet (1798–1874) remained one of the very few notables in Europe whom he never met. It was just as well: their democratic impulses ran divergently. Michelet lacked Bancroft's cosmopolitanism, though his missionary work on behalf of Vico suggested that he wanted to do more than magnify France.[34] Yet Michelet's

---

34   See Michelet 1833, which has a 'Discourse sur le système et la vie de Vico'.

achievement lay so close to a vision of the French people's achievement that the two do not readily separate. The involvement with the state so evident in the other writers we have discussed is not replicated here, except negatively when Michelet was sacked from his position as keeper of the national archives at the restoration as a reprisal for having welcomed the revolution of 1848. Unlike the others he held academic positions: he had been a professor of ancient history at the Ecole Normale before moving to the *Archives* in 1831. Rather than silhouette the recent French state as an embodiment of liberality (as a Macaulay or Bancroft might have done), Michelet's version of democracy made him face the other way and conceive a different trajectory – one that had its rise but also its fall.

The reason takes little finding. Behind him Michelet had at half a century's remove the most spectacular revolution of the modern world, one in which he identified the French soul. He had no 1688 or 1776 since when the world had grown better and better. He had 1789 since when the world had retarded into the mediocrity and compromise of the empire which even the eruptions of 1830 and 1848 had failed to avert. And he had predecessors like Mignet who had already plotted a path towards welcoming the Revolution.[35]. Like Carlyle, he could not baptize the results of Whig complacency. Unlike him, he found no pleasure in blaming the people. Michelet therefore presents a parabola to the retrospect of France and his commentators do not readily forgive him the excesses which he displays in conceiving of a period of greatness followed by a collapse into a diseased state. For Gooch, half a century later, the disease was not France's but Michelet's: we have the first six volumes of his early *History of France* rated as his 'most perfect and enduring work ... written before his genius had reached its fullest development and before his imagination had become diseased' (Gooch 1913: 178). But *The French Revolution* shows him in decline: a peddler of disgusting scandal, incest and unwholesomeness. One sees what Gooch had in mind. But he misses the point that for Michelet France had been wrong in failing to seize the day; she had fallen away from the highest of ideals and succumbed to restoration through the human frailties that he narrates. Even the frailest – Danton and especially Robespierre – he loved with a passion that left him bereft on completing the book.[36]

Yet Hayden White's brilliant investigation of the innerness of Michelet's volumes substantiates an alternative view: that the sense of disease and corruption after 1789 inhered in Michelet's historical judgement which went far beyond the

35 'Long before Michelet, Mignet's work struck many as preaching both the acceptance of the whole Revolution and the acceptance of the *necessity* for the whole Revolution' (Ben-Israel 1968: 61).
36 His widow published in 1888 a fragment in which he grieves for his loss. 'Le plus grand vide à cette table de bois blanc, d'où mon livre s'en va maintenant et où je reste seul, c'est de n'y plus voir mon pâle compagnon, le plus fidèle de tous, qui, de 89 en thermidor, ne m'avait point quitté; l'homme de grande volunté, laborieux comme moi et pauvre comme moi, avec qui, chaque matin, j'eus tant d'âpres [bitter] discussions. Le plus grand fruit de mon étude morale, physiologique, c'est justement cette dispute, c'est d'avoir serieusement anatomisé Robespierre' *Histoire de la révolution francaise* (2 vol. edn, Paris, 1952), II, 995).

sources that he brought into play. This going beyond is what gives Michelet the sense of romance as well as the touch of greatness as an artist. His listening for 'words that were never spoken' and determination to 'make the silences of history speak' (see White 1973: 158) turn him all too readily into a spokesman for unborn *annalistes* or into some proto-Derrida. He sits more naturally, perhaps, with a volume of Romantic poetry or a canvas by Delacroix. On the other hand, he represents the ambiguities of romance in the period when it had become uncomfortable. If Michelet did not study in Göttingen and Berlin, his source-criticism suggested that German method had not been lost on the French. If his intellect made him the French Vico and his passion the French Carlyle, he had done enough in his excavation of national archives to pass muster as the French Ranke.

RANKE

Romance had not escaped the Germans. They applied it, however, to a culture that had a past but little history. To read their rediscovered *Volk* backwards into the blurredest origins in folk-tale plainly acted as an important imperative and it produced new histories of a peculiar (and to the modern ear all too familiar) kind. So we find the nine volumes of Voigt's *History of Prussia* dedicated 'To the Fatherland'[37] or one stumbles over Luden and his 'wish that we Germans would study like children the life of our beloved parents, dominated by the holy thought of the Fatherland.'[38] Compared with the great narratives created in England, France and America, such work nevertheless made little impact outside Germany: the romantic form found more authentic expression in poetry, music and the philosophy of the spirit. Instead, the main line of German historiography discovered an antidote to intuition in theorizing about historical method. Humboldt's lecture 'On the Tasks of the Historian' (1821) talks in a sophisticated way about history's function of finding form within chaos, of designating events as parts of organic wholes, of going deeper than the flow of occurrence in order to locate in some more fundamental sense the 'form of history per se'.[39] A second prophylactic against intuition already existed, of course, in the source-based *œuvres* of figures such as Niebuhr and Eichhorn[40] whose thrust lay in protecting the intellect from romantic subversion rather than encouraging its attack on the 'march of mind' in the manner of Carlyle. Together, these elements helped promote an approach to history which we associate inevitably with its greatest emblem – Leopold von Ranke – but which

---

37   'The supreme prize in research is when the spirit is raised to reverence and the heart is filled with enthusiasm at the sight of great and good men.' (see Gooch 1913: 73).

38   Heinrich Luden (1778–1847). The remark comes from his lectures at Jena in 1808, quoted in Gooch 1913: 72. His *magnum opus* was to be a *History of the German People* (12 vols, 1825–37).

39   Wilhelm von Humboldt, *On the Tasks of the Historian* (1821), quoted in White 1973: 180. For a study of Humboldt in English, see Sweet 1978–80.

40   Karl Friedrich Eichhorn ranks with Savigny as an interpreter of the history of German public and private law. See his *Deutsche Staats- und Rechtsgeschichte* (3rd edn, 1821–3).

has dimensions larger than Ranke's own contribution and amounts to a cultural identity.

Georg Iggers has analysed that identity through a lifetime's reflection on the distinctiveness of German historicism and it may be helpful to summarize his central findings (Iggers 1983). Most obviously in the century of Ranke, Droysen, von Sybel, Treitschke and a mass of lesser-known apologists for the *Machtstaat*, one can see a pervasive concern with the state, not only as an agency of authority domestically and power externally but as an ethical end in itself. Second, ethics become a product of that theatre of action which history considers. German historians reject the imposition of an ethical code from above the events and allow the events to announce their own morality. What ought to succeed becomes a function of what has succeeded – a doctrine with direct implications for the foregoing theory of the state. Third, one needs to be aware of historism, an agreement that historical knowledge will not emerge by applying conceptual schemata to the past but only through the analysis of individual instances and concrete events. To these guidelines we should, perhaps, add a fourth. German historical thinking did not remain static during the nineteenth century. It becomes important, therefore, to distinguish styles of thought prevalent between 1820 and 1870 from those that were to gain ascendancy between the foundation of the Empire and the cataclysm of 1914. In the first half of that period, for example, German historians made much of a supposed affinity with the British: they often visited England, as Ranke himself did.[41] In the later decades the Wilhelmine historians turned in on themselves and generated a distaste abroad which the First World War seemed to confirm and which convicted all German historians of views held by a few of a particular generation. This helps explain why no new edition of Ranke's work appeared in Britain or France until the 1960s.[42]

Yet Ranke's date of birth – he was born in Thuringia in 1795 – ought in itself to exonerate him from allegations of this kind. Indeed only his amazing longevity colludes with them, for had he died before 1871 he might never have been associated with the imperial spirit. His classical education and formative years as a historian during the 1820s took place outside a formalized state system, though his admiration for Prussia – reinforced in 1831 by his return to Berlin from his work in the Italian archives – left a permanent mark on his idea of political history. Thereafter the prodigious output and swings of mood left behind him a range of history so vast that it confutes any notion of *précis* and presents all students of his work with an unclimbable mountain. The image of his sitting in old age editing the first forty-five volumes of his own writing is enough by itself to loosen any serious grasp on the part of a general reader, unless he or she elevates Ranke to an obsession quite as pronounced as the one he made of the history of Europe between the

---

41 For the relationship with Britain, see McClelland 1971.

42 See Leopold von Ranke, *The Theory and Practice of History*, ed. G. G. Iggers and Konrad von Moltke (Indianapolis, 1973), xvii. In the United States after 1918 the distaste assumed more strident proportions: cf. Novick, 1988: 140–4.

Renaissance and the French Revolution. Even in old age he foxed those who knew him well. Lord Acton looked back in 1895 on their last meeting:

> I saw him last in 1877, when he was feeble, sunken, and almost blind, and scarcely able to read or write. He uttered his farewell with kindly emotion, and I feared that the next I should hear of him would be the news of his death. Two years later, he began a Universal History, which is not without traces of weakness, but which, composed after the age of eighty-three, and carried, in seventeen volumes, far into the Middle Ages, brings to a close the most astonishing career in literature.[43]

In order to penetrate the sheer mass of this material, we need to ask questions about at least four of its aspects: its epistemology or view of historical knowledge; its idea of historical understanding; its doctrines about explanation; and its implications about method. And with Ranke quite as much as with the context of his work, we shall need to be sensitive about change over time. The man who confronted the universe at the age of 83 was not the one who attracted an offer from the University of Berlin with his *History of the Latin and Teutonic Peoples* of 1825.

Two celebrated remarks take one close to the centre of Ranke's position on historical knowledge. The preface to the *Latin and Teutonic Peoples* contains the now notorious injunction to reconstruct the past 'wie es eigentlich gewesen'. The need to say what 'really' happened encouraged an entire branch of historiography – the American – to persist with its cult of objectivity.[44] It also misread Ranke's intention. The word 'eigentlich' had a nineteenth-century connotation resembling the English word 'essentially'; but when Ranke used it he seems to have had in mind a literal meaning – not 'mainly' or 'preponderantly' or 'in outline', but rather 'in essence', a term he used repeatedly. 'We ... desire to root tradition in our knowledge of actual existence,' he wrote to his brother in 1838, 'and in our insight into its essence.'[45] Because that essence lies below a number of surfaces, moreover, the historian can never reach it through the mere adducing of evidence; in fact he rarely reaches it at all. Hence the second *bon mot*: 'Man bemüht sich, man strebt, am Ende hat man's nicht erreicht' – one tries and strains, but in the end one has not achieved that entering into the essence of the past which is the point of historical effort.[46] More accurate than a sense of Ranke's composition as a form of unthinking *pointillisme* is therefore one that depicts him as a frustrated van Gogh, never quite able to render the mimesis authentic. The thought also gives the lie to Ranke's scientific empiricism and supposed rejection of conceptual views.[47]

---

43 Inaugural lecture at Cambridge, quoted in McNeill 1967: 336.
44 This misunderstanding has been clearly identified by Iggers: see his *The German Conception of History* (1983).
45 Ranke to Ferdinand von Ranke, 9 Aug. 1838, quoted in Krieger 1977: 37. It will be obvious how much this section owes to Professor Krieger's elucidations of Ranke's texts.
46 See Gilbert 1990: 36. The quotation also comes from the preface to the *Latin and Teutonic Peoples*.
47 Krieger 1977 argues persuasively for a distinction between Ranke's 'method of knowledge', where he is interested in particulars, and his 'substance of knowledge', where he seeks universal truths – leaving him with 'an operational solution for a problem which he left unresolved in its own theoretical terms' (1977: 15).

His understanding owed more to Herder and Hegel than he himself allowed. His division of Western civilization into Latin and Teutonic types proved only the beginning of an analysis of European peoples along the lines of language and among categories of *Völker* which are then dovetailed into the state system and the emergent balance of power which comments on the ethical virility of the states involved in it.[48] When he thinks about the heart of the impulse towards modernity, he points to an individual or national mind in preference to armies; and on numerous occasions Ranke sounds as though he were a pupil of Hegel more than a critic, as when he speaks of 'the profound necessity of the inner course of things' or sees '[e]very power ... moved by the inherent drive of the ideas lying at its base'.[49] The difference lay in the relationship envisaged between particular events and the generalizations which Ranke made to embrace them. He reads the unique and the common as working in tension rather than complementing one another in the synthetic process envisaged by Hegel. 'On the *opposition* of the particular and the general all European history is based'.[50] That sense of generality had entered Ranke's writing from the later part of his *History of the Popes* (1840), for all the detailed examination of events and personalities in that archival *tour de force*, and he defined it there not merely as the general context within which historians have to situate events in order to understand them but also as a style of history in its own right showing 'the inner changes of the spiritual–earthly tendencies of the world as they appear from epoch to epoch'.[51] These inner changes form the kernel of his study of *German History in the Age of the Reformation* (1839–52) and his comparative accounts of France and England in the seventeenth century (Ranke 1852–6; 1859–69).

Understanding Ranke's overall vision is especially important because he has traditionally struck students of historiography as deserving their attention for his having been the father of a method. He used primary sources in archives with a zest and thoroughness quite new to historical scholarship. He taught his students by making them read primary sources under his guidance: the origin of the 'special subject' in the university curriculum and the beginning of the 'seminar', albeit of a kind very different from those operating today. Both of these novelties in research and teaching had the most far-reaching consequences and historians of education have a strong case in dwelling on them. But one misses too easily the part of Ranke that had little claim to scientific method: the pre-archival mind that brought its own structures to bear on the material. In this sense Ranke had close affinities with the Romantic historiography that he wanted to disown because his very mode of constituting his thousands of pages of text had implications that he could not discern:

> What Ranke did not see was that one might well reject a Romantic approach to history in the name of objectivity, but that, as long as history was conceived to be *explanation by*

48 See the very helpful exploration of these themes in White 1973: 176ff.
49 These remarks come from the late 1840s and 1850s when Ranke is portrayed by Krieger as undergoing a 'second synthesis' in the development of his ideas: see Krieger 1977: 202–45.
50 From a private lecture to King Maximilian, 1850s: ibid. 241. (emphasis added).
51 Ranke to Ritter, Feb./Nov. 1835, quoted in Krieger 1977: 152.

narration, one was required to bring to the task of narration the archetypal myth or plot structure, by which alone that narrative could be given a form. ... His objectivity, critical principles, and sympathy for all sides of the conflicts he encountered through the historical record were deployed within the sustaining atmosphere of a metahistorical prefiguration of the historical field as a set of conflicts that must necessarily end in harmonious resolutions, resolutions in which 'nature' is finally supplanted by 'society' that is as just as it is stable.[52]

Ranke believed that the Prussia of his day embodied that just and stable society. He rejoiced in the loss of momentum of revolutionary ideas quite as much as Michelet grieved over them. In explaining the past, his problem lay simply in finding the generalizations – they seem often to work as historical laws – that joined together a fragmented and unhappy past with an organic and satisfactory present.

All these characteristics lend Ranke his distinctive voice in German historiography in the first half of the nineteenth century. It goes without saying that there were other voices, some of them as powerful as Ranke's. His pupil Georg Waitz (1813–86) developed at Göttingen techniques of *Verfassungsgeschichte* or constitutional history that some have seen as superior to Ranke's in their precision.[53] His younger contemporary, Theodor Mommsen (1817–1903), has many claims to standing closer to the centre of a 'German school' in its supposed acknowledgement of a historical 'science' and through his prosecution of Roman history on a Rankean scale. (His *curriculum vitae* is supposed to have contained 1,500 publications.) Certainly these and other German authors will make their presence felt later in this account. What has helped focus attention on Ranke at this point is a collection of characteristics that make him relevant to our theme. He was the most self-conscious writer of history in the modern age; he consequently reflects helpfully on the climates of opinion around him. He has attracted a battery of modern criticism and exegesis because of that reflection, so we can gain closer access to him than would be possible for others. He manifests, most importantly, his generation's ambiguities about thought and method. Where those ambiguities disappear, he loses them in God. He places events under God's hand and sees in their tendency God's moving finger. In that respect he points not forwards but backwards. Those historians who were not convinced Lutherans like Ranke had come to fear by 1840 that God, too, had become ambiguous.

THE VOICE OF SCIENCE

Ranke's Lutheranism, Arnold's Anglicanism and Bancroft's Congregationalism form elements in a common sensibility through the 1820s and 1830s. Theirs was the last

---

52   White 1973: 167. The implications of White's views about the nature of narrative are further discussed in two collections of his essays: *Tropics of Discourse: essays in cultural criticism* (1980), and *The Content of the Form: narrative discourse and historical representation* (1987). For a recent philosophical treatment, see Ricœur 1984–8.

53   He undertook a great deal of editing of sources for the *Monumenta* but the large-scale original works are *Deutsche Verfassungsgeschichte* (1844–78) and *Deutsche Kaiser von Karl dem Grossen bis Maximilian* (1864).

generation for whom divine guidance and intervention remained obvious and crucial aspects of historical explanation. Even within that generation, however, notable inroads had already been made. The development of classificatory science associated with Linnaeus (1707–78), Buffon (1707–88) and Lamarck (1744–1829) made available a new descriptive vocabulary which could transcend that of orthodox Christianity less by opposing than ignoring it. Some could even see the two things as entwined, science as the godfather of religion. 'The reading of *histories*, my dear Sir,' Samuel Taylor Coleridge addressed his audience,

> may dispose a man to satire; but the science of HISTORY – History studied in the light of philosophy, as the great drama of an ever-unfolding Providence has a very different effect. It infuses hope and reverential thoughts of man and his destination.
>
> (Coleridge [1830] 1976: 32)

From mid-century the new language gained currency from the work of Charles Darwin and Alfred Russel Wallace with highly significant results in the 1870s and 1880s. Seen as a whole, indeed, the nineteenth century saw a process of 'secularization' within the Western intelligentsia which brooked no denial.[54] In the case of its historians, on the other hand, we need to exercise care for the rush towards the secular in this sector by no means reflected that discovered among those committed to various forms of 'social science'. Geographically it lacked all symmetry: French and American historians made more of it, for example, than the British. Indeed one could make a case for British singularity in witnessing a surprising persistence of religious category and assumption as the basis of its historiography (see Bentley 1993). Nor did the 'scientific' impetus carry the same message to all parts of Europe. In France it became, for a time, a cult of generalization about historical method. In Germany it advanced a new school of economic history. In Britain it has to be sought, as ever, in a subtle change of climate that is better associated with the forensic work of an extraordinary collection of medievalists than with those who wanted to turn the world upside down. Yet for all those differences of emphasis, the spread of scientific language and method exercised a compelling influence in making the second half of the century very different from the first.

France provided much impetus for the new approach. The scientific approach to documentation that we associate with Germany had made its mark in France also through the efforts of Guizot, Mignet, Thierry and others to press forward the establishment of the Ecole des Chartes in 1829 and to publish French historical sources as a sort of counterblast to the *Monumenta Germaniae Historica*. But their conception of scientific advance took a form unknown to Berlin. The Revolution had brought in its train a systematic rethinking about the nature of society and how modern political structures might be reconstructed. This mood is evident in the writings of Saint-Simon and Louis Blanc. It underpins the astonishing vision of Auguste Comte, whose treatise on positive philosophy (see Comte 1830–42; cf.

---

54   The *locus classicus* for this process is Chadwick 1975.

Standley 1981 and Freund 1992) divided the history of the world into three phases and interpreted everything in terms of what the phases required. None of these writers considered himself a historian. Perhaps Guizot was the first to appropriate these surgical techniques for the writing of history rather than for social prophecy. He saw the corpus of material on which historians worked as literally a corpus – a body – and he certainly had been exposed to the analogy during the Revolution. When he was seven years old in 1794 his father, a Girondin lawyer, went to the guillotine in Nîmes. He fled with his mother to Geneva and spent formative years there, returning home during the Napoleonic period and becoming Professor of Modern History in the *faculté des lettres* in Paris in 1812 where he remained until his retirement in 1849. There he taught that historical science ought to assume the categories of autopsy. One must study anatomy (the collecting of the facts) and physiognomy (the individual features of events) with a view to constructing a physiology (the laws that govern historical events). These formed the tools with which Guizot went to work on the *History of Civilization in France* (1829–32), which the second revolution of 1830 truncated because of his political involvement. The result was arresting all the same and betrayed a commitment to analytical method that marked all his writing and suffused the frequent whispering in the reader's ear about what had to be done.

> I would like to follow in their totality the destinies of feudalism ... I would not wish to divide it up, but keep it constantly under your eyes, and make you thus see its successive transformations at a single glance. ... Unfortunately this cannot be. In order to study, the human mind is obliged to divide, to analyse; it only acquires knowledge successively and in pieces. It is then the work of imagination and reason to reconstruct the demolished edifice, to resuscitate the being destroyed by the scientific scalpel. But it is absolutely necessary to pass through this process of dissection ...[55]

Men closely identified with the fortunes of the new French democracy, such as Guizot and Thiers, articulated one mood. But the next generation had its own tone, perhaps because its background was different but also because it had available and unavoidable the new biblical criticism coming out of Germany in the work of Schleiermacher and Strauss[56] and the climate of extreme scientism engendered by Darwin's discoveries. It appears in one of the century's great teachers whose influence proved more wide-ranging than his writing: Numa Denis Fustel de Coulanges. He died before his sixtieth birthday in 1889 but Fustel's command over a generation of young French intellectuals became prodigious. His career as one of the new professionals in the historical field certainly helped him acquire authority. He had been an admirer of Guizot in his youth and had proceeded via the Ecole Normale and a teaching position in Amiens to a doctorate on Polybius. But social institutions interested him more than personalities or texts; and having moved to a chair at Strasbourg in 1860 – the year after Darwin's *Origin of Species* appeared –

---

55 *Histoire de la civilisation en France*, quoted in Crossley 1993: 84.
56 There is comparatively little in English on David Strauss and Friedrich Schleiermacher. For the former, see Lawler 1986. For Schleiermacher, see Richardson 1991; Forstman 1977.

he worked on *La Cité antique*, which, when it was published in 1864, invigorated discussion about religion because it identified the function of religion in the ancient city as one of binding together a given society with the institutions of the state.[57] His removal to the Ecole Normale on the strength of his book in 1870 and to a chair at the Sorbonne in 1875 gave him an opportunity radically to remould the opinions of the young.

Gabriel Monod (1844–1912) was not so young: he belonged to the highly talented group who straddled the two centuries and who help explain the shift from an orthodox historiography in France in the mid-nineteenth century to a subversive one after the First World War, as we shall see. Fustel strongly contributed to his education all the same and Monod applied to his own work on the early Franks the same concern with institutions displayed by his teacher (Monod 1895; 1896). More than any other historian working in France in the later nineteenth century, he wanted to drag French thinking into line with German advances in the subject and placed himself at the vortex of a movement to start a major professional journal that could rival the *Historische Zeitschrift*, begun in 1859. The *Revue Historique* owed its foundation in 1876 to Monod's drive. He also took a keen interest in historiography. His *Les Maîtres de l'histoire* (1894) ranks among the first modern studies of other historians. And his choice of subject matter – Michelet, Renan and Taine – has its own suggestiveness.

The force of Renan made itself felt less in historical circles than in theological because his *Vie de Jésus* (1863) caused all the furore in France that David Strauss's *Leben Jesu* had precipitated in Germany in 1835 and Sir John Seeley's *Ecce Homo* was to generate in English intellectual circles in 1865. But Taine's determination to alter the nature of historical thinking without his having initially the professional advantages possessed by Fustel or Monod succeeded, at least temporarily, by sheer muscle. Indeed in his case the new 'science' offered the opportunity, seized by a number of nineteenth-century failures, to turn the tables on those who had not seen their genius. Hyppolite Taine (1828–93) had been a flop at school. He failed his Ph.D. He became a schoolteacher, like Fustel, and then moved to Paris where he became a professional writer with a view about everything. Only in 1865, when he was nearly 40, did the Ecole des Beaux Arts offer him a chair in aesthetics; and from there he ruminated about neither aesthetics nor *Beaux Arts* but about the history of France and what had controlled it. *Les Origines de la France contemporaine* (1874–93) did not have three phases as Comte might have wished: it had instead three forces or moments which, between them, explained how history worked.

Few authors capture better than Taine the nightmare of pseudo-science elevated into a philosophy of history. The past became for him literally 'a geometry of forces' (quoted in Chadwick 1975: 205). His analysis of a major event in France's past would look rather like an engineer's drawing that depicts the various moments and thrusts operating on a bridge or a building. Taine would look first, perhaps, at race

---

57 Fustel de Coulanges 1864. His work is analysed in Hartog 1988.

because his typology of races would suggest a framework within which action took place. He would add in data from the relevant *milieu* (another of his categories) which would provide material to enable him to allow for local peculiarity. Most important of all would then be the *moment* pressing on the event in question; and he defined that, with an impressive imprecision, as the impetus given to the present by the past. In his later years these three forces left Taine with little to laugh about and his correspondence became a review of current degeneration as he saw dogs going for the world out of unstoppable instinct. He insisted to Guizot in 1873:

> Science, as soon as she becomes exact, ceases to be revolutionary, becoming even anti-revolutionary. Zoology shows us man's carnivorous teeth; – let us beware of awakening in him his carnivorous and ferocious instincts. Psychology shows us that human reason is based on words and images; – let us beware of provoking in him hallucination, madness. We are told by political economy that there is continual disproportion between population and sustenance; – let us not forget that even in a time of peace and prosperity, the struggle for life is ever going on, and remember not to exacerbate it. History proves to us that the state, government, religion, church, all public institutions, are the only means by which wild and animal man obtains his small share of reason and justice; – let us beware of destroying the flower by cutting at the root.
>
> In short, it appears to me that general science tends towards prudence and conservatism, not towards revolution and for proof of this we need but to study the delicate complexity of the social body.
>
> (Sparvel-Bayly 1908: III, 123–4)

Perhaps it seems harder to think of an English facet to this world of scientific laws and cosmic forces, yet one existed, albeit eccentrically. Henry Thomas Buckle gave ground to no Frenchman in eccentricity: seven miles walked every day, seven hours' reading every day, bread and fruit for lunch every day, master-strength at chess, nineteen languages, 22,000 books, dead by the time he was 41. He lived the life of a gentleman-scholar who had received little academic training but, like Taine, saw this disability as his edge over rival historians. It gave him an overview of several forests where others could only see trees. So in the *History of Civilisation in England* (1857–61), which he never lived to complete, he intended to supply a fresh version of British history by studying systematically what his predecessors had approached randomly and 'accomplish[ing] for the history of man something equivalent, or at all events analogous, to what has been effected by the enquiries for the different branches of natural science'. He needed to wrest the discipline from 'the hands of biographers, genealogists and collectors of anecdotes, chroniclers of courts and princes and nobles, those babblers of vain things'.[58] In practice, he created a deterministic world like Taine's where the explanation for historical events becomes a mechanical exercise in applying the laws of change that Buckle imagined himself to have discovered; and his text reminds a modern reader, as it did de Tocqueville, of what happens when investigations 'end up *at the machine*' (quoted in Semmel 1984: 138). Since religion went the way of everything else in this account, Acton

---

58 Buckle 1894, 6ff. Antonella Codazzi considers his historiographical significance and relation to Taine in *Hyppolyte Taine e il progetto filosofico di una storiografia scientifica* (1985).

gave the book one of its stormiest reviews. He, too, noted that Buckle 'look[ed] at men not as persons, but as machines' which enabled him to agglomerate them into bogus collectivities:

> The true historian takes the individual for his centre. ... If he treats of mobs, or armies, or bodies of men, he invests this multitude with a kind of personality of its own – its own wishes, passions, character, will, and conscience. Mr. Buckle's history, if he *could* write a history according to this programme, would be the reverse of all this: he would merge the individual in the company, the person in the body, wishes, passions, character, conscience, all would be abstracted. ... History would consist in tabular views of births, deaths, marriages, diseases, prices, commerce and the like; and the historian would be chiefly useful in providing grocers with cheap paper to wrap up butter in.
>
> (quoted in McNeill 1967: 17)

It was magnificently unfair and not a little prescient.

Nevertheless, the impact of scientific aspiration if not of execution could not be gainsaid, except by those such as Herbert Spencer who could gain by saying it. His allegation that historians were not only incapable themselves of developing social science but guilty of denying its possibility when others attempted it (Spencer 1904: II, 253) has more to do with his vainglory than what historians thought and wrote. Politically correct critics such as Henry Sidgwick disapproved of the violence which Buckle had met in the reviews. 'Abuse him as you like,' he wrote to a friend, 'he is the first Englishman who has attempted to write scientific history.'[59] A book like Walter Bagehot's *Physics and Politics* (1872) said volumes in its title about this gathering mood[60] and by 1875 the economist (and historian) J. E. Cairnes had reached conclusions quite different from Spencer's about the acceptance of science:

> There is a certain sense in which, I presume, the doctrine of 'Social Evolution' would be now pretty widely accepted, at least among those who have concerned themselves with the philosophy of history and kindred speculations. I mean the sense in which it expresses the fact that each stage in human progress is the outcome and result of the stage which has immediately preceded it, and that the whole series of stages ... represents a connected chain, of which the links are bound together as sequences in precisely the same way as in the instances of causation presented by other departments of nature. Some such assumption as this must necessarily form the basis of all attempts at a rational interpretation of history.
>
> (Cairnes 1875: 64)

That such support should come from an economist reminds us of one crucial area of 'scientific' history that responded especially well to the climate of the late nineteenth century. Germany perhaps began the swing towards economic history, not least because of her own industrial revolution and the presence of a Marxist understanding of economic processes, and the story was taken up strongly in Britain where classical 'political economy' had fallen prey by the 1870s to the mathematical

---

59 Sidgwick to Dakyns, 24 Aug. 1861, in Sidgwick and Sidgwick 1906: 68.
60 It also reflected expressly on history which '[e]very one now admits ... is guided by certain laws': Bagehot 1872: 42.

models of Stanley Jevons and the revolution in economic ideas spearheaded in Cambridge. The economic history pioneered by W. J. Ashley and William Cunningham[61] began an important national tradition that would mature only after the Second World War. In Germany the 'national' economic history revolving around Hildebrand, originally, and then Roscher, Knies and Schmoller[62] continued the project of dissection, rejecting economic theory with its cardboard models of human practice and insisting on the need for substantive accounts of real processes – on the need, in other words, for historical method. Here explanation took its power from actuality and history took its shape from experience revealed in detailed historical research. Problems would appear at the point, evident by the 1880s, when economics wished to take leave of 'political economy' and become its own science.

The sheer definitiveness of dealing in hard data caught the imagination of historians overpowered by the loss of familiar reference-points or tormented by the *Methodenstreit* in Germany, which we shall examine shortly. But of course the need to clarify social action by analysis and comparison would not stop there, especially when the late nineteenth century had seen the spawning of new intellectual fields of enquiry such as sociology, psychology and anthropology. If the second half of the century was the apogee of Marx, then it was also the epoch of Frazer and Tylor, of Croce and Dilthey, of Emile Durkheim and Gustave Le Bon. It combats credibility to see all historians of the period immolated behind an unthinking empiricism, even if many of them continued to see themselves in the tradition of a Rankean objectivity, looking for more facts to unearth. If there were an example of that myopia, perhaps America might best suggest it. Certainly John Higham was less than generous about the American commitment to 'science'. 'Scientific history tended towards a rigid factualism everywhere in the late nineteenth century,' he wrote,

> but perhaps nowhere more strongly than among American professionals. Unlike their contemporary colleagues in England, France and Germany, the Americans made not a single sustained effort to discuss the nature of historical knowledge. Even in the handbooks they wrote on historical method, American scholars dispensed with the theoretical sections of the European treatises – chiefly Ernst Bernheim's *Lehrbuch der historischen Methode* (1889) – on which they otherwise relied.
>
> (Higham *et al.* 1965)

---

61 William Cunningham (1849–1919) can be approached through Audrey Cunningham, *William Cunningham, Teacher and Priest* (1950). Among the more important of his books one might count *The Growth of English Industry and Commerce* (1882) and *Modern Civilisation in Some of its Economic Aspects* (1896). W. J. (later Sir William) Ashley (1860–1927) was impressively prolific across a chronological range that would overwhelm most modern scholars. The most seminal of the larger studies was *An Introduction to English Economic History and Theory* (1888–93).

62 The phenomenon as a whole is considered in Winkel 1977 and Krüger 1983. Bruno Hildebrand (d. 1878) had founded the *Jahrbücher für Nationalökonomie und Statistik* but Carl Knies and Wilhelm Roscher recommended the specifically historical treatment of the subject in their respective works, perhaps most significantly in Knies's *Die politischen Oekonomie vom Standpunkte der geschichtlichen Methode* (2nd edn, 1883). Gustav Schmoller carried these perceptions into a variety of social and political studies, as well as one major historical work, *Umrisse und Untersuchungen zur Verfassungs-Verwaltungs- und Wirtschaftsgeschichte besonders des preussischen Staates im 17. und 18. Jahrhundert* (1898).

In this sense the scientific spirit of enquiry might lead in directions which no apostle of 'processes' and 'phases' had the imagination to conceive. The early work of Wilhelm Dilthey had concerned itself with psychological investigation: he changed to thinking about history only when he decided that history was the true psychology. The disreputable young scholar of Leipzig, Karl Lamprecht, likewise found his scientific inclinations taking him further down the road of a comparative history that would interest itself not with quantifiable data generated by past societies, but with their *Weltanschauungen*, for the analysis of which historians would need to master more than one discipline. Working on a journal called the *Archiv für Kulturgeschichte*, he became ever more deeply involved in a new element in historical enquiry that would lead him and his generation towards a further broadening of the subject. But there was nothing inevitable about that turn. Nor was it clear that historians ought to take it.

CULTURE AND *KULTUR*

The need for a history of 'culture' sprang from deep roots in German historical consciousness. Lamprecht's journal of 1894 merely retitled an existing one, the *Zeitschrift für deutsche Kulturgeschichte*, which two men in particular, Johannes Falke and Johann Müller, had helped inaugurate as early as 1856. (Gilbert 1990: 84). An insistence on the Germanic character of *Kultur* followed predictably enough from the search for origins which we have noticed in the generation of Humboldt and the young Ranke; and its meaning proved limited in practice to a form of social history that tried to press exploration beyond the elites on whom historians normally concentrated. By the time Karl Lamprecht went up to Göttingen as an undergraduate in 1874, however, the connotations of a cultural history had begun the series of shifts which would eventually make two distinct patterns discernible. One of them reflected an interest in a new historical form arising from the history of art and literature as keys to understanding social perception and the limits of a period's sense of itself. This tendency prowled around the edge of the German Empire in Switzerland, Belgium and Holland. The other predilection saw in *Kultur* a concept that associated intellectual and aesthetic prowess with a definite understanding of state-ascendancy and tied its analysis of German thought to the development of the Bismarckian Reich. Even Lamprecht, who dissociated himself from some aspects of this reduction of *Kultur* to *Macht*, found himself amid the dislocations of 1914 looking back on what he saw as an 'extraordinarily strong distinction between west European cultural formation [*Kulturverhalten*] and the central European, especially German, one'; and he saw in the latter's peculiarity 'a close connection between state and nation' (Lamprecht 1914: 9, 11).

Few inhabitants of continental Europe were to escape that peculiarity between 1870 and 1914, and the rationale adopted by Berlin for German policy had an explicit cultural content. When Western cartoons satirizing the German army appeared during the First World War, a favourite theme lay, therefore, in depicting babies skewered on German bayonets over a caption exclaiming 'Another Example of German *Kultur*!' Nor was it accidental that the celebration among European historians of high culture as a resistance against the evils inherent in mass industrialized society reached its apogee among those at once close to the German *Kulturnation* yet nervous of its potential for harm. Lamprecht's journey, from a notion of culture to a modified acceptance of *Kultur* as his nation went off to war with full and pure hearts in search of a rich future[63], symbolized one way in which these categories elided. An alternative itinerary, one infinitely more significant for the future of cultural historiography, started in Basle, went to Berlin and came back again.

Quite what to make of the writings of Jacob Burckhardt (1818–97) poses more problems today than it might have done fifty years ago. The recluse who refused Ranke's chair to live alone above a baker's shop in his home town seems attractive to the modern understanding of what an intellectual ought to be. Conversely, his anti-Semitism, loathing for the masses and cultural pessimism does not endear him to modern liberals.[64] Most of these worries turn on Burckhardt's later work and one readily forgets just how much he had swallowed *Kultur* as a young student in Ranke's Berlin. 'I have Germany to thank for everything!', an early letter reported. 'What a people! What a wonderful youth! What a land – a paradise!'[65] But the revolution had dismayed him in 1848:

> The word freedom sounds rich and beautiful, but no one should talk about it who has not seen and experienced slavery under the loud-mouthed masses, called 'the people', seen it with his own eyes and endured civil unrest ... I know too much about history to expect anything from the despotism of the masses but a future tyranny, which will mean the end of history.
>
> (quoted in White 1973: 235)

In returning to Switzerland, he largely turned his back on the German dream and immersed himself in Renaissance art and literature, perhaps looking for that 'intoxication' or 'consolation' which Croce (1941: 104–5, 107) saw at the heart of Burckhardt's historical thought. Whatever his motivation, the book that ultimately resulted – *The Civilization of the Renaissance in Italy* (*Die Kultur der Renaissance in Italien*) – would come to have an importance quite overlooked at the time of its publication in 1860.

It was not his first book. Contact with Droysen in Berlin and Gottfried Kinkel at Bonn had taken his mind towards classical Greece and he had later written both a life of Constantine and *Cicerone* (1855), a guide to Italian painting. The rediscovery of that world in the Renaissance marked the awakening of spirit that he sought and

---

63   'Unsere Herzen waren rein and waren gross, und sie waren voll des Gedankens an eine reiche Zukunft unserer Nation' (Lamprecht 1914: 15).

64   Even so gifted a critic as Hayden White has a mild fit of modernity when presenting Burckhardt's world-view and his essay does not have the conviction of those on Ranke and Michelet. Cf. White 1973: 230–64.

65   Quoted in Hugh Trevor-Roper's introduction to Jacob Burckhardt, *On History and Historians* (1965), xiii. Cf. Trevor-Roper 1984.

missed in the Germany he had come to know; and it offered an opportunity to write about the state in a new way. Not that political history takes up much of his time: it is dispatched in a first chapter which shows the preconditions in state development that would allow the Italian Renaissance to happen. But the *Leitmotif* of those changes – the emergence of the 'individual' – he sees as both an ingredient in cultural arousal and a matter for personal celebration. Before the reader's eyes Burckhardt then exposes a series of what he calls 'cross-sections' dealing with aspects of the Renaissance environment: the revival of antiquity, the discovery of the world and its encapsulation in a new literature concerned with 'the daily course of human life':

> The comical and satirical literature of the Middle Ages could not dispense with pictures of every-day events. But it was another thing, when the Italians of the Renaissance dwelt on this picture for its own sake – for its inherent interest – and because it forms part of that great, universal life of the world whose magic breath they felt everywhere around them. Instead of and together with the satirical comedy, which wanders through houses, villages and streets, seeking food for its derision in parson, peasant and burgher, we now see in literature the beginnings of a true *genre*, long before it found any expression in painting.
>
> (Burckhardt n.d.: 181)

From here he heads towards society and festivals, morality and religion. Not only did such a structure mark a new departure in content, moreover, but it also has claims to constitute the first attempt in Western historiography to write a book in a non-narrative way. For although it makes use of chronology within its various sections to organize the presentation of argument, the book as whole lacks a chronological origin and terminus. *Die Kultur der Renaissance in Italien* made use, moreover, of categories of material that never before had been systematically deployed for a historical, rather than aesthetic, purpose – especially the visual arts and poetry, 'one of history's most important, singular [*allereinste*] and beautiful sources' (Burckhardt [1905] 1955: 69).

In the short term, Burckhardt's conspectus won little acclaim. Ruskin knew about him in England; perhaps Acton also helped to promote his name there (Kaegi 1962: 81). It was rather towards the end of the century, when current moods about decadence in Western civilization helped stimulate interest in cultural literature, that the book began to acquire a readership and Burckhardt his first disciples. It must have been in the early years of the twentieth century that a Dutch schoolboy or young student, Johan Huizinga, first read him and became persuaded of the need for a new form of historical statement.[66] But by then of course the world had changed radically and Burckhardt's *Weltgeschichtliche Betrachtungen* (1905) showed that he had changed too. He had been offended by the willingness of German apostles of *Kultur* to receive Darwinist teaching into their definition of cultural development; and the Bismarckian invasion of France in 1870 left him profoundly disturbed. In the Europe of the second industrial revolution he was left lamenting that everything would soon *'business* werden wie in Amerika'.[67] He became to

---

66   Huizinga's intellectual debts are traced in Collie 1964.
67   Reflection dated March 1873 in Burckhardt [1905] 1955: 203 (emphasis added).

historiography what Nietzsche had become to Germanic philosophy: the achievement lost itself in a clutch of catch-phrases. His later work shows a closer approximation, in fact, to the drift of his generation in seeing the state as a critical element in explanation and places *language*, rather than art or high culture, at the centre of the picture, together with race and blood.[68]

Race and blood had meanwhile darkened their stain in Lamprecht's Germany. In the year he went to Göttingen, Heinrich von Treitschke (1834–96) succeeded Ranke in the Berlin chair, having already moved away from his earlier liberalism to a state-led conception of society reflected in his history of Germany (Treitschke 1879–94). His pupil Friedrich Meinecke (1862–1954) helped Treitschke become chief editor of the prestigious *Historische Zeitschrift* on the death of Sybel in 1895; and when Treitschke himself died in the following year, Meinecke took over and held the position until the Nazis deposed him in 1935. In all these writers, as with Gustav Droysen and Ernst Troeltsch, the mood of Wilhelmine Germany infected their histories with a sense of Prussian triumphalism and a rethinking of the basis of ethics away from individual volition and towards the state as its own 'ethical unit of will'.[69] The idea of a *Kulturnation* had begun its trajectory towards a *Staatsnation* or, worse, the one had become subsumed in the other. Now Lamprecht, established since 1891 in a chair at Leipzig which he was to hold until his death in 1915, reacted archly against all forms of mysticism, whether in the form of Kantian Idealism or Treitschkian elegiacs about the Fatherland. His own *Deutsche Geschichte*, which began to appear from 1891, implied a different perspective. To be sure, Lamprecht felt a commitment to German *Kultur*. But his historical method had more to do with the comparative analysis of various kinds of culture than with the promotion of a particular one. He accepted that the state must lie at the centre of the analysis but taught that the Rankians had erred in missing the degree to which broad cultural forces determine outcomes rather than localized intentions. As a pupil of Roscher, he understood economies to play a salient role, as his early book on German economic life in the Middle Ages attested (Lamprecht 1885–6). And the enormous project he conceived on the history of German culture, for all its dwelling on political narrative, would come to manifest a commitment to a moral undertow in the narrative, as his biographer explains:

> Lamprecht did not define this concept [of culture] in the *German History* ... but his account made it clear that culture was foremost an ethical matter. It related to the regulation of behavior. Cultural progress meant the transition from collective to individual constraint, from external compulsion to internal discipline and freedom. Primitive civilizations were 'ruled by dark drives,' which were bridled by the collective compulsion exerted by family, clan and tribe. The development of culture then passed, in Lamprecht's analysis, through stages characterized successively by the appearance of legal order, the discipline of social convention, and the emergence of a sense of individual

---

68 ibid. 57–8. He saw culture finally as one of three 'Potenzen' in the world; religion and the state formed the other two. But he retained a commitment to 'die Gesellschaft im weitersten Sinne'.
69 Ernst Troeltsch, quoted in Iggers 1983: 186.

moral duty. It was no coincidence that culture developed through the same stages, marked out by the same historical periods, as did national consciousness, for the two were ultimately the same[70]

In all of this, most of all in his decision to establish a chronology in accordance with supposed aesthetic and symbolic transformations, he recalls Burckhardt, whom we know him to have studied. But the Treitschkian side also remained with him. He recognized that different states would produce different cultural formations with a scientific value of their own. That is why he commissioned Henri Pirenne to write a history of Belgium for his series on the history of European states.[71]

The two men had corresponded since 1894 and one of the sadnesses of increasing chauvinism in the twentieth century lay in its disruption of their relationship. Without having known Lamprecht, on the other hand, Pirenne would in any case have acquired a clear grasp of methodological trends in Germany where he spent a year after his graduation from Liège. He also worked with Monod and Fustel in Paris for a year: fulfilling the logic of his country's history so that he became neither French nor German. His own contribution to the idea of cultural history did not, like Lamprecht's, have the state at its core. Neither did it turn on an aesthetic perception, as Burckhardt's had done. Pirenne's historical writing had affinities with an earlier understanding of culture as the presentation of a global social and economic account. In his hands, however, it would become so much more than that.

Belgium itself – its geography, its linguistic and cultural blend – does something to explain the thrust of Pirenne's interests and career. In the late nineteenth century Belgian intellectual life had discovered a new self-confidence, especially in the University of Liège where Emile de Laveleye (1822–92) taught economics but also established a reputation in the higher journalism of western Europe, including England, for his contribution to the 'socialism of the chair'. He strongly influenced a young colleague, Paul Fredericq, who taught in Liège for a few years before moving back to his home environment at Ghent where he had completed his doctorate. Fredericq's passion was for *teaching*: he studied it as others researched their sources. While teaching at Liège, he began his expeditions to other universities in Germany and England to discover how they taught history; and his conclusions appeared in a book about *Better Teaching in History* at the turn of the century (Fredericq 1899). As a working historian, he developed an expertise on the Spanish Inquisition in the Low Countries.[72] All of this impinged greatly on Pirenne because he took three courses with Fredericq as an undergraduate. Like Fredericq, moreover, Pirenne wanted to travel. His two years spent in Germany and France gave him a sharp sense of how historical work might be approached from radically divergent directions. His own studies often display the stronger qualities of each.

---

70   Chickering 1993: 136. I draw on this important study at a number of points in my account.
71   The background to the *Europäische Staatengeschichte* is presented in Chickering 1993: 166. Lamprecht outlined his own approach in his *Die Kulturhistorische Methode* (1900).
72   For information on Fredericq, see Lyon, 1974: 40ff.

434

Pirenne's period was the early Middle Ages, his territory the Pays-Bas. But his definition of both defied convention. If his name is now associated particularly with the economic and social structures of northern Europe and the towns and institutions that arose there, it is typical of him that he should have seen the rise of Islam as contributing centrally to the creation of his subject matter.[73] Similarly, the Pays-Bas connoted for him a tract of territory stretching from northern France, through Flanders and into modern Holland. Even so wide a perspective, moreover, never occludes Pirenne's assumption that he is speaking about 'l'Europe occidentale' against which all subsets of information must be gauged. Within those categories he concerned himself less with the interaction of geography and social formations than with administrative boundaries and political questions. The exception that proved the rule happened to be his masterpiece, the *Histoire de Belgique*, but there the constraints of Lamprecht and his fellow editors sometimes feel fairly strong. The idea of depicting Belgium as a cohesive culture that thrived on internal difference rather than suffering atrophy from it was the central perception that only a mind like Pirenne's would have seen. Having announced it, he proceeds in fairly conventional terms; he spends time on literature and art − more than would be usual at the time he wrote − but the political account leads strongly once he is out of his own period and presumably relying on secondary sources that have a mostly political orientation.

In his own period Pirenne studied cultures in the way a biologist does: under the microscope. But because he believed that results can be applied across territories, his work always had an implicit commitment to *comparative* study. Here is an example from a page in *Les Anciennes Démocraties des Pays-Bas* which appeared in 1910. The French is retained to illustrate Pirenne's economy and simplicity, which often verges on the terse:

> En France et en Angleterre, le pouvoir royal fut assez puissant pour s'opposer tout d'abord aux tentatives urbaines, puis pour en triompher. En Italie et en Allemagne, sa faiblesse le condamna au contraire à capituler devant elles, et une riche floraison de villes libres s'épanouit bientôt des deux côtés des Alpes. Quant aux Pays-Bas, ils présentent une situation intermédiaire ... [Ses grandes communes] diffèrent tout à la fois des *freie Reichstädte* de l'Empire ou des républiques municipales de la Toscone et des communes de France étroitement surveillées par les prévôts and les baillis du roi.
>
> (Pirenne 1910)

Pirenne's own story runs through into the 1930s and his unfinished *Muhammad and Charlemagne*. But long before 1914 he had contributed enough to show how the history of a national or regional culture might be attempted and he had done so in face of an *étatisme* which had begun to turn Europe into an armed camp.

Burckhardt never saw much of that except in his mind's eye; he died in 1897. Pirenne would see too much of it in his internment camp in Germany during the

---

73   The so-called 'Pirenne thesis' identified the rise of Islam in the seventh century as the cataclysm which disrupted the economic life of southern Europe and turned the northern periphery into the centre of a new Carolingian civilization. For a recent re-evaluation see Hodges and Whitehouse 1983.

First World War. Culture as an ambition had not died, but then neither had *Kultur*: an unknown schoolteacher in Wilhelmine Germany had already committed himself to saving the latter, if only to follow the logic of History as its great wheel turned once more to crush the declining 'civilization' of the West (Spengler [1918–23] 1926–9). The two senses of cultural history came together more poignantly in the life of another schoolteacher who became a professional academic and eventually Holland's greatest historian of the twentieth century. For Huizinga maintained much of the Burckhardtian legacy, looking for his material in poetry, encapsulating the *Geist* of an entire period, seeing no difficulty in discussing *The Waning of the Middle Ages* as though an epoch could lose its sense of itself (Huizinga [1919] 1924). Culture continued in his hands to mean intellectual and aesthetic cultivation; and social elites were necessary for sustaining it. Like Toynbee, he saw barbarism as the natural ally of democracy. Like Burckhardt, he avoided the dwelling on materialism that he saw as characteristic of his day by transporting himself to more propitious periods in his private imagination. In 1940 his country felt the force of *Kultur*: the experience of Huizinga re-ran the narrative of Pirenne in 1915 with the patriotic self-closure of his university and his internment at the hands of the invading Germans. He was not taken to a field and shot, like Marc Bloch; he died along with thousands of his countrymen in the ravaging Dutch winter of 1944–5 when no food could be found. So there was an acrid irony. He was killed by the very element that his history had always excluded. 'Culture' in his sense survived him in the history of art and music, but as a force in historical research it underwent a definitional (and generational) transformation. *Kultur* became an embarrassment or a capitalist symptom. The next thirty years would bring cultural history to a new height of popularity and influence only when it turned itself into an intellectual form that neither Meinecke nor Huizinga would have appreciated.

THE ENGLISH 'WHIGS'

At first sight, the British avoided the rise of cultural history. The symptoms of a historiographical mood which they shared in the Romantic period with France and Germany and America seem to have disappeared thereafter. Of course, there remained 'influences'. Ranke became a model for many historians who were engaged in serious work and held his popularity until the German Empire began its change of direction towards an assertive imperialism after 1871 and lost its veneration for British practice.[74] The more cosmopolitan historians in Britain, with Acton at their head, read widely in French and German and presumably sensed changes afoot on the Continent. For the most part, however, Britain, like the United Sates, went its own way. The result was a distinctive and remarkably time-specific tendency which focused on British experience at the expense of the world outside, one that concentrated on types of constitutional history rather than on social, cultural or

---

74 For this development see McClelland 1971; cf Sheehan 1978.

intellectual studies, and that often imbued that study with linear logic leading from past to present, so that history became a matter of identifying broad processes working themselves out over hundreds of years and connecting the present of Victorian Westminster with a past running back through the Glorious Revolution, Magna Carta, the Witanagemot and eventually towards the forests of Saxony. The doctrines associated with this history were congratulatory: the story celebrated English (as opposed, mostly, to Scottish, Welsh or Irish) liberty and the institutions that it deemed central to the widening of English freedom through the ages. And they were *colligatory*.[75] Events across long spans of time could be sewn together in a common story of success as though the historian's thread were as strong and endless as his tapestry. For Edward Freeman (1823–92) William the Conqueror and William III who 'delivered' England in the Revolution of 1689 attracted comparison as though the 600 years between them only heightened their mutual relation.

> In the one case the invader came to conquer, in the other he came to deliver; but in both cases alike the effect of his coming was to preserve and not to destroy; the Conqueror and the Deliverer alike has had his share in working out the continuous being of English law and of English national life ... [B]oth revolutions have worked for the same end; the great actors in both were, however unwittingly, fellow-workers in the same cause.[76]

In 1931 Herbert Butterfield published a typology of such approaches under the title *The Whig Interpretation of History* which gained a great vogue during the next two or three decades and fixed the nineteenth century, to its detriment, with a ready-made critique which lesser historians than Butterfield have applied mechanically to several generations of writers. Butterfield's short meditation – it was hardly more than an essay – singled out no particular men for attack; it offered no index. It took its starting-point from discomfort in the face of writers (and here he plainly had Acton in mind) who used historical work as a way of executing judgement on the past and exacting vengeance on malefactors. Instead, 'research' had a different task. It should illuminate the past as it appeared to those for whom it was the present, rather than treating historical persons as though they were apprentice-figures, trying and often failing to be modern:

> Real historical understanding is not achieved by the subordination of the past to the present, but rather by our making the past our present and attempting to see life with the eyes of another century than our own. It is not reached by assuming that our own age is the absolute to which Luther and Calvin and their generation are only relative; it is only

---

75   A very useful term reinvented by W. H. Walsh from its origin in the nineteenth-century Cambridge mathematician and philosopher, Whewell. See Walsh [1951] 1992: 23–4. Colligation is the activity of binding together a narrative (and thus rescuing it from mere sequence) by deciding how events in a given story can be made to tie in with one another. A permanent problem for philosophers of history lies in establishing whether colligation is something that historians achieve despite the incoherence of their subject matter or whether colligation is already inherent in the world that they merely describe and report. For divergent readings of this difficulty, cf. Carr 1986 and White 1987.
76   Quoted in Burrow 1981: 196. This section draws heavily on Professor Burrow's work.

reached by fully accepting the fact that their generation was as valid as our generation, their issues as momentous as our issues and their day as full and vital to them as our day is to us.

(Butterfield [1931] 1973: 20–1)

This says little more than Ranke had said. Where Butterfield went further was in his perception that bad history functioned by abridgement: it simplified a complex story and bent its inner linkages by leaving out all those facts that got in the way of the moral:

> for both the method and the kind of history that results from it would be impossible if all the facts were told in all their fullness. The theory that is behind the whig interpretation – the theory that we study the past for the sake of the present – is one that is really introduced for the purpose of facilitating the abridgement of history; and its effect is to provide us with a handy rule of thumb by which we can easily discover what was important in the past. ... No one could mistake the aptness of this theory for a school of writers who might show the least inclination to undervalue one side of the historical story; and indeed there would be no point in holding it if it were not for the fact that it serves to simplify the study of history by providing an excuse for leaving things out.

(ibid. 25–6)

Leaving aside the problems raised by Butterfield's own implied views about selection in history, a difficulty has emerged from labelling as 'Whigs' his disliked historians. Since Whigs appear in British and not European political history, his doctrines have come to be seen as a commentary on a school of British historians, though not, oddly, on American ones where the term 'Whig' also came into prominence during the Reconstruction period. They are held to have their origin in the reaction against Hume's 'Tory' version of the seventeenth century in Hallam and Macaulay and to persist as a tradition in historical writing until at least the high period of George Macaulay Trevelyan in the 1920s and 1930s. Between those terminal dates a canon of historians comprising, among others, William Stubbs, James Anthony Froude, E. A. Freeman, J. R. Green, W. E. H. Lecky, Lord Acton, J. R. Seeley, S. R. Gardiner, C. H. Firth and J. B. Bury come into focus all too often as embodiments of 'Whig' attitudes with no sense of what made them different from one another or any idea of how the nineteenth century changed in its assumptions. But then, that is what the Whig theory has done: it provides insight into 100 years of historiography by telling posterity what all historians had in common rather than establishing criteria that might help differentiate them. That commonality, moreover, reached far beyond those who could be held guilty of 'Whig' attitudes. Indeed the only nineteenth-century British historian who was *not* a Whig, on Butterfield's understanding, was Carlyle, unless one extends the title of historian to the Tory firebrand Sir Archibald Alison.[77] Recent writing has proved more astringent and it seems possible both to separate out chronological phases in

---

77 Sir Archibald Alison (1792–1867) wrote many vast books informed by invincible Toryism. The best-known and most vast are the *History of Europe during the French Revolution* (1833–42) and the *History of Europe from the Fall of Napoleon in 1815 to the Accession of Louis Napoleon in 1852* (1853–9). He reflected on his achievements in *Some Account of my Life and Writings: an Autobiography* (1883).

nineteenth-century writing and to see the role of religion within them as an important determinant of attitude.

Religion remained central to the intellectual environment in Britain during the nineteenth century in a way and to a degree that continental experience did not replicate. Britain did not possess, to be sure, the confessional complications of Belgium and France; nor did the established Church retain that mastery over secular institutions that the Roman Catholic Church continued to enjoy in Spain and Italy. But the insecurities and the questions that gave rise to them invigorated religion as an intellectual domain and contributed in a major fashion to historical understanding. Carlyle apart, the so-called Whigs were predominantly Christian, predominantly Anglican, thinkers for whom the Reformation supplied the critical theatre of enquiry when considering the origins of modern England. When they wrote about the history of the English constitution, as so many of them did, they approached their story from the standpoint of having Good News to relate. Sometimes (since some of these authors were bishops or ordained priests) their commentary edged over into direct homily. More often it took the form of eternal breeziness, thankfulness and oblique reference to universal truth.[78] They registered their gratitude for the British way of life, following the example of Freeman who, as John Burrow acutely observes, spoke of his medieval people and institutions like 'a proud or anxious relative'. (Burrow 1981: 199). They wrote, too, in an age innocent of tragedy on the scale known to the century that followed. If they could not have found the grandeur that they developed had they been writing half a century earlier, neither could they have supported their optimism had they lived to endure the barbarisms of the Somme and Passchendaele. In a remarkably stark fashion, the tone of English constitutional history in the second half of the nineteenth century spoke to a specific condition of place and time.

The year 1849 marks a point of origin because in that year appeared John Mitchell Kemble's account of the Saxons and their role, as he conceived it, in the foundation of British political institutions (Kemble 1849). His work reflected the *völkisch* mood of the Germans (he had spent time working with Jakob Grimm) but it also signalled the end of a willingness to see Magna Carta as *fons et origo* for British constitutional development. Macaulay and his contemporaries pressed backward Hume's concern with the seventeenth century to the events of the thirteenth century in their search for the beginning of modernity: Runnymede in 1215, the baronial wars in 1258–65, the calling of the knights to Parliament in 1295. They had begun to outgrow Hume's characterization of the pre-Norman period which is delicious enough to stand recollection:

> With regard to the manners of the Anglo-Saxons we can say little, but that they were in general a rude, uncultivated people, ignorant of letters, unskilled in the mechanical arts, untamed to submission under law and government, addicted to intemperance, riot and disorder. ... Even the Norman historians, notwithstanding the low state of the arts in their own country, speak of them as barbarians.
>
> (Hume 1754–62: I, 305–6)

---

78 I have commented on their proclivities elsewhere: see Bentley 1993.

But despite the efforts of Sharon Turner (1768–1847)[79] and Benjamin Thorpe (1782–1870)[80] the Anglo-Saxon period retained its image of bone-gnawing savagery until Kemble advanced the suggestion of a fundamental continuity between the world of the Saxons and that of the Norman kingdom that followed. Kemble disliked the Saxons on a number of grounds but a recent scholar sees him as having given 'very balanced accounts of the Roman contribution to the conversion of the Saxons, of the influence of Canon Law, and of the previously notorious career of St. Dunstan' (Smith 1987: 199). Yet what might be termed a 'continuity thesis' received its strongest support from Edward Augustus Freeman (1823–92) in his account of the Norman conquest (Freeman 1867–9), which, together with the more generous appreciation of the relationship between Saxon and Norman England in his *Select Charters* of 1860, marks a high point in mid-Victorian constitutionalism. Between them, Stubbs, Freeman and John Richard Green (1837–83), whose *Short History of the English People* (1874) may be added to the litany, helped establish a climate of composition in which British history assumed a particular shape: 'England' emerged from the Teutonic migrants from northern Germany; it was confirmed in the events of the Norman invasion, sullied by the Angevins, rescued by the barons. Then, Maitland said in recalling Stubbs,

[s]omewhere about the year 1307 the strain of the triumphal march must be abandoned; we pass in those well-known words 'from the age of heroism to the age of chivalry, from a century ennobled by devotion and self-sacrifice to one in which the gloss of superficial refinement fails to hide the reality of heartless selfishness and moral degradation'.

(Maitland [1901] 1957: 272–3)

The way was open for the factious wars of the fifteenth century, the Tudor Tyranny and the rescue-bid of William III. Stubbs was too discerning a historian and too considerable a Tory to swallow much of this prospectus; but in Freeman's hands it became a hallowed story of aspiring and inspiring liberty within which William the Conqueror and William the Deliverer became equally Gladstonian in their consequences.

Hallam and Macaulay had commented on some facets of this picture in the 1820s and 1830s. But the generation of Stubbs and Freeman hated the rhetoric and lack of documentation which they associated with the romantics and loaded their accounts with evidence from primary sources. Because James Anthony Froude did that, too, his work provided constitutional historians with an unsavoury problem. His *magnum opus* covered a period of the sixteenth century that touched the nerves of Protestantism and provided a key element in the history of repression (Froude 1856–70). Froude's account made no attempt to camouflage his defence of the Reformation; nor did he

---

79 Principally a philologist, he had studied Icelandic and Anglo-Saxon. The four volumes of his *History of England from the Earliest Period to the Norman Conquest* (1799–1805) drew for the first time on manuscripts in the Cottonian Library.

80 Thorpe, like Kemble, had studied abroad. He spent four years in Copenhagen working with R. C. Rask. His central text on the Anglo-Saxon period is *Ancient Laws and Institutes of England* (1840).

mitigate his almost pathological defence of Henry VIII. He used new primary material, moreover, to strike out on his new path and (according to critics) mistranscribed and corrupted it.[81] Between Froude and Freeman, therefore, the journals rang with abuse and counter-claim as the volumes proceeded. Only with Freeman's own excoriation at the hands of John Horace Round in the 1890s did the dismissal of Froude's writing lessen in its severity. Far more acceptable to historical opinion was the mammoth research project of S. R. Gardiner (1829–1902), whose sixteen volumes (Gardiner 1883–4; 1886–91; 1894–1901) on the constitutional history of the seventeenth century (eighteen if one counts the continuation by Stubbs's pupil, Charles Harding Firth[82]) lent renewed force to the idea of a Puritan revolution having marked an outbreak of liberation against the forces of darkness.

But of course figures other than Froude posed a challenge to 'Whig' notions of constitutional change by the turn of century. Those notions' essential connectedness and vaunted continuities suffered from Round, who destroyed key items of Freeman's understanding of the Norman Conquest in a series of articles beginning in 1891 and collected in his *Feudal England* (1895), and Frederic William Maitland whose enquiries into the bases of English law rendered untenable the Stubbsian analysis of, in particular, the nature and status of the English Parliament at the beginning of the fourteenth century.[83] In the later part of the chronology, meanwhile, J. R. Seeley's teaching on the nature of the state and the degree to which its growth must be sought in external considerations rather than some internally generated efflorescence did little to help the model provided in the 1860s and 1870s (see Seeley 1883 and 1895). Even Froude's dyspeptic defence of the sixteenth century came to have a more sophisticated champion in the work of A. F. Pollard (1869–1948), who was later to found London's Institute of Historical Research.[84] Indeed the faithful themselves had come by the turn of the century to reflect on how different 'Whig' history had become since the time of Macaulay:

> [T]he politics of the seventeenth century, when studied for the mere sake of understanding them, assume a very different appearance from that which they had in the eyes of men who, like Macaulay and Forster,[85] regarded them through the medium of their own

---

81 Much of the criticism of Froude seems small-minded in retrospect when one considers his assiduity in researching archives in Spain and his determination to write history from authentic primary material. His mistakes have not been found to compromise his argument (though many other weaknesses have done so) and although his history was infected with doctrines that he did not pretend to hide, so were the thoughts of his critics.

82 *The Last Years of the Protectorate 1656–58* (2 vols, 1909) was a self-conscious extension and one 'undertaken with Dr Gardiner's wishes' (ibid. 5).

83 Maitland's beautifully constructed critique, which devastates through its relentless civility, forms the introduction to his edition of the *Records of the Parliament holden at Westminster, on the 28th day of February, 1305* (Rolls Series, 1893) reprinted in *Selected Essays* (1936).

84 For Pollard's significance and the impact of anti-'Whig' sentiment generally, see Blaas 1978: 274–344.

85 John Forster, barrister (1812–76). He was best known to Victorians for his lives of Goldsmith and Dickens, but Gardiner is thinking here presumably of the early biographical studies of Pym, Vane and Eliot (all published in 1831) and his life of *Oliver Cromwell 1599–1658* (1839).

441

political struggles. Eliot and Strafford were neither Whigs nor Tories, Liberals nor Conservatives. As Professor Seeley was, I believe, the first to teach directly, though the lesson is indirectly involved in every line written by Ranke ... the constant or unavowed comparison of [the past] with the present ... is altogether destructive of real historical knowledge.

(Gardiner 1883–4: I, vi)

Far from presenting a constant picture of advance towards Protestant liberty, British history had come to have a more complicated aspect by 1900. Why, though, did the complication leave British historiography still looking very different from that in the rest of Europe? Why, with the partial exception of Green, did it produce no social historian? Why no English Burckhardt or Pirenne?

A facile answer might rely on Britain's political and economic supremacy in the nineteenth century and see in historical constitutionalism a simple enjoyment of its status through a relishing of its past.[86] One might speak, less clumsily, of the awareness of a distinctive antiquity surrounding the British polity and the resolution by 1800 of those assimilative problems in regard to Scotland, Wales and Ireland with whose analogues countries like Germany, Italy and Belgium had only recently come to terms. Nineteenth-century historians were willing to see the British *state* appearing as long ago as the thirteenth century and to focus their work on a concept that would have struck an Italian or Belgian as fanciful in respect of his own state. Certainly this line of thought gives a clue; but one can take it further. Perhaps British historiography took its constitutional turn from a sense common to many of its adherents that in writing the history of the state they *were* writing precisely the kind of history that later times deem absent: a form of indirect social history. For men such as Stubbs, the attraction of law and constitutional practice lay in their ability to reflect the lives of thousands of anonymous people and thus provide access to those who could never be reached via direct oral testimony. One can sense in him a 'fascination with the structures fabricated, coral-like, by countless almost imperceptible creatures'. (Burrow 1981: 107). In this sense the constitutional history so despised by twentieth-century social historians had attempted to embrace society by absorbing it into the history of the state. It followed that a radical social history would only emerge in Britain when the pretensions of the state as an avatar of social harmony came into question after 1914.

TOWARDS A HISTORICAL 'PROFESSION'

We are entitled to retain the quotation marks until some point after the First World War. The years from 1860 to 1914 saw considerable change none the less and an observer surveying the background, working conditions, sources, production, expectations and theoretical sophistication of Western historians on the eve of Sarajevo could hardly miss significant developments engendered over the past half-century.

---

86 Some of this message appears in Martin Wiener's account of *English Culture and the Decline of the Industrial Spirit* (1985).

Leisured dilettantes who held university posts by virtue of their birth or in spite of their reluctance to prosecute 'research' had decreased as a proportion of the whole. In England one was less likely to run into a Buckle on his daily constitutional or on the way to his club, though one might well encounter Frederick York Powell (1850–1904) on his way to a boxing match as late as the 1890s. Indeed York Powell confutes many suppositions about professionalization understood as a process among historians. As Regius Professor at Oxford he struck the fastidious R. L. Poole as betraying 'an excessive hostility to all things German, an awkward archaic style, and an extreme dilatoriness in carrying out engagements'.[87] Doubtless the impression had gained some currency through his having arrived late for his own inaugural lecture which he had then failed to protract beyond twenty minutes (Slee 1986: 142). And of course once the mind sets out on this track, the quaintnesses rush into view: 'Sligger' Urquart of Trinity College, Oxford, and his chic reading holidays for attractive young men in his Swiss chalet; Oscar Browning of King's College, Cambridge, and his violence against the idea of research; Acton himself who insisted on research while avoiding publishing much of it and whose career had been built on an expensive personal library, an eccentric education at the hands of Dr Döllinger in Germany and the social cachet that helped him become Earl Granville's son-in-law.[88] Even in America, where the *idea* of treating the past in a 'professional' way had entwined itself with a peculiar doctrine about 'objectivity', the main strides in recruiting historians from those of non-notable background had still to come. Peter Novick's recent examination of American historians reveals, for example, that around a quarter of them still came from 'privileged' backgrounds before 1914 (Novick 1988: 171). The thought brings back a wonderful New Year's Resolution – George Bancroft's on the first day of 1821. 'I think it would be highly useful', he wrote in his diary, 'to take lessons in dancing for the sake of wearing off all awkwardness and uncouthness': (Howe 1908: I, 94). Social mobility mattered then far more than professional ascendancy.

While thinking about sociological tendencies among historians, perhaps we do better, indeed, to consider age rather than class or status as a guide to change. For what is apparent in the generation maturing by 1900 is the boost given to the young by the development of the university system in many Western countries and by the spread of the research thesis as both an academic rite of passage and a first rung on the ladder of publication. In France a veritable 'revanche de la jeunesse' seems evident in retrospect.[89] Both there and in

---

87   R. L. Poole to Lord Acton, 25 Oct. 1896, in Blaas 64 n. 253.

88   For Urquart, see Bailey 1936. Cf. Browning 1910. Acton has a rough ride in Kenyon 1983; but then Kenyon's account has had a rough ride. Ironically, when Mandell Creighton declared himself pleased that Acton would collaborate on the project that would become the *English Historical Review*, he plainly thought that Acton would supply some professionalism. 'We must confess that we are not strong on historical method in England. Our work has all the advantages and all the disadvantages of amateur work' Creighton 1904: I, 334.

89   The phrase comes from Charles-Olivier Carbonell's important study of French historians in the 1860s and 1870s. 'Une vocation les appelle, parfois à l'origine d'un métier.' See his *Histoire et Historiens* (1976): 170.

America, new opportunities opened before those with the talent to seize them:

> Before 1914 the professionalization of history [in America] had served as a dramatically successful ladder of personal social and economic mobility for dozens of small-town boys of lower-middle class backgrounds. In the rapidly expanding university world of prewar America, it was not unusual for a bright young man to become a full professor within a few years of receiving the doctorate, and to achieve national eminence before he was out of his thirties. Salaries, for the most successful, compared favourably with those of many other professionals. In the more difficult to measure area of status, the college professor was a figure of consequence in the local community.
>
> (Novick 1988: 169)

Carbonell finds in the French case, similarly, that the *thèse* helped generate historical scholars who, before they were 30, had achieved their first step in a professional world and written a text that would become their first book or series of articles. (Carbonell 1976: 172). On the other hand, the intellectual substance of the Ph.D. qualification, then as now, soon becomes inflated. It helps perspective to recall that Michelet's thesis had amounted to 26 pages of generously spaced text, or to bring to mind Edward Channing's much later Harvard Ph.D. which took eighteen months to produce and comprised 78 pages of unintelligible handwriting (ibid. 265; Novik 1988: 265). Still, with the American universities alone turning out more than 200 of them each year by 1900, the doctoral graduates presented a new feature of an increasingly professional scene and had in effect made the doctorate a precondition of appointment to many university and college posts. First-degree graduates enjoyed a parallel expansion in their number. The Honours school at Oxford expected to see over 100 candidates graduating each year – far larger than the twenty-odd at Cambridge but minuscule in comparison with the 1,000 students of history registered at the Sorbonne by the turn of the century.[90]

A few years earlier, one would have looked less to the University of Paris than to Berlin, Göttingen, Leipzig, Munich, Kiel and Jena for such statistics. The German universities easily outranked French institutions up to the 1880s as vehicles for teaching history. In 1878, for example, there were still only two chairs in history at the Sorbonne, as opposed to eight each in Berlin and Leipzig (Keylor 1975). Indeed, much of the apparatus of professionalism, from social status to professional journals and attitudes to source-criticism, seemingly began in Germany and then spread outwards. Appearances may deceive, however, and it should be stressed that the German case presents substantial ambiguity. Youth, for example, achieved less rapid advancement there because of the two-tier doctoral system which required not only the normal doctorate, often under the impress of a near-feudal *Doktorvater*, but the more demanding *Habilitation* which made it harder for those under 30 to achieve the meteoric careers sometimes seen in the United States. On the other hand, the availability of junior posts for historians in the system of *Privatdozenten* enabled talented younger people to achieve employment and a salary. Again,

---

90 Slee 1986: 125. For the Sorbonne, see Gerard 1983: 81.

structural considerations of this kind sometimes camouflage the degree to which the German norms of co-option and promotion could turn on nepotism and the need to find a powerful patron. The ambiguities soon appear if one reflects on the career of one of the greatest 'professional' historians of the nineteenth century.

Theodor Mommsen's life, after all, spanned most of it: he had reached his mid-eighties when he died in 1903. He achieved, even more than Ranke, the professional dream by out-writing everyone around him. Yet Mommsen's struggles to reach Berlin and the character of his work thereafter comment on the limits of 'professionalization' as a process. He came from Schleswig, the son of a pastor, as so often among German historians, and following his schooling in Altona went to his *Heimatuniversität* at Kiel where he read law and came into contact with Gustav Droysen, Georg Waitz and in particular Otto Jahn.[91] His doctorate in 1843 opened no academic doors; he elected to become a schoolteacher in a girls' school in his home town. It was the serendipity of a royal appointment as Master of Latin Inscriptions that took him on his three years of travel in France and Italy between 1844 and 1847 and which formed the foundation of his epochal work on Roman history. But when his mission ended, he still had no job and went back to teaching schoolchildren, a fate from which the offer of a chair in jurisprudence at Leipzig rescued him, but only because Jahn had used his influence to prompt it. The appointment went wrong almost at once. Mommsen had more on his mind than jurisprudence in 1848 and so did his employers. His liberalism and support for the new political mood soon sent him elsewhere: to Zurich for a while and then Breslau. So he was 41 before a chance of moving to Berlin arose in the editorship of the *Corpus Inscriptionum Latinarum*; and 44 before he became professor of ancient history at the university there. Once having arrived, his academic output became astonishing in the fields of Roman history and law, though the first three volumes of his *Römische Geschichte* had already appeared. His daughter put it down to genius but she reports Mommsen's ominous reply: 'Nein, mein Kind. ... Ich habe ein Organisationstalent, das ist aber alles.'[92] Whatever the form of his ability, however, there were those then and since who have alleged that Mommsen's method consisted in reading back the ethos of 1848 into the Roman world and discussing imperial Rome as though it were a reflection of Bismarckian Germany (and vice versa), despite his protestations to the contrary.[93]

Mommsen was a scholar of international repute and a political figure of some weight. Waitz, who had taught him, was a great teacher as well as a luminous collaborator of Pertz at the *Monumenta*: he probably exercised more direct influence on recruitment to the profession in the later years of the century. But both men show the significance of a new style of source-criticism and of one strand of German

---

91 Otto Jahn (1813–69). Principally interested in archaeology and classical philology but also a distinguished musicologist.

92 'No, my child ... I have a talent for organization, but that's all.' Quoted in Kuczynski 1978: 14.

93 Wücher in particular sees him in this light as 'ein viel zu zeitverbundener Mensch': see Wücher 1956. Cf. Mommsen's denial in a letter to Jahn (1854), quoted in Kuczinski 1978: 85.

academia during the Wilhelmine period. One can identify others and Otto Hintze (1861–1940) could act as a cameo for one of them. He had sat under both Mommsen and Waitz, not to mention Droysen, Treitschke and a philosopher, Wilhelm Dilthey, who would prove more significant in the twentieth century than anyone at the time understood. A combination of Treitschke and the economic historian Schmoller as supervisers of his *Habilitation* must have left Hintze bifocal; but the economic and social thrust certainly overpowered the nationalistic and although he became known for his history of Prussia, Hintze's work developed affinities with Lamprecht's, while Weber would later prove an influence. Indeed Christian Simon has recently seen the Berlin professoriate as divisible into three groups: the older political historians of the Treitschke stamp; a younger group interested in *Kultur* more widely defined and in the notion of comparative history; and a further section of the younger men, typified in Max Lenz, who absorbed a Diltheyan concept of *Verstehen* (understanding resting on empathy rather than deductive science) and wanted to graft it on to a Rankean sense of source-criticism (Simon 1988: I, 138–9). Possibly Friedrich Meinecke falls into this latter group but if so his presence only underlines the impossibility of effecting precise divisions. Both he and Hintze contributed greatly to German historiography before 1914[94] – Meinecke particularly through his editorship of the *Historische Zeitschrift* from 1895. Both names take one forward also to a darker period when they would feel the weight of what German nationalism might mean.

These various forms of precocity became thinkable in no small degree because the continuity of Germany's higher educational system had not suffered any severe interruption in the wake of the French Revolution. In France the universities could hardly have suffered more. Abolished by the revolutionaries, they made a limited re-appearance under Napoleon in 1808 as *facultés* which had a social as much as an academic function in offering courses open to the public and lacking any infrastructure on the German model. Only after the coming of the Third Republic in 1871 did the pace of change begin to increase; but – the crucial point – once having begun, it increased exponentially and soon placed France ahead of Germany in the construction of a historical profession. In 1877 the establishment of a new post, the *maître de conférences*, gave young French historians the chance of obtaining positions similar to the *Privatdozenten* in Germany, while the Ferry ministry's introduction of the *agrégation* in history (1881) produced a first-degree structure to rival that of competitor countries. In 1896 'universities' returned. By 1903 the Ecole des Chartes, the Ecole Pratique des Hautes Etudes and the Ecole Normale Supérieure had become part of the University of Paris. The complex of institutions in Paris proved able to mount each year at least fifty courses in history by the early 1880s.[95] Nor did

---

94 Otto Hintze wrote predominantly on Prussia and the Hohenzollerns: see esp. his *Hohenzollern in ihr Werk* (5th edn, Berlin (1915)). Meinecke's early work examined elements of *Staatsgesechichte* though he turned to historiography in his influential *Rise of Historism* (*Die Entstehung des Historismus* (1936) and after the war reflected courageously on *Die deutsche Katastrophe* (1946).

95 For all these developments, see the very helpful exposition of Keylor 1975.

significant change limit itself to expansion. Qualitative shifts also became apparent in the French writing of history from the 1860s. The German approach to textual analysis and apparatus made a clear impact, not least through the example of those who, like Gabriel Monod, had spent time working in Germany. Their editions started to *look* German:

> ces gros livres prennent l'allure savante que leur donnent les longues et prudentes préfaces, le scrupuleux apparat critique qui dévore le rez-de-chaussée, les index et autres outils de travail.
> En trente ans, on est passé de l'édition passive, simple copie et paresseuse réproduction, à l'édition critique ... et pratique.
>
> (Carbonell 1976: 116)

The new rigour informed Monod's *Revue Historique* of 1876 whose much-quoted manifesto is often taken as a significant departure in Western historiography generally but which might more plausibly be seen as a counterblast to the rival *Zeitschrift* of 1859.[96] It committed itself to the conception of scientific history that had dominated French historical thought since the Enlightenment. More importantly, it found itself over the next thirty years operating as a critical forum for discussion of how to teach the subject. When Monod looked back on the journal in 1907 he discovered that he had included no less than thirty-seven articles dealing with some aspect of teaching (Gerard 1983: 80).

If this tendency distanced French experience from the German one, so did the relative conservatism of its preferred historical subject matter. It shared, to be sure, an entire generation's fascination with the ancient world – one in which the republican aspirations of France, the imperial certainties of Germany and the effortless absence of mind celebrated in England could all find some reflection. Carbonell's sample of historical works published in France between 1866 and 1875 suggests that well over half concerned themselves with antiquity, broadly defined (Carbonell 1976: 269). They also show, however, a far stronger presence of religion in their content than might have been guessed in a culture so committed to analysis. Of that economic history so prominently displayed in the school of Knies, Roscher and others in Germany, there seems comparatively little. More evident is the weight accorded to geography as the true ancillary domain of the historian. This close *Zusammenhang* reached the young at an early point in their education and often continued into the university, as it did with notable effects in the history/geography syllabus followed by the young Marc Bloch at the Ecole Normale in the 1900s. It persisted via the scattered documentation of French history which perhaps helped engender a concentration on the region as a focus of study – not quite in the formalized fashion followed in German *Landesgeschichte* but a pervasive tradition none the less.

Where Germany and France had led, England followed but slowly and with a distinctive twist. The singular relationship between class structure and educational

---

96 For these and other journals of the period, see Stieg 1986.

opportunity continued to starve the universities of talent from those born to unprivileged parents. To speak of a historical profession committed to teaching in the 1860s may be arguable for Oxford (Slee 1986: 100–2) but it seems unpersuasive as an overall picture. Plainly the reforms imposed on Oxford and Cambridge in the second half of the nineteenth century went some way to developing a new sense of purpose. Certainly the foundation of the *English Historical Review* in 1886 marked an important staging-post in the transformation of professional attitude: its first number printed pieces of considerable distinction from men well known across Europe. The expansion of the university system in a context of economic downturn after the mid-1870s also acted as a catalyst in providing a career structure for those unsuccessful in or stifled by the competition in Oxford and Cambridge. London may have lacked a *Monumenta* or an Ecole des Chartes but her centralized public records had the greatest continuity in Europe. Eventual governmental interference in their management, of which the Public Records Act of 1838 was symptomatic (see also Martin and Spufford 1990), and improved access to primary-source collections helped fuel a concern for precise scholarship of the kind practised by Round and encouraged the annihilation of imprecise scholars also practised by Round. Yet by 1900 the model for precise historical work was best embodied in Maitland, whose background hardly emphasized the contours of a self-conscious profession, bringing, like Mommsen, a training in the law to history rather than any steeping in a common training or social catchment. The Royal Historical Society, which theoretically united disparate elements after 1869, in fact acted as a loose manifold for a collection of isolated notables interested mainly in the editing and printing of frequently arcane primary sources.

In those countries where the university system remained nascent, the individuals who wrote history suffered far greater isolation. Spain and Italy present examples where the twentieth century has thrown up far more distinguished historians than did the nineteenth. Spain had its own move towards a systematization of educational institutions, as in the Institución Libre de Enseñanza (Free Institute of Education) in 1876. But Spanish universities entered their era of major development only in the first third of the twentieth century, stimulated by what Julian Marías has called the 'tectonic' effect of the lost war against America in 1898 (Marías 1990: 380–4). One finds there significant 'researchers' such as Ramón Menéndez Pidal[97] rather than a school of history. Spaniards in the twentieth century, especially during their crisis of identity in the 1930s, turned back to nineteenth-century authors such as Menendez y Pelayo for their home truths. 'On the subject of the essence or genius of Spain,' Peter Linehan writes,

> a Spain forever stuck in the sixteenth century, a Spain oblivious of the disasters caused by 'bad Spaniards' from 1640 to 1898 and beyond, Menendez y Pelayo was inexhaustible. In 1910, towards the end of his life, he had lamented in words which were to become famous what he called 'the slow suicide' of the Spanish people.
>
> (Linehan 1992: I, 11–12)

---

97 Pidal covered almost all aspects of Spanish culture in a wide-ranging *œuvre*. For historians, the most significant are his *Historia de España* (4 vols, 1940–54) and his earlier study of *La España del Cid* (2 vols, Madrid, 1929).

Likewise in Italy, the developments we have been considering in northern Europe were not replicated until after 1914 and even then the notion of a 'professional' history sits uncomfortably within the Italian university system. Not that this most historical of cultures failed to make major contributions to historical thought in the revised Idealism associated with Benedetto Croce. Nor was it without distinguished historians, though the acid of fascism corroded the vision and achievement not only of those who embraced it, among whom Volpe stood supreme,[98] but also of those who, like Salvemini, found their careers destroyed because of their opposition, as we shall see later. But the point at issue is a different one. Despite the work of particular individuals, Italian historiography does not reflect the pattern found further north. It required a Ranke to write the history of their popes, a Burckhardt to celebrate their art. Perhaps Italian self-identity was too young a phenomenon and her state-formation too retarded to permit an easy transition to a professionalized packaging of her past. Yet here and in Spain and in tsarist Russia, no sooner had that transition become feasible than state-formation rolled forward at spectacular speed, crushing the resistance of all before it and re-writing accounts of all behind it.

CRISIS OVER METHOD

Radical approaches to history depended to some extent on the burgeoning professionalization of the discipline because a systematic understanding of source materials helped generate new questions about their use and limitations. But larger developments played their part, too. The growth and new concentrations of population in cities, the scale of immigration into the United States in particular, the pace of industrialization in North America and western Europe after 1850, the shrinkage of the world in space and time[99] – these implications of a mass society caught in a period of technological turmoil could not escape historians looking for interesting ways to think about the past. The new context implied that economic issues had lain for too long at the margin of enquiry. It asked how the histories of economies and the social groupings that interacted with them should be constructed. It raised with renewed force the Enlightenment's questions about history's relation to social science. Nor did historians need to frame all their own questions *ab initio*. For the second half of the nineteenth century became so heated with argument about social theory that even if historians had never read a word of Marx or Dilthey or Pareto or Durkheim or Weber, even if they had turned their backs on

---

98   Gioachimo Volpe (1876–1971). Professor of Modern History, Milan 1905–24; Rome 1924–40. Official historian of the regime: *Storia del movimento fascista* (1939). He had begun as a medievalist (*Eretici e moti ereticali sociale dal XI al XIV secolo* (1907), but then wrote on modern Italian political and diplomatic history, as in his study of *Guerra, Dopoguerra, Fascismo* (1928). After the collapse of fascism he wrote a two-volume account of *L'Italia moderna* (1943–52). For perspectives on post-war Italian historiography, see Chapter 22.
99   For a stimulating introduction to this theme, see Kern 1983.

the sour *Methodenstreit* which so disfigured German historical discussion in the 1890s, they could hardly remain immune from the contagion of self-awareness and self-criticism which infected most areas of intellectual enquiry.[100] It did not help those seeking isolation that they comprised the last generation of universalists who expected to find the time to read about the latest developments in biology and geology, physics and philosophy as well as to sustain their historical projects. Epidemics travelled quickly.

We have to ask why a sensitive observer like Lamprecht had become convinced by 1896 that issues of method, rather than wider outlook or assumption, had divided historians into two armed camps.[101] The question takes one back to mid-century and the role that German Idealism had come to play in historical writing, on the one hand, against the claims of science, voiced especially in France, on the other. In the wake of Darwinist argument among social theorists and internal developments within inductive science itself, those latter claims gained ground in the 1870s and 1880s. Perhaps scientific approaches did not often translate in a literal way: the past offers few laboratories. But the need to categorize, systematize and above all to *reduce* became paramount in a culture bewildered by its own volume. Reduction took a number of forms but one motif ran through much of it. The past became, as it had been in *dix-huitième* Paris, a series of predictable transitions organized less as a finite number of ages in the style of Vico or Condorcet than as a progression from one conceptual state to another. For Sir Henry Maine, whose *Ancient Law* (1861) attracted widespread notice in Britain, the journey through time witnessed a transition from a society based on status to one based on contract.[102] For Herbert Spencer, Maine's contemporary, it reflected a universal grain in organic and inorganic matter that required an unstable condition of homogeneity always to differentiate itself over time into a more sophisticated and permanent one of heterogeneity; and that process inhered in everything from the evolution of the galaxy to the organization of the brain and the social division of labour.[103] For the German sociologist Tönnies the journey for all societies wound through a landscape always dominated by the conceptual norms of *Gemeinschaft* on the one side and *Gesellschaft* on the other with the latter producing the stronger polarity.[104] And of course each of these progressions anticipated or echoed in some way the more famous, but more catastrophic, transitions envisaged by Marx.

---

100 See the seminal, though now dated, analysis of Hughes 1959.

101 ... 'ein Unterschied der Methode, nicht der Weltanschauung, ... der die Vertreter des Faches in zwei Heerlager spaltet' (*Alte und neue Richtungen* (1896): 4).

102 Maine 1861. The longest chapter in the account is on 'The Early History of Contract', pp. 252–304.

103 For Herbert Spencer's ideas, see in particular *Social Statics* (1855) and his *Autobiography* (1904). Among recent commentaries are Peel 1971 and Andreski 1971. For the wider issues in social theory, see Taylor 1992.

104 Ferdinand Tönnies produced a considerable body of writing among which the most indicative for his historical ideas are probably *Gemeinschaft und Gesellschaft* (1926) and *Einführung in die Soziologie* (1931). He can be contextualized through Bickel 1991.

It seems paradoxical that the theorist who shaped historical thinking more than any of his contemporaries should never have written any substantial history himself, unless *Das Kapital* (which began to appear in German in 1867 and was translated into English in 1887) be conceived as an implied history of industrial society. We have 'The Eighteenth Brumaire of Louis Bonaparte' as one example of the style and a series of forceful theoretical postulates in the preface to the *Critique of Political Economy* of 1859. Yet for the most part Marx's view of historical change remains a retrospective construction that continues to engross his theologians and critics.[105] His retention of the Hegelian dialectic as a fundamental explanation of change and his turning of it 'downside up' by grounding the dialectic in correspondences and frictions between the forces of production and the relations of production offered a new way of conceiving how societies worked:

> In the social production which men carry on they enter into definite relations that are indispensable and independent of their will; these relations of production correspond to a definite stage of development of their material powers of production. The sum total of these relations of production constitutes the economic structure of society – the real foundation, on which rise legal and political superstructures and to which correspond definite forms of social consciousness. The mode of production in material life determines the general character of the social, political, and spiritual processes of life.

Implicit in this picture of social change one can sense a view of historical processes – almost a programme for the past:

> No social order ever disappears before all the productive forces for which there is room ... have been developed, and new, higher relations of production never appear before the material conditions of their existence have matured in the womb of the old society.[106]

Phrases such as the 'social order' betokened a radical reorientation of what historians might study and led in that direction for reasons that were to prove of fundamental significance. It was not simply that a new emphasis emerged when 'society' became its own unit of analysis rather than a collective noun for all the individuals who composed it. ('The history of all hitherto existing *society* is the history of class struggles.')[107] Marx's point thrust far deeper. His allegation was that individuals did not make up societies at all. Societies rather made individuals by providing the framework from which they took their meaning. One of the most arresting thoughts in the whole of Marx's writing – certainly one of the most challenging to conventional historical method – emerges in his bald remark that 'society does not consist of individuals; it expresses the sum of connections and relationships in which individuals stand.'[108] This idea was to become an organizing concept for several

---

105   For modern assessments, see Rigby 1987 and Cohen 1979. Dr Rigby considers the impact of Marxism on recent historiography later in this volume: see Chapter 36.
106   Both quotations come from the preface to the *Critique of Political Economy*, quoted by R. V. Daniels in Cahnman and Boskoff 1964: 65, 68.
107   The all too well-known first sentence of the *Communist Manifesto* of 1848 (my emphasis).
108   From his *Grundrisse*, quoted in Cohen 1979: 37.

strains of social theory in the late nineteenth century and the starting-point for new departures in an authentic 'social' history in the twentieth.

In presenting a social theory that reflected Marx's concern with 'social holism' or 'social realism', none took the concept further than the French sociologist Emile Durkheim (1858–1917). Possibly his origins in a Jewish family with long rabbinical traditions increased his sensitivity to societies as living organisms that had the power to dictate what individuals did or thought. He certainly acquired the power to make his own contemporaries do his bidding, especially following his promotion from Bordeaux to Paris in 1902 where he exercised a formidable influence over a generation of research students and terrorized those whom he failed to persuade. The rival cults of Durkheim and Bergson preoccupied Parisian students in the years before the First World War and each was to bring to historical work a distinctive voice. Like Marx, Durkheim was not a historian but a soi-disant 'sociologist'; his reputation had been made in the explication of social variables – suicide, famously, in the 1890s and then, more controversially, religion.[109] He nevertheless legislated for historians by redefining their method until it resembled his own. In a debate with the grotesquely maligned French historian Seignobos, who had co-authored one of the least-loved manuals of historical method in modern times, Durkheim reacted against any attempt to see history and sociology in contrasted categories, 'as if they were two disciplines using different methods.'[110] Historians should approach the history of society in the way sociologists analysed its present: in accordance with major axes along which all social formations could be placed. Here Durkheim outflanked Marx in regarding the social fabric as so 'real' as to empower the observer to speak of its physical attributes, just as a physicist might talk about the gaseous content of a flask – its volume, its concentration, the ability of the molecules to communicate energy to one another. Taken together, these and other attributes enabled the analyst to move away from the 'why?' questions that turned into a request for information about origins, and turn towards those 'how?' questions that would reveal the *function* of variables within a given social system which would in turn throw up a more satisfying understanding of what it is that compels societies to change and present reasons for not seeing their transitions as arbitrary. In order to unearth these functions the historian must analyse those 'coercive' elements in a society's make-up that exercise obvious control and definition over the individual. From 1898 Durkheim referred to such elements as *représentations collectives* and directed students to look for them in language, group customs and practices, legislation, works of art and literature and, more portentous for the future of historical method, in statistical abstracts free from the contamination of partiality.[111]

---

109   *Elementary Forms of the Religious Life* appeared in 1912 and presented the thesis that religion should be understood as 'primarily a system of ideas with which individuals represent to themselves the society of which they are members, and the obscure but intimate relations which they have with it.' For a brilliant modern critique of some of the implications for historians, see Bossy 1982.

110   Quoted by R. N. Bellah, in Cahnman and Boskoff 1964: 86. Cf. Langlois and Seignobos 1898; the English translation has a preface by York Powell.

111   These aspects of Durkheim's approach are lucidly presented in Lukes 1973.

The tissue of ideas associated with Durkheim had yet to find an historical application. In Germany the situation was more complicated: practice and theory ran in grooves that sometimes separated but occasionally converged. Not that the Germans lacked ideologues willing to drive theoretical precepts through historical material. Indeed the young Durkheim had gained some of his insights from the wild writings of the pioneer psychologist Wilhelm Wundt (1832–1920). 'Everything occurs mechanically,' Wundt had said,[112] and he found many to follow him in his determinism. Most thinkers and researchers looked for a different route, none the less, and in their arguments we can see the beginning of the controversy over method in the humanities that was to dog speculation in Germany for a generation. That this response characterized Germany in particular we may ascribe to two central conditions in German intellectual life. First, the economic surge which characterized the years after 1870 produced a form of economic history which posed important theoretical questions of a kind which, for example, the British school of William Cunningham and W. J. Ashley did not. This assault from 'scientism' in method had to direct itself, second, at the most formidable philosophical establishment in Europe and one which still cleaved to its Idealist heritage. It will help the logic and chronology surrounding these points if we consider them in reverse order.

To a unique extent the purchase of Kantian and Hegelian ideas remained firm in Germany despite the aggression of scientific assumptions and methodologies after 1860. The United States never experienced it, outside a few individuals; the British played with it in their academic philosophy but less so in their histories; the Italians retained significant features of it but diverted much of it into their own special brew of nationalism and Marxism; the French largely eschewed it. When, therefore, Wilhelm Dilthey took his place in Lotze's chair of philosophy in Berlin from 1882 he spoke to an audience considerably larger than the university and to a constituency which, beyond Germany, he would have been denied. Between 1882 and his death in 1911 Dilthey produced a critique of scientific method in its application to the humanities which only now are we fully discovering. Like Vico, he has had to wait a century to receive the reading he requires; and, like Vico, he has become regarded as a father-figure for a number of persuasions among succeeding generations. Since he conceived a particular interest in and sympathy for historical thought, moreover, his ideas invite more than a moment's consideration.

Dilthey's quarry was a special form of inner experience that he called *Erlebnis*. In his early days an exposure to Ranke's seminar and a dose of Buckle had left him convinced that history moved according to laws and was less explanatory when considering the lives of individuals than psychology – a view he retained until about 1894. The breakthrough in his understanding lay in deciding that psychology could not give an account of how individuals revealed their essential selves *over time*; the true psychology was therefore history. But the history could not be that nomothetic

---

112   Quoted in Lukes 1973: 91.

or law-based enquiry he had once envisaged. It would need to be ideographic, in Windelband's terminology, certainly; but it ought to be viewed as a discipline in itself, a *Geisteswissenschaft* with its own techniques and assumptions. It would seek not the law-based 'explanation' required in science, but a form of *Verstehen*, by which Dilthey intended not merely 'understanding' but a series of procedures for achieving it. One of them consisted of using one's *own* sense of lived experience to discover it in past figures, to 'locate the I in the Thou'. This sense of historical *Einfühlung* has come into English as 'empathy' and it is now one of the most used, many would say over-used, concepts in the modern teaching of history. 'We understand', Dilthey said,

> when we restore life and breath to the dust of the past out of the depths of our own life. ... The general psychological condition for this is always present in the imagination; but a thorough understanding of historical development is first achieved when the course of history is re-lived in imagination at the deepest points at which the movement forward takes place.[113]

The last clause has all the blurredness that dogs Dilthey's formulations, but it seems to imply the possibility of using one's vantage point as a historian to observe transformations invisible to contemporaries. Events can be placed in a total continuum: the parts of the story make more sense in the context of the whole, which in turn becomes clearer because one knows the parts better, which in turn gives the whole an expanded perspective, which in turn illuminates other parts, and so on. Dilthey thus invents a dialectical way of thinking about how history can be approached. It is a deeply humanistic account – history is a domain where 'life grasps life' (Dilthey 1976; cf. Rickman 1979) – to which British Idealist thinkers such as Collingwood would respond. And it offered a way for historians to think of their practice as autonomous, even though Dilthey never wrote the Kantian *Critique of Historical Reason* that was going to establish these thoughts in a systematic way.[114]

If such notions recommended one style of method in the *Geisteswissenschaften*, then the school of economic history associated with Knies, Roscher and Schmoller was already employing a very different one. For the use of economic models and the abstractions of economic theory called into question not only the method of Dilthey but the entire genre that they regarded as history. Friedrich Tenbruck well suggests the distance between a discipline based on reviving the inner experience of individual actors and a new one in which such revivals, even when feasible, seemed irrelevant to the project 'Here', he writes,

> the formless mass of data did not permit an ordering by the traditional methods because what was at issue was a concern with overall conditions (*Zustände*) as opposed to actions. Procedures were therefore developed that worked with 'evolutionary stages' or even 'evolutionary laws' to bring order to the disparate plurality of individual facts.
>
> (Tenbruck 1987: 236)

---

113   Quoted in Plantinga 1980: 109–10.
114   For this theme and for Dilthey generally, see Michael Ermarth's valuable study, *Wilhelm Dilthey: the Critique of Historical Reason* (1978). A recent account is Owensby 1994.

For some that distance seemed too far to travel because it blurred the distinction between science, as an environment in which it made sense to speak of regularities and laws, and human behaviour which, if only because of freedom of the will, would always beggar consistency. Indeed the so-called *Methodenstreit* opened with a controversy between Gustav Schmoller and Carl Menger which centred on that precise point. Often in intellectual circles a trivial occasion becomes a platform for ideas long in circulation but somehow inarticulate. Some unanticipated enhancement of the kind must have affected a lecture by Wilhelm Windelband who commented on these controversies in 1894 in *Geschichte und Naturwissenschaft*. The separation of subject matter in the humanities into those that rewarded treatment by scientific techniques and those that did not had dominated discussion for a decade. But Windelband invented new words for it and thereby gained immortality. His distinction between 'nomothetic' aspects of reality (those which are subject to the operation of laws and regularities) and 'ideographic' areas where laws do not apply has entered academic language. It was Windelband's lecture that influenced Wundt's colleague at Leipzig, Karl Lamprecht, when he turned against his critics in 1896 after he had been goaded beyond endurance by bitter reviews of the first five volumes of his *Deutsche Geschichte* from a collection of neo-Rankian historians.[115] It was a combination of Windelband and Dilthey that stimulated Heinrich Rickert into defending Idealist history from the attack of science in 1902.

As a teacher of philosophy at Freiburg, Rickert became dismayed through the 1890s at the incursion of 'science' into historical work – dismayed and surprised, as he recalled a decade later:

> In these days ... I would have considered it the least possible of all possibilities that even in historical circles, the old idea of the 'elevation of history to the status of a science' by means of the method of natural science would reappear so soon and prove itself capable of attracting attention; for at that time, the belief in Buckle and related thinkers seemed to be thoroughly discredited in the province of history and retained a role only in naturalistic philosophy. Today, nevertheless, the old speculations of the Enlightenment are treated as the most novel and important achievements of history. For this reason, I thought it necessary to demonstrate the conceptual confusions that lie at the basis of these views ...
>
> (Preface to Rickert [1896] 1986: 4)

His unappealing title – *Die Grenzen der naturwissenschaftlichen Begriffsbildung* – and his less than animated prose perhaps denied Rickert's volume the impact it might have had, for the argument is powerful and often crushing. He regarded concepts as abstracted constructs with no basis in actuality; individual events do not generate such constructs; at the individuated level of analysis it followed that the concepts on which science rested could not reach and explain individual actions and events. There existed, therefore, what he called a *hiatus irrationalis* between concept and

---

115 The context of this debate is presented very fully in Chickering 1993: 146–253. Raphael Lutz has seen broad parallels – '[t]hematische Übereinstimmungen und zeitliche Parallelität' – between this debate and what occurred in France when Berr's *Revue de synthèse* raised the issue of nomothetic explanation in the humanities. Cf. Lutz 1990.

reality (ibid. xvi), and it would of necessity remain unbridgeable. These views, reflecting in some respects a Kantian vision of the world, mattered on their own account but they mattered also on a more particular one. Rickert's colleague at Freiburg during the gestation of these ideas was the young economist Max Weber; and Rickert's critique of 'scientism' proved crucial in undermining Weber's juvenile theories and turning his mind towards framing a synthesis of the two dispositions that we have been considering. Indeed, the point of labouring this dialectical swing between two poles of argument has consisted partly in providing an adequate framework within which to understand the importance and contribution of Weber.

By 1904, when Weber entered a two-year period of intense meditation on the problems of methodology, he had grasped the reins of two horses travelling in opposite directions. One of them galloped towards a view of 'social science' that insisted at the very least on the patterning and replicability of human behaviour. The other headed towards a form of individualism that conceded Rickert's neo-Kantian positions about the unknowability of the world in general and individual whim in particular – a position that would always leave a gap between a researcher trying to make sense of social behaviour and the imponderables of individual choice and perception that helped constitute it.[116] Faced with this tension within his thinking – one informed by the specific discussions of method in economics, economic history, the philosophy of 'value' and the role of historical enquiry that had dominated German speculation through the 1890s – Weber moved towards a position that maintained the tension rather than eased it and positioned himself within a context quite as *zeitbedingt* as any contemporary writer. With those other writers no subsequent problem has ensued: nobody thinks that Lamprecht or Simmel or Rickert can be understood outside the paradigms of their day. But Weber has been, partly through his own ambition to transcend context, turned into a minor prophet speaking to all ages; he has become dehistoricized. As a consequence critics find fault with Weber's answers without properly understanding the questions that, mostly, were not his in the first place.

He wanted to go beyond both Dilthey and Rickert. Dilthey would not do because his notion of *Verstehen* seemed to Weber a weak, descriptive activity based on individual intuitions that would often prove simply aesthetic. Empathy no doubt helped historians, but empathy was not explanation. Rickert valuably corroded scientistic certainties and showed why a nomothetic concept of social behaviour would not work. But to leave matters there would be to relegate social enquiry to a form of historism in which detailed description of specifics would exhaust the possibilities. His resolution, amended and embattled between 1906 and the appearance of *Wirtschaft und Gesellschaft* at the end of the war, lay in insisting on the importance of *concepts* in social (and therefore historical) thought. Most observers agreed that researchers

---

116 The relationship between Weber and Rickert is persuasively analysed by Burger 1976. Although many other studies have been undertaken since Burger's, usually from a sociological or philosophical stance, I have found Burger's study the most helpful for historians since he makes a clear effort to locate Weber's thinking within a precise context of time and space.

should look for common characteristics in the phenomena that they studied and try to form classifications – *Klassenbegriffe* – based on those perceptions. These were concepts of a kind; but they were not *gattungsmässig* or generic: they identified common denominators but they did not help over issues of significance and essence. In order to form a view of the world, one had to move beyond what the world itself would yield up in trivial description: one needed a more powerful sense of concept and only the observer could frame it. It was this enriched, authorially generated, organizing concept to which Weber gave the name 'ideal type', which has suffered ever since from the ambiguities inherent in the German understanding of 'ideal' for this generation. Weber's notion had elements of both the Kantian sense of ideal, in that it represented an imposition of mind on the unassimilable complication of the external world, but also of a utopian meaning of the term, for ideal types gave an understanding of how particular individuals, groups or social formations would behave in an ideal world of rationality and consistency. Unravelling the problems of conceiving the relationship between observer and world in this way ultimately passed by or defeated Weber and it has never been fully achieved, though Burger's account dispenses with many problems of *ignoratio elenchi* (see Burger 1976, esp. 115–30). For immediate purposes we need rather to recognize that Weber had devised a methodological instrument, whose use he tried to exemplify in his construction of a model[117] of early modern 'Protestantism' and 'capitalism' in order to show how one implied the other (Weber 1958), on which historians of recent times have seized as a way of manipulating complexity or, not infrequently, providing a safe haven from Marxism.

Between the death of Marx in 1883 and that of Weber in 1920, the place of history in the humanities had shifted and the humanities themselves had undergone redefinition. To one historian in the inter-war period, indeed, it seemed as though Weber and his kind of history had turned into nothing less than sociology (Antoni 1962). If some historians persisted in the older patterns of thought they did so defensively by 1914. Others were more likely to ask, as Lamprecht had wondered in 1896, where these new movements would take the subject (Lamprecht 1896). Some had already gone further than Lamprecht would ever want to go. Currents would shortly drag on Western historiography in ways that, particularly in America and France, might widen the scope of historical enquiry in ways that would have seemed revolutionary, even arcane, two decades earlier. Reviewing them from a distance of almost a century, it becomes plainer that these radical waves had their own weight and significance but rolled in the grip of a yet stronger tide.

FROM THE NEW WORLD

As much in historiography as in music, Dvořák's visit to America in 1892 echoed a

---

117 This is the closest modern term to what Weber had in mind and will suffice for most practical purposes; but readers are reminded that Weber's epistemological position is quite distinct from and considerably more profound than that cheerfully adopted by most of the historians who use it.

broadening contact between Europe and the New World. Weber and Schmoller could hardly have missed it when at least one of their pupils in Berlin in the early 1890s had been both American and black. It is not one's first thought about W. E. B. Du Bois: he fits into memory more naturally as part of a fabric of American Negro Marxism woven around Fisk and Harvard, the universities of Pennsylvania and Atlanta (where he developed into the confrontational author of *The Souls of Black Folk* (1903)) and the New York ambience that would later give rise to *Black Reconstruction* 1935.[118] Yet Du Bois's two years in Europe remain important in retrospect for the illumination of a common strand in American graduate experience. One could exemplify it under a less glaring light. Consider John William Burgess, the political scientist who did so much to remodel Columbia University's faculty system in the 1880s but who clung to his Hegelian ideas and became the first Roosevelt Professor in the University of Berlin in 1906. Or, among historians, recall the two Adamses: Henry Brooks Adams (1838–1918) and Herbert Baxter Adams (1850–1901). The first, as scion of a great Boston family, enjoyed the cosmopolitanism inevitable in one whose grandfather and great-grandfather had held the greatest office in the land; and doubtless felt driven by a similar imperative to write the histories of formative administrations in the American past – volumes of careful scholarship that American historians still see as the pillar of his historical writing (Henry Brooks Adams 1889–90). For others the masterpiece of *Mont-Saint-Michel and Chartres*, which did not appear until 1904, his Grand Tour, after Harvard, at the end of the 1850s and his commuting between Washington and Paris from the 1880s enabled him to stamp a particular European influence on those around him, even if his tenure of a university chair had been a short one and his subsequent life broken by events that he excised from his famous autobiography.[119] The second Adams, also a New Englander, brought to his post-doctoral appointment at Johns Hopkins in 1876 the fruits of two years in Heidelberg and Berlin, a questionable regard for his *Doktorvater*, an energizing earnestness about the German seminar system and a dangerous historical theory about Teutonic dissemination.[120]

American students went to Germany in order to pursue doctoral work because before 1880 they had very little choice. When Baxter Adams went to Johns Hopkins on his return from Germany, he joined the first graduate school in history in the United States. Columbia's in New York had stuck at the planning stage for a number of years; it opened only in 1880–1. Gradually the pull of German academia lost its strength in the last two decades of the century. There were those,

---

118 Du Bois (1868–1963) came originally from New England and developed his racial consciousness at Fisk. He later became so embittered over this issue that he renounced his American citizenship and departed in voluntary exile to Ghana, where he died. There is a recent perspective on his racial ideas in Hae-song 1992. Cf. Andrews 1985 and Moore 1981.
119 *The Education of Henry Adams* (1917) omits, among many other things, his marriage into a family of depressives and the subsequent suicide of his wife following the death of her father in 1885.
120 Baxter Adams retained his faith in the 'germ theory' which assumed the dissemination of the *Markgenossenschaft* into modern Western institutions. Cf. his *The Germanic Origins of New England Towns* (1882). His devotion to Johann Kaspar Bluntschli issued in a privately printed memoir.

certainly, who continued the tradition after the need for it had disappeared: witness the man most credited with the origins of a 'new history' in America, James Harvey Robinson (1863–1936). He could have remained in the United States after graduating from Harvard but a combination of private means and *Wanderlust* took him to Freiburg where he worked with the constitutional historian Hermann E. von Holst who later himself moved to America. Robinson returned to appointments at the University of Pennsylvania and later Columbia with an admiration for Lamprecht and a devotion to German techniques of source-criticism that he imposed on his students. He therefore fits an older model, but variants in the year-abroad syndrome become apparent as one examines others. The rampant radical Charles Beard went to (of all places) Oxford and was supervised by (of all people) York Powell. Charles Haskins, the prodigy who entered college at 13, graduated at 17 and took his Ph.D. at Johns Hopkins at 19, went to both Berlin and Paris but gained more from Langlois and Lot, as his future research interest in Normandy would imply. Carl Becker, Beard's moderate twin, embraced the new model by going nowhere at all: Wisconsin, *cum* Turner and Haskins, Columbia, *cum* Robinson, and then into his first post at Pennsylvania State University on a career that would wind through Kansas and Minnesota to Cornell.

Becker and his inspirational teacher, Frederick Jackson Turner, help suggest through the distinctiveness of their backgrounds an important new sociology among those born into the era of Reconstruction. Turner instantiated his own thesis about the frontier. His parents had come from traditional New England stock but his father had gone west, to Portage, Wisconsin, where he ultimately became owner of the local newspaper and instilled in his son a regard for things American in their own right rather than as copies from a European original. Turner never lost that sense of aggression, as Becker recalled:

> If he knew that Europe was infinitely richer than the United States in historic remains and traditions, I never heard him mention the fact. ... It was as if some rank American flavor ... kept the man still proud to be an American citizen, contentedly dwelling in Madison, quite satisfied with the privilege of going every day to the State Historical Society Library where the Draper Manuscripts were.
>
> (Becker 1935: 11)

Becker and Beard reinforce the trend away from the Atlantic and towards the Midwest. Both were brought up on farms, Becker in Iowa, Beard in Indiana. James Harvey Robinson's father reflected the social prestige of banking and left his son with private means; yet Robinson, too, originated not in New England but in Bloomington, Illinois. Add Haskins's connection with Meadville, Pennsylvania, and a tendency becomes sufficiently clear. The 'middle group' of American historians – those sandwiched between the pioneers and the young Turks of the *fin-de-siècle* – had headed for Harvard as a matter of course: George Bancroft, John Lothrop Motley, Francis Parkman and William H. Prescott all fitted this model (see Novick 1988: 72–3; cf. Bassett 1917). Their work had striven for the heroic treatment of heroic themes and evolved into a literary formalism redolent of the English romantic school. The new generation looked elsewhere, if not to the textual analysis familiar in German seminars then to the slogans of Freeman and Acton or the inner pulse of American experience with acknowledgement to no one.

The latter diagnosis came first. But then Turner (1861–1932), who effected it, was a couple of years older than James Harvey Robinson (1863–1936) and escaped the complications of a European entanglement. He left his undergraduate university (Wisconsin) only for a short period at Johns Hopkins and by the age of 28 had rejoined Wisconsin as an assistant professor. In completing his apprenticeship so quickly by American standards he gave himself the opportunity of benefiting intellectually from the census of 1890, one of whose conclusions he was about to place before the historical public as a major structural change in American society. For this census could be interpreted to imply the closure of the American frontier and the removal of what Turner had come to see as the most important single feature of American democracy and character: the availability of a new world to conquer and the transforming consequences for those who tried. Life on the boundary of the known world had thrown up unique challenges and met with responses whose story should be seen as the spine of American history. Other elements played their role, naturally; but the frontier had supplied the decisive factor, the catalyst that made American society distinctive and that held the key to understanding its past. The argument seems not to have impressed those who heard it in Chicago in 1893. Thirty years later a schoolboy historian could hardly avoid coming across 'The Frontier in American History'[121] or escape the sense of breakthrough that accompanied the idea's popularity. It was not Turner's only idea, for he had two. A second major thesis turned on sectionalism: the clash of regional and sociological cultures and interest groups – which Turner alleged had complemented the frontier in providing an explanation for the track of American experience (Turner 1932). All the same, his career remained one of promise unfulfilled, short not only on published work but on imaginative fluidity because of his penchant for patterns and schemata. But his teaching struck those who received it as special in its quality and openness. Among its most prominent beneficiaries was a scholar who would shrink from schemata and develop his own hesitations about method.

Whether the Carl Becker who made the journey to Madison in 1893 ever resembled the 'prairie country boy' he liked to recall in later years (Becker 1935: 191), it brooks no denial that he came to admire Frederick Turner intensely and to share his dismissiveness over theoretical nit-picking and Europhilia. Becker's homespun quality has two sorts of camouflage: his concern with intellectual history and his famous scepticism about historical 'fact' that was to link him with Beard's relativism in the 1930s.[122] Both of these attributes had appeared before the First World War. His doctoral thesis had dealt with American political parties in New

---

121　The lecture is reprinted in *The Frontier in American History* (1921).

122　For an introduction, see Dray 1980. The issue of relativism and the place of Becker and Beard within it preoccupies much of Peter Novick's analysis of the inter-war period in Novick 1988, esp. 250ff.

York (Becker 1901), without any intimations of that 'new' history which he always considered merely the latest of many fashions. By the time of his first general book, *The Beginnings of the American People* in 1915, he had espoused the frontier as a major part of the explanatory apparatus (Becker 1915: 180–1, 184) and had also begun to grope his way towards what he would later call, after Whitehead, a climate of opinion. For the moment it came out in isolated remarks which tried to fix *mentalité* in a diffuse phrase, as when he doubted whether colonial aristocrats 'had permitted the dissolvent philosophy of the century to enter the very pith and fiber of their mental quality' (ibid. 171). There was no suggestion that this pith and fibre lay beyond recovery, for all those initial doubts about factuality that had emerged in an article of 1910. (Becker 1935: 1–34) He retained a belief in the possibility of 'imaginative reconstruction of vanished events' (Becker 1932: 88) long after he had disproved for himself the coherence of the 'facts' which the 'reconstruction' would require. This awkwardness does not argue that Becker's views about factuality were trivial (though in comparison with, say, Oakeshott's systematic treatment of the issue they certainly look amateur).[123] It rather implies that 'the objectivity question' may not have so much edge on it in Becker's case than observers imagine. His affinity to Turner's starting-points and his antipathy to all 'new' or 'scientific' history, even to the idea of historiography itself ('labelling'), come closer to the core. He would have regarded this paragraph about him as not so much a criticism as an intrusion on intellectual privacy.

Harry Elmer Barnes, who wrote a distinguished account of modern historiography, stung Becker repeatedly by counting him among the New Historians in whose novelty Becker disbelieved (see Barnes 1962: 373ff.; Becker 1935a, esp. 36–40; cf. Becker 1935b: 132–42). The laurel rested better on Robinson and Beard. They had collaborated at Columbia, once Beard had finished his Ph.D. in 1904, on a textbook covering modern European history (Robinson and Beard 1907–8) and contrived to present an account that spent less time on political history than conventional books in order to treat 'the more fundamental economic matters' (ibid. I, 4). In practice this meant that Beard would be allowed to write a polemical piece at the end about Marx, social reform, trade unions, Booth, Rowntree and the paraphernalia of Ruskinism with which Beard had surrounded himself in Manchester and London during his bad-tempered stay in England. Apart from that, the book had eight pages on English trade in the eighteenth century, ten on science and a twelve-page chapter in volume 2 on the Industrial Revolution. This hardly made a manifesto for Weber. Indeed, the opening lament that 'our historical manuals ... have ordinarily failed to connect the past with the present' (ibid. I, iii) sounded more like an invocation of Freeman. It was rather Robinson's *The New History* of 1912 that placed the message in a more European key, though the volume has a slighter feel than its reputation might imply. Most of the

---

123 Michael Oakeshott, *Experience and its Modes* (1932) appeared in the same year as Becker's Storrs Lectures on the eighteenth century (see Becker 1932) and assaulted common-sense understanding of factuality from an explicitly Idealist direction, whereas Becker left behind a probably inadvertent Kantianism for others to find. See Smith 1956: 53–4.

'manifesto' was announced through a short, introductory essay in a volume that collected together a number of disparate papers. Its burdens were four: that historians should broaden the terms of their enquiry and move away from a narrow political history; that they should seek what Robinson called a 'genetic' approach to their problems, pressing back causation through time, seeking the oak in the acorn, as it were; that they should, third, apply the tools developed within the various social sciences to historical enquiry and seek to blur the boundaries of the subject with sociology, psychology, economics and so on; and lastly – a point seized on later by Richard Hofstadter – that historians should make their subject an instrument for social progress (Robinson 1912; cf. Hofstadter 1968).

Yet the 'new history' as an American genre never quite happened. 'I waited hopefully', Becker once reminisced, 'for the appearance of one of these new histories ... None appeared.' (Becker 1935a: 36–7). It was not that Robinson, for one, swerved away from his commitment so much as that he read into the changed conditions of post-war America different imperatives—the same ones seen by Becker. All had become new and changed; the world of Einstein and Eddington and Jeans and Whitehead had established the wonder, but also the tyranny, of fact, just as President Harding's normalcy had reified the American dream of business. One's priority lay in transcending both with an expanded sense of mind:

> So novel are the conditions, so copious the knowledge, that we must undertake the arduous task of reconsidering a great part of the opinions about man and his relations to his fellow-men which have been handed down to us by previous generations who lived in far other conditions and possessed far less information about the world and themselves. We have, however, first to create an *unprecedented attitude of mind to cope with unprecedented conditions and to utilize unprecedented knowledge.*[124]

But this programme produced in Robinson a series of books that had less to do with history than with cosmology. He sought to replace conventional understandings of change over time by a general morphology of the kind developed by Oswald Spengler whose criticisms of modern historians Robinson came to accept. 'They have told how things *have been*,' he argued in his italicized way, 'rather than how they *came about*' (Robinson 1937: 11). Retailing how they came about left him sounding metaphysical and windy. Then he developed mental blocks, apparently, and finished few of the projects he set himself in later life. There persists in his post-war work a sense of diminuendo.

His erstwhile collaborator, Charles Beard, never knew this mood: his sole alternative to forte had long been fortissimo. His 'new history' developed its own theme after 1912 and it turned not on mind but on capitalism. In effect, the Beards

---

124 Robinson 1921: 4–5 (emphasis in original). For business, see ibid. 173. Robinson's book became a best-seller. Compare Becker's complaint against positivist ideas about 'facts', presented as a description of the post-war intellectual environment: 'We start with the irreducible brute fact, and we must take it as we find it, since it is no longer permitted to coax or cajole it, hoping to fit it into some or other category of thought on the assumption that the pattern of the world is a logical one. Accepting the fact as given, we observe it, experiment with it, verify it, classify it, measure it if possible, and reason about it as little as may be. The questions we ask are "What?" and "How?" ... Our supreme object is to measure and master the world rather than to understand it.' (Becker 1932: 16–17).

(for Mary Beard contributed as a significant historian in her own right) wrote a three-volume history of economic causes and consequences in American history from the 1770s to the industrialization of the nineteenth century (Beard and Beard 1913; 1915; 1927). Of these the first remains memorable for the outrage it provoked. *An Economic Interpretation of the Constitution* offended through the directness of its prose but also because people read it as a rubbishing of the American heritage hidden within a tight and logical exposition. Property in the eighteenth century fell under two heads: 'realty', by which Beard meant authentic landholding by farmers, and 'personalty', by which he wanted to identify speculation for gain; the latter group believed their interests compromised by the Articles of Confederation and they supplied the central figures of the Constitutional Convention of 1787 since they benefited from an absurdly small electorate among white males. In their hands the new Constitution became, inevitably, an expression of particular anxieties and purposes which married democratic argument to economic interest. 'The Constitution was essentially an economic document based upon the concept that the fundamental rights of property are anterior to government and morally beyond the reach of popular majorities' (Beard and Beard 1913: 324). It was 'essentially' so because 'great movements in politics' were understood generally as suffering conditioning by 'real economic forces' (ibid. v). Had Beard remained central to the academic historical establishment, his message might perhaps have escaped the marginalization it encountered after the First World War. His courageous resignation from Columbia in 1917, when he refused to accept the treatment handed out to faculty members who opposed the war, rendered this impossible and he drifted into the role of a non-Marxist *enfant terrible*, an existence eased after he inherited his father's money and bought a large house at New Milford, Connecticut, from where he could scream dissent like an American Jacobin or score clever points in the manner of Sidney Smith.

If, indeed, anyone succeeded in implementing a new history after 1918, the only candidate strong enough would be one who eschewed the manifestos of 1907–13, who continued his annual visits to Europe through that period, patiently amassing a mastery of Norman and English archives and whose critical contribution to the understanding of *Norman Institutions* (1918) still commanded a readership half a century later. And the significance of Charles Homer Haskins went further as his interests and expertise widened to include the twelfth-century Renaissance and the medieval university (Haskins 1923; 1927). Prominent though Haskins's history remains in the historiography of the West between the wars, however, his very singularity leaves behind a conundrum. The United States had become the richest country in the world; its graduate schools had become the best resourced, its professors the most favourably endowed.[125] Where were its new social historians

---

125 When Becker went to Cornell in 1917 his interviewers felt unable to tell him what the requirements of the post might be. 'We have assumed', he was told, 'that whatever you found convenient and profitable to do would be sufficiently advantageous to the university and satisfactory to the students' (quoted in Smith 1956).

promised in the braver days of 1912? The war plainly made some difference and Peter Novick's thesis of a collapsing ideal of objectivity comments on a substantial malaise. Perhaps more crushing was a sense of lost cultural optimism that had so readily fired the progressivism of the pre-war period. Rather than think concurrently of the French, perhaps one ought to recall the English and the Whig tradition that had at least as much to do with American historiography as anything happening in Berlin or Paris. Baxter Adams hung on a banner in his new seminar room at Hopkins the chant of Edward Freeman: 'All history is past politics and all politics present history.' Just as Freeman's liberalism left his successors unprepared for crisis in 1914, so Adams's found the various catastrophes of 1917 too confusing to accommodate and too dispiriting to challenge.

ANNALES: THE FRENCH SCHOOL

Thinking concurrently about the French remains a major imperative, despite the distance between Columbia and the Sorbonne. The need for doing so does not disappear in the absence of a manifest *Methodenstreit*, for the French had their own version; nor does the lack of a Pirenne or a Lamprecht in pre-war France provide a case for its marginality. As one looks forward into the period of European disaster between 1918 and 1939, the impression strengthens that the *belle époque* concealed a time of transition that would provide the groundwork for a series of developments that would make France the most exciting forum of historical thought between the great wars of the twentieth century. The date of fundamental importance within that period is one known to everyone who studies historiography at all: 1929, the year when Marc Bloch and Lucien Febvre founded a new periodical to which they, under pressure from their publisher, gave the title *Annales d'histoire économique et sociale*. Though the subtitle has changed, *Annales* has remained an avatar for one approach and become the name not only of a publication but also of a major school of historical enquiry, the most celebrated and admired, lamented and despised school of historiography to which the present century has given rise. Much of the resonance of *Annales*' foundation derives from the conditions of the inter-war period, as we shall see. But no small degree of influence attaches to developments within French historiography in those crucial years of transition before 1914 that we have observed in the cases of Germany, Britain and the United States. *Annales* has a history *avant la lettre*.

How far back this fuller perspective requires one to reach depends on which characteristics seem most urgent in the range of tendencies that would eventually emerge in *Annales*. For an American observer such as Carlton Hayes, writing in 1920, the mood represented by Henri Berr (a figure often taken to be an inspiration for the thinking of Bloch and Febvre) appeared as anti-*belle époque* as Lytton Strachey's recent *Eminent Victorians* had been anti-Victorian. Hayes juxtaposed Berr's views with the ones he associated with Robinson's New History: 'their ideas represent[ed] a profound reaction on the part of the twentieth century against the narrow specialization of the nineteenth and the attempt to return to the interests of the eighteenth century.'[126] Set in a larger frame, on the other hand, those ideas have more of the nineteenth century in them than caught his eye. This is true, not only because challenges to existing orthodoxies contained in ventures such as Vidal de la Blache's *Annales de géographie* and Durkheim's *Année sociologique* began in the 1890s but, more importantly, because those challenges were posed to an orthodoxy that its critics badly misunderstood and caricatured. Out of their misunderstanding has grown a later one: that the mood of *Annales* came out of the rejection of traditional, often diplomatic, history symbolized by the profession's flagship journal, the *Revue historique*, which remained wedded to the approaches proclaimed by Langlois and Seignobos in their notorious manual of method published in 1898.[127] All effective cartoons contain something genuine, but this one stands in need of refinement.

Perhaps the influence and outlook of Gabriel Monod in his later career have been especially undervalued. Editor of the *Revue historique* until 1912, he presided over the empire that Berr and Febvre and Bloch sought to undermine; and certainly his acute sense of German source-criticism and relentless pursuit of a form of professionalization could be depicted as part of the target for radical social historians after 1900. Yet the historian of the *Revue*, Alain Corbin, finds Monod in retrospect 'complex, ambiguous, even perplexing': a man caught between his devotion to the tradition of Michelet and his admiration for what German scholarship had achieved in the nineteenth century (Corbin 1983: 106). Rather than oppose the synthesis of disciplines or the framing of hypotheses for historical testing – a crucial call among the young Turks – he believed in doing both, but *only* when the discipline had reached a point at which it had sufficient solidity in its professional practice to benefit from and exercise control over the thrust of radical initiatives. His Turks, moreover, were quite as young as those belonging to the opposition camp: the *Revue* was a product of overwhelmingly young historians rather than a vehicle for the elderly conservatives, as it is often implied to have been. Here he is in 1896 with his own criticisms of feeble approaches among historians and an agenda that Febvre himself could almost have written:

> On s'est trop habitué en histoire à s'attacher surtout aux manifestations brillantes, retantissantes ou éphémères de l'activité humaine, grands événements ou grands hommes, au lieu d'insister sur les grands et lents mouvements des institutions, des conditions

---

126   Quoted in Siegel 1983. This volume of research papers (Carbonell and Livet (1983)), on which the present section draws heavily, offers much the best overview currently available of the condition of French historiography in the early twentieth century. It is a great pity that it is not more generally available outside the larger university collections that hold the 'Recherches et Documents' series of the Société Savante d'Alsace et des Regions de l'Est (*Tome* XXI). Meanwhile there is some relief from the appalling sycophancy attaching to the historiography of the *annalistes* in a recent critical study by Dosse 1987.

127   Langlois and Seignobos 1898. The lack of attention accorded these scholars under the influence of *annaliste* orthodoxies persists even in the most recent studies. It is arresting that so distinguished an historian as Peter Burke allows Seignobos, 'the symbol of everything the reformers opposed', a little more recognition than orthodoxy permits while granting him insufficient attention to spell his name properly; Burke 1990: 10.

économiques et sociales qui sont la partie vraiment intéressante de l'évolution humaine, celle qui peut être analysée avec quelque certitude et, dans une certaine mesure, ramenée à des lois.

(quoted in Rebérioux 1983: 219–20)

Similar points could be made about Langlois and Seignobos. Certainly their approach to factuality would prove far too constraining for radical social historians, but the bulk of their insistence on accurate source-criticism and documentation, drawn from Seignobos's period in Germany in the 1870s, rather as Monod's had been acquired a decade earlier, would have struck Bloch, with his own German experience behind him, as unexceptionable. The point lay not in deriding documentary scholarship but in transcending it by extending the subject's comparative and disciplinary base.

Pressures in this direction came largely from outside the profession; and their effects insist that French historiography in the early twentieth century be conceived as a fragment from a more general intellectual history. The arrival of Paul Vidal de la Blache as a teacher at the Ecole Normale Supérieure in 1877 ensured, for example, that the teaming of geography with history would become a powerful and permanent feature of French undergraduate education, while his own *Annales de géographie*, appearing from 1891, gave those longing for a more research-grounded history a model of how to proceed. Instead of reading a landscape as the conditioner of a passive population – the thing that shapes them – Vidal insisted that the relationship was reciprocal at its weakest and that, argued in its stronger sense, a physical landscape should be viewed as having been formed by those who live in it so that the latter becomes an artefact bearing the picture of its creators, 'une médaille', as his resonant remark goes, 'frappée à l'image d'un peuple'. Only a small degree of exaggeration informed Febvre's recollection in 1953 that 'la géographie vidallienne' had engendered an approach that evolved into the *Annales* style of history (see Baker 1984: 5). If anything, the comment became more appropriate as time passed and especially following the appearance of Vidal's study of France in 1903. One sees the impression that this might have made on the young Marc Bloch whose degree at the Ecole Normale took the form of a dual-subject study of history and geography. By the time the first Congress of Historical Geography met at Brussels in 1930, those writers associated with the *Annales* impetus had been deploying geographical insights for a generation in their historical questions and research. 'It is somewhat absurd,' a leading historical geographer has conceded recently, 'that *annalistes* seem to have both learned and practised Paul de la Blache's principles of human geography more soundly and faithfully than have many French geographers' (Baker 1984: 2). Nor need one restrict the comment to geography: it seems hardly less relevant to refer to the sociology of Durkheim or Maurice Halbwachs, whom Bloch and Febvre encountered at Strasbourg after the war, or the anthropology of Marcel Mauss. Closer still to what became the *annaliste* home lay the development of specialist economic history with the first number in 1908 of the *Revue d'histoire économique et sociale*, a precursor in some ways of the *Economic History Review* (1927) and Luigi Einaudi's *Rivista di storia economica* (1936).[128]

That future *annalistes* should have sought to run rival disciplines together into a common cause owed little to chance associations. It followed the logic established by an academic mood of synthesis which no one enhanced more consistently than Henri Berr (1863–1954). Despite his enormous output, Berr never achieved the intellectual stardom of Bloch and Febvre, but his intellectual role in shifting historical enquiry in France was quite central. He was not a historian, primarily, but a philosopher whose doctoral thesis in the University of Paris had focused on the prospect of synthesizing historical knowledge in order to reverse the fragmentation of the subject that recent developments seemed to threaten.[129] The project ruined his career: he was rejected, together with Simiand, by the Collège de France in 1912 and his refusal to espouse any singular discipline left him marooned between all of them. But his *Revue de synthèse historique*, which began its appearance from the turn of the century, represents a remarkable monument to an original mind. It attracted, moreover, some of the brightest historians of their generation: we find Febvre writing for it by 1905, Bloch from 1912. And the alliances formed in these years carried through into the post-war era to become the basis for much new thinking in the Strasbourg period after 1919. A modern definition of the *Annales* movement – 'the attempt by French scholars to adapt economic, linguistic, sociological, geographical, anthropological, psychological, and natural science notions to the study of history and to infuse a historical orientation into the social and human sciences' (Stoianovich 1976: 19) – shows if nothing else the length of Berr's shadow.

We see it in his series 'L'Evolution de l'humanité', in which books by Febvre and Bloch would later appear, each with an enthusiastic introduction by Berr himself. Febvre was Bloch's senior by eight years. He had come to Paris from Nancy, where his father taught, and spent a formative four years at the Ecole Normale astride the new century (1898–1902). His doctoral thesis on Philip II and the Franche-Comté (a district of south-western France close to the Swiss border) took many years to complete: he was 33 when the work finally emerged in 1911. Through Berr's journal he had already begun, however, both to manipulate some of his data and to think about method, so that the complete thesis contained some of the constituents of *annaliste* approaches. From there he moved towards writing one of his most important books, a *Geographical Introduction to History*. It appeared some years after the First World War and one thinks of it as an inter-war project; but he had put together some of the material and started writing before the war changed Febvre's perspective. It did so partly because he, like Bloch, served in the army. Febvre spent the war years in a machine-gun company and rose to the rank of captain. But the experience inevitably brought with it an anti-Teutonic backlash, perhaps the greater

---

128 For an account of these, see Allegra and Torre 1977: 276, 303.
129 'L'avenir de la philosophie: esquisse d'une synthèse de la connaissance de l'histoire' (Paris, 1898). In the published version he wrote of the need 'd'unifier l'histoire et la sociologie, les deux pôles de la même réalité, de l'individu et des institutions' (see Siegel 1983: 206).

467

for Febvre's never having studied in Germany as had so many of his contemporaries. This came through in his analysis of the German nationalistic geographer Friedrich Ratzel (1844–1904) whose association of soil and people Febvre found disturbing in the light of the past four years; he countered with his plea for a human geography that drew on history for its explanations rather than race or *Vaterland*. The collaboration with Bloch in the University of Strasbourg began in 1920 and Febvre was intensely preoccupied with establishing the credibility of their method not only in the foundation of *Annales* in 1929 but in his explosive reviewing, which was prodigious, and his direction of research students. His best-known work, on Rabelais and the possibility of religious unbelief in the sixteenth century, did not appear until the middle of the Second World War (Febvre 1942).

So much is impressive about Febvre that one loses sight of what is not. A feeling sometimes creeps over the reader that Febvre's interest lies in a rather self-indulgent form of historical propaganda. The *Combats pour l'histoire* (1953) seem everywhere, leaving a nostalgia for forms of history that do not begin with combat. It is as though his mind would not turn unless he could find a straw figure to bayonet, which is why reviewing became a natural outlet. Even the major books have to be understood in this way. The bland title of his book about historical geography barely conceals the attack, of which it essentially consists, on German conceptions, with a balancing defence of Vidal's method enshrined in the *Tableau*, 'a unique book, with a character of its own, a masterpiece, but devoid of all dogmatism and quite inimitable.' (Febvre 1925: 18). The study of Rabelais likewise takes the form of a reply to Abel Lefranc's account of him.[130] In affirming the unavailability of unbelief to a sixteenth-century writer Febvre made an intelligent, original point and opened a channel of enquiry that has been assiduously followed in post-war political theory. Whether it needed 450 pages to express it raises a different question. Indeed Febvre's discourse which, quite as much as his language, is implacably, untranslatably French, can provoke the fantasy that he may have taken a bet with someone to see how many pages he could write without stating a substantive historical proposition. For some historians the result approximates to playful wit: they applaud his innovative qualities, admire his lightness of touch (see e.g. Burke 1973). Readers outside his culture may none the less be forgiven for believing that there is too much of Febvre. They agree from Madrid to Oslo, whatever their nationality or historical orientation or poetic sensibility or sense of humour, that there is too little of Bloch.

More lies behind this recognition than Bloch's murder by the Nazis when he was 57. It rests on the character of his work, which left the rhetoric to his partner and concentrated on turning an ungovernable enthusiasm for knowing about past people into texts that almost seem over-silted out of a compulsion to demonstrate, elucidate, interrogate. There is a near-tangible aversion to posture and a level of

---

130 Abel Lefranc had written a series of studies including *Le Visage de François Rabelais* (1925) and *L'Œuvre de Rabelais d'apres les recherches les plus récentes* (1932). For a very different view of Febvre, see Chapter 35 below.

commitment that pervades the text in its perpetual dialogue between contention and source. And each study feels like a report on work in progress, as though the future will change the past as a matter of course and require its constant rewriting. For that reason, the erasure of Bloch's personal future, known to the reader but not to the author, gives each text a special poignancy.

His Jewishness carries much of the imprint of that unknown future: one wonders whether, without it, he would not have seen out the war in his library, like Febvre. In Lyon his father, Gustave Bloch, had become a distinguished scholar as professor of ancient history and an expert on Roman Gaul; he returned to the Ecole Normale to teach almost immediately after Bloch's birth and the family moved to Paris. And to the extent that the younger Bloch also made his way to the Ecole Normale, there is an echo of Febvre's biography. From 1904 onwards their paths diverged. Bloch made geography part of his degree and, following his graduation in 1908, he spent a year in Germany – at Berlin and Leipzig, where he came across Lamprecht. His return to Paris and the Fondation Thiers between 1909 and 1912 helped lay his own foundation for much later research and gave rise to his study of the *Île de France* (1913), but his life, like Febvre's, was to undergo fundamental disruption: first in provincial schoolteaching but then through the war which affected him more, possibly, than most historians by teaching him how to look instead of read. Separated from his books, he found himself inserted into the countryside, albeit one scarred from perpetual shelling. He took to noticing field sizes and shapes; he listened to those soldiers from peasant backgrounds who knew the rhythms of rural life. A process of intense speculation about using landscape as a source has its origins, probably, in these years, between acts of conspicuous gallantry in the front line. Bloch realized the degree to which historians, because they are often so tied to documentation, begin at the earliest point of their story and look for relics that lead up to their point of interest. He came to believe that much could be done by reversing this procedure – starting with what exists now as a matter of certainty and then working backwards in the manner of the genealogist towards a less certain past. The point would not lie in making the past a vehicle for the present, in the style of British Whig history, but rather in seeing parts of it, usually aspects of physical geography, as a reliable and unused source from which to extrapolate bygone structures of landowning and settlement.

None of this bore fruit immediately. Teaching and participation in the work of a new department preoccupied him after his appointment in 1919 to the chair of medieval history at the new University of Strasbourg. His contact with the Febvrian inferno, as well as with those working in parallel fields such as the sociologist Maurice Halbwachs, generated an intense and self-conscious historiographical radicalism which had its first expression in *Les Rois thaumaturges* (1924), a study of the environment and *mentalité* which gave rise to 'the king's touch' as a healing device. But the commitment to building up a knowledge of the patchwork-quilt of rural society and to seeing the whole within a comparative perspective, such as Pirenne urged at Brussels in 1923, carried on at the quieter level of note and docket. Some of the printed regional material he plainly read at home; there were days, too, in the archives in Paris, producing material for the bottom drawer. Without his summons from Oslo, he always said, the book would probably have remained a mental patchwork. Certainly it was an invitation from the Institut pour l'Etude Comparative des Civilisations for a course of lectures to be delivered in the Norwegian capital in the autumn of 1929 that compelled the conversion of intimation to text. For all its tone of pre-emptive apology, the book that would emerge under a clumsy and prosaic title – *Les Caractères originaux de l'histoire rurale française* (1931) – shows better than any other the calibre of Bloch's thought and his originality of vision over what he believed the subject to be about. Together with the better-known two volumes of *La Société féodale* (1939–40), it gives an indication of what the *Annales* tendency might have become had he lived.

What remains striking about Bloch's historical thinking in the 1930s is its commitment to the analysis of change over long periods and the search for structures which would make temporal and geographical variety reducible to intelligible patterns. *Les Caractères* had both dimensions: it surveyed the chronology from the early medieval *seigneurie* to the agricultural revolution of the eighteenth century; and it proposed ideal types of 'agrarian regimes' which reduced the complexity of French rural experience to three forms of field-shape intersected by two types of plough, the *araire* or scratch-plough of the south and the wheeled *charrue* of the north. There are Durkheimian flourishes. In the middle of a structural meditation in the chapter on 'Agrarian Life' one can meet a one-sentence paragraph arranged as a *pensée*: 'As in the regions of open fields, these material manifestations [enclosures] were the outward expression of underlying social realities' (Bloch [1931] 1966: 57). Later, in the less-remarked section called 'Social Groupings', the stirrings of a possible social history of medieval civilization occasionally come to the surface. 'To sum up' (his detailed discussion of the *manse*),

> it seems that a number of weighty if slightly mysterious happenings lie behind the superficially trivial fact that in the eleventh century estate surveys are arranged by *manses*, in the thirteenth or seventeenth centuries by fields or households: the reduction of the family to a narrower and more changeable compass, the total disappearance of public taxation, and a radical transformation in the internal organization of the *seigneurie* must all have played their part.
>
> (ibid. 163)

Ideas of this kind were developed in a systematic way in the two volumes of *Feudal Society*. Bloch concerned himself with an entire civilization: its economic structures, its social stratification, its sources of power. He saw a division within it by period. The earlier had a character determined by insecurity in the wake of Islamic and Scandinavian threats. Because no unified social structure could congeal in such circumstances, ties of local dependency became common, marked by military obligation operating as a *quid pro quo* for protection: the crucial background to the development of 'feudalism'.[131] In the later period particular cultural and technological developments conflicted with the original *raison d'être* of the social system; but that system had established itself in so profound a way that only certain forms of adaptation

---

131 For a penetrating modern critique of these assumptions, see Reynolds 1994, esp. ch. 3.

could remain possible – a key to how feudalism became a sclerotic way of organizing social and military resources.[132] Like Pirenne's understanding of the development of medieval trade, the image perhaps suffered from too sharp a resolution; but that must always happen to innovative conceptualization and Bloch always knew that it did.

By the time Bloch's volumes appeared, he had finally succeeded in making the move back to Paris. Since 1936 he had held the chair of economic history at the Sorbonne: truant had turned prefect. The new journal had meanwhile dominated much of the research time of both Febvre and Bloch in its early years. They imposed on it a tone calculated to *épater les bourgeois*, especially bourgeois professors. They invited scholars from all over Europe and America to contribute, especially where they could write on subjects that joined together past and present in the way that the Strasbourg mood deemed appropriate. In practice this meant that *Annales* soon lost its ancient and medieval contributions and became more securely located in the period since 1500.[133] Differences of approach between the editors made themselves felt. Febvre wanted to use *Annales* as a weapon against the establishment, deploying radical contemporary history with a minimum of academic apparatus; Bloch had more interest in printing imaginative history of all kinds. Febvre's move to the Collège de France in 1933 made communication that much harder to sustain and by the time of Pirenne's death in 1935 fissures had appeared that threatened the future of the enterprise. Bloch's famous piece examining the history of the watermill began life as one attempt to resuscitate *Annales*; and it was during the 'second wave' of the journal's life that he and Febvre attempted a definition of *annaliste* method. Seen against the background of the previous fifty years, it seems not so very different from what Monod had tried to achieve, though the surface-texture has a Febvrian choppiness:

> Préoccupation du general, goût de l'histoire totalitaire, scrutée par alliance entre les disciplines; refus de soumettre aux routines alternées d'une historiographie oratoire et d'une érudition sans horizon; décisions très fermes de n'attaquer le sujet qu'après avoir tout d'abord dressé un questionnaire assez serré pour que rien d'important ne risque de glisser entre ses mailles, assez simple pour s'adapter, chemin faisant, aux révélations de l'enquête elle-même; dans l'établissement de ce premier schema comme dans le choix des instruments d'investigation ou d'expression – cartes ou statistiques par exemple – le sense le plus juste à la fois de la réalité concrète et des phénomènes de profondeur: si vraiment ces traits composent la méthode des 'Annales'.[134]

---

132 I follow here Daniel Chirot's characterization of Bloch's argument: see Chirot 1984: esp. pp. 24–5.
133 Carole Fink has a helpful chapter, on which I have drawn, analysing the content of *Annales* in her biography of Marc Bloch, Fink 1989: 128–65.
134 Editorial statement in 1937, quoted in Allegra and Torre 1977: 303–4. 'A preoccupation with the general, a taste for global history examined in an inter-disciplinary way; a refusal to stumble into the twin pitfalls of a rhetorical historiography on the one hand or pointless demonstrations of erudition on the other; very firm decisions never to approach the subject until one has first asked questions which are both sufficiently precise as to avoid allowing anything of importance to slip through the net, but also flexible enough to be adjusted as one goes along in response to what the investigation throws up; a refined sense both of concrete reality but also of deeper, less visible phenomena when drawing up the plan of action and its various tools – maps or statistics, for example: truly, these are the characteristics which inform the method of the "Annales".' On the watermill piece and the importance of Bloch's revisions of early positions through the 1930s, see Davies 1967.

But, as Alain Corbin (1983: 109–10) rightly reminds a generation that may have become over-fascinated by *Annales*, this mood should be seen as only one part of a more general 'turn' in the intellectual direction of the 1930s – a mood that included in France the Marxist critiques of Mathiez,[135] Lefebvre,[136] Simiand[137] and others, and an anthropological surge associated among French thinkers preponderantly with the writing of Marcel Mauss.[138]

The ascendancy gained by *Annales* historians in the post-war years when Braudel became their wayward guru masks just how fragile the project seemed during those first ten years. There were times when Febvre, in particular, felt like throwing in the towel; times when publication dates passed with the copy not ready (Fink 1989: 144, 149). The more telling threat came, for all that, from outside academia. During the middle years of the decade *Annales* began, in its zest for contemporary history, to run articles on Nazism. By the spring of 1939 it became apparent to those with a finger on the political pulse that scholarship was about to be overtaken by events. Certainly none of their implications were lost on Bloch who, as a Jew and a former soldier, felt an overwhelming sense of concern and duty. The young Braudel, safe in the University of São Paulo, came home to enlist and spent much of the war in a prison camp as a consequence. For each of the 'Big Three' the years after 1939 proved momentous. Febvre's survival placed him at the forefront of the new *Sixième Section* and allowed him guidance of the journal whose new title he inaugurated: *Annales: économies, sociétés, civilisations*. Bloch's promise ended among a group of fellow members of the Resistance in a spatter of machine-gun fire in a field outside Lyon on 16 June 1944. Braudel took with him into German captivity a collection of ideas for a book about the history of the Mediterranean Sea. He

---

135 Albert Mathiez (1874–1932). Socialist from a peasant family in Franche-Comté. Taught by Monod and supervised by Alphonse Aulard, of whom he became a life-long critic. Member of the Communist Party for three years (1920–3). Main appointments Besançon (1911–19) and Dijon (1919–26). Achieved lectureship at Paris but a stroke terminated his career. Main field French Revolution and especially Robespierre: *La Revolution Française* (1922–7); *La Réaction thermidorienne* (1929); *Le Directoire* (1934).

136 Georges Lefebvre (1874–1959). Flemish: father a bookkeeper. Taught by Petit-Dutaillis at Lille. Schoolteacher before and during war. Marxist from mid-1930s. Chair in history of the French Revolution at the Sorbonne (1937). Concentration on what he called 'L'influence intermentale' during the years of revolutionary upheaval and anxiety. See *Les Paysans du Nord pendant la Revolution française* (1924); *La Grande Peur de 1789* (1932); *Foules historiques* (1934); *Les Thermidoriens* (1937).

137 Françcois Simiand (1873–1935). Economic historian who read philosophy at Ecole Normale; influenced by Durkheim and Lévy-Bruhl. Socialist voicing admiration for Jaurès and Blum; friend of Péguy and Daniel Halévy (younger brother of Elie). Ran a socialist publishing company and then became librarian at the new Ministry of Labour (1906). Preoccupation historically with workers' wages. From 1910 lectured on history of economic theory at Ecole Pratique des Hautes Etudes; head of history department by 1924. Central work: *Le Salaire: l'évolution sociale et la monnaie* (1932).

138 Marcel Mauss (1872–1950). Durkheim's nephew. Possibly under his influence rejected religion of Jewish parents. Avid Dreyfusard. One of the pre-eminent ethnographers of his generation; chairs at Ecole Pratique (until 1930) and then Collège de France (1931–9). His early work on magic may have contributed to Durkheim's view of the sociology of religion. Classic study of *Le Don* (1925), a transcultural account of gifts and their function.

emerged, famously, with a manuscript which was to provide him with a doctorate and a chair at the Collège de France within five years. When we look back over the historiography of twentieth-century France, as of Germany or Russia or Italy or Spain, these events remind us of the centrality of military forces in their shaping, which were quite as important as intellectual ones, and recall the frequent presence of ideological repressions and threats far beyond the imagination of the despised professors of the Sorbonne.

REPRESSION AND EXILE

So consuming and notorious was the repression of historical scholarship by agents of the Third Reich that we readily overlook earlier evidence of intellectual control by other states seeking to starve curiosity as a means of leaving awkward questions unanswered. Take the case of Russia. Long before the rise of Bolshevism as a major force, the destabilization of tsarist society left some sensitive Moscow intellectuals reflecting whether they could remain in the country as the interference of the authorities increased over curricula and public attitudes in the universities. One such – perhaps in a sense the first émigré historian of the twentieth century – was Paul Vinogradoff. He had known about Europe's attractions for many years for his original subject had turned on the nature and significance of English villeinage.[139] A pupil of Mommsen's in Berlin in the late 1870s, he went on to make the acquaintance of the formidable British legal and constitutional historian Frederic Maitland when he worked on British material in the Public Record Office in 1883. But only in 1901 did he make the decision to leave Russia for good and it was during his tenure of the chair of jurisprudence at Oxford that he acted in turn as an influential teacher, bridging the divide between the generation of Mommsen and that of highly significant medievalists such as Frank Stenton and Helen Cam.[140] M. I. Rostovtzeff came closer to their generation than to Vinogradoff's: he had been born near Kiev in 1870. His peregrinations round Europe came in the 1890s; the decision to go he delayed until after the 1917 Revolution. In his case the emigration led from St Petersburg to the Sterling Chair of Ancient History at Yale by way of Oxford and

---

139 *Villainage* [sic] *in England* (1892) was followed by *The Growth of the Manor* (1905). For a collection of papers examining the entire relationship indicated here, see Kozicki 1993.

140 Frank Merry Stenton (1880–1967) spent most of his academic life at University College, Reading, until it became a university in 1926. He was professor of modern history there from 1912 until 1946 when he became vice-chancellor for the four years before he retired in 1950. The seminal works are *The First Century of English Feudalism 1066–1166* (1932) and *Anglo-Saxon England* (1943). Helen Maud Cam (1885–1968) spent the early part of her career at Royal Holloway College, London, where she had been an undergraduate, apart from a year at Bryn Mawr. But she spent the period from 1921 to 1948 at Girton College, Cambridge, before taking a chair at Harvard for the last six years preceding her retirement in 1954. Most of her output is to be found in articles and essays, collected in *Liberties and Communities in Medieval England: Case Studies in Administration and Topography* (1944) and *Law Finders and Law Makers in Medieval England* (1962). She became a Fellow of the British Academy in 1945 and was the first woman to deliver the Raleigh Lecture.

Madison, Wisconsin. In his case, moreover, the relationship between his experience and how he conceived the past in his historical writing became more demonstrable than in that of Vinogradoff. His determination that civilization should win and barbarism, defined to look very like Bolshevik ideals, should fail, informed and energized his earlier works, especially the *Social and Economic History of the Roman Empire* (also Rostovtzeff 1926–7; 1941; cf. Wes 1990).

Much the same deployment of experience as a touchstone for historical interpretation lies embedded in the work of one of the most serious historical thinkers of the century, a Polish-Russian who was sent to England for his education in order to avoid the threat of further Russian oppression in the region of Galicia. One wonders what sort of figure Lewis Bernstein Namier would have cut had he remained in his own country, because it seems overwhelmingly clear that his year at the London School of Economics, where he was impressed by the geopolitical perspectives of Halford Mackinder, and then the stimulus of Balliol College, Oxford, where he came into contact with the mind of Arnold Toynbee, played a critical role in fathering the man. And the migration to England, once achieved, would never be reversed. First in Oxford but then, after a period in business in the United States, in Manchester where he became professor of modern history, Namier brought to the study of both British and recent European history a formidable forensic intelligence which he used to celebrate the past of Britain's elites and the future of Europe's Jews, seeing, like Rostovtzeff, a fragility in civilization which barbarism would always threaten and, like so many Jewish intellectuals of the twentieth century, suspecting a predisposition in European society to marginalize and victimize Jews. The first theme came out strongly in the early work on eighteenth-century politics, which Namier so powerfully reoriented that he gave the language a new verb: to Namierize. His method turned on a severe reliance on the scrutiny of individuals as central historical actors and the power of individual biography to explain events without recourse to sociological or ideological structures. *The Structure of Politics at the Accession of George III* (1929) showed that explanatory structures in the eighteenth century could be identified but they had to be understood at an atomized level of individual agents and families, not as an engagement between Whig and Tory principles which he largely disbelieved and announced that his protagonists did also. His second thrust appeared in his studies of Europe in the age of the dictators, especially *Europe in Decay* (1950) and *In the Nazi Era* (1951). For all his lifelong attachment to 'English' values, his émigré status never quite left him and certainly never left his sense of which historical problems ought to be studied (see J. Namier 1971; Rose 1980; Colley 1989).

It follows that a sophisticated sense of the period should resist an instinct that fascism and Nazism supplied the only vehicles for intellectual repression and resettlement in this most repressive of periods. They nevertheless do supply contexts of spectacular importance in explaining why the historiographies of Italy and Germany developed (or failed to develop) as they did; and they give luminous examples of displaced persons who would take their historical talents away from central Europe and towards Britain or – especially in the case of displaced

Germans – towards the United States, with significant consequences for the enrichment of two cultures and the impoverishment of several others.[141] Detailed treatments of the Italian and German cases appear in Chapters 21 and 22 of this volume and we need not reconnoitre ground that will come under review later. Yet in thinking about the global weight that we need to accord the phenomenon of displacement, certain points occur naturally here.

One of them is a thought about generations. Not only did mature, working historians find their lives uprooted by circumstances beyond all prediction and control, but they took with them into exile their children, some of whom would in turn emerge as major historians in their own right but as persons who now had an entirely different identity: people who might have taken into adult life only a shadowy recollection of the Soviet Revolution or of fascist politics in the 1930s but whose entire perspective would nevertheless be dominated by the experience. The Russian future Byzantinist, George Ostrogorski, was still in his teens when his family left St Petersburg. But the trajectory through Germany, where Percy Schramm taught him at Heidelberg, and Paris, where he met the influential Byzantinist Charles Diehl, propelled him in the direction of Yugoslavia and his chair at Belgrade after 1933. For British medievalists, by the same token, Michael Postan seemed an emblem of the Soviet Revolution which had driven his family away but whose prehistory nevertheless left in Postan a permanent concern with the medieval economy, issues of trade and social structure which would lead him to a chair in economic history at Cambridge, and a hardly less significant marriage to the distinguished medievalist Eileen Power.[142] For relicts of fascist and Nazi displacement, think only of two major historical personalities of the years after the Second World War, G. R. Elton and Franco Venturi. The first we associate with Cambridge and the Tudors, the second with a number of Italian universities and the Enlightenment in Italy in the eighteenth century.[143] Yet the story of each has a common thread wound around the history of Mussolini and Hitler. Venturi's father was an art historian who took his son into exile with him in 1931; so the teenager's environment shifted from Rome to Paris. The removal did not prevent his internment during the war but doubtless coloured his view of a special Italian past characterized by the best elements of the Enlightenment, a repeated concern in the volumes of his series on

---

141   The phenomenon of intellectual exile has given rise to a substantial literature of which that treating Europe's historians should be seen as a complement. Some examples of the wider lens include Lixl-Purcell 1988; Tucker 1991; Krohn 1993.

142   Her life has recently been assessed by the economic historian, Maxine Berg (1996).

143   G. R. Elton (1921–94) wrote a very large collection of books and papers. The latter he assembled as *Studies in Tudor and Stuart Politics* (1974–84). Among the more significant work on British history one might mention *England under the Tudors* (3rd edn, 1991); *The Tudor Constitution* (2nd edn, 1982); *Policy and Police* (1972); *The Parliament of England 1559–1581* (1986). Franco Venturi (b. 1914) has been likewise prolific, with an interesting division of interest between Italy and Russia and an impressive range of languages: *Il populismo russo* (1952); *Utopia and Reform in the Enlightenment* (1971); *Italy and the Enlightenment* (1972); *Les intellectuels, le people* (1977); *Venezia nel secondo settecento* (1980); *Giovinezza di Diderot (1713–53)* (1988).

the *Settecento riformatore* and elsewhere in an impressive body of writing. 'Elton' was an English invention imposed by the army to prevent confusion over his real name – Ehrenburg – and became an alternative identity which masked the background in Prague until excitement or relaxation revived his trilled 'R's. The Ehrenburgs had left Czechoslovakia under threat of Nazi occupation and thus precipitated Elton's future sense of himself as an adoptive Englishman who believed that continentals had too much awareness of the past for their own good and who preferred the cooler perspectives of British empiricism and national forgetfulness.

A second point also concerns geography. Entire sections of continental Europe lost their Jews in the black smoke of Himmler's vision. But some did not; and for students of intellectual history, within which Jewish historians have always played a particular part, a radical disjunction becomes apparent in post-war Europe. It has been well observed by a historian of the *Annales*, for example, that the role of Jewish scholars in giving that persuasion a strong cosmopolitan, anti-nationalist flavour should be seen as an element in its post-war complexion, for all the tragedy of Bloch's murder.[144] Equally, one can argue that the systematic snuffing-out of Jewish brilliance in Germany and Austria has brought about a long-term, possibly permanent deadening of the intellectual cultures once supported in those countries. Perhaps the impact on social theory and philosophy comes most quickly to mind in the repression of the Frankfurt and Vienna schools of thought—an impact not lost on history because many of the more penetrating questions available to inter-war historians had their origins in critical social thought.[145] Thus a Karl Popper might be projected from Vienna and end up, via New Zealand in his case, in the London School of Economics. But the lesson is equally valid for historians. The distance from Vienna to Rome reduced, as a result of policies associated with Hitler and Mussolini, to the few hundred yards between the London School of Economics and University College, London, when that College accepted Arnaldo Momigliano as professor of ancient history in 1951. Few careers better make the point. The greatest historiographer of the twentieth century was an Italian Jew who had been a pupil of Gaetano de Sanctis at Turin and was deprived of his chair in Rome by Mussolini's race laws. Brief stays in Oxford and Bristol prefaced Momigliano's tenure of a post in which he was to produce the volumes of *Contributi* which have become the greatest landmark of classical and antique learning witnessed since the Second World War.[146] London had no more right to Momigliano than to Popper; it benefited immeasurably from both.

---

144 Stoianovich 1976. He notes, however, that the *annalistes* have never made Jewish studies, or any form of ethno-history, central to their outlook (ibid. 51–6).
145 For the Frankfurt School, see Wolin 1992; Wiggershaus 1994. Much has been written on the Vienna circle, e.g. Coffa 1991; Menger 1994.
146 *Contributi alla storia degli studi classici (e del mondo antico)* (9 vols, Rome, 1955–92). Momigliano (1908–87) can be approached in English through his *Studies in Historiography* (1966) and his *Essays in Ancient and Modern Historiography* (1977), though they barely touch the surface of an output of more than 1,000 titles. Commemorative volumes include Weinberg 1988; Steinberg 1988; Dionisotto 1989.

Where this notion of a global redrawing of mental maps makes itself overwhelmingly felt is in the diaspora of Jews from Nazi Germany itself after 1933 and in particular the common destination of so many of them. Immigration restrictions in Britain and possibly a discomfort about British culture felt by German intellectuals after their humiliation in 1918 helped them contemplate a bolder uprooting whose effect would be radical and often permanent. For someone like Wilhelm Levison, who worked on English and European history in the early medieval period, America seemed too great a wrench when the tightening of the racial laws in Germany forced him from his chair in Bonn. The University of Durham had given him an honorary degree, doubtless under the recommendation of his friend, Bertram Colgrave, some years before; it took him in when he arrived in England in 1939 and he stayed there till his death in 1947, delivering his highly regarded Ford Lectures on England and the Continent in the eighth century in 1942.[147] Yet for many others America presented the more attractive alternative and the westward shift of Jewish historians from Germany seems in retrospect one of the more significant intellectual migrations of the twentieth century that now attracts serious scholarly attention.[148]

To an uncanny degree, many of them had originally been, or had turned into, pupils of Friedrich Meinecke. He shared the disillusion with Weimar felt by former nationalists but his pluralism and humanity led him to help colleagues in trouble as easily as it led to his sacking from the editorship of the *Historische Zeitschrift* by the Nazis. One should not over-press Meinecke's liberality: his preoccupation with the history of ideas had a Prussian twist and amounted to a metaphysical and sometimes mystical notion of the state as the outcome of moral endeavour. He placed the needs of the state on a supra-ethical plane, particularly in his study of *raison d'état* (Meinecke 1924). His pupils reflected his period and his leanings and they constituted a formidable group of émigrés, from Dietrich Gerhard (b. 1896) to Felix Gilbert (b. 1905), by way of Hans Baron, Hajo Holborn, Eckhart Kehr, Gerhard Masur and Hans Rosenberg.[149] The effect on American research and teaching in the modern history of Europe turned out to be prodigious and corrected, through the most painful of mechanisms, a serious imbalance left by the more inward-looking generation headed by Turner. And once the movement had begun, it did not halt with the end of hostilities in 1945. The post-war period saw a continued influx that raised the world-profile of American expertise (see Novick 1988: 378).

The concern with ideas emerges also from two of the most prominent medievalists driven from Berlin by the Nazis, not from the university lectures and seminars of Meinecke in their cases but from the *Monumenta Germaniae Historica* when it was still housed there. In Ernst Kantorowicz and Theodore 'Ted' Mommsen,

---

147 The lectures were published after the war: see Levison 1946.

148 See in particular the very helpful volume of essays produced by the German Historical Institute in Washington: Lehmann and Sheehan 1991.

149 See Wolfgang Mommsen's superb portrait of 'Historiography in the Weimar Republic' in Lehman and Sheehan 1991, esp. 52ff.

Germany lost two of its more famous historical names: the first because his strange, romantic, atavistic and (far worse in Berlin) unfootnoted life of Frederick II (1927) had given rise to waves of abuse and enthusiasm; the second because no grandson of the great ancient historian could have escaped fame, even if he had not been Max Weber's nephew. An ability in the one to think freshly through the problems of myth and symbol in modern thought, in the other to present small-scale essays investigating specific contexts in the intellectual history of the Middle Ages were lost to the German universities as they departed, in the case of Kantorowicz for the Institute for Advanced Study in Princeton (eventually) and for Princeton and Cornell in the case of Mommsen.[150] Kantorowicz had the greater intellect and his work had an innovative quality that would have made him comfortable among the future *annalistes* of Strasbourg. Indeed *The King's Two Bodies* (1957) could be placed on the same shelf as Marc Bloch's *Les Rois thaumaturges*, though it attempted a very different project. Kantorowicz had become preoccupied by the dual status of medieval kings: as owners of a human body with an ordinary existence but also as custodians of a body politic with a constitutional, social and sometimes mystical existence. The first could suffer, sin and die; the second drew its sustenance from without, enjoyed various forms of immaculacy and could not arrange its own death. His section on 'The Crown as Fiction' travels quite as far in its imaginative drive as anything projecting from Braudellian Paris (see Kantorowicz 1957: 336–83).

Most of these émigrés did not develop new genres: they wrote in a familiar frame of post-Lamprechtian *Kulturgeschichte* or persisted in that Rankian emphasis on foreign policy and international relations that is reflected in a phrase such as *der Primat der Aussenpolitik*. The work of perhaps the best-known of the established émigrés, Hans Rothfels, may be taken as symptomatic of the group as a whole.[151] Sometimes, however, the task of one of these expatriates might include acting as a mediator in presenting to a transatlantic audience the more adventurous ideas of one who stayed. Otto Hintze was to remain largely unknown except among specialists working on the Hohenzollern until Felix Gilbert edited his shorter pieces in the mid-1970s (Gilbert 1975; cf. Simon 1968). His lack of self-advertisement, which often came across as icy superiority, had doubtless contributed to the isolation and sadness of this lapsed *Weltpolitiker*; but we readily forget that he had resigned his chair in Berlin rather than submit to the racial inquisitions of the Nazis and died in lonely and miserable obscurity in 1940. Hintze's case underlines the point that staying in Germany should not be read as a form of collaboration: much depended on situation, temperament and stage of life, as well as political conviction or racial background. These latter characteristics could, of course, make remaining a sheer

---

150 Their intertwined careers are helpfully reviewed by Robert Lerner in Lehmann and Sheehan 1991: 188–205. For Kantorowicz, see Boureau 1990.

151 Hans Rothfels's *œuvre* significantly includes a book on the German resistance (*Die deutsche Opposition gegen Hitler* (1949), but its previous emphasis is in the Meineckian tradition of state and diplomatic history: *Carl von Clausewitz* (1920); *Bismarcks englische Bündnispolitik* (1924); *Bismarck und der Osten* (1934); *Ostraum, Preussentum und Reichsgedanke* (1935).

impossibility. One thinks of the difficulties of Veit Valentin, whose outspoken defence of liberal values under the Weimar Republic prevented him from achieving a post worthy of his scholarship and brought about his dismissal even from that, once the Nazis came to power.[152] Or one might recall the clouds gathering over the Warburg Institute in Hamburg by 1933.

Warburg's story pulls together a number of themes from these years of mounting anxiety for Jews.[153] As a member of a distinguished Jewish banking family, Aby Warburg (1866–1929) never had to worry about money. His passions were different: he adored art and collected books, financed by the family. He did so in order to pursue his own studies in art history, which resulted in many papers on the Renaissance and the impact on it, in particular, of classical modes of thought. There was a book on Botticelli. But the library that Warburg began to amass in his house in Hamburg began to take on a life of its own, not merely because of its size – there were much larger private libraries – but because its concentration on cultural history in the Burckhardtian sense and its relationship with Warburg's own intellectual priorities gave it a special coherence and utility for historians of art and Renaissance culture. Scholars would come to the house and try to make sense of the Byzantine cataloguing system invented by Warburg himself. By the 1920s the reputation of the collection had become so widespread that the ambitions of Warburg and his assistants turned towards the establishment of a major institute which could contain the books and offer civilized surroundings for visiting historians. Unfortunately these years also saw Warburg's obsession, for only an obsessive could have driven the collection forward, turning to neurosis; he became confined in a hospital for the mentally ill. He made a partial recovery – sufficient for him to see the inauguration of his dream of an Institute, under the aegis of the University of Hamburg, in 1924 and the move of the library into an adjacent and larger space in 1925. The death of Warburg in 1929 did not, therefore, destroy what he had made, for it had a financial and institutional framework that would permit the Institute's work to continue and expand. Far more crippling was the coming of the depression, which subverted the Warburg family's wealth, and then the arrival of the Nazis in power at the beginning of 1933. The 'solution' turned out to be an English one. Underpinned by Samuel Courtauld and the American wing of the Warburg family, the Warburg Institute transformed itself into a pile of boxes and moved to London in 1933; it was incorporated in the University of London during the Second World War. In this way the deranged new powers of Nazism cost Germany a new kind of history together with the prestige of the Institute and the

---

152 He had been sacked at Freiburg for holding incorrect views about German foreign policy and Tirpitz. For Valentin's subsequent problems, see Mommsen in Lehman and Sheehan 1991: 44–7: 'His fate as a determined democratic liberal, who in spite of respectable research achievements was never considered acceptable by official academic historiography, was in many ways representative of the trends prevailing in the German historical profession in the 1920s and 1930s.'
153 For the history of Warburg and his institute, see Ernst Gombrich's seminal account *Aby Warburg: an Intellectual Biography* (1970), which also contains an account of the library's migration by Warburg's assistant, Fritz Saxl.

journal that it launched in 1937. With the Institute went people, moreover, and the talents in particular of two young art historians, Erwin Panofsky and Ernst Gombrich, the latter of whom still, at the time of writing (1996), has a room at the Warburg Institute and whose vestigial Viennese accent still makes its mark on public radio.[154]

Mapping these many moves in the age of communism, fascism and Nazism produces false impressions as well as necessary and important ones. For every historian obliged to seek refuge from repression, many more sat it out, kept their heads down and continued working amid difficult and uncertain circumstances. Nor should the historiography of the period come into focus as one dominated by responses to extreme doctrines. Seen in the round, the historical writing of the period between 1919 and 1945 seems as much conservative as radical; and when it *does* seem radical it often appears so in countries that were not repressive: the France of Febvre and Bloch, the America of Becker and Beard. Even within free societies, innovative thinking easily masks the face of traditional scholarship. Febvre comes to mind before Ferdinand Lot (1866–1952). Yet Lot's books (close to forty of them) and his persistent presence at the Sorbonne from 1909 to the beginning of the Second World War may eventually prove a greater influence on the historiography of the twenty-first century than anything Febvre said. Lot certainly thought so. Alphonse Aulard may have lacked the divine spark of a Bloch; but he reached the top sooner and stayed there longer. The Britain that nursed the radical futures of Christopher Hill, Eric Hobsbawm (himself a refugee from Berlin), Rodney Hilton and Edward Thompson also nursed the present of Bruce Macfarlane's Oxford and G. M. Trevelyan's Cambridge (see Cannadine 1993), neither of which threatened revolution. Yet the immediate future seemed to confirm that the torch had passed to a generation for whom the desperate realities of inter-war life played a major role. Few of those displaced went back. One finds occasional exceptions, such as the determined anti-fascist Salvemini[155] who had been driven out of Italy and had campaigned against Mussolini from America. He returned to his chair in Florence after the war when he was long past the age of retirement. But such stories are few. The centre of gravity in historical thought and writing had shifted not for one decade but for several.

POST-WAR MOODS

The resolution of the Second World War presents itself to memory in the 1990s as both an end and a beginning for some forms of historical writing. Some historians would go further and assert that 1945 is now the wrong place to start, inviting as it

---

154 For Panofsky (1892–1968), see in particular his *Meaning in the Visual Arts* (1970) and the account by M. A. Holly of *Panofsky and the Foundation of Art History* (1984). Gombrich's wide-ranging publications can be scrutinized in and supplemented by Onians 1994.
155 Gaetano Salvemini (1873–1957) had been professor of modern history at Florence between 1916 and his expulsion by the fascist government in 1925. He was eventually awarded a chair at Harvard (1934), but returned to Florence in 1949 at the age of 76.

does the picture of a century riven in its centre when perhaps, even in German history, the continuities between the world of the 1930s and that of (say) the 1960s appear more compelling thirty years on than the sharp disjunctions of *die deutsche Katastrophe*.[156] At one level of logic, continuity can always be proved, of course: no one – not even if he or she suffered exile or persecution – could disown a personal past and all the conditioning elements associated with it. Yet there seems little doubt that historiography after 1950 did go in new directions in order to fit itself to a different world order and a series of intellectual and political shifts. Many of the chapters in the first half of this book have already reflected those shifts by discussing developments in recent historical thinking about classical, medieval and early modern subjects. Many of those in the second half address themselves precisely at determining what the shifts have been about. To describe all the significant changes that have taken place since 1950 would not only fill its own book, therefore, but disturb the balance of the chapters found elsewhere in this one. An opportunity should be taken none the less to indicate some broad lines of development across the chronology and to catch up with some styles of historiography not treated in depth in this volume.

Because the Second World War and its global aftermath embraced hardly less than the world and because it therefore threw into historical awareness the cultures of Japan, Australasia, Russia and the United States as well as those of Europe, the fortunes of world history as a form of enquiry became fashionable again after 1945. The so-called Cold War between the United Sates and Soviet Russia and the Maoist revolution in China, with the Korean War to follow, helped assert a view of history that made conventional approaches to international history seem dated and lop-sided. Only a view of world history, rather than the study of relations between two or three states within the system, seemed to have scale enough to cope with these new perspectives and to underline the degree to which everyone was now living in a different world. Few historians felt the weight of this thought so severely as the British historian Geoffrey Barraclough, who by 1956 had come to see the historiography of Europe as so provincial that

> it would not be difficult to argue that we should be better off if we could scrap our histories of Europe and free our minds from their myopic concentration on the West. For such history, while it may conceivably serve to harden our prejudices and fortify us in our belief in the superiority of our traditions and values, is liable to mislead us dangerously about the actual distribution of power and the forces actually operative in the world in which we live. Moreover it inculcates a false sense of continuity, against which experience rebels, and obscures the fact that we are living in a world totally different, in almost all its basic preconditions, from that which Bismarck bestrode. ... The questions we have to ask today have changed; and the past we look back upon from the small, surviving rock which still protrudes from the upheaval is totally different from the smooth expanse we saw stretching behind us before 1939.
>
> ('The Larger View of History', *Times Literary Supplement*, 6 January 1956)

---

156   For the continuity thesis, see an excellent collection of essays, Lehmann and Van Horn Melton 1994. *Die deutsche Katastrophe* (1946) was the title of Friedrich Meinecke's seminal attempt after the war to make sense of the Nazi past in a longer view of German historiography.

Ten years later one American historian could regret that the number of books directed at world history was probably still smaller than the volume of works dealing with (say) seventeenth-century England (Erwin 1966; 1189).

These irritations were real enough; but the comments belie the degree to which subterranean movement had already begun. Two multi-volume works designed to reassess world perspectives had already appeared. One of them was French – the *Histoire générale des civilisations*, the other a German-inspired compilation, the *Historia Mundi*. Yet a paradox quickly emerged. Both in these publications and in those that followed in Germany, France, Britain and America, world history came into focus through a persistent national lens. In the *Histoire générale* we learn that 'l'histoire n'est pas choix, mais reconstitution de tous les aspectes de la vie'; and these turn out to be 'surtout ... les formes economique et social',[157] just as Braudel would have wished. For Jacques Pirenne, in his *Tides of History*, the problem was Barraclough's.

> Confronted by the abyss into which humanity has fallen, should we not take stock and examine our consciences? There is no other way to do so, in my opinion, than to follow, through the universal history of the first six thousand years of man, the long adventure of humanity.
>
> (Pirenne [1944–56]: 9–10)

The language, however, was not Barraclough's but, again, that of post-*Annales* inclusiveness, with a nod at Vico and Comte and even – he was searching for 'scientific and moral conclusions' – at Voltaire. The German studies similarly found that they could no more forget Sybel and Treitschke than Hitler; or at least they clung to a form of *Weltgeschichte* whose starting-point was novel – the sinking of the *Mutterkontinent* (see Randa 1954) – but whose vocabulary echoed traditional exponents of the art such as Hans Delbrück whose monumental series of lectures in Berlin had appeared in print as his five-volume *Weltgeschichte* during the 1920s.[158] In Britain the subject had become so stained by the speculations of Arnold Toynbee about the presence of cycles in world development that professional historians, as John Roberts complained when he turned to the subject of world history in 1976, had simply let it alone.[159] For Americans, meanwhile, the subject degenerated often into a bland 'World Civs' module through which generations of students were required to plough until William McNeill grasped the subject and pulled it away towards an interesting and challenging way of thinking, not about the history of the world but rather about an enquiry called world history which had its own distinctive purpose and method—a story told expertly by R. I. Moore in Chapter 38 of this book. The recent establishment of a seminar in London entitled 'Global History in the Long Run' implies that this story is far from over.

---

157 *Histoire générale des civilisations*, ed. Maurice Crouzet (7 vols, Paris, 1955–7), ix, xi. Cf. *Historia Mundi: ein Handbuch der Weltgeschichte*, ed. Fritz Valjavec (10 vols, Berne, 1952–61).
158 Delbrück 1924–8. He had been a pupil of Sybel. See above, Chapter 11.
159 Roberts 1976: 9. For Toynbee, see Toynbee 1934–61 and McNeill 1989.

If the war reconfigured the historians' sense of geography, it also transformed their awareness of technology. Partly this expanding horizon emerged from the progress made in communications generally: it became harder to pretend that Latin America or India or China needed no history when their images appeared regularly on television or documentary film. But overwhelmingly the harbinger of major change appeared through a revolution in computer technology driven by the need to counter Hitler's rocket programme and acquire a master-weapon in the atomic bomb. The genius of Alan Turing, the advanced calculations brought to the United States by Hitler's propulsion scientists, and the need to control and manipulate massive banks of data pressed forward the construction of computers whose utility for historians was as yet dimly perceived but which would make possible types of enquiry which no previous generation had been in a position to attempt. And from the mid-1950s onwards, these opportunities have given rise to styles of analysis which have altered the shape of historical argument in some fields. Three of these have proved especially remarkable: the 'new' economic history; the analysis of demography and family reconstitution; and the rise of a retrospective psephology which has given the conventional world of political history a distinctive turn.

We have seen that economic history had been part of the historiography of the West since at least the rise of the German school in the last third of the nineteenth century. It had shaken hands with Marxism, encouraged the theoretical models of Weber and had a shot in the arm from the economic catastrophes of 1929–33. When Bloch finally fought his way to a Parisian chair, it was a chair of economic history that he acquired.[160] The proliferation of professional periodicals such as the *Economic History Review* (1927) and others in Europe had already, by 1945, given the subject status and made it possible for the establishment of separate departments of economic history in the universities with a stress on the history of modern industrialization. In Britain this would give rise to prominent names that became quite as familiar as those of political historians : Clapham, needless to say, but also C. R. Fay, W. H. B. Court, Sidney Pollard. In France the thrust of *Annales* ran alongside economic investigation in the tradition of Simiand and Labrousse. Where a significant departure occurred in the 1950s was in the United States where some articles by Conrad and Meyer helped prompt a style of analysis that would attract the unlovely label 'cliometrics'. This approach had two central features: the collection of economic data covering long periods and in forms that a computer could manipulate; and the building of models against which to test hypotheses about economic variables within certain historical problems. The models attracted criticism and indeed notoriety for their being 'counter-factual'. They claimed to present a picture of what would have happened, if particular items in a historical complex had not been present or had been phased differently – a form of speculation that gave rise to indigestion among empiricists but which has also caused theorists some insomnia.[161] For its enthusiasts, the ability to control vast

160 For the circumstances surrounding Bloch's appointment at the Sorbonne, see Fink 1989: 185–7.
161 Some of the problems and opportunities are critically reviewed by Hawthorne 1991: 1–37.

flows of quantitative information rendered conventional economic history out of date and immediately questioned all forms of history that could not provide precise quantification for their evidence. 'How many?', 'Have you counted?': these became the 1960s questions.

But of course the new mood went beyond that. Sir John Clapham (d. 1946), the doyen of British economic historians, had always insisted on quantitative precision; computers merely made the task easier in one sense. Quite different from Clapham's teaching, indeed contrary to it, was a fashion in the United States for linking economic history to economic theory in a sub-Weberian way. There were to be ideal types, but the computer was to generate them, taking the historian's mind away from conventional reliance on isolated accounts (these were 'anecdotal') and supplementing historical portraiture ('impressionistic') with a quantitative method that ought to yield objective results through their very mass, rather in the way that Durkheim had thought that statistics contained a true history if only it could be divined. No sharp divide marks off 'old' from 'new' economic history; but one could certainly nominate as highly symptomatic of its central tenets an article by Conrad and Meyer in 1958. This aimed to show whether slave-ownership on Southern plantations was profitable in the *ante-bellum* period, but it performed this task by using statistical and computational techniques that had gained currency over the previous few years and on the basis of historical sources that seemed to many as random as they were slight. In retrospect, however, the article took on a pioneering quality because it seemed to adumbrate the more celebrated enquiry prosecuted by Fogel and Engerman in 1974, which appeared under the title *Time on the Cross*.

Fogel came at the subject of slavery from the direction of more conventional problems relating to the economic structure of America during the nineteenth century. His study of the railway system's impact on growth deployed the model-building and counter-factual propositions that were to become integral to his later work (Fogel 1964; compare, on the methodologies involved, Fogel 1966). But the book on slavery touched nerves that the earlier publications had not – partly because of the obvious technical problems facing anyone trying to reconstruct a balance sheet using data derived from so oral and informal a society, yet more, perhaps, because historians wedded to history as a *Geisteswissenschaft* found themselves reacting almost out of aesthetic revulsion in seeing an area of human tragedy and humiliation reduced to a spreadsheet evaluated by 'systematic statistical tests' (Fogel and Engerman 1974: I, 10) rather than the educated eye. It seemed a history untouched by human hand. This was undoubtedly unfair and Fogel was right to see such criticisms as missing the point of the enquiry. In a later debate with G. R. Elton, he rounded on critics of cliometrics with an argument that we can take as a definition:

> The common characteristic of cliometricians is that they apply the quantitative methods and behavioral models of the social sciences to the study of history. ...Cliometricians want the study of history to be based on explicit models of human behavior. They believe that historians do not really have a choice of using or not using behavioral models since all attempts to explain historical behavior – to relate the elemental facts of history to each

other – ... involve some sort of model. The real choice is whether these models will be implicit, vague, incomplete and internally inconsistent, as cliometricians contend is frequently the case in traditional historical research, or whether the models will be explicit, with all the relevant assumptions clearly stated, and formulated in such a manner as to be subject to rigorous empirical verification.

(Fogel and Elton 1983: 24–6)

This clarity of exposition did not prevent the savaging of *Time on the Cross*: indeed its very starkness helped stimulate a battery of assaults on and defences of the idea of cliometrics through the 1970s and 1980s.[162]

The debate between Fogel and the arch-empiricist Elton proved that they believed basically the same thing: they disagreed about the place of social science but they agreed that the point of historical work was to uncover some historical 'truth' by a process of discovery and reconstruction. Curiously, the French historical establishment, by now a virtual tyranny of *bien pensants* dominated by Braudel, went in the same direction. This was odd because much of the theoretical underpinning of the *annaliste* enterprise turned on representing history as an act of imaginative construction rather than the reporting of a given state of affairs that historical work somehow uncovered. Yet in their enthusiasm for the computer (who can forget Le Roy Ladurie's remark that the historian of the future will be a programmer or he or she will be nothing?) the *dévôts* of Paris moved towards a development of cliometrics which their guru, Pierre Chaunu, decided to call 'serial history'. Building on the methodological recommendations of a sociologist, Jean Marczewski, in 1965, this approach seeks to go beyond the archive and extend the base from which historians can work by constructing series or runs of data calculated at regular intervals, say at yearly logging-points, over long periods – often a century or more. The point seems to be the resurrection of a hidden 'historical reality' which can only be grasped quantitatively and only tested statistically. Here is François Furet in definitional mood:

[T]he most general and at the same time the most elementary ambition of quantitative history is to set out historical reality in temporal series of homogeneous and comparable units, and in that way to measure the evolution of that reality at given intervals, usually annual. This fundamental logical operation is definitional of what Pierre Chaunu has called serial history ... [This] has the decisive advantage from a scientific point of view of replacing the ineffable 'events' of positivist history with the regular repetition of data selected and constructed because of their comparable nature. ... The distribution of historical reality into series presents the historian with materials broken up into different levels, into different subsystems, and he is then free to establish or not to establish connections between these levels.

(Furet 1984: 14)

Needless to say, the empowered historians have indeed 'established' connections and produced a formidable historiography relating to climate and demography as well as to economic history. The problem remains the one that arose in the United

---

162 For an excellent introduction to the material available, see Fogel 1964: 24–6, n. 17.

States – one about the fundamental ambitions of historical work and the conceptual thought-world in which they are set.[163]

This objection did not operate in the domain of demography. For here the ability of a computer designed to make use of silicon-chip technology rather than punch-cards[164] to handle the vast runs of data available in, for example, modern census reports operated as an extension of human memory to allow a form of analysis that no human could perform. Beginning in France in the 1950s, the impetus reached Britain with the foundation in 1964 of the Cambridge Group for the History of Population and Social Structure.[165] Those connected with that group such as Peter Laslett, whose *The World We Have Lost* made a considerable stir when it appeared, and E. A. Wrigley, whose work has reorientated understanding of British demographic history since the early modern period, have made a major difference to the way in which problems not only of global demographic data but also of the microcosm of family reconstitution are approached.[166] Similarly social historians such as Michael Anderson have transformed the way in which nineteenth-century population history is tackled through their insistence on sophisticated quantification. Anderson's sample of the 1851 census in Britain comments on the astonishing detail that the computer makes available to researchers, because of the ability to code data in ways that make retrieval not only possible but simple in styles of search that would have taken previous generations years to attempt and which they would have ruled out of the enquiry on that ground.[167]

Some of the same thrust has become apparent in political analysis, too, though historians have not always found it possible to feel enthusiastic. Psephology – the study of elections and voting behaviour – certainly has benefited. British experience in particular suggests a clear future for such work in face of the use made by analysts such as Frank O'Gorman (1989) and the American scholar John A. Philipps (1982) of quantitative method as a way of investigating the pre-1832 British electorate. Presented with 'poll books', which are collections of printed information about how people voted in the years before the secret ballot was introduced in 1872, the historian can do little with the naked eye: the columns of material form too complex a block of information to allow one to see patterns in it. A simple software package into which the information may be keyed allows one to go beyond this confinement; the machine is able to search along axes established by the author, identify cases that fit the stated criteria and present the information in accordance with any variable named. Even the most Luddite of archival scholars finds it hard to resist the usefulness of such a device when once it is demonstrated. Of course the familiar GIGO – garbage in, garbage out – applies in political

---

163 For an American perspective on the French developments, see Tilly 1972.

164 Non-initiates are guided to Hull 1992. Cf. Lukoff 1979; Evans 1983 for a history of the computer.

165 For some details see Barraclough 1978: 77f.

166 Peter Laslett's central work in demography, apart from *The World We Have Lost*, is *A Fresh Map of Life; the Emergence of the Third Age* (1996). Cf. Bonfield *et al.* 1986. For E. A. Wrigley, see Wrigley 1987; 1988; Wrigley and Schofield 1989.

167 See Anderson's guide to the records: Anderson 1987. See also Anderson 1980.

history quite as strongly as elsewhere. Roderick Floud, whose work in quantitative history has been of seminal importance in Britain over the past two decades (Floud 1979; cf. Floud and McCloskey 1994) rightly remarks that it may well be the case that one could correlate parliamentary division lists with phases of the moon. Achieving the correlation would not turn it into an intelligent operation (Floud 1979: ch. 7) – a thought some would like to see translated into French. For this reason one wonders sometimes about the point of focusing on sources such as division lists in the British Parliament as the source for quantitative analysis, though that has not prevented extensive work from being done on them (see e.g. Aydelotte 1971; 1972; 1977). As in other areas where quantification has become fashionable, much depends on a personal reading of the 'scientific' nature of history. And as in other areas of personal experience, the national often determines the personal: it is no accident that American scholars still turn more readily to the silicon chip than do scholars working in more conventional cultures.

THE HISTORY OF THE PRESENT

The 1960s acquired a historiographical mood. It was nothing so tight as an agenda, far less a list of specified topics or approaches. But it wanted answers, crystalline conclusions, whether they came as numbers or prosaic certainties. Like most moments that imagine themselves to have found keys to long-closed doors, it welcomed science and baptized various styles of positivism: *annaliste*, *marxisant*, anthropological, archaeological, sociological, ideologically correct, emotionally committed. It was a self-conscious decade in a way and to a degree that the despised 1950s had never aspired to be; and it nurtured an earnest view of its own importance that the 1970s and 1980s never sought. Amid the trials of Cuba and Vietnam, the Prague Spring and the Paris Spring, it depicted itself as the beginning of something significant in social and historical enquiry. It was right about its significance, wrong about its beginning. For the 1960s seem from the 1990s not a departure but an arrival. The decade became the terminus of modernism.

Understanding 'modernism' matters if only to help sort out what we ought to understand by 'postmodernism', which has become the slogan for so much since. Modernist views may perhaps best be seen as a cluster of positions relating to philosophy, literary analysis, aesthetics and all the social sciences between, very roughly, 1910 and 1970. The views themselves ranged widely in content and application, but they seem united by a particular tone that implied the availability of truth, the undesirability of metaphysics and all forms of blurredness, the necessity for rationalism of an Enlightenment kind. From the two theories of relativity to the double helix of DNA, from the sociology of Talcott Parsons to the anthropology of Claude Lévi-Strauss, the texts of modernism breathed the excitement of discovery, the identification of hidden structures, the digging-up of clues and Sutton Hoos.[168]

---

168 Sutton Hoo in Suffolk, England, is a well-remarked archaeological site containing a longboat of *circa* the seventh century, discovered in 1939.

Historians did not believe themselves to be modernists because they rarely believe themselves to be anything worth a label. But their enquiries, beyond the subversion of a few sceptics like the brilliant but baffling Michael Oakeshott, had the modernist feel for realizable truth and a consistent implication that the past was out there as a visitable place. 'The past is a foreign country; they do things differently there.'[169] This modernist remark says exactly what modernists believed and what postmodernists do not.

The certainties and the discoveries extended to politics. Chief among the 1960s certainties came a from-the-heart leftism which denounced imperialist wars, espoused a youth culture in dress and music, and dallied with soft drugs. In West Germany sizeable proportions of the undergraduate population removed themselves from any form of democratic politics and threatened radically to destabilize the most hierarchical academic system in Europe. This mood intersected in Britain with what in retrospect seems the high point of historical Marxism. Most of the original members of the Communist Party Historians' Group, formed just after the war, had left the party after the crushing of Hungary's liberation movement in 1956. But the message of Christopher Hill, Eric Hobsbawm and above all E. P. Thompson, whose *The Making of the English Working Class* (1963) became the cynosure of its generation, mixed easily with the 1950s populism of Richard Hoggart and Raymond Williams,[170] maintaining through the incendiary pages of the *New Left Review*, meanwhile, a dialogue with Perry Anderson in the United States and Louis Althusser in France (for more detail, see Chapter 36). It was a time to *épater les bourgeois*. Sometimes those doing the shocking found themselves shocked in turn by a form of 'revisionism' that reversed the prevailing colours; and it is noticeable how some very fundamental rethinking of historical problems took place in reaction to the changed mood, whether it was A. J. P. Taylor's (1961) denial of Hitler's 'blueprint' for a war in 1939, or the denial by Ronald Robinson (1961) and John Gallagher of the Marxist thesis of imperialism in Africa (Robinson *et al.* 1961), or the denial by Maurice Cowling (1967) of the Marxist thesis about the importance of the English working class in 1867. It even provoked a clever book denying certainty itself (Letwin 1965).

At some point in the 1970s, whatever held together a prevalent intellectual environment of this sort changed and changed utterly. Chronologically the shift ran alongside a major political one in the West away from socialist planning and towards free-market economics associated with political leadership such as that of Ronald Reagan and Margaret Thatcher. Perhaps the relation between these two levels of discussion went beyond fellow-travelling; certainly some observers found in the new mood an outgrowth of a particular stage of late capitalism (Jameson 1991; 1981). Yet whatever its initial conditions may have been, a developing sense of a 'turn' – the 'postmodern turn' – began to make itself felt in the social and

---

169   The often-recalled opening words of L. P. Hartley's novel *The Go-Between*. Cf. Lowenthal 1985.
170   Richard Hoggart (b. 1918) became best known for *The Uses of Literacy* (1957) and Williams (1921–88) for *Culture and Society* (1958).

literary theory of the period, strengthening and redefining through the 1980s and beyond. At first it may have seemed to practical historians that people had turned against 'science' (again). This is what Michael Postan seems to have picked up in 1971:

> Except for Marxists, most historians writing about the philosophy of history, most philosophers concerned with the methodology of historical and social study, and even some influential social anthropologists, have in recent years ranged themselves against the supposed fallacies of 'scientism'. They accept, however unconsciously, the idealistic dichotomy of 'physical' and 'humanistic' studies of that of pure and practical reason, and consequently decry all attempts to use the methods of natural science in the study of history or of human affairs in general.
>
> (Postan 1971: ix)

But of course it went further than that. New words appeared: 'post-structuralism'; 'deconstruction'; 'alterity'; 'textuality'; many others. Historians chose normally not to use them; indeed few of them knew what any of them meant. Yet their periodicals, their weekly reviews and magazines, and, in increasing numbers, their monographic literature began to reflect a changing climate. It is witness to the pervasiveness of that environment that the chapters in this volume, when they discuss changes in the historiography of this recent period, often say little explicitly about postmodernism while implying volumes between their lines about its impact. The reticence is completely understandable. Postmodernism has made a major difference to historical projects now underway but does not yet itself have a historiography: we shall see much more clearly its historical ramifications in thirty or forty years' time. It has, all the same, a presence and a vocabulary that readers need to encounter and we ought not to conclude this survey of historiographical developments without considering them.

'Postmodern' is an adjective most helpfully attached to a particular phase or period of thought, as Jane Caplan suggests, rather than to a specific collection of tools or approaches.[171] Like 'enlightened' or 'romantic', it signals a persuasion that has obtained a partial grip on the speculations of a particular epoch. And like those designators, it provides only a broad clue to what any person falling within its ambit may believe. Some of the more obvious characteristics common among 'postmodern' writers include: a rejection, philosophically, of the self as a 'knowing subject' in the form presented in European thought after Kant and before Heidegger; an allied rejection of the possibility of finding a singular 'true' picture of the external world, present or past; a concern to 'decentre' and destabilize conventional academic subjects of enquiry; a wish to see canons of orthodoxy in reading and writing give way to plural readings and interpretations; a fascination with text itself and its relation to the reality it purports to represent; a drive to amplify previously unheard voices from unprivileged groups and peoples; a preoccupation with gender as the most immediate generator of underprivileged or

---

171 I follow in this section the untangling of 'postmodern' from 'poststructural' in Professor Caplan's thoughtful and stimulating paper, Caplan 1989.

unempowered status; a dwelling on power and lack of it as a conditioner of intellectual as much as political configurations within a culture. Each of these has begun to nibble at, sometimes bite on, the assumptions of working historians whose conscious activity may betray no shadow of interest in theoretical matters. To review each of them here would take the discussion away from the focus of this volume; but four clusters of questions have none the less impinged forcefully enough to warrant a word here, those surrounding poststructuralism and language, textuality and narrative, a feminist reading of the history of women, and the project of a 'new' cultural history.

Poststructuralism differs from postmodernism because it addresses itself to a specific mode of criticism arising out of linguistics and then tries to reverse and supersede it. It does not connote an atmosphere promoted by a particular period – its central ideas became available before the onset of a distinctive 'postmodern' environment – but rather a collection of insights provoked by a reaction against the idea that language consists of 'closed' structures. This latter view is normally associated with Saussure, though the writers we think of as structuralists ran far beyond Saussure's contentions. The insistence in Saussure that language operates as a constantly modifying but always complete system which generates meaning through complicated internal codes and symbols (instead of a one-to-one correspondence between words and things, signifier and signified) was expanded outside the sphere of linguistic and literary analysis to imply, in Caplan's words, that 'all cultural systems represent coded systems of meaning rather than direct transactions with reality' (1989: 265). But one could go further than that, and in doing so social theorists often exposed their modernist roots by claiming that these puzzles of meaning and codification could be solved. One could extract an answer; it was a question of cracking the code. It is not possible to read a structural anthropologist like Claude Lévi-Strauss, for example, without picking up that fundamental optimism and many of the historical works of the 1960s reflect some of the same tone. This was the position against which poststructuralists reacted. Among historians perhaps the most influential thinker involved in this reaction was the Parisian guru, Michel Foucault. It is not that Foucault was a historian himself or, if he were, he was a very bad one. Rather, his assertion of a relationship between power and knowledge reversed the familiar one – power is knowledge rather than vice versa because power determines the conditions in which particular knowledge-forms ('epistemes', as he called them) come into being and find sustenance. And by doing so it brought into question the familiar forms of knowledge brought to bear on the past by historians, forms which he implied reflected the power-distributions of their own societies to the detriment of plural readings of the past.[172] No one observer can ever encompass the 'truth' of a situation, this line of criticism alleged, which will appear differently to people with distinctive cultures imposing different

---

172 For Foucault on power, see in particular Foucault 1966 and 1980. Cf. Megill 1985; Grumley 1989; Barker 1993.

points of view. Historiography has to make space, therefore, for the 'truths' of women, black people, Asian people, the inarticulate and dispossessed. In Caplan's formulation,

> [t]he poststructuralism advanced by the later [Roland] Barthes, [Jacques] Derrida, Foucault and others rejects the stability and closure of the structuralist system ... and the proposition that the truth of a system is intelligible to an observer or reader who occupies the appropriate vantage point.
>
> (Caplan 1989: 266)

In so far as an historical truth is available at all, it becomes one whose validity can only apply in relation to the particular and limited vantage point from which it derives. The past disappears as an object and turns into a construct which must allow the validity of alternative constructions which can be tested only by criteria internal to the cultural and intellectual frameworks that generate them.

These alternative constructions do not take the form of structures fixed in time, as many pre-1970 texts might have displayed, but rather become narratives over time. In some ways, indeed, poststructural history can resemble in its textuality the historiography of the 1860s more closely than that of the 1960s. Yet there remains a crucial difference. Victorian narrative arranged itself as a fundamental story-line that gave an account of some great and overarching theme: the rise of the nation; the coming of greatness; the history of liberty. Postmodern narratives begin with the proposition that all such grand architecture is suspect at best. At worst, it confines historical accounts to an established canon of interpretation in order to prove by implication the presence of some persistent undertow. When Jean Lyotard wrote *The Postmodern Condition* (1984), possibly the first book self-consciously to announce the beginning of a new era, he provided the shortest known definition of postmodernist assumption as a 'disbelief in metanarratives'; and certainly the dismissal of historiography devoted to proving the reality of a single *Leitmotif* has become a theme of much poststructural criticism. There should be stories, lots of them. But they are to reflect a plurality of 'truths', not a single Authorized Version. Historical narrative is to be distinguished from fiction, moreover, by nothing so trivial as truth. Of course, historical narrative takes its form and content from certain controls implicit in the sort of material historians use; but it is not, in its postmodern raiment, to be seen as having a one-to-one correspondence with historical truth. It will function simply as one form of 'discourse' (Foucault's over-used and often misunderstood term) that one can place against other forms but never against the thing that all historical discourses consider: the past itself.[173] Peter Munz has given the issue a pungent formulation:

> We cannot glimpse at history. We can only compare one book with another book. ... Historians alone among all scientists still believe that the only reason why truth eludes them is that they show too much bias, or that their sources do, or that there are missing

---

173   Cf. Palmer 1989. Peter Munz deals with some of the issues in more detail in Chapter 34, in this volume.

'facts'. But this is all wrong. The real reason why it must forever elude us is that it is not there. There is nothing the case over and above what people have thought (ie., the sources) and think (ie., the narratives), so that we can have no statement of which we can say that it is true if and only if what it asserts is the case.

(Munz 1977)

For this reason, among others, the power of literary theory as a critique of common historical practice has become very noticeable since the 1970s.[174] Historians have watched or actively aided the unravelling of their discipline in order to cope better with new currents of thought and to bring their more recent subject matter into a better fit with modern thought.

One subject has exemplified this movement particularly clearly. The rise of 'gender' as an historiographical category has been as remarkable as it is recent, beginning with a politicized history of women on the back of the female emancipation movement of the 1960s but turning into a genre that seeks to address the problem of female and male roles in past societies and thereby to unlock doors into a number of historical areas that conventional political and social history had left closed. To see the transition in this light offends those who deem 'this field ... a dynamic study in the politics of knowledge production' (Scott 1992: 44) but there seems no obligation to think about the story in that way. It undoubtedly is the case that accounts of male–female relations in past societies now flourish without the patina of overt political recommendation that the early literature tended to deploy. All history has, ultimately, a political propulsion in that all stories begin from a standpoint. The tone of postmodernist speculation about gender seems no more political, on the other hand, than most other sectors of historical writing and it has recently adopted a mood of sub-scientific enquiry that would not so easily consort with an overt political stance.[175] The literature none the less concerns itself heavily with issues of identity which in turn raise painful questions about who should write history in this sphere. People sometimes say that only women, perhaps only some kind of women, are qualified to write women's history. The thought echoes in the proposition that only black people can write the history of black people; and so on in an infinite progress or regress. Each of these narratives, moreover, will take its place as another slab of discourse within which, seen from one modernist or structuralist direction, criticism will be internalized. It is hardly surprising that for one wing of the argument this kind of development marks a significant and necessary liberation from the tyranny of unsympathetic historical method. For another, it heralds the collapse of historical method of any kind, the dissolution of an intellectual discipline (in both senses) and a 'descent into discourse', as Bryan Palmer complains in his book of that title (1989). In Chapter 37 of this volume, Olwen Hufton offers a

---

174 Literary theory has affected historical thought in too many indirect ways to note here, but see Barthes 1977; Canary and Kozick 1978; Gossman 1990. See also n. 176 below.

175 Fletcher 1995; Hufton 1995. Of course to some extent the divide may reflect an Anglo-American contrast. For bibliographical guidance on recent developments in this area of study, see Dauphin *et al.* 1986; Vickery 1993. I am grateful to Julia Smith for these latter references.

personal reflection of some of this story while in Chapter 9 Janet Nelson shows how these perspectives come into play when historians look at a particular problem.

A similar concern with discourse, readings and texts dominates a strand of historiography to which the label of 'new cultural history' has been attached by the American scholar, Lynn Hunt (1989). Unlike the case of the new economic history, this mode is not a self-conscious one and it rather pulls together a series of disparate initiatives through the 1980s: work on reading, literacy and the history of the book (especially in the hands of the subject's first master, Roger Chartier (1987; 1993; 1994); analysis of narrative texts as a form, particularly the innovative thinking of Hayden White, Paul Ricoeur and Dominick LaCapra;[176] anthropological views of micro-historical events, such as Robert Darnton's famous *The Great Cat Massacre* or Natalie Zemon Davis's well-known book *The Return of Martin Guerre*;[177] and the beginning of a theme dealing with social 'memory'.[178] Even these few instances suggest how different this approach to the study of a 'culture' is from the classical origins of *Kulturgeschichte* in Burckhardt and Huizinga. New cultural historians reflect often a cultural optimism and a picture of the proper concerns of social history that is avowedly 'inclusive' both socially and intellectually. They stand far away from the celebration of elites and the vision of a hierarchical society as the last bastion of civilization. Nor do they appear blind to some economic determinants, as both Burckhardt and Huizinga tended to be: witness the success of Martin Wiener's *English Culture and the Decline of the Industrial Spirit* (1981). Their methods and topics, equally, suggest innovation rather than the working-out of a former tradition; and these have an intercontinental as much as an inter-disciplinary feel. Just as one wing of new sensibility announced itself in a volume such as Quentin Skinner's influential *The Return of Grand Theory* in 1985, another threw off theory in order to pursue what became known in Italy as *microstoria*, which sometimes took the form of local or regional social history but which came to take on the character of a non-spatial concentration on a particular event or source in order to elucidate wider contexts. Carlo Ginzburg's *The Cheese and the Worms* of 1980 famously reconstructed the thought-world of a sixteenth-century miller and opened a decade of Italian concern with specific contexts reflected in the work, for example, of Giovanni Levi.[179] This work echoes the

---

176 For Hayden White see in particular White 1973; 1987. Paul Ricoeur's reputation was made in hermeneutics: for a representative selection, see Valdes 1991. There is a rather unsatisfactory published lecture on *The Reality of the Historical Past* (1984); but the main source for historians should be *Temps et recit*, which has been translated as *Time and Narrative* (1984–8). The thrust of LaCapra has been literary as much as historical, but there are helpful pieces in LaCapra 1983; 1985.

177 Robert Darnton's techniques of *microstoria* can be seen in *The Great Cat Massacre* (1984). Cf. his study of *The Corpus of Clandestine Literature in France 1769–89* (1995) and its sister volume, *The Forbidden Bestsellers of Pre-Revolutionary France* (1995). The fame of Natalie Zemon Davis was made by *The Return of Martin Guerre* (1983), but see also *Society and Culture in Early-Modern France: Eight Essays* (1975) and *Women on the Margins: Three Seventeenth-Century Lives* (1995).

178 Social 'memory': Fentress and Wickham 1992; Roth 1995.

179 Ginzburg 1980; 1983; 1991; Levi 1988. Cf. Ginzburg's essays collected in English as *Myths, Emblems, Clues* (1990) and Levi's reflections 'On Microhistory' in Burke 1992: 93–113. I am grateful to Professor Chris Wickham for his guidance here. For the wider context of Italian Historiography, see Chapter 22, this volume.

best-selling account of *Montaillou* by the *annaliste*, Emmanuel Le Roy Ladurie (1978), (cf. Le Roy Ladurie 1984), which likewise showed what might be wrung from a collection of tightly organized material relating to a single series of events in a locality. The American version of cultural history took much of its tone originally from France, also; and as one thinks across territory in considering the historiography of the 1980s a fault-line seemingly wanders across it, dividing the historical approaches of France, Italy and America but uniting parts of those environments in a common tendency.

French tendencies affected Britain less markedly and Germany hardly at all. Perhaps the British case makes sense when one considers not only its traditional empiricism and hostility to over-conceptualized argument, but also the lack of *Kulturgeschichte* as a national trait, beyond the history of art pioneered in the Warburg Institute. The German resistance to this new mood is harder to explain. In a tradition of scholarship that included Lamprecht, and his long-standing friendship with Pirenne, one might expect to find a readier response. Yet in fact the Rhine, as one observer pointed out a decade ago, became an intellectual frontier just as it had functioned as a territorial one since 1870. The lack of mutual interest between French and German historiography after 1945 seems little less than astonishing. It is not that Germany persisted in a state-dominated, political historiography: one could argue that West Germany gave rise to a school of important social history based in Bielefeld, inspired by Werner Conze and Hans-Ulrich Wehler and drawing on a depth of work in social history that ran back into Weimar and the Nazi period.[180] But the questions asked never moved in the direction of *annalisme*; and the various emphases of *le monde Braudelien* found little sympathy from Berlin and Heidelberg. The French, conversely, did not write about Germany to nearly the extent that British and American historians have done – a point stressed by Hartmut Kaelble in a revealing analysis of the difference between the two cultures. In seeking the distinctiveness of the German experience he notes a number of points of contrast, three of which seem fundamental: the German concern with history as a form of political education – unavoidable granted German memories since 1933—contrasting with the French mood of transcending traditional categories in a way that leaves its historians '*politikfern*', distant from political concerns; a German interest in change and process, contrasting with a growing French stress on unchanging or slowly changing structures, on *durée* rather than *l'histoire événementielle*; and finally a German preoccupation with theory as a leading category rather than what often seems a romantic or rhetorical decoration for the hands-on practices of the *Annales*. If the Germans have failed to find a Braudel or a Duby, the French have not sought to produce a Reinhart Kosellek or Jörn Rüsen.[181] For all these reasons the structuralist ideas associated with a

---

180   Conze 1963; 1964; 1967; his later work on social history has mostly been editorial, though voluminous. Wehler's output has been enormous and centres currently on his continuing *Deutsche Gesellschaftsgeschichte*. But see also the *Festschrift* for his sixtieth birthday: Hettling *et al.* 1991.
181   Koselleck *et al.* 1982; Koselleck 1985; Rüsen 1983–6. An exception on the French side is the late Michel de Certeau: see esp. Certeau 1988.

'modernist' disposition better suited the temperament and background of German historians, especially granted the powerful Marxist tradition of analysis which, of course, was mandatory in East Germany until the coming of unification. Even when the Berlin Wall came down in 1989, the ensuing euphoria produced not a ripple of cultural history in the *Historische Zeitschrift*.

Historiography is not a form of prediction and only a fool would assert where these various trends will go. The best platform for speculation perhaps lies in studies of concrete instances and some of the contributors to this volume have taken the opportunity to think ahead and wonder about the direction of their specialism over the next few years. Meanwhile so much in the current context appears undigested. Postmodernism as an intellectual form is already provoking a backlash. The consequences for the writing of history of the crash of communism in 1989 have not yet begun to work themselves out, though we can certainly remain sceptical in face of arguments about the End of Ideology, the End of History and the Beginning of Post-History (see Bell 1960; Fukuyama 1992; Niethammer, 1992). The discipline has survived several political revolutions and two world wars: it ought to be able to cope with Mr Gorbachev. National identities still inform all versions of historiography, sometimes in indirect ways. Indeed we seem still to be using history as the early nineteenth century did, as a vehicle for locating groups and peoples and giving them a past that suits their present or encourages their sense of a future. All of these things may alter. But one development in the history of the present looks likely to be both permanent and valuable. Historians have never been so *aware* of what they are attempting as they have become over the past two decades. Always a reflective form of writing, history has become (as they say) 'reflexive': it is self-conscious to a degree and to a level of sophistication that no previous generation can match with the partial exception of that of Carlyle and Humboldt. Possibly historians will become morbid and self-destructive as a result. Not a few have already become self-important. Yet the move towards a deliberately constructed history gives critics of all persuasions the opportunity and the duty to keep their swords sharp against a moment when contingencies may threaten to destroy the discipline or subvert an interest in the past at all. We shall do well to remember that historiography forms the stone that whets the blade.

REFERENCES

Adams, Henry Brooks (1889–90) *History of the United States during the Jefferson and Madison Administrations*, 9 vols, New York.
—— (1904) *Mont-Saint-Michel and Chartres*, London.
—— (1917) *The Education of Henry Adams*, Boston and New York.
Adams, Herbert Baxter (1882) *The Germanic Origins of New England Towns*, Baltimore.
Alison, A. (1833–42) *History of Europe during the French Revolution*, 10 vols, Edinburgh.
—— (1853–9) *History of Europe from the Fall of Napoleon in 1815 to the Accession of Louis Napoleon in 1852*, 8 vols, Edinburgh.
—— (1883) *Some Account of my Life and Writings: An Autobiography*, ed. Lady Alison, 2 vols, Edinburgh.

Allegra, L. and Torre, A. (1977) *La nascità dalla storia sociale in Francia dalla Commune alle Annales*, Turin.
Anderson, M. (1980) *Approaches to the History of the Western Family 1500–1914*, London.
—— (1987) *The 1851 Census: A Guide to the National Sample of the Enumerators' Returns*, Cambridge.
Andreski, S. (ed.) (1971) *Herbert Spencer*, London.
Andrews, W. L. (1985) *Critical Essays on W. E. B. Du Bois*, Boston.
Antoni, C. [1940] (1962) *From History to Sociology*, ed. H. White, New York.
Ashley, W. J. (1888–93) *An Introduction to English Economic History and Theory*, 2 vols, London.
Aydelotte, W. O. (1971) *Quantification in History*, Reading, Mass.
—— (ed.) (1977) *The History of Parliamentary Behavior*, Princeton.
—— *et al.* (eds) (1972) *The Dimensions of Quantitative Research in History*, London.
Bagehot, W. (1872) *The English Constitution*, 2nd edn, London.
Bailey, C. (1936) *Francis Fortescue Urquart: A Memoir*, London.
Baker, A. R. H. (1984) 'Reflections on the relation of historical geography and the *Annales* school of history', In A. R. H. Baker and D. Gregory (eds) *Explorations in Historical Geography*, Cambridge.
Bancroft, G. (1882) *History of the Formation of the Constitution of the United States of America*, 2 vols, New York.
Bann, S. (1984) *The Clothing of Clio: A Study of the Representation of History in Nineteenth-Century Britain and France*, Cambridge.
Barker, P. (1993) *Michel Foucault: Subversions of the Subject*, New York and London.
Barnes, H. E. [1937] (1962) *A History of Historical Writing*, New York.
Barraclough, G. (1978) *Main Trends in History*, New York.
Barthes, R. (1977) 'Introduction to the structural analysis of narrative', in R. Barthes, *Image, Music, Text*, London.
Bassett, J. S. (1917) *The Middle Group of American Historians*, New York.
Beard, C. and Beard, M. (1913) *An Economic Interpretation of the Constitution*, New York.
—— (1915) *The Economic Origins of Jeffersonian Democracy*, New York.
—— (1927) *The Rise of American Civilisation*, New York.
Beck, L. W. (ed.) (1963) *Kant on History*, Indianapolis.
Becker, C. L. (1901) *The Growth of Revolutionary Parties and Methods*, New York.
—— (1915) *The Beginnings of the American People*, New York.
—— (1932) *The Heavenly City of the Eighteenth-Century Philosophers*, New Haven, CT.
—— (1935a) *Detachment and the Writing of History*, New York.
—— (1935b) *Everyman his own Historian*, New York.
Bell, D. (1960) *The End of Ideology*, Glencoe, IL.
Ben-Israel, H. (1968) *English Historians on the French Revolution*, Cambridge.
Bentley, M. (1993) 'Victorian historians and the larger hope', in M. Bentley (ed.) *Public and Private Doctrine: Essays in British History Presented to Maurice Cowling*, Cambridge.
Berg, M. (1996) *A Woman in History: Eileen Power 1889–1940*, Cambridge.
Berlin, I. (1976) *Vico and Herder*, London.
Bickel, C. (1991) *Ferdinand Tönnies: Soziologie als skeptische Aufklärung zwischen Historismus und Rationalismus*, Opladen.
Blaas, P. B. M. (1978) *Continuity and Anachronism: Parliamentary and Constitutional Development in Whig Historiography and in the Anti-Whig Reaction between 1890 and 1930*, The Hague.
Bloch, M. [1931] (1966) *French Rural Society: An Essay on its Basic Characteristics*, Berkeley and Los Angeles.
Bonfield, L., Smith, R. and Wrightson, K. (eds) (1986) *The World we have Gained: Histories of Population and Social Structure. Essays Presented to Peter Laslett on his Seventieth Birthday*, Oxford.
Bossuet, J. B. (1681) *Discours sur l'histoire universelle*, Paris.

Bossy, J. (1982) 'Some elementary forms of Durkheim', *Past and Present* 95: 3–18.

Boureau, A. (1990) *Histoires d'un historien: Kantorowicz*, Paris.

Breisach, E. (1983) *Historiography: Ancient, Medieval, and Modern*, Chicago.

Browning, O. (1910) *Memories of Sixty Years at Eton, Cambridge and Elsewhere*, London.

Buckle, H. T. [1857–61] (1894) *The History of Civilisation in England*, 3 vols, London. [2 vols, 1857–61.]

Burckhardt, J. [1860] (n.d.) *The Civilization of the Renaissance in Italy*, New York.

—— [1905] (1955) *Weltgeschichtliche Betrachtungen*, ed. J. Oeri, Stuttgart.

—— (1965) *Judgements on History and Historians*, New York.

Burger, T. (1976) *Max Weber's Theory of Concept Formation*, Durham, NC.

Burke, P. (1973) *A New Kind of History from the Writings of Lucien Febvre*, London.

—— (ed.) (1992) *New Perspectives on Historical Writing*, Philadelphia.

—— (1990) *The French Historical Revolution: The Annales School 1929–89*, Stanford.

Burrow, J. W. (1981) *A Liberal Descent: Victorian Historians and the English Past*, Cambridge.

—— (1985) *Gibbon*, Oxford.

Butterfield, H. [1931] (1973) *The Whig Interpretation of History*, Harmondsworth.

Cahnman, W. J. and Boskoff, A. (eds) (1964) *Sociology and History: Theory and Research*, New York.

Cairnes, J. E. (1875) *FR* 23/17 (Jan.).

Cam, H. M. (1944) *Liberties and Communities in Medieval England: Case Studies in Administration and Topology*, Cambridge.

—— (1962) *Law Finders and Law Makers in Medieval England*, London.

Campbell, I. (1993) *Thomas Carlyle*, Edinburgh.

Canary, R. H. and Kozick, H. (eds) (1978) *The Writing of History: Literary Form and Historical Understanding*, Madison.

Cannadine, D. (1993) *G. M. Trevelyan: A Life in History*, New York.

Caplan, J. (1989) 'Postmodernism, poststructuralism and deconstruction: notes for historians', *Central European History* 22: 260–78.

Carbonell, C.-O. (1976) *Histoire et historiens*, Toulouse.

—— and Livet, G. (eds) (1983) *Au Berceau des Annales*, Toulouse.

Carlyle, T. [1830] (1956) 'On history', in Stern 1956.

—— (1833–42) *The French Revolution*, 3 vols, London.

—— [1858–65] (1897) *History of Friedrich II of Prussia, called Frederick the Great*, 8 vols, London.

Carr, D. (1986) *Time, Narrative and History*, Bloomington.

Certeau, M. de (1988) *The Writing of History*, NY.

Chadwick, O. (1975) *The Secularization of the European Mind*, Cambridge.

Chartier, R. (1987) *The Cultural Uses of Print in Early-Modern France*, Princeton.

—— (1993) *Cultural History: Between Practices and Representations*, Cambridge.

—— (1994) *The Order of Books: Readers, Authors and Libraries in Europe between the Fourteenth and Eighteenth Centuries*, Cambridge.

Chickering, R. (1993) *Karl Lamprecht: A German Academic Life (1856–1915)*, Atlantic Highlands, NJ.

Chirot, D. (1984) 'The social and historical landscape of Marc Bloch', in T. Skocpol (ed.) *Vision and Method in Historical Sociology*, Cambridge.

Codazzi, A. (1985) *Hyppolyte Taine e il progetto filosofico di una storiografica scientifica*, Florence.

Coffa, J. A. (1991) *The Semantic Tradition from Kant to Carnap: To the Vienna Station*, ed. L. Wessels, Cambridge.

Cohen, G. A. (1979) *Karl Marx's Theory of History: A Defence*, Oxford.

Coleridge, S. T. [1830] (1976) *On the Constitution of the Church and State*, ed. J. Colmer, London.

Colley, L. (1989) *Lewis Namier*, London.
Collie, R. (1964) 'Johan Huizinga and the task of cultural history', *American Historical Review* 69: 607–30.
Collingwood, R. G. (1946) *The Idea of History*, ed. T. M. Knox, Oxford.
Comte, A. (1830–42) *Cours de philosophie positive*, 6 vols, Paris.
Condorcet, Marquis de (1795) *Esquisse d'un tableau des progrès de l'esprit humain*, Paris.
Conrad, A. H. and Meyer, J. R. (1958) 'The economics of slavery in the ante-bellum South', *Journal of Political Economy* 66: 95–130.
Conze, W. (1963) *Die deutsche Nation*, Göttingen.
—— (1964) *Die Zeit Wilhelm II und die Weimarer Republik*, Tübingen.
—— (1967) *Das deutsch–russische Verhältnis*, Göttingen.
Corbin, A. (1983) '*La Revue historique*: analyse de contenu d'une publication rivale des *Annales*', in Carbonell and Rivet 1983.
Coulanges, F. de (1864) *La Cité antique*, Paris.
Cowling, M. (1967) *1867: Disraeli, Gladstone and Revolution*, Cambridge.
Creighton, L. (1904) *Life and Letters of Mandell Creighton*, 2 vols, London.
Croce, B. (1941) 'History complete and incomplete', in B. Croce, *History as the Story of Liberty*, London.
Crossley, C. (1993) *French Historians and Romanticism: Thierry, Guizot, the Saint-Simonians, Quinet, Michelet*, London.
Culler, A. D. (1985) *The Victorian Mirror of History*, New Haven.
Cunningham, A. (1950) *William Cunningham, Teacher and Priest*, London.
Cunningham, W. (1882) *The Growth of English Industry and Commerce*, Cambridge.
—— (1896) *Modern Civilisation in some of its Economic Aspects*, London.
Darnton, R. (1984) *The Great Cat Massacre and Other Episodes in French Cultural History*, London.
—— (1995a) *The Corpus of Clandestine Literature in France 1769–89*, New York.
—— (1995b) *The Forbidden Bestsellers of Pre-Revolutionary France*, New York.
Dauphin, C., Farge, A., Fraisse, G. *et al.* (1986) 'Culture et pouvoir des femmes: essai d'historiographie', *Annales ESC* 41: 271–93.
Davies, R. R. (1967) 'Marc Bloch', *History* 52: 265–82.
Davis, N. Z. (1975) *Society and Culture in Early-Modern France: Eight Essays*, Stanford.
—— (1983) *The Return of Martin Guerre*, Cambridge, MA.
—— (1995) *Women on the Margins: Three Seventeenth-Century Lives*, Cambridge, MA.
Delbrück, H. (1924–8) *Weltgeschichte*, 5 vols, Berlin.
Dilthey, W. (1976) *Wilhelm Dilthey: Selected Writings*, ed. H. P. Rickman, Cambridge.
Dionisotto, C. (1989) *Ricordo di Arnaldo Momigliano*, Bologna.
Dosse, E. [1987] (1994) *New History in France: The Triumph of the Annales*, Chicago.
Dray, W. (1980) *Perspectives on History*, London.
Du Bois, W. E. B. (1903) *The Souls of Black Folk*, Chicago.
—— (1935) *Black Reconstruction*, New York.
Dunn, W. H. (1961–3) *James Anthony Froude: A Biography*, 2 vols, Oxford.
Eichhorn, K. F. (1821–3) *Deutsche Staats- und Rechtsgeschichte*, 3rd edn, Göttingen.
Elton, G. R. (1972) *Policy and Police*, Cambridge.
—— (1974–84) *Studies in Tudor and Stuart Politics*, 3 vols, Cambridge.
—— (1982) *The Tudor Constitution*, 2nd edn, Cambridge.
—— (1986) *The Parliament of England 1559–1581*, Cambridge.
—— (1991) *England under the Tudors*, 3rd edn, London.
Ermarth, M. (1978) *Wilhelm Dilthey: The Critique of Historical Reason*, Chicago.
Erwin, R. (1966) 'Civilization as a phase of world history', *American Historical Review* 71: 1181–98.
Evans, C. (1983) *The Making of the Micro: A History of the Computer*, Oxford.

Febvre, L. (1925) *Geographical Introduction to History*, New York.

—— (1942) *Le Problème de l'incroyance au XVIe siècle: la religion de Rabelais*, Paris.

—— (1953) *Combats pour l'histoire*, Paris.

Fentress, J. and Wickham, C. (1992) *Social Memory*, Oxford.

Fink, C. (1989) *Marc Bloch*, Cambridge.

Fletcher, A. (1995) *Gender, Sex and Subordination in England*, New Haven, CT.

Floud, R. (1979) *An Introduction to Quantitative Methods for Historians*, 2nd edn, London.

—— and McCloskey, D. (eds) (1994) *The Economic History of Britain since 1700*, 2nd edn, Cambridge.

Fogel, R. W. (1964) *Railroads and Economic Growth: Essays in Economic History*, Baltimore.

—— (1966) 'The new economic history: its findings and methods', *Economic History Review*, 25, 19: 642–56.

Fogel, R. W. and Elton, G. R. (1983) *Which Road to the Past? Two Views of History*, New Haven, CT.

Fogel, R. W. and Engerman, S. L. (1974) *Time on the Cross*, 2 vols, Boston and Toronto.

Forbes, D. (1952) *The Liberal Anglican Idea of History*, Cambridge.

Forster, J. (1839) *Oliver Cromwell 1599–1658*, 2 vols, London.

Forstman, J. (1977) *A Romantic Triangle: Schleiermacher and Early German Romanticism*, Missoula.

Foucault, M. (1966) *Les Mots et les choses*, Paris.

—— (1980) *Power/Knowledge: Selected Interviews and Other Writings 1972–77*, ed. C. Gordon, New York.

Frédèricq, P. (1899) *L'Enseignment supérieure de l'histoire*, Ghent.

Freeman, E. A. (1867–79) *The Norman Conquest of England*, 6 vols, Oxford.

Freund, J. (1992) *D'Auguste Comte à Max Weber*, Paris.

Froude, J. A. (1856–70) *The History of England from the Fall of Wolsey to the Defeat of the Spanish Armada*, 12 vols, London.

Fukuyama, F. (1992) *The End of History and the Last Man*, London.

Furet, F. (1984) *In the Workshop of History*, Chicago.

Galston, W. A. (1975) *Kant and the Problem of History*, Chicago.

Gardiner, P. (ed.) (1959) *Theories of History*, New York.

Gardiner, S. R. (1883–4) *History of England from the Accession of James I to the Outbreak of the Civil War*, 2 vols, London.

—— (1886–91) *History of the Great Civil War*, 3 vols, London.

—— (1894–1901) *History of the Commonwealth and Protectorate*, 3 vols, London.

—— (1909) *The Last Years of the Protectorate 1656–58*, London.

Gay, P. (1975) *Style in History*, New York.

Gerard, A. (1983) 'À l'origine du combat des *Annales*: positivism e historique et système universitaire', in Carbonnel and Livet 1983.

Gibbon, E. [1776–88] (1909–14) *The History of the Decline and Fall of the Roman Empire*, ed. J. B. Bury, 7 vols, London.

Gilbert, F. (1990) *History: Politics or Culture?*, Princeton.

—— (ed.) (1975) *The Historical Essays of Otto Hinze*, Oxford.

Ginzburg, C. (1980) *The Cheese and the Worms: The Cosmos of a Sixteenth-Century Miller*, Baltimore.

—— (1983) *Night Battles: Witchcraft and Agrarian Cults in the Sixteenth and Seventeenth Centuries*, London.

—— (1990) *Myths, Emblems, Clues*, London.

—— (1991) *Ecstasies: Decyphering the Witches' Sabbath*, Harmondsworth.

Goldstein, L. J. (1976) *Historical Knowing*, Austin.

Gombrich, E. (1970) *Aby Warburg: An Intellectual Biography*, London.

Gooch, G. P. (1913) *History and Historians in the Nineteenth Century*, London.

Gossman, L. (1990) *Between History and Literature*, Cambridge, MA.

Gray, J. (1995) *Isaiah Berlin*, London.

Grumley, J. E. (1989) *History and Totality: Radical Historicism from Hegel to Foucault*, London.

Guizot, F. (1829–32) *Histoire de la civilisation en France*, 5 vols, Paris.

Haddock, B. (1980) *An Introduction to Historical Thought*, London.

Hae-song, H. (1992) *Booker T. Washington and W. E. B. Du Bois: A Study in Race Leadership. 1895–1915*, Seoul.

Hartog, F. (1988) *Le XIXe siècle et l'histoire: le cas Fustel de Coulanges*, Paris.

Haskins, C. H. (1923) *The Rise of Universities*, New York.

—— (1927) *The Renaissance of the Twelfth Century*, Cambridge, Mass.

Hawthorne, G. (1991) *Plausible Worlds: Possibility and Understanding in History and the Social Sciences*, Cambridge.

Hay, D. (1977) *Annalists and Historians: Western Historiography from the Eighth to the Eighteenth Centuries*, London.

Hettling, M. *et al.* (1991) *Was ist Gesellschaftsgeschichte? Positionen, Themen, Analysen*, Munich.

Higham, J., Krieger, L. and Gilbert, F. (1965) *History*, Englewood Cliffs.

Hintze, O. (1915) *Hohenzollern und ihr Werk*, 5th edn, Berlin.

Hodges, R. and Whitehouse, D. (1983) *Charlemagne and the Origins of Europe: Archaeology and the Pirenne Thesis*, London.

Hofstadter, R. (1968) *The Progressive Historians*, New York.

Hoggart, R. (1957) *The Uses of Literacy*, London.

Holly, M. A. (1984) *Panofsky and the Foundation of Art History*, Ithaca, NY.

Howe, M. A. de Wolfe (1908) *The Life and Letters of George Bancroft*, 2 vols, London.

Hufton, O. (1995) *The Prospect before her: A History of Women in Western Europe*, 1: *1500–1800*, London.

Hughes, H. S. (1959) *Consciousness and Society: The Reorientation of European Social Thought 1890–1930*, New York.

Huizinga, J. [1919] (1924) *The Waning of the Middle Ages*, London. (Tr. of: *Herfstij der Middeleeuven*, 1919.)

Hull, R. (1992) *In Praise of Wimps: A Social History of Computer Programming*, Hebden Bridge.

Hume, D. (1754–62) *History of England from the Invasion of Julius Caesar to the Revolution of 1689*, 6 vols, London.

Hunt, L. (ed.) (1989) *The New Cultural History*, Berkeley.

Iggers, G. G. (1983) *The German Conception of History: The National Tradition of Historical Thought from Herder to the Present Day*, Middletown, CT.

Jacobitti, E. E. (1981) *Revolutionary Humanism and Historicism in Modern Italy*, New Haven, CT.

Jameson, F. (1981) *The Political Unconscious: Narrative as a Socially Symbolic Act*, London.

—— (1991) *Postmodernism, or, the Cultural Logic of Late Capitalism*, London.

Jann, R. (1985) *The Art and Science of Victorian History*, Columbus, OH.

Kaegi, W. (1962) *Europäische Horizonte im Denken Jacob Burckhardts. Drei Studien*, Basle and Stuttgart.

Kantorowicz, E. H. (1957) *The King's Two Bodies: A Study in Medieval Political Theology*, Princeton.

Kemble, J. M. (1849) *The Saxons in England*, London.

Kenyon, J. (1983) *The History Men: The Historical Profession in England since the Renaissance*, London.

Kern, S. (1983) *The Culture of Time and Space 1880–1920*, London.

Keylor, W. R. (1975) *Academy and Community: The Foundation of the French Historical Profession*, Cambridge, Mass.

Knies, C. (1883) *Die politischen Oekonomie vom Standpunkte der geschichtlichen Methode*, 2nd edn, Brunswick.

Koselleck, R. (1985) *Futures Past: On the Semantics of Historical Time*, Cambridge, MA.

——, Lutz, H. and Rüsen, J. (eds) (1982) *Formen der Geschichtsschreibung*, Munich.

Kozicki, H. (ed.) (1993) *Western and Russian Historiography: Recent Views*, Basingstoke.

Krieger, L. (1977) *Ranke: The Meaning of History*, Chicago.

Krohn, C.-D. (1993) *Intellectuals in Exile: Refugee Scholars and the New School for Social Research*, Amherst.

Krüger, D. (1983) *Nationalökonomie in wilhelminischen Deutschland*, Göttingen.

Kuczynski, J. (1978) *Porträt eines Gesellschaftswissenschaftlers*, Berlin.

LaCapra, D. (1983) *Rethinking Intellectual History: Texts, Contexts, Language*, Ithaca, NY.

—— (1985) *History and Criticism*, Ithaca, NY.

Lamprecht, K. (1885–6) *Deutsches Wirtschaftsleben im Mittelalter*, 3 vols, Leipzig.

—— (1896) *Alte und neue Richtungen in der Geschichtswissenschaft*, 2 vols, Berlin.

—— (1900) *Die kulturhistorische Methode*, Berlin.

—— (1914) *Krieg und Kultur: Drei vaterländische Vorträge*, Leipzig.

Langlois, C. V. and Seignobos, C. (1898) *Introduction to the Study of History*, London.

Laslett, P. [1965] (1971) *The World we have Lost*, 2nd edn, London.

—— (1996) *A Fresh Map of Life: The Emergence of the Third Age*, Basingstoke.

Lawler, E. G. (1986) *David Friedrich Strauss and his Critics: The* Life of Jesus *Debate in Early Nineteenth-Century German Journals*, New York.

Le Quesne, A. C. (1982) *Carlyle*, Oxford.

Lefebvre, G. (1924) *Les Paysans du Nord pendant la Révolution française*, 2 vols, Paris and Lille.

—— (1932) *La Grande Peur de 1789*, Paris.

—— (1934) *Foules historiques*, Paris.

—— (1937) *Les Thermidoriens*, Paris.

Lefranc, A. (1925) *Le Visage de François Rabelais*, Melun.

—— (1932) *L'Œuvre de Rabelais d'après les recherches les plus récentes*, Groningen.

Lehmann, H. and Melton, J. Van Horn (eds) (1994) *Paths of Continuity: Central European Historiography from the 1930s to the 1950s*, Cambridge.

Lehmann, H. and Sheehan, J. L. (eds) (1991) *An Interrupted Past: German-Speaking Refugee Historians in the United States after 1933*, Cambridge.

Le Roy Ladurie, E. [1978] (1982) *Montaillou: Cathars and Catholics in a French Village 1294–1324*, London.

—— (1984) *Love, Death and Money in the Pays d'Oc*, Harmondsworth.

Letwin, S. R. (1965) *The Pursuit of Certainty*, Cambridge.

Levi, G. (1988) *Inheriting Power: The Story of an Exorcist*, Chicago.

Levison, W. (1946) *England and the Continent in the Eighth Century*, Oxford.

Liebel, H. P. (1963/4) 'Philosophical idealism in the *Historische Zeitschrift* 1859–1914', *History and Theory* 3: 316–30.

Lilla, M. (1993) *G. B. Vico: The Making of an Anti-modern*, Cambridge, MA.

Linehan, P. (1992) *Past and Present in Medieval Spain*, Aldershot.

Lixl-Purcell, A. (1988) *Women in Exile: German-Jewish Autobiographies since 1933*, New York.

Loewenberg, B. J. (1972) *American History in American Thought*, New York.

Lowenthal, D. (1985) *The Past is a Foreign Country*, Cambridge.

Luden, H. (1825–37) *Geschichte des deutschen Volkes*, 12 vols, Gotha.

Lukes, S. (1973) *Emile Durkheim: His Life and Work*, London.

Lukoff, H. (1979) *From Dits to Bits: A Personal History of the Electronic Computer*, Portland, OR.

Lutz, R. (1990) 'Lamprecht-Streit und französischer Methodenstreit: der Jahrhundertwende in vergleichender Perspektive', *Historische Zeitschrift* 251: 325–63.

Lyon, B. (1974) *Henri Pirenne*, Ghent.
Lyotard, J. (1984) *The Postmodern Condition*, Manchester.
Macaulay, T. B. [1828] (1956) 'History', in Stern 1956.
—— (1849–61) *History of England*, 5 vols, London.
McClelland, C. E. (1971) *German Historians and England: A Study in Nineteenth-Century Views*, Cambridge.
McClelland, P. D. (1975) *Causal Explanation and Model Building in History, Economics and the New Economic History*, Ithaca, NY.
McNeill, W. H. (ed.) (1967) *Essays in the Liberal Interpretation of History* by Lord Acton: *Selected Papers*, Chicago.
—— (1989) *Arnold J. Toynbee: A Life*, New York.
Maine, H. J. S. (1861) *Ancient Law*, London.
Maitland, F. (1936) *Selected Essays*, Cambridge.
—— [1901] (1957) 'William Stubbs, Bishop of Oxford', in H. Cam (ed.) *F. W. Maitland: Historical Essays*, Cambridge.
Maner, J. R. (1982) 'Theory and practice of history in the French and German Enlightenment', unpublished Ph D. thesis, Chapel Hill, NC.
Marías, J. (1990) *Understanding Spain*, Ann Arbor.
Martin, G. H. and Spufford, P. (1990) *The Records of the Nation: The Public Record Office 1838–1988*, Woodbridge.
Mathiez, A. (1922–7) *La Révolution française*, 3 vols, Paris.
—— (1929) *La Réaction thermidorienne*, Paris.
—— (1934) *Le Directoire*, Paris.
Mauss, M. (1925) *Essai sur le don*, Paris.
Megill, A. (1985) *Prophets of Extremity: Nietzsche, Heidegger, Foucault, Derrida*, Berkeley.
Meinecke, F. (1924) *Die Idee der Staatsräson in der neueren Geschichte*, Berlin.
—— (1936) *Entstehung des Historismus*, Munich and Berlin.
—— (1946) *Die deutsche Katastrophe*, Wiesbaden.
—— (1972) [1936] *Historism: The Rise of a New Historical Outlook*, London.
Menger, K. (1994) *Reminiscences of the Vienna Circle and the Mathematical Colloquium*, ed. L. Golland, B. McGuiness and A. Sklar, Dordrecht.
Meyer, J. (1993) *Bossuet*, Paris.
Michelet, J. (1833) *Principes de la philosophie de l'histoire, traduits de la Scienza Nuova de J. B. Vico par Jules Michelet*, Brussels.
Millgate, J. (1973) *Macaulay*, London.
Mink, L. O. (1969) *Mind, History and Dialectic*, Indianapolis.
Momigliano, A. (1955–92) *Contributi alla storia degli classici (e del mondo antico)*, 9 vols, Rome.
—— (1966) *Studies in Historiography*, London.
—— (1977) *Essays in Ancient and Modern Historiography*, Oxford.
Mommsen, W. J. and Osterhammel, J. (eds) (1987) *Max Weber and his Contemporaries*, London.
Monod, G. (1895) *Du Rôle de l'opposition des races et des nationalités dans la dissolution de l'empire carolingien*, Paris.
—— (1896) *Études critiques sur les sources de l'histoire carolingienne*, Paris.
Montesquieu, C.-L. de (1749) *De l'esprit des lois*, Geneva.
Moore, J. (1981) *W. E. B. Du Bois*, Boston.
Munz, P. (1977) *The Shapes of Time: A New Look at the Philosophy of History*, Middletown, CT.
Muratori, L. A. *Antiquitates italicae medii aevi*, Milan.
Namier, J. (1971) *Lewis Namier: A Biography*, London.
Niethammer, L. (1992) *Posthistoire: Has History Come to an End?*, London.

Novick, P. (1988) *That Noble Dream: The 'Objectivity Question' and the American Historical Profession*, Cambridge.
Oakeshott, M. (1932) *Experience and its Modes*, Cambridge.
—— (1983) *On History*, Oxford.
O'Gorman, F. (1989) *Voters, Patrons and Parties: The Unreformed Electoral System of Hanoverian England 1734–1832*, Oxford.
Onians, J. (ed.) (1994) *Sight and Insight: Essays on Art and Culture in Honour of E. H. Gombrich at 85*, London.
Owensby, J. (1994) *Dilthey and the Narrative of History*, Ithaca, NY.
Palmer, B. (1989) *Descent into Discourse: The Reification of Language and the Writing of Social History*, Philadelphia.
Panofsky, E. (1970) *Meaning in the Visual Arts*, Harmondsworth.
Peardon, T. P. (1933) *The Transition in English Historical Writing, 1760–1830*, New York.
Peel, J. D. Y. (1971) *Herbert Spencer*, London.
Phillips, J. A. (1982) *Electoral Behavior in Unreformed England: Plumpers, Splitters and Straights*, Princeton.
Pidal, R. M. (1929) *La España del Cid*, 2 vols, Madrid.
—— (1940–54) *Historia de España*, 4 vols, Madrid.
Pirenne, H. (1910) *Les Anciennes Démocraties des Pays Bas*, Paris.
Pirenne, J. (1945–56) *Les Grands Courantes de l'histoire universelle*, 7 vols, Neuchâtel.
Plantinga, T. (1980) *Historical Understanding in the Thought of Wilhelm Dilthey*, Toronto.
Popper, K. (1957) *The Poverty of Historicism*, London.
Porter, R. (1988) *Edward Gibbon: Making History*, London.
Postan, M. (1971) *Fact and Relevance*, Cambridge.
Randa, A. (1954) *Handbuch der Weltgeschichte*, 2 vols, Olten and Freiburg im Breisgau.
Ranke, L. von (1824) *Geschichte der romanischen und germanischen Völker von 1494 bis 1535*, Berlin.
—— (1840) *The Ecclesiastical and Political History of the Popes of Rome during the Sixteenth and Seventeenth Centuries*, 3 vols, tr. S. Austin, London. (First published as: *Die römischen Päpste, ihre Kirche und ihr Staat im 16. und 17. Jahrhundert*, 3 vols, Berlin, 1834–6.)
—— (1852–6) *Französische Geschichte vornehmlich im sechszehnten und siebzehnten Jahrhundert*, Stuttgart and Tübingen.
—— (1859–69) *Englische Geschichte vornehmlich im siebzehnten Jahrhundert*, Berlin.
—— (1973) *The Theory and Practice of History*, ed. G. G. Iggers and K. von Moltke, Indianapolis.
Rebérioux, M. (1983) 'Le Débat de 1903: historiens et sociologues', in Carbonell and Livet 1983.
Reill, P. H. (1975) *The German Enlightenment and the Rise of Historicism*, Berkeley.
Reynolds, S. (1994) *Fiefs and Vassals: The Medieval Evidence Re-interpreted*, Oxford.
Richardson, R. (ed.) (1991) *Schleiermacher in Context: Papers from the 1988 International Symposium on Schleiermacher at Herrnhut*, Lewiston, NY and Lampeter.
Rickert, H. [1896] (1986) *The Limits of Concept Formation in Natural Science: A Logical Introduction to the Historical Sciences*, ed. G. Oakes, Cambridge.
Rickman, H. P. (1979) *Wilhelm Dilthey: Pioneer of the Human Studies*, London.
Ricœur, P. (1984) *The Reality of the Historical Past*, Milwaukee.
—— (1984–8) *Time and Narrative*, 3 vols, Chicago.
Rigby, S. H. (1987) *Marxism and History: A Critical Introduction*, Manchester.
Roberts, J. (1976) *The Hutchinson History of the World*, London.
Robertson, W. (1759) *History of Scotland*, 2 vols, London.
—— (1777) *History of America*, 2 vols, London.
Robinson, J. H. (1912) *The New History*, New York.

—— (1921) *The Mind in the Making*, New York.
—— (1937) *The Human Comedy*, New York.
—— and Beard, C. A. (1907–8) *The Development of Modern Europe*, 2 vols, New York.
Robinson, R., Gallagher, J. and Denny, A. (1961) *Africa and the Victorians*, London.
Rose, N. (1980) *Lewis Namier and Zionism*, Oxford.
Rosenberg, J. D. (1985) *Carlyle and the Burden of History*, Oxford.
Rostovtzeff, M. (1926) *Social and Economic History of the Roman Empire*, Oxford.
—— (1926–7) *A History of the Ancient World*, 2 vols, Oxford.
—— (1941) *The Social and Economic History of the Hellenistic World*, 3 vols, Oxford.
Rotenstreich, N. (1987) *Time and Meaning in History*, Dordrecht and Boston.
Roth, M. (1995) *The Ironist's Cage: Memory, Trauma and the Construction of History*, New York.
Rothfels, H. (1920) *Carl von Clausewitz*, Berlin.
—— (1924) *Bismarcks englische Bündnispolitik*, Stuttgart.
—— (1934) *Bismarck und der Osten*, Leipzig.
—— (1935) *Ostraum, Preussentum und Reichsgedanke*, Leipzig.
—— (1949) *Die deutsche Opposition gegen Hitler*, Krefeld.
Rüsen, J. (1983–6) *Grundzüge einer Historik*, 2 vols, Göttingen.
Schmoller, G. (1898) *Umrisse und Untersuchungen zur Verfassungs-, Verwaltungs- und Wirtschaftsgeschichte besonders des preussischen Staates im 17. und 18. Jahrhundert*, Leipzig.
Schön, M. (1987) 'Gustav Schmoller and Max Weber', in Mommsen and Osterhammel 1987.
Scott, J. (1992) 'Women's history', in Burke 1992.
Seeley, J. (1883) *The Expansion of England*, London.
—— (1895) *The Growth of British Policy*, 2 vols, Cambridge.
Semmel, B. (1984) *John Stuart Mill and the Pursuit of Virtue*, New Haven.
Sheehan, J. J. (1978) *German Liberalism in the Nineteenth Century*, Chicago.
—— (1989) *German History 1770–1866*, Oxford.
Sidgwick, A. and Sidgwick, E. M. (eds) (1906) *Henry Sidgwick: A Memoir*, London.
Siegel, M (1983) 'Henry Berr et la *Revue de synthèse historique*', in Carbonell and Livet 1983.
Simiand, F. (1932) *Le Salaire. L'évolution sociale et la monnaie*, 3 vols, Paris.
Simon, C. (1988) *Staat und Geschichtswissenschaft in Deutschland und Frankreich 1871–1914*, 2 vols, Berne.
Simon, W. M. (1968) 'Power and responsibility: Otto Hintze's place in German historiography', in L. Krieger and F. Stern (eds) *The Responsibility of Power: Historical Essays in Honor of Hajo Holborn*, London and Melbourne.
Skinner, Q. (ed.) (1985) *The Return of Grand Theory in the Human Sciences*, Cambridge.
Slee, P. R. H. (1986) *Learning and a Liberal Education: The Study of Modern History in the Universities of Oxford, Cambridge and Manchester 1800–1914*, Manchester.
Smith, C. W. (1956) *Carl Becker: on History and the Climate of Opinion*, Ithaca, NY.
Smith, R. J. (1987) *The Gothic Bequest*, Cambridge.
Sorensen, D. (1983) *Carlyle's Method of History in 'The French Revolution'*, Edinburgh.
Sparvel-Bayly, E. (ed.) (1902) *Life and Letters of H. Taine*, 3 vols, n.p.
Spencer, H. (1855) *Social Statics*, London.
—— (1904) *Autobiography*, 2 vols, London.
Spengler, O. [1918–23] (1926–9) *The Decline of the West*, 2 vols, London.
Standley, A. (1981) *Auguste Comte*, Boston.
Steinberg, M. P. (1988) *The Presence of the Historian: Essays in Honour of Arnaldo Momigliano*, Middletown, CT.
Stenton, F. M. (1932) *The First Century of English Feudalism 1066–1166*, Oxford.
—— (1943) *Anglo-Saxon England*, Oxford.
Stern, F. (ed.) (1956) *Varieties of History: From Voltaire to the Present*, New York.
Stieg, M. F. (1986) *The Origin and Development of Scholarly Historical Periodicals*, Alabama.

Stoianovich, T. (1976) *French Historical Method: The 'Annales' Paradigm*, Ithaca, NY.

Sweet, P. R. (1978–80) *Wilhelm von Humboldt: A Biography*, 2 vols, Columbus, OH.

Taine, H. (1874–93) *Les Origines de la France contemporaine*, 6 vols, Paris.

Taylor, A. J. P. (1961) *The Origins of the Second World War*, London.

Taylor, M. (1992) *Men versus the State*, Oxford.

Tenbruck, F. H. (1987) 'Max Weber and Eduard Meyer', in Mommsen and Osterhammel 1987.

Thorpe, B. (1840) *Ancient Laws and Institutes of England*, 2 vols, London.

Tilly, C. (1972) 'Quantification in history, as seen from France', in V. R. Lorwin and J. N. Price (eds) *The Dimensions of the Past: Materials, Problems and Opportunities for Quantitative Work in History*, New Haven.

Tönnies, F. (1926) *Gemeinschaft und Gesellschaft*, 7th edn, Berlin.

—— (1931) *Einführung in die Soziologie*, Stuttgart.

Toynbee, A. (1934–61) *A Study of History*, 12 vols, London.

Treitschke, H. von (1879–94) *Deutsche Geschichte im neunzehnten Jahrhundert*, 5 vols, Leipzig.

Trevor-Roper, H. (1984) 'Jacob Burckhardt', *Proceedings of the British Academy* 70: 359–78.

Tucker, M. (ed.) (1991) *Literary Exile in the Twentieth Century: An Analysis and Biographical Dictionary*, New York.

Turner, F. J. (1921) *The Frontier in American History*, New York.

—— (1932) *The Significance of Sections in American History*, New York.

Turner, S. (1799–1805) *History of England from the Earliest Period to the Norman Conquest*, London.

Valdes, M. (1991) *A Ricœur Reader: Reflection and Imagination*, London.

Venturi, F. (1952) *Il populismo russo*, 2 vols, Turin.

—— (1971) *Utopia and Reform in the Enlightenment*, Cambridge.

—— (1972) *Italy and the Enlightenment*, London.

—— (1977) *Les Intellectuels, le peuple*, 2 vols, Paris.

—— (1980) *Venezia nel secondo settecento*, Turin.

—— (1988) *Giovinezza di Diderot (1713–53)*, Palermo.

Vickery, A. (1993) 'Golden Age to separate spheres? A review of the categories and chronology of English women's history', *Historical Journal* 36: 383–414.

Vico, G. B. (1708) *De nostri temporis studiorum ratione*, Naples.

—— (1710) *De antiquissima Italorum sapientia ex linguae latinae originibus eruenda*, 3 vols, Naples.

—— (1982) *Selected Writings*, ed. L. Pompa, Cambridge.

Vinogradoff, P. (1892) *Villainage in England*, Oxford.

—— (1905) *The Growth of the Manor*, London.

Voegelin, E. (1975) *From Enlightenment to Revolution*, Durham, NC.

Volpe, G. (1907) *Eretici e moti ereticali sociale dal XI al XIV secolo*, 2 vols, Milan.

—— (1928) *Guerra, dopoguerra, fascismo*, Venice.

—— (1939) 'Storia del movimento fascista', in B. Mussolini (ed.) *La dottrina del fascismo*, Rome.

—— (1943–52) *L'Italia moderna*, Florence.

Waitz, G. (1844–78) *Deutsche Verfassungsgeschichte*, 8 vols, Kiel.

—— (1864) *Deutsche Kaiser von Karl dem Grossen bis Maximilian*, 5 vols, Berlin.

Walsh, W. H. (1976) 'The logical status of Vico's ideal eternal history', in G. Tagliacozzo and D. Verene (eds) *Giambattista Vico's Science of Humanity*, Baltimore.

—— [1951] (1992) *An Introduction to the Philosophy of History*, Bristol.

Waugh, E. (1962) *Ronald Knox: A Biography*, London.

Weber, M. (1958) *The Protestant Ethic and the Spirit of Capitalism*, New York.

Weinberg, J. (1988) *Where Three Civilizations Meet: A Tribute to the Life and Work of Arnaldo Dante Momigliano*, London.

Wes, M. A. (1990) *Michael Rostovtzeff, Historian in Exile*, Stuttgart.

White, H. (1973) *Metahistory: The Historical Imagination in Nineteenth-Century Europe*, Baltimore.

—— (1980) *Tropics of Discourse: Essays in Cultural Criticism*, Baltimore.

—— (1987) *The Content of the Form: Narrative Discourse and Historical Representation*, Baltimore.

Whitrow, C. J. (1988) *Time in History: Views of Time from Prehistory to the Present Day*, Oxford.

Wiener, M. (1981) *English Culture and the Decline of the Industrial Spirit*, Harmondsworth.

Wiggerhaus, R. (1994) *The Frankfurt School: Its History, Theories and Significance*, Cambridge.

Wilcox, D. F. (1987) *The Measure of Times Past: Pre-Newtonian Chronologies and the Rhetoric of Relative Time*, Chicago.

Williams, R. (1958) *Culture and Society*, London.

Windelband, W. (1894) *Geschichte und Naturwissenschaft*, Strasbourg.

Winkel, H. (1977) *Die deutsche Nationalökonomie im 19. Jahrhundert*, Darmstadt.

Winter, E. J. (1961) *August Ludwig v. Schlözer und Russland*, Berlin.

Wolin, R. (1992) *The Terms of Cultural Criticism: The Frankfurt School, Existentialism, Poststructuralism*, New York.

Wrigley, E. A. (1987) *People, Cities and Wealth: The Transformation of Traditional Society*, Oxford.

—— (1988) *Continuity, Chance and Change: The Character of the Industrial Revolution in England*, Cambridge.

—— and Schofield, R. S. (1989) *The Population History of England 1541–1871*, Cambridge.

Wücher, A. (1956) *Theodor Mommsen. Geschichtsschreibung und Politik*, Göttingen.

Yovel, Y. (1980) *Kant and the Philosophy of History*, Princeton.

IV.1 REVOLUTION AND IDEOLOGY

19

THE HISTORIOGRAPHY OF THE FRENCH REVOLUTION

Jacques Solé

Georges Lefebvre's academic work, *La Révolution française* (The French Revolution), published in its definitive form in 1951, serves as an ideal introduction to the present study. This is because the Parisian historian produced in this work both the book of a lifetime and at the same time the fruits of half a century's research. His work remains the culminating point of the historiography of the French Revolution: even if he has been justly surpassed or criticized, historiographers of the French Revolution almost always take his work as their starting-point.[1] Apart from his personal talents, Georges Lefebvre owes this exceptional situation to the fact that his work, taken as a whole, reflects the meeting point of a triple tradition which has shaped and dominated the historiography of the French Revolution in the twentieth century.

The first of these traditions, by far the most important in French national history, and whose influence has extended beyond France, is constituted by the intellectual mythology of a Republican Party for whom the event of 1789 represents an act of foundation. Published the day before the Revolution of 1848 and fed on its passion, the work of Michelet, based largely on oral tradition, powerfully contributed to the mythologization of the revolutionary spirit.[2] As an expression of a democratic trend, this history only served to broaden, by enriching without contradicting its leading ideas, the liberal tradition inaugurated by Mignet, Thiers or Guizot since the time of the Restoration. From this perspective, and according to this type of bourgeois interpretation, the French Revolution, in short, marks the end of French history. If he added a more populist hope and an even more nationalist exaltation, Michelet changed nothing that was fundamental to the optimistic overall view shared, at the same time, in Lamartine's *L'Histoire des Girondins* (History of the Girondins).

---

1 Lefebvre 1951. The subsequent editions and numerous translations have not altered the position of this classic text.

2 Michelet 1952. This Georges Walter edition is recommended for the historian.

Some of his friends or adversaries, in the republican camp, no doubt had a slightly different point of view. Edgar Quinet, who was less dramatic and more analytical, definitely took a more pessimistic stance on the subject of the 'religious' failure of the French Revolution. Both, however, were in agreement with the future founders of the Third Republic in blaming the useless excesses of the Reign of Terror. On the other hand, Louis Blanc, a socialist and an admirer of Robespierre, took the opposite view. In spite of such divergence in individual opinion the fundamental presupposition of the whole historiographical movement of the nineteenth century, liberal then republican, remains an apology for a French Revolution that liberated individuals and the nation and founded modernity. The richness of this intellectual movement was to prove considerable in so far as the new political regime, definitively established in France from the 1880s, proclaimed itself to be both its heir and servant (Quinet 1866).

With this we touch upon the second factor which helps to explain the position of Georges Lefebvre. The end of the nineteenth century, during which time he had perfected his craft, witnessed a triumph for the Republic: new critical, objective methods allowed historical science to show that it could be justified. Alphonse Aulard symbolizes the change in atmosphere. While his work as a historian is significant, it is less important than his influence as a teacher, organizer or editor. At the same time that, thanks to him, the French Revolution was becoming less a complex series of dramatic events than the progressive assertion of democratic ideas, doctoral theses, review articles and other vast projects begun at his initiative ended in making the split with the *ancien régime* the threshold of the beginning of contemporary France. France's republican certainties, from this point onwards, were established.[3]

Following a century of controversies, this new beginning finally gave rise to an atmosphere of respectability, symbolized by university chairs at the Sorbonne and elsewhere, and by teachers' textbooks at primary, secondary and higher-education levels due to the initiative of Ernest Lavisse and his peers. From then on, the official history of the French Revolution took on the appearance of objective, scientific research that was none the less in the hands of the political regime whose ideology it legitimized. Georges Lefebvre was at first but a modest servant to this official version of the French Revolution. Above him, Albert Mathiez, exceptionally brilliant and pugnacious, was the brightest star of this new chapter in the historiography of the French Revolution. Initially passionate, as was Aulard, about the political and religious aspects of the French Revolution, the ideas of Mathiez developed, in parallel with those of other French intellectuals of his time, from the sort of liberalism familiar in the days of radicalism, to socialism along the lines of the current Left bloc. Despite the fact that it was his cult of Robespierre which enabled him to demonstrate this development, the focus of attention was his concept of the popularization of the French Revolution. This popularization was

---

3   Aulard 1901. This text, even more 'dated' than the two preceding ones, was not, as they were, republished for the bicentenary.

central to his lively overview, which depicted the events from 1789 to 9 Thermidor [the time of Robespierre's fall in July 1794] and in which the keynotes were revolutionary determinism and the apologia of Jacobinism. After 1930, Mathiez's account of the French Revolution began to assume the status of a sort of vulgate for those who approached the subject with sympathy. Quick to distrust Russian communism, Albert Mathiez had none the less seen to it that his readers (such as Romain Rolland or André Malraux, Jean-Paul Sartre or the Progressive Christians) were primed to identify, in the French Revolution, the starting-point, albeit interrupted, of a movement that others still desired to imitate.

Even more than Mathiez, Georges Lefebvre was finally influenced by a third historiographic source, namely the *Histoire socialiste de la Révolution française* (Socialist History of the French Revolution) by Jean Jaurès which was published at the beginning of the century and which Mathiez had reissued. Although an amateur, Jaurès was an extraordinary intellectual. Perfectly fitting in with trends in opinion that were currently so popular with the French Left, his work effectively synthesized the views of the Marxist analysts, the democratic traditions in the manner of Michelet, and the transfiguration of the revolutionaries in the manner of Plutarch. This fine orator and socialist philosopher provided Aulard's pupils with new intellectual material. These preoccupations of Jaurès increasingly extended abroad to foreign historians, Russians in particular, who placed the situation, the destiny and intervention of the masses, at the forefront of their studies.

With Jaurès, the peasantry truly played a vital role in the French Revolution as did the organization and conveyance of property, and social and economic development in general. Political history is not so much forgotten as replaced in this general context. As a faithful pupil of Marx and his *Manifesto*, the author of this *History* is revealed, moreover, as a great admirer of the French bourgeoisie at the end of the eighteenth century. On the model of Barnave, Jaurès attributes the revolutionary action to the general progress of capitalism of that time and in doing so shows himself to be far less 'miserabilist' than Michelet in his *Révolution française*.

Jaurès was naturally more sensitive than Michelet to the phenomenon of class struggle, which further complicated an already complex historical picture. Jaurès does, however, fall in with the romantic and liberal tradition in viewing the class struggle from an optimistic angle. This explains his regret when confronted with terrorist acts which took place during the French Revolution, and his attempts to minimize and excuse them. But above all it explains his preoccupation with celebrating the conquering optimism of the revolutionary bourgeoisie (so as to heighten the contrast with the cold egoism of its heirs), and his belief that by a process of historical continuity, the proletariat of the twentieth century would logically complete, through the next socialist revolution, the work begun in 1789 (Jaurès 1968–73).

Thus we have observed a doctrinal credo, more or less implicit, which dominated the Left's historiography of the French Revolution, before or after 1914 or 1945, and which only began to lose its stature little by little from the 1960s. This is not to suggest that this point of view was the only one that was presented to the public. Commentators from overseas have always had a tendency to overestimate the reputation – notably at the current time – of academic or 'republican' authors involved in the internal debate on the French Revolution. On the contrary, the Counter-Revolution victorious in 1814–15, 1851 and 1871, inspired constantly both works and a trend that were hostile to the inspiration, characteristics and consequences of the French Revolution.

This monarchist and Catholic tradition did not limit its ambitions to producing volumes of political or religious writings. Instead, it sustained a voice that was both remarkably informed and resiliently anti-terrorist. Beyond clericalism or even positivism, it led, at the very beginning of the Third Republic, to Taine's synthesis. Although his pessimism probably condemned alike the *ancien régime* and the French Revolution, his pamphleteer's gifts and his sense of the present tragedy in history enabled him to relate events from the decade beginning in 1789 to the absurd triumph of anarchy; then to the bloody dictatorship of the revolutionary militants over their frightened compatriots. By finishing with Napoleonic centralization, Taine showed that this nightmare in history had, moreover, prevented France, unlike England, from taking the path to true liberalism.

Nietzsche admired Taine as much as he admired Burckhardt. Censured by the Sorbonne, who rightly reproached him, for example with Seignobos, for having ignored, at least from 1792, the significance of external circumstances, the author of *Les Origines de la France contemporaine* (The Origins of Contemporary France) had none the less produced the secret Bible of conservative opinion covering the Third Republic. The work had a double posterity which turned on the *Action française*, a French nationalist and royalist group founded in the late nineteenth century, whose intellectual influence at the end of this political regime was profound (Taine 1986).

Beside Jacques Bainville, Pierre Gaxotte, from the 1920s, offered a commentary on the history of the French Revolution which was not only very well written and academic, but was also powerful in tone. If the French Revolution remained, in his opinion, the bloody and absurd farce that Taine had described, the French Right now reproached him, after 1917, of having initiated a 'communist' experience. They objected to the portrayal of a marvellous *ancien régime* the foolish destruction of which was nothing short of a historical catastrophe. Enriched now by a realist analysis of eighteenth-century France, the destruction of the *ancien régime* was to become the subject of much historical debate (Gaxotte 1988).

This was equally the case with the original opinions of Augustin Cochin, who was a disciple of Taine, opposed Aulard and corresponded with Mathiez. For he believed that responsibility during the political and intellectual crisis, which began at the end of the *ancien régime* and continued with the destruction of the monarchy and the advent of the Jacobin Republic, lay with intellectual societies. This was not so much a question of reconstructing Barrvel's thesis on the masonic origins of the French Revolution as a sociological interpretation of the mechanisms of the conquest of militant opinion, then of bureaucratic power, between 1789 and 1794, by the 'revolutionary' party (Cochin 1979).

Brutally interrupted by his death during the First World War, Cochin's influence was real but limited. The popularization of academic history, thanks to the authors linked with the *Action française*, was, on the other hand, considerable. Their readership comprised large sectors of the so-called cultivated public whereas Mathiez only had left-wing militants and other secular teachers. Republican textbooks were outweighed by the Right's best-sellers which certainly reflected better (by the significance of their print-runs between the two World Wars) Catholic opinion of the French Revolution than, for example, the effort made by the Christian Democrats who sought to reconcile it with their Church's traditions. This conflict was not finalized until after 1945 with the publication of André Latreille's impressive work (Latreille 1946–50).

The work of Georges Lefebvre, then, has to be seen in the wake of this legacy and these conflicts. An original disciple of Jaurès, he had taught for a long time in a secondary school and had begun to work on farming communities in northern France during the Revolution. Lefebvre was very interested in the study of mentalities, and he collected late on in life, from the 1920s onwards, specific studies (on the Great Fear, the Thermidorians, the Directory, and so on) and acquired large works (on Napoleon, first of all, then on the French Revolution itself). Lefebvre presented French academia and the international scholarly world with a classic interpretation of the French Revolution in which, in Marxist theory, it had naturally arisen from that development which immediately preceded it within economic infrastructures. The evolution of capitalism had thus undermined, in France, feudal relations and created the bourgeoisie's political and social power. At the very most, Georges Lefebvre added to this thesis the recent views of Ernest Labrousse (1933) relating to the disastrous effects of the economic crisis which hit the kingdom of Louis XVI from the 1770s.

However, Lefebvre's great history of the French Revolution, consistent with his initial research, insisted on the multiplicity of forms in which the French Revolution had manifested itself. Notable in his account was the large part he attributed to the originality and relative autonomy of the peasant revolts of 1789 and the following years. As for the rest, however, Georges Lefebvre described the French Revolution, from the end of the *ancien régime* to the Reign of Terror, as a series of logical links whose progressive radicalization ensued essentially from the mechanisms of class struggle.

Thus Lefebvre attributed the origin of the political events of the revolutionary decade to internal divisions within the bourgeoisie and to the different relations that various sections of the bourgeoisie held with the working classes. He linked this to his conclusion which was relatively pessimistic since the proclamation of the rights of man had ended in the Thermidorian reaction, then, in accordance with bourgeois fears and egoism, in Napoleonic dictatorship.

The Napoleonic dictatorship, which was like the French Revolution as a whole essentially centralizing (because unitarian and egalitarian with regard to the law), none the less has a long-term place in France's social and political history. Tocqueville had asserted this from 1856 and Lefebvre, who had also considered it, like Tocqueville, united a sense of revolutionary split with that of institutional and mental continuities. Lefebvre's keen interest in military and diplomatic history meant he was familiar with the work of Albert Sorel who had rightly insisted, at the end of the nineteenth century, on the influence of the *ancien régime*'s foreign policy on that of the French Revolution (de Tocqueville 1952–3; Sorel 1885–1901).

A resolute apologist for the global benefits of the French Revolution, Georges Lefebvre was no less sensitive to its contradictions or terrorist perversions, even if he did not highlight all of them for the reader's attention. Like Jaurès, he read the French Revolution first of all, and fundamentally, as a seizure of power by an enlightened bourgeoisie, who in doing so produced the crowning point in French history. Through revolutionary violence the bourgeoisie had got rid of a monarchist state (which had shown itself to be incapable of adapting to their reasonable demands) and an archaic nobility (which had become anachronistic in the wake of historical progress). The bourgeoisie had achieved this by employing, in a limited and self-interested way, the blind upsurge of working-class forces to which the future belonged.

This concept of the history of the French Revolution was dominated by the idea of a progressive *embourgeoisement*, at both the top and bottom ends, of political, cultural and social development in France. Other trends that were present in the development of history of that time – the intervention of working-class forces, the upholding of the economic importance of the aristocracy, the power of Catholic-inspired ideological conservatism – were hardly given their due by historians of this camp. By merely implicitly reproaching the revolutionary bourgeoisie for its narrow-mindedness and class egoism, Georges Lefebvre, in the tradition of Jaurés and Mathiez, interpreted the decade which began in 1789 – and the events which he recounted in his apologetic history – as a significant preparation. This preparation was for the subsequent reign of an equality of a more fundamental nature and towards which, since the end of the nineteenth century, the most advanced of French republicans worked. In an overview written on the basis of his own research and that of Lefebvre, Ernest Labrousse (1953), a committed militant socialist, celebrated Year Two of the French Revolution as an epoch which was probably 'ephemeral' but certainly 'prophetic'.

The assumption that there is historical continuity between the sequence of events in France during the period 1789–94 and that which began in Russia in 1917 does indeed dominate this apparently objective historical science. Proponents of this theory have contributed considerably to the various unforeseen turn of events of the French Left during the first half of the twentieth century: hopes that sprang from the era of coalition of left-wing parties or the Popular Front; disappointments engendered by the First World War or the Germano-Soviet pact. But, after the Liberation of France in 1944 and the accession of the Communist Party to the highest rank in the French Left where they enjoyed power for more than one-third of a century, once again everything seemed clearer. The thread which had been interrupted in 1794, and which nothing since had succeeded in renewing, was again about to be renewed. For many young historians who, attracted by the Soviet model, had opted to study the history of the French Revolution, their mentor Albert Soboul soon symbolically succeeded Georges Lefebvre as leader.

Published in 1958, his broad thesis on the social and political movement of the Parisian *sansculottes* of Year Two of the French Revolution is by no means a testimony to ideological conformism. If the writer has no difficulty in showing the superficiality of Daniel Guérin's reconstructions (he had taken pains to paint, in the Paris of 1793, a class struggle between the manual workers and the revolutionary bourgeoisie, taking all political persuasions together), Albert Soboul's work is above all valued for its fine and sensitive portrait of revolutionary militancy in the Paris of those days. His *sansculottes* are first and foremost the *petits-bourgeois*, independent producers whose horizons did not stretch beyond that of their own shop or workshop. The vicissitudes of '*Hébertisme*' (the leftist wing of the Parisian revolutionary movement in 1793–4) which the *sansculottes* were to experience pointed up for Soboul the deep political incompatibility that then existed between the working-class movement and the revolutionary government who, despite having been endorsed by the *sansculottes*, were quick to abandon them. Their fall, in this respect, contributed to a general process of bureaucratization of the Jacobin Revolution (Soboul 1973).

Albert Soboul's activity as a more popular writer took him into the domain of social or 'cultural' history; these works were perhaps less prolific. His works on general history did not add significantly to the views of Georges Lefebvre. In his last work, an idiosyncratic trilogy written in the 1970s, Soboul depicted again in the French Revolution the inevitable political outcome of the events that had taken place in eighteenth-century France. The class struggle alone, which he presented mechanically in this work, explains the French Revolution as it accounts for the different stages of the revolutionary movement or its Napoleonic setting. Although a well-informed piece of national bibliography, this partisan representation had neither the nuance nor the open-mindedness which were typical of research going on at that time outside France. This research was already of a stimulating nature and being conducted on a large scale.

Albert Soboul was unfortunate in that the official part of his career coincided with the progressive collapse of the ideological universe to which he was attached. No doubt this development was only fully appreciated posthumously, during the 1980s, when both the Communist party's hold on the Left and the methodological respectability specific to Marxism were gradually disappearing. An entire generation of historians, influenced by these two factors, and for obvious reasons attracted towards the French Revolution, were hard hit by these changes. The death of Soboul, and of the doctrinal world and scientific milieu which had affected him, left this generation abandoned in the middle of the academic world (university departments, research centres, journals and so on), and of other notable activities that it had inspired. At the time when political hope, which had justified this intellectual investment, gradually began to disappear, it became even more necessary to confront the formidable academic challenge which originated from both overseas and within France (Soboul 1970–83).

Indeed history is first indebted here to the English historian Alfred Cobban for his conclusive analysis of the dominant pattern of interpretation of the French Revolution. This was based on the works of Georges Lefebvre and was extremely influential right up to the 1970s. Alfred Cobban's findings were made known in 1954 and published the following year in his famous *Myth*, the title of which at once attracted Lefebvre who died soon afterwards. The English historian's contribution to the historiographical debate was not immediately given its due merit for the importance of Cobban's work was overshadowed by another quarrel with which academics were more preoccupied during the Cold War period.

The important American historian Robert Palmer and his colleague from Toulouse, Jacques Godechot, had insisted, at this time, on the common character of the serious ideological, political and social weakening which affected the American and European continents in the last third of the eighteenth century. These two historians asked whether this period had not witnessed a vast Atlantic revolution taking place, marked by, in particular, a confrontation between the bourgeoisie and the aristocracy, and implicating traditional monarchies and oligarchies. This view, which was the inspiration for vast and impressive overviews, was opposed, by Marxist historians or those influenced by them, as a historiographical variant of the Atlantic Charter. The views of Palmer and Godechot, however, probably do not merit such a prestigious interpretation. Their work, as evinced by volume two of Palmer's book or Godechot's entire output (before or since that time), have barely added anything to Lefebvre's interpretations. Content to remain where Lefebvre or Jaurès had left off, they integrated the phenomenon of the revolutionary decade into the general development of the West at the end of the eighteenth century. In doing so they were less influenced by French short-sightedness which had preoccupied critics from Michelet to Soboul. After Palmer (1964) and Godechot (1965), Hobsbawm (1969) and Venturi (1971) did likewise. One can hardly accuse these authors of being revisionist.

The same cannot be said of the critic Alfred Cobban, whose work quickly brought him to the fore in the 1960s. His studies and larger works soon transformed his London seminars into a laboratory for new ideas on the subject of the 1789 French Revolution. The considerable number of pupils trained in this school and under Cobban's influence were soon to contribute to an, as yet, unpublished interpretation of the 1789 French Revolution. With the advantage of a precise knowledge of French sources and strong in that they were without innate French prejudice, their work marks, at the same time, the emancipation of foreign historiography from French models and the affirmation of a typically Anglo-Saxon hypercriticism which was no less sparing of its own heritage. From Macaulay to Hill, liberal or Marxist readings of seventeenth-century English revolutions were subjected to as rigorous a reinterpretation as were their Gallic counterparts.

Cobban above all reproached Lefebvre for a sociological analysis which was wrongly simplistic and reductive in its approach to the events which led to 1789. He could not discern, in the lawyers who served to illustrate his analysis, the emergence of a bourgeoisie merchant and industrial, anti-feudal and capitalist. Even more sensitive to the regional and social diversity of revolutionary phenomena than the French critics he refuted, Cobban believed study should be conducted without recourse to anachronistic conceptualizations and vocabularies. He asked that the French Revolution be examined in its authentic historical context to reveal the role of the micro-conflict and the weight of local traditions which were sometimes very old. At each stage in the French Revolution the London historian considered the split between town and country to be its single most important factor. He was critical of traditional views for having reproduced the language and justifications of actors rather than replacing these representations with concrete and complex conditions which would have been genuine. Obsessed by a need to glorify or abominate the fundamental events that brought about the French Revolution, contemporary French commentators had transformed it. They had read into the French Revolution what they wanted it to reflect, whether that be an Assumption, an Annunciation or an Apocalypse. They refused to see elements that were banal, everyday and derisory and which were present on a very large scale. Obsessed by either enthusiasm or disgust, they had singled out the forces behind the movement, choosing to forget the importance of resistance that was made to it. To illustrate his points, Cobban drew on his knowledge of a nineteenth-century France in which he could find no trace of the beginning of a decisive transformation at the economic, social or cultural levels. He therefore concluded there had only been a 'revolution' in the areas of the law and political life.[4]

Accused of supporting the contrary view, Lefebvre, in fact, had himself been very sensitive to the phenomena of continuity which were still evident in France in 1789. In this he followed, and surpassed, de Tocqueville. Lefebvre, with his extensive knowledge of the documents and many local or regional studies which had been produced since the end of the nineteenth century, knew only too well that the Revolution of liberty, equality and fraternity had been more of a promise than a realization and that the rupture and rebirth which it sang contained, in fact, much that was old. Lefebvre also defended himself with humour against Cobban who accused him of clinging on to outdated myths. This serenity not only stemmed from the detachment that comes with age, or the light irony that a French person of distinction delights in using when he encounters someone from Britain. The truth of the matter was that Georges Lefebvre was well aware that the London historian's work was based on incontestable realities already brought to light by numerous national works of research, from both Right and Left. Above all he knew that one could never better criticize the predominant interpretation of the French Revolution than by departing from one's own analyses relating to the agrarian, bourgeois, noble or mental continuity of France. Had Cobban, in fact, done anything beyond that?

---

4 Cobban 1984. With this edition, Cobban's views could finally be directly accessed by the French public.

His fertility, at any rate, has been remarkable thanks to his influence (from the end of the 1960s up to today) on a group of historians mainly British but also Canadian, Australian and increasingly American. Without entirely renewing the subject, their grasp of the concrete and regional diversity replaced the reigning historiography (which depicted revolutionary France as a nation in which everyone drew his or her identity from a national model) with the geopolitics of the division of land. They drew on a multitude of regional or local socio-political developments, sometimes contradicting national phenomena. This realist vision, where the monolithic abundance of minutely detailed prosopography supplanted the colourful cult of heroes and great men, granted less space to ideological justifications and more to the complex motivations of individuals and groups. The new historians' interpretations responded less to the logical links involved in the radicalization of the revolutionary period than to the mass of contradictions with which the French Revolution was riddled. Having carefully considered the time factor, they associated the specifics of 1789 as much with chance as with the weight of determining factors. They eschewed dogmas, social or political theories, preferring instead concrete analysis; they did not subscribe to the long-standing belief that the French Revolution was inevitable nor did they accept its imaginary unity.

Combining numerous individual works of research, often of French origin, two significant Anglo-Saxon works, published in the 1980s, symbolize the new interpretations of the French Revolution. Drawing on his knowledge of the institutions of the *ancien régime*, William Doyle's (1980) interpretation of the origins of the French Revolution broke with the mechanistic determinism which was still dear to Jaurès or Mathiez, Lefebvre or Soboul. An accidental political rupture for Doyle, the events of 1789 were not rooted in earlier cultural, social or economic developments, which were still rich in other potential outcomes. Like Taine in his disapproval of a monarchy in decline, Doyle shows that the monarchy's responsibility stemmed above all from its abdication which left a socio-political void to be filled by a new elite. The new elite's irruption to head the state was not so much prepared in advance over a long period of time as sudden and unexpected. According to the analyses of Taylor (1967) or Lucas (1973), this bourgeoisie (which was not rooted in an important capitalist development and whose advancement did not match the wishes of a country that had remained deeply conservative) were not so much the catalyst to revolutionary outburst as a by-product of it. Surprising for everyone, the Revolution was rationalized, justified and legitimized afterwards by those who had triumphed. Historians influenced by this interpretation took up the theme.

The context of the revolutionary event itself resembles much less the familiar majestic succession of the liberal upper middle class to the Jacobin lower middle class, and then to the Thermidorian reaction, than the authentic and relentless conflicts which took place at every level. The progressive aggravation behind the radicalization of the French Revolution is explained by these conflicts: farmers angered by inadequate land reform; taxpayers dissatisfied by tax reform; Catholics protesting against irresponsible ecclesiastical reform. The inability to run a 'normal' constitutional regime was soon compounded by a foreign war triggered by domestic overblown promises but which ended none the less by spreading, in revolutionary France, the spirit and reality of civil war. The power from then on belonged, right up to the era of Napoleon, to a small group of militants and profiteers, fiercely determined above all else to maintain their position even if it meant becoming bitterly divided over how to achieve that end. This led to constant instability which was reflected in the improvised proclamation of the French Republic; the blind leap into the black hole of the Reign of Terror; opposition, under the Directory, between the official and the real state of the country; the frightened flight to safety in Bonapartist dictatorship. Donald Sutherland, originally specializing in the inconsistencies of counter-revolutionary France in the West, offers the best overall picture of the historic development between 1789 and 1799 (Sutherland 1985). To begin with, the scene is dominated by the uncertainty of the leaders and the gradual swelling of the anti-revolutionary movement. Far from being the privileged field from which contemporary political ideas ensued, the French Revolution in the first place was a blood-soaked theatre of institutional chaos and economic, if not cultural, regression.

Older than the proponents of this interpretation, another historian of British origin, Richard Cobb, did not refute it in a work that was long considered as on the fringe of the dominant French school (Cobb 1970). Cobb's experience provided him with a knowledge of the sources of the French Revolution that was both first-hand and surprisingly internalized. His work focused on working-class mentalities, the obscure fate of militants, the deep motivations of the masses already examined by Lefebvre or Rudé (1959), but he was less convinced than Soboul about the vast political mechanisms of the elite and illustrated, even more clearly than Mathiez, the socio-economic continuity between the people of the French Revolution and those of the *ancien régime*. The great players of the French Revolution which dominate his work are no longer the Rights of Man or the Republic but hunger and misery. Agnostic and realist, this interpretation (the work of probably in 1995 the greatest living historian of the French Revolution, and one who so impressively understood Georges Lefebvre's status) relates less to dominant French historiography, which had at first welcomed him as a fellow-historian, than to two other schools of thought. These were the traditions of Counter-Revolution, to which Cobb greatly contributed, and that of his compatriots and successors, for whom he has been something of a patriarch.

The myth of the French Revolution was first destroyed, therefore, outside France, mainly as a result of the impetus given by Cobban. The historiographical and ideological debate in France which took place in the period 1960–80 also contributed but in a manner that might be considered less profound and professional. François Furet typifies this group, which is much more concerned with representing and interpreting events and the intellectual motivations of the actors than with their concrete actions, especially where they are not intellectual men. This is clearly a type of historian very different from the majority of those who comprised the Anglo-Saxon school.

When Furet began his work on the subject in the mid-1960s, it was in the form of an overview written in collaboration with Denis Richet (Furet and Richet 1973).

These two former Communists were none the less apprehensive about abandoning the impressive global picture that Georges Lefebvre had passed on. If they had little difficulty in presenting it to the public in a more original way than Soboul, they none the less could not break from Lefebvre's substantive interpretation of the origins and unfolding of the French Revolution. In some chapters, written generally by Richet, they insist only on the fertility of the Thermidorian era or cautiously present the hypothesis of two revolutions, the second, the Jacobin, having succeeded the first, liberal revolution, in accordance with a loss of control, which could have been better contained if not avoided altogether.

However, in an atmosphere of great excitement when France was marching towards 'victory for the Left', and where the Communist Party continued to give universal lessons and carefully cultivate its intellectual territories, Furet and his colleague were accused of excessive iconoclasm. Between the end of the 1970s and the early 1980s, precisely at the time when the French Left was triumphing, and at the same time its traditional view of the world was beginning to disintegrate, the historian of *Annales* launched a frontal attack against the interpretation of the French Revolution to which the Left had been so closely linked since the second half of the nineteenth century (Furet 1978).

This lively calling into question of the pro-Jacobin catechism was more noted for its polemic or stylistic successes than for anything of substance in the interpretative outline proposed in place of the one it undermined. Although he had contributed to the relative popularization, among French historians, of the works of Anglo-Saxon historians specializing in the French Revolution, Furet did not share their preference for first-hand study of archive sources. To justify his main preoccupations (opposition between the elite that existed prior to the French Revolution and that which was created by the events that followed 1789; analysis of the loss of control; condemnation of the terrorist aberration) he focused on de Tocqueville and even, more curiously, on Cochin.

From this perspective, the linking of events from the period prior to the French Revolution to 9 Thermidor would owe less to the interplay of external circumstances (political, institutional and financial crises, social and economic difficulties, confrontation between political parties and their interests, counter-revolution of the people and its consequences, foreign war and its consequences), than to the development of all the implications contained in the speech which are proper to intellectual societies. This curious echo of Taine, the final metamorphosis of a structuralism which was at that time dying away, no doubt contributed to the fascination of historians of the twentieth century by the language and its virtues. Furet's work is also in keeping with a long-term tradition of ideological interpretations. But in reading his work it is difficult to understand how, at the fall of Robespierre, we switch all of a sudden from Cochin's influence to that of de Tocqueville.[5]

---

5 Colin Lucas drew attention to this point at the opening of a seminar dedicated to the memory of Robespierre, in Arras, in April 1993 given by the Université Charles de Gaulle de Lille.

In the hands of Furet and his colleagues the tendency to single out the history of political ideologies in the development and analysis of the era of the French Revolution was increased during the 1980s. At the time of the bicentenary this worried Denis Richet who, shortly before his death, sought to distance himself from it because it had transformed the French Revolution and its preparations into a kind of course in constitutional law unfortunately interrupted by periods of upheaval. This failing, which found authority among Anglo-Saxon writers such as John Pocock, was in addition reinforced by the distinguished research of Keith Baker from Chicago (Pocock 1985).

In 1989 the *Dictionnaire historique et critique de la Révolution française* (Critical and Historical Dictionary of the French Revolution), edited by François Furet and Mona Ozouf, was published in France for a domestic readership but in fact created a considerable international stir. The *Dictionnaire* embodies, for those French specialists of the French Revolution who separated from it, the dominant opposition to the 'authorized' version, derived from Georges Lefebvre and Albert Soboul. Written in the scattering style that is now dear to French historiography, under the leadership of Pierre Nora, these disorganized points of view present a fragmented picture of the French Revolution where its actors are closer to what Taine had said than to what Mathiez had thought; where theories are more valued than facts, ideas and interpretations more than actual events and documents. It is not difficult to see why this 'outrageous' work provoked the virtuous indignation expressed by Palmer's committed heirs in the *American Historical Review*.

Even so, the United States were, in turn, influenced by revisionist repercussions. The successful sales of *Citizens* (1989) by the eminent historian Simon Schama symbolized this calling into question of earlier Marxist and liberal overviews of the French Revolution. *Citizens*, which is a work of humour, has the distinction of focusing attention on the tragic, often absurd, cataclysm, in which, since Aulard, the French Left had seen only beauty and order. These myths were being gradually abandoned at the same time as the real-life politics of the Left were collapsing so that the horrific republican events of La Vendée or the harrowing futility of the Reign of Terror could now be looked at in a realistic light.

The bicentenary of 1789 could not, therefore, resemble its centenary. Curiously subsidized (apart from the French government) by the plutocrat Robert Maxwell, for whom it was to be a swan-song, its chief merit as far as international academia is concerned was the publication of three majestic volumes dedicated to the correlations between the French Revolution and sources of modern political culture. Successfully combining diverse French opinion (whether revisionist or those more traditional in interpretation) and excellent Anglo-Saxon analyses (derived from Cobban or close to Baker), this book was testimony to the new tendencies already published in Furet's *Dictionnaire*: giving primacy to the long-term tradition of ideological interpretations; giving up the notion of an apocalyptic rupture that prepared an outstanding future; insisting on cultural continuity heralding, through the French Revolution, a de Tocqueville-type of democratic society (Baker and Lucas 1987–9).

Anglo-Saxon or French, the most eminent contemporary historians, whether Roger Chartier (1991) or Robert Darnton, are responding more and more to these themes and less and less to the old ones: class struggle; confrontation between parties and individuals; significance of circumstances; and so on. Just as their liberal or Marxist precursors did when they referred to the progress of the Enlightenment or to economic determinism, they readily amalgamate the political, institutional or legal changes which took place from 1789 onwards into some kind of logical outcome of a great cultural displacement which supposedly preceded and accompanied them. Such a view, more clever than original, hardly explains the French exception, the phenomena of rupture or reaction which marked it or its Napoleonic outcome.

Concrete studies, derived from Alfred Cobban or Richard Cobb, who were distinguished within the Anglo-Saxon school as specialists of the French Revolution, had more success. Michel Vovelle, Albert Soboul's heir at the Sorbonne, has gradually reached such a conclusion. Eccentric Communist, this great historian of mentalities had moved, together with his first wife, from an analysis of the de-Christianization of the French Revolution to an analysis of the evolution of long-standing religious beliefs. Like Maurice Aguihon, he thus painted in the Provence of the second half of the eighteenth century the elements of a process of secularization and laicization of consciousness and behaviour (Vovelle 1978). Returning to the study of the French Revolution, he naturally singled out in the first place the evolution of mentalities. However, political and academic circumstances made him scholarly patron of the bicentenary and saviour of the intellectual reputation of the traditional interpretation of the French Revolution. He was capable of integrating this interpretation more and more with both the political inventiveness of the Revolution and the uncanny fragmentation of the national landscape which the French Revolution had caused. Published at the end of 1992, his last book presents the geopolitics of the events of the French Revolution and its immediate consequences which lead one to think more of Siegfried than Aulard. Jaurès and Mathiez would scarcely recognize this picture of the people's France often overwhelmingly counter-revolutionary. Diametrically opposed to the ideological interpretations dear to Furet, this representation of socio-political realities owes a great deal to Anglo-Saxon research, and at the same time to scientific scholarship conducted in France. This scholarship, while taking into account the importance of local sources, does so today with far less ideological prejudice (Vovelle 1992).

To get at the true revisionism of the French Revolution one has to look not so much to Cochin or de Tocqueville as to the archives. The archives were thoroughly re-examined – which was the bicentenary's chief merit – at the countless seminars and conferences held at the end of the 1980s. The main precepts of Anglo-Saxon works of the previous twenty years were confirmed: the great extent of regional diversity in the phenomena of the French Revolution and the importance of local resistance. The west of France was a theatre of choice of these contradictions and conflicts: Roger Dupuy for the Chouans and Jean-Clément Martin (1987) for La Vendée have notably illustrated this for us.

Georges Lefebvre had never been a total stranger to what lay behind these new trends. Everything has happened then, from the beginning of the 1990s, as if, along with the intoxications of cultural and ideological history and reactionary recriminations, a new overview is developing which is capable of preserving the best of traditional precepts while allowing for necessary revisions. We know only too well what the revisions entail.

The French Revolution was not born uniquely out of the material and cultural development of the preceding epoch. A political transformation, the French Revolution appeared to the people of that time as the conquest of power by individuals essentially new to such a level of responsibility. The bitter rifts among their groups were not solely due to personal or ideological rivalries. These also stemmed from their reactions, often irrational, to the tremendous resistance met (in a France that was extremely diverse, particularly with regard to the heavy influence of traditional religiosity) by the phenomena associated with the French Revolution. Thus recent historians, all too aware of the traditional interpretation which insists on the dynamism of those who led the movement of 1789, such as the American Lynn Hunt (specialist in politics and culture) and the British P. M. Jones (specialist in agrarian problems), paint a French Revolution which no longer resembles in any way that of Mathiez: authority is endlessly fragmented and the balance between positive and negative aspects is considerably modified. Born of an opinion falsely unanimous and apparently dominant, the French Revolution has often ended up accumulating contradictions; produced by unprecedented hope, it passed on in turn weariness and disappointment (Hunt 1984; Jones 1985).

As might be expected, our epoch in particular has replaced the old historical vision of the French Revolution with one that is more complex, therefore made commonplace and demythologized. If the French Revolution continues to be an important source of modern political culture, it no longer functions, after the demise of communism, as a fundamental myth. In France, Bastille Day is now less celebrated and the French are more interested in the event that followed 14 July 1790: the split six months later in January 1791 when half of France through the intermediary of its priests refused the civil Constitution of the clergy. Timothy Tackett (1986) fully appreciated the significance of this revelation which illustrates for his readership's benefit the depth of the ruptures that the French Revolution was destined to confront.

Our predecessors described the French Revolution notably as the profound unity of a movement of collective liberation. Since that interpretation we have come to decipher above all the immense social and mental diversity which arose from the multi-faceted phenomena of individual regions. Far distant from those historians who summed up the French Revolution in narrow terms, the most extensive research into the subject reveals contradictions to be found in all individuals and groups in real-life situations. Echoing the psychological development of the last decades, the current historiography of the French Revolution sets little store by over-generalized explanations, whether these relate to its origins, unfolding or consequences. On the contrary, historiographers today are increasingly at pains to interpret the interactive systems which produced, in a context of the utmost complexity, the mechanisms distinctive to the epoch of the French Revolution.[6]

REFERENCES

Aulard, A. (1901) *Histoire politique de la révolution française*, Paris.
Baker, K. M. (1981) 'Enlightenment and Revolution', *Journal of Modern History*: 297ff.
Baker, K. and Lucas, C. (eds) (1987–90) *The French Revolution and the Creation of Modern Political Culture*, 3 vols, London.
Chartier, R. (1991) *Les Origines culturelles de la révolution française*, Paris.
Cobb, R. (1970) *The Police and the People: French Popular Protest, 1789–1820*, Oxford.
Cobban, A. (1955) *The Myth of the French Revolution*, London.
—— (1984) *Le Sens de la révolution française*, Paris.
Cochin, G. (1979) *De l'esprit du jacobinisme: une interprétation sociologique de la Révolution Française*, Paris.
Darnton, R. (1968) *Mesmerism and the End of Enlightenment in France*, Cambridge.
Doyle, W. (1980) *Origins of the French Revolution*, Oxford.
Dupuy, R. (1988) *De la Révolution à la Chouannerie: Paysans en Bretagne 1788–1794*, Paris.
Furet, F. (1978) *Penser la Révolution Française*, Paris.
—— and Ozouf, M. (eds) (1989) *Dictionnaire critique de la Révolution Française*, Paris.
—— and Richet, D. (1973) *La Révolution Française*, Paris.
Gaxotte, P. (1988) *La Révolution française*, Paris.
Godechot, J. (1965) *Les Révolutions (1770–1799)*, Paris.
Hobsbawm, E. (1969) *L'Era des révolutions*, Paris.
Hunt, L. (1984) *Culture and Class in the French Revolution*, Berkeley.
Jaurès, J. (1968–73) *Histoire socialiste de la Révolution Française*, 7 vols, Paris.
Jones, P. M. (1985) *Politics and Rural Society: The Southern Massif Center: 1750–1880*, Cambridge.
—— (1996) *The French Revolution in Social and Political Perspective*, London.
Kaplan, S. L. (1993) *Adieu 1989*, Paris.
Labrousse, E. (1933) *Esquisse du mouvement des prix et des revenus en France au 18ième siècle*, 2 vols, Paris.
—— (1953) *Le XVIIIième siècle (1715–1815)*, Paris.
Lamartine, A. M. L. (1847) *Histoire des Girondins*, Paris.
Latreille, A. (1946–50) *L'Église catholique et la Révolution Française*, 2 vols, Paris.
Lefebvre, G. (1951) *La Révolution Française*, Paris.
Lucas, C. (1973) 'Nobles, bourgeois and the origins of the French Revolution', *Past and Present*: 46–73.
Martin, J. C. (1987) *La Vendée et la France*, Paris.
Mathiez, A. (1934–40) *La Révolution Française*, 3 vols, Paris.
Michelet, J. (1952) *Histoire de la Révolution Française*, 2 vols, Paris.
Palmer, R. (1964) *The Age of the Democratic Revolution*.

---

6 It is a pity that Steven L. Kaplan (1993) reduced the significance of the bicentenary to the anecdotal level by focusing on accounts of personal rivalries among French historians. Inspired on the whole by the same concern to arbitrate in favour of the 'Jacobin' tradition, the recent synthesis by Jones 1996, besides curious omissions (the influence of Jaurès, the importance of religious problems), claims, in a debatable manner, that a new orthodoxy, typically 'revisionist', would predominate today in the historiography of the French Revolution. On the contrary, that recent work of revision has replaced a dominant and justifying model by a plurality of interpretations more respectful of the variety of the realities.

Pocock, J. G. A. (1985) *Virtue, Commerce and History*, Cambridge.
Quinet, E. (1866) *La Révolution*, Paris.
Rudé, G. (1959) *The Crowd in the French Revolution*, Oxford.
Schama, S. (1989) *Citizens: A Chronicle of the French Revolution*, London.
Soboul, A. (1970–83) *La Civilisation et la Révolution Française*, 3 vols, Paris.
—— (1973) *Mouvement populaire et governement révolutionnaire de l'an II*, Paris.
Sorel, A. (1885–1901) *L'Europe et la Révolution Française*, 8 vols, Paris.
Sutherland, D. M. G. (1985) *France, 1789–1815: Revolution and Counter-Revolution*, London.
Tackett, T. (1986) *Religion, Revolution, and Regional Culture in Eighteenth-Century France: The Ecclesiastical Oath of 1791*, Princeton.
Taine, H. (1896) *Les Origines de la France contemporaine*, 2 vols, Paris.
Taylor, G. V. (1967) 'Non-capitalist wealth and the origins of the French Revolution', *American Historical Review*: 469–96.
Tocqueville, A. de (1952–3) *L'Ancien Régime et la Révolution*, 2 vols, Paris.
Venturi, F. (1971) *Europe des Lumières: recherches sur le XVIIIième siècle*, Paris.
Vovelle, M. (1978) *Piété baroque et déchristianisation en Provence au XVIIIième siècle*, Paris.
—— (1992) *L'Invention du politique: Géopolitique de la Révolution Francaise*, Paris.
Woloch, I. (1996) *The New Regime: Transformations of the French Civic Order, 1789–1820*, Norton.

20

THE SOVIET REVOLUTION

Catherine Merridale

There is no historical consensus about the Russian Revolution of 1917. Few events in modern history provide such a vivid picture of the relationship between contemporary political attitudes and the range of historical interpretation. Russia's history – which is stormy enough – is not the only issue at stake. Debates about socialism, economic development and the potential for an alternative to Western capitalism are all involved. The fate of the Soviet Union itself has influenced the historical perspective; its collapse in 1991 exacerbated a crisis in scholarship which had already been perceptible a decade earlier. This is a field whose development in the next ten years is likely to be controversial, unexpected and vigorous. In the following pages we shall examine the history of the debate and the most important points of controversy before discussing its prospects in the post-Soviet world.

The debate began while the February slush was still wet on the Petrograd demonstrators' boots (see e.g. Miliukov 1967 and Sukhanov 1955). Winners and losers of all kinds had their stories, as did observers of all nationalities and political persuasions. What they were all clear about was that the Russian Revolution would have implications for the rest of Europe, and possibly also for the future of the developed world.[1] In this assumption they were correct. The Russian Revolution did more than overturn one of the longest-established autocratic regimes in Europe. Russia became the country in which the nineteenth-century positivist hope that society could be perfected by enlightened human effort was put to the test. Eventually, too, it was to witness an attempt to accelerate economic 'modernization', the introduction of large-scale mechanized industry, without the human costs witnessed in other European countries.

These utopian pretensions have attracted fierce controversy. They have

---

1 'It has fallen to the Russian proletariat to have the great honour of beginning a series of revolutions', declared Lenin in February (*Polnoe sobranie sochinenie* (=*PSS*), vol. xxxi, p. 91). An opponent, Yu. V. Got'e, regretted in July that 'we are only fit to be manure for the peoples of higher culture' (1988: 28).

influenced assessments of the entire history of the USSR. The world-wide reaction to the fall of the Soviet communist regime indicates how closely linked its reputation has always been to that of the socialist ideal. For some commentators, the very idea of an explicit ideology informing politics has always been unacceptable; they condemn the Revolution outright for its flawed ambition.[2] But other assessments have been influenced by the subsequent history of the Soviet Union. These do not dismiss the whole project out of hand, but trace a direct line through 1917 to the evils of Stalinism and to Brezhnevite stagnation, attributing the continuities to a range of strategic political errors or to pathological flaws in Russian political culture.[3]

The result of this outlook has been a series of changing fashions in historical appraisal. The first reaction of most developed countries after 1917 was to reject the Bolshevik regime out of hand.[4] Hostility and suspicion remained the dominant responses throughout the 1920s. But by the 1930s, when most Western economies were in deep recession, it was also possible to admire the Soviet Union for its rapid economic growth and pretensions to full employment and a just social system.[5] Details of the privations involved in the collectivization of agriculture appeared only slowly, as did the reality behind the much-publicized show trials of 1936–8; all contributed to an unfavourable picture of the regime. The war hushed this criticism for a time. By 1942, when Russian troops were bearing the brunt of the Nazi military effort, British and American publications began to praise Stalin and his patriotic supporters in a language unthinkable five years before. The Cold War would change all this within three years, but even at the time of Stalin's death the man's reputation as a war hero and socialist pioneer exercised as strong a hold on many people's imaginations as did the allegations of his brutality. Depending on one's position in these controversies, the Russian Revolution could be seen as a dramatic act of popular liberation or the first in a series of disastrous steps to repression and social regimentation.

The horrors of collectivization and famine and the appalling excesses of Stalin's purges remain a stumbling-block for any historian writing about the revolutionary period. Conservative historians are correct to point out how rapidly they followed the Revolution, and how many continuities exist between Leninism and its murderous successor. No one seriously disputes that Stalin's was a brutal polity, its values distorted by suspicion and violence. The difficulty has been to transcend this judgement in order to arrive at a better understanding of the processes involved. Studies which fail to dwell on the horrors of Stalinism are too easily accused of

---

2 A recent example is provided by Pipes 1990: 132–3. For a Russian statement to the same effect, see Shcherbakh on Russian political culture (1987).

3 This is a theme pursued in the second volume of Robert Tucker's biography, *Stalin in Power. The Revolution from Above, 1928–1941* (1990).

4 As Lenin predicted, 'terrible clashes between the Soviet republic and the bourgeois states are inevitable', *PSS*, vol. xxiv, p. 122.

5 The most famous example is Webb and Webb 1935.

apologizing for it. The debate about the appropriate weight to be given to the 'moral' questions of Soviet history, which racked American historians of the early Soviet period in the 1970s and 1980s, has yet to be resolved.[6] Some of the most exciting new research complements the question of high politics and political manipulation by exploring political and social history 'from below'. As we shall see, historians of this school have raised vital questions about the origins and course of the Revolution, as well as developing a comparative sense of labour and revolutionary history in the twentieth century.[7] This school's ethos has rightly been described as 'libertarian' rather than pro-Leninist (see Acton 1991). But while the Cold War critics of Soviet communism remain locked in their belief that those who do not condemn the regime must be apologists for it,[8] the subtlety of the distinction will escape the average textbook reader. Indeed, the most widely marketed of the recent crop of textbooks on 1917 deliberately ignores the whole school, thereby depriving its readers of the fruits of the best recent research (Pipes 1990).

For historians outside the former Soviet Union, ideological considerations like these have complicated the study of 1917 and its aftermath. But until recently it was inside the Soviet Union that the problems were most severe. Official censorship and control of research funds compounded the difficulty – shared by Western scholars – of access to archival records. There was almost no contact between Soviet and Western specialists. From the late 1920s to the 1960s, little scholarly work on the modern period was possible in the USSR. The scope for original thinking was so narrow that serious historians often preferred to study medieval or ancient history, on which the ideological restrictions were more lax. A brief 'thaw' in the late 1950s and early 1960s saw the preparation of a number of more serious pieces of work, but the gradual resumption of censorship after 1964 meant that much of this material remained unpublished. With few exceptions, history-writing remained shackled to official formulae until the late 1980s.

The eclipse of the Communist Party changed all this in two or three years.[9] Since 1988, it has become possible for historians in Russia to question virtually every aspect of their revolutionary past, including Lenin's role and the viability of the tsarist system. Attention initially focused on the alternatives to Stalinism in the 1920s and 1930s. The Communist leadership encouraged historians to look again at such figures as Bukharin, Rykov and even Trotsky. A major national effort went

---

6 See, for example, the debate in *Russian Review*, 1986, vol. 45.

7 As Diane Keonker points out, this applies above all to social historians of the family and of urbanization; Keonker *et al.* 1989: 54.

8 An outrageous example of this kind of criticism appeared in the *Times Literary Supplement*'s commemoration of the seventy-fifth anniversary of the October Revolution. In the lead article, Richard Pipes wrote that 'revisionist' academic monographs, 'as unreadable as they were irrelevant to the understanding of the subject', were the fruit of a deliberate policy of academic manipulation by the Communist Party of the Soviet Union, the object of which was 'to have western historians accept the cardinal principle of Communist dogma, namely the legitimacy and inevitability of the October Revolution and the regime that issued from it.' *TLS*, 6 November 1992, p. 3.

9 One of the finest accounts of this 'mental revolution' is given by Davies 1989.

into commemorating the victims of the purges.[10] Scholarship was still used as a political tool. It was vital for the future of perestroika that the so called 'blank pages' of Russian history be filled in such a way as to rescue Soviet socialism from the stigma of its past.[11] At the same time, history enjoyed a period of genuine public prominence. For a year or so, controversies about the foundations and history of the Soviet system appeared on the front pages of popular newspapers and featured in television chat shows.

The fall of communism changed the whole picture. It provoked a new interest in pre-revolutionary culture and history, a fascination with the Romanov dynasty and with nobility, the Orthodox Church and traditional customs.[12] At the popular level, much of this was escapism; economic and social conditions in Russia were growing steadily worse, and in most national republics the search for a non-Soviet identity inevitably evoked a pre-industrial, 'traditional' culture.[13] Some of it was also an understandable reaction to the monotony of the recent past. Romantic images of tsarist Russia were accompanied by a rejection of the Soviet period as a failed experiment. But as the country's political and economic difficulties worsened, the widespread popularity of history gave way to a preoccupation with survival. Serious historical research alone has benefited from the change. Censorship is not a problem at the moment. It is low wages, high production costs and the paper shortage which now hold back the publication of new work in Russia.

The end of the communist era in the USSR and Eastern Europe must encourage a reappraisal of 1917 among scholars of all persuasions. But for now, the most lively historical controversies in East and West focus on one cluster of questions. These have a marked teleological emphasis. Explicitly or not, and whether their emphasis is on high politics or history 'from below', they concentrate on the overall picture of Russian 'modernization' and on the implications of the Revolution for what followed it. Was 1917 'necessary'? Could the tsarist regime have reformed itself from within, and could Russian economic development have brought sufficient prosperity to avert disaster if the war had not intervened? And if revolution could not have been avoided, might not some more humane outcome have been possible than the establishment of a one-party state, the repression of minorities and the mass murder of millions of peasants?

The question of the 'necessity' of 1917 is fundamental to all these debates. The counter-argument rests on the idea that tsarist Russia was showing signs of reforming itself successfully from within from the late nineteenth century onwards.

---

10   The Union-wide organization, Memorial, attracted large numbers of supporters in 1989–90, many of whom participated in its campaign to set up memorials to the victims and perpetrators of Stalin's purges and to establish a photographic and memoir record of them.

11   The delicate position of historians expected to defend the Communist Party while condemning Stalinism is illustrated by the contributions to the Round Table on Soviet history, *Voprosy istorii KPSS*, 1989, no. 2.

12   For an article praising the pre-revolutionary value of charity, see Granin 1987.

13   The exception is the Baltic republics, which were absorbed into the Soviet empire after the Second World War.

About the reforms themselves there is no doubt. Prompted by defeat in the Crimean War in 1856 and by Russia's perceived backwardness compared with Britain, France and, later, Germany, successive tsarist ministers attempted to modernize the Russian economy, beginning with the emancipation of the serfs in 1861.[14] Constitutional reform, which had accompanied economic growth in western Europe, followed much more slowly. It took the crisis of the 1905 revolution to force the Tsar to accept change in the form of the October Manifesto (see Harcave 1965 and Hosking 1973). Although the concessions this granted were limited (and many of them were subsequently revoked), the argument runs that a crucial step had been taken. The autocracy was finally compromised, and if circumstances had permitted a peaceful evolution, some form of just constitutional monarchy would eventually have emerged.

No one (except perhaps extreme monarchist politicians in Russia today) has seriously argued that the Tsar himself was an intelligent or capable head of state. The historians who hold that the tsarist regime had the potential to reform itself from within point to 'tendencies' which might have blossomed in 'normal' conditions. Whatever the limitations of the Tsar, several of his ministers displayed dedication and energy, often in the face of hostility from their monarch and colleagues. Sergei Witte in the late nineteenth century and Pyotr Stolypin in the early twentieth both introduced significant reforms aimed at encouraging economic growth and social stability.[15] Stolypin in particular has emerged from the recent literature as an enlightened statesman whose reform programme, including a scheme for the gradual creation of a yeoman peasantry in place of the post-emancipation commune, puts him in a direct line with current thinking about the need for privatization in the countryside. His efforts appeared to bear fruit; the Russian economy enjoyed a period of rapid growth between 1909 and 1914.[16] Some of this growth was financed by Russian, as opposed to foreign, capital. In some sectors this had largely replaced the foreign investment which had driven earlier boom periods.[17] The growth of domestic funding was a positive economic development, while in social and political terms it signalled the emergence, at last, of a native Russian bourgeoisie, the potential backbone for a constitutional monarchy. It is possible to conclude from this information that a stable social and political structure was snatched from the Russian people only by their involvement in the war.

The problems with this line of argument are obvious. However successful Russian industry may have become by 1914, major problems, amounting to a

---

14   Excellent essays on the emancipation of the serfs, together with an overview by the editor, are given in Emmons 1970.

15   The best biography of Witte remains von Laue 1963. A recent reappraisal of Stolypin, entirely laudatory, appears in Pipes 1990: 166–94. See also *Voprosy istorii*, 1988, no. 3.

16   Figures are analysed in Gregory 1982: 56–7.

17   The most optimistic assessment is that of Gerschenkron 1965a. More recently, see McKay 1970: 28.

potential political crisis, were all too apparent. Historians disagree about the rate of growth of the entrepreneurial class in tsarist Russia. Most new industry was still financed by foreign capital. And the bourgeoisie which had established itself may have had little reason to support the regime by 1914, denied as it was from participating in a democratic process, hindered as often as it was aided by tsarist regulations.[18] Outside the narrow ranks of the Petersburg elite, peasant discontent and working-class radicalism threatened to boil over into rebellion at any time.[19] The peasants' problems do not seem to have been resolved by the Stolypin reforms.[20] The take-up for his private farms varied from region to region, but in general, fewer than 20 per cent of peasant households had left the commune by 1914. Of these, less than half had succeeded in consolidating their holdings. The rest continued to farm scattered strips of land (Pipes 1990: 175–6; figures from Dubrovskii 1963). Partly for this reason, there was little sign that Russian agriculture was transforming itself along the desired west European lines. While overall agricultural output was rising in the decade before 1914, grain production far outstripped that of livestock, farming methods remained primitive and chronic rural over-population threatened peasants' livelihoods (Wheatcroft 1990). The boom of 1909–14 should be attributed primarily to a coincident world-wide economic surge rather than to domestic Russian policies.

In the cities, rapid and uneven economic development had created new industries, new factories and a greatly expanded workforce without the infrastructure to support them. The literature on the working class in this period is voluminous; historians even disagree about the applicability of the term 'class' to so heterogeneous a social group (for a discussion, see Haimson 1988). Some were 'hereditary' workers from families which had lived in the city for more than one generation. Some were highly skilled. But others were rural migrants, not all of whom lived permanently in the city. Many workers of all types retained ties with the village, either holding land there or returning seasonally to help with the harvest.[21] Whatever word is used to describe this workforce, however, all historians agree that its living and working conditions were among the worst in Europe. By 1905 there were many people in Russia who were not content to let this situation continue unchallenged. The last decade of tsarism was marked by frequent and coherent expressions of worker protest. The regime's response, which was usually to use troops, was inflammatory and brutish.[22] Sooner or later, it can be argued, some kind of confrontation on a large scale was almost inevitable.[23]

---

18 This less optimistic view of the period may be found in Gattrell 1986.

19 The seminal article on this subject was Haimson 1964–5. On peasant unrest, see Atkinson 1983.

20 Again, this is the subject of controversy, with historians discussing 'tendencies' rather than achieved results. For a more 'optimistic' appraisal of the Stolypin reform, see Gregory 1982.

21 A description of the workforce in the textile industry in the early 1920s appears in Ward 1990.

22 The most infamous use of troops, likened in impact to 'Bloody Sunday' in 1905, was the Lena goldfields massacre of 1912.

23 The classic presentation of this view is Pokrovsky 1933.

The nature and mainsprings of this worker protest have been the subject of intensive historical debate. The traditional Soviet view, crudely based on Lenin, was that Russia's urban workers were 'conscious' or 'unconscious', depending on their willingness to accept a Bolshevik political programme. 'Consciousness' came with a reading of the Marxist classics, an appreciation that revolution was the only solution and a willingness to make sacrifices to achieve it. The professional revolutionaries' role was to encourage this consciousness and prevent compromises from being struck which might defer the ultimate achievement of the Revolution. The 'vanguard party of a new type' plays a central role in all traditional Soviet accounts. Without it, the argument runs, the elemental forces of proletarian discontent would have remained incapable of concerted political action.[24]

Paradoxically, this view was accepted in broad outline by the Soviet Union's bitterest critics, many of whom presented the Russian Revolution as an exercise in Jacobin putschism.[25] It is only in the last thirty years or so that the research of social historians has challenged this position seriously. Studies of the Russian factory confirm that conscious working-class radicalism was a prominent feature of late tsarist society.[26] Historians disagree about the extent of its political purposiveness. Some have argued that the revolutionary parties, and above all the Bolsheviks, played a negligible role in the growth of working-class activism.[27] But the idea that the whole movement was 'spontaneous' or undirected is unconvincing. Scholars who have studied workers' demands and the politics of the strike movement in detail reveal that it was far more complicated than schematic Soviet accounts allowed (see, in particular, Keonker and Rosenberg 1989). But they point to a number of collective goals, such as a consensus about certain issues of social justice. They also challenge the 'revolution from above' model by pointing out that skilled workers, and above all those in the metal industry, were becoming increasingly radical by 1914, and that their demands were no longer limited to 'economic' goals, such as better wages or working conditions, but extended to a radical political programme.[28]

All this suggests that the tsarist system was in difficulties before 1914, and that the war may even have deflected criticism away from the regime for a while at the outset. But the war was not a *deus ex machina* in Russian affairs.[29] From the

---

24 For a relatively recent re-statement of this line, see *Velikii oktyobr'* 2: 1987.

25 This view was restated in *TLS*, 6 November 1992, articles by Richard Pipes and Lescek Kolokowski.

26 To list every contribution to this debate would be impossible in this short review. However, in addition to Leopold Haimson's seminal articles of 1963–4, attention should be drawn to Bonnell 1984; Engelstein 1982; Glickman 1984; and Johnson 1979.

27 This is the thread running through R. McKean's massive *St. Petersburg between the Revolutions* (1990).

28 Russian historians (and indeed Lenin himself) would agree about skilled workers' consciousness. The difference is the weight they would give to the role of the party. For two accounts, one Soviet and one western, see Volobuev 1964 and Haimson 1964–5.

29 The contrary view is suggested by Gerschenkron 1965b: 141.

nineteenth century onwards (and certainly throughout the Brezhnev years), Russia's commitment to great-power status influenced its diplomatic policy and its economic development. In neither case was the country's domestic political life made more secure. It was tsarism's great-power pretensions which involved the country in the Russo-Japanese War of 1904–5, defeat in which provided the spark for the 1905 Revolution. The same pretensions encouraged a concentration on military-related industries (such as arms and machinery) where wider diversity might have provided a more secure base for industrial growth and social stability. Russia's involvement in the First World War was not accidental; the crisis it provoked was a crisis of the tsarist system as a whole.[30]

The February Revolution brought down the autocracy and opened the way for an alternative style of government as well as alternative policies. The brief interlude of the Provisional Government left historians with a problem: was there ever a moment when democracy might have triumphed in Russia, and if not, why? Clearly this is a question invested with considerable wishful thinking. Especially at the time, liberal historians expressed frustration that first the Provisional Government and then the freely elected Constituent Assembly (which the Bolsheviks dissolved in January 1918) failed to take hold in Russia (Ulam 1981). Underlying their remarks was a belief that democratic institutions might in some way have been the 'normal' development for Russia if the war and revolutionary crisis had not blocked their path. Latterly this view has been expressed by Russian historians too; the Kerensky regime is enjoying a new popularity in a country eager to find alternatives to chaos or dictatorship (for a discussion, see Startsev 1990).

The most pessimistic riposte has been to suggest that Russia was somehow destined to be ruled by autocrats. This explanation comes in several degrees of determinism. At its mildest, it consists of an assumption that countries without democratic traditions have difficulty in establishing elected institutions, and that the moment for doing so in Russia was also one of the most troubled in her history (Ulam 1981: 69–70). But stronger versions also exist, in many cases attributing to Russians a desire to be ruled by despots and an inability to resist 'Tsar' figures. Such explanations are often couched in racist terms; Russians are seen as 'feeling uncomfortable' if they are offered 'too much freedom' (Laqueur 1989: 8). Adherents of this school often make connections with the distant past which are tenuous, speculative and unproven.[31] But the explanation has considerable appeal, for it maintains a sense of Russia's exoticism and excuses current and recent generations for seventy years of Bolshevism.

Seductive though these overarching explanations of Russian authoritarianism may be, reality, as always, was more subtle. The Provisional Government's failure has to be explained in terms of Russia's economic and military collapse, and of its own devotion to a system of property ownership and parliamentary elitism which

---

30 The case is made eloquently in R. W. Davies's introduction to Davies 1980: 20.

31 For a classic example, see Tucker 1991.

held no charm for the bulk of the population. By 1917 it was too late to ask the Russian peasant to wait for land legislation. It was also no time for a government to array itself behind the small industrial class against the underfed, insecure and frustrated workforce. By August, the fear had become widespread that the prime minister, Alexander Kerensky, intended to institute some form of dictatorship, and his involvement with Kornilov's attempted coup appeared to prove the point. It was not the lack of democratic tradition which brought down the Provisional Government (and how any government can appeal to tradition in a revolutionary situation is a moot point) but a combination of external disasters, short-sightedness, mismanagement and a growing impatience – among soldiers and sailors as well as civilians – with the continuing war. All these difficulties, moreover, were symptoms of a greater structural crisis. As early as February 1917, the Provisional Government had been only one of two potential loci of power in Russia. 'Dual power', the other element of which was the Petrograd Soviet, deprived it of the ability to build legitimacy. By October, it was the Soviet, and not Kerensky's, government which commanded mass, multiparty support (see Ferro 1980).

The Provisional Government's collapse, therefore, hardly came as a surprise. The Executive Committee of the Petrograd Soviet had been a credible alternative for several months. But was the October 'revolution' really a *coup d'état?* This view, a staple of a certain type of Western historiography for many years, would have been unthinkable for a Soviet historian of the old school. But now it is openly expressed in Russia – with more conviction, if anything, than it has been recently in the West.[32] The argument rests on three sets of assumptions. The first – that the Bolsheviks created the revolutionary situation from above – we have already examined. The second, to which it is related, is that Bolshevism was an alien ideology smuggled into Russia by a tiny group of revolutionaries, an ideology, moreover, which commanded very little grass-roots support. And the third is that Lenin's party (or rather, a fraction of its leadership) pre-empted a democratic coalition of the popular socialist parties from assuming power on behalf of the Petrograd Soviet.

The idea that Leninism was an alien system is especially popular among the new Slavophiles in Russia today. Marxism can be made to appear technocratic, industry-obsessed, out of keeping with the Russian peasant soul.[33] And it is true that it had little to offer to peasants determined to remain on the land, wedded, as Marx would put it, to 'the idiocy of rural life'. It also, in practice, had little appeal for women, even factory workers, who generally felt excluded and overawed by the atmosphere generated at party meetings (Glickman 1984). But Marxism undoubtedly attracted thousands of Russians from the late nineteenth century onwards. In the variant

---

32 As Alan Wood explained in the introduction to the special anniversary edition of the *European History Quarterly*, vol. 22, October 1992, 'The Bolsheviks, the Baby and the Bathwater'.
33 Marxism was a German product, of course, and Lenin, by the same token, may have been the recipient of 'German gold' in 1917. This is a point which continues to fascinate his detractors. For a recent example, see *Argumenty i fakty*, August 1992, nos 29–30, p. 5.

debated and refined by dozens of exiled revolutionaries in the cafés of Vienna, Paris and Geneva, it fitted admirably with pre-existing millenarian ideas, with a desire to see wholesale changes to a regime which no longer made any kind of sense, with a belief that Russia, which Lenin came to see as the 'weakest link' in the world imperialist chain, was special, that its sufferings would eventually make it the beacon of world socialism.[34] For Russia's workers, discussing their collective future in very different circumstances, Marxism made sense of a bewildering present while offering a vision of the future built on the sacrifices they were making and the lessons they had learned in city and factory. It did not seek to escape from industrialization. Rather, like the science fiction which workers were so avid to read (Stites 1989, esp. ch. 1), it offered a cleaner, more just version of capitalism.

Latterly, as the Russian workers' world has begun to come to life for historians, a good deal has been written about the relationship between the émigré revolutionaries' vision of Marxism and that of the workers back in Russia. One school shows them as largely separate; its advocates point to the 'unreality' of much émigré thinking (including Lenin's). And there is no doubt that revolutionaries who remained active in Russia, such as Tomskii and Rykov, had frequently to remind their comrades in Vienna and Geneva about the needs and priorities of the people whom they sought to guide (McKean 1990). There were points where the émigrés and the Russian workers disagreed, for example about party discipline, about participation in the Duma, and in many cases, about the correct response to the outbreak of war. Moreover, tensions were created by the fact that émigré intellectuals spent their lives discussing politics and designing general schemes (and resenting, in many cases, the fact that they were exiled from their country), while activists at home, who ran a daily risk of arrest, had to deal with a living working-class movement in the factories. But the two movements were not sealed off from each other. There was a genuine interaction between the different segments of the revolutionary movement.[35]

The events of 1917 itself accelerated and emphasized the political radicalization of Russia's workers, soldiers, sailors and peasants. Bolshevik opposition to the war had seemed like unpatriotic lunacy in April. By October it was one of the most popular planks of Lenin's platform. The Bolshevik image of 'extremism', particularly unattractive after the abortive July uprising in Petrograd, was one of their most compelling features after the Kornilov putsch. It is true that Lenin's policy was not generally understood in all its details, that part of the Bolsheviks' appeal was that they were not identified with a government whose policies were all

---

34 For a discussion of these theories, see Harding 1977–81, especially vol. 2, ch. 3, 'The Theoretical Basis.'
35 For an account of how the 'Russian' section of the party began to take the initiative after 1909, see Geoffrey Swain's introduction to *Protokoly soveshchaniya rasshirennoi redaktsii 'Proletariya': iyun' 1909* (1989). A different approach is adopted by William Chase and J. Arch Getty, who have demonstrated, by quantitative analysis, that in Moscow at least the Bolshevik Party had come to represent the bulk of the working population by 1917 (Chase and Getty 1978).

too clearly apprehended by the average citizen, but the fact remains that the Bolsheviks' popularity was rising by October to a point where they commanded majorities in the local and city soviets in many industrial areas (Keonker 1981: 208–27).

That there was widespread – even mass – support for the Bolsheviks in October 1917 is no longer in doubt. It is unlikely, however, that this support extended to the idea of single-party rule. Recent Russian research confirms the Western social historians' finding that the overwhelming majority of trade-unionists opposed the 'dictatorship of the proletariat' throughout the revolutionary period (Kiselev 1991). Even workers who favoured the Bolsheviks over the so-called 'moderate' socialist parties did not, as far as can be established, imagine that the latter would be excluded from government and ultimately outlawed. Many of the Bolsheviks' own rank and filers did not advocate this solution. The split between the Bolshevik and Menshevik factions, for example, had always been less emphatic inside Russia than among the leaders in emigration. In some towns, 'combined' socialist parties still operated in the summer of 1917.[36] Life may have been difficult for these alliances, but where activists were thin on the ground, some kind of general co-operation was preferable to isolation and enmity. After October, the Bolsheviks were to be castigated repeatedly for the vigour with which they excluded and even persecuted members of the other parties. A recent study of the Mensheviks shows how rapidly support for them grew after the Revolution as the reality of Leninist single-party rule began to emerge (Brovkin 1987). It was not so much that voters wanted to see the implementation of the Mensheviks' policies (if indeed they understood what these were); the vote was an overwhelming demand for the fulfilment of revolution- ary promises, including soviet democracy.

The rank and file was not alone in resisting the imposition of one-party rule. It is likely that the majority of the Bolshevik elite had little idea that Lenin proposed to circumvent the Soviet entirely in October. Within the Bolshevik Central Commit- tee, Lev Kamenev, Grigorii Zinoviev and several others deplored the direction Lenin's policy took from September. Their resistance overflowed from the closed meetings of the Central Committee to the national press before the insurrection, and for several days after it Kamenev and others worked to secure a coalition government (Bone 1974). These negotiations, and the general possibility of coalition after October 1917, demand more attention from historians. At the same time, however, there can be no escaping the conclusion that the odds were heavily stacked in favour of the Leninist solution. One of the main barriers to coalition was the attitude of the socialist parties themselves. Their leaders entrenched themselves in positions from which there was no obvious retreat. A condition stipulated at the negotiations by the 'minority' socialist parties, for example, was that Lenin and Trotsky be excluded from any future government. While Kamenev, eager to prolong the talks, appeared to entertain this idea for several days, it was clearly

36 According to O. V. Volobuev (1964), as late as 1917 10–20 per cent of local Social-democratic party organizations remained 'unified'.

unacceptable to the people who had successfully organized and carried out the insurrection. Trotsky took advantage of the impasse to abandon the talks and further humiliate the minority parties.[37] But even if the talks had succeeded, the minority parties did not have workable solutions to the major issues which confronted them, beginning with the pressing question of the war. These were serious problems, although they might not, on their own, have excluded the possibility of co-operation altogether.

The core of the Bolshevik leadership, however, was bent on single-party rule. Their record after 1917 was a grim one. Within three years of taking power, the Bolsheviks had dissolved, at bayonet-point, the only national body ever elected by universal suffrage, they had initiated a state-directed 'red terror' and they had subjected the mass of the population to coercive economic regulation, either through grain requisitioning or through labour regimentation and rule by ration card. Few Russian historians would now claim that there was anything laudable about 'War Communism'. Most see it as a makeshift response to crisis. Some would go further, and might emphasize the opportunism with which Lenin's government pre-empted future opposition while securing victory over its overt political enemies (Buldakov 1992). Newly released evidence suggests that Lenin himself perceived the importance of terror as a state-building tool; what we know of his enthusiasm for the summary execution of priests, for example, is hardly consonant with traditional 'Soviet' accounts of the ultimate humanitarian and father of his people. More research into this period is necessary, for it was a formative stage in Soviet history.[38] Many of the institutions hastily formed in 1917–18 (and believed by some Bolsheviks to be temporary) were to survive for the next seventy years.

These new discoveries will encourage the view, traditionally held by communism's bitterest opponents, that Stalin's murderous policies of mass collectivization and mass terror were the logical sequel to Leninist rule.[39] The argument proceeds through several stages. First there is the evidence of the pre-revolutionary Leninist party. Lenin was well known as an intolerant factional leader; his quarrel with the influential Bolshevik philosopher, Bogdanov, for example, developed into a full-scale party split in 1909, and some of the language used by members of Lenin's wing calling for the extirpation of Bogdanovism from the party now has a sinister echo (Swain 1989). But from this intolerance and faction-fighting to Stalin's purges was a very large step indeed. Bogdanov was not 'purged' in the Stalinist sense. Other dissidents were tolerated,[40] and in many cases Lenin had no effective control over his disparate and egotistical faction. The image of Lenin the puppet-master manipulating his followers is greatly overdrawn.

The second stage in the argument is based on the evidence of the coup itself. As

---

37 For a recent account of the negotiations before and after the insurrection, see Service 1991: 251–79.

38 For a preliminary discussion, see Keonker *et al.* 1989: section III.

39 The main lines of this debate are discussed in Tucker 1977.

40 Kamenev, for example, was reinstated within days of his public denunciation of the coup.

we have seen, Lenin and Trotsky deliberately circumvented the democratic process; it may never have been part of their scheme to share power with the other socialist parties. Like the factional intolerance of the pre-revolutionary period, this decision indicates that Lenin's goals were in no way democratic. From his point of view, only a Bolshevik dictatorship could ensure the future of the world proletarian revolution. It was not a matter of power for its own sake. But if he had wanted co-operation, alternatives did exist, albeit on a local scale. Not all the rebel regimes in the former empire were dictatorships, though the long-term prospects for such bodies as the Committee of Members of the Constituent Assembly in Samara were questionable without some form of economic or political coercion and centralization. Power-sharing with members of the other revolutionary parties, as we have seen, might also have been an option, but for the lack of faith (and sometimes active treachery) on both sides which ruled it out in practice.

Despite the criticisms and costs, however, there were good reasons why Lenin chose to rule by dictatorship in the first years after the seizure of power. The empire was falling apart, transport, and therefore supply and industry, was in chaos, and the country was losing a major war. One of his first tasks was to build some kind of state structure through which to impose order. Critics are correct to point to the fact that the force employed was occasionally excessive.[41] They might insist that the price paid for maintaining the empire was extortionate; a better solution, as recent history suggests, might have been to allow peripheral states to secede, to consolidate a core of European Russia and thus, because the need for centralization would have been less, to open the way for possible democracy.[42] But no revolutionary regime has managed to establish itself peacefully; reactions to the Treaty of Brest-Litovsk demonstrated how unpopular the ceding of territory might be, and the behaviour of the White forces in the areas under their control suggests that the most credible alternative to Bolshevism would not have been more merciful. To base an argument about the next twenty years of Soviet power entirely on decisions taken in the country's deepest crisis is futile.

The most serious evidence for the assertion that, had Lenin lived, something akin to Stalinism would inevitably have been established in Moscow is based on the leader's behaviour in the 1920s, when the revolutionary crisis appeared at last to be under control. The most important issues are the maintenance and even tightening of party discipline and the continuation, under another name, of the secret police. In the past three years, the story of the prison camps on the Solovetsky Islands in the extreme north of Russia, camps which held political prisoners condemned by Lenin's government, has been explored in Russian literature and film. The Bolshevik mentality, even under Lenin, was not a tolerant one. Their political experience inured them to measures which other politicians would have avoided;

---

41 Very different accounts of the Bolsheviks' first years in power are given by Service 1979 and Leibman 1975.

42 This view, associated with a good deal of anti-Islamic and Great Russian chauvinism, can be found in the political statements of Alexander Solzhenitsyn.

they also knew that their tenure of power was uncertain and that reprisals awaited them if they failed. The stakes were high, for they believed that they were acting on behalf of a greater cause; extreme measures were justified to secure the future of the Revolution. The Civil War left many Bolsheviks and other combatants traumatized for life,[43] but the memory of its more heroic moments encouraged a feeling, especially among those who did not see active service, that quick executive decisions at gun-point were the best way to solve intractable social and economic problems.[44] All this helps to explain the political atmosphere which facilitated the emergence of Stalinist autocracy.

There is little justification for taking the case one stage further and arguing that Stalinism was somehow 'inevitable', however. In the first place, Lenin's last years were characterized by a search for less violent paths to growth. Within the party elite, this search was accompanied by vigorous debate; the introduction of the New Economic Policy (NEP), for example, was heatedly opposed by some politicians, few of whom suffered in the short term for their views.[45] Second, the options facing the Soviet government were more varied than has sometimes been supposed. The main impetus behind Stalin's final victory in the party was the decision to embark on rapid industrialization and the state-directed collectivization of agriculture. Whatever the economic rationality of this course, there were genuine alternatives as late as 1928. And after the four desperate years of the 'great turn' of 1928–32, there was no clear 'necessity' for the Moscow trials and massive purge of 1936–8.

There is probably no controversy about the Revolution more complex than the debate about the Soviet economy in the 1920s. To understand it, the different strands of the argument must be separated. The first concerns the long-term viability of NEP as a strategy for economic growth. Even if it were possible to agree on that, there would remain the difficulty of setting the whole debate in the context of the Bolsheviks' priorities and world-view. The picture is also clouded by the historian's judgement about the costs of the 'great turn', costs which few Bolsheviks could calculate as they debated their country's future in the winter of 1927–8.

Three basic positions characterize the debate about the economy. The first is that NEP was a viable system and that its abandonment in 1928–9 was, from a purely economic perspective, unnecessary. The market economy which emerged in the 1920s, in this view, showed potential for medium-term stability, although most would agree that relations between town and countryside remained problematic. This was the view so enthusiastically aired in the West by Stephen Cohen in the 1970s (Cohen 1973), and again in Moscow in 1988, the year in which Bukharin

---

43 Surveys conducted in the 1920s confirmed that large numbers of former members of the Red Army suffered from nervous and respiratory disorders, some connected with poor living conditions and others with the stress of the revolutionary years; Merridale 1990: 132.

44 Evidence for this is abundant; the language used by the new generation of activists, mostly too young to have fought, in 1928–31 was almost entirely drawn from the Civil War era.

45 As Bukharin put it, 'everyone argued, searched for ways and means, quarrelled and made up and moved on together.' Cited in Merridale 1990: 21.

became a posthumous national hero. A second school suggests that NEP was not viable because of the havoc wrought during the Civil War (Gershenkron 1965b: 144–60). While the tsarist economy may have shown signs of peaceful evolution, in other words, its successor was doomed because confidence had been shattered, and the infrastructure destroyed, in the upheavals of 1914–21. A third group argues that NEP was collapsing by 1928, with the potential for co-operation between town and country exhausted and industry on the verge of a capital investment crisis from which there was no escape within the existing economic structure.[46] Large quantities of evidence have been marshalled in support of all three versions and their variants, for economists working on the pre-Stalin period, enjoyed a relative abundance of archival material even during the Brezhnev years.

To some extent, however, the long-term economic viability of NEP is less important than the way in which it was perceived at the time. From its inception, it was never a policy which appealed to the Bolshevik cast of mind. Fears that the peasant countryside was holding the socialist city to ransom were voiced repeatedly in the 1920s. And the pace of economic growth appeared painfully inadequate. Heavy industry, the home of the most advanced technology and the most conscious proletarians, could hardly make progress if the constant peasant demand for consumer goods had to be met. Stalin was correct to insist that his colleagues take note of the gap between Soviet and Western levels of industrial development. At the heart of the debate was the danger that the Soviet Union could not protect itself from a second round of foreign aggression.[47] Heavy industry was the first prerequisite for a thriving arms-production sector. The force of these priorities is clear from contemporary material. Not only the Bolshevik leadership, but also a large section of the urban working class believed that rapid growth would be necessary in the relatively short term if the revolutionary regime were to survive (Merridale 1990: 59–67).

Stalinist industrialization, and the collectivization of the peasantry which preceded it, was not inevitable in 1917, then, but some form of state-directed growth was a likely solution to the problems faced by the USSR from about 1926 onwards. The manner in which the great turn was conducted, including such measures as the deportation of supposed 'kulaks' (an official category which bore little resemblance to the real victims of the campaign), owed much to Stalin's style of leadership and priorities, but much also to the desperation of local officials.[48] Stalin's aides occasionally criticized the brutality or waste involved in the collectiviz- ation campaigns, and there was a good deal of discussion about the correct plan for industry by 1931, but the broad strategy of state-sponsored growth was accepted almost universally, and with it, with gritted teeth, many of its excesses.

It is when the other major aspect of Stalinism is examined – the purges of 1936–8 – that the continuities with Leninism look thinnest. Such widespread

---

46   This view is most concisely argued in Nove 1969.

47   This argument is developed in Davies 1980: Part III.

48   On this, see Davies 1980: conclusion.

brutality might not have been possible if the way had not been prepared by two decades of political violence, if there had not been scores to settle, and story-tellers to be silenced from the Revolution, the Civil War and the 'great turn'. But the Moscow trials of 1936–8 and the accompanying great purge, unleashed in 1937, owe much to Stalin's personal direction. Recent biographies confirm this using newly released material.[49] We may never fully understand the Soviet leader's psyche, but there is no doubt that ruthlessness, vengefulness and a tendency to paranoia were prominent features of it.[50] He may not have planned the purges from the outset, but his desire for revenge and personal insecurity led him first to remove his major rival, Sergei Kirov, murdered in 1934, and then to implicate his former allies, Zinoviev and Kamenev, in the plot. By the end of 1938 virtually no member of Lenin's Politburo (except Stalin himself and Trotsky) was still alive. Stalin's responsibility for the wider purge is less clear; he did not personally order every death, nor did he stipulate in detail where every enquiry should be made. But he took advantage of the whirlwind to dispose of enemies and rivals and to break the resistance of powerful institutions. His signature appears on hundreds of lists of condemned victims, and conversely his word was sufficient to spare someone who might otherwise have died.[51]

There remain, however, a large number of unanswered questions. If the Soviet experience is compared with those of other societies in revolution, the picture changes immediately. For almost all revolutions are followed by a purge of some kind – and often by more than one. The reasons for this must be sought in the problems of post-revolutionary state-building and in the social psychology of populations which have undergone rapid change at the hands of millenarian regimes. The answers remain tentative.[52] But it is clear that the purges cannot be understood purely in terms of Stalin's personality. This is an area where new archival material must be used with imagination, for the obvious sources can tell us only who signed which warrants and how many died. In the end the most satisfying global explanations are likely to come from setting the best new research in a broader, and possibly comparative, framework. Before this can be done, moreover, it is vital that historians agree to a reduction of the moral temperature. The language of the Grand Inquisitor, which flows so easily on this topic, was not designed for the furtherance of scholarship.

The question of historical imagination demands discussion now. The sudden availability of so much new material has led to a scramble for archives; buyers are being sought, officially and unofficially, for the juiciest material, and the rush is on to publish exciting findings. The secret police files remain closed to all but a few, but the material already released will occupy historians for decades. Among the

---

49 The best of these is probably Tucker 1990.

50 Tucker (1990) develops the 'psycho-history' theme in his biography, as does Roy Medvedev in his outstanding *Let History Judge: the Origins and Consequences of Stalinism* (1989).

51 New evidence about the extent of his responsibility appears in Tucker 1990: 443–52.

52 The best single comparative study is still Skocpol 1979.

archives now opened, those of the Central Committee and Politburo, and many local or institutional archives, offer new vistas of understanding, not only about the elite, but also about the opinions and priorities of ordinary people. And the mere fact that the archives have opened and that Russian scholars can discuss their work freely has created a bolder intellectual atmosphere for everyone involved.

But all this is taking place against a background of crisis in the subject. Even before the Communist Party collapsed in 1991, the writing of Soviet history had reached an impasse; the debates tended to circle around the group of questions which we have discussed here. These were, and remain, central issues, but they are not the only ones which demand attention. The re-emergence of the 'nationalities' problem reminds us that a whole area of Soviet development was largely neglected until recently. Other 'blank pages' were blamed on the shortage of material, and this was a genuine problem, but as an excuse it may sound a little thin to archaeologists and students of the pre-modern world. Another difficulty was the isolation in specialist departments of historians in Russia and of Sovietologists in the West. This isolation restricted everyone's horizons. The Soviet Union came to be seen as a 'black box', as a remote and special case, separate from Europe. Fortunately, this state of affairs cannot continue. Parts of the former empire, after all, may well become member states of NATO or the European Community.

There will be many responses to this crisis. In Russia itself, history is at a crossroads. The Brezhnev generation must adapt to the new freedom of debate or retire, while the young historians currently training have received little guidance from teachers as confused about historical techniques, and even about the basic facts of their own past, as they are. Many of the most talented have left the universities for more lucrative employment in commerce and industry. Those who remain are hearing from their colleagues in the West that archives are sovereign and ideology perilous. But is that all we have to offer them? Our own profession is as much in need of an infusion of new thinking as is theirs. If we are to benefit from the availability of documents and the ready co-operation of Russian and other former Soviet historians, it is surely time to start asking new questions.

The writing of history is heavily dependent on the priorities and disposition of individual historians, and all have their own agendas for the future. But at this stage, there are several obvious areas for new research. Some are provided by the priorities of the present itself; the nationalities problem, racism, humane alternatives to socialism in a world where capitalism faces another serious crisis. But others arise from the general rethinking of historical writing outside the Soviet field since the Second World War; the rise of social history, broadly interpreted; the study of cultural history; comparative history; the history of ideas. Many of the questions which need to be asked about twentieth-century Russia – such as those dealing with its social history or the world-view of its citizens – will cut across the political and economic issues which we have dealt with here. They may not focus as sharply as traditional historians might wish on the ethical problems raised by Stalinism. But in the end they may help to make more sense of the Soviet experiment and more generally of the twentieth-century history of the countries of what is now called the Commonwealth of Independent States than the narrow range of issues which has for so long been under such intensive discussion.

REFERENCES

Acton, E. (1991) *Rethinking the Russian Revolution*, Sevenoaks.
Atkinson, D. (1983) *The End of the Russian Land Commune, 1905–1930*, Stanford.
Bone, A. (trans.) (1974) *The Bolsheviks and the October Revolution. Central Committee Minutes of the RSDLP (bolsheviks), Aug. 1917–Feb. 1918*, London.
Bonnell, V. E. (1984) *Roots of Rebellion*, Berkeley.
Brovkin, V. (1987) *The Mensheviks after October*, Ithaca, NY.
Buldakov, V. P. (1992) 'The October Revolution: seventy-five years on', *European History Quarterly* (October) 22.
Chase, W. and Getty, J. A. (1978) 'The Moscow Bolshevik cadres of 1917: a prosopographic analysis', *Russian History* 5(1).
Cohen, S. F. (1973) *Bukharin and the Bolshevik Revolution*, New York.
Davies, R. W. (1980) *The Socialist Offensive. The Collectivisation of Soviet Agriculture, 1929–1930*, London.
—— (1989) *Soviet History in the Gorbachev Revolution*, London.
Dubrovskii, S. M. (1963) *Stolypinskaya zemel'naya reforma*, Moscow.
Emmons, T. (ed.) (1970) *The Emancipation of the Russian Serfs*, London.
Engelstein, L. (1982) *Moscow 1905: Working-Class Organisation and Political Conflict*, Stanford.
Ferro, M. (1980) *October 1917*, London.
Gattrell, P. W. (1986) *The Tsarist Economy, 1850–1917*, London.
Gerschenkron, A. (1965a) 'Agrarian policies and industrialisation. Russia 1861–1914', in *Cambridge Economic History of Europe* 6.2, Cambridge.
—— (1965b) *Economic Backwardness in Historical Perspective*, New York.
Glickman, R. L. (1984) *Russian Factory Women*, Berkeley.
Got'e, Yu. V. (1988) *Time of Troubles, the Diary of Iurii Vladimirovich Got'e*, tr., ed. and annotated by T. Emmons, London.
Gregory, P. R. (1982) *Russian National Income, 1885–1913*, Cambridge.
Haimson, L. (1964–5) 'The problem of social stability in urban Russia, 1905–1917', *Slavic Review* 23–4.
—— (1988) 'The problem of social identities in early twentieth century Russia', *Slavic Review* 47(1).
Harcave, S. (1965) *First Blood. The Russian Revolution of 1905*, London.
Harding, N. (1977–81) *Lenin's Political Thought*, 2 vols, London.
Hosking, G. (1973) *The Russian Constitutional Experiment*, London.
Johnson, R. E. (1979) *Peasant and Proletarian: the Working Class of Moscow in the Late Nineteenth Century*, New Brunswick.
Keonker, D. P. (1981) *Moscow Workers and the 1917 Revolution*, Princeton.
—— and Rosenberg, W. G. (1989) *Strikes and Revolution in Russia, 1917*, Princeton.
—— Rosenberg, W. G. and Suny, R. G. (1989) *Party, State and Society in the Russian Civil War*, Bloomington.
Kiselev, A. F. (1991) *Profsoyuzy i sovetskoe gosudarstvo*, Moscow.
Laqueur, W. (1989) *The Long Road to Freedom*, London.
Laue, T. H. von (1963) *Sergei Witte and the Industrialisation of Russia*, New York.
Leibman, M. (1975) *Leninism under Lenin*, London.
McKay, J. P. (1970) *Pioneers for Profit: Foreign Entrepreneurship and Russian Industrialisation, 1885–1913*, Chicago.

McKean, R. (1990) *St Petersburg between the Revolutions*, New Haven, CT and London.

Medvedev, R. (1989) *Let History Judge: the Origins and Consequences of Stalinism*, rev. and expanded edn, New York.

Merridale, C. (1990) *Moscow Politics and the Rise of Stalin*, London.

Miliukov, P. (1967) *Political Memoirs 1905–1917*, Ann Arbor.

Nove, A. (1969) *An Economic History of the USSR*, Harmondsworth.

Pipes, R. (1990) *The Russian Revolution*, London.

Pokrovsky. M. N. (1933) *Brief History of Russia*, tr. D. S. Mirsky, London.

Service, R. (1979) *The Bolshevik Party in Revolution, 1917–1923*, London.

—— (1991) *Lenin, a Political Life*, 2: *Worlds in Collision*, London.

Skocpol, T. (1979) *States and Social Revolutions*, Cambridge.

Startsev, V. (1990) 'Al'ternativa: fantazii i real'nost'', *Kommunist* 15.

Stites, R. (1989) *Revolutionary Dreams*, Oxford.

Sukhanov, N. N. (1955) *The Russian Revolution*, Oxford.

Swain, G. (1989) Introduction to *Protokoly soveshchaniya rasshirennoi redaktsii 'Proletariya': iyun' 1909*, New York and London.

Tucker, R. (ed.) (1977) *Stalinism*, New York.

Tucker, R. (1990) *Stalin in Power. The Revolution from Above, 1928–41*, London and New York.

—— (1991) 'What time is it in Russia's history?', in C. Merridale and C. Ward (eds) *Perestroika: The Historical Perspective*, London.

Ulam, A. (1981) *Russia's Failed Revolutions*, London.

Volobuev, P. P. (1964) *Proletariat i burzhuaziya v 1917 godu*, Moscow.

Ward, C. (1990) *Russia's Cotton Workers and the New Economic Policy*, Cambridge.

Webb, S. and Webb, B. (1935) *Soviet Communism: A New Civilisation?*, London.

Wheatcroft, S. G. (1990) 'Agriculture', in R. W. Davies (ed.) *From Tsarism to the New Economic Policy*, London.

21

THE HISTORIOGRAPHY OF NATIONAL SOCIALISM

Jane Caplan

The Nazi period is in many ways unique as a historical epoch, since there are virtually no defenders of or apologists for a regime that has become a synonym for political infamy in the modern world. But this does not mean that there has ever been universal scholarly consensus about the history of National Socialism or its 'meaning', either in German history or in any wider historical or cultural context. On the contrary, intense and sometimes acrimonious debates about the sources, nature and consequences of National Socialism have been common since the Nazi movement emerged in the 1920s. And although an enormous scholarly literature on the history of the Nazi movement and regime has accumulated since 1945, these arguments have not been exclusively academic in character. Some of the earliest interpretations of Nazism were advanced by its political opponents, and enduring debates about the relationships among fascism, totalitarianism, capitalism and mass society have their origins in the intense political climate of the 1920s and 1930s. The political controversies of the inter-war epoch persisted beyond 1945 as well, their contours revised and sharpened by the impact of Germany's partition, by the Cold War and by the two successor states' competitive claims to legitimacy: a polemical context that sometimes had the effect of exaggerating the distinctions between theories that in practice shared some common origins and revealed certain overlaps. Most recently, the unification of Germany has shattered one of these post-war historiographical traditions, and presented new challenges of confrontation and reintegration, though it is still hard to see what will emerge from this process. The political realities of the past seventy-odd years have thus established the context within which native and foreign historians alike have negotiated the meaning of the German nation's recent history.

If the tenacious divisions of twentieth-century politics have marked one of the critical fault-lines in the interpretation of National Socialism, another derives from the texture and status of historiography itself in German scholarly culture. As

Georg Iggers (1968: 3) has pointed out, few national historiographies have been as self-consciously theoretical as Germany's has since the nineteenth century.

The Germans, as Marx once noted, were a nation whose capacity for philosophical self-creation outran its ability to establish itself politically. The same idea recurs, more delphically, in Hagen Schulze's recent comment that 'the identity of the Germans lies not in their present but in their past and their future simultaneously' (Schulze 1987: 1014). Both observations point, across a span of 150 years, to an original project of imaginative national self-creation; in the hands of early nineteenth-century thinkers like Herder, Fichte and Humboldt, this was an act of quintessential historical Idealism, and set the terms of the enduring German historicist tradition. Historicism, in its broadest meaning as a modern historical sensibility, was nowhere more at home or more pervasive in nineteenth-century Europe than in Germany, whose intellectual culture was saturated with debates about history and historical theory, especially as they applied to the Germans themselves. Historicism in its narrower sense – as a philosophy of historical interpretation that calls for empathetic understanding rather than law-bound explanation, and that has characteristically been applied in the narrative reconstruction of state-formation and policy-making – was even more essentially Germanic. Virtually without effective challenge, this paradigm dominated German historiography from the 1830s until well after 1945, and determined its research priorities: state rather than society, foreign policy rather than internal affairs, the sequence of historical events rather than the analysis of structures and systems. Only the experience of National Socialism dislodged historicism from its pedestal in West Germany, and that belatedly. In the German Democratic Republic, the historicist tradition was challenged more dramatically by Marxist dialectical and historical materialism, though even there it took time for historiography to respond to the new political agenda established there in the early 1950s.

The inheritance of historicism, which will be discussed in more detail below, provides an important key to post-1945 developments in the German historiography of National Socialism. In the early years of both the Federal Republic (Bundesrepublik Deutschland; BRD) and the Democratic Republic (Deutsche Demokratische Republik; DDR), though for somewhat different reasons, the historicist tradition exercised a negative influence on the reconstruction of academic history, and inhibited the emergence of new methods and approaches for a generation after 1945. Despite the radical change of political direction in the DDR, academic history there was simply unequal to the challenge of developing a new historiographical tradition. The absence of historians who were in political or intellectual sympathy with socialism left the DDR without an appropriate professional historical culture between the late 1940s and the early 1950s. This strengthened the strategy, adopted by the leadership of the SED (Sozialistische Einheitspartei), of conflating the academic history of Nazism with the politics of popular antifascism. As a cadre of academic historians schooled in socialism emerged in the 1960s, the tasks of the profession became more defined, yet remained subordinate to the SED's political priorities. Whatever its value in helping to legitimize the new state and in criticizing authoritarian traditions in Germany's history, this political agenda also obstructed internal disciplinary innovation in the DDR. The SED version of Marxism was, in effect, superimposed upon method-ological traditions that otherwise remained curiously conventional and undisturbed. It was not until the 1970s that the practice of history as such began to acquire a critical, self-reflective dimension in the DDR, and that research themes, objectives and debates began to emerge from the internal disciplinary process of intellectual exchange rather than from external instructions.

In post-war West Germany, meanwhile, professional and public resistance to 'coming to terms' with the immediate past meant that there, too, 1945 was less of an intellectual rupture than might have been expected. Most West German historians, like other intellectuals, appeared to be sufficiently free of direct responsibility for the intellectual and political climate of the Third Reich that they could resume their work undisturbed – the more so once the brief flourish of denazification came to an abrupt halt in the Cold War. With few exceptions, West German historians, in the words of one critic, resumed the practice of 'a politically and morally tamed historicism' between 1945 and 1960 (Ernst Schülin, cited in Klessmann 1987: 116). A critical historiography of National Socialism emerged in West Germany only in the 1960s, by which time the contours of debate had already been established by international scholarship. Actually, the research that is usually taken as the evidence of this transition – Fritz Fischer's controversial interpretation of Germany's responsibility for the outbreak of the First World War – may have been interpreta-tively iconoclastic, but methodologically it was quite traditionalist in its dense archival reconstruction of the governmental decision-making process. It was the impact of theoretical models from mainly non-German scholarship that from the 1960s transformed both West German historiography in general, and research into National Socialism in particular. The irony here was that these models to some extent represented a reimportation of Weberian socio-structural scholarship that had previously been rejected by the German historical profession. and that had found a more congenial home in other cultures and disciplines. And even though the pattern of West German research into National Socialism since the 1960s testifies to a profound breach with earlier methodology in some circles, the historicist tradition has never been entirely abandoned, but has broken forth from time to time in renewed debates that have been as much political as methodological. In this story, we shall see how debate about National Socialism has oscillated between integration into broader explorations of the nature of modern European society, and confinement to narrower questions about German national identity. In a related move, debate has also fluctuated between the historicist concept of a 'German path' (*deutsche Weg*), and the comparative concept of Germany's 'special development' (*Sonderweg*).

The task of summarizing the vast interpretative literature on National Socialism poses, of course, considerable challenges of thematization and periodization, and every student will have his or her preferred solution. My own somewhat idiosyn-cratic response represents an attempt to highlight what I regard as the two most intellectually engaging analytical literatures. First, there is the largely theoretical analysis of National Socialism as a form of fascism. This approach emerged simultaneously with the rise of National Socialism itself in the 1920s; originally politico-theoretical in cast, it has since become partially incorporated into historiographical debate, although not without controversy as to its scholarly status. The second major body of literature – German post-1945 scholarship on National Socialism – is more conventionally historiographical and professional in character, but also raises, as I have suggested, important questions about historical methodology and intellectual politics. Into this basically two-part structure of my chapter I have inserted a brief discussion of the German historical profession under National Socialism, a topic often neglected in surveys of this kind; and I have also aimed to integrate as appropriate the research agendas developed in non-German scholarship since 1945. My emphasis will lie on the broad intellectual issues of interpretation. I will not rehearse in detail the numerous academic debates about specific aspects of the period, for these have already been the subject of a number of admirable, up-to-date and easily accessible surveys.[1]

FROM POLITICS TO HISTORY: THE CHALLENGE OF NATIONAL SOCIALISM IN INTERNATIONAL SCHOLARSHIP 1920s–1950s

Witnesses to the rise of National Socialism found it hard to resist the conclusion that Nazism was a symptom of some wider crisis in the European system: that National Socialism was to Germany what fascism was to Italy, and what similar hyper-nationalist, anti-Bolshevik and anti-democratic movements and regimes were to Spain and a number of central European states. But while this concept of a European fascism was widely shared in the 1920s and 1930s, and was to remain the guiding theme of Marxist historiography well into the 1970s, it always circulated in relation to two other powerful theses which commanded respect in liberal and conservative circles. One emphasized the specifically German origins and character of National Socialism, seeing in it the culmination of deep-laid weaknesses and failures in Germany's historical development. A second school identified Bolshevism as a related anti-democratic movement which was symptomatic of the same tensions from which fascism arose, including the weakening of liberalism and of the bourgeois social and cultural order in Europe at the turn of the century, the political mobilization of the masses, the *fin-de-siècle* intellectual crisis, and finally the drastic dislocations in European politics and society brought about by the First World War.

---

1 See Kershaw 1989, which includes in ch. 1 a valuable summary of the major historiographical issues; Hiden and Farquharson 1989, which concentrates on topical historical debates, and includes an extensive bibliography of works in English and German; Ayçoberry 1981, which is particularly useful on the theoretical debates since the 1920s; and Hildebrand 1991, which includes an extensive bibliography of mainly German publications. Erdmann 1976 = vol. 2, Part 4 of Gebhardt's *Handbuch der deutschen Geschichte* (9th edn) offers a useful synthesis of the German literature to that date. See also Kehr and Langmaid 1982.

In its most coherently expressed form, this equation of fascism and Bolshevism developed into the theory of totalitarianism that emerged in the 1940s and survived in the academic literature of the West until the 1960s. I will survey in turn these interpretations of National Socialism as a version of fascism, as a German peculiarity and as a form of totalitarianism.[2] However, it should be borne in mind that these distinctions are partly a matter of convenience: in practice, theories grew up alongside one other, often sharing common origins, premises and conclusions, yet also repudiating these affiliations in the light of intellectual or political antagonism.

Within the theory of fascism as a comparative concept, the clearest divide lies between interpretations which draw on some variant of Marxist class theory, and those that do not. What all these theories share, however, is a strong sense of crisis that had been building in European society since the late nineteenth century, of which the fascist movements, ideologies and regimes that emerged after 1918 were the climactic manifestation. Important here are the different roles played by the concept of the 'irrational' in these theories. For Marxists, this crisis was the inevitable and predictable consequence of the structural irrationality internal to the capitalist mode of production at its imperialist apogee, an irrationality that was, however, subsumed into the larger rationality of the logic of history, which was hastening towards the final revolutionary epiphany heralded by the crisis. By contrast, most non-Marxist theories tended to emphasize the irrationality of the popular *responses* to the undeniably profound strains on European society between the 1890s and the 1930s, but hoped for an eventual restoration of the basically sound principles of the liberal social and political order. This divergence persisted in the academic literature after 1945. Non-Marxist theorists and historians saw their judgement vindicated by the restabilization of capitalism and liberalism in Europe, and believed on the whole that the era of fascism was over. Marxists, on the other hand, continued to look for evidence of the ultimate instability of monopoly capitalism, and to see fascism as an endemic resource for capitalism in crisis.

Marxist theories of fascism first developed in the context of the direct confrontation between Europe's communist parties and the fascist movements and regimes of inter-war Europe. Their primary objective was to discover the social location and logic of the fascist movements, within an overarching theory of capitalism and class struggle on the one hand, and of the conjunctural politics of post-war revolutionary stalemate on the other. Structurally, orthodox Leninist theory held that capitalism

---

2   This does not exhaust the full range of interpretations of National Socialism, far less of fascism, but identifies the approaches that have sponsored the most important historical research into National Socialism. Ayçoberry 1981 is a valuable and wide-ranging summary of the major theories of Nazism since the 1920s. Comparative accounts of fascism include Nolte 1966; 1967; Carsten 1967; Woolf 1968a and 1968b; Kedward 1969; Lubasz 1973); Laqueur 1979; Payne 1980; Kitchen 1976; Larsen *et al.* 1980; Wippermann 1972; Poulantzas 1974; Schulz 1974; Cassels 1975; Saage 1976; Schieder 1976; de Felice 1977; O'Sullivan 1983; Mühlberger 1987; Kühnl 1990; Brooker 1991; and two issues of the *Journal of Contemporary History* devoted to fascism, 1(1) (1966), and 11(4) (October 1976). See also Rees 1984.

had entered its final period of crisis in 1914, marked by the ripening of its economic contradictions and the growth of the revolutionary working-class movement. Conjuncturally, after the end of the war, capital faced a worsening crisis of economic restabilization and political representation in all European nations, yet at the same time the revolutionary momentum had been blocked by the collapse of working-class unity in 1919, and by the Left's failure to gain the support of the social classes intermediate between capitalists and the proletariat. Nowhere was this alignment clearer after 1918 than in the defeated ex-power Germany, and in the quasi-loser nation of Italy. Fascism entered the political and historical scene in these countries as a mass counter-revolutionary movement of the socially disorganized classes, mobilized by capital in a bid to recover its political hegemony.

A crucial element in contemporary Marxist analyses of Italian fascism and German National Socialism was thus the distinction they drew between the class composition of the movements, and the class interests they served. As the Comintern theorist Karl Radek put it in 1934

> Marxist analysis cannot of course disregard the social composition of any political organization, but it does not admit that the social composition is the decisive factor in determining the social character of a given movement; it asks what class interests in the last analysis are directing this movement.
>
> (quoted in Cammett 1967: 158)

In the 1920s, Comintern worked through various versions of this basic interpretation, drawing first on the Italian experience of fascism in the agrarian sector, and castigating social democracy as fascism's helpmate. From the point of view of the German resistance to National Socialism, it was little short of catastrophic that the rise of the NSDAP after 1928 coincided with the climax of Comintern's attack on social democrats, in which the entire social and political spectrum from social democracy to National Socialism was characterized as 'one reactionary mass'.[3] It was not until the disaster of National Socialism's seizure of power in 1933 that Comintern took official notice of alternative voices within its ranks, and developed an analysis that, belatedly, recognized the need for a defensive front of all antifascist forces. It was this shift that produced what became the classic Marxist definition of fascism, first formulated by Dmitrov at the ECCI Plenum in December 1933, and formally adopted at the 7th Comintern Congress in August 1935. Here fascism was characterized as 'the open terrorist dictatorship of the *most* reactionary, *most* chauvinistic and *most* imperialist elements of finance capital [my emphases]' – a formula whose crucial superlatives finally opened the way to political collaboration with any groups short of these extreme 'elements' (Dmitrov n.d.: 40). It was this formulation that, as we shall see, was to preside over the bulk of post-1945 historiography in the German Democratic Republic, where it did service not only in accounts of the rise of National Socialism, but also in the explanation of the

---

3 For the role of the KPD in Germany, see Fowkes 1984; Fischer 1991; Rosenhaft 1983 explores the tension in the communist movement between official and rank-and-file views on resisting the Nazis; on SPD attitudes to fascism, see Sturm 1986; Breitman 1989; Pyta 1989; Winkler 1990.

relationship between the Nazi regime and industrial capitalism after 1933, and of German aims in the Second World War.

It is, however, important to remember that these 'official' Comintern interpretations of fascism were by no means the sole contribution by Marxist theorists in this period. The 1920s and 1930s saw a wide range of alternative theories that used Marxist theoretical tools to probe the nature of fascism and the means of resistance to it. For example, the Austrian Marxist Otto Bauer explored the way in which the extensive industrial rationalization of the inter-war years had provoked social crisis by intensifying the contradictions between social production and private accumulation; the young German crypto-Marxist Alfred Sohn-Rethel also stressed the significance of the rationalization process, and identified fascism as an attempt to solve the consequent crisis of profitability by means of a return to the production of absolute instead of relative surplus value. Also important were the so-called 'Bonapartist' interpretations of fascism, which drew upon Marx's well-known analysis, in *The Eighteenth Brumaire of Louis Bonaparte*, of the stalemate of class forces that had permitted Bonaparte's seizure of power in 1851; this interpretation of fascism was most famously developed by Trotsky, but it was first advanced by Bauer and by the dissident German communist August Thalheimer.[4] And just as Comintern's 1933/5 formula was taken over into East German and Soviet orthodoxy after the war so also it was the rediscovery of these heterodox interpretations from the 1920s and 1930s that fuelled the revival of fascism theory in the West in the 1960s and 1970s.

Beyond the official and dissident Marxist theories of fascism, a third important strand in German leftist thought was the attempt to synthesize the theories of Marx and Freud. Here Marxism offered, roughly speaking, a structural analysis of the dynamics of social process and historical change, and psychoanalysis a theory of the production, introjection and function of ideology in human agents. Wilhelm Reich, for instance, explored the relationship between patriarchal ideology, sexual repression and fascism and racism, using Marxist and psychoanalytic methods in increasingly heretical fashion; in the 1940s Erich Fromm developed an interpretation of the relationship between domination and submission in the psychology of the modern individual; and, most systematically, members of the Frankfurt School, notably Theodor Adorno and Max Horkheimer, began the intellectual journey that led to their theory of the authoritarian personality and also to their pessimistic explorations of the repressed relationship between Enlightenment rationality and the irrational, which reached its perverse climax in the extermination of the Jews.[5]

---

4 See Bauer 1967; Sohn-Rethel 1987; Kitchen 1973; Trotsky [1930–40] 1971. Translations of contemporary Marxist writings can be found in Beetham 1984; Bottomore and Goode 1978; see also Ceplair 1987. The best discussion of these theories is Saage 1976, and see also Kitchen 1976.

5 Reich [1934] 1975; Fromm 1941; Adorno *et al.* 1950; Horkheimer and Adorno [1944] 1990; on Frankfurt School interpretations of Nazism, see Jay 1973; Dubiel and Söllner 1981; Wilson 1982; and Held 1980. Despite the importance of sexual identity and pathology in these studies, they have very little to say about women and the feminine in fascism; see Macciocchi 1976, also Theweleit 1987–9.

From the left reaches of the Frankfurt milieu came too Franz Neumann's powerful analysis of Nazi Germany as a quadripartite power system, built upon the competing pillars of party, army, bureaucracy and industry; first published in 1942, his study *Behemoth* remains one of the most compelling and insightful accounts of the regime. It was the Frankfurt School tradition that, although interrupted and redirected by exile and dispersal during the 1930s and 1940s, recovered after 1945 to become the strongest link between pre- and post-Nazi German theory; and its most eminent heir, the philosopher Jürgen Habermas, became deeply involved in the bitter historiographical controversy of the mid-1980s known as the *Historikerstreit* (historians' dispute), as we shall see.

The principal contemporary alternative to Marxist analyses of fascism, the 'mass society' thesis, had emerged towards the end of the nineteenth century as a description of the spiritually anomic, socially amorphous, and ideologically irrational tendencies of post-traditional European societies. While class antagonisms played a part in this image of mass society, they did not occupy the same determining role as they did in Marxist analysis; anti-Semitism, for example, which Marxist theory tended to see in instrumental terms, was here given an ideological autonomy of its own. The imagery came into its own in the 1930s and 1940s as a plausible explanation for fascism's appeal to the popular experience of loss, displacement and disillusion in the post-war period.[6] Nazism, in this view, was an extreme irrationalist response to the intolerable pressures of post-war German life, pressures which the Weimar state proved incapable of relieving. This approach reappeared in the postulate of a cultural and spiritual crisis of European civilization that was a popular recourse of West German historians immediately after 1945, as we shall see. Later interpretations of fascism as a form of resistance to modernization were also essentially refinements of this initial view; and Ernst Nolte's important study *Der Faschismus in seiner Epoche* (1963), with its thesis of fascism as a movement of 'resistance to transcendence', was another heir to this tradition.[7] Parallel to the attempted convergence of Marx and Freud, the mass-society thesis offered its own synthesis of sociological and psychological theories to explain both the nature of social distress in the post-war period and the susceptibility of certain social groups to fascism's solutions. Such interpretations echoed Marxism's emphasis on the crucial role of the petty bourgeoisie in fascism, but pressed beyond the question of its material status to examine the specific psychosocial pressures experienced by this most liminal of social groups (Geiger 1930; Parsons 1942/3a; 1942/3b; Lipset 1960). And with psychology as the new science in the early twentieth century, the

---

6 Biddis 1977; and see on fascism and mass society Ortega y Gasset 1932; Parsons 1942/3a; Arendt 1952; Bendix 1952; Kornhauser 1959; Hagtvet 1980.
7 For discussions of the relationship between National Socialism and modernization, see Gregor 1969; Peukert 1991, which applies the alternative concept of 'pathological modernity' to the Weimar period; Baumann 1989; Herf 1984; among recent German contributions to the modernization issue see especially Matzerath and Volkmann 1977. Mommsen 1990; Rauh 1987; Zitelmann 1990; Prinz and Zitelmann 1991.

idiom of pathology could also be directly applied to Hitler and his followers: 'What is involved [in Hitler's ideology] is an *idée fixe* of atavistic origin, which does away with the complexity of reality and replaces it with the uniformity of primitive combat', wrote the *Frankfurter Zeitung* in 1928. 'At bottom, Hitler is a dangerous madman' (cited from Ayçoberry 1981: 76). This psychopathological interpretation has obvious attractions to biographers seeking to understand Hitler's personality, and has been developed academically through the genre of psychohistory.[8]

Whether Marxist or non-Marxist, these theories begged the question of why it was Germany that apparently exhibited the most extreme symptoms of crisis. The idea of a particularly German susceptibility to fascism was not necessarily incompatible with Marxist theory; even the idea that National Socialism was a phenomenon of German backwardness was accommodated into Marxist thought, despite the logic of a theory that depended upon capitalism reaching its most *advanced* stage as the prelude to its final collapse. Intellectually, the transitional figure here was the Austro-German Marxist Ernst Bloch, who in the 1930s developed the concept of 'asynchronism', or the coexistence of 'non-contemporaneity and contemporaneity' (*Ungleichzeitigkeit und Gleichzeitigen*), to explain the strength of pre-capitalist survivals in Germany, 'the classic land of anachronism'.[9] And as the world divided in war in the 1940s, and the evidence of the barbarous inhumanity of National Socialism accumulated, the search for the specifically German sources of National Socialism was further stimulated among its political and ideological enemies. Historians from the Allied nations (e.g. Rohan Butler (1941), Edmond Vermeil (1944) and A. J. P. Taylor (1946)), and German émigrés (e.g. Hermann Rauschning (1939), Peter Viereck (1941), later Fritz Stern (1961) and George Mosse (1964)), traced the roots of National Socialism back into earlier German history, and confected a logic of German development, or misdevelopment, that led almost ineluctably to Hitler.[10] Many of these authors shared a tendency to emphasize the ideological origins and logic of National Socialism, as well as its peculiarly German quality, though they offered varying chronologies for its origins and rise, and differed in their explanations of this tradition of German political extremism. Typically, they focused on such issues as the shallowness of the Enlightenment in Germany; the uncontested power of authoritarian statism; the consequent weakness of rationalist, liberal and emancipatory values among the German elite, and a broader openness to ideas of aggressive nationalism, anti-Semitism and civic quietism among the popular classes; the anti-modernist, often nihilist 'cultural pessimism' that characterized *fin-de-siècle* German thought; and

---

8   See, e.g. Waite 1977; Binion 1976; Stern 1975; see also Ayçoberry 1981: ch. 10.

9   Ernst Bloch [1935] 1962: 45–204. The Hungarian Marxist philosopher George Lukács developed the idea that German philosophy provided uniquely fertile soil for the flourishing of irrationalism in *Die Zerstörung der Vernunft* (1953); for further comments on the German backwardness thesis in Marxist thought, see Evans 1985, and Caplan 1986.

10   See also Barraclough 1949; Kohn 1960; Glaser 1978, and Plessner 1959. Shirer 1960 is probably the most widely read popularization of this approach.

the alleged susceptibility of the masses to seductive political mythologies and defensive bigotry. Although these political and intellectual tendencies could be found throughout pre-1914 Europe, Germany – strained morally and socially by the particularly intense pressures it experienced from industrialization and the rise of mass society – was seen as offering the most fertile soil, so that it only took the further crises of war and revolution to convert this latent extremism into the overt form of National Socialism. In this way, the pathology of modern society was reinterpreted as a visitation concentrated in its most virulent strain on Germany.

Totalitarianism theory was in some respects a derivation from the mass-society thesis, though it abandoned the latter's previous broad interest in social dynamics for a more limited obsession with the mechanics of power. It emerged as a systematic political analysis in the 1950s, though the term itself had first been coined in the 1920s, in application to fascism and National Socialism. The term's earlier currency among leftist analysts of fascism – including Franz Neumann (1942), Herbert Marcuse (1967) and Ernst Fraenkel (1941) – has largely been forgotten in the wake of its later appropriation as a generic description for both communism and fascism. This usage, which developed during the Cold War, deliberately challenged the Left's claim that there was an absolute antithesis between the two ideologies – because fascism was, in class terms, a variant of capitalism, while communism was the overcoming of capitalism.[11] Totalitarianism theory does not necessarily deny the existence of major differences between communist and fascist political systems, but concludes that in the final analysis these differences are less significant than either what the systems have in common, or what distinguishes them from liberal democracy. The classic formulation, originally advanced by Carl Friedrich in the 1950s, identified six characteristics of totalitarian regimes:

> an official ideology . . . a single mass party . . . a system of terroristic police control . . . a technologically conditioned near-complete monopoly of control . . . of all means of effective mass communication [and] of all means of effective armed combat . . . a central control and direction of the entire economy.[12]

Marxism's emphasis on the class character of fascism was thus discounted, and in general the social-structural approach characteristic of both the Marxist and Weberian traditions of political analysis was discarded in favour of a narrower focus on the political apparatus alone. A powerful exception was Hannah Arendt's *The Origins of Totalitarianism*, first published in 1949, whose thesis depended upon a devastating argument about the relationship between mass populations and mass murder: that the *raison d'être* of the true totalitarian regime was its capacity for the annihilation of its unintegrated superfluous populations. Arendt's arguments

---

11 Kershaw 1989: 20–3, 30–5 offers an informed and judicious summary of the term and its applications; see also Ayçoberry 1981: ch. 8.
12 Friedrich and Brzesinski [1956] 1961: 9–10; see also Talmon 1952; Friedrich 1954; Buchheim [1962] 1968; Schapiro 1972. Neumann 1942 confined the term 'totalitarianism' to National Socialism alone.

derived from her profoundly pessimistic assessment of the potential for responsible politics in modern class societies, which she saw as an incoherent assemblage of atomized masses on the one hand and an elite of leaders on the other. She traced the historical emergence of this deformed polity, until its ultimate perversion as the totalitarian state of her own day, in which terrorist domination became its own logic and legitimation. Yet like other theorists of totalitarianism, Arendt found it easier to apply her model to Nazi Germany than to Stalinist Russia, even though she saw both of them as equally utopian (or rather dystopian) projects of social transformation in the name of history, freed from the constraints of divine, natural or human law alike.

Although in the 1920s and 1930s the concepts of totalitarianism and fascism were not seen as belonging to mutually irreconcilable theories, by the 1950s a polemical distance had been established between them by the exigencies of Cold War scholarship. Irrespective of their intellectual merits, both theories got taken up as political weapons in the stand-off between West and East, and were often grossly over-simplified by proponents and caricatured by opponents. In practice, academic historians in the West had little to contribute to this political stalemate – unlike their counterparts in the East, or their own colleagues in Western political science departments, both of whom were heavily engaged in it. Nevertheless, when scholarly research into the history of National Socialism began to take shape in the 1960s, it was this debate that formed the initial framework – though it was not long, as we shall see, before this research undermined the theoretical structures within which it first emerged. But before turning to this, it will be helpful to review the character of the historical profession under National Socialism, and the re-emergence of academic history after 1945.

HISTORIANS UNDER NATIONAL SOCIALISM

The history of the profession and practice of history between 1933 and 1945 is one neither of principled resistance to the pressures of the National Socialist regime, nor of enthusiastic political capitulation.[13] Before 1933, academic historians, conservative politically as well as methodologically, were no more moved by the radicalism, not to mention anti-intellectualism, of Nazism than they had been by any other ideology or theory that threatened to disturb their own traditions.[14] But these traditions also predisposed them to powerful reservations about the Weimar Republic, and to an inner sympathy with National Socialism once it came to power. Like the professoriate in general, academic historians were politically inclined to a conservative nationalism that made them mistrustful of republican democracy.

---

13 On historiography in Nazi Germany, see Gilbert 1947; Heiber 1966, which is much more than a history of the Reichsinstitut für die Geschichte des neuen Deutschlands alone; Werner 1967; Werner 1974; Werner 1968; Franz 1981; Schreiner 1985; Burleigh 1988; Schulze 1989: ch. 3.
14 On academic historiography in the Weimar Republic, see Faulenbach 1980; also Hammen 1941; Iggers 1968: ch. 8; Oberkrome 1991.

Their intellectual practice privileged the history of the state, the role of the 'world-historical' individual and the peculiarity of Germany's history by contrast with that of western Europe. Weimar appeared to them as an ahistorical imposition, a deviation from the path of German national assertion; anxious to see that continuity re-established, they had little interest in embedding the republic in any alternative logic of historical development. Thus a tendency to look for the emergence of a new German leader to overcome the political and spiritual crisis of the age was clearly discernible in 1920s historiography. On the whole, it seems hard to argue with the applicability to this group of German historians of the cynical observation made about an earlier generation, that 'they easily lose the ability to move their heads because of their always looking backwards, so that if any movement at all is possible, only movement to the right remains'.[15]

Still, the fit was not necessarily a close one. Despite the status ascribed to history in Hitler's world-view (see Wippermann 1989: 98–105), the regime's own priorities lay more in mass indoctrination through popular propaganda and the lower echelons of the educational system. The esoteric researches of academic historicism were not much use there. For their part, academic historians were not directly attracted by the Nazis' insistence on the primacy of biological racism as the key to history; they preferred to preserve their traditional standards of intellectual integrity, if more for narrow and self-interested professional reasons than out of political principle. Like other members of the bourgeois elite, their sights were set more on the restoration of a familiar social and political conservatism than on the kind of radical changes promised by the Nazis. But it was this very narrowness of perspective that made most historians – again, like members of other professions – willing to shut their eyes to Nazi radicalism, and to compromise with the regime as long as their own professional activities were not too intrusively politicized. Few had been or became enthusiastic members of the NSDAP, but at the same time few showed any scruples about continuing their scholarly work with appropriate gestures to the new political dispensation. On the whole, academic research remained relatively undisturbed, and there was no sharp break in publishing practices (though Meinecke was forced out of the editorship of the *Historische Zeitschrift*). In this sense the profession was not thoroughly purged or Nazified – yet this was hardly necessary, given the underlying sympathy among historians for the regime. As Schreiner comments in his discussion of academic research on the concept of the German 'Reich', historians after 1933 presented evidence of 'historical connections [that] lent recognition and legitimacy to the third foundation of the Reich. ... Academic language coincided with the language of party propaganda. The lecture hall became a forum for *völkisch* ideology' (Schreiner 1985: 189–9).

Given this widespread stance, it was not surprising that the profession as a whole did little to protect those of its colleagues who did fall foul of the regime, most of whom were by definition already intellectual, political or racial 'outsiders' in this

---

15 Quoted in Schreiner 1985: 224; this translation in Burleigh 1988: 46.

conservative milieu. A number of liberal historians whose heterodox ideas had found little acceptance in the profession in the 1920s were forced into emigration, among them Eckart Kehr, Hans Rosenberg, Arthur Rosenberg, Hajo Holborn, Georg Hallgarten and Veit Valentin. Even though most continued to study the history of their homeland, few returned to it after 1945, and thus most of the discipline's liveliest and most imaginative minds were permanently lost to the German historical profession.[16] Some historians who were not professionally or politically radical, such as Ernst Kantorowicz and Hans Rothfels (both men of impeccable conservative credentials), were obliged to flee as Jews. Others, such as Hermann Oncken and the *Vernunftrepublikaner* Friedrich Meinecke, remained in Germany and tried to distance themselves from the regime (and protect themselves from their critics) as best they could. Only a handful of those who remained, including Fritz Kern and Walter Markov, can be said to have resisted National Socialism either intellectually or politically.

On the other side, a minority of historians offered more active intellectual support to National Socialism. A handful of established scholars – for example Heinrich Dannenbauer and Otto Westphal – aligned themselves enthusiastically with the racial and geopolitical perspectives of the Nazi regime. Some younger scholars looked to the new regime for career openings beyond the frustrating limits of Germany's narrowly hierarchical academic system. Among these were the lesser or marginal scholars who were responsible for the political revision of educational textbooks.[17] Others found a niche in Walter Frank's Reichsinstitut für die Geschichte des neuen Deutschlands, established in 1935 under the patronage of the Nazi ideologue Alfred Rosenberg. The ambitious and unprincipled Frank and his colleagues saw themselves as the intellectual pacesetters and political watchdogs for the profession, but they were pretty much discounted by their fellow-historians and ignored by the Nazi leadership.[18] Strangled by political and administrative intrigues that he had courted but was incompetent to control, Frank was evicted from his position in 1941, though the institute struggled on until 1945. More baleful was the contribution by historians to *Ostforschung*, or the academic study of eastern Europe, which had a more central role to play in Nazi policy. By nature interdisciplinary, *Ostforschung* included specialists in fields such as archaeology, anthropology and political economy, as well as history. Working often in close collaboration with the

---

16 Though they did influence the post-war generation of academic historians; see below p. 559. For the émigré historians, see Iggers 1974: a fuller list of those who either left as historians or trained in the discipline during exile includes some of the most eminent scholars in the field of modern German history, among them Felix Gilbert, Theodor Mommsen, Fritz Epstein, Golo Mann and Francis Carsten, also the younger Georg Mosse, Fritz Stern, Peter Gay, Fritz Ringer and many others: an outstanding harvest of talent, garnered mainly by the United States. Women historians, virtually ignored in existing studies of émigré scholars, are discussed by Epstein in a volume of essays based on the conference 'Women in the Emigration after 1933' held in November 1991 (Epstein 1993); see also in this series Lehmann and Sheehan (eds) 1991 and Lehmann and van Horn Melton (eds) 1994.

17 On school textbooks, see Blackburn 1985, especially ch. 3.

18 See Heiber 1966 for a summary see Vierhaus 1968.

SS, and through organizations such as the Nordost-Deutsche Forschungsgemein-schaft, the Bund deutscher Osten, and other research institutes based in occupied Poland, the *Ostforscher* were deeply complicitous with the implementation of Nazi *Lebensraum* policies, as well as with the intellectual sink-hole of racism (see Burleigh 1988; Klessmann 1985; also Kater 1974). Their major intellectual contributions to the regime were 'the production of a leaden stream of propaganda literature justifying German hegemony in the occupied East', and research into the ethnic identity and composition of Germany's new subject peoples – all in the service of racial discrimination, resettlement and ultimately extermination (Burleigh 1988: 206).

The tendency in West Germany after 1945 was to argue that academic historiography had remained more or less marginal to the activities of the Nazi regime, and that historians as a group had not deeply compromised themselves. However, as Klaus Schreiner has pointed out, the question of who complied with, who resisted National Socialism is more than a matter of individual biography. The significant question is how historians collectively allowed their intellectual principles to be replaced by or subordinated to the ideological agenda of National Socialism, and here it is impossible to ignore the importance of pre-1933 profes-sional and political values in helping the historical profession to come to terms with the Nazi regime (Schreiner 1985: 167). In the words of the most recent student of the German historical profession, 'The discipline's basically national-conservative consensus and its acquired willingness to adopt "völkisch" perspectives in general created an effective web of internal relationships with the aims of National Socialism' (Schulze 1989: 40).

MASTERING THE PAST IN POST-WAR GERMANY

West Germany

The renewal of West German historiography after 1945 was conditioned by a series of somewhat negative factors: by a strong reaction against the disparaging image of Germany conveyed by Nuremberg and the Allies' denazification efforts, by the profession's own desire to assert its freedom from contamination by Nazism, and, consequently, by a return to traditional historiographical standards rather than the development of new critical approaches.[19] Moreover, so successfully had the historical profession excluded heterodoxy in the 1920s and conformed to the political pressures of the 1930s that it had few internal resources upon which to

---

19 The most useful sources on the post-war development of West German historiography in general are Mommsen 1973; Conze 1977; Mommsen 1981a; Faulenbach 1981; Rüsen 1984; Wehler 1984; Mommsen 1984; Faulenbach 1974; Klessmann 1987; Hein 1986; Schulin 1989; Iggers 1975: ch. 3. For a detailed examination of the immediate post-war period, see Schulze 1989; and see also Ritter 1950. Useful surveys of the early post-war historiography of National Socialism include Kwiet 1989; and Wippermann 1976.

draw for a critical reconstruction of its practice. And in 1945, even more than in 1933, continuity in academic appointments was the rule: only about 20 out of the 110 professors of history lost their university positions due to denazification efforts, and even some of these found reappointment in the 1950s.[20] Thus the *Historische Zeitschrift*, the profession's journal of record, published but a single article on National Socialism before 1950, and picked up the historical themes favoured before 1933, such as the 1848 revolutions, the tradition of local self-government, or Bismarck and unification. These were subjected to re-evaluation in the light of the failure of liberalism in Germany, but the framework of interpretation remained basically historicist, motivated primarily by intellectual and moral concerns, and not theoretically informed or interested in structural analysis (Mommsen 1973: 127). To a great extent it was the émigré generation of historians – notably George Mosse, Peter Gay, Hajo Holborn and Fritz Stern – who took up the challenge of reinterpreting the German past, fortified by the right of the victors to tell the story on their own terms. By the same token, the surviving generation of senior West German historians was reluctant to address directly in their research or teaching a history in which their own part had been less than glorious.

Yet German reluctance to address the Nazi past should not be exaggerated, for the immediate post-war years saw a spate of publications on National Socialism and the war, by journalists and independent authors as well as historians; it was not until the 1950s that fuller rein was given to popular desires to repress the recent past.[21] The titles of early works bristled with a vocabulary of national self-recrimination and moral bafflement – 'catastrophe', 'guilt', 'wrong turning', 'fate' and the like.[22] Among the most celebrated examples of this genre were two works by spokesmen for two generations of German academic history: the 85-year-old Friedrich Meinecke, and Gerhard Ritter, at twenty years his junior the new leader of the profession. Meinecke's *Die deutsche Katastrophe* (1946, trans. 1950) interpreted National Socialism as a manifestation of deep faults in *European* society, and ascribed its success in Germany to a series of avoidable accidents. Not dissimilarly, Ritter's *Europa und die deutsche Frage* (1948) also emphasized the European scope of the crisis of modernization that led to National Socialism, and viewed the Third Reich as an unpredictable moment of rupture in the course of German history (see also Ritter 1955). These titles also suggest that, perhaps unsurprisingly, the earliest publications in West Germany were concerned more with the moral implications of National Socialism than with the search for broader political or social explanations. This was true too of the émigré Hans Rothfels's early study of the German resistance first published in English in 1948 and based on a

---

20 Schulze 1989: 124–5. The continuity in the profession and methodology of *Ostforschung* was even more blatant and reprehensible: see Klessmann 1985: 370–4 and Burleigh 1988: 300–21. For the lineage of the historical profession in general, see Weber 1984.

21 Wippermann 1976 argues that the immediate post-war years saw a lively debate, a point often missed in reviews of the academic literature; for the retreat from history, see Heuss 1959.

22 See the catalogue in Schulze 1989: 47; also comments by Faulenbach 1981: 31–2.

lecture delivered in Chicago in 1947.[23] Rothfels credited the moral achievement of the national-conservative resistance in spite of its evident political failure, and thus reversed the normal historicist criteria for judging success; to that extent his book represented a rejection of the inherited traditions of historical evaluation (Mommsen 1981: 153). Yet this emphasis on values and traditions perpetuated another element of the historicist tradition, and was evidence of a wider professional reluctance to embrace social and structural approaches to history.[24] In addition, Rothfels's exclusive emphasis on the national-conservative resistance ignored the contribution of the communist opposition, reflecting a broader tendency in West Germany to dismiss the leftist resistance to the Nazis as essentially traitorous – a conservative position that was given new force by the emergence of Cold War polarities in the 1950s.

As research gathered steam in the 1950s, it did not shun genuine and difficult questions about the origins of and responsibility for National Socialism, yet pursued these in a somewhat limiting interpretative context which emphasized the ideological, criminal and anomalous character of the regime. This had the double effect of limiting research into the specific political and sociological circumstances of the Nazi rise to power, and of protecting the broader span of German history from a more probing and critical re-evaluation. Thus Hans Buchheim's Hitler was portrayed as a demonic and more than Machiavellian character; the sources of his power were located above all in his ideological and manipulative skills, as the Führer himself had claimed (Buchheim 1958; 1962). In a similar reflection of the Nazis' own imagery, the regime after 1933 was depicted as monolithic and totalitarian in structure, and its policies as the logical implementation of the leadership's ideological programme. While foreign and émigré historians, as we have seen, traced the roots of National Socialism far back into German history, the dominant West German historical interpretations insisted, with Meinecke and Ritter, on the character of the Nazi regime as an unforeseeable rupture in the course of German history, and/or as one local expression of common perils shared by the post-Enlightenment world. In so far as the triumph of National Socialism was not explained as the accidental victory of a conspiracy of brutal political thugs, German responsibility was broadly assessed in terms of the cultural weakness of German liberalism, rather than being assigned, as Brecht put it in his *Kriegsfibel*, to 'dunkle Mächte' – dark powers – who were not the anonymous emanations of fate, but had identifiable names and addresses. As Gerhard Ritter (1965: vii) pointed out, the intended readership of these early publications was less the Germans themselves than a hostile world of foreign critics addicted to the concept of collective guilt. In Hans Mommsen's phrase, Germany was represented as if it had been 'occupied' by National Socialism; the question of the specific institutional and social sources of

23 Translated into German as *Die deutsche Opposition gegen Hitler. Eine Würdigung* (1949); a revised edition was published in Frankfurt in 1961, and an English translation in London the same year.
24 The same can be said of Gerhard Ritter's masterwork, the four-volume *Staatskunst und Kriegshandwerk. Das Problem des Militarismus in Deutschland* (1954–68).

National Socialism within Germany itself was thereby occluded. At the same time, historians were willing to contribute to the construction of a positive foundation for the new West German state, even if their temperament meant that they saw this less as a democratic than as an ethical project.[25]

This period saw the foundation of the Munich Institut für Zeitgeschichte (Institute for Contemporary History), a research foundation that pioneered West German historical scholarship on National Socialism.[26] It is significant that this initiative took place outside the traditional university structure, and was even opposed as insufficiently scholarly by some members of the academic establishment, Ritter included. But the Institute has remained the premier centre for research into National Socialism and contemporary history in general, and has sponsored a string of extremely important research and bibliographical projects, the publication of both primary sources and secondary research, and the issue from 1953 of the *Vierteljahrshefte für Zeitgeschichte* (first edited by Rothfels), which immediately established itself as the journal of record for research into the history of National Socialism.[27] The first short popular account of the National Socialist period aimed at a domestic readership was issued by the Institute's first head, Hermann Mau, in collaboration with Helmut Krausnick (1953); it was followed by a number of similar studies by Buchheim (1958), Helga Grebing (1959), and – harbinger of a new generation – Martin Broszat (1960), who was to become one of the most prominent historians of National Socialism and retained a lifelong association with the Institute.[28] Mau, who had written his *Habilitation* thesis on the use of the Nuremberg documentation as a historical source, also played an important role in the process by which the Allies agreed to return most captured documents to German archives more speedily than they had originally envisaged.[29] Under the editorship of Rothfels, and with an international editorial committee, the publication of the important series of *Akten zur deutschen auswärtigen Politik 1918–1945* began in 1950, to be followed in 1958 by the independently published series *Ursachen und Folgen*; the first popular edition of selected documents on National Socialism was published in 1957 by Walter Hofer (300,000 copies were in circulation by 1961) (see Kwiet 1989: 186). In general, the major themes of the first

---

25   For these points see Mommsen 1973: 129–33.
26   For the origins and work of the Institute, which until 1952 bore the name 'Institute for Research into the National Socialist Period', see Gimbel 1965; Auerbach 1970; and Schulze 1989: 229–42. A second non-university institute, the Hamburg Forschungsstelle für die Geschichte des Nationalsozialismus (led for many years by Werner Jochmann), was established after much delay in 1960.
27   It is impossible in the limits of this chapter to discuss the periodicals in the field of contemporary history; the most important for contemporary history are, apart from the *Vierteljahrshefte*, *Geschichte in Wissenschaft und Unterricht*, *Internationale Wissenschaftliche Korrespondenz* and the more recent *Geschichte und Gesellschaft*. Important English-language periodical sources for the period include *Central European History*, *German History*, *Journal of Modern History*, *New German Critique*.
28   Mau and Krausnick 1959 – parts were originally published in Rassow 1953; Buchheim 1958; Grebing 1959; Broszat 1960. For a broader listing of early publications, see Kwiet 1989: 186–7.
29   For the capture and return of German records, see Wolfe 1974; Henke 1982.

scholarly publications, German and foreign alike, were the war and foreign policy, and the ideological origins of National Socialism, notably in modern anti-Semitism. The internal structure and domestic policies of the Third Reich did not become the object of intense study before the mid-1960s, and until then the interpretation of the domestic structure of the regime was dominated by totalitarianism theory. Interestingly enough, despite the influence ascribed to Hitler as the demonic power in the regime, there was no major biography of the Nazi leader by a German historian until Helmut Heiber's 1960 study, and even this was more workmanlike than inspired. Alan Bullock's (1952) magisterial study remained the canonical work, and there was nothing comparable in German until 1973, when Joachim Fest's biography appeared.

The turning-point in the development of post-war West German historiography came in the early 1960s, with the publication of the Hamburg historian Fritz Fischer's research on the origins of the First World War.[30] Fischer's central arguments – that there was a significant continuity in German foreign policy between 1914 and 1939, even between Bismarck and Hitler, and that foreign policy emerged from domestic rather than geopolitical considerations – had been anticipated to some extent in the early 1950s, notably by Ludwig Dehio, but the difference now was the presence of a new generation of historians willing to pick up this iconoclastic note and develop it systematically. Fischer's thesis, which was enthusiastically embraced by his younger colleagues, also aroused a storm of controversy among his own contemporaries, and for much the same reasons: because he shattered the prevailing academic view that 1933–45 could be safely cordoned off as an anomaly in Germany's history, and because he was engaging in a form of national and professional self-criticism that was deeply antagonizing to his more conservative colleagues.

The broad impact of the Fischer controversy on the reorientation of German historiography is beyond the scope of this chapter, but it was crucial in initiating that process of critical historiographical reflection which had been evaded by the German profession in the immediate post-war era.[31] In elaborating (and hardening) his position in the course of a widely publicized and increasingly vituperative debate, Fischer moved away from his originally ideological and diplomatic interpretation and towards a more socio-structural analysis of causation. In this, he echoed calls already issued by colleagues such as Theodor Schieder, Otto Brunner and Werner Conze for a new institutional and structural approach to historical studies in general, but invested them with a new moral energy that was also highly attractive to the rising generation of young historians. Fischer's analysis of German foreign policy was thus extended by his students and disciples into a radically revisionist interpretation of modern German history.

---

30   Fischer 1959. For its significance, see e.g. Iggers 1975: 89ff.
31   See the references in n. 19 above, especially Mommsen 1973: 138ff.

Inevitably, this centred largely on Wihelmine rather than Nazi Germany, yet the approach was massively overdetermined by the desire to explain why National Socialism had been able to come to power in Germany: a project which, in the eyes of this new generation, had been deliberately and culpably neglected by the majority of their teachers. Influenced partly by American models of sociological and political analysis (domesticated in Germany most notably through the work of Rainer Maria Lepsius and Ralf Dahrendorf) and partly by the reimported influence of the émigré generation of German historians, a new and prolific generation of historians began their publishing careers in the 1960s. Including Hans-Ulrich Wehler, Jürgen Kocka, Hans-Jürgen Puhle, Peter-Christian Witt and Heinrich August Winkler among others, this group reconfigured the cultural and intellectual interpretation of German uniqueness into a new focus on the peculiar structure and continuities of social and political institutions and practices in modern Germany.[32]

Characteristically, the work of these historians focused less on the ideological origins of antidemocratic tendencies than on the medium-term social and political consequences of the German experience of industrialization and modernization. According to this approach, German history has followed since the rise of industrial capitalism a 'special path' or *Sonderweg* by comparison with the nations of western Europe and the United States. Its development was peculiar in that it proved unable to develop the modern social and political institutions, ideologies and relationships that have normally been concomitant with the transition to industrial capitalism: a politically powerful bourgeoisie, parliamentary institutions, a modern class structure and set of social practices. Though Germany undoubtedly acquired an economically powerful bourgeoisie in the course of the nineteenth century, this class failed to identify itself with liberal social and political values, or to assert its political leadership over the aristocracy and working classes. Instead, the pre-industrial economic (agrarian) and social (aristocratic-military) elites continued to exercise power in Wilhelmine Germany by means of the political repression of the working class, and the manipulation of the intermediate petty bourgeoisie. In this way the old elites blocked the development of liberal and democratic institutions, and saturated society with their pre-industrial authoritarian values. Repression sharpened social hostilities, so that when the Wilhelmine system finally collapsed in 1918/19, the bitterly antagonistic, mutually fearful and politically frustrated classes confronted each other directly, without the mediating influence of democratic and emancipatory traditions or a liberal consensus. The Weimar Republic was thus saddled with a virtually fatal baggage of anachronistic institutions and expectations, with which heritage it faced the recurrent climate of crisis in the 1920s and early 1930s. National Socialism was the mass political expression of this unbalanced socio-political structure, in that it capitalized on the fears of the lower middle

---

32 Dahrendorf 1965; Lepsius 1969; 1973. For discussions of this literature, see Blackbourn and Eley 1984; Moeller 1983/4; Evans 1985; Iggers 1975: ch. 3.

classes caught between traditionalism and the pressures of modernization. In this sense, as critics of this school have argued, imperial German history was rewritten as the prehistory of National Socialism, and National Socialism was seen as the outcome of a peculiarly German failure to accomplish a balanced process of social and political modernization.[33]

This revisionist interpretation of pre-Nazi history as a crisis of modernization developed in tandem with a new historiography of National Socialism that also took shape in the 1960s. German historians themselves were thus recovering the initiative that had been forfeited to émigrés and foreigners in the immediate post-war period. In an important sense, from the mid-1960s the writing of Germany's recent history became a shared international project for the first time, engaging British and US historians in particular and presenting a new convergence of research perspectives and objectives. Behind this process stood the momentous generational transition that took place in the 1960s, not only in Germany. Following hard on the emergence of the post-Fischer school of critical historiography came the cohort of the 1960s, the first truly post-war generation, who enjoyed a freedom to question conventions that had been unavailable to their parents. Not least, they insisted on challenging openly the absence of serious public education in the reasons for the success of the Nazi movement and the impact of the regime on German society.[34] The Eichmann trial in Israel in 1960 and the beginning of West Germany's first major prosecutions of war criminals in 1964 also stimulated the desire to make up for the deficit of public knowledge and debate.[35] More prosaically, the opening of the West German archives from the late 1950s and the expansion of the university systems in Germany, western Europe, the United States and Canada presented both opportunity and necessity for successive waves of doctoral candidates to embark on intensive monographic research projects. The result was an unprecedented outpouring of academic publications on the history of National Socialism, which began appearing in the mid-1960s and which has continued to the present.

This extension of research was also the beneficiary of an expansion and re-orientation of historical perspectives and methodologies which, coming thick and fast upon the international scene in the 1970s and 1980s, influenced Germans and non-Germans alike. The process was initiated by the revival of debate about Marxist theory, which opened up in the later 1960s along with the emergence of a New Left as critical of the legacy of Stalinism as it was of the Cold War rigidities of Western politics. Marxist theories of fascism underwent a major process of

---

33   For a critical discussion of the implication of this argument for the study of fascism, which discusses the work of Kocka and Winkler in particular, see Eley 1989.

34   See e.g. Haug 1967; Uhe 1972. Kühnl 1973 is highly critical of West German textbooks, but does not cover National Socialism as such.

35   See Krausnick *et al.* 1968, which was originally presented as historical evidence in the 1963 Auschwitz trial; and for German prosecutions of war criminals see Rückerl 1980.

recovery and re-evaluation in this period, reaching far beyond the repetitive orthodoxy of official communist analysis.[36] In West Germany, left analyses of National Socialism drew much of their vitality from the claim that fascism was an endemic recourse of capitalism in crisis – not least in contemporary West Germany itself, in which many on the Left saw troubling anti-democratic tendencies. These leftist critiques and histories were repudiated by liberal and conservative historians alike, for being too politicized or too abstract, in either sense too distant from the 'real' history of Nazi Germany (see especially Winkler 1978; Bracher 1976). These academic and political debates became very heated, reflecting a tense political climate in which democratic institutions in West Germany appeared to be under threat – though whether from the Right or from the Left depended upon one's perspective.

The revival of interest in Marxist theories of fascism, and the growth of empirical research into the history of National Socialism, were between them bound to put into question the claims of the main existing contender in the theoretical field, totalitarianism theory. This approach had been developed mainly by sociologists and political scientists rather than historians, yet with the eclipse of fascism theory in the 1950s it had presided over early interpretations of National Socialism, notably those advanced by Hans Buchheim and Karl Dietrich Bracher, and the early work of Martin Broszat.[37] Yet having developed in something of an empirical vacuum, totalitarianism theory itself was vulnerable to the corrective onslaught of detailed research into the history of Weimar and Nazi Germany. Critics of the theory claimed that it depended upon on an illicitly retrospective reading of the history of National Socialism from regime back to movement; on an exaggerated estimate of the Nazi regime's capacity for integration and functional rationality; and on a highly selective comparison that reduced Soviet Russia to Stalinism alone, and established too simple a polarity between democracy on the one hand and all forms of dictatorship on the other. In turn, advocates of this model attacked Marxist versions of fascism theory for subordinating empirical research to distorting political and theoretical premises, and especially for ignoring the substantial differences between National Socialism and Italian fascism – especially

---

36   For the revival of Marxist theories in West Germany, see, apart from the sources cited in n. 4 above, Rabinbach 1974. Pioneering the new Marxist work on National Socialism was the exchange of articles in the Berlin left periodical *Das Argument*, 1964–70. Numerous analyses of fascism from the left appeared in the late 1960s to the 1970s: for a sympathetic survey see Kühnl 1990; for more critical surveys, see Wippermann 1975, and Thamer and Wippermann 1977. Among the representative German texts of the 1960s and 1970s: Kühnl 1971; Alff 1971; Clemenz 1972; Kuhn 1973; Kühnl 1974; Backhaus 1976; Pozzoli 1976; Hennig 1977. Poulantzas 1974, originally published in France in 1970, was an influential re-evaluation of Third International theories; see also Caplan 1976. The West German periodicals *Geschichte in Wissenschaft und Unterricht*, *Neue Politische Literatur* and *Politische Vierteljahresschrift* reviewed the new German literature extensively in the 1970s; see also *International Journal of Politics*, Winter 1972–3 – issue on critiques of fascism theory from West Germany.
37   Buchheim 1962; Broszat 1960; Bracher 1955; [1969] 1970.

the far greater significance of racism in Nazism, as well as the extraordinary political dynamism of the Hitler-led regime.[38]

The renewal of interest in fascism theory was not confined to the Left alone. It received a highly influential reworking in the conservative philosopher Ernst Nolte's phenomenological analysis of fascism as an independent 'metapolitical' movement with a novel revolutionary ideology.[39] Nolte's interpretation turned on his difficult concept of fascism as 'resistance to transcendence': an ideology that was opposed to the practical movement of emancipation and the spiritual striving of 'freedom towards the infinite' offered by Enlightenment tradition. Nolte based his account on a comparative analysis of the Italian, French and German fascist movements, but the philosophical magnitude of his interpretation stood in some tension with his claim that fascism was also, as the German title of his book proclaimed (*Der Faschismus in seiner Epoche*), an epochal event which was peculiar to the brief inter-war period alone. Curiously, Marxist interpretations of fascism were at the same time embarking on a reverse journey: from excessively prescriptive statements about the nature and function of fascism, to a new concern with the historically specific conjunctures of its origins and success. Among the most prominent issues for Marxists was one that, for obvious reasons, had already engaged the Left's attention in the 1920s and 1930s: the relationship between capitalism and fascism, both theoretically and in terms of industry's contributions to the Nazi rise to power. Much new Marxist scholarship was devoted to exploring this relationship, often in highly abstract terms that allowed its critics to contend not only that no such relationship could be demonstrated, but also that Marxism as a method was incompatible with the conventions of empirical history. Partly in response to this criticism, and partly because of their own dissatisfaction with excessive theoretical abstraction, historians on the Left took up the empirical research which would test, and potentially support, the validity of the theories. Characteristically, they investigated such key questions for Marxist theory as the class composition of the Nazi movement, the socio-political circumstances of its rise to power, the position of labour under Nazi rule, and the relationship between economics and politics in the Third Reich.[40]

The generation of West German historians who came of age in the 1960s thus inaugurated a remarkable period of research into the history of National Socialism.

---

38   The debate can be followed in *Totalitarismus und Faschismus* 1980, also in Kershaw 1967: 20–3, 30–5, and Ayçoberry 1981: ch. 8; for a critique, Mommsen 1971; for a defence, Bracher 1976.

39   Nolte 1966. This was one of a series of studies of fascism by Nolte, the others being *Die faschistische Bewegungen* (1966) and *Die Krise des liberalen Systems und die faschistischen Bewegungen* (1968).

40   Important examples of this neo-Marxist literature include the works of Tim Mason, e.g. 'The Primacy of Politics – Politics and Economics in National Socialist Germany', in Woolf, ed.. *The Nature of Fascism*, pp. 165–95; Mason 1995, 1993. Hennig 1973; Stegmann 1973 and 1976; Abraham [1981] 1986 and 1984. For a sustained criticism of the claims of Marxist history, see the work of Henry Turner, especially Turner 1975b: Preface; 1980; 1985; and see the exchange between Turner 1975a and Stegmann 1977.

The range of work published in the past thirty years has been enormous, and it is impossible to review it in detail here.[41] Much of it has revisited older themes, including the social sources of mass support for the NSDAP before 1933, the role of the political and industrial elites in the rise of Nazism and in the Third Reich, the political structure and functioning of the Third Reich, Hitler's role and policies, ideology and the propaganda system, foreign policy and the origins of the war, the economic system and rearmament, resistance, the legal and judicial system, and anti-Semitism and the 'Holocaust' – the latter began to attract serious attention from German historian for the first time in the 1970s. By this date, a younger generation of historians, often influenced by the Marxist debates of the 1960s, was also opening up new issues to investigation, such as the social structure of Nazi Germany, the texture of everyday life (*Alltagsgeschichte*), the experience of marginalized social groups including women, youth and sexual minorities, culture and science under National Socialism, eugenic policies, and the persecution of groups other than Jews and political opponents of the regime.

The debate generated by new work on the political organization of the Nazi regime can be taken as symptomatic of the clash of the different theoretical and political perspectives adopted by those engaged in this research. Led by Martin Broszat and Hans Mommsen, historians subjected the structure and functioning of the Nazi state to intensive re-examination, and concluded that the Third Reich, far from being a totalitarian monolith, was a kind of disorganized 'polyocracy' in which power was in practice fragmented and decentralized, and policy-making was unsystematic and improvised. The much-vaunted Nazi *Volksgemeinschaft* in fact masked rather than reconciled antagonistic social and political interests; these emerged in distorted and displaced forms, and created a factious and competitive political system in which rational policy-making was impossible.[42] This claim led to further arguments about the role of Hitler, especially the issue of whether the policies of the Nazi regime were the planned implementation of the Führer's fixed ideology and programme, or whether they arose far less predictably and consistently from the anarchic and friction-ridden way in which the regime actually functioned.[43] This debate between an 'intentionalist' interpretation of Hitler's motives

---

41   The reader is referred again to Kershaw 1989, and Hiden and Farquharson 1989 for more exhaustive summaries of this research. A number of references are also given in the footnotes that follow below.

42   See Mommsen 1966, and see also his collected essays: Mommsen 1991; Peterson 1969; Broszat [1969] 1981; Hüttenberger 1969; Diehl-Thiele 1969; Hüttenberger 1976. The full range of literature is reviewed in Kershaw 1989: ch. 4, Hiden and Farquharson 1989: ch. 3, and Hildebrand 1991: Part II. The debate about Hitler is extensively examined in Schreiber 1984; and see Kater 1981.

43   The terms 'intentionalist' and 'functionalist' were put into circulation by Mason 1981. For the functionalist argument, see in addition to references in the previous footnote, the important essay by Broszat 1970; Kershaw [1980] 1987; and most recently Kershaw 1991; Mommsen 1979. For the intentionalist argument, see Bracher 1979 and 1978; Jäckel 1979 and 1984, and the linked studies, Jäckel [1969] 1972 and 1988; also Hildebrand 1981. Other critical surveys of the literature from an intentionalist point of view include Hofer 1957 and Hillgruber 1982.

and role, and the 'functionalist' or 'structuralist' arguments advanced by Broszat, Mommsen and others echoed an older argument between the British historians A. J. P. Taylor and Hugh Trevor-Roper about the extent to which the outbreak of the Second World War was the effect of Hitler's deliberately calculated policy.[44] In its new form, however, the argument came to a climax on the horrific but crucial question of the extermination of the Jews and Hitler's role in it. The intentionalist argument is that the 'Holocaust' represented the planned climax of a fixed policy of genocide conceived by Hitler in the early stages of his political career, and systematically put into practice under his direction after 1933: from the boycotts, purges and legalized discrimination of the early years, to the total exclusion of Jews from Germany's economic and social life by the end of the 1930s, to the deportations, ghettoization and Europe-wide 'Final Solution' of the war years; also that it was Hitler himself who orchestrated this sequential process. The 'functionalists', on the other hand, have argued that Nazi anti-Semitic policies were far more *ad hoc* than the intentionalist model allows, that the documentary record shows that different leaders and agencies in the regime took the initiative at different times and for varied motives, and that the liquidation of the Jews was neither planned in advance of its initiation in mid-1941 nor personally directed by Hitler. Rather, anti-Semitic policies are seen as mostly improvised responses to a variety of political pressures; the move to physical annihilation is represented not as the barbaric climax to a systematically planned policy of anti-Semitism, but as the outcome of a haphazard process of radicalization which translated Hitler's metaphors of racial cleansing into a terrifying reality.[45]

This repositioning of an older argument from the conduct of foreign policy and war to the project of genocide signalled both the durability of the major issues in the historiography of National Socialism and the radically changing context of interpretation. The personality and role of Hitler have continued to occupy a prominent position in the historiography of Nazism, to an extent unequalled for any other 'world-historical' individual except perhaps Napoleon. And it is the most destructive and horrifying 'achievements' of the Third Reich – war and genocide – that have attracted lasting attention. But the angle of vision has tended to shift from the external policies and relationships of the regime to its internal organization and functioning. The evaluation of Nazi racism lies at the heart of this debate, calling into question the centrality of anti-Semitism, the primacy of foreign over domestic policy and the choice of a comparative framework of interpretation for National

---

44   This debate is most easily followed in Robertson 1971, which reprints some of the major contributions, but see also Taylor 1961; and see Kershaw 1989: ch. 6, and Hiden and Farquharson 1989: ch. 5.

45   The literature here is of course enormous; a judicious summary is Marrus 1987b; see also Marrus 1987a, Kulka 1985 and Friedländer 1984a. Intentionalist accounts include Dawidowicz 1975 and Fleming 1986. Major contributions to the functionalist debate include Broszat 1985 (originally published 1977) – a devastating exposé of Irving 1977; Mommsen 1986; Adam 1972; see also the important mediating works by Christopher Browning: Browning 1986a, 1986b, 1989 and 1992.

Socialism. First, recent research has greatly strengthened the case for seeing racial politics as definitive of the Nazi regime; yet opinions differ sharply on whether this racism was essentially anti-Semitic, or whether it embraced a broader regime of eugenic and 'biopolitical' manipulations, involving assaults on women as a sex, and on a whole range of 'asocials' and other people judged 'unworthy' of life according to Nazi criteria: homosexuals, Romani/Sinti, the hereditarily diseased, habitual criminals, alcoholics and so on.[46] Second, Nazi racism can be construed as an effect of either external or domestic policy, an ambiguity that allows for very different interpretations of its logic. Intentionalist historians have generally argued that Nazi anti-Semitism derived its strength from Hitler's own fanatical ideology, and that its ultimate logic was to power a war launched by Hitler as a campaign of territorial imperialism and racial extermination.[47] Structuralists, as we have seen, argue that racist policy arose essentially out of the internal dynamics of the regime, and that its evolution was characteristic of the conduct of a system that was functionally as well as substantively irrational; some also take the view that the decision to go to war in September 1939 was the outcome of domestic pressures that forced an economically and militarily adverse choice on Hitler.[48] Third, the extraordinary significance of Hitler's personal rule, together with the unprecedented enormity of the 'Holocaust', symbolized by the horror of Auschwitz, make the choice of a comparative framework very delicate. To compare National Socialism with other dictatorial regimes could lead to accusations of apologetics, relativization and trivialization; but to see the regime as somehow *sui generis*, as so to speak uniquely unique, risks removing it from historical explanation altogether.

The attempt to reposition the interpretation of National Socialism as a debate about internal structures and policies rather than the state and its leading personalities reflects one of the major new paths taken by post-war Western historiography in general, i.e. the turn from broadly political and narrative history to broadly social and analytical history. This was bound to be a hot issue in Germany, given the tenacious historicist legacy of concern with narratives of the state and its leaders, and with the interpretation of political motives by means of insight and empathy. Intentionalist analysis was recognizably historicist in its concentration on Hitler's political leadership and the primacy of high politics, especially foreign policy. By claiming too that Hitler and his anti-Semitic ideology were the keys to National Socialism, intentionalists also sought to argue that Nazism was not a variant of generic 'fascism': if anyone was comparable to Hitler, it was the twentieth century's

---

46   This research is now too extensive to be noted here, but there is an excellent discussion and lengthy bibliographical essay in Burleigh and Wippermann 1991. Important examples of the new literature include on asocials, Peukert 1982; on biopolitics and euthanasia, Klee 1983 and 1985, Schmuhl 1987, Aly 1989, Aly and Roth 1984, Pross and Aly 1989. On women and sexual politics, see Bock 1986, Czarnowski 1991; on homosexuals, Schoppmann 1991, Stümke and Finker 1981; on Romani and Sinti, Rose and Weiss 1991.

47   See, e.g. Hildebrand 1977 and Hillgruber 1972; the debate is surveyed by Thies 1978.

48   See Mason 1975 and 1995.

other totalitarian dictator, Stalin.[49] (Hence Ernst Nolte's argument, to be discussed below, that the murderous results of Stalinist policies anticipated the extermination of the Jews: Stalin and Hitler become comparable as equal architects of genocide.) The questions of the uniqueness of National Socialism, of Hitler's role in its history and of Germany's path towards it thus continue to occupy an absolutely central place, posing great challenges to contemporary historians, and repeatedly returning arguments to the topography of historicism.

The post-Fischer school of historians had, as we have seen, no argument with the view that modern Germany had undergone a special process of development that set it apart from the model of Western industrial capitalist democracy. Whatever the merits of this approach, it did function as an explanation of the course of German history up to 1933; on the other hand, it left unanswered the question of the status of German history *after* the end of National Socialism. At the same time it displaced to an unspecified future the issue of whether an eventually 'normalized' *post*-Nazi history would also permit the renormalization of modern German history as a whole: a re-evaluation, in other words, of the 'peculiarity' of German history. That time came in the mid-1980s, when, fifty years after the Nazi seizure of power, a concerted attempt began to reconfigure the position of the Third Reich in the history of contemporary Germany. As on previous occasions, this was as much a political as an academic debate. In political terms, the mandate in the earliest years of the Federal Republic's existence had been to legitimize and anchor a newly constructed constitutional identity, under the reassuring rubric 'Bonn ist nicht Weimar' – Bonn is not Weimar. Then the opening-up of West Germany's political and intellectual life in the late 1960s and 1970s led to an intensive engagement with the history and legacy of National Socialism, motivated in part by the belief that only by confronting this past could West Germans develop a critical perspective on their own national identity and, as some believed, resist the renewed threat of fascism. But the late 1970s witnessed another so-called *Tendenzwende*, or change of direction, in West German political life, moving the centre of the spectrum rightwards as the decade of reformism faltered and lost authority. The resulting debate among intellectuals was enacted as quintessentially a confrontation with Germany's past; and this *Vergangenheitsbewältigung* ('mastery of the past') was to be construed, in Hans Mommsen's telling argument, not simply as a moment of catharsis or a single act of historical enlightenment, but as a continuous process of 'confrontation with the causes and operating mechanisms of fascist domination' (quoted in Habermas 1984: xxiii). Mommsen's injunction implied that the Germans would never be 'rid' of their Nazi past, and that any refusal to face this fact carried risky implications for the political present. It was against this image of a past that eternally dominated the present that reaction gathered in the 1980s, breaking out

---

49   The comparison has been most recently drawn in biographical form by Bullock 1991.

into a glare of publicity in the so-called *Historikerstreit*, or historians' dispute, in 1986.[50]

What sparked the most intense phase of public debate was a press article by Ernst Nolte that suggested that Auschwitz was essentially a technically improved successor to the 'Asiatic deeds' of extermination carried out by the Turks against the Armenians and by the Bolsheviks in the collectivization campaign and the purges. This was not the first time Nolte had made these arguments, which consummated his retreat from fascism theory by equating Nazi genocide with Stalin's 'Asiatic deed'.[51] But, as with the Fischer debate twenty years earlier, it was the existence of a receptive context that propelled the issue into public controversy. Nolte's ideas seemed consonant with reinterpretations of Nazi history then being advanced by other conservative historians, notably Michael Stürmer (1988) and Andreas Hillgruber (1986; Hildebrand 1987). A raging dispute erupted which engaged virtually all the leading historians in the field, and was conducted through the newspapers and popular publications as well as in the specialist scholarly press. Essentially, it turned on two issues: the uniqueness of Germany's history, and the question of whether it could be made into a 'usable' past – usable, that is, in the construction of a sense of national continuity and historic German identity. Should Auschwitz, for all its distilled horror, continue to be the bench-mark against which Germans measured their national consciousness? Against Mommsen's argument that 'mastering the past' was a continuous process, Stürmer contended that 'We cannot live by making our own past . . . into a permanent source of endless guilt feelings' (quoted in Evans 1989: 103–4).

The *Historikerstreit* revealed the strength of the historicist tradition in Germany, the durability of basic epistemological questions about interpretation and explanation, and the intricate and passionate inflection of history and politics in West Germany. But its undoubted public political prominence was not entirely matched by its historiographical significance. In terms of its direct contribution to the agendas and methodologies of historical research, as opposed to political argument,

---

50   The background to open controversy included the Bitburg episode, discussions about a new German museum of history, and a newly acceptable consensus among conservative politicians and commentators that Germany had spent enough time regretting its guilty past and now deserved to develop a new sense of national identity and pride; see Hartman 1986; on the museum issue, see Heuser 1990. There are two excellent accounts of the *Historikerstreit* in English: Evans 1989, which offers a clear and comprehensive reading of the historical and political issues and a useful bibliographical essay, and Maier 1988, which takes a more philosophically reflective approach; see also Kershaw 1989: chs. 8 and 9, for a briefer but valuable summary. Baldwin 1990 is an important collection of German and English essays, but from the anti-Nolte side only; for Nolte's original essay, see Nolte 1985; but otherwise most of this literature remains untranslated. See also Habermas 1989; for the political background, see Eley 1988. Among the more important German contributions and surveys, see Backes 1990; Broszat 1988; Diner 1987; Habermas 1987; Hennig 1988, 1987; Meier 1987; Nolte 1987 and 1988; Senfft 1990; Wehler 1988.

51   For a careful evaluation of Nolte's arguments, and a discussion of his shift from Nazism/fascism to Nazism/Bolshevism comparisons, see Evans 1989: ch. 2.

the debate was somewhat sterile; it revisited ground that had already been opened up by historians and it lacked the energizing intellectual quality of the Fischer controversy twenty-five years earlier.[52] The major antagonists were members of the now dominant generation of historians – born in the 1920s and 1930s for the most part – who had already spent lifelong careers in the study of German history (the same had been true of contributors to Habermas's important 1979 conspectus of intellectual trends). To be sure, younger historians were far from silent in the *Historikerstreit*, yet their perspectives were often at odds with those of their senior colleagues, and the scholarly and political divisions were multiple rather than simply dualist.

The dominant generation of German historians had been formed in the context of the Fischer debate, which had pitched historicism against structural analysis in a first confrontation between West Germany's political and intellectual inheritances. But the younger generation had grown up among the diverse new political movements of the 1970s and 1980s – leftism, feminism and sexual politics, the civic initiative and the green movements – and many became politically and academically interested in topics quite foreign to that older confrontation. One particularly striking and innovative result has been the recent convergence of academic and popular interest in history from below, women's history and the history of everyday life (*Alltagsgeschichte*).[53] These new departures in a traditionally elitist historical culture have been strongly influenced by the British history workshop movement. They naturally raise special questions about the responsibility of a popular history of Nazism not simply to pander to public and commercial tastes for entertainment, as allegedly was the case with popular responses to the 1970s 'Hitler-wave' and the TV series *Holocaust* and *Heimat*.[54] The reception of women's history is also problematic in an academic culture which remains notoriously inhospitable to women, who occupy a mere handful of university positions, and who have developed this field virtually without support from the academy and largely outside it.[55] And *Alltagsgeschichte* has raised the ire of the previous generation of radical revisionists, who see in it a risk that the enormity of National Socialism will be trivialized if subjective individual experience is granted as much authority to generate 'meaning' in history as the reflected knowledge and theorized explanations

---

52 This point is made in Childers and Caplan 1992: Introduction.
53 For these new trends, see Crew 1989; Hull 1989; Jarausch 1989; Gerstenberger and Schmidt 1987; Niethammer 1983–5; Peukert 1986; 1987a; 1987b. The work of Martin Broszat has been the crucial crossover between generations here, notably the major project on the history of Bavaria under National Socialism led by him under the sponsorship of the Institut für Zeitgeschichte (1977–83); see also the essays in Broszat 1988, and his contributions to Baldwin 1990: 77–134.
54 See the special issues of *New German Critique* on the 'Holocaust'-reception, nos. 19 and 20.
55 See Hull 1989. The absence of women is registered for instance in Schulze 1989, whose ten-page index of names lists not a single substantive reference to a woman historian; further, its unremarkableness is attested in Weber 1984, a sociological analysis of the profession that ignores the category of gender. For a relatively sympathetic discussion of the issue, see Puhle 1981.

produced by the traditional professional historian.[56] At the same time, the practitioners of the new social history (among others) are troubled by the latest 'postmodernist' turn in intellectual circles with its implications – disturbing to the Marxist and the liberal traditions alike – for a retreat from objective rationality and grounded explanation. These newer questions about the claims of subjectivity and representation emerged first out of a largely US intellectual debate, and while the philosophical issues are familiar in Germany, their historical dimensions remain to be explored.[57]

Prominent in these recent debates are two major challenges to the writing of German history which are likely to remain unanswered in any final sense for the immediate future: how the country's Nazi past can be 'historicized' without normalizing or trivializing it; and whether current critiques of Enlightenment rationalism and its regime of truth are compatible with the critical assessment of this most 'irrational' of political ideologies. Neither of these issues on its own is peculiar to the history of National Socialism: 'historicization' in a neutral sense is the inevitable product of all historiographical work, while philosophical debates about the criteria of historical truth are scarcely new in themselves. Yet we should not be surprised that their bearing on the history of Nazi Germany has become so problematic at just this moment. The passage of time, in bearing away Nazism's last surviving witnesses, leaves behind a new field for historical interpretation. For some, this change threatens to abandon the meaning of Nazi history to those who would apparently revise or deny the truth of lived experience.[58] For others, it is precisely this inevitable shift of perspectives that is posing new historical challenges that can neither be forestalled nor ignored, however onerous the responsibility of meeting them.

German Democratic Republic

The development of the historiography of National Socialism in the DDR shows some parallels with that in West Germany, but rather more differences. First, as Günther Heydemann has pointed out, there was for long periods an unequal relationship between the two historiographies: West German historians virtually ignored their East German counterparts until the 1970s, while the East Germans

---

56 See, e.g. Kocka 1984, and the counter by Tenfelde 1984.
57 One exception is Niethammer 1989; see also Caplan 1989; Hull 1989 and Jarausch 1989; some comments in Maier 1988: 168ff. The issues are most directly addressed in Friedländer 1992; Friedländer 1984 now appears as a forerunner to this debate. See also Lyotard 1988. It is not accidental that the two most public controversies on this issue – the cases of Paul de Man and Martin Heidegger – turn on the problem of National Socialism: see de Man 1988; Hamacher et al. 1988; Derrida 1988, and the symposium of responses in *Critical Inquiry* 15(4) (Summer 1989): 765–874; Farias 1989; Lyotard 1990; 1989.
58 For the problem of 'revisionist' history proper, i.e. the denial of Nazi genocide as a historical event, see Vidal-Naquet 1989 and 1992.

engaged in a continuous though inevitably one-sided polemic with West German historiography.[59] Second, both historiographies took time to develop in new directions after the end of the war, but their characters differed, and so did the periodization and sources of change. Third, although these shifts in historiographical disposition were related to broader changes in the political and intellectual climate in both countries, the linkage to the political was looser in West than in East Germany, where the political leadership established the goals and frameworks for historical research at least into the 1970s. Finally, the Nazi period was the overriding issue in DDR historiography, occupying a status that reflected the importance of antifascism in defining the logic and character of the new state. For both these latter reasons, the historiography of National Socialism occupied a more public and dominant role in the DDR than in the Federal Republic.

The tendency to dismiss all DDR historiography as the polemical expression of an undifferentiated and unchanging political dogma has fortunately been replaced by a more nuanced sense of the relationship between the political/theoretical line set by the SED (Sozialistische Einheitspartei) and the academic profession. With some differences of detail, commentators on DDR historiography agree that there were three distinct phases of development between 1945 and the 1980s: a post-war transitional period between 1945 and 1948/9; a period of political construction and consolidation up to the end of the 1960s; and a period beginning in the 1970s in which a degree of professional independence was achieved and debates internal to the discipline began to emerge.[60]

The immediate post-war period, preceding the constitution of the DDR as a state, saw comparatively little direct political intervention into academic historiography, and not much systematic research into contemporary history either, given the more pressing tasks of institutional and curricular refoundation. Inevitably, the historical profession was still dominated by non-Marxist academics, and an antifascist consensus rather than a specifically Marxist orientation was the order of the day. Political and intellectual leaders tended to the view that Germany's history was so negative as to be virtually useless to the project of socialist construction (Heydemann 1987: 18). To a greater extent than in the West, historians and other academics in the Soviet zone conceded not only Germany's responsibility for the war, but also the fatality of a German past that had culminated in National Socialism; in this sense, their views were closer to those of their non-German than their German colleagues.[61]

This rather open situation dissipated once the DDR had been founded as a state, and from the beginning of the 1950s through to the mid-1970s central direction by

---

59 Heydemann 1987. Other major Western surveys include Riesenberger 1973; Kwiet 1976; Thamer 1987; Dorpalen 1988; Fischer and Heydemann 1988; Kuppe 1987; Jarausch 1991; Iggers 1992: Introduction. For surveys by DDR historians, see Berthold *et al.* 1973; Lozek 1989; Bramke 1988.

60 This follows Heydemann's (1987) periodization; Iggers offers a similar three-phase process, while Jarausch and Kuppe suggest five roughly decadal phases.

61 For examples of early publications, see Lozek 1989: 200–2.

the political leadership was far more visible. The SED claimed, in the name of Marxism-Leninism, a monopoly of intellectual leadership; non-Marxist academics were eliminated from the universities as far as possible, and compulsory courses in dialectical and historical materialism were instituted.[62] In 1951 the party, after consultation with members of the historical profession, declared the opening of a new phase of ideological-political struggle: in a speech to the October Central Committee meeting, Walter Ulbricht proposed in effect a dual reading of German history, leading up to the divided nation of the present. The Federal Republic was represented as the embodiment of the reactionary element in German history, carried by Junkers, industrialists, militarists, anti-Semites, fascists and the like. Against this stood the positive and progressive strand in German history, identified with the peasant wars, the war of liberation, 1848, the origin of the working-class movement, the foundation of the KPD and the anti-fascist resistance, and culminating in the foundation of the DDR as the first German socialist state. The SED initiative obviously reflected the intensification of the Cold War, and set the scene for a growing organizational and intellectual divergence between the professions in East and West (the East Germans left the Verband der Historiker to found their own association in 1958, after some years of increasing friction). It was accompanied by other specific moves to establish a new historical tradition which would assist the legitimation of the East German state. These included an official injunction against historicism, and the substitution of historical materialism as the theoretical underpinning of historical scholarship; the establishment of a museum of German history in Berlin (opened in 1952), of historical institutes at the universities in Berlin, Leipzig and Halle, and of the Deutsche Akademie der Wissenschaften; the decision to embark on new canonical histories of the German people and of the German working-class movement; and the inauguration (in 1953) of the *Zeitschrift der Geschichtswissenschaft* as the journal of record for the DDR historical profession (Lozek 1989: 202–7). Through the 1960s, most scholarship was carried out in these research institutes by collectives of historians charged with the production of definitive official texts – a structure that was not conducive to debate, innovation or resistance to the official line.

As far as East German research on National Socialism was concerned, these were the years of domination by 'Stamokap' theory, and of maximum polemic with Western scholarship.[63] The presiding concept of fascism in the continuing era of state monopoly capitalism was taken from Dmitrov's classic formulation in his 1935 speech to the 7th Comintern Congress, as 'the open terrorist dictatorship of the most reactionary, most chauvinistic and most imperialist elements of finance capital' (Dmitrov n.d.: 40). The success of National Socialism was represented as the effect of the interests of monopoly capitalism, an approach that focused attention less on

---

62 For the shift in appointments practices, see Weber 1984: 314–18.
63 'Stamokap' is the German contraction of 'state monopoly capitalism', i.e. the existing stage of capitalist development. For critical surveys of DDR theory, see Thamer 1987; Dorpalen 1988: ch. 8; Jarausch 1991.

the *form* of the Nazi dictatorship than on the *function* it performed for capital. Consequently, a strong element of continuity was asserted between Weimar and the Third Reich, and between the Third Reich and its alleged successor state in West Germany. The major themes in DDR historiography were the relationship between the state and economic interests before and after 1933, the role of the antifascist resistance, and the political economy of the Second World War. Each of these topics was the subject of monographic publications which drew on, and sometimes reprinted, documentary sources not readily available to Western scholars (see e.g. Eichholtz and Schumann 1969; Eichholtz 1969; Eichholtz 1974– ; Bartel 1956). By contrast, topics which depended upon a different conceptualization of the relationship between the economic and the political than that offered by historical materialism, or which treated social history as an autonomous sphere, were largely neglected: these included important themes which were beginning to attract Western scholars in the 1960s, including the precise trajectory of the transition from Weimar to the Third Reich, the internal political structure of the Nazi system, the centrality of racism and genocide to Nazism, and the structures of social integration and control in the Third Reich. For more contingent political reasons, some specifically difficult topics such as the Nazi–Soviet Pact, or the full complexity of resistance and collaboration after 1933, were also barred from critical assessment. Research was also designed to refute the claims of West German 'bourgeois' historiography, in a context in which genuine debate was, unfortunately, rare on either side.[64]

The recovery of disciplinary independence and the emergence of internal historiographical debates were products of the consolidation of a politically secure historical profession in the universities in the 1970s, as well as of shifts in official political ideology. The SED was obliged to acknowledge the fact that the rigidity of the party's ideological stance had so sterilized official history that it was neither creative nor popular, and was forfeiting the legitimatory political role it had been assigned. The party's 7th congress in 1967 established the new goal of creating a 'socialist consciousness', and this inaugurated a new period of debate about the tasks of history – a debate which, as Günther Heydemann (1987: 21) has pointed out, reinvigorated the concept of debate itself as a scholarly method. At a more remote but extremely important level of political determination, the succession of Erich Honecker to the DDR leadership in 1971, and the opening of a new era of East–West *détente*, marked a highly significant shift in the DDR's self-representation and legitimation. Politically, this was signalled in an abrupt and unexpected declaration of German national unity at the SED's 8th party congress in 1971, and the deletion from the constitution of all references to political unification. These decisions acknowledged the reality that the DDR was not to be 'a brief transitional phase' (Fulbrook 1989: 199) before the establishment of a socialist state on all

---

64 The official *Zeitschrift für Geschichtswissenschaft* carried critical reviews of West German publications. The contributions by DDR historians to the fascism debate in the West Berlin journal *Das Argument* in the 1960s were unusual; see also Czichon 1967.

German soil, but that it was a nation in its own right, with its own future and its own history. The meaning of nation was premised on a shared experience of class and social structure, rather than on language and ethnicity. The dual heritage of the German past that prior orthodoxy had assigned on the one hand to the BRD (seen as reactionary) and on the other hand to the DDR (seen as progressive) was reconceptualized, and the hindrances to the achievement of socialism in the DDR were no longer represented as residues of a soon-to-be-superseded past. Instead, the complexities and contradictions of German history were conceded a constructive status within the history and prehistory of the DDR itself, which in this sense could now claim all German history as its own. Cast into the mould of a semantic distinction between 'Erbe' (heritage: the undifferentiated historical past) and 'Tradition' (the selective elements of 'our' national identity), this history now became the source for a new construction of national identity which embraced Luther, Frederick the Great and Bismarck, as well as Marx, Engels and the SPD.[65]

As Georg Iggers has pointed out, the *Erbe/Tradition* debate was not in itself methodologically innovative, for it exhibited more associations with traditional German historiography than with the genuinely new trends then gaining ground in the West. Yet it did encourage an expansion of the range and depth of historical enquiry, including into National Socialism. With the admission of previously discounted points into the historical compass, it became possible to explore seriously for the first time topics such as the role of the non-communist resistance, including its bourgeois and conservative participants, or the history of racial persecution under National Socialism (see e.g. Bramke 1988, and refs. therein; Bramke 1989; Buuck 1988; Finker 1989; Groehler and Drobisch 1989; Drobisch *et al.* 1973; Petzold 1983). The wider sweep of this more recent historiography was well illustrated in the important volume *Faschismusforschung*, edited in 1978 by two of the senior historians of the period, which included essays on Nazi ideology, the Nazi state, anti-Semitism and genocide, and comparative fascism.[66] By the 1980s, contacts between DDR and Western historians were becoming closer and more frequent, with joint conferences and seminars and a growing sense of dialogue. As a result partly of this, and partly of the internal move towards a more popularly accessible historiography, DDR historians began to take up some of the innovative approaches that had been at work in the West since the 1970s, notably *Alltags-geschichte*.[67] Yet this growing interest in social history was most characteristic of nineteenth-century studies, and was only just beginning to make headway into the

---

65 Discussions of this important and ramified debate can be found in Iggers 1992: Introduction; Jeismann 1988; Küttler and Schleier 1983; Meier and Schmidt 1989 – the latter two titles are by DDR historians.
66 Eichholtz and Gossweiler 1980; see also e.g. Petzold 1983, and Gossweiler 1986. For a critical review of this literature, see Pätzold 1992.
67 For reviews of the progress of social history, see Iggers 1992: Introduction (where the range of contacts between DDR and Western historians in the 1980s is also briefly reviewed on p. 36); Kocka 1973; Handke 1986.

Nazi period when the DDR collapsed.[68] Feminist history, the history of sexuality, the new history of eugenics, the reconceptualization of the relationship between power and ideology: these most recent tendencies in Western history had encountered few parallels across the border before the unification of the two Germanies coercively transformed the context of scholarly exchange.[69]

EPILOGUE

It is easy enough to point out that the late 1980s political revolutions in the Soviet Union and central Europe, and the unification of East and West Germany, have transformed the tasks and conditions of research into the history of National Socialism. Less simple is to predict what the results will be, but I will offer a few hostages to fortune. First, the specific history of Weimar and Nazi Germany is likely to lose some of its immediate interest as the 'lost' history of the last forty-five years claims a greater share of academic and popular interest – a trend that will be strengthened by the passing on of the last generation with direct personal experience of the 1930s and 1940s.[70] This too is likely to reinforce an already visible tendency for more research questions to emerge out of the process of scholarly exchange as such, rather than from political and moral agendas, and this will be more practically effective in 'historicizing' the Nazi past than was possible by means of the agonized debates of the 1980s. The history of eastern Germany and eastern Europe under National Socialism will be reconsidered as new archival sources become available, and this may generate new conclusions about the nature of the German imperium in the East, the process of German military defeat, the liberations and the experience of the Germans under the advancing Allied armies. This is likely to lead to new insights into the relationship between wartime and immediately post-war Germany. As research into the history of the DDR and of the other communist states expands, the nature of totalitarianism will also be opened to scrutiny once again. This will no doubt stimulate renewed debates about the generic concept of totalitarianism: to what extent should it be based on the Soviet model, and what would be the relationship between such a model and the nationally specific histories of the DDR, Poland, Hungary, Czechoslovakia and the rest? As a result, fascism theory too may well undergo a revival and revision, especially given the grim likelihood that nationalist movements and regimes in the new Europe reveal their own dictatorial, racist or imperialist tendencies. Indeed, as I write, the brutal campaigns of 'ethnic cleansing' being carried out upon the body of the ex-Yugoslavian state are already

---

68   Jacobeit 1992 is a rare example of this.

69   For initial reports of the effects of unification on historians and historical studies in the erstwhile DDR, see Iggers 1991 and Eckert 1991; also Küttler 1992; Blaschke 1992; Eckert 1992; and Mommsen 1992. For a critical view, see Bridenthal 1992.

70   Let Martin Broszat (d. 1989) speak for his generation: 'If I myself had not been a member of the generation of Hitler Youth, if I had not lived through its very specific experiences, then I probably would not have felt such a need after 1945 to confront the Nazi past so critically' (Baldwin 1990: 122).

being widely compared with anti-Semitic genocide, and numerous European countries, including Germany itself, yield horrifying examples of racist and nationalist intolerance. And as the 'developed' world faces, or more likely tries to evade or resist, the twin challenges of world economic inequalities and new patterns of international population movements, the equally grim precedent of the Nazi state's management of its own surplus populations may, as Hannah Arendt feared, be revealed as a harbinger of the future rather than as a lapse into barbarism.

REFERENCES

Abraham, D. [1981] (1986) *The Collapse of the Weimar Republic*, 2nd rev. edn, New York.
—— (1984) 'Debate: David Abraham's *The Collapse of the Weimar Republic*', *Central European History* 17: 159–293.
Adam, U. D. (1972) *Judenpolitik im Dritten Reich*, Düsseldorf.
Adorno, T. *et al.* (1950) *The Authoritarian Personality*, New York.
Alff, W. (1971) *Der Begriff Faschismus und andere Aufsätze zur Zeitgeschichte*, Frankfurt.
Aly, G. (ed.) (1989) *Aktion T4, 1939–1945. Die 'Euthanasie' Zentrale in der Tiergartenstrasse 4*, Berlin.
—— and Roth, K. (1984) *Die restlose Erfassung, Volkszählen, Identifizieren. Aussondern im Nationalsozialismus*, Berlin.
Arendt, H. [1949] (1952) *The Origins of Totalitarianism*, Glencoe, IL.
Auerbach, H. (1970) 'Die Gründung des Instituts für Zeitgeschichte', *Vierteljahreshefte für Zeitgeschichte* 18: 529–44.
Ayçoberry, P. (1981) *The Nazi Question. An Essay On the Interpretations of National Socialism 1922–1975*, New York.
Backes, U. *et al.* (eds) (1990) *Die Schatten der Vergangenheit. Impulse zur Historisierung des Nationalsozialismus*, Berlin.
Backhaus, H. (ed.) (1976) *Gesellschaft. Beiträge zur Marxschen Theorie*, vol. 6, Frankfurt.
Baldwin, P. (ed.) (1990) *Reworking the Past. Hitler, the Holocaust and the Historians' Debate*, Boston.
Barraclough, G. (1949) *The Origins of Modern Germany*, Oxford.
Bartel, W. (ed.) (1956) *Deutschland in der Zeit der faschistischen Diktatur, 1933–45*, Berlin.
Bauer, O. (1967) 'Der Faschismus', in Bauer *et al.* 1967.
—— *et al.* (1967) *Faschismus und Kapitalismus. Theorien über die soziale Ursprünge und die Funktion des Faschismus*, ed. W. Abendroth, Frankfurt.
Bauman, Z. (1989) *Modernity and the Holocaust*, Ithaca, NY.
Beetham, D. (ed.) (1984) *Marxists in Face of Fascism. Writings by Marxists on Fascism in the Inter-war Years*, Totowa, NJ.
Bendix, R. (1952) 'Social stratification and political power', *American Political Science Review* 46: 357–75.
Berthold, W. *et al.* (eds) (1973) *Kritik der bürgerlichen Gesetzschreibung. Handbuch*, Cologne.
Biddis, M. (1977) *The Age of the Masses*, Harmondsworth.
Binion, R. (1976) *Hitler among the Germans*, New York.
Blackbourn, D. and Eley, G. (1984) *The Peculiarities of German History*, Oxford.
Blackburn, G. W. (1985) *Education in the Third Reich. Race and History in Nazi Textbooks*, Albany.
Blaschke, K. (1992) 'Geschichtswissenschaft im SED-Staat', *Aus Politik und Zeitgeschichte* B17–18/92 (17 April): 14–27.
Bloch, E. [1935] (1962) *Erbschaft dieser Zeit*, in E. Bloch, *Gesamtausgabe*, vol. 4, Frankfurt. (Eng. tr.: *Heritage of our Times*, Cambridge, 1991.)

Bock, G. (1986) *Zwangssterilisation im Nationalsozialismus. Studien zur Rassenpolitik und Frauenpolitik*, Opladen.

Bottomore, T. and Goode, P. (eds) (1978) *Austro-Marxism*, Oxford.

Bracher, K. D. (1955) *Die Auflösung der Weimarer Republik. Eine Studie zum Problem des Machtverfalls in der Demokratie*, Villingen.

—— (1969) *Die deutsche Diktatur. Entstehung, Struktur und Folgen des Nationalsozialismus*, Cologne. (Tr. as: *The German Dictatorship*, New York.)

—— (1972) 'Stages of totalitarian "integration" (*Gleichschaltung*): the consolidation of National Socialist rule in 1933 and 1934', in Holborn 1972.

—— (1976) *Zeitgeschichtliche Kontroversen um Faschismus, Totalitarismus, Demokratie*, Munich.

—— (1978) 'Tradition und Revolution im Nationalsozialismus', in Funke 1978.

—— (1979) 'The role of Hitler: perspectives of interpretation', in Laqueur 1979.

—— Sauer, W. and Schulz, G. (1959) *Die nationalsozialistische Machtergreifung. Studien zur Errichtung des totalitären Herrschaftssystems in Deutschland 1933/4*, Cologne.

Bramke, W. (1988) 'Der antifaschistische Widerstand in der Geschichtsschreibung der DDR in den achtziger Jahren. Forschungsstand und Probleme', *Aus Politik und Zeitgeschichte*, B 28: 23–33.

—— (1989) 'Terror und antifaschistischer Widerstand in der regionalgeschichtlichen Forschung der DDR. Forschungsstand und Probleme', in *Deutscher Faschismus – Terror und Widerstand. Zur 2. Tagung der IREX-Unterkommission 'Faschismus – Theorie und praxis' von Historikern der USA und der DDR in Princeton, N.J., in Mai 1989*, ed. Akademie für Gesellschaftswissenschaften beim ZK der SED, Berlin.

Breitman, R. (1989) 'Nazism in the eyes of German social democracy', in M. N. Dobkowski and I. Walliman (eds) *Radical Perspectives on the Rise of Fascism in Germany, 1919–1945*, New York.

Bridenthal, R. (1992) 'The meaning of unification for German history and historiography: an introduction', *Radical History Review*, 54 (Fall): 81–6.

Brooker, P. (1991) *Faces of Fraternalism. Nazi Germany, Fascist Italy, and Imperial Japan*, Oxford.

Broszat, M. (1960) *Der Nationalsozialismus. Weltanschauung, Programm und Wirklichkeit*, Stuttgart.

—— (1970) 'Soziale Motivation und Führer-Bindung des Nationalsozialismus', *Vierteljahreshefte für Zeitgeschichte* 18(4): 392–409.

—— (ed.) (1977–83) *Bayern in der NS-Zeit*, 6 vols, Munich.

—— (1978) 'Tradition und Revolution in Nationalsozialismus', in Funke 1978.

—— [1969] (1981) *The Hitler State*, London. (First published as: *Der Staat Hitlers*, Stuttgart, 1969.)

—— [1977] (1985) 'Hitler and the genesis of the "Final Solution": an assessment of David Irving's theses', in Koch 1985.

—— (1988) *Nach Hitler. Der schwierige Umgang mit unserer Geschichte*, Munich.

Browning, C. (1986a) 'Nazi ghettoization policy in Poland 1939–41', *Central European History*, Dec.: 434–68.

—— (1986b) 'Nazi resettlement policy and the search for a solution to the Jewish Question 1938–1941', *German Studies Review* 11(3) (Oct.): 497–520.

—— (1989) 'The decision concerning the Final Solution', in F. Furet (ed.) *Unanswered Questions. Nazi Germany and the Genocide of the Jews*, New York.

—— (1992) 'Beyond "intentionalism" and "functionalism": a reassessment of Nazi Jewish policy from 1939 to 1954', in Childers and Caplan 1992.

Buchheim, H. (1958) *Das Dritte Reich*, Munich.

—— [1962] (1968) *Totalitarian Rule. Its Nature and Characteristics*, Middletown, CT. (First published as *Totalitäre Herrschaft*, Munich, 1962.)

—— (1972) 'The position of the SS in the Third Reich', in Holborn 1972.

Bullock, A. (1952) *Hitler. A Study in Tyranny*, London.

—— (1991) *Hitler and Stalin. Parallel Lives*, New York.

Burleigh, M. (1988) *Germany Turns Eastward. A Study of* Ostforschung *in the Third Reich*, Cambridge.

—— and Wippermann, W. (1991) *The Racial State. Germany 1933–1945*, Cambridge.

Butler, R. (1941) *The Roots of National Socialism*, London.

Buuck, G. (1988) 'Auswahlbibliographie. Neuere Veröffentlichungen der DDR–Forschung zum Thema "Faschismus – Terror – Widerstand"', in *Deutscher Faschismus – Theorie und Widerstand. Zur 2. Tagung der IREX-Unterkommission 'Faschismus – Theorie und praxis' von Historikern der USA und der DDR in Princeton, N.J., in Mai 1989*, ed. Akademie für Gesellschaftswissenschaften beim ZK der SED, Berlin.

Cammett, J. (1967) 'Communist theories of fascism', *Science and Society* 31: 148–63.

Caplan, J. (1976) 'Theories of fascism: Poulantzas as historian', *History Workshop Journal* 3: 83–100.

—— (1986) 'Myths, models and missing revolutions: comments on a debate in German history', *Radical History Review* 34: 87–99.

—— (1989) 'Postmodernism, poststructuralism, and deconstruction: notes for historians', *Central European History* 22 (Sept./Dec.): 260–78.

Carsten, F. (1967) *The Rise of Fascism*, Oxford.

Cassels, A. (1975) *Fascism*, Arlington Heights, IL.

Ceplair, L. (1987) *Under the Shadow of War. Fascism, Anti-fascism and Marxists 1919–1939*, New York.

Childers, T. and Caplan, J. (eds) (1992) *Reevaluating the Third Reich*, New York.

Clemenz, M. (1972) *Gesellschaftliche Ursprünge des Faschismus*, Frankfurt.

Conze, W. (1977) 'Die deutsche Geschichtswissenschaft seit 1945. Bedingungen und Ergebnisse', *Historische Zeitschrift* 225: 1–28.

Crew, D. (1989) 'Alltagsgeschichte: a new social history "from below"?', *Central European History* (Sept./Dec.): 394–407.

Czarnowski, G. (1991) *Das kontrollierte Paar. Ehe- und Sexualpolitik im Nationalsozialismus*, Weinheim.

Czichon, E. (1967) *Wer verhalf Hitler zur Macht? Zum Anteil der deutschen Industrie an der Zerstörung der Weimarer Republik*, Cologne.

Dahrendorf, R. (1965) *Gesellschaft und Demokratie in Deutschland*, Munich.

Dawidowicz, L. (1975) *The War against the Jews 1933–1945*, London.

Derrida, J. (1988) 'Like the sound of the sea deep within a shell: Paul de Man's war', *Critical Inquiry* 14 (Spring): 590–652.

Diehl-Thiele, P. (1969) *Partei und Staat im Dritten Reich: Untersuchungen zum Verhältnis von NSDAP und allgemeiner und innerer Staatsverwaltung*, Munich.

Diner, D. (ed.) (1987) *Ist der Nationalsozialismus Geschichte? Zur Historisierung und Historikerstreit*, Frankfurt.

Dmitrov, G. (n.d.) *Report to the 7th Congress Communist International 1935*, London.

Dorpalen, A. (1988) *German History in Marxist Perspective. The East German Approach*, Detroit.

Drobisch, K. *et al.* (eds) (1973) *Juden unterm Hakenkreuz. Verfolgung und Ausrottung der deutschen Juden 1933–1945*, Berlin.

Dubiel, H. and Söllner, A. (eds) (1981) *Wirtschaft, Staat und Recht im Nationalsozialismus. Analysen des Instituts für Sozialforschung*, Frankfurt.

Eckert, R. (1991) 'Geschichtswissenschaft in der ehemaligen DDR: Ein ostdeutsche Sicht', *German Studies Association Newsletter* 16(1) (Winter): 38–50.

—— (1992) 'Entwicklungschancen und -barrieren für den geschichtswissenschaftlichen Nachwuchs in der DDR', *Aus Politik und Zeitgeschichte* B17–18/92 (17 April): 28–34.

Eichholtz, D. (1969) *Geschichte der deutschen Kriegswirtschaft 1939–1945*, Berlin.

—— (ed.) (1974–) *Deutschland im Zweiten Weltkrieg*, 6 vols, Berlin.

—— and Gossweiler, K. (eds) (1980) *Faschismusforschung. Positionen, Probleme, Polemik*, Berlin.

—— and Schumann, W. (eds) (1969) *Anatomie des Krieges. Dokumente über die Rolle des deutschen Monopolkapitals bei der Vorbereitung und Durchführung des Zweiten Weltkrieges*, Berlin.

—— (1988) 'Nazism, politics and the image of the past', *Past and Present* 121: 171–208.

—— (1989) 'What produces fascism: preindustrial traditions or a crisis of the capitalist state?', in M. N. Dobkowski and I. Walliman (eds) *Radical Perspectives on the Rise of Fascism in Germany, 1919–1945*, New York.

Epstein, C. (1993) *A Past Renewed. A Catalog of German-Speaking Refugee Historians in the United States after 1933*, Cambridge.

—— (forthcoming) 'Fashioning fortune's whim: German-speaking emigrant historians in the United States after 1933', Washington.

Erdmann, K. D. (1976) *Die Zeit der Weltkriege*, Stuttgart. (=vol. 2 of Gebhardt (ed.) *Handbuch der deutschen Geschichte*, 9th edn.)

Evans, R. (1985) 'The myth of Germany's missing revolution', *New Left Review* 149: 67–94.

—— (1989) *In Hitler's Shadow. West German Historians and the Attempt to Escape from the Nazi Past*, New York.

Farias, V. (1989) *Heidegger and Nazism*, Philadelphia.

Faulenbach, B. (ed.) (1974) *Geschichtswissenschaft in Deutschland. Traditionelle Positionen und gegenwärtige Aufgaben*, Munich.

Faulenbach, B. (1980) *Ideologie des deutschen Weges. Die deutsche Geschichte in der Historiographie zwischen Kaiserreich und Nationalsozialismus*, Munich.

—— (1981) 'Deutsche Geschichtswissenschaft nach 1945', *Tijdschrift voor Geschiednis* 94: 29–57.

Felice, R. de (1977) *Interpretations of Fascism*, Cambridge, MA.

Fest, J. (1973) *Hitler. Eine Biographie*, Berlin and Frankfurt. (Tr. as: *Hitler. A Biography*, New York, 1974.)

Finker, K. (1989) 'Zum Widerstandskampf kleinbürgerlicher und bürgerlicher Nazigegner in Deutschland', in Meier and Schmidt 1989.

Fischer, A. and Heydemann, G. (eds) (1988) *Geschichtswissenschaft in der DDR*, 2 vols, Berlin.

Fischer, C. (1991) *The German Communists and the Rise of Nazism*, London.

Fischer, F. (1959) 'Deutsche Kriegsziele, Revolutionierung und Separatfrieden im Osten 1914–1918', *Historische Zeitschrift* 188: 129–310.

Fleming, G. (1986) *Hitler and the Final Solution*, New York.

Fowkes, B. (1984) *Communism in Germany under the Weimar Republic*, London.

Fraenkel, E. (1941) *The Dual State*, New York.

Franz, G. (1981) 'Das Geschichtsbild des Nationalsozialismus und die deutsche Geschichtswissenschaft', in O. Hauser (ed.) *Geschichte und Geschichtsbewusstsein*, Göttingen.

Friedländer, S. (1984a) 'From anti-Semitism to extermination. A historiographical study of Nazi policies towards the Jews and an essay in interpretation', *Yad Vashem Studies* 16: 1–50.

—— (1984b) *Reflections of Nazism: An Essay on Kitsch and Death*, New York.

—— (ed.) (1992) *Probing the Limits of Representation. Nazism and the 'Final Solution'*, Cambridge, MA.

Friedrich, C. J. (ed.) (1954) *Totalitarianism*, Cambridge, MA.

—— and Brzesinski, Z. [1956] (1961) *Totalitarian Dictatorship and Autocracy*, New York.

Fromm, E. (1941) *Escape from Freedom*, New York.

Fulbrook, M. (1989) 'From "Volksgemeinschaft" to divided nation: German national identities and political cultures since the Third Reich', *Historical Research* 62: 93–213.

Furet, F. (ed.) (1989) *Unanswered Questions. Nazi Germany and the Genocide of the Jews*, New York.

Geiger, T. (1930) 'Panik im Mittelstand', *Die Arbeit* 10: 637–54.

Gerstenberger, H. and Schmidt, D. (eds) (1987) *Normalität oder Normalisierung? Geschichtswerkstatt und Faschismusanalyse*, Münster.

Gilbert, F. (1947) 'German historiography in the Second World War', *American Historical Review* 53(1): 50–8.

Gimbel, J. (1965) 'The origins of the *Institut für Zeitgeschichte*. Scholarship, politics, and the American Occupation, 1945–1949', *American Historical Review* 70(3): 714–31.

Glaser, H. (1978) *The Cultural Roots of National Socialism*, Austin.

Gossweiler, K. (1986) *Aufsätze zum Faschismus*, Berlin.

Grebing, H. (1959) *Der Nationalsozialismus*, Munich.

Gregor, A. J. (1969) *The Ideology of Fascism. The Rationale of Totalitarianism*, New York.

Groehler, O. and Drobisch, K. (1989) 'Der 20. Juli 1944', in Meier and Schmidt 1989.

Habermas, J. (ed.) (1984) *Observations on 'The Spiritual Situation of the Age'. Contemporary German Perspectives*, Cambridge, MA.

Habermas, J. (1987) *Eine Art Schadensabwicklung*, Frankfurt.

—— (1989) *The New Conservatism. Cultural Criticism and the Historians' Debate*, Cambridge, MA.

Hagtvet, B. (1980) 'The theory of mass society and the collapse of the Weimar Republic. A re-examination', in Larsen *et al.* 1980.

Hamacher, W. *et al.* (eds) (1988) *Responses: On Paul de Man's Wartime Journalism*, Lincoln.

Hammen, O. (1941) 'German historians and the advent of the national socialist state', *Journal of Modern History* 13 (June): 161–88.

Handke, H. (1986) 'Zur sozialgeschichtlichen Forschung in der DDR', *Zeitschrift für Geschichtswissenschaft* 34: 291–302.

Hartman, G. (ed.) (1986) *Bitburg in Moral and Political Perspective*, Bloomington.

Haug, W. F. (1967) *Der hilflose Antifaschismus. Zur Kritik der Vorlesungen über Wissenschaft und NS an deutsche Universitäten*, Frankfurt.

Heiber, H. (1960) *Adolf Hitler. Eine Biographie*, Berlin.

—— (1966) *Walter Frank und sein Reichsinstitut für die Geschichte des neuen Deutschlands*, Stuttgart.

Hein, D. (1986) 'Geschichtswissenschaft in den Westzonen und der Bundesrepublik 1945–1950', in C. Cobet (ed.) *Einführung in Fragen an die Geschichtswissenschaft in Deutschland nach Hitler 1945–1950*, Frankfurt.

Held, D. (1980) *Introduction to Critical Theory. Horkheimer to Habermas*, London.

Henke, J. (1982) 'Das Schicksal deutscher zeitgeschichtlicher Quellen in Kriegs- und Nachkriegszeit', *Vierteljahreshefte für Zeitgeschichte* 30: 557–620.

Hennig, E. (1973) *Thesen zur deutschen Sozial- und Wirtschaftsgeschichte 1933 bis 1938*, Frankfurt.

—— (1977) *Bürgerliche Gesellschaft und Faschismustheorien in Deutschland. Ein Forschungsbericht*, Frankfurt.

—— (1988) *Zum Historikerstreit. Was heisst und zu welchem Ende studiert man Geschichte?*, Frankfurt.

Herf, J. (1984) *Reactionary Modernism: Technology, Culture, and Politics in Weimar and the Third Reich*, Cambridge.

Heuser, B. (1990) 'Museums, identity and warring historians, observations on history in Germany', *Historical Journal* 33(2): 417–40.

Heuss, A. (1959) *Verlust der Geschichte*, Göttingen.

Heydemann, G. (1987) 'Geschichtswissenschaft und Geschichtsverständnis in der DDR seit 1945', *Aus Politik und Zeitgeschichte* B 13.

Hiden, J. and Farquharson, J. (1989) *Explaining Hitler's Germany. Historians and the Third Reich*, London.

Hildebrand, K. (1977) 'Nationalsozialismus oder Hitlerismus?', in M. Bosch (ed.) *Persönlichkeit und Struktur in der Geschichte*, Düsseldorf.

—— (1981) 'Monokratie und Polykratie? Hitlers Herrschaft und das Dritte Reich', in Hirschfeld and Kettenacker 1981.

—— (ed.) (1987) *Wem gehört die deutsche Geschichte?*, Cologne.

—— (1991) *Das Dritte Reich*, Munich.

Hillgruber, A. (1972) 'Die "Endlösung" und das deutsche Ostimperium als Kernstück des rassenideologischen Programme des Nationalsozialismus', *Vierteljahreshefte für Zeitgeschichte* 18: 133–53.

—— (1982) *Endlich genug über Nationalsozialismus und Zweiten Weltkrieg? Forschungsstand und Literatur*, Düsseldorf.

—— (1986) *Zweierlei Untergang. Die Zerschlagung des deutschen Reiches und das Ende des europäischen Judentums*, Berlin.

Hirschfeld, G. and Kettenacker, L. (eds) (1981) *The 'Führer State': Myth and Reality. Studies on the Politics and Structure of the Third Reich*, Stuttgart.

'Historikerstreit'. (1987) *Die Dokumentation der Kontroverse um die Einzigartigkeit der nationalsozialistischen Judenvernichtung*, Munich.

Hofer, W. (1957) *Der Nationalsozialismus. Dokumenten 1933–1945*, Frankfurt.

Holborn, H. (ed.) (1972) *Republic to Reich: The Making of the Nazi Revolution: Ten Essays*, New York.

Horkheimer, M. and Adorno, T. [1944] (1990) *Dialectic of Enlightenment*, New York.

Hull, I. (1989) 'Feminist and gender history through the literary looking glass: German historiography in postmodern times', *Central European History* 22 (Sept/Dec.): 279–300.

Hüttenberger, P. (1969) *Die Gauleiter. Studie zum Wandel des Machtgefüges in der NSDAP*, Stuttgart.

—— (1976) 'Nationalsozialistische Polykratie', *Geschichte und Gesellschaft* 2: 417–42.

Iggers, G. (1968) *The German Conception of History*, Middletown, Conn.

—— (1974) 'Die deutschen Historiker in der Emigration', in Faulenbach 1974.

—— (1975) *New Directions in European Historiography*, Middletown, Conn.

—— (1991) 'The reorganization of historical studies in the new German Bundesländer', *German Studies Association Newsletter* 16(1) (Winter).

—— (ed.) (1992) *Marxist Historiography in Transformation. New Orientations in Recent East German History*, New York and Oxford.

Irving, D. (1977) *Hitler's War*, London.

Jäckel, E. (1969) *Hitlers Weltanschauung. Entwurf einer Herrschaft*, Tübingen. (Tr. as: *Hitler's Weltanschauung. A Blueprint for Power*, Middletown, Conn., 1972.)

—— (1979) *The Meaning of Hitler*, Cambridge, Mass.

—— (1984) *Hitler in History*, Hanover, NH.

—— (1988) *Hitlers Herrschaft. Vollzug einer Weltanschauung*, Stuttgart.

Jacobeit, S. (1992) 'Clothing in Nazi Germany', in Iggers 1992.

Jarausch, K. (1989) 'Towards a social history of experience: postmodern predicaments in theory and interdisciplinarity', *Central European History* 22 (Sept./Dec.): 427–43.

—— (1991) 'The failure of East German antifascism: some ironies of history as politics', *German Studies Review* 14(1): 85–102.

Jay, M. (1973) *The Dialectical Imagination. A History of the Frankfurt School and the Institute of Social Research, 1923–1950*, Boston.

Jeismann, K.-E. (1988) 'Die Einheit der Nation im Geschichtsbild der DDR', in Fischer and Heydemann 1988.

Kater, M. (1974) *Das 'Ahnenerbe' der SS 1935–1945. Ein Beitrag zur Kulturpolitik des Dritten Reiches*, Stuttgart.

—— (1981) 'Hitler in a social context', *Central European History* 14(3) (Sept.): 243–72.
Kedward, H. R. (1969) *Fascism in Western Europe 1900–1945*, London.
Kehr, H. and Langmaid, J. (eds) (1982) *The Nazi Era 1919–1945. A Select Bibliography of Published Works from the Early Years to 1980*, London.
Kershaw, I. (1987) *The 'Hitler Myth'. Image and Reality in the Third Reich*, Oxford. (First published as: *Der Hitler-Mythos. Volksmeinung und Propaganda im Dritten Reich*, Stuttgart, 1980.)
—— [1967] (1989) *The Nazi Dictatorship. Problems and Perspectives of Interpretation*, London.
—— (1991) *Hitler*, London.
Kitchen, M. (1973) 'August Thalheimer's theory of fascism', *Journal of the History of Ideas*: 67–78.
—— (1976) *Fascism*, London.
Klee, E. (1983) *'Euthanasie' im NS-Staat. Die 'Vernichtung lebensunwerten Lebens'*, Frankfurt.
—— (1985) *Was sie taten – was sie werden*, Frankfurt.
Klessmann, C. (1985) 'Osteuropaforschung und Lebensraumpolitik im Dritten Reich', in Lundgreen 1985.
—— (1987) 'Geschichtsbewusstsein nach 1945. Ein neuer Anfang?', in Weidenfeld 1987.
Koch, H. W. (ed.) (1985) *Aspects of the Third Reich*, London.
Kocka, J. (1973) 'Zur jüngeren marxistischen Sozialgeschichte. Eine kritische Analyse unter besonderer Berücksichtigung sozialgeschichtlicher Ansätze in der DDR', in P. C. Ludz (ed.) *Soziologie und Sozialgeschichte*, Opladen.
—— (1984) 'Zurück zur Erzählung? Plädoyer für historische Argumentation', *Geschichte und Gesellschaft* 10: 395–408.
Kohn, H. (1960) *The Mind of Germany: The Education of a Nation*, New York.
Kornhauser, W. (1959) *The Politics of Mass Society*, New York.
Krausnick, H. *et al.* (1968) *Anatomy of the SS State*, London.
Kuhn, A. (1973) *Das faschistische Herrschaftssystem und die moderne Gesellschaft*, Hamburg.
Kühnl, R. (1971) *Formen bürgerlicher Herrschaft. Liberalismus – Faschismus*, Hamburg.
—— (ed.) (1973) *Geschichte und Ideologie. Kritische Analyse bundesdeutscher Geschichtsbücher*, Reinbek.
—— (ed.) (1974) *Texte zur Faschismusdiskussion*, Reinbek.
—— (1990) *Faschismustheorien. Ein Leitfaden*, Heilbronn.
Kulka, O. D. (1985) 'Major trends in German historiography on National Socialism and the "Jewish Question" (1924–1984)', *Yearbook of the Leo Baeck Institute* 30: 215–42.
Kuppe, J. (1987) 'Das Geschichtswissenschaft in der DDR', in Weidenfeld 1987.
Küttler, W. (1992) 'Neubeginn In der ostdeutschen Geschichtswissenschaft', *Aus Politik und Zeitgeschichte* B17–18/92 (17 April): 3–13.
—— and Schleier, H. (1983) 'Die Erbe-Konzeption und der Platz der preussischen Geschichte in der DDR-Geschichtswissenschaft', *German Studies Review* 6: 535–57.
Kwiet, K. (1976) 'Historians of the German Democratic Republic on antisemitism and persecution', *Leo Baeck Institute Year Book* 21: 173–98.
—— (1989) 'Die NS-Zeit in der westdeutschen Forschung 1945–1961', in Schülin 1989.
Laqueur, W. (ed.) (1979) *Fascism. A Reader's Guide*, Harmondsworth.
Larsen, S. U. *et al.* (eds) (1980) *Who were the Fascists? Social Roots of European Fascism*, Bergen.
Lehmann, H. and Sheehan, J. J. (eds) (1991) *An Interrupted Past. German-Speaking Refugee Historians in the United States*, Cambridge.
Lehmann, H. and van Horn Melton, J. (eds) (1994) *Paths of Continuity: Central European Historiography from the 1930s to the 1950s*, Washington, DC.
Lepsius, M. R. (1969) 'Demokratie in Deutschland als historisch-soziologisches Problem', in T. W. Adorno (ed.) *Spätkapitalismus oder Industriegesellschaft*, Stuttgart.

Lepsius, M. R. (1973) 'Parteisystem und Sozialstruktur: zum Problem der Demokratisierung der deutschen Gesellschaft', in G. A. Ritter (ed.) *Deutsche Parteien vor 1918*, Cologne.

Lipset, S. N. (1960) *Political Man. The Social Bases of Politics*, New York.

Lozek, G. (1989) 'Die deutsche Geschichte 1917/18 bis 1945 in der Forschung der DDR (1945 bis Ende der sechziger Jahre)', in Schülin 1989.

Lubasz, H. (1973) *Fascism: Three Major Regimes*, New York.

Lukács, G. (1953) *Die Zerstörung der Vernunft*, Berlin.

Lundgreen, P. (ed.) (1985) *Wissenschaft im Dritten Reich*, Frankfurt.

Lyotard, J.-F. (1988) *The Differend. Phrases in Dispute*, Minneapolis.

—— (1989) 'Symposium on Heidegger and Nazism', *Critical Inquiry* 15(2): 407–88.

—— (1990) *Heidegger and the Jews*, Minneapolis.

Macciocchi, M.-A. (1976) 'Les femmes et la traversée du fascisme', in *Élements pour une analyse du fascisme. Séminaire de Maria A. Macciocchi. Paris VIII Vincennes 1974–1975*, Paris.

Maier, C. (1988) *The Unmasterable Past. History, Holocaust and German National Identity*, Cambridge, MA.

Man, P. de (1988) *Wartime Journalism: 1939–1943*, ed. V. Hamacher *et al.*, Lincoln, NE.

Marcuse, H. (1967) 'Der Kampf gegen den Liberalismus in der totalitären Staatsauffassung', in Bauer *et al.* 1967.

Marrus, M. (1987a) 'The history of the Holocaust: a survey of recent literature', *Journal of Modern History* 59: 114–60.

—— (1987b) *The Holocaust in History*, New York.

Marx, K. (1973) 'The eighteenth brumaire of Louis Bonaparte' [1852], in K. Marx, *Surveys from Exile* (Pelican Marx Library, vol. 2), Harmondsworth.

Mason, T. (1975) 'Innere Krise und Angriffskrieg 1938/39', in F. Forstmeier and H.-E. Volkmann (eds) *Wirtschaft und Rüstung am Vorabend des Zweiten Weltkriegs*, Düsseldorf.

—— (1981) 'Intention and explanation: a current controversy about the interpretation of National Socialism', in Hirschfeld and Kettenacker 1981.

—— (1992) 'The domestic dynamics of Nazi conquests: a response to my critics', in Childers and Caplan 1992.

—— (1993) *Social Policy in the Third Reich: The Working Class and the 'National Community' 1918–1939*, ed. J. Caplan, Providence, RI and Oxford.

—— (1995) *Nazism, Fascism and the Working Class. Essays by Tim Mason*, ed. J. Caplan, Cambridge.

Matzerath, H. and Volkmann, H. (1977) 'Modernisierungstheorie und Nationalsozialismus', in J. Kocka (ed.) *Theorien in der Praxis des Historikers. Forschungsbeispiele und ihre Diskussion*, Göttingen.

Mau, H. and Krausnick, H. (1959) *German History 1933–45. An Assessment by German Historians*, London.

Meier, C. (1987) *Vierzig Jahre nach Auschwitz. Deutsche Geschichtserinnerung heute*, Munich.

Meier, H. and Schmidt, W. (eds) (1989) *Erbe und Tradition in der DDR. Die Diskussion der Historiker*, Cologne.

Meinecke, F. (1946) *Die deutsche Katastrophe. Betrachtungen und Erinnerungen*, Wiesbaden. (Tr. as *The German Catastrophe. Reflections and Recollections*, Boston, 1950.)

Michaelis, H. *et al.* (eds) (1958–79) *Ursachen und Folgen. Vom deutschen Zusammenbruch 1918 und 1945 bis zur staatlichen Neuordnung Deutschlands in der Gegenwart*, 26 vols, Berlin.

Moeller, R. (1983/4) 'The *Kaiserreich* recast? Continuity and change in modern German historiography', *Journal of Social History* 17(4): 655–83.

Mommsen, H. (1966) *Beamtentum im Dritten Reich*, Stuttgart.

—— (1971) 'Nationalsozialismus', in C. Kernig (ed.) *Sowjetsystem und demokratische Gesellschaft*, Freiburg.

—— (1973) 'Betrachtungen zur Entwicklung der neuzeitlichen Historiographie in der Bundesrepublik', in G. Alföldy *et al.* (eds) *Probleme der Geschichtswissenschaft*, Düsseldorf.

—— (1979) 'National Socialism – continuity and change', in Laqueur 1979.

—— (1981a) 'Gegenwärtige Tendenzen in der Geschichtsschreibung der Bundesrepublik', *Geschichte und Gesellschaft* 7: 149–88.

—— (1981b) 'Stellung im nationalsozialistischen Herrschaftssystem', in Hirschfeld and Kettenacker 1981.

—— (1984) 'The burden of the past', in Habermas 1984.

—— (1986) 'The realization of the unthinkable: the "Final Solution of the Jewish Question" in the Third Reich', in G. Hirschfeld (ed.) *The Politics of Genocide. Jews and Soviet Prisoners of War in Nazi Germany*, London.

—— (1990) 'Nationalsozialismus als vorgetäuschte Modernisierung', in W. Pehle (ed.) *Der historische Ort des Nationalsozialismus. Annäherungen*, Frankfurt.

—— (1991) *From Weimar to Auschwitz*, Oxford.

Mommsen, W. J. (1992) 'Die Geschichtswissenschaft in der DDR. Kritische Reflexionen', *Aus Politik und Zeitgeschichte* B17–18/92 (17 April): 35–43.

Mosse, G. (1964) *The Crisis of German Ideology. The Intellectual Origins of the Third Reich*, New York.

Mühlberger, D. (ed.) (1987) *The Social Basis of European Fascist Movements*, London.

Neumann, F. (1942) *Behemoth. The Structure and Practice of National Socialism*, London.

—— (1963) *Der Faschismus in seiner Epoche*, Munich.

Neumann, S. (1942) *Permanent Revolution. The Total State in a World at War*, New York.

Niethammer, L. (1989) *Posthistoire. Ist die Geschichte zu Ende?*, Reinbek.

Niethammer, L. (ed.) (1983–5) *Lebensgeschichte und Sozialkultur im Ruhrgebiet 1930 bis 1960*, 3 vols, Bonn.

Nolte, E. (1966) *Die faschistischen Bewegungen*, Munich.

—— (ed.) (1967) *Theorien über Faschismus*, Cologne and Berlin.

—— (1968) *Die Krise des liberalen Systems und die faschistischen Bewegungen*, Munich.

—— (1985) 'Between myth and revisionism? The Third Reich in the perspective of the 1980s', in Koch 1985.

—— (1987) *Das europäische Bürgerkrieg 1917–1945. Nationalsozialismus und Bolschewismus*, Berlin.

—— (1988) *Das Vergehen der Vergangenheit. Antwort an meine Kritiker im sogennanten Historikerstreit*, Berlin.

O'Sullivan, N. (1983) *Fascism*, London.

Oberkrome, W. (1991) 'Reformansätze in der deutschen Geschichtswissenschaft der Zwischenkriegszeit', in Prinz and Zitelmann 1991.

Ortega y Gasset, J. (1932) *The Revolt of the Masses*, New York.

Parsons, T. (1942/3a) 'Democracy and social structure in pre-Nazi Germany', *Journal of Political and Legal Science* 1: 96–114.

—— (1942/3b) 'Some sociological aspects of the fascist movements', *Social Forces* 1: 138–47.

Pätzold, K. (1983) *Verfolgung, Vertreibung, Vernichtung. Dokumente des faschistischen Antisemitismus 1933 bis 1942*, Leipzig.

—— (1992) 'Research on fascism and antifascism in the German Democratic Republic: a critical perspective', *Radical History Review* 54: 87–109.

Payne, S. (1980) *Fascism. Comparison and Definition*, Madison.

Peterson, E. N. (1969) *The Limits of Hitler's Power*, Princeton.

Petzold, J. (1983) *Die Demagogie des Hitlerfaschismus*, Frankfurt.

Peukert, D. (1982) *Volksgenossen und Gemeinschaftsfremde. Anpassung, Ausmerze und Aufbegehren unter dem Nationalsozialismus*, Cologne.

—— (1986) 'Das "Dritte Reich" aus der "Alltags"-Perspektive', *Archiv für Sozialgeschichte* 26: 533–56.

—— (1987a) 'Alltag und Barbarei. Zur Normalität des Dritten Reiches', in D. Diner (ed.) *Ist der Nationalsozialismus Geschichte?*, Frankfurt.

—— (1987b) *Inside Nazi Germany. Conformity, Opposition and Racism in Everyday Life*, New Haven.

—— (1991) *The Weimar Republic. The Crisis of Classical Modernity*, London.

—— (1992) 'The genesis of the "Final Solution" from the spirit of science', in Childers and Caplan 1992.

Plessner, H. (1959) *The Rise and Fall of the Third Reich*, London.

Poulantzas, N. (1974) *Fascism and Dictatorship*, London.

Pozzoli, C. (ed.) (1976) *Jahrbuch Arbeiterbewegung*, 4: *Faschismus und Kapitalismus*, Frankfurt.

Prinz, M. and Zitelmann, R. (eds) (1991) *Nationalsozialismus und Modernisierung*, Darmstadt.

Pross, C. and Aly, G. (eds) (1989) *Der Wert der Menschen. Medizin in Deutschland 1918–1945*, Berlin.

Puhle, H.-J. (1981) 'Warum gibt es so wenige Historikerinnen? Zur Situation der Frauen in der Geschichtswissenschaft', *Geschichte und Gesellschaft* 7: 364–93.

Pyta, W. (1989) *Gegen Hitler und für die Republik. Die Auseinandersetzung der deutschen Sozialismus mit der NSDAP in der Weimarer Republik*, Düsseldorf.

Rabinbach, A. (1974) 'Toward a Marxist theory of fascism and National Socialism: a report on developments in West Germany', *New German Critique* 1(3) (Fall): 127–53.

Rassow, P. (ed.) (1953) *Deutsche Geschichte in Überblick*, Stuttgart.

Rauh, M. (1987) 'Anti-Modernismus im nationalsozialistischen Staat', *Historisches Jahrbuch* 107: 94–121.

Rauschning, H. (1939) *Germany's Revolution of Destruction*, London and Toronto.

Rees, P. (ed.) (1984) *Fascism and Pre-fascism in Europe 1890–1945. A Bibliography of the Extreme Right*, Brighton.

Reich, W. [1934] (1975) *The Mass Psychology of Fascism*, Harmondsworth.

Riesenberger, D. (1973) *Geschichte und Geschichtsunterricht in der DDR*, Göttingen.

Ritter, G. (1948) *Europa und die deutsche Frage. Betrachtungen über die geschichtliche Eigenart des deutschen Staatsdenkens*, Munich.

—— (1950) 'Gegenwärtige Lage und Zukunftsaufgaben deutscher Geschichtswissenschaft', *Historische Zeitschrift* 170: 1–22.

—— (1954–68) *Staatskunst und Kriegshandwerk. Das Problem des Militarismus in Deutschland*, 4 vols, Munich.

—— (1955) 'The historical foundations of the rise of National Socialism', in G. Ritter, *The Third Reich*, London.

—— (1965) *The German Problem*, Columbus, OH.

Robertson, E. M. (ed.) (1971) *The Origins of the Second World War*, London.

Rose, R. and Weiss, W. (1991) *Sinti und Roma im 'Dritten Reich'*, Göttingen.

Rosenhaft, E. (1983) *Beating the Fascists? The German Communists and Political Violence 1929–1933*, Cambridge.

Rothfels, H. (1948) *The German Opposition to Hitler*, Hinsdale, IL. (Tr. into German as: *Die deutsche Opposition gegen Hitler. Eine Würdigung*, Krefeld, 1949.)

—— et al. (eds) (1950–) *Akten zur deutschen auswärtigen Politik 1918–1945*, Göttingen.

Rückerl, A. (1980) *The Investigation of Nazi Crimes 1945–1978. A Documentation*, Hamden, CT.

Rüsen, J. (1984) 'Theory of history in the development of West German historical studies: a reconstruction and overview', *German Studies Review* 7: 11–25.

Saage, R. (1976) *Faschismustheorien. Eine Einführung*, Munich.

Schapiro, L. (1972) *Totalitarianism*, London.

Schieder, W. (ed.) (1976) *Faschismus als soziale Bewegung. Deutschland und Italien im Vergleich*, Göttingen.

Schmuhl, H.-W. (1987) *Rassenhygiene. Nationalsozialismus und Euthanasie*, Göttingen.

Schoppmann, C. (1991) *Nationalsozialistische Sexualpolitik und weibliche Homosexualität*, Pfaffenweiler.

Schreiber, G. (1984) *Hitlerinterpretationen 1923–1983: Ergebnisse, Methoden und Probleme der Forschung*, Darmstadt.

Schreiner, K. (1985) 'Führertum, Rasse, Reich. Wissenschaft von der Geschichte nach der nationalsozialistischen Machtergreifung', in Lundgreen 1985.

Schülin, E. (ed.) (1989) *Deutsche Geschichtswissenschaft nach dem Zweiten Weltkrieg (1945–1965)*, Munich.

Schulz, G. (1974) *Faschismus – Nationalsozialismus. Versionen und theoretische Kontroversen 1922–1972*, Frankfurt.

Schulze, H. (1987) 'The "German Question" and European answers', *Historical Journal* 30(4): 1013–22.

Schulze, W. (1989) *Deutsche Geschichtswissenschaft nach 1945*, Munich.

Senfft, H. (1990) *Kein Abschied von Hitler: Hinter den Fassaden des Historikerstreits*, Hamburg.

Shirer, W. (1960) *The Rise and Fall of the Third Reich*, London.

Soth-Rethel, A. (1987) *The Economy and Class Structure of German Fascism*, London.

Stegmann, D. (1973) 'Zum Verhältnis von Grossindustrie und Nationalsozialismus 1930–1933', *Archiv für Sozialgeschichte* 13: 399–482.

—— (1976) 'Kapitalismus und Faschismus 1929–1934: Thesen und Materialien', in Backhaus 1976.

—— (1977) 'Antiquierte Personalisierung oder sozialökonomische Faschismus–Analyse? Eine Antwort auf H. A. Turners Kritik an meinen Thesen zum Verhältnis von Nationalsozialismus und Grossindustrie vor 1933', *Archiv für Sozialgeschichte* 17: 275–96.

Stern, F. (1961) *The Politics of Cultural Despair*, Berkeley.

Stern, J. P. (1975) *Hitler: The Führer and the People*, London.

Stümke, H.-G. and Finker, R. (1981) *Rosa Winkel, Rosa Listen. Homosexuelle und 'Gesundes Volksempfinden' von Auschwitz bis heute*, Reinbek.

Sturm, R. (1986) 'Faschismusauffassungen der Sozialdemokratie in der Weimarer Republik', in R. Saage (ed.) *Solidargemeinschaft und Klassenkampf. Politische Konzeptionen der Sozialdemokratie zwischen den Weltkriegen*, Frankfurt.

Stürmer, M. (1988) *Dissonanzen des Fortschritts. Essays über Geschichte und Politik in Deutschland*, Munich.

Talmon, J. H. (1952) *The Origins of Totalitarian Democracy*, Boston.

Taylor, A. J. P. (1946) *The Course of German History*, London.

—— (1961) *The Origins of the Second World War*, London.

Tenfelde, K. (1984) 'Schwierigkeiten mit dem Alltag', *Geschichte und Gesellschaft* 10: 395–408.

Thamer, H. U. (1987) 'Nationalsozialismus und Faschismus in der DDR-Historiographie', *Aus Politik und Zeitgeschichte* B 13: 27–37.

—— and Wippermann, W. (1977) *Faschistische und neofaschistische Bewegungen*, Darmstadt.

Theweleit, K. (1987–9) *Male Fantasies*, 2 vols, Minneapolis.

Thies, J. (1978) 'Hitlers "Endziele": zielloser Aktionismus, Kontinentalimperium oder Weltherrschaft?', in W. Michalka (ed.) *Nationalsozialistische Aussenpolitik*, Darmstadt.

Trotsky, L. [1930–40] (1971) *The Struggle against Fascism in Germany*, New York.

Turner, H. A. (1975a) 'Grossunternehmen und Nationalsozialismus 1930–1933', *Historische Zeitschrift* 221: 18–68.

—— (1975b) *Reappraisals of Fascism*, New York.

—— (1980) *Faschismus und Kapitalismus in Deutschland. Studien zum Verhältnis zwischen Nationalsozialismus und Wirtschaft*, Göttingen.

Turner, H. A. (1985) *German Big Business and the Rise of Hitler*, New York.
Uhe, E. (1972) *Der Nationalsozialismus in den deutschen Schulbüchern. Eine vergleichende Inhaltsanalyse von Schulgeschichtsbüchern aus der Bundesrepublik Deutschland und der Deutschen Demokratischen Republik*, Berne and Frankfurt.
Vermeil, E. (1944) *Germany's Three Reichs*, London.
Vidal-Naquet, P. (1989) 'Theses on revisionism', in Furet 1989.
—— (1992) *Assassins of Memory. Essays on the Denial of the Holocaust*, New York.
Viereck, P. (1941) *Metapolitics. From the Romantics to Hitler*, New York.
Vierhaus, R. (1968) 'Walter Frank und die Geschichtswissenschaft im nationalsozialistischen Deutschland', *Historische Zeitschrift* 207: 617–27.
Waite, R. (1977) *The Psychopathic God. Adolf Hitler*, New York.
Weber, W. (1984) *Priester der Klio. Historisch-sozialwissenschaftliche Studien zur Herkunft und Karriere deutscher Historiker und zur Geschichte der Geschichtswissenschaft 1880–1970*, Frankfurt, Berne and New York.
Wehler, H.-U. (1984) 'Historiography in Germany today', in Habermas 1984.
—— (1988) *Entsorgung der deutschen Vergangenheit? Ein polemischer Essay zum 'Historikerstreit'*, Munich.
Weidenfeld, W. (ed.) (1987) *Geschichtsbewusstsein der Deutschen. Materialien zur Spurensuche einer Nation*, Cologne.
Werner, K. F. (1967) *Das NS-Geschichtsbild und die deutsche Geschichtswissenschaft*, Stuttgart.
—— (1968) 'On some examples of the National Socialist view of history', *Journal of Contemporary History* 3: 193–206.
—— (1974) 'Die deutsche Historiographie unter Hitler', in Faulenbach 1974.
Wilson, M. (1982) *Das Institut für Sozialforschung und seine Faschismusanalysen*, Frankfurt.
Winkler, H.-A. (1978) *Revolution, Staat, Faschismus*, Göttingen.
—— (1990) *Der Weg in die Katastrophe. Arbeiter und Arbeiterbewegung in der Weimarer Republik 1930 bis 1933*, Bonn.
Wippermann, W. (1972) *Faschismustheorien*, Darmstadt.
—— (1975) *Faschismustheorien. Zum Stand der gegenwärtigen Diskussion*, Darmstadt.
—— (1976) '"Deutsche Katastrophe" oder "Diktatur des Finanzkapitals"? Zur Interpretationsgeschichte des Dritten Reiches in Nachkriegsdeutschland', in H. Denkler and K. Prümm (eds) *Die deutsche Literatur im Dritten Reich, Themen, Traditionen, Wirkungen*, Stuttgart.
—— (1989) *Der konsequente Wahn. Ideologie und Politik Adolf Hitlers*, Gütersloh and Munich.
Wolfe, R. (ed.) (1974) *Captured German and Related Records. A National Archives Conference*, Athens, OH.
Woolf, S. J. (ed.) (1968a) *European Fascism*, London.
—— (1968b) *The Nature of Fascism*, London.
Zitelmann, R. (1990) 'Nationalsozialismus und Moderne. Eine Zwischenbilanz', in W. Süss (ed.) *Übergänge. Zeitgeschichte zwischen Utopie und Machtbarkeit*, Berlin.

22

MODERN ITALY – CHANGING HISTORICAL PERSPECTIVES SINCE 1945

John A. Davis

INTRODUCTION

From the fall of Mussolini in 1943 to the dramatic political changes of recent years, debate on Italy's future has been driven by reinterpretation of its past. Fascism has been the single most important issue in these debates even when it has not been addressed directly, and much of the debate on unification and the liberal state has revolved around the search for the roots of fascism and the collapse of Italy's parliamentary democracy after the First World War.

This chapter will chart briefly the ways in which these debates have developed, with particular reference to the contributions of non-Italian (especially British and American) historians. As a broad generalization, in the first two and a half decades after the fall of Mussolini the concern was to set fascism in the context of what had preceded it. More recently the focus has shifted to relate fascism to what came after, not least because as Italy began to acquire a history since the fall of Mussolini it has made increasingly less sense to assume – as earlier studies necessarily did – that 1943 had been the end of an era in Italian history.

Historiographical shifts are not easily pinned down to neat dates, but in this case 1968 and the wave of protests against Italy's post-war political system are more than a bench-mark. Until then, at least some of the optimism that had accompanied the founding of the Republic survived, and with it the notion that the collapse of the regime, the struggles of the Resistance and the founding of the Republic had marked a new beginning – *anno zero*, 'Year Nought'. But the political and cultural climate in Italy changed significantly in the 1960s and 1970s. On the Left, Stalinism was losing its appeal, while the papacy of John XXIII and the first openings towards the Left signalled profound changes. The decade ended with the protest movements of 1968 and 1969. The terrorist attacks inspired by the extreme Right that began with the Piazza Fontana bombing in Milan in 1969 in turn triggered the response of the Red Brigades and the spiral of violence that gripped Italian society throughout the 1970s.

It was in this climate that Italian historians began rethinking the longer-run patterns in Italian history, posing new questions and challenging formerly persuasive interpretations and models. New perspectives in historical research and writing played a part in this, as did an awareness that the problems of Italy's post-war democratic Republic seemed to have little to do with economic failure. Indeed, post-war Italy had experienced perhaps the most dramatic economic and social transformation of any western European state. This meant that the emphasis on Italy's relative backwardness that permeated much of the earlier debates on Liberal Italy and fascism became questionable too. In this new climate, the continuities between fascist Italy and post-war Italy began to attract closer attention.

POST-WAR PREMISES: FASCISM AND THE RISORGIMENTO

History and politics were inseparable in the painful process of political reconstruction in Italy after the fall of fascism. Each of the political parties that had been part of the antifascist Resistance and participated in the founding of the Italian Republic in 1946 sought to establish its particular identity and democratic legitimacy by appealing to the past. Gaetano Salvemini, a distinguished antifascist exile, former militant socialist and a professional historian, opened a debate in the constitutional Consulta in 1946, for example, with the question 'Was Pre-fascist Italy a Democracy?'. This set an agenda for historical debate for over a decade that focused on the political programmes of Giovanni Giolitti, who had dominated Italian politics in the decade before the First World War. Had Giolitti been working to strengthen Italian democracy by introducing welfare and franchise reforms? Had his overtures to the Socialist Party been genuine or merely a new variant of the traditional cross-party gerrymandering known as *trasformismo*? How did the invasion of Libya in 1911 and the introduction of universal suffrage fit into this picture? Had Italy's entry into the First World War in 1915 against the wishes of the parliamentary majority signalled the collapse of parliamentary government in Italy even before the post-war crisis? Had fascism, in other words, overwhelmed a 'democracy in the making', or was liberal democracy in deep crisis well before the advent of Mussolini's blackshirts?

Arguing that, despite Giolitti's unprincipled and corrupt management, Italian political institutions had in these years become more democratic, Salvemini was endorsing the reformist strategies of the pre–1914 Socialist Party – although at the time he had been amongst their most bitter critics. In one of the first English-language studies to appear after the fall of fascism the Italian-American scholar A. W. Salamone supported Salvemini's interpretation. The Communists naturally disagreed, and their leader Palmiro Togliatti argued that although Giolitti had been a genuinely progressive bourgeois liberal, his attempts at reform had been blocked by Italy's backward and reactionary capitalist classes. Togliatti's purpose was of course to discredit the reformist policies of the Socialist Party (PSI) earlier in the century while endorsing the revolutionary programme advocated by the Communists (PCI) who had broken away from the PSI in 1921.

More moderate and conservative liberals took their lead from the philosopher-historian and antifascist of international renown, Benedetto Croce, whose *History of Italy from 1870 to 1915* (1929) had refuted Mussolini's claim that fascism was the true heir of the Risorgimento. Arguing that fascism was simply a 'parenthesis', a phenomenon without roots in Italian history and a product of the terrible upheavals and trauma caused by the First World War, Croce emphasized the achievements of the Liberal state, which he believed had reached its highest levels in the years of Giolitti's political supremacy before 1914.

The debate took on wider dimensions when the prison writings of Antonio Gramsci were published. A co-founder of the Italian Communist Party and one of the major Marxist thinkers of the twentieth century, Gramsci's reflections on the Risorgimento were written in fragmentary notes to avoid detection in fascist jails. For Gramsci, the struggle for Italian unification had resulted in a 'passive' or 'missing revolution' (*'rivoluzione mancata'*) because Italy's small and immature bourgeoisie of landowners and professionals had been unable to carry through a political revolution on their own. To overthrow the absolutist Italian rulers, Gramsci argued, the middle classes were forced to make an alliance with the reactionary Piedmontese monarchy and its army (Gramsci 1971).

Italy's relative backwardness – in economic and social terms – also explained why the Risorgimento radicals had failed to offer a democratic alternative. Lacking a significant following among the middle classes, in Gramsci's view the radicals could only have created a social base by harnessing the force of peasant unrest in Italy. That would have meant adopting reforms to meet the peasants' demand for land, something that Gramsci acknowledged the radicals were unable to do because it would have threatened their own class interests. Cavour's more moderate political programme was, therefore, unbeatable. But for Gramsci the alliance between the propertied classes and the reactionary Piedmontese monarchy on which Cavour's strategy was based compromised Italy's liberal revolution from the outset in ways that hindered the development of modern capitalism, left the working classes as well as the bourgeoisie divided and hence opened the way to fascism.

The historical debate on the strengths and merits of the rival radical and moderate political programmes in the Risorgimento moved back to the reform movements of the Enlightenment in Italy. Croce had always insisted that nineteenth-century moderate liberalism was heir to eighteenth-century reformism, while socialist and communist historians now looked to the more radical figures of the Enlightenment for the origins of an alternative Italian democratic tradition. But this field was soon to be dominated by the towering intellectual figure of Franco Venturi, who warned against simplistic attempts to turn the Enlightenment into an intellectual prehistory of nineteenth-century Italian politics. For Venturi, the openness and richness of the intellectual, political and economic debates of the eighteenth century were symptoms of the disintegration of the *ancien régime* world. This was a unique moment of cosmopolitan enquiry that moved backwards and forwards between abstract ideas and practical proposals and across territorial and dynastic frontiers. Venturi's decision to bring his studies to a close before the French Revolution underlined his conviction that no subsequent political movement or philosophy could claim to be the sole 'heir of the Enlightenment' (Venturi 1971; 1972).

The first major reworking of Croce's defence of the Risorgimento came from Rosario Romeo's study of the Risorgimento in Sicily (Romeo 1954). Romeo's central theme was that Sicily had been too backward to achieve political or economic progress unaided in the nineteenth century. Neither the peasants nor the middle classes had sufficient influence or vision to formulate new political programmes capable of commanding broad support. For Romeo, only the inspiration provided by the liberal values inherent in the broader movement for Italian independence and unity had made it possible for Sicilians to overcome Sicily's social and material backwardness.

In his later and monumental three-volume biography of Cavour (Romeo 1969–84), Romeo elaborated this defence of the progressive and constructive force of Risorgimento liberalism. Understanding that liberalism offered the only alternative to the political extremes posed by the Jacobin legacy of the French Revolution and the equally destructive reactionary and absolutist politics of the Restoration, Cavour came to accept that constitutional government was the essential premise for political stability on the Italian peninsula. Since a constitutional monarchy proved difficult to consolidate within the narrow confines of the Kingdom of Savoy, above all because of opposition from the Church, Cavour's determination to press forward with liberal reforms led him to seek the wider support of the propertied classes of northern and central Italy and hence to adopt the nationalist cause against Austria. Refuting categorically the claim that the Liberal state had been flawed from birth, Romeo insisted that Cavour's policies were the necessary prerequisites for Italy's political, economic and cultural modernization: the falling-off had come later and had resulted from the failure of Cavour's successors to understand and uphold the original values of Italian liberalism.

Denis Mack Smith (1954) was the first British historian to enter this new debate with his study of the relations between Garibaldi and Cavour. This was conceived as a critique of the heroic terms in which G. M. Trevelyan had depicted the struggles for Italian unification for British audiences at the beginning of the century (Trevelyan 1907; 1909; 1911). For Trevelyan, the struggle for Italian independence had been one of the great, if not the greatest, achievements of nineteenth-century liberalism and individualism. But that interpretation was discredited by fascism, and Mack Smith's study told a very different tale. As A. J. P. Taylor noted, 'with brilliant, though well-founded perversity, Mr. Mack Smith turns everything upside down' (Taylor 1967: 83). Although sharing Trevelyan's admiration for Garibaldi, Mack Smith contrasted Garibaldi's idealism with the wily but more effective *Realpolitik* of Cavour. For Mack Smith, Cavour's triumph in 1860 fatally compromised the liberalism of the new state and in his *Italy: A Modern History*

(1955) he drew out the broader consequences. In Cavour's misuse of parliamentary procedures Mack Smith saw the origins of the weaknesses of Liberal Italy and continuities that linked Cavour to Mussolini.

Mack Smith's study spoke to two quite different audiences. For British readers, it explained how Italian fascism was rooted in the failings of the Risorgimento, while for Italians it offered a coherent critique of Italian liberalism that was not tainted by Marxism. In Italy, however, Mack Smith's most severe critics – most notably Rosario Romeo – were on the Right not the Left. But his work also drew responses from non-Italian historians and in 1968 Christopher Seton-Watson published a detailed history of Italy from liberalism to fascism that challenged Mack Smith's analysis at every turn. Arguing that Italy had succeeded in strengthening its liberal institutions and politics at least until the crisis after 1918, Seton-Watson's conclusions came closer to those of Salvemini and Croce (Seton-Watson 1968).

While other British historians turned to examine the ways in which British diplomacy shaped Italian unification (Beales 1961), the debate on the politics of the Risorgimento was also taken up by American scholars. They were influenced less by Trevelyan than by earlier American studies such as the pre-First World War study of Cavour by J. A. Thayer but above all Kent R. Greenfield's remarkable 1934 study of economics and liberalism in Lombardy in the Risorgimento (which was republished with an introduction by Romeo in 1965). Greenfield's book was written as a critique of the Marxist claim that Italian nationalism was linked to the emergence of a new capitalist bourgeoisie, and showed that the demands for political reform and independence from Austria had come from intellectuals rather than from the Lombard commercial and entrepreneurial classes.

The study of Austrian administration in Lombardy after the Restoration of 1814 was taken up by R. J. Rath (1969), who showed how the exclusion of the Italian propertied classes from power soured relations with the Lombard patriciate. In his important study of the Italian National Society, Raymond Grew (1963) also examined the ways in which the propertied classes of Northern and Central Italy influenced the political outcome of the struggle for independence. The National Society was founded in 1857 by Cavour's supporters in central Italy to prevent the radicals gaining control of the Italian Revolution. Grew showed how the 'success' of its conservative supporters 'spoiled' the broader democratic ideals present in the struggles for independence. The radicals and their programmes were the subject of three books by Clara M. Lovett, which included biographies of Carlo Cattaneo (1972) and Giuseppe Ferrari (1979), the leading advocates of federalist solutions for an independent Italy, and a more general study of the social and cultural background of the Risorgimento radicals and their destinies after Unification (Lovett 1982).

Interest in the political programmes of the Risorgimento radicals also drew attention to the ideas of Antonio Gramsci, and following the pioneering work of John Cammet (1967) these were the subject of a growing bibliography. This included H. Stuart Hughes's (1958) masterly study of European intellectual history in the late nineteenth century, a useful brief essay by James Joll (1977) and more recently detailed studies of Gramsci's political thought by Joseph Femia (1981) and Walter Adamson (1980). Two studies of the Italian revolutions of 1848 were directly inspired by Gramsci's notion of the 'missing revolution'. Taking another of Trevelyan's subjects, Manin and the Venetian Revolution of 1848, Paul Ginsborg (1979) argued that Manin's leadership of the Venetian Revolution well illustrated Gramsci's analysis of the political weakness of the radicals. Ginsborg's claim that the refusal to arm the peasants and adopt a programme of agrarian reform had wrecked Manin's attempts to join forces with the constitutional regimes in Milan, Turin, Florence and Rome was contested, however, by Alan Sked (1979) who approached the revolutions from an Austrian perspective. David LoRomer (1987) adopted a similar Gramscian analysis in his study of the 1848 revolution in Livorno.

MOVING FORWARD: LIBERALISM AND MODERNIZATION

The debate on Liberal Italy that began with the post-war exchanges on Giolitti came to focus on the relationship between liberalism and economic growth, or – in broader terms – liberalism and modernization. This was partly because of Gramsci's insistence on the immaturity of the Italian bourgeoisie as a class and his claim that the 'missing revolution' of 1860 was reflected in the reactionary alliance between the northern industrialists and the southern landowners that took shape in the late 1880s in support of tariff protection for agriculture and industry. For Gramsci this alliance was the key feature of the Liberal state and remained the principal obstacle to both political and economic development down to the 1920s. The rejoinder came once again from Rosario Romeo, for whom unification had been the premise for Italy's economic as well as political modernization. Arguing that after 1860 agriculture, through taxation, demand and invested profits, had financed the infrastructures (roads, railways, banks) on which Italy's industrialization depended, Romeo claimed that an agrarian reform would simply have preserved an outdated peasant agriculture and hence have retarded Italy's economic modernization (Romeo 1961).

The response to Romeo came not from the Left, but from Alexander Gerschenkron (1966) who claimed that Italy's relatively late and internally patchy industrialization was the result of state intervention and the creation of new mixed investment banks (the Banca Commerciale Italiano and the Credito Italiano) in the 1890s and not of capital transfers from agriculture. What was at stake in this debate was nineteenth-century Italy's capacity for independent economic growth. Gerschenkron believed that in Italy, as in other industrial latecomers (such as Germany and Russia), spontaneous economic growth had been weak. Like Germany's notorious *Sonderweg*, Italy's path to the twentieth century was as a result marked by a process of industrialization from above that was not accompanied by broader forms of social modernization and indeed exacerbated the existing internal dualisms between an industrializing North and the still backward and predominantly agrarian South. It was to these internal contrasts that Gerschenkron attributed the political disasters that would beset all the industrial latecomers – Russia, Germany, Italy and Japan – in the twentieth century, thereby offering a non-Marxist explanation of the structural weaknesses of Italian liberal democracy (Gerschenkron 1966).

Gramsci's notion of an incomplete bourgeois revolution and Gerschenkron's inclusion of Italy in the category of industrial latecomers were in many ways complementary, and both linked the problems of Italian liberalism to incomplete and imbalanced modernization. These arguments established a broader context for debate, much of which focused on the limits of Italian liberalism – one of the central themes in the essays published in the volume on *Gramsci and Italy's Passive Revolution* (Davis 1979). But the economic record of Liberal Italy also found defenders and F. J. Coppa's (1971) detailed study of the renegotiation of Italy's protectionist tariff regime in the early twentieth century put up a stout defence of Giolitti's economic and political liberalism.

The other principal field of debate was foreign policy and nationalism. Had Italy's entry into the Triple Alliance in 1882 distanced her from liberal Britain as well as from republican France, or was the German–Austro-Hungarian axis dictated purely by diplomatic considerations? The terms of the debate were set by Federico Chabod (1953), who emphasized how the new Italian state had been born in the shadow of the Paris Commune and hence at a moment when European liberalism as a whole was rapidly losing its progressive and constructive features. Reconstructing the tensions between liberal and nationalist aspirations and the links between domestic and foreign policy, Chabod underlined the narrow constraints within which the new Italian state had to steer its foreign policy after unification.

Studies by Decleva, Di Nolfo, Vigezzi and others focused on the diplomatic and ideological aims of Italian foreign policy before 1914 and the contrast between the cautious diplomacy of Visconti-Venosta and the more aggressive and anti-Austro-Hungarian policies adopted by Di San Giuliano. Industrialization and its influence on foreign policy became a major issue in this field as well. Were the first colonial initiatives of Crispi's government linked to Italy's industrial expansion? Did the social legislation of the Giolittian era go hand in hand with the emergence of new forms of industrial imperialism? The American historian Richard Webster (1974), for example, argued that Italian colonialism before 1914 had been driven by the network of financial and industrial interests that converged at the beginning of the twentieth century around the Banca Commerciale Italiana, although this has been challenged. In *Italy Least of the Great Powers* (1979), the Australian historian Richard Bosworth argued that Italy's economic backwardness made it impossible for her to sustain her pretensions as a Great Power. Bosworth saw this as the principal cause of the adventurist tendencies in Italian foreign policy that he believed were present from Crispi's early and disastrous bid for colonial expansion in the 1890s, to Giolitti's invasion of Libya in 1911 and finally to Mussolini's imperialism in the 1930s. In parallel with this, the studies by J. A. Thayer, A. Saladino, A. De Grand and Richard Drake explored the origins and influence of nationalist ideas in Italy before 1914.

FASCISM

It was in the 1960s that the debate on fascism itself began in earnest. The first studies based on extensive archival sources began to be published, while in international terms a broader debate on the cultural roots and sociological contexts of totalitarianism was stimulated by the publication of studies like Barrington Moore Jr. *Social Origins of Dictatorship and Democracy*, and Ernst Nolte's *Three Faces of Fascism*. The two volumes edited by Stuart Woolf (*European Fascism* and the *Nature of Fascism*) and the launch of the *Journal of Contemporary History* are all indications of this widening interest.

In Italy, Alberto Aquarone's study (1965) of the institutional organization of the fascist regime, Roberto Vivarelli's analysis of the post-war crisis, and the first volume of Renzo De Felice's biography of Mussolini appeared in quick succession. De Felice's work in particular aroused great controversy. Like Romeo, De Felice chose biography as a means to write a general study of the period and the evolution of Mussolini's regime, but whereas Romeo had stressed the European breadth of Cavour's ideas and culture, De Felice insisted on the essentially Italian character of fascism, although denying that fascism and Mussolini-ism were identical. Many historians on the Left saw the claim that Mussolini's politics were rooted in his experience as a revolutionary socialist (De Felice 1965) as an attack on the integrity of the antifascist alliance on which the post-war Italian Republic was founded. But De Felice's arguments also offended a historian like Vivarelli (1967) who blamed the revolutionary rhetoric of the Socialist Party for heightening the political crisis in Italy after 1918, but insisted that the ideological matrix of fascism lay in the pre-fascist nationalist movement.

The controversy grew as successive volumes of De Felice's biography set out an interpretation that many believed sought to rehabilitate and 'relativize' Italian fascism. The claim that Mussolini's regime had in its heyday commanded the active support ('consensus') of the majority of Italians and that the regime reflected the aspirations of a rising political class that had previously been excluded from the patrician politics of the old elites sparked off a particularly heated controversy (see also M. Ledeen *Interpretations*). The later volumes continue to cause controversy, not least because of De Felice's insistence that fascism had firm roots in Italian society, was not in every respect negative (although he denounced its dictatorial and imperialist aspects) and bore no substantial similarities to German National Socialism.

English translations of general studies on the origins of fascism like Salvemini's *Origins of Italian Fascism*, Angelo Tasca's *Rise of Italian Fascism* and Paolo Spriano's *Occupation of the Factories* attracted non-Italian historians to study the post-war crisis and the fascist seizure of power. Many focused on the failure of the Left, and Martin Clark's *Antonio Gramsci and the Revolution that Failed* examined how the fragile unity of the industrial workers, the unions and the socialists collapsed during the factory occupations in the summer of 1920.

Paul Corner's study of fascism in Ferrara (1974) was concerned to explain the collapse of the militant agricultural labour unions in the Po Valley after 1918. Much to Mussolini's astonishment, it was here that fascism first found a mass following and Corner reconstructed the ways in which fascism emerged as a response to a class war that had been endemic in the rural Po Valley since the beginning of the century. During the war, the highly organized and militant labourers' unions had made great conquests, but once the war was over the landowners looked to claw back the concessions they had made and the incursions of black-shirt squads into the agrarian landscape provided the means. Despite its rural setting, Corner's study points firmly to the links between fascism and capitalist modernization in rural Italy. Other regional studies, by Anthony Cardoza (1982) (the province of Bologna), Frank Snowden (1989) (Tuscany and Apulia) and Alice A. Kelikian (1986) (Brescia), developed these arguments and showed how the fascist movement inserted itself in a variety of different local conflicts.

At stake was the claim that fascism had developed after 1920 as a form of capitalist counter-revolution to destroy labour organizations and reformist political parties (including the new Catholic Popular Party) at the behest of big business and the landowners. Charles S. Maier's *Recasting Bourgeois Europe* (which deals with Italy in detail, as well as France and Germany) questioned that interpretation, while setting Italian fascism in the context of a broader abandonment by the European bourgeois and managerial elites of pre-war liberalism for new corporatist strategies. The timing of the crisis in Italy in Maier's view was determined by the relative weakness of the economic and political institutions of the Liberal state. Douglas Forsyth (1993) has recently argued that the financial and economic demands of the war made it impossible for Italy's post-war governments to maintain or develop the welfare programmes and social legislation adopted before 1914 by Giolitti. In these terms, fascism is seen as a consequence of the failure of post-war Italian liberal governments to adapt to modernization, social and economic change in conditions when it was no longer possible to pursue a model of welfare consensus, in ways that anticipated the later fate of Weimar Germany.

Relations between the fascists and Italian industrialists were the subject of a detailed study by Roland Sarti (1971), who argued that although Italian business leaders were not opposed to Mussolini, many remained wary of the movement's revolutionary tendencies and kept their distance. But once the dictatorship was in place, Sarti claimed that the Italian industrialists proved better able to retain their corporate autonomy than any other interest group.

Of the principal political groups and tendencies that converged in the fascist movement, David D. Roberts (1979) has examined the role and influence of the revolutionary syndicalists and shown how Mussolini never supported a genuinely syndicalist programme. Alexander De Grand's study (1978) of the nationalist movement from the founding of the Italian Nationalist Association in 1911 to the merger with the fascists in 1923 reveals how the Nationalists played an often critical and conservative role in shaping the fascist state. Christopher Duggan's *Fascism and the Mafia* (1989) examines the ways in which the regime attempted to establish a political base in western Sicily and the political alliances that this involved.

Adrian Lyttelton's *Seizure of Power* (1974) offered a model for these approaches, emphasizing the heterogeneous nature of different local situations while seeking to explain how these converged into the fascist movement, how they held together and how this cohesion was preserved in the transition from political movement to regime. Critical of De Felice's argument that the creation of the fascist state entailed no major break with the past, the underlying theme of Lyttelton's study is that fascism resulted from the failure of the liberal ruling classes to adapt to the realities of mass politics. Accepting that the regime was in essence 'Mussolini's personal dictatorship' (p. 432), Lyttelton shows how Mussolini played different factions off against one another but avoids identifying the dictator and the regime too closely. Lyttelton also describes the ways in which the Fascist Party was gradually subordinated to Mussolini and the state bureaucracy in the power struggles after 1925, although Emilio Gentile (1984) has recently suggested that the Party retained important functions within the fascist state.

A central theme in Lyttelton's study is the degree to which fascism was a political movement driven by clear yet often competing political and economic interests, rather than an exercise in mere political eclecticism, opportunism and chicanery. The staunchest champion of the second interpretation – which had also been Salvemini's – was Denis Mack Smith, whose biography of Mussolini appeared in 1981. Directed primarily against De Felice's insistence on the rationality of Mussolini's politics, Mack Smith portrayed the Duce as a bombastic artist in propaganda, self- and national deception whose power ultimately rested on graft and corruption.

Mack Smith's critics believed he exaggerated the incoherence of fascist policy, and the recent revival of right-wing political ideologies in both Europe and the United States explains why historians have tended to take the ideologies of fascism more seriously now than in the past (see Griffin 1993). But even amongst those who argue that fascism did have a coherent ideology there is still disagreement. The Israeli historian Zeev Sternhell (1993) has recently revived an argument first suggested by Ernst Nolte (1966) that the ideological matrix of Italian fascism lay in the ideas of the pre-1914 French Action Française and French syndicalism, but his critics argue that fascism drew on wider ideological and cultural sources. The Italian historian Emilio Gentile (1990), for example, has developed George Mosse's argument that fascist ideology was part of a wider reaction against the secularization of European societies in the nineteenth century and can be interpreted as an attempt to forge new forms of secular religion through nationalism, myth and public display. On similar lines, Walter Adamson (1993) has also argued that the avant-garde of anti-liberal and anti-positivist writers and artists associated with the pre-1914 Florentine journal *La Voce* prefigured much of the content and thrust of later fascist ideology.

The role of ideology is also the central question addressed in studies on the regime's policies once in power. For the American historian, A. J. Gregor (1979),

Mussolini's regime was a 'developmental dictatorship' bent on modernizing the Italian economy and society. Jon Cohen (1988), however, has cogently argued that such an interpretation risks taking the regime's claims too much at face value and is not substantiated by Italy's economic performance in the 1920s and 1930s. Indeed, it is still far from clear whether it is possible to define a 'fascist' economic policy. Some argue that the regime did have a clear policy and that the revaluation of the lire in 1927 intentionally precipitated a deflationary trend that sacrificed consumption and consumer goods industries to strengthen Italy's chemical, iron, and steel sectors, marking the beginning of a bid for economic autarchy and the restructuring of Italian industry that laid the basis for Italy's post-war economic miracle. Others claim that changes in the Italian economy owed more to the Depression and the international economy than to Mussolini's policies, that after revaluation Italy's dependence on US loans increased, and that massive increases in state intervention in the economy through the rescue of the banking system and the creation of state holding companies (IRI, IMI) in the early 1930s were crisis measures that did not form part of any longer-term or coherent economic plan. Both those interpretations are rejected by those who argue that Mussolini, like Hitler, subordinated economic policy to his imperialist ambitions, forcing Italy into disastrous economic subordination to Germany and dragging the country into a war that it lacked the resources to fight. Vera Zamagni's recent *Economic History of Italy 1860–1990* (1993) offers a clear and balanced guide to these debates.

Lack of reliable data makes generalizations about the performance of the economy in the 1930s difficult, and this has caused debate on the role of ideology to focus on the regime's social and cultural policies. A recent general study by D. Thomson (1991) in some respects updates Tannenbaum's older book (1972) on fascist social and cultural policies, but the best insights come from detailed studies. Philip Cannistraro's research on the Ministry of Popular Culture, for example, shows clearly the limited success of the regime's attempts to generate consensus through propaganda (*La Fabbrica del Consenso*) (1975). Marla Stone's analysis of the 1932 exhibition to commemorate the anniversary of the Fascist Revolution emphasizes how the regime at this time was attempting to project a pluralist and inclusive image of fascism (1993). A rapidly expanding bibliography in English on the cinema explores the ways in which the regime deployed propaganda and the broader question of whether there was a 'fascist' culture. The relationship between the regime and Italian artists and intellectuals has been the subject of major studies by Italian historians, and the recent biography of Margherita Sarfatti, Mussolini's Jewish mistress, by B. R. Sullivan and P. Cannistraro (1993) contains much information on intellectual life and the arts in fascist Italy. This is also the subject of a recent article by Ruth Ben Ghiat (1995) that examines the ways in which many leading Italian writers and artists who subsequently disclaimed any contact with the regime were more closely and actively associated with official fascist culture than they chose to remember after 1943.

The debate on the cultural policies of the regime has always been closely linked to De Felice's claim that in the early part of the 1930s Mussolini's regime achieved broad consensus amongst Italians. Shifting the focus from high to popular culture, Victoria De Grazia's *Culture of Consent* (1981) examined the relationship between the regime and the working classes in the broader context of the search throughout the capitalist economies for ways to respond to the advent of mass society. De Grazia argued that the regime's objectives in establishing the network of workers' recreational associations (*Dopolavoro*) were an offshoot of principles of scientific management pioneered by industrialists like Henry Ford and adopted in Italy by leading Italian industrialists like Giovanni Agnelli after the war. Fascist attempts to redraw the boundaries of private and public life by bringing the state directly into the leisure activities of Italian workers were one variant on a wider range of responses to the advent of mass society.

Early optimism soon gave way to more realistic aims partly, De Grazia argued, because Mussolini's Italy lacked the material resources to attempt anything comparable to the later Nazi 'Strength through Joy' organizations, but also because its policies were fundamentally contradictory. The regime never decided whether it wanted to exploit a nascent consumer economy or to block its growth (on the grounds that it was not 'fascist'), while its strategy of mobilization ran up against the fascist emphasis on obedience, hierarchy and deference: as De Grazia pointed out, it proved difficult to mobilize the masses to be passive. Early aspirations to turn Italians into fanatical fascist men, women and children soon gave way, therefore, to more minimalist but not ineffective attempts to associate everything that was traditionally Italian – sports, pastimes and entertainment – with fascism. A recent article by Emilio Gentile (1993) also shows how the regime's ambivalence over consumerism was reflected in fascist attitudes to America.

Fascist education has been studied by T. Koon (1985), while following earlier studies by Alexander De Grand (1976), Leslie Caldwell (1986) and Emiliana Noether (1982), Luisa Passerini (1979) has studied women's memories of the regime and the Duce. A recent study by Perry Willson (1993) offers a detailed reconstruction of the work and experiences of the mainly female workforce of a leading Milanese engineering company that was also deemed to be a model 'fascist' enterprise. But the broadest study of the regime's policies towards women is Victoria de Grazia's *How Fascism Ruled Women* (1992), which again sets the regime's policies in the broader comparative context of the ways in which all advanced industrial societies were responding to fears that the advent of mass society would cause birth-rates to fall. In the Italian case, De Grazia emphasizes how the regime's policies evolved hesitantly and, despite a deep-seated misogyny, ambiguously. On the one hand, the regime wanted to remove women from the workplace, deprive them of freedom of choice and bend them to its demographic needs. But at the same time fascist attempts to push back the boundaries of the private gave many Italian women a new freedom to lead lives outside the family and enter into a consumer culture unknown to their mothers. As in its attempts to organize leisure, the regime's specific objectives were not achieved (the birth-rate did not increase and the number of women in the workforce did not decline) and provided a further illustration of the contradictions inherent in the fascist desire to achieve economic modernity within a context of traditional social values and institutions.

De Grazia's study also deals at length with the conflicts with the Church that resulted from the regime's policies on education, the family, maternity, gender, race and eugenics. Relations between the regime and the Church have been the subject of studies by Jemolo (1960), Binchy (1941), R. Webster (1960) and most recently by J. F. Pollard (1988), while R. Kent has written on the Vatican's policies towards the dictators. Attention has also focused on the relationship between racism and fascism, and in a recent comparative essay Maria Quine (1996) has argued that racial theories and eugenics influenced the regime's policies more deeply than has been recognized. The regime's anti-semitism has also attacted new attention. The Jewish communities and their role in Italian intellectual life have been studied by H. Stuart Hughes (1983) while Alexander Stille (1991) has vividly described the contrasting political outlook and fortunes of five Jewish families in fascist Italy. The background to the racial laws of 1938 and the origins of fascist anti-Semitism are the subject of Meir Michaelis's *Mussolini and the Jews* (1978), while the idea that Italian fascism was free of anti-Semitism and racism and that the racial laws of 1938 were imposed by the alliance with Germany has found many critics. Esmonde Robertson, for example, has emphasized the importance of racism in Italian imperialism and the links between racism and anti-Semitism. On the other hand, both Susan Zucotti (1987) and Jonathan Steinberg (1990) have shown that the 1938 legislation against the Jews was deeply unpopular among many Italians, and that down to 1943 the Italian authorities refused to co-operate with their German allies in deporting Jews either from Italy or from the Italian-occupied territories in Croatia and southern France. But for Meir Michaelis (1989) the regime's open advocacy of imperialism, racism and violence made fascist Italy no less an accomplice in the destruction of European Jewry.

The regime's policies on Jews, minorities, workers and women raise the issue of opposition to fascism, which has attracted little attention in English since Charles Delzell's pioneering book on Mussolini's enemies (1961). Paul Corner (1990) has explored the reasons for the lack of opposition amongst industrial workers in Italy before 1943, while Luisa Passerini (1979) has studied forms of covert working-class opposition to the regime. Both J. P. Diggins's study *Fascism: The View from America* (1972) and H. Stuart Hughes's *Italy and America* (1979) contain extensive reference to Italian political exiles in America, as does the biography of Margherita Sarfatti. The Italian antifascist diaspora in Europe has not yet been studied, although interest is growing in the ideas of Carlo Rosselli (1994) and the Justice and Liberty movement which he and his brother Nello helped to found in Paris in the late 1920s.

Debates on racism and imperialism take us back to the regime's foreign policy, a topic on which contributions by non-Italians have understandably been particularly numerous. The earliest studies focused on the origins of Mussolini's alliance with Germany and the diplomatic relations between Rome and Berlin (Elizabeth Wiskemann 1949; 1966 and F. W. Deakin 1962; 1966). The debate on the coherence of Mussolini's foreign policy was taken up by Alan Cassels in his study (1970) of Mussolini's early diplomacy, where he argued that Mussolini's expansionist objectives were present from the beginning but were held in check by Italy's old guard professional diplomats in the Foreign Ministry. Once the dictatorship was secured and the rise of Hitler had thrown the Versailles settlement into question, Mussolini was able to adopt increasingly overt revisionist strategies.

Esmonde Roberston (1977) also stressed the internal consistency of Mussolini's policies, which he argued found their logical outcome in the bid to create a new Roman Empire, whereas Denis Mack Smith (1976; 1981) depicted Mussolini's foreign policy as a series of improvisations determined by the regime's need to maintain its popularity at home. This argument was extended in his biography of Mussolini which echoes Gaetano Salvemini's earlier description of Mussolini as a 'sawdust Caesar' (1927; 1936) and argues that the Duce's foreign policy was throughout an extension of domestic propaganda. Admitting that Mussolini's North African ventures after 1935 were motivated by the need to strengthen the regime's image in Italy, Renzo De Felice (1990) rejected the claim that Mussolini's policies lacked consistency and argued that Mussolini looked to achieve his revisionist aims by playing off the Western allies against one another, a task that was initially made easier by the rise of Hitler. De Felice's claim that Mussolini's foreign policy was driven by revisionist rather than ideological considerations is supported by the conclusions of John Coverdale's study of Italy's intervention in the Spanish Civil War (1975), a move that was dictated not by ideological affinity with the National-ists in Spain but by the need to protect Italy's established interests in the western Mediterranean.

MacGregor Knox's *Mussolini Unleashed* (1982; 1984) offers an interpretation that differs from all these, however, and insists that Mussolini's foreign policy was throughout guided by the clear intention of establishing Italian domination over the entire Mediterranean. Rejecting the idea that Mussolini's foreign policy was incoherent or dictated by domestic considerations, Knox argues that as soon as the opportunities arose Mussolini attempted to implement this plan even at the risk of alienating public opinion and exhausting Italy's fragile resources. However, Mussolini's 'parallel war' failed precisely because of those inadequate resources, inadequate preparation and planning. With little or no inter-service co-ordination, Mussolini's generals proved reluctant to take risks and indeed even to take the offensive. In this light, Italian fascism appears no less aggressively imperialist than German National Socialism, although Italy lacked Germany's material resources. Mussolini proved less successful than Hitler in bending Italy's armed forces to his will – not because the Italian generals, navy and air-force commanders were hostile to fascism but because they were beset with internal rivalries and unwilling to innovate.

Rivalries within the fascist leadership are the subject of other recent studies. Segre's biography of Italo Balbo (1987), an early leader of the fascist movement who became the head of the air-force before being sent virtually into exile as governor of Libya by a jealous Mussolini in 1934, throws light on the internal politics of Mussolini's Roman Empire (like Segre on the colonization of Libya), and on the growing opposition to Mussolini's leadership amongst leading figures in the regime that was fuelled by the alliance with Germany. But jealousy amongst the fascist hierarchies and fear of the Duce meant that this opposition was never articulated. The rivalries and tensions within the fascist leadership in the late 1930s are also the subject of a detailed essay by Alexander De Grand (1991).

Mussolini's decision to declare war on France and Britain in June 1940 began the process that led to his fall in July 1943 following the Allied landings in Sicily. The armistice of 8 September then marked the beginning of a two-year tragedy which turned Italy into both a lingering battlefield and the theatre of a violent civil war as fascists and antifascists fought one another against the background of resistance to the Nazi occupation in central and northern Italy.

English-language studies have concentrated primarily on the military operations and the allied administration of Italy down to the liberation of Milan in April 1945. Carlo D'Este's studies (1988; 1991) of the Allied landings in Sicily and Anzio show that personal rivalries and poor military planning were by no means a monopoly of Mussolini's regime. David Ellwood's analysis (1985) of the Allied administration in Italy underlines the areas of dissent between the British and the Americans, not least in their attitudes towards the Resistance in the North. Denis Mack Smith's study of the Italian monarchy (1989) – although covering the entire period from Unification – also describes how Victor Emanuel III's abrupt abandonment of Rome, the army and the administration in 1943 contributed to the opprobrium that resulted in the abolition of the monarchy in 1946.

American economic relations with fascist Italy have been studied by G. G. Mignone, while the United States' role in the economic and political reconstruction of Italy at the end of the war is the subject of excellent books by James E. Miller (1986) and John Harper (1986). Acknowledging the impact of the Cold War and Washington's hostility to the Italian Communists, both suggest that the Christian Democrats and the Vatican needed little external assistance to defeat their political rivals on the Left. This confirms the conclusions of Sidney Tarrow's earlier analysis of the ways in which after 1945 the Christian Democrats outmanoeuvred the Left and in particular the Communists by exploiting widespread peasant unrest in the South. An earlier but still valuable collection of essays on Italian reconstruction edited by Stuart Woolf (1972) is now supplemented by a more recent volume edited by C. Wagstaff and C. Duggan (1995), while Paul Ginsborg's *History of Contemporary Italy* (1990) offers English readers a comprehensive guide to this period.

British and American historians have understandably tended to focus on the military, political and diplomatic contexts of the war, and have shown less interest in the internal history of Italy during the war. F. W. Deakin's *Last Days of Mussolini* (1966) is the only study of the Republic of Salò in English, and is concerned primarily with Mussolini's relations with Hitler. There is a wealth of first-hand documentary and fictional writing on the war, including works of outstanding literary merit like John Horn Burns's *The Gallery*, Norman Lewis's *Naples '44* and Eric Newby's *Love and War in the Apennines*. The trials of leading figures in the fascist regime after the fall of Mussolini are the subject of a new book by Roy Palmer Domenico (1991). Another recent study by Roger Absalom on the ways in which Tuscan peasants helped – often at great personal risk – to shelter Allied POWs also touches on an issue that has been most fiercely debated in recent years by Italian historians. In a remarkable book published in 1990 the Communist historian and former Resistance militant, Claudio Pavone, argued that it was time to make a new and dispassionate assessment of the Resistance and its political legacies in post-war Italy. His book attempts to reconstruct the choices made by those Italians who after Italy's surrender on 8 September 1943 chose to join the Resistance. He challenges the long-held claim that the Resistance was a combination of a patriotic war against the German forces of occupation and a class war to create the basis for the revival of democracy in Italy. While accepting that both elements were present, Pavone argues that the Resistance was also part of a more confused civil war in which alignments and loyalties were more accidental, and which gave rise on both sides to acts of systematic violence and mass executions.

For many historians on the Left, Pavone's study was seen as a timely coming to terms with the realities of the past, one that was particularly relevant at a moment when the fortunes of the Italian Communist Party were declining and the whole orientation of Italian politics seemed to be moving towards something new. But Renzo De Felice (1995) and other critics seized on Pavone's conclusions to argue that the Resistance's claim to represent the most constructive, progressive forces in Italian society was a myth. According to De Felice, only a minority of Italians had been actively militant for either the Resistance or Mussolini's Republic of Salò. The majority constituted what he termed a 'grey zone' of uncertainty and confusion, in his view because Italy's military defeat on 8 September 1943 had brought with it a crisis of national identity. That argument has become the subject of heated recent debate in Italy, since implicit in De Felice's argument is the idea that Mussolini's regime did claim to represent the Italian people and that in failing to acknowledge this the Left has weakened the sense of Italian national identity and has been responsible for the political failings of post-war Italian politics.

Like the French historian François Furet, De Felice believed that the Russian Revolution of 1917 brought about the crisis from which fascism and National Socialism emerged and also gave rise to a left-wing political mythology that in his view has choked off liberalism and individualism. There are echoes here of the German *Historikerstreit* and in Italy champions of the contemporary new-right look to reassess fascism in ways that underline the 'relativist' character of Mussolini's regime, challenging the 'myth' of the antifascist Resistance and blaming the political shortcomings of the Italian Republic on the political parties that drew their legitimacy from the Resistance. At this point the historiographical wheel seems to have come full circle: after 1945 Italy's post-war political parties looked to the pre-fascist past to establish their legitimacy and roots in Italian democracy. In the crisis that since 1990 has overwhelmed the political parties that had dominated Italy since 1945, claims for political legitimacy must once more be established by reinterpreting Italy's more recent past.

BACK TO THE NINETEENTH CENTURY: NEW QUESTIONS IN NEW PERSPECTIVES

The recent debates on fascism and its place in Italian history since the 1970s have also brought new questions to bear on the history of nineteenth-century Italy. One of the first debates focused on the labour movement and was partly an offshoot of the heated controversies within the Italian Left in the 1960s and 1970s over the leadership and policies of the PCI. The terms of the debate were set by the studies on the origins of the industrial proletariat by Stefano Merli and the German labour historian Volker Hunecke. Louise Tilly's study of class formation in Milan (1992) (although published much later) was written in the context of these debates, as was Donald Bell's analysis (1986) of labour and politics in the Milanese industrial suburb of Sesto San Giovanni before 1914. But the unique importance of the Italian Communist Party in post-war Italy, and then in the 1980s the re-emergence of the Italian Socialist Party under Bettino Craxi, also drew the attention of non-Italian historians to the history of the Italian Left. Studies by Spencer Di Scala (1980), James E. Miller (1990) and Alexander De Grand (1986; 1989b) re-examine the achievements of the PSI's pre-1914 reformist strategies and explore the alternative paths of Italian socialism. Since the end of the Cold War, the ideas of anti-Marxist socialists such as Carlo Rosselli have also begun to attract new interest.

The debate on the Italian labour movement and politics was also about modernization and the emergence of new social forces, themes that have dominated recent research on nineteenth-century Italy much more widely. The idea that fascism was linked in some way to Italy's experience of 'difficult modernization' called into question notions of 'backwardness' and began to reshape debate on nineteenth-century Italy in ways that were clearly signalled in the Introduction to Raffaele Romanelli's 1979 *History of Liberal Italy* (*Italia Liberale* 1979). The highly differentiated realities of Italian society were in many ways best approached through local or regional studies, Romanelli argued, and were difficult to reconcile within a framework determined by national unification. While not denying its importance, Romanelli also acknowledged that the history of the Italian 'state' was essentially a history of the political projects of the Italian ruling classes, almost an 'autobiography of the Italian bourgeoisie', and hence only one of many possible histories of Italy and of the Italians (C. Rosselli 1994).

Instead of assuming that the creation of a nation-state was the natural outcome of political unification, Italian historians –like historians more generally – were now beginning to explore how social and political identities were shaped, how nations were 'constructed', how the relationship between state and society, state and nation, nation and state have developed over time. As well as asking new questions this meant doing new types of history. The multi-volume Einaudi *Storia d'Italia* that was published in the 1970s reflected a growing interest in Italian social history that was captured in the subtitle of Stuart Woolf's *History of Italy 1700–1860: The Social Constraints of Political Change* (1979) (which first appeared in Italian in vol. 3 of the Einaudi *Storia*). A number of new journals came into being to promote research on social history (*Quaderni Storici*, *Movimento Operaio*, later *Passato e Presente*, *Società e Storia*, *Donna-Women-Femme*, *Memoria*, *Richerche Storiche* and most recently *Meridiana*), and in the 1980s the multi-volume Einaudi *Storia delle Regioni* offered important new outlets for this research.

Accepted images were soon called in question, not least that of nineteenth-century Italy's social and economic 'backwardness'. Economic historians pointed out that earlier assessments of Italy's economic performance had taken too much account of the most advanced sectors of Italian industry and too little account of less spectacular but broader and in the end equally effective forms of economic growth. Luciano Cafagna (1973), for example, has argued that agriculture, and especially the cultivation and production of silk (nineteenth-century Italy's most valuable export), sustained capital accumulation, commercial expansion and new manufacturing enterprises that by the end of the century had generated relatively dynamic and spontaneous economic expansion throughout much of northern and central Italy.

The dramatic success of many small family-based firms like Benetton in the 1980s focused attention on the longer-term role of small enterprise in Italy's modern economic growth, and Paul Corner has explored the role played by peasant farms in the transition from agriculture to dynamic small family-based enterprises. Italian entrepreneurial capacity has also been reconsidered in ways that stress the rationality and 'modernity' of entrepreneurial strategies. Rather than a sign of backwardness, for example, the ruralization of Italian industry can be seen as a rational entrepreneurial strategy that enabled Italian manufacturers (especially in the textile sector) to respond to constantly unstable external markets by exploiting a cheap rural labour force composed mainly of women and children. Others have emphasized the aggressively modernizing and self-sufficient features of the rural capitalist entrepreneurs in the Po Valley and the Veneto in the late nineteenth century (Davis 1996a). Nineteenth-century Italy, in other words, was not backward although its experience of capitalist development and modernization had taken a path that was in many respects distinctive and modernization had always been 'difficult'.

Social historians were making similar points, and focused above all on Italy's hitherto much-maligned but until recently virtually unexplored middle classes. Abundant new studies now reveal the presence of a self-conscious new class with tastes and values that differed little from their counterparts in other western European societies, which in turn reopens the debate on the relationship between politics and society. Challenging the idea that 'modern' capitalism and liberalism were necessarily interdependent, Silvio Lanaro (1979) and Alberto Banti (1989) have argued that modernization bred a particularly assertive and self-sufficient form of capitalist enterprise in Italy. If Italian capitalists showed little interest in liberalism, this was because many successful Italian capitalists in the late nineteenth century and early twentieth century believed that nationalist and corporatist programmes were more 'modern' than liberalism and offered more effective solutions to political and social conflict in advanced industrial societies.

From a different perspective, Raffaele Romanelli has also challenged the idea that the Italian political system (or any other) should necessarily have imitated that of Great Britain as some historians had always implied. Whereas Prussian iron and steel forged the new German state on terms dictated by Bismarck and the Prussian elites, Piedmont had never played a similar role in Italy and as a result, Romanelli has argued, Italian unification took the form of a settlement negotiated with the regional elites. The Italian political system was not then an aberration from some general (yet never defined) European norm, but rather the product of Italy's history and the particular balance of political and social forces on the Italian peninsula: a system that was not necessarily 'good' or 'bad', 'better' or 'worse' than others, merely different.

The essays in the volume on *Society and Politics in the Age of the Risorgimento* (1991) show how the debates on the social history of nineteenth-century Italy have in recent years become increasingly international in ways that make it difficult to distinguish clearly between 'Italian' and 'non-Italian' approaches. This is partly the result of new international debate and research projects (for example, on the comparative study of the European bourgeoisie), and also because more Italian studies are now appearing in English. One of the principal themes has been the bourgeoisie, and recent studies are discussed by Meriggi (1993) and Adrian Lyttelton (Davis and Ginsborg 1991). The upper boundaries of the post-Unification middle classes are charted by Anthony Cardoza's work on the Piedmontese aristocracy (1993), that looks to validate Arno Mayer's thesis on the 'persistence of the Old Regime' in Italy down to 1914. In the other direction, Jonathan Morris's study of Milanese shopkeepers (1993) draws boundaries at the other end of the social scale and defends the petty bourgeoisie against the charge that their politics were inherently anti-liberal. A new collection of essays in English edited by Maria Malatesta (1995) on the professions explores the middle ground.

There are also many studies that touch on the emergence of new middle-class tastes and life-styles: John Rosselli's book on the opera industry (1984), for example, provides a particularly vivid description of the new theatre-going urban middle classes. Mary Jane Phillips-Matz's biography (1993) of Giuseppe Verdi and Roberta Olson's study on the iconography of Risorgimento art (1992) offer additional insights into the politics of nineteenth-century Italian bourgeois culture. The volume on *Italian Art in the 20th Century* (Braun 1989) also contains essays and culture and society by Lyttelton on the Giolittian era, by Cannistraro on the fascist period and by Woolf on post-war Italy.

The distinctive role of the family in the development of Italian society and politics has also begun to attract attention, and in addition to the general study by David Kertzer (1991), Marzio Barbagli offers a useful overview (Davis and Ginsborg 1991). The history of the family in Italy is closely linked to regional differences and especially those between the North and the South. Here, too earlier theories of modernization have come under concerted attack in ways that are well illustrated in recent studies devoted to the origins of the Mafia. The anthropologists Anton Blok (1975) and Jane and Peter Schneider (1976) were among the first to link the emergence of the Mafia in Sicily in the late nineteenth century to the development of commercial capitalism, while an important recent study by the sociologist Diego Gambetta (1994) emphasizes the economic rationale of Mafia enterprise. Rather than a form of 'primitive rebellion' or an example of the social and cultural backwardness of the South, these studies link the emergence of the Mafia to the economic modernization of the South. Marta Petrusewicz's recent re-evaluation (1996) of what has long been considered the epitome of the backwardness, the vast latifundist estates, argues that what made economic activity and behaviour in the South different was not the lack of modern management but the chronic insecurity and uncertainty of the markets on which Southern producers depended. Robert D. Putnam (*Making Democracy Work. Civic Traditions in Modern Italy*, 1993), on the other hand, has revived the older claims that the disparities between North and South have been rooted in cultural differences. For Putnam, the key differential lies in the lack of civic traditions in the South, where from an early date feudalism and foreign rule precluded the development of the 'civic' cultures typical of northern and central Italy from the time of the Renaissance. But this theory of cultural determinism extending over centuries runs counter to the principal thrust of recent research on the Southern economy.

The role of the South and the 'Southern Problem' in the formation of an Italian national identity has been explored by Daniel Pick (1989) and John Dickie (1992), who argue that the negative stereotyping of the South after 1860 formed part of a conscious strategy of cultural standardization and constituted the 'otherness' against which Italy's new elites sought to establish new collective identities and cultural norms (see also Davis in Levy 1996). The 'construction' of national identities in wider terms is also the subject of an important recent study by Silvana Patriarca (1996) on statistics and nation-building, while Adrian Lyttelton (1993) has suggested new perspectives on Risorgimento nationalism.

The emphasis on the processes of state-formation and changing social and political identities has kept the relationship between state and society at the centre of the debate on nineteenth-century Italy. But by focusing on the emergence of modern forms of bureaucracy and administration and the ways in which this changed the distribution of power between rulers and elites and redefined the contours of public and private, Unification ceases to be the isolated miracle portrayed by Trevelyan to become a variant of a broader European historical process of state-formation.

This is the central theme of Stuart Woolf's *Napoleonic Integration of Europe* (1991a), which measures the impact of Napoleonic rule and reform on the Italian states, and of my own study on *Conflict and Control: Law and Order in Nineteenth Century Italy* (1988), which is concerned with the changing distribution of power between the elites and the state from the crisis of the *ancien régime* rulers in the late eighteenth century to the political crisis of the 1890s. Confrontations between local elites and rulers are also centre stage in Steven Hughes's study (1994) of policing in Bologna, which shows how the Papal government's assumption of new powers to put down public disorder clashed with the interests of the propertied classes and contributed to the political crisis of the Papal States. For the period after

610

Unification, Mary Gibson's study (1986) of prostitution reconstructs an important chapter in the history of Italian working-class women and the development of the Liberal state, and sets the Italian debates on public health, gender and crime in a broader European context. Women's history in nineteenth- and twentieth-century Italy is the subject of a recent essay by Michela De Giorgio (1996), while Alice Kelikian (1996) and Margherita Pelaja (1996) have explored new aspects of the history of women, gender and family in Italian society and culture both before and after Unification.

Thanks to these studies we can for the first time begin to map out the contours of social change in nineteenth-century Italy, to see how social forces and politics were related, and so set Italy's social and political developments down to 1914 in their broader comparative European perspective. This does not mean that the political history of unification has been neglected. Denis Mack Smith returned to the fray in 1985 with a study of Cavour in which he challenged the positive assessment of the Piedmontese statesman in Rosario Romeo's biography. Harry Hearder (1994) has also written a new biography of Cavour. The second volume of A. J. Reinerman's *magnum opus* (1979; 1989) on Austrian policy in Italy, and especially the relations between Vienna and the Papacy, has now also been published, while F. J. Coppa (1990) has made important reassessments of the politics of the curia of Pius IX.

Denis Mack Smith's recent biography of Mazzini (1993) shows how contemporary concerns are also setting new perspectives for the political history of the Risorgimento. His is the first major English biography of the prophet of Italian nationalism since Bolton King's study written at the turn of the century (and still worth reading) and the translation of Salvemini's more complex work. Indeed, Mazzini has long been out of favour, in part because Mussolini unjustly appropriated him as the prophet of fascism, but also because Mazzini had quarrelled furiously with the Risorgimento socialists. It is partly for this reason that Mazzini's search for a form of democracy that was not tainted by Jacobinism has recently begun to attract new interest (Urbinati 1996). Mack Smith, not surprisingly, finds Mazzini a more sympathetic subject than his political rival Cavour. As well as underlining the impact of Mazzini's contacts with English politicians and intellectuals during his exile in England, Mack Smith emphasizes how Mazzini's programme anticipated the more contemporary idea of a united Europe composed of independent nations.

As in the case of fascism, the debates on nineteenth-century Italy have opened out to accommodate new questions and new agendas. Social and cultural history has made its mark in ways that have drawn Italy into more general comparative debates on the processes of modernization and state-building in nineteenth-century Europe. But as Lucy Riall (1994) has rightly pointed out, this has meant that issues such as nationalism and the reasons why Italy achieved political unification have tended to be sidelined. However, a number of important recent studies have attempted to set cultural and social history more firmly in the context of political processes (for example, Patriarca 1996). But this also owes much to the rapidly expanding literature devoted to Italy's history since the Second World War (see especially

Ginsborg 1990 and McCarthy 1995) which has reopened debate on the longer-run 'peculiarities' of Italy and the Italians. The deconstruction of the older stereotypes that linked the peculiarities of Italian history to 'backwardness and under-development' has served to bring into sharper profile the specific features that in the longer term seem to have epitomized Italy's particular path to the twentieth century – features that include the particular character of the Italian state, and its political systems and administrative structures from its origins in the nineteenth century down to the present (Romanelli 1995), the complex relationship between centralism and regionalism (Levy 1996), the development of a 'national' identity, the problems posed by Italy's generally vulnerable position in changing international markets, the nature and role of its bourgeoisie, the specific role of the family in Italian society and politics, and not least the long-term role and influence of the Catholic Church and religion. It is around these themes that the attempt to understand the nature of Italy today in terms of its more recent past is currently focused.

REFERENCES

Absolom, R. (1991) *A Strange Alliance. Aspects of Escape and Survival in Italy 1943–1945*, Florence.
—— (1995) *Italy since 1980: A Nation in Balance*, London.
Adamson, W. A. (1980) *Hegemony and Revolution. Antonio Gramsci's Political and Cultural Theory*, Berkeley.
Adamson, W. L. (1989) 'Fascism and culture: avant-gardes and secular religion in the Italian case', *Journal of Contemporary History* 24: 411–35.
—— (1990) 'Modernism and fascism: the politics of culture in Italy 1903–1922', *American Historical Review* 95: 359–90.
—— (1993) *Avant-garde Florence: From Modernism to Fascism*, Cambridge and London.
Aquarone, A. (1965) *L'organizzazione dello stato totalitario*, Turin.
Arlacchi, P. (1983) *Mafia, Peasants and Great Estates: Society in Traditional Calabria*, Cambridge.
Azzi, S. C. (1993) 'The historiography of Italian foreign policy', *Historical Journal* 36(1): 187–203.
Banti, A. (1989) *Terra e denaro: una borghesa padana dell'Ottocento*, Venice.
Barbagli, M. (1991) 'Marriage and the family in Italy in the early nineteenth century', in Davis and Ginsborg 1991.
—— and Kertzer, D. I. (1991) *The Family in Italy from Antiquity to the Present*, New Haven, CT.
Beales, D. (1961) *England and Italy*, London.
—— (1981) *The Risorgimento and the Unification of Italy*, London.
Bell, D. H. (1986) *Sesto San Giovanni. Workers, Culture, and Politics in an Italian Industrial Town 1880–1901*, New Brunswick.
Bell, R. M. (1979) *Fate and Honor, Family and Village: Demographic and Cultural Change in Rural Italy since 1800*, Chicago.
Ben Ghiat, R. (1995) 'Fascism, writing and memory. The realist aesthetic in Italy 1930–1950', *Journal of Modern History* 67(3): 627–65.
Bernadini, C. (1977) 'The origins and development of racial anti-Semitism in fascist Italy', *Journal of Modern History* 29: 431–53.
Bessel, R. (ed.) (1996) *Fascist Italy and Nazi Germany*, Cambridge.
Binchy, D. A. (1941) *Church and State in Fascist Italy*, Oxford.

Blok, A. (1975) *The Mafia of a Sicilian Village 1860–1960. A Study of Violent Peasant Entrepreneurs*, Oxford.

Bosworth, R. J. (1979) *Italy, the Least of the Great Powers: Italian Foreign Policy before the First World War*, London.

—— (1983) *Italy and the Approach of the First World War*, London.

Braun, E. (1989) *Italian Art in the 20th Century*, London.

Bull, A. and Corner, P. (1993) *From Peasant to Entrepreneur. The Survival of the Family Economy in Italy*, Oxford.

Cafagna, L. (1973) 'The Industrial Revolution in Italy 1830–1914', in C. Cipolla (ed.) *The Fontana Economic History of Europe*, vol. 4, London.

Caldwell, L. (1986) 'Reproducers of the nation: women and family in fascist policy', in D. Forgacs (ed.) *Rethinking Italian Fascism*, London.

Cammett, J. (1967) *Antonio Gramsci and the Origins of Italian Communism*, Stanford.

—— (1972) 'Mussolini's cultural revolution: fascist or nationalist?', *Journal of Contemporary History* 7: 115–39.

Cannistraro, P. V. (1975) *La fabricca del consenso: fascismo e mass media*, Bari.

—— (1982) *The Historical Dictionary of Italian Fascism*, Westport, Ont. and London.

—— and Sullivan, B. R. (1993) *Il Duce's Other Woman*, New York.

Cardoza, A. L. (1982) *Agrarian Elites and Italian Fascism. The Province of Bologna 1901–1925*, Princeton.

—— (1993) 'The long good-bye: the landed aristocracy in north-western Italy, 1880–1930', *European History Quarterly* 23(3): 323–58.

Cassels, A. (1968) *Fascist Italy*, London and New York.

—— (1970) *Mussolini's Early Diplomacy*, Princeton.

Chabod, F. (1953) *Storia della politica estera italiana dal 1870 al 1896*, 1: *Le premesse*, Bari.

—— (1996) *Italian Foreign Policy: the Statecraft of the Founders*, Princeton.

Chadwick, O. (1981) *The Popes and European Revolution*, Oxford.

Chubb, J. (1996) 'The Mafia, the market and the state', *Journal of Modern Italian Studies* 1(2): 273–91.

Clark, M. (1977) *Antonio Gramsci and the Revolution that Failed*, New Haven, CT.

—— (1985) *Modern Italy 1871–1982*, London.

Cohen, J. S. (1988) 'Was Italian fascism a developmental dictatorship? Some evidence to the contrary', *Economic History Review* 2nd ser., 41(1): 95–113.

Coppa, F. J. (1971) *Planning, Protectionism and Politics in Liberal Italy: Economics and Politics in the Giolittian Age*, Washington, DC.

—— (1985) *Dictionary of Modern Italian History*, Westport, Ont. and London.

—— (1990) *Cardinal Giacomo Antonielli and Papal Politics in European Affairs*, Albany, NY.

—— (1992) *Origins of the Italian Wars of Independence*, London.

Corner, P. (1974) *Fascism in Ferrara*, Oxford.

—— (1990) 'Italy', in S. Salter and J. Stevenson (eds) *The Working Class and Politics in Europe and America 1929–1945*, London.

—— (1993) 'Women in fascist Italy. Changing family roles in the transition from an agricultural to an industrial society', *European History Quarterly* 23: 51–68.

Coverdale, J. F. (1975) *Italian Intervention in the Spanish Civil War*, Princeton.

Craig, A. (ed.) (1970) *The Diplomats 1919–1939*, vol. 1, Princeton.

Croce, B. (1929) *A History of Italy 1870–1915*, tr. C. A. M. Ady, Oxford.

Davis, J. A. (ed.) (1979) *Gramsci and Italy's Passive Revolution*, London.

Davis, J. A. (1981) *Merchants, Monopolists and Contractors; Economy and Society in Bourbon Naples 1815–60*, New York.

—— (1988) *Conflict and Control. Law and Order in Nineteenth-Century Italy*, London.

—— (1989) 'Socialism and the working classes in Italy before 1914', in D. Geary (ed.) *Labour and Socialist Movements in Europe before 1914*, Oxford.

—— (1991) 'Innovation in an industrial late-comer: Italy in the nineteenth century', in P. Mathias and J. A. Davis (eds) *Innovation and Technology in Europe: From the Eighteenth Century to the Present Day*, Oxford.

—— (1994) 'Remapping Italy's path to the twentieth century', *Journal of Modern History* 66: 291–320.

—— (1996a) 'Enterprise and labour Italy 1860–1929', in P. Mathias and J. A. Davis, *Enterprise and Labour from the Eighteenth Century to the Present*, Oxford.

—— (1996b) 'Changing perspectives on Italy's "Southern Problem"', in C. Levy (ed.) *Italian Regionalism*, Oxford.

—— and Ginsborg, P. (eds) (1991) *Society and Politics in the Age of the Risorgimento*, Cambridge.

De Felice, R. (1965) *Mussolini il rivoluzionario*, Turin.

—— (1966–8) *Mussolini il fascista*, 2 vols, Turin.

—— (1974–81) *Mussolini il Duce*, 2 vols, Turin.

—— (1976) *Fascism: An Informal Introduction to its Theory and Practice: An Interview with M. Ledeen*, New Brunswick.

—— (1990) *Mussolini l'Alleato: I. L'Italia in guerra*, 2 vols, Turin.

—— (1995) *Rosso e Nero*, ed. P. Chessa, Milan.

De Giorgio, M. (1996) 'Women's history in Italy', *Journal of Modern Italian Studies* 1(3): 411–29.

De Grand, A. (1976) 'Women under Italian fascism', *Historical Journal* 19(4): 947–68.

—— (1978) *The Italian National Association and the Rise of Fascism in Italy*, Lincoln, NE.

—— (1986) *In Stalin's Shadow: Angelo Tasca and the Crisis of the Left in Italy and France.*

—— (1989a) *Italian Fascism: Its Origins and Development*, Lincoln, NE.

—— (1989b) *The Italian Left in the Twentieth Century: A History of the Socialist and Communist Parties*, Bloomington.

—— (1991) 'Cracks in the facade; the failure of fascist totalitarianism in Italy 1935–9', *European History Quarterly* 21: 515–35.

—— (1995) *Fascist Italy and Nazi Germany. The Fascist Style of Rule*, London.

De Grazia, V. (1981) *The Culture of Consent. Mass Organization of Leisure in Fascist Italy*, Cambridge.

—— (1992) *How Fascism Ruled Women: Italy 1922–1945*, Berkeley.

Deakin, F. W. (1962) *The Brutal Friendship*, London.

—— (1966) *The Last Days of Mussolini*, London.

Decleva, E. (1971) *Da Adua a Sarajevo. La politica estera italiana e la Francia (1896–1914)*, Bari.

—— (1987) *L'incerto alleato*, Milan.

Delzell, C. (1961) *Mussolini's Enemies: The Italian Anti-fascist Resistance*, Princeton.

D'Este, C. (1988) *Bitter Victory. The Battle for Sicily 1943*, London.

—— (1991) *Fatal Decision: Anzio and the Battle for Rome*, London.

Di Nolfo, E. (1960) *Mussolini e la politica estera italiana (1919–33)*, Padua.

—— (1972) 'L'Europa fra Russia e America', *Quaderni Storici*, 20.

Di Scala, S. (1980) *Dilemmas of Italian Socialism: The Politics of Filippo Turati*, Amherst.

Dickie, J. (1992) 'A world at war. The Italian army and brigandage', *History Workshop Journal* 33: 1–24.

Diggins, J. P. (1972) *Mussolini and Fascism: the View from America*, Princeton.

Domenico, R. P. (1991) *Italian Fascists on Trial 1943–8*, Chapel Hill, NC.

Drake, R. (1980) *Byzantium for Rome: The Politics of Nostalgia in Umbertian Rome 1878–1900*, Chapel Hill, NC.

Duggan, C. J. (1989) *Fascism and the Mafia*, London.

—— (1994) *A Concise History of Italy*, Cambridge.

—— and Wagstaff, C. (eds) (1995) *Italy in the Cold War. Politics, Culture and Society 1948–58*, Oxford.

Ellwood, D. (1985) *Italy 1943–45*, Leicester.

Femia, J. (1981) *Gramsci's Political Thought. Hegemony, Consciousness and the Revolutionary Process*, Oxford.

Forgacs, D. (ed.) (1987) *Rethinking Italian Fascism*, London.

Forgacs, D. (1990) *Italian Culture in the Industrial Era. Cultural Industries, Politics and Public*, Manchester.

Fornari, H. (1971) *Mussolini's Gadfly*, Nashville, TN.

Forsyth, D. (1993) *The Crisis of Liberal Italy: Monetary and Financial Policy 1914–1922*, Cambridge.

Gambetta, D. (1994) *The Sicilian Mafia, the Business of Private Protection*, Cambridge, MA.

Gentile, E. (1984) 'The problem of the Party in Italian fascism', *Journal of Contemporary History* 19: 251–74.

—— (1986) 'Fascism in Italian historiography: in search of an individual historical identity', *Journal of Contemporary History* 21: 179–208.

—— (1990) 'Fascism as political religion', *Journal of Contemporary History* 25: 229–51.

—— (1993) 'Impending modernity: fascism and the ambivalent image of the United States', *Journal of Contemporary History* 28: 7–29.

Gerschenkron, A. (1966) 'Rosario Romeo and the original accumulation of capital', in A. Gerschenkron, *Economic Backwardness in Historical Perspective*, Cambridge, MA.

Gibson, M. (1986) *Prostitution and the State in Liberal Italy*, New Brunswick.

Ginsborg, P. (1979) *Daniele Manin and the Venetian Revolution of 1848–9*, Cambridge.

—— (1990) *A History of Contemporary Italy, Society and Politics 1943–1988*, London.

Gramsci, A. (1971) 'Notes on Italian history', in Q. Horae and G. Nowell Smith (eds) *Selections from the Prison Notebooks of Antonio Gramsci*, London.

Greenfield, K. R. [1934] (1965) *Economics and Liberalism in the Risorgimento. A Study of Nationalism in Lombardy 1814–1848*, 2nd edn, with Introduction by R. Romeo, Baltimore.

Gregor, A. J. (1979a) *Italian Fascism and Developmental Dictatorship*, Princeton.

—— (1979b) *Young Mussolini and the Intellectual Origins of Fascism*, Berkeley.

Grew, R. (1963) *A Sterner Plan for Italian Unity. The Italian National Society in the Risorgimento*, Princeton.

—— (1986) 'Catholicism and the Risorgimento', in F. J. Coppa (ed.) *Studies in Modern Italian History. From the Risorgimento to the Republic*, New York.

Griffin, R. (1993) *The Nature of Fascism*, London.

Gundle, S. and Parker, S. (eds) *The New Italian Republic. From the Fall of the Berlin Wall to Berlusconi*, London.

Harper, J. L. (1986) *America and the Reconstruction of Italy 1945–1948*, Cambridge.

Hay, J. (1987) *Popular Film in Fascist Italy*, Bloomington.

Haycraft, J. (1985) *Italian Labyrinth*, London.

Hearder, H. (1983) *Italy in the Age of the Risorgimento 1790–1870*, London.

—— (1994) *Cavour*, London.

Holmes, G. (ed.) (1997) *Oxford Illustrated History of Italy*, Oxford.

Hughes, H. S. (1955) 'The aftermath of the Risorgimento in four successive interpretations', *American Historical Review* 61(1): 70–6.

—— (1958) *Consciousness and Society: The Reorientation of European Social Thought 1890–1930*, New York.

—— (1970) 'The early diplomacy of Italian fascism 1922–32', in G. A. Craig (ed.) *The Diplomats 1919–1939*, vol. 1, Princeton.

—— (1979) *United States and Italy*, 3rd edn, Cambridge, MA.

—— (1983) *Prisoners of Hope. The Silver Age of Italian Jews 1924–1974*, Cambridge.
Hughes, S. C. (1994) *Crime, Disorder and the Risorgimento. The Politics of Policing in Bologna*, Cambridge.
Jemolo, A. C. (1960) *Church and State in Italy 1850–1950*, Oxford.
Joll, J. (1977) *Gramsci* (Fontana Modern Classics), Glasgow.
Kelikian, A. A. (1986) *Town and Country under Fascism*, Oxford.
—— (1996) 'Science, gender and moral ascendancy in Liberal Italy', *Journal of Modern Italian Studies* 1(3): 377–89.
Kertzer, D. I. (1984) *Family Life in Central Italy 1880–1910: Sharecropping, Wage-Labor and Co-residence*, New Brunswick.
—— (1993) *Sacrificed for Honor: Italian Infant Abandonment and the Politics of Reproductive Control*, Boston.
King, B. (1902) *The Life of Mazzini*, London.
Knox, M. (1982) *Mussolini Unleashed 1939–41: Politics and Strategy in Fascist Italy's Last War*, London.
—— (1984) 'Conquest, foreign and domestic, in fascist Italy and Nazi Germany', *Journal of Modern History* 56: 1–57.
Kogan, N. (1956) *Italy and the Allies*, Cambridge.
Koon, T. (1985) *Believe, Obey, Fight: Political Socialization of Youth in Fascist Italy 1922–1943*, Chapel Hill.
Lanaro, S. (1979) *Nazione e lavoro: Saggio sulla cultura borghese in Italia, 1870–1925*, Marsilio.
Landy, M. (1986) *Fascism in Film. The Italian Commercial Cinema 1931–43*, Princeton.
Ledeen, M. (1976) 'Renzo De Felice and the controversy over Italian fascism', *Journal of Contemporary History* 11: 269–83.
Levy, C. (ed.) (1996) *Italian Regionalism, History, Identity and Politics*, Berg.
LoRomer, D. (1987) *Merchants and Reform in Livorno 1814–1868*, Berkeley.
Lovett, C. M. (1972) *Carlo Cattaneo and the Politics of the Risorgimento*, The Hague.
—— (1979) *Giuseppe Ferrari and the Italian Revolution*, Chapel Hill, NC.
—— (1982) *The Democratic Movement in Italy 1830–1876*, Cambridge, MA.
Lyttleton, A. (1974) *The Seizure of Power*, London.
—— (1976) 'Italian fascism', in W. Laqueur (ed.) *Fascism: A Reader's Guide*, London.
—— (1993) 'The national question in Italy', in M. Teich and R. Porter (eds) *The National Question in Europe in Historical Context*, Cambridge.
McCarthy, P. (1995) *The Crisis of the Italian State. From the Origins of the Cold War to the Fall of Berlusconi*, New York.
Mack Smith, D. (1954) *Cavour and Garibaldi, 1860. A Study in Political Conflict*, Cambridge.
—— (1955) *Italy: A Modern History*, Ann Arbor.
—— (1971) *Victor Emanuel, Cavour and the Risorgimento*, Oxford.
—— (1975) *Garibaldi*, London.
—— (1976) *Mussolini's Roman Empire*, London.
—— (1981) *Mussolini*, London.
—— (1985) *Cavour*, London.
—— [1968] (1988) *The Making of Italy 1796–1866*, 2nd edn, Cambridge.
—— (1989) *Italy and its Monarchy*, New Haven, CT and London.
—— (1993) *Mazzini*, London.
Macry, P. (1988) *Ottocento: Famiglia, elites e patrimoni a Napoli*, Turin.
Maier, C. S. (1975) *Recasting Bourgeois Europe*, Princeton.
Malatesta, M. (ed.) (1995) *Society and the Professions in Italy 1860–1914*, Cambridge.
Meriggi, M. (1993) 'The Italian *borghesia*', in J. Kocka (ed.) *Bourgeois Society in Nineteenth Century Europe*, Oxford.

Merli, S. (1976) *Proletariato di Fabbrica e capitalismo industriale*, Florence.
Michaelis, M. (1978) *Mussolini and the Jews: German-Italian Relations and the Jewish Question in Italy*, New York and London.
—— (1989) 'Fascism, totalitarianism and the Holocaust: reflections on current interpretations of national socialist anti-Semitism', *European History Quarterly* 19: 85–103.
Migone, G. (1980) *Gli Stati Uniti e il fascismo. Alle origine dell' egemonia americana in Italia*, Milan.
Miller, J. E. (1986) *The United States and Italy 1940–1950: The Politics of Diplomacy and Stabilization*, Chapel Hill, NC.
—— (1990) *From Elite to Mass Politics. Italian Socialism in the Giolittian Era*, Kent.
Molony, J. N. (1977) *The Emergence of Political Catholicism in Italy*, London.
Morris, J. (1993) *Political Economy of Shopkeeping in Milan 1886–1922*, Cambridge.
Mosse, G. L (1990) 'The political culture of Italian futurism: a general perspective', *Journal of Contemporary History* 25: 253–68.
Noether, E. P. (1982) 'Italian women under fascism: a reevaluation', *Italian Quarterly* (Fall): 69–80.
Nolte, E. (1966) *Three Faces of Fascism: Action Française, Italian Fascism, National Socialism*, New York.
Olson, R. J. M. (1992) *Ottocento. Romanticism and Revolution in 19th Century Italian Painting*, New York.
Painter, B. (1990) 'Renzo De Felice and the historiography of Italian fascism', *American Historical Review* 95: 391–405.
Passerini, L. (1987) *Fascism in Popular Memory: The Cultural Experience of the Turin Working Class*, Cambridge.
—— (1979) 'Work, ideology and consensus under fascism', *History Workshop Journal* 8: 82–108.
Patriarca, S. (1996) *Numbers and Nationhood. Writing Statistics in Nineteenth Century Italy*, Cambridge.
Pavone, C. (1990) *Una guerra civile. Saggio storico sulla moralità nella Resistenza*, Turin.
Pelaja, M. (1996) 'Marriage by exception: marriage dispensations and ecclesiastical policies in nineteenth century Rome', *Journal of Modern Italian Studies* 1(2): 223–44.
Pernicone, N. (1993) *Italian Anarchism 1864–1892*, Princeton.
Petrusewicz, M. (1996) *Latifundium: Moral Economy and Material Life in a European Periphery*, Ann Arbor.
Phillips-Matz, M. J. (1993) *Verdi: A Biography*, Oxford.
Pick, D. (1989) *Faces of Degeneracy: A European Disorder 1814–1918*, Cambridge.
Pollard, J. F. (1985) *The Vatican and Italian Fascism 1929–32. A Study in Conflict*, Cambridge.
Putnam, R. D. (1993) *Making Democracy Work. Civic Traditions in Modern Italy*, Princeton.
Quine, M. S. (1996) *Population Politics in Twentieth-Century Europe*, London.
Rath, R. J. (1969) *Provisional Austrian Rule in Lombardy Veneto*, Austin.
Reinerman, A. J. (1979–89) *Austria and Italy in the Age of Metternich*, 2 vols, Washington, DC.
—— (1991) 'The failure of popular counter-revolution in Risorgimento Italy: the case of the centurions 1831–47', *The Historical Journal* 34: 21–41.
Riall, L. (1993) 'Elite resistance to state formation: the case of Italy', in M. Fulbrook (ed.) *National Histories and European History*, London.
—— (1994) *The Italian Risorgimento. State, Society and National Unification*, London.
Roberts, D. (1979) *The Syndicalist Tradition in Italian Fascism*, Chapel Hill, NC.
Robertson, E. M. (1977) *Mussolini as Empire Builder: Europe and Africa 1932–36*, London.

—— (1988) 'Race as a factor in Mussolini's policy in Africa and Europe', *Journal of Contemporary History* 23, 37–58.

Romanelli, R. (1979) *L'Italia liberale*, Bologna.

—— (1988) *Il commando impossibile: stato e società nell' Italia liberale*, Bologna.

—— (1991) 'Political debate, social history and the Italian *borghesia*: changing perspectives in historical research', *Journal of Modern History* 63(4): 717–39.

—— (ed.) (1995) *Stona dello Strato italiano dall' Unità a oggi*, Donzelli, Rome.

Romeo, R. (1954) *Il Risorgimento in Sicilia*, Bari.

—— (1961) *Risorgimento e capitalismo*, Bari.

—— (1969–84) *Cavour e il suo tempo*, 3 vols, Bari.

Rosselli, C. (1994) *Liberal Socialism*, ed. N. Urbinati, Princeton.

Rosselli, J. (1984) *The Opera Industry in Italy from Cimarosa to Verdi: The Role of the Impresario*, Cambridge.

Saladino, S. (1970) *Italy from Unification to 1919: Growth and Decay of the Liberal Regime*, New York.

Salamone, A. W. (1945) *Democracy in the Making. The Political Scene in the Giolittian Era*, Philadelphia.

—— (ed.) (1970) *Italy from Liberalism to Fascism. An Inquiry into the Origins of the Totalitarian State*, New York.

Salvemini, G. (1927) *The Fascist Dictatorship in Italy*, New York.

—— (1936) *Under the Axe of Fascism*, London.

—— (1973) *The Origins of Fascism in Italy*, with an Introduction by R. Vivarelli, New York.

Sarti, R. (1971) *Fascism and Industrial Leadership in Italy 1919–1940*, Berkeley.

—— (ed.) (1974) *The Ax Within: Italian Fascism in Action*, New York.

—— (1985) *Long Live the Strong: A History of Rural Society in the Apennine Mountains*, Amherst.

Sassoon, D. (1986) *Contemporary Italy. Politics, Economics and Society since 1945*, London.

Schneider, J. and Schneider, P. (1976) *Culture and Political Economy in Western Sicily*, New York.

Segre, C. (1974) *Fourth Shore. The Italian Colonization of Libya*, Chicago.

—— (1987) *Italo Balbo: A Fascist Life*, Berkeley.

Seton-Watson, C. (1968) *Italy from Liberalism to Fascism*, London.

Sked, A. (1979) *The Survival of the Habsburg Empire: Radetzky, the Imperial Army and Class War in 1848*, London.

Snowden, F. M. (1986) *Violence and the Great Estates in the South of Italy 1900–1922*, Cambridge.

—— (1989) *The Fascist Revolution in Tuscany 1919–1922*, Cambridge.

Spriano, P. (1975) *The Occupation of the Factories: Italy 1920*, London.

Steinberg, J. (1990) *All or Nothing. The Axis and the Holocaust 1941–43*, London and New York.

Sternhell, Z. (with M. Sznajder and N. Asheri) (1993) *The Birth of Fascist Ideology: From Cultural Rebellion to Political Revolution*, Princeton.

Stille, A. (1991) *Benevolence and Betrayal. Five Italian Jewish Families under Fascism*, London.

Stone, M. (1993) 'Staging fascism: the Exhibition of the Fascist Revolution', *Journal of Contemporary History* 28: 215–43.

Tannenbaum, E. (1972) *The Fascist Experience: Society and Culture 1922–1945*, New York and London.

Tarrow, S. (1967) *Peasant Communism in Southern Italy*, New Haven, CT.

Tasca, A. [Rossi, A. 1938] (1966) *The Rise of Italian Fascism*, New York.

Taylor, A. J. P. (1967) *Europe: Grandeur and Decline*, Harmondsworth.

Thayer, J. A. (1964) *Italy and the Great War. Politics and Culture*, Madison.

Thomson, D. (1991) *State and Control in Fascist Italy: Culture and Conformity*, London.
Tilly, L. (1992) *Politics and Class in Milan 1881–1901*, New York.
Toniolo, G. (1990) *An Economic History of Liberal Italy 1815–1918*, London.
Trevelyan, G. M. (1907) *Garibaldi's Defence of the Roman Republic*, London.
—— (1909) *Garibaldi and the Thousand*, London.
—— (1911) *Garibaldi and the Making of Italy*, London.
—— (1923) *Daniele Manin and the Venetian Revolution of 1848*, London.
Urbinati, N. (1996) 'A common law of nations. Giuseppe Mazzini's democratic nationality', *Journal of Modern Italian Studies* 1(2): 197–222.
Venturi, F. (1971) *Utopia and Reform in the Enlightenment*, Cambridge.
—— (1972) *Italy and the Enlightenment. Studies in a Cosmopolitan Century*, ed. S. J. Woolf, London.
Vigezzi, B. (1966) *L'Italia di fronte alla prima guerra mondiale*, 1: *L'Italia neutrale*, Naples.
Visser, R. (1992) 'Fascist doctrine and the cult of Romanità', *Journal of Contemporary History* 27: 5–22.
Vivarelli, R. (1967–91) *Storia delle origine del fascismo*, 1: *Dalla fine della guerra all'impresa di Fiume*; 2: *L'Italia dalla Grande Guerra alla Marcia su Roma*, Bologna.
—— (1991) 'Interpretations of the origins of fascism', *Journal of Modern History* 63: 29–44.
Wanrooij, B. (1987) 'The rise and fall of Italian fascism as a generational revolt'. *Journal of Contemporary History* 22: 401–11.
Webster, R. (1960) *The Cross and the Fasces: Christian Democracy and Fascism in Italy*, Stanford.
—— (1974) *Industrial Imperialism in Italy 1908–1915*, Berkeley.
Willson, P. R. (1993) *The Clockwork Factory: Women and Work in Fascist Italy*, Oxford.
Wiskemann, E. (1949) *The Rome-Berlin Axis*, London.
—— (1966) *Europe of the Dictators 1919–1945*, London.
Woolf, S. J. (ed.) (1968a) *European Fascism*, London.
—— (1968b) *The Nature of Fascism*, London.
—— (1972) *The Rebirth of Italy 1943–50*, London.
—— (1979) *A History of Italy 1700–1860. The Social Constraints of Political Change*, London.
—— (ed.) (1983) *Fascism in Europe*, London.
—— (1986) *The Poor in Western Europe in the Eighteenth and Nineteenth Centuries*, London.
—— (1991a) *Napoleon's Integration of Europe*, London.
—— (1991b) 'The poor and how to relieve them: the Restoration debate on poverty in Italy and Europe', in Davis and Ginsborg 1991.
Zuccotti, S. (1987) *The Italians and the Holocaust: Persecution, Rescue and Survival*, New York.

23

THE CRITIQUE OF ORIENTALISM[1]

Ulrike Freitag

The Orient is in our minds.

(Thierry Hentsch)

In 1978, Edward Said, an American-Palestinian professor of English and comparative literature, published *Orientalism*, a book which became the focal point of a broad international and interdisciplinary debate.[2] It was a provocative study of Western discourses, academic and other, on the Islamic Orient which, Said claimed, can be regarded 'as a Western style for dominating, restructuring, and having authority over the Orient' (Said 1991: 3). Although many of Said's arguments had already been voiced by earlier critics, none had discussed such a wide range of materials from different fields and disciplines to demonstrate the basic features and continuities of this discourse.[3] And it was precisely the polemic nature of Said's book, the fact that 'he unceremoniously dumps every Westerner who has ever studied the Arabs into one big basket', as one of his reviewers remarked sourly,[4] which ensured the success of the book.

In part, Said's success can be measured by a change in terminology. 'Orientalism', which had, in English, hitherto been a more or less neutral denotation for 'Oriental scholarship; knowledge of Eastern languages',[5] has taken on a pejorative

---

1   I would like to thank Gabriele vom Bruck, Gerhard Dannemann, Christoph Herzog, Jamal Malik and David Morgan for their comments on earlier drafts of this paper.

2   Edward Said (1991), *Orientalism. Western Conceptions of the Orient*. Penguin (London etc.). 1st edn, Routledge & Kegan Paul 1979. For an analysis of the early debate on Said's book, see Mani and Frankenberg 1985.

3   Ahmad 1922: 173. Said himself acknowledges some predecessors of this debate in Said 1985: 4.

4   Little 1979: 118. Little refers to Said 1976. For a more detailed discussion of Said, see p. 628f.

5   *The Oxford English Dictionary*, vol. 10, 2nd edn, Clarendon Press (Oxford) 1989, p. 931. Its other meaning in English refers to 'Oriental character, style, or quality', whereas the German term 'Orientalismus' signifies the preoccupation of nineteenth-century artists with Oriental motifs. It is not mentioned in *La Grande Encyclopédie* (Librairie Larousse) of 1975.

connotation and is now mainly used 'to refer to older European scholars who combine a conservative methodology with what is felt to be a contemptuous or prejudiced attitude towards the peoples of the Near East'.[6] Incidentally, Said's book has thus accelerated the process of replacing the term 'Orientalism' by 'human sciences in Asia and North Africa', as had been suggested by the Orientalists themselves at least since their international congress in Paris in 1973. A similar, and probably somewhat earlier, transformation can be observed for the Arabic term, *istishrāq*, as a result of extensive discussions about the – in many Arab eyes redoubtable – merits of Western scholarship.[7]

From the beginning, Orientalism has been discussed with a number of aims and has addressed widely varying issues. This chapter, which gives an overview that by no means claims to be comprehensive, will concentrate on three broad aspects. First, it suggests reading the debate historically, as an expression of the cultural encounter – or should one say confrontation? – between the 'West' and the 'East'; second, it will discuss major issues which were raised by Said and some of his predecessors; and finally, it will look at some of the more profound problems the debate poses for scholarly work on the 'Orient'.

It seems in order to clarify some terminological problems before embarking on the debate itself. Not least as a result of the increased discussion of Orientalism, recent scholarship has elaborated on the imaginary quality of such terms as 'Orient' and 'Occident', 'Easterner' and 'Westerner', pointing out that geopolitical boundaries are hardly objectively definable but remain very dependent on historically changing collective identities and perceptions. Furthermore, their heuristic value is limited in that they tell us more about our self-image through the definition of the 'other' than about the 'other' him- or herself (Hentsch 1992: ix–21, 159–205; Carrier 1992: 197; cf. Chandhuri 1990: 22–8). If these terms are used in the present chapter, albeit with reservations, it is not only for the sake of convenience but also because they form the frame of reference, indeed the key, to much of the debate on Orientalism. The geographical imaginary 'Orient' has greatly varied within scholarly Orientalism, from wide definitions including all of Asia to a rather more limited interest in the area closest to the imaginary boundary which is now often known as the Near East (Waardenburg 1993: 735; al-ʿAyyād 1965: 161–4; Hentsch 1992: xi), as have the preoccupations and developments of scholarly activity on various parts of the 'Orient'. The following discussion limits itself mostly to that part of the debate from within and without which deals with North Africa and West Asia, for which the terms 'Orient' or 'Middle East' will henceforth be used. It should at least be mentioned, however, that many of the problems inherent in Orientalism have also been discussed with regard to Western

---

6 Malti-Douglas 1979: 724. For a history of the term, see Waardenburg 1993: 735f. and Reig 1988: 9–15.

7 The term and its history in the Arabic language are discussed in al-Bustānī 1977: 11–14. For an overview of the discussions about Orientalism in Arabic, see Rudolph 1991. A useful anthology of texts on Arab perceptions of the West from 1870 to 1990 is al-Kaṭīb 1991.

scholarship of Africa, showing the similarities and discrepancies in the general approach.[8]

Similarly, with regard to the term 'Orientalism', certain reservations are in order. Not only did it undergo the aforementioned change in meaning, it is also debatable whether the discourse on the Orient has actually been as congruous as Said wants us to believe, or whether, as Maxime Rodinson claims, there always was 'a multiplicity of issues coming under the jurisdiction of many general disciplines. These issues emerge from varied phenomena found in certain countries previously grouped under the questionable rubric of the East' (Rodinson 1987: 81). What is fairly undisputed, however, is the predominance, in older Western scholarship on the Orient, of philology. This has increasingly been challenged by scholars who argue that in order to understand historical, sociological or economic developments, a scholar needs to be equipped with the methodological tools of these respective fields instead of relying exclusively on the knowledge of Oriental languages. Another prominent feature of traditional Orientalism has been the concentration on 'Islam', often seen as an unchanging phenomenon, as a key to the understanding of Middle Eastern societies. (Halliday 1993: 1512–7; Philipp 1994: 166–9). 'Orientalism' will be used with reference to scholarship marked by these characteristics, rather than making more problematic assumptions about the general attitudes of the scholars involved.

HISTORICAL ROOTS OF A MODERN DEBATE

Although the European interest in and scholarly examination of the Orient can be traced back to the Middle Ages,[9] what concerns us here is the nineteenth century, when the European expansion brought an altogether new dimension into the relationship between East and West, and when, mostly as a consequence of the imperial project, Oriental and Islamic Studies became established as an independent field of studies (Johansen 1980: 88). To what extent even apparently innocent publications could feed into imperial ideology becomes clear in the case of Volney (1757–1820), author of a travel report on Syria and Egypt and an opponent of the French involvement in Egypt. By analysing the Ottoman Empire in Syria and Egypt as foreign despotism, enhanced by reliance on a religion that aimed at the absolute rule of the Prophet, he concluded that a change in political control was in the interest of the local populations as well as in that of the preservation of the historical monuments (Volney 1959: 156). Thus, Volney provided the arguments used by Napoleon when he invaded Egypt in 1798, and can be seen as the founding father of a liberal and republican version of the French *mission civilisatrice* (Laurens 1987: 78).

8 For the difference and similarities between Orientalism and discourses on Africa, see Miller 1985, particularly pp. 14–23. For Western discourse on Africa, cf. Mudimbe 1988. Andreas Eckert kindly drew my attention to these references.

9 For overviews of the development of Oriental Studies, one may consult Waardenburg 1993; Rodinson 1987; Hourani 1991: 7–60; and Fück 1955.

Consequently, the perception of the Europeans in general, and of the Orientalists in particular, underwent a major change in the eyes of the people they studied. In 1798, the Egyptians clearly recognized the French as foreigners, mainly characterized by their different religion, but otherwise considered them on a basically equal footing as normal human beings with their weaknesses and strengths. The French interest in science and knowledge, manifested in the enormous effort of the Institut d'Égypte which had been established in Cairo, was commented upon very positively by the Egyptian historian al-Jabartī. However, at that time the European presence did not have any major impact on the wider Egyptian society.[10] This changed in the second half of the nineteenth century with the increasingly direct European involvement and the establishment of more permanent forms of rule and influence in the Middle East. (Ende 1965: 86–8). More and more, the Europeans came to be regarded by the Arabs as the 'other' in relation to whom they tried to define themselves, to the extent that, according to the Moroccan historian Abdallah Laroui, the question of 'who is the other and who am I' became a major preoccupation for the Arabs (Laroui 1967: 15), in a vein similar to other 'Oriental' societies.[11] Although this was somewhat analogous to the function 'the Oriental' fulfilled for those Europeans concerned with the Orient, the situation cannot be fully compared. The very real difference in power relations and the depth of European penetration forced the encounter upon Oriental societies on a scale unknown in Europe, where the consideration of the 'Orient' as the relevant 'other' remained, in the nineteenth and twentieth centuries at least, to some degree a matter of choice (Said 1991: 204).

Although the Europeans might not, at large, have realized this until the second half of the twentieth century, they came under intensified scrutiny by the supposedly so passive 'Orientals' (cf. Abu-Lughod 1963 and Lewis 1982a). It is not intended to give a detailed overview of how the perception of Europeans in the Middle East changed.[12] It is worthwhile noting, however, that from the inter-war period, the peak of direct European domination and growing cultural influence in the Middle East, the belief in basic common humanity, upheld in spite of many criticisms of the Europeans, began to be replaced by a more outright rejection of things European, culminating in the period of struggles for independence and political self-determination.

Orientalists formed an integral part of the Europeans observed. An interesting early account of such a personality, characterized by his knowledge of Arabic, is given by the Egyptian writer 'Alī Bāshā Mubārak in his novel '*Alam al-Dīn* which was published in 1882 (Wielandt 1980: 48–72 and Alleaume 1982: 6–9). The Orientalist in his novel was an intermediary between Orient and Occident, a propagator of European ideas in the East and an advocate of Orientals in Europe.

---

10   Wielandt 1980: 17–33. Wielandt's book gives a very wide-ranging and differentiated overview of how the perception of Europeans changed from the early nineteenth century to the 1960s.

11   For a similar argument concerning India see Inden 1990: 3.

12   Cf. Wielandt 1980 and Alleaume 1982. The best background study on the development of Arabic thought in more general terms is still Hourani 1983.

He continuously enhances particular judgements and the world-view deemed important by 'Alī Bāshā, thus playing an inherently positive role.[13]

Around the same time, however, some Oriental intellectuals started to respond more critically to Orientalists, and, more specifically, to their writings. Although they were, at first, isolated individuals, they are significant in that they challenged, albeit on a modest scale, the Orientalist claim to an explanatory monopoly about 'the Orient'. Thus, they are predecessors of the 'writing back' of the 'objects' of European observation[14] that set in with the more systematic and general critique of Orientalism which started in the 1950s.

One of the earliest instances of such a response to an Orientalist interpretation of Islam, aimed not only at pointing out minor errors to an author but at openly opposing his views in front of a wider public, is the famous exchange between the French Orientalist Ernest Renan and the pan-Islamist activist Sayyid Jamāl al-Dīn al-Afghānī.[15] Renan had argued in a lecture at the Sorbonne, published in the *Journal des Débats* in March 1883, that Islam constituted a severe obstacle to progress. The Arab lack of scientific advancement was, in his eyes, enhanced by the inherent hostility of the Arab race – as opposed to the Aryan one – to science. What was known as Arabic science was, according to Renan, either pure linguistics or else due to the influence of Christians (taken not to be Arabs) and Persians. While al-Afghānī accepted the limiting influence of religion on scientific exploration, he stressed that this was an intrinsic problem of narrow religious thought – as opposed to philosophy – which could be found in all faiths, rather than being a characteristic trait of Islam. Al-Afghānī also rejected Renan's racist approach, opting instead for an evolutionary explanation which underlined that all people underwent various developmental stages before adopting science and philosophy.

Among the Arab authors who obtained wide-ranging knowledge of Orientalists and their works and thus came to a differentiated evaluation was the Syrian scholar and journalist Muḥammad Kurd 'Alī (Hermann 1990: 83–94 and Escovitz 1983: 95–109). Kurd 'Alī held many Orientalist works in high esteem because their concern with and their editions of classical Arabic works had contributed largely to the renaissance or *nahda* of the Arab language and literature in the second half of the nineteenth century. For his history of Syria, *Khiṭaṭ al-Shām*,[16] Kurd 'Alī consulted Orientalist scholarship and made a conscious effort to write a modern,

---

13 This function has been termed 'europäischer Bestätiger vom Dienst' by Wielandt 1980: 57.

14 Clifford 1980. The term 'writing back' was coined by Michel Leiris in an article called 'L'Ethnographe devant le colonialisme', *Les Temps Modernes* 58 (1950). Clifford 1980: 205. For an overview, cf. Rudolph 1991: 14–30 and al-Mūsawī 1993: 149–82.

15 Renan 1883. For comments on this debate, cf. Hourani 1983: 120–3 and Keddie 1983: 84–95 and 181–7, for an English translation of al-Afghānī's answer to Renan. There had been earlier instances of minor criticisms, often with regard to philological errors committed by Orientalists. Cf. Rudolph 1991: 15.

16 6 vols, first published Damascus 1926–8, 2nd edn Damascus 1983. About this work, cf. Freitag 1991: 144–56.

secular, emancipatory history, discarding old taboos and employing an analytical style. Kurd ʿAlī encountered criticism for his alleged adoption of the Orientalist method and the fact that he at times openly recommended Orientalist scholarship to his fellow Arab scholars. It has to be noted, however, that he himself employed it almost subversively to write from an Arab perspective against the neglect of Arab history by Arabs, regretting that most accounts of Syrian history so far – and by this Kurd ʿAlī seems to refer to the kind of analytical Syrian history he tried to provide – had been written by Westerners (Kurd ʿAlī 1983: I, 3). Kurd ʿAlī maintained no illusions about the innocence of at least part of Orientalism. He recognized colonialism as one of the three factors which had stimulated the growth of Oriental Studies, the other two being religion and scholarly curiosity. Furthermore, he realized that many Orientalists, while their training enabled them to mediate between Orient and Occident, put their knowledge at the disposal of the political interest of their respective countries. This however, did not occur to him as something morally inappropriate but rather as normal, because, he argued in 1935, Muslims did the same thing. (Kurd ʿAlī 1935; quoted after Reid 1987: 58). In a similar vein, his Egyptian contemporary, the writer Zakī Mubārak, defended Orientalism in a public newspaper discussion entitled 'Did Orientalism do more harm than good?'[17] by arguing that even those Orientalists who wrote negatively about Islam still often contributed worthy publications and, in any case, spurred public interest in this religion.

Such a line of argument shows clearly that the thought of Kurd ʿAlī and some of his contemporaries, while being more critical of the Orientalists than ʿAlī Bāshā Mubārak had been, was based on a strong self-confidence. Kurd ʿAlī's controversy with Henri Lammens over the latter's book on Syrian history (Lammens 1921) shows in an exemplary way this tolerance towards other interpretations, provided they comply with basic rules of fairness, something which Kurd ʿAlī misses in Lammens:

> We do not demand that the author should write about the Islamic scholars without criticism and comment, or that he should curtail his freedom of judgement. We also do not expect that he believes in the religion [Islam] in the same way as its followers do. What we do expect, however, is that he judges fairly and distances himself from emotions which are brought forward under the pretext of scholarship. ... He has said things about the Quran ..., its interpretation and language that were first brought up by medieval fanatics in monasteries. We had hoped that he would not follow their opinions, after his non-Muslim contemporaries have already rejected them. His words degrade a religion of approximately 300 million followers.
>
> (Kurd ʿAlī 1922: 275)

Kurd ʿAlī was neither the first nor the only Arab scholar who came under attack from conservative circles for following Orientalist methodology. When the new Egyptian University was established in 1908, it extended invitations to Italian,

---

17 Mubārak 1934. Quoted from al-Khaṭīb 1991: II, 577f. The opposite view was taken by Ḥussain al-Hrāwī.

French and German Orientalists to give lectures on topics such as early Oriental languages, Egyptology and classical studies. At the same time, an increasing number of Egyptian students were sent to Europe for higher education. Attacks on those who, under the influence of Orientalist methodology and scholarship, started to question time-honoured historical and religious interpretations led to a series of controversies and affrays over personalities such as Jurjī Zaidān (1910), Ṭaha Ḥussain (1926) and Muḥammad Aḥmad Khalaf Allāh (1947).[18]

Although the end of the Second World War was accompanied by widespread independence in the Arab World, the establishment of Israel and the Cold War in the Middle East increased rather than decreased the heat of the cultural confrontation. Numerous books on Orientalism as a discipline and its deeds came to be published in Arabic for an Arab audience, attacking Orientalism as a mode of cultural imperialism, that is, as an attempt to exercise control even after formal political independence had been achieved. This criticism came partly from a religious, partly from a Marxist perspective. While it can be argued that the critique in Arabic countries constituted at least partly an internal debate about the future orientation of the respective societies now that independence had been achieved (Rudolph 1991: 9), the same arguments were taken up by Oriental scholars in the West and published in European languages. These publications were clearly directed at a wider European – and scholarly – audience, a sign that the 'writing back' had reached a new phase.

The first major critique of Orientalism in English was by the London-based Palestinian scholar Abdel-Latif Tibawi and came from a religious perspective.[19] Many of Tibawi's arguments can be found in similar writings in Arabic and other languages (Algar 1971; al-Sibāʿī[1968] 1971; Rudolph 1991: 30–42). His argument is based on the assumption that Orientalist scholarship was, in its early phase, inspired by religious hatred, coupled with a Christian desire to proselytize among Muslims. With the imperial expansion, and the development of anti-colonial nationalist movements, these movements became the new focus of the West's feud with Islam. While acknowledging the contribution of Orientalists to the editing of Oriental manuscripts, Tibawi bitterly accused Western students of Islam of doubting its inherent value by presenting it mainly as a deviation from Judaism and Christianity. This was not only a defamatory, Eurocentric approach, Tibawi claimed, but also distorted Islamic history. Besides scrutinizing the work of some British Orientalists such as W. M. Watt, K. Cragg, B. Lewis and P. M. Holt from this perspective, Tibawi makes some further points worth mentioning.

The first might be considered as providing some insight into the motives of the 'writing back'. While Arabs held, Tibawi notes, high respect for Westerners, they were not treated on an equal footing and had no chance, at least in Great Britain, of

---

18 For a discussion of these controversies, cf. Reid 1987, Rudolph 1991: 24–30 and Nagel 1978: 23–37.
19 Tibawi 1963: 1979; 1980. For comments on Tibawi, cf. Little 1979: 111–15, Rudolph 1991: 34f. and Ḥamīs 1981: 93–6.

obtaining equally high academic positions. Hamid Algar (1971: 104–6) developed the point further by suggesting ways in which Muslims could, in such a position of hierarchical inferiority, react to Orientalist scholarship by challenging the Orientalist's claim to objectivity. Underlying both authors' criticisms are strong doubts about the possibility of any outsider's capacities for understanding things 'Islamic'.

Tibawi's second argument raises a major methodological issue: the author claims that many Orientalists not only had insufficient knowledge of the Oriental languages they claimed to master, but also lacked the training in social sciences required to justify their judgements on the Middle East.

This latter argument is taken up at great length by socialist critics of Orientalism such as Anouar Abdel-Malek.[20] Abdel-Malek argues that the 'crisis of Orientalism' came about because of the independence not only of the countries but also of the people who had formerly been the 'objects' of Orientalists' studies. This development had challenged the Western assumptions about the essential difference between 'Westerners' and 'Orientals' who had been regarded as passive, non-autonomous and non-sovereign, ideas which often had been conflated with racism. Although Abdel-Malek noted that since 1945, (neo-)Orientalism had somewhat adapted itself to the changing conditions, for example by legitimizing the study of modern developments, the Orientalist's 'Orient' still remained the passive object of a field that did not admit 'Orientals' into its ranks.[21]

Abdel-Malek (1963: 120–30) contrasted this with the approach chosen by socialist countries. He outlined as its characteristics, first of all, a critique of Euro-centrism; second, political solidarity and co-operation – including on the academic level – with the peoples of Asia, Africa and Latin America, thus transforming them from 'object' into 'subject'; and third, a new focus on contemporary sociological and political problems. Such studies were carried out by professionals trained in social sciences and humanities with additional linguistic skills – as opposed to the primarily philological training of traditional Orientalists.

At this level, Abdel-Malek's arguments tied in with paradigmatic changes in mainly, but not exclusively Western leftist and anti-imperialist circles which had been, as Abdel-Malek had already noted, deeply influenced by the independence of the formerly colonized peoples after the Second World War and further stimulated by the opposition to the Vietnam War.[22] This critique of conventional scholarship started in disciplines which were much more directly confronted with political changes than the more textually oriented Orientalists. Thus, in 1950 Michel Leiris had analysed the relationship between anthropological knowledge and colonialism and had provoked a debate about how European knowledge about other parts of the

---

20   Abdel-Malek 1963. About his criticism, cf. Little 1979: 115–18; Rudolph 1991: 47–9 and Johansen 1980: 71f. For more immediate answers to Abdel-Malek, see Cahen 1965 and Gabrieli 1965.
21   This latter point was also criticized by Tibawi 1979: 25f.
22   The following discussion draws on Clifford 1980: 204f., Halliday 1993: 148f., Johansen 1980 and Waardenburg 1993: 749–51, all with further bibliographical references.

world had been structured by a will to power (Clifford 1980: 205). In the political sciences, the critique of the Eurocentric traditional and behaviouristic approaches in the 1960s encouraged the development of a more comparative, theoretical, humanistic and problem-orientated approach which was 'Third World'-centred and can be classified as 'post-behavioural' (Chilcote 1981: 57). This debate spilled over into the domain of Orientalism, primarily on the level of studies directed at the contemporary world, stimulated by political concerns as much as by a desire to reorientate research in a way that was linked more directly with mainstream scholarship in specific disciplines (Ḥamīs 1981: 63–88). For example, historicism began to loose its paradigmatic influence on German Oriental Studies in the 1960s (Johansen 1980: 93f.). In France, Maxime Rodinson had suggested that general questions pertaining to social, economic and political development and inspired by Marxism should be considered for Muslim countries, thus breaking free from the paradigm of religious specificity and integrating the discussion into a global context (Rodinson 1979; cf. Turner 1978). Also, Orientalist studies came under scrutiny from younger Orientalist academics, as Jacques Waardenburg's study exemplifies, which analyses the approaches of five Western scholars to Islam in view of the problematic relationship relation between subject and object (Waardenburg [1963] 1970). The already mentioned debate about the future name of international gatherings of scholars working on the Orient was just another reflection of the extent to which the debate had reached the scholars concerned.

EDWARD SAID: THE RENEWAL OF A DEBATE

With regard to *Orientalism*, one of the critics remarked that 'Like the title, the very act of writing the book is a political statement and a literary fact which may prove to be more important than the author's arguments themselves' (Malti-Douglas 1979: 724). Many of the criticisms of 'Orientalism', for Said a field encompassing virtually all Western expressions about the (Middle) East, from politicians' statements such as Balfour's to poetic works by Goethe and Flaubert and to treatises by scholars as far apart as d'Herbélot and Louis Massignon, well as the collective effort of societies and scholarly institutions, can indeed be found in much of the critiques outlined above, as well as in others that were in print at the time when Said was writing his book.[23] In a way, Said popularized and polemicized the earlier debate and carried it from the relatively isolated field of academic discourse into the expanse of popular Western discourse—an area which this debate, I would argue, had already reached with regard to an Arabic speaking audience in the context of the debate about decolonization and neo-imperialism. The publication of Said's initial articles on the topic, as well as his exchange with Bernard Lewis in the *New York Review of Books*, indicate the kind of public he was aiming at (Said 1976 (for comments, cf. Little 1979: 118–31); Lewis 1982b; Said 1989).

---

23   Ahmad 1992: 173. Ahmad refers in this context to Alatas 1977 and Turner 1978.

However, what was new in Said's analysis was that he made use of the analytical framework of theories of discourse and power to integrate such a wide-ranging body of material. This allowed him to reformulate some of the questions raised by earlier contributors to the debate in more fundamental terms. While the link between Orientalist knowledge and imperial power had already been recognized, Said expressed more serious doubts about the possibilities of Westerners obtaining knowledge about the Orient, arguing 'that political imperialism governs an entire field of study, imagination, and scholarly institutions – in such a way as to make its avoidance an intellectual and historical impossibility' (Said 1991: 14). He problematizes the counter-argument, i.e. that individual scholars were trained in various disciplines and not by necessity linked immediately to the imperial project, by locating such supposedly individual discourses within the more general context of their time, pointing to the fact that 'each work on the Orient affiliates itself with other works, with audiences, with institutions, with the Orient itself' (ibid. 20; cf. p. 96). Furthermore, he observes a historical continuity from traditional Orientalism to modern political thinking which conceives of cultural differences as essential, thus, in the final analysis, resulting in a confrontational desire to contain, and possibly rule, the 'other' (ibid. 47f.).

In accordance with the observations made by Abdel-Malek, Said recognizes the changes which took place within Orientalism, namely the influence of the Western cultural crisis in the inter-war period which led to a re-examination of 'the Orient' in search of a new Western self-definition, and of the social sciences after the Second World War (ibid. 257, 284). Whereas in most humanities this caused a serious rethinking of Western superiority, Said claims that this did not happen in Orientalism. In spite of sympathy for the 'Orientals', scholars such as Gibb and Massignon nevertheless upheld the claim to speak for 'the Oriental', whom they considered to be inherently unable to represent himself (ibid. 260–3, 271). In contrast to Abdel-Malek, who perceives the socialist approach as a viable alternative, Said's tone is more pessimistic. He sees little room for change in the 'discursive consistency' (ibid. 273) of Orientalism, the cause for which Said locates in the constant reproduction of a culturally hegemonic discourse (ibid. 321–4). This has prompted the Syrian philosopher Ṣādiq Jalāl al-'Aẓm to reproach Said for a renewed essentialism in the form of an 'Orientalism in reverse'[24] although Said himself emphasizes that he is highly critical about conceptions pre-supposing such essentially different entities (Said 1991: 322).

REACTIONS TO SAID'S ARGUMENT

Said's work has received a mixed response. This has been facilitated by his very wide definition of 'Orientalism' as well as by his sometimes contradictory and often

---

24 al-'Aẓm 1981. A shorter English version was published under the title 'Orientalism and Orientalism in Reverse', *Khamsin* 8 (1981: 5–26). For affirmative comments on al-'Aẓm's as well as other Arab critics of Said, cf. Sivan 1977; and 1985: 133–54.

less than systematic and methodologically rigorous approach.[25] Much of this criticism moves on the level of the correction of particular errors and a discussion of his omission of German and Russian scholarship,[26] points which are of little interest within the current context.

Bernard Lewis, who himself was attacked by Said for his pro-Zionist stance, polemically compared the criticism of Orientalism to a situation

> in which a group of patriots and radicals from Greece decides that the profession of classical studies is insulting to the great heritage of Hellas, and that those engaged in these studies, known as classicists, are the latest manifestation of a deep and evil conspiracy...
> (Lewis 1982b: 49)

and concluded that 'The most rigorous and penetrating critique of Orientalist scholarship has always been and will remain that of Orientalists themselves' (ibid. 56). Thus Lewis reiterated the exclusivist Orientalist stance already criticized by Tibawi and Abdel-Malek, implicitly reconfirming once more the idea that only outsiders – that is, Orientalists – could really represent 'the Orient' and were the only ones competent to review their own scholarship.[27] Such a position, as well as the continuing topicality of cultural essentialism in international politics, as exemplified in Samuel Huntington's recent article on the confrontational nature of civilizational differences,[28] might alone suffice to underline the ongoing importance of works such as Said's which provide the basis for a widespread, broad and critical debate.

However problematic many of Said's generalizations may be, what seems important is not only the popularization of the debate about Orientalism, and thus a spreading awareness of certain problems, but also the new kind of research and questions which it has instigated in the field of Oriental Studies. Besides critical investigations into the state of the art which might have been on the agenda in any case (e.g. Kerr 1980; Reig 1988), and alternative accounts of Orientalism, Said's work has prompted more detailed research into the history of the discipline and its relationship with the imperial project (e.g. Hourani 1992; Rodinson 1987; Ḥamīs 1981; Juhā 1982; 1983; al-Munaẓẓama and al-Khalīj 1985). On the level of discourse analysis, such varied topics as the intellectual origins of Napoleon's expedition to Egypt, the development of studies on Algeria, and the Western imagination of the Middle East have been investigated (Laurens 1987; Leimdorfer 1992, Hentsch 1992), to give but a few examples.

Besides adding to our knowledge, such studies have also allowed us to reformulate the questions which were raised by the critics of Orientalism in a more precise manner. 'How true is it that Orientalists were the main ideological authorities of

---

25 This has been pointed out most systematically in the critique of Said by Ahmad 1992: 159–219. Cf. Halliday 1993, Malti-Douglas 1979 and Mani and Frankenberg 1985.

26 e.g. Irwin 1981–2. For a classification of reviews, cf. Mani and Frankenberg 1985.

27 This latter position had been criticized by Ḥamīs 1981: 8.

28 Huntington 1993, for comments cf. the contributions by Ajami, Mahbubani, Barthey, Binyan and Kirkpatrick in *Foreign Affairs* 72. 4 (1993).

Orientalism in nineteenth-century Germany?', asks Johansen in his seminal study of German Orientalism, only to come to an analytical distinction between 'Orientalism as the imagination or scholarly judgement that produces the Orient as an object of knowledge and domination that is clearly separated from the Occident' and the scholarly field of Oriental Studies (Johansen 1980: 75). While Johansen's study shows the manifold links between these two categories, the distinction allows him to differentiate between the two and analyse their relationship. Thus he can show that while early representatives of Oriental Studies in Germany, such as Friedrich Rückert and Joseph von Hammer-Purgstall, became the main authorities of romanticist Orientalism, and while German Oriental studies since the 1830s came under the paradigm of classical philology, Orientalism became embodied in the views of Leopold von Ranke, the leading German historian of the time. He adhered to a particular kind of historicism, then the leading paradigm in historical and political studies, which held, *inter alia*, that 'a history of the human kind does not and cannot exist' and that 'only some peoples form part of world history' (ibid. 80).

On this basis, and against the background of the 'Eastern Question', Ranke developed the idea that Europe, and more specifically the Germanic and Romanic peoples as embodiments of civilization, had to control the barbarous Ottoman Empire. Ranke became the main historical and political 'expert adviser', to use the modern terminology, on the 'Eastern Question' or, in Said's terms, 'the leading authority in the field of Orientalism'.[29] 'It is', Johansen pointedly argues, 'for this reason that he did not care for the results of Oriental studies research' (Johansen 1980: 82). In a very similar vein, one can observe even nowadays that public opinion about the 'Orient' in countries like Germany is dominated by self-styled 'experts' who have little, if any, knowledge of the field of Oriental Studies.[30]

It has been remarked that because Said limits his critique to studies of the Middle East, the usage of 'Orientalism' implies that there is something special about the Middle East, and thus reiterates the very notions Said set out to attack, while many of the methodological approaches chosen by Orientalists, as well as the notions of superiority and inferiority, racism and even particular stereotypes can be found in much of the writing about anything 'non-Western' (Halliday 1993: 158). Said's claim that Europe's experience with the Middle East or Islam has been in many ways specific (Said 1991: 17), did not deter scholars in fields related to the study of other parts of Asia from a critical scrutiny of their own scholarly traditions in the light of his work, and thus incited further debates about scholarly traditions and their consequences. Thus, Ronald Inden (1990) has set out to destroy the notion of an essential, passive India locked in its unchanging caste system and often described by metaphors such as female, dream or jungle (see also Inden 1986). Similarly, Richard Minear (1980), has demonstrated that Said's analysis of Orientalists' use of

---

29 Ibid 82. On the question of Ranke's view of the Orient, cf. Schülin 1958.
30 This is particularly true of the mass media. Cf. the profound critiques of the two leading German TV journalists, Gerhard Konzelmann and Peter Scholl-Latour: Rotter 1992, and Klemm and Hörner 1993.

the abstractions 'Oriental' and 'European' with its prejudice in favour of the latter and the ideas about past Oriental greatness and present degradation can provide a fertile basis for a critique of Western studies of Japan.

Minear's investigation points to another field of enquiry that has received renewed attention in the wake of Said's study, which involves fundamental epistemological questions about the conditions, possibilities and limits of obtaining knowledge about other cultures. Said, and a number of his adherents, have linked the specific picture painted by Orientalism to the imperial project. Minear, however, argues that very similar results emerged from scholarship on Japan in the absence of a similarly long-standing relationship with the West, Western participation in the Japanese rediscovery of its own past and, most importantly, in the absence of actual Western domination. Minear suggests, therefore, 'to focus less on the specific historical setting – be it Said's Orient or our Japan – than on the general one: the encounter between Europe and America on the one hand and the "non-Western world" on the other' (Minear 1980: 515). Thus, Orientalism points once more to questions that had already been asked by anthropologists, namely, as J. Clifford put it,

> the key theoretical issue raised by *Orientalism* concerns the status of all forms of thought and representation for dealing with the alien. Can one ultimately escape procedures of dichotomizing, restructuring and textualizing in the making of interpretative statements about foreign cultures and traditions?
>
> (Clifford 1980: 209f.)

It may well be, as has been elaborated on the basis of these questions, that in the final analysis, this problem is not even limited to intercultural communication, as has been pointed out by James Carrier: 'Essentialization appears to be inherent in the way Westerners, and probably most people, think and communicate. After all, to put a name to something is to identify its key characteristics and thereby essentialize it' (Carrier 1992: 207). However, this is almost certainly aggravated in situations of intercultural contact through the mutual definition of the 'other' in opposition to the 'self' through 'Orientalism in reverse' or, as Carrier has called it, 'ethno-Orientalism' (ibid. 198). It has been feared that the recognition of such a fundamental issue might easily lead either to a relieved or a resigned attitude in view of an apparently insoluble problem (Mani and Frankenberg 1985). However, the epistemological impasse plays the ball back into the field of politics: 'The problem, then, is not of essentialism itself. Instead, the problem is a failure to be conscious of essentialism, whether it springs from the assumptions with which we approach our subjects or the goals that motivate our writing' (Carrier 1992: 207; cf. Clifford 1980: 221).

CONCLUSION: CONSEQUENCES FOR THE STUDY OF THE MIDDLE EAST

Although it is certainly true that reflections of this kind do not add anything to our factual knowledge about the Middle East (Halliday 1993: 151), they are nevertheless, in my view, of great importance in that they stimulate not only a certain self-reflection among Orientalists but contribute, as a body of discussion, to an increasing awareness of the historicity of knowledge in Oriental Studies. This need not be confounded with the absolute arbitrariness of any knowledge in the humanities and social sciences that Hamid Algar (1971: 105) seems to imply when he writes with regard to Oriental Studies 'that the whole claim to objectivity, academic method, impartiality and so forth ... is basically false. After all, the whole concept of objectivity is in this case inapplicable'. However, if one assumes the existence of a reality, one has, in its investigation, not only to comply with certain rules, commonly thought to be the academic method, but also to accept that such an endeavour is by definition an open and unfinishable enterprise.[31] Thus, a certain scepticism about uncritical reliance on the academic *silsila* or chain of transmission, so well described by Albert Hourani,[32] and a critical reconsideration of earlier scholarship in the light of the circumstances surrounding its production are in place. While this may, by now, be regarded as self-evident in disciplines such as history (cf. Koselleck 1977), Said's study provides ample evidence that such a reminder might still be well in place in Oriental Studies, as well as in any field, West or East, that is dominated or influenced by the search for an essential, timeless 'truth'.

This problem is all the more real because so much of Orientalist scholarship is conducted on the basis of texts. This is particularly problematic for those who are working on discourses of identity, be they inspired by secular or religious ideologies. More often than not, the sources themselves reflect the notions of identity held by their authors and are thus, by the very nature of this particular genre of texts, predominantly rooted in essentialist and exclusivist notions. Scholars can be easily tempted into uncritically reproducing these notions, and thus easily perpetuating old prejudices of essential differences between various groups of humankind.[33] The following example of Huntington shows in an exemplary way how such notions of Orientalists and Orientals alike can be used – and, for political purposes, misused – very conveniently to reinforce each other, when he writes,

> On both sides the interaction between Islam and the West is seen as a clash of civilizations. The West's 'next confrontation,' observes M. J. Akbar, an Indian Muslim, 'is definitely going to come from the Muslim world. It is in the sweep of the Islamic nations from the Maghreb to Pakistan that the struggle for a new world order will begin.'
> (Huntington 1993: 32)

It thus seems that the current trend to consider the analysis of discourses as the methodological *non plus ultra* harbours a certain danger of backfiring so as to bolster old prejudices in a new disguise (cf. al-Azmeh 1993: 19). This danger is enhanced by the criticism of ignoring or diminishing the importance of authentic self-

---

31 In this I agree with Halliday 1993: 145 and 163. As for the possibilities and limits of (historical) knowledge, cf. Kocka 1977.
32 Hourani 1992: 32f. and 61f. The same point was made by Abu-Lughod 1987, who speaks of Orientalist '*isnād*' (p. 155).
33 See, for example, the criticism of al-Azmeh 1993: 1–28 and Prakash 1990.

expressions which Oriental adherents of various brands of essentialism direct at those Orientalists who try to avoid this trap by looking to other paradigms for an explanation of these ideologies. This 'Scylla of the secularists and Charybdis of the religious', as it has been called (Fähndrich 1988: 183), can probably not be entirely avoided. It might, however, be more important than ever in such a context to integrate 'Oriental studies' into the relevant humanities and social sciences to avoid the tautology of treating something as 'Oriental' simply because it originated in 'the Orient'.[34] On this basis, topics such as Islamic history can be fruitfully reconsidered in the light of the critique of Orientalism.[35]

Another important aspect is certainly that discourses and their analysis can be approached in different ways. Gyan Prakash (1990: 384) has made a strong case for treating the Third World (and, one should add, all other worlds as well) 'as a variety of shifting positions which have been discursively articulated in history' instead of seeking a new 'nativist romanticization' (ibid. 406). While such positions are easily exposed to criticism on the grounds that they seem to threaten the unity of the anti-imperialist camp, a critical exchange about and constant review of scholarly results seems to be one of the main prerequisites for a further deconstruction of Orientalist conceptions. To realize this, a crucial condition is the globalization of the field to encompass not only Western Orientalists, or scholars of Oriental origin who are integrated into the Western system, such as Edward Said, but also scholars, Eastern and Western, who are based in 'the Orient'.[36] While Said is certainly correct in observing a Western-dominated hegemonic discourse, it is certainly no longer true – if indeed it ever was – that Western scholars can afford to ignore academic developments in the Middle East or elsewhere,[37] in spite of the often serious problems, such as a lack of resources or the widespread and lamentable absence of academic freedom.[38]

Besides the gains and stimulation for scholarly insight, such a co-operation may be regarded as a necessary corrective of Occidentocentrism. Although this might seem to be a small step considering the practical and epistemological problems of intercultural understanding outlined above, it might nevertheless prove to be a significant one, as the Syrian author Mikhā'īl Rustum already observed in 1895. During his travels in the United States, he had come across the books of a certain Dr Henry Jessup whom he had known as a Christian missionary in Syria. Disappointed and outraged by Jessup's descriptions of Syria, Rustum wrote: 'I believe that had he known that the Syrians will read his book, he would have desisted [from his defamatory statements], and instead written the truth.'[39] It is

---

34 Besides earlier cited advocates of this strategy, cf. al-Azmeh 1981. A slightly different Arabic version was published under the title Ifṣāḥ al-istishrāq. *al-Mustaqbal al-'arabī* 32 (1981), pp. 43–62.
35 See, for example, the suggestions made by Schulze 1990.
36 This has been vehemently demanded by Benaboud 1982: 12; Djait 1985: 171; and Ḥamīs 1981: 88.
37 Said 323. This point has been strongly made by Malti-Douglas 1979: 731.
38 This is being extensively discussed in the Arab literature, e.g. al-Nabī Iṣṭaif 1982; and Ḥamīs 1981: 120f. For a study of the problems of Arab academics, cf. Sabour 1988.
39 Rustum 1895: 88. The episode is related by Musallam 1979: 22.

true that, as Musallam (1979: 22) observes, Said is separated from Rustum by the Balfour Declaration, the Sykes–Picot Agreement and other historical events, as well as by current unequal power relations which have severed the optimism expressed in Rustum's words. On the other hand, the increasingly general global experience, exemplified by such travellers between cultures as Said, might well improve the chances for the development of a shared imagination of 'Orient' and 'Occident' amongst those concerned with the human past, be they from the 'East' or the 'West'.

REFERENCES

Abdel-Malek, A. (1963) 'Orientalism in crisis', *Diogenes* 44: 103–40.
Abu-Lughod, I. (1963) *Arab Rediscovery of Europe. A Study in Cultural Encounters*, Princeton.
Abu-Lughod, J. L. (1987) 'The Islamic city – historic myth, Islamic essence, and contemporary relevance', *International Journal of Middle East Studies* 19: 155–76.
Ahmad, A. (1992) *In Theory. Classes, Nations, Literatures*, London and New York.
al-'Ayyād, M. K. (1965) 'Ṣafaḥāt min tārīkh al-istishrāq', *Revue de l'Académie Arabe de Damas* 40: 161–70.
al-'Aẓm, S. J. (1981) *al-Istishrāq wa-l-istishrāq ma'kūsan*, Beirut.
al-Azmeh, A. (1981) 'The articulation of Orientalism', *Arab Studies Quarterly* 3(4): 398–400.
—— (1993) *Islams and Modernities*, London.
Alatas, S. H. (1977) *The Myth of the Lazy Native. A Study of the Image of the Malays. Filipinos and Javanese from the 16th to the 20th Century and its Function in the Ideology of Colonial Capitalism*, London.
Algar, H. (1971) 'The problems of orientalists', *Islamic Literature* 17: 95–106.
Alleaume, G. (1982) 'L'Orientaliste dans le miroir de la littérature arabe', *British Society of Middle Eastern Studies Bulletin* 9: 5–13.
Benaboud, M. (1982) 'Orientalism and the Arab elite', *Islamic Quarterly* 26: 3–15.
al-Bustāni, F. A. (ed.) (1977) *Dā'irat al-ma'ārif, Qāmūs 'āmm li-kull fann wa-maṭlab*, vol. 12, Beirut.
Cahen, C. (1965) 'To the editor', *Diogenes* 49: 135–8.
Carrier, J. L. (1992) 'Occidentalism: the world turned upside down', *American Ethnologist* 19(2): 195–212.
Chandhuri, K. N. (1990) *Asia before Europe. Economy and Civilisation of the Indian Ocean from the Rise of Islam to 1750*, Cambridge.
Chilcote, R. H. (1981) *Theories of Comparative Politics, The Search for a Paradigm*, Boulder, CO.
Clifford, J. (1980) 'Orientalism', *History and Theory* 19(2): 203–23.
Djait, H. (1985) *Europe and Islam, Cultures and Modernity*, Berkeley.
Ende, W. (1965) *Europabild und kulturelles Selbstbewußtsein bei den Muslimen am Ende des 19. Jahrhunderts, dargestellt an den Schriften der beiden ägyptischen Schriftsteller Ibrahim und Muhammad al-Muwailihi*, Hamburg.
Escovitz, J. H. (1983) 'Orientalists and Orientalism in the writings of Muhammad Kurd Ali', *International Journal of Middle East Studies* 15: 95–109.
Fähndrich, H. (1988) 'Orientalismus und *Orientalismus*: Überlegungen zu Edward Said, Michel Foucault und westlichen "Islamstudien"', *Die Welt des Islams* 28: 178–86.
Freitag, U. (1991) *Geschichtsschreibung in Syrien 1920–1990. Zwischen Wissenschaft und Ideologie*, Hamburg.

Fück, J. (1955) *Die arabischen Studien in Europa bis in den Anfang des 20. Jahrhunderts*, Leipzig.
Gabrieli, F. (1965) 'Apology for Orientalism', *Diogenes* 50: 128–36.
Halliday, F. (1993) '"Orientalism" and its critics', *British Journal of Middle Eastern Studies* 20(2): 145–63.
Ḥamīs, S. (1981) *al-Istishrāq fī' ufq insidādih*, Rabat.
Hentsch, T. (1992) *Imagining the Middle East*, Montreal and New York.
Hermann, R. (1990) *Kulturkrise und konservative Erneuerung. Muhammad Kurd Ali (1876–1953) und das geistige Leben in Damaskus zu Beginn des 20. Jahrhunderts*, Frankfurt.
Hourani, A. (1983) *Arabic Thought in the Liberal Age 1798–1939*, Cambridge.
—— (1992) *Islam in European Thought*, paperback edn, Cambridge. (Hardback edn, 1991.)
Huntington, S. P. (1993) 'The clash of civilisations?', *Foreign Affairs* 72(3): 22–40.
Inden, R. (1986) 'Orientalist constructions of India', *Modern Asian Studies* 20(3): 401–46.
—— (1990) *Imagining India*, Oxford and Cambridge, MA.
Irwin, R. (1981–2) 'Writing about Islam and the Arabs', *Ideology and Consciousness* 9 (Winter): 101–12.
Johansen, B. (1980) 'Politics and scholarship: the development of Islamic studies in the Federal Republic of Germany', in T. Y. Ismael (ed.) *Middle East Studies. International Perspectives on the State of the Art*, New York, Westport, Ont. and London.
Juḥā, M. (1982) *al-Dirāsāt al-'arabīya wa-l-islāmīya fī Aurūbā*, Beirut.
—— (1983) *al-Fikr al-'arabī* 5: 31–2.
Keddie, N. R. (1983) *An Islamic Response to Imperialism, Political and Religious Writings of Sayyid Jamal ad-Din 'al-Afghani'*, Berkeley.
Kerr, M. H. (ed.) (1980) *Islamic Studies: A Tradition and its Problems*, Malibu.
al-Khaṭīb, M. K. (ed.) (1991) *al-Sharq wa-l-gharb*, 2 vols, Damascus.
Klemm, V. and Hörner, K. (eds) (1993) *Das Schwert des 'Experten': Peter Scholl-Latours verzerrtes Araber- und Islambild*, Heidelberg.
Kocka, J. (1977) 'Angemessenheitskriterien historischer Argumente', in Koselleck *et al.* 1977.
Koselleck, R. (1977) 'Standortbindung und Zeitlichkeit', in Koselleck *et al.* 1977.
——, Mommsen, W. J. and Rüsen, J. (eds) (1977) *Objektivität und Parteilichkeit in der Geschichtswissenschaft*, Munich.
Kurd 'Alī, M. (1922) "Ali, Baḥt intiqādī fī mukhtaṣar tārīkh Sūrīya', *Revue de l'Académie Arabe de Damas* 2: 271–81.
—— [1926–8] (1983) *Khiṭaṭ al-Shām*, 6 vols, 2nd edn, Damascus.
—— (1935) 'Aghrāḍ al-mustashriqīn', *al-Risāla*, 9 September.
Lammens, H. (1921) *La Syrie, précis historique*, 2 vols, Beirut.
Laroui, A. (1967) *L'Idéologie arabe contemporaine*, Paris.
Laurens, H. (1987) *Les Origines intellectuelles de l'expédition de l'Égypte. L'Orientalisme islamisant en France (1698–1798)*, Istanbul and Paris.
Leimdorfer, F. (1992) *Discours académique et colonisation. Thèmes de sur l'Algérie pendant la période coloniale*, Paris.
Lewis, B. (1982a) *The Muslim Discovery of Europe*, London.
—— (1982b) 'The question of Orientalism', *New York Review of Books*, 24 September: 49–56. (Repr. in Lewis 1993.)
—— (1993) *Islam and the West*, New York and London.
Little, D. P. (1979) 'Three Arab critiques of Orientalism', *The Muslim World* 69: 110–31.
Malti-Douglas, F. (1979) 'Re-orienting Orientalism', *The Virginia Quarterly Review* 55: 724–33.
Mani, L. and Frankenberg, R. (1985) 'The challenge of Orientalism', *Economy and Society* 14: 174–92.

Miller, C. L. (1985) *Blank Darkness. Africanist Discourse in French*, Chicago and London.
Minear, R. H. (1980) 'Orientalism and the study of Japan', *Journal of Asian Studies* 39(3): 507–17.
Mubārak, Z. (1934) 'Hal ḍarrar al-mustashriqqūn akṭar min naf 'ihim? Naf 'uhum akṭar min ḍarrarihim', *al-Hilāl*, January.
Mudimbe, V. Y. (1988) *The Invention of Africa. Gnosis, Philosophy, and the Order of Knowledge*, Bloomington, Indianopolis and London.
al-Munaẓẓama al-'arabīya li-l-tarbiya wa-l-ṭaqāfa wa-l-'ulūm, and Maktab al-tarbiya al-'arabī li-duwal al-Khalīj (eds) (1985) *Manāhij al-mustashriqīn fī'l-dirāsāt al-'arabīya wa-l-islāmīya*, 2 vols, Riyad.
Musallam, B. (1979) 'Power and knowledge', *MERIP-Reports* 79: 19–26.
al-Mūsawī, M. J. (1993) *Al-Istishrāq fī'l fikr al-'arabī*, Beirut.
al-Nabī Iṣṭaif, A. (1982) 'Naḥnu wa-l-istishrāq', *Revue de l'Académie Arabe de Damas* 57: 648–65.
Nagel, T. (1978) 'Gedanken über die europäische Islamforschung und ihr Echo im Orient', *Zeitschrift für Missionskunde und Religionswissenschaft* 62: 21–39.
Philipp, T. (1994) 'Geschichtswissenschaft und die Geschichte des Nahen Ostens', *Saeculum* 45(1): 166–78.
Prakash, G. (1990) 'Writing post-Orientalist histories of the Third World: perspectives from Indian historiography', *Comparative Studies in Society and History* 32: 383–408.
Reid, D. X. (1987) 'Cairo University and the Orientalists', *International Journal of Middle East Studies* 19: 51–76.
Reig, D. (1988) *Homo orientaliste, La Langue arabe en France depuis le XIXe siècle*, Paris.
Renan, E. (1883) *Der Islam und die Wissenschaft. Vortrag gehalten in der Sorbonne am 29, März 1883. Kritik dieses Vortrags vom Afghanen Scheik Djemmal Eddin und Ernest Renans Erwiderung*, Basel.
Rodinson, M. (ed.) (1979) *Marxism and the Muslim World*, London.
Rodinson, M. (1987) *Europe and the Mystique of Islam*, London.
Rotter, G. (1992) *Allahs Plagiator: Die publizistischen Raubzüge des 'Nahostenexperten' Gerhard Konzelmann*, Heidelberg.
Rudolph, E. (1991) *Westliche Islamswissenschaft im Spiegel muslimischer Kritik, Grundzüge und aktuelle Merkmale einer innerislamischen Diskussion*, Berlin.
Rustum, M. (1895) *Kitāb al-gharīb fī'l-gharb*, New York.
Sabour, M. (1988) *Homo Academicus Arabicus*, Joensuu.
Said, E. (1976) 'Arabs, Islam and the dogmas of the West', *The New York Times Book Review*, 31 October: 4–5, 35–7.
—— (1985) 'Orientalism reconsidered', *Race and Class* 27(2): 4.
—— (1989) 'Orientalism. An exchange', *New York Review of Books*, 12 August: 44–6.
—— (1991) *Orientalism, Western Conceptions of the Orient*, Harmondsworth. (First published London, 1979.)
Schülin, E. (1958) *Die weltgeschichtliche Erfassung des Orients bei Hegel und Ranke*, Göttingen.
Schulze, R. (1990) 'Das islamische 18. Jahrhundert. Versuch einer historiographischen Kritik', *Die Welt des Islams* 30: 140–59.
al-Sibā'ī, M. [1968] (1979) *al-Istishrāq wa-l-mustashriqīn. Mā lahum wa-ma'alaihim*, Beirut.
Sivan, E. (1977) 'Orientalism, Islam and Cultural Revolution', *Jerusalem Quarterly* 5: 84–94.
—— (1985) *Interpretations of Islam. Past and Present*, Princeton.
Tibawi, A. L. (1963) 'English-speaking Orientalists. A critique of their approach to Islam and Arab nationalism', *The Muslim World* 53: 185–204, 298–313.
—— (1979) *Second Critique of English-Speaking Orientalists and their Approach to Islam and the Arabs*, London.

—— (1980) 'On the Orientalists again', *The Muslim World* 70: 56–61.

Turner, B. (1978) *Marx and the End of Orientalism*, London.

Volney, C.-F. (1959) *Voyage en Egypte et en Syrie*, Paris and The Hague.

Waardenburg, J. D. J. [1963] (1970) *L'Islam dans le miroir de l'Occident*, 3rd edn, Paris and The Hague.

—— (1993) 'Mustashriqūn', *Encyclopedia of Islam*, vol. 7, 2nd edn, Leiden and New York.

Wielandt, R. (1980) *Das Bild der Europäer in der modernen arabischen Erzähl- und Theaterliteratur*, Beirut and Wiesbaden.

IV.2 AREA STUDIES

24

THE HISTORIOGRAPHY OF
MODERN CHINA

Pamela Kyle Crossley

Less than a quarter-century ago it was still customary in American and European scholarship to begin 'modern' China at the Opium War (1839–42). In American scholarship this approach is now associated with the late John King Fairbank. Both as a scholar and as a trainer of scholars at Harvard University, Fairbank created the foundation of a literature dominated by an interest in commercial and political institutions, heavily (though by no means exclusively) dependent upon original documentation in European languages (and generated by American and European agencies), and informed by an implicit assumption that successive wars and partial colonization in nineteenth-century China represented a clash between the declining Chinese order and the modernizing influences of the 'West'.[1] At bottom the premises of Fairbank and a majority of his students were not unlike those that were being simultaneously institutionalized in the historical profession of the People's Republic of China. This partly explains why, as historical circles in the United States, Europe and their kindred academic communities are moving sharply away from the Fairbank style of periodization, from the preoccupation with the role of the West in China, and from the privileging of institutional history and the cultural view of the elite, many of the most basic ideas that had been characteristic of Fairbank continue to be influential in the Chinese academic world.

The influence of the view institutionalized by the Harvard group persists, but now competes with a variety of other historical and methodological approaches. Some of these approaches are closely connected to the Fairbank school, but others find their sources in Marxism, in literary theory and in feminist critique. The great

---

1 Space does not permit an examination of the reified 'West' embedded in this style of scholarship, and the reader will, I am afraid, have to accept it as a conceit of the genre under discussion. On the model for clashing political cultures as an explanation for the Opium War, see Fairbank and Têng 1942; Fairbank 1953; 1 vol., Stanford University Press, 1969); 1968 (see especially Fairbank's introduction). See also Evans 1988.

change that has resulted is that few younger specialists on China would now make a disciplinary identification of themselves as 'sinologists',[2] believing that the objectification of 'foreign' cultures as imaginary disciplines is a practice of 'Orientalism' (Said 1978; 1993; 1995), or similarly alterizing ideologies. It is, as a consequence, more likely that those writing the history of China now identify themselves with a discipline of the social sciences or humanities.

PERIODIZATION

Under the terms of Fairbankian scholarship modernity was introduced in China through the agency of Western missionaries, merchants and militarists; a second-order modernizing influence came through Japan, which had already been affected by the West. China before exposure to the West had been in 'decline,' and thus vulnerable to being penetrated by Western influence, but had not itself been capable of generating transformative energies. The road to epochal change in China had been opened through the country's 'response' to the West (Têng and Fairbank [1954] 1963). More precisely, a series of responses was perceived, in the earliest of which (initiation of the Opium Wars, suppression of the Taiping Rebellion) reactionary forces had prevailed and in the latter of which (the nationalist and communist revolutions) revolutionary forces had prevailed.

The 'decline' – or, as contemporary Chinese scholars would yet have it, the 'decadence' or 'corruption' (*fubai*) – of imperial China forms the backdrop to the Fairbankian conception of the meaning of the arrival of the 'West'. This decline is understood as a function of the 'dynastic cycle', an idea that was well established in traditional Chinese scholarship and was adapted by Western historians (see Yang 1961). According to this paradigm, all dynasties inescapably underwent the process of formation, maturation and decay. Though all dynastic regimes were understood to decline in time, the longevity of any dynasty was not predetermined. The institutional character of the regime was a significant factor, as were the personal qualities of any ruler. Most critical, however, was the question of whether in its late maturity any particular regime could effect a 'restoration' (*weixin*), which is to say the moral as well as the institutional revitalization of the regime. Without restoration all dynastic traditions would be hopelessly tethered to finite cycles, some of short duration, and political stability would remain elusive. The profound importance of restoration as a political ideal and as a historical concept was perhaps most dramatically expressed in the nomenclature applied to the Meiji 'restoration' (*Meiji ishin*) in Japan in 1868, which was regarded as a successful traditionalist revitalization. In China at roughly the same time the search for a genuine restoration was seen to motivate the reconstruction of the political order in the aftermath of the Taiping War (1853–66) and during the Tongzhi (1862–75) era. Fairbank's student Mary Clabaugh Wright's study, *The Last Stand of Chinese Conservatism* (1971), is

---

2   On the decline of Sinology, see Crossley 1990.

both a classic statement of the Fairbankian tradition and a thorough examination of the ideal and practice of 'restoration.'

Even with restorations, dynastic cycles are obviously models of a closed and self-perpetuating political culture, in which only new dynasties are generated. Fairbank's explanation of the final end of the dynastic cycle in China – and the birth of modernity – was that there came a point of 'secular' change in the nineteenth century, when the traditional institutions could no longer revitalize themselves, a new dynasty could not be generated and the imperial era was superseded by the republican era. Though Fairbank and those influenced by him recognized many factors contributing to the fatal weakness of the Qing dynasty, the determinative factor, for them, was the West. On all fronts – economic, technological, political and cultural – the West was capable of overwhelming the Qing state. This occurred in stages during the nineteenth century, with the result that China was unwillingly brought into the 'modern' world.

Modernization and Westernization are not invariably equated in this scholarship, but the clarity with which this analysis is able to pinpoint the first Opium War as the threshold of 'modern' China is based upon a number of ideas about the relationship of economic and social development to culture. Fairbank himself cannot be considered Marxist,[3] but his ideas about the absence of social and economic dynamism in traditional China shares many assumptions with nineteenth- and early twentieth-century ideas regarding an 'Asiatic mode of production.'[4]

Though Fairbank was not inclined to frame his arguments regarding the end of imperial history in China in terms of relations of production, he was as impressed as Hegel and Marx had been with the idea of China as a closed and unchanging system. Much weight is put, in the Fairbankian paradigm, upon the role and conditioning of the elite. Scholars and officials of nineteenth-century China were characterized as, with few exceptions, unflinching clients of the patron court, who subscribed entirely to the imperial view of China as central, superior and self-sufficient. The insistence of much traditional Chinese rhetoric respecting the civil and ethical values of the elite were taken rather literally by the Fairbankian school. In sum the fundamental tension between China and the West by the early nineteenth century was understood to be cultural. Where the West determined to insist upon commercial freedom and diplomatic equality in relations, the Chinese court and literati were monolithically committed to refusing diplomatic relations with the West in favour of superior–inferior 'tributary' relations, and determined

---

3 For recent interpretations of Marx's writings on India and China see Sawer 1977, Krader 1975; Ghosh 1984. It is also important to note that in the case of China, Wittfogel 1957 was long an influential rumination on Marx's concept of the 'Asiatic mode'. In this respect, note Mote 1961. Finally, one should mention that in Marx's own time historical knowledge that contradicted the interlocking theses of an 'Asiatic mode of production' and 'Oriental despotism' was already available. See for instance Anquetil 1800 and commentary in Anderson 1974.

4 For recent discussions of the 'Asiatic mode' see Dunn 1982; O'Leary 1989; Geertz 1984; Jaksic 1985; Maisels 1987; Mehdi 1988; Jaksic 1990. For a rendition of Chinese writing on the Asiatic mode question, see Brook 1989.

to refuse free economic exchange between China and the West.[5] The result was the Opium War.

The concomitant changes in China were all to be directly connected to the presence and persistence of the West. The Taiping movement was a traditionalist peasant rebellion galvanized by Western millenarian religious influences, empowered by Western arms and encouragement, and ultimately quelled by Western intervention.[6] The reconstruction efforts after the war were spearheaded by progressive Westerners, many employed by the Chinese court (see Fairbank *et al.* 1975; Banno 1964). Western missionaries and doctors took knowledge of Western technology and culture into remote Chinese provinces. Western imperialists exposed the Chinese urban populations to Western literature, entertainment, transportation and education. Western support was critical to the sustenance of Sun Yatsen's nationalist movement at the turn of the twentieth century, and Western education was fundamental to the maturation of the generation that would lead the communist revolution of 1949 (see Wright 1968).

Fairbank and his colleagues were aware that among those Western influences was Marxism, and they were often at pains to explain why Marxism should have been among the most successful of all Western influences in China. Their solution was that Marxism was really only the rhetorical veneer on a twentieth-century political movement that was in fact traditionalist and nationalist.[7] The political culture of post-1949 China was rendered in terms reminiscent of the eighteenth- and nineteenth-century characterizations of 'oriental despotism' – as a milieu hostile to private property and the personal liberties that were extensions of it, and friendly to state domination of society and culture. The implication of much of this scholarship is that 'modern' China has not yet fully arrived, and that the periodization marking the 'modern' period is really that marking the history of modernizing influences in China.

The great teleological problem for the generation of Fairbank was the success of the communist revolution and the establishment of the People's Republic of China in 1949. The Harvard school tended to find the antecedents of communist political culture in the putative authoritarianism of 'Confucianism', in which individuality and liberty had no value. An interesting alternative to this line of thinking was offered at the University of Washington, where Wittfogel had popularized the 'oriental despotism' thesis. Wittfogel's student Franz Michael, in his work on the Taiping Rebellion,[8] suggested that the Taiping movement had in fact been a

---

5   Fairbank 1968 and the influence in works such as Kim 1980. See also Iriye 1988. For a recent Chinese response to Fairbank's views see Tao 1992.

6   See Têng 1971; there is a large literature on Charles Gordon published before 1950, but see, more recently, Carr 1992.

7   For an overview of this general analysis see Graebner 1977. For China, see Johnson 1962. An early and still very influential study in this vein on China – and much more philosophically based than many studies of this subject – is Schwartz 1951.

8   Michael and Chang 1971. There is a large literature in English on the Taiping Rebellion. Among the more recent works one might mention Zhongguo 1976; Clarke and Gregory 1982; Weller, 1994.

precursor of the communist revolution – a zealous dictatorship based on an ostensibly egalitarian philosophy, fuelled by popular resentment of the elitist, paternalist, Confucian social orthodoxy. Thus Michael offered a key to understanding the 'secular' change by which the dynastic cycle was broken. Mass politics, arising from the progressive debilitation of the Qing regime at the hands of the West, had in successive waves washed away the Chinese political structure, culminating at length in the establishment of a communist state.

The Fairbankian schema for periodizing and analysing modern China has been modified by several intellectual generations subscribing to the general framework. Nevertheless, the idea has been the matrix in which a new academic specialization has formed, and its simplicity may not be irrelevant to its success in this respect. Moreover, it has (as has been suggested) a credible pedigree in twentieth-century historical positivism, which at more than one juncture has permitted it to facilitate ostensibly comparative discussions of other East Asian societies with Confucian political traditions – particularly Japan, Korea and Vietnam – and nineteenth-century confrontations with European or American powers.[9] Like all good intellectual ideologies, Fairbankianism has sufficient obtrusive teleology (in this case, the suggestion of the inevitable conflict with and domination by the 'West') to stimulate vigorous opposition from its own progeny. The great rejection of Fairbankianism occurred in the United States during the period of opposition to the war in Vietnam, which profoundly factionalized China studies – and by extension Asian studies. Though by no description a political conservative, Fairbank himself led the forces which attempted to quash the influence of younger scholars who saw scholarship and politics as naturally joined and viewed the claim of 'objective', apolitical scholarship as delusional or hypocritical. In ensuing decades this contest has carved a deep methodological divide, which will be discussed below.

Before we leave the subject of periodization it should be noted that the Fairbank schema had both antecedent and postcedent rivals, neither of which has disappeared from international scholarship on Chinese history. From the earlier part of the twentieth century the 'Kyōto school' of historical scholarship, based primarily upon the ideas of Naitō Torajirō, had dominated much of Japanese scholarship on Chinese history, particularly during the 1950s and 1960s (Miyakawa 1955; Fogel 1984). Drawing in a rather loose way upon the ideas of Marx, Naitō proposed that the end of feudalism in China occurred during the Song period (tenth to twelfth centuries), when a large private economic sector arose and the legal delimitation of private property occurred. The Kyōto paradigm leaves some obscurity in the

---

9   This is very much the message of the most famous textbook ever used in the field of East Asian studies. In its current incarnation its authors are listed as John King Fairbank, Edwin O. Reischauer and Albert M. Craig: *East Asia: Tradition and Transformation* (Revised Edition), (Houghton Mifflin Company, 1989). This book succeeds a former two-volume series, the first of which was Fairbank and Reischauer, *A History of East Asian Civilization* (Houghton Mifflin [1960–65]), and the second of which was Fairbank, Reischauer and Craig, *East Asia, the Modern Transformation* (Houghton Mifflin, 1965). Free-standing volumes of the China and Japan portions of 1989 text are also in print. See also Nahm 1988.

645

periodization and analysis of the centuries from about 1200 to the present, and has been primarily of importance to specialists of the Song period. Nevertheless, it has the appeal of portraying a dynamic, historically generative China that was well on its way to 'modernity' before the arrival of the West. The Kyōto thesis has remained prominent, due primarily to the work of Miyazaki Ichisada, Shiba Yoshinobu and Mark Elvin, whose *Pattern of the Chinese Past* (1973; see also Elvin 1986) remains one of the most influential theses on the early development and late undevelopment of the Chinese economy.

Another hypothesis from Japanese scholarship, that of the 'Tōkyō school' (associated in modern Chinese studies with Sudō Yoshiyuki, particularly), has been more influential in China, Europe and the United States. Adhering rather more closely to the theories of Marx, the Tōkyō school places the end of feudalism in China in the sixteenth century, at the end of the Ming period, rather than four or five centuries earlier. The interpretation is based on a close analysis of land use, the growth of small enterprises and the development of a private economy. It is the inspiration in China for the 'sprouts of capitalism' thesis made famous by Shang Yue.[10] According to the Shang hypothesis, early capitalism was well rooted in late Ming China, but was smothered by the calamities of the Qing conquest of the mid-seventeenth century, and never grew to full height. Though the particulars of the thesis can be debated, its influence on periodization – primarily through the influence of the Tōkyō school – has been very strong, and it is now common for authors in America, Europe and Australia to mark the beginning of 'modern' China in the seventeenth century. Thus the claim of Western agency in the introduction of modernity to China is obviated by a major change in periodization.[11]

CRITICAL SCHOLARSHIP

'Modernism', like functionalism, commissioned itself to strip away the camouflage of decoration, symbolic distortion and cultural self-reference to expose the 'reality' of beams, pipes, pulleys; to construe language not in metaphor but in grammar; to interpret culture as the facilitation of patterns of exchange that were necessary to the security, perpetuation and economic development of communal humankind. But modernism earned its name because it was based upon a self-referencing teleology, raised upon the following tenets. It is progressive to see through cultural flesh to the social and economic bones beneath. It is the final goal of all historical, linguistic, religious, political and literary study. And most important, the infrastructural objects of modernist analysis are real, in a way that the cultural layers covering them are not.

Historical 'modernism' is as paradigmatic in its understanding of history as it is in its programme for itself. It posits stages of development, and it shows in this respect

---

10   For a summary in English, see Feuerwerker 1968: 228–35 and Wang 1982.

11   A possible exception here lies in new studies of Jesuit influence. There is a large literature on the Jesuits in East Asia, but for important new reassessments see Waley-Cohen 1993; Du and Han 1992.

its debts both to Marxian social science and to Freud. Whether in its manifestation in the '*Annales*' styles of history, or in structuralist literary scholarship and cultural anthropology, or in its enthusiasm for studies of peasants, women and other non-elites, or in its studies of revolutionary movements, modernism affirmed the priority of epochal historical forces over the romantic or elitist histories of the past, which had emphasized biographical studies and intellectual history.[12] In China studies the self-conscious modernist movement coincided with the rise of critical scholarship inspired by opposition to American involvement in the war in Vietnam and opposition to those in the field who were viewed as apologists for imperialism. Scholarship on Chinese history, it was argued, had been informed by the desire to explain and excuse the depredations practised upon Asia by the 'West', and not by the putative objectivity of the historians themselves.

Not surprisingly, early critical scholars revisited the Opium War. The question of causes of the Opium War had not been deeply investigated since the publication of Chang Hsin-pao's brilliant and enigmatic *Commissioner Lin and the Opium War* in 1964. Chang was a student of Fairbank, and the book was published with a foreword by Fairbank himself. In its salient features the work seemed to adhere to the Fairbankian model, opening with a discussion of the 'world order' under the Qing Empire, with a history of failed diplomacy, and following with analyses of the Confucian world-view of Lin Zixu. Large portions of the study, however, fell outside the model, and provided fodder for later work that would emphasize the details of the opium market, the growing British dependence on the drug to balance their trade with China, and the nationalist orientation of Lin Zixu and others who opposed opium import.[13] Instead of the inevitable cultural clash with the West caused by 'sinocentrism' among the Qing elite, the modernist scholars – in the early 1970s, most visibly the Committee of Concerned Asian Scholars – concluded that the opium in the Opium War was not after all an incidental factor.[14] Instead, the crisis precipitated by the Chinese decision to ban the import of opium could be linked to a hunger of the international capitalist system for markets, including those that could be exploited only through the forced distribution of deleterious substances.[15] Capitalism and imperialism were the overriding elements in the paradigms, and they were dynamically opposed by nationalism, which became a prominent subject of the modernist scholars (Friedmann 1974). Through nationalism, Asian populations regained the independence and the dignity – indeed their literal standing as human beings – of which they had been systematically deprived by the imperialist system.

---

12 For comment on the same subjects from a different angle see Skinner 1985.

13 The author died in 1965 at the age of 33, and it is impossible to know how his later thought on these and related topics would have developed.

14 A significant work in this respect is Polachek 1992. Though published at a date when interest in many areas of critical scholarship and in the Opium War itself has waned, the work was originally conceived and written in the heyday of Fairbankian influence, and would have represented a distinct departure from conventional treatments of the war if published earlier.

15 Many post-Fairbank studies have been anticipated by Epstein 1964 and Kuo 1935. For recent work on the Opium War see Fay 1975; Beeching 1975; Inglis 1976; Tau 1978.

With their emphasis upon systems and structure, those working in a modernist style were able to seek more subtle explanations for the political transformation of twentieth-century China than the action–response model of Fairbank. Philip A. Kuhn's (1970) seminal study of nineteenth-century China established a new chronology of increasing social disorder and deepening militarization to find the roots of civil war as early as the White Lotus Rebellion of 1796. Kuhn's emphasis upon local development paralleled the thinking of the sociologist G. William Skinner (1964–5), whose schema of 'macro-regions' (based on central-place theory) offered historians of China new ways of conceptualizing internal changes in Chinese economy, society and culture (Skinner 1964–5). The two studies together created the foundation for a flourishing literature on the roles of local elites in the training and mobilization of militias, in the utilization and development of agricultural land, in economic management, in education, and finally in the local political movements that ended the Qing Empire and created the nationalist republic (Zelin 1985; Schoppa 1982; Rowe 1984; Rankin 1986; Mann 1987; Duara 1988, Rowe 1989; Strand 1989; Will 1990).

The interest in structural analysis has extended far beyond the elites themselves, and produced multi-layered studies of natural resources, elite management or mismanagement, popular responses to natural disasters and economic privations. In many of these studies, political narrative has been eschewed as distracting and less important than the structural underlay that is regarded as truly causative. Some of the studies connected with this general stream of writing and analysis, particularly that of the demographic historians,[16] have also declined to attempt explanations larger than what their particular database will support. Others, however, have offered new paradigms of late imperial China derived from structural analysis of the interplay of demographics, agriculture and agricultural technologies, environment, and the interactions among local government, central government and society (Rawski 1972; Huang 1985; Rawski 1989; Huang 1990; Rawski and Li 1992; Myers 1991). In general, they propose that the imperial state was a competent manager of economic and social difficulties until it was disastrously weakened by a series of financial crises in the mid-nineteenth century, after which there was a progressive devolution of political initiative and credibility away from the imperial centre to the localities (see also Rawski 1991).

Some portion of the modernist group has retained its original interest in rebellion, protest, revolution and dispossession. Joseph Esherick's *Origins of the Boxer Uprising* (1987) is in many ways a critical, modernist response to the Fairbankian paradigm.[17] Where the Harvard school had sought the sources of contemporary Chinese political culture in the imperial era of authoritarianism,

---

16 For recent studies in demography and history see Perdue 1987; Will 1990; Wong 1991; Li 1991; Lavely 1990.

17 Esherick's earlier *Reform and Revolution in China: The 1911 Revolution in Hunan and Hubei* (1976) can be described as a structured and structuralist interpretation of the nationalist movements (both stratified and localized leading to the destruction of the Qing political order).

hierarchy, insularity, ethnocentrism and resentment of the more technologically advanced West, Esherick suggested that the Boxer Uprising was more symptomatic of the political culture that ended the Qing dynasty and created the first republic: popular discontent sparked by profound, if recent, social disruption, easily focused on secondary targets such as foreigners or officials, resulting in disastrous upheavals that left the elites permanently distrustful of popular involvement in politics. A similar theme was sounded in Esherick's former CCAS colleague Andrew Nathan's *Chinese Democracy* (1985), which describes a twentieth-century China in which nervous elites have failed to develop mechanisms for popular participation, and have instead propounded a theory of 'democracy' in which the state enunciates the people's will and serves popular ends by placating majorities and ignoring or eradicating minorities. The critical themes remain strong: Under the structural pressures of population overload, economic underdevelopment, imperialist exploitation and military aggression, nationalism in China has worked to inhibit the distinction between state and society that would have fostered the development of institutions of liberal political participation. The result, in this view, has been instability, insecurity and periodic radicalization.

NARRATIVE AND ETHNOGRAPHY

If modernist historians can be characterized as those who see the past as conditioning the present, a broad group of 'postmodern' scholars might be characterized as those who see the past as conditioned by the present. While critical scholars of the early 1970s were using Marxist or structuralist paradigms to create new understandings of modern Chinese change, another group was re-establishing the importance of narrative as a tool for understanding historical experience. By relativizing the establishments of taste, hierarchy and the role of some literature as archetypical, 'new historicist' literary scholars reopened the eyes of contemporary readers to styles, subjects and cultural perspectives that would under the old criteria have been dismissed as minor or meaningless.

One can in addition discern a modernist/postmodernist watershed in the study of 'myth' (which means different things in these two contexts). Modernists tend to categorize motivated narratives as 'myths', as in Paul Cohen's (1992) recent study of the Boxers, with the clear implication that there is an oppositional non-myth to be revealed by the historian. Those influenced by postmodern literary influences, on the other hand, see mythicizing as a necessary feature of all narrative – indeed, of all culture – and do not posit a higher or more real 'truth' to which 'myth' can be compared; it is Foucault's 'effect of truth' that is of concern. Thus the content of what modernists might call 'myths' tends to be of less interest to historians working in the postmodern style than does the process of mythicizing, or, to put it another way, narrating.

The diminution of narrative was a characteristic of modernist historians, who were sceptical of the self-glamorizing, power-affirming histories of the elites. Structural analyses – whether Marxian class analysis, economic analysis, political analysis, or studies focused on urbanization, industrialization or that mysterious process of 'modernization' itself – were the preferred foundation for historical works, and narrative was to be economically and judiciously employed to establish the chronology behind the structural analysis. But under the influence of postmodernism, narrative returned. It was much celebrated in the general field of historical writing when Natalie Zemon Davis published *The Return of Martin Guerre* after her involvement with the film of that name, and it is important that the return of narrative meant precisely the openness to ambiguity that is at the centre of the Martin Guerre story.[18]

In historical writing on China, narrative had already returned in the late 1970s. Its primary practitioner was Jonathan Spence, whose *The Death of Woman Wang* was a rumination on history and subjectivity that openly acknowledged the influence of Harold Bloom on its author. The interplay of narrative and ambiguity has become something of a hallmark for Spence.[19] It would be regrettable, however, if this combination of narrative and ambiguity were to be seen as an eccentricity or peculiarity of Spence's own vision. In the post-structuralist view of which Spence is exemplary, all narratives are meaningful inventions whose purposes, processes and reception are fields dominated by conflicting and sometimes ineluctable forces.[20]

Narrative as self-invention, for individuals as well as for peoples, has been a primary insight of the 'new historicism'. In their search for the least 'authorized' or mainstream sources the new historicists have found and institutionalized sources that some historians were inclined to dismiss as trivial, though most recognize both the vastness and the quality of the materials that have been neglected for centuries. In Asian studies the influence of the new historicism has been felt, too, as increasingly scholars turn not only to the imperial and local archives but also to private writings, and oral traditions as sources of narrative.

It is partly through these sources that new views on the cultural complexity of China have reshaped our understanding of minority cultures and 'minority nationalities' in China's history. The Fairbankian emphasis on a monolithically 'Confucian' China had never been unopposed; the work of Wolfram Eberhard (see particularly Eberhard 1982), for instance, has always depicted China as the sum interaction of vital local cultures. More recent scholarship, however, has stressed not only the historical importance but the relevance to China's modern experience of

---

18   For specific comment on narrative and subjectivity see Davis 1988.

19   Among Spence's works see particularly *Ts'ao Yin and the K'ang-hsi Emperor: bondservant and master* (1966); *The Death of Woman Wang* (1978); (1984); *The Question of Hu* (1988).

20   Jonathan Spence and the general milieu of Yale University in the 1970s were both influences on another seminal work of this period, Susan Naquin's *Millenarian Rebellion in China: the Eight Trigrams Uprising of 1813* (1976), a work remarkable for its attention to alternative cultural traditions, orality and ideology. Naquin's work was not only strongly narrative, but in its approach to its primary source – the forced deposition of Lin Qing – grappled with the problems of personal narrative authority and the politicization of narrative. Charles Curwen had also dealt with this problem of narrative transformation in his *Taiping Rebel: The Deposition of Li Hsiu-ch'eng* (1976).

the identity issues confronted by minority populations. There has been concomitant re-examination of the Qing Empire – founded by Manchus and encompassing Mongolia, Tibet and Turkestan as well as China itself – and its political culture. Considering the Qing order as a multinational and multicultural 'empire' (not the 'dynasty' of Fairbankian scholarship) gives a new understanding of the emergence of Chinese nationalism at the end of the nineteenth century, and casts some doubt upon the confident pronouncements of earlier scholars who considered the racism (or 'anti-Manchuism') of the period as a mere 'veneer' over more substantial political rhetoric. The tendency of postmodern scholarship to depose established narratives presents a new opportunity to explore local identities in China, including the 'ethnic', urban, religious and political. Equally significant, the processes of ethnicization of identity in China are now more visible and open to exploration (Crossley 1990; Gladney 1991; Honig 1992).

Closely related to this interest in narratives that relativize the established views is scholarship on women's experience. Until very recently, sustained work on women in China was represented primarily by the Japanese historian Ono Kazuko (some of whose writing is now available in English translation – Ono 1989) and by the work of Marilyn Young (1973), Margery Wolf (1984) and Roxane Witke (Wolf and Witke 1975). Historical scholarship on women in China is increasingly well developed, though its distribution is still perhaps not well formed, since writers, revolutionaries and prostitutes tend to be over-represented (see e.g. Andors 1983; Stacey 1983; Honig and Hershatter 1988; Franklin 1989; Tseng 1993; Gilmartin *et al.* 1994; Judd 1994; Jaschok and Miers 1994). Obviously, a major portion of women's experience in China of the past two centuries is still unexamined, but the way has been opened to those studies, and only the acquisition and study of sources remains an obstacle. As gender has become institutionalized in the historiography, so has its variations. Gay and lesbian experience, for instance, has become increasingly visible with the emphasis upon alternative narratives (e.g. Hinsch 1990).

It is interesting that the exploration and analysis of women's experience and of the standardization of behaviour has led back to an attention to institutional history, particularly as it relates to law (e.g. Ng 1987; 1990; 1994). This is partly a result of the recent utilization of legal archives for the study of culture and society, and partly a development abreast of increasing interest in the social impact of legal development in all fields of historical enquiry. Earlier scholarship on Chinese law tended to emphasize the extent to which law was used to enforce 'Confucian' norms in Chinese behaviour (Bodde and Morris 1967). More recent work has emphasized legal documentation as a source for understanding changes in economic relationships, in social standards and in state development.[21]

---

21   As examples see Hom 1994; Benson 1993; the special issue of *Law and Contemporary Problems* 52 [Spring/Summer 1989] edited by Jonathan Ocko; and Bernhardt and Huang 1994. There is in addition a large literature on various aspects of law and legal development in the People's Republic of China.

CULTURAL STUDIES

A second-wave development in postmodern influences has featured a more self-conscious group of scholars professing 'cultural studies', and declaring a strong theoretical affinity with a handful of European scholars, foremost among them Pierre Bourdieu and Roger Chartier. These scholars tend to see cultural manifestations as textual, and to see culture as subject to the process of 'reading' – that is, the imposition of order on perception, or ideology on practice. Because of the distinctive claims to special identity made by many of these scholars, and because of the strong allegiance on the part of many to a highly stylized vocabulary, there is some scepticism regarding the depth and breadth of their contribution to the field. Nevertheless, there is the possibility of lasting impact on China studies. Certainly, the movement already has a number of achievements to its credit. Among them has been the sharper definition and improved methodology of discursive studies. These efforts have proved invaluable in the illumination of the workings of systems of reference both within China and also within the field of China studies. They have begun to explore not only reading as a culturally dynamic process, but also emphasize the process through which any culture 'reads' its own past and those of other cultures – including museums, zoos, exhibitions, institutes of oriental research and imperialism itself. Cultural studies has also made these subjects readily visible to beginning students, so that from the beginning of training China specialists are now forced to confront their own subjectivities and the plasticity of what they 'know'.

Material culture becomes in this sense a continuous decipherable surface, part of the expressive process of which culture is composed. Chinese material culture has recently been explored in Craig Clunas's *Superfluous Things* (1991), a study of taste in early modern China that is in some ways close to the studies of European taste done by Richard Goldthwaite, and which challenges the assumptions of the modernists that consumption in this style was the exclusive property of the capitalizing and mercantilizing societies of Europe. The 'reading' of culture is not limited to material things, however, and encompasses rituals both religious and secular – including manners, professional conventionalities, sartorial customs, mating habits. This is a facet of the cultural restorationism of cultural studies, which sees custom and ritual not as activities representing higher realities, but as 'texts' whose meanings come from their allusiveness, self-characterization, layers of repetition and improvisation. In order to 'read' behaviour postmodernists must construct imaginary spaces in which behaviours are given dimension and delimitation. Bourdieu's 'field' (*champs*) is one of these postmodernist imaginary spaces, but most cultural scholars have to deal in one way or another with the contextualization of subjects.

These 'spaces', which encompass time and narrative as well as, in some cases, actual space, are difficult to define, but one of the handiest ways to do it is with ritual, which generally takes as its fundamental concerns the enveloping of the past and present, movement, allusiveness and the immanence of the supernatural in the physical. Studies of ritual in China have the additional charm of reviving interest in well-documented and patently important activities that modernists lost interest in some time ago. They have also cast ritual in a new light from that previously thrown on it by sinologists, who adopted the view that all ritual was an extension of Confucian language, and by the modernists, who saw ritual as representing (that is, symbolizing) fundamental communal imperatives. For cultural-studies specialists, ritual is performance, to be read for its grammar and its ideological integrity.[22]

The differences between the postmodern approach and others is demonstrated in the rescue from neglect of a famous ritual episode: Lord Macartney's mission of 1793, which in its cultural dimensions has been most thoroughly explored by James Hevia (1995).[23] Until very recently, scholarship strongly influenced by the Fairbank 'world-order' concept has regarded Ming and Qing tributary practices as opaque rites of subordination to supreme Chinese imperial status – political representation-alism, with a little supernatural language. With respect to the incidents of 1793, discussion has focused on Lord Macartney's denial that he had kowtowed to the representatives of the Qianlong emperor. It has long been recognized that the preponderance of the evidence supports Macartney's claim and for some time this subject has dropped from the view of the field. With a revival of interest in ritual, the Macartney question has reappeared and yields more to the gaze of the cultural historian than it had to the scrutiny of the diplomatic historian. Hevia reminds the reader that the British were as highly ritualized as the Chinese in these matters and notes the significant deviations from ordinary tribute ritual that the Qing granted Macartney. Most significantly, Hevia characterizes the audience with the Qianlong emperor and attempts afterwards to narrate it as a struggle over whether one centre or 'two' would be represented in the ceremony – a question in which the imperial ideology of the British and the universalist ideology of the Qing were equally invested.

Finally, cultural studies are impatient with the 'essentialist' assumptions of past generations of scholars, many of which were incorporated by structuralist social science. The opposition to essentialism and the argument that race, ethnicity and gender are all constructions of the hegemonic ideology has been familiar to all Asian scholars since the publication of Edward Said's *Orientalism* in 1978. A burgeoning literature examines the processes behind construction of racial, national and ethnic identities in modern China (Dikötter 1992; 1994; see also Crossley 1997). Gender has no more essentialist grounding than race or nationality in the view of cultural studies, and thus it, too, is increasingly subject to analysis (Dikötter 1995).

For purposes of discussion, this chapter has suggested four dominant styles in writing on Chinese history by American and European scholars in recent years. These four – the Fairbank style, the 'critical' or modernist style, the postmodern style and the cultural-studies style – are not meant to be posed in a successive or

---

22 For recent work in this style see Zito and Barlow 1994.
23 A further recent treatment of the Macartney expedition is also Peyrefitte.

evolutionary relation to one another. All are represented in the current field of China studies, and all are in a continuous process of mutual influence and interaction. Nevertheless, the epistemological and methodological premises of each of these styles is distinct, and has a distinctive product. It is hoped that this chapter has provided a meaningful introduction to those who are not specialists in the field, and has stimulated the thinking of those who are.

REFERENCES

Anderson, P. (1974) *Lineages of the Absolutist State*, London.

Andors, P. (1983) *The Unfinished Liberation of Chinese Women, 1949–1980*, Bloomington, IN.

Anquetil, L.-P. (1800) *A Summary of Universal History ... Exhibiting the Rise. Decline, and Revolutions of the Different Nations of the World, from the Creation to the Present Time*, London.

Banno, M. (1964) *China and the West, 1858–1861*, Cambridge, MA.

Beeching, J. (1975) *The Chinese Opium Wars*, New York.

Benson, L. (1993) 'A much married woman: marriage and divorce in Xinjiang 1850–1950, with historical, social, and juridicial commentaries, *Muslim World* 83 (July/October): 227–47.

Bernhardt, K. and Huang, P. C. (eds) (1994) *Civil Law in Qing and Republican China*, Stanford.

Bodde, D. and Morris, C. (1967) *Law in Imperial China, Exemplified by 190 Ch'ing Dynasty Cases. Translated from the Hsing-an hui-lan*. Cambridge, MA.

Brook, T. (ed.) (1989) *The Asiatic Mode of Production in China*, Armonk, NY.

Carr, C. (1992) *Devil Soldier: The Story of Frederick Townsend Ward*, New York.

Chang, H-C. [1964] (1970) *Commissioner Lin and the Opium War*, Cambridge, MA.

Clarke, P. and Gregory, J. S. (eds) (1982) *Western Reports on Taiping: A Selection of Documents*, Honolulu.

Cohen P. (1984) *Discovering History in China: American Historical Writing on the Recent Chinese Past*, New York.

—— (1992) 'The contested past: the Boxers as history and myth', *Journal of Asian Studies* 51 (February): 82–113.

Craig, C. (1991) *Superfluous Things: Material Culture and Social Status in Early Modern China*, Cambridge.

Crossley, P. K. (1990a) *Orphan Warriors: Three Manchu Generations and the End of the Qing World*, Princeton.

—— (1990b) 'Thinking about ethnicity in early modern China', *Late Imperial China* 11(1): 1–35.

—— (1997) *A Translucent Mirror: History and Identity in Qing Imperial Ideology*, Berkeley.

Curwen, C. (1976) *Taiping Rebel: The Deposition of Li Hsiu-ch'eng*, Cambridge.

Davis, N. Z. (1988) 'History's two bodies', *American Historical Review* 93: 1–30.

Dikötter, F. (1992) *The Discourse of Race in Modern China*, Stanford.

—— (1994) 'Racial identities in China: context and meaning', *China Quarterly* 38 (June): 404–12.

—— (1995) *Sex, Culture and Society in Modern China*, London.

Du, S-R. and Han, Q. (1992) 'The contributions of French Jesuits to Chinese science in the seventeenth and eighteenth centuries', *Impact of Science on Society* 167: 265–75.

Duara, P. (1988) *Culture, Power, and the State: Rural North China, 1900–1942*, Stanford.

Duberman, M. B., Vicinus, M. and Chauncey, G. (eds) (1989) *Hidden from History: Reclaiming the Gay and Lesbian Past*, New York.

654

Dunn, S. (1982) *The Fall and Rise of the Asiatic Mode of Production*, London and Boston, MA.

Eberhard, W. (1982) *China's Minorities: Yesterday and Today*, Belmont, CA.

Elvin, M. (1973) *The Pattern of the Chinese Past: A Social and Economic Interpretation*, Stanford.

—— (1986) 'A working definition of "modernity"?', *Past and Present* 113 (November): 209–13.

Epstein, I. (1964) *From Opium War to Liberation*, 2nd, enlarged revised edn, Peking.

Esherick, J. (1976) *Reform and Revolution in China: The 1911 Revolution in Hunan and Hubei*, Berkeley.

—— (1987) *The Origins of the Boxer Uprising*, Berkeley.

Evans, P. (1988) *John King Fairbank and the American Misunderstanding of China*, Oxford and New York (Chinese translation, Shanghai, 1995).

Fairbank, J. K. (1953–69) *Trade and Diplomacy on the China Coast: The Opening of the Treaty Ports, 1842–1854*, 2 vols, Cambridge, MA.

—— (ed.) (1968) *The Chinese World Order: Traditional China's Foreign Relations*, Cambridge, MA.

Fairbank, J. K. and Reischauer, E. O. (1960–5) *A History of East Asian Civilization*, Cambridge, MA.

Fairbank, J. K. and Têng, S-Y., T. (1942) 'Tributary trade and China's relations with the West', *Far Eastern Quarterly* 1(2): 129–49.

Fairbank, J. K., Banno, M. and Yamamoto, S. [1955] (1971) *Japanese Studies of Modern China: A Bibliographical Guide to Historical and Social-Science Research on the 19th and 20th Centuries*, Cambridge, MA.

Fairbank, J. K., Bruner, K. F. and Matheson, E. M. (1975) *I.G. in Peking: Letters of Robert Hart, Chinese Maritime Customs, 1868–1907*, 2 vols, Cambridge, MA.

Fairbank, J. K., Reischauer, E. O. and Craig, A. M. (1965) *East Asia, the Modern Transformation*, Cambridge, MA.

Fairbank, J. K., Reischauer, E. O. and Craig, A. M. (1989) *East Asia: Tradition and Transformation*, rev. edn, Cambridge MA.

Farquhar, J. and Hevia, J. L. (1993) 'Culture and postwar American historiography of China', *positions* 1(2) (Fall): 486–525.

Fay, P. W. (1975) *The Opium War, 1840–1842: Barbarians in the Celestial Empire in the Early Part of the Nineteenth Century and the War by which they Forced her Gates Ajar*, Chapel Hill, NC.

Feuerwerker, A. (ed.) (1968) *History in Communist China*, Cambridge, MA.

Fogel, J. (1984a) 'A new direction in Japanese sinology', *Harvard Journal of Asiatic Studies* 44 (June): 225–47.

—— (1984b) *Politics and Sinology; The Case of Naitō Kōnan (1866–1934)*, Cambridge, MA.

Franklin, M. A. (1989) *The Chinese Sex-Gender System, Party Policy, and the Education of Women*, East Lansing, MI.

Friedmann, E. (1974) *Backward Toward Revolution: The Chinese Revolutionary Party*, Berkeley and Los Angeles.

Geertz, C. (1984) 'Culture and social change: the Indonesian case', *Man* 19 (December): 511–32.

Ghosh, S. K. (1984) 'Marx on India', *Monthly Review* 35 (January): 39–53.

Gilmartin, C. K. *et al.* (eds) (1994) *Engendering China; Women, Culture, and the State*, Cambridge, MA.

Gladney, D. C. (1991) *Muslim Chinese: Ethnic Nationalism in the People's Republic*, Cambridge, MA.

Gordon, L. and Shulzan, F. J. (1972) *Doctoral Dissertations on China: A Bibliography of Studies in Western Languages, 1945–1970*, Seattle.

Graebner, N. A. (ed.) (1977) *Nationalism and Communism in Asia; The American Response*, Lexington, MA.

Hershatter, G. (1993) 'The subaltern talks back: reflections on subaltern theory and Chinese history', *Positions* 1(1) (Spring): 103–30.

Hevia, J. (1995) *Cherishing Men from Afar: Qing Guest Ritual and the Macartney Embassy of 1793*, Chicago.

Hinsch, B. (1990) *Passions of the Cut Sleeve: The Male Homosexual Tradition in China*, Berkeley.

Hom, S. K. (1994) 'Engendering Chinese legal studies: gatekeeping, master discourses, and other challenges', *Signs* 19 (Summer): 1020–47.

Honig, E. (1992) *Creating Chinese Ethnicity: Subei People in Shanghai, 1850–1980*, New Haven, CT.

—— and Hershatter, G. (1988) *Personal Voices: Chinese Women in the 1980s*, Stanford.

Horowitz, D. (1971) 'Politics and knowledge: an unorthodox history of modern China studies', *Bulletin of Concerned Asian Scholars* 3(3–4).

Huang, P. C. (1985) *The Peasant Economy and Social Change in North China*, Stanford.

—— (1990) *The Peasant Family and Rural Development in the Yangzi Delta, 1350–1988*, Stanford.

Inglis, B. (1976) *The Opium War*, London.

Iriye, A. (1988) 'Reischauer, Fairbank and American East Asian relations', *Diplomatic History* 12 (Summer): 329–39.

Jaksic, M. (1985) 'The theory of modes of production and changes in international economic relations', *Journal of Contemporary Asia* 5(3): 361–74.

—— (1990) 'Exploitation in the model of capitalism and in the Asian mode of production', *Journal of Contemporary Asia* 20: 224–38.

Jaschok, M. and Miers, S. (eds) (1994) *Women and Chinese Patriarchy: Submission, Servitude, and Escape*, Hong Kong.

Johnson, C. (1962) *Peasant Nationalism and Communist Power: The Emergence of Revolutionary China, 1937–1945*, Stanford.

Judd, E. R. (1994) *Gender and Power in Rural North China*, Stanford.

Kim, K.-H. (1980) *The Last Phase of the East Asian World Order: Korea, Japan, and the Chinese Empire, 1860–1882*, Berkeley.

Krader, L. (1975) *The Asiatic Mode of Production: Sources, Development and Critique in the Writings of Karl Marx*, Assen.

Kuhn, P. A [1970] (1980) *Rebellion and its Enemies in Late Imperial China: Militarization and Social Structure, 1796–1864*, Cambridge, MA.

Kuo, P.-C. (1935) *A Critical Study of the First Anglo-Chinese War, with Documents*, Shanghai.

Lavely, W. (1990) 'Chinese demography: the state of the field', *Journal of Asian Studies* 49: 807–34.

Li, L. M. (1991) 'Life and death in a Chinese famine: infanticide as a demographic consequence of the 1935 Yellow River flood', *Comparative Studies in Society and History* 33 (July): 466–510.

Maisels, C. K. (1987) 'Models of social evolution: trajectories from the Neolithic to the state', *Man* 22 (June): 331–59.

Mann, S. (1987) *Local Merchants and the Chinese Bureaucracy, 1750–1950*, Stanford.

Marks, R. (1985) 'The state of the China field: or, the China field and the state', *Modern China* 11(4) (October): 461–509.

Mehdi, M. (1988) 'A review of the controversy around the Asiatic mode of production', *Journal of Contemporary Asia* 18(2): 207–19.

Michael, F. and Chang, C-L. (1971) *The Taiping Rebellion*, 3 vols, Seattle.

Miyakawa, H. (1955) 'An outline of the Naïto hypothesis and its effects on Japanese studies of China, *Far Eastern Quarterly* 14: 533–52.

Mote, F. W. (1961) 'The growth of Chinese despotism: a critique of Wittfogel's oriental despotism as applied to China', *Oriens Extremus* 8: 1–41.

Myers, R. H. (1991) 'How did the modern Chinese economy develop? – a review article', *Journal of Asian Studies* 50 (August): 604–33.

Nahm, A. C. (1988) *Korea: Tradition and Transformation: A History of the Korean People*, Elizabeth, NJ.

Naquin, S. (1976) *Millenarian Rebellion in China: The Eight Trigrams Uprising of 1813*, New Haven, CT.

Nathan, A. J. (1985) *Chinese Democracy*, Berkeley.

—— (1993) 'Is Chinese culture distinctive? – a review article', *Journal of Asian Studies* 52 (November): 923–36.

Ng, V. (1987) 'Ideology and sexuality: rape laws in Qing China', *Journal of Asian Studies* 46 (Feb.): 57–70.

—— (1990) *Madness in Late Imperial China: From Illness to Deviance*, Norman, OK.

—— (1994) 'Sexual abuse of daughters-in-law in Qing China: cases from the *Xing'an huilan*', *Feminist Studies* 20: 373–91.

O'Leary, B. (1989) *The Asiatic Mode of Production: Oriental Despotism, Historical Materialism, and Indian History*, Oxford.

Ono, K. (1989) *Chinese Women in a Century of Revolution, 1850–1950*, ed. J. A. Fogel, Stanford.

Perdue P. C. (1987) *Exhausting the Earth: State and Peasant in Hunan, 1500–1850*, Cambridge, MA.

Peyrefitte, A. *et al.* (1922) *The Immobile Empire*, New York.

Polachek, J. M. (1992) *The Inner Opium War*, Cambridge, MA.

Rankin, M. B. (1986) *Elite Activism and Political Transformation in China: Zhejiang Province, 1865–1911*, Stanford.

Rawski, E. S. (1972) *Agricultural Change and the Peasant Economy of South China*, Cambridge, MA.

—— (1991) 'Research themes in Ming–Qing socioeconomic history – the state of the field', *Journal of Asian Studies* 50 (February): 84–111.

Rawski, T. G. (1989) *Economic Growth in Prewar China*, Berkeley.

—— and Li, L. M. (eds) (1992) *Chinese History in Economic Perspectives*, Berkeley.

Roberts, M. (1971) 'The structure and direction of contemporary China studies', *Bulletin of Concerned Asian Scholars* 3(3–4) (Summer–Fall).

Rowe, W. T. (1984) *Hankow: Commerce and Society in a Chinese City, 1796–1889*, Stanford.

—— (1989) *Hankow: Conflict and Community in a Chinese City, 1796–1895*, Stanford.

Said, E. (1978) *Orientalism*, New York.

—— (1993) *Culture and Imperialism*, New York.

—— (1995) 'East isn't East: the impending end of orientalism', *Times Literary Supplement* 4792 (3 February): 3–6.

Sawer, M. (1977) *Marxism and the Question of the Asiatic Mode of Production*, The Hague.

Schoppa, R. K. (1982) *Chinese Elites and Political Change: Zhejiang Province in the Early Twentieth Century*, Cambridge, MA.

Schwartz, B. (1951) *Chinese Communism and the Rise of Mao*, Cambridge, MA.

Shulman, F. (1978) *Doctoral Dissertations on China 1971–1975: A Bibliography in Western Languages*, Seattle.

Skinner, G. W. (1964–5) 'Marketing and social structure in rural China', *Journal of Asian Studies* 24: 3–43.

—— (1985a) 'Presidential address: the structure of Chinese history', *Journal of Asian Studies* 44 (February): 271–92.

—— (1985b) 'Rural marketing in China: repression and revival', *China Quarterly* 103 (September): 393–413.

Spence, J. (1966) *Ts'ao Yin and the K'ang-hsi Emperor; Bondservant and Master*, New Haven, CT.
—— (1978) *The Death of Woman Wang*, New York.
—— (1984) *The Memory Palace of Mattee Ricci*, New York.
—— (1988) *The Question of Hu*, New York.
Stacey, J. (1983) *Patriarchy and Socialist Revolution in China*, Berkeley.
Strand, D. (1989) *Rickshaw Beijing: City, People and Politics in the 1920s*, Berkeley.
Tan, C. (1978) *China and the Brave New World: A Study of the Origins of the Opium War (1840–42)*, Durham, NC.
Tao, W-Z. (1992) 'John King Fairbank and Sino-US relations', *Beijing Review* 35 (25 May): 33–5.
Têng, S-Y. (1971) *The Taiping Rebellion and the Western Powers: A Comprehensive Survey*, Oxford.
—— and Fairbank, J. K. (eds) [1954] (1963) *China's Response to the West: A Documentary Survey 1839–1923*, Cambridge, MA.
—— and Knight, B. [1950] (1969) *An Annotated Bibliography of Selected Chinese Reference Works*, Cambridge, MA.
Torchinov, E. A. (1992) 'Philosophical studies (Sinology and Indology) in St. Petersburg (Leningrad), 1945–1990', *Philosophy East and West* 42 (April): 327–33.
Tseng, Chi-fen (1993) *Testimony of a Confucian Woman: The Autobiography of Mrs. Nie Zeng Jifen, 1852–1942*, tr. and ed. T. L. Kennedy, Atlanta, GA.
Waley-Cohen, J. (1993) 'China and Western technology in the late eighteenth century', *American Historical Review* 98 (December): 1525–44.
Wang, Y-C, (1982) 'Notes on the sprouts of capitalism' in Albert Feuerwerker (ed.) *Chinese Economic and Social History from Song to 1800*, Ann Arbor: Unversity Center for Chinese Studies.
Weller, R. (1994) *Resistance, Chaos, and Control in China: Taiping Rebels, Taiwanese Ghosts, and Tiananmen*, Seattle.
Will, P.-E. (1990) *Bureaucracy and Famine in Eighteenth-Century China*, tr. E. Forster, Stanford.
Wittfogel, K. (1957) *Oriental Despotism: A Comparative Study of Total Power*, New Haven, CT.
Wixted, J. T. (1993) *Japanese Scholars of China: A Bibliographical Handbook*, Princeton.
Wolf, M. (1984) *Revolution Postponed: Women in Contemporary China*, Stanford.
—— and Witke, R. (eds) (1975) *Women in Chinese Society*, Stanford.
Wong, R. B. (1991) *Nourish the People: The State Civilian Granary System in China, 1650–1850*, Ann Arbor.
Wright, M. C. (ed.) (1968) *China in Revolution: The First Phase, 1900–1913*, New Haven, CT.
Wright, M. C. (1971) *The Last Stand of Chinese Conservatism: The T'ung-chih Restoration, 1862–1874*, New York.
Yang, L-S. (1961) 'Toward a study of dynastic configurations in Chinese history', in Y. Lien-sheng, *Studies in Chinese Institutional History*, Cambridge, MA.
Young, M. B. (ed.) (1973) *Women in China: Studies in Social Change and Feminism*, Ann Arbor.
Zelin, M. (1985) *The Magistrate's Tale: Rationalizing Fiscal Reform in Eighteenth-Century Ch'ing*, Berkeley.
Zhongguo jindai shi congshu bianxiezu [Compilation Group for the 'History of Modern China' Series] (1976) *The Taiping Revolution*, Peking.
Zito, A. and Barlow, T. E. (eds) (1994) *Body, Subject and Power in China*, Chicago.

25

THE ENGLISH-LANGUAGE HISTORIOGRAPHY OF MODERN JAPAN[1]

Alan Smith

It is widely accepted by historians that modern Japanese history begins with the Meiji Restoration of 1868 when the government of the Tokugawa shoguns was ended and direct imperial rule – in theory at least – restored. A few scholars, for example Professor Hane (1983), argue that the majority of the Japanese people, the peasants and women, were so underprivileged and oppressed until the reforms of the American Occupation of Japan between 1945 and 1952 that modern Japanese history only begins after the Second World War. Others would see the Occupation as the beginning of 'contemporary' rather than modern Japan, but in any event stress on the Occupation makes a point with which few historians would disagree; the Occupation is one of the two greatest turning-points of recent Japanese history, the Meiji Restoration being the other.

If we argue that the Meiji Restoration was the beginning of modern Japan, a survey of modern Japanese historiography should begin with discussion of the Restoration's origins. There would be a good deal of agreement among Western historians that the Restoration was a result of three interlocking sets of factors: of long-term social and economic developments within Japan – notably changes in the composition and wealth of the samurai and merchant estates and of the peasantry; of the intrusions of Western powers from the 1850s onwards; and of political disputes within the ruling elite, the samurai. The same historians would, of course, differ greatly as to the relative importance to be attached to each of these sets of factors. The political disputes, though they came to a head during the 1850s and 1860s, were longstanding. The domains of Choshu and Satsuma, which took the lead in the overthrow of the shogunate, had been its traditional enemies since the battle of

---

1 This chapter deals with works written in English or translated from Japanese into English and, with rare exceptions, with scholarship published since 1945. The very high percentage of books published in the United States reflects the continuing importance of Japanese history in America since the Occupation of 1945–52.

Sekigahara in 1600, though it was the circumstances of the Western intrusion in the mid-nineteenth century which gave their long-term political resentments an opportunity to make themselves felt. The social and economic developments were centred on the rise of the merchants (Sheldon 1958) and the changing composition of the peasantry (Smith 1959), with the growth of a wealthy peasant elite which by the early nineteenth century had become a body of entrepreneurs, often referred to as rural merchants. The bulk of the peasantry have traditionally been seen as existing in a state of increasing immiseration during the Tokugawa period, but persuasive revisionist work notably by Hanley and Yamamura (1977), has painted a very different picture, suggesting that most peasants were becoming more prosperous even while the rural elite of peasant entrepreneurs considerably outstripped the others in growing wealth. Meanwhile the samurai were becoming relatively – though probably not absolutely – poorer (Yamamura 1971). The ruling group within the shogunate was therefore already under severe pressure when the Western powers made their appearance from 1853 onwards, and the difficulties already described were compounded by the lack of really able shoguns – there was no outstanding ruler between Yoshimune in the early eighteenth century and Keiki who got his chance, too late, only in the last year of shogunal rule; by disputes within the shogunal bureaucracy; by the growing threat from the imperial institution, deprived of all power during the Tokugawa period but, at any rate in Japanese theory, representing an unbroken line of emperors going back for two millennia and, since the eighteenth century, the subject of analyses by men like Motoori Norinaga and Hirata Atsutane who stressed imperial legitimacy and drew attention to the delegated role of the shogun (Webb 1968; Earl 1964; Harootunian 1970). The Western powers, which entered this scene of political, social, economic and intellectual instability in the 1850s, demanded the opening of Japan to Western trade and settlement, and the upheavals which resulted from their demands led in 1867/8 to the overthrow of the shogunate and the theoretical restoration of direct imperial rule. The splendid syntheses of Totman (1980) and Beasley (1972) which discuss these events in detail, though from rather different angles, stress the strands in historical thinking which see the Restoration as essentially a nationalist revolt against the Western intruders. This interpretation, which goes back to a notable article published in 1956 (Yoshio and Hall 1956) and which has received and continues to receive wide support from Western (and now as well from some Japanese) experts on the Restoration, can incorporate work like that of Craig (1961) on Choshu, which stresses the local particularism which still existed amidst this growing Japanese nationalism, but other historians like Norman (1940) and Huber (1981) have laid more emphasis on internal social and economic developments in explaining the events of 1867/8. Norman, much influenced by Marxist theory, saw the Restoration as a revolt by lower samurai and merchants at a time of serious peasant unrest against a 'feudal'[2] system dominated by shogun and samurai, while

---

2   There has been vigorous debate among historians about the nature and, indeed, the very existence of Japanese feudalism. A good introduction is Hall 1968.

Huber argues that these lower samurai should be regarded as a merit intelligentsia excluded by their relatively undistinguished birth from the upper reaches of a social and political system dominated by high-born samurai who were often of limited abilities.

While vigorous debate continues about the relative weight to be attached to each of the major sets of factors which led to the Restoration, it is also unabated about the Restoration's consequences. The new ruling elite of lower-ranking samurai dominated by men from the Choshu and Satsuma domains were determined to strengthen Japan in order to achieve as soon as possible both domestic security and equality with the Western powers in international affairs. As a result they embarked on a major programme of reforms which so transformed Japan's domestic and international situation that the country emerged by the end of the Meiji emperor's reign in 1912 secure at home and a colonial power in its own right, which treated on terms of equality with the West, an equality symbolized by the Anglo-Japanese treaty of 1902, which has been discussed in a fine work of scholarship by Ian Nish (1966).

The Japanese word *ishin*, usually translated into English as 'restoration', should more properly appear as renovation and it is significant that the latter term, which points to the future as well as to the past, is pleasing to those historians who see the Restoration as a revolution, stressing the long-term political, social, economic, military and intellectual changes which flowed from it.[3] A powerful school of Japanese historians, influenced by the Marxist thought which became so widespread among Japanese intellectuals in the period between the two World Wars, have debated, both during the 1920s and 1930s and in the years after the Second World War, whether the Restoration should be regarded as a successful or as a failed bourgeois revolution. The question had practical implications for the attitudes of left-wing political activists between the wars, as historians of the Rono-ha school, who believed that the Restoration was a successful bourgeois revolution, were able to dream of an immediate socialist revolution, while those of the Koza-ha school, who believed that it was a failed revolution, maintained that both bourgeois and socialist revolutions were still necessary in Japan's historical evolution. Some of these debates came to be conducted in highly theoretical terms but the dispute also produced a flood of detailed research on nineteenth-century Japanese social and economic history. This has until recently been largely inaccessible to those Western scholars who do not read Japanese, but a recent book by Germaine Hoston (1986) now provides a good English introduction to the literature.

It is hardly surprising that these Marxist interpretations had little appeal for the empirically minded American historians who came to the forefront in Western studies of Japan in the years after the Second World War, a period dominated by the 'Cold War' against the Soviet Union. In the 1960s, following a conference at Hakone in Japan, they launched a series of studies based on modernization theory,

---

3   In this connection, the subtitle of a recent collection of interpretative essays is significant, Nagai Michio and Miguel Irrutia, *Meiji Ishin: Restoration and Revolution* (1985).

which, they hoped, would enable them to produce 'value-free' work on post-Restoration history.[4] During the Meiji period Japan not only entered the mainstream of international life but also recast many of its domestic institutions along Western lines. This was, in the eyes of both Japan's rulers and of foreign observers, an attempt to catch up with the great modern powers of the West, and the modernization school of Western historians which has been so influential since the 1960s has had plenty of material to work upon: the creation of a centralized nation-state to replace the divided Tokugawa polity; the abolition of samurai privileges and the introduction of a conscript army; effective reform of the taxation system; education reforms which created an almost entirely literate population; the creation of a constitution and of political parties; fundamental legal reforms based on Western models; the creation of a national civil bureaucracy and of a modern military establishment; the development of Japanese industry, so that by the end of the nineteenth century Japan had made the 'take-off' into self-sustaining industrial growth. These domestic reforms, in turn, enabled Japan to transform her international position between 1868 and 1912 from one of weakness and inferiority to the Western powers to one in which she dealt with them on broadly equal terms.

By examining these dramatic changes in terms of modernization theory the historians involved undoubtedly added to knowledge and understanding of post-Restoration history. On the other hand, from the 1970s onwards critics mounted increasing attacks upon their judgements, pointing out that they tended to take a far more favourable view of Japanese developments not only in the Meiji years but over the whole period from 1868 to 1945 than the majority of their Japanese colleagues working in the same fields. Critics challenged above all the claims of members of the modernization school that they had gone far in introducing value-free judgements in their studies. Dower (1975) and Hane (1982), especially, have produced powerful critiques of their methods and conclusions, arguing that they have implicitly if not explicitly favoured the elite groups who controlled Japanese society at the expense of the mass of the population: the peasants, the industrial workers, women and outcasts, all groups which, Hane (1982) argues, led lives which varied from the barely tolerable to the totally wretched. No reader of his descriptions of the conditions of the poorest peasants or of female textile workers can fail to appreciate the very heavy costs which modernization imposed on the most vulnerable sections of the Japanese community, but it is perhaps also fair to point out that wretched conditions were also common within advanced Western nations during the processes of industrialization and modernization.

English-language scholarship, so full of the ideas of the modernization school, is,

---

4 A number of influential volumes were published by Princeton University Press as a result of the researches of the modernization school: M. B. Jansen (ed.) *Changing Japanese Attitudes Toward Modernization* (1965); W. W. Lockwood (ed.) *The State and Economic Enterprise in Japan* (1965); R. P. Dore (ed.) *Aspects of Social Change in Modern Japan* (1967); R. E. Ward (ed.) *Political Development in Modern Japan* (1968); D. H. Shiveley (ed.) *Tradition and Modernization in Japanese Culture* (1971); J. W. Morley (ed.) *Dilemmas of Growth in Prewar Japan* (1971).

as we have seen, only beginning to absorb the details of the Marxist debates of the 1920s onwards about the course and meaning of the country's modern history. It is only beginning, too, to absorb the ideas of the 'people's history' which has been influential in Japan since the 1960s but has only recently begun to appear in English translations,[5] though it was drawn to the attention of English-language scholars over a decade ago in a notable article by Carol Gluck (1978–9). About the same time as the American modernization theorists were launching their views in the scholarly world a group of Japanese historians, rejecting both Marxist and modernization theory, began to search for what they called an 'integral' or 'indigenous' approach to Japanese history, centring on 'the people'. People's historians divide society into two parts, the elite and the rest of the population. In their concentration on the bulk of the population they are obviously closer to the Marxists than to the modernization theorists, but they criticize Marxist historiography as being too concerned with endless ongoing debates, such as that over the nature of the Meiji Restoration. They themselves have traditionally concentrated on rural history, seeing the real Japan as village Japan, and stress the importance of studying everyday life in the localities. They have devoted special attention to village communities, symbols of the interdependence of rural people, and have shown their rejection of Marxist theory by abandoning analytical frameworks in favour of the accumulation of descriptive material about the people and communities which they study. As Professor Gluck emphasizes, because the Western world in a general sense and Western historians in particular are so often identified with the establishment and the elites in Japan, people's history, by de-emphasizing that establishment and these elites, also de-emphasizes the role of the West in Japan's modern history.

The American modernization theorists, in contrast, who so often stress the role of the West as exemplar, can point, *inter alia*, to the creation of the Meiji constitution of 1889 as a clear example of extensive borrowing from Europe. The detailed studies which have been published about the events preceding and surrounding the drafting and promulgation of the constitution (Beckmann 1957; Akita 1967; Pittau 1967; Siemes 1966) have revealed especially the strong German influences throughout the process, influences very obvious during the mission to Europe in 1882–3 of Ito Hirobumi – soon to be Japan's first prime minister – to survey Western models. He visited Austria, France and Britain as well as Germany, but after he returned to Japan it became obvious that the major foreign impact would be German. When the actual drafting of the constitution began in 1885, six men played major roles. Four of them, including Ito himself, were Japanese; the other two were Germans. The final document has been appositely described by one Western scholar as 'a remarkable combination of western political technology and traditional Japanese political ideas' (Hall 1970: 297). The political theory behind it was firmly Japanese: it was freely granted by the divinely descended and sovereign emperor to his loyal subjects. There was only one slight

---

5 Notably, Irokawa Daikichi, *Meiji no bunka* (1970), translation edited by Marius B. Jansen as *The Culture of the Meiji Period* (1985).

loophole in this implied absolutism. Article 4 provided that the government should be conducted 'according to the constitution' and this opened the way for theorists to discuss the possibility that there might be a law above the emperor. The prime minister and members of the new Cabinet, which had been created in 1885, were responsible to the emperor alone and not to the Diet. The constitution provided the legal framework for what scholars have come to describe as 'the emperor system', the pre-1945 Japanese political system within which the emperor theoretically wielded supreme power. In reality, though everything was done in the emperor's name, he himself did not normally make political decisions. In that situation a number of elites competed for power in the state and important scholarship has been produced analysing these elites and debating their respective influences at different times during the fifty or so years before the Second World War. There were at least five elites: party politicians; the civil bureaucracy; the military; big business; and the imperial advisers, with whom can be associated the peerage and the Privy Council. In addition, there has been debate about how much influence Emperor Hirohito did exercise and could have exercised in the dramatic events of 1931 to 1945.

The beginnings of political parties in Japan can be traced to the popular-rights movement of the 1870s, but throughout the period up to the end of the First World War cabinets, though they might contain party politicians, were dominated by ministers drawn from the bureaucracy. From 1913 onwards, however, when there were two major competing parties in the Diet, pressure for government through party cabinets grew, and between 1918 and 1932, with the exception of the period 1922–4, Japan had party cabinets, with the premiership passing between the leaders of the two main political parties. During this period too the previously very small electorate was substantially expanded, first of all in 1920 and then, much more significantly, in 1925, when all men over 25 were given the vote. From 1932 onwards, however, with serious economic difficulties and growing violence within Japan and with Japanese military ventures on the Asian mainland, which brought international condemnation, there was a reversion to non-party cabinets, headed by either military men or civilian bureaucrats. Finally, in 1940, all political parties were dissolved. This rise and fall of the parties in the late nineteenth and early twentieth centuries has been described and analysed in some excellent works (Scalapino 1962; Duus 1968; Berger 1977), and it should be noted that it was underpinned on the theoretical side by Minobe's theory of the constitution, often referred to as the 'emperor organ theory'. Minobe, a law professor at Tokyo imperial university, argued that sovereignty lay not in the emperor personally but in the state and that the emperor ruled as the highest organ of the state. The Diet, he maintained, was an organ representing the people and grounded directly in the constitution, an idea which both encouraged and legitimated party cabinets. Minobe's theory was very influential – though never universally accepted – in academic circles during the 1920s, but in the mid-1930s ultranationalists mounted a ferocious campaign against his ideas, accusing him of *lèse-majesté*. He was driven out of academic life and narrowly escaped assassination in 1936. The career of Minobe, which has been well dissected by Frank Miller (1965), provides a vivid commentary on the varying fortunes of Japanese political parties during the 1920s and 1930s.

A second elite was the civil bureaucracy. Tokugawa Japan had a long tradition of bureaucratic rule, both in the shogun's lands and in the daimyo domains and after the Restoration, in the 1880s and 1890s, a national civil service recruited by competitive examinations was established. This meritocracy, responsible to the emperor and subject to only limited control by the political parties, conducted the day-to-day government of the country. The highly trained upper civil servants numbered about 15,000 in 1927 and scholars who have analysed their role all agree on their vital importance in the government of Japan between the late Meiji period and the end of the Second World War (Quigley 1932: ch. 9; Silberman 1974; Spaulding 1971).

The power of the third elite, the military, was entrenched, first of all, in the 'right of autonomous command' and, second, in the effective veto which the leaders of the army and the navy held over the formation of cabinets. The first of these rights, which dated from the creation of a General Staff System in 1878, meant that generals in the field could take operational decisions there without consulting the cabinet, even though these operations might have the most important political consequences. This right, when it was exercised in China in the 1930s, had the most profound consequences for Japan. The veto over the formation of cabinets arose from the right of the armed services to approve the choice of war and navy ministers, who were always generals and admirals. These huge powers, exercised at the expense of civilian politicians, seem even more dramatic in view of the very limited influence of the party politicians in military affairs. The whole situation was complicated further by the endemic rivalries both between and within the army and navy, and the work which has been done on the military has, therefore, revealed an elite which was both immensely powerful and very divided (Maxon 1957; Crowley 1962; Hackett 1964).

A further elite was big business. The great zaibatsu cartels, huge conglomerates with financial, industrial and commercial interests, which reached the height of their power in the inter-war years, had important connections with both the bureaucracy and the political parties. Bureaucrats in post who provided help to businessmen could expect sinecure jobs in business when they retired, and the zaibatsu contributed large sums to the campaign funds of the political parties, with the two greatest zaibatsu, Mitsui and Mitsubishi, being traditionally linked with the two main political parties, the Seiyukai and the Minseito (Tiedemann 1971; Roberts 1973; Hirschmeier and Yui 1981).

Finally, the emperor's advisers wielded great influence. They consisted of the *genro* and the leading members of the imperial household, and there is some excellent scholarship on their roles. The *genro* (or elder statesmen) were the most important of the Meiji oligarchs. Until 1901 one or other of them headed the government of the day. After that they acted as elder statesmen, advising the emperor on the appointment of prime ministers as well as on other important affairs of state. After 1924 only one *genro*, Prince Saionji, was left alive and in the 1930s he fought an increasingly hopeless battle against the increasing power of the military.[6] The imperial household ministry, set up in 1885, not only served the emperor's personal needs but provided him with advice on political and military affairs and Titus, in an important book (Titus 1974), has shown how its higher officials carried out their duties. A Western-style peerage had been created in 1884 and a Privy Council, an advisory body to the emperor, had been set up in 1888. Both can be regarded as part of the imperial establishment.

One subject which has provoked considerable debate in the West as well as in Japan is the role of Emperor Hirohito in the events of 1931–45. Some scholars, like Sheldon, stress that he saw himself as a constitutional monarch, normally obliged to follow the recommendations of his ministers and other advisers, but argue that in private he consistently advocated a moderate line of action, always doing his best to curb the more reckless ambitions of the military. When the political machinery of the state was in disarray in August 1945 and he had to make a personal decision he voted for Japan's unconditional surrender to the Allies at a time when the preservation of the imperial institution itself seemed to be endangered by the wrath of the victors. Other historians, like Bix (1992) in a recent article, have been much more ready to assert his war responsibilities and it is clear that the issue will provoke continuing debate.

Another subject of controversy is the precise balance of power within the elite groups at any given moment during the pre-1945 era. In the Meiji period attention has usually been focused on the *genro*, in the 1920s the political parties are often seen at the centre of the stage and in the 1930s the armed forces seem predominant. The interpretation of the 1920s as 'Taisho democracy' (the Taisho emperor reigned between 1912 and 1926) has been understandably attractive to Western historians, who have stressed that this was the era of party governments and who have seen the introduction of universal male suffrage in 1925 as a pivotal event. It has also been argued, however, that the political parties of the Taisho period were corrupt, selfish and limited in their conceptions of democracy – they were unwilling to widen it to envisage social and economic justice for the peasants and the urban proletariat. In this latter line of argument the 'democracy' of the 1920s was largely a sham and there was much more continuity between that decade and the militaristic 1930s than the proponents of 1920s democratization would allow.[7]

What does seem clear is that the elite structure persisted throughout the Pacific war. Professor Shillony (1981) has demonstrated this beyond much doubt. He draws attention to the restraints placed on Tojo's power during the war years by the bureaucracy, the Diet, big business and the imperial institution. Japan never became a totalitarian state and Tojo's position never remotely resembled that of Hitler or Mussolini. Shillony's picture undoubtedly gives comfort to the large band of Western historians who are uncomfortable with descriptions – commonplace

---

6 Hackett 1968; Hackett 1971 – Yamagata was one of the most important of the *genro* until his death in 1922; Connors 1987.

7 For discussions of the controversy, Wray and Conroy 1983: 171–98; Hoston 1986: 11ff.

among Japanese historians (e.g. Masao 1969) – of Japan as a fascist state during the 1930s and early 1940s. In a particularly notable and convincing essay in scepticism Professors Duus and Okimoto (1979–80) argue that it is meaningless to speak of a fascist political system in Japan – the emperor's position ensured that no supreme leader like Hitler or Mussolini could come to the fore and there was no mass fascist party – and suggest that 'we should stop pondering why democracy failed in pre-war Japan, and consider instead why fascism failed'.

If the constitution of 1889, which provided the legal framework of Japan's pre-1945 political system, was part of the Meiji oligarchs' modernizing measrures, so in a sense was their embarkation on an imperialist policy in Asia. When the oligarchs looked at the modernized nations of the West which they wished to emulate they saw that all of them were imperialist powers. It is hardly surprising, therefore, that imperialism seemed a natural as well as an attractive path to follow. Japanese imperialism was so bound up with the country's foreign policy that it is artificial to separate the two and Western historians have written with distinction both on Japan's foreign policy in a general sense – here we have, especially, Professor Nish's (1977) analysis – and on the motives, chronology and results of Japanese imperialism in a narrower sense, where Professors Beasley (1987), Myers, Peattie and Duus have made notable contributions (Myers and Peattie 1984; Duus *et al.* 1989). These authors agree that Japan's imperialist ambitions were derived from a variety of motives among which questions of economics and security inevitably loomed large, and in that judgement they echo the views of the writers of more specialized monographs, such as Professors Crowley (1966) and Barnhart (1987). Barnhart's recent book, for example, is a good demonstration of the mingling of economic needs, foreign policy and the quest for empire during the 1920s and 1930s, leading up to the dramatic confrontation with the United States at the beginning of the 1940s.

Japan's constant interactions with the outside world in the years between 1868 and 1945, such a contrast to the isolationism of the Tokugawa period, continued after the Second World War, but on a very different basis. There was almost as dramatic a discontinuity in the country's foreign policy in the years after 1945 as in the period after 1868. Japan's pursuit of an imperialistic and independent foreign policy between 1868 and 1945 was replaced by a clear rejection of all imperialist ambitions and, at least for a time, by an almost complete dependence on the United States in international affairs. Japan's new rulers set out to achieve world respectability through economic strength and the measure of their success can be seen in Japan's crucial position in the world today. The exhausted and impoverished state of 1945 has become the economic superpower of the early 1990s, poised between East and West. As such, Japan has established itself as a new world power centre and found a role for the twenty-first century (Saito 1990; Drifte 1990).

The dramatic discontinuity of Japanese foreign policy in the post-1945 era was one result of the country's defeat in war and of the American occupation. The extent of Japan's plight in 1945 has been well described by Thomas Havens (1978). The war had had a steadily increasing effect on the life of the Japanese people, with mounting inflation, poor, scarce and rationed food, fewer consumer goods each year, higher and higher taxes, forced labour, separated families, long casualty lists from both the war zones and the home front and, from 1944, carpet bombing by American 'planes of the Japanese home islands which left swathes of destruction in almost all the major cities. The Occupation which followed has been described in many general studies, of which Kazuo Kawai's (1960) is probably the best. The American authorities were determined to achieve both the demilitarization and democratization of the country. Japan was deprived of all of the great empire which she had acquired since 1868, her armed forces were dissolved and there was a purge from positions of leadership of those who were believed to have 'participated in Japanese expansion'. On the creative front a new constitution, based on entirely different principles from the Meiji constitution of 1889, was promulgated in 1946, and, among many other reforms, the most important were probably those in land tenure and education.

The constitution completed the theoretical demythologizing of the emperor's position which had begun in early 1946, when he personally renounced any claims to divine or quasi-divine status. Now the constitution vested supreme authority in the people 'with whom resides sovereign power'. The emperor was merely the 'symbol of the state', deriving his position from the will of the people. This was a revolution in the traditional concept of the Japanese polity and the emperor's new role has been well analysed by Titus (1980), though it should be noted that not all Japanese have been happy with the reduced status of the imperial institution, and Hirohito's death in January 1989 produced much speculation both in Japan and abroad about the future of the throne (Crump 1989). The constitution created a Cabinet system with ministers responsible to the Diet, guaranteed the vote to women on the same basis as men (over the age of 20), provided for an independent judiciary, decentralized local government, gave elaborate guarantees of human rights and in the most famous (or notorious) of all its clauses formally renounced the right of Japan to wage war. The establishment of responsible ministerial government seemed to decide once and for all the major problem which had plagued the pre-1945 political system: where did effective power in the state lie? Two of the pre-1945 elites, the military and the imperial advisers, were abolished. Big business was temporarily in eclipse (it revived to rejoin the elite system later), but the civil bureaucracy remained throughout the Occupation and thereafter as a functioning elite. In theory it was now firmly subordinated to the politicians, but in practice things were not so simple and scholars are still discussing vigorously today the actual balance of power between bureaucrats and politicians (Koh 1989).

There was also a fundamental reform of land tenure. Following the creation of a new taxation system for the land at the start of the Meiji period the amount of land held in tenancy rose steadily, reaching about 45 per cent of the total by the early 1940s. The traditional picture of tenant farmers has stressed the difficulties and hardships of their lives as part of that 'underside' of modern Japan about which Hane (1982) has written so eloquently, and recent attempts to present their fate in a more favourable light (Waswo 1977, and especially Smethurst 1986) have not met with general acceptance. That debate seems certain to continue but, whatever its outcome, there is no doubting the fundamental importance of the 1946 land reform, well described by Dore (1959). The abolition of absentee landlordism and the selling of large quantities of land to tenant farmers at easy prices meant that within a few years only about 10 per cent of land was held by tenants. The reform created a group of independent, prosperous farmers who were to be a fundamental support of the conservative political forces which have dominated Japan since the war.

The education reforms built on the very high level of basic literacy which prevailed in pre-war Japan. Already during the Tokugawa period literary levels were high among men (Dore 1965), and the introduction of universal primary education for both boys and girls during the Meiji period produced an almost wholly literate population by the early twentieth century, although advanced secondary and university education was confined to a small minority (Roden 1980). The whole pre-war system was closely controlled by the Ministry of Education in the interests of the state (Hall 1973) and pupils were taught, in ethics courses, the virtues of loyalty to the emperor. The post-war education reforms, in contrast, stressed education for all on a decentralized basis. The school-leaving age was substantially increased, the control of the Education ministry over schools was drastically curtailed and the content of education fundamentally altered, especially at the primary level, with the elimination of the old ethics courses and stress on the values of democratic citizenship.[8] Since the war a higher percentage of children have stayed on at school beyond the compulsory leaving age and more of these have continued their education to a further stage within the vastly expanded university system. Many authorities now argue that the Japanese are the best-educated people in the world and 'objective' tests in subjects like mathematics seem to confirm this view. On the other hand, much of the education consists of hard memory-work and the pressures for achievement clearly have implications for the psychological development of individual Japanese. Recent books by Rohlen (1983) and Duke (1986) stress the efficiency of and striking results obtained by Japanese schools, but Cummings's (1980) argument that the post-war school system has created a more egalitarian society has been strongly challenged. Rohlen, for example, has argued powerfully that the school system creates a good deal less social mobility than is sometimes thought.

Such divisions of opinion about the specific results of the educational reforms are part of a wide-ranging debate about the significance of the Occupation as a whole, a debate which Ward has surveyed in his introduction to a recent volume of essays (Ward and Yoshikazu 1987). As he points out, most historical judgements on the Occupation, especially those by Western scholars, have been favourable; but while the essays confirm this in general they also show the extent to which experts differ over how far the Occupation realized its full potential, especially where democratization is concerned. Here the position of women in modern Japan is clearly relevant.

---

8   Passin 1965 provides an excellent survey of educational developments from the Tokugawa period to the early post-war years.

Late Tokugawa Japan was a patriarchal society in which women's inferiority to men was clear in both theoretical and practical terms, with a woman subject successively during her lifetime to the authority of her father, her husband and her oldest son. In the period after 1868, despite the growth of a feminist movement which has been chronicled by Sharon Sievers (1983), basic attitudes were little changed. The Meiji constitution excluded women from direct participation in the political process, and the civil code of 1898, in all its clauses relating to women, 'reinforced their subordinate, subservient position in Japanese society' (Hunter 1989: 143). This legal inferiority, which was maintained throughout the pre-1945 period, was in theory transformed during the Occupation. Women were given the vote in 1945 and their right to the franchise was enshrined in the 1946 constitution, which guaranteed sexual equality. The new civil code of 1948 formally ended women's subordination to men, asserting their equal rights in all areas of life. Here, however, the words of the Occupation decrees and social realities have remained very far apart. Study of the contemporary Japanese rural scene shows how hard the life of a farm woman can still be, and Alice Cook and Hiroko Hayashi, concentrating on urban life, have concluded that the modern Japanese employment system 'probably exploits women more extensively than is the case in any other industrialized country' (Cook and Hayashi 1980: 2). An important book on middle-class Japanese women shows that, though they are certainly less confined to the house than their mothers were, their primary role continues overwhelmingly to be that of wife and mother; all other daily activities have to be fitted in around that central task (Imamura 1987).

The early post-war years, the period of the Occupation, were a time of severe economic difficulties for the prostrate Japan of 1945, but the greatest historical phenomenon of recent Japanese history has been the 'economic miracle' of the second half of the twentieth century which has transformed the country into the second largest capitalist economy in the world (Japan achieved that position in 1968 when she overtook West Germany in Gross National Product) and arguably the most successful. Since the 1950s her economic performance has continually outstripped that of the other major powers, and during the 1980s experts were debating when rather than if she would overtake the United States in total economic output. This dramatic economic advance has inevitably led to a huge Western literature, both describing the phenomenon and seeking to explain it.

It is worth noting that the remarkable economic growth of the period between the end of the Second World War and 1990 was the accelerated phase of a trend which has been evident throughout the twentieth century. Except for the collapse during the Second World War and for some minor blips during the early 1990s Japan's economy has grown continuously since the Meiji period and historians, in detailing the advances of the second half of the century, are now stressing as well the more modest growth of the first half.[9] One major study which emphasizes continuity between pre-war and post-war developments is Nakamura's (1981) balanced and lucid discussion, which tells the story until the end of the 1970s. The

---

9 See Duus 1988: 14ff., especially the references in note 22.

collective works edited by Patrick and Rosovsky (1976) on the one hand and Yamamura and Yasuba (1987–) on the other are very comprehensive and between them cover the period to the 1980s, while Minami's (1986) important volume adopts a quantitative approach. Among a wide range of valuable studies which discuss more specific aspects of the Japanese economy and also throw light on the general reasons for Japan's success are Cusumano's (1985) study of the automobile industry, which shows, *inter alia*, how sharply Nissan and Toyota have differed from each other in their development, a point which may give pause to those who have talked too glibly of a single 'Japanese management system'; Gordon's (1985) work on labour relations, which shatters some myths about relationships between managers and workers; MacMillan's (1985) study of the workings of the industrial system, stressing its positive aspects; and Chalmers Johnson's (1982) book on the role of the Ministry of International Trade and Industry in economic development. These very different books, taken together, demonstrate beyond much doubt the number and complexity of the factors which explain the economic successes of the post-war years and the difficulty of assigning primacy to any one of them. An interesting additional perspective is provided by Morishima (1982) who believes that in searching for the secrets of Japan's modern economic success it is necessary to go back to religious and cultural developments in the very early periods of Japanese history. Such studies emphasize the success story, but in recent years some authors have begun to question the reality or the endurance of the economic miracle. The works of such sceptics as Woronoff (1986) and Reading (1992) are doubtless useful antidotes to the Japanophile writings of Vogel (1979) and Kahn (1970,) but their more extreme scenarios, notably Reading's prediction of a coming Japanese 'collapse', will not – despite the economic difficulties of the early 1990s – readily convince those who find their work very one-sided.

Most commentators would agree that Japan's remarkable economic success in the post-war period was a major reason for the dominance of Japanese politics by conservative forces from 1945 to the 1990s. That dominance was symbolized by the Liberal Democratic Party, formed in 1955, which only yielded power in 1993, and then to a coalition composed of seven opposition parties. There are good studies of the Liberal Democrats and the reasons for their success by Thayer (1969) and Fukui (1970). Books by Ward (1978) and Stockwin (1982) are among the best studies of the general workings of the political system, while a recent volume of essays, edited by McCormack and Sugimoto (1986), takes as its theme what the contributors see as the gaps between the democratic theories of Japan's 1946 constitution on the one hand and the authoritarian and nationalistic realities of present-day Japanese society on the other; this is a book which will give much comfort to historians who wish to stress that the Occupation had only limited long-term success.

The broad history of modern Japanese politics can, therefore, be seen as a story of stability achieved, then lost, then achieved once more, and then lost again: the control of the Meiji oligarchs was succeeded by the competing elites of the early twentieth century. These in turn were replaced by the dominant Liberal Democrats of the post-war years. They themselves have been succeeded by unstable coalitions and whether a genuine multi-party system will develop from the present situation remains to be seen.

The dominance of the Liberal Democrats for a period of about forty years in what is, avowedly at least, a democratic state is unusual, but certainly not unique – the Christian Democrats dominated the post-war political scene in Italy to almost the same extent, and also lost power in 1993 – but many Japanese are fond of the word 'unique' to describe their history and culture. They use the term *nihonjinron*, which can be translated as 'theorizing about the Japanese', to describe the huge Japanese literature which is devoted to what the authors see as the very special qualities of their customs, history and beliefs. The general message which *nihonjinron* is intended to convey is one of marked contrasts between most things Japanese and most things Western with usually the added point, made either implicitly or explicitly, that Japanese ways are better. In such thinking the Japanese economic miracle could never have happened in a Western country because so much of it stemmed from Japan's own peculiar cultural attributes, such as the pre-eminence of the group rather than the individual. A good deal of Western literature on Japan has absorbed, sometimes almost unconsciously, the less extreme ideas of *nihonjinron*, but the concept has also been attacked head on by some scholars, not least by Dale (1986) in a recent book.

It is probably best to steer a path midway between the extreme views of the most enthusiastic proponents of *nihonjinron* – it is unlikely, for example, that Japanese brains work in an entirely different way from their Western counterparts! – and the equally extreme views of diehard sceptics like Dale. There is a powerful argument to be made that, in the broad context of world history, modern Japan *is* unique. Meiji Japan was the only non-Western country successfully to copy the Western great powers of the day, transforming itself into an industrialized, imperialist power, and the industrialized Japan of the second half of the twentieth century has consistently outstripped these same Western rivals in economic growth over a period of forty years. Moreover, studies of Japanese society, of which those by Nakane (1979), Smith (1983) and Hendry (1987) are among the best, stress the continuing importance of the group as opposed to the individual to an extent which would be unthinkable in similar studies of a Western society. Supporters of *nihonjinron* can also point to the peculiarities of Japanese religion. It is true that contemporary Japan, just like so many Western countries, is often described as a 'secularized society', but, whatever the truth of this judgement, its whole religious background, a mixture of Shinto, Buddhism, Taoism, Confucianism and folk religion, with additions of 'new religions' which were derived from Buddhism and Shinto and came to the fore in the nineteenth and twentieth centuries, is very different from that of any of its economic rivals. Christianity has never been a powerful force in Japan and today only a very small minority of the population are Christians.[10]

---

10 Good surveys of the Japanese religious scene are Kitagawa 1966; Ellwood and Pilgrim 1985; Byron Earhart 1982; Thomsen 1963.

The works mentioned in this survey represent a tiny fraction of the historical research and scholarship which has been published on modern Japan – a recent and avowedly select bibliography contains nearly 3,000 items in English on the period from the 1860s to the 1980s, the vast majority of them published since 1945 (Perren 1992) – and some scholars have taken time from their more specialized work to produce general surveys of modern Japan, incorporating both their own researches and those of fellow-scholars. Among the best are books by Beasley (1990), Duus (1976), Storry (1982) and Hunter (1989). Beasley is especially strong on the mid-nineteenth century, a reflection of his expertise in the Meiji Restoration; Duus, a specialist on Taisho political parties, deserves special mention for his treatment of the politics of the inter-war period; Storry, who wrote a notable book on right-wing politics in the 1930s (Storry 1957), has a brilliant general chapter on that decade; and Hunter, who eschews the essentially chronological approach of the other three writers in favour of a thematic treatment, is especially good on economic and social history, in which she has research interests. Very recently *The Cambridge History of Japan* has begun to appear, with volumes on the nineteenth and twentieth centuries, published in 1989 and 1988 respectively (Jansen 1989; Duus 1988). The primary purpose of the work, as described by the general editors, is 'to put before the English-reading audience as complete a record of Japanese history as possible', though it is also stated that a decision was taken to leave out 'the history of art and literature, aspects of economics and technology and science, and the riches of local history'. The volumes undoubtedly have great merit – they sum up much scholarship on the topics with which they deal as well as presenting readers with a good deal of new research and ideas – but it is also fair to point out, as Hunter has done, that they were commissioned about twenty years ago and that the history which they contain is mostly 'mainstream history as it was broadly accepted in the early 1970s ..., the history of national politics, macro-economics and international relations' (Hunter 1990: 286). Where, she asks, are the women, the workers, the underdogs? This is fair comment, even though it says no more than that the volumes are works of their time, which means the time of commissioning rather than the time of publication. Despite that perhaps inevitable drawback they will be of considerable value to students of Japanese history in the years to come.

REFERENCES

Akita, G. (1967) *Foundations of Constitutional Government in Modern Japan: 1868–1900*, Cambridge, MA.

Barnhart, M. A. (1987) *Japan Prepares for Total War: The Search for Economic Security, 1919–1941*, Ithaca, NY.

Beasley, W. G. (1972) *The Meiji Restoration*, Stanford.

—— (1987) *Japanese Imperialism 1894–1945*, Oxford.

—— (1990) *The Rise of Modern Japan*, London.

Beckmann, G. M. (1957) *The Making of the Meiji Constitution: The Oligarchs and the Constitutional Development of Japan, 1868–1891*, Lawrence, KS.

Berger, G. M. (1977) *Parties out of Power in Japan, 1931–1941*, Princeton.

Bernstein, G. L. (1983) *Haruko's World: A Japanese Farm Woman and her Community*, Stanford.

Bix, H. P. (1992) 'The Showa emperor's "Monologue" and the problem of war responsibility', *Journal of Japanese Studies* 18: 295–363.

Connors, L. (1987) *The Emperor's Adviser: Saionji Kinmochi and Pre-war Japanese Politics*, London.

Cook, A. H. and Hayashi, H. (1980) *Working Women in Japan*, Ithaca, NY.

Craig, A. M. (1961) *Choshu in the Meiji Restoration*, Cambridge, MA.

Crowley, J. B. (1962) 'Japanese army factionalism in the early 1930s', *Journal of Asian Studies* 21: 309–26.

—— (1966) *Japan's Quest for Autonomy*, Princeton.

Crump, T. (1989) *The Death of an Emperor*, London.

Cummings, W. K. (1980) *Education and Equality in Japan*, Princeton.

Cusumano, M. A. (1985) *The Japanese Automobile Industry: Technology and Management at Nissan and Toyota*, Cambridge, MA.

Daikichi, I. (1970) *Meiji no bunka*, Tokyo. (Tr. as *The Culture of the Meiji Period*, ed. M. B. Jansen, Princeton.)

Dale, P. N. (1986) *The Myth of Japanese Uniqueness*, London.

Dore, R. P. (1959) *Land Reform In Japan*, London.

—— (1965) *Education in Tokugawa Japan*, Berkeley.

—— (ed.) (1967) *Aspects of Social Change in Modern Japan*, Princeton.

Dower, J. W. (ed.) (1975) *Origins of the Modern Japanese State: Selected Writings of E. H. Norman*, New York.

Drifte, R. (1990) *Japan's Foreign Policy*, London.

Duke, B. (1986) *The Japanese School: Lessons for Industrial America*, New York.

Duus, P. (1968) *Party Rivalry and Political Change in Taisho Japan*, Cambridge, MA.

—— (1976) *The Rise of Modern Japan*, Boston, MA.

—— (ed.) (1988) *The Cambridge History of Japan*, 6: *The Twentieth Century*, Cambridge.

Duus, P. and Okimoto, D. I. (1979–80) 'Fascism and the history of pre-war Japan: the failure of a concept', *Journal of Asian Studies* 39.

Duus, P., Myers, R. H. and Peattie, M. R. (eds) (1989) *The Japanese Informal Empire in China, 1895–1937*, Princeton.

Earhart, H. B. (1982) *Japanese Religion*, 3rd edn, Belmont, CA.

Earl, D. M. (1964) *Emperor and Nation in Japan: Political Thinkers of the Tokugawa Period*, Seattle.

Ellwood, R. and Pilgrim, R. (1985) *Japanese Religion*, Englewood Cliffs, NJ.

Fukui, H. (1970) *Party in Power: The Japanese Liberal Democrats and Policy-Making*, Berkeley.

Gluck, C. (1978–9) 'The people in history: recent trends in Japanese historiography', *Journal of Asian Studies* 38: 25–50.

Gordon, A. (1985) *The Evolution of Labour Relations in Japan: Heavy Industry, 1853–1955*, Cambridge, MA.

Hackett, R. F. (1964) 'The military' in R. E. Ward and D. A. Rustow (eds) *Political Modernization in Japan and Turkey*, Princeton.

—— (1968) 'Political modernization and the Meiji genro', in R. E. Ward (ed.) , *Political Development in Modern Japan*, Princeton.

—— (1971) *Yamagata Aritomo in the Rise of Modern Japan*, Cambridge, MA.

Hall, I. P. (1973) *Mori Arinori*, Cambridge, MA.

Hall, J. W. (1968) 'Feudalism in Japan – a reassessment', in J. W. Hall and M. B. Jansen (eds) *Studies in the Institutional History of Early Modern Japan*, Princeton.

—— (1970) *Japan from Prehistory to Modern Times*, London.

Hane, M. (1982) *Peasants, Rebels and Outcasts: The Underside of Modern Japan*, New York.

674

—— (1983) 'Agrarian Japan and modernization', in H. Wray and H. Conroy (eds) *Japan Observed*, Honolulu.

Hanley, S. B. and Yamamura, K. (1977) *Economic and Demographic Change in Preindustrial Japan, 1600–1868*, Princeton.

Harootunian, H. D. (1970) *Toward Restoration*, Berkeley.

Havens, T. R. (1978) *Valley of Darkness: The Japanese People and World War II*, New York.

Hendry, R. J. (1987) *Understanding Japanese Society*, Beckenham.

Hirschmeier, J. and Yui, T. (1981) *The Development of Japanese Business*, London.

Hoston, G. A. (1986) *Marxism and the Crisis of Development in Prewar Japan*, Princeton.

Huber, T. M. (1981) *The Revolutionary Origins of Modern Japan*, Stanford.

Hunter, J. L. (1989) *The Emergence of Modern Japan*, London.

—— (1990) Review of the *Cambridge History of Japan*, vols 5 and 6 (1989), *Japan Forum* 2: 284–6.

Imamura, A. E. (1987) *Urban Japanese Housewives: At Home and in the Community*, Honolulu.

Jansen, M. B. (ed.) (1965) *Changing Japanese Attitudes toward Modernization*, Princeton.

—— (1989) *The Cambridge History of Japan*, 5: *The Nineteenth Century*, Cambridge.

Johnson, C. (1982) *MITI and the Japanese Miracle: The Growth of Industrial Policy 1925–1975*, Stanford.

Kahn, H. (1970) *The Emerging Japanese Superstate*, Englewood Cliffs, NJ.

Kawai, K. (1960) *Japan's American Interlude*, Chicago.

Kitagawa, J. M. (1966) *Religion in Japanese History*, New York.

Koh, B. C. (1989) *Japan's Administrative Elite*, Berkeley.

Lockwood, W. W. (ed.) (1965) *The State and Economic Enterprise in Japan*, Princeton.

McCormack, G. and Sugimoto, Y. (1986) *Democracy in Contemporary Japan*, Armonk, NY.

McMillan, C. J. (1985) *The Japanese Industrial System*, Berlin and New York.

Masao, M. (1969) *Thought and Behaviour in Modern Japanese Politics*, expanded edn, ed. I. Morris, London.

Maxon, Y. C. (1957) *Control of Japanese Foreign Policy: A Study of Civil Military Rivalry*, Berkeley.

Michio, N. and Irrutia, N. (1985) *Meiji Ishin: Restoration and Revolution*, Tokyo.

Miller, F. O. (1965) *Minobe Tatsukichi, Interpreter of Constitutionalism in Japan*, Berkeley.

Minami, R. (1986) *The Economic Development of Japan: A Quantitative Survey*, London.

Morishima, M. (1982) *Why has Japan 'Succeeded'? Western Technology and the Japanese Ethos*, Cambridge.

Morley, J. W. (ed.) (1971) *Dilemmas of Growth in Prewar Japan*, Princeton.

Myers, R. H. and Peattie, M. R. (eds) (1984) *The Japanese Colonial Empire, 1895–1945*, Princeton.

Nakamura, T. (1981) *The Postwar Japanese Economy: Its Development and Structure*, tr. J. Kaminski, Tokyo.

Nakane, C. (1979) *Japanese Society*, London.

Nish, I. (1966) *The Anglo-Japanese Alliance: The Diplomacy of Two Island Empires, 1894–1907*, London.

—— (1977) *Japan's Foreign Policy, 1868–1942*, London.

Norman, E. H. (1940) *Japan's Origins as a Modern State*, New York.

Passin, H. (1965) *Society and Education in Japan*, New York.

Patrick, H. and Rosovsky, H. (eds) (1976) *Asia's New Giant: How the Japanese Economy Works*, Washington.

Perren, R. (ed.) (1992) *Japanese Studies from Pre-history to 1990: A Bibliographical Guide*, Manchester.

Pittau, J. (1967) *Political Thought in Early Meiji Japan: 1868–1889*, Cambridge, MA.

Quigley, H. S. (1932) *Japanese Government and Politics*, New York.

Reading, B. (1992) *Japan: The Coming Collapse*, London.

Roberts, J. G. (1973) *Mitsui: Three Centuries of Japanese Business*, New York.

Roden, D. J. (1980) *Schooldays in Imperial Japan: A Study in the Culture of a Student Elite*, Berkeley.

Rohlen, T. P. (1983) *Japan's High Schools*, Berkeley.

Saito, S. (1990) *Japan at the Summit: Its Role in the Western Alliance and in Asian-Pacific Co-operation*, London.

Scalapino, R. A. (1962) *Democracy and the Party Movement in Prewar Japan*, Berkeley.

Sheldon, C. D. (1958) *The Rise of the Merchant Class in Tokugawa Japan, 1600–1868*, Locust Valley, NY.

—— (1976) 'Japanese aggression and the Emperor, 1931–1941, from contemporary diaries', *Modern Asian Studies* 10: 1–40.

—— (1978) 'Scapegoat or instigator of Japanese aggression? Inouye Kiyoshi's case against the emperor', *Modern Asian Studies* 12: 1–35.

Shillony, B.-A. (1981) *Politics and Culture in Wartime Japan*, New York.

Shiveley, D. H. (ed.) (1971) *Tradition and Modernization in Japanese Culture*, Princeton.

Siemes, J. (1966) *Hermann Roesler and the Making of the Meiji State*, Tokyo.

Sievers, S. L. (1983) *Flowers in Salt: The Beginnings of Feminist Consciousness in Modern Japan*, Stanford.

Silberman, B. S. (1974) 'The bureaucratic role in Japan, 1900–1945: the bureaucrat as politician', in B. S. Silberman and H. D. Harootunian (eds) *Japan in Crisis: Essays in Taisho Democracy*, Princeton.

Smethurst, R. J. (1986) *Agricultural Development and Tenancy Disputes in Japan, 1870–1940*, Princeton.

Smith, R. J. (1983) *Japanese Society*, Cambridge.

Smith, T. C. (1959) *The Agrarian Origins of Modern Japan*, Stanford.

Spaulding, R. M. (1971) 'The bureaucracy as a political force, 1920–1945', in Morley 1971.

Stockwin, J. A. A. (1982) *Japan: Divided Politics in a Growth Economy*, 2nd edn, London.

Storry, R. (1957) *The Double Patriots*, London.

—— (1982) *A History of Modern Japan*, rev. edn, London.

Thayer, N. B. (1969) *How the Conservatives Rule Japan*, Princeton.

Thomsen, H. (1963) *The New Religions of Japan*, Westport, Conn.

Tiedemann, A. E. (1971) 'Big business and politics in prewar Japan', in Morley 1971.

Titus, D. A. (1974) *Palace and Politics in Prewar Japan*, New York.

—— (1980) 'The making of the "Symbol Emperor System" in postwar Japan', *Modern Asian Studies* 14: 529–78.

Totman, C. (1980) *The Collapse of the Tokugawa Bakufu, 1862–1868*, Honolulu.

Vogel, E. F. (1979) *Japan as Number One: Lessons for America*, Cambridge, MA.

Ward, R. E. (ed.) (1968) *Political Development in Modern Japan*, Princeton.

—— (1978) *Japan's Political System*, 2nd edn, Englewood Cliffs, NJ.

—— and Yoshikazu, S. (eds) (1987) *Democratizing Japan: The Allied Occupation*, Honolulu.

Waswo, A. (1977) *Japanese Landlords: The Decline of a Rural Elite*, Berkeley.

Webb, H. (1968) *The Japanese Imperial Institution in the Tokugawa Period*, New York.

Woronoff, J. (1986) *The Japan Syndrome: Symptoms, Ailments and Remedies*, New Brunswick.

Wray, H. and Conroy, H. (eds) (1983) *Japan Examined*, Honolulu.

Yamamura, K. (1971) 'The increasing poverty of the samurai in Tokugawa Japan, 1600–1868', *Journal of Economic History* 31: 378–406.

—— and Yasuba, Y. (eds) (1987–) *The Political Economy of Japan*, 3 vols, Stanford.

Yoshio, S. and Hall, J. W. (1956) 'The motivation of political leadership in the Meiji Restoration', *Journal of Asian Studies* 16: 31–50.

26

MODERN INDIAN HISTORIOGRAPHY

C. A. Bayly

In all former European colonies intellectual elites have sought in history a body of myths of origin to legitimate their independence. This has been the most powerful influence on the development of post-colonial historiography. Yet Indian historical writing has a deeper lineage than this might suggest. At several points over the last two centuries India edged from the margins towards the centre of international historical interest. The discovery of the Enlightenment that Sanskrit was an Aryan language and interest in oriental despotism as a mirror of Western absolutism ensured that late Mogul India engaged the attention of the international scholarly community. Ironically, it was the British conquest of the subcontinent, and particularly James Mill's ferocious denunciation of the barbarities of Indian society in his *History of British India* (1817), which pushed it out to the margins again. Fifty years later, Sir Henry Maine's *Village Communities in East and West* (1871) initiated a discussion about the status of village, commune and property right in historic civilizations which drew upon some of the arcane lore of the Indian district officers. In the 1960s, again, the debate about preconditions and 'take-off' in industrialization generated an interest in Indian economic history which was matched by a fickle admiration among the Western intelligentsia for Nehru and the Non-Aligned Movement.

Generally, however, Indian history has seemed exceptional, mainly because it fitted into no obvious paradigm of development, whether liberal or Marxist. It seemed to have failed to follow the 'right' form of industrial development under both Raj and Republic. Neither the Raj nor the Indian National Congress had been able to forge a solid and economically effective modern state above the *mêlée* of factions, castes and local bosses. Fierce disputes between Hindus and Muslims, or between Sikhs and the central government, seemed still to mark it out as a fragile civil society always on the edge of being wiped out by ethnic violence, religious obscurantism and 'amoral familism'. Every decade since the death of the Mogul Emperor Aurangzeb in 1707 seemed to have been 'the most dangerous decade' for

India, and its historical writing, too, limped from the examination of one peak of famine, slaughter and civil unrest to another.[1]

Now we all seem to be in the same boat. The capacity of the modern state and international economy to erode localism, to supress inter-ethnic violence and religious extremism seems everywhere in doubt. The collapse of the Soviet Union, the West's crises of deindustrialization and the rapid rise of Asian economies towards global dominance (though not, as yet, India's), eroded many of the old teleological certainties of economic history. Now, too, we all live in plural societies balanced on the edge of ethnic and religious violence. We have all become citizens of little Indias.

These changes in the world outside have been mirrored in the cultural battles of the media and the academy. While cultural and historical discourse remained 'centred', India with its myths and ballads, linguistic and semantic complexities, seemed like some worn old Afghan patchwork, eye-catching but impractical as an area of study. Even the Marxists despaired, and invoked the 'Asiatic' and 'colonial' modes of production to explain why India seemed different.[2] But now that 'decentred discourses', 'thick description', 'cultural self-representation' have become the norm in the academy, particularly in America, India has come into its own again. Indian historians were postmodernists before their time, though often unknowingly or unwillingly. It is not surprising therefore that able young expatriate Indians have entered the historical and literary culture-wars of the United States with great vigour. This revolution of the Green Card-holders has begun to surface in Europe and New Delhi. Indian novelists writing in English have produced texts bursting with historical comment, while, at their head, Salman Rushdie has himself become an exercise pit for international cultural combat. Yet despite its slow advance to international significance, Indian historical writing is still deeply immured in the debates and controversies of the past. This chapter seeks to uncover both the continuities and discontinuities in the writing of modern Indian history.

THE ORIGINS OF MODERN INDIAN HISTORY

It is often said that India, and in particular Hindu India, lacked a strong tradition of historical writing. For Hindus, time is supposed to have been 'fuzzy' or even 'cyclical'. History in its modern form, according to this view, came with the modern state or in India with the colonial state. These statements are dubious at best. Hindu India expressed its historical memory through legends and ballads, a true representation of popular constructions of the past. Yet even Hindu kingdoms had elaborate records, genealogies and annals which could be as precise as those found in other early modern societies (Tod [1819] 1982: I, 1–3). Likewise, an Indo-Muslim tradition of historical writing, drawing on the precision and concern for

---

1 Harrison 1960 was a classic of this genre.
2 For a discussion of these concepts and the concept of feudalism in Indian history see Byres and Mukhia 1985.

correct testimony of Arabic and Persian exemplars, developed under the patronage of the Mogul and other Indian Muslim courts. This tradition continued to flourish during the late seventeenth and eighteenth centuries.[3] Persian histories of dynasties and religious teachers, biographical dictionaries of writers and poets, local histories of landed clans and small towns were written in great numbers, often by Hindus of the scribal classes who had taken Mogul service.

While one of the main themes of these histories was the evanescence of human might in the face of God's greatness, other more 'secular' themes emerged (Hardy 1960). Eighteenth-century indigenous historians were deeply concerned about the corruption of Mogul public office and the decline of virtue. Such writers were by no means innocent of historical explanation; it is simply that their explanations differed from twentieth-century predilections, though not necessarily from eighteenth-century European ones. The Mogul conquerors had lost their virtue, it was said, in the great well-watered and well-provisioned cities of the Indian plains; their place was usurped by hard men, usually Hindus from the dry, unwatered parts of the Empire. The Empire was like a human organism; its humours were out of balance, with the dry and choleric overwhelming the damp and bilious.[4]

These themes were quickly adapted to the new conditions created by the rise of British power after Robert Clive's seizure of the revenues of Bengal in 1765. Persian histories, notably Ghulam Hussain Tabatabai's *Siyyar al-Muta 'akhkhirin* (1790), chronicled the gradual British takeover of the Mogul domain by stealth. This and similar works sometimes lauded the stability the 'Franks' brought, but often denounced their brutality and incivility. These historians wrote of a revolution in power which had brought the 'drunken and licentious butlers' of the English to power. In the early nineteenth century grand chronicles were matched by large numbers of local histories, often produced by the old literati under British direction. These works informed the new British collectors and land-revenue managers, but they also embodied claims for status and land-rights on behalf of particular groups of landlords and local government servants in the new British districts.

Indians were, therefore, consciously producing their own histories of 'modern times' during the very period of British conquest. Over recent years, these have provided the primary materials for a number of histories which have sought to portray the Indian eighteenth and early nineteenth centuries in a more rounded and complex light than the old stereotypes of the Time of Troubles. These works, many of American origin, have shown how dynasties created local and regional states, how these states functioned through the redistribution of resources and honour, and

---

3 Abul Fazil's 'Akbar Namah' was a model, as was Inayat Khan, 'Shahjahan Namah', tr. W. Begley and Z. Desai, Delhi, 1990; some eighteenth-century representatives of this tradition were Mustajab Khan Bahadur, 'Gulistan-i-Rehmat' tr. C. Elliot as *The Life of Hafeez-ool-Moolk*, London, 1821; Abu Talib Isfahani, 'Tafzih-ul Ghafalin', tr. W. Hoey as *History of Asaf'ud Dawlah, Nawab Wazir of Oudh*, Allahabad, 1885; Mahomed Faiz Baksh, 'Tarikh-i Farah Baksh', tr. W. Hoey as *Memoirs of Delhi and Faizabad*, Allahabad, 1889.
4 Ghulam Ali Azad Bilgrami, 'Khazana-i-Amira'; large parts of this are translated in Rao 1963, esp. p. 227.

how they in turn provided much of the scaffolding for the East India Company's rule, both in the areas it controlled directly and in the princely states under British Paramountcy (e.g. Barnett 1980; Fisher 1987; Cole 1988).

IMPERIAL HISTORIES AND THE CIVILIZING MISSION

Early British writing on India drew heavily on the indigenous historians either directly through their writings or from verbal informants. The local histories passed into the body of genealogical and revenue lore which were later embodied in the British *District Gazetteers*, *Reports on Revenue Settlements* and other statistical and topographical enquiries which remain the staple of Indian social historians. But by the 1830s there was a sea change of mood. The new vigour and arrogance associated with the anglicizing bureaucracy of Macaulay's period had less time for Indian histories and their pretensions. Sir Henry Elliot, of course, fathered a twelve-volume work, *The History of India Told by its Own Historians* ([1869] 1958). But his aim was specifically to disabuse the 'bombastic young baboos [English-educated gentry of Calcutta]' of the idea that Mogul times had been superior to British rule. After James Mill's *History*, Anglo-Indian historians voiced few objections to the British conquest of India and were content to chronicle the divisions, disorganization and depravity of a society which seemed to them to have invited foreign conquest. It is true that the Mutiny Rebellion of 1857 resulted in violent disagreements between those who blamed the military authorities and those who claimed the civil authorities were to blame (Stokes 1986: 1–35) but no one of significance doubted the legitimacy of Britain's civilizing mission in the East.

On the surface, Anglo-Indian historical writing in the later nineteenth century followed the same plan. Social history was rendered down into 'folklore' and disquisitions on 'tribes and castes' or bottled up in gazetteers. Economic history was severed from political and immured in land-revenue settlement reports and statistical minutes. British Indian political history was ensconced in Oxford University Press's *Rulers of India Series* which memorialized a succession of British men of action, prayer and thought, in direct succession to the Great Mogul Emperors. Yet Anglo-Indian history, whether written in a bureaucratic or public mode, was already under pressure. Since the 1840s Indian historical writing had revived, especially in Bengal. In the early days much of this writing was sycophantic and the most interesting development was the increasing blackness with which Hindu writers portrayed the period of Muslim (though not yet British) rule. Many of these histories were produced under the auspices of the newly formed Committees of Public Instruction. But even here many small barbs were beginning to be stuck into the carcass of the Raj.[5] The tools of scientific historical criticism which were being used by Western orientalists to dissect India's past could quickly be turned against the presumption of Britain's civilizing mission.

---

5   e.g. Prasad 1851, which is largely a précis of Cunningham's *History of the Sikhs*, 1852.

INDIAN HISTORIES AND THE NATIONALISTS

The foundation of the Indian National Congress and the emergence of 'economic nationalism' in the 1890s was accompanied by a spate of works which denounced the British for loading the peasant with intolerably heavy revenue demands. They also attacked the government for repatriating the wealth of India in the form of the Home Charges levied by the government of India. In the realm of political history, there was an increasing desire to show that the Moguls and regional dynasties, such as the Hindu Maratha states which preceded the British, were wise and humane. Indian nationalism was now matched by the growth of regional feeling, especially in Bombay and western India. But the seminal work in the new Nationalist history did not appear until 1908 when young radicals in the Congress had made a lurch towards more radical and insurrectionary types of politics. This was V. D. Savarkar's *The Indian War of Independence 1857* (finally published in 1947), which portrayed the movement of that year not as a mutiny, but as a justified response to British tyranny and racism. At this point the main lines of historical debate both for the last days of the Raj and for the years after Independence were already laid.

In British writing about India, the early twentieth century saw a slow adjustment to the growing power of the Indian National Congress and its rival, the Muslim League, which had precipitated mass civil disobedience and the constitutional reforms of 1909, 1919 and 1935. Yet the *Cambridge History of India* and Vincent Smith's *Oxford History of India* both remained remarkably British-centred and colonialist in their basic premises. Even radical histories such as Edward Thompson and G. T. Garrett's *The Rise and Fulfilment of British Rule in India* (1934) continued to laud Britain's initial civilizing mission and also to assign to her a residual role in arbitrating between the supposedly homogeneous blocs of Hindu and Muslim opinion.

More interesting was the emergence of Indian social and economic history during these years. Much of the best work was based on official and local sources and hidden away in the growing number of local historical journals such as *Bengal Past and Present*, *The Indian Antiquary* or *The Journal of the Andhra Research Society*. The dominant figure here was W. H. Moreland, whose *The Agrarian System of Moslem India* (1924) was the founding text of pre-colonial and, by default, early colonial Indian economic history. Moreland's work arose from his period as Director of Land Records in the United Provinces (see Moreland 1912), and it was in direct descent from the history of Sir Henry Elliot sixty years before in that it sought to show that the pre-British economy was small and hampered by poor transport, and that its long-distance internal trades and external commerce dealt in little more than luxury commodities. Indian historians connected with Aligarh Muslim University have worked hard to correct these stereotypes (notably Habib 1963), but they are still dominated by Moreland's influence in the topics they choose. Indeed, despite the emergence of self-consciously Marxist, Gramscian and anthropological schools of history in the last twenty years, the ideas and material accumulated by the historians and sociologists of the Indian Civil Service remain critical to the writing of Indian history. Hardly a single argument or idea which has emerged from increasingly sophisticated writing on Indian history in the last generation lacks its precursor in the musings of a revenue official or the writings of a district judge. Yet Indian historiography is not yet mature enough to admit this debt, since a facile anti-colonialism flourishes throughout the academy in India and abroad. Alongside Moreland should be mentioned another founder of modern Indian history who also wrote on the immediate pre-colonial period. This was Sir Jadunath Sarkar (1901; 1919; 1955, etc.; see Gupta 1957) who initiated a dispassionate and largely apolitical strain of national history which had many imitators among the next generation of historians of the colonial period. The most typical work of this generation of 'grand old men' was *The History and Culture of the Indian People* (1951–69) produced by R. Majumdar and his collaborators.

Radical nationalist Indian history was taking shape faster in the 1920s and 1930s against the background of the struggle for freedom. The 'economic nationalist' interpretation of Indian history which had arisen amongst the bourgeois nationalists of Bombay and Calcutta in the 1880s and 1890s was now crossed with a more self-consciously Marxist strain, though before Independence this was banned in schools and universities. M. N. Roy (see Bhattacharjee 1971) and R. Palme Dutt (1940), orthodox Marxists, laboured alongside Fabian socialists, notably Jawaharlal Nehru (1965), to show that India's struggle against the British was part of an international struggle against capitalism. Their assumption that British-imposed free-trade wiped out the Indian textile industry in the early nineteenth century and stunted the growth of Indian-owned machine milling in the later nineteenth century provided a historical justification for the economic autarchy which Marxists of all hues argued should constitute the policy of an independent India. 'Landlordism' was identified as the problem in the internal economy. Historical evidence was brought forward to show that the British had favoured their collaborators among the great landholders, while poor peasants and small landholders had been expropriated.

This dominant leftist and Marxist tendency within Indian historical writing did not go unchallenged, however. Regional history flourished in the last years of the Raj, partly, one suspects, because the Education Department smiled on a history which appeared to fragment India into provinces, castes and cultures in a manner which matched the official political discourse. Regional patriotisms did, however, have a life of their own. In western India scholars put in train a large programme of publication from the records of the erstwhile Maratha rulers of the seventeenth and eighteenth centuries (e.g. Ranade 1900; Kincaid and Parasnis 1918–25; Sardesai 1946–8). Their interpretation of the Maratha kings and their ultimate fight to the death against the British was significantly different from the treatment accorded them by Bengali historians, who tended to see the Marathas as 'predators'. In the south, the Tamil literary revival gave rise to a historiography which claimed that the brahmins had subverted the cultural and political independence of southerners, a stance which matched that of the Justice Party, a non-brahmin conservative alliance which dominated the Madras Presidency in the inter-war years and proved to be a precursor of modern southern regionalism (Irschick 1986). This theme of 'brahmin dominance' was taken up in the caste and community histories of low-caste workers which were beginning to be written as labouring people and the poor began to be mobilized into politics in the 1920s and 1930s (Gooptu 1991). In these histories the British played an ambiguous role. Sometimes they were depicted as foreigners who had begun to break the yoke of brahmin priesthood; equally often they were held to have perpetuated it by educating brahmins in science and the English language.

The most politically important challenge to the writing of secular, leftist and nationalist history came, of course, from a section of the Muslim leadership. In the 1860s and 1870s Sir Syed Ahmed Khan, founder of the Aligarh College, had asserted that Hindus and Muslims were 'two nations' who merely shared the soil of India (Robinson 1974). An inheritor of the eighteenth-century traditions of local and dynastic history, he argued both from Islamic history and the history of 'modern times' that Muslims had an identity which set them apart from the Hindus, and that this entitled them to separate representation and separate leadership within imperial India. Many, but by no means all, Muslim leaders and literati elaborated these themes in the next generation. The celebration of the Islamic and west Asian cultural and racial heritage of India's Muslims reached its apogee in the work of Maulana Muhammad Iqbal, a Persian and Arabic scholar, who argued on historical precedent that they should have a separate 'homeland' within the redrawn map of post-colonial south Asia (Hussain 1971). Ultimately, the creation of a separate history for Muslims resulted in the virtual abandonment of historical writing in the future Pakistan. If Islam, rather than the historical experience of Muslim people living amongst their Hindu neighbours, was to be the touchstone of national memory, then history was itself a valueless category. In Pakistan, modern history has largely been dropped in favour of the vacuous 'Pakistan Studies'.

THE POLITICAL CONTEXT OF POST-INDEPENDENCE HISTORICAL WRITING

All new nations work to consolidate their myths of foundation and India was no exception. To a surprising extent history remains a fundamental constituent of contemporary political debate. Controversies ranged from banal polemic generated by the decision to remove the statues of British conquerors from public places to esoteric debates about the balance between exogenous and endogenous factors in India's nineteenth-century growth rate. This latter debate has remained lively. The reason is that the position scholars take on the historical record tends to be reflected in their stance on whether India should deregulate, liberalize the economy and plunge naked into the storms of the international market, unprotected by the regime of controls established by Nehru's Congress. When the American economic historian Morris D. Morris proposed in the early 1960s that colonial rule may not have been as dire for the Indian economy as commonly thought, he stirred up a massive controversy which still echoes on, partly for political reasons.

Resistance to the British also remains a hot issue. The Ministry of Tourism in

Uttar Pradesh now offers tours to see the locations of the glorious deeds of the Indian 'martyrs' of the 1857 rebellion. Political parties jostle to appropriate the heroes who died on the scaffold or in hails of British bullets during the Independence movements. Subhas Chandra Bose, 'Netaji', who took up arms against the British alongside the Japanese in 1942, has become a national hero who dwarfs the pacific and saintly Gandhi. Ironically, the fact the India did not throw up a mass anti-colonial revolutionary movement, like Vietnam or Algeria, has served to radicalize its history. New village Hampdens are discovered lurking in every colonial police file.

Institutional changes inside the country and outside have also moulded the new historiography of post-Independence India. Indian educational institutions and centres of advanced study have increased immeasurably since Independence. Dedicated historical institutes such as the Nehru Memorial Museum and Library or the National Archives of India have co-operated with the Indian Historical Manuscripts Commission and the Indian Council of Historical Research to breed a new professional academic community. The 'golden triangle' runs between the Nehru Library, the campus of Jawaharlal Nehru University and the offices of the *Economic and Political Weekly* in Bombay. Congress patronage and the political stance of Indian youth has tended to ensure that this new professional community of Indian scholars has remained in the mode of its Nehruvian predecessors. The effort has been Marxist, anti-imperialist, anti-capitalist and more recently directed to 'history from below'. A glance at the articles in the most innovative of the historical journals, *The Indian Economic and Social History Review*, will show that the majority of them continue the tradition of anti-imperialist historical writing which was pioneered by Dadhabhai Naoroji's *Poverty and un-British rule in India* (1893; see Masani 1939) and was consolidated by Bipan Chandra's *History of Economic Nationalism in India*. The concern of Jawaharlal Nehru with the peasantry, manifested in his *Discovery of India* (1935), has spawned a huge number of books and theses in recent years, seeking to reconstruct, largely from colonial records, the history of the 'people without history'. But it would be a grave injustice to believe that the domestic historical profession represented a kind of historical establishment of the sort that existed once in the Soviet Union and now exists in China. The vitality of Indian historiography in recent years reflects deep internal contradictions as much as the growing influence of historiographical changes overseas, notably in the United States, but to a lesser extent in Britain and Europe. Before we go on to deal with several important areas in recent historical writing, we will outline some of these fissures and influences.

While Indian historiography has been generally leftist, the Indian Left has been a house minutely divided against itself. Distinct pro-Chinese and pro-Soviet schools of historical writing loosely matched the political parties which espoused these causes. The Congress right and left also saw different lessons in the history of the nationalist struggle. All the while, regional political parties and their ideologies subtly influenced the style of history being written. There is no sense in which these political divisions were directly reflected in historical writing. But a tendency to study the working class as against the peasantry, a predilection for *jacquerie*-like peasant movements, as opposed to Congress-led nationalism, often betray the political assumptions which Indian authors bring to bear on their work.

The issues of religion and region are only now beginning to surface in elite historical discourse. There has been an enormous gap between the professional, cosmopolitan, English-speaking elite and the vernacular schools of historical writing and teaching in which 95 per cent of the country's historical effort is concentrated. Some of these non-elite institutions still use translations of old British textbooks. But others, particularly in states where anti-centre, non-Congress parties are in power, have begun to propagate forms of local chauvinist and fundamentalist religious historiography which have alarmed and galvanized the historical establishment. Most significantly, the country's main rightist Hindu party, the Bharatiya Janata Party, has over the last decade made an organized effort to infiltrate professional institutions and to propagate its own version of history. This version holds that Nehru's socialist secularism is a distortion of India's true Hindu identity, and no more than a continuation of the anti-Hindu agenda of India's British rulers. They depict Muslim rule as a scourge, Muslims as foreigners in India, and the partition of India in 1947 as a betrayal by Gandhi and Nehru. Some of India's leading 'secular' historians have taken up arms against this revival by the Hindu Right of the nineteenth-century Muslim assertion that Hindus and Muslims in India were 'two nations'. It was colonial rule, they say, which 'constructed communalism', that is Hindu–Muslim conflict. It is too early to say where this cultural struggle will lead, but it has already influenced the writing of Indian history to the extent that 'communalism', that is Hindu–Muslim and other types of religious conflict, has become a critical area of research, overtaking an earlier obsession with anti-colonial nationalism.[6]

Finally, what are the international professional influences that have come to bear on the domestic Indian historical scene since Independence? The most important development has, perhaps, been its emancipation from the influence of British historiography (cf. Kumar 1989). While many young Indian historians still come to Britain for postgraduate studies (almost exclusively to Oxbridge and London), the colonial monopoly has been broken. A significant number now follow MAs in Jawaharlal Nehru University with doctoral work in the United States, Australia, France and Germany. In Chicago, Pennsylvania and Berkeley they come into direct contact with the tradition of historical anthropology which has dominated Indian studies in America since the 1960s. As disciplinary boundaries break down in US academia, they are much more likely to exchange ideas with the new generation of literary theorists and 'discourse analysts'. Besides this, most US orientalists come out of a tradition of study in literature and civilization which insists that doctoral work has a strong component of indigenous language material. This was never the case in Britain, or, ironically, in India itself, where many capable dissertations were written without benefit of any indigenous language sources.

6 See the recent collection by Pandey 1993.

On balance, this pedagogical tilt towards America, and the matching awareness of French historical and social theory (the *Annales* School, Foucault, Derrida, etc.), has been invigorating, not least to the writing of Indian history in Britain. Yet some things have also been lost alongside gross British historical empiricism. Few students have much knowledge or understanding of the political and social theories which the colonial rulers brought to bear in Indian life, let alone any grasp of British social and economic history. Similarly, for all the antediluvian emphasis on constitutional history and sturdy narrative, the old school of British imperial history did at least provide a framework for studying issues of imperialism and resistance at a global level. Now one often gets the impression that authors believe that India was the only country to have been colonized, while naive essentializations of 'the British' or the 'colonial state' have replaced the alleged orientalist reduction of India to a pot-pourri of essences. Another measure of the internationalization of Indian historiography has been the relative decline of economic history. While India produces some of the best economists in the world, economic history, especially quantitative economic history, has recently suffered a distinct loss of status as the brightest young minds in India hitch their colours to the standard of an ill-defined concept of 'culture'.

PRESENT DEBATES AND OBSESSIONS

It would be wrong, it must be said again, to think that contemporary Indian historiography has succumbed completely to political or intellectual fashion. Both inside India and outside an equally powerful force has been the growth of professionalization of history. In the United States and India, regional studies associations have come into being. Their annual conferences and newsletters chart the development of the history of Bengal, the Punjab or Tamilnadu. Urban history has its own Indian association,[7] while the Indian Council of Historical Research, the Indian Historical Records Commission and the National and state archives have continued programmes of documentary publishing. Environmental history, while clearly responding to contemporary worries, has become established as a serious branch of Indian historical writing.[8] The history of science in India now shows signs of throwing off its early need to show that all major scientific discoveries in the West were anticipated in India.

Some of the older fields of study have continued to grow without scholars very obviously looking over their shoulders at contemporary political disputes. One area which has moved from strength to strength since the 1960s has been the study of the British conquest and initial impact on India.[9] Echoes of the broader debates on imperialism and British motivations in conquest, spurred to life again in the 1960s by Robinson and Gallagher's *Africa and the Victorians*, took some time to reach

---

7 For urban history see Banga 1991.
8 An excellent new synthesis of this work is Guha and Gadgil 1993; see also Guha 1989.
9 Two decades of studies have been commented on by Fisher 1993; see also Fisher 1991.

India's shores. When they did, interesting variations were discovered. Some historians continued to argue that the British conquest was essentially one part of a geopolitical battle for supremacy in the wars with the French. Others argued for an expansion dominated by economic interests, whether it be the interests of the East India Company itself, or private merchants in cloth, raw cotton and opium, or the interests of the Indian merchant entrepreneurs who financed much of the British trade. More sophisticated studies of the politics and motivations of the East India Company officials and Indian rulers produced arguments that stressed the indirect influence of political or economic crises. For instance, it has been argued that the key to British expansion was 'military fiscalism'. The eighteenth-century British had to finance their colonial armies with local resources. In India this meant forcing or cajoling Indian powers to pay for the Company's presence through the mechanism of the so-called subsidiary alliance system. The need to pay out so much cash to foreigners forced Indian states either to resist – and be conquered – or to hand over large tracts of their territory. In either case the British frontier inexorably expanded both across the map and down into Indian society. This was a local variant of Galbraith's notion of the uneasy frontier. At all events, the recent emphasis on local agents of expansion, whether the British official, private traders, the East India Company's army or the Indian communities which served and financed the expansion, has proved productive of much new material and argument.

Indian resistance to British colonial expansion, as well as to the mature Raj, has been another topic which has attracted great interest. In the eighteenth century the emphasis has generally fallen on the last independent Indian states. As in the case of Africa, the propensity of post-Mogul Indian rulers to resist or capitulate has been closely calibrated to the social politics, resources and ideologies of their ruling elites. At the same time the stark dichotomy between 'collaboration' and 'resistance' has been eroded. For the nineteenth and twentieth centuries resistance has been seen to be the response of specific communities on the land, fortified by their sense of space, their symbols of kingship and their indigenous definitions of proper government. Indian historians' debts to international peasant studies, especially to the works of Eric Hobsbawm, E. Le Roy Ladurie, E. P. Thompson and James Scott, have been very great. There have been many academic scuffles about the social and economic status of the resisters. Were the rebels of 1857 rich peasants, or small landlords? Or, on the other hand, were they the wretched of the earth, the impoverished smallholder or dispossessed rural labourer?[10] The same sorts of arguments have been raging about the peasant movements of the later nineteenth century and those of the Gandhian era. In the world of industrial labour there have been interesting investigations of the origins of the extraordinary stamina with which Indian working people pursued their disputes in the twentieth century (see Chandavarkar 1994; Chakrabarty 1986).

However, in the last few years an important group of historians has switched away from social structural and economistic arguments about the origins of peasant

---

10   Mukherjee 1984, who took issue with Stokes 1986, etc.

and working-class resistance. Disillusionment with orthodox Marxism and with the notion that the Indian National Congress ever really played a leading role in the 'mobilization of the Indian masses' have been rife, as Congress and the Communist parties themselves seem to come to represent the new establishment in the Republic of India. The so-called *Subaltern Studies* group of mainly younger Indian historians have consciously employed the arguments of Gramsci to stress the role of culture in domination and resistance, and to loosen the grip of social-structural understandings of the motivations of the poor and the oppressed.[11]

This work has been productive of most interesting details and observations about the life and struggles of peasants, rural labour, Indian 'tribal groups' and the underclasses of the towns and many sophisticated arguments. Yet the *Subaltern Studies* Group of historians and their imitators have had considerable difficulty in integrating their histories from below into a picture which accounts for historical continuities and change. Despite a Gramscian agenda, the dominance of the ruling elites, and indeed of the imperial state itself, remains unexplained. There also appears to be a clash of agendas. One part of the project stresses the anti-imperial heroism of the 'subaltern', and tends to essentialize and even romanticize resistance. Another, influenced by literary deconstruction, is sceptical of the existence of anything outside 'discourse' in an ultra-Foucauldian mould. The etiolation of conjunctural economic history has made it difficult to discover why anything occurred when it did. Another set of problems arise when historians attempt to combine standard archival sources with increasingly sophisticated collections of oral traditions. Meanwhile, a growing number of studies of Indian women from a feminist perspective have argued that even history from below has tended to ignore the role of Indian women, denying them agency and 'alternative discourses' of resistance to male oppression.

One of the reasons why history from below has found it difficult to come into focus is the relative neglect of the role of elites and nationalism in recent scholarship. This in turn is a reaction against the heavy focus on these themes that characterized the 1960s and 1970s. During those years biographies and analyses of the regional politics of nationalism were written in great numbers. The majority of works produced in the United States saw Indian nationalism as an aspect of the 'modernization' of Indian society. Works produced in Britain, especially those of the so-called called Cambridge School, emphasized the factional struggle for power and office among a very fragmented set of regional and local Indian elites. Indian historiography naturally tended to be dominated by the idea of nationalist struggle and failed to address the many things that imperialists and nationalists had in common across the divide of race and power.

There are some signs that a more nuanced history of the thought and social life of the nationalist elites is coming into being now. Their construction of an Indian ideal family life, their understandings of modern science, and of their conceptions of new 'public' Hinduism and Islam, have begun to appear. But it must be admitted that

---

11 Guha 1981–92; for comments see O'Hanlon 1988 and C. A. Bayly 1988.

modern Indian intellectual history hardly exists, let alone a history which tries to situate and contextualize ideas in society. On the contrary, the 'anti-elitist' bias of the younger generation of historians, and their attempts to dismantle 'foundationalist' historical narratives which are supposedly complicit with capitalism and the modern state, have deflected attention from this very important need. While the new history of 'decentred discourses' persistently evokes the concept of power, the sophistication of its treatment of those without power contrasts strangely with its simple-mindedness about the sources and projection of that power.

One area where this attempt has been more successfully made is in the history of religious conflict, and especially of Hindu–Muslim communalism. In part this is because there has been a steady accretion of excellent works on modern Indian religious life (e.g. Jones 1992; S. Bayly 1989). The personalities and institutions of the nineteenth-century religious revival in the major Indian religions have been portrayed with great success, as has been the continuing syncretic culture of many localities. The emergence of religious conflict in public space can thus be situated against a much clearer understanding of how religions were taught and learned. A lively if somewhat crude controversy has also arisen about the extent to which conflicting religious identifications were products of colonial policies and structures, and how far these competing identities grew out of older ideological and social roots. The vitality of this writing clearly reflects the immediacy of the experience of Hindu–Muslim and Hindu–Sikh rioting to both Indians and foreigners. Yet this remains a baffling and difficult area of study. The precise relations between the 'high politics' of communalism in the councils of the Congress, Muslim League and Hindu Mahasabha, and the conflicts in the streets and villages is yet to be satisfactorily explained. If anything, the rise of contemporary Hindu militancy has made that task harder. Much of the secular elite among Indian historians is working so hard to show that communalism is modern and politically inspired that it cannot bear to consider evidence of older and deeper imbalances, ambivalences and conflicts among Indian religious groups. The result is that the most obtuse religious chauvinist can often appear to win the argument by default, simply by showing, for instance, that Muslim monarchs did sometimes destroy Hindu temples.

This last example explains some of the strengths and weaknesses of modern Indian historiography. The closeness of religious conflict to the ordinary citizen of Ajodhya or New Delhi – and even Birmingham or New York – makes of Indian history a powerful political artefact. Indian debates are now immediately relevant to those general cultural questions about representation and self-representation which are being raised in all fields of history. Should the historian point to pre-colonial religious conflict if this might indirectly feed into the armoury of the Hindu and Sikh right-wing or Muslim fundamentalists? Can Westerners represent Indians? Can elite, English-speaking Indians represent the peasants and the poor simply by appealing to an implicit racial solidarity? Such questions have given a powerful stimulus to historical research and controversy. Equally, they have given rise to an

inordinate amount of political posturing which has distracted attention from our
continuing ignorance about great swathes of the Indian past.

REFERENCES

This is not a full bibliographical list, only a sample of relevant works. More comprehensive
bibliographies are provided in the volumes of the *New Cambridge History of India*, ed. G.
Johnson, Cambridge, 1986– ; see also, C. H. Philips (ed.) *Historians of India, Pakistan and
Ceylon*, London, 1962, and J. S. Grewal, *Muslim Rule in India: The Assessments of British
Historians*, Calcutta, 1970. Oxford University Press India's 'Themes in Indian History'
series, ed. N. Bhattacharya *et al.*, also provides bibliographical essays and a sample of
important articles.

Bahadur, Mustajab Khan (1821) ['Gulistan-i-Rehmat'] *The Life of Hafeez-ool-Moolk*, tr. C.
　Elliot, London.
Baksh, M. F. (1889) ['Tarikh-i Farah Baksh'] *Memoirs of Delhi and Faizabad*, tr. W. Hoey,
　Allahabad.
Banga, I. (ed.) (1991) *The City in Indian History. Urban Demography, Society and Politics*,
　Delhi.
—— (1992) *Ports and their Hinterlands 1700–1950*, New Delhi.
Barnett, R. (1980) *North India between Empires. Awadh, the Mughals and the British*,
　Berkeley.
Bayly, C. A. (1988) 'Rallying around the subtaltern', *Journal of Peasant Studies* 16(3).
Bayly, S. (1989) *Saints, Godesses and Kings: Muslims and Christians in South Indian Society
　1700–1900,* Cambridge.
Bhattacharjee, G. P. (1971) *Evolution of the Political Philosophy of M. N. Roy*, Calcutta.
Byres, T. J. and Mukhia, H. (eds) (1985) *Feudalism in Non-European Societies*, London.
Chakrabarty, D. (1989) *Rethinking Working Class History: Bengal 1890–1940*, Princeton.
Chandavarkar, R. (1994) *The Origins of Industrial Capitalism in India*, Cambridge.
Cole, J. R. I. (1988) *The Roots of North Indian Shi'ism in Iran and Iraq*, Berkeley.
Cunningham, J. (1852) *History of the Sikhs*, London.
Dutt, R. P. (1940) *India Today*, London.
Elliot, H. M. [1869] (1958) *The History of India Told by its own Historians. The Muham-
　madan Period. The Posthumous Papers of Sir H. M. Elliot*, Calcutta.
Fisher, M. H. (1987) *A Clash of Cultures: Awadh, the British and the Mughals*, New Delhi.
—— (1991) *Indirect Rule In India. Residents and the Residency System, 1764–1858*, Delhi.
—— (ed.) (1993) *The Politics of British Annexation of India, 1757–1857*, Delhi.
Gooptu, N. (1991) 'The political culture of the urban poor in U.P., 1920–47', unpublished
　Ph.D. thesis., University of Cambridge.
Guha, Ramchandra (1989) *The Unquiet Woods. Ecological Change and Peasant Resistance*, Delhi.
—— and Gadgil, M. (1992) *This Fissured Earth*, Delhi.
Guha, Ranajit (ed.) (1982) *Subaltern Studies*, 8 vols., Delhi.
Gupta, H. R. (ed.) (1957) *The Life and Letters of Sir Jadunath Sarkar*, Hoshiarpur.
Habib, I. (1963) *The Agrarian System of Mughal India*, Bombay.
Hardy, P. (1960) *Historians of Medieval India. Studies in Indo-Muslim Historical Writing*,
　London.
Harrison, S. S. (1960) *India. The Most Dangerous Decade*, Princeton.
Hussain, R. (1971) *The Politics of Iqbal*, Lahore.
Irschick, E. (1986) *Tamil Revivalism in the 1930s*, Madras.
Isfahani, Abu Talib (1885) ['Tafzih-ul Ghafalin'] *History of Asaf ud Dawlah, Nawab Wazir
　of Oudh*, tr. W. Hoey, Allahabad.

Jones, K. (ed.) (1992) *Religious Controversy in British India*, New York.
Kincaid, C. A. and Parasnis, D. B. (1918–25) *History of the Maratha People*, 3 vols, Bombay.
Kumar, R. (1989) *The Making of a Nation: Essays in Indian History and Politics*, Delhi.
Maine, H. S. (1871) *Village Communities in East and West*, London.
Majumdar, R. C. *et al.* (eds) (1951–69) *The History and Culture of the Indian People*, 14 vols, Delhi.
Masani, R. P. (1939) *Dadhabhai Naoroji. The Grand Old Man of India*, London.
Mill, J. [1817] (1975) *History of British India*, Chicago.
Moreland, W. H. (1912) *The Agriculture of the United Provinces. An Introduction for the Use of Landholders and Officials*, Allahabad.
—— (1924) *The Agrarian System of Moslem India*, London.
Mukherjee, R. (1984) *Awadh in Revolt, 1857–8. A Study of Popular Resistance*, Delhi.
Naoroji, D. [1893] (1962) *Poverty and un-British Rule in India*, Delhi.
Nehru, J. (1965) *Glimpses of World History*, repr. Bombay.
O'Hanlon, R. (1988) 'Recovering the subject; subaltern studies and the history of resistance in south Asia', *Modern Asian Studies* 22(1).
Pandey, G. (ed.) (1993) *Hindus and Others. The Question of Identity in India Today*, Delhi.
Prasad, B. S. (1851) *Sikhiyon Ka Udaya aur Asta*, Benares.
Ranade, M. G. (1900) *History of the Maratha Power*, Bombay.
Rao, P. S. M. (1963) *Eighteenth Century Deccan*, Bombay.
Robinson, F. C. R. (1974) *Separatism among Indian Muslims*, Cambridge.
Sardesai, G. D. (1946–8) *New History of the Marathas*, 3 vols,
Sarkar, J. N. (1901) *The India of Aurangzeb*, Calcutta.
—— (1919) *Studies in Mughal India*, Calcutta.
—— (1955) *The House of Shivaji*, Calcutta.
Savarkar, V. D. (1947) *The Indian War of Independence 1857*, Bombay.
Smith, V. (1958) *Oxford History of India*, 3rd edn, Oxford.
Stokes, E. (1986) *The Peasant Armed. The Indian Rebellion of 1857*, Oxford.
Tabatabai, Ghularn Hussain (1790) ['Siyar al-Muta 'akhkhirin'] *Seir Mutaqherin*, tr. 'Haji Mustapha', Calcutta.
Thompson, E. and Garrett, G. T. (1934) *The Rise and Fulfilment of British Rule in India*, London.
Tod, J. [1829] (1982) *Annals and Antiquities of Rajast'han*, 2 vols, repr. Delhi.

691

27

HISTORY IN AFRICA

David Birmingham

The discovery of the African past has been the most important advance in historical study since the Second World War. It has flourished when scholars have seen Africans as the creators of their own history and have relied on sources which Africans have produced: their material remains, languages, traditions, institutions and written documents, Whenever the subject has deserted those principles, its vitality has waned.

John Iliffe, Professor of African History,
University of Cambridge, in *History Today*,
September 1992

MATERIAL EVIDENCE AND THE MILLION-YEAR PERSPECTIVE

One of the first and most famous pieces of African historical popularization was titled 'Old Africa Rediscovered' and in 1959 it explored the archaeological researches into the African Iron Age and emphasized the often-neglected fact that Africa, like Europe, did have a history and even a prehistory (Davidson 1959). In that same year, 1959, the most notable of Africa's archaeologists (or palaeo-anthropologists) went even further back in time and captured the front page of the *East African Standard* with the banner headline 'Leakey Discovers The Missing Link' (Leakey 1961). The reference was to Darwin's theory of evolution from ape to man, and thereafter no scholar seriously doubted that Africa was the probable location in which the origins of the human species should be sought. Olduvai Gorge, in what was to become the Republic of Tanzania, was the first site where early hominid fossils and footprints were discovered, but soon others were to be found in Kenya and Ethiopia as well, thus reinforcing Africa's claim to be the cradle of mankind and pushing the origins of the species back beyond the million-year threshold (Richard Leakey 1981). The times were exciting as academics discussed Davidson's book and listened to Leakey on the subject of hominid dentition and diet.

Historiography in Africa had to develop a whole series of new scientific tools and techniques to cope with the questions that historians began to ask. From being the backwater of the historical sciences Africa became the pioneer, using new forms of dating. The relative chronology of archaeological layers and geological time-spans was strengthened by the development of absolute dating through physics and chemistry. The discovery of potassium-argon dating enabled inorganic materials with human associations to be dated, and what is more it enabled them to be dated for much earlier periods than was permitted by the radio-carbon dating of organic material. Radio-carbon dating itself was refined so that errors of measurement created by sun-spot activity or other influences could be discounted and 'calibrated'; dates could be given with higher degrees of probable accuracy. The development of dendrochronology meant that patterns of tree-ring growth could be recognized in old timbers to provide an even more accurate absolute dating in given vegetational and climatic zones. The African Stone Age was mapped out from the development of regular patterns of human tool-making and tool-using to the origins of spoken language (Clark 1970; Ki-Zerbo 1981).

The study of language in Africa, and the associated study of material and social culture, involved the development of yet further historical skills, this time in the field of statistics. Glottochronology, the measuring of the time over which languages evolve and diverge, was never a precise science but it enabled historians to create patterns of human association over the last 10,000 years that were far more plausible than those based on earlier concepts of 'race'. The 'Hamitic Hypothesis', which the first generation of anthropologists had fed into African history, had imagined the swarthy sons of Noah invading the land of their wholly black brethren, bringing light into darkness (Seligman c.1930). The linguistic statisticians were much more refined in their cultural partitioning of the continent into zones of very ancient common ancestry such as northern Africa and the Middle East and zones of relatively recent linguistic colonization such as central and southern Africa (Greenberg 1963). In the north it was recognized that the languages of the Middle East had their roots in Africa long before the emergence of the Egyptian dynasties. Later these very old African languages returned to Africa in their new Semitic forms of Ethiopic and Arabic. Meanwhile quite different languages evolved in the Niger basin of West Africa and, during the the first millennium before Christ, spilled over into the Congo basin as well. In central Africa, and in southern and eastern Africa as well, the great Bantu family of languages evolved at much the same time as the Germanic family of languages evolved in northern Europe (Guthrie 1967–71; Dalby 1970; Ehret and Posnanski 1982). It was among the older communities of the north and the west of tropical Africa, however, that a food-producing revolution began during the new Stone Age. From there it was diffused throughout Africa, requiring historians to turn to yet another branch of scholarship, palaeobotany.

The history of agriculture became and remained one of the central themes of African studies. Although food foraging has remained of greater or lesser import-ance to many peoples in many places over the past 10,000 years, the development of regular patterns of food production affected the majority of African peoples and has attracted the attention of large numbers of historians. Explanations for the change no longer assume that the farming way of life was naturally more secure than the foraging one, but where population densities grew, or reliable rainfall dwindled, the intensification of land-use evolved. Old ideas of agricultural diffusion from a cradle in the fertile crescent of the Middle East had to be modified as botanists established that many of the food crops of Africa evolved from indigenous plants (Harlan *et al.* 1976) The concept of 'vegeculture' emerged among the societies which had discovered that wild tubers such as yams could renew themselves if carefully tended. Tree harvesting for oil seeds developed in both palm groves of the forest and orchards of the savanna (Davies 1967). But above all the domestication and ennoblement of the wild grasses of Africa provided the basis for the cultivated cereal crops of millet, eleusine, sorghum and teff, which formed the staple ingredients for beer, for porridge and for bread (Lewicki 1974; Miracle 1966).

Historians have always been interested in differentials of wealth and ostentation, and in Africa such differentials were often associated with the supply of protein to supplement the diet of foraged and farmed vegetable foods. The history of fishing, fish-drying, fish-marketing and fish-transporting dominates the history of many African societies over the last 10,000 years. One archaeologist went so far as to refer to the 'fish-stew revolution' that occurred along the streams of the southern Sahara as former hunters began to settle down and wait for a riverine prey to swim past their villages rather than themselves living as hunters constantly on the move (Sutton 1974). On the lower Niger river fishermen became so adept at the carving and manning of heavy transport canoes that they became large-scale entrepreneurs in carrying crops and salt over long distances (Northrup 1978). On the middle Niger, above the rapids where Mungo Park met his death, other fishermen developed a naval might that enabled them to challenge the land-based rulers of empire and create a military kingdom of their own which linked the rice plantations of the upper river with desert gateways of the caravan routes to the Mediterranean (Rouch 1954). On the lower Congo (or Zaïre) river large states did not evolve, but the management of economic opportunity created a network that spread ideas, technologies and ornaments along a thousand-mile chain of villages (Harms 1981). On the upper Congo (or Lualaba) fishermen did create an early empire whose wealth was based on the management of lakes and waterways that supplied dried fish that could be sold over long distances. The fishermen bought preserving salt from the dried-lake pans of East Africa and adopted currencies that had evolved from the eighth-century AD copper mines of the Zambezi watershed (Birmingham and Martin 1981; Reefe 1981).

Domestic animals were as important as fish in the creation of new prosperity in Africa and have attracted the same attention from historians. Household cats, ferrets and hunting dogs were followed by domesticated sheep, goats, pigs and hens which spread readily to become an essential part of the agricultural way of life of most African societies. Of even greater if more localized importance was the development of cattle ranching, which can be traced through art history as well as bone middens. Those parts of the Sahara that had adequate pasture 6,000 or more years ago saw wild cattle become tamed herds, and the herdsmen drew magnificent pictures of their prize beasts on the walls of their rock shelters (Lhote 1959). Smaller cattle, often herded by nomadic specialists, were taken south to the very fringes of the tsetse-infested forest, and in the highlands of East Africa long-horned cattle and humped cattle spread through the highlands to reach South Africa during the early centuries of the Christian era (Phillipson 1977).

The history of cattle became intimately linked to the history of social organization among many Bantu-speaking peoples. In the highlands of East Africa the Iron Age kingdoms were associated with the management of herds and pasture. The ownership of cattle gave the wealthy a better diet, better health, a taller stature and political status (Karugire 1971). Cattle were the primary form of wealth in the fourteenth-century AD empire of Zimbabwe whose 'barons' leased out their livestock to their 'villains'. The royal Zimbabwe court was surrounded by a curtain wall 60 feet high topped by chevron decorations that were built in the thirteenth century. Provincial governors quarried granite or alternative local stone to build imitation courts where they tended herds of cattle right up to the margins of the disease-infested lowlands. The royal regalia were ornamented with leopard skins and the royal banquets were served on Chinese celadon, paid for with gold dust quarried from deep pits by women and children while men devoted themselves to the prestige task of nurturing and protecting the herds (Garlake 1973). Further south, cattle played a key role in clan relations and cows became the preferred form of bride-wealth when women passed from one community to another in marriage (Kuper 1982). Cattle also played an important role in the history of transport. Bullocks drew carts across the Roman Sahara several centuries before the introduction of the pack camel and 2,000 years before Boer waggons, spanned with sixteen oxen apiece, were drawn across the South African high veld (Bulliet 1975; Walker 1934).

RECORDED HISTORY AND ORAL EVIDENCE

African historiography is even better known for its pioneering work on the use of oral evidence than it is for its innovative use of material evidence to recreate early history (Vansina 1985; Henige 1982; Miller 1980). One of the first historians to collect oral evidence from Africa was Herodotus, who gained knowledge of the interior from the Greek colonies of modern Libya. The Carthaginians had oral accounts of epic voyages down the African coast and perhaps even heard of a circumnavigation of the continent. The Roman senator Pliny exclaimed that something new was always coming out of Africa. A thousand years later it was the interface between literate Muslim travellers and oral chroniclers that brought details of the medieval empires of West Africa to the world of Mediterranean scholarship. (Levtzion and Hopkins 1981). Timbuktu and Kano became centres of historical learning as the Arabic alphabet spread into Africa and caused orally transmitted legal precedents, constitutional agreements, dynastic successions and international

695

peace treaties to be committed to writing. In the fourteenth century the emperor of Mali made the pilgrimage to Mecca to enhance his credentials as a Muslim and his caravan was so lavishly endowed with West African gold that its passage through Cairo caused turbulence on the money markets (Bovill 1933; Levtzion 1973).

The northern interface between oral historical records and written ones was matched by a similar interface in eastern Africa, along the monsoon lanes of the Indian Ocean. East Africa's early history was recorded in boat-building technology brought from Indonesia, along with the Indonesian languages still spoken in Madagascar, Indonesian crops such as the vegetable-banana, Indonesian diseases such as elephantiasis and most dramatically Indonesian music as played on huge wooden xylophones with gourds for resonance chambers (Jones 1964; Kent 1970). The first literate observers to report on the exotic wealth of East Africa came from Rome, in the first Christian century, and later ones came from Persia, from Arabia, from India and from Muslim Spain until in 1415 a Chinese embassy arrived in Africa and went home to parade a live giraffe before the Ming emperor (Freeman-Grenville 1962; Snow 1988). Some of the visitors used, wrote and diffused the local Swahili language of the north Kenya coast until it became a lingua franca along 2,000 miles of sea-shore and eventually spread into parts of the interior as well. Historical legends were recorded in Swahili, long-distance traders wrote their autobiographies in Swahili and eventually German conquerors adopted Swahili as the official language of modern colonial government (Nurse and Spear 1985; Whiteley 1969; Pauwels 1987). The oral and literary records are supplemented by the inscriptions on the foreign and local coin which numismatists decipher and by the artwork on the coral palaces of sultans in the medieval city-states of the coastal islands and enclaves (Chittick 1974; Garlake 1966).

Africa's third frontier, the western one facing the Atlantic, was very different from the northern and eastern frontiers in that it did not have open communication with the classical world of antiquity or with the culture and literature of Islam and of the Asian empires. The historiographical dialogue between the custodians of oral information and literate visitors from across the seas began at a much later date, in the fifteenth century, and some societies did not meet literate observers until the colonial period of the twentieth century. It was therefore here, in Guinea and West Central Africa and also in the deeper interior of eastern Africa, that the modern skills of the oral historian were perfected. The first oral historians thought that they were collecting individual memories handed down by old men and women from generation to generation. Later they realized that the oral records could be more formalized, structured or coded accounts of social and political systems. The traditions could be passed on for centuries where the institutions to which they related survived with such longevity. But formal oral records also needed to be modified by their custodians so that each generation understood its society's history in ways that made sense to the current political or cosmological view of the world. Moreover the explanations of oral tradition could become stylized and stereotyped, making their interpretation by outsiders particularly difficult. Episodes of historical change became cloaked in conventional stories of migration, epitomizing a remote and prestigious ancestry, or of hunting and salt-gathering, epitomizing power and success in times of hardship, or of cruelty and barbarity, epitomizing domination by force and ritual. Capuchin missionaries of the seventeenth century and Belgian anthropologists of the twentieth each perfected their own way of interpreting the oral records which they heard in Central Africa (Cavazzi 1687; Vansina 1978; Ogot 1967).

The most extensively collected and printed oral records from Africa relate to political systems, and historians of Africa have been accused of being excessively preoccupied with the history of states and empires, of kingdoms and chiefdoms. The majority of Africans, it was pointed out, lived in villages and hamlets with few overarching institutions to connect them. Part of the historian's preoccupation with states derives from the nature and richness of the oral chronicles relating to institutions which need to prove their legitimacy and pedigree. Some of the oldest known oral records, for instance, belong to the rain priests of the Angolan grassland whose magico-religious authority evolved into structured chiefdoms and then kingdoms. The power of prayer, and the control of the supernatural, preceded the military mobilization of regiments of drilled archers, and the economic domination of mines of iron and salt, in the fourteenth- and fifteenth-century origins of the kingdom of Angola (Miller c.1974). Elsewhere states kept records relating to their constitutions, their legal systems, their boundaries, their property-ownership, their dynasties, their kinship alliances and their wars. African historiography has taught the historical profession how to decode material which at one time or another has been conveyed by oral means. Classical scholars now look at the interface between the spoken and the written form in Greece and Rome with new eyes, and modern historians have made strides in recovering the invisible past of women and men who did not take part in the literate culture of decision-making.

One of the great problems of oral tradition, like that of material evidence, has been the problem of supplying absolute as opposed to relative dating. Where generations are counted some help is available, but in polygynous societies the children of young wives may be very much younger than their fathers, and in matrilineal societies heirs may be brothers or nephews and not sons at all. Average reign-lengths may provide rough guidance, though with the same variables, but an excessive concern with rulers can lead to the padding of king-lists and the confusing of proper names with titles. Attempts to identify remembered and datable natural phenomena, such as total or annular eclipses of the sun, have not carried the matter very far. Thus the dating of social events, wars, accessions and droughts has lagged behind the dating of material artefacts in Africa. Absolute dating, like literacy, has come largely with outside contact, and the most pervasive outside contact has come with the spread of world religions from the Near East. Although Islam and Christianity have been extensively studied, the history of Judaism in Africa is one of the more neglected of the continent's historiographical fields. In Ethiopia the black Falasha long practised Judaism and subsequently gained admission to the state of Israel. In Morocco Jewish communities prospered and were enriched by refugees from Spain when Castile conquered Granada in 1492. In medieval Cairo Jews provided a class of merchants who retained their beliefs and practices alongside

697

their Christian and Muslim neighbours. Yet Judaism did not gain the hold over Africa that Islam and Christianity were to have, nor has it yet gained its rightful place in the scholarly literature.

The birth of Christ in Nazareth, and the flight of Muhammad from Mecca 622 years later, provide the fixed points around which most Africans have built their calendars. Christianity reached into Africa at much the same time it reached into late Roman Europe. It spread down the Red Sea, up the Nile, along the Mediterranean coast, into the desert oases. The Coptic Church flourished in Egypt and became the state Church of Ethiopia for more than 1,000 years. In North Africa the Donatist Church, named after a fourth-century bishop of Carthage, gave the region a distinctive religious style, albeit one that others would consider heretical. In the person of Saint Augustine of Hippo, Africa also provided the Western Church with one of its most influential theological fathers. Islam, however, spread farther and faster than early Christianity and in many places overwhelmed it, in North Africa, up the Nile and in the lowlands surrounding the mountain core of Christian Ethiopia. Eventually Islam even overwhelmed Christianity in the last bastion of the Roman Empire, Constantinople, which was conquered in 1453. Thereafter Islam was given a new stimulus in Africa by the rise of the Ottoman Empire and its confrontation with the new Christian empire of Portugal at the opposite end of the Mediterranean (Groves 1948; Holt ed. 1970; Lewis 1966; Trimmingham 1962; Doresse 1957).

FOREIGN EMPIRES AND ARCHIVAL RECORDS

There are two great repositories of early modern archives for Africa, and neither of them has been fully exploited. The first is in Istanbul and relates to the spread of Ottoman imperial influence through northern Africa in the sixteenth century. It has rarely attracted the attention of historians interested in Africa. The second set of archives is in Lisbon and was seriously disrupted by the earthquake of 1755. Only slowly did historians come to recognize the wealth of materials relating to the Atlantic face of Africa with some material on the India Ocean as well (Ryder c.1965). The two spheres of early imperial influence in Africa overlap and interact both on land and at sea in Morocco and in the Red Sea basin. Both empires sent diplomats deep into the African interior and both created creolized African elites who spoke Turkish or Portuguese and became the local agents of colonial administration. The archival records of the Portuguese literate urban cultural enclaves around the African shore have been partially quarried by historians and the surviving creole communities have been studied by anthropologists. The most striking surviving cultures are to be found on the islands which were used as pioneering bases for the European development of colonial plantations growing wine, cotton and sugar in the tropics (Boxer 1964; Russell-Wood 1992; Mercer 1980; Duncan 1972; Hodges and Newitt 1988). Hard on the heels of the Ottomans and the Portuguese came a third wave of merchants and settlers from The Netherlands. They gained access to the gold emporia of West Africa, the slave and ivory grounds of Central Africa, and the temperate farmlands of South Africa, creating ordered historical records which the first generation of modern African historians used to sharpen their historiographical skills and write their doctoral theses (Daaku 1970; Martin 1972).

Planters and merchants were followed by Muslim and Christian preachers who spread literacy, ethics, jurisprudence and belief along the long-distance trade routes and settled missionaries in the great urban centres of politics and commerce. The city of Kano in West Africa became a centre of learning as well as a focus for the trade in textiles, metals, livestock and slave labour. One travelling scholar provided the city-state with constitutional guidelines for good governance and another hoped to buy a literate slave to take home to Muslim Spain as his secretary. In the nineteenth century one British visitor was asked if he could supply copies of the Greek works of mathematics missing from the sultan's library. Victorian scholar-adventurers became profoundly interested in African Islam and their awe passed to both British and French administrators of the next generation (Bovill 1964–6; Fisher and Fisher 1970). In the Christian sphere of influence the sixteenth-century kings of Kongo hired clerks who kept their ledgers and wrote on theological matters to the popes of Rome. A royal archive was steadily built up until a column of marauding colonists from Portugal burnt it to the ground in the mid-nineteenth century. The loss of the Kongo archive facilitated the dissemination of the European myth that Africa had no history and, by implication, that conquest in the name of 'civilization' was morally justified (Hilton 1985; Thornton 1983).

The early attempts to Christianize Africa gradually subsided as European interest in the continent became increasingly dominated by the slave trade. The rise of the modern slave trade became a major preoccupation of historians. The trade was not a new phenomenon when Europeans entered it in the fifteenth century. In the north of Africa black slaves were bought by Romans to supplement the white slaves who came from the eponymous Slav territories in Europe. The Carthaginians probably also had black slaves, and the name Guinea which came to be applied to the west coast of Africa derives from the Carthaginian word for black. Arabs developed more reliable routes across the Sahara and bought not only male labourers but also attractive young women who could fetch high prices in the harems if they survived the ordeal of the desert crossing. The Turkish Empire went on buying slaves into the nineteenth century and in exchange supplied West Africa with firearms for its infantry and chain-mail for its cavalry. The first Portuguese also bought slaves for their newly conquered Muslim estates in the Algarve and paid for them with metal goods and horses (Thompson and Ferguson 1969; Boahen 1964; Saunders 1982). The trade in people from eastern Africa was as varied as the northern trade but has been less well illustrated in the literature. Ethiopian slave wives seem to have been prized in Persia and child pearl-divers were taken to the Persian Gulf in large numbers. Colonial regiments in India were sometimes reinforced by black slave soldiers from Africa, though the scale of the trade to India has not been adequately quantified (Clarence-Smith 1989; Austen 1987; Russell-Wood 1992).

The modern extension of the slave trade to the Americas became a topic of virulent academic controversy. Much of the early writing about the slave trade came from the pens of polemicists who wished either to condemn its morality or to justify it as a means of redeeming souls from the perceived barbarism of indigenous society. Historians were slow to adopt a properly critical approach to this data and to delve into the archives to find authenticated evidence about such a sensitive subject. When they eventually did so, driven by American scholars rather than by either European or African ones, they unleashed a spate of new research and publication. Measuring the Atlantic slave trade has been the concern of polemicists for two centuries, but it was not until 1969 that serious scholarship prevailed and Philip Curtin, a founder of the American school of African history, published his historiography of slave statistics and his own estimate of the scale of the Atlantic trade. His evidence was subjected both to emotive condemnation and to statistical refinement, culminating in a consensus that 11 or 12 million people had been taken from Africa to the Americas in less than four centuries (Curtin 1969; Klein 1978; Inikori 1982). One of the great controversies over the slave trade was the measuring of its impact on Africa not only in statistical terms but also in terms of demographic change, commercial initiative, military destruction and political innovation. Several diaries of slaves and of slaving captains were discovered, edited and published. In the South Atlantic the evidence of the Brazil trade shed light on how slaves were procured, on the methods of credit used in the trade, on the ownership of slaves during the middle crossing and on the rivalries of shipping interests (Lovejoy 1983; Miller 1988; Curtin 1975; Edwards 1967; Grant 1968). The other great debate among historians concerned the reasons for the outlawing and suppression of the African slave trade by the future colonial powers. Economic, moral and political factors were debated with increasingly sophisticated intellectual passion (Williams c.1944; Anstey 1975; Drescher 1977).

Traders, missionaries and slavers were followed by cohorts of invaders, settlers and conquerors, each of which acquired a specialist accompaniment of historians. The history of this imperialism was treated with some reserve by the post-war generation of new historians of Africa who were concerned to understand the African experience rather than to study the activities of Europeans in Africa. Yet the questions had to be raised concerning the reasons for the 'scramble for Africa', its diplomatic partition and the subsequent imposition of 'effective rule' by foreigners. An acrimonious debate occurred between those who saw imperialism as 'uneconomic', an extension of nineteenth-century European nationalism into colonial provinces, and those who saw it as a search for minerals and *Lebensraum* (Hammond 1966; Clarence-Smith 1985). 'My map of Africa', Bismarck was purported to have proclaimed in 1885, 'is in Europe', but Leopold, the king of the Belgians, would hardly have agreed as he carved out his million-mile fief in the Congo. Anglo-French rivalry over spheres of influence and methods of financing services for traders was another source of sharp disagreement that led to the creation of formal colonies with boundaries and tariff regimes. France won the upper Niger and Britain the lower Niger in a series of military expeditions. Further south treaty makers and mineral prospectors sought land, labour and local alliances with African rulers (Slade 1962; Hargreaves 1974–85; Kanya-Forstner 1969; Oliver 1957). Beyond the debates over local circumstance and agency was the wider debate about the world partition and Africa's place within it as a dark continent separating the two economic giants of South Africa and Egypt and providing a barrier on the sea-road from Europe to Asia (Robinson and Gallagher 1961; Penrose 1975).

THE CHANGING FACE OF SOUTH AFRICAN HISTORIOGRAPHY

The African territory that required the most intense military effort to conquer it was South Africa. The second Anglo-Boer War of 1899–1902 was, with the possible exception of the Crimean War, the most brutal and expensive British war to be fought between Waterloo in 1815 and the Great War in 1914. British soldiers died of wounds and diseases, African auxiliaries disappeared without trace or concern, Afrikaner women and children were rounded up in desolate concentration camps, farmhouses were fired, heirlooms were looted, war reports were forged, fortunes were made (Warwick 1980; Cammack 1990). Despite the profound impact which the conquest of South Africa had on Britain and on British historians, the post-1945 generation of 'new' African historians found South Africa almost invisible. It did not feature in their syllabuses and did not attract their research students. South African history was an enclave of European history, a political debate among white males. Only two non-European politicians feature in the entire index to a history of South Africa put out by the English Universities Press in 1946, and one of those was the 'diabolically ingenious' Mr Gandhi who caused Mr Smuts so much grief (Williams 1946). The history of race relations in South Africa was more commonly an account of the relations between the British and the Dutch races than an historical analysis of the so-called 'native' question or even of the 'Indian' question. Indeed it was officially put about in school texts and government publications that the black population of South Africa consisted of 'hordes' of 'warriors' who had come down from the north to try to wrest South Africa from the legitimate white settlers who had turned the wilderness into a garden. The beginnings of an effective challenge to this historical propaganda came not from a historian but from an anthropologist who traced back the records of the societies she was studying to discover that there were well-documented accounts of sixteenth-century shipwrecked mariners being cared for by African farmers a century before the first Dutch settlers came on the scene (Wilson 1959; Boxer 1959).

A turning-point in South African historiography came in 1969–71 with the appearance of the *Oxford History of South Africa* (Wilson and Thompson 1969–71). Not only was the history of first-millennium AD cereal farming, cattle-raising and iron-working brought into focus, but archaeological evidence of trade with China was unearthed to demonstrate at least limited medieval contact with the outside world. Not only was the history of modern African society shown to be a long one, but the organization of the society was shown to be more complex and sophisticated than the colonial conquerors had been willing to acknowledge. An Oxford chapter on nationalism compared the aspirations of white Afrikaans-speaking nationalists with those of black Bantu-speaking nationalists, inviting a debate which the South African government did its best to stifle by censorship. From 1969 onwards, however, South African historiography began to grow apace. Afrikaner nationalists, it emerged, were not the only ones to be critical of the 'liberal' tradition of South African historiography. A new school of 'revisionist' historians were anxious to bring the experience of the black majority into the mainstream of historical writing. These radical historians included both Afrikaner and British scholars, though at first few Africans had access to the new centres of academic research. In 1982 a two-volume social history of the Witwatersrand provided a path-breaking collection of essays on poor whites who came to the city, on Zulu guilds of washermen and rickshaw peddlers, on the role of alcohol and prostitution in attracting black and white workers respectively to the gold mines, on the distilling of Boer farm produce into hard liquor, and on the efforts of the Kruger government to meet the competing demands of farm capital and of mine capital, thereby revising received ideas about the causes of the Boer War (van Onselen 1982). Labour history replaced financial history as the core subject of the mineral revolution in South Africa and studies focused not only on the mining demand for segregation, mine compounds and rural reserves for migrants' families, but also on the supply of cheap workers from outside South Africa and indeed from as far away as China (Wilson 1972; Turrell 1987; Richardson 1982; Levy 1982).

Although the nineteenth-century mineral revolution and its legacy provided an early focus of revisionist historiography among South Africa's émigré historians, rural life, and often a very uncertain life at that, remained the experience of the majority of South Africans and attracted the attention of the growing historical profession. Introductions to the emerging themes appeared in a three-volume set of essays edited by Shula Marks and others (1980; 1982; 1987). Zulu history emerged from the colonial and anthropological mystification of the conquest to become a subject of thrusting historical controversy (Marks 1970; 1986; Guy 1979). The history of the rise and fall of modern black farming in the Cape concentrated on the competition between black and white farmers over access to land, transport and markets. As landless proletarianization advanced, so historians turned to studying social, political and trade union organization (Bundy 1979; Beinart 1982; Bradford 1987). The drama of rural South Africa reached its nadir in the Bantustans which bore the brunt of South Africa's labour policy and had to carry the social costs of reproducing a labour force with minimal expense to industry or the state. Some of the heaviest burdens were borne by women whose men had gone off to the mines and plantations as they had done under slavery or colonialism in other times and other parts of Africa. Some women followed men into the labour market, but often under conditions of great poverty and isolation. In the 1980s the lives of many of these women were brought into the light in a new branch of South African historiography (Marks 1987; 1994; Walker 1990; Berger 1992; Cocks 1980).

Despite its pockets of racially confined wealth and its great development potential, much of South Africa remained poor and prone to disease. The history of disease was slow to catch the imagination of historians and yet it is one of the prevalent experiences of South Africans. The mining industry brought new diseases to the continent and accentuated the effects of old ones. Disease brought poverty and death to former workers who had neither medication nor security. The great pandemic of Aids appeared to spread in the male hostels of mine workers and the old plague of tuberculosis revived to become again one of the world's great killers (Packard 1989). Disease affected rural people and also their livestock. At an earlier date South Africa suffered a severe epidemic of rinderpest, and in East Africa cattle disease cleared whole areas of herders and led to ecological changes of deep importance to human activity and the encroachment of colonial conquest (Kjekshus 1977). In French equatorial Africa sleeping sickness killed many workers in the logging camps and led to acute shortages of labour and the harsh recruitment of forced conscripts (Coquery-Vidrovitch 1972). In Angola an epidemic of smallpox swept through village society in the early twentieth century and disrupted the expansion of the colonial coffee plantations. River blindness affected those who lived near snail-infested rivers and malaria killed more people than any other disease in all the lowland areas. Drought and famine became increasingly oppressive as the population of Africa increased in number during the twentieth century and caused a new wave of historical investigation of ecological factors. As deprivation and stress grew so the history of mental health became a preoccupation and records of the colonial attitude to psychiatry began to be investigated. The history of public health, of sanitation and and of medical science in Africa began to explore the change and lack of change brought by the twentieth century (Iliffe 1987; Vaughan 1987; Lyons 1992).

THE PROFESSIONALIZATION AND POPULARIZATION OF AFRICAN HISTORY

The first major steps in the formalizing and disseminating of African history were taken in 1948. In that year the University of London took measures to bring Africa into the mainstream of the discipline by creating a quaintly archaic 'lectureship in the history of the tribal peoples of East Africa' at the School of Oriental and African Studies. London distanced itself from the old British Academy tradition which insisted that scholarship was exclusively literate and that Africa was only of reputable academic interest where it interacted with the civilizations of Greece and Rome, or Mecca and Jerusalem. The London initiative led to the hosting of two international conferences on African history in 1954 and 1961, to the founding of a Cambridge journal devoted to African history, and coincided with the establishment of history departments in the University's new colonial colleges on the Gold Coast, in Nigeria and in Uganda. Local journals of historical scholarship were established in Africa and local history degrees gradually introduced Africa into their syllabuses. London itself concentrated on postgraduate teaching and encouraged the publication of hundreds of hardbound monographs that began life as doctoral theses. In 1961 London University began teaching African history at an undergraduate level and in 1966 it launched

703

American-style masters degrees as well. In 1962 the London pioneers published a Penguin history of Africa which has been in print in numerous editions and several languages ever since. They also began commissioning work for an eight-volume Cambridge history (Oliver and Fage 1962; 1975–85). Each author was awarded a chair in African history and within twenty years no less than fourteen British history chairs were held by Africa specialists. During those years African historical studies spread from British Africa to the ex-colonial universities of Belgian and French Africa as well. The African universities also sponsored new research by hosting international conferences and publishing the proceedings, with the help of the International African Institute, the Pan-African Congress of Prehistory and Archaeology, the Leverhulme Foundation and UNESCO. UNESCO also launched an ambitious *General History of Africa* which aimed to encourage African scholarship and disseminate it into educational syllabuses. The eighth and last volume was published in 1993 and abridged paperback editions have begun to appear (Mazrui 1993). African schools, however, were slow to change their neo-colonial customs and adopt even subsidized new textbooks. African history made better progress in American schools where many teachers had gained familiarity with Africa through their Peace Corps service.

In the 1960s historians of Africa were almost overwhelmed by the demand that they explain the surge of anti-colonialism that was presumed to herald the advent of nationalism in Africa, on the model of the nationalism that had grown in Europe during the unification of Italy or the dismemberment of Austria. The first tide of nationalist history was informed by an American school of political science that developed its own language and its own interview materials (Apter 1955; Coleman 1958; Young 1963). The second development in nationalist historiography was more profoundly historical as scholars sought to find the roots of nationalism in the early colonial experience by recovering the submerged 'authentic voice' of Africa. Historians looked at the history of primary resistance, as Africans struggled against the advent of imperialism, and at secondary resistance as they tried to maintain their identity under the colonial yoke (Ranger 1967; 1970; Iliffe 1969; Crowder 1971; 1968). The third phase of nationalist history came later, once the colonial archives had been opened to scrutiny, after judicious shredding by the departing powers. Historical documentation significantly challenged the triumphalism of the 1960s and brought a more nuanced interpretation to the controversial conflicts of decolonization. The anti-colonial war in Kenya was revisited by British scholars while remaining virtually a taboo subject for Kenyans, and even the profoundly traumatizing war of independence in Algeria began to be studied with liberated hindsight in France (Kanogo 1987; Throup 1987). One way in which the popularization of history was expected to grow was through the publication of national histories on the European model, but in fact very few of the fifty-odd ex-colonial nations in Africa have been covered by single-volume, single-author histories that are both scholarly and readable. A few notable exceptions include Tanzania, Nigeria, Zambia, Ethiopia, South Africa and Algeria (Iliffe 1979; Isichei 1983; Zewde 1991; Thompson 1990; Ageron 1991).

When the history of Africa began to be studied and written in the 1950s it was reasonable to expect that its popularization would include the publication of biographies of leading Africans, just as biography became a major branch of wider history in Europe. One of the first great classics of the new historical school was just such a life-and-times biography (Shepperson and Price 1958). This path was not followed by many later historians and the great African biographies were more commonly devoted to the lives of the colonial proconsuls than to their indigenous partners and protagonists. (Perham 1956–60; Flint 1974). In South Africa the biographical tradition was stronger and covered both black and white South Africans (Willan 1984; Thompson 1975; Paton 1964). In tropical Africa some of the heroes of the anti-colonial resistance have yielded up documentation that has led to studies of a quasi-biographical kind. (Robinson 1985; Person 1968–75). Modern political leaders have been the subject of biography or of autobiography that may be more or less ghost-written. (Murray-Brown 1972; Nkrumah 1957). The biographies of common individuals are even more scarce than those of leaders but those that have been published are richly illuminating (Smith 1954; Crowder 1988).

By the 1990s African history had gained its place in the mainstream of the historical profession, even though the current work devotes only one chapter to the continent as compared to four devoted to Asia. African history has been presented on television in two eight-part series, one made by the pioneering Basil Davidson and the other by the Kenyan scholar and Reith Lecturer, Ali Mazrui. In Africa itself historical publishing has suffered grievously from closed frontiers, restricted currencies, paper shortages, impecunious students; and much historical work prepared in the 1970s and 1980s therefore still awaits an outlet. In Britain, however, two of the founding fathers of African historiography reviewed their life work in books of enormous vision and vitality (Oliver 1992; Davidson 1992). At the younger end of the historical profession students throughout Europe and North America continue to turn to Africa as a source of new evidence, ideas and methods through which to perfect their training.

REFERENCES

Ageron, C. R. (1991) *Modern Algeria*, tr. M. Brett, London.
Anstey, R. (1975) *The Atlantic Slave Trade and British Abolition*, London.
Apter, D. (1955) *The Gold Coast in Transition*, Princeton.
Austen, R. (1987) *African Economic History*, London.
Beinart, W. (1982) *The Political Economy of Pondoland 1860–1930*, Cambridge.
Berger, I. (1992) *Threads of Solidarity: Women in South African Industry*, Bloomington.
Birmingham, D. and Martin, P. M. (1981) *History of Central Africa*, vol. 1, Harlow.
Boahen, A. A. (1964) *Britain, the Sahara and the Western Sudan*, Oxford.
Bovill, E. W. (1933) *Caravans of the Old Sahara*, London.
—— (1964–6) *Missions to the Niger*, 2 vols, Cambridge.
Boxer, C. R. (ed.) (1959) *The Tragic History of Sea*, Cambridge.
Boxer, C. R. (1964) *Portuguese Society in the Tropics*, Madison.
Bradford, H. (1987) *A Taste of Freedom: The ICU in Rural South Africa*, New Haven, CT.
Bulliet, R. W. (1975) *The Camel and the Wheel*, Cambridge, MA.

Bundy, C. (1979) *The Rise and Fall of the South African Peasantry*, London.
Cammack, D. (1990) *The Rand at War*, London.
Cavazzi, G. (1687) *Congo Matamba e Angola*, Bologna.
Chittick, N. (1974) *Kilwa*, London.
Clarence-Smith, W. G. (1985) *The Third Portuguese Empire: A Study in Economic Imperialism*, Manchester.
—— (ed.) (1989) *The Economics of the Indian Ocean Slave Trade*, London.
Clark, J. D. (1970) *Prehistory of Africa*, London.
Cocks, J. (1980) *Maids and Madams: A Study in the Politics of Exploitation*, Johannesburg.
Coleman, J. (1958) *Nigeria*, Berkeley.
Coquery-Vidrovitch, C. (1972) *Le Congo au temps des grandes compagnies concessionaires*, The Hague.
Crowder, M. (1968) *West Africa under Colonial Rule*, London.
—— (ed.) (1971) *West African Resistance*, London.
Crowder, M. (1988) *The Flogging of Phineas McIntosh: A Tale of Colonial Folly and Injustice*, New Haven.
Curtin, P. D. (1969) *The Atlantic Slave Trade: A Census*, Madison.
—— (1975) *Economic Change in Precolonial Africa*, Madison.
Daaku, K. Y. (1970) *Trade and Politics on the Gold Coast*, Oxford.
Dalby, D. (1970) *Language and History in Africa*, London.
Davidson, B. (1959) *Old Africa Rediscovered*, London.
—— (1992) *The Black Man's Burden: Africa and the Curse of the Nation State*, London.
Davies, O. (1967) *West Africa before the Europeans*, London.
Doresse, J. (1957) *L'Empire du prêtre Jean*, Paris.
Drescher, S. (1977) *Econocide: British Slavery in the Era of Abolition*, Pittsburgh.
Duncan, T. B. (1972) *Atlantic Islands*, Chicago.
Edwards, P. (ed.) (1967) *Equiano's Travels*, London.
Ehret, C. and Posnanski, M. (1982) *The Archaeological and Linguistic Reconstruction of African History*, Berkeley.
Elphick, R. and Gilliomee, H. (1988) *The Shaping of South African Society*, Middletown.
Fisher, A. G. B. and Fisher, H. J. (1970) *Slavery and Muslim Society in Africa*, London.
Flint, J. (1974) *Cecil Rhodes*, London.
Freeman-Grenville, G. S. P. (1962) *The East African Coast*, Oxford.
Garlake, P. S. (1966) *The Early Islamic Architecture of the East African Coast*, Oxford.
—— (1973) *Great Zimbabwe*, London.
Grant, D. (1968) *The Fortunate Slave*, Oxford.
Greenberg, J. H. (1963) *Languages of Africa*, The Hague.
Groves, C. P. (1948–58) *The Planting of Christianity in Africa*, 4 vols, London.
Guthrie, M. (1967–71) *Comparative Bantu*, 2 vols, Farnborough.
Guy, J. (1979) *The Destruction of the Zulu Kingdom*, Harlow.
Hammond, R. (1966) *Portugal and Africa: A Study in Uneconomic Imperialism*, Stanford.
Hargreaves, J. D. (1974–85) *West Africa Partitioned*, 2 vols, London.
Harlan, J. R. *et al.* (1976) *Origins of African Plant Domestication*, The Hague.
Harms, R. (1981) *River of Wealth, River of Sorrow*, New Haven.
Henige, D. (1982) *Oral Historiography*, London.
Hilton, A. (1985) *The Kingdom of Congo*, Oxford.
Hodges, T. and Newitt, M. (1988) *São Tomé and Príncipe*, Boulder, CO.
Holt, P. M. (ed.) (1970) *The Cambridge History of Islam*, Cambridge.
Iliffe, J. (1969) *Tanganyika under German Rule*, Cambridge.
—— (1979) *A Modern History of Tanganyika*, Cambridge.
—— (1987) *The African Poor*, Cambridge.
Inikori, J. E. (ed.) (1982) *Forced Migration*, London.

706

Isichei, E. (1983) *A History of Nigeria*, Harlow.
Jones, A. M. (1964) *Africa and Indonesia: the Evidence of the Xylophone*, Leiden.
Kanogo, T. (1987) *Squatters and the Roots of Mau Mau*, London.
Kanya-Forstner, A. S. (1969) *The Conquest of the Western Sudan: A Study in French Military Imperialism*, Cambridge.
Karugire, S. R. (1971) *The Kingdom of Nkore*, Oxford.
Kent, R. K. (1970) *Early Kingdoms in Madagascar*, New York.
Ki-Zerbo, J. (1981) *Methodology and African Prehistory* (vol. 1 of the *UNESCO General History of Africa*), Paris.
Kjekshus, H. (1977) *Ecology, Control and Economic Development in East African History*, London.
Klein, H. S. (1978) *The Middle Passage*, Princeton.
Kuper, A. (1982) *Wives for Cattle*, London.
Leakey, L. S. B. (1961) *The Progress and Evolution of Man in Africa*, London.
Leakey, R. (1981) *The Making of Mankind*, London.
Levtzion, N. (1973) *Ancient Ghana and Mali*, London.
—— and Hopkins, J. F. P. (1981) *Corpus of Early Arabic Sources for West African History*, Cambridge.
Levy, N. (1982) *The Foundations of the South African Cheap Labour System*, London.
Lewicki, T. (1974) *West African Food in the Middle Ages*, Cambridge.
Lewis, I. M. (1966) *Islam in Tropical Africa*, Oxford.
Lhote, I. (1959) *The Search for the Tassili Frescoes*, London.
Lovejoy, P. E. (1983) *Transformations in Slavery: A History of Slavery in Africa*, Cambridge.
Lyons, M. (1992) *The Colonial Disease: A Social History of Sleeping Sickness in Northern Zaire*, Cambridge.
Marks, S. (1970) *Reluctant Rebellion*, Oxford.
—— (1986) *The Ambiguities of Dependency in South Africa*, Baltimore.
—— (1987) *Not Either an Experimental Doll: The Separate Worlds of Three South African Women*, London.
—— (1994) *Divided Sisterhood: The Nursing Profession and the Making of Apartheid*, London.
—— et al. (1980) *Economy and Society in Pre-industrial South Africa*, Harlow.
—— et al. (1982) *Industrialisation and Social Change in South Africa*, Harlow.
—— et al. (1987) *The Politics of Race, Class and Nationalism in Twentieth Century South Africa*, Harlow.
Martin, P. M. (1972) *The External Trade of the Loange Coast*, Oxford.
Mazrui, A. (1993) *General History of Africa*, vol. 8, Paris.
Mercer, J. (1980) *The Canary Islanders*, London.
Miller, J. C. (1976) *Kings and Kinsmen*, London.
—— (1980) *The African Past Speaks*, Folkestone.
—— (1988) *Way of Death: Merchant Capitalism and the Angolan Slave Trade*, London.
Miracle, M. (1966) *Maize in Tropical Africa*, Madison.
Murray-Brown, J. (1972) *Kenyatta*, London.
Nkrumah, K. (1957) *Ghana*, Edinburgh.
Northrup, D. (1978) *Trade without Rulers*, Oxford.
Nurse, D. and Spear, T. (1985) *The Swahili*, Philadelphia.
Ogot, B. A. (1967) *A History of the Southern Luo Peoples*,
Oliver, R. (1957) *Sir Harry Johnstone and the Scramble for Africa*, London.
—— (1992) *The African Experience: Major Themes in African History from Earliest Times to the Present*, London.
—— and Fage, J. D. (1962) *A Short History of Africa*, Harmondsworth.
—— (eds) (1975–85) *The Cambridge History of Africa*, 8 vols, Cambridge.
Onselen, C. van (1982) *Studies in the Social and Economic History of the Witwatersrand*, Harlow.

Packard, R. (1989) *White Plague, Black Labor: Tuberculosis and the Political Economy of Health and Disease in South Africa*, Pietermaritzburg.

Paton, A. (1964) *Hofmeyer*, Cape Town.

Pauwels, R. L. (1987) *Horn and Crescent*, Cambridge.

Penrose, E. F. (ed.) (1975) *European Imperialism and the Partition of Africa*, London.

Perham, M. (1956–60) *Lugard*, 2 vols, London.

Person, Y. (1968–75) *Samori: une révolution dyula*, 3 vols, Paris.

Phillipson, D. W. (1977) *The Later Prehistory of Eastern and Southern Africa*, London.

Ranger, T. (1967) *Revolt in Southern Rhodesia*, London.

—— (1970) *The African Voice in Southern Rhodesia*, London.

Reefe, T. Q. (1981) *The Rainbow and the Kings*, Berkeley.

Richardson, P. (1982) *Chinese Labour in the Transvaal*, London.

Robinson, D. (1985) *The Holy War of Umar Tal*, Oxford.

Robinson, R. and Gallagher, J. (1961) *Africa and the Victorians: The Official Mind of Imperialism*, London.

Rouch, J. (1954) *Les Songhai*, Paris.

Russell-Wood, A. J. R. (1992) *A World on the Move*, Manchester.

Ryder, A. F. C. (1965) *Materials Relating to Africa in the Archives of Portugal*, London.

Saunders, A. C. de C. M. (1982) *A Social History of Black Slaves and Freedmen in Portugal*, Cambridge.

Sautter, G. (1966) *De l'Atlantique au fleuve Congo: une géographie du sous-peuplement*, Paris.

Seligman, C. G. (1930) *Races of Africa*, London.

Shepperson, G. and Price, T. (1958) *Independent African*, Edinburgh.

Slade, R. (1962) *King Leopold's Congo*, Oxford.

Smith, M. (1954) *Baba of Karo: A Woman of the Moslem Hausa*, Oxford.

Snow, P. (1988) *The Star Raft: Chinese Encounter with Africa*, London.

Sutton, J. E. G. (1974) 'The Aquatic Civilization of Middle Africa' in *Journal of African History*, xv. 4, Cambridge.

Thompson, L. (1975) *Survival in Two Worlds: Moshoeshwe of Lesotho*, Oxford.

—— (1990) *A History of South Africa*, New Haven, CT.

Thompson, L. A. and Ferguson, J. (eds) (1969) *Africa in Classical Antiquity*, Ibadan.

Thornton, J. K. (1983) *The Kingdom of Kongo*, Madison.

Throup, D. W. (1987) *Economic and Social Origins of Mau Mau*, London.

Trimmingham, J. S. (1962) *A History of Islam in West Africa*, Oxford.

Turrell, R. V. (1987) *Capital and Labour on the Kimberley Diamond Fields*, Cambridge.

Vansina, J. (1978) *The Children of Woot*, Madison.

—— (1985) *Oral Tradition as History*, London.

Vaughan, M. (1987) *The Story of an African Famine: Gender and Famine in Twentieth-Century Malawi*, Cambridge.

Walker, C. (ed.) (1990) *Women and Gender in Southern Africa*, Cape Town.

Walker, E. A. (1934) *The Great Trek*, London.

Warwick, P. (1980) *The South African War*, Harlow.

Whiteley, W. (1969) *Swahili: The Rise of a National Language*, London.

Willan, B. (1984) *Sol Plaatje: South African Nationalist*, London.

Williams, B. (1946) *Botha, Smuts and South Africa*, London.

Williams, E. (1944) *Capitalism and Slavery*, London.

Wilson, F. (1972) *Labour in South African Gold Mines*, Cambridge.

Wilson, M. (1959) 'The Early History of the Transkei and Ciskei', *African Studies*, 18, IV.

Wilson, M. and Thompson, L. (eds) (1969–71) *The Oxford History of South Africa*, 2 vols, Oxford.

Young, C. (1963) *Politics in the Congo*, Princeton.

Zewde, B. (1991) *A History of Modern Ethiopia*, London.

28

MODERN AMERICAN HISTORIOGRAPHY

Carl N. Degler

Probably the written history of few peoples has been so influenced by the present as that of Americans. As a people admittedly more tuned to the future than the past, they have, none the less, found it necessary to draw upon history to explain themselves. All nations, of course, do that; few, however, need it as much as Americans. From the beginning Americans have been a heterogeneous people, and their relatively brief national existence fits entirely within the confines of 'modern times'. The sources of American nationality, unlike those, for example, of England or France, are not lost in the mists of time; rather, they seem to have been laid down only yesterday.

These forces that have shaped American historiography have never been more obvious and potent than over the last three decades when a minor revolution has reshaped historians' conception of the American past. Part of that renovation derives from a problem inherent in all historical study, namely, the tension between the collective and the individual. We want and need a history that describe groups of all sizes from clubs and organizations to cities and states, to nations and empires. Yet the larger the group the more diverse are the individuals who make it up. By what means can a historian generalize about a large diverse nation like the United States? That problem occasioned the first turn of the wheel of American historiography. The object of attack was the American Studies or consensus approach to the past.

Ever since the beginning of American history, like that of most nations, a history of the whole country has been both necessary and commonplace. Usually the story has been shaped around politics or government. During the 1930s and 1940s, however, some venturesome students of the American past moved beyond that narrow conception of the past; they sought to integrate American literature, sociology, psychology and even some economics into the nation's story; they called their approach 'American Studies'. By taking such a multidisciplinary view of American history, they believed they could more accurately encompass the breadth and diversity of that past. Among historians that approach came to be called a 'consensus' view since it sought to identify the values and attitudes that character-ized Americans in the course of their history.

Several of those studies are worth examining briefly because they provide concrete examples of the approach. Perhaps the best-known and certainly the most influential was Richard Hofstadter's *The American Political Tradition and the Men Who Made It*, which appeared in 1948. Hofstadter's point was that deep and enduring social divisions had been absent from the American past, a historical homogeneity that he seemed mildly to deplore. Daniel Boorstin's *The Genius of American Politics*, which appeared ten years later in 1958, happily argued that the central clue to appreciating and understanding the American past was its lack of ideology or dogma. Instead of conflict, he contended, Americans had been primarily concerned with what worked, with responding to the moment, with adjusting to the unexpected. Some historians interpreted this to mean that Boorstin discerned no principles, no ideological commitment in the American story. A less explicitly provocative effort to explain a large part of the American past by discerning a central theme was advanced in David M. Potter's *People of Plenty* (1954). His contention was that the American experience could best be understood by recognizing the central role played by material abundance in the making of American history. By abundance Potter meant more than just the fertile land, and plentiful mineral and plant resources; he also pointed to the immense amount of wealth produced by Americans beginning soon after the first settlements. Because they had lived amidst so much wealth, as compared with other nations of the past and present (he was writing, of course, after the devastating destruction of Europe's wealth during the Second World War), many of their characteristics, such as wastefulness, emphasis upon privacy, individualism and democracy could be explained or accounted for by that abundance.

Like all efforts to explain a society and its history through a single operating force or consensus, Hofstadter's, Boorstin's and Potter's efforts were criticized for ignoring those events and developments not easily accounted for by central principles or values. But the objection most frequently raised against the consensus approach to the past was the absence of any depiction or even recognition of conflict or diversity in that history. To be sure, that was precisely what the approach intended to do: to move beyond conflict and contradictions by articulating what that past had meant in general once whatever passing conflicts there may have been had been resolved by time or events. Though probably not intended by the several authors to be a justification of the American way, in practice their books could easily be read as such, especially since the United States at that time was at the peak of its economic abundance as well as being the only untouched victor in the most devastating war in history.

As we will see in a moment, self-satisfaction with national achievement was not the only sentiment emerging from the Second World War. But before we turn to that, one other aspect of David Potter's *People of Plenty* is worth noting in any discussion of American historiography: the attention Potter paid to the social sciences in the course of his effort to uncover the sources of the American character. Among other things, he turned to social psychology, particularly that of Karen Horney, a contemporary neo-Freudian psychologist. In fact, in this book and throughout his career in subsequent years, Potter looked to social sciences such as anthropology, political science as well as psychology in seeking to understand the American past. That part of Potter's work, unlike his attempt to identify American national character, proved to be only the beginning of a broad interest among American historians in turning to the social sciences for new insights into the nation's past. Thus Stanley Elkins in his 1959 study of American slavery depended heavily upon the interpersonal psychology of Henry Stack Sullivan, Lee Benson in 1961 deliberately looked at Jacksonian Democracy through the lenses of political scientists, while Charles Strozier (1982) boldly employed psychoanalysis in trying to understand Abraham Lincoln. Herbert Gutman's *Black Family in Slavery and Freedom, 1750–1924* (1976a) drew upon the insights of cultural anthropology in analysing the history of black families. Probably more than any other field of history, recent students of the American past have worked to bridge the otherwise broad gap between their discipline and the social sciences. One additional measure of that continuing interest was the founding in the 1960s and 1970s of scholarly journals such as *Historical Methods Newsletter* (1967), *Journal of Interdisciplinary History* (1970) and *Social Science History* (1976), all of which continue to be published.

Important as these new methods were in reshaping American historiography, they did not constitute what needs to be seen as a minor revolution: the transformation of the historians' conception of the American past. That derived, as suggested already, from a fundamental dissatisfaction with the absence of conflict in the history presented by historians such as Boorstin, Potter and Hofstadter. Two forces seems to have given rise to those criticisms.

The first was the altered nature of the America of the 1960s. Rather than an America of wealth, international power and internal progress, which had spawned the American studies or consensus approach, the United States of the 1960s was a society in turmoil. The struggle on behalf of equal rights for blacks that had begun in 1954 with the Supreme Court decision outlawing segregation had become by the early 1960s a fully-fledged struggle to eradicate discrimination against minorities and women. At the same time, the growing war in Vietnam had spawned an opposition that was increasingly vocal and effective, particularly among students and faculties at colleges and universities. In such a climate, a history that lacked depictions of a contentious past seemed unrealistic at best and hypocritical at worst. Besides, at a time when ethnic and sex discrimination were increasingly seen as unAmerican, it was hard to deny that such discrimination must have been present in the past as well as in the present; surely such strongly held feelings could not have sprung forth without antecedents.

The second development standing behind that minor revolution was the changes in the composition of the historical profession itself. For most of the twentieth century academic historians were much more likely to have been recruited from among 'old' Americans, that is, middle- or upper-class, white Protestants of English or northern European background, than were the scholars in some of the social sciences, such as anthropology and sociology. After the Second World War, however, when many veterans took advantage of federal stipends and tuition for graduate education, the traditional demographic composition of the historical profession changed dramatically; sons and some daughters of working-class America, whose parents may well have also come from eastern or southern Europe backgrounds, joined the historical profession. They began to see their country's past with different eyes from those who had come from traditional backgrounds.

The emerging view of the American past was, as might be anticipated, more varied, and more detailed. It was therefore less willing to draw broad conclusions about the nature of Americans in general; it was the diversity of America that now seemed central to the nation's past. Americans had long been aware of their diversity of peoples, of their being a nation of immigrants. Yet behind that traditional view stood the anticipation that in due time the immigrants would melt into the general population, that a composite American population would emerge from the 'melting pot'. Beginning in the 1950s, however, some historians began to recognize that the 'melting' had not yet been completed, even though the massive immigration of the decades before the First World War had been almost entirely shut off by the immigration law of 1924. In 1952, for example, Samuel Lubell's *Future of American Politics* documented the ways in which immigrant background still shaped electoral politics in the United States, setting a pattern for subsequent historians and political scientists when they sought to explain American political behaviour. Lubell pointed out, for example, that much of the isolationist areas of the country just prior to the entrance of the United States into the Second World War coincided geographically with concentrations of voters with German or Scandinavian ancestry.

Traditional historians of immigration may have looked towards a 'melting pot' as the future of American diversity, but they had also begun to recognize, as in Oscar Handlin's *Uprooted* (1953), the difficulties encountered by European peasants seeking to make their way in the strange and threatening United States of factories and cities. Scholars who came after Handlin did not ignore the newcomers' difficulties, but in line with their new vision of a revised American past, they shifted from seeing immigrants as victims to emphasizing the newcomers' group solidarity and ability to make a life to their own liking. Thus Tamara Hareven's *Family Time: Industrial Time* (1982) demonstrated the way in which co-operation among immigrants could shape the work patterns in a modern factory situation, while Virginia Yans-McLaughlin's (1977) investigation of Italian immigrant families revealed how family behaviour varied according to ethnic or immigrant origins. In place of a 'melting pot', many historians began to give recognition to the persistence of ethnic differences by invoking instead the symbol of the 'salad bowl'.

Nowhere is the recognition of the persistence of immigrant diversity more strikingly measured than in a recent essay by Frederick C. Luebke, a historian of German immigration. In his *Germans in the New World* (1990) he called for the study of the ways in which immigration shaped American society outside the political sphere, where, ever since Samuel Lubell's book, it has long been recognized. 'Would the United States have been a different society if the largest immigrant group had been French instead of German?' he asked.

What Luebke was referring to in regard to changes in political history as a result of a new recognition of American cultural diversity was the emergence in the 1960s of what came to be called an ethno-cultural interpretation of political history. Traditionally, historians had been most inclined to uncover economic interests in explaining the policies of political parties and the winning of elections. Beginning with Lee Benson's pioneering work, *The Concept of Jacksonian Democracy* (1961), political analysis took a new turn. After Benson argued for cultural values and religion as sources of division between the major political parties and their voters, historians delved more consistently than ever into the cultural differences within the American electorate. Notable in taking an ethno-cultural approach to politics was Paul Kleppner, *The Cross of Culture: A Social Analysis of Midwestern Politics, 1850–1900* (1970) and Ronald P. Formisano, *The Birth of Mass Political Parties: Michigan, 1827–1861* (1971).

Over the years historians of labour have also been acutely aware of the diversity of peoples when attempting to explain why unions have been weak in the United States as compared with other industrial nations. Sometimes the emphasis has been placed upon employers' exploiting ethnic antagonisms in order to control workers; at other times historians have argued that in certain periods class has been able to unite even a workforce composed of diverse ethnic allegiances. But the divisive power of ethnic diversity rarely remained far beneath the surface when historians endeavoured to account for the relatively low proportion of industrial workers in the United States who actually joined labour unions. It is that historical heterogeneity of the workforce, contended Gary Marks (1989) in his comparative study of unions in politics in Britain, Germany and the United States, that has been a 'recurring, dynamic process' in keeping American unions from reaching the level of membership achieved by workers in Germany or Great Britain. Ethnic diversity has also been a well-recognized explanation as to why the United States has historically lacked a socialist movement comparable to those in the major industrial countries. One recent historian of labour, Lizabeth Cohen,[1] has described this lack of socialism as a measure of the conservative character of American labour, which she summarizes as workers' belief in a 'moral capitalism'. This outlook, Cohen contends, has differentiated the American working class from the more anti-capitalist outlook of European labour traditions. In a sense, Cohen and Marks are reviving an older interpretation of American labour and American historiography in general, namely, the idea that America is 'an exception' to a European pattern of development. Most recent historical writings have stayed away from, or even denied outright any kind of 'exceptionalism' but, as Cohen's and Marks's books

---

1 Cohen 1990. Cohen uses the term 'moral capitalism' to describe the American worker's view that 'capitalism could be made fair.' (p. 317).

make clear, exceptionalism still occupies a useful place in the minds of historians of the American past.

The new social or demographic diversity of the American historical profession has caused scholars to be interested in more than simply documenting the way in which immigration has affected the working class or impeded the spread of labour unions. Labour historians of late have been especially concerned to describe and analyse the worker's life in the workplace. Traditional American historians had been principally concerned with the structure and nature of labour organizations. The more recent labour historians, who are frequently imbued with sympathy for the workers' lot, want instead to portray the lives of workers on the shop floor or in the community. The late labour historian, Herbert Gutman, led the way with a series of articles on nineteenth-century workers, now collected in his *Work, Culture, and Society in Industrializing America* (1976b). Following in the footsteps of E. P. Thompson's *Making of the English Working Class* (1963), Gutman stressed the role of social values, such as religion, in shaping the American worker's conception of his role and his work. By combining labour and immigrant history, Gutman also broke down the academic barriers that had once artificially separated historical investigations of the working class into different fields. Gutman's approach is exemplarily carried forward in Lizabeth Cohen's *Making a New Deal*, where she breaks fresh ground in depicting the interactions among immigrants, natives and employers in creating during the Great Depression a modern, politically conscious American working class.

Less social and more ideological in interpreting labour's place in the American past has been the work of the Yale professor David Montgomery, whose approach culminated in his *Fall of the House of Labor. The Workplace, the State, and American Labor Activism, 1865–1925* (1987). The ideological and social approaches to working-class life and work are apparent, too, in Alan Dawley's *Class and Community: the Industrial Revolution in Lynn* (1976) and in Sean Wilentz's *Chants Democratic: New York City and the Rise of the American Working Class, 1788–1850* (1984), both of which treat as well the transition from pre-industrial society to factory life. Both studies exemplify, too, the new emphasis upon the detailed study of individual communities or cities rather than of states, regions or nation.

An additional reason why the 'melting pot' interpretation of American ethnic diversity or cultural pluralism came under criticism was its failure to recognize that the different races in the United States never 'melted' into the mainstream. Blacks, Amerindians, Japanese, and Chinese were always set apart, either by law, as in the case of African-Americans in the American South, or by custom. Here, too, the political and social changes set in motion by the Great Depression, and its offspring, the New Deal, along with the social changes in the course of the Second World War, radically reshaped historians' conceptions.

The Supreme Court's repudiation of legal segregation in 1954 unleashed an unprecedented academic inquiry into the history of African-Americans. Black historians had long been pursuing that story, but largely without either much assistance or interest from white historians. But once racial discrimination became a primary political as well as legal and social concern, the social roots of discrimination and racism took on a new urgency among historical researchers. By the time the excitement and interest had subsided in the mid-1980s, American social history in general, not only African-American history, had been transformed.

The transformation began in connection with the writing of the history of slavery in the United States, a subject that seemed to many observers to lie at the heart of the question of why blacks had been kept apart from whites for all of American history. Slavery, after all, had begun the separation, and in the works of some early historians provided the primary justification for the separation: Africans were naturally suited to be slaves. By the 1950s, however, a simple racial justification for either slavery or social and economic discrimination was no longer acceptable to most citizens. What, then, was the role of slavery in shaping the position of blacks in a white-dominated America? Should it be seen as simply a historical institution that had been eliminated and could therefore be forgotten, or had its impress been so deep that it continued to shape the fate of African-Americans in the present? Kenneth Stampp in his study of *ante-bellum* Southern slavery, *Peculiar Institution* (1954), meticulously depicted the harshness, even the cruelty, of bondage, while emphasizing the essential similarity of whites and blacks. It was this last point – the lack of inherent differences between the races – that clearly marked his study as fitting into the post-Second World War conception of US history. Earlier students of US slavery had not begun their enquiries from that point of view; they had generally accepted the idea that African-Americans were inherently different from other Americans. After the 1950s, no historian would start from that position.

Stampp's emphasis upon the harshness of slavery opened up a quite new exploration of the nature of human bondage in the American past. 'Harshness' of treatment is a relative, not a precise term. Harsh in relation to what: freedom, or other kinds of oppression? Obviously slavery was harsh, not to mention horrible, when compared with freedom, but that was not the real issue since earlier discussions about slavery had recognized that only black people – forced immigrants from Africa – were slaves. From that recognition the contention had arisen that slavery was not so horrible because only a people who were not considered the same as white people fell within it. So the question became: was US slavery harsh as compared with slavery in other parts of the world?

A beginning had been made in this regard even before Stampp's book appeared. In 1946 a Latin American historian named Frank Tannenbaum drew a comparison between slavery in certain Latin American countries and in the American South, from which he concluded that American slavery was harsher because it denied blacks many of the protections and life conditions which the law and the Roman Catholic Church provided in certain Latin American societies.

Tannenbaum's book had little impact upon American historians, for it came too early on to the political and social scene. But a student of Tannenbaum, Stanley Elkins, picked up Tannenbaum's comparison in 1959, and elaborated upon it. By that date, popular concern over the history and fate of blacks in American society, past and present, had reached a high point. Elkins's contention was that the denial of the essentials of humanity to the slave by the American system had been so severe that it had reshaped the psyche of the African-Americans who lived under its weight. As a consequence of slavery's almost total repression, black people had became infantile, irresponsible, happy-go-lucky and generally incapable of mounting serious resistance or protest against their bondage. The conclusion, in short, was that American slavery had been the most burdensome form of human bondage in the New World. It had psychologically unfitted blacks for life in freedom. Throughout the book Elkins made clear that he was not talking about a racial or biological difference, only a psychological or cultural transformation of Africans under the impress of US slavery, a transformation that was seen to be an accurate, if horrendous, measure of that institution's profoundly evil character. Since, at the time, many historians and citizens alike were struggling to understand the background of the social and legal movement on behalf of equal rights for blacks through which the society was then moving, Elkins's imaginative depiction of the enormities of slavery found a wide acceptance among both white and black historians. The acceptance was reinforced by the publication of Winthrop Jordan's monumental documentation of English-speaking white people's hostility towards people of African descent from the sixteenth to the nineteenth centuries, *White Over Black: American Attitudes Toward the Negro* (1968).

Yet, as often happens with interpretations of historical events, persons or institutions, a change in social context soon raised doubts about Elkins's interpretation. If one was only interested in the severity of the impact of slavery on American black people, then Elkins's view might be convincing. But if one also wanted to know how blacks reacted to their burden of slavery, Elkins's interpretation left them largely victims, people unable to resist or to challenge their bondage. Elkins's conception of US slavery might help to account for the very few slave rebellions that broke out during the *ante-bellum* years, but it had no place for the many examples of individual resistance slaves exhibited throughout those years, nor for the hostile communal and social reactions of the slaves to their bondage. So a whole new historical literature on slavery began to emerge, depicting slaves not as victims, but as vibrant, often courageous and resourceful resisters and survivors of bondage.

Some of these historians were of African descent themselves, like John Blassingame, who wrote *The Slave Community: Plantation Life in the Antebellum South* (1972), in which he traced the everyday life of the slave in 'the quarters' and in the fields, using that depiction, quite explicitly, to refute Elkins's conception of the black slave as a complaisant victim. Some other critics of Elkins were white, like Eugene Genovese, whose *magnum opus*, *Roll, Jordan, Roll: The World the Slaves Made* (1974), ranged over the whole life pattern of the slaves, portraying them as engaged in continual struggle with their masters to win a life of their own, to obtain sufficient 'social space' to escape that total control which Elkins had contended the masters exercised over them.

One consequence of the widespread interest in the history of slavery was a new willingness to use sources once seen as 'tainted' or improper for scholarly exploitation, namely, the hundreds of slave reminiscences, which had been recorded during the 1930s, some sixty years after the abolition of slavery. Kenneth Stampp, for example, in his book *The Peculiar Institution*, had refused to draw upon those sources because they were so dependent upon admittedly fallible, partisan and highly selective memories. He relied primarily, as had his racially orientated predecessors, upon contemporaneously written documents by white men and women. By the 1960s and 1970s, however, the need and the desire to have sources from the slaves themselves, and the recognition that all sources are partisan and always require critical examination made the slave reminiscences quite acceptable as an entry into the everyday life of slaves. Genovese relied heavily upon those particular sources in his *Roll, Jordan, Roll* (1974), and George Rawick based his picture of life in the quarters, *From Sundown to Sunup* (1972), largely upon them.

Probably the most imaginative effort at uncovering insights into the spiritual and mental life of slaves, who had few chances to leave written documents of their own, was Lawrence W. Levine's *Black Culture and Black Consciousness: Afro-American Folk Thought from Slavery to Freedom* (1977), in which he gave an imaginative reading of the slaves' spirituals, religious rituals and folk-tales. In a sense, Levine's book was the definitive cultural answer to Elkins's contention that slavery in America had been so oppressive as to obliterate the essential humanity of the Africans who had been forced to endure it. Herbert Gutman, whom we had last encountered in regard to labour history, provided a *social* response to Elkins's interpretation of the impact of slavery that almost equalled in definitiveness of Levine's cultural response. Gutman's retort to Elkins was his book *The Black Family in Slavery and Freedom. 1750–1925* (1976a).

Like so much else, as we have seen, in the historiography of American slavery, Gutman's book on the African-American family was the direct outgrowth of a contemporary public concern, in this case a controversy over a social policy of the American government. In the 1960s, partly under the influence of Elkins's work on slavery's devastating effect upon black people, the administration of President Lyndon Johnson initiated a social programme to prevent the break-up of black families, a social phenomenon that was seen as a direct legacy of slavery. The most common measure of the disruption of families was the presence of mother-headed households, something that was thought to be characteristic of families under slavery since it was known that marriage between slaves was without legal support, and within families, fathers were thought to lack economic or psychological authority. Contrary to these widely held views, Gutman's research showed that long-standing marriages between couples were characteristic of slave households. Moreover, by following former slave couples after emancipation, Gutman demonstrated that the idea of enduring marriages was something cherished by the slaves themselves rather than being an institution imposed on the slaves by masters or the cultural pressure of the white social order. Through a deft analysis of slave children's names, Gutman was able to show that fathers were more than solely generators of offspring; they held positions of authority within the family not unlike those occupied by white husbands. Finally, by carefully uncovering the lines of kinship that ramified among members of slave communities, Gutman revealed in

717

yet another way the complex lives the slaves had managed to create and maintain even under the oppression of bondage.

If the awakening of historians to the need for a new history of African-Americans began with the enormous outpouring of studies of slavery, it did not stop there. New biographies of historically important African-Americans began to appear, among which was a monumental study in two volumes (1972, 1983) of the former slave who became a noted educator and black leader, Booker T. Washington, by Louis Harlan, and a study of twentieth-century black leaders (Franklin and Meier 1982). The Harlem Renaissance of the 1920s, the establishment of black communities (the so-called 'ghettoes') in northern cities and the story of the economic success of African-Americans also became the subjects of scholarly works. (e.g. Osofsky 1966; Spear 1967; Huggins 1971; Lewis 1981; Schweninger 1990). The whole field of Southern Reconstruction history, which had been long interpreted as a measure or sign of the grievous errors of a too rapid and too egalitarian emancipation, now came under fresh scrutiny. This time around the emphasis was placed upon the achievements of former slaves in and out of the governments of the Southern states with full recognition of their long history of exclusion from a free life. The new emphasis was especially well displayed in Eric Foner's thoroughly documented *Reconstruction: America's Unfinished Revolution, 1863–1877* (1988), in which, for the first time in an academically accepted volume by a white historian, the story is told more from the standpoint of blacks than from that of whites.[2]

At the root of the burgeoning interest in black history lay the assumption that the proper history of the United States required the bringing into the mainstream of historical writing the activities of all minorities, not simply blacks. African-Americans, it is true, constituted the largest minority in both the American present and the American past. But as young men and young women worked together in the 1960s on behalf of the civil rights of blacks, it soon became apparent to some of the young women, at least, that there was an analogy between the limits that were placed upon women's roles in society and those against which they were protesting on behalf of the freedom of African-Americans. Obviously, the analogy was not precise: women, for example, had never been segregated. On the contrary, because they were a sex, they had been intimately 'integrated' with the dominant group. Yet historically it was true that, like blacks, women had been kept from voting, or participating in government, and denied access to certain kinds of jobs, and even a college education. When, in more modern times, higher education, politics and the vote had been opened to them, custom and family obligations had still confined most women to limited roles in life compared with those open to men. It was not far-fetched, then, for women in general and women in the historical profession in particular to ask that they, too, along with blacks and other minorities, begin to bring their past into the mainstream of US history. Unlike the situation that

---

2 Much is revealed about the changes in Reconstruction historiography over the last half-century when it is recognized that the black historian W. E. B. Du Bois had published his *Black Reconstruction* as long ago as 1935, and that it had been ignored by the great majority of white historians.

prevailed in regard to African-Americans, who had been segregated throughout American history until very recent times, women themselves were ready to take on the task of writing their own history. Their historic 'integration' with men meant that many already possessed the necessary educational and scholarly preparation for the job.

Some women, it needs to be said, had been writing for decades about women in the past, but their work had not been acknowledged as a part of the general historiography of the United States. That changed in the course of the 1960s. The earliest work in the new women's history, during the 1960s, followed a path not unlike that which Elkins had sparked when he depicted blacks as primarily victims under slavery. For women that meant emphasizing the ways, particularly during the nineteenth century, by which familial domesticity limited women's lives. The classic article that inspired many subsequent studies was Barbara Welter's 'The Cult of True Womanhood: 1820–1860', which appeared in 1966. Notable among those subsequent studies was Nancy Cott's *Bonds of Womanhood: 'Woman's Sphere' in New England, 1780–1835* (1977). Some authors found within 'woman's sphere', as others had found within black bondage, signs of restlessness or outright resistance. Nina Baym identified it through an examination of *Woman's Fiction: A Guide to Novels by and about Women in America, 1820–1870* (1978), where she showed how women writers and readers created a symbiotic relation that sustained their gender-identity. Domesticity itself could well provide a strong sense of identity, Kathryn Kish Sklar showed in her sympathetic biography of the leading home economist of her time, *Catharine Beecher* (1975). Firmly convinced of the strength of women even in the nineteenth century, Gerda Lerner made her point early in her vigorous biography of the anti-slavery and women's rights advocates, *The Grimke Sisters* (1967). Anne Firor Scott documented women's strength even within the domestic sphere in the South in her *Southern Lady: From Pedestal to Politics, 1830–1930* (1970), but Suzanne Lebsock (1984), writing later about the *ante-bellum* women of Petersburg, Virginia, was not so sure that Southern women were that independent. Lebsock also included black women in her story, taking a broader approach than some of the first books on women's history, which dealt primarily with middle-class white women. The problem of the division which class inevitably produced among women was well explored in Barbara Epstein's *Politics of Domesticity* (1980). By the late 1980s the sharp change that had taken place in women's conception of domesticity was thoughtfully documented in Glenna Matthews's *'Just a Housewife'. The Rise and Fall of Domesticity in America* (1987).

By the 1980s it had become abundantly clear that the category 'women' was a much more divided category than 'African-American'. Black people after all, had been largely confined to poverty because of their long history under slavery, but women from the beginning had been spread evenly throughout the social structure. In addition to class and ethnic divisions among women, historians began to explore those parts of women's past that differed from men's. John Mack Faragher, *Women and Men on the Overland Trail* (1979) and Julie Ray Jeffrey, *Frontier Women: the Trans-Mississippi West, 1840–1880* (1979) not only documented women in the west,

719

but stressed as well their commitment to the separate sphere for females. The quite different experience of black women at work and in families was dramatically and sympathetically told in Jacqueline Jones, *Labor of Love, Labor of Sorrow* (1985).

Perhaps the most striking ways in which women's lives in the past differed from men's was in their work outside the home, and so numerous studies soon appeared documenting their experiences. The once familiar 'Lowell Girls' received a fresh and more realistic analysis from Thomas Dublin (1972), while domestic service, the most common form of women's work, was analysed by David M. Katzman (1978). The inequalities and limitations that women encountered in the workforce are historically considered in Alice Kessler-Harris, *Out to Work; a History of Wage-earning Women in the United States* (1982). The primary social reason for the expansion of women's work was the growth of the factory and the city, which not only found a need for women's labour, but often provided as well an escape for women from the restrictions imposed by the traditional family. These aspects of the opportunities cities provided women were insightfully presented in Joanne J. Meyerowitz's imaginative *Women Adrift: Independent Wage Earners in Chicago, 1880–1930* (1988) and, for an earlier period, in Christine Stansell, *City of Women. Sex and Class in New York, 1789–1860* (1987). The traditional 'trade' of women is scrutinized in Ruth Rosen, *Lost Sisterhood: Prostitution in America, 1900–1918* (1982).

Virtually all white women in the nineteenth century who worked outside the home were unmarried, but that pattern began to change dramatically in the 1930s and 1940s, and then became a revolution after the 1950s. Winifred Wandersee's *Women's Work and Family Values, 1920–40* (1981) began the story. The movement of married women into the workforce in great numbers after the Second World War and the movement against job discrimination is well analysed by a professional economist in Claudia Goldin, *Explaining the Gender Gap* (1990) and with fewer economists' equations in the later chapters of Julie A. Matthaei, *An Economic History of Women in America: Women's Work, the Sexual Division of Labor, and the Development of Capitalism* (1981).

Prostitution became a subject of importance in women's history because it touched on a fact that must always distinguish women's past from that of men. Sexuality, we must not forget, is the historical as well as the social link between men and women. Indeed, it is not at all radical to see sex as the source of women's subordination to men and, as such, to be a subject historians need to explore if they are to create a history of women. One of the earliest efforts to re-examine the nature of women's sexuality was a 1974 article of mine, which was based on a turn-of-the-century questionnaire answered by forty-five middle-class women on their sex habits.[3] The subject of sexuality has been expertly traced throughout American history in John D'Emilio and Estelle Freedman, *Intimate Matters: A History of Sexuality in America* (1988). The shift among historians from thinking about sex to thinking about 'gender', the socially constructed difference between the sexes, is

---

3 Degler 1974. All of the forty-five individual questionnaires have been published in Mosher 1980.

elucidated in important articles contained in Carroll Smith-Rosenberg, *Disorderly Conduct: Visions of Gender in Victorian America* (1985).

Given the reasons why women's history has generated a novel subject like sexuality, it can come as no surprise that the content of history, under the prodding of women's history, has now expanded to include the history of childbirth and birth control. Excellent in the first regard is Judith Walzer Leavitt, *Brought to Bed: Childbearing in America, 1750–1950* (1986) and equally rewarding in the second is James Reed, *From Private Vice to Public Virtue: The Birth Control Movement and American Society Since 1830* (1978). And if contraception has been added to history, one must expect that the addition of abortion is not far behind, as James Mohr's *Abortion in America: the Origins and Evolution of National Policy, 1800–1900* (1978) demonstrates.

The unfolding of the once hidden subject of sexuality has added the history of homosexuality to the historiography of the United States, the pioneering work of Jonathan Katz, *Gay American History*, appearing as early as 1976. John D'Emilio's important scholarly study of the origins of homosexual political and communal activity appeared in 1983, to be followed a few years later by Allan Berube's (1990) thoroughly researched story of homosexual men and women during the Second World War.

Finally, as a further offshoot from the upsurge in women's history, there needs to be mentioned the beginnings of a history of manhood. The aim of this most recent field of study is to do for men's past what the study of women's history brought to women's past: the discovery of the social construction of sex or gender, that is, in the case of men, to ascertain what it meant to be a man at various times and occasions in the past. Several such studies appear in the collection entitled *Meanings for Manhood. Constructions of Masculinity in Victoria America* (1990), edited by Mark C. Carnes and Clyde Griffen, and in Carnes's book, *Secret Ritual and Manhood in Victorian America* (1989), where he seeks to delineate the feelings of men nurtured by the highly popular adult fraternal organizations of the nineteenth century.

The growing recognition of the diversity of the American past carried one other group into the mainstream of the country's historiography: a people who had been present for the longest time of all: the First Americans or Indians. A few historians and many anthropologists had been studying and writing about Amerindians as long ago as the mid-nineteenth century, but most historians generally pushed aside their works, much as the Europeans had pushed the Amerindians aside as they moved westward across the continent. Just as blacks were often seen in traditional history as a source of conflict and ultimately civil war, so Amerindians came to be perceived as a source of problems, and, then, as their numbers declined and they were confined to reservations, as outside the American story. Indeed, in 1959, in writing a general interpretation of American history that took as its focus the relevance of the past to the present (Degler 1959), I deliberately omitted any discussion of Amerindians on the ground that in the 1950s they were not of contemporary concern! Within a matter of years, that perception was dramatically changed because in California and in South Dakota Amerindians staged large public protests that soon brought their plight and the nation's neglect to the attention of daily newspaper readers.

Today, the history of the First Americans is a burgeoning field of scholarship that draws heavily upon conventional historical sources as well as the more traditional anthropological sources. What has changed dramatically, of course, has been the point of view. Whether written by Amerindians themselves (who happen not to be active in the field compared with, say, women in the field of women's history or of African-Americans in black history[4]) or by non-Amerindians, the writing of Native American History today has abandoned the 'white man's' approach to the indigenous peoples, as Wilbur R. Jacobs's pioneering book, *Dispossessing the American Indian* (1972), makes clear. Sometimes these new historians do not even attempt to conceal their indignation, as in Francis Jennings, *The Invasion of America: Indians, Colonialism, and the Cant of Conquest* (1975). The aim, as James Axtell's *The European and the Indian* (1981a), emphasizes, is to understand, not to judge, the divergent cultures that clashed on the North American continent in the course of some 300 years. One of the most striking discoveries of the new history of Amerindians is the devastating demographic consequences of the arrival of the Europeans, as Russell Thornton, *American Holocaust and Survival* (1987) summarizes in horrifying detail.

As one might anticipate, the rapid increase in historical subjects has also meant that some fields now begin to overlap as they cross-fertilize one another. A notable example of this is William Cronon's *Changes in the Land* (1983), a magnificent study of the effects of the physical environment of New England on the life of the indigenous population, and their impact, in turn, on the physical landscape. In another example of cross-fertilization, Theda Perdue brought together Amerindian history and Southern slavery in her wide-ranging book *Slavery and the Evolution of Cherokee Society, 1540–1866* (1979). Or take James Axtell's intelligent integration of the history of women and of Amerindians in his collection of primary sources, *Indian Peoples of Eastern America. A Documentary History of the Sexes* (1981b).

Up to now in delineating the variety of new fields and approaches in recent American historiography, I have been emphasizing the influence of ethnic and national diversity in American society. That influence is real, but it should be perceived also as a surrogate for a less obvious, but no less significant influence, namely, concerns about the distribution of power in American society. By historical experience and definition minorities and women lack power and to a substantial degree still do in the present. The new emphasis on telling the story of minorities and women is a way of calling into question the power hierarchy of the present as well as that of the past. It takes the place, in part at least, of similar tendencies among European historians to emphasize class differences, for in their pasts class is the traditional identification of differences in power. Among Americans, however, class has always had less salience than ethnic and racial minorities as a means for criticizing the distribution of power in the past and the present.

---

4   De Loria 1969 is an exception, but it was not a scholarly work. Brown 1971 was not an academic work, either, but it measures the sudden upsurge of interest in Amerindian history in that it was a Book-of-the-Month-Club selection.

In conclusion, there remains one other aspect of the American past that has been sharply redefined as a result of changes in the society in which historians live. That is the field of American diplomatic history. As with social history, the dividing line that cuts across the foreign-relations history of the United States is the Second World War. Before that event, most historians of foreign relations manifested a largely sympathetic understanding of the United States' dealings with other nations. The main dissent from that outlook had been objections to American involvement in the First World War, an enduring proponent of that dissent being the well-known historian and political scientist Charles A. Beard. Unlike the great majority of his professional colleagues, Beard resisted the Roosevelt administration's frank support of the Allies in their war against Germany before the bombing of Pearl Harbor. Beard interpreted the European war as without immediate significance to the vital interests of the United States. Beard thought that the American 'national interest', which most official and unofficial supporters of Britain and France invoked in justification, was largely a euphemism for the economic interests of American business and finance. After the war, Beard continued to denounce Franklin Roosevelt for having put the United States in such an international position in the late 1930s as to have made the Japanese attack in 1941 very likely. Beard's heavily economic – really anti-business – interpretation of the motives behind US foreign policy and action won few supporters until the 1960s, when it began to be taken up in different forms by a substantial number of young historians of American diplomacy. The issue around which the revival turned was the question of how the 'Cold War' between the two Second World War allies – the United States and the Soviet Union – had begun. The generally accepted view was that it grew out of the Soviet Union's truculence and lack of co-operation with the Western allies, particularly Great Britain and the United States, in settling the many difficult questions that were left by the political as well as the physical devastation of Europe in the course of destroying Hitler's Germany.

Perhaps the first systematic effort to call that interpretation into question was D. F. Fleming, *The Cold War and its Origins* (1961). Fleming did not follow the Beard economic explanation, but he did raise questions about the fairness of the Allies' dealings with the Soviet Union and that unfairness, he contended, threatened the kind of sound world order that Woodrow Wilson had sought to achieve after the First World War. Even before Fleming had published his critique, the ground had been laid for bringing the old Beardian interpretation into the discussion. A young diplomatic historian at the University of Wisconsin opened the new path with his *Tragedy of American Diplomacy*, published in 1959. Williams was not only an admirer of Beard's approach, but also a historian who focused that interpretation on the idea that at least from the end of the nineteenth century, US foreign policy had been shaped, if not dominated, by a search for markets abroad for the goods pouring out of the expanding American industrial economy. The chief American policy instrument for accomplishing that goal, according to Williams, was the 'Open Door', or open competition for international markets, a policy that had been proclaimed at the onset of the twentieth century and which became a centrepiece of US international economic policy thereafter.

Both Williams's and Fleming's books appeared just as the United States was entering upon what American leaders of both political parties later came to see as a world struggle to contain the influence of the Soviet Union and its ideology of communism. Not all Americans accepted the view that the United States was without fault or responsibility in bringing about that struggle. This was especially true of many historians who were already critical of many actions and policies of the American government and society as they examined the social and political history of their country. Again and again the point was made by Williams and by those who followed in his footsteps that the antagonists in the Cold War were socialist and capitalist countries. N. Gordon Levin's *Woodrow Wilson and World Politics* (1968) developed this theme for the years when the Soviet Union was being founded, as a conflict between Woodrow Wilson's and Vladimir Lenin's conception of world order. In short, there is a fairly obvious connection to be discerned between the changes in the social historiography we have already examined, and the emerging critical or revisionist historiography of American foreign policy influenced by William Appleman Williams. Both were critical of the distribution of power in American society, past and present.

Gar Alperovitz was not a student of Williams, but his book *Atomic Diplomacy: Hiroshima and Potsdam* (1965) made an argument similar to Williams's in contending that nuclear bombs had been dropped on Japan principally to bring the war to an end before the Soviets could enter in force against Japan, and to demonstrate to the world, and to the Soviet Union in particular, the enormous power in the hands of the United States as it prepared to shape the post-war world. Walter LeFeber's *America, Russia, and the Cold War 1945–1967*, appearing in 1967, pressed a much clearer economic or market-seeking interpretation of US diplomatic behaviour, that left the motives of the Soviet Union as largely defensive and even fearful of the dangers of capitalist intrusion into the socialist economy of eastern Europe. Joyce Kolko and Gabriel Kolko, *The Limits of Power: The World and United States Foreign Policy, 1945–1954* (1972) provide the most extreme example among scholarly efforts to follow single-mindedly an economic determinist interpretation of US foreign policy. Although these revisionist interpretations were derived from examination of many internal – often once top secret – documents of the United States government, no United States historians had access to comparable documents of the Soviet government. Nevertheless, the revisionist view of the Cold War was widely accepted, though not in all particulars, as the widely praised book by Daniel Yergin, *Shattered Peace: The Origins of the Cold War and the National Security State* (1977), makes evident.

The generally critical approach to recent foreign policy, which the revisionists on the Cold War began, has continued in studies on the origins of the Korean War, as exemplified in Bruce Cumings's two-volume *Origins of the Korean War* (1983, 1990), and numerous monographs on the roots and policies of the war in Vietnam.

The magnificent efflorescence of historical studies as a result of the social and ideological changes in American society since the Second World War does have a little shadow over it. That is the difficulty of integrating this diversity of subjects and interpretations into a fresh and useful picture of the American past. No agreement has been reached on the meaning of the newly revealed America. Obviously it cannot be said that the United States is simply a collection of diverse groups that the new social history has brought so forcefully and fruitfully to everyone's attention. The old political history that once provided a coherent theme, a line of development to the American past, is clearly no longer sufficient. Yet the complexities spread before us by the new studies provide no obvious theme or pattern. Certainly one of the central purposes of national history is to display to the nation's people the story of who they are. That, however, requires some focus, some identification that is more than a patchwork of events and ideas. Most likely, in time and in line with the changing historiography of the last thirty years, that synthesis, that focus will emerge from the present, which, in the end, is the ultimate shaper of history since most written history is composed largely of responses to questions the present asks of the past.

REFERENCES

Alperovitz, G. (1965) *Atomic Diplomacy: Hiroshima and Potsdam*, New York.

Axtell, J. (1981a) *The European and the Indian*, New York.

—— (1981b) *Indian Peoples of Eastern America. A Documentary History of the Sexes.*

Baym, N. (1978) *Woman's Fiction: A Guide to Novels by and about Women in America, 1820–1870*, Urbana.

Benson, L. (1961) *The Concept of Jacksonian Democracy: New York as a Test Case*, Princeton.

Berube, A. (1990) *Coming Out Under Fire. The History of Gay Men and Women in World War Two*, New York.

Blassingame, J. (1972) *The Slave Community: Plantation Life in the Antebellum South*, New York.

Boorstin, D. (1958) *The Genius of the American People*, Chicago.

Brown, D. (1971) *Bury my Heart at Wounded Knee. An Indian History of the American West*, New York.

Carnes, M. C. (1989) *Secret Ritual and Manhood in Victorian America*, New Haven, CT.

—— and Griffen, C. (eds) (1990) *Meanings for Manhood. Constructions of Masculinity in Victorian America*, Chicago.

Cohen, L. (1990) *Making a New Deal. Industrial Workers in Chicago, 1919–1939*, Cambridge.

Cott, N. (1977) *Bonds of Womenhood: 'Woman's Sphere' in New England, 1780–1835*, New Haven, CT.

Cronon, W. (1983) *Changes in the Land*, New York.

Cumings, B. (1983–90) *The Origins of the Korean War*, 2 vols, Princeton.

Dawley, A. (1976) *Class and Community: The Industrial Revolution in Lynn*, Cambridge, MA.

D'Emilio, J. (1983) *Sexual Politics, Sexual Communities, the Making of a Homosexual Minority in the United States 1940–1970*, Chicago.

—— and Freedman, E. B. (1988) *Intimate Matters: A History of Sexuality in America*, New York.

Degler, C. N. (1959) *Out of Our Past. The Forces that Shaped Modern America*, New York.

Degler, C. N. (1974) 'What ought to be and what was: women's sexuality in the nineteenth century', *American Historical Review* 79: 1467–90.

De Loria, Jr, V. (1969) *Custer Died for your Sins. An Indian Manifesto*, New York.

Dublin, T. (1972) *Women at Work. The Transformation of Work and Community in Lowell, Massachusetts, 1826–1860*, New York.

Du Bois, W. E. B. (1935) *Black Reconstruction*, New York.

Elkins, S. (1959) *Slavery. A Problem in American Institutional and Intellectual Life*, Chicago.

Epstein, B. (1980) *Politics of Domesticity*, Middletown.

Faragher, J. M. (1979) *Women and Men on the Overland Trail*, New Haven, CT.

Fleming, D. F. (1961) *The Cold War and its Origins*, New York.

Foner, E. (1988) *Reconstruction. America's Unfinished Revolution, 1863–1877*, New York.

—— (ed.) (1990) *The New American History*, Philadelphia.

Formisano, R. P. (1971) *The Birth of Mass Political Parties; Michigan, 1827–1861*, Princeton.

Franklin, J. H. and Meier, A. (eds) (1982) *Black Leaders of the Twentieth Century*, Urbana.

Freedman, E. B. (1988) *Intimate Matters: A History of Sexuality in America*, New York.

Genovese, E. (1974) *Roll, Jordan, Roll: The World the Slaves Made*, New York.

Goldin, C. (1990) *Understanding the Gender Gap*, New York.

Gutman, H. G. (1976a) *Black Family in Slavery and Freedom, 1750–1925*, New York.

—— (1976b) *Work, Culture, and Society in Industrializing America*, New York.

Handlin, O. (1953) *Uprooted*, London.

Hareven, T. (1982) *Family Time; Industrial Time*, Cambridge.

Hofstadter, R. (1948) *The American Political Tradition and the Men who Made it*, New York.

Huggins, N. I. (1971) *Harlem Renaissance*, New York.

Jacobs, W. R. (1972) *Dispossessing the American Indian*, Norman, OK.

Jeffrey, J. R. (1979) *Frontier Women. The Trans-Mississippi West, 1840–1880*, New York.

Jennings, F. (1975) *The Invasion of America; Indians, Colonialism, and the Cant of Conquest*, Chapel Hill, NC.

Jones, J. (1985) *Labor of Love, Labor of Sorrow*, New York.

Jordan, W. (1968) *White over Black; American Attitudes toward the Negro*, Chapel Hill, NC.

Kammen, M. (ed.) (1980) *The Past before us. Contemporary Historical Writing in the United States*, Ithaca, NY.

Katz, J. (1976) *Gay American History*, New York.

Katzman, D. M. (1978) *Seven Days a Week: Women and Domestic Service in Industrializing America*, New York.

Kessler-Harris, A. (1982) *Out to Work; a History of Wage-Earning Women in the United States*, New York.

Kleppner, P. (1970) *The Cross of Culture. A Social Analysis of Midwestern Politics, 1850–1900*, New York.

Kolko, J. and Kolko, G. (1972) *The Limits of Power: The World and United States Foreign Policy, 1945–1954*, New York.

Leavitt, J. W. (1986) *Brought to Bed; Childbearing in America, 1750–1950*, New York.

Lebsock, S. (1984) *Free Women of Petersburg. Status and Culture in a Southern Town, 1784–1860*, New York.

LeFeber, W. (1967) *America, Russia, and the Cold War, 1945–1967*, New York.

Lerner, G. (1967) *The Grimke Sisters*, New York.

Levin, N. G. (1968) *Woodrow Wilson and World Politics*, New York.

Levine, L. W. (1977) *Black Culture and Black Consciousness; Afro-American Folk Thought from Slavery to Freedom*, New York.

Lewis, D. L. (1981) *When Harlem Was in Vogue*, New York.

Lubell, S. (1952) *The Future of American Politics*, New York.

Luebke, F. C. (1990) *Germans in the New World*, Urbana and Chicago.

Marks, G. (1989) *Unions in Politics. Britain, Germany, and the United States in the Nineteenth and Early Twentieth Centuries*, Princeton.

Matthaei, J. A. (1981) *An Economic History of Women in America: Women's Work, the Sexual Division of Labor, and the Development of Capitalism*, New York.

Matthews, G. (1987) *'Just a Housewife'. The Rise and Fall of Domesticity in America*, New York.

Meier, A. and Rudwick, B. (1986) *Black History and the Historical Profession, 1915–1980*, Urbana.

Meyerowitz, J. J. (1988) *Women Adrift: Independent Wage Earners in Chicago, 1880–1930*, Chicago.

Mohr, J. (1978) *Abortion in America: The Origins and Evolution of National Policy, 1800–1900*, New York.

Montgomery, D. (1987) *Fall of the House of Labor. The Workplace, the State, and American Labor Activism, 1865–1925*, Cambridge.

Mosher, C. D. (1980) *The Mosher Survey*, New York.

Osofsky, G. (1966) *Harlem: the Making of a Ghetto*, New York.

Perdue, T. (1979) *Slavery and the Evolution of Cherokee Society, 1540–1866*, Knoxville, TN.

Potter, D. M. (1954) *People of Plenty*, Chicago.

Rawick, G. (1972) *From Sundown to Sunup*, Westport, Ont.

Reed, J. (1978) *From Private Vice to Public Virtue: The Birth Control Movement and American Society since 1830*, New York.

Rosen, R. (1982) *Lost Sisterhood: Prostitution in America, 1900–1918*, Baltimore.

Ross, D. (1991) *The Origins of American Social Science*, Cambridge.

Schweninger, D. (1990) *Black Property Owners in the South, 1790–1915*, Urbana.

Scott, A. F. (1970) *Southern Lady: From Pedestal to Politics, 1830–1930*, Chicago.

Sklar, K. K. (1975) *Catherine Beecher*, New York.

Smith-Rosenberg, C. (1985) *Disorderly Conduct: Visions of Gender in Victorian America*, New York.

Spear, A. H. (1967) *Black Chicago*, Chicago.

Stampp, K. (1954) *The Peculiar Institution*, New York.

Stansell, C. (1987) *City of Women. Sex and Class in New York, 1789–1860*, Urbana and Chicago.

Strozier, C. B. (1982) *Lincoln's Quest for Union. Public and Private Meanings*, New York.

Tannenbaum, F. (1946) *Slave and Citizen: the Negro in the Americas*, New York.

Thompson, E. P. (1963) *The Making of the English Working Class*, New York.

Thornton, R. (1987) *American Holocaust and Survival*, Norman, OK.

Tyrrell, I. (1986) *The Absent Marx. Class Analysis and Liberal History in Twentieth Century America*, New York.

Wandersee, W. (1981) *Women's Work and Family Values, 1920–40*, Cambridge, MA.

Welter, B. (1966) 'The cult of true womanhood: 1820–1860', *American Quarterly* 18: 151–74.

Wilentz, S. (1984) *Chants Democratic: New York City and the Rise of the American Working Class, 1788–1850*, New York.

Williams, W. A. (1959) *The Tragedy of American Diplomacy*, Cleveland, OH.

Yans-McLaughlin, V. (1977) *Family and Community: Italian Immigrants in Buffalo, 1880–1930*, Ithaca, NY.

Yergin, D. (1977) *Shattered Peace: The Origins of the Cold War and the National Security State*, Boston.

29

LATIN AMERICA

Alan Knight

THE LABYRINTH

Like the labyrinth of King Minos, Latin America is big, complicated and easy to get lost in.[1] The first task of any tour-guide is therefore to give the traveller some bearings. Latin America covers nearly 8 million square miles (more than twice the area of the United States, sixteen times that of the United Kingdom). Historically underpopulated, it has experienced a demographic explosion in the twentieth century and now contains a population approaching half a billion. This population is divided among twenty sovereign states and the 'self-governing commonwealth' of Puerto Rico. All these states save one (Cuba)[2] have enjoyed independent existences since they emerged from the dissolving Spanish and Portuguese empires in the 1810s and 1820s. As such, they are older than most European states and almost all African states. Latin America is ethnically diverse: large Indian populations live in what once were the heartlands of the Aztec, Maya and Inca civilizations, in Middle America and the Andean highlands. Black slaves, brought in droves to the slave plantations of Brazil, the Caribbean, and some coastal regions of the Spanish American mainland, added to the region's rich ethnic and cultural blend. And the original Spanish and Portuguese immigrants of the colonial period – conquistadores and clerics, merchants and officials – were later followed by millions of the late nineteenth- and early twentieth-century migrants, who left southern Europe and came – particularly to Argentina, Uruguay and southern Brazil – to 'make America' (*hacer América*), thus creating Latin versions of the US 'melting pot'.

---

1 The labyrinth, as a metaphor, has a particular Latin American – especially Mexican – association: Paz 1961.
2 Cuba did not gain its independence from Spain until 1898, following two massive wars of national liberation and Spain's defeat at the hands of the United States – which promptly installed a quasi-protectorate over the island.

Ethnically mixed, Latin America has also experienced contrasting processes of economic development, class conflict and state-formation. Argentina, in 1914, ranked among the ten richest countries in the world.[3] Haiti was and remains among the poorest. If the colony (*c*.1500–1800) was a period of relative political calm, independence unleashed the demons of instability. Bolivia, it has been calculated, experienced 185 revolutions between 1826 and 1903; 1848 – a 'red year' in Bolivia as in Europe – witnessed fifteen of them (Dunkerley 1992: 153). Mexico similarly suffered instability and territorial loss; yet, following the Mexican Revolution of 1910, the country acquired a 'revolutionary' government which achieved stable, one-party, civilian rule for over two generations. Uruguay, the 'Switzerland of South America', pioneered a precocious welfare state in the early twentieth century; while neighbouring Paraguay, in contrast, languished under the personal dictatorship of General Alfredo Stroessner for thirty-five years (1954–89).

Powerful political leaders of this kind, usually hung with the loose label of 'caudillos',[4] punctuate Latin American history and – traditionally and excessively – dominate the region's historiography:[5] Bolívar and San Martín, the architects of South American independence; the renegade priests, Morelos and Hidalgo, who established a tradition of Mexican popular insurgence in the 1810s which Villa and Zapata would reprise a century later; Toussaint L'Ouverture, who helped forge the first independent black republic from the ashes of the French slavocracy in Haiti; José Martí, the Cuban nationalist leader, and Máximo Gómez, his black guerrilla chief, who drove Spain from its last colonial possession – the 'ever faithful' (*siempre fiel*) island of Cuba in the 1890s. These insurgent caudillos may be contrasted with the hard-headed, state-building caudillos of the nineteenth century – Portales in Chile and Páez in Venezuela; Paraguay's Dr Francia; Rosas and Roca in Argentina; Juárez and Díaz in Mexico. Finally, we encounter the 'populist'[6] caudillos of the twentieth century, who captained new mass movements and confronted an ideologically turbulent world in which socialism and fascism, liberal capitalism and economic nationalism, contended for power: Calles and Cárdenas in Mexico; Argentina's Perón; Brazil's Vargas; Chile's Allende (the world's first democratically elected Marxist president); the Cuban president/dictator Fulgencio Batista and his nemesis Fidel Castro; and their Nicaraguan counterparts, Somoza and the Sandinistas, who set the stamp of history on their struggle by assuming the

---

3 Useful analyses of Argentina's subsequent fall from grace are: Ferns 1973 and Lewis 1990.

4 Roughly, caudillos were warlords, capable of mobilizing a clientelist following, and often dependent on a provincial base: see Wolf and Hansen 1966–7. A good recent study is Lynch 1992.

5 It is sometimes worth making the distinction between 'history' (what happened) and 'historiography' (what historians have written about what happened). However, it would be rather pedantic and long-winded to insist on this distinction throughout, so I have sometimes used 'history' to denote 'historiography', particularly where no ambiguity exists.

6 'Populism' is another common but contentious term: it can denote a general political style or, more often, a specific type of movement/regime/leader which, it is argued, flourished in Latin America during the middle of this century – i.e. from the Depression to the 1970s. A useful symposium is Connif 1982.

name of the great patriot and political martyr of the inter-war years, Augusto César Sandino.

These, of course, are but a handful of examples drawn from a political universe remarkable for its diversity (hence the very term 'caudillo' may disguise huge contrasts). Furthermore, as I shall try to show, historians have rightly moved away from the 'Great Man' approach to history (there never was a 'Great Woman' theory, certainly not in *macho* Latin America); Carlyle's 'history [as] the biography of great men' (Carr 1964: 49) has given way to forms of local, regional, social, economic and cultural history, in which individuals appear as products as much as creators of their historical environments. This does not mean the annihilation of biography, but rather the interweaving of biography – or that form of collective biography which is jawbreakingly labelled prosopography[7] – with these other analytical approaches. The goal, as in the case of nineteenth-century Mexico, has been to avoid 'explaining Mexico in terms of Santa Anna rather than Santa Anna in terms of Mexico';[8] that is, to locate key individuals within their political, cultural and socio-economic contexts, without entirely sacrificing their individuality. The result, at national as well as regional and local level, has been a retreat from simplistic stereotypes (providential national histories, crude teleologies, the 'distorting dichotomies' of colony/nation, conservative/liberal, hero/villain)[9] and a renewed stress on diversity and variation. Contrasting political histories mirrored – or created? – contrasting political cultures in Latin America. Colombia, it was once said, was ruled by lawyers, Ecuador by priests and Venezuela by soldiers: a neat rule of thumb, conveying a simple truth about contrasting national experiences, but one that requires almost infinite qualification both by region (Guayaquil and coastal Ecuador were not 'ruled by priests' in the way that Quito and the highlands were) and by period (Venezuela, a bastion of militarism and authoritarianism up to the 1940s, has been consistently – if at times a little precariously – democratic since 1958).

Thus, despite its superficial unity – a shared Iberian colonial background, a powerful Catholic Church, a dominant linguistic tradition[10] – Latin America is notable for its great internal variety. To claim to be a historian of Latin America – or to try to summarize historiographical trends for Latin America as a whole – is to

---

7　That is, the compilation and analysis of data covering a range of individuals (usually elite individuals) and their relationships – political, factional, familial. A good example is Guerra 1985: vol. 1. On Brazil: Barman and Barman 1978; Lewin 1987; Graham 1990.

8　The phrase of Moisés González Navarro, quoted in Stevens 1992: 2.

9　Taylor 1985: 117. I acknowledge a considerable debt to this excellent article, particularly as regards my risky references to the colonial period.

10　Although the dominance of Spanish and Portuguese affords the historian unusually wide access to sources – primary and secondary – throughout the continent, it should not be forgotten that Indian languages are widely spoken in Mexico and Central America (Nahuatl and Maya especially) and in the Andean region (chiefly Aymara and Quechua); colonial historians and contemporary practitioners of oral history have both used these to good effect. A classic example – in which Nahuatl is used not just as a tool of research but also as a means to calibrate social change – is Lockhart 1991.

display a vaulting ambition, and to ride for a fall. Nowadays most 'Latin Americanists' are, first and foremost, historians of a particular country, increasingly of a particular region, class or topic within a particular country, especially when it comes to their 'primary', archival work. Some historians, driven by the urge to generalize (a dying impulse, one sometimes feels) or by the need to supplement meagre academic salaries, attempt grand syntheses, i.e. textbooks. But the latter do not make – although they may help break – academic reputations, which depend, particularly at the outset, on narrow monographic work, based on archival research. Hence, as I shall suggest in conclusion, a combination of professional command of the archives, coupled with a territorial imperative to defend one's own patch, can lead to a certain narrowness of vision, and a resulting fragmentation of historical scholarship. It follows that any discussion of Latin American historiography – where it's at, where it's going – must try to encapsulate a field which, by virtue of sheer divergent detail and infinite variation, presents enormous problems.

In some particular areas – for example, my own field of Mexican revolutionary studies – it is difficult for the individual scholar to keep up with the exponential growth of articles, theses, monographs and the occasional synthetic work.[11] In Mexico, as elsewhere in Latin America, archives have grown and improved. In Mexico City the old Lecumberri prison – a Benthamite panopticon – has been turned into an outstanding national archive, where, no doubt, scholars of the fashionable Foucaultian persuasion feel particularly at home. Agrarian reform programmes, by confiscating properties, have released estate archives into the public domain. Regional research centres have boosted the output of regional and local history – of which more anon. Today's novice historians of Latin America, while they may have to master a bewildering array of published sources, at least face a happier archival fate than that of previous generations, whose primary work sometime resembled a cross between an obstacle race and a tribal *rite de passage*. (I refer not just to the primitive or non-existent photocopiers, but also, more importantly, to inadequate catalogues, filthy conditions, unpredictable hours and eccentric archivists, such as the gentleman responsible for the old Casa Amarilla – an ex-convent in Mexico City which once housed the labour department papers – where researchers wore surgical masks and the archivist, fond of taking potshots at the pigeons fluttering in the rafters, served hot *tacos de paloma* (pigeon sandwiches) to hungry researchers at the end of a long morning.)[12]

Primary sources are now more abundant, accessible, catalogued, sometimes microfilmed. The raw material of historical research has therefore expanded and,

---

11 Bailey 1978 made the point nearly twenty years ago, since which time the volume of historiography has further mushroomed.

12 I am indebted to Barry Carr for this anecdote. The 'hands-on' knowledge and expertise of some old-style archivists should not be disdained. 'Don Goyo', as he was generally known, was for years the best guide to the Guatemalan national archive in Guatemala City. Conversely, gung-ho new archivists can foul up functioning systems with their unthinking innovations (e.g. at the ecclesiastical archive of Morelia, Michoacan, Mexico).

while twentieth-century sources may be most prolific (at least for the heyday of the written word, c.1900–50),[13] the mixed blessing of abundance also affects the colonial period, when a bureaucratic administration churned out paper, particularly relating to administrative, fiscal and judicial matters. Where the archives are abundant, the historians assiduous and the techniques advanced, complex 'professional' debates have developed, concerning, for example, the fluctuating population of the Americas, race mixture in colonial New Spain (Mexico), Bourbon fiscal reforms and tax yield (e.g. Seed 1982; McGaa 1984; Ouweneel and Bijleveld 1989). By virtue of their complexity – the engaged historian needs to understand colonial procedures as well as modern statistical techniques – these debates are resistant to quick résumés, and may even prove impenetrable to the 'lay' historian.

I mention these points partly to stress that Latin American historiography is, like most other historiographies today, multifaceted – or, to use a more negative term, fragmented. The drive towards professionalism, expertise and archival research – fuelled by graduate programmes and productive of an enormous volume of historiography (good, bad and indifferent) – makes synthesis difficult and liable to any amount of subjective bias. As a modern (twentieth-century) historian, chiefly of Mexico, I write with rather more authority about this century than preceding periods, and about Mexico rather than the rest of Latin America. However, for an overview of this kind to be of use, it must strive for broad coverage, venturing into different corners of the labyrinth, with all the risks that that entails. I shall, therefore, try to avoid an excessive focus on my own place and period – though it is not, I think, personal bias to suggest that the historiography of Mexico, both colonial and modern, has certainly been the most voluminous and probably been the most penetrating in the last generation: Mexico, in other words, leads the Latin American pack as it tries to cut back the long lead established by European and North American historiographies.[14] And I shall attempt some coverage of the colony, despite my lack of expertise; not only because the colony was the cradle of modern Latin America,[15] but also because colonial historiography has, in some areas, proved more innovative and sophisticated than its modern counterpart – proof, were it needed, that historiography, like the past itself, does not advance and

---

13 It is my informed guess that the combination of literacy, state-building and technology made the first half of this century a golden age for the production of written information, not least official documents. More recently, I suspect, the growth of non-written communication (telephone, radio, TV, e-mail) has resulted in a relative reduction in the quantity of useful written material which future historians may be able to consult.

14 It is worth stressing that, despite its rapid advance in recent years, Latin American historiography remains some way behind its European and US counterparts, in respect of volume, archival resources and number of practitioners. While this can make for an apparent lack of sophistication – Latin American historians are to be found hacking clearings out of the jungle rather than cultivating neat market gardens – it also imparts a certain raw, outdoor vigour to the enterprise.

15 Of course, pre-conquest Native American societies were also 'cradles' of colonial society, and colonial historians have often stressed the continuities which spanned the trauma of the Iberian conquest. However, it would break the back of an already overloaded llama if I attempted to cover pre-conquest history in this brief résumé.

unfold in a neat, unilinear fashion. However, it would be self-defeating to try to cover everything, to cite every trend and drop every name. I shall therefore concentrate on two themes and a deficiency; *en route* through the labyrinth, I shall also touch upon – without abstracting – the eternal question of periodization.[16]

THREADS THROUGH THE LABYRINTH: REGIONS AND LOCALITIES

The two salient themes in recent Latin American historiography are closely intertwined and readily recognizable to those who have contemplated the leafy branches of Clio as they spread across other countries and continents: first, regional/local history (history 'from-the-periphery-in', as it were) and popular/ subaltern history (history 'from-the-bottom-up', the history of *los de abajo*).[17] These, clearly, represent a reaction against earlier emphases which stressed nation-states, national elites, political and military narratives, political and constitutional evolution (or retrogression) (Taylor 1985: 142). In part because these earlier works suggested – but did not much investigate – regional variation, political Balkaniz-ation and provincial resistance to centralization, recent historians have tended to quit the capital for the provinces, addressing questions of local or regional economic development, political organization and collective identity. Thus, the once bland façade of the colony – or the independent nation-state – has, on closer inspection, come to resemble a Baroque exterior, rich in detail, contrast and eccentricity. The process has been made possible by the growth of regional archives and research centres, by the better organization of national archives already mentioned, and by the proliferation of graduate programmes, particularly in the United States and Latin America itself.[18] Thus, a new generation of young regional and local historians has assumed the mantle once worn by venerable 'amateur' historians of the *patria chica*, the chroniclers of local events and customs. Sometimes these newcomers have even acquired a touch of local chauvinism ('my *patria chica* right or wrong') to go with it. As in Europe, they have often taken the utility and rationality

---

16 I am aware of a third theme which may merit special treatment: the Latin American state, in its colonial and post-colonial forms. While this is an enduring historiographical issue – to which I refer in passing – it is less useful as an 'organizing concept' with which to make sense of recent historical research: for that reason, and because of pressure of space, I have chosen to concentrate on two other concepts, or approaches: (1) regions/localities and (2) popular history.

17 'The underdogs', as in the title of Mariano Azuela's classic (1915) novel of the Mexican Revolution.

18 The output of Latin American history by Latin Americans has been remarkable in recent years. Furthermore, as Latin American universities and research institutes have – often in the face of severe financial and political difficulties – developed innovative historical programmes, periodicals and career structures, so the historiography produced within the continent has come to conform to the US/ European model, the older bellelettrist tradition though far from dead, has given way to a more 'professional' approach, in which archival research, graduate degrees and specialist journals figure prominently. In seeking to limit the number of bibliographical references – and in aiming at an English-language readership – I have regrettably excluded most Spanish/Portuguese sources; hence Latin American historians of Latin America are sadly underrepresented.

of regional or local history for granted: justifications of the unit of analysis (why choose to study a state, province, district, municipality or community?) do not bulk large; the very notion of 'regionalism' – the tissue of relationships which ties people together, politically, economically, culturally, in subnational units – is rarely explored, even though the centrality of the concept in contemporary historiography (not to mention contemporary *history*) makes the 'region' almost as deserving of conceptual clarification today as the 'nation' was in the past.[19]

Given the volume of regional/local studies, any résumé must be partial and arbitrary. Colonial regional studies have illuminated the process of conquest and settlement, particularly in the old heartlands of Mexico and Peru. The pioneering work of Charles Gibson (1952; 1964) on the Indian communities of Tlaxcala and the Valley of Mexico has paved the way for subsequent studies of colonial regions, northern and mestizo as well as central/southern and Indian (Altman and Lockhart 1976). The richness of colonial archives has made possible sophisticated analyses of the structures of the colonial economy, including its mining centres at Guanajuato, Zacatecas (both Mexico) and Potosí (Upper Peru/Bolivia) (Brading 1971; Bakewell 1971; 1984); its mercantile networks (Oaxaca and Mexico City; New Granada; Buenos Aires);[20] its commercial farming, particularly as practised by the entrepreneurial Jesuits (Morelos and Guadalajara, Mexico; Cochabamba, Upper Peru/ Bolivia; Quito and coastal Peru) (Martin 1985; Van Young 1981; Larson 1988; Cushner 1980; 1982); and – a theme to which I will return – its abiding, enduring, peasant communities (Oaxaca and Yucatan; Huamanga and Huarochirí, Peru) (Taylor 1972; Farriss 1984; Stern 1982; Spalding 1984). Colonial research has also helped us understand the tensions of late colonial society – aggravated by the Bourbon administrative and fiscal reforms, already mentioned, and the brisk commercialization of the late eighteenth-century economy – which in turn contributed to the independence struggles of the 1810s (Hamnett 1986; O'Phelan Godoy 1988).

This research, dominated by the regional approach, has made possible new – but still few – syntheses, which try to integrate regional studies, weaving local, provincial and (proto-)national stories together: John Tutino's ambitious overview of Mexican agrarian history;[21] James Lockhart's (1992) masterly analysis of cultural and linguistic assimilation in colonial New Spain; Nancy Farriss's (1984) outstanding study of the Yucatec Maya and their long struggle for survival through three centuries of colonial rule. Given the nature of colonial society – ordered, orderly,

---

19   Taylor 1985: 178, makes a similar point, asking why a diocese should be used as a unit of socio-economic analysis (save for the fact that it happens to contain a diocesan archive). For a useful discussion and examples, see Van Young 1992.
20   Hamnett 1971; Kicza 1983; Twinam 1983; Socolow 1978. Note the preponderance of studies on the Bourbon eighteenth century, especially post-1750; 'studies of merchants in the mid-colonial period', as Catherine Lugan (1986: 73) observes, 'are rare'.
21   Tutino 1986. It should be added that many of the Mexican regional studies which Tutino, for example, synthesizes were themselves stimulated by an earlier seminal synthesis which, though qualified by later research, remains a classic: Chevalier [1952] 1970.

bureaucratic and legalistic – these studies are particularly good at describing methods of rule and modes of production over time (they can also, I shall later suggest, probe deeper into popular 'mentalities' and beliefs). They can also bite off big chunks of time, giving a sense of – and what historiographical analysis dare omit the phrase? – the *longue durée*.[22] Eric Van Young (1981) charts Guadalajara's socio-economic evolution over a century and a half; Brooke Larson does the same for Cochabamba over 350 years. These are chronological chunks which few modern (nineteenth/twentieth-century) historian could bite off, without risk of severe indigestion or frustrating superficiality: in part because the modern archives are, in general, more voluminous (though not necessarily more revealing); and in part because, following independence, the tempo of political change quickens and the staccato story of events – of *l'histoire événementielle* – interrupts the slower socio-economic cadences of colonial history.[23]

Thus, as we leave the (relatively) orderly and bureaucratic colony,[24] to enter the rowdy, caudillesque era of independence, the emphases shift. Regional and local studies still prevail, and with good reason: they alone can subvert, question and qualify the grand old simplicities of national history. But the cast and the plot are rather different, hence the historiography differs too. Bureaucratic actors – viceroys, audiencias, mercantilist monopolies – give way to political animals: caudillos and their motley followers; embryonic political parties (or their counter-parts, the masonic lodges); regular armies, freelance financiers and cliques of local notables; and a Catholic Church which, no longer subject to royal patronage, now becomes politically as well as spiritually and socio-economically salient. Local and regional studies tend to contract in chronological scope and, particularly for the earlier nineteenth century, to admit the novel importance of politics. For some, this is largely a story of caudillos, clients and local cliques/camarillas: politics is a Namierite struggle for place and privilege, requiring a Namierite analysis of family ties and patronage network (Balmori *et al.* 1982, esp. chs 3 and 4; and on Brazil, see Lewin 1987 and Graham 1990). Others – continental Europeans, as it happens – prefer to stress a more genuine and precocious politicization, involving ideological

---

22 In fact, Braudel's *longue durée* is misquoted as much as quoted, including in this instance. I use it (as many seem to do) to denote long periods of – usually slow, incremental – socio-economic change, spanning a century or more. As I understand Braudel, however, such a span corresponds to the Braudelian 'secular trend', *longue durée* being reserved for yet longer phases of almost glacial, geographical change: Braudel 1984: 76–7, 620–1.

23 Of course, colonial history started with a bang – the Spanish Conquest, which offers ample scope for classic *histoire événementielle*, as William Prescott demonstrated in the 1840s. Concrete proof that *histoire événementielle* is alive and well and living in the British House of Lords is afforded by Hugh Thomas's readable but nitpicking narrative, *The Conquest of Mexico* (1993). A contrasting contemporary study, illustrating where historiography is going rather than coming from, is Gruzinski 1993, which discusses the conquest in terms of cultural domination and resistance.

24 The colony was not uniformly tranquil, of course; but revolts and riots were sporadic and, more important, often formed part of a broad spectrum of popular protest, litigation and petitioning; they were as much parts of, as threats to, the colonial system, at least until the later eighteenth century. See Taylor 1979 and Cope 1994: ch. 7.

debate, elections and participation; for them, the Spanish-American revolutions bear comparison with the French, for both serve as midwives of a new political culture (Guerra 1994). All agree – implicitly if not explicitly – on the central importance of the state, whose workings and rationale were transformed by independence.[25] But few agree as to the nature of this transformation. The strength or weakness, legitimacy or illegitimacy, class affiliation or relative autonomy of the post-colonial state are as difficult to evaluate in the case of Latin America as they are in the case of Africa; and the regional studies of the period remain too few and scattered to admit of an imminent synthesis.

In economic terms, however, the break at independence is less marked. If the colonial mining and mercantile economy partly collapsed, this did not – historians now stress – result in a dramatic breakthrough to a vigorous free-market capitalism. Foreign – chiefly British – investment was limited and often unsuccessful; the old notion that Latin America exchanged formal Iberian colonialism for informal British imperialism has been severely qualified (Platt 1980). Latin American markets remained shallow and politically unpredictable; recalcitrant regions – such as the Argentine interior – blocked the best-laid plans of enlightened urban reformers (Ferns 1960; Gootenberg 1991). Trade remained patchy, liberal reforms and foreign loans sank without trace in a quicksand of protectionism, subsistence and caudillo politics. Many (social and economic) historians would therefore see a certain unity in the 'Bourbon' period, c.1750–1850. Political revolution, for them, did not imply social or economic revolution; the lineaments of the colonial order – merchant and artisan guilds, big haciendas, corporate peasant communities – remained, stressed but surviving.[26]

Thereafter – and the timing would vary from place to place – the tempo of economic change quickened, as Latin American countries boosted exports, acquired an infrastructure (ports, railways), and began to participate more vigorously in the world division of labour. Regional studies have offered numerous and crucial examples of this process of economic extraversion: wheat farming and stockraising in Argentina (Scobie 1964; Sabato 1990); sugar in north-eastern Brazil, coastal Peru and Cuba (Eisenberg 1974; Klarén 1977; Knight 1970); henequen in Yucatan (Joseph 1982: chs 1, 2; Wells 1985); silver, later tin, in Bolivia (Langer 1989); copper in the Peruvian highlands (Mallon 1983); rubber in the Amazon basin (Weinstein 1983); oil in Mexico and Venezuela (Brown 1993, esp. chs 1, 2; McBeth

---

25 As Taylor 1985: 144–5 points out, the question of the colonial state remains contentious: was it a 'nearly omnipotent' Leviathan, relatively autonomous of society, or, rather, 'weak and fragmented', a 'passive arena of competing interests'? As indicated above (n. 16), I shall duck any direct discussion of this issue. Interestingly, similar debates arise in the context of twentieth-century Latin American states, to the extent that colonial labels – 'Habsburg', 'Bourbon' – can be pressed into service for the construction of contemporary typologies: Knight 1993b: 42ff.

26 Taylor 1985: 122–3 entertains doubts about this – by now almost conventional – periodization of socio-economic history in terms of a rough 'Bourbon' century, c.1750–1850. For good examples, see Jacobsen 1993: part 1, and Andrien and Johnson 1994, the introduction to which discusses the question of periodization.

1983); and coffee – cultivated on small plots or big estates, by peasants, peons, slaves and proletarians – throughout the hemisphere, from Puerto Rico through Guatemala, Venezuela, and Colombia down to the great coffeetropolis of São Paulo in southern Brazil (Bergad 1983; McCreery 1994; Roseberry 1984; Legrand 1986; Palacios 1980; Stein 1957; Holloway 1980; Dean 1976).

While not all socio-economic studies of the later nineteenth century – what Tulio Halperin (1993) terms the 'neo-colonial' era of Latin American history – are precisely regional in approach (some, for example, attempt broader national analyses of export staples, such as Chilean copper; Monteon 1982), most in effect are, and have to be. First, because patterns of socio-economic development tended to be regionally specific: 'modernization' thus served to Balkanize, socio-economically, rather than to homogenize – it hardened divisions between, for example, the port metropolis of Buenos Aires and the Argentine interior; between the declining Brazilian north-east and the dynamic south; between a buoyant, free-labour northern Mexico, a more torpid 'traditional' centre and a coercive, plantocratic south.[27] And, second, because the primary sources, though ample, are often intractable: nineteenth-century historians, lacking the ordered bureaucratic archives of the late colony, are driven to resort to the rich but recalcitrant archives of courts, lawyers, landed families, foreign companies, state/provincial governments and municipal authorities.

Nevertheless, great strides have been made and, as usually occurs when case studies multiply, the old certitudes are called into question. The infant Latin American states did not, as I mentioned, exchange formal Spanish – or Portuguese – rule for informal British rule; foreign commercial penetration was slow and partial; even in the late nineteenth century, as penetration accelerated and export markets became the motor of development, patterns of regional diversity remained. It was not just that some regions benefited from trade and investment while others suffered from neglect (this may seem a banal statement, but it begs some thorny theoretical questions).[28] These studies also show how the nature of capitalist development varied significantly from place to place. In some regions, the market displayed its presumed affinity with free-wage labour, sucking migrant workers from peasant communities locally, nationally, and, of course, internationally.[29] But elsewhere it either reinforced 'traditional' forms of peonage or created new forms of coerced labour. In Cuba and Brazil, slavery flourished until the supply of slaves was cut off by British action in the second half of the nineteenth century (Bethell 1970; Murray 1980). In the old Indian heartlands of Middle and Andean America,

---

27   Katz 1974 offers a good résumé of the Mexican case.

28   Extreme versions of dependency theory suggest that any integration into capitalist world markets produces underdevelopment, while development can be achieved only by shunning such integration – whether deliberately, by means of radical policies of economic nationalism, or fortuitously, because of external market failure, as during the 1930s: see Frank 1969. A perceptive critique of (simplistic) dependency theory is provided by Halperín 1982.

29   A useful symposium is Duncan and Rutledge 1977.

landlords resorted to the coercion of Indian and mestizo populations to secure labour for their enterprises. Guatemala's coffee boom involved dragooned labour and a hardening of ethnic divisions (McCreery 1994; Smith 1990). In Mexico, a coercive, plantocratic south confronted a more liberal, free-labour north (the parallel with the United States may be pursued: the Mexican Revolution saw the victory of the north and the irruption of reformist northern carpetbaggers into the recalcitrant south; Knight 1986: II, 236–51). Yet in Brazil it was the declining sugar-producing north, unable to retain its dwindling slave population, which pioneered abolition, in the face of opposition from that great bastion of slavery – and modernity – São Paulo (Conrad 1972; Toplin 1972). Highly divergent in its regional and rural impact, export-orientated economic development (*desarrollo hacia afuera*) did tend consistently to promote major cities – Buenos Aires, São Paulo, Río de Janeiro, Mexico City – where a rich elite and growing literate middle class were the chief beneficiaries of economic growth, of urban infrastructure and cultural florescence.[30]

Regional and local studies, while particularly revealing of patterns of socio-economic development, also shed light on political trends and events. In most Latin American countries export-led growth facilitated the rise of stronger, more solvent states; and, into the twentieth century, as the continent experienced a series of external shocks – the First World War, the Depression, the Second World War – so the role of the state increased.[31] States intervened increasingly in economic life: regulating, taxing, even expropriating. Especially during and after the 1930s, 'inward-orientated' development (*desarrollo hacia adentro*) came to prevail over the older export-led strategy (see Thorp 1984). Regional studies therefore pay great attention to the impact of national – and international – events on the provinces, and to the latter's interaction with centralizing forces, both political and economic. Brazil's Old Republic (1889–1930) – a polity based on a delicate balance of states' rights and interests – is a classic example (Love 1971; Wirth 1977; Levine 1978; Topik 1987).

So too, in a different way, is the Mexican Revolution. Despite the existence of some new syntheses (Knight 1986; Hart 1987), the thrust of 'revolutionary studies', broadly defined, has been toward regional and local history. If Mexico was a sprawling, variegated country before the Revolution – 'Many Mexicos' in Simpson's (1941) phrase, now a mantra for Mexicanists – so there were many revolutions, in respect of both causes, course and outcome.[32] Zapatista Morelos

---

30 Morse 1958 pioneered big-city history, which was further developed by Scobie 1974 and Needell 1987. Holloway 1993 stresses the class dimension of urbanization; Scobie 1988 reminds us that urbanization was not confined to metropolises.

31 On the growth of the state, see Whitehead 1994. Knight 1993: 39–42 makes the obvious – but sometimes overlooked – point that the 'strength of the state' is a vague concept which may involve different and even contradictory criteria: e.g. on the one hand, the state's capacity to mould society and, on the other, its durability, longevity and capacity for self-reproduction over time.

32 Brading 1980, and Benjamin and Wasserman 1990 are useful collections. Note also Carr 1980 and the articles by Linda Hall and Paul Vanderwood in *Mexican Studies/Estudios Mexicanos* 3.2 (summer 1987).

differed from Villista Chihuahua; Sonora, cradle of the triumphant Sonoran dynasty of the 1920s, was different yet again.[33] For Yucatan, in the south-east, the revolution came 'from without', carried by northern carpetbaggers who descended on the peninsula in 1915 (Joseph 1982). A decade later, the great Catholic uprising known as the Cristiada – Mexico's Vendée – represented a regional repudiation of revolutionary anticlericalism and centralization in the centre-west states of Jalisco, Guanajuato and Michoacan.[34]

Yet even these broadbrush regional distinctions require further spatial disaggregation. In Michoacan, for example, clerical/Cristero communities existed cheek by jowl with revolutionary/anticlerical counterparts. Local politics often revolved around such historic enmities, which were successively redefined according to the political terminology of the day: liberal and conservative in the nineteenth century; revolutionary and Cristero in the 1910s and 1920s.[35] Hence the importance of genuine *microhistoria* – the history of individual communities, painstakingly reconstructed on the basis of local archives and oral accounts – which, in the Mexican case, has been pioneered by Luis González (1983). Though some antediluvian historians of the Revolution still cling to the crude notion of an undifferentiated popular insurgency (Hart 1987), most now recognize the infinite local variety of revolution. In some communities, the Revolution was eagerly espoused; some had revolution thrust upon them; in Luis González's community, San José de Gracia, 1910 was not the *annus mirabilis* of the Revolution, but rather the year when Halley's Comet blazed in the night sky and the village eccentric tried unsuccessfully to soar from the roof of his house, flapping wings made of straw matting.

THREADS THROUGH THE LABYRINTH: THE COMMON PEOPLE

Such centrifugal historiography – the historian's flight from the centre to the provinces – has its social or class counterpart. Apart from fleeing the centre, historians have tried to plumb the neglected depths of the societies they study. 'Centre-out' historiography is therefore complemented by 'bottom-up' historiography, the historiography, we might say, of *los de abajo*, of 'groups such as women, servants, children, peasants, vagrants, and criminals' (Taylor 1985: 119; cf. Guha and Spivak 1985) – Latin America's equivalent of India's 'subaltern studies' school.

33 Womack 1969 is a classic of interpretative narrative: it can be supplemented by Warman 1980, which builds on oral accounts and locates the Zapatista rebellion within a wider chronological framework and Brunk 1985, a good recent biography. By way of comparison note Katz 1980 and Aguilar Camín 1980: 59–75, 92–123. Katz's pioneering work on Villismo will soon culminate in a major study of the northern caudillo and his movement.
34 Meyer 1976 is a major revisionist study, a translation and abridgement of the author's three-volume *La Cristiada* (1973).
35 The broad debate between 'traditional' and 'revisionist' interpretations of the Cristero revolt has – as we might have hoped and expected – begun to take into account such local variations: see Jrade 1985 and Purcell 1994, which forms part of a very promising research project on local politics in 'counter-revolutionary' western Mexico.

Such a trend is apparent throughout the five centuries of post-conquest history. The viceroys and prelates of the colony have ceded ground to the Indian peasant (especially the hard-drinking, rock-throwing, protesting Indian peasant), to the city mob and the urban artisan, to the petty official and the rabble-rousing cura, the counterpart of medieval Europe's 'hedge-priest'.[36] The colonial archives have, in particular, facilitated enquiries into Latin America's subalterns; and they have enabled historians to go beyond purely political or socio-economic categories – the straitjackets which so often confine 'popular' subjects – and to penetrate the minds and morals of the common people. We now know about their drinking and carousing (Taylor 1979); their resort to sporadic violence, in both city and countryside;[37] their formulation of a 'syncretic' religion which embraced aspects of both Catholicism and Precolumbian religion, the messianic and millenarian beliefs which coursed like subterranean streams beneath the baroque edifice of Tridentine Catholicism.[38] If rebellions – and even early industrial strikes – have naturally captured historians' imagination, increasing attention has also been paid to daily life, to the normal and unexceptional, or to forms of 'resistance' which were slippery, discreet and anonymous – rather than overt and violent.[39]

Such an approach, involving careful research into largely illiterate, frequently evasive, social groups is not easy, and places particular demands upon both historians and archives (Taylor 1985: 155; Van Young 1990). The latter, necessarily the product of literate 'superordinate' classes, admit the subaltern only at particular moments: during – or after – rebellions and popular protests; at court trials or church investigations of immorality or blasphemy. (Menocchio, Ginzburg's heretic miller, now has his Latin American counterparts.)[40] None of these situations encourages transparent revelation – they are not, in Habermas's term, 'ideal speech situations'. On the contrary, arraigned plebeians may have every incentive to dissimulate. Nevertheless, the colonial bureaucracy, both lay and clerical, generated ample material which may be sensitively dissected. The same, alas, is not true of the often unstable governments of the nineteenth century; hence, when it comes to 'history-from-below', especially history which seeks to go beyond simple socio-economic categories, the post-independence period presents particular problems.

Again, wars and revolts may offer brief moments of revelation, moments when the

---

36 On the role of the curas, see Taylor 1985: 149–52.

37 Taylor 1979 deals with the countryside; on the city, see Cope 1994: ch. 7. Valuable symposia, which span the colonial and national periods, are: Katz 1988 and Stern 1987.

38 Gruzinski 1989; Van Young 1989. Taylor 1985: 155–62 provides a suggestive analysis of Mexico's Virgin of Guadalupe cult. Note also Platt 1993.

39 The turn away from overt revolt to quotidian resistance is, of course, a global shift, influenced, in particular, by James Scott's south-east Asian anthropological study, *Weapons of the Weak, Everyday Forms of Peasant Resistance* (1985). A concrete example, relating to the plantation peons of Yucatan, is Joseph 1994: 145. Brazilian slave studies (see n. 43 below) have taken a similar turn.

40 Van Young 1989 offers a foretaste of a major forthcoming study of popular insurgency in Mexico, 1810–21, in which questions of mentality, heterodox religion and political dissent are broached, with court records supplying much of the empirical and Freudian psychology some of the analytical tools.

'public transcript' of popular deference and caution is torn up and subaltern groups speak – by their deeds as well as their words – with greater clarity and forthright-ness.[41] Thus, Florencia Mallon infers a vigorous proto-patriotism among peasants of the central sierra of Peru at the time of the War of the Pacific (1879–81): far from languishing in anti-national parochialism, Huancayo's peasants resisted the Chilean invader with greater commitment and resolution than Peru's 'national bourgeoisie' – who, according to some theoretical scenarios, were the designated carriers of early nationalism (see Mallon 1983; 1987; Bonilla 1987). Peasant patriotic consciousness, Mallon (1995) argues, was not peculiar to Peru – indeed, one may even talk of an emergent school of peasant-nationalist studies, involving, for example, Mexico and Nicaragua (Grossman 1992). Nor was it confined simply to questions of national identity: rather, it exemplified a broader *crise de conscience* among nineteenth-century popular groups who, Mallon (1995) argues, mobilized, politicked and – according to today's fashionable jargon – developed a 'national-democratic discourse' which blended universal appeals with particular, local concerns.

Mallon's bold claims, some might say, outrun her empirical data. But she rightly stresses two related points: first, that popular groups – even during the murky nineteenth century – entertained ideas, theories and projects, they displayed ingenuity, autonomy and creativity; they were neither the inert primitives of conservative historiography, nor – E. P. Thompson (1978) has reminded us – the prisoners of grand historical structures, as structural Marxism suggest. In this respect, peasants – as well as other popular groups – are no longer equated to Pavlov's dogs, but rather to Aristotle's political animals, possessed of ideas, goals and knowledge, including knowledge of the world beyond the village. The study of elite cultural history and elite proto-nationalism is an established – and still productive – field;[42] now, however, themes once confined to elite studies have invaded 'popular' history, and 'the people' are credited with agile brains as well as empty bellies. Of course, popular culture and consciousness differ from their elite counterparts. The latter can – to a degree – be culled from printed sources; for largely illiterate communities the transmission of ideas and symbols requires alternative approaches. Thus, historians have recently looked at symbolic violence (Szeminski 1987), at rituals and fiestas (see the innovative symposium, Beezley *et al.* 1994), at nineteenth-century brass bands and twentieth-century comic books (Thomson 1994; Hinds and Tatum 1992).

In particular, Latin American historians have discerned a kind of historic compromise linking popular groups with nineteenth-century liberalism (especially patriotic liberalism). Liberalism was not simply an ideology of free-trading

---

41   Scott 1990. Joseph and Nugent 1994 is an interesting attempt to marry Scott's thesis to Mexican revolutionary history.

42   Lafaye 1976 helped initiate a course of enquiry into (elite) proto-nationalism which has been carried to fruition by Brading 1991. Shumway 1993 offers an interesting but contentious analysis of Argentina's foundation myths. Hale 1989 is another good example of recent elite intellectual/cultural history.

mercantile elites. This may seem banal to students of European – or United States – history, for whom the notion of popular liberalism is no oxymoron. But Latin American historians – and social scientists more generally – have consistently seen liberalism as imposed, elitist and anti-popular (while Catholicism and conservatism, conversely, have often been seen as popular and organic) (Burns 1980; Tutino 1986). The latter perspective is certainly not all wrong. But recent attempts to grapple with popular politics and belief in the nineteenth and early twentieth centuries clearly demonstrate the vigour of popular, even peasant, liberalism, the product less of calm ratiocination than of pressing historical events and conflicts: the Chilean invasion of Peru (1879), the French invasion of Mexico in the 1860s, the US invasion of Nicaragua and pursuit of Sandino in the 1920s. Tristan Platt (1987: 285–6) sees the Indian peasantry of the Bolivian highlands linked to the liberal state by means of a political and symbolic pact, whereby the payment of tribute implied the recognition of community autonomy. But, in all these cases, wide local variations prevailed. If peasants – the greater part of the Latin American population – were more plugged into national politics than was previously thought, it is perhaps not surprising that they – like more literate, more studied, elite groups – should display important divisions and contrasting allegiances: thus, the more we study popular culture, the more rich and variegated it appears, the less valid seem the old stereotypes of bland uniformity (Knight 1994).

The rescue of 'subaltern classes' from historiographical neglect – from the 'enormous condescension of posterity' (Thompson 1968: 13) – is not simply a matter of Indian peasants or of proto-patriots. Brazil, for example, witnessed a series of messianic movements, some of remarkable scale and duration: the most celebrated, Canudos, was ruthlessly – and gratuitously? – repressed by the army in 1897 (Levine 1992). Although messianism affected other Latin American societies, it flourished most vigorously in backwoods Brazil, for reasons which historians hotly debate (Pessar 1981; Queiroz 1985; Diacon 1992). Brazil was also a prolific source of another controversial and characteristically Latin American phenomenon: banditry. Hence, Eric Hobsbawm's notion of 'social banditry' – the bandit as Robin Hood and banditry as a form of surrogate social protest – has been extensively tested in the Latin American context (Joseph 1990; Slatta 1991; Singelmann 1991; Birkbeck 1991; Joseph 1991). But Brazilian – and, to a lesser extent, Cuban – historiography has, necessarily, focused on a third issue, no less relevant for comparative analysis: the peculiar institution of slavery – its rise and fall, economic and political rationale, its inner workings. The suggestive – but questionable – broadbrush studies of Gilberto Freyre have therefore given way to a range of specialist approaches: studies of slave economics, some of distinctly cliometric sophistication; of abolition, both domestic and international; and, most significantly in recent years, of slave protest, culture and daily life.[43] The collapse of Brazilian slavery, we now know, derived not just from the

---

43 See the useful survey in Schwartz 1992. Varieties of slave resistance are analysed in Reis and Silva 1989.

British naval tourniquet, internal economic contradictions or high-minded middle-class abolitionism; the slaves themselves played a part, especially during the final *débâcles* of the last slavocrat bastion, São Paulo (Conrad 1972: ch. 16; Toplin 1972). Cuban and Peruvian slaves, too, played an important part in their own incremental emancipation (Blanchard 1992; Scott 1985). But slave resistance, in Brazil particularly, had punctuated the nineteenth century, sometimes assuming the form of overt protest (Reis 1993), sometimes deploying the covert 'weapons of the weak'. As the spectrum of 'resistance' expands, so historians of slavery have now begun to recapture subaltern experiences which are less violent and eye-catching. Court archives reveal the lives of female slaves and domestic servants; we are learning more about the daily live of slaves and freedmen; and biographers, traditionally enamoured of white male elites, have begun – sources permitting – to cast their net more widely (Lauderdale Graham 1988; Silva 1993 is a rare biography). The 'faces in the crowd' – once an indistinct and anonymous mass – have begun to acquire individual features.

Slavery ended in the later nineteenth century, although forms of coerced labour – peonage (debt-slavery) and contract labour – survived and even flourished well into the twentieth century.[44] But as we enter the latter, it is the growing urban working class who command increasing attention. Until quite recently this attention was excessively coloured by grand theory and crude assumptions. If, as I have suggested, casual students of Latin America regarded the peasantry as marginal, illiterate and parochial, they often paid disproportionate attention to the (small) urban working class, seeking – though not usually finding – a revolutionary vanguard, and pondering questions of somewhat bastard European origin.[45] Was the labour movement revolutionary? If not, why not? Did the Latin American state – especially the 'populist' state of the mid-twentieth century, the state of Perón, Cárdenas or Vargas – co-opt the workers, thus drawing the sting of revolution? Did the workers sell their revolutionary birthright for a mess of populist pottage?

These are loaded, though not wholly pointless, questions, and they are still being

---

44 An interesting, though inconclusive, debate on the character of debt-peonage has developed, involving – roughly – revisionists who would stress the rural workers' relative freedom and bargaining power as against traditionalists who would tend to equate peonage with slavery. See Bauer 1979b and Loveman 1979 in *Hispanic American Historical Review*, pp. 478–89. Knight 1988 offers a brief overview.
45 'Bastard' in the sense that they were probably illegitimate questions even in the original European context. Thus, Latin American labour historians have wrestled with the 'problem' of their continent's 'non-revolutionary' working class, assuming that any decent, self-respecting working class ought to be 'revolutionary'; yet the European – not to mention the North American – experience hardly confirms that assumption. A similar bastard Eurocentrism is evident in the study of revolutions, where European exemplars (e.g. France, 1789) are assumed to be rapid, root-and-branch transformations, whereas their Latin American counterparts (e.g. Mexico, 1910) are feeble compromises; again, the European yardstick is hopelessly crooked. A third and final example: the syncretic – 'pagan/Christian' – religions of Latin America are sometimes taken to be unusual hybrids, compared to the orthodox and consistent Catholicism of Europe – which was itself, of course, a heterodox – 'pagan/Christian' – hybrid.

743

debated, more so by political scientists than by historians.[46] However, they encouraged an excessively top-down, macropolitical approach to labour history. Workers were seen as political clients (or occasionally subversives), not as social, economic – and cultural – actors. They were also seen, too often, as essentially reactive, easily manipulated by conniving populist caudillos, particularly by caudillos who supposedly capitalized on the clientelist tendencies of first-generation urban workers who had recently migrated from the 'traditional' countryside to the 'modern' city.[47] Political in its focus, Latin American labour history concentrated on organized – as opposed to non-organized – labour, on men rather than women, and on major unions and confederations, especially those linked to left-wing political parties, rather than on informal groups and relationships. The only good worker was a red worker; the union hall and the Internationale counted for more than the tavern and the tango. Some analyses – even some good ones – sank into an alphabet soup of impersonal acronyms.[48]

Now, just as peasants and slaves have received more sympathetic – and empathetic – attention, so, too, labour historians are disaggregating the acronyms, skirting the simplistic old questions (were the workers revolutionary and, if not, why not?) and descending from the sindicato office to the shopfloor – even, in some cases, to the bar, poolroom and football field. The result is not – to quote Trevelyan's old description of social history – 'history with the politics left out', but history in which politics is located within a social, economic and cultural context, in which unorganized as well as organized workers figure, women as well as men, artisans as well as industrial workers, and in which rather more subtle questions of protest and accommodation, 'resistance and integration' are debated. This shift is not entirely confined to the twentieth century. The colony had its working class, notably in the mines: Mexico's first major strike, the subject of a recent study, dates back to 1766.[49] Historians have also begun to investigate the key role of artisans in nineteenth-century urban politics and society, notably in Peru and Colombia; they have uncovered traditions of organization, protest and culture which long antedated the rise of industry and the 'social question' of the 1900s (Gootenberg 1989; Sowell 1992; note also Thomson 1989). But, given the resistance of written sources to detailed investigation of working-class culture, it has been the recent – post-1930 – period which has benefited most from oral history, from the unpacking of bland acronyms, and from the development of the 'new labour history'. Such approaches

---

46 Collier and Collier 1991 is a compendious study of state–labour relations in the twentieth century; but, from a labour-history perspective, some of the questions look a bit dated. Roxborough 1994 is similarly useful, but conventional.

47 Germani 1965 proposed this thesis for Argentina; Murmis and Portantiero 1971 challenged it, pretty successfully.

48 Barnard 1992 is one of the best chapters in a good symposium, but it seems unable to escape from the dance of the acronyms (e.g. p. 75 'the PS set aside its animosity toward the PCCh in order to collaborate with the ADCh parties and the CTCh').

49 Ladd 1988. On colonial artisans, see the useful overview by Johnson 1986.

are evident in Jeffrey Gould's (1990) pioneering study of Nicaraguan sugar workers, in Daniel James's (1988) seminal work on Peronist workers in Buenos Aires and in Peter Winn's (1986) influential history of the textile workers of Yarur, Chile, in the 1970s.[50]

Oral history, of course, is no *passe-partout*. It presents particular problems. Subaltern spokespeople, like their elite counterparts, have – to employ a useful Mexicanism – their own *rollo*, their own – often unconsciously – prepared script.[51] They may also be understandably wary of talking to inquisitive gringos. Additional problems – not to say risks – may attend this form of research, and they go rather beyond surgical masks and pigeon-potting archivists. Peter Winn (1986: viii) was pulled in by the Chilean military and, after three days' interrogation, warned: 'we have no proof that you have committed a crime exactly ... but talking with our workers, interviewing union leaders, all this is very suspicious. We do not want anyone talking to our workers'; after which he was summarily expelled from the country. Nevertheless, when the risks and problems can be surmounted, oral history, complementing archival work, can provide a fuller picture of the 'lives of labour', one that is neither one-dimensionally political nor excessively coloured by crude Eurocentric suppositions.

I have left till last the biggest victim of posterity's condescension: women. (What is more, my brief and belated reference will seem to some like abject tokenism.) The traditional history of Latin America was, by and large, history with the women left out. Political historians could of course, plead that women usually played a minor role in politics, especially if 'politics' meant 'high' politics – the politics of presidents, generals, caciques and caudillos.[52] But this was not an absolute rule and, during the twentieth century, as universal suffrage and mass parties developed, the political role of women expanded (Lavrin 1994). Much more important, however, has been the shift in historiographical emphasis, as a result of which historians have begun to investigate women in colonial nunneries, in nineteenth-century metropolises, in the coffee fields of São Paulo or in the ranks of Mexican revolutionary armies.[53] If, initially, articulate feminist minorities attracted attention, the latter has now switched to more numerous – and socially significant? – groups, hitherto the victims of historiographical neglect: the prostitutes of Buenos Aires, the women schoolteachers who sought to bring 'socialism' to the *macho* Mexican countryside in

---

50 A more traditional – broad, structural and comparative – approach is evident in Bergquist 1986. For a useful review of recent labour history, see Viotti de Costa 1989, and ensuing comments by Barbara Weinstein, Perry Anderson, Hobart Spalding and June Nash (*International Labor and Working Class History* 36 (1989): 25–50).

51 This is even more true of elite scripts, which can reduce – though not negate – the usefulness of elite oral history: e.g. Wilkie and de Wilkie 1969.

52 Even here there are exceptions, most obviously Eva Perón; studies of Evita, however, are notable more for their quantity than their quality.

53 Lavrin 1986; Graham 1988; Stolcke 1988; Salas 1990, although the latter is rather stronger on myth than history.

the 1930s.[54] Furthermore, as these examples suggest, research into the role of women involves a broader enquiry into issues of gender, affecting men no less than women. In a continent and culture where – witness the stereotype of the Latin American *macho* – notions of patriarchy have been unusually strong, historians have set about unravelling 'gendered' structures of work and warfare, nationalism and religion (Fowler-Salamini and Vaughan 1994: xix–xx; Mallon 1995: xix, 69, 79).

THREADS THROUGH THE LABYRINTH: THEORY

The new labour history – like the 'new peasant history' and the 'new local history' – necessarily tends to be finely focused. Pioneering investigation cannot be done with a wide-angle lens. Occasionally, the fine focus leads to a certain myopia. The historian of a community becomes immersed in its every detail; the meticulous quest in the archives becomes an obsessive end in itself; the local historian even acquires a kind of petty local chauvinism – a means, perhaps, to warn off interlopers from his/her chosen terrain. As a result we may lose not only the wood for the trees, but even the trees for the twigs. Fortunately, the better and more broad-minded practitioners keep an eye on the big picture. While remaining faithful to their case studies, they try to link them to grander debates – they may, indeed, initiate grand debates. One – the putative peasant patriotism of Florencia Mallon – has been mentioned. Steve Stern (1988a) has drawn on his pioneering research on colonial Peruvian peasants to contest the sublime simplicities of Wallerstein's world-system theory. Eric Van Young (1990 and 1989) links his work on peasant insurgency to broader comparative questions and brings to bear theoretical insights as diverse as psychoanalysis and geographical space theory: Freud and von Thünen connect in the halls of Clio. In the field of modern labour history, case studies have been located within wider debates about state–civil society relations; and, if these involve reprises of older questions (e.g. did the state co-opt the workers?), at least the questions are posed with greater sophistication and answered with greater empirical evidence than in the past. Of course, debates of this scope are rarely resolved: the character of the Mexican Revolution – which in turn hinges a good deal on the nature of Mexican peasant life and politics – remains a polemical issue; recent studies of Brazilian labour have generated vigorous debate concerning working-class attitudes towards government and the respective roles of class and gender in worker mobilization (Wolfe 1991a, 1991b; French 1991).

This is as it should be. Historiography does not involve a gradual, peaceful and consensual process of frontier expansion. Like the real frontier, the historiographical frontier is jagged, irregular and sometimes violent. (There is also, we should note, a massive 'internal' frontier: i.e. large chunks of ignorance within areas we once thought securely settled, especially with regard to the period *c.*1820–70.) The

---

54 Guy 1989; Vaughan 1990 and 1994 (which appears in an excellent new symposium). A good example of the more traditional political history, which pioneered the study of women, is Hanner 1980.

historians' advance is governed not only by the logic of the archives – the onward march of time,[55] the slow process of archival rescue and reorganization – but also by the prevalent questions of the day. As I have stressed, provincial, local and popular history has been dramatically developed, partly in response to changing historiographical fashions that extend far beyond Latin America. Latin America has also shared – to a lesser degree – in the more sophisticated 'cliometric' economic history and in the cross-fertilization which has occurred in the social sciences more generally. One obvious – and very positive – example is the fusion of history and anthropology, brought about, on the one hand, by the historian's sharp focus on small communities and their inner cultural and symbolic life, and, on the other, by the anthropologist's departure from a static ('synchronic') structural functionalism and growing interest in both historical ('diachronic') analysis and non-Indian societies. Thus, anthropological concepts such as the 'closed corporate peasant community' are now earnestly debated by historians of the Mexican Revolution (here, as elsewhere, the powerful and generally beneficient influence of Eric Wolf is evident);[56] and studies are written – be they monographs or broader analyses – in which the 'history' cannot be disentangled from the 'anthropology' and, indeed, the dual disciplinary inspiration is acknowledged: Paul Friedrich's (1977; 1986) arresting analysis of the revolutionary pueblo of Naranja; Daniel Nugent's (1993) comparable study of Namiquipa, in the Villista north; and Antonio García de León's (1985) monumental history of colonial and modern Chiapas, to which recent events have given an additional relevance.

The anthropological turn is matched by the switch to semiotics, the – postmodern? – concern for decyphering texts and deconstructing discourse. I speak of this with both caution and ignorance. In one sense, historians have always deconstructed discourse (whether they did it well or badly is another matter). Some, it is true, may have placed an excessively positivistic faith in the dicta of documents; but it is nothing new to warn students about the need to 'interrogate' documents and to display a due scepticism as regards their writers' motives. E. H. Carr (1964: 22–7) was, in this respect, a semiotician *avant la lettre*. However, this is not to say that historians work with nothing more than free-floating texts which are capable of infinitely variable interpretation, and behind which 'historical reality' remains utterly elusive. The recognition of textual bias and autonomy is compatible with a cautious commitment to an 'objective' historiography (meaning by that a historiography which strives for as close an approximation to 'reality' as can be achieved,

---

55   The criteria which determine when and which official documents are lodged in accessible archives vary from country to country, institution to institution – and, to my knowledge, there is no comprehensive guide. Britain's 'Thirty Year Rule' is unusually precise; in Latin America the rules vary, or are indeterminate. However, it usually takes at least a generation for documents to find their way to the archives and many – for reasons relating to security, inefficiency and lack of resources – never make it. At local and municipal level the attrition rate is probably much greater.

56   Wolf 1957; Vanderwood 1990. Note also the recent symposium edited by Schneider and Repp 1995 and Wolf 1982, which departed from the premise (p. ix) that 'anthropology needed to discover history'.

while recognizing that such a goal is unattainable). And this recognition is nothing new: old-timers like Max Weber (1970) and Jack Hexter (1971) said as much decades ago. Thus, just as M. Jourdain spoke prose for decades without realizing it, so many historians (I do not say all) have practised intelligent and sceptical discursive deconstruction – if that is what we wish to call it – without falling into the black hole of utter relativism.

Delivered in small doses, deconstructionism may sensitize historians to textual nuances. An overdose, however, can lead to a surreal detachment from reality, as texts – sometimes remarkably few texts – are subjected to merciless torture and, like the witches of Salem, yield up the 'subtexts' which their interrogators want to hear, morbid imagination triumphing over solid good sense. In this respect, deconstructionism – and the postmodernist turn of which it forms part – revels in multiple meanings, ambiguities and intellectual fancies: again, a useful antidote – were it needed – to bullish positivism, but also a solvent of grand theory, or even middle-range hypotheses.[57] Such an approach has its drawbacks, the defects of its sceptical virtues. Bullish positivism and fey postmodernism may be poles apart, but they share a common hostility to general theories and grand paradigms which, to both schools, appear as delusive engines of intellectual authoritarianism. And it is here that the historiography of Latin America – again following global trends – is currently deficient.

Almost all the recent historiographical trends, mentioned above, conspire to produce narrow, usually highly expert, but sometimes myopic history (Taylor 1985: 120). Rigorous professionalism, intimate acquaintance with the archive(s), immersion in the text, even an admixture of anthropology – all tend to encourage narrow focus and to deter broad comparison. The hypotheses generated by such work – and historiography depends on hypotheses, whether explicit or implicit[58] – are liable to be low-level: they are limited to a narrow range, spatially and temporally. They tell us about historical processes in this place or that period, but rarely establish links across space and time, and, if they invoke 'grand theory' – the 'organizing concepts' whereby the minute clutter of history can be usefully ordered – they do so either cursorily or dismissively.[59] Thus, we are lead to believe, the grand paradigms which

---

57 By positivism I mean that approach to history which believes that historical enquiry can approximate the rigour, precision and certitude of the natural sciences (for example, by means of cliometrics – sophisticated economic and statistical methods). Needless to say, this begs the question of the rigour, precision and certitude of the natural sciences.

58 Hypotheses, concepts and assumptions about causality underlie even the most basic narrative statement. A random example: 'The failure of the magicians to unsettle the Spaniards of course disturbed Tenochtitlan' (Thomas 1993: 205, referring to Cortés's arrival in Mexico in 1519). This simple statement, itself a hypothesis, raises questions about 'magicians', 'Spaniards' and 'Tenochtitlan': collective nouns which, however superficially self-explanatory, in fact embody layers of meaning which in turn – depending on how they are understood – determine the meaning of the sentence.

59 A common pattern is for a work of history to invoke grand theory – Marxism, modernization or dependency theory – at the outset, and perhaps again in conclusion, while maintaining a rigorously empirical and atheoretical approach through the long middle. Theory and data do not engage; hence the theory cannot help organize the data, nor the data qualify the theory.

748

once stalked the savannahs of Latin American history – modernization theory, structural Marxism, dependency – have lumbered off to die; their bleached bones are to be found in dog-eared texts of the 1960s or in dismissive footnotes of the 1990s. Like all extinctions, this had its positive side: lumbering paradigms which could not withstand predatory criticism deserved to die. Thus, simplistic notions of national character, Hispanic-Catholic backwardness and racial stereotypes have been justifiably killed off (though note Dealy 1992). No historian worth his or her salt interprets Brazilian society in terms of Gilberto Freyre's tropical lasciviousness. The simple 'distorting dichotomies' into which historians once shoehorned a complex historical reality have been severely qualified, if not altogether discarded.[60] Few historians would now regard modernization theory as a *passe-partout* to historical understanding (although, I shall note, modernization theory has made a regrettable comeback, thinly disguised, in today's 'neo-liberal' discourse).

On the other hand, some extinctions were arguably premature. Dependency theory, which posited a Latin America detrimentally conditioned by its subjection to successive imperialist metropolises – Spain, Britain, the United States – was certainly simplistic and sometimes plain wrong. It exaggerated external stimuli, created simple dichotomies (metropolis/satellite), and depicted an almost timeless and undifferentiated capitalism (Frank 1969). But, despite severe disparagement (Platt 1980; and, by way of reply, Stern and Stein 1980); it retains some limited analytical utility. There are times and places – such as Porfirian Yucatan – for which 'dependency', suitably interpreted, is usefully applicable (Joseph 1982: 41–65, 299). In what is probably the best general overview of post-independence Latin America, Tulio Halperín (1993: chs 4, 5; note also Taylor 1985: 123–4, 132) sees the period 1850–1930 as one which witnessed the emergence and maturity of a 'neocolonial order'.

Structural Marxism, which chose to see Latin American history in terms of unfolding modes of production,[61] has also been eclipsed by a widespread – and often unthinking – dismissal of Marxism as a system of intellectual enquiry. (I do not refer, of course, to Marxism, or communism, as a system of government, which is a different matter.) By dismissing – or simply neglecting – grand theory of this kind, historians tend to encourage an excessive fragmentation of their discipline, while leaving the difficult, but important, task of high-level hypothesizing to those – sociologists, political scientists, journalists, instant pundits and self-appointed gurus – whose indifferent grasp of history seems to encourage, rather than deter, stratospheric generalizations (on Wallerstein, see Stern 1988b (reply to Wallerstein 1988); cf. Fukuyama 1992: 21–2, 103–6). Even at lower levels of generalization – where, if you like, 'middle-range hypotheses' enter in – historians have probably too readily abdicated the field, too generously ceded it to non-historians. It has

---

60 The phrase is Taylor's (1985: 117; and, for a useful set of examples, p. 169).
61 Examples would include Semo 1993 and Cardoso 1980. Mallon 1983 combines a fairly traditional structural Marxist framework with rich empirical data – a somewhat unusual combination which also manages to avoid the intellectual schizophrenia mentioned in n. 59 above.

fallen to the Colliers – political scientists – to attempt the most ambitious recent synthesis of Latin American labour history.[62] The application of Barrington Moore to Latin America – and the interesting comparison with Balkan Europe which Moore's scheme suggests – has been undertaken, rather well, as it happens, by a sociologist, not a historian (Mouzelis 1986).

Thus we come to the recent period of political 'democratization' and neo-liberal economics. Historians have played no more than a bit-part in the booming industry of 'democracy' studies which has flourished in recent years.[63] As a result, political scientists – and others – have played fast and loose with history, with relative impunity. They have hailed a brave new democratic world which is far from new and may not be so brave. Historians, in contrast, would stress recurrent cycles, rather than outright novelty, underlying structures of power rather than superficial transformations, local variations rather than bland national aggregations. They would query, perhaps, how 'new' the 'new social movements' of the 1980s really were, and whether the whipping boy of 'economic populism' really bears any relation to the classic 'populist' regimes of the 1930s.[64] They would, in other words, subject today's fashionable assumptions to a sceptical and informed historical critique.

Unfortunately, they have rarely done so. The imperatives of the historical profession – archival expertise, narrow research, specialist publication – have militated against a broad encounter with current trends in social enquiry and policy-making. As a result, the major transformation which Latin America has undergone in the last fifteen years – years of economic crisis, structural adjustment, neo-liberal experiment, and halting democratization – has proceeded in an intellectual ambience of mild amnesia. Freewheeling social scientists – economists first and political scientists second – have dispensed advice and analysis; but, with a few notable exceptions, theirs has been a short-term, ahistorical, 'immediatist' per-spective. The same is true of many of today's ruling technocrats in Latin America, who believe that the timeless logic of the market must transcend messy historical traditions, and that, where necessary, historiography can be painlessly rewritten to suit that logic.[65] They are not the first generation of technocrats to subscribe to such

---

62 Collier and Collier 1991. It is interesting to note that the most recent volumes in the monumental *Cambridge History of Latin America*, vol. VI, parts 1 and 2, entitled *Latin America since 1930: Economy, Society and Politics*, which deal with thematic issues (the state, organized labour, the Left, the military), are largely written by non-historians, who outnumber the contributing historians by four to one; one relevant factor is no doubt historians' diffidence about broad, contemporary syntheses; one consequence is a marked emphasis on formal organizations, salient events and political leadership (what might be called *cupular* history).

63 Linz 1978; O'Donnell 1986; Higley and Gunther 1992; Mainwaring *et al.* 1992 are among the major studies.

64 These happen to be two of my own bugbears: Knight 1990 and 1993a.

65 Hence Ernesto Zedillo, now President of Mexico, tried, as Minister of Education, to have the country's school textbooks rewritten to accord more with today's neo-liberal technocratic ethos: traditional (nationalist) heroes were excised or written down; the 1910 Revolution was deflated; the pre-revolutionary regime of Porfirio Díaz – itself loosely liberal and technocratic – was rehabilitated. Popular and pedagogic opinion was offended; in the ensuing *brouhaha* the new texts had to be withdrawn.

beliefs, although their collective amnesia prevents them from being aware that they are trading in second-hand goods. Hence the collective bewilderment which ensues when history rears its ugly head: when, now as in the past, financial crisis overwhelms the best-laid plans of economic wizards, or when popular revolt, redolent with historical allusion, rises up in the Lacandon forest of Chiapas to challenge the overweening presumptions of First World 'modernity'.[66]

My conclusion to this rapid and subjective résumé is therefore ambivalent. In terms of its volume, sophistication and intrinsic interest, the historiography of Latin America is alive and kicking. New themes have been broached (gender, subaltern studies) and new approaches have been tried (cliometrics, deconstructionism, 'anthrohistory', 'microhistory'). The 'condescension of posterity' has been corrected, though not eliminated; and the resulting 'democratization' of history has involved 'finding seats at the banquet of history for great gatherings of forgotten people' (Taylor 1985: 121). Historians of Latin America have been alive to historiographical trends and fashions elsewhere, particularly in Europe and the United States. (Needless to say, this has not been reciprocated: historiography is an industry in which core–periphery relations correspond to the good old, crude, dependency model.) But growing volume and expertise have often been accompanied by excessive focus and introspection; historians have tended to turn in on themselves, to pride themselves on their narrow professionalism, thus to cede the broader field of comment and comparison to non-historian social scientists. Historiography has therefore suffered from a certain intellectual constriction; and, perhaps more important, the social sciences have cut loose from their historical anchors. Yet, at a time of social, political and economic flux such as this, historical anchors are crucial: not to inhibit advance, but to ride out storms without coming spectacularly to grief.

REFERENCES

Aguilar Camín, H. (1980) 'The relevant tradition: Sonoran leaders in the Revolution', in Brading 1980.

Altman, I and Lockhart, J. (eds) (1976) *Provinces of Early Mexico. Variants of Spanish American Regional Evolution*, Los Angeles.

Andrien, K. J. and Johnson, L. L. (eds) (1994) *The Political Economy of Spanish America in the Age of Revolution, 1750–1850*, Albuquerque.

Bailey, D. (1978) 'Revisionism and the recent historiography of the Mexican Revolution', *Hispanic American Historical Review* 58(1): 62–79.

---

66 The Zapatista revolt erupted in southern Mexico on 1 January 1994, the day when the North American Free Trade Agreement came into effect; it provoked widespread surprise, consternation and applause and contributed to Mexico's subsequent financial crisis. Despite its sophisticated use of the electronic media, and its condemnation of recent political and economic abuses in the region, the Zapatista Army of National Liberation draws heavily on historical memory, invoking the revolutionary agrarian hero Emiliano Zapata, as well as five centuries of colonial oppression of the Maya Indians. For some perceptive comments on recurrent financial crises, see Dawson 1991, a review of Marichal 1989.

Bakewell, P. J. (1971) *Silver-Mining and Society in Colonial Mexico: Zacatecas 1546–1700*, Cambridge.

—— (1984) *Miners of the Red Mountain*, Albuquerque.

Balmori, D., Voss, S. F. and Wortman, M. (1982) *Notable Family Networks in Latin America*, Chicago.

Barman, R. J. and Barman, J. (1978) 'The prosopography of the Brazilian Empire', *Latin American Research Review* 13(2): 78–97.

Barnard, A. (1992) 'Chile', in L. Bethell and I. Roxborough (eds) *Latin America between the Second World War and the Cold War, 1944–48*, Cambridge.

Bauer, A. (1979a) 'Rural workers in Spanish America: problems of peonage and oppression', *Hispanic American Historical Review* 59(1): 34–63.

—— (1979b) 'Reply', *Hispanic American Historical Review* 59(3): 486–9.

Beezley, W. H., English, C. M. and French, W. E. (eds) (1994) *Rituals of Rule, Rituals of Resistance: Public Celebrations and Popular Culture in Mexico*, Wilmington.

Benjamin, T. and Wasserman, M. (eds) (1990) *Provinces of the Revolution. Essays on Mexican Regional History, 1910–1929*, Albuquerque.

Bergad, L. (1983) *Coffee and the Growth of Agrarian Capitalism in Nineteenth-Century Puerto Rico*, Princeton.

Bergquist, C. (1986) *Labor in Latin America. Comparative Essays on Chile, Argentina, Venezuela and Colombia*, Stanford.

Bethell, L. (1970) *The Abolition of the Brazilian Slave Trade: Britain, Brazil and the Slave Trade Question, 1807–1869*, Cambridge.

—— (ed.) (1994) *The Cambridge History of Latin America*, vol. 6, Cambridge.

Birkbeck, C. (1991) 'Latin American banditry as peasant resistance: a dead-end trail?', *Latin American Research Review* 26(1): 156–60.

Blanchard, P. (1992) *Slavery and Abolition in Early Republican Peru*. Wilmington.

Bonilla, H. (1987) 'The Indian peasantry and "Peru" during the war with Chile', in Stern 1987.

Brading, D. A. (1971) *Miners and Merchants in Bourbon Mexico*, Cambridge.

—— (ed.) (1980) *Caudillo and Peasant in the Mexican Revolution*, Cambridge.

—— (1991) *The First America: The Spanish Monarchy, Creole Patriots and the Liberal State*, Cambridge.

—— et al. (1989) 'Comments', *Hispanic American Historical Review* 69(3) (August): 479–558.

Braudel, F. (1984) *Civilization and Capitalism, 15th–18th Century, 3: The Perspective of the World*, London.

Brown, J. C. (1993) *Oil and Revolution in Mexico*, Berkeley.

Brunk, S. (1995) *Emiliano Zapata. Revolution and Betrayal in Mexico*, Albuquerque.

Burns, E. B. (1980) *The Poverty of Progress: Latin America in the Nineteenth Century*, Berkeley.

Cardoso, C. (1980) *Mexico en el siglo XIX*, Mexico City.

Carr, B. (1980) 'Regional aspects of the Mexican Revolution', *Latin American Research Review* 15(1): 3–14.

Carr, E. H. (1964) *What is History?*, Harmondsworth.

Chevalier, F. [1952] (1970) *Land and Society in Colonial Mexico*, Berkeley. (First published in French, 1952.)

Collier, R. B. and Collier, D. (1991) *Shaping the Political Arena*, Princeton.

Connif, M. (ed.) (1982) *Latin American Populism in Comparative Perspective*, Albuquerque.

Conrad, R. (1972) *The Destruction of Brazilian Slavery, 1850–1888*, Berkeley.

Cope, R. D. (1994) *The Limits of Racial Domination. Plebeian Society in Colonial Mexico City, 1660–1720*, Madison.

Cushner, N. P. (1980) *Lords of the Land: Sugar, Wine and the Jesuit Estates of Coastal Peru, 1600–1767*, Albany.

—— (1982) *Farm and Factory: The Jesuits and the Development of Agrarian Capitalism in Colonial Quito, 1600–1767*, Albany, N.Y.

Dawson, F. G. (1991) Review of Marichal 1989, *Journal of Latin American Studies* 23(2): 467–9.

Dealy, G. (1992) *The Latin Americans: Spirit and Ethos*, Boulder, CO.

Dean, W. (1976) *Rio Claro: A Brazilian Plantation System 1820–1920*, Stanford.

Diacon, T. A. (1992) *Millenarian Vision, Capitalist Reality. Brazil's Contestado Rebellion, 1912–1916*, Durham, NC.

Dunkerley, J. (1992) *Political Suicide in Latin America and Other Essays*, London.

Eisenberg, P. L. (1974) *The Sugar Industry in Pernambuco, 1840–1910: Modernization without Change*, Berkeley.

Farriss, N. (1984) *Maya Society under Colonial Rule. The Collective Enterprise of Survival*, Princeton.

Ferns, H. S. (1960) *Britain and Argentina in the Nineteenth Century*, Oxford.

—— (1973) *The Argentine Republic 1516–1971*, Newton Abbot.

Frank, A. G. (1969) *Capitalism and Underdevelopment in Latin America: Historical Studies of Chile and Brazil*, New York.

French, J. D. (1991) 'Practice and ideology; a cautionary note on the historian's craft', *Hispanic American Historical Review* 71(4): 847–55.

Friedrich, P. (1977) *Agrarian Revolt in a Mexican Village*, Chicago.

—— (1986) *The Princess of Narania: An Essay in Anthrohistorical Method*, Austin.

Fukuyama, F. (1992) *The End of History and the Last Man*, Harmondsworth.

García de León, A. (1985) *Resistencia y utopía*, 2 vols, Mexico City.

Germani, G. (1965) *Política y sociedad en una época de transición*, Buenos Aires.

Gibson, C. (1952) *Tlaxcala in the Sixteenth Century*, New Haven, CT.

—— (1964) *The Aztecs under Spanish Rule: A History of the Valley of Mexico, 1519–1810*, Stanford.

González, L. (1983) *San José de Gracia. Mexican Village in Transition*, Austin.

Gootenberg, P. (1989) *Between Silver and Guano: Commercial Policy and the State in Postindependence Peru*, Princeton.

Gould, J. L. (1990) *To Lead as Equals: Rural Protest and Political Consciousness in Chinandega, Nicaragua, 1912–1979*, Chapel Hill, NC.

Graham, R. (1990) *Patronage and Politics in Nineteenth-Century Brazil*, Stanford.

Grossman, R. (1992) 'Patria y libertad: Sandina and the development of peasant nationalism in northern Nicaragua', paper given at the 17th International Congress of the Latin American Studies Association, Los Angeles, September 1992.

Gruzinski, S. (1989) *Man-Gods in the Mexican Highlands, 16th–18th Centuries*, Stanford.

—— (1993) *The Conquest of Mexico*, Cambridge.

Guerra, F.-X. (1985) *Le Méxique de l'ancien régime à la révolution*, 2 vols, Paris.

—— (1994) 'The Spanish-American tradition of representation and its European roots', *Journal of Latin American Studies* 26(1) (February): 1–17.

Guha, R. and Spivak, G. C. (1985) *Selected Subaltern Studies*, New York.

Guy, D. J. (1989) *Sex and Danger in Buenos Aires: Prostitution, Family and Nation in Argentina*, Lincoln, NE.

Hale, C. A. (1989) *The Transformation of Liberalism in Nineteenth-Century Mexico*, Princeton.

Halperin Donghi, T. (1982) '"Dependency theory" and Latin American historiography', *Latin American Research Review* 17: 115–30.

—— (1993) *The Contemporary History of Latin America*, Durham, NC.

Hamnett, B. (1971) *Politics and Trade in Southern Mexico 1750–1821*, Cambridge.

—— (1986) *Roots of Insurgency: Mexican Regions, 1750–1824*, Cambridge.

Hahner, J. (1980) 'Feminism, women's rights and the suffrage movement in Brazil', *Latin American Research Review* 16(1): 41–64.

Hart, J. M. (1987) *Revolutionary Mexico*, Berkeley.

Hexter, J. H. (1971) *Doing History*, London.

Higley, J. and Gunther, R. (eds) (1992) *Elites and Democratic Consolidation in Latin America and Southern Europe*, New York.

Hinds, H. E. and Tatum, C. M. (1992) *The Mexican Comic Book in the Late 1960s and 1970s*, Westport, Ont.

Hoberman, L. S. and Socolow, S. M. (eds) (1986) *Cities and Societies in Colonial Latin America*, Albuquerque.

Holloway, T. H. (1980) *Immigrants on the Land: Coffee and Society in São Paulo, 1886–1934*, Chapel Hill, NC.

—— (1993) *Policing Rio de Janeiro: Repression and Resistance in a Nineteenth-Century City*, Stanford.

Jacobsen, N. (1993) *Mirages of Transition: The Peruvian Altiplano, 1780–1930*, Berkeley.

James, D. (1988) *Resistance and Integration: Peronism and the Argentine Working Class, 1946–76*, Cambridge.

Johnson, L. (1986) 'Artisans', in Hoberman and Socolow 1986.

Joseph, G. M. (1982) *Revolution from Without: Yucatan, Mexico and the United States, 1880–1924*, Cambridge.

—— (1990) 'On the trail of Latin American bandits: a reexamination of peasant resistance', *Latin American Research Review* 25(3): 7–53.

—— (1991) '"Resocializing" Latin American banditry', *Latin American Research Review* 26(1): 161–74.

—— (1994) 'Rethinking Mexican revolutionary mobilization: Yucatán's seasons of upheaval', in G. M. Joseph and D. Nugent (eds) *Everyday Forms of State Formation*, Durham, NC.

Jrade, R. (1985) 'Inquiries into the Cristero insurrection against the Mexican Revolution', *Latin American Research Review* 20(2): 53–69.

Katz, F. (1974) 'Labor conditions on haciendas in Porfirian Mexico: some trends and tendencies', *Hispanic American Historical Review* 54(1): 1–47.

—— (1980) 'Pancho Villa, peasant movements and agrarian reform in northern Mexico', in Brading 1980.

—— (ed.) (1988) *Riot, Rebellion and Revolution: Rural Conflict in Mexico*, Princeton.

Kicza, J. E. (1983) *Business and Society in Late Colonial Mexico*, Albuquerque.

Klarén, P. (1977) 'The social and economic consequences of modernization of the Peruvian sugar industry, 1870–1920', in K. Duncan and I. Rutledge (eds) *Land and Labour in Latin America: Essays on the Development of Agrarian Capitalism in the Nineteenth and Twentieth Centuries*, Cambridge.

Knight, A. (1986) *The Mexican Revolution*, 2 vols, Cambridge.

—— (1988) 'Debt bondage in Latin America', in L. Archer (ed.) *Slavery and Other Forms of Unfree Labour*, London.

—— (1990) 'Historical continuities in social movements', in A. Craig and J. Foweraker (eds) *Popular Movements and Political Change in Mexico*, Boulder, CO.

—— (1993a) 'El abrigo de Arturo Alessandri: populismo, estado y sociedad en América Latina, siglo XX', in M. L. Tarrés (ed.) *Transformaciones sociales y acciones colectivas: América Latina en el contexto internacional de los noventa*, Mexico City.

—— (1993b) 'State power and political stability in Mexico', in N. Harvey (ed.) *Mexico: Dilemmas of Transition*, London.

—— (1994) 'Popular culture and the revolutionary state in Mexico, 1910–40', *Hispanic American Historical Review* 74(3): 393–444.

Knight, F. W. (1970) *Slave Society in Cuba during the Nineteenth Century*, Madison.

Ladd, D. (1988) *The Making of a Strike: Mexican Silver Workers' Struggles in Real del Monte, 1766–1775*, Lincoln, NE.

Lafaye, J. (1976) *Quetzalcóatl and Guadalupe: The Formation of Mexican National Consciousness, 1521–1813*, Chicago.

Langer, E. (1989) *Economic Change and Rural Resistance in Southern Bolivia, 1880–1930*, Stanford.

Larson, B. (1988) *Colonialism and Agrarian Transformation in Bolivia: Cochabamba 1550–1900*, Princeton.

Lauderdale Graham, S. (1988) *House and Street. The Domestic World of Servants and Masters in Nineteenth-Century Rio de Janeiro*, Cambridge.

Lavrin, A. (1986) 'Female religious', in Hoberman and Socolow 1986.

—— (1994) 'Women in twentieth-century Latin American society', in Bethell 1994.

Legrand, C. (1986) *Frontier Expansion and Peasant Protest in Colombia*, Albuquerque.

Levine, R. M. (1978) *Pernambuco in the Brazilian Federation, 1889–1937*, Stanford.

—— (1992) *Vale of Tears: Revisiting the Canudos Massacre in Northeastern Brazil, 1893–1897*, Berkeley.

Lewin, L. (1987) *Politics and Parentela in Paraíba: A Case Study of Family-Based Oligarchy in Brazil*, Princeton.

Lewis, P. H. (1990) *The Crisis of Argentine Capitalism*, Chapel Hill, NC.

Linz, J. (1978) *The Breakdown of Democratic Regimes*, Baltimore.

Lockhart, J. (1991) *Nahuas and Spaniards: Postconquest Central Mexican History and Philology*, Stanford.

—— (1992) *The Nahuas after the Conquest*, Stanford.

Love, J. L. (1971) *Rio Grande do Sul and Brazilian Regionalism, 1882–1930*, Stanford.

Loveman, B. (1979) 'Critique of Arnold Bauer's "Rural workers in Spanish America"', *Hispanic American Historical Review* 59(3): 478–85.

Lugan, C. (1986) 'Merchants', in Hoberman and Socolow 1986.

Lynch, J. (1992) *Caudillos in Spanish America, 1800–1850*, Oxford.

McBeth, B. (1983) *Juan Vicente Gómez and the Oil Companies in Venezuela, 1908–35*, Cambridge.

McCaa, R. (1984) '*Calidad, clase* and marriage in colonial Mexico: the case of Parral, 1788–90', *Hispanic American Historical Review* 64(3): 477–501.

McCreery, D. (1994) *Rural Guatemala, 1760–1940*, Stanford.

Mainwaring, S., O'Donnell, G. and Valenzuela, J. S. (eds) (1992) *Issues in Democratic Consolidation*, Notre Dame.

Mallon, F. E. (1983) *The Defense of Community in Peru's Central Highlands: Peasant Struggle and Capitalist Transition, 1860–1940*, Princeton.

—— (1987) 'Nationalist and antistate coalitions in the War of the Pacific: Junín and Cajamarca, 1879–1902', in Stern 1987.

—— (1995) *Peasant and Nation: The Making of Postcolonial Mexico and Peru*, Berkeley.

Marichal, C. (1989) *A Century of Debt Crises in Latin America*, Princeton.

Martin, C. E. (1985) *Rural Society in Colonial Morelos*, Albuquerque.

Meyer, J. (1976) *The Cristero Rebellion: The Mexican People Between Church and State: 1926–1929*, Cambridge.

Monteon, M. (1982) *Chile in the Nitrate Era. The Evolution of Economic Dependence, 1880–1930*, Madison.

Morse, R. (1958) *From Community to Metropolis: A Biography of São Paulo*, Gainsville.

Mouzelis, N. (1986) *Politics in the Semi-periphery: Early Parliamentarism and Late Industrialization in the Balkans and Latin America*, London.

Murmis, M. and J. C. Portantiero (1971) *Estudios sobre los orígines del peronismo*, Buenos Aires.

Murray, D. (1980) *Odious Commerce: Britain, Spain and the Abolition of the Cuban Slave Trade*, Cambridge.

Needell, J. (1987) *A Tropical Belle Epoque: Elite Culture and Society in Turn-of-the-Century Rio*, Cambridge.

Nugent, D. (1993) *Spent Cartridges of Revolution: An Anthropological History of Namiquipa, Chihuahua*, Chicago.

O'Donnell, G., Schmitter, P. and Whitehead, L. (eds) (1986) *Transitions from Authoritarian Rule: Prospects for Democracy*, Baltimore.

O'Phelan Godoy, S. (1988) *Un siglo de rebeliones anticoloniales: Perú y Bolivia, 1700–1783*, Cuzco.

Ouweneel, A. and Bijleveld, C. (1989) 'The economic cycle in Bourbon central Mexico: a critique of the *recaudación del diezmo liquido en oesos*', *Hispanic American Historical Review* 69(3): 479–530.

Palacios, M. (1980) *Coffee in Colombia, 1850–1970: An Economic, Social and Political History*, Cambridge.

Paz, O. (1961) *The Labyrinth of Solitude: Life and Thought in Mexico*, tr. L. Kemp, New York.

Pessar, P. (1981) 'Unmasking the politics of religion: the case of Brazilian millenarianism', *Journal of Latin American Lore* 7(2): 255–78.

Platt, D. C. M. (1980) 'Dependency in nineteenth-century Latin America: an historian objects', *Latin American Research Review* 15(1): 113–30.

Platt, T. (1993) 'Simón Bolivar, the Sun of Justice and the Amerindian Virgin: Andean conceptions of the *patria* in nineteenth-century Potosí', *Journal of Latin American Studies* 25(1) (February): 159–85.

Purcell, J. (1994) 'The politics of identity: Cristeros and Agraristas in revolutionary Michoacan', paper presented at the 18th International Congress of the Latin American Studies Association, Atlanta.

Queiroz, M. I. P. de (1985) 'Messiahs in Brazil', *Past and Present* 31 (July): 62–86.

Reis, J. J. (1993) *Slave Rebellion in Brazil. The Moslem Uprising of 1833 in Bahía*, Baltimore.

—— and Silva, E. (eds) (1989) *Negociacao e conflito: A resistância negra no Brasil escravista*, São Paulo.

Roseberry, W. (1984) *Coffee and Capitalism in the Venezuelan Andes*, Austin.

Roxborough, I. (1994) 'The urban working class and labour movement in Latin America since 1930', in Bethell 1994.

Sabato, H. (1990) *Agrarian Capitalism and the World Market: Buenos Aires in the Pastoral Age, 1840–1890*, Albuquerque.

Salas, E. (1990) *Soldaderas in the Mexican Military: Myth and History*, Austin.

Schneider, J. and Repp, R. (1995) *Articulating Hidden Histories: Exploring the Influence of Eric R. Wolf*, Berkeley.

Schwartz, S. (1992) *Slaves, Peasants and Rebels. Reconsidering Brazilian Slavery*, Urbana.

Scobie, J. R. (1964) *Revolution on the Pampas: A Social History of Argentine Wheat, 1860–1910*, Austin.

—— (1974) *Buenos Aires: Plaza to Suburb, 1870–1910*, New York.

—— (1988) *Secondary Cities of Argentina: The Social History of Corrientes, Salta and Mendoza, 1850–1910*, Stanford.

Scott, J. (1985) *Weapons of the Weak. Everyday Forms of Peasant Resistance*, New Haven, CT.

—— (1990) *Domination and the Arts of Resistance: Hidden Transcripts*, New Haven, CT.

Scott, R. J. (1985) *Slave Emancipation in Cuba: The Transition to Free Labor, 1860–1899*, Princeton.

Seed, P. (1982) 'Social dimensions of race: Mexico City, 1753', *Hispanic American Historical Review* 62(4) (November): 569–606.

Semo, E. (1993) *The History of Capitalism in Mexico: Its Origins, 1521–1763*, Austin.

Shumway, N. (1993) *The Invention of Argentina*, Berkeley.

Silva, E. de (1993) *Prince of the People: The Life and Times of a Brazilian Freeman of Color*, New York.

Simpson, L. B. (1941) *Many Mexicos*, Berkeley.

Singelmann, P. (1991) 'Establishing a trail through the labyrinth', *Latin American Research Review* 26(1): 152–5.

Slatta, R. W. (1991) 'Bandits and rural social history: a commentary on Joseph', *Latin American Research Review* 26(1): 145–51.

Smith, C. A. (1990) 'Origins of the national question in Guatemala: a hypothesis', in C. Smith (ed.) *Guatemalan Indians and the State, 1540 to 1988*, Austin.

Socolow, S. M. (1978) *The Merchants of Buenos Aires, 1778–1810*, Cambridge.

Sowell, D. (1992) *The Early Colombian Labor Movement: Artisans and Politics in Bogotá, 1832–1919*, Philadelphia.

Spalding, K. (1984) *Huarochiri: An Andean Society under Inca and Spanish Rule*, Stanford.

Stein, S. J. (1957) *Vassouras: A Brazilian Coffee County, 1850–1900*, Cambridge, MA.

Stern, S. J. (1982) *Peru's Indian People and the Challenge of Spanish Conquest: Huamanga to 1640*, Madison.

—— (ed.) (1987) *Resistance, Rebellion and Consciousness in the Andean Peasant World, 18th to 20th Centuries*, Madison.

—— (1988a) 'Feudalism, capitalism and the world-system in the perspective of Latin America and the Caribbean', *American Historical Review* 93(4): 829–72.

—— (1988b) 'Reply: "ever more solitary"', *American Historical Review* 93(4): 886–97.

—— and Stein, B. H. (1980) 'D. C. M. Platt: the anatomy of "autonomy"', *Latin American Research Review* 15(1): 131–46.

Stevens, D. F. (1992) *Origins of Instability in Early Republican Mexico*, Durham, NC.

Stolcke, V. (1988) *Coffee Planters, Workers and Wives. Class Conflict and Gender Relations on São Paulo Plantations, 1850–1980*, London.

Szeminski, J. (1987) 'Why kill the Spaniard? New perspectives on Andean insurrectionary ideology in the 18th century', in Stern 1987.

Taylor, W. (1972) *Landlord and Peasant in Colonial Oaxaca*, Stanford.

—— (1979) *Drinking, Homicide and Rebellion in Colonial Mexican Villages*, Stanford.

—— (1985) 'Between global process and local knowledge: an inquiry into early Latin American social history, 1500–1900', in O. Zunz (ed.) *Reliving the Past: The Worlds of Social History*, Chapel Hill, NC.

Thompson, E. P. (1968) *The Making of the English Working Class*, Harmondsworth.

—— (1978) 'The poverty of theory', in E. P. Thompson, *The Poverty of Theory and Other Essays*, London.

Thomson, G. P. C. (1989) *Puebla de los Angeles. Industry and Society in a Mexican City*, Boulder, CO.

—— (1994) 'The ceremonial and political role of village bands, 1846–1974', in Beezley *et al.* 1994.

Thorp, R. (ed.) (1984) *Latin America in the 1930s: The Role of the Periphery in World Crisis*, London.

Topik, S. (1987) *The Political Economy of the Brazilian States, 1889–1930*, Austin.

Toplin, R. (1972) *The Abolition of Slavery in Brazil*, New York.

Tutino, J. (1986) *From Insurrection to Revolution in Mexico: Social Bases of Agrarian Violence, 1750–1940*, Princeton.

Twinam, A. (1983) *Miners, Merchants and Farmers in Colonial Colombia*, Austin.

Van Young, E. (1981) *Hacienda and Market in Eighteenth-Century Mexico*, Berkeley.

—— (1989) 'Quetzalcóatl, King Ferdinand and Ignacio Allende go to the seashore; or messianism and mystical kingship in Mexico, 1800–1821', in J. E. Rodríguez O. (ed.) *The Independence of Mexico and the Creation of the New Nation*, Los Angeles.

Van Young, E. (1990) 'To see someone not seeing: historical studies of peasants and politics in Mexico', *Mexican Studies/Estudios Mexicanos* 6(1): 133–69.

—— (1992) 'Introduction: are regions good to think?', in E. Van Young (ed.) *Mexico's Regions: Comparative History and Development*, La Jolla.

Vanderwood, P. (1990) 'Explaining the Mexican Revolution', in J. E. Rodriguez O. (ed.) *The Revolutionary Process in Mexico. Essays on Political and Social Change, 1880–1940*, Los Angeles.

Vaughan, M. K. (1990) 'Women school teachers in the Mexican Revolution: the story of Renya's braids', *Journal of Women's History* 2(1): 143–68.

—— (1994) 'Rural women's literacy and education during the Mexican Revolution. Subverting a patriarchal event?', in H. Fowler-Salamini and M. K. Vaughan (eds) *Creating Spaces, Shaping Transitions: Women of the Mexican Countryside, 1850–1990*, Tucson.

Viotti da Costa, E. (1989) 'Experience versus structures: new tendencies in the history of labor and the working class in Latin America – what do we gain? What do we lose?', *International Labor and Working Class History* 36: 3–24.

Wallerstein, I. (1988) 'Comments on Stern's critical tests', *American Historical Review* 93(4): 873–85.

Warman, A. (1980) *'We Come to Object': The Peasants of Morelos and the National State*, Baltimore.

Weber, M. (1970) *From Max Weber, Essays in Sociology*, tr. and ed. H. H. Gerth and C. Wright Mills, London.

Weinstein, B. (1983) *The Amazon Rubber Boom, 1850–1920*, Stanford.

Wells, A. (1985) *Yucatan's Gilded Age: Haciendas, Henquén and International Harvester, 1860–1915*, Albuquerque.

Whitehead, L. (1994) 'State organization in Latin America since 1930', in Bethell 1994.

Wilkie, J. and Wilkie, E. M. de (1969) *Mexico visto en el siglo XX: entrevistas de historia oral*, Mexico.

Winn, P. (1986) *Weavers of Revolution: The Yarur Workers and Chile's Road to Socialism*, New York.

Wirth, J. D. (1977) *Minas Gerais in the Brazilian Federation, 1889–1937*, Stanford.

Wolf, E. R. (1957) 'Closed corporate peasant communities in Mesoamerica and central Java', *Southwestern Journal of Anthropology* 13(1): 1–18.

—— (1982) *Europe and the People without History*, Berkeley.

—— and Hansen, E. C. (1966–7) 'Caudillo politics: a structural analysis', *Comparative Studies in Society and History* 9: 168–79.

Wolfe, J. (1991a) 'Anarchist ideology, worker practice: the 1917 general strike and the formation of the São Paulo working class', *Hispanic American Historical Review* 71(4): 809–46.

—— (1991b) 'Response to John French', *Hispanic American Historical Review* 71(4): 856–8.

Womack, Jr, J. (1969) *Zapata and the Mexican Revolution*, New York.

V CONTEXTS FOR THE WRITING OF HISTORY

V.1 HINTERLANDS

30

PHILOSOPHY AND HISTORIOGRAPHY

William Dray

CRITICAL PHILOSOPHY OF HISTORY

As many historians still think of it, philosophy of history has as its central aim the discovery of some overall meaning in the human past. This has generally been considered a rather dubious enterprise, engaged in chiefly by speculative metaphysicians, such as Hegel, whose grasp of the details of the patterns they claim to discern often seems rather sketchy, or by superhistorians, such as Toynbee, whose erudition tends to outstrip their capacity for coherent system-building.[1] But the task of philosophy of history is seldom conceived nowadays in that way, at any rate by English-speaking philosophers. Calling upon a distinction popularized by W. H. Walsh (1951: 13ff.), most would now describe what they do as 'critical' rather than 'speculative' philosophy of history, by which they mean not a search for ultimate meanings in the record of the past but an analysis of the kind of thinking required for the past's recovery. The terminology is vaguely Kantian, and expresses an interest in examining the philosophical foundations of history as a type of knowledge and enquiry somewhat as the Kantian philosophy undertook to examine the categories and presuppositions of scientific knowledge. Critical philosophers of history also sometimes characterize their approach as epistemological rather than metaphysical. In fact, questions about history as knowledge or enquiry can hardly be considered for long without getting involved also in questions about the general nature of history's subject matter, questions which are ultimately metaphysical. In considering them, however, there is no need to raise the question of the overall pattern of the past.

Critical philosophy of history, self-consciously and systematically pursued, is of comparatively recent date, although its concerns are prefigured, if only in occasional

---

1 The term is used by Barker 1982.

and fragmentary ways, in the writings of earlier philosophers like Vico or Hegel, and more substantially in the work of late nineteenth-century authors like Dilthey and Croce. In English thought its antecedents amount to little more than scattered observations in some of the lesser-known writings of Hume,[2] some afterthoughts on the social sciences in J. S. Mill's *System of Logic* and a single essay by F. H. Bradley published in 1874, perhaps the first considerable piece of philosophical writing on history by an English philosopher.[3] The real foundations of the subject as currently conceived were laid in the 1920s and 1930s, notably in the voluminous writings of the philosopher-historian-archaeologist R. G. Collingwood, and to a lesser extent in those of his contemporary Michael Oakeshott. However, Collingwood's work was largely ignored until the posthumous appearance in 1946 of what is now probably his best-known book, *The Idea of History* (see also Collingwood 1939). This event happily coincided with a new readiness of English philosophers to move beyond a narrow preoccupation with problems of sense perception and of scientific knowledge, which the logical positivism of the 1930s and early 1940s had made *de rigueur*, to consider philosophical issues raised by art, religion, law, morals, politics and finally history.

The new readiness showed itself first in a modest trickle of writings in the late 1950s, most of them responding in one way or another to a widely read article by a philosopher of science, C. G. Hempel, which denied any need for a philosophical examination of history as a possibly distinctive intellectual endeavour.[4] By the late 1960s, this trickle had become a flood, spreading from debate about the nature of explanation in history to an ever-widening circle of questions about historical thinking. Many of these questions, like that of the degree to which historical studies can reasonably aspire to objectivity, were ones that historians themselves had often raised and discussed, and philosophers sometimes took what they had to say as a point of departure: for example, the wrestlings of Beard and Becker with the problem of relativism, or Bury's elucidation of the sense in which history can be considered a science. Critical philosophy of history gained an important platform with the appearance in 1960 of *History and Theory*, a journal devoted entirely to problems in the theory of historiography and philosophy of history, and one to which both philosophers and historians were encouraged to contribute.[5] Fruitful interaction between the two groups has nevertheless been the exception rather than the rule. Respected members of the historical guild, such as J. H. Hexter and Geoffrey Elton, have complained that the work of critical philosophers is generally too remote from the realities of historical practice to be of much interest to

---

2 For Hume's view of history, see Norton and Popkin 1965.
3 *The Presuppositions of Critical History*, reprinted in Bradley 1935: 1–53.
4 'The Function of General Laws in History,' reprinted in Gardiner 1959: 344–56.
5 The tables of contents of this journal (and the bibliographical issues of 1961, 1967, 1971, 1974, 1979, 1984, 1989) offer a useful overview of the problems that have interested critical philosophers of history in recent decades. Another excellent bibliographical source, citing writings by both philosophers and historians, is Ritter 1986.

historians (see e.g. Hexter 1971: 7–8, 15; Elton 1970: 113–14). And some philosophers, such as R. F. Atkinson (1978: 8), have returned the compliment by observing that when philosophers raise questions about historical knowledge, it must be understood that they have their own agendas, which are not designed to serve the needs of another discipline.

In fact, the reservations that historians have frequently expressed about the relevance of critical philosophy to their own activities often seem at least partly traceable to misconceptions about the problems it aims to address. Its goal is not, for example, methodological in the sense of offering practical advice about doing historical research, something that few critical philosophers know at first hand. It is rather to clarify and, where it seems appropriate, to offer a critique of the framework of basic concepts and assumptions within which historians conduct their enquiries, and which they expect their readers to share. These include quite everyday, but often surprisingly problematic ideas like fact, event, interpretation, understanding, explanation, cause, reason, probability, point of view, relevance, importance, narrative, period, process and the like. As was noted above, the study of such ideas shades easily into a consideration of the general character of the historian's subject matter. It may raise problems about human nature, for example, or about the meaning of temporality, or about the relation of value to reality, or about the legitimacy of assuming determinism, or holism, or naturalism in interpreting the relics of the past. As for philosophers having their own agendas, that is, of course, true to some extent. What they want ultimately to be able to do is to locate history on the map of knowledge, to integrate a satisfactory view of historical enquiry into a general theory of human knowledge, something which few past epistemologies have made very serious attempts to do. There is common ground with historians interested in reflecting on their own activities, however, in the need of philosophers first to understand how historical thinking characteristically goes, a need which has increasingly led them to undertake analyses of actual historical argumentation, and especially of ongoing controversies, the presuppositions and conceptual frameworks of historians often being found to emerge most clearly where they cannot agree about what conclusions to draw.[6]

It is not easy, in a short space, to convey much sense of the breadth and liveliness of recent discussion in critical philosophy of history, not only because it has often proceeded at a somewhat technical level, but also because the problems are sufficiently complex to render summaries or abstracts, at best, half-truths. What follows is an attempt mainly to illustrate philosophical interests and methods, eschewing technicalities as much as possible, and being prepared to make claims which might require some modification given a more extended treatment. Three main issues will be addressed, all of which have generated a considerable philosophical literature. The first is the kind of explanation that is required or acceptable in historical studies, where this means, chiefly, what kind of formal

---

6 For examples of such analyses, see Goldstein 1976: ch. 4, or Martin 1989: chs 3, 4.

features or logical structure it should exhibit. The second is the extent to which historical reasoning should be, or can be, value-free, in view of the structural role that value judgements often appear to play in historical accounts. The third is the kind of case that can be made for narrative as a way of expressing historical conclusions, this calling for some analysis of the idea of narrative. In considering these questions, I shall not try to conceal my own positions with respect to them; but my main aim will be less to argue a position than to make clear, in each case, the nature of a problem.

HISTORICAL EXPLANATION

What general form should an explanation in a subject like history take? Exactly the same form that it takes in the natural sciences, and should take in any serious form of enquiry, it has sometimes been replied. Assuming that what is to be explained is an occurrence, what must be sought is some earlier occurrence or occurrences given which what is to be explained necessarily followed. And the only way to show that it did so, it has often been argued, is to subsume it under laws which govern the subject matter: to show that, in the light of those laws, what happened was, in principle, predictable (see e.g. Hempel 1959: 347ff.). Doubtless anything very close to strict predictability and to exceptionless laws will be hard to come by in history; even the merely statistical generalizations that historians are sometimes prepared to assert are seldom formulated very precisely. What is important for present purposes, however, is not how tight or how loose historical argumentation generally is, but the idea of explanation that functions in it, the standard by which proffered explanations are to be judged. From that standpoint, the law-instantiating, or nomological, view of explanation is not without plausibility. Historians themselves sometimes seem, in effect, to accept it, as when they criticize explanations offered by others for leaving it open that what is said to be explained might as easily not have occurred. If an explanation is to be considered complete, the argument goes, it must show that what happened *had* to happen. And that, defenders of the nomological theory will insist, can only be accomplished by appeal to laws.

One common response to such considerations is to say that, since genuine laws are seldom available in history, all that historians can realistically aim at is approximations to explanation, perhaps the subsumption of events under less-than-universal generalizations which would at least show the probability of what occurred, and to that extent, its predictability. But responses have also taken a more theoretical turn, pointing to alleged peculiarities of the historian's subject matter which make the idea of explaining things in the nomological way simply inapplicable. One consideration sometimes stressed is that what historians largely concern themselves with is human actions, which are not mere happenings, but the expressions, and possibly the unpredictable expressions, of reason, purpose and will. Another is that what especially interests historians is occurrences and states of affairs which may be unique and unrepeatable, this excluding any possibility of bringing them under laws. Those who have found the nomological theory of

766

explanation antecedently convincing may argue that, if historians really do have to deal with a subject matter displaying such features, there is little in it they will be able to explain. Others, however, have responded to the same apparent difficulty by looking more closely at what might appropriately be meant by explanation in historical studies.

Collingwood is well known for having insisted that any account of explanation in history must start from the recognition that the main concern of historians is with human actions, which are always, in a broad sense, expressions of thought. If such things are to be understood, he maintained, what one must do is, not relate what was done to antecedent conditions which rendered it predictable, but show rather how various thoughts which are ascribable to the agents afforded them reasons for acting as they did (see especially Collingwood 1946: 213ff.). To take one of his own examples: the expedition of Caesar to ancient Britain can be said to have been explained, in a sense appropriate to history, when one can see that it was an expression of his determination to conquer the country (rather than, say, to carry out a punitive expedition or a mere raid). Human activities are to be understood, in other words, not by reference to their probability, but by reference to their point. Collingwood often expresses this idea by saying that the historian must 'think himself into the action' and, in imagination, 're-enact' the agent's thoughts. Critical philosophers who have regarded such an account as essentially correct have generally preferred to put Collingwood's point in a way that draws attention less to the experience of the investigator than to the logical structure of the explanatory assertion. To explain an action, they have maintained, involves attributing to the agent a practical argument which enjoins its performance. One can claim to understand what was done when it can be seen as the appropriate thing to have done, given the agent's beliefs about the situation and the goals he was trying to achieve.[7]

Such an account of the way explanations may proceed in history has been variously criticized. It has been argued, for example, that since agents could have had good reasons for acting in certain ways without in fact acting in those ways, merely showing that they had those reasons cannot be said completely to explain what they did. Collingwoodians have replied that although this may not explain it completely in the sense of showing that what was done would necessarily be done, it may still explain it completely in the sense of showing that it was precisely what the agents' goals and assessment of the situation required – sometimes, indeed, the one and only thing they required. What is at issue, in other words, is whether only one sort of thing counts as explanation: whether the concept of explanation is univocal. It has also been objected that, even if acceptable in cases like Caesar's invasion, explanation of this kind would have a very restricted application to the range of things historians normally study, which is hardly confined to what was done by highly self-conscious or fully rational individuals. By way of reply, it has sometimes

---

7 For two different ways of putting this thesis see Donagan 1962: 192–6, and Dray 1980: ch. 1.

been pointed out that explanation by reference to agents' reasons is by no means limited to actions of a reflective sort. Even explanation in terms of unconscious motives, if really explanatory, would take the form, not of identifying determining antecedent conditions, but of reconstructing implicit justificatory arguments. Like a conscious motive, an unconscious one will only explain if it can be seen as having afforded the agent a reason for acting as he did. Collingwood's theory has also been criticized as inapplicable to any object of study transcending the actions of particular persons, and, more particularly, to attempts to understand institutional structures and developments. But to this sort of objection, too, Collingwoodians are not without means of reply. The rationale of institutional arrangements, they may point out, can often be made clear without mentioning the actions of any of the participating individuals. Lawrence Stone (1967: 149–50) does this convincingly, for example, when he explains the popularity of landholding by'beneficial lease' in seventeenth-century England by reference to its meeting obvious psychological and economic needs at a time of great social uncertainty and risk.

The objection that the uniqueness of what historians characteristically study makes it impossible for them to explain things in the law-instantiating way is associated especially with the name of Oakeshott (1933: 154), who declared that once historical events are brought under laws 'history is dismissed.' A common response to this has been that, although no two historical events may ever be identical in all respects, no historian would set out to explain such events 'in all their uniqueness.' Any actual enquiry would necessarily bring its objects of interest under general concepts: wars, Acts of Parliament, economic depressions and the like. And that is deliberately to ignore ways in which they may in fact differ from other things falling into the same classes: it is to study them as members of their class. Or, to put the point in another way, one cannot, in history or in any other kind of enquiry, simply explain 'what happened'; one can only explain what happened as one chooses to conceptualize or describe it. Explanation is relative to description; we explain things 'under descriptions'; and descriptions necessarily generalize in the sense of bringing things under concepts.

Against this, as a consideration allegedly supporting nomological theory, it has been argued that, although historical enquiry may require generalization in the sense of bringing a subject matter under concepts, that is not equivalent to bringing it under laws. Laws connect classes of things, and that presupposes the application of concepts; but events, as conceptualized, may still not be of kinds that follow events of certain other kinds in predictable ways. So far as their relations to other things is concerned, they may still thus be unique. But can events which are unique in this sense be explained? An answer sometimes given is that to bring things under concepts is itself a way of explaining them: it is to make them more intelligible by representing them as things of the indicated kinds.[8] And when historians talk of giving explanations, this does appear sometimes to be what they mean. A set of

---

8 See, for example, Dray in Gardiner 1959. Note also the mention of 'colligatory' concepts on p. 777 below.

actions or occurrences is explained 'as a revolution' or 'as a renaissance'. It needs to be emphasized, however, that explanation, so conceived, does not tell us why anything happened. What it tells us is what something under study really amounted to; it is 'explanation what', not 'explanation why'. The question remains whether explanation in the sense of explaining why something happened can be given if what happened, as described, was unique in the sense of not falling under universal laws.

There is in fact a kind of explanation that is frequently offered in history which neither brings things under mere concepts nor subsumes them under laws, at any rate as laws have generally been conceived. Historians often explain what happened or was done as characteristic of the period, society, institution or movement which they have in view. Such explanations bring things under generalizations, but under generalizations the envisaged scope of which is limited in space and time.[9] To explain a certain activity as characteristic of feudal barons, for example, is not to call upon a general law of behaviour which is applicable to all human beings of a certain kind; it is to bring it under a generality which applies only to people living at designated places and times. As such it leaves open the possibility, and may be intended to leave open the possibility, that the ways of acting in question were unique to those places and times. There is a logical analogue of such limited-law explanations, as they have sometimes been called, in the even more strictly individualized explanations that historians sometimes give of the actions of particular historical agents. A certain action, for example, may be explained as characteristic of Luther or of Disraeli, explained as being the sort of thing that the established patterns of behaviour of these individuals would lead one to expect, without anything being implied about how similar historical agents might act in similar situations. Both limited-law and individual-character explanations represent something as explicable because typical, but typical of a particular context, or group, or person, not typical of a class.

The currency in history of reason-attributing and of highly individualized explanations is a matter of considerable importance for its eventual characterization as a type of knowledge and enquiry. Neither corresponds to what would normally be considered explanation in the natural sciences. Natural events cannot be understood as expressions of purposes – or, at any rate, have not been so understood since the demise of Aristotelian physics. And explaining things in terms of what may well turn out to be their individual idiosyncrasies, if ever acceptable at all in natural science, would clearly be considered there as no more than a step toward explaining them by reference to unlimited generalizations. In history, by contrast, this sort of explanation may function as the terminus of the enquiry.

And besides this point about the distinctive logical structure of some kinds of explanation in history, there is a further, more practical consideration to be noted. For along with the conceptual argument that historical explanations must display nomological necessities of a sort familiar in science has commonly gone the

9 The first critical philosophers to stress the logical implications of this point were Joynt and Resches 1966.

methodological claim that history is, in consequence, dependent in a crucial way upon the other social sciences. For it is generally conceded that historians have neither much interest in trying to discover universal laws of human affairs, nor the kinds of expertise required to do so, if indeed any exist. If such laws are logically required for the explanations they want to give, historians will therefore have to derive them ready made from some other source: if not (dubiously) from the common wisdom, then from sociology, economics, political science or some other ostensibly generalizing social science. However, if discovering the rationale of actions and recognizing something done as characteristic of a certain time and place are acceptable modes of explanation in history, there is a theoretical basis for regarding the explanatory inquiries of historians as 'autonomous' (to use a term favoured by Collingwood). Which is not, of course, to say that historians should never exploit the findings of other disciplines where these appear to be well founded and happen to serve their purposes.

VALUE JUDGEMENT IN HISTORY

When philosophers have raised the question of how far historical accounts can aspire to objectivity, the more particular issue they have often had in mind is how far they can be value free. In fact, the varying perspectives that have been brought by different historians to the study of the same subject matter have often consisted of much more than schemes of values. They have generally included, for example, varying metaphysical preconceptions: different views of what is possible or impossible in human affairs, of whether everything must be conceived as having been fully determined, of whether all human motivation is ultimately economic, of the extent to which social entities and forces can have a life of their own. However, it is differences of values that have most often been seen as putting the objectivity of history in question. And a sharp contrast has generally been drawn in this connection between history and the natural sciences, which are commonly supposed to be value free.

The argument that history is inescapably value judgemental has often turned on the consideration that, in elaborating their accounts, historians have to select. Their obligation with regard to a chosen subject matter is presumably to tell us what is important about it. And importance seems to be a category of value, although a very general one which may well, in the end, incorporate all the others: moral, aesthetic, prudential and so on. Some philosophers have sought to find a place for objectivity in history by maintaining that, even if the way historians select expresses value judgements in the form of judgements of importance, what they select need not itself be represented or even conceived in value-loaded ways (of which more below). Others, with similar intent, have denied that, as it enters into historical thinking, the idea of importance is in fact a category of value. To call something important in history, declares Arthur Danto (1965: 11), is implicitly to refer to its consequences, to imply that it is a matter of consequence. And consequences are to be discovered by causal analysis, not stipulated by value judgement.

There is doubtless an element of truth in this contention, but there is something misleading about it too. For an event in history can only be judged important by virtue of its consequences if its consequences are themselves considered important. And the latter cannot be considered important only in the same consequential sense without the original judgement of importance becoming empty. If the incoherence of an infinite regress is to be avoided here, something must be considered important not because of its consequences, but because of its nature. In other words, consequential importance presupposes intrinsic importance; and unless historians are prepared at some point to make judgements of the latter kind, they cannot meaningfully make judgements of importance at all. But they do, of course, quite routinely, and at many points, make judgements of intrinsic importance. The importance that most historians of the United States would ascribe to the American Civil War will not be based only on such considerations as its having led to the abolition of slavery or to the reduction of Southern political power. It will be based also on its having been a traumatic American experience, something that mattered a great deal for those who fought it and suffered through it. The art of Michelangelo will similarly not be considered important by historians of the Renaissance only because of what it led to.

The structural role played by intrinsic value judgements in historiography is most easily seen where there have been large-scale shifts over time in what historians have tended to make central in their accounts: shifts from religious to secular emphases, for example; from political and military to social and economic ones; from the activities of social elites to more everyday concerns; from exclusively European ways of looking at things to the viewpoints of other regions and cultures as well. The recent impact of feminism on historiography well illustrates the point. The main thrust of feminist revisionism has not been a complaint that the causal efficacy of women in the past has been missed; it has been rather that their distinctive experiences and concerns have been given less attention than their intrinsic importance warrants. If it is necessary now to rewrite the history of the French Revolution or of the settling of Australia 'with the women in it', that need not be because women are now seen as having had a larger share than was previously recognized in bringing these things about. What makes their activities and experiences important, and selectable, may not be less what they helped to produce than what they had to endure.

Most of those who have stressed the value-relative character of historical enquiry would find little to quarrel with in what has just been said. But many of them have written as if the question of how value judgements may enter into historical thinking is to be answered entirely by reference to the historian's need to select. Beard (1956), for example, was inclined to exclude from the value-relative aspects of history the ascertaining of particular facts and the discovery of causal connections between them. He saw value judgements as functioning largely at the level of interpretation, not at the levels of ordinary description and explanation. In fact, there are features of both description and explanation in history that raise in special ways the problem of how value free historical enquiry can reasonably hope to be.

For one thing, the descriptive language which historians in fact use is, of course, frequently value loaded. Historical accounts are replete with references to foolish enterprises, acts of statesmanship, cruel repressions and looming catastrophes. But many of the value judgements thus expressed seem to be decorative rather than structural, gratuitous rather than required. Are there any reasons for holding that historians are actually obliged to make value judgements simply in characterizing what they study? Some philosophers have insisted that there are (see e.g. Winch 1958: ch. 3, or Strauss 1953: ch. 2). For many of the things into which historians enquire, they maintain, are in their very nature partly value constituted, and cannot be adequately represented in abstraction from those values. Historians of art, for example, must not only to be able to distinguish more important works of art from less important ones; they must be able to judge whether something is a work of art at all, and thus even a candidate for such further appraisal. And that, in itself, will require of them an aesthetic judgement made on their own authority. Historians of religion, science or philosophy may similarly have to make religious, scientific or philosophical judgements simply in recognizing certain activities as being of a relevant kind, that is, as answering to certain criteria.

Nor is the possibility that even relevance will have to be established in value-judgemental ways a feature only of cultural histories. The same problem can arise, if less frequently, in military, political and other kinds as well. Let us say that the task is to write a history of twentieth-century warfare. Do certain acts of violence committed by the PLO belong to the subject matter? How one answers surely depends on whether one adopts the standpoint of the Arabs or the Israelis. What the former will categorize as an act of warfare the latter will describe rather as an act of terrorism. And that not because they disagree about who shot whom on what occasions, but because they disagree about where political legitimacy lies. The conceptual logic of the enquiry may oblige the historian to address that issue too. Similar considerations may arise with regard to a notion like revolution. English historians who have questioned whether the so-called English Revolution of the mid-seventeenth century was really a revolution have not been expressing doubt about whether certain well-known political and social changes actually took place. What they have been questioning is whether an upheaval which leaves power in the hands of the class that had it at the beginning represents a sufficiently important change (i.e. changes sufficiently important things) to be called a revolution.

It has been maintained by some philosophers that causal judgements, as historians commonly make them, are also vehicles of value judgement, and, once again, not accidentally or gratuitously, but necessarily, by virtue of the very logic of the concept employed. In abstract discussion, it is frequently assumed that by a cause is meant a condition or set of conditions sufficient for the occurrence of an effect. In fact, what is considered a cause in history is seldom more than a necessary condition of it. But not all necessary conditions are plausibly regarded as causes. The fact that the German army was ready to obey Hitler's orders in 1939, and the fact that Hitler was determined to achieve mastery in Europe, may both have been necessary conditions of the outbreak of the Second World War; but only the second would get serious consideration as a possible cause of it. Any attempt to explicate the concept of causation as it is employed in history must, among other things, address the problem of the principles upon which such discriminations are made.

There have been many theories of how genuinely causal conditions are to be distinguished from merely necessary ones. One which currently enjoys a good deal of support is that the conditions which can be regarded as causes are those which were either abnormal in the circumstances or were voluntary interventions by one or more of the human agents involved.[10] This seems at any rate to correspond to ways in which we often think about causation in ordinary life. If I return home one evening by my usual route and, as I pass a neighbour's house, a slate falls off the roof and strikes me, the cause of my injury is the slate's being loose, not my being at the point of impact when it fell, although the latter was a condition as necessary for what occurred as was the former. By contrast, if the building has been condemned and pedestrians are barred from the area, and I act in a similar way with similar results, the cause is more likely to be seen as my own intrusion, now regarded as an abnormal way of behaving under the circumstances. If the intrusion was deliberate, perhaps an act of bravado on my part, the voluntariness of my own contribution to what ensued would make it even more likely that causal status would be assigned to it rather than to the contribution of the slate.

The idea that what makes certain relevant conditions distinctively causal is their abnormality or voluntariness has been elaborated in ways too subtle and complex to be reproduced here. Some of the nuances may be suggested, however, by a brief glance at a disagreement between two historians about the causes of the Second World War. A few years ago, A. J. P. Taylor (1961) challenged received accounts of the war's outbreak by denying that its causes could be traced to Hitler.[11] In support of this thesis, he maintained that Hitler's part in the preceding train of events consisted of actions which were only to be expected from the leader of a great power placed in a position like Germany's after the Peace of Versailles. What really caused the catastrophe, he alleged, was the strange failure of the leaders of Britain and France to take the counter measures that, until quite late in the day, were so obviously available. Both the actions of Hitler and the inaction of the British and the French were doubtless necessary conditions of what ensued; but, as Taylor sees it, it was the latter condition, not the former, that was abnormal, and hence identifiable as the cause. Taylor also argued that, while it was Hitler who ultimately unleashed the war, that was something he was forced into doing by the actions of others, a series of provocations culminating in the intransigence of the Polish premier, Beck, in the summer of 1939. Both on the ground that Hitler's actions were relatively normal, and that he had little choice but to act as he did, we are directed to look elsewhere for the causes of the war.

Some philosophers have gone on to argue that, if causal judgements in history

---

10   The best presentation of this position is by Hart and Honoré 1959, esp. ch. 2.
11   I select only one of several not clearly consistent causal analyses offered by Taylor. His position and those of several of his critics are examined in greater depth in Dray 1980: ch. 4.

depend in some such way upon prior judgements of abnormality and voluntariness, value judgements will necessarily enter into the causal conclusions drawn. It may perhaps seem that whether something is abnormal or not is a purely factual matter, a matter of relative frequency of occurrence, and that whether an action is voluntary is a matter of psychological fact. But a judgement of abnormality requires the choice of a standard of comparison, and regarding one standard rather than another as appropriate in a given instance may express a value judgement. When Taylor describes Hitler as a normal great-power statesman, the implied comparison is with the way powerful political figures have behaved from time immemorial. When one of Taylor's critics, H. R. Trevor-Roper, rejects his causal conclusion, one of his grounds is that, for the post-Versailles world, this is no longer an acceptable way of judging political normality. Thus a decision as to how normality is to be measured may incorporate a value judgement into a causal judgement. The question whether Hitler's actions were voluntary raises value issues in an even more obvious way. Like Hitler himself, Taylor represents the refusal of a series of European statesmen to accede to German demands as having forced Hitler to march. Trevor-Roper (1961: 89ff.) finds morally frivolous any such notion of what the German dictator 'had' to do. Whether a person acted non-voluntarily in the sense of being forced or coerced to act is thus not just a psychological issue; it raises the question of what justifies a person's saying 'I had to do it.' Further analysis along similar lines has been held by some philosophers to highlight a network of connections between the language of causation and the language of responsibility in historical work that makes the historian's concept of cause not a scientific, but a thoroughly humanistic notion.

THE NATURE AND ROLE OF NARRATIVE

The place that narrative ought to occupy in historiography has long been a matter of controversy among historians. Critical philosophers of history had little to say about it before the mid-1960s, but their quite extensive treatment of it since then, although relatively independent of ongoing discussion by historians, has tended to reflect the same concerns. The way narrative initially presented itself as a problem to philosophers was an outgrowth of their well-established interest in the question whether history is an explanatory discipline, and if so in what way. The common wisdom echoed the view of historians like Beard (1956: 325) that a narrative was merely a particular historian's 'selection and organization of facts': in other words, that the narrative form of a historical work was mainly of literary significance. Thus anti-narrativists like Maurice Mandelbaum insisted that narrative construction does not belong to history as enquiry; and even philosophers friendly to narrative like Morton White held that if a narrative can be regarded as explanatory, that can only be because of the discrete explanations it contains.[12] In a way that might have appealed to historians of the *Annales* school, Mandelbaum further criticized

12 See, for example, Mandelbaum 1967, and replies by Ely, Gruner and Dray 1969; and White 1965: 221ff.

narrative as in fact diverting attention from the explanatory purpose of historical work, there being a logical tension, almost a logical incompatibility, he argued, between the goals of explaining and of story-telling. More recently, philosophers like Louis Mink (1987, esp. chs 2, 3, 6, 9) and Hayden White (1987, esp. chs 1, 2, 7), influenced by narrative theory in literary studies, have come close to embracing the view that narrative has no cognitive significance at all: that the way it structures its materials does not convey, and is not intended to convey, the way the past really was.

The question whether the relationships that structure narratives are explanatory, and may reflect reality, drives one back to an examination of the nature of narrative form. This turns out to be a complicated matter, but discussion of the topic has generally begun with a recognition of the time-honoured contrast between narrative and mere chronicle. Like a narrative, but unlike, say, mere annals, a chronicle has to be *about* something: it must have a central subject. And like both narrative and annals, it will express or betray judgements of value through the selection and characterization of its materials. But whereas a chronicle merely describes how one thing succeeded another, a narrative, ideally at least, describes how one thing led to another. A narrative, in other words, is a chronicle with explanation added; a chronicle is a narrative with the explanation left out.

Some philosophers have assumed that the explanations incorporated into a narrative would necessarily be causal, and that a completely explanatory narrative would trace out the links of a causal chain. Others have alleged that what provides the detailed explanatory texture of narratives may be explanations exhibiting a myriad of forms. These would certainly include, besides an occasional causal sequence, the kind that was represented earlier as Collingwoodian, and also limited-law and individual-character explanations. But some have stressed also the way in which yet another kind of explanatory connection often plays a role in binding the elements of narratives together. Transitions in narratives, declared W. B. Gallie (1964: chs 4, 5), are often made understandable by showing how one thing made another possible rather than showing how one thing brought another about. In other words, drawing attention to opportunities as well as to reasons or causes can help to make a series of actions or events intelligible. If the early departure of Rupert's cavalry from the field of Naseby is said to explain Cromwell's winning the battle, it will not be in the sense of showing what brought it about, but in the sense of showing what cleared the way for it. Gallie notes the way explanation of this kind reserves a place in narrative intelligibility for the idea of contingency: the idea of the unintended and even the possibly not fully determined. In fact, some room may be left for a degree of contingency even where the ingredient explanations of a narrative are of a causal kind. For, as Danto (1965: ch 11) has noted, even narratives which are overtly causal seldom set out to show each component event as the effect of the last and the cause of the next, the paradigmatic structure of a causal chain. As was suggested above, causes are typically intruding conditions; they often enter narratives from outside the primary series of events being narrated; they may explain without always themselves being explained.

But is a narrative's containing particular explanations, causal or otherwise, or even its consisting of a series of them, the only way in which it makes its subject matter more intelligible? Is the explanatoriness of a narrative simply a function of the explanations it contains? Philosophers who have resisted this conclusion have sometimes emphasized two other structural features that narratives characteristically display.

The first is that, although they typically refer back at various points to what happened earlier with a view to explaining what happened next, they also frequently refer to what is still to come. When Veronica Wedgwood (1966: 408) reports the organization of the New Model Army, she remarks that this is the army that 'would win the war'. When Lawrence Stone (1967: 221) describes the hopes of the young nobles who joined the Essex Rebellion as 'vain', there is a similar, if more covert, forward reference. Narrative histories refer constantly, of course, to the future as it was envisaged by those whose actions are being explained, their expectations being an indispensable part of any explanation given of what they did in terms of what they thought. But they frequently make reference also to what was actually in store, something which the historian, unlike the original agents, is in a position to know by grace of hindsight. Narrative construction might indeed be described as, in part, a systematic exercise in being wise after the event. More precisely, it could be said to be Janus-faced, moving constantly between the forward-looking standpoint of the agents and the retrospective standpoint of the hindsighted observer. Only from the latter's vantage point can the full significance of what was happening at any particular time be made clear; and judgements of significance are as much the stuff of narratives as are constituent explanations. Some historians have thought it their primary duty to construct narratives, as far as possible, from the standpoint of the agents.[13] But even if explicitly forward-pointing assertions of significance are eschewed, judgements of that genre will be ingredients in the organization of the narrative, guiding both its content and its structure. If these judgements are not visible on a first reading, they should be visible enough on a second.

It might be noted, in passing, that the hindsighted nature of historical reconstruction offers a constant temptation to historians to think about their objects of study in a deterministic way. What happened in the past is now clearly fixed and unchangeable; what the original agents regarded as an open future will now quite properly be seen by the historian as closed. But the sense in which we may legitimately think of the past as necessarily the way it was must be distinguished carefully from the idea that past happenings were brought about necessarily by their antecedents. Being determined in the sense of being predictable from antecedents and being determined in the sense of being unchangeable after the fact are entirely different notions, which, however, are easily confused. One wonders, for example, which of them Geoffrey Elton has in mind when he remarks that the really superior

---

13 Wedgwood inclines this way, despite the remark attributed to her above: see, for example, her introduction to Wedgwood 1956.

historian is the one who not only knows what his subjects thought and did, but also what they are going to think and do next.[14]

A second relevant feature of much narrative history is its having a synoptic or holistic aspect. What it does, by means of its forward and backward references, is bring gradually into view what might be called a whole of non-simultaneous parts: a single development, perhaps, with a beginning, middle and end. As Mink (1987: 56–7, 83–4) has put it, a good narrative enables us to rise above the 'river of time' and take an 'aerial view' of what happened. The kind of understanding which is thus attained rests upon, but also goes beyond, the particular explanations and judgements of significance a narrative may contain. It is a moot point whether such a synoptic grasping of a whole should itself be considered a mode of explanation; some have thought it less confusing to call it interpretation. But it is not easy to maintain a firm distinction in historical studies between interpretation and explanation.[15] And if the underlying question is how narratives make things intelligible – what their cognitive function is – it will be clear at any rate that merely to say that they may contain explanations is not enough. Mink has usefully described what a narrative may ultimately achieve as configurational understanding; and he contrasts this with the understanding to be gained by bringing things under laws or under concepts, which he calls theoretical and categoreal, and sees as typical of science and philosophy respectively. Scientists try to bring what they study under general theories; philosophers seek to discern the general natures of things; historians endeavour to locate things in their contexts.

It should perhaps be remarked that configurational understanding, so conceived, is not the goal only of narrative history. For cross-sectional histories also configure, although mainly in space rather than mainly in time. Both enterprises reinforce the idea that the interest of historians is with the particular and even the unique. The more detailed a configuration, the more it becomes the grasping of a concatenation of relationships which, taken as a whole, may have no other instances. Yet, Mink's trichotomy notwithstanding, historians do sometimes, in the end, bring the configurations they claim to descry under general concepts. After exploring a vast interconnection of happenings, attitudes, actions, dispositions, states of affairs, they may, for example, refer to them collectively as 'the Enlightenment' or 'the Industrial Revolution', thus superimposing categoreal understanding upon configurational. Concepts of this kind, however – 'colligatory' concepts, as Walsh and some others have called them[16] – tend to function as much like proper names as like indications of classes into which designated details are thought to fall. Many of them, too, are clearly metaphorical, this adding a further problematic element to their logical status.

---

14 Elton 1965: 30. Presumably it ought to be the second, since Elton appears to be a historical indeterminist.
15 For an interesting attempt to maintain the distinction between explanation and interpretation, see Levich 1985.
16 For good reading suggestions on colligation see Ritter 1986: 50–5.

But what of the complaint that narratives impose upon their materials a structure which is arbitrary, or at any rate does not reflect the original reality? What of the claim that narratives apply distinctions and assert relationships that are mainly of literary interest? One focus of much criticism of this kind has been on the 'closure' that narratives typically seek to achieve. The very notion of a beginning, middle and end, narrative sceptics like Hayden White (1987: x, 23–4) have asserted, is artificial, a product of the aesthetic and/or moralizing imagination. The real world, White avers, has no beginnings or endings; these are imposed upon an accommodating subject matter for purposes which, since they cannot reflect reality, can only, in the end, be ideological. It is hard to see, however, how, in any sense that is relevant to the problem, this can be accepted as true. The end of something like the First World War is, of course, not the end of the world: things of interest to historians continued to happen after 1918. But it can surely be concluded, on grounds that have nothing to do with the deliverances of the aesthetic imagination or the serving of ideological ends, that these further happenings were not further episodes of the war. It can be a matter simply of seeing that the concept of a world war, a concept that is not particularly obscure, was no longer instantiated. It is true that discerning beginnings and endings in history will sometimes require an exercise of value judgement, as, perhaps, in narrating the decline of Victorian piety or the rise of impressionistic art. But the involvement of value judgement in such cases will not be traceable to the exigencies of narrative structuring; it will be due rather to the fact that what is said to begin and end was (in the sense explicated earlier) partly value constituted. Concern with value-impregnated subject matters is a general feature of historiography, not a special feature of narrative history.

Another focus of criticism of the idea that narratives might adequately reflect reality has been on the retrospective judgements they characteristically contain. To describe something partly in terms of its future, it has sometimes been contended, is not to describe it 'as it actually was', but only as it may later appear in the context of a narrative. It is only in the story, declares Mink (1987: 60), that Columbus discovered America. Presumably, what he discovered, in reality, was some nameless islands which he mistook for a gateway to the Orient. But to tie the notion of historical truth in such a way to what could be known at the time is surely disputable. One is inclined at least to say that, if it was not yet true in 1492 that what Columbus discovered was America, it is certainly true now, and now is when the historian's judgement is being made. But deep problems about the nature of truth and of time will obviously need further consideration before an entirely satisfactory resolution of this problem can be claimed.

More relevant to the current fashion of downgrading narrative as something of chiefly literary significance is Mink's further charge that narrative construction is arbitrary. There are, he complains, no 'rules' for constructing a narrative one way rather than another, this leaving in limbo what it can mean to call a narrative true or false, considered as a whole. There are, of course, ways of testing its constituent statements. But how, in addition, are we to test the truth of the whole, Mink asks. One reply might be that to test the details of a narrative is at the same time to test the viability of its overall structure, excluding its purely literary features. As was argued above, narratives are not simply selections and arrangements of discrete facts; they have a logical structure; their constituent claims interconnect. If some later event that was taken to show that an earlier one was important, or was part of a development of some kind, is found not to have been as was believed, that will at the same time bring into question the structure to which it was thought to contribute. A narrative can be considered true as a whole to the extent that it survives such challenges. Of course, there are no rules for 'thinking up' promising narrative structures; only for testing them. But that is as true of theories in the most prestigious of the sciences as it is of historical narratives.

HISTORIANS AND PHILOSOPHERS

Should historians be interested in the reflections of critical philosophers of history on questions like those aired in this chapter? One relevant consideration is that, although sometimes expressed in an idiom not naturally employed by historians, their content is to a considerable extent continuous with that of historians' own reflections on historiography. No absolute distinction can be drawn between theory of historiography as practised by historians, and critical philosophy of history. When Hexter calls upon his colleagues to pay more attention to the 'rhetoric' of their discipline, what he sometimes has in view is problems that arise chiefly for history as a branch of literature, as when he raises the question of when a narrative needs to change scale. But they are just as often problems about what philosophers would call history's conceptual logic, as when he raises the question of what is involved in a search for origins, a problem on which the analysis of causes as interventions might be expected to throw some light, or when he laments the absence in current historiographical writing of any well-thought-out account of the idea of historical importance (Hexter 1971: 171, 166; 1979: 196).

It might be noted, too, that, although critical philosophers of history are not historical methodologists in the ordinary sense of the word, many of the issues they discuss do have a bearing on historical practice. Historians who accept the common view that narration and adequate explanation are incompatible, for example, may either feel obliged to abjure narrative, or to apologize for continuing to write it. Showing how a narrative may function as a distinctive vehicle of explanation, showing that it has a logic as well as a rhetoric, puts the case for narration in an entirely different light. Historians who feel on some general ground, that they should avoid value judgement to whatever extent human weakness allows, may similarly be freed from a false constraint if it can be shown that, in the study of human affairs, facts may be partly value constituted, and even causal judgement may logically require an exercise of value judgement. The bearing on practice may sometimes be still more direct. Philosophers, whose interest is more in the form than in the content of a historical controversy, can sometimes see more easily than those engaged in it that the disputants are to some extent talking past one another because of different presuppositions or conceptual commitments. This seems to be what happened at times in the controversy between Taylor and Trevor-Roper, who never asked how much their differences over what were causes in the particular case may have owed to their having significantly different notions of what counts as a historical cause.

Historians themselves, of course, sometimes discuss fundamental historio-graphical ideas in ways that take them well past the blurred distinction between theory of historiography and philosophy of history. A good example is E. H. Carr, whose *What is History?* (1961) can be read with profit by both historians and philosophers. But although Carr's discussion is stimulating, it tends to whet the appetite without satisfying it. What he has to say about the idea of chance in history may illustrate the point. According to Carr, to ascribe something to chance is just a 'way of exempting oneself from the tiresome obligation to investigate its causes' (ibid. 96). He evidently thinks this follows from his acceptance of historical determinism, which seems to make the occurrence of anything by chance a theoretical impossibility. But it is highly doubtful that the concept of chance is ever used in history, as it would be in science, to indicate what was less than fully determined, and was therefore inexplicable in principle. In historical contexts, chance generally signifies the unexpected, the coincidental or the accidental. So understood, it does not imply an absence of explanation, but only of explanation of certain kinds – for example, explanation in terms of agents' intentions and beliefs. The point is even clearer if one accepts (as Carr, strangely, seems to do) the more positive analysis of the idea of chance as what occurs 'at the intersection of relatively independent causal sequences', an analysis which has found favour with theorists ranging from positivists to Marxists (se e.g. Nagel 1969 and Plekhanov 1959). For on such a conception, what happens by chance is explicitly represented as something which is fully explicable, but explicable in an unusual, bifurcated way. The moral would seem to be, first, that it is not only philosophers who raise philosophical issues about history, and, second, that once such issues are raised, better philosophy may be required to drive out worse.

Not least of the reasons why the reflections of critical philosophers of history should be of interest to historians is the contribution they may make to presenting the case for the discipline of history in the intellectual community at large. History has often come under attack as a kind of enquiry which is logically rather loose, which continues to ask old-fashioned questions and which tends to give answers in overly intuitive ways. Although historians have often given the lie to such accusations by their actual performances, they have not been conspicuously successful in explaining in theoretical terms what the distinctive nature and value of their sort of enquiry is. While justifying the discipline of history is not, as such, part of the critical philosopher of history's goal, it can be one of the by-products of a careful explication and appraisal of the concepts and presuppositions of historical work. In that connection a final remark might be made about a feature of recent philosophical discussion of history, as illustrated by this chapter, that some may consider a weakness, namely, that it has been largely concerned with elucidating the framework of ideas within which traditional historiography has been conducted.

This is to some extent accidental, a consequence of what those active in the subject happen to have been interested in: there is no reason why more recent historical techniques, subject matters and kinds of questioning should not be equally the object of philosophical analysis. As a matter of priorities, however, the present emphasis may not be so inappropriate. For most of the more recent departures in history have come already equipped with a formidable body of theory. The theoretical case for traditional history has generally gone by default.

REFERENCES

Atkinson, R. F. (1978) *Knowledge and Explanation in History*, Ithaca, NY.

Barker, J. (1982) *The Superhistorians: Makers of Our Past*, New York.

Beard, C. A. [1935] (1956) 'That noble dream', repr. in F. Stern (ed.) *The Varieties of History*, New York.

Bradley, F. H. (1935) *Collected Essays*, vol. 1, Oxford.

Carr, E. H. (1961) *What is History?*, London.

Collingwood, R. G. (1939) *An Autobiography*, London.

—— (1946) *The Idea of History*, Oxford.

Danto, A. (1965) *Analytical Philosophy of History*, Cambridge.

Donagan, A. (1962) *The Later Philosophy of R. G. Collingwood*, Oxford.

Dray, W. H. (1980) *Perspectives on History*, London.

Elton, G. R. (1965) *The Practice of History*, London.

—— (1970) *Political History*, Ithaca, NY.

Ely, R. G., Gruner, R. and Dray, W. H. (1969) 'Mandelbaum on historical narrative: a discussion', *History and Theory* 8: 275–94 ('1. by Richard G. Ely', 274–83; '2. By Rolf Gruner', 283–7; '3. By William H. Dray', 287–94).

Gallie, W. B. (1964) *Philosophy and the Historical Understanding*, London.

Gardiner, P. (ed.) (1959) *Theories of History*, New York.

Goldstein, L. (1976) *Historical Knowing*, Austin.

Hart, H. L. A. and Honoré, A. M. (1959) *Causation in the Law*, London.

Hempel, C. G. (1959) 'The function of general laws in history', repr. in Gardiner 1959.

Hexter, J. H. (1971) *The History Primer*, London.

—— (1979) *Reappraisals in History*, 2nd edn, Chicago.

Joynt, C. B. and Resches, N. (1966) 'The problem of uniqueness in history', *History and Theory* 1: 150–62.

Levich, M. (1985) 'Interpretation in history: or what historians do and philosophers say', *History and Theory* 24: 44–61.

Mandelbaum, M. (1967) 'A note on history as narrative', *History and Theory* 6: 413–19.

Martin, R. (1989) *The Past Within Us*, Princeton.

Mink, L. O. (1987) *Historical Understanding*, Ithaca, NY.

Nagel, E. (1969) 'Determinism in history', in R. H. Nash (ed.) *Ideas of History*, New York.

Norton, D. F. and Popkin, R. H. (eds) (1965) *David Hume: Philosophical Historian*, New York.

Oakeshott, M. (1933) *Experience and its Modes*, Cambridge.

Plekhanov, G. (1959) 'The role of the individual in history', repr. in Gardiner 1959.

Ritter, H. (ed.) (1986) *Dictionary of Concepts in History*, New York.

Stone, L. (1967) *The Crisis of the Aristocracy*, abbr. edn, Oxford.

Strauss, L. (1953) *Natural Right and History*, Chicago.

Taylor, A. J. P. [1961] (1964) *The Origins of the Second World War*, Harmondsworth.

Trevor-Roper, H. (1961) 'A. J. P. Taylor and the war', *Encounter* 17–74: 88–96.

Walsh, W. H. (1951) *An Introduction to Philosophy of History*, London.
Wedgwood, C. V. (1956) *The King's Peace 1637–1641*, New York.
—— (1966) *The King's War 1641–1647*, London.
White, H. V. (1987) *The Content of the Form*, Baltimore.
White, M. G. (1965) *Foundations of Historical Knowledge*, New York.
Winch, P. (1958) *The Idea of a Social Science*, London.

31

HISTORY AND ANTHROPOLOGY[1]

Jordan Goodman

People know what they do; they frequently know why they do what they do; but what they don't know is what what they do does.

(Michael Foucault, quoted in Dreyfus and Rabinow 1982: 187)

Stretching before me is a landscape of problems. Whose history? Whose anthropology? Histories? Anthropologies? Which historians? Which anthropologists? Disciplinarity is a curse to some, a blessing (and a crutch) to others. Defining and defending disciplinary boundaries is an exercise in identity politics. Travelling along boundaries, crossing boundaries, operating on the fringe, in the shadow of canons: seeing from the outside in, the inside out: these are exercises in identity dynamics.

This chapter is not about a lot of things, of which three are perhaps most important. First, it is not about disciplines. That is, it is not an excursion into the relationship between history and anthropology, in the sense of an exercise in epistemology. Issues arising in the philosophy of history are treated elsewhere in this volume (Chapter 30). As for practice, that is another matter. The whole issue of discipline(s) and disciplinarity is covered elsewhere, to which the reader is referred (Messer-Davidow *et al.* 1993). Second, the chapter does not list names *qua* names, except in the references and footnotes; nor does it privilege one practitioner (historian and anthropologist) and one practice (history and anthropology) over another. That has already been done on many occasions and, in the opinion of this author, has been – certainly for the practice of history – a distinctly unhelpful exercise.[2] Finally, it is not prescriptive. It is not a guide as to how to do history with

---

1 Eric Hirsch, Ludmilla Jordanova and Steve Smith read this chapter and made very many valuable suggestions and criticisms. To each of them I would like to express my thanks for their time and friendship. Michael Bentley gave me important pointers at the start and helped me bring the chapter into shape – I thank him for that.
2 See the remarks by Ludmilla Jordanova in her review of Burke's book, 'Resisting reflexivity' *History of the Human Sciences* 5 (1992): 59–67.

anthropology. What the chapter *is* about and how it gets that message across is intimately related to this author's own standpoint. This may be summed up in the following short assertive statements.

1 Those historians who have gone fishing in anthropological waters have been timid, reserved and pre-selective. They have made the cardinal sin of following an anthropologist, not anthropologists and certainly not anthropology.
2 Anthropology is a gateway. Anthropology and the writings of anthropologists offer boundary-crossers an enormous theoretical/abstract/problematized literature that opens onto other literatures. These literatures may appear bounded and mutually exclusive but that is an image of disciplinarity, no more. From the viewpoint of practice, however, the literatures are hybrid creations and they are as much part of the practice as are the practitioners.
3 Neither discipline stands/has stood still. In practice they are two-way avenues. Some historians worry about anthropology; some anthropologists worry about history. In both cases, knowledges are contingent.

The chapter is divided into three sections. The first looks at how some historians and anthropologists have attempted to make sense of each other's practices. The focus will be on an exchange in the *Journal of Interdisciplinary History* published in 1981 but the discussion will move both backwards and forwards in time from this date. The second section will explore the disciplinary hybrids, cultural history, historical anthropology, ethnographic history and others. The final section concentrates on the issue of the right tools for the job. The chapter concludes with a discussion of disciplinary intersections as evidenced by what has been called science, technology and medicine studies. Some of the most perceptive insights in this area of study offer ideas simultaneously to both history and anthropology.

BOUNDARY ISSUES AND THE RAPPROCHEMENT LITERATURE

Bernard Cohn (1980: 216) stated it clearly and unambiguously: 'history can become more historical in becoming more anthropological, ... anthropology can become more anthropological in becoming more historical'. This statement was made after a playful but caustic rendering of nearly a quarter of a century of historical and anthropological practice and definition, leading to what the author described as 'epistemological anarchy'. To save the situation, Cohn recommended a 'conjuncture between history and anthropology' in the shape of an anthropological history.

The central problem for this reassertive hybrid would be the process of cultural construction, constitution and representation. Moreover, it would restore the common subject matter – otherness – while dispensing with the dualism of time and space, the former assigned to history and the latter to anthropology. The choice of place and time in which anthropological history could be studied would be neither arbitrary nor a product of an overarching or metanarrative. Rather, the specification of place and time would emerge in the dialogue between question and subject. The units of study Cohn envisioned for the project of anthropological history included power, authority, exchange, systems of social classification, rituals, and the construction of time and space.

One interesting call, and one which I shall refer to later in this chapter, was for anthropological history to open up its black boxes, one of which contains the concept of an event. Cohn argued that a specific analytical field is not necessarily defined by what may be perceived as temporal unity. As examples, Cohn referred the reader to labels such as 'Age of Enlightenment' and 'Age of Revolution'. Events, he argued, are not of equal value. Some have structural consequences not apparent within the event itself. Only with hindsight can events be ranked in some scale of importance, for example. Some actions which, at the time they were taken, had specific contexts and explanations, could be thoroughly transformed from what Cohn termed a dependent to an independent variable. Though he did not provide an example of this phenomenon, the 'killing' of Captain Cook by the Hawaiians is a case in point: what was being killed in this 'killing' was different for the Hawaiians who performed it and the English who witnessed it – the latter responded by setting in motion events that finally transformed the Hawaiian world (Sahlins 1985).

Cohn's article appeared without citations. In the following year, he was invited to comment on the relationship between history and anthropology in a symposium on history in the 1980s (Cohn 1981). This time, Cohn provided a full scholarly arm-amentarium, an academic landscape of names and topics, references to the works of many historians and anthropologists who had, over time, crossed disciplinary boundaries. This article did not, unsurprisingly given its timing, offer any substantive theoretical additions to the earlier article. It did, however, cast a wide, non-Eurocentric net, as far as the writing of history is concerned.

Readers of the 1981 issue of the *Journal of Interdisciplinary History* who had just finished reading Cohn's contribution might have been forgiven for thinking that furthering relations between history and anthropology, between historians and anthropologists, was a matter of finding common and fertile epistemological ground. But nothing could be further from the truth. Turn the page and there is a contribution to the debate by John Adams (1981).

Adams set his sights on how historians, particularly the 'new breed' of social historians of colonial America, had engaged with anthropology and anthropologists over the past decade and more, and his verdict was both disturbing and damning. He chastized historians for dabbling with anthropology. He attacked them for misunderstanding the issue by thinking that anthropologists studied exoticism and that historians should do so as well. He almost seems to have lost patience when he reproached them for searching out social equivalents in their patch of the Balinese cockfight, Kula ring or potlatch.[3]

All was not destructive criticism in Adams's account, however. A lifeline was thrown out at the end of the article. In trying to understand the nature of social relations, he advised historians to attend to the 'mundane, with its pettiness and

---

3   Adams 1981: 257–8. For another view of the impact of the example and analysis of the Balinese cockfight on anthropology see Roseberry 1989b.

dissensions, as well as its cooperativeness', rather than dwelling on the exotic and, thereby, creating fantasies of Golden Ages (Adams 1981: 265). As for how historians should engage with anthropology, his advice was at once surprisingly conciliatory and possibly unattainable. 'If historians borrow from anthropology', he writes, 'it should be with the intention of developing the concepts borrowed and of *making, in return, a contribution to anthropology* [my italics]' (ibid.). His parting shot should also be recorded here, for it is an insight that intersects historians' practices generally. 'History', Adams warns,

> must become more reflexive about its goals and about the means it uses to realize its ends. To anthropologists the lack of interest in theory among historians still seems great. But borrowing concepts from another discipline does not hold out much promise either if the concepts are simply misused in a thoughtless way.
>
> (ibid.)

One can imagine a whole set of reactions to Adams's comments, from 'Right on!' to 'Mind your own business!'. Ironically, as an anthropologist, Adams did not let on that the theoretical turmoil in his own discipline, as heretofore seemingly invincible theoretical standpoints, networks and institutional positionings, was being prodded, tested and assaulted.

Next in turn in the section on Anthropology and History in the 1980s was a key witness to and practitioner of history with anthropology. While not directly responding to Adams, Natalie Davis outlined the historian's engagement with anthropology from the former's point of view. The anthropological literature, she implied, liberates historians from a metanarrative that had ranked past phenomena by importance, marginalizing some events (and types of events) and privileging others (Davis 1981). How this metanarrative was constructed and how events were valorized she didn't say. What is important is that anthropology is useful, according to Davis, because of four features that the discipline brings to bear on its objects of study: 'close observation of living processes of social interaction; interesting ways of interpreting symbolic behavior; suggestions about how the parts of a social system fit together; and material from cultures very different from those which historians are used to studying' (ibid. 267).

For Davis, the key word is culture, about how it is constructed, how it is reproduced and how it is represented. To meet these objectives, she implored historians to 'slice into a culture through texts, pictures and artifacts' (ibid. 272). Davis did not deal with the issue of exoticism as raised by Adams; instead she made out a case for using ethnographic texts as comparative material. In studying oral cultures in the European past, for example, she suggested that an understanding of present-day African language practices might help reveal to the historian 'how things were said in sixteenth-century villages' (ibid.).

The prescriptions appear to be delivered and, presumably, self-administered effortlessly. Before bringing her article to an end, Davis alerted historians to some possible pitfalls in drawing upon anthropology. The key comment is that

> anthropology is not ... some kind of higher vision of social reality to which historians

should convert, but a sister discipline *with increasingly close ties to our own* [my italics] ... . We should not only be borrowing from them with discernment, we should also be prepared to offer advice about their own work and about anthropological theory.

(ibid. 274)

Right here lies the problem. Davis's article is richly referenced, taking in a wide range of historical and anthropological writings: not surprisingly, given her keen interest in the nature of culture, the key anthropological guides to expanding historical awareness for her are Clifford Geertz, Victor Turner, Roy Rappaport and Mary Douglas.[4] She asks historians to read these works, understand the arguments and evidence in ethnographies, make themselves aware of different schools of anthropological interpretation, integrate them into the historian's 'own vision of social organization': but not to 'import all the special reservations that anthropologists have about each other's work or all their infighting' (Davis 1981: 273).

Lying behind this seemingly commonsensical – in other words, no longer controversial – statement, is a deep and damaging contradiction. How can historians advise anthropologists about their theory without getting into the mess with them? Yes, anthropology is concerned with and anthropologists write about culture, but that is a bit like saying that Hamlet is a play about a Danish prince. Before slicing into a culture, historians need to be able to find their way into and around cultures, to be able to pose cultural questions, to understand how culture constitutes itself – and that of course includes its objects, texts, etc. What Davis calls infighting may, at one level, be nothing more than departmental politics, but to turn it into nothing more than this is insulting. Rather, historians need to understand that the infighting is a reflection of reflexivity about profound issues of interpretation of culture and its meaning.

The choice by Davis – and for that matter many historians writing about culture in history at the time – of Geertz, Turner, etc. is not surprising because these anthropologists and their works came to prominence precisely as a consequence of special reservations and infighting. Their canonization and that of their writings as revered texts must be understood as the end of a process of disciplinary argument. Though to an outsider it may have the characteristics of closure, closure itself is how the victors to an argument declare they have won – the arguments, though, are not closed. Not recognizing this has very serious consequences for a broad engagement of history and anthropology. Davis's advice that historians should stay away from anthropologists was wrong.

How many historians hold this view is, of course, unknown and beside the point, though Davis could not possibly be alone. One historian, in print at least, took issue with Davis. Darrett Rutman was invited to comment on the relationship between history and anthropology in a short collective exegesis on dialogue between the two disciplines (Rutman 1986). The piece is quite remarkable – disturbing in several senses – in that it was written in the form of an extended metaphor, in which

---

4   Davis refers to several works by these authors including Geertz 1973; Turner 1967; Rappaport 1979; and Douglas 1966.

Rutman recounts Clio's practices as a lover, both enticing and being seduced by disciplinary suitors, in which 'anthropology is only the latest object of her ardor' (ibid. 121). The sexual explicitness of the text, of the gender assumptions behind the actions are quite revealing.[5] They also resonate in quite interesting ways with those E. P. Thompson (1972) used earlier in his review of Keith Thomas's *Religion and the Decline of Magic* and Alan Macfarlane's *The Family Life of Ralph Josselin, a Seventeenth-century Clergyman*, two books that were prominent in their explicit use of anthropological perspectives.

It is very difficult to read Rutman's article without becoming engaged in the gender politics of his choice of metaphor. Nevertheless, through his dubious attributions of character to Clio – that she is a shallow figure, that she flirts widely and that the satisfaction of her sexual activities are primarily for herself – he makes the important argument that, far from avoiding the reservations and infighting of anthropologists, historians wishing to engage with anthropology need to begin right at this point, with the fundamentals (Rutman 1986: 122). Conjuring up his metaphor of choice, though now treating the sexuality of the suitor ambiguously, Rutman concludes by urging historians 'to enter anthropology widely and deeply, allowing its fundamentals to affect their doing of history' (ibid. 122–3).

At the start of this chapter, I stated that I would not be listing names *qua* names. I would like to offer two reasons for this. First, naming particular anthropologists has the effect of reinforcing privilege in one place where such privilege is likely to be contested in another place. Second, naming is not quite the same as engaging and on that I have already made some comment. Take, for example, the distinct infatuation that some historians have had for some anthropologists. Of course, I am referring here to Clifford Geertz. I do not intend to analyse why Geertz has had the impact he has had on some historians: others have done this admirably (see e.g. Walters 1980 and Kertzer 1984). I just want to note that one of the reasons for Geertz's reception and elevation to a 'paradigm for the entire discipline' for historians had to do precisely with historians' reservations about each other's works; with infighting over what some believed was the encroachment into history of the positivistic social sciences, especially economics and quantitative analysis; and with a search for a saviour in the shape of a towering figure from another discipline.[6]

That Geertz is an 'obligatory point of passage' (Latour 1988: 43–9) for historians is still being reinforced in a recent collection of essays by Peter Burke (1991a). One of the reviewers of this collection makes this a central concern of her essay when she writes: 'a Martian, sent to investigate the state of historical knowledge on the late 20th-century Earth, might be forgiven for thinking that anthropology was a discipline with only one practitioner – Clifford Geertz!' (Jordanova 1992: 62).

---

5 See Martin 1991 for a discussion of the constitutive functions of metaphors.

6 See the comments in Walters 1980, Kertzer 1984 and Kertzer 1986. Further insights into the Geertzian influence can be gained from Darnton 1990, especially chapters 10 and 15; Clark 1983. For anxiety over the social sciences, see Stone 1977 and 1979.

Geertz is not, of course, the first or last obligatory point of passage.[7] He has, however, made his own analysis of the relationship between the two disciplines (Geertz 1990; see also Rosaldo 1990).

The position of Geertz takes us back to the issue of what was going on and had gone on in anthropology when Cohn, Adams and Davis contributed to the debate about anthropology and history in the 1980s. The relational issue is picked up by the anthropologist Paul Rabinow. He writes:

> There is a curious time lag as concepts move across disciplinary boundaries. The moment when the historical profession is discovering cultural anthropology in the (unrepresentative) person of Clifford Geertz is just the moment when Geertz is being questioned in anthropology.
>
> (Rabinow 1986: 241–2)

It is not, however, just a one-way street. An anthropologist on history:

> Just as we were turning to history for guidance, at the moment when our early paradigmatic foundations were crumbling, many historians began to repay the compliment. Just as we were inclined to see history as 'good' – as if time might cure everything – they seemed to see ethnography as a panacea. This should have warned us that they were in as much theoretical trouble as we were ourselves.
>
> (Comaroff and Comaroff 1992: 17)

A sense of what this statement means can be gained from an essay by Sherry Ortner (1984) surveying the debates within anthropology from the 1960s to the early 1980s. It is a crucial paper for historians wishing to engage with anthropology. Ortner takes the reader on a voyage beginning with symbolic anthropology – in which Geertz is located temporally and theoretically – then to cultural ecology, structuralism, structural Marxism, political economy and finally to practice theory, drawing specifically on Pierre Bourdieu's (1978) key work.

Ortner, to be sure, provides historians with a rich landscape of theoretical developments within anthropology together with a check-list of required readings. For that alone, the essay is critical. But it also has a more subtle offering. Specifically, and not accidentally, she turns to the question of history and its meaning for anthropologists in the final pages of her review. Reference is made to the historic turn in anthropology, or, as she terms it, the 'move to diachrony', evident certainly in the early 1980s, and associated at the time principally with Marshall Sahlins, Renato Rosaldo, Anthony Wallace and John Comaroff.[8] While she applauds the historical turn, Ortner is careful to argue that the fundamental issues in anthropology thrown up by the theoretical insights of the previous decade cannot be pursued simply by bolting on history—by which she means a temporal

---

7 Keith Thomas, in an earlier discussion of history and anthropology, implicitly placed Evans-Pritchard (and by implication British social anthropology) in this position – see Thomas 1963. See also the comments in H. Geertz 1975.

8 Apart from Sahlins 1981, see Sahlins 1985, especially chapters 2 and 5; Rosaldo 1980; Wallace 1996; Comaroff 1982. For a survey of history and anthropology from an anthropologist's point of view see Faubion 1993. Some earlier comments on these disciplines can be found in Schapera 1962 and Smith 1962.

process which happens to people. Placing practice at the centre of anthropological concerns, she argues, will also rebound on history, in the sense of thinking of history as being made through practice. 'A practice approach', she states,

> attempts to see this making, whether in the past or present, whether in the creation of novelty or in the reproduction of the same old thing. Rather than fetishizing history, a practice approach offers, or at least promises, a model that implicitly unifies both historical and anthropological models.[9]

What is so important about Ortner's statement is that it offers a way forward *simultaneously* for history and anthropology – I will return to this point later in the chapter. Before leaving this section, it would be well to draw attention to two historians who have attempted to travel across much of the anthropological terrain covered by Sherry Ortner and who share many of the same sentiments. Both William Reddy (1992) and William Sewell (1992) have attempted to outline what a theory of change would have to be like if it were to intersect with the historically minded anthropologists at the same time as it cohered with the idea of social practice. Sewell's insistence on adopting an understanding of society which is at the same time multiple, contingent and fractured has enormous implications for how history is done; Reddy's analysis of the public sphere as being historically constituted and constitutive of society raises fundamental issues about the possibilities of a historical ethnography of the present.

HYBRIDS AND PARTIAL CONNECTIONS

The discussions about history and anthropology and the metaphors employed to describe the relationship need to be seen in the context of the creation and proliferation of hybrids: anthropological history, historical anthropology, ethnographic history, historical ethnography and cultural history. What these hybrids are or should be are, of course, negotiable and, not surprisingly, in view of the many different accounts of the history and anthropology relationship, ambivalent. To give no more than just a flavour of this, let us tune into two quite different imaginings of historical anthropology.

The first is given by the historian Peter Burke (1987: 3–4) in the introduction to a set of essays on early modern Italy. Burke lists a number of features of historical anthropology that define its concerns and practice and which, according to the author, distinguish this discipline from social history. Historical anthropology rests on qualitative evidence and concentrates on local practices in small communities; the historical anthropologist seeks to uncover and understand social interaction – particularly through apparently trivial actions – in precisely the same terms as they were constructed locally, that is, following Geertz's 'thick description'; as for theory, historical anthropologists seek inspiration from figures such as Arnold van Gennep, Marcel Mauss, Clifford Geertz, Victor Turner and Pierre Bourdieu.

---

9 Ortner 1984: 159. See also Comaroff 1982 and Comaroff 1984.

By contrast, the anthropologists Jean and John Comaroff offer a different historical anthropology, one that makes the version by Peter Burke appear parochial and theoretically naive. Theirs is a call for a theoretically principled historical anthropology. Interestingly, they draw some inspiration from cultural history (as practised by historians) and on the methods for uniting the disciplines, but argue that neither amounts to a historical anthropology. In something that is very much like a call to arms, they assert their historical anthropology to be 'anti-empiricist, anti-objectivist, anti-essentialist ... anti-statistical and anti-aggregative' (Comaroff 1992: 20).[10] The challenge for this historical anthropology is

> to address the equations of structure and indeterminacy, of form and incoherence, involved in tracking the movement of societies and peoples through time; to disinter the endogenous historicity of local worlds, both perceptual and practical, in order to understand better their place within the world historical processes of which they are a part; and to rupture the basic tropes of Western historiography – biography and event – by situating being and action, comparatively, within their diverse cultural contexts.
>
> (ibid. 27)

Whatever the topic under analysis, they argue, it should be approached in the same way: 'as meaningful practice, produced in the interplay of subject and object, of the contingent and the contextual' (ibid. 32).

It is not possible here to give more than just this short statement of historical anthropology as advanced by Jean and John Comaroff. The entire richly layered and nuanced argument needs to be treated with concentrated attention. Theirs has not been the only call for such a hybrid. Marshall Sahlins (1993), Terence Turner (1991) and Sherry Ortner (1989), to name but a few anthropologists, have thrown their lot in with others to argue for a historical ethnography.[11]

Historical practice that seeks to produce a historical ethnography explicitly is an exciting project. Its relationship with other forms of historical practice that focus on local matters, such as local history, microhistory and *Alltagsgeschichte*, would be useful to analyse.[12] Yet, as the anthropologist Renato Rosaldo (1986) has shown in a critique of Emmanuel Le Roy Ladurie's *Montaillou*, the claim of ethnographic authority is not unproblematical. Indeed, Rosaldo takes Ladurie to task for being too textualized, perhaps even contrived. As recent anthropological literature has shown, ethnography as an authoritative referent is problematical for anthropologists, and, by implication, should be so for historians (see also Clifford 1988, esp. ch. 1).

---

10   The insistence on the anti-statistical and the anti-aggregative has an interesting resonance in recent literature which seeks to deconstruct social science disciplines (and subdisciplines) which are positivism-driven. The literature is burgeoning. Some sense of what's going on can be gained from the following: Megill 1994; Greenhalgh 1996; Nelson 1996.

11   See also Schieffelin and Crittenden 1991; Gewertz 1983; Ortner 1995. For an interesting volume covering areas of interest to both anthropologists and historians see Dirks *et al.* 1994.

12   On microhistory, the reader is advised to pursue the following references: Levi 1991; Ginzburg 1993; and Revel 1994. I discuss *Alltagsgeschichte* later on in this chapter (pp. 794–5).

Perhaps the charge frequently made by anthropologists (and others, including historians) that historians are not particularly interested in – or do not understand – theory, is one that will be made whenever historians attempt to participate in a hybrid adventure. Many historians would, without a moment's hesitation, resist and rebut either characterization with vigour. Yet it is interesting that the hybrids with history and anthropology have been particularly exploited and analysed primarily by anthropologists. Rather than engage in the theoretical fracas, it would seem that history is more interested in producing its own in-house hybrids and then allowing the monster to go in search of prey.

This indeed seems to be the case with cultural history. I am fully aware that using this expression runs the risk of effacing a substantial literature that dates back more than a century (Burke 1991b). But as it is commonly used today, cultural history refers at least to a body of work that began to appear mostly during the 1970s.

History needs a sustained critique of cultural history: perhaps it will appear soon. Whenever it does, it will need to engage with cultural studies as it is and has been developing. This is not the place to begin, though there have already been beginnings.[13] The only point I wish to make here is that cultural history as a subdiscipline occupies two sites simultaneously: one of these is cultural history *qua* cultural history; the second is cultural history in the sense of 'the cultural history of X', where X can stand for anything.

The first of these brands of cultural history (re-)emerged in the 1980s as 'the new cultural history'. Theoretically, as the editor of a volume of papers locating the field stated, the new cultural history drew inspiration from anthropology and literary criticism, superseding the sociology which framed issues in social history until then (Hunt 1989: 10–11). As for which anthropologist speaks the theoretical arguments, one should not be surprised to know that it was Clifford Geertz, though Aletta Biersack (1989) solicits theoretical advice from Marshall Sahlins, signalling for the reader that there may be more than one anthropologist around. Historians meeting the requirements for inclusion/identification as cultural historians are those such as Natalie Zemon Davis, Roger Chartier and Robert Darnton, though these are not meant to be exclusive. Pierre Bourdieu and Michel Foucault are the theorists at the centre of discussion.

While the first kind of cultural history appears to be the core, there is the second kind, where cultural history operates at a site of practice. As I have suggested, the site can be almost anything.[14] To give some sense of this, I list some—only a tiny proportion—of the topics that have been submitted for a cultural history analysis.

---

13 See for example and only the most recent: *Cultural History/Cultural Studies*, special issue, number 65, *New German Critique* (1995); McCrum 1995; Mainardi 1995; Miller 1995. A good beginning as far as cultural studies is concerned is Grossberg *et al.* 1992.

14 François Furet has criticized the school of French history concerned with *mentalités* precisely along these lines, arguing that the study of *mentalités* is fragmentary, lacking in discipline, a factory of topics – see Furet 1983.

In recent years there have been cultural histories of:[15] science and technology;[16] consumption;[17] landscape;[18] labour;[19] the body;[20] the senses (Camporesi 1994; Corbin 1995; 1986; Classen *et al.* 1994); disease (Delaporte 1986; Patterson 1987; Gilman 1995; Barnes 1995; Bates 1992; Rothman 1994); advertising (Lears 1994); popular culture;[21] clothing;[22] colour;[23] food;[24] sugar (Mintz 1985); tobacco (Goodman 1993); drugs (Camporesi 1989; Goodman *et al.* 1995); the tele-

---

15   In what follows, I have decided to present either review articles that, in themselves, guide the reader through a wealth of material; or, in the absence of such valuable bibliographical works, I have chosen what I feel are representative works, preferably of recent vintage that include some overview of the field.

16   For a recent overview of literature, problems and insights see Dear 1995. For thoughts on cultural historical approaches to technology see Bijker 1995 and the bibliography to which he refers. See also MacKenzie and Wajcman 1985. A recent exploration of the history of the computer that is framed by tropes familiar to cultural history is Edwards 1996. Anthropological perspectives on technology are neatly summarized in Pfaffenberger 1992. See also Pfaffenberger 1988. As for science, a review of anthropological concerns is available in Franklin 1995. On the intersection between cultural studies and science and technology studies see Rouse 1992. Excellent overviews of the burgeoning field of the anthropology of science and technology can be found in Hess 1995, and Hess and Layne 1992. Strict cultural histories of technology in a general, rather than particular, sense are rare. For interesting suggestions of how this might proceed and of the theoretical areas into which one might venture, see Scranton 1995.

17   Brewer and Porter 1993. A recent overview of how anthropologists (and some historians) have been treating consumption is given in Miller 1995.

18   Schama 1995. For the anthropologist's perspective, see Hirsch and O'Hanlon 1995. Related to the interest in landscape is a burgeoning literature in the history of the environment, much of it bordering on, if not within, the cultural history mode. See, for example, 'A round table: environmental history' *Journal of American History* 76 (1990): 1087–1147; Cronon 1992; Demeritt 1994; Merchant 1995. Spatial history is also making a break for recognition – see the special section 'Spatial history – rethinking the idea of place', *History Workshop Journal* 39 (1995): 137–92. See also the quite remarkable work on perceptions and representations of the sea, a topic that cuts across other concerns of this mode of cultural history, particularly popular culture: Corbin 1994.

19   Rancière 1989 and Reid 1991. For an overview of the problems encountered in engaging with theoretical 'turns' in the last few decades, as far as labour history is concerned, see Berlanstein 1993. Although it is ostensibly about 'social history', much of the debate recently aired about its future can be reconstructed as a debate about the cultural history of labour – see Joyce 1995 and the response by Eley and Nield 1995.

20   Feher *et al.* 1989; Gallagher and Laqueur 1989; Laqueur 1990; Sennett 1994. An interesting study that investigates the body not only as a site of social practice but as an object of economic – investment – practice is Rabinbach 1990. A possible rich area for investigation is the history of the body at work, specifically, in what has been termed a workplace ecology, of the interactions between technology, the social relations of production, and the mediation of biology and manufacture. Some interesting ideas on this can be found in McEvoy 1995. For an anthropological perspective see Martin 1994 and Lock 1993. See also the fascinating and very suggestive essay by Martin 1992.

21   Levine 1993. See also Levine 1992a and the responses to it by Kelley 1992, Davis 1992 and Lears 1992. See also Levine's response: Levine 1992b. Though Levine's primary concern is American popular culture during the 1930s, what he has to say goes well beyond the United States at the time: comparative perspectives, from Europe and Africa are also on offer from Davis. See also Susman 1984. A recent study that incorporates a wide range of representational tropes and which promises to be a model for work in other areas is Ross 1995. Another recent work, recalling an earlier generation of work on the study of the crowd in history and the work of historians such as Emmanuel Le Roy Ladurie, is Corbin 1992.

phone;[25] electricity and lighting (Nye 1990; Schivelbusch 1988); plastic (Meikle 1995); and the pencil (Petroski 1993).

In attempting to clear an area for historical investigation into which theoretical or methodological approaches from other disciplines can be folded, historians have pursued other kinds of hybrids and webs of partial connections, particularly the latter. The two that come most into view at the moment are *Alltagsgeschichte* and microhistory.

The latter has been a historical practice which has enjoined its adherents to reduce the scale of observation but nothing else. Teleology and ethnocentrism are two of its enemies. The event becomes a lens for gazing at an entire landscape of processes, some within view and others in the distance. The important point is that the reduction of scale is not a reduction to the particular (see Ginzburg 1993). It shows possibilities and with it offers up the past as more contingent and less monolithic than frequently portrayed by the macro-practitioners.[26] One of the frequent charges against microhistory is that its attention to the object in the reduced scale of vision precludes an engagement with the larger tapestry from which the object has been approached. Interestingly, this problem has also been raised by anthropologists, especially John and Jean Comaroff (see particularly J. L. Comaroff 1982). John Comaroff has offered dialectics – an internal dialectic, a set of systematic contradictions of the local that shape and are shaped by historical outcomes of complex arrangements, and a dialectic of articulation, the contradictory principles that underlie the interaction between the local and its encompassing context – not only as a solution to the problem but, more importantly, as the unit of study itself (ibid. 146).[27] Natalie Davis has responded to this charge in an interesting way by turning the problem on its head: namely, by arguing that macrohistorians must accommodate the microhistorical disclosure.[28]

Microhistory, or to be more precise, those who practise or speak for those who practise microhistory, frequently elide it with *Alltagsgeschichte* (see Davis 1990; also Medick 1994; 1987). Geoff Eley (1989) has recently shown that to define it as a uniform programme of study would be to obscure much of its lively diversity. Put plainly, and certainly oversimply, *Alltagsgeschichte* is the history of everyday life, in

---

22 Roche 1994; Perrot 1994; Weiner and Schneider 1989. For a review of the anthropological literature, see Schneider 1987.

23 Gage 1993; Pastoureau 1988; 1987; Medick 1995. Anthropologists have had much to say about colour. See, for example, Sahlins 1976. For a review of some of the issues, see Saunders 1995.

24 Camporesi 1993; Mennell 1985; Mintz 1993. See also Camporesi 1992. An overview from other perspectives can be found in Mennell *et al.* 1992.

25 Fischer 1992. See also the highly original and deeply interdisciplinary Ronell 1989.

26 See the point made in Medick 1995. A longer discourse on this point is made in Medick 1994.

27 One of the key attempts to write a local historical anthropology set within a world-systems approach is Wolf 1982. For a recent review of the problems see Abu-Lughod 1995. See also Appadurai 1990.

28 Davis 1990. For a recent and very interesting collection of essays that examine the encounter of different cultures in different historical contexts, see Schwartz 1994.

whatever circumstances the analyst chooses. Though it has a specific German pedigree, the formulation of this historical approach reaches beyond national boundaries and specificities. Eley's synthesis of the writings of Alf Lüdtke, whom he takes as typifying the approach, makes this clear. In particular, he draws out five main methodological diktats: a history from below of cultural practice; an emphasis on subjectivity and experience;[29] decentralization of analysis and interpretation; a new formulation of the big questions through the latter turn; and finally, the rendering of the political as an expression of the intersection of public and private. (Eley 1989: 322–3).

If, as Eley argues, the theoretical debt (especially to anthropologists) is more implicit than explicit, nevertheless the intersection of *Alltagsgeschichte* and historical ethnography has been noted by others, including Lüdtke himself.[30] One interesting question that *Alltagsgeschichte* raises is the possibility of finding an analytical route towards an understanding of social formations as historical agents involved in cultural practices. Here, there is another intersection, but one that has not been noticed: the increasing interest in the concept of hegemony, among those cultural historians and anthropologists who are committed to a political engagement.[31] As Eve Rosenhaft (1987: 105) has so clearly stated it:

> 'Hegemony' directs us more clearly than any other term in current use to examine 'culture' as an arena of class domination and negotiation, but it does not instruct us as to what we will find or even how to go about it. In this sense, Gramsci has bequeathed us not a philosopher's stone for the perfect fusion of history and anthropology, but a credo for combining methodological diversity with coherence of purpose in any social study.

RIGHT TOOLS FOR THE JOB: THE HISTORIAN AS *BRICOLEUR* AND *CHIFFONIER*

It is often said that historians eschew theory, preferring a world of facts. Who exactly says this is uncertain, but whatever the provenance, there seems to be a confusion over the word 'theory'. The question is: which theory? Certainly historians in their practice do not engage with the theory of history in the way that anthropologists, for example, engage with cultural and social theory. On the other

---

29 This turn resonates particularly with debates within labour history, especially those taking place in the United States. On experience and on the possibility of the historian 'knowing' this, see the important article by Scott 1991. An interesting discussion of the relationship between language and experience and of both with that of historical practice can be found in Reid 1993.

30 See Eley 1989: 252–3. For another and much shorter perspective on *Alltagsgeschichte* see Rosenhaft 1987.

31 For some recent thoughts see Comaroff and Comaroff 1992: chs 1 and 10. See also Lears 1985. One anthropologist who has made the return to the political his *cri de cœur* is William Roseberry. See, especially, Roseberry 1996; 1992; and 1989a, especially chs 5 and 6. Nicole Polier and William Roseberry have provided a stinging critique of the representational turn in ethnography, as demonstrated particularly in Clifford and Marcus 1986, and a plea to return ethnographic knowledge to the rich contexts in which it is produced and consumed – see Polier and Roseberry 1989.

hand, it would be untrue to say that historians do not engage with social or linguistic theory. It is just that not all of them do all of the time. The other statement that is often made of historians is that they are eclectic in their choice of who or what theory to follow. Historians are best described as *bricoleurs* or *chiffoniers* (Wohlfarth 1986), pursuing their interests, picking up little theoretical titbits here and there, knowing this name and that theory; but essentially driven by the pragmatist's credo – the right tools for the job.

Despite appearances, this credo is deeply problematic. What is the job? How does a tool become right?[32] These are reflexive questions. Confronting them effaces the dangerous dualism of theory and practice that haunts the historical discipline. The object here is not to harangue but rather to provide signposts for the profitable engagement of history with anthropology. To bring this chapter to an end, I want to return to an earlier point – that is, for the need of concerns that *simultaneously* call forth an anthropological and historical response – and to look briefly at the field of science, technology and medicine studies where such simultaneity is, I think, especially clear.[33]

In a recent article concerned with the predicament of social history, particularly with respect to its failure to engage with contemporary social and cultural theory, the argument was made that the historian's terrain is not only being invaded but interpreted and offered to postmodernity by those not practising history themselves (Joyce 1995: 73). In other words, not only is the past contested terrain, but the terrain itself is contested with historians as the spectators. Patrick Joyce, the author of the article, is thinking especially that postmodernism 'must project a "modernism" by means of which its own image can be made ... there is a tendency to invent a modernism which acts as postmodernism's founding concept' (ibid.). In other words, if historians hang around while 'postmodernism' is performing its dastardly deed, they will find the past foreclosed; that is, the past will appear as an assemblage of elements acting as one into which it will be difficult, if not impossible, to enter. Gone too will be the cherished but often unstated principle that history is open-ended; or as Carolyn Steedman put it, the 'implicit understanding that *things are not over*, that the story isn't finished, can never be finished, for some new item of information may alter the account that has been given' (Steedman 1992: 614; see also Miller 1995). One might add: some new insight, theory, or even off-the-cuff remark.

This is not the place to debate history and postmodernism,[34] but rather to add to

32 A whole volume of essays in science and technology studies (including historical ones) has been devoted to this very issue. See Clarke and Fujimura 1992.
33 A recent overview of the intersections of science, technology and medicine studies, though with little reference to historical material, is Traweek 1993. This article also surveys feminist perspectives and intersections, but for material relating to history see Jordanova 1993.
34 The question is where to begin in following the ongoing debate. A good place to start would be Stone 1991 followed immediately by Joyce and Kelly 1991, and Stone and Speigel 1992. Going around the problem from another direction, one can begin with Kirk 1994: and working backwards through the same journal. See also Eley 1993 and Appleby 1994.

Joyce's concern a more positive or (pro)active turn. Namely, that there are others, historians none of them, who are in the middle of the skirmish about history, not on the sidelines with the practitioners. They are allies. They can help historians with terrain problems. And what is more, and by very good fortune, they are also in the skirmishes in anthropology, in philosophy, in science and technology studies, and in gender studies. Historians should get to know these voices.

Though I said at the start of the chapter that I would not be mentioning names, I would like to offer Marilyn Strathern, Bruno Latour, Donna Haraway and Andrew Pickering.[35] Instead of symbolic interpretative anthropology and thick description, these analysts offer partial connections, irreducibility, hybrids and post-humanism. As a historian, I offer them as tropes, as ways of thinking about the past, about historicizing the tropes themselves.

What appears to me as central to much of this work and what should appeal to historians is the primacy of practice, performance and time. To take one example, historians, and many others as well, choose, for instance, between writing about people or things. When the choice is people, things seldom appear: when the choice is things, then the problem of agency pops up, often solved (or thought to be solved) by resorting to the principle that things only have meaning when used by people. This is, of course, analytically asymmetrical, but most historians would not give it a second thought. By contrast, Donna Haraway challenges with the following:

> what counts as human and nonhuman is not given by definition, but only by relation, by engagement in situated, worldly encounters, where boundaries take shape and categories sediment. ... Human and non-human, *all* entities take shape in encounters, in practices; and the actors and partners in encounters are not all human, to say the least. Further, many of these nonhuman partners and actors are not very natural, and certainly not original. And all humans are not the same.
>
> (Haraway 1994: 64–5)

In this passage, Haraway, it seems to me, has in one stroke offered historians an unmissable opportunity to historicize the entire package. Together with her repertoire of the webs of culture studies, feminist, multicultural and antiracist theory, Haraway clears a terrain for a 'new' new cultural history; a cultural history of categorization, of classification or, to put it another way, how we make sense of everything.[36] Following a suggestion from Zygmunt Bauman (1991), this must include not only the anomalies but the practices devised to confront and manage them. Needless to say, an analysis of the management of anomalies must extend to

---

35 I only list here either the most recent – with citations to earlier work – or particularly significant contributions. Strathern 1991; 1995; Latour 1993; 1988; 1994 – for a clear exposition of the ingredients of actor-network theory, in whose construction Latour has played a key role see Law 1992; Haraway 1991; 1992; Pickering 1995.

36 Ludmilla Jordanova has recently made a similar argument concerning the use of the word reproduction in a non-problematized, presentist sense – see Jordanova 1995. Jordanova's essay is a perfect example of how historians can put the brake on runaway presentism by working from the inside – that is, in the historically specific – out.

include non-human actors. Marilyn Strathern (1990 and 1992) does a similar job on the idea of an 'event'. By analysing, or as she puts it, decomposing the event, Strathern confronts how time and identity are constructed through an encounter. Event becomes an analytical category through which relations and definitions become theorized. Bruno Latour (e.g. 1988; 1993) has quite a bit to say about time, about metaphors of time, and about chronology and its construction. But he also makes a powerful argument in favour of the irreducibility of phenomena and the attack on it by analysts. 'The smallest AIDS virus', he writes,

> takes you from sex to the unconscious, then to Africa, tissue cultures, DNA and San Francisco, but the analysts, thinkers, journalists and decision-makers will slice the delicate network traced by the virus for you into tidy compartments where you will find only science, only economy, only social phenomena, only local news, only sentiment, only sex.
>
> (Latour 1993: 2)

In all of his writings, Latour has insisted on following the actors wherever they may take us. This has two main objectives. The first is simply to follow the actors in the same way as a biographer might perform her/his task. The second is much more subtle; that is, to treat the traces left by the actors' movements as constituting the analytical field itself. Rather than prejudging the nature of the analytical project, the researcher allows the subject/object of the study to perform that function.[37] Ironically, this method is superbly suited to a historical ethnography, in which the choice of which actor (human or non-human) is entirely open, in which classifications and categories are not pre-selected. Recently George Marcus (1995) has advocated just such an approach in order to help anthropology out of its commitment to single-sited ethnography.

In a way, the chapter has now come full circle. Anthropology throws a very wide net for its theoretical catch. Getting in on this act allows the historian to be taken into an unexpected landscape. I have been talking about engaging with anthropology, in the key sense of following it as it spins its web. The patterns left behind it, but especially the nodes of greatest density, are what should interest the historian. Slicing through the nodes will reveal areas of inter- and multidisciplinary practice, include those of history itself. As a model discipline, anthropology foregrounds interrelationships between things that appear to be unconnected. Historians should learn to listen to these voices and the echoes in their own practices.

REFERENCES

Abu-Lughod, J. L. (1995) 'The world-system perspective in the construction of economic history', *History and Theory*: 86–98.

Adams, J. W. (1981) 'Consensus, community, and exoticism', *Journal of Interdisciplinary History* 12: 253–65.

---

37 The historian Thomas Hughes has done precisely this in his analysis of electrification, using Thomas Edison as his guide – see Hughes 1983. See also Hughes 1986.

Appadurai, A. (1990) 'Disjuncture and difference in the global cultural economy', *Public Culture* 2: 1–24.
—— (ed.) (1993) *The Social Life of Things*, Cambridge.
Appleby, J., Hunt, L. and Jacob, M. (1994) *Telling the Truth about History*, New York.
Barnes, D. S. (1995) *The Making of a Social Disease: Tuberculosis in Nineteenth-Century France*, Berkeley.
Bates, B. (1992) *Bargaining for Life: A Social History of Tuberculosis, 1876–1938*, Philadelphia.
Bauman, Z. (1991) *Modernity and Ambivalence*, Cambridge.
Berlanstein, L. R. (ed.) (1993) *Rethinking Labor History*, Urbana.
Biersack, A. (1989) 'Local knowledge, local history', in L. Hunt (ed.) *The New Cultural History*, Berkeley.
Bijker, W. E. (1995) 'Sociohistorical technology studies', in S. Jasanoff, G. E. Markle, J. C. Petersen and T. Pinch (eds) *Handbook of Science and Technology Studies*, Thousand Oaks, CA.
Bourdieu, P. (1978) *Outline of a Theory of Practice*, Cambridge.
Breward, C. (1995) *The Culture of Fashion: A New History of Fashionable Dress*, Manchester.
Brewer, J. and Porter, R. (eds) (1993) *Consumption and the World of Goods*, London.
Burke, P. (1987) *The Historical Anthropology of Early Modern Italy: Essays on Perception and Communication*, Cambridge.
—— (ed.) (1991a) *New Perspectives on Historical Writing*, Cambridge.
Burke, P.(1991b) 'Reflections on the origins of cultural history', in J. H. Pittock and A. Wear (eds) *Interpretation and Cultural History*, Basingstoke.
Camporesi, L. (1989) *Bread of Dreams: Food and Fantasy in Early Modern Europe*, Cambridge.
—— (1992) *Le Goût du chocolat*, Paris.
—— (1993) *The Magic Harvest: Food, Folklore and Society*, Cambridge.
—— (1994) *The Anatomy of the Senses: Natural Symbols in Medieval and Early Modern Italy*, Oxford.
Clark, S. (1983) 'French historians and early modern popular culture', *Past and Present* 100: 62–99.
Clarke, A. E. and Fujimuru, J. H. (eds) (1992) *The Right Tools for the Job: At Work in Twentieth-Century Life Sciences*, Princeton.
Classen, C., Howes, D. and Synnott, A. (1994) *Aroma: The Cultural History of Smell*, London.
Clifford, J. (1988) *The Predicament of Culture: Twentieth-Century Ethnography, Literature and Art*, Cambridge, MA.
—— and Marcus, G. (eds) (1986) *Writing Culture: The Poetics and Politics of Ethnography*, Berkeley.
Code, L. (1995) *Rhetorical Spaces: Essays on Gendered Locations*, New York.
Cohn, B. S. (1980) 'History and anthropology: the state of play', *Comparative Studies in society and History* 22.
—— (1981) 'Toward a rapprochement', *Journal of Interdisciplinary History* 12: 227–52.
Comaroff, J. L. (1982) 'Dialectical systems, history and anthropology: units of study and questions of theory', *Journal of Southern African Studies* 8: 143–72.
—— (1984) 'The closed society and its critics: historical transformations in African ethnography', *American Ethnologist* 11: 571–83.
Comaroff, John and Comaroff, Jean (1992) *Ethnography and the Historical Imagination*, Boulder, CO.
Corbin, A. (1986) *The Foul and the Fragrant: Odor and the French Social Imagination*, New York.
—— (1992) *The Village of Cannibals: Rage and Murder in France, 1870*, Cambridge.

799

Corbin, A. (1994) *The Lure of the Sea: The Discovery of the Seaside in the Western World*, Cambridge.

—— (1995) *Time, Desire and Horror: Towards a History of the Senses*, Cambridge.

Cronon, W. (1992) 'A place for stories: nature, history, and narrative', *Journal of American History* 78: 1347–76.

Darnton, R. (1990) *The Kiss of Lamourette*, London.

Davis, N. Z. (1981) 'The possibilities of the past', *Journal of Interdisciplinary History* 12.

—— (1990) 'The shapes of social history', *Storia della storiografia* 17: 28–34.

—— (1992) 'Toward mixtures and margins', *American Historical Review* 97: 1409–16.

Dear, P. (1995) 'Cultural history of science: an overview with reflections', *Science, Technology, and Human Values* 20: 150–70.

Delaporte, R. (1986) *Disease and Civilization: The Cholera in Paris*, Cambridge, MA.

Demeritt, D. (1994) 'The nature of metaphors in cultural geography and environmental history', *Progress in Human Geography* 18: 163–85.

Dirks, N., Eley, G. and Ortner, S. (eds) (1994) *Culture/History/Power: A Reader in Contemporary Social Theory*, Princeton.

Douglas, M. (1966) *Purity and Danger*, London.

Dreyfus, H. L. and Rabinow, P. (1982) *Michel Foucault: Beyond Structuralism and Hermeneutics*, Chicago.

Edwards, P. N. (1996) *The Closed World: Computers and the Politics of Discourse in Cold War America*, Cambridge, MA.

Eley, G. (1989) 'Labor history, social history, *Alltagsgeschichte*: experience, culture, and the politics of the everyday – a new direction for German social history?', *Journal of Modern History* 61: 297–343.

—— (1993) 'Is all the world a text? From social history to the history of society two decades later', in T. McDonald (ed.) *The Historical Turn in the Human Sciences*, Ann Arbor.

—— and Nield, K. (1995) 'Starting over: the present, the post-modern and the moment of social history', *Social History* 20: 355–64.

Faubion, J. D. (1993) 'History in anthropology', *Annual Review of Anthropology* 22: 35–54.

Feher, M., Naddaff, R. and Tazi, N. (eds) (1989) *Fragments for a History of the Human Body*, New York.

Fischer, C. S. (1992) *America Calling: A Social History of the Telephone to 1940*, Berkeley.

Franklin, S. (1995) 'Science as culture: cultures of science', *Annual Review of Anthropology* 24: 163–84.

Furet, F. (1983) 'Beyond the *Annales*', *Journal of Modern History* 55: 389–410.

Gage, J. (1993) *Colour and Culture: Practice and Meaning from Antiquity to Abstraction*, London.

Gallagher, C. and Laqueur, T. (eds) (1989) *The Making of the Modern Body: Sexuality and Society in the Nineteenth Century*, Berkeley.

Geertz, C. (1973) *The Interpretation of Cultures*, New York.

—— (1990) 'History and anthropology', *New Literary History* 21: 321–35.

Geertz, T. and Geertz, H. (1975) 'An anthropology of religion and magic', *Journal of Interdisciplinary History* 8: 71–109.

Gewertz, D. B. (1983) *Sepik River Societies: A Historical Ethnography of the Chambri and their Neighbors*, New Haven, CT.

Gilman, S. L. (1995) *Picturing Health and Illness: Images of Identity and Difference*, Baltimore.

Ginzburg, C. (1993) 'Microhistory: two or three things that I know about it', *Critical Inquiry* 20: 10–35.

Goodman, J. (1993) *Tobacco in History: The Cultures of Dependence*, London.

—— Lovejoy, P. E. and Sherratt, A. (eds) (1995) *Consuming Habits: Drugs in History and Anthropology*, London.

Greenhalgh, S (1996) 'The social construction of population science: an intellectual, institutional, and political history of twentieth-century demography', *Comparative Studies in History and Society* 38: 26–66.

Grossberg, L., Nelson, C. and Treichler, P. (eds) (1992) *Cultural Studies*, London.

Haraway, D. J. (1991) *Simians, Cyborgs, and Nature: The Reinvention of Nature*, New York.

—— (1992) 'The promises of monsters: a regenerative politics for inappropriate/d others', in Grossberg *et al.* 1992.

—— (1994) 'A game of cat's cradle', *Configurations* 2: 64–5.

Hess, D. J. (1995) *Science and Technology in a Multicultural World: The Cultural Politics of Facts and Artifacts*, New York.

—— and Layne, L. (eds) (1992) *Knowledge and Society*, 9: *The Anthropology of Science and Technology*, Greenwich, CT.

Hirsch, E. and O'Hanlon, M. (eds) (1945) *The Anthropology of Landscape: Perspectives on Place and Space*, Oxford.

Hughes, T. P. (1983) *Networks of Power: Electrification in Western Society, 1880–1930*, Baltimore.

—— (1986) 'The seamless web: technology, science, etcetera, etcetera', *Social Studies of Science* 16: 281–92.

Hunt, L. (ed.) (1989) *The New Cultural History*, Berkeley.

Jordanova, L. (1992) 'Resisting reflexivity', *History of the Human Sciences* 5: 59–67.

—— (1993) 'Gender and the historiography of science', *British Journal for the History of Science* 26: 469–83.

—— (1995) 'Interrogating the concept of reproduction in the eighteenth century', in F. D. Ginsburg and R. Rapp (ed.) *Conceiving the New World Order*, Berkeley.

Joyce, P. (1995) 'The end of social history?', *Social History* 20: 73–9.

—— and Kelly, C. (1991) 'History and post-modernism, I and II', *Past and Present* 133: 204–13.

Kelley, R. (1992) 'Notes on deconstructing the folk', *American Historical Review* 97: 1400–8.

Kertzer, D. I. (1984) 'Anthropology and family history', *Journal of Family History* 9: 201–16.

—— (1986) 'Anthropology and history', *Historical Methods* 19: 119–20.

Kirk, N. (1994) 'History, language, ideas and post-modernism: a materialist view', *Social History* 19.

Laqueur, T. (1990) *Making Sex: Body and Gender from the Greeks to Freud*, Cambridge, MA.

Latour, B. (1988) *The Pasteurization of France*, Cambridge, MA.

—— (1993) *We Have Never Been Modern*, Cambridge, MA.

—— (1994) 'Pragmatogonies: a mythical account of how humans and nonhumans swap properties', *American Behavioral Scientist* 37: 791–808.

Law, J. (1992) 'Notes on the theory of the actor-network: ordering, strategy, and heterogeneity', *Systems Practice* 5: 379–93.

Lears, T. J. (1985) 'The concept of cultural hegemony', *American Historical Review* 90: 567–93.

—— (1992) 'Making fun of popular culture', *American Historical Review* 97: 1417–26.

—— (1994) *Fables of Abundance: A Cultural History of Advertising in America*, New York.

Levi, G. (1991) 'On microhistory', in Burke 1991a.

Levine, L. W. (1992a) 'The folklore of industrial society, popular culture and its audience', *American Historical Review* 97: 1369–99.

—— (1992b) 'Levine responds', *American Historical Review* 97: 1427–30.

—— (1993) *Unpredictable Past: Explorations in American Cultural History*, New York.

Lock, M. (1993) 'Cultivating the body: anthropology and epistemologies of bodily practice and knowledge', *Annual Review of Anthropology* 22: 133–55.

McCrum, A. (1995) 'Theories, methods and concepts in social and cultural history – report on the social history society conference, York', *International Labor and Working-Class History* 48: 165–7.

McEvoy, A. F. (1995) 'Working environments: an ecological approach to industrial health and safety', *Technology and Culture* 36 (Supplement): S145–72.

MacKenzie, D. and Wajcman, J. (eds) (1985) *The Social Shaping of Technology*, Milton Keynes.

Mainardi, P. (1995) 'Impertinent questions (issues surrounding and arising from research on sensitive subjects in French cultural history)', *French Historical Studies* 19: 165–7.

Marcus, G. E. (1995) 'Ethnography in/of the world system: the emergence of multi-sited ethnography', *Annual Review of Anthropology* 24: 95–117.

Martin, E. (1991) 'The egg and the sperm: how science has constructed a romance based on stereotypical male–female roles', *Signs* 16: 485–501.

—— (1992) 'The end of the body?', *American Ethnologist* 19: 120–38.

—— (1994) *Flexible Bodies: Tracking Immunity in American Culture from the Days of Polio to the Age of AIDS*, Boston, MA.

Medick, H. (1987) '"Missionaries in the row boat"? Ethnological ways of knowing as a challenge to social history', *Comparative Studies in Society and History* 29: 76–98.

—— (1994) 'Mikro-Historie', in W. Schulze (ed.) *Sozialgeschichte, Alltagsgeschichte, Mikro-Historie*, Göttingen.

—— (1995) 'Una cultura delle apparenze: i vestiti e i loro colori a Laichingen (1750–1820)', *Quaderni Storici* 89: 515–37.

Megill, A. (ed.) (1994) *Rethinking Objectivity*, Durham, NC.

Meikle, J. L. (1995) *American Plastic: A Cultural History*, New Brunswick, NJ.

Mennell, S. (1985) *All Manners of Food: Eating and Taste in England and France from the Middle Ages to the Present*, Oxford.

—— Murcott, A. and Otterloo, A. H. van (1992) 'The sociology of food: eating, diet and culture', *Current Sociology* 40: special number, issue 2.

Merchant, C. (1995) *Earthcare: Women and the Environment*, New York.

Messer-Davidow, E., Shumway, D. R. and Sylvan, D. J. (eds) (1993) *Knowledges: Historical and Critical Studies in Disciplinarity*, Charlottesville, VA.

Miller, A. H. (1995) 'Prosecuting arguments: the uncanny and cynicism in cultural history', *Cultural Critique* 29: 163–82.

Miller, D. (1995) 'Consumption and commodities', *Annual Review of Anthropology* 24: 141–61.

Mintz, S. (1985) *Sweetness and Power: The Place of Sugar in Modern History*, New York.

—— (1993) 'The changing role of foods in the study of consumption', in Brewer and Porter 1993.

Nelson, J. A. (1996) *Feminism, Objectivity and Economics*, London.

Nye, D. E. (1990) *Electrifying America: Social Meanings of a New Technology*, Cambridge, MA.

Ortner, S. (1984) 'Theory in anthropology since the sixties', *Comparative Studies in Society and History* 26: 126–66.

—— (1989) *High Religion: A Cultural and Political History of Sherpha Buddhism*, Princeton.

—— (1995) 'Resistance and ethnographic refusal', *Comparative Studies in Society and History* 37: 173–93.

Pastoreau, M. (1987) 'Vers une histoire de la couleur bleu', *Sublime indigo*, catalogue of an exhibition held at the Musée de Marseilles, Fribourg.

—— (1988) *Couleurs, images, symboles: études d'histoire et d'anthropologie*, Paris.

Patterson, J. T. (1987) *The Dread Disease: Cancer and Modern American Culture*, Cambridge, MA.

Perrot, P. (1994) *Fashioning the Bourgeoisie: A History of Clothing in the Nineteenth Century*, Princeton.

Petroski, H. (1993) *The Pencil*, New York.

Pfaffenberger, B. (1988) 'Fetishized objects and humanised nature: towards an anthropology of technology', *Man* 23: 236–52.

—— (1992) 'Social anthropology of technology', *Annual Review of Anthropology* 21: 491–516.

Pickering, A. (1995) *The Mangle of Practice: Time, Agency, and Science*, Chicago.

Polier, N. and Roseberry, W. (1989) '*Tristes tropes*: post-modern anthropologists encounter the other and discover themselves', *Economy and Society* 18: 245–64.

Rabinbach, A. (1990) *The Human Motor: Energy, Fatigue, and the Origins of Modernity*, New York.

Rabinow, (1986) 'Representations are social facts: modernity and post-modernity in anthropology', in Clifford and Marcus 1986.

Rancière, J. (1989) *The Nights of Labor: The Worker's Dream in Nineteenth-Century France*, Philadelphia.

Rappaport, R. (1979) *Ecology, Meaning and Religion*, Berkeley.

Reddy, W. M. (1992) 'Postmodernism and the public sphere: implications for an historical ethnography', *Cultural Anthropology* 7: 135–68.

Reid, D. (1991) *Paris Sewers and Sewermen: Realities and Representations*, Cambridge, MA.

—— (1993) 'Reflections on labor history and language', Berlanstein 1993.

Revel, J. (1994) 'Microanalisi e costruzione del sociale', *Quaderni Storici* 29: 549–75.

Roche, D. (1994) *The Culture of Clothing: Dress and Fashion in the Ancien Régime*, Cambridge.

Ronell, A. (1989) *The Telephone Book*, Lincoln, NE.

Rosaldo, R. (1980) *Ilongot Headhunting, 1883–1974*, Stanford.

—— (1986) 'From the door of his tent: the fieldworker and the inquisitor', in Clifford and Marcus 1986.

—— (1990) 'Response to Geertz', *New Literary History* 21: 337–41.

Roseberry, W. (1989a) *Anthropologies and Histories: Essays in Culture, History, and Political Economy*, New Brunswick, NJ.

—— (1989b) 'Balinese cockfights and the seduction of anthropology', in Roseberry 1989a. (First published in *Social Research* 49 (1982): 1013–28.)

—— (1992) 'Multiculturalism and the challenge of anthropology', *Social Research* 59: 841–58.

—— (1996) 'The unbearable lightness of anthropology', *Radical History Review* 65: 5–25.

Rosenhaft, E. (1987) 'History, anthropology, and the study of everyday life. A review article', *Comparative Studies in Society and History* 29: 99–105.

Ross, K. (1995) *Fast Cars, Clean Bodies: Decolonization and the Reordering of French Culture*, Cambridge, MA.

Rothman, S. M. (1994) *Living in the Shadow of Death: Tuberculosis and the Social Experience of Illness in American History*, New York.

Rouse, J. (1992) 'What are cultural studies of scientific knowledge?', *Configurations* 1: 1–22.

Rutman, D. B. (1986) 'History and anthropology: Clio's dalliances', *Historical Methods* 19.

Sahlins, M. (1976) 'Color and culture', *Semiotica* 16: 1–22.

—— (1981) *Historical Metaphors and Mythical Realities: Structure in the Early History of the Sandwich Islands Kingdom*, Ann Arbor.

—— (1985) *Islands of History*, Chicago.

—— (1993) 'Goodbye to *Tristes Tropes*: ethnography in the context of modern world history', *Journal of Modern History* 65: 1–25.

Saunders, B. (1995) 'Disinterring *Basic Color Terms*: a study in the mystique of cognitivism', *History of the Human Sciences* 8: 19–38.

Schama, S. (1995) *Landscape and Memory*, New York.

Schapera, I. (1962) 'Should anthropologists be historians?', *Journal of the Royal Anthropological Institute* 92: 143–56.

Schivelbusch, W. (1988) *Disenchanted Night: The Industrialization of Light in the Nineteenth Century*, Berkeley.

Schieffelin, E. L. and Crittenden, R. (1991) *Like People You See in a Dream*, Stanford.

Schneider, J. (1987) 'The anthropology of cloth', *Annual Review of Anthropology* 16: 409–48.

Schwartz, S. B. (ed.) (1994) *Implicit Understandings: Observing, Reporting, and Reflecting on the Encounters between Europeans and Other Peoples in the Early Modern Era*, Cambridge.

Scott, J. (1991) 'The evidence of experience', *Critical Inquiry* 17: 773–97.

Scranton, P. (1945) 'Determinism and indeterminacy in the history of technology', *Technology and Culture* 36 (Supplement): S31–S52.

Sennett, R. (1994) *Flesh and Stone: The Body and the City in Western Civilization*, New York.

Sewell, W. H. (1992) 'A theory of structure: duality, agency, and transformation', *American Journal of Sociology* 98: 1–29.

Smith, M. G. (1962) 'History and social anthropology', *Journal of the Royal Anthropological Society* 92: 73–85.

Steedman, C. (1992) 'Culture, cultural studies, and the historians', in Grossberg *et al.* 1992.

Stone, L. (1977) 'History and the social sciences in the twentieth century', in C. Delzell (ed.) *The Future of History*, Nashville, TN.

—— (1979) 'The revival of narrative: reflections on a new old history', *Past and Present* 85: 3–24.

—— (1991) 'History and post-modernism', *Past and Present* 131: 217–18.

—— and Spiegel, G. M. (1992) 'History and post-modernism, III and IV', *Past and Present* 135: 189–208.

Strathern, M. (1990) 'Artefacts of history: events and the interpretation of images', in J. Siikala (ed.) *Culture and History in the Pacific*, Helsinki.

—— (1991) *Partial Connections*, Savage, MD.

—— (1992) 'The decomposition of an event', *Current Anthropology* 7: 244–54.

—— (1995) 'Nostalgia and the new genetics', in D. Battaglia (ed.) *Rhetorics of Self-making*, Berkeley.

Susman, W. J. (1984) *Culture as History: The Transformation of American Society in the Twentieth Century*, New York.

Thomas, K. (1963) 'History and anthropology', *Past and Present* 24: 3–24.

Thompson, E. P. (1972) 'Anthropology and the discipline of historical context', *Midland History* 1.

Traweek, S. (1993) 'An introduction to cultural and social studies of sciences and technologies', *Culture, Medicine and Psychiatry* 17: 3–25.

Turner, T. (1991) 'Representing, resisting, rethinking: historical transformations of Kayapo culture and anthropological consciousness', in G. W. Stocking (ed.) *Post-colonial Situations: The History of Anthropology*, vol. 7, Madison.

Turner, V. (1967) *The Forests of Symbols: Aspects of Ndembu Ritual*, Ithaca, NY.

Wallace, A. F. C. (1996) *Rockdale: The Growth of an American Village in the Early Industrial Revolution*, Norwalk, CT.

Walters, R. G. (1980) 'Signs of the times: Clifford Geertz and historians', *Social Research* 47: 537–56.

Weiner, A. B. and Schneider, J. (eds) (1989) *Cloth and Human Experience*, Washington, DC.

Wohlfarth, I. (1986) 'Et cetera? The historian as *chiffonier*', *New German Critique* 39: 143–68.

32

ARCHAEOLOGY AND HISTORIOGRAPHY

Guy Halsall

INTRODUCTION

Archaeology is the study of the human past through its material remains,[1] yet even this straightforward definition produces problems. Are not manuscripts and books material remains? Are other objects, such as inscriptions or coins, which bear writing, the province of the archaeologist or the documentary historian? We might hive these classes of material off into the disciplines of epigraphy or numismatics, but the problem remains, with, for example, graffiti on pottery, and so on. Acknowledging these blurred areas leaves us with an admittedly problematic and provisional, but nevertheless useful, definition of archaeology as the study of the unwritten, material records of the human past; it also, of course, raises the question of the interrelationship between the disciplines of documentary history and archaeology.

The two are separate disciplines, in that the types of evidence dealt with, written records on the one hand and excavated data on the other, require, at a technical level at least, the acquisition of different skills for their evaluation and interpretation. Nevertheless, as they are both concerned with the human past, archaeology and documentary history ought to be natural allies. However, over recent decades there has been something of an estrangement between the two. In some areas of historical writing, like the early medieval period, where the volume of archaeological work and the comparative absence of documentary data highlight the problems of integrating written and excavated evidence, there is a disturbing lack of dialogue between archaeologists and historians. To give one current example: within the University of London a regular Wednesday-evening 'earlier medieval' seminar meets at the Institute of Historical Research, while on Thursday evenings, a few

---

1 For introductions to archaeology, see Rahtz 1991; Greene 1995; Bahn and Renfrew 1991. Bahn 1989 is extremely entertaining and contains a surprising amount of serious information.

hundred yards away at the Institute of Archaeology, the 'Postgraduate Seminar in Medieval Archaeology' convenes. Yet, in spite of the chronological, geographical and thematic overlaps between the two seminars, the personnel in attendance are almost entirely different. This lack of dialogue is particularly ironic as most schools of archaeological theory currently stress the importance of the close interrelationship between history and archaeology.

This chapter will not be concerned with the methodologies of archaeological fieldwork which, it is worth stating, deals with a much wider range of activities than excavation alone, including aerial prospection, field-walking, and methods of site evaluation and survey such as electronic 'geophysical' technology, enabling subsurface remains to be charted to some extent without excavation.[2] It should also be made clear that archaeological theory and practice do not stand as opposed entities. The theory-bound nature of even the most apparently mundane aspects of archaeological fieldwork have been known for some time, even if there often remains a self-conscious opposition between 'dirt archaeologists' and 'theorists'. In recent years, the lack of practical integration of theory and fieldwork has preoccupied several leading archaeologists (see Hodder 1992; Carver 1993; Bradley 1993; Barrett 1995).

Nor is it the concern of this chapter to provide an introduction to specialist scientific aspects of archaeological enquiry such as metallurgical, ceramic or petrological analyses, scientific dating methods, palaeobotany, or the study of animal or human bone (see Aitken 1990). Instead the chapter will provide a guide, in rough chronological order, to the ways in which archaeologists have approached the past.[3] The main focus will be that of the present writer's research, the immediately post-Roman period of the Middle Ages.[4]

CULTURE-HISTORY

The concept of an archaeological 'culture', 'certain types of remains – pots, implements, ornaments, burial rites, house forms – constantly recurring together' (Childe 1929: v–vi), emerged at the end of the nineteenth century. This led to narratives of the succession of such cultures within a particular area, or the movement of 'cultures' from one area to another. This ensuing 'Culture-History' (not to be confused with cultural history!) is today something of a dirty term in

2 On excavation, the best introduction remains Barker 1993. For fieldwalking, see Fasham, *et al.* 1980, and for 'geophysics', see Clark 1990.

3 For an excellent history of archaeology, the reader is referred to Trigger 1989. See also Renfrew and Bahn 1991: 17–40; Daniel 1967.

4 I reject absolutely the assertion that 'historical archaeology' means the archaeology of the modern world, recently made by Orser 1996: 26–8. Orser's view appears to be that 'history' only began when the New and Third Worlds came into contact with the Old. Although intended, laudably, to counter Eurocentrism, this formulation seems to me to do precisely the opposite. It also, of course, makes the title of his book tautological! Here, the tight schedule required for the production of this chapter has forced me to ignore historical archaeology outside Europe. This is a significant lacuna. *Mea culpa.*

archaeological circles. As examples of Culture-History in the historical period we might note the excavations of Sir Mortimer Wheeler which aimed at elucidating and illustrating the conquest of Britain by the Romans, best known at Maiden Castle. Similarly we might cite the use made of archaeological material to track the invasion and settlement of the 'Angles, Saxons and Jutes',[5] and the similar plotting of the migration of Franks into Gaul from the distribution of grave-types and their associated forms of artefact.[6] Change in archaeological culture was usually interpreted as resulting from either 'diffusion' (the spread of cultural forms but not necessarily of people) or migration (where the appearance of new cultural forms in a region represented the immigration of new people 'bearing' that culture), or even invasion. It was within the Culture-History paradigm that most classical and biblical archaeology operated, attempting to link sites into a particular political-historical narrative. As one example of this, and of how it affected the publication of fieldwork, we might cite the example of the French Romanist Jean-Jacques Hatt, who reduced most of the sites upon which he worked to unilinear sequences of 'layers', each identified with a particular historical phase, and punctuated by burnt levels which he associated with historically attested 'sacks'.[7]

Culture-History, by presenting the possibility of tracing 'peoples' through time, and especially backwards from their first appearance in written records, lent itself to abuse and manipulation in the service of nationalist and racist beliefs, and soon acquired some fairly nasty connotations (Trigger 1989: 148–206, esp. 163–7). The Nazis made much use of the interpretations of Gustaf Kossinna (1858–1931), who argued for the supremacy of the Aryan race and the Germanic origins of Indo-European civilization; whereas Stalin (until 1950) employed the ideas of Nikolai Marr (1865–1934), which, in total opposition to Kossinna's migrationism argued that material cultural and even linguistic changes represented internal socio-political change, thus allowing Slavic dominance in eastern Europe to be projected far back into prehistory.

FUNCTIONALISM

In the 1930s and particularly after the Second World War, with the ensuing awareness of the horrific extent to which ideas of 'national characteristics' could be pushed, Culture-History fell out of vogue, to be replaced, gradually and far from universally, by functionalist archaeology.[8] Influenced by structural-functionalist anthropology, such as the (admittedly diverse) work of Malinowski and Radcliffe-Brown, this approach saw 'cultures' as functional systems, wherein internal components served a particular purpose for the maintenance of the whole (whether

---

5 Leeds 1913, which, as has recently been noted, used the concept of an archaeological culture over a decade before its more famous 'introduction' by V. G. Childe: Dark 1995, 5–6.

6 For critique, see James 1979.

7 Hatt's approach can be seen clearly at his excavations near St-Médard, Strasbourg: Hatt 1953.

8 Culture-history in effect remained the dominant paradigm in medieval archaeology until the 1970s.

or not acting towards biological imperatives). Each component of a culture, or social institution, could be explained in terms of its function, rather like the organs of the body. This led to environmental determinism; cultural components functioned in an adaptive way to cope with the natural environment, and could thus be explained in terms of the latter. To understand the function of a given element of the archaeological record, it needed to be interpreted in relation to other parts of that 'culture'. Thus developed the archaeological subdiscipline of environmental archaeology and the study of settlement patterns, increasingly using aerial archaeology, some practitioners of which had noticed the potential of aerial photographs during wartime service in the RAF.

Functionalist archaeology could encompass diverse views, such as the later writings of V. Gordon Childe (Childe 1936; 1949; 1951; 1956a; 1956b; 1958; on Childe himself, see Trigger 1980) and the earlier work of Grahame (J. G. D.) Clark (Clark 1932; 1939 (3rd edn of 1957 cited here); 1940; 1952; 1954). Whereas Childe's functionalist work began within an economically determinist perspective, he gradually became more interested in social organization, the contradictions inherent in the 'functioning' of society, and eventually the ways in which social evolution was advanced or retarded by the use and control of knowledge. Clark, on the other hand, in opposition to Childe's Marxist views, saw functionalism as meaning that societies operated primarily to maintain stability and their continued existence in their specific environment. Childe's actual archaeological work remained somewhat limited and constrained within the field of typology, but Clark, most famously in his excavation of the Neolithic site of Star Carr in Yorkshire, was one of the pioneers of environmental archaeology.

Another influential outcome of the functionalist phase in western European archaeology was 'Hawkes's ladder' (Hawkes 1954), a hierarchy according to the difficulty with which archaeologists could investigate topics without recourse to historical texts or oral tradition (Clark, for example, made much use of folklore). Technology, according to Hawkes, was the easiest subject to examine archaeologically, followed by economics; socio-political organization was at best recoverable with difficulty, and religious belief more or less impossible to study. This provided some justification for functionalist archaeology's major concern with the environment, settlement patterns, technology and economy, the latter three of which were seen as very heavily constrained by the first. Environmental archaeology within the functionalist perspective produced works of overtly environmentally, or ecologically, determinist character, such as that of Claudio Vita-Finzi and Eric Higgs. During this period, advances in scientific dating, most notably in carbon (C^{14}) dating, produced a huge revision of prehistoric chronology, which was dramatically lengthened.[9] For all its potential diversity, however, functionalist archaeology still relied, like Culture-Historical archaeology, on factors such as diffusion and migration for much of its explanation of change.

9   On which see Renfrew 1973.

THE NEW ARCHAEOLOGY (OR PROCESSUAL ARCHAEOLOGY)

In the 1960s archaeology significantly altered the way in which it conceived of itself as a discipline. These developments are usually bracketed together as 'the New Archaeology'. This was not the first time a 'New Archaeology' had been proposed (see e.g. Wissler 1917; Caldwell 1959), but the name has become fixed to the movement generally associated with the American archaeologist Lewis Binford.[10] Binford believed that archaeology should recover general aspects of human behaviour, and strive to be a science. Binford resolutely opposed what he conceived of as the 'particularist' tendencies of history (his view of which discipline was decidedly bizarre and outmoded). Instead, archaeology should be concerned with looking for cross-cultural generalities, and the proposal, testing and establishment of general laws (nomothetic interpretations). Explanation was thus equated with prediction.

Binford conceived of society as a functioning system, responding adaptively to its natural environment. This led to a certain ecological or environmental determinism, and a view of social relations as essentially tending towards stasis. Again change was viewed as produced by agents external to the system. Such change could, however, only really be understood in relation to the effects it had on the workings of the system, so internal relationships had to be studied. This in turn meant that one had to study the whole of a social system, and all its remains. Binford was uninterested in diffusion, and the New Archaeological approach to change has been termed 'neo-evolutionism'. Although humans were capable of adapting to such things as environmental change (adaptation), the forces driving change were largely non-human.

The English archaeologist David (D. L.) Clarke came to similar conclusions as Binford at about the same time.[11] Clarke, however, was influenced more by the New Geography and less opposed to the use of history. Clarke, like Binford, believed that archaeology needed to formulate its own technical terms to describe and analyse its data more efficiently. This led to a growth of what traditional archaeologists, and specialists in other disciplines, regarded as excessive jargon. Reading his and Binford's early work can be hard work, and the posthumous second edition of *Analytical Archaeology* carried out by R. Chapman has even been termed 'the Chapman translation'. One of Clarke's principal interests, arising naturally from the approaches outlined, was in the spatial distribution and

---

10   Binford's early work is collected in Binford 1972. Within this volume, his essays 'Archaeology as anthropology' (originally *American Anthropology* 28 (1962: 217–25), 'Smudge-pits and hide smoking: the use of analogy in archaeological reasoning' (originally *American Antiquity* 32 (1967): 1–12) and 'Some comments on historical versus processual archaeology' (originally *South-Western Journal of Anthropology* 24 (1968): 267–75) are of particular importance. See also Binford 1983 and 1989.

11   As has often been noted, Clarke's influential *Analytical Archaeology* (1968) appeared in its first edition in the same year as Binford's equally important edited volume (with S. R Binford), *New Perspectives in Archaeology* (1968). Clarke died tragically early, and his essays are collected in Clarke 1979. Particularly important essays by Clarke were Clarke 1972 and Clarke 1973.

relationships observed within the archaeological record, and the means by which such patterns could be tested for statistical relevance, predicted and explained. This was followed up in the early work of his student, Ian Hodder (Clarke 1977; Hodder and Orton 1976).

New Archaeology rapidly, and unsurprisingly, became interested in 'systems theory' to study of the workings of cultural systems, using models derived from geography and biology. This allowed New Archaeologists, rather than seeing systems as simply reproducing themselves in a straightforward functional way, to examine the relationships between different elements of the system and seek processes which tended towards change, which they termed structure-elaborating, or morphogenetic, processes, as well as those which tended towards stability (homeostatic processes). This was accomplished through the use of the idea of feedback. When change occurred in one element of the system it would produce related change, adaptation or feedback in the others. Negative feedback by counteracting the initial change, would tend towards stability, whereas positive feedback, by amplifying it, would produce greater and irreversible change.

Systems theory produced two further developments. The first was the use of Immanuel Wallerstein's (1974; see Champion 1989) notion of the world system, and the second was the idea of 'peer-polity interaction', developed by Colin Renfrew (see Renfrew and Cherry 1986). Whereas the first developed ideas of 'core and periphery' in the interrelationship of different cultures, the second theory was designed to explain comparable changes in different, more or less equal, cultures. In a system of units of roughly equal socio-political and economic power or geographical extent (peer polities), changes in one unit would, through processes of emulation and competition (agents of which being warfare, competitive monumental architecture and so on), lead to comparable and more or less contemporary change in the other units.

New archaeologists were interested in long-term developments, such as the development of social organization, or the collapse of complex societies. These they perceived as processes which could be studied in general cross-cultural perspective (hence this approach is generally now referred to as processual archaeology). They made use of theories of the 'stages' of social development, such as the progression from band, through chiefdom, to state (see e.g. Sahlins and Service 1960; Service 1962; Fried 1967; Claessen and Skalnik 1978).

In order to test the hypotheses proposed and arrive at the desired general laws of human behaviour, various archaeologists proposed different means of relating archaeological remains to actual human behaviour. Binford argued that archaeologists tend to 'confirm the consequent',[12] by which he meant that since the archaeological record does not speak for itself, and thus we approach the archaeological record with particular views in mind (the 'feudal' nature of Maya economics, for example), any testing of these ideas against the data will simply tend

---

12   Binford 1981: Though the quote is comparatively late within Binford's *œuvre*, the idea can be traced back through his writings to the 1960s. See also Sabloff *et al.* 1987.

to reaffirm them. Binford instead argued for the use of 'middle-range theories' from outside archaeology, which would demonstrate general aspects of human behaviour. These would then be used to find such regularities within the data, and act as a kind of bench-mark against which to judge interpretations. These external theories would come from, for example, ethnographic observation or the use of written records which reveal such general observations. These provide externally validated laws, and archaeological data can be examined with them in mind. Thus Binford stimulated 'middle-range research'.[13]

With the same general goal in mind, Clarke (1973) defined five types or levels of theory in which archaeologists were engaged: pre-depositional and depositional theory, dealing with the human and natural processes which led to the deposition and initial patterning of archaeological data; post-depositional theory, concerned with what happened to this data once it was in the ground, how processes of decay and disturbance would affect the archaeological record; retrieval theory, simply enough theorization of excavation, sampling procedures and so on; analytical theory, covering the treatment of the material recovered, its classification, experimental studies, etc. and interpretative theory, which involves the recovery of the original social, behavioural, environmental patterns and activities (bringing us full circle to the processes studied by pre-depositional theory). Clarke argued that archaeology had to develop adequately scientific theory to deal with all these levels. Otherwise, he argued, archaeology would remain 'an irresponsible art form' (Clarke 1973: 16).

In the United States, Michael Schiffer (1976) argued that archaeologists would have to understand certain processes involved in the formation of archaeological sites, which give the data their observable patterning. First, one identified 'correlates', relating artefacts and patterns to specific human activities, or behaviour (so a certain patterning of material will be the correlate of gift exchange, for example). Then one had to study the ways in which this material record had been altered by two kinds of process. The first he called 'C-transforms', 'cultural transformation processes' or the means by which the archaeological record is formed in the course of normal human activities, loss patterns and so forth, but also things which would come under Clarke's heading of post-depositional theory, such as subsequent ploughing. N-transforms, on the other hand, 'non-cultural transformation processes', determined how the material record would be altered by its relationships with the natural environment. If archaeologists could reconstruct these transformation processes and eliminate them, they would arrive at a 'reality' of the material record, and the basis for its interpretation.

Seen in the light of much of the functionalist archaeology of the mid-twentieth century, especially that of Grahame Clark, or similar work in the United States, much of the New Archaeology does not look particularly revolutionary, or even new. Binford was, however, reacting not so much to functionalist archaeologists

---

13 See Binford 1978, which produced comparative data on discard patterns around hearths, and so on, for testing against palaeolithic evidence of hunter-gatherer communities.

such as Clark as to the Culture-Historical archaeology which predominated over much of the United States. Clarke, as a student of Clark, proposed a way forward from earlier functionalism and especially away from the text-dominated or art-historical archaeology which was still to be found all too often in Britain. New Archaeology did add to earlier paradigms the concern with historical processes, the quest for general laws, and the attempts to make archaeology a more rigorous and scientific discipline. The latter concern brought the introduction of mathematical formulas, computerized techniques of statistical evaluation and modelling, and spatial analysis. It also produced a more formal concern with the processes of site formation and the problems of archaeological sampling. These ideas together produced the concept of the 'research design', which should be set up to evaluate current knowledge of a subject, and establish sampling procedures at various levels, theoretical frameworks and the questions to be asked, before any fieldwork was undertaken.

New Archaeology was slow to catch on in historically documented periods, although spatial analysis of the distribution of Roman towns was undertaken by Hodder (Hodder and Hassall 1971). It took even longer to make an impact on medieval archaeology. In 1982, at the twenty-fifth anniversary conference of the Society for Medieval Archaeology, Philip Rahtz proposed a 'New Medieval Archaeology' (published as Rahtz 1983). In the same year, Richard Hodges published a lengthy paper which similarly argued for the application of the methods and theory of New Archaeology to medieval data. (Hodges 1982b). Ironically, by 1982, when New Archaeology found its way on to the stage of medieval studies,[14] it was already beginning to be rejected by a significant body of theoretical archaeologists.

AFTER THE NEW ARCHAEOLOGY: CURRENT APPROACHES[15]

'New Archaeology' always had its critics, and these were by no means all the traditionalists and reactionaries which writers like Binford liked to portray them as being. As early as 1974, an anthropologist, R. Adams, had, quite rightly, criticized some New Archaeologists for their 'behaviouristic gradualism and biological reductionism' (Adams 1974: 249), and for failing to recognize the sometimes decisive 'conscious diversity of actions' (ibid.). This provided a foretaste of what was to come in the 1980s. Ironically, Ian Hodder, pioneer of spatial analysis and student of David Clarke, spearheaded the reaction against the New Archaeology (Hodder 1982a; 1982b; 1986; 1992).

14 For major processual works in the historical period, we may cite Rondsborg 1980; 1991; Hodges 1982a.

15 For an unusually reader-friendly overview of current theoretical archaeological approaches to diverse subjects, the reader is referred to Dark 1995. A degree of caution is, however, necessary, as the conceptualization of various topics becomes increasingly vague as the book progresses. For example, the effective difference between his economic categories of 'feudalism' and 'render-systems' (pp. 139–40) will remain quite opaque to any medievalist.

A number of general criticisms of New Archaeology can be made.[16] Prominent among these are its removal of the individual from history. Human beings simply responded in predictable ways to 'system needs', or to changes beyond their control; social systems were essentially stable; change brought about by conflict within the 'system' was ignored.[17] The issue of ideology was almost entirely absent from processual archaeology. New Archaeology was excessively functional; from components of a 'social system' down to individual artefact forms, everything was explained in terms of its function; there was little symbolism in New Archaeology, and that which there was saw symbolism, predictably, as functional.[18] The idea that societies could be divided up into neatly compartmentalized interrelating 'boxes', is also questionable. Gordon Childe had long before said that humans reacted only to their *perception* of environmental needs, and this point was repeated in opposition to the environmentally or ecologically determinist aspects of processual archaeology. Middle-range theory and its analogues also faced a barrage of criticism. Schiffer's C- and N-transforms were attacked by Binford, but his own ideas of externally verifiable general aspects of human behaviour were rightly condemned as being every bit as theoretically contingent as any other aspect of archaeology. Further-more, the value of ethnographic analogies was called into question, particularly where the cultures under study, rather than being in some pristine state, could be shown to owe much of their character to their relationship to other types of society, or to their contacts with the Western world. The anti-historicism of New Archaeology also caused problems, and even processualists condemned refusals to deal with written data in historic periods. Perhaps most importantly of all, the New Archaeology was still only really interested in the lower rungs of 'Hawkes' ladder'.

Response to these criticisms of New Archaeology produced an alternative and antithetical theoretical framework and a development within the processual paradigm. The first of these is what is known as post-processual archaeology. Rather than being a closely defined and more or less unified 'school' of thought, post-processual archaeology is essentially defined simply by its opposition to processual archaeology, in accordance with the points made above.[19] The starting-point of post-processualism is that material culture is actively and meaningfully constituted. It creates as well as reflects social relationships, so that, for example, the particular costume deemed appropriate for a young woman does not simply reflect that social category (of 'young woman'), but also actively creates it, in that the mental image of someone of that age and gender will largely be conditioned by that costume which symbolizes it. People

---

16   For a lengthy statement, see Courbin 1988. Whilst Courbin's criticisms of New Archaeology are entirely convincing, his subsequent proposal that archaeology return to a sole concern with the collection of facts is reactionary and theoretically untenable. See the review of his work by Moreland 1991b.

17   For the reactionary political undertones of this stance, see Trigger 1989: 312–15, 322–6.

18   Binford acknowledged the 'ideotechnic' aspect (note the term!) of artefacts; Binford 1965.

19   For the essential statements of post-processualism, see Hodder 1982a; 1982b; 1986; 1992; Shanks and Tilley 1987; 1991.

use material culture actively within social relations, so that material culture can be read as a discourse. However, to understand this symbolism we need always to place it in context. Not only might different symbols mean different things in different cultures, but their meanings might change from one context to another even within the same society. The often-cited example of this would be the priest's costume, which is white in some circumstances, symbolizing good : bad/white : black oppositions, yet black in others. At the same time, however, post-processual archaeologists argued that objects were polysemic (had more than one meaning) or even deliberately ambiguous, within contexts as well as between them. One might be able to arrive at one meaning, perhaps even the dominant meaning, by examining the context within which a material cultural symbol was found, but one should always remember that other people might have read the symbol in a quite different way.

These statements were also the product of a particular view of society and of social change. Post-processualism reacted against the slow, long-term systemic change envisaged by the New Archaeology, seeing social change instead as dynamic. Social structure could be seen as a mental image of rules or norms, or appropriate codes of behaviour, and of the ways in which material culture was used in these. This kind of 'structure', while in some ways inhibiting action, nevertheless also enables it, and individuals can play *with* these rules as well as within them. Social structure thus never quite reproduces itself exactly. These theories drew heavily upon the anthropologist Pierre Bourdieu's (1977) notion of the 'habitus', the Marxist sociologist Anthony Giddens's (1984) concept of structuration and Noam Chomsky's 'generative grammar'.

Some post-processualists, such as Hodder (1986: 1; 1982a: 1–16, repr. in 1992: 92–121), have been quite open in stressing the conscious 'steps backwards' involved in post-processual archaeology, reviving the importance of historical context (and thus even of Culture-History), and several of Gordon Childe's views. Many of their ideas were based initially upon a reading of structuralist thought, especially from linguistics (e.g. Saussure) and anthropology (e.g. Lévi-Strauss). The flaws in structuralist theory were rapidly taken on board, so that post-processualists quickly became poststructuralists too. Given that processualists were also interested in structuralism (the comparisons between 'structure' and 'system' are obvious), structuralism and the critiques of it provided the bridge from processualism to post-processualism. The influence of Marxist thought, particularly that of the 'Frankfurt school' (e.g. Althusser) was also to be seen in post-processualism, although the Marx-influenced rather than Marxist theory behind much of post-processualism has led other Marxist archaeologists to describe it as 'ersatz Marxism' (Trigger 1989: 369). The other major source of theory drawn upon by post-processualists was that of literary criticism and 'critical theory'. In the early days of post-processual archaeology, thinkers such as Foucault, Barthes and Derrida came to be cited almost as often as archaeological writers.[20]

---

20 For introductions to structuralist and post-structuralist writers, and applications of their thinking to material culture, see Tilley (ed.) 1990.

Post-processualists rejected absolutely the opposition between data and theory. Following work by Mark Leone (1978; 1982) they argued that interpretations of the past are entirely dependent upon the ideological standpoint and socio-political context of the researcher in question. This led to arguments for a 'plurality' of archaeologies, with each interpretation as valid as the others. This was an attempt to evade the elitism of academic archaeology, to make the subject more democratic, and to try to avoid imposing modern, Western capitalist 'pasts' on other societies. At the same time, in line with some at least of these views, post-processualists proposed that archaeologists take an active political stance, to combat the appropriation of the past by dominant ideologies. Archaeologists should consciously reflect on what they are doing, and use it actively to shape the present. Thus feminist archaeologists have been attracted by the post-processual approach.[21]

Some processualists had come to some similar conclusions about the shortcomings of old-style processualism, a point which radical post-processualists often forgot. This led to the establishment of 'cognitive processualism', which reinstates symbolism, ideology, the active use of material culture, and internal conflict into the study of the past.[22] It is also far more open to the use of written sources than earlier processualist work. Nevertheless, it retains an obsession with long-term process and general laws. Some have claimed that that cognitive processualism represents a new consensus (Bahn and Renfrew 1991: 431–4), although post-processualists have denied both that this 'consensus' owes much to processualism or, indeed, that there is consensus at all (Hodder 1992: 147). The focusing on laws has led to a somewhat fruitless positivist search for laws of the mind. A further development mainly within processualist archaeology has been the (to a historian) rather belated rediscovery of *Annales* school history (Bintliff 1991a). One could say that the *Annales* school shares many features with processual archaeology, not least its inability to cope with historical change. However, post-processualists have also taken up certain *annaliste* ideas about the *longue durée* and *mentalités* (Hodder 1987). Needless to say, historians have been more than a little bemused by this, as they see it, reinvention of the wheel.[23] There still seem, in spite of Renfrew and Bahn's claims for a consensus, to be major differences between cognitive processualists and even 'new' post-processualists.

The term 'new' post-processualists is used because there were developments within this loosely defined body of theorists, or steps backwards from some of the extreme positions adopted in the mid- to late 1980s. The principle line of attack was against the 'disabling relativism' of the 'hard-line' post-processualism of, for example, Shanks and Tilley. This attack was spearheaded by feminist archaeologists, who rightly saw that it was not feasible for post-processualists to argue that

---

21   On feminist archaeology in general, see: Gero and Conkey 1990; Gilchrist 1991; Engelstad 1991. For an application to a historical period, see Gilchrist 1994.

22   The origins of this movement can be traced to Renfrew 1982. For cognitive processual studies in the historical period, see Mytum 1991; Hedeager 1992; Hodges 1989.

23   See reviews of Bintliff 1991a, by Dyer 1992 and by Delano-Smith 1992.

archaeology be used actively in the present and at the same time claim that one reading of the past was as good as any other. If the latter was the case, then chauvinist readings of the past overtly aimed at the subjugation of women would have to be admitted as equally permissible as views of the past designed to empower women. How could archaeologists use their discipline to silence neo-Nazi abuse of the past, other than through the 'naked' use of academic power which post-processualists claimed to oppose? At the same time, the irony of lectures on the evils of elitism and the opening-up of the past to the masses delivered from the high table of Peterhouse, Cambridge, was apparent even to one of their Cambridge school proponents (Hodder 1991). The realization of the impossibility of maintaining both pluralism and a politically active stance led to a reassessment of the early post-processual insistence upon the inextricability of data and theory (see Graves 1991). The difference between 'facts' and the body of data whence facts are selected, to paraphrase E. H. Carr (1987: 10ff.) was realized. Dark (1995: 36) has conveniently referred to this as the difference between data and evidence. Although the evidence we choose to study and cite in our research is entirely contingent upon the researcher, although, in archaeology, the way in which the data is observed, excavated, recorded and (above all) published is heavily dependent upon the theoretical stance of the excavator, and although the formation of the data itself is hardly unbiased, there nevertheless remains a body of data out there, which exists independently of our theoretical viewpoint, whether we choose to study it or not. It has frequently been possible to use data collected for one purpose to study quite different questions and arrive at conclusions entirely alien to the original excava-tor.[24] It ought to be possible to accept or reject hypotheses about the past according to how well they 'fit' that body of data. For example, it is no longer possible to accept ideas linking particular types of weapons in graves to particular social classes, because closer examination of the data simply does not support them (Samson 1987; James 1989). If this were not the case, we would never be surprised in our encounters with history. So, as Hodder (1992: 175) has most recently argued, we are not locked in a hermeneutic vicious circle, but rather our work represents a 'hermeneutic spiral', a dialogue with the past, where our experience of the data shapes our conceptions, as well as being structured by them. There may be no 'right answers', but we can establish that some answers are less wrong than others.

Marxist approaches have to some extent stood to one side of the theoretical approaches outlined above. Marxism has its own theoretical basis and discourse, independent of the discipline of archaeology (see Chapter 36, this volume). It has also, however, been able to adapt in some way or other to each of these trends. Childe was a Marxist who worked within a generally functionalist paradigm. Although Marxist explanations of change were radically different from those of generally conservative processualists, there was something recognizable in pro-

---

24 See, for example, the use of old cemetery data to propose reinterpretations of Frankish social structure which would have never occurred to the excavators of the site in question, in Halsall 1995: chs 3–4. A similar point is made by Bintliff 1991b.

cessualist 'stagist' views of social development for Marxists used to theorizing about sequences of modes of production. Structural functionalism or even systems theory could also be modified to represent contradictions within society, and especially the oppositions between infrastructure and superstructure. Structuralism has been closely bound up with Marxist thinking and post-processual archaeology has very largely been proposed by theorists heavily dependent upon Marxist thought and, in some cases, self-consciously proclaiming their stance to be Marxist, although, as noted, more traditional Marxists have rejected this.[25]

Some overall remarks can be made about archaeological approaches to the past. The first is that the sequence of fashionable paradigms is far more obvious, and paradigmatic changes are accompanied by far more polemic and posturing than appears to be the case in documentary history. Another is that for all the usual disparagement of the previous theoretical fashion, most new approaches in fact owe a substantial amount to their precursors. Referring to archaeology's tendency to borrow often obsolescent ideas from other disciplines Bintliff has written that archaeological theory always 'reappears in clean but borrowed finery'.[26] This borrowed finery is almost always worn over at least some of the garb of previous theory.

RELATIONSHIPS BETWEEN HISTORY AND ARCHAEOLOGY

There is an emerging consensus among archaeologists that closer links with documentary history ought to be forged. Yet, for all these good intentions, there is still far too little meaningful dialogue between historians and archaeologists. The usual situation has been well summed up by Ian Morris:

> [those] who rely mainly on texts and those who rely mainly on archaeological evidence often act as if they were two sides in a competition, and one day an impartial observer will judge whose evidence is the best and who wins the game.
>
> (Morris 1992: 200)

As instances of this 'competitive' attitude we may turn to work on the early medieval era:

> It has been said that the spade cannot lie but it owes this merit in part to the fact that it cannot speak.
>
> (Grierson 1959: 129)

But for the first millennium the written sources are primarily chronicles, biographies, letters and poems. Few wills and charters survive before about 950, and virtually no records of village life. The historian is at an obvious disadvantage. With these personal

---

25 On Marxist archaeology, see Trigger 1989: ch. 6, *passim*, pp. 259–63, 338–47; McGuire 1992. For Marxist archaeology applied to a historical period, see, recently, the two chapters by Steve Roskams in Christie and Loseby 1996.

26 Bintliff 1991b: 275 It should be said that Bintliffs 'discovery' of *Annales* puts him very much in the same category.

sources only at his disposal, it is not surprising that the result commonly amounts to what Colin Renfrew has termed the 'Dark Age myth', ...

(Hodges 1989: 6)[27]

Archaeology can help, at least in terms of the description of the material culture of the Scandinavian societies, but there are strict limits to the types of questions which it is competent to answer.

(Collins 1991: 313)[28]

The roots of the problem lie in archaeology's development as an academic discipline in western Europe. Culture-History, by simply attempting to flesh out, illustrate or extend political historical narratives, and by being conducted, usually, by researchers trained as historians, posed few problems for disciplinary relationships. History was dominant; archaeology was simply auxiliary or ancillary. These attitudes are still to be found today; in the University of London's Institute of Historical Research, archaeology is still classified under 'auxiliary sciences'.[29] Functionalism, by being essentially a prehistorian's approach, and by concentrating on topics such as environment and economy which were not readily confronted through written sources, similarly did not rock the boat.

The problems came with New Archaeology, which, as stated, tried consciously to distance itself from history. Partly this was based upon a rather strange view of documentary history; partly, too, it stemmed from an understandable and justifiable desire by archaeologists to rid their discipline of the tag, 'handmaiden of history' (Hume 1964). New Archaeological polemic, especially in the medieval period, did not help interdisciplinary relations. Picking up on critical reassessments of certain texts (most notably, Dumville 1977), some archaeologists decided that written sources simply had nothing very interesting to say. It was unfortunate for their case that, rather than having sufficient courage in their convictions, or faith in the explanatory power of their evidence, to produce alternative studies entirely drawn from the material data, they often fell back on the written sources whenever they ran into difficulties, especially with issues higher up 'Hawkes's ladder'.[30] Moreover, the use made of such sources was frequently crude, and counter to historians' critical assessments. The perceived jargon of the New Archaeology heightened the

---

27 One wonders if Hodges has actually read many early medieval written sources!

28 Collins's total ignorance of archaeology is best illustrated by the astonishing 'clanger' dropped on n. 47 to p. 323 (note on p. 419), where he claims that no archaeological evidence has ever been found of Viking Dublin, in spite of many documentary references, thus ignoring the major discoveries at Wood Quay and Fishamble St. On the latter, see, for example, Wallace 1985.

29 Hobsbawm 1979: 249 implies that he thinks archaeology is an 'ancillary discipline to history'.

30 For example, R. Hodges's appeal to Bede's account of a political marriage to provide a context for archaeological evidence of cross-Channel contact. 'There is a firm historical foundation for these contacts, since Charibert I, who reigned at Paris from 561 to 567, gave his only daughter Bertha in marriage to Ethelbert of Kent' (Hodges 1982: 35). Bertha was not Charibert's only daughter; the marriage almost certainly took place in the 580s; thus Charibert did not 'give' her in marriage. See Wood 1983 for examination of how this forces a complete revision of Hodges's view of Kentish–Merovingian relations.

problems of dialogue (Wormald 1982). This is the context within which Morris's 'game' is played.

In trying to move forward we need to address traditional uses of archaeology by historians. These usually fall into three categories:

1 Illustrative. Archaeological data, mainly artefacts, are used to provide illustrations of the appearance of people, or settlements and 'daily life' (see Collins 1991).
2 Justificatory. Usually crude and off-the-shelf use of archaeology is made to 'prove' history. Documents attest the existence of X and here it is, proved by excavations at Y.
3 'Filling in the gaps'. Where documents do not tell us anything about a given problem, it is valid to use archaeology to probe these areas.

These categories are also to be found in archaeological work. The third, in particular, gives rise to what Ian Morris calls the 'zero-sum' view of archaeology, that the importance of archaeology is inversely proportional to the number of written documents. An explicit view of this statement can be found from the pen of Grahame Clark (1957: 20–1). This is a view which must be abandoned by historians and archaeologists if we are ever meaningfully to integrate written and material cultural evidence.

When we look more closely at previous attempts to use history and archaeology together, we usually see a three-stage process. In the first stage, an assumption drawn from written sources is used to structure the archaeological data, or the excavated data are themselves collected to answer a question drawn from the written sources. In the second phase, these neat correlations and illustrations are rapidly shown to be flawed, both by re-examining the archaeological sources and by more sophisticated consideration of the documents. As a result of the problems raised, in the third stage the idea that the two types of evidence can be used together at all is rejected. This can take the form of disparagement of one or other evidential form,[31] and thus Morris's competitive interdisciplinary 'game'. Where this is not the case, it is simply assumed that the two types of evidence relate to wholly different things and thus cannot be used together. Sometimes this attitude is summed up in the epigram, 'archaeology tells you what people did, while history tells you what they thought', which of course implies that people did not usually think about what they were doing! The whole process is founded on the premises that one-to-one correlations ought to exist, and that the two evidential forms ought to relate to the same aspect of a given problem if they have anything at all to contribute to its study.

---

31 See, for example, Hodges's comments on the failure (by 1982) of archaeology to find any confirmation of the existence of the thriving emporium at York mentioned in written sources: 'At some stage we have to accept the power of this kind of negative evidence' (Hodges 1982a: 74). This, needless to say, is the opposite view to that of Collins 1991. Within a few years of the writing of these lines excavations at Fishergate revealed the 'missing' town!

A concrete example may be seen in the examination of religion in post-Roman Gaulish cemeteries. Written sources provided the idea that there was a dichotomy between Christianity and paganism, especially in rural areas, in this period. Thus, in archaeology, graves with grave-goods and those without were assumed to be the graves of pagans and Christians respectively. Signs on artefacts were read as religious indicators; west–east orientated burials and even burials in sarcophagi were assumed to be of Christians. The flaws in these ideas were swiftly revealed. The Church did not ban grave-goods; documentary and archaeological instances of burial in church with grave-goods were cited; whether or not one was provided with grave-goods was shown to be governed to some extent by age and gender; general anthropological work showed that grave-goods were not indicative of a particular view of the afterlife; west–east burial became common before widespread conversion to Christianity; the symbols on artefacts were rarely to be read in straightforward ways. Closer study of the documents even questioned the idea of this kind of religious opposition. As a result of this barrage of criticism, some archaeologists decided that this served as a 'cautionary tale' about using history and archaeology together.[32]

The despairing view of integration now seems mainly to be held by historians.[33] Certainly the combative stance, and rather silly mistakes in the use of written sources, of New Archaeologists like Richard Hodges served to obscure in historians' eyes the very real advances and significant contributions to understanding which their work represented. Some historians still refuse to accept that archaeology has explanatory value. Many others see it as very difficult to produce independent hypotheses from archaeological evidence because that evidence does not take written form. Whilst it is true that the movement from 'data' to 'evidence' is, initially, more difficult, and requires more theoretical involvement (Dark 1995: 36), it is a long time since documentary historians drew their interpretations purely from the overt, face-value statements of their texts.

The movement away from New Archaeology produced attempts to bring about a *rapprochement* between the disciplines. Yet although much sense has been spoken about the need to reopen dialogue, break down disciplinary barriers and find common theoretical approaches, no workable methodology has been proposed which allows archaeology to retain an equal and independent explanatory voice, and thus to move on from the 'zero-sum' view. In 1988 a collection of studies of early medieval Britain and Ireland was published (Driscoll and Nieke 1988) with the expressed intention of examining the integration of historical and archaeological

---

32 P. Périn, 'La confrontation des données écrites et archéologiques est toujours délicate et parfois il y a peu de rencontres, comme j'ai pu les vérifier, avec des autres, pour les questions de paganisme et de christianisme' (personal communication, 14 June 1988).

33 Dumville 1989: 213. The comments of Cornell 1995: 26–30, esp. 29, seems to stem from a despair at precisely the same sort of crass one-to-one correlations as are described above. The conclusion, though, is unduly negative.

evidence from different theoretical perspectives.[34] Worthy though the aims were, there was little methodological advance. Documentary evidence still set the agenda and there was not much attempt to use the archaeology to question or refine the picture drawn from often problematic written sources. Partly the problem arose from an absence of papers by historians which might have served to question the applicability of these types of document to the periods, places and problems under study. The concluding essay by Driscoll (1988) begins with valuable and important comments about the value of interdisciplinary study and the historiography of historical archaeology. However, the case study intended to illustrate the potential of interdisciplinary work remains disappointing. The analysis is flawed by being structured around particular views of conversion to Christianity, the Pictish state and the expanding power of the latter, all drawn from late and problematic sources. In the end the material remains, Pictish symbol stones, are used simply to illustrate these notions rather than to interrogate them.

More recently, the post-processual archaeologist John Moreland has written extensively on the relationships between history and archaeology. Moreland makes excellent points about how material culture may be read as text, and how texts may be seen as a kind of material culture. This permits us to use material culture and texts to examine the same kinds of power relationships and discourses.[35] However, while Moreland's work provides a valid means of using material cultural studies with work on the use and form of texts and literacy, he does not offer a framework for the use of archaeology with the contents of documents, which is, after all, what most historians work with.

To progress, we need to take a step backwards. The problems in previous attempts to integrate historical and archaeological sources stem from two key issues. The first is a continuous hopping back and forth from one discipline to the other, using off-the-shelf interpretations from one to shape interpretations of the other. This is exacerbated by the ignorance of specialists in one discipline of the problems involved in the use of data in the other. This has resulted in the borrowing of 'facts' from unreliable documents, or simplistic use of archaeological data.[36] We therefore need to do two things. We have to eliminate the cross-disciplinary comparisons and borrowings from all but the highest and most sophisticated levels of interpretation, and we have to rebuild the walls between disciplines, even if as low walls respected only in particular stages of analysis. In practice this means separating different categories of data within the disciplines (i.e. keeping settlement data separate from cemetery evidence, and the study of saints' lives distinct from that of charters) as well as simply keeping written data distinct from excavated.

---

34 Such as Leslie Alcock's culture-history, Chris Arnold's processualism, Richard Hodges's (by then) cognitive processualism and Stephen Driscoll's post-processualism.

35 Moreland 1991a. For more consideration of common theoretical approaches to written and excavated material, see Tabacynzki 1993. The article's excessively impenetrable style is not helped by bad proof-reading.

36 See, e.g., B. S. Bachrach's (1970) use of cemetery archaeology to evaluate the numbers of mounted warriors.

If we see all our data in context and as meaningfully and contingently formed by active individuals, analogous processes of enquiry are presented. These become clearer still if we see all our evidence, whether written document, decorated artefact, settlement or house plan or grave, as textual, conveying symbolic, coded 'messages' to an audience. The stages of enquiry can be set out as follows:

1 Frame questions.
2 Collect data.
3 Evaluate the data. This means assessing its reliability, to what extent archaeological sites were reliably excavated or published and what potential features were not recorded, or the extent to which a historical text is interpolated.
4 Examine the context of the data. This implies not only the geographical and chronological provenance of the material but also more general questions of who formed the data, why and for whom. Textual scholars need to consider the questions of genre; archaeologists analogous issues such as what the data represents: votive pit, midden, grave and so on. Archaeologists also need to consider such questions as how easy of access was this evidence, how visible was it, and for how long?
5 Establish patterning within the data. In documentary terms this simply means reading the document, and reconstructing internal semantic patterns, ranges of meaning, narrative strategies and so forth. For archaeologists it means looking at spatial distributions, patterns of correlation and so on. In both cases it involves reconstructing the message of the data, as opposed to the context within which that message was made.
6 Produce detailed conclusions from this body of data. Alternative explanations should be kept open.

This process is not purely linear. For example, stage 5 must sometimes precede stage 4; sometimes we can only establish who created a body of evidence, for whom, and how visibly, once we have considered what the overt message of the data is. Moreover, the process is recursive, as ideas emerge during the investigation of the data at stages 4, 5 or 6; we often return to our data to examine aspects of it which did not at first seem important, or we collect more data.

Each body of data should be studied separately. Although at stage 1 we come at that evidence with preconceived ideas drawn from the usual *bricolage* of history and archaeology (including parallels from other periods and places), geography, anthropology, ethnography, linguistics, literature, sociology and philosophy, as well as personal experience, we ought to be asking what that particular type of data, when analysed on its own merits, can say in answer to those questions. I would also argue that questions at stage 1 be framed in as general a way as possible. Posing questions which are too specific, or too closely based upon ideas drawn from another discipline, can lead at best to the abandonment of the examination of potentially interesting sources of information, or, at worst, hammering the data to fit these preconceptions. During stages 2–6 we should rule out any interference from the study of other categories of data. It has been this kind of criss-crossing between the study of different kinds of material at these stages which has obscured the potential of so many sources.

We must always remember that different kinds of evidence might have different things to say about different aspects of particular problems. This method allows us to abandon questions which do not seem to be answered, or answerable, from that kind of data, to frame new ones. It also allows us to determine those issues, or aspects of questions, which that material *does* confront. In spite of a widespread scepticism, the analysis of different bodies of data can realistically be kept distinct at these stages. Just as, recently, students of hagiography have been able to study their source material without trying to make it fit preconceptions drawn from work on narrative histories, and as settlement archaeology (especially urban) has often been studied in total separation from cemetery studies, it is quite feasible to study a body of archaeological material without constantly framing one's questions or structuring the data and its patterning according to preconceptions from documentary history. The approach recommended here not only falls into line with the contextualism of post-processual archaeology, but also chimes with more rigidly contextual studies of written texts proposed recently by historians (see Fouracre 1990; Wood 1992).

Moreover, it permits each body of data to question, as well as to confirm or complement, the others[37] because once we have studied these bodies of evidence separately, we can and must merge the conclusions drawn from each (stage 6) at a higher level.[38] We ought to be able to see more clearly where genuine correlations do exist, but where, as is usually the case, such direct links are absent, it allows us to confront the questions of why they do not, by looking at the purposes served by the creation of each kind of data. It also allows meaningful integration to be made at a more sophisticated level, by looking at common purposes or mentalities involved in the creation of data. It should enable us to identify significant social change, which unidisciplinary studies have either ignored or dismissed as mere 'fashion'.[39] This approach should also allow us to choose between alternative explanations of one body of data on the grounds of sophisticated study of the others, not by pre-conceived ideas of the supremacy of one kind of data, but by the production of hypotheses which explain all sets of data equally. If different kinds of evidence are approached in this way, via analogous stages of analysis, posing comparable kinds of question, and arriving at independent conclusions, fruitless old questions of whether history or archaeology is dominant, ancillary or auxiliary are sidestepped.

This 'multidisciplinary' methodology does however require either that people be more specifically educated in more than one discipline or at least that disciplinary

---

37 I would argue that none of the post-processual examples of interdisciplinary integration cited approvingly by Moreland 1991a uses archaeology or material culture to provide a voice independent of the written sources. Some seem only to justify or illustrate the latter.

38 Thus whilst I agree with Richard Reece (1984) that archaeologists should keep their data separate from historical ideas, I do so only when considering preliminary stages of analysis.

39 For an attempt to put this methodology into practice, see Halsall 1995, although, like all who would be jack of all trades, the author suffers from being a master of none. For a subsequent rejection of the only neat, direct correlation identified in this work, see Halsall 1996: 18.

specialists be prepared to engage in the kind of dialogue which allows such conclusions, rather than vacuous one-to-one similarities or competitive attempts to prove one set of data better than the other. As far as future developments are concerned, it requires academics to educate their students in the possibilities of such dialogue, and to stop perpetuating the disparaging or confrontational states of mind discussed above.

If we can carry out this methodology, we will produce much more rounded views of the past. Binford (1977: 13) once wrote that historical archaeology would one day be at the forefront of archaeological theory. With a more thoughtful integrative methodology this might at last be possible, but just as archaeologists ought to benefit from the existence of documentary evidence, historians ought to be prepared to accept the benefits of independent material cultural research, and not just for illustrative, justificatory or 'zero-sum' purposes. The recognition that archaeology has an equal and independent explanatory voice will allow a fuller understanding of all historical periods, from the Bronze Age Near East to the present day, by allowing us to challenge 'the primacy of the articulate and the articulated from the perspective of the embedded and the silent' (Miller 1985: 205).

REFERENCES

Adams, R. M. (1974) 'Anthropological observations on ancient trade', *Current Anthropology* 15: 239–58.
Aitken, M. J. (1990) *Science-Based Dating in Archaeology*, London.
Bachrach, B. S. (1970) 'Charles Martel, the stirrup, mounted shock combat and feudalism', *Studies in Medieval and Renaissance History* 7: 49–75.
Bahn, P. (1989) *Bluff Your Way in Archaeology*, Horsham.
—— and Renfrew, C. (1991) *Archaeology. Theory, Methods and Practice*, London.
Barker, P. A. (1993) *The Techniques of Archaeological Excavation*, 3rd edn, London.
Barrett, J. C. (1995) *Some Challenges in Contemporary Archaeology*, Oxbrow Lecture 2, Oxford.
Binford, L. R. (1965) 'Archaeological systematics and the study of culture process', *American Antiquity* 31: 203–10.
—— (1972) *An Archaeological Perspective*, New York.
—— (1977) 'Historical archaeology: is it historical or archaeological?', in L. Ferguson (ed.) *Historical Archaeology and the Importance of Material Things*, Tucson.
—— (1978) *Nunamiut Ethnoarchaeology*, New York.
—— (1981) *Bones, Ancient Men and Modern Myths*, New York.
—— (1983) *Working at Archaeology*, New York.
—— (1989) *Debating Archaeology*, New York.
—— and Binford, S. R. (eds) (1968) *New Perspectives in Archaeology*, Chicago.
Bintliff, J. (ed.) (1991a) *The* Annales *School and Archaeology*, Leicester.
Bintliff, J. (1991b) 'Post-modernism, rhetoric and scholasticism at TAG: the current state of British archaeological theory', *Antiquity* 65: 274–8.
Bourdieu, P. (1977) *Outline of a Theory of Practice*, tr. R. Nice, Cambridge.
Bradley, R. (1993) 'Archaeology: the loss of nerve', in N. Yoffee and A. Sherratt (eds) *Archaeological Theory: Who Sets the Agenda?*, Cambridge.
Caldwell, J. (1959) 'The new American archaeology', *Science* 129: 303–7.
Carr, E. H. (1987) *What is History?*, 2nd edn, Harmondsworth.

Carver, M. O. H. (1993) *Arguments in Stone. Archaeological Research and the European Town in the First Millennium*, Oxbow Monograph 29, Oxford.

Champion, T. C. (1989) 'Introduction', in T. C. Champion (ed.) *Centre and Periphery. Comparative Studies in Archaeology*, One Word, London.

Childe, V. G. (1929) *The Danube in Prehistory*, Oxford.

—— (1936) *Man Makes Himself*, London.

—— (1949) *Social Worlds of Knowledge*, Oxford.

—— (1951) *Social Evolution*, New York.

—— (1956a) *Piecing together the Past: The Interpretation of Archaeological Data*, London.

—— (1956b) *Society and Knowledge: The Growth of Human Traditions*, New York.

—— (1958) *The Prehistory of European Society*, Harmondsworth.

Christie, N. and Loseby, S. T. (eds) (1996) *Towns in Transition. Urban Evolution in Late Antiquity and the Early Middle Ages*, Aldershot.

Claessen, H. J. M. and Skalnik, P. (eds) (1978) *The Early State*, The Hague.

Clark, A. (1990) *Seeing Beneath the Soil*, London.

Clark, J. G. D. (1932) *The Mesolithic Age in Britain*, Cambridge.

—— [1939] (1957) *Archaeology and Society*, 3rd edn, London.

—— (1940) *Prehistoric England*, London.

—— (1952) *Prehistoric Europe: The Economic Basis*, London.

—— (1954) *Excavations at Star Carr*, Cambridge.

Clarke, D. L. (1968) *Analytical Archaeology*, London.

—— (1972) 'Glastonbury lake village. A provisional model of an Iron Age society and its settlement pattern', in D. L. Clarke (ed.) *Models in Archaeology*, London.

—— (1973) 'Archaeology: the loss of innocence', *Antiquity* 47: 6–18.

—— (ed.) (1977) *Spatial Archaeology*, New York.

—— (1979) *Analytical Archaeologist, Collected Papers of David L. Clarke*, London.

Collins, R. J. H. (1991) *Early Medieval Europe*, London.

Cornell, T. (1995) *The Beginnings of Rome. Italy and Rome from the Bronze Age to the Punic Wars (c.1000–264 BC)*, London.

Courbin, P. (1988) *What is Archaeology?*, Chicago.

Daniel, G. E. (1967) *The Origins and Growth of Archaeology*, Harmondsworth.

Dark, K. R. (1995) *Theoretical Archaeology*, London.

Delano-Smith, C. (1992) 'The *Annales* for archaeology?', *Antiquity* 66: 539–41.

Driscoll, S. T. (1988) 'The relationship between history and archaeology: artefacts, documents and power', in Driscoll and Nieke 1988.

—— and Nieke, M. R. (eds) (1988) *Power and Politics in Early Medieval Britain and Ireland*, Edinburgh.

Dumville, D. N. (1977) 'Sub-Roman Britain – history and legend', *History* 62: 173–92.

—— (1989) 'The origins of Northumbria: some aspects of the British background', in S. Bassett (ed.) *The Origins of Early Anglo-Saxon Kingdoms*, Leicester.

Dyer, C. (1992) Review of Bintliff 1991a, *Medieval Archaeology* 36: 361.

Engelstad, E. (1991) 'Images of power and contradiction: feminist theory and post-processual archaeology', *Antiquity* 65: 502–14.

Fasham, P. J., Schadla-Hall, R. T., Shennan, S. J. and Bates, P. J. (1980), *Fieldwalking for Archaeologists*, Andover.

Fouracre, P. (1990) 'Merovingian history and Merovingian hagiography', *Past and Present* 127: 3–38.

Fried, M. H. (1967) *The Evolution of Political Society*, New York.

Gero, J. M. and Conkey, M. W. (1990) *Engendering Archaeology. Women and Prehistory*, Oxford.

Giddens, A. (1984) *The Constitution of Society: Outline of the Theory of Structuration*, Cambridge.

Gilchrist, R. (1991) 'Women's archaeology? Political feminism, gender theory and historical revision', *Antiquity* 65: 495–501.

—— (1994) *Gender and Material Culture: The Archaeology of Religious Women*, London.

Graves, P. (1991) 'Relative values? Criticisms of critical theory', *Archaeological Review from Cambridge* 10: 86–93.

Greene, K. (1995) *Archaeology, An Introduction*, 3rd edn, London.

Grierson, P. (1959) 'Commerce in the Dark Ages: a critique of the evidence', *Transactions of the Royal Historical Society*, 5th ser., 9: 123–40.

Halsall, G. (1995) *Settlement and Social Organization. The Merovingian Region of Metz*, Cambridge.

—— (1996) 'Female status and power in early Merovingian central Austrasia. The burial evidence', *Early Medieval Europe* 5(1): 1–24.

Hatt, J.-J. (1953) 'Les fouilles de la Ruelle St-Médard à Strasbourg', *Gallia* 11: 225–48.

Hawkes, C. F. C. (1954) 'Archaeological theory and method: some suggestions from the Old World', *American Anthropologist* 56: 155–68.

Hedeager, L. (1992) *Iron Age Societies. From Tribe to State in Denmark, 500 BC–AD 700*, Oxford.

Hobsbawm, E. J. (1979) 'An historian's comments', in B. C. Burnham and J. Kingsbury (eds) *Space, Hierarchy and Society. Interdisciplinary Studies in Social Area Analysis*, British Archaeological Reports (Supplementary Series) 59, Oxford.

Hodder, I. (ed.) (1982a) *Symbolic and Structural Archaeology*, Cambridge.

—— (1982b) *Symbols in Action. Ethnoarchaeological Studies of Material Culture*, Cambridge.

—— (1986) *Reading the Past*, Cambridge.

—— (ed.) (1987) *Archaeology as Long-Term History*, Cambridge.

—— (1991) 'To interpret is to act. The need for an interpretive archaeology', *Scottish Archaeological Review* 8: 8–13.

—— (1992) *Theory and Practice in Archaeology*, London.

—— and Hassall, H. (1971) 'The non-random spacing of Romano-British walled towns', *Man* 6: 391–407.

—— and Orton, C. (1976) *Spatial Analysis in Archaeology*, Cambridge.

Hodges, R. (1982a) *Dark Age Economics. The Origins of Towns and Trade, 600–1000*, London.

—— (1982b) 'Method and theory in medieval archaeology Part 1', *Archaeologia Medievale* 9: 7–38.

—— (1989) *The Anglo-Saxon Achievement. Archaeology and the Beginnings of English Society*, London.

Hume, I. N. (1964) 'Archaeology: handmaiden to history', *North Carolina Historical Review* 41: 215–25.

James, E. (1979) 'Cemeteries and the problem of Frankish settlement in Gaul', in P. H. Sawyer (ed.) *Names, Words and Graves*, Leeds.

—— (1989) 'Burial and status in the early medieval West', *Transactions of the Royal Historical Society*, 5th ser., 29: 23–40.

Leeds, E. T. (1913) *The Archaeology of the Anglo-Saxon Settlements*, Oxford.

Leone, M. P. (1978) 'Time in American archaeology', in C. Redman *et al.* (eds) *Social Archaeology*, New York.

—— (1982) 'Some opinions about recovering mind', *American Antiquity* 47: 742–60.

McGuire, R. H. (1992) *A Marxist Archaeology*, San Diego.

Miller, D. (1985) *Artefacts as Categories, A Study of Ceramic Variability in Central India*, Cambridge.

Moreland, J. (1991a) 'Method and theory in medieval archaeology in the 1990s', *Archaeologia Medievale* 18: 7–42.

—— (1991b) Review of Courbin 1988, *History and Theory* 30: 246–61.

Morris, I. N. (1992) *Death-Ritual and Social Structure in Classical Antiquity*, Cambridge.

Mytum, H. C. (1991) *The Origins of Early Christian Ireland*, London.

Orser, Jr, C. E. (1996) *A Historical Archaeology of the Modern World*, New York.

Rahtz, P. A. (1983) 'New approaches to medieval archaeology Part 1', in D. A. Hinton (ed.) *25 Years of Medieval Archaeology*, Sheffield.

—— (1991) *Invitation to Archaeology*, 2nd edn, London.

Randsborg, K. (1980) *The Viking Age in Denmark*, London.

—— (1991) *The First Millennium in Europe and the Mediterranean. An Archaeological Essay*, Cambridge.

Reece, R. (1984) 'Sequence is all: or archaeology in an historical period', *Scottish Archaeological Review* 3(2): 113–16.

Renfrew, C. (1973) *Before Civilization, The Radiocarbon Revolution and Prehistoric Europe*, London.

—— (1982) 'Towards an archaeology of mind', inaugural lecture, Cambridge.

—— and Cherry, J. F. (eds) (1986) *Peer-Polity Interaction and Socio-Political Change*, Cambridge.

Sabloff, J. A. and Binford, L. R. and McAnany, A. (1987) 'Understanding the archaeological record', *Antiquity* 61: 203–9.

Sahlins, M. D. and Service, E. R. (1960) *Evolution and Culture*, Ann Arbor.

Samson, R. (1987) 'Social structures in Reihengräber: mirror or mirage?', *Scottish Archaeological Review* 4(2): 116–26.

Schiffer, M. B. (1976) *Behaviorial Archaeology*, New York.

Service, E. R. (1962) *Primitive Social Organization*, New York.

Shanks, M. and Tilley, C. (1987) *Social Theory and Archaeology*, Cambridge.

—— (1991), *Re-constructing Archaeology*, 2nd edn, London.

Tabacynzki, S. (1993) 'The relationship between history and archaeology: elements of the present debate', *Medieval Archaeology* 37: 1–12.

Tilley, C. (ed.) (1990) *Reading Material Culture. Structuralism, Hermeneutics and Post-structuralism*, London.

Trigger, B. G. (1980) *Gordon Childe. Revolutions in Archaeology*, London.

—— (1989), *A History of Archaeological Thought*, Cambridge.

Wallace, P. (1985) 'The archaeology of Viking Dublin', in H. B. Clarke and A. Simms (eds) *The Comparative History of Urban Origins in Non-Roman Europe*, British Archaeological Reports (Supplementary Series) 255, Oxford.

Wallerstein, I. (1974) *The Modern World System*, vol. 1, New York.

Wissler, C. (1917) 'The new archaeology', *American Museum Journal* 17: 100–1.

Wood, I. N. (1983) *The Merovingian North Sea*, Alingsas.

—— (1992) 'Continuity or calamity: the constraints of literary models', in J. F. Drinkwater and H. Elton (eds) *Fifth-Century Gaul: A Crisis of Identity?*, Cambridge.

Wormald, C. P. (1982) Review of Hodges 1982a, *London Review of Books*, 21 October–3 November: 22–3.

33

THE HISTORY OF WESTERN ART HISTORY

Nigel Llewellyn

DEFINITIONS AND CONTEXTS

There is no single, linear, progressive history of Western art history; rather there are several parallel traditions of writing about art, some of them truly historical. Indeed, it is hard to separate the history of art history from the history of art theory; the historiographic boundary in relation to art history is somewhat blurred. Nevertheless, if we adopt the working definition that art history is a historical account of the existence and form of works of art and if we bear some important contextual points in mind, a historiographic analysis of art writing is possible.

The first necessary cognizance is of the common ground between writing about art and writing about other historical phenomena, for example, the adoption by art history of models used by historians to describe religion or diplomacy; second, an awareness of the links between historical writing and the current practice of art itself (Gaehtgens 1990 and Belting 1987); third, a recognition of the actual state of knowledge, in the senses of access or archaeology, for example, how much of an artist's work is known and available for study, what is the state of its conservation and restoration?;[1] fourth, an awareness of the role of technology, to capture a memory of a work of art, by sketching or using a camera, to reproduce a work of art or overcome the difficulty of understanding colour or paint via a line engraving (Haskell 1987; 1976: 168ff.; Lloyd 1975); fifth, an appreciation of the political context for historical discussions about art, since its high symbolic potential, understood since antiquity, means that art's history is not written in ideologically

---

1 See the history of the Laocoon for the politics of restoration over several generations in Haskell and Penny 1981: 243–7; for discussions of the condition of a work of art affecting the judgement of the historian see Roscoe 1846: 316; or the long-benighted state of Giotto studies, with many fresco cycles under whitewash, for which see Schneider 1974.

neutral terms, for example, the eighteenth-century rationalists who referred to their own times when addressing the historical problem of art under absolutist tyranny, or the German-Jewish art historians of the 1930s who were obliged to rethink long-standing racialist assumptions about artistic development;[2] sixth, an awareness of the role of taste, those shifting emphases towards and away from particular artists, genres and objects, for example, the changing critical and historical fortunes of various artists such as Piero della Francesca or Vermeer;[3] seventh, an understanding of the role of ideology in shaping an art historian's view and writing, his or her class, gender and national interests; and lastly, an awareness of the use of language (M. D. K. Baxandall, in Kemal and Gaskell 1991: 67–85).

Art history shares some of its terms with other histories, especially concepts used to describe the shapes of time. Repeated patterns include a periodic, cyclical model (London under George III as a new Periclean Athens, Augustan Rome or Medicean Florence), models of decline and fall, assumptions about progress, biological models with stages of growth, maturity and decay, and eras divided into mega- and sub-periods.[4] The Hegelian form of dialectical development, a style-period in art as a statement (thesis), subsumed and answered by another style (antithesis) out of and between which a third style (synthesis) appears, is no longer fashionable, but was highly influential over several generations.[5] Style-periods can be labelled in various telling ways: for example, after place, race or culture (Gothic, Early Christian); following negative criticism (Archaic, Mannerism); or consequent upon style rather than period (Realism, Romanesque) (Frankl 1960; Gombrich 1966: 19–106). Gombrich has argued that all styles are in essence either classical or anti-classical (Gombrich 1966: 81–98). There are many tensions between these labelled concepts, for example, the work of an artist might represent a style counter to that prevailing in the mega-period.[6] Is the Baroque a late corrupt phase, a version or the antithesis of the Renaissance? (Kurz 1963 and Dempsey 1977). In addition, these style-period labels are also anachronistic and undesirable in their application to non-Western art.

---

2 Friedländer 1969: 51: 'Racial mixture seems to be good for the intellect.'

3 Haskell 1976: 147 and Meltzoff 1942 on the rediscovery in the 1840s–1860s of Vermeer by Thoré (b. 1807). [Lord] Alexander Lindsay (1812–80) was one of the first to celebrate Piero della Francesca, see Lindsay 1847. Piero is much beloved of the English and regarded as rational and unpopish in northern Europe. For his changing reputation see Longhi 1963: 116–69 and Carrier 1987; for Lindsay see Brigstocke 1981. No one wrote much about Botticelli until the later nineteenth century when a taste developed for his art, see Haskell 1976: 51 and Levey 1960. For a recent attempt to chart changing fortunes, see Turner 1993.

4 For periodic cycles see Potts 1985 and Janson 1973: 331. The inevitability of decline was long recognized as a problem, see the comments of the Abbé Laugier (1753) 'the moment we arrive at perfection ... we are fallen again', see Herrmann 1962: 12 and Wölfflin [1888] 1964: Preface 'The subject of this study is the disintegration of the Renaissance'.

5 Wind 1963 is perhaps the best-known modern development of Hegelianism.

6 Andrea Palladio (1508–80), regarded in some quarters as an arch-classicist, lived in the Age of Mannerism.

FOUNDERS

In antiquity there was no self-standing body of literary discourse called art history. In general, ancient histories of any subject tended to be based on the writers' observations of distinctions and categories, which could then be arranged in a developmental pattern. Given the valuable models offered by the political historians in the Roman canon – Livy, Plutarch, Tacitus – and the Roman tradition of writing historical accounts, we can only regret what has been lost in the field of art history. Recurrent themes in the ancient historiography of art include certain models for the shaping of historical time; the tendency for historians to take a point of view (Pliny stresses the Roman achievement, the triumph of naturalism and the end of Greek art) and utilize their personal observations; the inclination towards functional analyses of art, to ponder the status of its practitioners, national stereotypes, artistic individuality, descriptions of style, classifications such as genres, and relations between art and society. Ancient art history was, however, produced in a range of literary genres. Encyclopaedists surveyed and compiled data, some of it art-historical, and the rhetoricians cited art objects.[7] Rhetoric, the science of speech-making, was so important that its principles and aims informed the total cultural experience of the educated ancient world and several Roman rhetoricians (Cicero, Quintilian) discussed the evolution of the style of visual art by analogy with verbal languages. The rhetoricians had a particular interest in style but could not really agree on the relative merits of early (simple) styles and later (complex) ones. The sublime work of Pheidias was given priority over the conquering of realism in the following century. Another group (Philostratus, Callistratus) used works of art as the objects of descriptive or ekphrastic writing giving a sense of the conceptual language applied to visual representation in the ancient world (James and Webb 1991).

A third group of ancient art-writers were practical people. The Greek concept of *techne* ('making') required the authors of treatises (Vitruvius and others), writing for practitioners and the patron class, to consider art and help solve technical problems by exploring historical accounts of the arts. Fourth, ancient aestheticians, concerned with the perception of beauty, have left a substantial group of fragmentary writings which assume the components of art-historical thought. The most influential figures in Greek thought – Socrates, Plato and Aristotle – all had ideas about visual representation and their Roman successors were especially concerned with the problem of art objects as symbols of decay and excessive luxury. These thoughts often resolved into historical comparisons and so reveal something of the art-historical assumptions of the day. There was also a lively ancient literary tradition in biography, although artists did not always enter the canons of 'Great Men'. Artistic biographies only appeared when their subjects had extraordinary capabilities; they were exceptionally ingenious or witty or employed by the rich and

---

7 Quintilian, *Institutio oratoria* XII 10; Cicero, *On Invention* and *Brutus*; Philostratus, *Imagines*; Callistratus, *Descriptions*. On Cicero, see Baxandall 1971: 34ff.

powerful. Finally, there were guide-book writers such as Pausanias, a Greek author and traveller of the second century AD, whose text includes art-historical material as a matter of intriguing but secondary significance.[8] Pliny appears to have made use of other topographical texts in his encyclopaedia, which is by some long measure the most substantial extant ancient art-historical source, and a survey of the *Natural History* will disclose themes that recur throughout the history of Western art history.[9]

The principle of Pliny's shaping of art-historical time is demonstrated in his treatment of the history of sculpture where he identifies a clearly determined starting-point – a creation myth of sorts – from which progress is slowly made (Pliny XXXIV. 54–65). Progress follows directly from the actions taken by a series of gifted artists who have individual skills and ingenuity to solve problems of representation in a series of shifts on the naturalistic scale towards the real. Individual, competing, male artists are Pliny's main historical concern, following contemporary Roman histories and biographies by writers such as Plutarch and Suetonius. The *Natural History* might be encyclopaedic but it is also partial and subjective and Pliny's history of art has been enormously influential for its schemata, giving straightforward models of historical development. His simple patterns edit out controversy about the nature of representation and about the means of achieving it, for it is very clear from other sources that the ancient world witnessed a lively debate about the principles upon which representation should be based. Such questions as those about the relative merits of drawing and colouring have recurred throughout history and have had a profound effect on critical historians. In painting, Pliny's narrative moves from the simple to the complex. The rigidity of his schemes for the history of sculpture and painting is clearly derived from his Greek sources and noteworthy and familiar is the assumption in the *Natural History* and elsewhere that the art of the past – a Golden Age – is superior to that of the present. Pliny's explanation for decline is rooted in the common Roman complaint about the close links between decadence and luxury: a certain softening of the Roman character, too many fancy ideas, mostly imported, and too many luxury goods. Some writers argued that over-elaborate drawing and excessive colour lay at the root of Roman decline – Pliny, Vitruvius and Dionysius of Halicarnassus – though not everyone agreed with them (Plutarch).

Pliny uses literary sources rather than works of art themselves, preferring to read Varro's antiquarian tracts than to study the huge numbers of Greek works available in the imperial collections and elsewhere. The idea that the history of art had to be written with the author having engaged directly with the objects is, in fact, a quite recent one: right into the nineteenth century, the Word controlled the Image in art's history. Pliny's account of bronze statuary reflects a widespread assumption in Roman society that art was primarily a functional phenomenon, to serve the state

---

8   Pausanius, *Description of Greece*, translated by P. Levi, 2 vols, Harmondsworth, 1971.
9   Pliny the Elder, *Natural History: The Elder Pliny's Chapters on the History of Art*, translated by K. Jex-Blake with a commentary by E. Sellars, London, 1896.

and commemorate great figures and events. In the *Natural History*, individual artists are responsible for the development of art and the text is full of biographical elements celebrating the skills of artists and their capacities for problem-solving. This, despite the fact that his primary subject was the materials worked into art – the intrinsic value of the bronze, even its transformation by skill.

The architectural theorist Vitruvius used history to address questions of style.[10] He explains three different forms of ancient architecture referred to since the sixteenth century as the Orders – as historical and ethnic phenomena. The Ionian people wanted to improve on the kind of columns used in Doria so they embellished that form with a volute and made it taller. All Pliny's colleagues used anecdotes to explain how new artistic forms evolved. An important consequence about these historical stories is that they gendered and enspecied styles, they imbued them with emotion and made them physically manifest. Such a history politicizes works of art.[11] Once a conceptual language for art was invented in antiquity, style itself became a historical tool. Criteria such as proportion, harmony, appropriateness and decorum, emotion and narrative could all be identified, measured and compared to register historical change. In Pliny's treatment of painters we are also shown categories of art and ways of prioritizing art and marking historical change unrelated either to materials or to authorship (Pliny XXXV. 117–18). The assertion that a decorative landscape fresco can never attain the reputation of an easel painting on a narrative theme or of a portrait ties in with Pliny's implicit admiration for expression in art. Amongst the ancient Greeks, he writes, painting became the exclusive art and practice of the freeborn, Aristeides was the first to paint the soul, and [give] expression to the soul of man ... and also the emotions' (Pliny XXXV. 98).

A final, influential theme in Pliny is that the standard of a society is matched by and (influences) the standard of its art (Pliny XXXV. 50). Some Romans were intensely suspicious of art as a foreign source of idleness and luxury associated especially with the decadence and effeminacy of conquered nations; some harked back to the legends of the earliest Roman state when sculpted or painted representations of the gods had been forbidden as it was only thought proper to contemplate the divine through the intellect; others took a sceptical view of images, believing that looted booty in the form of works of art endangered the body politic (Livy reporting Cato in Pollitt 1966: 33). Amongst a few, there was an intellectual yearning for moments of quiet contemplation before the work of art (Pliny XXXVI).

Hardly any of these ideas can be found in Western medieval writing about art. The artist, as an individual, was accorded a low social status and was therefore not worthy of biography. To medieval historians, the makers of art were usually the

---

10   Vitruvius, *De architectura* (ed. F. Granger, Loeb edition) IV. i. 9–10; for the Orders, see Rykwert 1980, esp. 5–9 and 33–9, and Onians 1988.

11   For racist attitudes in art-historical writing about the Renaissance see C. Farago's essay in her edited volume, Farago 1996.

patrons, not the artists; educated ecclesiastics had little time for the skilled manipulation of the material world in comparison with the contemplation of the world of ideas. Science, in the sense of knowledge, was regarded as far superior to art in the sense of skill with the hand. The ancient conceptual vocabulary of stylistic change and historical development was largely abandoned, thus discouraging the comparison of past art with that of the present. The medieval Christian world regarded itself as superior to the pagan past. We can trace some intellectual parallels with ancient attitudes towards art, but these were insufficient to supply the context that would nurture art history (Panofsky 1951). In biographies of the saints, art objects were considered for their material value but not for the way those materials were worked into art (Panofsky 1946). The least ambitious ancient kind of art-historical writing did recur: the topographical guides to places and collections, for example, *Mirabilia Urbis Romae* ('Marvels of the City of Rome') was written and often rewritten for pilgrims. This treated the surviving ancient works of art as vehicles for allegorical commentary and in so doing negated the pagan aspect of antiquity for Christian pilgrims. Secular works of art were hardly written about and religious art was considered first and foremost in terms of function – either as an aid to devotion or as a sign of grace. As the late eleventh-century monk wrote in his description of an abbey church at Dijon 'it seems to have been achieved through some mystic intuition being attributable rather to divine inspiration than to the experience of any master', a convention of approval that would have disappointed the architect and mason responsible.

RENAISSANCE RE-FOUNDERS

Key changes in Italian Renaissance historiography, from the earliest biographers, through Ghiberti (1378–1455) to Vasari (1511–74), followed the invention of printing and the drawing of tighter parallels between visual art and verbal communication (Cochrane 1981; Soussloff 1990; Joost-Gaugier 1982; Norman 1983: 223). The very structures of Latin prose historians were adopted as models for composition and style (Goldstein 1992). In line with Roman historiography, Renaissance histories of art were primarily didactic, great artists became great men and were treated like other great men, for example, generals, statesmen and poets.[12] Pliny's powerful causal links between change in art and the innovative and inspired solutions of gifted individuals was undoubtedly an influential model, as was the medieval tradition of saintly lives as exemplary primers for human behaviour.[13] The best-known biographies of all, the Gospel accounts of the life and ministry of Christ, were also influential.[14] In his Tuscan vernacular manuscript *Commentaries*, an eccentric mixture of history (some a précis of Pliny) and technical advice,

---

12 See Vespasiano de' Bisticci's *Lives of Illustrious Men*, available in several modern editions after 1839.
13 Pliny's MSS circulated widely and the text was printed over a dozen times by 1500.
14 See the opening paragraph of Vasari's 'Life of Michelangelo' and Barolsky 1990.

Ghiberti, a practising sculptor and metalworker, stressed that artists had to be learned ('instructed in all the Liberal arts') (von Schlosser 1912; Krautheimer 1969: 257; Gombrich 1966: 1–10). Working with the hands alone would deprive them of authority, although learning to draw was presented as a sign of civility and intellectual progress. Ghiberti described the period between antiquity and his own day as an age of dark iconoclasm, resulting from bigotry in the Church. As with all his contemporaries, he knew next to nothing about ancient statues and pictures; however, his scheme of renewal requires that the classical be assumed to be unsurpassable. But Ghiberti's ambitious, unfinished project was unmatched in Renaissance Italy or anywhere else.

The long Renaissance tradition of biography and scholarly and theoretical discussions of the *paragone*, or critical comparison, between poetry and painting evidences that intellectual advancement which slowly improved the social status of artists, who even became autobiographers (Cellini, Bandinelli), although it has saddled artists with a peculiar, gendered-male, 'outsider' heroism ever since.[15] Only gradually did more scientific approaches to art-history writing, based on archival or archaeological evidence, enter Italian historiography. An important theme in the peninsula was regional rivalry, for art was politicized and local historians were disinclined to concede to their rivals. Vasari's great *Lives* is precisely not a compilation of factual material; nevertheless, many subsequent readers have had just those expectations. His politics – the servant to an ambitious dynast and absolutist – were immediately recognized and challenged by his followers, although the self-congratulatory, autobiographical element in the book took longer to identify.[16] An important device was to use anecdote when historical material ran out, for example in the 'Life of Giorgione' whom Vasari rightly identifies as important to the history of style but poorly documented.[17] He adopted an extremely subtle and even polemical critical position, for Vasari was not simply a hoarder or compiler but a real historian, with a point of view and capable of sifting evidence to support it. He used descriptive writing to reconstruct the form and style of the pictures discussed and worked within a historical model of revival after decline. He set out artistic periods and identified those periods' leading protagonists. Most of all, his history of art is also dedicated to honouring the achievements of his prince, hence the politicization of artistic renewal and standards as based on Tuscany and the virtual deification of Michelangelo (1475–1564).

The non-biographical thread in Renaissance historiography had less of an impact. The literary critics sometimes drew on their historical knowledge of art and Renaissance treatises also contain historical material, for example Alberti's influential works on architecture, painting and sculpture (Grendler 1969a; Zimmermann 1976; Morisani 1953). Palladio's much-published *Four Books* (1570) on architecture

15 See the *proemi* to Vasari's *Lives* for a taste of the *paragone* debate.
16 Amongst the substantial literature on Vasari several texts stand out: Kallab 1908; Alpers 1960; Belting 1987.
17 Haskell 1971. Little positive progress was made in Giorgione studies until Morelli in 1880.

has a chapter on Roman archaeology that was influential for several generations afterwards and written as a result of time-consuming, dangerous and demanding scholarship. As with Ghiberti and others, Palladio assumes a decline from ancient standards into 'barbarian abuses', rescued by the Renaissance enterprise of which he is a part. The topographers also had to have some sense of the historical development of art. This genre is typified by Francesco Sansovino in Venice (1581), who was extremely well connected, as part of a small learned circle within the Venetian patron class and the son of the great sculptor-architect to the *Serenissima*, Jacopo Sansovino (1486–1570) (Grendler 1969b). Early printed art history outside the Italian peninsula is very patchy, although examples in all genres exist and have to be understood against the context of political and religious tension in Renaissance and Reformation Europe (Filipczak 1993).

EARLY MODERN ART HISTORY

Art-historical literature from the mid-sixteenth to the late eighteenth century was initially dynamized by a politicized reaction to Vasari's Tuscano-centric view of artistic standards and progress. In *Il Riposo* (Florence, 1584), Borghini states an opposing but equally biased point of view stressing the roles of Venetian artists and a Venetian theory of art (arguing for the primacy of colouring) to counter the Tuscan emphasis on drawing (Hope 1983–4; Sohn 1991). This polemical literature typifies an explosion of historical writing about art across Europe, very little of which is sufficiently well known. Many writers followed by generations of editors produced collections of biographies which tended to include theoretical or polemical prefaces and revealed the interests of their authors simply through their selection of artists (Goldberg 1988). All European cultures and languages saw exercises in this manner of writing and the production of a set of great artists became a matter of national pride.[18] For the increasingly paradigmatic art of Bologna there is Malvasia (1678; Perini 1986; 1988; 1990): north of the Alps the key work is the *Schilderboeck* by Karel van Mander, a scholar of the noble class (a parallel with Alberti here).[19] Van Mander's history is more synthetic than Vasari's; it is fully cross-referenced and closely integrated but has no periodic model, no scheme of history and no single hero. As with some Italian forebears and French successors, van Mander pursues the analogy between painting and poetry (Dubos 1719). He uses the Vasarian device of a claimed antique inheritance and standard, but celebrates the particular northern creative achievements of landscape and portraiture. Each painter is treated as an

---

18   For France see Roger De Piles (1635–1709), *Abrégé de la vie des peintres* (Paris, 1699), for whom see Puttfarken 1985 and Descamps 1753–63. For Spain, Francisco Pacheco (?1564–1654), *Arte de la pintura, su antigüedad y grandezas ...* (Seville, 1649) and [Antonio] Palomino (1655–1726), *El Museo Pictórico y Escala Óptica*, 3 vols (Madrid, 1715–24).

19   *Schilder-boeck ...* (1603–4), 2nd edn with supplementary biography of van Mander, 1616–18; newly edited by H. Miedema as Karel van Mander, *Lives of the Illustrious Netherlandish and German Painters* (Doornspijk, 1994), the first of a projected six-volume project. See also Melion 1991.

individual specialist (Vasari had described this as their each having a *maniera* or 'manner') operating within a particular niche.

All his successors had to confront the harsh logic of Vasari's model. If standards had peaked with Michelangelo, what might happen subsequently? Was decline inevitable or could art be redirected? Might standards be maintained? Bellori, following Baglione's book of lives and describing seventeenth-century art with unabashed partisanship, was highly manipulative in his historical presentation of the seventeenth century and set up Raphael and Poussin (a new Raphael) as alternative high points to Michelangelo (Bellori 1672; 1695; 1664; Baglione 1642). These arguments, presenting artists such as Michelangelo or Raphael as heirs to the ancients, were paralleled in other scholarly discourse by philosophers such as Francis Bacon and literary historians such as Perrault in France, protagonists in the Ancients versus Moderns debate (Félibien 1685–8; Perrault 1688). In the 1600s there was also an increasing interest in establishing a framework for writing a critical history of art by establishing the authenticity of the very materials themselves, an interest which became known as 'connoisseurship', the exercising of judgement to establish authenticity and the definitive *œuvre* of particular artists. The listing of pictures in collections, for example in the third part of von Sandrart, as a historical source has continued into our own day.[20]

In the 1700s, the subject markedly opens out. Walpole (1717–97) attempted a history of the unfashionable art of England and in his encompassing of all schools and artists he was matched in due course by Dézallier d'Argenville and Seroux d'Agincourt in France and by J. D. Fiorillo (1748–1821) in Germany.[21] For the theory of history, the most important eighteenth-century development was an increasingly ambitious description of stylistic change without recourse to analogy with literature and in terms of evolution rather than in Vasarian, modular terms. Gradually, a broad range of art came to be considered, rather than the exemplary peaks and standard-setting yardsticks. During this period, serious books on Chinese temples, gardens or Gothic cloisters were published, as were more and more studies of classical monuments, although the established historiography was boosted by an increased reliance on new archaeology. In Enlightenment circles, there were deep-rooted assumptions that 'under a minor prince, and amidst a struggle of religion, we are not likely to meet with much account of the arts' (Walpole 1762–71 (1862 edn): I, 135). The Risorgimento offered further encouragement to this kind of speculation, one contemporary editor wondering whether national unity might return Italian art to the standards established elsewhere in Europe (Kugler 1842). Amongst

---

20   ... *Teutsche Academie ...*, 8 vols (Nuremburg, 1768–75). The labelling of objects on the basis of ownership is an important historical procedure, for example, the Farnese Hercules, the Apollo Belvedere.

21   Walpole 1762–71; Dézallier d'Argenville 1745–52; Seroux d'Agincourt 1823; Leopoldo Cicognara (1767–1834), *Storia della scultura ... in Italia fino al secolo di Napoleone ...*, 3 vols (Venice, 1813–18) (with a 2nd edn in 7 vols, Prato, 1823–4); Fiorillo 1796–1808. Seroux was influenced by Gibbon's *The History of the Decline and Fall of the Roman Empire* (London, 1776–88), especially in the blame for decline as residing with the Byzantines and other 'eastern' Mediterranean cultural powers.

this ever-increasing published output, Cicognara's celebration of neo-classical taste signals the tendency of history-writing to parallel taste in the production of visual art itself. Systematic and enlightened accounts by Winckelmann (1717–68) of the style and development of ancient art greatly influenced historians, artists and an international, well-informed public. He imposed an objective of philosophical idealism on his historical judgements and set a new standard in the scholarly use of literary sources.[22] Winckelmann firmly established fixed points and standards in a way unseen since Vasari, setting Greek art in a quadripartite periodic scheme: the ages of the archaic, the sublime, the beautiful and of imitation and his underlying cyclical conceptions link these stages to periods in the modern era, namely, the Renaissance before Raphael, Raphael to Michelangelo, Correggio to Guido Reni and the death of art from the Carracci to Maratti (e.g. Rousseau 1755). Winckelmann also engages in a rich homoerotic, discursive fantasy to explore the impact of a selection of key antique works, mostly male nudes. His explanation for their form lies partly in his account of their context, for example, in the practices of ancient religion, in the moral economy of the ancient Greeks and even in the workings of the weather, which allowed the naked body to be revealed in sport and exercise to the beneficial effect on watching artists.[23] Modern scholarship on Winckelmann has shown that he had less genuine knowledge of Greek originals but a great deal of poetic inspiration. Like all eighteenth-century historians of art, he was deeply interested in taste and expected the study of past art to have an impact on current practice. Another key eighteenth-century figure was Luigi Lanzi (1732–1810), an *abbé*, curator and scholar who set out to revise Vasari's account, reduce its gossip and offer a comparatively democratic account of the whole Italian achievement (Lanzi 1792). He confirmed the pattern of schools of art (seen earlier in the early seventeenth-century manuscript *Considerazione* of the papal physician Giulio Mancini) and was immediately influential amongst European collectors who wanted exemplary works of each class and genre.[24] In Lanzi, each School is divided into a series of epochal divisions and he argued consistently that all the regional arts required intervention from academies to effect a revival of standards. For Piemonte, the first epoch covers 'The Dawn of Art and Progress to the Sixteenth Century', the second frames the seventeenth century and the establishment of an academy, and the third covers the court painter Beaumont and the restoration of the academy in the eighteenth century. Throughout this period, European art history remained a matter of national pride.[25] Late in the 1700s, public museums developed as sites for the presentation of new art-historical taxonomies (see McClellan 1994).

---

22 Winckelmann 1755; 1764. For Winckelmann see Potts 1994.

23 For climate as a determinant in early modern historical writing see Cardy 1976: 73.

24 For schools see too Moyer [1752] 1966 and J. F. Christ (1700–56), for whom see Kultermann 1993: 72ff. On Mancini see Marucchi and Salerno 1956–7.

25 de Dominici 1742–63; Ratti 1766, for whom see Collu 1983; dal Pozzo 1718. For examples of nationalistic art-historical writing see Harvey 1948; J. Meier-Graefe (1867–1935), for whom see Moffett 1973.

WRITING ART HISTORY IN THE NINETEENTH CENTURY

During the nineteenth century important technical advances and changing institutional practices transformed the way that art history was illustrated and increased the range of art-historical publication (Haskell 1976). Connoisseurship, well established in the eighteenth century, became a dominant mode of art-historical writing over the next 100 years.[26] It is an approach to art history which assumes the primary evidence of the art historian to be the work of art itself, words being unable fully to describe a work's qualities (Pope-Hennessy 1980: 11–38; Offner [1927] 1972). In important ways, especially in attempts to reconstruct the artistic 'personality', connoisseurship depended on Freudian psychology, although this has often been refuted by its practitioners (Wollheim 1973: 177–200; Spector 1969): '[c]onnoisseurship is not a poor substitute for knowledge, but provides ... means by which our limited state of knowledge can be broadened' (Offner, quoted in Pope-Hennessy 1980: 35). Important contributions to this historical method were made in early nineteenth-century Germany by Waagen and others (Waagen 1842–5; 1837–9; see too Bickendorf 1985; Schröter 1990): Rumohr (1785–1843), whose interests were curatorial – the originality and authenticity of works – made extensive use of documents in the positivist manner (Rumohr 1832); Kugler was a state employee and the author of an influential handbook on painting from late antiquity to the present day (see n. 20 above); J. D. Passavant (1787–1861) established a new tone by discussing art as a public act and responsibility, not as the plaything of the private collector (Passavant 1833). Morelli's method is particularly interesting: anatomy and the camera in use for the first time (Morelli 1897). The reputation of Berenson's published output, often vivid and memorable as criticism but now poorly regarded by historians, has been damaged by his commercial interests.[27]

With its origins in antiquarianism, documentary research developed apace in the 1800s, for example in the production (1878–83) of a definitive edition of Vasari's *Lives* by Gaetano Milanesi, sub-director of the Florentine archives.[28] In various ways since the nineteenth century, art historians have learned to deploy the document in their arguments, led by Ranke and other professional 'positivists', and a tension between such a documentary approach and connoisseurship has existed since. Cavalcasselle's work in the 1850s depended on his own drawings, exhaustive archival work and the democratic treatment of any artists about whom information could be found (Crowe and Cavalcasselle 1864–6; 1877; Levi 1985; Crowe 1885).[29]

---

26 For the eighteenth-century origins of connoisseurship see Gibson-Wood 1984 and Llewellyn (forthcoming).

27 Key Berenson texts are: the essays later collected as *Italian Painters of the Renaissance*, which originally appeared separately in New York in 1894, 1896, 1897 and 1907; *The Study and Criticism of Italian Art* in three series (1901–16); *The Arch of Constantine; or, the Decline of form* (1954); on Berenson see Mostyn-Owen 1972; Samuels 1979 and Brown 1979.

28 For antiquarianism and the Enlightenment see Thornton 1963: 24–7.

29 J. A. Crowe (1825–96); G. Cavalcaselle (1817–97).

Such enterprises tended to be flawed by a disinclination or inability to distinguish between second-hand accounts and genuine original documents. Access to sources of documents and exemplary works of art was patchy, for most of the art was in private ownership, although public access slowly increased as more museums and galleries opened and the first academic posts were filled in history of art.[30] There were also new non-empirical theories of art history, for example the materialism of Taine (1828–93), which showed his interests in the ethnic and climatic contexts for picture-making and a system based on an analogy between art and natural science, especially botany. Any particularity is only a variation in terms of classification and therefore of limited significance, a methodological assumption precisely opposed to connoisseurship. The determinism of Burckhardt related particular phenomena to general trends (Burckhardt 1855; 1878; Gossman 1988). Although he claimed otherwise, his famous book on the cultural history of the Renaissance represented a current of nineteenth-century thinking that was based on Hegelian metaphysics, a system sheltering two ideas, that art has a certain autonomy and that history was growing in its values. In such *Kulturgeschichte*, the changing styles of art became an index of the spirit of the age, the *Zeitgeist*.[31] Other streams of art history continued to be didactic and several prominent English authors stressed religious teaching in relation to art history. For example, Anna Jameson had a Protestant audience in mind when she opened her survey of religious iconography with an observation that papist '"hero-worship" had become, since the Reformation, strange to us ... as if it were antecedent to the fall of Babylon' (Jameson 1890: 1; see also Holcomb 1983: 171). Others celebrated the value of art history to comment on contemporary mores. William Roscoe (1753–1831), an autodidact interested in the impact of patronage, made extensive use of engravings and literary sources rather than visit Italy itself (Roscoe 1795; Compton 1960). His *Life of Lorenzo de' Medici* contains a political and moral subtext, that culture was morally and politically beneficial and the role of commerce was to fund it. Roscoe's study of Renaissance Florence analysed this system, arguing that Lorenzo 'il Magnifico' had supported a number of initiatives 'from which Europe derives its present advantages', such as printing, geographical discovery, the established principles of taste, etc.

DEVELOPMENTS FROM THE 1880s

Connoisseurship, developed initially to establish a taxonomy of Renaissance painting, has continued to evolve and has broadened its range in the twentieth century. Historians of ancient art have turned their attention to Greek pots, arguments about which reveal essential conflicts in art-historical practice. The connoisseurs, conscious of the absence of any other Greek 'painting', have established artistic

---

30 Gustav Waagen was appointed professor at Berlin in 1844; for comment on a proposed expansion in provision the UK in the 1960s see the editorial to the *Burlington Magazine* 103 (May 1961).
31 For an interesting angle on Burckhardt see Rüsen 1985.

personalities and traced hands while the social historians have emphasized trade and argued that the pots were worth less than the goods they carried. The answer to the standard art-historical question: why did a style develop from one point in art-historical time to another, is one of immense theoretical complexity and has dominated much twentieth-century art-historical writing. The formalists set out to answer it. Formalism, based on the assumption that art is a closed discourse, reliant on intuition and revealing an inner meaning, was established by Wölfflin (1864–1945) and his followers and has become a powerful theme in twentieth-century historiography.[32] A characteristic English school of formalism, shaped by German philosophical arguments about the impossibility of objectivity, linked both to the taste for post-Impressionist painting and early Italian painting and the first English translation of Wölfflin's *Classic Art* (1903), was exemplified by Roger Fry (1866–1934) (Smart 1966; Maginnis 1996; Falkenheim 1980). Formalists are now more rarely heard, whether complaining about 'naive historicism', condemning oversimplifications of cause and effect, or continuing to celebrate the role of the artist as gifted innovator, confronted by the critic.[33]

Increasingly, questions of psychology have entered the art historian's purview. Freud's own historical essays tend to be treated with caution since he uses Leonardo's pictures to offer an analysis of Leonardo's brain; however, his influence has been enormous and is growing (Wollheim 1973: 202–19; Damisch 1971–2; Schapiro 1956). Psychoanalytic accounts of art-historical phenomena appear from the 1920s. Aby Warburg is an example of an innovative figure whose influence has vastly exceeded his published output.[34] Other German-speaking scholars developed a school of writing especially directed at explanations of expression: for example, Max Dvorak (1874–1921) whose key interest was art history as the history of the spirit (*Kunstgeschichte als Geistesgeschichte*, 1928), Wilhelm Worringer (1881–1965) and Alois Riegl (1858–1905).[35] Some early twentieth-century scholars interested in expression started to reassess unfashionable schools such as the northern and Spanish artists of the sixteenth century, like Grünewald and El Greco, who themselves worked in an expressive vein.[36] This art-historical method depends on the concept of a *Kunstwollen*, an era's collective, psychic state with respect to artistic creation, and an inherently obscurantist term. Gombrich's influential book *Art and Illusion* takes a more mechanical line and argues for perceptional explanations for artistic understanding.[37]

---

32 The key Wölfflin texts are *Renaissance und Barok* (1888); *Die Klassische Kunst* (1899); and *Kunstgeschichtliche Grundbegriffe* (1915). For Wölfflin see Iversen 1981.

33 An exception is found in the 'Preface' to Freedberg 1983: 'what I say about these artists derives almost altogether from my confrontation with the visual substance of their art'.

34 The key collection of essays is in *Gesammelte Schriften* (1932), to be read with Gombrich 1970 and Ferretti 1990) (1st Italian edn, 1984).

35 Dvorak 1967; Donahue 1995. On Riegl see, Iversen 1993 and Olin 1993.

36 See the chapter on El Greco in Dvorak 1967 and Haskell 1976: 163–4.

37 Gombrich 1959, a book which exemplifies but one strand of Gombrich's work. For Gombrich's method see Kemp 1984 and Podro 1989.

The direct challenge to formalism came initially from iconography, the earliest versions of which took an approach analogous to the establishment of definitions in a dictionary, identifying the subject matter of works and objects by certain signs.[38] Panofsky later formulated a new theory of iconography, and an adjunct methodology 'iconology', as a historical approach that conceives of the visual arts as part of the 'universe of culture' including other creative manifestations of human enterprise.[39] Iconology effected 'synthetic intuition', a way of examining the mentality which governs the self-reflexive viewing of humankind, in groups. The artistic experiences of groups of humans have also been the concern of social histories of art based on ideas about class and the established means of production. A more recent variant of social history of art raised questions about gender, not only in the sense of the practitioner (male and female artists) but as a filter for understanding production and for understanding meaning, as a context for both seeing and making. Marx never completed his proposed description of art in its social setting, although his materialist followers have attempted an analysis, working in two distinct waves (Williams 1980: 48). First, an older German-speaking generation led by Antal, who published little: 'it is the content of art which clearly shows its connection with the outlook of different social groups for whom it was created',[40] and Hauser (1951; 1965)[41] who promulgated a sociological law connecting and explaining both aesthetic pleasure and the popularity of certain works and artists. For Hauser, the way art changes was a direct consequence of social conditions. The second wave comprised a younger group formed in the 1960s and 1970s, with T. J. Clark as its leading voice.[42] According to Marxist theory, art exists as a phenomenon of the superstructure inextricably linked and dependent upon the activities of the economic and social base; art therefore shows the direct trace of ideology; however, art is not merely its reflection, nor is it its expression merely as a passive recipient, but as an active force.

The human sciences offered art history a set of methods understood in the Anglo-Saxon world as relying on a *mélange* of French thinkers such as Althusser, Barthes, Foucault, Lacan (none of them art historians), in opposition to Anglo-Saxon empiricism. Such approaches assume that the world, as perceived by humankind, is an artificial construction rather than a natural phenomenon and they extend this principle to all human creativity, establishing meaning through a process using inversion and differentiation, defining humankind not by thought but by language.[43]

---

38 Cesare Ripa, *Iconologia* (Padua 1611 is a full early edition); B. de Montfaucon, *L'Antiquité expliquée et représentée en figures* (1717), for whom see Haskell 1993: 131–5.

39 Accessible examples of Panofsky's art history can be found in *Meaning in the Visual Arts: Papers in and on the Humanities* (1955); *Studies in Iconology* (1962; 1st edn 1939); *Albrecht Dürer* (1949). On Panofsky see Bialostocki 1963; Gombrich 1973: 1–22; Lavin 1995; Klein 1979: 143–60; Holly 1984; Mitchell 1986; Argan 1975. Against Panofskian iconology see Hope 1981.

40 Antal 1966: 2, an argument further developed in Antal 1948: 4.

41 For Hauser see Werckmeister 1984 and Orwicz 1985.

42 Clark 1974; 1973: 9–20; Werckmeister 1991. For an account of Clark see Carrier 1990.

43 For adaptations of the Lacanian method see Bryson 1983 and Leeks 1996.

Semioticians understood visual motifs by analogy with language as signs operating within systems, the meanings of which require decoding and have to be understood as conventions, their relations one to the other arbitrary, not fixed in nature.[44] These kinds of histories do not result in explanation in a conventional, historical sense and from some quarters they are dismissed as 'mere formalism'.[45]

EPILOGUE

Finally, current methodological and institutional difficulties and issues in art history need to be signalled. Academic art history is now a major international concern and describes a host of differing (sometimes conflicting) interests. There is a struggle over the definition of the art historian's material as there is over what constitutes the practice of art history itself. Many art historians have acquired new methodological tools developed over the last decades without necessarily subscribing to all the conditional theoretical apparatus. It is likely that additional significant advances will be possible in empiricist art history resulting from technological development, especially as manipulated by museum curators and conservators. Discoveries made by these means are likely to transform the sciences of attribution, classification, dating and the eliciting of meaning. On the level of theory, two basic schools seem to be developing: one which explains the form of the object through its analysis within one of a number of historical contexts, as determinants of its meaning; the second which stresses, often from quite wildly different standpoints, the autonomy of the text itself. This second group criticizes cultural history for its interest in finding in art objects equivalents to the ideas already formed about the 'spirit of the age' or about the patron and, in turn, it tends to be criticized for its lack of objectivity. In turn, its opponents are condemned for their claim to empirical objectivity. Social anthropology, dealing with ritual and performance and social structures, has become more influential, matching moves made by the *Annaliste* historians who have moved from merely quantifying to an understanding of values and attitudes via a study of linguistics and anthropology (Bull 1988).

The most recent trend is towards multiculturalism, that is, a dissatisfaction with a scholarly canon comprising the art of the West. Resistance to this approach to art history is voiced through concerns that such a shift of focus, away from the statues of the ancients, the frescoes of the Renaissance and the oil paintings of Rembrandt and the masterpieces of cubism towards tribal masks, sand-paintings and Chinese manuscripts, is vulnerable to mere tokenism. The counter-accusation that the maintenance of the Western canon is intellectually indefensible is formulated in the aftermath of feminism, which has raised central questions of the role of 'artists'. For art historians to raise questions about gender is part of an inherently complicating

---

44 Bal and Bryson 1993; Schapiro 1973 and articles on Schapiro's semiotics in *Social Research* 45 (1978); Iversen 1990.

45 For a challenge to the possibility of interpretation see Elkins 1993. For the dangers of such a dismissal, see Llewellyn 1984.

process, for it creates and encourages histories by challenging the notion of a single paradigm. Gender issues do not equate precisely with feminism, although some argue that the materials of traditional and radical art historical analysis are irretrievably polluted by patriarchy (Pollock and Parker 1981). In keeping with a general mood of postmodern pessimism, serious philosophical scepticism has been voiced that histories of art can be anything other than histories of the literature on art (Thompson 1993). Some of the historical approaches rehearsed in this chapter claim exclusivity and truth, as manifestations of an attitude to life, not methods to be selected as if from a menu. However, there is no evidence that any of them can claim mastery; there is and never has been a single true art history, only a range of interconnected problems and possibilities.

REFERENCES

Allsopp, B. (1970) *The Study of Architectural History*, New York.
Alpers, S. (1960) 'Ekphrasis and aesthetic attitudes in Vasari's Lives', *Journal of the Warburg and Courtauld Institutes* 23: 190–215.
Antal, F. (1948) *Florentine Painting and its Social Background*, London.
—— (1949) 'Remarks upon the method of art history', *Burlington Magazine* 91: 49–52 and 73–5.
—— (1966) *Reflections on Classicism and Romanticism*, London.
Argan, G. C. (1975) 'Ideology and iconology', *Critical Inquiry* 2: 297–305.
Baglione (1642) *Le Vite de pittori, scultori ... del 1572. In fino a' ... 1642*, Rome.
Bal, M. and Bryson, N. (1993) 'Semiotics and art history', *Art Bulletin* 73: 174–208.
Barolsky, P. (1990) *Michelangelo's Nose: A Myth and its Maker*, University Park, PA.
Baxandall, M. D. K. (1971) *Giotto and the Orators*, Oxford.
Bellori, G. P. (1664) *Idea*, also in Bellori 1672.
—— (1672) *Le vite de' pittori, scultori ed architetti moderni*, Rome.
—— (1695) *Descrizzione delle imagini dipinte de Rafaelle d'Urbino nelle Camere del Palazzo Apostolico Vaticano*, Rome.
Belting, H. (1987) *The End of the History of Art?*, Chicago and London.
Berenson, B. (1901–17) *The Study and Criticism of Italian Art*, London.
—— (1930) *Italian Painters of the Renaissance*, Oxford. (Repr. London 1952.)
—— (1954) *The Arch of Constantine: or, the Decline of Form*, London.
Bialostocki, J. (1963) 'Iconography and iconology', in *Encyclopaedia of World Art*, vol. 7, New York.
Bickendorf, G. (1985) *Der Beginn des Kunstgeschichtschreibung unter dem Paradigm 'Geschichte' in G. F. Waagens Frühschrift 'Über Hubert und Jan van Eyck'*, Worms.
Brigstocke, H. (1981) *Bulletin John Rylands Library* 65(1).
Brown, D. A. (1979) *Berenson and the Conoisseurship of Italian Painting*, exhibition catalogue, Washington.
Bryson, N. (1983) *Vision and Painting: The Logic of the Gaze*, London.
Bull, M. (1988) 'The iconography of the Sistine Chapel ceiling', *Burlington Magazine* 130 (August): 597–605.
Burckhardt, J. (1855) *Der Cicerone*, Basle. (Tr. into English as: *The Cicerone: Or, Art Guide to Painting in Italy*, London, 1873.)
—— (1860) *Die Kultur der Renaissance in Italien*, Basle. (Tr. into English: London, 1878.)
Cardy, H. (1976) 'Discussion of the theory of climate in the *querelle des anciens et des modernes*', in *Studies on Voltaire and the Eighteenth Century* 163: 73–88.

Carrier, D. (1987) 'Piero della Francesca and his interpreters: is there progress in art history?', *History and Theory* 26: 150–65.

—— (1990) 'Art history in the mirror stage', *History and Theory* 29: 296–320.

Cicognara, L. [1813–18] (1823–4) *Storia della scultura ... in Italia fino al secolo di Napoleone*, 2nd edn, 7 vols, Prato.

Clark, T. J. (1973) *Image of the People*, London.

—— (1974) 'The conditions of artistic production', *Times Literary Supplement*, 24 May: 561–2.

Cochrane, E. (1981) 'The lateral disciplines', book 6, esp. ch. 14, 'Biography', in E. Cochrane, *Historians and Historiography in the Italian Renaissance*, Chicago.

Collu, R. (1983) *Carlo Giuseppe Ratti: pittore e scenografo d'arte*, Savona.

Compton, M. (1960) 'William Roscoe and early collectors of Italian primitives', *Bulletin of the Walker Art Gallery Liverpool* 9: 27–51.

Crowe, J. A. (1885) *Reminiscences of Thirty-Five Years of My Life*, London.

—— and Cavalcasselle, G. (1864–6) *A New History of Painting in Italy, from the Second to the Sixteenth Century*, 3 vols, London.

—— and —— (1877) *Titian: His Life and Times*, 2 vols, London.

Damisch, H. (1971–2) 'Le gardien de l'interpretation', *Tel Quel* 44: 70–84; 45: 82–96.

De Piles, R. (1699) *Abrégé de la vie des peintres*, Paris.

Dempsey, C. (1977) *Annibale Carracci and the Beginnings of the Baroque Style*, Glückstadt.

Descamps, J. B. (1753–63) *La Vie des peintres flamands, allemands et hollandais*, 4 vols, Paris.

Dézallier d'Argenville, A. J. (1745–52) *Abrégé de la vie des plus fameux peintres*, Paris.

Dominici, B. de (1742–63) *Vite de' pittori*, 3 vols, Naples.

Donahue, N. H. (ed.) (1995) *Invisible Cathedrals. The Expressionist Art History of Wilhelm Worringer*, University Park, PA.

Dubos, J.-B. (1719) *Réflexions critiques sur la poésie et sur la peintre*, Paris.

Dvorak, M. (1928) *Kunstgeschichte als Geistesgeschichte*, Munich. (English edition: London, 1984.)

—— (1967) *Idealism and Naturalism in Gothic Art*, Notre Dame.

Elkins, J. (1993) 'On monstrously ambiguous paintings', *History and Theory* 32: 227–47.

Falkenheim, I. V. (1980) *Roger Fry and the Beginnings of Formalist Art Criticism*, Ann Arbor.

Farago, C. (ed.) (1996) *Reframing the Renaissance: Visual Culture in Europe and Latin America 1450–1650*, New Haven, CT. and London.

Félibien, A. (1685–8) *Entretiens sur les vies et sur les ouvrages des plus excellents peintres anciens et modernes*, 2nd edn, 2 vols, Paris.

Fernie, E. (ed.) (1995) *Art History and its Methods: A Critical Anthology*, London.

Ferretti, S. (1990) *Cassirer, Panofsky and Warburg: Symbols, Art and History*, New Haven, CT. and London. (First published in Italian, 1984.)

Filipczak, Z. Z. (1993) 'Selective importation of Italian theories of art into the Netherlands', in J. R. Brink and W. F. Gentrup (eds) *Renaissance Culture in Context: Theory and Practice*, London.

Fiorillo, J.-D. (1796–1808) *Geschichte der zeichnenden Künste*, Hamburg.

Frankl, P. (1938) *Das System der Kunstwissenschaft*, Brünn and Leipzig.

—— (1960) *The Gothic: Literary Sources and Interpretations through Eight Centuries*, Princeton.

Freedberg, S. J. (1983) *Circa 1600. A Revolution of Style in Italian Painting*, Cambridge, MA.

Friedländer, M. (1969) *Reminiscences and Reflections*, ed. R. M. Heilbrunn, New York.

Gaehtgens, T. (1990) 'Les rapports d'histoire de l'art et de l'art contemporain en Allemagne à l'époque de Wölfflin et de Meier-Graefe', *Revue de l'Art* 88: 31–8.

Gibson-Wood, C. (1984) 'Jonathan Richardson and the rationalisation of connoisseurship', *Art History* 7(1): 38–56.

Goldberg, E. L. (1988) *After Vasari: History, Art and Patronage in Late Medici Florence*, Princeton.

Goldstein, C. (1992) 'Rhetoric and art history in the Italian Renaissance and Baroque', *Art Bulletin* 74: 520–1.

Gombrich, E. H. (1959) *Art and Illusion. A Study of the Psychology of Pictorial Representation*, Oxford.

—— (1966) *Norm and Form*, Oxford.

—— (1970) *Aby Warburg: An Intellectual Biography*, London.

—— (1973) *Symbolic Images*, London.

Gossman, L. (1988) 'Jacob Burckhardt as an art historian', *Oxford Art Journal* 11(1): 25–32.

Grendler, P. F. (1969a) *Critics of the Italian World 1530–60*, Madison.

—— (1969b) 'Francesco Sansovino and Italian popular history', *Studies in the Renaissance* 16: 139–80.

Grinten, E. F. van der (1952) *Enquiries into the History of Art Historical Writing*, Amsterdam.

Harvey, J. (1948) *Gothic England*, 2nd edn, London.

Haskell, F. (1971) 'Giorgione's 'Concert Champêtre' and its admirers', *Journal of the Royal Society of Arts*: 543–55.

—— (1976) *Rediscoveries in Art. Some Aspects of Taste, Fashion and Collecting in England and France*, Oxford.

—— (1987) *The Painful Birth of the Artbook*, London.

—— (1993) *History and its Images*, New Haven, CT. and London.

—— and Penny, N. (1981) *Taste and the Antique*, New Haven, CT. and London.

Hauser, A. (1951) *The Social History of Art*, London.

—— (1965) *Mannerism. The Crisis of the Renaissance*, London.

Herrmann, W. (1962) *Laugier and Eighteenth-Century French Theory*, London.

Holcomb, A. M. (1983) 'Anna Jameson: the first professional English art historian', *Art History* 6: 171–87.

Holly, M. A. (1984) *Panofsky and the Foundations of Art History*, Ithaca, NY and London.

Hope, C. (1981) 'Artists, patrons and advisers in the Italian Renaissance', in G. F. Lytle and S. Orgel (eds) *Patronage in the Renaissance*, Princeton.

—— (1983–4) 'The historians of Venetian painting', in J. Martineau and C. Hope (eds) *The Genius of Venice 1500–1600*, Exhibition Catalogue, Royal Academy, London.

Iversen, M. (1981) 'Politics and the historiography of art history: Wölfflin's "Classic Art"', *Oxford Art Journal* 4(1): 31–4.

—— (1990) 'The vicissitudes of the visual sign', *Word and Image* 6(3): 212–16.

—— (1993) *Alois Riegl: Art History and Theory*, Cambridge, MA.

James, E. and Webb, R. (1991) 'To understand ultimate things and enter secret places: art and ekphrasis in Byzantium', *Art History* 14: 1–17.

Jameson, A. (1890) *Sacred and Legendary Art*, vol. 1, 3rd edn, London.

Janson, H. W. (1973) 'Criterion of periodisation in the history of European art', in H. W. Janson, *Sixteen Studies*, New York.

Joost-Gaugier, C. L. (1982) 'The early beginnings of the notion of "Uomini famosi" and the "De viris illustribus" in Graeco-Roman literary tradition', *Artibus et Historiae* 6(3).

Kallab, W. (1908) *Vasaristudien*, ed. J. von Schlosser, Vienna.

Kemal, S. and Gaskell, I. (eds) (1991) *The Language of Art History*, Cambridge.

Kemp, M. (1984) 'Seeing and signs. E. H. Gombrich in retrospect', *Art History* 7: 228f.

Klein, R. (1979) *Form and Meaning*, Princeton.

Kleinbauer, W. E. (1971) *Modern Perspectives in Western Art History*, New York.

—— and Slavens, T. P. (1982) 'Determinants of writing art history', in *Research Guide to the History of Western Art*, Chicago.

Krautheimer, R. (1969) *Studies in Early Christian, Medieval and Renaissance Art*, New York.

Kris, E. and Kurz, O. (1979) *Legend, Myth and Magic in the Image of the Artist*, New Haven and London.

Kugler, F. (1842) *A Hand-Book of the History of Painting*, London. (First published in German, 1837.)

Kultermann, U. (1993) *The History of Art History*, rev. English edn, Pleasantville, NY. (First published in German as: *Geschichte der Kunstgeschichte*, Vienna, 1966.)

Kurz, O. (1963) 'Barocco: storia di un concetto', in V. Branca (ed.) *Barocco europeo e barocco veneziano*, Venice.

Lanzi, L. (1792) *La storia pittorica*, Florence. (Translated into French, German and English in the 1820s and 1830s.)

Lavin, I. (ed.) (1995) *Meaning in the Visual Arts: Views from the Outside*, Princeton.

Leeks, W. (1996) 'What's love got to do with it?', *Oxford Art Journal* 19(1): 103–6.

Levey, M. (1960) 'Botticelli and nineteenth-century England', *Journal of the Warburg and Courtauld Institutes* 23: 291–306.

Levi, D. (1985) *Cavalcassalle ... della conservazione dell'arte italiana*, Turin.

Lindsay, A. (1847) *Sketches of the History of Christian Art*, 3 vols, London.

Llewellyn, N. (1984) Review of Bryson 1981, *The Modern Language Review* 74(4): 937–40.

—— (forthcoming) 'Une science du regard. Les connaisseurs', in *Histoire de l'histoire de l'art* (4e partie), Paris.

Lloyd, C. (1975) *Art and its Images*, exhibition catalogue, Oxford.

Longhi, R. (1963) *Piero della Francesca*, London.

McClellan, A. (1994) *Inventing the Louvre. Art, Politics, and the Origins of the Modern Museum in Eighteenth-Century Paris*, Cambridge.

Maginnis, H. B. J. (1996) 'Reflections on Formalism: the Post-Impressionists and the early Italians', *Art History* 19(2): 191–207.

Malvasia, C. C. (1678) *Felsina Pittrice. Vite de pittore bolognesi*, 2 vols, Bologna.

Mander, K. van (1994) *Lives of the Illustrious Netherlandish and German Painters*, vol. 1, Doornspijk.

Marucchi, A. and Salerno, L. (eds) (1956–7) *Considerazione sulla pittura*, 2 vols, Rome.

Melion, W. (1991) *Shaping the Netherlandish Canon. Karel van Mander's Schilder-Boeck*, Chicago.

Meltzoff, S. (1942) 'The rediscovery of Vermeer', *Marsyas* 2: 145–66.

Mitchell, W. J. T. (1986) *Iconology – Image, Text, Ideology*, Chicago.

Moffett, K. (1973) *Meier-Graefe as Art Critic*, Munich.

Montfaucon, B. de (1717) *L'Antiquité expliquée et représentée en figures*, 10 vols, Paris.

Morelli, G. (1897) *Della pittura italiana*, Milan.

Morisani, O. (1953) 'Art historians and art critics III. Cristoforo Landino', *Burlington Magazine* 95: 267.

Mostyn-Owen, W. (1972) *Bibliografia di Bernard Berenson*, 2nd edn, New York.

Moyer, J. B. de [1752] (1966) *Réfléxions critiques sur les différentes écoles de peinture*, Paris.

Norman, D. (1983) 'History and historiography', *Art History* 6(2): 223–7.

Offner, R. (1927) 'An outline of a theory of method', in R. Offner, *Studies in Florentine Painting*, New York. (Repr. 1972.)

Olin, M. (1993) *Forms of Representation in Alois Riegl's Theory of Art*, University Park, PA.

Onians, J. B. (1988) *Bearers of Meaning*, Princeton.

Orwicz, M. R. (1985) 'Cultural discourse on the formation of a social history of art: Anglo-American response to Arnold Hauser', *Oxford Art Journal* 8: 52–62.

Pacheco, F. (1649) *Arte de la pintura, su antigüedad y grandezas*, Seville.

Pächt, O. (1980) *Methodisches zur kunsthistorischen Praxis*, Munich.

Palomino, A. (1715–24) *El Museo Pictórico y Escala Optica*, 3 vols, Madrid.

Panofsky, E. (ed.) (1946) *Abbot Suger on the Abbey Church of St. Denis*, Princeton.

Panofsky, E. (1949) *Albrecht Dürer*, 3rd edn, Princeton.

—— (1951) *Gothic Architecture and Scholasticism*, New York.

—— (1955) *Meaning in the Visual Arts: Papers in and on the Humanities*, Garden City.

—— [1939] (1962) *Studies in Iconology*, 2nd edn, New York.

Passavant, J. D. (1833) *Kunstreise durch England und Belgien*, Frankfurt.

Perini, G. (1986) 'Central issues and peripheral debates in seventeenth-century art literature', *Acts of the 26th Congress of the International Committee for the History of Art*, vol. 1, Washington.

—— (1988) 'Carlo Cesare Malvasia's Florentine letters: insight into conflicting trends in seventeenth-century art historiography', *Art Bulletin* 70: 273–99.

—— (1990) 'Malvasia's connections with France and Rome', *Burlington Magazine* 132: 410–12.

Perrault, C. (1688) *Paralelle des Anciens et des Modernes*, 4 vols, Paris.

Podro, M. (1981) *The Critical Historians of Art*, New Haven, CT. and London.

—— (1989) 'Michael Podro in conversation with Sir Ernst Gombrich', *Apollo* 130: 373–8.

Pollitt, J. J. (1966) *The Art of Rome. c.753 B.C.–A.D. 337*, Englewood Cliffs, NJ.

—— (1990) *The Ancient View of Greek Art: Sources and Documents*, Cambridge. (=rev. edn of *The Art of Greece, 1400–31 B.C.*, Englewood Cliffs, NJ, 1965.)

Pollock, G. and Parker, R. (1981) *Old Mistresses. Women, Art and Ideology*, London.

Pope-Hennessy, J. (1980) *The Study and Criticism of Italian Sculpture*, Princeton.

Potts, A. D. (1985) 'Winckelmann's construction of history', in *Art History* 5(4): 386–407.

—— (1994) *Flesh and the Ideal. Winckelmann and the Origins of Art History*, New Haven and London.

Pozzo, B. dal (1718) *Le Vite de' pittori ... Veronesi*, Verona.

Puttfarken, T. (1985) *Roger De Piles' Theory of Art*, New Haven and London.

Ratti, C. G. (1766) *Istruzioni di quanto può vedersi di più bello in Genova*, Genoa.

Roscoe, W. [1795] (1846) *The Life of Lorenzo de' Medici called the Magnificent*, 8th edn, London.

Rousseau, J.-J. (1755) *Discours sur les origines de l'inégalité*, Amsterdam.

Rumohr, C. F. (1832) *Drey Reisen nach Italien*, Leipzig.

Rüsen, J. (1985) 'Jacob Burckhardt: political standpoint and historical insight on the border of post-modernism', *History and Theory* 24: 235–46.

Rykwert, J. (1980) *The First Moderns*, Cambridge, MA. and London.

Salerno, L. (1963) 'Historiography', in *Encyclopaedia of World Art*, vol. 7, New York.

Samuels, E. (1979) *Bernard Berenson. The Making of a Connoisseur*, London.

Sandrart, J. von (1768–75) *Teutsche Academie der Bau-, Bildhauer- und maler-Kunst*, 8 vols, Nuremburg.

Schapiro, M. (1956) 'Leonardo and Freud: an art-historical study', *Journal of the History of Ideas* 17: 147–78.

—— (1973) *Words and Pictures*, Paris.

Schlosser, J. von (1912) *Lorenzo Ghibertis Denkwürdigkeiten*, Berlin.

—— (1962) *La letteratura artistica*, Florence.

Schneider, L. (ed.) (1974) *Giotto in Perspective*, NJ.

Schröter, E. (1990) 'Raffael-Kult und Raffael-Forschung: Johann David Passavant und seine Raffael-Monographie im Kontext der Kunst und Kunstgeschichte seiner Zeit', *Römisches Jahrbuch der Kunstgeschichte* 26: 303–97.

Seroux d'Agincourt, J. B. L. G. (1823) *Histoire de l'art par les monuments*, 6 vols, Paris.

Smart, A. (1966) 'Roger Fry and early Italian art', *Apollo*: vol. 83, 262–71.

Sohn, P. (1991) *Pittoresco*, Cambridge.

Soussloff, C. M. (1990) 'Lives of poets and painters in the Renaissance', *Word and Image* 6(2): 154–62.

Spector, J. J. (1969) 'The method of Morelli and its relation to Freudian psychoanalysis', *Diogenes* 66: 63–83.

Tafuri, M. (1987) 'Introduction: the historical project', in M. Tafuri, *The Sphere and the Labyrinth*, Cambridge, MA.

Thompson, M. P. (1993) 'Reception theory and the interpretation of historical meaning', *History and Theory* 32: 248–72.

Thornton, R. D. (1963) 'The influence of the Enlightenment upon eighteenth-century British antiquaries, 1750–1800', *Studies on Voltaire and the Eighteenth Century*, 24: 1593–1618.

Turner, A. R. (1993) *Inventing Leonardo. The Anatomy of a Legend*, New York.

Venturi, L. (1964) *The History of Art Criticism*, New York.

Waagen, G. F. (1837–9) *Kunstwerke und Künstler in England und Paris*, 3 vols, Berlin.

—— (1842–5) *Kunstwerke und Künstler in Deutschland*, 2 vols, Leipzig.

Walpole, H. (1762–71) *Anecdotes of Painting in England*, Strawberry Hill.

Warburg, A. (1932) *Gesammelte Schriften*, Leipzig.

Werckmeister, O. K. (1984) 'The depoliticised, attenuated version', *Art History* 7: 345–8.

—— (1991) 'A working perspective for Marxist art history today', *Oxford Art Journal* 14: 83–7.

Williams, R. (1980) 'Base and superstructure in Marxist cultural theory', in *Problems in Materialism and Culture. Selected Essays*, London.

Winckelmann, J. J. (1755) *Gedanken über der Nachahmung der griechischen Werke*, Dresden. (English edn: *Reflections on the Painting and Sculpture of the Greeks*, tr. H. Fuseli, London, 1765–7.)

—— (1764) *Geschichte der Kunst des Altertums*, Dresden.

Wind, E. (1963) *Art and Anarchy*, London.

Wölfflin, H. (1888) *Renaissance und Barok*, Munich.

—— (1899) *Die Klassische Kunst*, Munich. (Tr. as: *Classic Art*, London, 1903.)

—— (1915) *Kunstgeschichtliche Grundbegriffe*, Munich. (Tr. as: *Principles of Art History*, London, 1932.)

—— [1888] (1964) *Renaissance and Baroque* [tr. of Wölfflin 1888].

Wollheim, R. (1973) *On Art and the Mind*, London.

Zimmermann, T. C. P. (1976) 'Paolo Giovio and the evolution of Renaissance art criticism', in C. H. Clough (ed.) *Cultural Aspects the Italian Renaissance*, Manchester.

V.2 APPROACHES

855-7
facts vs story
865+
generalizations
make historistic.
not facts

868
metahistory
metanarratives
+ White

34

THE HISTORICAL NARRATIVE

Peter Munz

There are a good many reasons why people are interested in the past. At one end of the scale there is idle curiosity and the fascination of the exotic; in the middle, there has always been the desire to learn from other people's experiences; and at the other end there is the assumption that one's past defines one's identity and that the perception, even though it may be spurious or imagined, of a shared past promotes a sense of community.[1] In addition to these various aesthetic, didactic and political reasons, there is the fact that we are the products of the past. Our anatomy and physiology are largely genetically determined and even socially and culturally we are the way we are because of our past. True, we must allow for freedom of choice; but the choices are always limited by the past and I venture to guess that while our capacity for choice has increased with evolution, that same evolution by now also precludes many choices we would have had in the past – supposing, of course, that that capacity had been available in the past. In any case, only the past explains why we are here and why we are the way we are.[2] Whether we start with the Big Bang or with the appearance of the first living cells, there are straight lines of causal sequences from the past to the present and if the past had been substantially or significantly different, we would not be the way we are. Our presence in the universe is a mystery which can be somewhat abated when we see ourselves and other people at the end of a long line of causes and effects. But the curious thing is that while we are quite certain that the past has taken place and that we stand at the

---

1   Tacitus and Thucydides were read for centuries as *magistri vitae*. For the therapeutic value of story-telling see Bruner 1990: 114–15. For the social cohesion produced by story-telling see Durkheim 1912: 610ff.
2   Gould 1989 tends to confuse this issue. He argues that, since there is no predetermination, everything is contingent. But this does not follow. The mutations and changes are contingent; but the selections made are not. In Darwinian selectionism, absence of predetermination and absence of contingency are combined.

end of it, the past does not lie out there or back there, for us to look at. If we want to know it and talk about it, it first has to be written up and turned into a story.[3] It has to be made ready for inspection. This is so not only for human history, but also for the history of living matter and for the history of the earth.[4] Only when it is laid out can we inspect it and gather from it how it has come about that we are here and that we are the way we are. As Fernand Braudel (1980: 27) put it, 'all historical work is concerned with breaking down time past'. The question is, of course, how it is to be broken down, i.e. described.

In order to do justice to time, it must be described in a narrative form. Any other form of description fails to take account of the fact that the past bears the mark of the arrow of time. Narrative is the only literary device available which will reflect the past's time structure. When historians are discussing whether narrative is the best or an acceptable form to represent the past and whether it should or should not be revived, they are engaging in an idle discussion and might as soon ask whether the universe out to be represented truthfully or falsely. The ineluctable reality of time and its arrow, pointing from the past to the future, has not always been appreciated or taken seriously, and at the present time there is vigorous resistance to it from, of all people, historians. It is true that there have been philosophers who have maintained that the passage of time is an illusion and in classical physics, time was reversible. But just when physicists and biologists are beginning to take time to be real and irreversible,[5] historians, probably over-reacting to the ancient religious belief that human history is governed by divine providence as well as to its more modern secular version that human history is a march towards progress, are retreating in the opposite direction. Instead of representing the past in its irreversible time structure, they have come to consider the past simply as a directionless heap of all the things that happen to be no longer here. It is no exaggeration to say that at the present time historians (and many anthropologists) are probably the only people around who think that human societies do not evolve out of each other but are so many entities, to be studied as configurations which have nothing much to do with what went before or came after, each, as Ranke used to put it, equidistant from God. Or if they do not think so, they believe it to be none of their business to take the arrow of time into account. When they do narrate they think that the sequences produced by their narratives are an illusion rather than a representation of reality.[6]

This attitude to the past as a jumble of events rather than as a series of events

---

3 History has to be written before it can be studied. See Munz 1985: ch. 2.

4 See Munz 1977: 44–5 for how the story is altered by the changes in generalizations used. This is well explored in regard to the story of the evolution of man by Landau 1991.

5 See Munz 1993: 194f. For a very readable introduction to the subject see Coveney and Highfield 1990.

6 Cf., e.g. the 1979 Chicago symposium 'Narrative: The Illusion of Sequence', the contributions to which were edited by Mitchell 1980.

where the earlier are the causes of the later has received strong confirmation from modern anthropologists, who are mindful of the fact that even quite primitive social orders like Papua New Guinea are now members of the United Nations with full voting rights, so that one ought to take it that all social orders and the behaviour they generate are so many equal variations on the same human theme. This careless attitude to the irreversible nature of time is reflected in the syllabuses of modern universities where odd spans of time are studied in no particular order and certainly not in the order in which they succeeded one another. Hence there is a resistance to orderly narration and a preference for the description of static structures. Those historians who nevertheless advocate narration are faint-hearted and do not consider narration to be a matter of principle related to the time structure of the past (see Stone 1979). Historians, rightly, hate thoughts of a Whig interpretation of history or of any other notion of progress. But there is no need to throw out the baby with the bath-water. One can accept the irreversibility of time and the fact that its representation requires narrative even though one is ignorant of the direction it is moving in.

Let us begin by looking at Fernand Braudel's *The Mediterranean and the Mediterranean World in the Age of Philip II* (1949), an influential example of this lack of interest in the irreversibility of time and of the consequent rejection of narrative which has become a veritable non-narrative paradigm of the representation of the past. Instead of telling a story and pursuing it along the path of the arrow of time, Braudel divides the events of the past into three categories. There are, first, the events of the long duration, such as the geographical setting. Then there are the events of the middle duration, such as technical inventions, birth-rates, trade relations. And finally, there are the events of the short duration, the politics of war and peace. There is nothing wrong with the classification as such. The flaw in Braudel's representation is that it fails to bring out the causal connections between the three classes of events, for it is precisely those causal connections which would oblige him to represent all the events in a narrative form. Instead he prides himself on having discarded narrative and on having revealed the 'structure' of events. But that structure, like all structures, is subject to the arrow of time and therefore crying out for a narrative in which the causal connections are brought out. It is a telling commentary on the change of paradigm and the decline of narrative that Braudel has replaced the old philosophers of history as a cultural hero.

But it is not necessary to go back to the old philosophers of history. Long before Braudel and at a time when historians had not yet formed an ideological opposition to the arrow of time, Tolstoy in his *War and Peace* produced a narrative in which the links between the three structures were revealed. There are the events of the long duration – Russia and her peasants, directly represented in the immobility of Kutuzov. If one then considers the events of short duration, it looks as if he were the leader. Then there are the events of the middle duration – family life, the economy of the agricultural holdings and the customs of marriage, attractive or reprehensible, as the case may be. And on the third level, there are the events of the short duration – political intrigues, the war and the battles. The latter are narrated

853

with stupendous virtuosity at Austerlitz from a bird's-eye view and at Borodino from a worm's-eye view. Tolstoy succeeded where Braudel failed. For Tolstoy showed, for example, how the financial fortunes of the Rostovs (middle duration) are influenced by the peasants' conditions (long duration) and how the lives of Natasha and Nicolai (short duration) are in part determined by the events in the middle and the long duration. Or take the narrative of the rebuilding of Moscow, which consists of the interaction of events of the long duration (Moscow, though in ruins, continues to 'exist') with events of the middle duration (builders have to keep on building and human beings have to have shelter) to give rise to the events of the short duration, the rebuilding of Moscow. Encouraged by Tolstoy's success and challenged by Braudel's failure, we should take a close look at the structure of narrative and its relation to the past with its arrow of time. Given the nature of time, narration is the only realistic representation of the past and we are not free to choose or reject it.

The meaning of the past is the way we are now, because if the past had been different, we too, would be different and if it had not happened at all, we would not be here. But that meaning cannot be gathered by looking at the past as it is in itself but only looking at the past as it has been written about or talked about by somebody. The distinction between the past as it is in itself and as it is narrated is old enough – we find it even in ancient times as the distinction between *res gestae* and *historia rerum gestarum*. But until quite recently, people have been unaware of the epistemological consequences of the distinction and of the philosophical problems it poses to all historians. The problem does not simply consist in the fact that the past is not readily remembered or frequently insufficiently recorded. If it simply amounted to this, then pedantic research could remedy the situation and one could eventually find out what happened in the past. If this were the case, one would presume that people at any stage of the past knew what was happening to them and that the reason why we do not know is that the records or traditions were lost. But the point is that even the people who were alive at any stage of the past had either little knowledge or perception of what was happening; or that such perceptions as they had were widely influenced by their personal interests and abstractions and therefore were in no sense 'correct' perceptions. They themselves had no knowledge of *res gestae* but, at best were making up stories about it and constructing *historiae rerum gestarum*. Which goes to prove the truth of an old saying, attributed (falsely, I believe) to Thucydides, that 'stories only happen to people who have the ability to tell them'.

It is therefore not just a matter of recovering all the facts, but of finding a way of incorporating past constructions of what people thought had happened to them into modern constructions or, possibly, the other way round. Once this is understood, there also breaks down the traditional convention that one can distinguish between primary and secondary sources. The primacy sources of the knowledge of the past are believed to be documents and remains which date from the part of the past to be investigated and are believed to be more genuine sources of information about what happened than later accounts. The secondary sources are those which have been constructed by later historians about that part of the past. In fact, even the so-called primary sources are not mindless records of *res gestae*; but they too are *historiae rerum gestarum*, so that the time honoured distinction disappears.

The distinction between the unknowable substance of events and the construction of stories about it by the enumeration of distinct facts comes from the realization that the events of the past are a seamless web of unidentifiably fluid happenings; and that stories are series of distinct facts which are related in some way to one another. There is a hiatus between story and the objects or events it claims to be about: the story must consist of facts the occurrence of which can be located in the substance; but the substance by itself does not lead into the story or its constituent facts. As I shall demonstrate below, the story is an artificial construction and it is not a portrait of the substance. One might almost conclude that that constructed story is an arbitrary construction. There is indeed a remarkable tradition which stretches from Rousseau to Simon Schama that what we call the past is a story of fables to which people, for some obscure reason or other, give their assent. Given the unknowability of the seamless substance, some people like Gore Vidal and Simon Schama have come to believe in the totality of fiction and end up by wiping out the difference between novels and history (see e.g. Vesser 1989 and Bennington *et al.* 1987). But this seductive conclusion cannot go without saying and when we take a closer look at the way narratives are constructed, we will be able to recognize that there are constraints on such arbitrariness and that stories, though constructions, are not arbitrary constructions, even though it is true that they are constructions which do not stand in a direct relationship to the substance of happenings they claim to represent. If the substance is seamless and events roll into each other without boundaries and are unidentifiably fluid, we have to take a closer look at the so-called facts, alleged to be the raw material of the narrative.

We start with the notion that there is no absolute size to any fact, and that the size we choose is not dictated by the substance it reflects. This denial of ultimate facticity follows from logical analysis. Unfortunately, it has been seized upon by postmodern historians, blown up into the view that all 'facts' are invented, and used to drive a coach and four through the conception of historical knowledge. In reaction to the absurdities of postmodernism, leading historians like Gertrude Himmelfarb (1992) keep persuading themselves, against all reason, that the past consists of hard-and-fast facts which the historian has to discover. My argument will steer clear of the modernist belief that there are facts which have to be discovered as well as of the postmodernist belief that there are no facts and that the past can be invented (Hurst 1981: 278).

Let us start with an example. It is a fact that the Second World War started on 1 September 1939. It is also a fact that it began when the first German soldier moved his right foot across the border of Poland. It is also a fact that the Second World War was the second round of the First World War which began in August 1914. Nobody would dispute the truth of these facts and yet it can be seen that although they reflect overlapping parts of the underlying substance of events, they differ enormously in size. This is so because none of them are given and all of them are constructed. This realization then leads immediately to the next observation, that the facts which will go to form a narrative do not succeed one another in time. If they could be seen as succeeding each other in time and if, therefore, the narrative could be seen as a description of the facts as they succeed one another in time, they all would have to be of the same size, that is, cover discrete and equal spans of time and not overlap.

As we are free to construct facts of any size, facts cannot be seen as chronologically contiguous. A narrative, therefore, is not a description of facts as they succeed one another in time. For any two facts can be broken up and subdivided to make myriads of other facts and in this way, for any two facts which appear chronologically close to one another, there can be constructed other facts which can, chronologically, be inserted between the two initial facts. The procedure is inexhaustible and shows us that any fact is infinitely subdivisible and that whatever narrative is, its structure is not given by the sequence of events in time.

Facts are artificial constructions. A large fact like 'the Second World War happened in the first half of the 1940s' is really a portmanteau term for lots of smaller facts and is to be seen as a summary narrative, rather than as a simple fact. Smaller facts do not readily appear as similar summaries, but they are. Even a small fact like the movement of the German soldier's foot across the Polish border in September 1939 is really a composite fact. Its constituent elements consist of the even smaller facts that the foot moved one inch and a little later it moved another inch, and so forth, until it was right across the border. For that matter if we happen not to be interested in constructing facts about the war, we could easily take the first constituent fact, the movement along the first inch, and link it to the insect it encountered on the road and make a fact out of that foot which stepped on an insect and killed it. We could then insert this fact into the natural history of insects and lose sight of all human wars. Alternatively, we could leave out the death of the insect and construct a fact to the effect that the movement of the foot injured the surface of an insect and produced a secretion of an acid nature. With this fact in mind, we would then look for the havoc caused by the acid on a pebble on that road and either tell a story about the chemical changes wrought on the pebbles by the steps of the foot or produce a more summary fact which states that on that September day there were chemical changes on a certain road leading into Poland. According to whatever our interest happens to be, we obtain for the same indivisible substance of events two quite different stories or summary facts. One leads to the Second World War and the other to molecular changes in the pebbles on the road. Whichever we pursue, the other is almost immediately lost below the horizon of our interest.

We can see now that the distinction between a fact and a story is not absolute. It is merely a matter of size and of the explicit mention of the constituent 'facts' into which any summary description of a fact is broken up. If the constituent facts are separately and explicitly mentioned, we speak of a story or a narrative. If they are not, we tend to remain with the notion of a single 'fact'. In the case of a summary fact which is very large, this is quite obvious; but it is equally true of a very small fact like the inch-long movement of the boot of the German soldier. Every fact is a mini-narrative; and, equally, any narrative can, summarily, be described as a fact. With this conclusion we can now see that there is no absolute distinction between facts and stories or narratives and that it would be quite wrong to think that a narrative is a composition made out of facts and that the facts in any sense whatever, are 'given'.

The construction of facts which are mini-narratives or 'narrative-laden' and the construction of genuine narratives which could also be summed up as large facts, is in all cases an artificial procedure controlled, in the first instance, and in the first instance only, by their compatibility with those other stories which we chose to regard as the 'sources' of our knowledge of the past.

In the nineteenth century and well into the twentieth century, it was believed that the hard-and-fast facts can be ascertained from the primary sources and that the narrative results from the chronological order in which these facts stand to one another.[7] But when it was discovered that the construction of a narrative is not just a simple process of culling facts from primary sources and of ordering them in their temporal succession, the pendulum swung soon in the opposite direction. There is now a school of postmodern historians who are telling their stories about the past on the assumption that there is no descriptive element in the sources, so that the facts culled from them contain no descriptive element. In the absence of this descriptive element, any story told is 'merely the expression of the authoritarian nature of that particular speech act'[8] In this postmodern view there are not three elements – the story, the historian and the event; but only two elements – the historian and the story. This postmodern view has gained an initial plausibility from the consideration that the story is constructed by the historian rather than copied from the reality of the events of the past. But when one investigates the way the story is constructed, one recognizes the constraints under which the historian is working and that these constraints exist in spite of the fact that the historian neither records the past seismographically nor copies from the sources. His construction, in spite of the high degree of artificially, is not arbitrary. There are quite solid constraints on the construction of narratives, even though they do not consist in the correspondence of what is being told to the facts – not even to the facts as contained in the 'sources'. What are they?

The real constraints come from a very stringent phenomenon. Whatever size fact we settle for, the next fact in its proper order must be linked to it via a generalization, not to say a general law. It is this generalization rather than temporal contiguity which leads from one fact to the next and thus establishes the form of

---

7 As examples see the famous École des Chartes and Lord Acton's Cambridge Modern History Project published from 1902 onwards. See Burke 1991: 5–6.
8 Barthes 1970: 154. Barthes considers all determinate meaning to be inherently 'terroristic'. Cf. Barthes 1976.

narrative. This may seem surprising and especially surprising in view of the fact that these connecting generalizations are almost always left out. They are understood tacitly and, in most cases, taken for granted. But without them, we would never get a sequence and see how one fact literally leads to the next. As E. M. Forster (1962: 93) once observed, when we are told 'the king died and then the queen died', we do not have a story or a narrative. We will at most be left with the impression that there was a strange coincidence. But as soon as the sequence is amended to read 'the king died and then the queen died of grief', we have a narrative in which the first fact leads to the second. Formally, what has happened is that the tacit generalization that people can die of grief was used to link the two facts. The first fact now becomes a cause and the second the effect. This cause–effect feature is the basic element in narration.

One might well ask why it is necessary to use a generalization in order to see the cause–effect relationship. We have known ever since Hume that causality is not something that can be observed the way we observe a table. It is a relationship which is postulated to hold between two facts and the only way it can be postulated is by using a generalization. We do not observe that setting of the sun *causes* darkness. All we can observe is that every time the sun is setting, darkness follows. In order to turn this sequence into a narrative in which the setting is the cause of the darkness, we need a general law about the light and the rays of the sun. With this general law at the back of our mind, the sequence becomes a causal sequence. We can then also see that the designation of both cause and effect is relative to a generalization and that whatever we designate as a 'cause' is a cause in terms of a generalization. Take the generalization away and the reason for designating an event as a cause disappears. This has led Karl Popper ([1935] 1959: 59ff.; also 1945: 248–52, 342–3) to formulate the minimum requirement for a causal explanation. We have a causal explanation, he wrote, when a prognosis is deduced from a generalization with the help of an initial condition. Take an example: the fact to be explained is that John broke his leg (*explanandum*). If we know that people who fall on ice tend to break their leg (generalization) and that John fell on ice (initial condition), we can deduce that John broke his leg. The initial condition *together* with the generalization become the *explanans* and the initial condition is seen to be the cause of the broken leg but only in virtue of the generalization. The initial condition by itself is not enough to be the *explanans* of the *explanandum*. (See this work, Chapter 30.)

Eventually Carl Hempel gave this analysis its classical expression in a famous paper (Hempel 1942) and applied it directly to the narrative structure of historical writing, so that it is sometimes referred to as Hempelian explanation. William Dray (1957) called it the Covering Law Model of explanation and, by implication, of narrative structure. It is under this name (CLM) that it is now mostly referred to. According to this model the minimum unit of narrative consists of three propositions – one generalization and two particular propositions which stand in a causal relationship in virtue of the generalization. This arrangement is not only the basic form of historical explanation but of all explanations as such. There is nothing specially historical about this form of explanation: for other, unhistorical, explanations are not possible. While the general law can be mentioned in any place and may even remain tacitly understood, the initial condition (*explanans*) must precede the prognosis (*explanandum*). This establishes the historical element in all explanations and it is this fact which enables us to use this arrangement as the minimum standard of explanation in history and as the model for the construction of narratives. This model of explanation does justice to the arrow of time because it reflects the temporal sequence of the explaining and explained facts. To be sure, this model is not a mirror or any other kind of portrait of a temporal sequence, because the facts which explain and the facts that are explained do not actually follow upon one another in time. They are not temporally contiguous.

It is no surprise that narrative and explanation coincide. A narrative has to be a story which listeners or readers can follow and the reason why it can be followed is precisely because the single facts it consists of are, in virtue of implicit or explicit generalizations, explained. Formally, the explained fact should become, in a longer narrative, the explaining, initial condition of the next fact. But no narrative is that orderly and no narrative need be that orderly. A lack of formal order can, on the contrary, increase the intelligibility of the narrative. Taking the example of the king's death, the intelligibility is enhanced by the intrusion of a second series. Thus: the proposition 'the king died' could be followed by the proposition 'the earth shook'. The generalization about death by grief which leads to the proposition about the death of the queen is here temporarily suspended. Instead there is a tacit generalization to the effect that when kings who are guarantors of fertility die, there is a cosmic disturbance. With this generalization, we now go from the death of the king to the earthquake and not immediately to the death of the queen. The death of the queen and the generalization that leads to it will be inserted after the cosmic-disturbance generalization and the earthquake.

Let us look, however, at a schematic representation of the structure of the narrative in order to determine the role played by generalizations and the problems raised by this role. Here is a sequence of facts in temporal order but not temporally contiguous. They are or could have been distilled from our knowledge of the sources and we will leave aside the question whether the sources could verify all or any of them.

1 Napoleon gets up.
2 Napoleon brushes his teeth.
3 Napoleon feels a slight pain in his cheek.
4 Napoleon received a message that the Austrian army is advancing.
5 Napoleon eats his breakfast.
6 Napoleon signs a marching order for his army.
7 Napoleon sees a doctor about his pain.
8 Napoleon's army begins to move.
9 Napoleon gets dressed.
10 Napoleon presides at a meeting of his generals.
11 Napoleon rebukes one of his generals.

This series is not an intelligible narrative because there is not only an absence of temporal contiguity of the eleven facts, but also a complete absence of a causal relationship even though a cursory glance will immediately suggest some causal relationships. This is because the required generalizations are so deeply and so tacitly ingrained in our minds that we are not always aware when we are using them. The point is that these causal relationships are not hard and fast, but depend on generalizations and will vary with them. With the help of generalizations, we can establish an intelligible relation between them and so turn some of these facts into a narrative. If we take the generalization that if a person is in pain, he will be irritable, we can see how 3 leads to 11 because with the help of our generalization, 3 will be the cause of 11. But try the generalization that if a person is in pain, he will see a doctor. Now we get a causal relationship between 3 and 7. Or try the generalization that a person at war with his enemies will seek to counteract the movement of their forces with a movement of his forces. This time we will get 4 and 6 into a causal relationship. There is no need to multiply examples. The point is that the sequence of events in the narrative will depend not on the facts they contain, but on the generalizations employed. Any narrative can be changed into a different narrative if the generalizations with the help of which it is composed are changed. In our example, one can see that it is possible to construct very different narratives about the same span of time at the same place. There are as many narratives about this span of time as there are generalizations or, to use Hayden White's more rhetorical terminology, 'narrative accounts of real events admit of as many plot structures as are available' (White 1986: 489). In short, what matters is not the facts, but the generalizations. This situation is made specially unstable because we have seen that facts can be constructed in any size and that therefore it is always possible, provided a generalization requires it, to insert additional facts into the series, either as initial conditions or as prognoses. Although, given the sources, this process is not infinitely elastic, it allows a wide measure of latitude.[9] The generalizations matter not only in that they determine the sequences of the facts but also in the sense that they determine which facts are to be mentioned and which are to be omitted as irrelevant. It is therefore necessary now to take a close look at these generalizations.

To begin with, there has been a lot of argument because it is clear that these generalizations differ from the general laws used in the natural sciences. A generalization is much more vague than a general law of unlimited universality. It states a tendency rather than a necessity and talks about expectations, rather than about hard causal determination. Above all, it is not and need not be universally valid. All that is required is that it should be valid or accepted as valid in a certain community. Critics of the CLM have assumed that generalizations are general laws and have had no difficulty in showing that in the social sciences there can be no such general laws and that all suggestion of determination and necessity is misleading.

---

9   There are at least four salutary postulates which restrict that latitude. See Munz 1977: 281–93.

But once the difference between a generalization and a general law is accepted, this criticism of the CLM falls to the ground. This difference also disposes of the frequent criticism that the general law, with its unlimited universality, provides a set of hard-and-fast rules which are atemporal and which make the whole of the past appear to be so many variations on a single set of atemporal themes. This criticism is rebutted by the fact that there is nothing atemporal about these generalizations. They are, on the contrary, very temporary, because they are general beliefs held in societies which have a very limited life and which are, even during that limited life, unstable.

It is nevertheless true that the employment of generalizations in the construction of a narrative creates an appearance of necessity and predictability. If one could manage a narrative in which it is an accident that Napoleon felt a pain and that he rebuked his generals, the rebuke would appear unpredictable because undetermined. But in that case, there would be no reason why the rebuke should form part of a narration which started with the pain and, if truly accidental, the rebuke would probably have been left out as irrelevant to the narrative.[10] As soon as it appears relevant and is mentioned, there must be an explanation of the relevance. The explanation of that relevance is the (possibly) tacit generalization that people in pain tend to be irritable. This seems to show that a properly constructed narrative always gives the impression of a necessary sequentiality of the narrated facts and makes the story told look more necessary and less accidental than it possibly was. But here we come to the crux of the matter. What does the expression 'than it possibly was' mean? It has no meaning at all; for there is no reality, no real order in which the facts stand over and above the order contained in somebody's story about these facts. The appearance of determination is therefore not an appearance in the sense that it is an illusion. It is an appearance in the sense that it appears as soon as somebody talks about the events in question and this appearance of determination comes as a package with the telling of the story. Somebody else might tell a different story about the pain and the rebuke; but in so far as that different story can be followed and in so far as it is intelligible, it will have been constructed with the help of a different generalization and therefore will have the appearance of a different predetermination. One can then compare the two stories. But one cannot compare either story with the objective reality as it is in itself. As Thomas Kuhn trenchantly put it: there can be no 'direct comparison with nature'.[11] And for this reason Ranke's old cliché that the historian has to tell it 'how it actually was' can have no meaning at all. The truth of a narrative, in other words, cannot depend on its correspondence

---

10   Thus we read a narrative with the expectation that each thing mentioned is *going to be important* (Danto 1985: 355). See also Gallie 1964: 29, 89.
11   Kuhn 1970: 77: 'No process yet disclosed ... resembles the methodological stereotype of ... direct comparison with nature.' Strangely and incomprehensibly Kuhn appears to exempt historical facts from this stricture. He writes on p. 96 that of all facts, 'historic' ones must be taken seriously and that it is those 'historic' ones which show that all others are constructed in terms of preconceived paradigms. I pointed this contradiction out to Kuhn and in a letter of 10 November 1976; he thanked me and admitted this inconsistency. Cf. Munz 1985: 111–29 and O'Hear 1989: 77.

with what actually happened and, for this reason, the expression 'more determined than it possibly was' has no meaning.

It has also been argued that these generalizations are not needed and that one can construct a historical series of facts which follow one upon another without them. It is possible, so the criticism goes, to produce a series of facts which are temporally sufficiently close together that one can see every antecedent fact as a cause of the fact that follows and that is all that is required for a sufficient – if not necessary – causal explanation. As Michael Oakeshott once put it, the narrower the gap between the facts, the more 'the mystery is abated'[12] The closer the facts are together and the smaller the temporal gap between them, the more sufficient the explanation why, say, my car had an engine seizure. The series starts with the fact that the oil ran out of a hole. Then nothing came into the cylinder to lubricate it, so that the movement of the dry pistons against the wall made it hot. And then the hot metal expanded and locked tightly. This is alleged to be a 'continuous series' of happenings in which one fact explains the next.[13] But without the generalizations about the way metal expands when hot and the generation of heat through friction, this series would not be continuous and the explanations would not even be sufficient, let alone necessary. It is admittedly not necessary to provide 'necessary' explanations. But the point is that such a series as it stands does not even yield a sufficient explanation. If one believes in the narrative efficacy of such continuous series, one would also have to accept Benjamin Franklin's ([1756] 1967: 49) explanation that the kingdom was lost for want of a horseshoe nail.

There are two reasons why such a series by itself is not a narrative, but a mere recital. First, there is no way in which the mentioned facts can be made to be temporally contiguous. No matter how we formulate them, it is always possible to break them up into subfacts and to point at events that come between them. The gap must remain and must keep crying out for a covering law so that we can get from one to the next. Second, since a fact like the oil running out of the hole is a construction, the same span of time in the same place could have led to the construction of a different fact such as that the piercing of the cylinder wall caused a pressure on the metal, and that at that point heat was formed which led to a chemical change in the steel, which caused a change in the viscosity of the oil that was running out, which changed the colour of the pebble on the road it fell upon and so on. The only reason why we construct a fact about the hole and not about the chemical changes and the changes in viscosity is that we have at the back of our mind a general law to the effect that the dryness in the cylinder will cause the friction, which will heat up the cylinder, which will cause the seizure, Or, to stand Oakeshott on his head, the only reason why the mystery is abated is that we have

---

12 Oakeshott 1975: 106. See also the many works on historical method by G. R. Elton in which the view that the thicker the accumulation of 'facts', the clearer the picture of the past, is constantly reiterated.
13 Dray 1957 maintains that particular facts can form a continuous series. See also Mink 1969 and 1978: 132 for the view that narrative form without generalizations represents 'uniquely'.

generalizations. Our entire attention must therefore be turned to the generalizations. What is their status? What is their truth?

These questions used to have a fairly simple answer until approximately the eighteenth century. Until that time it was held or tacitly assumed that human nature was uniform[14] and that there were generalizations about it which were true and accepted by all human beings at all times and in all places. If somebody constructed a narrative with the help of 'untrue' generalizations, the narrative would have to be rejected as untrue because the way it presented the sequence of events was a way which was unintelligible. Consider for example the generalization that a brutal tyrant tends to disregard conspiracies. Such a generalization is against human nature and therefore cannot be used to construct a narrative. It would link facts which a true generalization about brutal tyrants would not link. But note that the rejection of the narrative does not depend on the facts; but on the falsity of the generalization employed. But when it came to be discovered in the course of the eighteenth century that there is no uniformity of human nature and that generalizations which are held to be true in one society are held to be untrue in another society, this easy way of distinguishing true narratives from untrue narratives disappeared (Meinecke [1936] 1972; see also Berlin 1991: 38, 52, 70; Geertz 1965: 94–5). Since then we have been inundated with an ever-increasing number of reports about the lack of the uniformity of human nature and have been made to confront the fact that there is a vast kaleidoscope of generalizations. For example, in the early Middle Ages it was widely believed that royal power depended on the number of relics possessed by the king (Southern 1970: 191), and then in our century, the Kwaio of the Solomon Islands believe that the dead return to the villages of the living and wreak mischief (Keesing 1982: 44–5). Today in modern Western societies we believe instead that in the Middle Ages royal power came from the ownership of land and that the dead do not return to our villages. Our generalization about the power of kings tends to be economic; and we seek to generalize about the mischief in villages by looking at the psyche of the living rather than at the travels of the dead. Since it is impossible to compare any of these generalizations with 'nature' and so decide on their truth, we are left with all these generalizations. Narratives about early medieval politics and contemporary Kwaio will very markedly differ according to which of these generalizations we use and especially whether we are using indigenous generalizations or our own generalizations. Historians writing about the past and anthropologists writing about far-away present-day societies face exactly the same problem, for, as David Lowenthal (1985) eloquently put it, the past is a foreign country.

Formally it is possible to distinguish between explanatory and interpretative narratives. An explanatory narrative is a narrative which is constructed with the help of generalizations which were available to or known by the people the narrative

---

14   Herodotus was aware of the difference of customs; but he did not suppose that human nature changes.

is about. When telling a story about ancient Romans, one is providing an explanatory narrative if the generalizations employed were known to or could have been used by the ancient Romans. A narrative becomes interpretative when the generalizations used were not known to the people one is writing about but belong to a different and, as a rule later period. Thus a narrative about ancient Romans which uses generalizations culled from modern economic theory would be interpretative: and a narrative which uses generalizations taken from Virgil's reflection (*Aeneid* 6.851f.) that the 'arts' the Romans are really good at are the arts of imperial domination would be explanatory. The choice of the two terms 'explanatory' and 'interpretative' is not altogether arbitrary. If one narrates other people in the terms in which they themselves would have told stories about themselves, one is explaining them. Whereas, if one is narrating in terms which they themselves would have rejected or been ignorant of, one is providing an interpretation.

The distinction, though formally rigid, is in practice not absolute. Take the case of Julius Caesar and the crossing of the Rubicon which led to his violation of Rome, symbolized as a mother figure even in ancient times. At the time generalizations about power and the desire for fame were available and this is how the story was told by Plutarch and by Suetonius. They produced explanatory narratives. Plutarch (*Caesar* 32) mentioned, gratuitously, as far as his story goes, that Caesar dreamed the night before crossing the Rubicon that he was sleeping with his mother. Suetonius (*Caesar* 32) does not mention this 'fact' but merely includes in his story that Caesar had a vision of aggressive power. But later on he mentions that young Caesar had planned writing a play about Oedipus (ibid. 56) Today we are all familiar with Oedipal desires and one could imagine a narrative which would fully exploit these 'facts' and incorporate them into the story of how Caesar intended to ravish Rome, his mother, by using generalizations culled from Freudian psychoanalysis. Such a narrative would be interpretative. But then comes the question as to whether Caesar, long before Freud, could or could not have known of incestuous desires and of the symbolic displacement of his mother by the city of Rome. A modern Freudian version of the story would be an interpretation. But given Caesar's dream and his plan to write about Oedipus, would it not be possible to suppose that he himself harboured a generalization about Oedipal wishes? Whatever the answer, it is clear that it would be difficult to decide with certainty whether a Rubicon narrative which made more of the dream than Plutarch did would be explanatory or interpretative.

The detection of the role of generalizations in narrative also helps to solve a problem which has been widely discussed by historians. Following upon Dilthey and Croce, Collingwood suggested that the ultimate effort of the historian should be directed towards empathy, that is, towards entering into the minds of the people he was writing about and of re-enacting what they had done. This, he argued, was the ultimate purpose of historical research.[15] The project, though temptingly desirable

---

15 Collingwood 1946: 282–3. See also the modern more vulgar version in Greenblatt (1988: 1): 'I began with the desire to speak with the dead.'

– what greater purpose of historical research was imaginable? – is unreasonable, at least in those terms. First, it would require an aptitude for intuition which we do not even have when it comes to members of our own family, let alone when we are dealing with strangers who lived hundreds of years ago. Second, there is no way of telling whether the results of any such pretended empathy are genuine or not. Collingwood might claim that he had entered the minds of Hengist and Horsa, but had he? Or was he just pretending? We can now give a more tangibly reasonable answer to these questions. 'Empathy' means that one succeeds in using those generalizations which Hengist and Horsa would have used. It will still be difficult to be sure which ones they would have used. But at least with this formulation the project is moved from the realm of psychic experience into the realm of rational epistemology and this is, I think, what Collingwood really meant. We should also note that even those modern historians who are most opposed to a narrative representation of the past make the recovery of generalizations or frames of mind (*mentalités*) the chief objective of research.

Ever since it was found that human nature is not uniform and that people differ in the generalizations they use to understand themselves and to tell stories about their pasts, historians have tended to favour explanatory narratives and if not narratives, then explanations and have regarded interpretations with suspicion. There are some very good reasons for this preference. Since the past does not lie ready for our inspection, a story about the past is a construction and as such it has no obvious truth value, for as a construction it cannot possibly simply correspond to what has actually happened. If one wants to discriminate between different narratives, one must do so without thinking some true and some false in terms of their correspondence to the past. But an explanatory narrative can be true or false in a sense in which an interpretative narrative cannot. An explanatory narrative can be true if the generalizations it uses are in fact the generalizations used by the people it is about. Such a truth criterion is not available to the mere interpreter. The interpreter, taking his generalizations from the twentieth century but writing about the fifteenth century, cannot claim to be truthful in the sense in which an explanatory narrative, using mostly fifteenth-century generalizations, can be truthful.

The difference between fiction and non-fiction or historicity does not depend on the degree of accuracy with which the separate facts are ascertained. It depends, on the contrary, on the generalizations employed to link the separate facts to one another. If the generalizations are generalizations used by the people the story is about, the story is not fiction. This is so even when the separate facts mentioned cannot be verified to have actually happened. Georg Lukács (1962, *passim*) has used this phenomenon to distinguish the specifically historical novel from the ordinary novel. A novel is genuinely historical if the generalizations and institutions used in the narrative are genuinely those of the time and place the story is about. A novel can, in this sense, be historical even when all the single and particular facts it is composed of are fictitious. Its historicity, like the truth of a more explicit historical narrative, depends on the verifiability of the generalizations, not on the verifiability of the separate facts. If one thinks of truth as the result of the correspondence of the story to reality, then the correspondence is to the generalizations, not to the particular facts. An interpretative narrative, clearly, can claim no such truth by correspondence. For this reason a historical novel like Anatole France's *Les Dieux ont soif* (1912), though its facts are fictitious, corresponds more truly to the reality of the French Revolution than some of the Marxist interpretations of Albert Soboul, even though the latter contains only verifiable facts. For the same reason, Conrad Ferdinand Meyer's *Jürg Jenatsch* (1876) though its separate facts are mainly fiction, has more historical correspondence to the Grison valley in the early seventeenth century than Le Roy Ladurie's (1979) acclaimed structuralist interpretation of the same social phenomenon in the French town of Romans even though Le Roy Ladurie's facts are no fiction.

There is an additional reason why the explanatory mode commends itself. Since the object of study, the people of the past, can speak for themselves and have often done so, it is ethically more acceptable to respect their views than to brush them aside and substitute generalizations they themselves would not have offered. Although ordinary historians were the first to prefer explanatory narratives to interpretative ones, the ethical advantage of their method has proved overwhelmingly and almost irresistibly attractive to anthropologists who have come to sponsor this preference under the grand-sounding term 'ethnomethodology'. In some schools of anthropology this has become real dogma and, when applied to people's pasts, goes under the name of 'ethno-history'. This term refers to a form of narrative which relies exclusively on generalizations provided by the people whose past is being studied. By contrast, the suggestion that one might use generalizations which modern historians or Western anthropologists believe to be true and apply them to the past of other people is considered a consequence of political imperialism, that is, something which only military conquerors would inflict on their victims. This revival of the historian's old-fashioned and well-founded preference for explanatory narratives has become a politically-motivated fashion. At the opposite end of the spectrum there stands the practice of a 'new science' which goes back to the eighteenth century and was first introduced by Giambattista Vico. By 'new science'[16] he understood a narrative which used nothing but eighteenth-century generalizations about religious belief, family habits, the acquisition of language and the practice of poetry and, in doing so, swept indigenous testimony about other generalizations under the carpet. The new science rested on the argument that people in the past did not know what they were doing and why they were doing it and that their own generalizations were therefore to be disregarded. What really happened, Vico argued, was what was being told in the narrative he constructed on the basis of his generalizations. The next great advocate of such a 'new science' was Karl Marx, who also offered to substitute his own (interpretative) generalizations for those which the people of the past had offered when he suggested that history is the history of class struggles and that people are divided into classes

---

16   For the concept 'new science', see Munz 1983.

even when they are not aware of being so divided. Since then, we have been treated to further such 'new' sciences by both Freud and Lévi-Strauss who, like Vico and Marx before them, keep maintaining that their generalizations about, e.g. patriotism and war and myths tell us what really happened, as against what the people who had told the myths and had been involved in the battles alleged about them.

The past is real enough. But the stories we tell about it are constructions. For this reason no amount of looking at the past can tell us whether we should pursue explanation or interpretation, or both. The one thing we can be sure about is that the dogmatists who advocate either a 'new' science which is overtly interpretative or an 'ethnomethodology' which is exclusively explanatory can have no leg to stand on. In the last analysis, an explanatory narrative which uses indigenous generalizations is as suspect as an interpretative narrative which uses generalizations framed by outsiders. There is at the present time a myth as rampant among anthropologists as it is among historians, that there is greater veracity in indigenous generalization than in generalizations provided by outsiders. The former have a purity and the latter look like the impositions of wicked imperialists (see, e.g. Fabian 1983; Said 1978 and 1989). But when one considers that the past is as closed a book to the people who were present when it happened as it is to later generations, the purity of the indigenous generalization vanishes. While it is true that the imperial conqueror and the modern historian may have a vested interest in their generalizations and the interpretative narratives they give rise to, it is equally true that the people on the spot have a vested interest in their generalizations. We have every reason to be suspicious of them because they are framed not because they are true accounts of what really happened, but in order to be idiosyncratically parochial, so that they can help to furnish a sense of identity to the community and help to distinguish it from other communities, the members of which have to be excluded from the division of labour and other co-operation (Munz 1989). For this reason there is a lot to be said for the idea of a 'new science' which sweeps indigenous explanations under the carpet and substitutes interpretative ones. Take the case of the old Ilongot from the Philippines who rejected the anthropologist's suggestion that his head-hunting, when there was a bereavement, was done as an exchange for the loss of the person who had died. This generalization, derived from Mauss and not indigenous, was an interpretation. It was rejected with indignation because, being applicable to people other than the Ilongot, it would not have served the purpose of demarcating the Ilongot from the rest of mankind. The generalization which the Ilongot preferred concerned 'rage' (Rosaldo 1989: 3ff.). But this generalization is suspect because it is held in order to distinguish the Ilongot from other tribes, not because it is the real reason. With this conclusion any initial preference for explanatory narratives as against interpretative narratives disappears.

In order to dispel the impression that this conclusion must lead to total relativism and that it might even support the postmodern fashion of looking upon narratives as nothing more than ideological constructions, I would like to show that there are at least two possible ways of maintaining a minimal objectivity. In view of what has been said about the construction of both facts and narratives, these ways must be very different from the traditional methodology in which objectivity is approached by source-criticism – a methodology reiterated and clung to by the late Geoffrey Elton (1983: 84). Given the argument that the facts which can be culled from the sources are narrative-laden and, as mini-narratives, not formally different from genuine narratives, source-criticism by itself remains a circular enterprise in which all one can achieve is a distinction between explanation and interpretation. I propose to explore two very different approaches to objectivity and in order to simplify matters I will drop the distinction between explanatory and interpretative generalizations because it served the very limited purpose of establishing nothing more than a minimal constraint on the historian.

The first possibility is to do what the old philosophies of history used to do and find a master discourse or a metanarrative which explains why different people at different times and places in the past used different generalizations. All traditional philosophies of history are attempts to discover master discourses which are designed to relate different generalizations to one another (Munz 1993: 132f.). Thus one would say, for example, that the old Ilongot's generalization about rage is a typical instance of the sort of generalization current in a well-structured closed society; and that the generalization about exchange theory is typical of modern cosmopolitan thinking promoted in an open society in which personal and religious considerations are pushed into the background. A master narrative would then tell of the ways in which some closed societies are being or have been transformed into open societies so that one could relate the indigenous Ilongot generalization to the modern Maussian sociological generalization. The purpose of the metanarrative is to explain why there are different generalizations and to use such explanation to transform the first-order incompatibilities into second-order compatibilities. The formulation of such metanarratives is beset by some real methodological difficulties[17] and there are many good reasons why we should replace the old conception of 'philosophy of history' by Hayden White's (1973; 1987) conception of 'metahistory'. It would lead too far to pursue this matter here, even though, unlike Hayden White, I do not believe that these difficulties are insuperable and that the only conceivable metahistory is one which confines itself to diagnosing the different rhetorical forms which control the stories.

The second possibility is simpler and more straightforward. It is based on a rule

---

17   There are countless criticisms of all philosophies of history; from Comte to Marx, from Hegel to Toynbee and Spengler, not to mention the less ambitious ones of Émile Durkheim and Max Weber. These criticisms have gained weight by Th. S. Kuhn's metanarrative of the history of science which shows that changes of paradigm are inexplicable and that incompatibilities are ultimate. His metanarrative is, in other words, a *reductio ad absurdum* or metanarrative. This argument has been further compounded by Foucault's insistence that people simply change their generalizations every hundred years for no reason at all; and by Lyotard's proclamation that an attempt at a metanarrative is nothing but an act of terrorism designed to intimidate past and present minorities to stop them from chanting whatever they choose to chant. In short, metanarratives or philosophies of history are at present out of fashion. For Kuhn, see this work, Chapters 14 and 15.

of thumb which states that if there is competition between conflicting generalizations, those with the greatest explanatory power are to be preferred (Munz 1993: 178f.). Generalizations which are clearly confined to the time and place in which they have been used have very little explanatory power, for they do little more than represent the people who have used them to themselves. In the above example, the Ilongot generalization about rage is the way in which the Ilongot identify themselves: Ilongot are people who hunt heads when they are driven by rage. As against this, generalizations like Mauss's exchange theory transcend the time and the place in which they are used and can be applied also to other situations.[18] Such generalizations have greater explanatory power than the local, indigenous generalizations. On the basis of this rule of thumb it becomes possible to order generalizations and the narratives they give rise to hierarchically. One starts at the bottom with narratives which use generalizations with low explanatory power and ends at the top with narratives which employ generalizations with greater explanatory power. As an example, let us consider some books on the history of the Puritan settlers in North America.

At one end of this scale there is a narrative the truth of which depends on the recovery of the generalizations employed by the early Puritans themselves. Theodore Dwight Bozeman's *To Live Ancient Lives: The Primitivist Dimension in Puritanism* (1989) is a case in point. Bozeman endeavoured to recover generalizations used by Puritans and the truth of his account consists entirely in the correspondence of these generalizations to those employed by the Puritans themselves. These particular generalizations have very little explanatory power outside the confines of the Puritanism of that time. Bozeman explains the Puritan Fathers as they explained themselves to themselves: they were biblical primitivists who were determined to undercut Anglican and other Protestant appeals to the instructions contained in the Bible and only managed to do so, in their opinion, by physically severing themselves from the body of less zealous Christians in England.

Next in line we come to a narrative in which generalizations contemporary to the historian who is writing, but no longer contemporary to the people he is writing about, are employed – to Samuel Rawson Gardiner's *The First Two Stuarts and the Puritan Revolution*, first published in 1876. Gardiner was writing in the heyday of English historical constitutionalism and used generalizations about representative government, self-determination and the rule of law very current in the Britain of his time and explained the Puritan migrants as an extremist section of the broader seventeenth-century movement towards such constitutionalism. He replaced the subjective generalizations used by the Puritans themselves in the seventeenth century by generalizations about political behaviour current in the nineteenth

---

18 It is frequently argued nowadays that Mauss's exchange theory or Einstein's theory of relativity are nothing but modern myths used in Paris or Princeton for people to represent themselves and that they do not differ from Ilongot myths. See, e.g. Feyerabend 1975, *passim*. Such arguments are red herrings, completely undermined by e.g. the considerations of Horton 1967, frequently reprinted.

century. Thus he made the Puritans more intelligible to his own readers, but was not able to claim truth for the generalizations he used in the sense that he had discovered them in the historical record. Moving forward, we come to Michael Walzer's *The Revolution of the Saints: A Study of the Origins of Radical Politics* (1965). Walzer used generalizations current in the first half of the twentieth century, replacing both the Puritans' own and Gardiner's nineteenth-century subjective generalization with yet another subjective generalization to the effect that the Puritans were the first self-disciplined agents of social and political reconstruction. In our own century, which has been replete with attempts at social reconstruction, Walzer is more intelligible than Gardiner, but, like Gardiner, cannot claim truth for his generalization in the sense that it is a 'true' discovery of the generalization the Puritans themselves used, that is in the sense in which Bozeman can claim truth.

Finally we come to the other end of the scale, to Andrew Delbanco's *The Puritan Ordeal* (1989). Delbanco uses generalizations about the phenomenon of migration. The Puritans, he writes, were 'immigrants', the first immigrants in the American immigrant culture. His description of their social order, their ideology and their personalities is derived from generalizations about immigration. Here we have new generalizations which, unlike those at the other end, transcend the beliefs of any one particular society or political culture. They were never used parochially in any one society as a form of self-understanding. For this reason, Delbanco's generalizations interpret not only the early Puritans, but also the way in which Russian, Polish, Italian, German and Irish immigrants made their way into the comparative wilderness of the North American continent, and are most probably also applicable to migrants to other continents.

In order to become an object for discussion and inspection, time has to be transformed into a causal sequence. The only way in which this can be done is by narration. But a narrative constructed with the help of generalizations is not a portrait of the span of time it represents. With this conclusion almost all historians have taken leave of the historical positivism which sought to tell what actually happened. But there is no justification for the hasty postmodern conclusion that such narratives do not represent time and that they, at most, represent their author. On the contrary. A correct understanding of the role played by generalizations leads us, when we are dealing with explanatory narratives, to a criterion of truth. An explanatory narrative is true if the generalizations it employs correspond to the generalizations used by the people it is about. And when we are dealing with interpretative generalizations, it helps us towards a critical transcendence of parochial and self-serving explanations.

REFERENCES

Barthes, R. (1970) 'Historical discourse', in M. Lane (ed.) *Structuralism*, London.
—— (1976) *The Pleasure of the Text*, London.

Bennington, C. *et al.* (eds) (1987) *Post-structuralism and the Question of History*, Cambridge.

Berlin, I. (1991) *The Crooked Timber of Mankind*, London.

Bozeman, T. D. (1989) *To Live Ancient Lives: The Primitivist Dimension in Puritanism*, Chapel Hill, NC.

Braudel, F. (1949) *La Méditerranée et le monde méditerranéen à l'époque de Philippe II*, Paris.

—— (1980) *On History*, Chicago.

Bruner, J. (1990) *Acts of Meaning*, Cambridge, MA.

Burke, P. (1991) *New Perspectives in Historical Writing*, Cambridge.

Collingwood, R. G. (1946) *The Idea of History*, Oxford.

Coveney, P. and Highfield, R. (1990) *The Arrow of Time*, London.

Danto, A. (1985) *Narration and Knowledge*, New York.

Delbanco, A. (1989) *The Puritan Ordeal*, Cambridge, MA.

Dray, W. H. (1957) *Laws and Explanations in History*, London.

Durkheim, E. (1912) *Les Formes élémentaires de la vie religieuse*, Paris.

Elton, G. R. (1983) 'Two kinds of history', in R. W. Fogel and G. R. Elton, *Which Road to the Past?*, New Haven, CT.

Fabian, J. (1983) *Time and the Other*, New York.

Feyerabend, P. K. (1975) *Against Method*, London.

Forster, E. M. (1962) *Aspects of the Novel*, Harmondsworth.

Franklin, B. (1967) *Poor Richard's Almanack*, ed. D. Valley, Kansas City.

Gallie, W. B. (1964) *Philosophy and the Historical Understanding*, London.

Gardiner, S. R. [1876] (1970) *The First Two Stuarts and the Puritan Revolution*, repr. of 1886 edn, New York.

Geertz, C. (1965) 'The impact of the concept of culture', in J. R. Platt (ed.) *New Views of the Nature of Man*, Chicago.

Gould, S. J. (1989) *Wonderful Life*, London.

Hempel, C. G. (1942) 'The function of general laws in history', *Journal of Philosophy* 39: 35–48.

Himmerlfarb, G. (1992) 'Telling it as you like it', *Times Literary Supplement*, 16 October: 12–15.

Horton, R. (1967) 'African traditional thought and Western science', *Africa* 37: 50–71 and 155–87.

Hurst, B. C. (1981) 'The myth of historical evidence', *History and Theory* 20: 278–336.

Keesing, R. M. (1982) *Kwaio Religion*, New York.

Kuhn, T. S. (1970) *The Structure of Scientific Revolutions*, 2nd edn, Chicago.

Landau, M. (1991) *Narratives of Human Evolution*, New Haven, CT.

Le Roy Ladurie, E. (1979) *Le Carneval de Romans*, Paris.

Lowenthal, D. (1985) *The Past is a Foreign Country*, New York.

Lukács, G. [1937] (1962) *The Historical Novel*, London.

Meinecke, F. (1936) *Die Entstehung des Historismus*, Munich. (Tr. as *Historism: The Rise of the New Historical Outlook*, London, 1972.)

Mink, L. O. (1969) 'History and fiction as modes of comprehension', *New Literary History* 1: 541–58.

—— (1978) 'Narrative form as a cognitive instrument', in R. H. Canary and H. Kozicki (eds) *The Writing of History*, Madison.

Mitchell, W. J. T. (1980) *On Narrative*, Chicago.

Munz, P. (1977) *The Shapes of Time*, Middletown, CT.

—— (1983) 'The idea of "new science" in Vico and Marx', in G. Tagliacozzo (ed.) *Vico and Marx*, Atlantic Highlands, NJ.

—— (1985) *Our Knowledge of the Growth of Knowledge*, London.

—— (1989) 'Taking Darwin even more seriously', in K. Hahlweg and C. Hooker (eds) *Issues in Evolutionary Epistemology*, Albany.

Munz, P. (1993) *Philosophical Darwinism*, London.

Oakeshott, M. (1975) *On Human Control*, Oxford.

O'Hear, A. (1989) *An Introduction to the Philosophy of Science*, Oxford.

Popper, K. (1945) *The Open Society and its Enemies*, London.

—— (1959) *The Logic of Scientific Discovery*, London. (First published as: *Logik der Forschung*, Vienna, 1935.)

Rosaldo, R. (1989) *Culture and Truth*, Boston.

Said, E. (1978) *Orientalism*, New York.

—— (1989) 'Representing the colonised', *Critical Inquiry* 15: 205–25.

Southern, R. (1970) 'Aspects of the European tradition of historical writing', *Transactions of the Royal Historical Society* 20: 173–96.

Stone, L. (1979) 'The revival of narrative', *Past and Present* 85: 3–24.

Veeser, H. A. (ed.) (1989) *The New Historicism*, New York.

Walzer, M. (1965) *The Revolution of the Saints*, Cambridge, MA.

White, H. V. (1973) *Metahistory*, Baltimore.

—— (1986) 'Historical pluralism', *Critical Inquiry* 12: 480–93.

—— (1987) *The Content of the Form*, Baltimore.

35

THE *ANNALES* EXPERIMENT

George Huppert

In spite of its awkward title, its esoteric content and the modest size of its subscription list, the French journal *Annales: Economies. Sociétés. Civilisations* began to reach a global audience in the 1960s. It has become, since then, probably the world's most talked about and most influential scholarly journal devoted to historical studies.[1] In Germany and in Britain, the *Annales* approach to history encountered incomprehension and resistance for some time,[2] but the triumph of *Annales* in American universities is indisputable, and this in spite of the fact that many of its American admirers cannot actually read the French journal and must remain content with anthologies of articles, in English translation, taken from *Annales*.[3]

Many books by *Annales* historians are now available in translation. Among these books there are celebrated doctoral theses, huge and little read, such as Braudel's *Mediterranean* or Le Roy Ladurie's *Peasants of Languedoc*; some exceptionally imaginative monographs, such as Febvre's *Religion of Rabelais*, Bloch's *Royal Touch* or Schmitt's *Holy Greyhound*; and outstanding works of synthesis as well, intended for a non-specialist audience, such as Bloch's *Feudal Society* or Lopez's *Birth of Europe*.[4]

It was only in the late 1960s that the reputation of the French historians, established earlier in much of Europe, especially in Italy, at last began to penetrate the English-speaking world. In 1968 I persuaded a major American commercial

---

1   For a selected bibliography, see Burke 1990. Burke focuses on the major works of the *Annales* historians and provides judicious analyses of these. My own chapter focuses on the journal itself. It may be read as complementary to Burke's book.

2   Erbe 1979. Erbe is especially astute in describing German resistance to *Annales* in the Cold War years. Erbe's monograph may well be the most careful and accurate assessment of *Annales* in any language. It includes a good bibliography.

3   Among a number of such anthologies, I would cite Ferro 1972. Another is Burke 1973.

4   Burke 1990 provides an up-to-date selective listing of the major *Annaliste* books in English translation.

publishing house to take on the monumental task of publishing an English-language edition of Fernand Braudel's *La Méditerranée et le monde méditerranéen à l'époque de Philippe II*. The book seemed virtually untranslatable. After rejecting seven or eight would-be translators, I found, at last, the person who could do it. I experienced the same, almost insurmountable difficulties when looking for a translator for Emmanuel Le Roy Ladurie's *Les Paysans de Languedoc*, until Professor John Day, an American medievalist and economic historian who had spent much of his career in Paris, volunteered for the job. Braudel's masterpiece finally appeared in its English version in 1972, Le Roy Ladurie's in 1974. The third *Annales* masterpiece, Lucien Febvre's *Philippe II et la Franche Comté*, originally published in 1912, has never been translated.

All three of these books happen to be enormous, but that is not the chief obstacle for the translator. It is their style, supremely attractive in the original, which is exceptionally difficult to render into English. Unlike the ordinary, garden-variety kind of French historical writing, which is not particularly inventive and which proceeds, as does most academic prose, by means of clichés whose equivalents are easy to locate in English or in German, the language created by Febvre and Braudel is idiosyncratic and poetic, full of archaic turns of phrase and of technical words lifted straight from the sixteenth-century sources. The effect is extraordinary, but it does not translate. Even the French reader is easily baffled by the oceanic murmur of those thousands of pages, exotic, authentic and exquisite though they are.

Not all the books associated with *Annales*, alas, are masterpieces: there is also a considerable proportion of rather dull academic productions and, increasingly, piles of textbooks, coffee-table books, ponderous volumes produced by committees and collections of less-than-scintillating occasional writings – the chaff, the spin-off, which reaches our bookshops and libraries because of the *Annales* label, much as ordinary and inferior wares bearing a famous couturier's trademark reach the market-place.[5]

First rate or not, these books can present a distorted picture of what the *Annales* experiment has been about. They tend to be written, almost exclusively, by Frenchmen whose concern is with pre-industrial France. The reason for this is that many of the weighty volumes which find their way into standard bibliographies were produced as doctoral theses. These overweight volumes, each of which represents ten to twenty years of hard labour in a French archive, display few of the qualities called for in *Annales*. They are rarely comparative or experimental and their style tends to be touched with the usual *rigor mortis* demanded of academic theses. It is also true that most of these *thèses* depend exclusively on French archival sources. Reading them, one could reasonably conclude, with Peter Burke (1990: 99,

---

5   An example among many: the multi-volume, multi-author *Histoire des femmes en Occident*, first prepared for an Italian publisher, then translated into French and eventually into English. The summer 1993 issue of *Annales* devotes much space to this consistently mediocre in-house product.

108), that the horizon of the *Annales* historians is limited to three centuries of French economic and social history.

Are the *annalistes* not interested in modern, contemporary or ancient history? Are they not curious about the world outside France? Outside Europe? You could not guess it from most of the books which make their way into English, but the truth is that *Annales*, from its beginnings, has always been ferociously, aggressively global in scope, both in its recruitment of contributors and in its choice of topics to pursue. Since the 1930s the journal has made a practice of commissioning articles and review essays from first-rate scholars not necessarily associated with the history departments of French universities: Americans, Italians, Poles, émigrés without academic posts, sociologists, anthropologists or colonial administrators. The editors made a practice of inquiring into topics not usually of interest to the Sorbonne, topics such as the collectivization of agriculture in the Soviet Union, the origins of railways, the function of Islamic universities, historical demography or attitudes towards death. Those were not subjects in which ordinary academic journals expressed much interest, until recently, when even the stodgiest of them began to imitate *Annales*.

I do not think of *Annales* as an academic publication among others. The special quality *Annales* possessed until recently is not easy to define. I remember my first encounter, in 1957 or 1958, with the thick, well-groomed volumes on the shelves of the reading room at the University of California at Berkeley, where I was an undergraduate student. I wandered in from the sunlight and the eucalyptus groves to pick up the latest issue of the journal, which had just acquired its peremptory new cover design. I came away, somehow, for better or worse, having found my vocation as a historian.

At the time, the journal was just beginning to attract attention in Cambridge, New York, Chicago and Berkeley, although it had been in existence for more than thirty years already – and long before that, before 1914, the future editors, Lucien Febvre and Marc Bloch, were already saying and writing pretty much what they would say and write in later years. The spirit of *Annales* is that of the early years of the century. If there is a single book, a single work of original scholarship, which embodies, more effectively than any other, the qualities venerated by those who admire the *Annales* kind of history, this book is Lucien Febvre's *Philippe II et la Franche Comté*, which was published in 1912.

The journal wished into existence by Febvre and Bloch in the 1920s did change in some important ways after 1945. It was to change again at various junctures in its history, each new departure spelled out in memorable manifestos written by Febvre – and eventually, after 1956, by his younger *alter ego*, Fernand Braudel. Still, anyone who undertakes to read, or at least to sample, the journal in its entirety, traversing some sixty years of continuous publication, is bound to be struck not so much by the editors' successive enthusiasms for new problems to be solved and new techniques to be applied, but rather by their rock-solid fidelity to the objectives defined by Febvre, with remarkable constancy, from the early years of the century up to the last year of his life. These objectives were reaffirmed by Braudel, right into the 1970s.

Some conclusions may be drawn from these observations. First, that the famous *esprit* of the *Annales* team was in large part the reflection of one man's mind. Lucien Febvre was seconded for some years by his younger colleague, Marc Bloch, and Bloch's contribution to the journal in its early years was important. But it was Febvre who wrote the editorials, it was his style and his role as impresario and talent scout which dominated *Annales* from the start and continued to do so beyond the grave.

Febvre was something of an anarchist. He rebelled, while still a student, against the cultural conventions of the nineteenth century and embraced revolutionary trends in art, music, psychology and literature. He proclaimed his distaste for everything bourgeois – by which he meant everything prudent, timid, lacking in passion and associated with the Sorbonne. In this, and in his fascination with non-Western cultures – the product, after all, of 'peoples so far removed from everything bourgeois' (*ces peuples si peu bourgeois*) (*Annales* 1948: 388), he belonged to the avant-garde. In harmony with the experimental painters, composers and novelists of his youth, he rejected established ways of doing history and ridiculed academic historians as laborious compilers of the obvious.

From the time when he was a student at the Ecole Normale, in 1902, to the time of his death, in 1956, he pursued his vision of what history as a discipline could become in the twentieth century – if it could only be rescued from the mortuary atmosphere of the university. It was Febvre's contention that historians had reached a dead end, that the books they wrote were mostly concerned with trivial surface effects (*histoire événementielle*) and that they ought instead to find ways of reaching deep down into the hidden forces which shape the destinies of human beings. To recount political events in chronological order seemed to Febvre as limited and pointless an activity as would be an attempt to understand landscapes without being aware of the geological forces which shaped them. His own *Franche Comté* was, among other things, an eloquent demonstration of the uses to which geology and geography could be put by historians.

Febvre's strategy for wresting historical research away from those he ridiculed as 'needle-point specialists' included alliances with geographers, sociologists and anthropologists, with students of comparative mythology, with economists and linguists. Not only were his friends in these fields more willing to support his heretical inclinations, but they were engaged in forms of inquiry which, by definition, favoured the search for long-term, hidden realities. It is really remarkable that Febvre, given his objectives, did not fall prey to the attractions of Marxism, to which some of his friends and associates did succumb. As early as 1920, however, Febvre set a course away from any kind of ready-made scenario for explaining everything.[6]

Annales was to steer away from ready-made formulas. It was not to espouse any doctrines. It was not to become a 'school'. It was to remain, as one of Febvre's

6   In his inaugural lecture at the University of Strasbourg, published in the *Revue de Synthèse historique*, 1920, vol. 30, pp. 1–15.

earliest and steadiest allies, the sociologist Georges Friedmann, put it, 'un chantier d'hommes libres' (*Annales* 1957: 4). Once it had rejected the old ways of doing history, the *Annales* group kept searching for an easily communicable way of defining their experiment. Febvre knew how to ridicule the Old Guard, the 'losers of 1870'. He saw what was wrong, what was missing, in the books he reviewed – a history of cities, for instance, whose author wrote about buildings and plans without mentioning human beings. But how was he to explain the kind of history he envisioned, since it did not as yet exist, since it was only an experiment in progress?

Any attempt to reduce the *Annales* approach to a formula is bound to proceed from a misunderstanding. Yes, the emphasis, in the 1930s, was said to reside in the pursuit of economic and social history, as the very title proclaimed: *Annales d'histoire économique et sociale*. But Febvre was quite clear in his own mind that 'economic and social history' was an expression vague enough to defy definition – and therefore especially useful for his purposes.[7]

The essence of what the *annalistes* were after was summed up most succinctly by the economic historian Ernest Labrousse: 'l'histoire est à faire,' that is, 'history has yet to be invented' (cited by Pierre Vilar, *Annales* 1973: 165). To invent a history suitable for the needs of the twentieth century, that has been the consistent programme pursued by the *Annales* group. This was the goal, proclaimed in an editorial manifesto of 1946 in which Febvre celebrated the resurrection of the journal after the difficulties of the war years: an experimental history quick to respond to the needs of the present.

That the needs of the present, rather than a university committee, should dictate the choice of problems to be investigated was a consciously heretical position, deeply at variance with academic practice. Febvre went so far as to declare that he could not countenance the notion of scholarship for scholarship's sake.[8] The Rankean – or Panglossian – hope, according to which each newly unearthed fact, like a modest brick, would join others, until the shape of the edifice revealed itself at last, struck Febvre as absurd. It made more sense to him that one should engage the services of an architect before employing bricklayers. *Annales* was not to publish simply whatever new research happened to come its way, as is the usual practice of academic journals. Instead, *Annales* was to commission research into problems of particular utility and act as a clearing house, matching problems requiring solution with appropriate specialists. The goal was that of a 'managed history', 'une histoire dirigée' (Febvre 1965: 55).

In some ways *Annales* may be considered a period piece. In recent years it has become more ordinary, more academic, but throughout its long life it was doing for historians what brash new quarterlies, art galleries, salons and cafés were doing for artists and poets in the 1920s: providing a home base for rebels who banded together, united in their opposition to official culture.

Not that the contributors to *Annales*, in the 1930s, and even less so in later years,

---

7 Febvre 1965: 19: 'Il n'y a pas, à proprement parler, d'histoire économique et sociale.'
8 'Et disons: l'érudition pour l'érudition, jamais,' cited by Erbe 1979: 48 n. 4.

were readily identifiable as rebels. They were mostly seasoned and middle-aged university professors, quite a few of them members of the narrowest elite imaginable, that composed of graduates of the Ecole Normale Superieure. *Annales* was founded in the wake of Febvre's appointment to the most coveted post in French higher education, a chair at the Collège de France, and Febvre made sure, eventually, that his chosen successor to head *Annales*, Fernand Braudel, would inherit the chair at his retirement, just as Braudel himself helped Le Roy Ladurie inherit the post in turn.

If, in spite of the indisputable elite status of its leadership, *Annales* had a reputation as a radical journal, the merit belongs entirely to the novelty of the ideas expressed in its pages, not to some imagined obedience to a political agenda, let alone a political party, although it is true that *Annales* was clearly on the Left, in a general sort of way, as long as Febvre dominated its editorial policy. Especially disturbing to conservative academics was the present-mindedness of the journal's editors, that is, their clearly expressed desire to influence events.

The defining moment for the journal and for Febvre himself came on the eve of the Second World War, when Febvre, it seems, broke with his publisher and almost ended the journal's life over the issue of the proper response to the triumph of the Nazi and fascist regimes (see Schöttler 1991). Taking sides against fascism was relatively easy, even if it meant publishing out of your living room. But to do it without being anchored in the Marxist constituency required rare independence of mind. Febvre identified the emergence of totalitarian mass movements as the most critical issue to face thinking men. It was therefore the duty of *Annales* to explain this phenomenon. 'Right next door to us', he wrote, 'a world has ended. A new world has taken its place.' To explain and therefore to counter this menace, one would have to develop new conceptual tools to replace worn-out theories, including Marxism: 'The old keys do not turn in the new locks' (ibid. 75).

In his search for new keys, Febvre turned to Franz Borkenau, a Viennese political refugee newly arrived in Paris. Trained as a historian, Borkenau was also intimately acquainted with both the Nazi movement and the Soviet system. He had been, until recently, a Comintern agent, working out of the Soviet embassy in Berlin, with full responsibility for the German communist youth movement. He would soon become known for his lucid reporting on the Spanish Civil War and for his authoritative analysis of totalitarian ideology. While in Paris, Borkenau served as a consultant to Febvre, pointing out the family resemblances between the Nazi and the Soviet regimes in a way which was simply unthinkable for the European Left. Borkenau's contributions to *Annales*, for all that, were somewhat pedestrian in character. It was Borkenau's wife, Lucie Varga, who turned out to be perfectly suited to the task of explaining the appeal of the new totalitarian ideologies. In her Febvre found the ideal partner. She was a medievalist by training and, among other things, an ethnographer, a linguist and a mountain-climber by avocation. It was Lucie Varga who fashioned the keys Febvre was looking for, in a series of articles in *Annales*. In these essays, full of intelligence and not in the least mindful of academic conventions, she reported on her fieldwork among Alpine villagers, both Austrian and Italian. She brought her experience as a student of medieval religious cults – as well as Freud, Marx and Malinowski – to her task, which was to understand what it was that prompted young people to discard the world-view of their parish priests in favour of the gospel preached by the black-shirted or brown-shirted purveyors of a different sort of salvation (ibid).

Lucie Varga's meteoric passage through the pages of *Annales* provides a concrete example of what Febvre was aiming at. He started by identifying an urgent problem. Then he cast about for the person most likely to bring a fresh solution to it. The historian, he believed ought always to begin with a problem, not with a set of documents which may or may not turn out to be significant. The Varga studies were concerned with popular belief systems (*mentalités*). Febvre's own *Religion of Rabelais* would pose the question: Was it possible, within the belief system of the sixteenth century, to be an atheist? This study was undertaken, originally, in collaboration with Lucie Varga. It may even be possible to detect the germ of Febvre's thesis, namely, that Rabelais was not an atheist, in Varga's dissertation (ibid.).

After the defeat of the Nazi and fascist regimes, the most urgent problems facing Europeans, in Febvre's analysis, were those created by centuries of rapacious colonial expansion in Africa, Asia and South America. *Annales* now began to make room systematically for articles and reports on the world outside Europe. A related problem which preoccupied the editors in the 1950s was that of a population explosion in the Third World, hence the journal's increasing interest in historical demography.[9] In those post-war years, under Febvre's leadership, the little heretical quarterly once known only to the *cognoscenti* experienced an irresistible ascension. Its size grew by leaps and bounds, it came out more frequently, the pool of its contributors widened, as did its subscription list and its influence.[10]

Febvre was able to participate in the general build-up of new research institutes initiated by the French government. He was appointed president of the newly created department of social sciences, the Sixième Section, within the old Ecole Pratique des Hautes Etudes. He established a Centre for Historical Research, headed by Fernand Braudel, and a number of other Centres, not lavishly funded, but capable of providing a modest institutional base for the *Annales* group. Alliances were established with the National Centre for Scientific Research (CNRS) and the National Institute for Population Studies (INED), among others. *Annales* now had a budget. Many of the historians and social scientists affiliated with *Annales* had opportunities now for permanent civil service appointments as researchers in the new institutes.

The Sixième Section was to grow prodigiously, especially under Braudel's

---

9   The interest in the Third World was initiated by Febvre in the 1930s and institutionalized under Braudel's editorship in a regular and increasingly important rubric under the heading of *le monde sauf l'Europe*.

10   Erbe 1979: 49. In 1946, 400 pages per volume; by 1958, 800; by 1960, 1,200 – and six issues yearly; by 1970, close to 1,800 pages.

shrewd management, threatening to swallow the other Sections, until it was eventually established as a separate institute, the Ecole des Hautes Etudes en Sciences Sociales, with its very own imposing glass-and-steel headquarters building on the Boulevard Raspail, the Maison des Sciences Humaines.

The resources were in place. It was time to move from prototype to production. It is at this point that controversy arises among those who pay close attention to the history of the *Annales* experiment. There are those who prefer to remain loyal to the original *Annales* (*Annales première manière*) and those who prefer *Annales* in its mature, fully developed stage, when it had become a highly publicized behemoth spewing out new journals and monograph series. This is when the *annalistes* began to achieve star-status. One now has to consult specialized and frequently updated bibliographies just to keep track of books and articles published each year *about* *Annales*, in several languages. A good illustration of the special place occupied by *Annales* in contemporary French culture is the reception accorded in the daily press, recently, to a serious monograph devoted to the work of Lucie Varga (Schöttler 1991). The author, Peter Schöttler, intimated, in passing, that Lucien Febvre had been in love with Dr Varga, in the 1930s. The daily press, papers such as *Libération*, saw fit to devote space, under lurid titles (Lucien et Lucie) to a putative romance involving two middle-aged historians sixty years earlier. Clearly, *Annales* is news in France.

Whether one is pleased or irritated by all the publicity surrounding *Annales*, the question remains: Did *Annales* deliver? Did it change the way history is written, when it acquired the means to influence historians on a large scale, when it moved on from provocation and exhortation to become the centre of a vast publishing empire? Personally, I preferred the original, combative stage, when the journal was full of possibilities and excitement and before it became the official mouthpiece of an entrenched bureaucracy. Braudel, too, at the end of his career, felt that way. But for all that, I am not quite as ready to close the books on *Annales* as Peter Burke appears to be.[11] I shall review the criticisms which have been directed at *Annales* since the 1960s before going on to describe the genuine achievements which, in my view, still make *Annales* stand out.

Perhaps the most commonly heard criticism has been that *Annales* adopted a naive positivist stance, claiming, in effect, that only those things which can be counted are worth studying. This is certainly a valid criticism. There was a time, in the 1960s and 1970s, when *Annales* appeared to focus almost exclusively on topics which lent themselves to quantification, the study of historical demography (for example), of grain prices, of the tonnage passing through Atlantic ports. Counting on a large scale was a technique applied also to less obviously suitable problems, the measuring of religious fervour, for instance, on the basis of very large numbers of testaments, or the study of literacy or book production.

There is nothing wrong with all this, and, in almost every instance, the tireless number-crunchers could rightly claim that they were only carrying out orders,

---

11   Burke 1990: 106–7: 'the movement is effectively over' and ' this is rather like writing an obituary'.

Febvre's marching orders, which did, indeed, specify team work, the search for long-term trends and the systematic use of evidence such as testaments to get at the history of collective *mentalités*. The problem with the way the late founders' orders were carried out is that it was done mechanically. As Franco Venturi pointed out in passing, rather gently, the *annalistes* of the 1960s, in their enthusiasm for 'scientific history', went to absurd lengths, 'using a cyclotron to crack a nut' (Venturi 1971: 9–10) and issuing theoretical pronouncements of a comical nature: 'from a scientific point of view, the only social history is quantitative history'.[12] It is hard to escape the feeling that the *normaliens* who found permanent employment in the Sixième Section, after an apprenticeship in the Communist cells of the École Normale, were conditioned to become doctrinaire followers and, as such, were the worst possible choice for carrying out the experiments envisioned by the founders.

It is worth noting in this connection that *Annales* is capable of self-criticism, on occasion. The fiftieth anniversary issue (1979) confesses, rather candidly, that the journal had been concentrating on methods for their own sake, in a routine fashion, while losing sight of its original mission. The editors were candid enough to admit that the journal was no longer what it had once been, that it was no longer dedicated to improving the world, as it had been under Febvre's direction, that the *annalistes*, no longer outsiders and critics, were securely integrated now and part of the academic establishment.

This self-criticism did not go far enough, to be sure. What needed to be said is that if Febvre or Bloch, by some miracle, were given the opportunity to scan their journal's pages now, they would die laughing at the fractured jargon which passes for French and the evident mediocrity of some of the contributors.[13] Some may wish to attribute the mechanical counting and the mechanical prose to the take-over of *Annales* by a new generation of salon-Marxists (Burke 1990: 24) but I do not believe that it was ideology alone which caused the *Annales* experiment to falter. I think that the problem is an institutional one, far too complex to describe in detail here, but, *grosso modo*, having to do with a new generation of *normaliens* who turned out to be civil servants first and historians last. When *Annales* had no paid staff and no offices and no more than 300 subscribers, the articles were signed Henri Pirenne, Marc Bloch, Georges Dumézil, Mircea Eliade, Roger Dion, Jacques Berque, Louis Gernet, Edouard Perroy – in a word, signed by giants, by scholars with towering reputations who endowed the struggling journal with the capital of their own well-earned reputations. As *Annales* was becoming the thriving house publication of a vast research institute, much of the journal's content was produced by staff members who, in some cases, had not even published a doctoral thesis, let alone a significant

---

12 Adeline Daumard and François Furet in *Annales* 1959: 676: 'scientifiquement parlant, il n'est d'histoire sociale que quantitative'.

13 Case in point: Lucette Valensi, who was to join the editorial board eventually, writes 'l'explicitation du non-événementiel suivant une perspective de longue durée.' In her pseudo-language, words like 'événementiel' and phrases such as 'longue durée' are transformed into 'scientific' concepts. Not surprisingly, she also speaks without inhibition of 'l'école des *Annales*' (*Annales* 1974: 1309).

work of scholarship. They began at the bottom, in the house that Braudel built, the Maison des Sciences Humaines, and moved, from cellar to attic, so to speak, working their way up through fierce office intrigues. They owed their entire reputations to their connection with *Annales*.

In spite of these changes, the price of success, one might say, *Annales* still retains a good deal of its original appeal. This is because of the extraordinary sense of continuity, of filial piety, of sectarian loyalty which holds the *Annales* group together. 'Les Annales continuent' was the title of Braudel's editorial, in 1957, implying that there was at least some question whether the journal could bring itself to continue to exist in the wake of Febvre's death, even though the *vie matérielle* of the journal was more secure than ever at this point. The continued spiritual presence of the founders is obvious in every issue of *Annales*. Bloch and Febvre are invoked at every turn, they are commemorated at every opportunity, and so are their peers and apostles. The editors' desire to change the journal's perspective as little as possible is clearly expressed. Braudel's sense of his apostolic mission never faltered and his authority remained firm until the events of May 1968 (and the *patron*'s temporary absence in Chicago) provided the opportunity for a little palace revolution which led to some sharing of authority and a *Directoire* style of governance which has since led to apocalyptic complaints about the empire's crumbling: *l'histoire en miettes*.

Actually, one need only study the composition of the editorial board over the years to see that Febvre's grip was hardly weakened, even after 1968. Twenty-five years after his death the board was still dominated by his closest comrades, some of whom had been in place since the 1930s. The choice of topics for research retained much of the old spirit. The 1960 volume, for instance, included studies of Yoruba farming practices, of Bosnian gold mines, of North African camels in the Roman period, of the Chilean economy in the eighteenth century, of technical experiments with mechanical harvesters in antiquity. In the same volume Jacques Le Goff published a first sketch of his study of medieval conceptions of time, Claude Lévi-Strauss reflected on history and anthropology, Lucien Goldmann wrote about Chagall, Robert Mandrou on the concept of the baroque, Alexandre Koyré on Newton, Galileo and Plato, Roland Barthes on Racine: altogether scintillating company and a roster which could have been chosen by Febvre. Perhaps it was, since most issues of *Annales* are painstakingly planned, sometimes years ahead of their deadlines.

Ten years later the 1970 volume remains just as rich and suggestive. It certainly was not planned by Febvre, but it was the creation of an editorial board unchanged since 1957. Etruscan city-planning, Indian gods, contemporary French schools, Peruvian cathedrals, rural Algeria, Sudanese gold, Bedouins, fairy-tales, probability theory, Freud, the history of climate, the physiology of the brain, the student movement of May 1968: another Febvrian cocktail with the power to intoxicate. What other publication dared to combine so many disciplines, continents and cultures? And in so rigorous and disciplined a way?

It may be true that some of the current *annalistes* lack both imagination and truly first-rate scholarly credentials, not to mention a sense of style, but even so, the journal as a collective enterprise continues to experiment, to invite experiment, to encourage collaboration between historians and social scientists, to engage the historical imagination in every conceivable way. It may be the case that the editors were more inclined to take risks, twenty years ago, by publishing, for instance, a wild but suggestive essay by a central Asian folklorist on the shamanistic significance of the Trojan Horse legend, or by publishing, under the rubric of 'comparative iconometry', an attempt to prove that the basic rules of artistic representation were invented in the Stone Age and would not change thereafter (see *Annales* 1963). One had the sense, in those years, that *Annales* was always ahead of everyone else, the first to make death, sexuality or climate objects of systematic historical study, for instance. Of late, *Annales* is more likely to feature articles on topics already discussed exhaustively in print elsewhere. That seemed to be the case when the journal hosted a conference on 'Vichy and the Jews' and published the proceedings in a special issue, with a somewhat defensive introduction (1993). For that matter, ten years earlier, in 1983, Fernand Braudel had already reached the sobering conclusion that *Annales* had given up on its original mission. In a letter dated 23 February of that year he wrote to explain why he had removed himself from all editorial functions at *Annales* in 1972, even though his name remained on the cover. His successors had disappointed him. They had blunted and diverted the journal's ancient course. For Braudel, *Annales* had lost its *raison d'être* when it ceased being an avant-garde journal: 'une revue d'avant-garde, donc de risque, et probablement hérétique'. The new *Annales* was trendy, following fashion rather than leading it. At the same time, the editors were in danger of departing from the philosophical perspective which had been 'essential since the journal's creation', namely the ambition to write total or global history by reconstituting 'all the social realities' which are in the background of any historical problem. (From an unpublished letter in the possession of Mrs Braudel.) It would be difficult to take issue with Braudel's authoritative assessment. The journal is certainly no longer an avant-garde quarterly, no longer self-consciously provocative and heretical. And it does seem to have given up on some of the more ambitious goals set by Febvre early in the century. One can point to articles, even to entire issues, already twenty years ago, which seem less than inspiring, but the basic ingredients of the *Annales* tradition remained present, in some sense.

At the most visible level this tradition manifests itself in the self-conscious engineering of each issue. It will contain, usually, two or three substantial *études*, finished articles based on new and usually exhaustive research. A separate category of *travaux en cours* reports on work in progress. Permanent rubrics such as *notes critiques* and *comptes-rendus* cast a wide, knowing and highly critical glance at what is being published in selected domains. The reviewing is coherent and follows thematic lines. Unlike those journals which simply review new books sent to the editor – those books which happen to fall within its specialized area of competence, medieval history, say, or Middle Eastern Studies – *Annales* assumes competence over absolutely everything. Of necessity, the journal's reviewing policy has to be highly selective. A topic is chosen and the critic or critics go on to review both books and articles in whatever languages may be relevant.

For instance, tucked away in the category of *Notes Brèves et Prises de Position*, in the 1965 volume, we find a characteristic series of critical notes held together by the topic 'Germany and its Neighbours after 1914'. In six closely packed pages the reviewers romp through an article in the *Historische Zeitschrift*, another in the East German *Zeitschrift für Geschichtswissenschaft*, a third in the *Československý Časopis Historický* (on the failure of Austrian social democracy). The reviewers take up an East German essay on the nature of the Nazi regime and blow it to smithereens: 'the author asks who was behind the Nazi system of control and repression. He replies, simply, big capital.' The next item is a book published by the Oxford University Press in 1963, Jürgen Gehl's *Austria, Germany and the Anschluss*. 'This work by a conscientious beginner will be of very little use to specialists' is the verdict and the reviewer never forgets that he is writing from a certain perspective, that of a Febvrian hostility, not to diplomatic history as such, but to diplomatic history as a lifeless routine in which ministers, ambassadors and other public figures 'spring up and disappear from the stage like the marionettes of old-fashioned diplomatic history'. Speaking of another article in the *Československý Časopis Historický*, the reviewer notes that the article's author waits until the last paragraph to ask the question which ought to have served as his guiding theme from the start.

What is striking about the reviewing policy at *Annales*, and this has been so since the beginning, when Febvre and Bloch did most of the reviewing, is that the judgements expressed, often rather brutally, about the published work of other historians are part and parcel of the *Annales* philosophy. The reviews often start by defining a problem, explain why the topic is an important one and then go on to do considerably more than bring a book to the readers' attention: they criticize and teach, always ready to show in what sense the book or article under review falls short of meeting the criteria for what historical research and historical writing ought to be, according to the editors of *Annales* and their friends and sympathizers. This pedagogical aspect of *Annales* criticism can of course be very irritating if you happen to be on the receiving end. Sharp reviews were a speciality of Marc Bloch's and the tradition was kept alive in the journal, although that quality too has become attenuated in recent years.[14]

The spirit of the early *Annales* was reverently maintained in the Braudel years, although the journal was constantly being refashioned to remain open to new developments, new opportunities, new interests. Established rubrics such as *Le Monde sauf l'Europe*, *Débats et Combats*, *Enquêtes en Cours* were joined by newer ones such as *Frontières Nouvelles*, *Domaines Contemporains*, *Inter-Sciences*, *Temps Présent*, *Mentalités*. Side by side with categories meant to be more or less permanent, increasingly, the editors put together special issues on topics such as *Famille*

---

14 For an example of Bloch's sarcasm, see, for instance, his review of Louis Battifol's *La Fortune de Richelieu*. Bloch writes: 'la fortune de Richelieu: beau sujet, assurément. Ayons le courage d'ajouter: après l'étude de M. Louis Battifol, presque autant qu'auparavant, sujet tout neuf' (*Annales* 1938: 459).

et Société, *Histoire et Psychanalyse*, *Histoire et Sexualité*, *Histoire et Environnement* or *Histoire Non-Ecrite* for instance.

'Pour une histoire anthropologique', in the 1974 volume, is a good example of the effort made by the editors to provide a reasoned foundation for cross-disciplinary explorations. I write 'reasoned foundation' so as to avoid the word 'theory'. The founders had no use for theory. As the sociologist Georges Friedmann was to recall, in 1953, on the occasion of Lucien Febvre's 75th birthday, it was their healthy contempt for theory, in the 1930s, which made the *Annales* group so attractive to those who had their fill of theorizing in the Marxist camp. Instead of the 'ratiocinations, the polemics, the scholastic disputes, the suspicion, the endless critiques in the absence of any attempts at originality', they found, in Febvre's camp, 'a spirit of research and cooperation'. 'We were in need of a team spirit,' wrote Friedmann, 'and we wanted no part of the *esprit de système* which prevailed among sociologists' (*Annales* 1957: 4).

Friedmann himself, Charles Morazé and Fernand Braudel constituted the core of the editorial board throughout most of the journal's history. They acted as a Board of Censors, keeping a watchful eye on the enthusiasms of the younger generation and, occasionally, they exposed the fragility of these constructs. Morazé and Friedmann, among others, prevented *Annales* from becoming a school, weighing in, from time to time, in editorial essays of a philosophical kind and providing a discrete corrective move of the tiller when the vessel showed signs of drifting into the Sargasso Sea of theory.

A fine example of this kind of intervention is Charles Morazé's essay on 'L'Histoire et l'unité des sciences de l'homme' in the 1968 volume. Sensing the danger *Annales* was in of becoming an object of idolatry – and wishing to puncture excessive claims made for the uniqueness of the *Annales* experiment, Morazé explained that 'the greatness of cities, their decadence … the poison and the vicissitudes called forth by prosperity, the ways in which anxiety can produce both vanity and wisdom, such considerations are to be found in Herodotus.' Lest under-educated technocrats mistake Febvre's call for 'économies, sociétés, civilisations' for a new formula ready to be patented, Morazé, who knew the sources of Febvre's thought, his *âme de papier*, wisely reminds his readers that 'no history worthy of the name was ever written in which the author neglected to consider societies, economies and psychologies'. In a word: the historian who writes for *Annales* belongs to a tradition of philosophical history which goes back to the very beginning of rational thought. The social sciences, writes Morazé, are 'anchored in the encounters between history and philosophy' (*Annales* 1968: 233). This is a formulation which would have made sense to Montaigne, four centuries ago, but it may be less meaningful to those who wish to believe that history is a science only recently developed in the laboratories of the Boulevard Raspail. The mental habits fostered by academic Marxism are not easily compatible with the humanist outlook of Morazé, Friedmann, Braudel, Febvre or Bloch. This, it seems to me, is the chief source of tension between one generation of *annalistes* and the next. It was the special merit of Fernand Braudel to bridge the gap between the cultivated and cosmopolitan Old Guard and the smooth technicians under his command.

Braudel was the keeper of the flame. He observed the directives laid down early in the century for the good management of the journal and of its adjunct activities: research seminars, conferences, monograph series. He preserved the spirit of those early years, making sure that history, a living history, as Febvre always insisted, reigned supreme within the family of the social sciences, fraternizing with the other disciplines, borrowing their methods and perspectives, but remaining in charge. The qualities which made Braudel so effective were those of an apostle, of the man who had absorbed the teachings of his master so completely that the spirit of Lucien Febvre lived on in Fernand Braudel. He made an art of his down-to-earth, Third Republic, up-from-the-ranks style, dismissing the species *homo academicus* in residence at the Sorbonne in pungent, unprintable, one-word judgements. He welcomed young disciples in a manner both lordly and informal, sweeping them up in his embrace and addressing them with an avuncular *tu*. He reminisced at every opportunity, evoking his long and close friendship with Febvre, sealed in the course of a slow passage across the South Atlantic, aboard the steamship *Campana*, in November 1937. His published tributes to Febvre, especially the luminous essay which, under the title of 'Presence de Lucien Febvre', serves as an introduction to the Festschrift of 1953, are the most authentic guides to the spirit of *Annales*.

Reading those pages, more than once, and listening to Braudel talk – he talked like a book, his lectures, stenographically recorded, could go straight to the printer – it was clear that his words preserved the style of a bygone era, the elegant, slightly archaic style of the French intellectual *circa* 1930. Listening to Fernand Braudel one could sometimes hear Lucien Febvre in the background, not Febvre alone, but the sound of that *belle époque*, already a historical memory, but alive, still, by special dispensation. Braudel understood that the substance of the *Annales* achievement was not to be found in the adoption of clever techniques, but in the personal credo Febvre shared with Bloch: a passion for scholarship framed by an equally deep involvement in the affairs of this world and close friendships with other 'esprits risqueurs et originaux'.

'To divide one's life into two parts: to assign one part to one's work, performed without love, and to reserve the other for one's deepest needs: that is abominable,' wrote Febvre, explaining his passion for his *métier*, which he could not separate from his deepest convictions. 'I am very much alone. I am working,' he wrote on more than one occasion. Ceaseless work, enforced solitude, the condition, in a word of the scholar's life. But when he was not at his desk, you would find Professor Febvre in brilliant company, motoring across France in a venerable Bugatti driven by Léon Werth and part-owned by Saint-Exupéry. Braudel's tribute reminds us of the large and exceptionally diverse and talented crowd of Febvre's friends, those to whom he remained 'romantically loyal' (Braudel 1953: I, 1–16).

This was more than a group of colleagues. It was a good sample of the French intelligentsia, including poets and politicians, psychologists and philosophers, brought together in part by their remarkable natural abilities which had catapulted many of them into the Ecole Normale in their youth, regardless of their social origins – and, in part, also, by a common attitude towards the grave political issues of their time. It was this attitude, opposed to all chauvinisms and deeply involved in the defence of the common man, in the spirit of Jules Michelet and of the anarchist Elisée Reclus – both of whom figure prominently in the construction of Febvre's *âme de papier* – it was this, and the sheer intelligence of their writing which passed like an electric current to reach young historians marooned in provincial universities as far away, spiritually, as Sardinia.

These are the qualities, perhaps muted now, which explain the triumph of the *Annales* experiment in a world recovering from the totalitarian nightmares which came so close to destroying the souls of western Europeans and still hovered over the East. Watching Fernand Braudel preside over the annual meeting of economic historians sponsored by the Communist municipality of the Italian city of Prato, watching the Communist Prince Doria, then deputy mayor of Genoa, standing elbow to elbow with a Braudel protégé from Warsaw, the medievalist Bronislaw Geremiek, who was on the way to prison and a leadership role in the Solidarity movement, one sensed that the *vita contemplativa* was never far removed from the *vita activa* in these quarters.

It was the great merit of the *Annales* group to enlarge the horizon of French historians, notoriously monolingual, by publishing the work of foreigners, both in the journal itself and in the various monograph series directed by Febvre, by Braudel and others after him. Italian, Polish or American historians in tune with the Parisian group became part of the French intellectual scene. Their books were published in translation, while French historians connected with *Annales* found their way into foreign journals, routinely, and the lists of publishing houses such as the Cambridge or Chicago university presses swelled with the names of French authors.

In the last twenty years, even while the tone of *Annales* has changed, and while the *annalistes* have come in for some tart criticism, the influence of the French group has grown to the point where *Annales* tends to assume pride of place in introductory methods courses in American graduate schools and even conventional textbooks include sections on *mentalités*. Social history with an anthropological twist in the *Annales* manner has become one of the most highly prized genres of historical writing. This is no ephemeral fashion. That is the point made in these pages: that the *Annales* experiment is with us for good. It has been in tune with our century. Whatever reservations one may harbour *vis-à-vis* this or that aspect of *Annales*, it remains true that a complete set of the journal is an indispensable tool for demonstrating the variety of twentieth-century historical practice and for showing how closely historians and social scientists mirror the tensions and the changes of our time.

REFERENCES

Braudel, F. (1953) 'Présence de Lucien Febvre', in F. Braudel, *Eventail de l'histoire vivante: hommage offert à Lucien Febvre*, vol. 1, Paris.

Burke, P. (ed.) (1973) *A New Kind of History and Other Essays*, tr. K. Folca, New York.
Burke, P. (1990) *The French Historical Revolution. The 'Annales' School 1929–1989.* Stanford.
Erbe, M. (1979) *Zur neueren französischen Sozialgeschichtsforschung*, Darmstadt.
Febvre, L. (1965) *Combats pour l'histoire*, Paris.
Ferro, M. (ed.) (1972) *Social Historians in Contemporary France. Essays from 'Annales'*, New York.
Huppert, G. (1994) Review of Schöttler 1991, *History and Theory* 33: 220–30.
Schöttler, P. (1991) *Lucie Varga: Les autorités invisibles*, Paris.
Venturi, F. (1971) *Utopia and Reform in the Enlightenment*, Cambridge.

36

MARXIST HISTORIOGRAPHY

S. H. Rigby

The value and extent of Marx's influence on modern historiography are rarely denied, even by those who reject his economics, politics and philosophy.[1] Yet the precise nature of Marx's impact influence on later Marxist historians or on historians in general is rather more difficult to specify. Too often Marx's theory of history ('historical materialism') is reduced to a general emphasis on the importance of class struggle or on the role of the 'economic factor'.[2] It is impossible in the space available here to provide a comprehensive survey of Marxist historiography, which would virtually amount to writing a history of the world. Instead, this chapter examines Marx's major claims about social structure and historical change, explores how and to what extent Marxist historical writing differs from orthodox historiography, and offers a general assessment of the Marxist approach.

MARX AND ENGELS'S 'HISTORICAL MATERIALISM'

One problem in specifying Marx's influence on later historians is that Marx and Engels themselves employed a number of different historical approaches and offered a variety of specific historical interpretations which were by no means necessarily mutually compatible.[3] In general, as Fleischer has shown, Marx and Engels worked within at least three overarching historical outlooks: the anthropogenetic, the pragmatological and the nomological. In their early works, Marx and Engels saw history in Hegelian, or 'anthropogenetic' terms. Here history is seen as the overarching, dialectical progression through which humanity comes to its full self-realization, passing through a necessary negative phase of self-alienation and social

---

1 Popper 1966: 106–10; Kolakowski 1978: I, 369–70, III, 524; Leff 1961: 7; Rigby 1992b: 14.
2 Hobsbawm 1972. As Marxists have been keen to point out, 'economic determinism' is not a sin which has been confined to Marxist historians: Hill 1968: 21; Thompson 1971: 78; Genovese 1972: 319.
3 On the contradictory nature of Marx and Engels's legacy, see Gouldner 1980.

atomization before achieving a fully human, free and rational community.[4] In their works of the mid-1840s, such as *The Holy Family*, *The Condition of the Working Class in England* and *The German Ideology*, Marx and Engels then shifted to a 'pragmatological' outlook, one more in line with orthodox notions of historical agency. Here the anthropogenetic conception of social development as a logical unfolding towards some particular goal is replaced by a view in which history is seen as 'the outcome, more blind than the result of any tendency to a specific goal, of the actions of individuals and of groups impelled by their needs in the situations in which they find themselves'.[5] Jon Elster has even claimed that the works of this period are characterized by a methodological individualism (the belief that all social phenomena are explicable 'in ways that only involve individuals', their properties, goals, beliefs and actions), although it should be stressed that Marx and Engels always insisted that 'real living individuals' were themselves the products of 'given historical conditions and relations'.[6] Finally, whilst never explicitly abandoning the pragmatological outlook, Marx and Engels's later works, such as *Capital* (1867) and *Anti-Dühring* (1878), also adopted a 'nomological' perspective in which historical development is seen as analogous to a natural process taking place in accordance with 'inner hidden laws' which it is the task of the historian to uncover.[7] Here the emphasis on human agency of the pragmatological outlook is replaced with a structuralist approach which sees the development of the economic formation of society as 'a process of natural history' and in which individuals are presented as 'the personifications of economic categories, the bearers of particular class-relations and interests'.[8] This outlook was generalized by later Marxists into the philosophi-

---

4   Marx and Engels 1975–6, II: 476, III: 172–4, 395, 419–42, 463–72, 475–6, 485, 491–2, 499; Fleischer 1975: 12–16; Adamson 1981; 1985: ch. 1; Tillich 1970; Rigby 1992a; Maguire 1972; Kain 1986.
5   Fleischer 1975: 13; see also Marx and Engels 1975–6, IV: 93, 298, 583; 1982: 12; V: 36–7, 39–41, 56–9, 88; 1962: 247; Rigby 1992a: 47–63; Benton 1977: 151–3; Miller 1979: 29–32; Kain 1986: ch. 2.
6   Marx and Engels 1975–6, V: 37, 39, 51–2, 76–8, 183, 215, 323, 329, 375–6, 378–9, 410, 413, 436–8, 442, 464, 479–80; Elster 1982; 1985: 5, 7, 109–10. For discussions of Elster see the articles in *Inquiry* 29 (1986): vol. 29, pp. 3–77 and *Theory and Society* 11 (1982): vol. 11, pp 483–539 and Callinicos, 1987. Carling presents Elster's methodological individualism as a central part of the emergence of 'rational choice Marxism', which has replaced French structuralism as the dominant paradigm within Marxism and which works from the assumption that 'actors decide what to do by applying principles of optimization to a set of alternatives for action' (Carling 1991: 27). See Carling 1986; Levine *et al.* 1987; Carling 1990; Callinicos 1990; Wood 1990; Rigby 1993.
7   Fleischer 1975: 13; Krieger 1953: 386–7, 403; Marx and Engels 1962: 246; 1949: 153, 354–5; Marx 1976–81: I. 90–3, 101–2, 928–30; Engels n.d.: 15, 147–61, 209–10, 305; Marx and Engels 1975: 442, 455; McLellan 1976: 423; Lichtheim 1964: 236, 243; Rigby 1992a: 187–95; Kain 1986: chs 3 and 4. This emphasis on history as a law-bound process was the basis of Soviet-Marxist historiography, see Acton 1990: chs 2 and 3.
8   Marx 1976, II: 92; Althusser and Balibar 1975: 180; Burris 1987. The debate between Miliband and Poulantzas on how to account for the class nature of the capitalist state provides a classic instance of the clash between the pragmatological and the structuralist concepts of agency. See Miliband 1973; Poulantzas 1973; Miliband 1973; Laclau 1979: ch. 2. See also the references in Miliband 1983: 26. A pragmatological emphasis on agency formed the basis for E. P. Thompson's attack on structuralist notions of class. See Wood 1982, and see the references in n. 102.

cal system of 'dialectical materialism', but it should be stressed that such dialectical materialism was neither chronologically nor logically prior to the empirical social theory developed by Marx and Engels in the mid-1840s: historical materialism is not an 'application' of dialectical materialism.[9]

Even in their analyses of particular historical conjunctures, it was inevitable, given that they were writing over a long period of time and in a variety of historical circumstances and literary genres, that Marx and Engels would produce a range of differing and even contradictory historical interpretations. There is, for instance, a contrast between the account of the transition from feudalism to capitalism offered in works such as *The German Ideology* (1845–6) and the *Communist Manifesto* (1848), where Marx and Engels focus on the rise of towns, trade and an urban bourgeoisie, and the increasing emphasis on the transformation of agriculture and the expropriation of the peasant producers contained in the *Grundrisse* (1857–8) and *Capital*.[10]

Yet, despite the ambiguous and often contradictory legacy bequeathed to later Marxists by Marx and Engels, and even though, as we shall see, Marxist historians often disagree violently with each other about specific issues, it is possible to identify a distinctive school of Marxist historiography. If, as E. P. Thompson (1978: 236) argued, the methodology and epistemology of historical materialism do not differ from the orthodox historical procedure of formulating hypotheses which can be tested against empirical evidence, Marxist historians can be distinguished from their non-Marxist colleagues in terms of their common vocabulary and concepts, and their shared body of interests, questions, hypotheses and historical emphases.

In *The German Ideology* (co-written with Engels in 1845–6) and the 'Preface' to *A Contribution to the Critique of Political Economy* (1859), Marx set out a comprehensive account of social structure and of historical change. For Marx, all social life is based upon the material production necessary to satisfy humanity's subsistence needs. This process involves the transformation of specific raw materials by means of particular instruments of production, human labour-power, and scientific and technological knowledge within a given specific technical division of labour, i.e. by means of society's 'productive forces'.[11] A particular level of development of these productive forces forms the basis for specific 'relations of production', i.e. relations between people (as in the case of the class relation between an employer and his employees), or between people and the productive forces (as in the case of the

9 Stalin 1951: 5; Dorpalen 1985: 35–45; Cornforth 1968: 126; Meikle: 1985: 1; Croce 1981: 3, 7–9; Hilferding 1981; Korsch 1938: 51–2, 168–71; Rigby 1992a: chs 6–8; Jordan 1967: 297. That historical materialism does not logically require dialectical materialism has not prevented Marxists identifying a 'dialectical progress of history' at work in events such as the French Revolution. See Lefebvre 1967: 360.
10 Marx and Engels 1975–6, V: 32, 64–74; VI: 485–90; Marx 1974b: 506, 508–12, 589; Marx 1976–81, I: chs 26–32; III: ch. 20; see Mumy 1978–9; Brenner 1977: 27, 33–8; Hilton 1976: 23.
11 Marx and Engels 1975–6, V: 41–2; Marx 1971: 19–23; Marx 1976–81, I: 284–90; 1974: 560, 699; McMurtry 1978: 55; G. A. Cohen 1978: 32.

employer's ownership of a factory). These relations of production, or property relations, determine people's access to the productive forces (for instance, the wage-labourer's access to the productive forces is dependent upon being employed by the capitalist) and to the products of the labour process (in the form of wages in the labourer's case, or as the ownership of those products which are to be sold for profit in the employer's case) (Hilferding 1981: 127–8; G. A. Cohen 1978: 3).

Although Marx's own terminology was by no means consistent, Marxists usually refer to a combination of specific relations of production with a specific level (or levels) of development of the productive forces as a 'mode of production', each mode of production being defined by its relations of production (feudal, capitalist, etc.).[12] For Marxists, the class relations of modes of production based on private property (as opposed to the communal property of primitive communism) are necessarily 'exploitative' since they involve the appropriation of specific forms of 'surplus labour' from the producers by a class of non-producers, as in the feudal landlord's appropriation of rent from his peasants.[13] Such exploitation inevitably generates class conflict as the producers seek to limit the level of exploitation and the non-producers seek to maximize it.[14]

Marx and Engels frequently claimed that society's relations of production 'corresponded' to the level of development reached by its productive forces,[15] a claim which they illustrated for each stage of historical development, from primitive communism,[16] through the ancient,[17] Asiatic,[18] feudal,[19] and capitalist[20] modes of production. As society acquires new productive forces, a transhistorical tendency which Marx and Engels largely took for granted[21] a stage is eventually reached

---

12 Mishra 1979. For Marx's own varying usage of the term 'mode of production', see Marx and Engels 1975: V, 43, 53; 1976: 175; Marx 1971: 203; Marx 1976–81: I: 505, 196; III: 373, 753, 734, 755, 759, 1019–1021; 1968: 429–30.

13 Marx 1976–81, I: 313, 324–5, 345–8, III: 763–5, 917–50; Marx and Engels 1975, V: 409. The concept of exploitation has been the subject of a highly abstract debate amongst Marxist theoreticians. See Roemer 1982, Lukes 1985 and M. Cohen *et al.* 1980. For bibliographical guidance see Geras 1985 and Carling 1991: chs 5 and 6. If, as Croce and Roemer have emphasized, the notion of exploitation implicitly involves the concept of some alternative, non-exploitative social arrangement, the concept of 'exploitation' as possessing an objective, measurable existence becomes a rather more problematical idea than Marx and Engels themselves realized. See Croce 1981: 127; Roemer 1989; Dalton 1974 (and see the subsequent debate, in *American Anthropologist* vols 77–9); Rigby 1992a: 214–19.

14 Marx and Engels 1975–6, VI: 482–5; 1975: 307; Marx 1976–81, I: 344, 553–4, 699–700; De Ste Croix 1984: 99–100.

15 Marx and Engels 1975–6, V: 35–6, 43, 59–60, 63, 81–2, 89, 231; Marx 1974b: 89; Marx 1971: 20, 220; 1976–81, I: 286, 325; 1970: 28; Marx 1973a: 95, 106–7, 156–7, 161, 171; Marx and Engels 1975: 356–441; McMurtry 1978: ch. 8; Rigby 1987: ch. 3; A. W. Wood 1981: 68–79.

16 Marx and Engels 1975–6, V: 32–3; Marx 1974b: 496; Engels 1968: 20–8.

17 Marx and Engels 1975–6, V: 33, 159; Engels n.d.: 182–3; 1968: 157–60.

18 Marx 1976–81, I: 173, 479; 1973: 83, 304–6.

19 Marx and Engels 1975–6, V: 74–5; Marx 1976–81, III: 929–30.

20 Marx 1969: 384; Marx 1974b: 277, 699.

21 Marx and Engels 1975–6, V: 52–3, 82–3, 89; Marx 1971: 20–1; Marx 1973a: 96, 107, 157; Cohen 1978: 31; Shaw 1978: 65; McMurtry 1978: 65.

where its relations of production lag behind its developing productive forces and become fetters upon them. In order that the productive forces may continue to develop, society's antiquated relations of production are cast aside and new relations of production brought into being, a process accompanied by social revolution, such as the bourgeois revolutions which marked the triumph of the capitalist class over the feudal aristocracy.[22]

If society's productive forces form the foundation for its relations of production, then, in turn, these relations of production form the 'economic base' for society's legal, political and ideological 'superstructure'.[23] The state and forms of social consciousness are 'determined' or 'created' by its relations of production or, more broadly, by its mode of production. The state and ideology are thus said to 'spring from', 'correspond' to, 'reflect', 'echo' or 'express' social relations.[24] More specifically, the state usually serves to defend the power and common interests of the propertied,[25] whilst specific forms of social consciousness are determined by the interests and position of particular social classes.[26]

Marx and Engels thus offered a three-tier model of social structure (the productive forces; the relations of production; and the political and ideological superstructure), and provided a 'functional explanation' of the relations between these three levels. A functional explanation is one which accounts for the existence of some particular arrangement or process in terms of its beneficial effects for something else, as when the long neck of the giraffe is explained by its advantages for the giraffe's survival and reproduction or the rain-dance performed by the Hopi Indians is explained by its tendency to promote social cohesion.[27] For Marx, society's relations of production are functionally explained by the development of the productive forces: 'in order that' society will not be deprived of the benefits of the growth of the productive forces, relations of production corresponding to the new level of development of social productivity have to be brought into existence (Marx 1973a: 197; 1971: 21). Similarly, Marxism offers a functional explanation of

---

22   Marx and Engels 1975–6, V: 33–4, 52, 74, 82; VI: 212, 33; Marx 1973a: 106–7; Marx 1974b: 540; Marx and Engels 1967: 85; Marx 1973b: 192–3; 1971: 21; 1976–81: I, 875; III: 449–52, 1023–4; Engels n.d.: 300; 1968: 6; 1978: 19–24; Bertrand 1979: 71–2, 185–6; Furet 1988: ch. 2; Löwy 1989.

23   Marx 1971: 20–1; Marx and Engels 1975–6, V: 53, 55, 57, 89, 329, 355–6, 373. The metaphor of base and superstructure is also implicit in Marx and Engels's critiques of the Hegelian 'inversion' of human consciousness and social activity. See, for example, Marx and Engels 1975–6, V: 30, 36, 61, 107–9, 126, 159.

24   Marx 1976–81, I: 95; 1974a: 335; 1973a: 156; 1973b: 250; Marx and Engels 1975–6, V: 36, 52, 59, 90, 193, 196, 250, 356, 410, 420, 463; 1975: 400.

25   Marx and Engels 1975–6, V: 52, 90, 92, 329, 355–6, 359, 361; Engels 1968: 168; Marx 1972a: 28, 30, 32, 35, 81, 102, 121–3; Marx 1972a: 28, 30, 32, 35, 81, 102, 121–3; Marx 1973a: 137; Marx and Engels 1967: 85, 100, 137; Marx 1973b: 261; Marx 1972b: 105.

25   Marx 1971: 20–1; Marx 1973a: 95, 100, 109; Marx and Engels 1975–6, V: 36–7, 74, 159, 183, 250, 438, 462; Marx 1974b: 540; Marx and Engels 1975: 401; Engels n.d.: 23; Marx 1972b: 37–8, 40; 1972a: 33, 48.

27   Rigby 1987: ch. 6. For functional explanation in Marx, see Giddens 1979a, esp. 210–14, and G. A. Cohen 1978, esp. chs 9 and 10. For functional explanation in general see Merton 1962: 19–84.

the political and ideological superstructure in terms of its benefits for society's class relations which the state and ideology help to stabilize and to legitimize.[28]

MARXIST HISTORIOGRAPHY

In accordance with the theoretical legacy bequeathed to them by Marx and Engels, Marxist historians have tended to concentrate their attention on a number of key issues: on tracing the growth – or lack of it – of society's productive forces; on characterising particular societies in terms of their dominant relations of production; on exploring the extent and nature of class conflict; on explaining the crises of particular modes of production and the transitions between them; and on establishing the relationship between class relations on the one hand and political power and social ideologies on the other.

Of all of Marx's historical theories, it is his claim for the social primacy of the productive forces which, despite its defence by Marxist theoreticians from Kautsky and Plekhanov, through Lenin, Trotsky, Bukharin and Stalin; to Cohen, Loone, Shaw, Callinicos and Sayer,[29] has proved least fruitful for later Marxist historians.[30] This is not surprising, since even within Marx and Engels's own works there is a contrast between their general, programmatic statements, such as Marx's '1859 Preface', and their actual analyses of specific historical periods. The former tend to emphasize the primacy of society's inexorably developing productive forces in explaining historical change; the latter recognized that, under the impact of particular relations of production, society's productive forces could stagnate or even regress and thus laid a far greater stress on the role of class relations and class struggle in bringing about social change.[31] Indeed, certain Marxists, unwilling to saddle Marx with views which they themselves cannot accept, have even attempted to deny that Marx ever claimed a social primacy for the productive forces in the first place.[32]

Far from emphasizing an inexorable tendency for the productive forces to expand and develop, Marxist historians have taken to heart Marx's warning that it is wrong

---

28 See references to the state and ideology above, and also G. A. Cohen 1978: 216–17, 278–80.

29 Kautsky n.d.: 120–37, 144–5, 161–71; 1988: xxxviii–ix, 227; Plekhanov 1972: 123–33, 147, 159–72, 216–18, 262; 1969: 49, 62, 64; Lenin 1969: 7, 21–3; Trotsky 1970: 9; Trotsky 1971: 169; Bukharin 1969: 120, 134, 140, 249, 257; Stalin 1951: 33–56; Cohen 1978: ch. 6; 1988: chs 1, 5, 6, 8, 9; Loone 1992: 163; Shaw 1978: ch. 2; 1979. See also Callinicos 1987: 91–5; Sayer 1987: 31–5.

30 For the attempt by the archaeologist V. Gordon Childe to apply this approach to historical development, see Childe 1947, esp. chs 2 and 7; 1941: 6; 1954: 23–6; Green 1981, esp. 78–83.

31 Marx 1971: 20–1; Miller 1991; Adamson 1980; Rigby 1987: 28–55, 144–60; Katz 1989: 3–4, 173–83; Lekas 1988: 105–6, 138, 153 and ch. 9, *passim*. For an attempt to reconcile these two approaches, see Miller 1981; Miller 1984.

32 Saville 1974: 7; Bettelheim, 1976: 23; J. S. Cohen 1978: 31; Rosenberg 1981; Levine 1987. T. McCarthy (1978: 24), though not a Marxist himself, also rejects the 'technological determinist' interpretation of Marx.

to apply to *all* modes of production the laws of development specific to capitalist society. Unlike capitalism, where there *is* a powerful, indeed historically unprecedented, tendency for the productive forces to develop, all pre-capitalist modes of production were, as Marx himself argued, inherently conservative.[33] In practice, it is the control which society's relations of production exercise over its productive forces and the class struggles which result from particular relations of production, rather than the autonomously developing productive forces, which enjoy pride of place in Marxist accounts of change and crisis within, and the transitions between, particular modes of production.[34]

Thus, for Walbank, it was precisely the failure of the productive forces to develop which underlay the decline of the Roman Empire. The level of the productive forces in the late Empire was essentially the same as it had been in the Greek world. Yet, from the second century AD, an Empire on the defensive faced the mounting costs of defending its frontiers, paying its bureaucracy, feeding Rome and so on. Once the Empire ceased to expand, the army was no longer a source of profit to the state but a burden which had to be supported by the population: the inevitable result of the *Pax Romana* was legalized extortion. In the short term, as under modern fascism, rulers such as Diocletian (284–305) turned to increased state regulation and control in an attempt to maintain a social system which was in crisis. In the long term, this ever more top-heavy political superstructure, with no adequate economic base of its own, was doomed to failure. The key to this failure of the productive forces to develop was the prevalence of relations of production based upon slavery, which deprived slaves of the incentive to innovate, induced a contempt for all forms of labour amongst the propertied and reduced much of the population to the edge of subsistence, thereby diminishing total demand and limiting the possibilities of economies of scale (Walbank 1946: 22; 1969: 40–80, 109–10; Engels 1968: 145). Thus, despite the obligation of historians in Stalinist regimes to explain the end of the Roman Empire by the universal law of the expansion of the productive forces (Oliva 1962: 171ff.; Gandy 1979: 29), most Marxist analyses of the ancient world have stressed the *failure* of the productive forces to develop and have given a historically specific explanation of such stagnation or regression in terms of society's relations of production (see also Konstan 1975: 149).

Robert Brenner's account of the crisis of feudalism also rejects any inherent tendency of the productive forces to develop and presents feudal social relations as a powerful brake on the growth of social productivity. For Brenner, feudal relations of production between peasants and lords inhibited agricultural innovation and thus

---

33 Engels n.d.: 167–8; Marx 1976–81, I: 101, 617; Wood 1995: 4, 110–27; Callinicos 1995: 101–2.

34 Hilferding 1981: 127–8; Hook 1934: ch. 12; Dobb 1951; Althusser and Balibar 1975: 235; Hindess and Hirst 1975: 9–12; Hilton 1976: 115; 1984: 88; Brenner 1976; Dockès 1982: 182; Joshua 1988, esp. 361–8; Rigby 1987: ch. 8; Larrain 1986: 82–9; E. M. Wood 1989b: 59–60; Katz 1989: 173–83; Jordan 1967: 94; J. S. Cohen 1982; Levine and Wright 1980; Smith 1984; Genovese 1972: 324.

generated the tendency towards over-population, declining living standards and demographic crisis which Malthusian or neo-Ricardian historians see as typical of feudalism. Unlike capitalism, which not only permits but, through competition on the market, positively encourages productive advance, feudalism offered little stimulus to investment or innovation. On the one hand, peasants lacked the resources or incentives to innovate. On the other, landlords, with the extra-economic coercive powers of serfdom and the manor available to them, were able to increase their share of the social product by enlarging their share of total production, through raising rents, tallages and entry-fines, rather than through increases in productive investment. In Marx's terms they resorted to 'absolute' rather than 'relative' surplus labour.[35] Similarly, for Genovese, the 'immanent contradictions' of the slave-economy of the American South meant that it too was destined for crisis, its low-level of labour productivity, lack of capital formation, limited home market and the restrictions which it imposed on the vitality of the mercantile and industrial bourgeoisie all retarded economic development and paved the way for political secession and, eventually, for military defeat (Genovese 1965: 3, 8–9, 43–61, 158).

Marxist historians still see a tendency towards productive advance as characteristic of capitalism, but they have abandoned such expansion as a universal historical law and have emphasized instead the need to identify the historically specific tendencies and laws of pre-capitalist modes of production.[36] As Perry Anderson (1977: 204) put it, far from vigorous forces of production bursting triumphantly through retrograde forces of production, 'forces of production typically stall and recede within the existing relations of production. ... The relations of production generally change *prior* to the forces of production in the epoch of transition and not vice versa'. What remains of Marx's claims is the idea of each mode of production being bound for crisis through its own inherent tendencies and, in particular, of social crisis as emerging from the clash of productive forces and the relations of production.[37] It is such *internal* problems and endogenous causal factors, rather than external forces, which create social crisis and transition. The Roman Empire, for instance, did not collapse because of the barbarian invasions but rather from its own internal contradictions.[38] Paul Sweezy was, therefore, rather unusual amongst Marxists when he sought an explanation of the dissolution of feudalism and the transition to capitalism in

---

35 Brenner 1976; 1982: 16–17, 24–41, 48–50; Brenner 1977: 42–6; 1989: 288–90. See also Hilton 1974: ch. 10 and Wickham 1981: 92–3. For Marx's distinction between 'absolute' and 'relative' surplus value, see Marx 1976–81: I, 643–72. On the crisis of feudalism, see also Kosminsky 1955; Dyer 1989: 6–7, 109–40; Bois 1976. For a critique of Bois, see Brenner 1982: 41–60.

36 Brenner 1977: 31–8, 52; Kula 1976: 54–6, 107–11; Wood 1984: 97–8, 101.

37 Wood 1995: 122–40. It was such fettering which, for Hobsbawm (1965), underlay the 'general crisis' of the seventeenth century, 'the last phase' of the transition from feudalism to capitalism.

38 J. S. Cohen 1978: 30–1; Wright *et al.* 1992: 57–8; Marx and Engels 1975–6, V: 32, 83–5; Dockès 1982: 159.

'causes external to the system', such as the rise of towns and trade.[39] Most Marxists have preferred to find some 'internal' prime mover of transition, such as the inefficiency of the feudal mode and its inherent tendency towards crisis, or the effects of feudal class struggle.[40]

Having abandoned Marx's claims for the primacy of the productive forces, Marxists have naturally paid little attention to Marx's claim that societies should be classified in terms of their characteristic productive forces and have concentrated, as Marx himself suggested, on distinguishing societies in terms of their relations of production (Marx 1976–81: I, 286, 325; II, 120). This is not to say that Marxist historians have necessarily agreed with Marx and Engels or with each other on the class-character of specific societies.[41] The very existence of an 'Asiatic' mode of production, where the state enjoys a monopoly of land so that the peasant producers hand over surplus labour in the form of tax, has proved extremely controversial.[42] In the early 1930s, the concept of the Asiatic mode was removed from the theoretical canon of Soviet Marxism whilst more recently Hindess and Hirst have denounced it as theoretically incoherent.[43] For Godelier, the Asiatic mode represents a form of the transition from primitive communism to class society, whereas Marx himself was happy to apply the term to Mogul India, a society which Godelier characterizes as a form of feudalism. Certainly, since defenders of this concept have seen societies in Africa or pre-Columban America as possessing 'Asiatic' relations of production, and since a state monopoly of land was by no means to be found in all pre-industrial Asian societies, 'Asiatic' may not be the best term for this mode of production (Godelier 1977: 64, 116–17; 1981: 264–7).

The class relations and dominant mode of production of the Ancient world have also proved a controversial issue amongst Marxist historians. Traditionally, despite Marx and Engels's references to the communal property of the ancient city-states, Marxists have placed a great emphasis on slavery as the class basis of the ancient world and, as in Walbank's analysis, as the chief obstacle to productive advance.[44]

---

39   Sweezy 1976; Hilton 1976: 115; Dobb 1963: 39–67, 124–6; Brenner 1977: 38–53; Brenner 1976: 31–2. Paradoxically, those who reject towns and trade as the prime movers of the transition to capitalism also tend to deny their external status with regard to feudalism. See Merrington 1976; Hilton 1985: ch. 13; Hilton 1992, esp chs 1, 2; Hibbert 1978: 91–104. For attempts to reconcile Sweezy's emphasis on the role of towns and trade in the transition to capitalism with those who stress the integral role of towns within feudal society, see Katznelson 1992: 161–3, 175–91 and Torras 1980.

40   Callinicos 1995: 116–25 argues that even inter-societal conflicts, such as military competition, can be related to the pattern of society's internal economic development and class relations.

41   The social character of the Soviet Union and other state-socialist societies proved to be a particularly contentious issue. See Bellis 1979 for a survey of views.

42   Marx 1976–81: III, 927. For Marx and Engels on the Asiatic mode, see Avineri 1964; Krader 1975; Anderson 1979; 473–83; Hobsbawm 1964b: 32–8; Sawer 1977; Lubasz 1984; Rigby 1987: 221–4; Rigby 1992a: 196–7. Marx's views are complicated by the red herring of his definition of the Asiatic mode in terms of the provision of agricultural irrigation by the state. See Marx 1973c: 303.

43   Dunn 1982; Hindess and Hirst 1975: ch. 4.

44   Marx and Engels 1975–6, V: 32–3, 84, 89; Marx 1976–81, III: 449–50; Engels 1968: 145–7; Walbank 1946: 24–7; 1969: 42–7, 104; Anderson 1977: 22.

Wood (1981) has challenged this approach on the grounds that the bulk of the population in the ancient world were peasant producers and independent craftsmen rather than slaves (see also Hilton 1977: 10; Marx 1976–81: III, 942). However, De Ste Croix, in an ambitious attempt to show the utility of Marxism for the study of the ancient world, argues that the key issue in characterizing the class nature of the ancient world is not simply the occupations of the majority of the population but rather that of the dominant form of surplus labour which provided the income of the propertied class.[45] His argument faces two main problems. First, it is by no means clear that slaves *were* the major source of surplus labour in antiquity; the prevalence of chattel slavery, even in ancient Athens, seems to have been rather limited in time and place.[46] Second, as Hindess and Hirst have argued, there is no need for us to identify an economic unity underlying antiquity. The cultural unity of the ancient world was perfectly compatible with a variety of relations of production, ranging from slavery and serfdom to the appropriation of surplus labour by right of citizenship.[47]

Feudal social relations have proved less controversial.[48] Nevertheless, Marxists have been divided over whether or not to accept Marx's claim that under feudalism the peasant producers *possessed* the means of production, and thus of their own subsistence, which meant that surplus labour in the form of rent could only be extracted by extra-economic means, by the landlords' legal, political and coercive powers embodied in serfdom and the manor. In this perspective, serfdom and extra-economic coercion become defining features of the feudal mode.[49] Other Marxists, by contrast, have argued that, since landed property assumes the monopoly of certain people over certain parts of the globe and the exclusion of others, the peasants' payment of rent should be seen as a result of their *separation* from the means of production and that serfdom, rather than constituting a universally defining feature of feudalism, requires a historically specific explanation.[50]

Marx's account of capitalism in terms of the labour theory of value has come in for much criticism, even from those who are sympathetic to his general outlook.[51]

---

45   De Ste Croix 1975: 16 (the whole of the 1975 issue of *Arethusa* is devoted to the question of Marxism and the ancient world); De Ste Croix 1984: 107; 1981, esp. 52, 54, 113, 173, 179. For appreciative reviews, see Browning 1981; Anderson 1983; Brunt 1982. Bois argues that, in the sense that slavery was the dominant relation of exploitation, if not the major form of production, 'Frankish society remained a slave-based society' until the end of the tenth century, although these were slaves settled on holdings: Bois 1992: 19–24, 157–8. Cf. this work, chapter 6.

46   Shaw 1984; Wickham 1988b: 183–93; E. M. Wood 1989a: 1–2, 39–40, 64–8, 78–80.

47   Hindess and Hirst 1975: 85–6; 1977: 40–1. Such cultural unity on the basis of diverse economic bases would, of course, pose problems for the metaphor of base and superstructure.

48   For a brilliant account of the short- and long-term dynamics of feudalism, see Kula 1976.

49   Marx 1976–81, III: 926; Dobb 1976: 165–6; Hilton *et al.* 1976: 165–6; Hilton 1985: 123; Anderson 1977: 147–8; Brenner 1993: 651.

50   Hindess and Hirst 1975: 236–7; Martin 1983: 16–17. For an empirical emphasis on the importance of free peasants in medieval England, see Kosminsky 1956: 92–4 and Hilton 1967; 140–3. Barg 1991 shows that many freeholders were non-peasants who must often have sub-let their land.

51   Böhm-Bawerk 1975; Robinson 1962: 34–46; 1966: 17; Steedman 1975; 1977; Steedman *et al.* 1981.

What Marxists have retained from Marx is his distinction between the 'manufacturing' period, which for Marx prevailed from the mid-sixteenth to the late eighteenth century, and the era of industrial capitalism, which followed. In the former, production remains on a handicraft basis but independent artisans are replaced by a number of wage-labourers concentrated in a single workshop. At first, workers still produce an entire product, although now under the supervision of a single capitalist (the 'formal' subsumption of labour to capital), although there is eventually a tendency for the concentration of production to be accompanied by the intensification of the division of labour by process. This 'real' subsumption of labour to capital reaches its extreme form with mechanization and the reduction of the worker to being an 'appendage of the machine'. In other words, a specific mode of production is defined by its invariant relations of production, but such relations may be compatible with a variety of forms of productive forces (Marx 1976–81: I, 429, 445–8, 453, 456, 480–1, 492, 590). More recent Marxists have emphasized that in the era of pre-industrial capitalism, the 'putting out' of raw materials to rural workers, so-called 'proto-industrialization', was more common than centralized manufacturing.[52] Furthermore, industrialization proper is now seen as a much more recent development. Only with the age of railway construction, from the mid-nineteenth century, did industrialization spread beyond textiles, the area of its initial breakthrough in the period 1780–1800. Even after 1850, mechanization, particularly in low-wage economies, made only slow progress.[53]

For Marxists, all of these modes of production are based on the appropriation of surplus labour by the propertied class, a process which inevitably generates class conflict as the propertied come into conflict with the producers. De Ste Croix (1981: 44) usefully reminds us that class struggle is not merely the product of the actions of slaves, peasants and workers, but that measures taken by the ruling class in its own interests are also forms of class struggle: the employer's lock-out is as much an instance of class conflict as the workers' strike. Nevertheless, in practice, Marxist historiography has tended to concentrate its attention on popular social movements and forms of unrest. For the medieval period, Hilton (1985: 7, 9, 11, 17; 1977: *passim*; 1975: ch. 4; 1967: 154–61; 1990: 183–4; 1992: ch. 6), Dyer (1981; 1992) and Razi (1979; 1983) criticize those historians who have seen feudal social relations in terms of consensus and argue that class conflict was the inevitable consequence of medieval social relations in both town and country. Similarly, Christopher Hill (1974: 181) has argued that class hostility was a 'simple fact' of the social world of sixteenth- and seventeenth-century England. Even in the American South, which lacked the slave rebellions found in Brazil and the Caribbean and where the slaves have often been seen as brutalized or bribed into submission, the overseers and plantation-owners did not have absolute power, since the Southern slaves *did* exhibit an 'impressive solidarity and collective resistance to their masters'. The slave-owners' 'paternalism' did not just mean obedience on the part of the slaves,

---

52 Kriedte *et al.* 1981: 1–11. For critiques, see Hudson 1981; Coleman 1983.
53 Hobsbawm 1962: 45–6; 1969: 68–72, 109–10; Samuel 1977.

but involved a negotiated set of practices which had to take account of the slaves' ability to frustrate their masters' wishes.[54]

Naturally, much Marxist historiography has been concerned with the emergence of the labour movement under modern capitalism. On the one hand, Marxists have been keen to show that the historical role which Marx and Engels ascribed to the proletariat was not sheer wishful thinking. Thus John Foster identified the existence of a revolutionary consciousness amongst the Oldham working class of the 1830s and 1840s, as the community's 'revolutionary vanguard' guided the workers from a trade-union defence of standards of living to a realization that what was needed was a 'total change of the social system'.[55] Likewise, Tim Mason (1981) argued that even after the Nazis had smashed the German labour movement, the actions of the working class, or the threat of such action, could force employers to give way and, even after the outbreak of war, disrupted economic activity. On the other hand, given the absence of revolution in the advanced capitalist countries, Marxists have sought some factor to explain the proletariat's failure to carry out its world-historic role, the emergence of a 'labour aristocracy', which 'implanted accommodationist responses to capitalism and subsequently transmitted them to a broader class movement', being a favourite candidate for this factor.[56]

In general, however, the Marxist historiography of popular struggle has been frankly celebratory, aiming, as E. P. Thompson famously put it, to rescue the 'obsolete' hand-loom weaver, the 'utopian' artisan and the 'deluded' follower of Joanna Southcott 'from the enormous condescension of posterity'.[57] Thus for Rodney Hilton, modern values of equality, liberty and freedom are a contribution to world history not of the bourgeoisie, but have their origins in peasant resistance to feudal subordination.[58] George Rudé has criticized those historians who see the 'crowd', the typical form of popular protest in the eighteenth and early nineteenth centuries, as an irrational mob made up of the socially marginal. The 'Swing' rioters in England or the Parisians who stormed the Bastille turn out to have been mainly

---

54   Kaye 1979: 413–14; Genovese 1974: 3–7, 585–660; 1979: xvi, xxii, 4–42. For the Caribbean, see James 1969; Blackburn 1988: 161–260; Campbell 1988.
55   Foster 1974: 6–7, 74, 99–100. For critique from Left and Right, see Jones 1987: 62–75 and Musson 1976, with a reply by Foster 1976.
56   Engels 1969a: 30–5; Lenin 1966a: 99–102; 1966b: 8–17; Hobsbawm 1964a: ch. 15; Hobsbawm 1970; Foster 1974: 203–4, 228–9, 237–8, 246, 254; Gray 1976: 1–4, 184–90; Crossick 1980: 14–20, 199–211, 251–4; Gray 1981. For critiques of the labour aristocracy thesis, see Moorhouse 1978 and Musson 1976.
57   Thompson 1972: 13. For the roots of this approach in a tradition of radical 'people's history' and of Communist Party populism, see Samuel 1980: 37–9 and Schwarz 1982: 55–6, 71. For an early version of this approach, see Morton 1938: whose achievement is praised in Kaye 1992: ch. 5. Marxist historians have thus tended to neglect popular political forms of which they disapprove, such as patriotism, even where patriotism provided a language of radical political opposition. See Cunningham 1981: 8–9.
58   Hilton 1977: 235; 1984: 97–8; Kaye 1985: 19.

respectable labourers and craftsmen of settled abode and fixed occupation.[59]
Similarly, for Thompson, the food riots of the eighteenth century were not simply
an excuse for crime or an instinctive reaction to hunger but constituted 'a highly
complex form of direct political action, disciplined and with clear objectives' in their
defence of a 'moral economy of the poor' against the emerging political economy of
the market place (Thompson 1971: 76−9, 131−6).

Nevertheless, the Marxist interest in class struggle is not simply the product of a
commitment to a 'history from below' and a political belief in the value of the
experience and struggles of the mass of the population. Rather, Marxists have
argued that class struggle is not only of interest to us today, but that it was also of
decisive importance in determining social change in the past. Thus Brian Manning
argues that whilst most accounts of the English Civil War have been dominated by
the aristocracy and gentry, it was in fact the 'middling sort', who expressed their
class consciousness through Puritanism, whose grievances and actions were 'the
main force behind events'. It was, for instance, fear of social protest and popular
movements which was decisive in splitting England's ruling elite in the period
1640−2, allowing Charles I to overcome his political isolation and to create a
Royalist party, and thus making civil war a practical possibility.[60] More broadly,
Marxist historians such as Hilton (1969: 32−43, 57), Brenner (1976: 47−75)
and Martin (1983: 56−7; see also Dyer 1981: 194; Rigby 1995a: 124−44) use the
class perspective to criticize the dominant historical orthodoxy which explains pre-
industrial social change in terms of the rise and fall of population. Instead, they
argue that it was the varying outcomes of the struggles between peasants and lords
that determined which path of social and economic development was taken in
particular regions of Europe in the late medieval and early modern periods: serfdom
in eastern Europe, an independent peasantry and absolutism in France, agrarian
capitalism in England (Lis and Soly 1982: 97−104).

A classic instance of Marxist claims for the epochal significance of class struggle is
Marx and Engels's interpretation of events such as the English Civil War and the
French Revolution as 'bourgeois revolutions', as movements through which, with
their destruction of feudal property relations, the bourgeoisie created a new social
order (see refs. on p. 893). Marxist historians have attempted to defend Marx and
Engels's views on such movements. Christopher Hill, for instance, argued that the
English Civil War was not just a constitutional conflict or a religious squabble but
was

> a class war, in which the despotism of Charles I was defended by the reactionary forces of
> the established church and feudal landlords. Parliament defeated the king because it could

---

59 Rudé 1959: 2−5, 186−9, 232; 1965: 179−84; 1964a: 5−7, 258−60; 1974b: 28−30; Hobsbawm and
Rudé 1973: 209−11; Kaye 1992: 36−8. For a sympathetic critique of Rudé, see Holton 1978.
60 Wood 1995: 52−3, 108−11; Manning 1976; Manning 1973: 76, 80, ibid. 82, 122−3; Manning
1970. See also Montgomery 1987: 1, 7 for an emphasis on the role of class conflict in the formation of
modern America.

appeal to the enthusiastic support of the trading and industrial classes in town and countryside, to the progressive gentry, and to wider masses of the population whenever they were able by free discussion to understand what the struggle was really about.

In a society that was still essentially feudal, revolution was essential in order to pave the way for the full development of capitalism.[61] Historians such as Lefebvre, Soboul, Rudé and Hobsbawm have offered a similar interpretation of the French Revolution as 'a conflict of social classes', as the product of the mismatch between the traditional social, political and legal pre-eminence of the aristocracy and clergy and the new reality of the economic power of the bourgeoisie. It was the latter, a 'rising new social force' based on the expansion of industry, commerce and finance, whose interests were met by the revolution, even if, as Engels argued, it was the radicalism of the popular movements of artisans and peasants which drove the revolution forward to the complete destruction of feudalism.[62] By contrast, it was the *weakness* of the Russian bourgeoisie, its reliance on the tsarist state and the importance of foreign capital in economic development, combined with a highly concentrated industrial working class, which meant that the Russian bourgeoisie would not lead its own revolution and that this revolution would not restrict itself to bourgeois aims but would become permanent and proceed immediately towards socialist goals.[63]

The Marxist fascination with the great historical revolutions has inevitably been accompanied by an interest in the social 'superstructure' of politics, the state and ideology. Indeed, despite the traditional Marxist claims for the determining role of society's mode of production, many of the most eminent Marxist historians, such as Christopher Hill, are better known for their accounts of religious and political change than for their original contributions to economic history.[64] Certainly, given this interest in society's 'superstructure', it would be wrong to portray Marxist historiography as simply 'history from below'. Hill, after all, has not only produced sympathetic analyses of the Diggers and the other radical sects of the English Civil War, but also a biography of Oliver Cromwell and a study of the economic problems of the Anglican Church and of how its attempts to solve such problems contributed

61   Hill 1940: 9, 25, 29–30; 1969: 132–4; 1958: 154–5; 1974b: 11–16; 1986: 111. See also Dobb 1963: 161–76; 1976: 62–4; Manning 1965: 252–4. Working with a similar general definition of bourgeois revolution, one modelled on the French experience, Perry Anderson found the English Civil War to be the 'least pure bourgeois revolution of any major European country' (Anderson 1992: 6,17). See, however, Thompson 1978: 47.

62   Lefebvre 1969: 1–3; 1962: xvii–xviii, 115–16; 1967: 360; Soboul 1974a: 3–9, 21, 110, 553–62; 1977: 1; 1981: 25, 29, 71, 73; 1978: 50–3, 63–9; McLennan 1981: ch. 9; Rudé 1964b: 71–2; 1974a: 314–15; 1974b: 63–81; 1989: 1–10; Hobsbawm 1962: 77–86; Hobsbawm 1990: x–xi, 6–15. Furet 1981: 81–131 offers a critique of Marxist interpretations of the French Revolution. For a further criticism of the Marxist position and general bibliographical guidance, see Blanning 1987.

63   Trotsky 1962; 1973; 1967: I, ch. 1; Deutscher 1954: 148–63; Liebman 1970: 29–33.

64   Johnson 1978: 80–1 (see, however, Thompson 1978: 396 n. 168; McClelland 1979: 104; Kaye 1984: 21–2). Marxist historiography shares this concentration on the social superstructure with Western Marxism in general. See Anderson 1976: 75.

to the alignment of the two sides in the Civil War (Hill 1972a; 1975; 1973; 1956: xi, 340–6).

As we have seen, Marx and Engels described the state and social consciousness as a superstructure which corresponds to society's economic base. In general they saw the state as the instrument of the propertied, the means by which the economically dominant class became the politically dominant class (see refs. on p. 893). Marx and Engels did, however, also argue that there were particular periods when the state could attain a certain degree of independence from the propertied, ruling class. This was particularly the case in those periods where two rival classes cancelled each other out, as in the absolutist states of early modern Europe whose rulers used the emergent bourgeoisie as a counterweight against the feudal nobility. Nevertheless, even though the state enjoys an abnormal social autonomy during such periods, such autonomy is itself socially determined.[65]

That the state is 'a class state, the state of the "ruling class"' is a commonplace of Marxist social theory and historiography (Miliband 1979: 74; Therborn 1980: 132). Thus, whilst constitutional and legal historians have placed great emphasis on the development of public authority in medieval England compared with the continued importance of private jurisdictions on the Continent, Hilton argues that it would be wrong to see this as a sign of the state's social neutrality. In England, a politically sophisticated baronage did not seek local independence from the Crown but rather sought to control the Crown through the royal council and Parliament whilst, at a local level, royal officials and justices were drawn from the gentry and nobility and many local courts were seigneurially controlled. The enforcement of law and order 'has never been a purely neutral act of government, especially when the power to do so is held exclusively in the hands of one social class'. What was important 'was not so much what the law was, as who administered it, and in whose interests' (Hilton 1967: 218–19, 240–1; 1977: 151). For Hill, the Tudor and early Stuart state was 'the main support of the propertied class' confronted with the threat of popular disorder (Hill 1974a: 186–7; 1976: 118–21). In a similar vein, Anderson even questioned Marx and Engels's claims for the autonomy of the absolutist states of early modern western Europe. Such states were not the product of the class-balance between aristocracy and bourgeoisie, but rather provided a 'political carapace' for a nobility which, with the decline of serfdom, had lost much of its local influence and so was increasingly reliant on the centralized extraction of surplus from the peasantry in the form of taxation.[66]

---

65   Marx and Engels 1975–6, V: 90, 92, 195, 200, 361; 1970: 102; Marx 1973b: 216; Marx and Engels 1967: 102; 1975: 166; Engels 1969b: 21–3, 33; Marx 1970a: 65–6, 72, 137, 162, 165, 167; 1972b: 39, 88–91, 103–5, 112–13; Engels 1968: 168–9; Elster 1985: ch. 7; Draper 1977: 327–9, 417–24.
66   Anderson 1979: 1. See also Kiernan 1965: 117, 150. For other Marxist interpretations of absolutism, see Littlejohn 1972; Lublinskaya 1972; Lublinskaya 1968 (criticized by Parker 1971); Porshnev 1963: 43, 563 (extracts from Porshnev's work are translated in Coveney 1977: 78–135); Parker 1990; Miliband 1983: 56–62; Brenner 1976: 68–72; Brenner 1982: 77–83.

Despite this emphasis on the state as a class state, E. P. Thompson has warned against the temptation to see politics and the law in simple instrumental terms as a conspiracy of the rich. To be sure, the law functioned as the central legitimizing ideology in eighteenth-century England and, more practically, reinforced contemporary class relations to the advantage of the ruling class, as shown by Thompson's own study of the Black Act of 1723, which, in response to forest disturbances in southern England, created more than fifty new capital offences. But, ironically, in order to serve such functions, the law did have 'to display an independence from gross manipulation'. In doing so, it helped to encourage the idea of the 'free-born Englishman' who enjoyed an equality before the law and a protection from absolutism, a conception which became a central part of the rhetoric of plebeian radicalism (Thompson 1975: 158–69; see also Hay 1975).

Just as Marxists have approached the state and law in class terms, so they have interpreted particular forms of social consciousness, from religious ideologies to political programmes and economic theories, in terms of the needs, interests and experiences of particular social groups. As Marx and Engels put it, there is no such thing as the history of ideas but only the history of the socially specific individuals who produce such ideas.[67] Marxists have therefore criticized those historians who see a religious ideology such as Puritanism as 'an obstinately religious phenomenon' adopted according to personal 'taste and choice' (see Collinson 1982: 241; 1983: 5–6). Instead, they have sought to identify the social basis and class-specific appeal of particular theologies. Protestantism, particularly in its Calvinist form, is seen as the expression of the interests of the bourgeoisie which 'arose when it did because it was the religion most suited to stimulating capitalist enterprise and enforcing labour discipline'.[68] Hill has argued that the social explanation of religious beliefs does not mean that such beliefs are simply a cynical cloak for vested interests. Protestantism was, after all, a system of thought for which men were willing to kill and be killed. Nevertheless,

> to understand Puritanism we must understand the needs, hopes, fears and aspirations of the godly artisans, yeomen, gentlemen and ministers and their wives, who gave their support to its doctrines. ... It seemed to point the way to heaven because it helped them to live on earth.[69]

Despite Marx's use of the metaphor of ideas as 'reflections' of social being, the Marxist theory of ideology does not mean that ideas are simply a passive product of

---

67 Marx and Engels 1975–6, V: 36–7, 154, 183, 250; Marx 1972b: 37.

68 Engels 1965: 41–2; 19–20; Marx 1976–81, I: 387, 882; 1974b: 232; G. A. Cohen 1978: 279.

69 Hill 1940: 44–5; 1958: 21; 1974a: 82, 89; 1969: 131, 142, 145, 494–5. Fromm, in contrast to Hill, argues that whilst Protestantism was a response to the social anxieties produced by the rise of capitalism, it was largely a conservative response and that, as Weber claimed, Protestantism's stimulus to capitalism was an unintended consequence of its doctrines. See Fromm 1975: 53, 62, 68, 74, 78, 86–8; Weber 1976: 90.

social conditions.[70] On the contrary, Hill argues that Puritanism was an active historical force, facilitating the transition from a society where poverty was no longer seen as a holy state but as a sign of wickedness and where the sin of avarice had become the virtue of thrift. Similarly, the upheaval of the English Revolution 'could not take place' without the ideals and new systems of thought needed if men were to risk their lives for the creation of a new order. For Hill, not only the individualistic faith of Calvinism but also the science of Sir Francis Bacon, the history of Sir Walter Ralegh and interpretation of law offered by Sir Edward Coke helped to pave the way for revolution (Hill 1958: 215; 1972b: 1–3).

The Marxist approach to ideology does not require that the intellectual 'representatives' of particular classes should themselves be members of that class (Hauser 1971: 137–8), although Marxists have, on occasion, taken this view of particular ideological outlooks (Howkins 1977: 158–9). It is rather that particular forms of ideology will appeal to specific groups and that such groups will interpret intellectual, religious or cultural traditions in their own, socially specific ways. Thus the Puritan insistence on inner faith proved useful to a range of social groups in their resistance to a variety of forms of traditional authority, to the rebellious gentry of Scotland or Hungary as well as to the English middle class; it could be used to justify social order and discipline as well as forming the basis of a radical individualism. Similarly, concepts such as God, Antichrist and the 'Norman Yoke' meant very different things to the different social groups of early modern England.[71]

In this perspective, even works of art can be seen as the expressions of particular forms of social being. Lucien Goldmann, for instance, offered a sociology of literature in which literary texts are seen as the embodiments of particular 'world visions' which, in turn, are the expressions of the interests and position of specific social groups, of which economic classes are the most important. Thus the philosophy of Pascal and the theatre of Racine express the tragic view of life of a particular group at a particular time: the *Noblesse de Robe* of the seventeenth century.[72] For Hilton, the ballads celebrating the deeds of Robin Hood, the ultimate 'social bandit' who engaged in a guerrilla struggle for justice on behalf of the poor and oppressed, expressed the social aspirations of the English peasantry in the century and a half of endemic agrarian discontent which preceded the revolt of 1381.[73] Even the poems of Andrew Marvell, which at first sight seem to bear little relation to the age in which Marvell lived, can be better appreciated when seen in

---

70 Kaye 1988: 37. The inheritance of the problematical metaphor of reflection combined with an awareness of the positive historical role of ideas has even led Marxists to posit the existence of 'active reflections'. See Dobb 1951: 4; John 1953: 4.

71 Marx 1972b: 40–1; Hill 1958: 92–3; 1974a: 99; 1971: 101; 1984: 19–20.

72 Laurenson and Swingwood 1972: 63–77; Forgacs 1986: 183–7; Goldmann 1972; Evans 1981: ch. 3.

73 Hilton 1981: 221, 232–5; 1977: 211; 1980; Coss 1985. For a critique of Hilton, which locates the ballads in an alternative social context, see Holt 1981 and 1989, esp. ch. 6. For Hilton's reply, see his review of Holt's *Robin Hood* in the *Times Literary Supplement*, 11 June 1982. For the concept of the 'social bandit', see Hobsbawm 1971: ch. 2 and 1982, esp. chs 1 and 3.

the political context of his time, not to mention the works of an active participant in the English Revolution such as John Milton (Hill 1958: 324–5; 1977: 4).

At times, Marx's own comments seem to imply that ideologies are simply cynical deceptions designed to defend particular vested interests (Marx 1972b: 37–8). Yet elsewhere, Marx himself denied that this was the case. As he said of the French petit-bourgeoisie of the mid-nineteenth century, classes tend to believe that the social conditions which are favourable to themselves are those which are most suitable for society as a whole.[74] Nevertheless, Marx and Engels did believe that the propertied classes would propagate ideologies which help to justify and maintain their power and privileges: feudal social relations were presented as ordained by divine will, or capitalism as the expression of human nature or of 'inviolable natural laws'.[75] Marx and Engels even went so far as to claim that 'the ruling ideas of each age have ever been the idea of the ruling class' (Marx and Engels 1975–6, V: 59), although this claim can be interpreted in two different ways. First, in its weaker form, it simply means that the ideas of the ruling class constitute the *official* ideas of the age, rather than that such ideas were widely adopted within society. After all, Marx and Engels were highly critical of those thinkers who believed that 'the rule of a certain class is only the rule of certain ideas' (Marx and Engels 1975–6, V: 52, 60–1, 292; 1982: 78). Thus, although the social doctrine of the essential harmony and mutual interdependence of the social orders was an intellectual commonplace throughout the Middle Ages, Hilton argues that the peasants' willingness to resist feudal exploitation was generally unaffected by priestly exhortation and justifications of 'the existing order in terms of celestially sanctioned harmony'. Indeed, as Marx and Engels themselves argued, it was precisely in those periods when the ruling class was threatened, as in the later medieval period, that the ideology of the ruling class was most forcefully expressed.[76]

Second, in its less-qualified interpretation, Marx and Engels's claim that the ruling ideas of the age are the ideas of the ruling class can be used as an explanation of the failure of the producing classes to rise up against their exploiters. In this perspective, it is the existence of a hegemonic, dominant ideology which forestalls the social conflict which would otherwise result. Ideology thus functions to conceal social contradictions in the interests of the dominant class.[77] As Althusser (1971: 139) put it, no ruling class can hold power over a long period purely by means of the Repressive State Apparatus 'without at the same time exercising its hegemony over and in the State Ideological Apparatuses'. His views had been anticipated, as Hill points out, by Francis Bacon, for whom there would be perpetual social disaffection

---

74   Marx and Engels 1975–6, V: 290, 410–14; Marx 1972b: 40. Hill argues that the view of ideas as either irrelevant to history or forms of hypocrisy and rationalization owes more to the historians of the Namier school than to the works of Marx. See Hill 1972: 3 and Brenner 1993: 645.

75   Engels n.d.: 353; Marx and Engels 1970: 100–2; 1975–6, V: 154; Engels 1965; 41–2; Marx 1974b: 85–7; 1973a: 105–6.

76   Marx and Engels 1975, V: 413–14; Hilton 1985: 251–2; 1977: 53–5; 1984: 92.

77   Abercrombie *et al.* 1980: ch. 1; Larrain 1979: 60–3, 210.

'except you keep men in by preaching as well as the law doth by punishing'.[78] In the Middle Ages, it was the Church which functioned as the main ideological state apparatus, its theology sanctifying and justifying feudal society, and subordinating the individual to the social system (Althusser 1971: 143–4; Gurevich 1985: 10, 299–301). Likewise, in Tudor and early Stuart England,

> it was the duty of the church to soften the bitterness of class hatred, to keep the lower orders peaceful and subordinate, to stress the religious considerations which united a hierarchical society against the economic facts which so visibly divided it, to console the desperate
>
> (Hill 1974: 189)

even if it was not always successful in this task. When E. P. Thompson (1972: 663) maintained that the growing radicalism of the English population meant that by 1816 'the English people were held down by force', Perry Anderson (1980: 37–8) replied that military repression, in itself, was insufficient to maintain the English *ancien régime*. The emergence of a counter-revolutionary nationalism, fostered by twenty years of war against the French Revolution and its successor regimes, which replaced religion as the dominant form of ideological discourse, was also crucial for social stability.

THE MARXIST TRADITION: AN ASSESSMENT

The influence of Marxism has been crucial in reminding historians, often caught up in the minutiae of local studies and the difficulties of their sources, of the need to study long-term social change, to examine social crisis and conflict not just functional reproduction, to be aware of the historical impact of class struggle, and to see the political institutions and forms of social consciousness in their broader social context. Nevertheless, despite its many positive contributions to the development of modern historiography, Marxism can be criticized on a number of fronts. One line of critique of Marxist historiography is to launch an empirical attack on its specific historical claims. For example, the Marxist interpretation of the English Civil War and the French Revolution as bourgeois revolutions has come in for much criticism. It is by no means clear that, in Charles I's England, a feudal aristocracy, hostile to capitalism, was confronted by a rising bourgeoisie. On the contrary, Marxist historians themselves, such as Brenner and Neale, have emphasized that the internal transformation of the English landed classes was the key to the transition to agrarian capitalism.[79] In France, 'revisionist' historians have questioned whether the aristocracy and bourgeoisie of the eighteenth century constituted economic classes with clearly opposed class interests and have denied that the Revolution led to a decisive breakthrough in French economic development in either the short or the long term.[80] As a result, many Marxists have abandoned or

---

78   Hill 1969: 111–12; Bergesen 1993; see also Genovese 1974: 597, 658.
79   Neale 1985: 85; Brenner 1993: 640–3, 648–9. For a general survey, see Hughes 1991: 3.
80   For a survey of the debate see Blanning 1987 and Lewis 1993.

modified the traditional Marxist account of the bourgeois revolutions. Hill now interprets the Civil War as a bourgeois revolution not in the sense that it was led by the capitalists against feudal aristocrats but because 'its *outcome* was the establishment of conditions far more favourable to the development of capitalism than those which had prevailed before 1640'.[81] Brenner doubts even this claim, arguing that, rather than constituting the decisive turning-point in the transition to capitalism, the Revolution was the political reflection of the fact that society was *already* capitalist (Brenner 1978; 1989: 296–304). Marxists such as Régine Robin and Althusser have raised similar doubts about the existence of an inherent class conflict between nobility and bourgeoisie in eighteenth-century France. The difficulty of identifying a capitalist bourgeoisie in pre-revolutionary France has even led Comninel to admit that the validity of the traditional Marxist interpretation of the French Revolution has been 'exploded'.[82] More generally, Wood (1991: 160) argues that the concept of bourgeois revolution 'conceals as much as it reveals. ... The formula tells us little about the causes of these revolutions or about the social forces that brought them about'. Increasingly the Marxist emphasis is on the *longue durée* of the transition to capitalism rather than the supposed breakthrough of the bourgeois revolution.[83]

Yet such empirical critiques are unlikely to shake the foundations of Marxist historiography. After all, Marxist historians have often disagreed amongst themselves about particular empirical issues. Opponents of historical materialism have thus been obliged to come up with a broader methodological critique of Marx's social theory. Four main theoretical issues have emerged in recent years: the legitimacy of functional explanation; the limited nature of the Marxist conception of social being; the 'interpenetration' of base and superstructure; and the problem of pluralism, i.e. of the 'interaction' of the so-called base and superstructure, each of which will be discussed in turn below.

First, as we have seen, the main claims of Marx's social theory, that the level of the productive forces explains the nature of society's relations of production, and that the nature of society's relations of production determines the nature of its

---

81 Hill 1980: 110–111; Kaye 1984: 116. As Hobsbawm said of the French Revolution, it was a bourgeois revolution, 'even though nobody intended it to be' (Hobsbawm 1990: 8; see also Morton 1978: 4). Callinicos thus defines bourgeois revolutions as ones which 'promote capitalism' rather than ones which are consciously made by capitalists. The French Revolution *was*, he believes, 'carried through under bourgeois leadership' but it is, in general, 'exceptional for the capitalist class to play the leading role in bourgeois revolutions' (Callinicos 1989: 122–5). Mooers also attempts to rehabilitate the notion of the French Revolution as a bourgeois revolution in terms of its beneficial consequences for capitalism even though his own analysis shows that the Revolution was a very mixed blessing in terms of the development of agrarian capitalism (Mooers 1981: 2–3, 61, 64–72, 176).

82 Grenon and Robin 1976, cited in Blanning 1987: 16; Althusser 1972: 99–106; Comninel 1987: 3, 19–20, 180, 195, 203, 205; Price 1993: 82. The orthodox view is defended by McGarr 1989. If even France is no longer seen as having experienced a classic bourgeois revolution, it follows that the specific course of modern German history can no longer be explained in terms of its failure to undergo such a revolution. See Blackbourn and Eley 1984: 7–21, 39–43, 51–9, 167–76, 287–8.

83 Corrigan and Sayer 1985: 85–6; Brenner 1993: 648–9; Blanning 1987: 16.

political and ideological superstructure, are both instances of 'functional explana-tion'.[84] For certain writers, functional explanations, whilst the norm in the theory of biological evolution, are invalid in the social sciences, a claim which would automatically invalidate historical materialism.[85] Nevertheless, as is shown by the example of the Chicago School's analysis of the market in terms very similar to those used by biologists to explain natural evolution, functional explanations are not, *per se*, invalid in the social sciences (Elster 1979: 31–2; G. A. Cohen 1978: 287–8). Their invocation in any particular instance can thus only be assessed empirically, and historical materialism is not inherently invalidated by their use.[86]

Second, even if we accept that social being can be defined independently of social consciousness, so that the former can be said to determine the latter, Marxism has been criticized for its equation of social being with class-position. Sociologists in the Weberian tradition have thus argued that economic class is simply one possible ground of 'social exclusion' and that other forms of exclusion, such as race, gender, status and order, which are by no means reducible to class inequalities, can be just as important. There are thus a number of forms and grounds of social power (economic, political and ideological), none of which can be assumed to have an automatic, universal or necessary social primacy.[87] It is not that Marxists have neglected such non-class inequalities. On the contrary, Marx and Engels themselves distinguished the estates and orders of pre-capitalist societies from the economic classes of capitalism (Marx and Engels 1975, V: 69, 73, 89–90; Godelier 1988: 245–52), whilst Marxist social theorists have produced a number of studies of non-class inequalities, particularly those of gender.[88] The problem is rather that, as feminist historians and sociologists have argued, Marxists have tended to offer a

---

84   G. A. Cohen 1978: chs 9, 10; 1980: 129–30; 1982a: 30; 1982b: 486; van Parijs 1993: 7, 29.

85   Giddens 1981: 17, 215; 1979a: 7, 110–17, 211–14; 1979b: 17, 25; Elster 1979: ch. 1; Halfpenny 1983. Halfpenny's article is also included in Wetherly 1992, along with a number of other articles on functional explanation and Marxism. For functional explanation and the biological sciences, see Frankfort and Poole 1966–7. A particular problem is that whereas the theory of evolution specifies the 'feedback mechanism' (random genetic variation and the survival of the fittest) which enables us to explain the evolutionary development of a particular species in terms of its functional effects, social scientists (Marxist or otherwise) have no equivalent, universally valid feedback mechanism. As a result, it is easier to explain why functional social arrangements persist than why they appear in the first place. See Elster 1980: 126–7; 1983b: 103–7; 1979: 34; G. A. Cohen 1980: 131; 1978: 269–70; 1983: 119, 24; Sztompka 1964: 140, 150, 151; Isajiw 1968: 127. For attempts to provide Marxism and the social sciences with a feedback mechanism, see G. A. Cohen 1978: 152; Stinchcombe 1975: 29; van Parijs 1982: 503–4; Torrance 1985: 388–9; Bertram 1990.

86   Rigby 1987: 90; 1992a: 184; Tännsjö 1990.

87   Weber 1978: I, 577, II, 926; Neuwirth 1969; Murphy 1988; Collins 1975; Parkin (ed.) 1974: 1–18; 1979a; 1979b; 1982: 100–2; Runciman 1969; 1974: 55–1; 1989: 2–24; Mann 1986; Giddens 1981. For Marxist responses, see Mackenzie 1980: 582–4; Barbalet 1982; Wright 1983; Wickham 1988a (on Mann); 1991 (on Runciman).

88   See, for instance, Middleton 1979; 1981; 1985; Hilton 1985: chs 15 and 16; 1975: ch. 6; Hobsbawm 1989: ch. 8. Many Marxist accounts of gender inequalities form an implicit or explicit debate with Engels 1968: For an assessment of Engels's approach, see the articles in Sayers *et al.* 1987; Coontz and Henderson 1986; Rigby 1992a: 198–204; Vogel 1983: ch. 6; Bloch 1983: 66, 75–6; Godelier 1988: 103.

functional explanation of patriarchal social relations in terms of their benefits for the reproduction of particular modes of production.[89] Patriarchy is thus viewed as secondary and derivative from society's mode of production rather than being presented as an autonomous form of social inequality in its own right,[90] or even, as some would prefer to see it, as in-built into society's mode of production as one of its defining features.[91]

Third, much criticism of historical materialism has centred on the issue of the interpenetration of base and superstructure, i.e on whether social being can be defined separately from (and thus presented as the basis of) social consciousness, politics and legal relations.[92] As we have seen, Marx's model of social structure assumes that the state, law and forms of social consciousness 'correspond' to the form taken by its relations of production. Critics such as Acton, Plamenatz, Leff and Lukes have countered such claims with the argument that so-called 'superstructural' phenomena such as politics and ideas do not merely reflect society's economic base or just interact with it; they are actually a constitutive part of society's economic 'base'. But if the distinction between base and superstructure is untenable, it is illegitimate to derive the latter from the former: one cannot say that x produces y if y is actually a part of x in the first place.[93] Furthermore, if it is impossible to locate some pure economic level of society, separate from politics, law and forms of social consciousness, it follows that the concept of the economic base is simply an analytical abstraction. To abstract a concept from reality, and then to invert this process and present this abstraction as the basis of reality, would seem to be a classic instance of the procedure which Marx and Engels themselves rightly condemned as 'idealist' when resorted to by the Hegelians. Ironically, what presents itself as the most materialist analysis of society turns out to be, with true dialectical irony, its exact opposite: pure idealism.[94]

In reply, certain Marxists have attempted to offer a defence of the

---

89   Middleton 1981: 151–2; Adamson *et al.* 1976; Gimenez 1987: 48; Barrett 1984: 132–3; Cockburn 1986: 81–2.

90   De Beauvoir 1974: 87; Firestone 1979: 15; Millett 1985: 38; Delphy 1984: 38–9, 74–5; McDonough and Harrison 1978: 31–2; Davin 1981: 180.

91   Hartmann 1981: 10–11, 17–19, 29: Middleton 1974; 1983: 13–14; Eisenstein 1979: 5, 28; Seccombe 1983: 19; Himmelweit 1991: 217–19; Hearn 1991: 239; Fox-Genovese 1982: 15.

92   Ironically, Engels himself advocated the notion of dialectical interpenetration in his philosophical works whilst adopting the more limited notion of the *interaction* of base and superstructure in his defence of historical materialism. See Engels n.d.: 28–9; 1964: 17, 63, 214–24, 264; Marx and Engels 1975: 394–5, 399, 401, 442; Jakubowski 1976: 38; Rigby 1992a: 112–13; 126–7, 132–4.

93   Acton 1955: 164–8, 177, 258; Plamenatz 1963: 283–9, 345; Leff 1969: 144–51; Wokler 1983: 231–7; Lukes 1983: 103–19. Graham usefully distinguishes two separate readings of the Acton–Plamenatz position. The first is that base and superstructure are conceptually inseparable; the second is that even if the two can be distinguished, they coexist and interact, which undermines the claim for priority of the so-called base (see the discussion of pluralism, pp. 911–15 below): Graham 1992: 52–4.

94   Marx and Engels 1975: 434; Marx and Engels 1975–6, IV: 7, 59–60, 82, 159, 192; V: 29, 36–7, 44–5, 55, 57, 59–62, 128–34, 144–5, 159–60, 168, 176, 236, 269, 274–5, 282, 287, 419, 434; Rigby 1992a: 174–5.

'traditionalist' Marxist distinction between the economic base and the political and ideological superstructure.[95] However, such traditionalist defences of the distinction between base and superstructure generally seem less than convincing, even to those within the Marxist tradition. After all, Marx and later Marxists have explicitly accepted the existence of such interpenetration,[96] as when they have presented the relations of production of the Asiatic mode of production and of feudal and ancient society as constituted by 'extra-economic' coercion[97] and have seen the state itself as a key extractor of surplus labour in a number of pre-capitalist societies.[98] Indeed, some Marxists have gone so far as to argue that far from the conception of society as an 'organic totality', in which the social parts are interdependent and mutually dependent, constituting a *challenge* to Marxism, it is historical materialism itself which (at least on its strongest reading) offers precisely this model of social structure.[99] The notion of society as an organic totality is, in certain respects, an attractive one (provided that it does not dissolve all analytical distinctions and causal claims). The problem with such holism, at least from a Marxist perspective, is simply that it is rather difficult to see what is specifically Marxist about it.[100]

Perhaps a more useful response to the problem of interpenetration of base and superstructure is Godelier's reformulation of Marx's metaphor of base and superstructure into a claim for the primacy of society's relations of production, conceived in their broadest sense, over those aspects of politics, the law and ideology which are not constitutive elements of class relations. Society's base thus includes those aspects of law and politics, such as the medieval landlords' manorial powers, which are defining elements of contemporary class relations. It is such broadly defined relations of production which constitute the base for those residual elements of the law, politics and ideology which make up the social superstructure. Base and superstructure are no longer seen as separate institutions but are instead defined by their different *functions* (Godelier 1978; 1988: chs 3–6; Wood 1981: 79).

Fourth, and finally, if Godelier's approach provides a response to those critics who raised the problem of the interpenetration of base and superstructure,

---

95   G. A. Cohen 1974: 88; 1970: 121–4; 1978: 223–4; 1988: chs 2 and 3; Lowe 1985.

96   Kautsky 1988: 228–30; Hilferding 1981: 131; Genovese 1972: 21, 32–3, 323–4.

97   Marx 1976–81; III, 926–7; Lekas 1988: 3, 81, 153, ch. 8; Hilton 1985: 123; 1984: 85–6; Gottlieb 1984: 4, 36; Bak 1980: 13–14; Amin 1976: 13–21; Hindess and Hirst 1975: 82–91; Given 1984: 11; Wickham 1988c: 76.

98   Wickham 1978: 72; 1984: 9, 20, 27–8; Brenner 1976: 68–9; Anderson 1979: ch. 1; De Ste Croix 1984: 105–6; Given 1984: 44.

99   For those who prefer the metaphor of society as a totality or an organic totality, as opposed to base and superstructure, see Rader 1979: ch. 2; Jay 1984; Gramsci 1977: 377; Jakubowski 1976: 102–3; Lukács 1974: 27; Korsch 1938: 241; Korsch 1938: 241; Althusser and Balibar 1975: 98; Hall 1977; 1972: 8–10; Kaye 1979: 405–19; 1984: 56–7, 107, 116–17, 159, 220; Genovese 1972: 322–3; Hill 1958: 39; J. S. Cohen 1978: 31; Sayer 1987: 145; Ryan 1986: 83–7, 98–100; Corrigan and Sayer 1985: 2; Ollman 1972: 15; Williams 1979: 118; Clarke 1979.

100   Williams 1973: 7; Rigby 1990: 829; Hellman 1979: 148–50, 161; Kiernan 1987: 107; McLennan 1979: 162).

historical materialism faces even greater difficulties when confronted with the far more straightforward issue of the *interaction* of base and superstructure. As early as *The German Ideology*, Marx and Engels had referred to the 'reciprocal action' of the productive forces, class relations, politics and ideology but, since they described society's superstructure as the 'expression' or 'reflection' of its economic base, it was easy for their critics to accuse them of presenting the economic factor as the only determining one and of ignoring the active historical role played by politics and ideas. From the time of Engels's famous letters on historical materialism of the 1890s, Marxists have thus been obliged to reject the charge of economic reductionism and to acknowledge the 'dialectical interaction' which takes place between base and superstructure (whether defined in the traditional sense or that of Godelier).[101]

The problem is how to acknowledge an awareness of the active role of politics and ideas without abandoning the primacy of society's mode of production which is, after all, the claim which gives Marxism its distinctiveness as a theory of the social world and of history. This dilemma can be seen in the structuralist version of historical materialism offered by Louis Althusser. Ironically, whilst Althusser's theory been attacked by E. P. Thompson for its economic reductionism, it would be truer to say that Althusser's theory actually founders (at least as a form of Marxism) on its recognition of the complex interaction involved in historical explanation. Far from reducing society to its mode of production, Althusser redefined the mode of production to include economic, political and ideological levels (or practices), each of which is 'relatively autonomous' and possesses its own chronology of development. Instead of positing a one-way determination of politics and ideology by economics, Althusser argues that specific relations of production may presuppose elements of the legal, political and ideological 'superstructure' as a condition of their existence.[102] Many historians and social theorists would be inclined to accept such a view. It is simply that, once more, it is rather difficult to see what is distinctively Marxist about it. In other words, the problem of reductionism cannot be solved simply by invoking the concept of the 'relative autonomy' of the state and ideology[103] (even if qualified by a determination by the economic 'in the last

---

101 Marx and Engels 1975–6, V: 40, 52–3; Marx and Engels 1975: 390–402, 433–5, 441–3; Rigby 1992a: 165–9; Kautsky 1988: 229, 232–3; Gramsci 1977: 407, 437; Genovese 1972: 322; Loone 1992: 164–5. Engels's letters are still appealed to today by Marxists keen to reject the accusation of reductionism. See Hilton 1990: 178; Thompson 1978: 261; Delany 1990: 43; Kirk 1994: 222, 227–8.

102 Lovell 1980: 27–8; Thompson 1978: 254, 355, 360; Althusser and Balibar 1975: 97, 100, 104–5, 177–8, 183, 187, 220–4; Althusser 1977: 96–101, 113; Gordy 1983. Althusser is presented as an *anti-reductionist* in Blackburn and Jones 1972: 369–74; Hall 1977; Bennett 1979: 40–1; Anderson 1980: 66–77; Hirst 1985: 22–3; Milner, 1981: 8. There is now a massive literature on Althusser, for which Elliot 1987 is a useful starting-point. For critiques of Althusser, see Clarke 1980; Geras 1978; Glucksmann 1978; Hindess and Hirst 1977; Rigby 1987: 194–8.

103 Miliband 1983: 56–62; Bennett 1979: 40–1; Althusser and Balibar 1975: 100–1; Eagleton 1991: 153; Williams 1983: 12–13, 32–3.

instance').[104] Neither is it a solution simply to abandon the metaphor of base and superstructure, perhaps by blaming it on Engels rather than on Marx himself.[105] It is not the *metaphor* of base and superstructure which is the problem but rather the idea which it seeks to express, i.e. the claim for a hierarchy of social elements or causal asymmetries which gave Marxism its specificity and separate identity as a form of social theory.[106]

Thus, in rejecting reductionism, Marxist theorists constantly slip towards an implicit pluralism by which Marxism dies the death of a thousand qualifications. This tendency is even more pronounced in the complex historical analyses offered by Marxist historians. For instance, Brenner's account of why the eastern European peasantry was enserfed in the late medieval period and early modern periods, when the peasantry in the West was winning its freedom, rejects explanations in terms of the population change and offers instead an analysis which is explicitly based on a Marxist claim for the primacy of class struggle. He argues that it was the strength of the western European peasant community which allowed it to resist the seigneurial offensive of the late medieval period and thus to win its freedom, whereas the weakness of the peasant communities in the East meant that they were unable to counter the landlords' pressure, thus opening the way to serfdom. The problem is that when he comes to explain why the peasant community was weaker in the East than in the West, Brenner lists a host of factors which cannot be reduced to expressions of class structure or class struggle, such as the absence of common land in the East, the prevalence there of individualistic methods of farming rather than of highly evolved common-field systems, the small size of eastern villages, the lack of villages of divided lordship, the effects of political conquest and the emergence of particular state-forms. The outcome of class struggle thus ceases to be simply an explanation and itself becomes something to be explained in terms of a variety of factors.[107] There is a comparable pluralism at work in Brenner's account of how strong peasant property and the absolutist state developed in early modern France 'in mutual dependence upon one another',

---

104   Marx and Engels 1975: 393–6, 399, 401–2, 441–2; Kautsky 1988: xlii, 3–4, 227, 232–3. As Althusser famously put it: 'From the first moment to the last, the lonely hour of the last instance never comes' (Althusser 1966: 113). However, Althusser developed his own reading of determination in the last instance by the economic level which he saw as assigning the other social levels their specific effectivity. Thus, in the feudal mode of production, the economic level 'determines' that the political level should be 'dominant' (Althusser and Balibar 1975: 97, 177–8, 220–4). For a critique, see Hindess and Hirst 1977: 55–6.
105   Colletti 1972: 65; Rader 1979: xx, 70, 75–6, 78, 82, 181, 183–4; Thompson 1978: 79–85, 119–121; Sayer 1987: 91–2, 148; Genovese 1969: ix; Kaye 1984: 117, 191–2, 205, 234.
106   Korsch 1938: 225, 230; Lovell 1980: 28; Geras 1990: 9–11; Anderson 1980: 66, 81; Genovese 1972: 19, 323; 1969: ix; Haldon 1991: 28; McDonnell and Robins 1980: 215; A. W. Wood 1981: 64–5; Miller 1991: 101; Genovese 1972: 324; van Parijs 1979: 87, 91; Kiernan 1987: 107; Hobsbawm 1984: 44–6; Wright *et al.* 1992: chs 3 and 6.
107   Brenner 1976: 57–60; 1982: 72–6. Guy Bois complains about Brenner's implicit pluralism in 'Against the neo-Malthusian orthodoxy' (1978: 67).

which suggests that absolutism was more than simply the 'expression' of social change, as Brenner also claims, but was itself an active agent in bringing such change about. (Brenner 1976: 71; 1982: 81).

Nor is such pluralism confined to the works of Brenner. Rather, it can be seen in Corrigan and Sayer's (1985: 85) explanation of why modern capitalism first triumphed in England in terms of 'the singularity of English state formation and state forms' and in Genovese's (1972: 322–3) attempt to square the circle by claiming that the social superstructure is 'generated' by the base of the mode of production but that it also develops according to a logic of its own and reacts back upon the base. Similarly, Parker, in an essay explicitly intended to *defend* the metaphor of base and superstructure, argues that the motor of historical change in the early modern period was not to be found in class struggle or in any aspect of the economy, 'but in the activities of the state', in particular, the rise of the absolutist state under the pressure of warfare and religious antagonisms.[108] In practice, such accounts present us with a multiplicity of interacting forces, an 'infinite variety of local factors',[109] which together bring about a particular historical outcome, a picture of history which is familiar from non-Marxist historiography and from Weberian sociology,[110] but which sits uneasily with the Marxist claims for the primacy of the economic base (even when redefined in Godelier's terms). As Kitching put it, commenting on the high quality of Marxist historiography: 'Engaging in a professional practice which is more sophisticated than its theorization is in fact very likely to coexist with a trained inability to either recognize or express that sophistication formally or explicitly'.[111]

The threat which such pluralism poses for Marxism cannot be avoided merely by changing historical materialism from a claim for the primacy of a narrowly defined 'economic' level to a more broadly conceived 'class determination'.[112] Nor is explanatory pluralism only implicit in the Marxist tradition which emphasizes

---

108   Parker 1990: 287, 297–8; 1983: 60–4, 74, 147–9. Parker thus recommends the application to western Europe of Anderson's account of the rise of Eastern absolutism in terms of international rivalry (Parker 1983: 297–8; Anderson 1979: 195–202, 212–16). See also the discussion of absolutism, p. 903 above.

109   Haldon 1991: 88–9. This variety of local factors can be seen in the treatment of the role of 'great men' in history, where the emphasis of Marxist historians on the indispensable role of particular individuals provides a contrast with Engels's (untestable) claim that 'if Napoleon had been lacking, another would have filled the place' (Marx and Engels 1975: 442; Deutscher 1954: vii; Rodinson 1973: ix–x, 298).

110   Bailey 1989: 1, 321–2; Glennie 1987: 300; 1988: 33–6; Holton 1985: 220–1.

111   Kitching 1988: 225. Breuilly (1987) makes a similar point about the pluralist-Marxist accounts of the making of the German working class offered by Jürgen Kocka and Hartmut Zwahr.

112   Wood 1995: 175; Genovese 1969: ix, 19, 103; 1972: 323–4; Kaye 1979: 415–19; Clarke 1979: 144; Williams 1979: 118; Kaye 1984: 232–41; Thompson 1972: 9–11; 1978: 85, 298–9. When class becomes an economic, social, political, psychological and cultural phenomenon (Genovese 1972: 323–4), there is a danger that this concept 'turns into a synonym for the social structure itself, occasionally masquerading as one of its principal parts' (Parkin 1979a: 8).

the primary role of the relations of production and of class struggle rather than of the productive forces (McLennan 1980: 39–40; 1989: 70–7). Rather, pluralism is an insoluble problem for *any* brand of Marxism which rejects reductionism and which seeks to explain historical change in terms of the interaction of a variety of historical forces.[113] As philosophers in the tradition of John Stuart Mill have argued, it is impossible to claim an objective explanatory primacy for any of the multiple factors which bring about a particular event. Causes have an objective existence in the real world, but which we choose to emphasize and which we take as given will largely depend upon our own subjective purposes, upon the knowledge which we think we can assume on the part of our audience, or on some new piece of the historical jigsaw which we have identified and to which we wish to draw attention.[114] In this perspective, it is not just the Marxist claim for the primacy of the economic which is doomed but *any* attempt to ascribe objective primacy in historical explanation. In other words, whatever our explicit theory may be, we cannot help, in practice, but be pluralists. It is precisely this fact which allows the piece of the historical jigsaw discovered by Marxist historiography to be so easily subsumed into orthodox history. As the high quality of Marxist historical writing suggests, Marxists have easily avoided the Scylla of reductionism, upon which its critics have usually seen it as foundering. Yet this danger has only been avoided at the expense of being drawn into the Charybdis of pluralism. I have argued here that there is no way in which Marxism can successfully navigate between these two fates.

REFERENCES

Abercrombie, N., Hill, S. and Turner, B. S. (1980) *The Dominant Ideology Thesis*, London.
Acton, E. (1990) *Rethinking the Russian Revolution*, London.
Acton, H. B. (1955) *The Illusion of the Epoch*, London.
Adamson, O. *et al.* (1976) 'Women's oppression under capitalism', *Revolutionary Communist* 5.
Adamson, W. L. (1980) Review of Cohen 1978, *History and Theory* 19: 186–204.

---

113 Johnston 1986: 8, 50, 66–7, 69, 80–1, 122. Since 'reductionism' is a term of abuse which no one applies to themselves, this means, in effect, all versions of Marxism. After all, even Stalin's *Dialectical and Historical Materialism* emphasized the 'reciprocal' influence of the social superstructure on the economic base and argued that, far from denying the role of the state and ideology in history, Marxism 'stresses the important role and significance of these factors in the life of society' (Stalin 1951: 26–97).

114 Mill 1970: 214–17; Hospers 1973: 292–6; Ryan 1974: 74–9; Skorupski 1989: 175–7; Ryan 1987: 41–50; Hart and Honoré 1985: xxxiii, 15–22, 28, 33–7; Ryle 1963: 50, 88–9, 113–14; Runciman 1983: 193; Gorovitz 1965: 701–2; Veyne 1984: 91–2, 101; Dretske 1972; Gardiner 1961: 10–11, 99–112; Dray 1957: 98–101; Putnam 1979: 41–4; 1983: 211–15; Garfinkel 1981: 3–5, 21–34, 138–45, 156–74; Anderson *et al.* 1986: 171; Brodbeck 1962: 239; Will 1974: 24, 273–5; Atkinson 1989: 159–64; Heller 1982: 159–60; McCullagh 1984: 208–11; Popper 1969: 151; Scriven 1966: 254–8; Rigby 1992a: 177–82; 1995a: 141–3; 1995b.

Adamson, W. L. (1981) 'Marx's four histories: an approach to his intellectual development', *History and Theory* 20.
—— (1985) *Marx and the Disillusionment of Marxism*, Berkeley.
Althusser, L. (1971) *Lenin and Philosophy and Other Essays*, London.
—— (1972) *Politics and History: Montesquieu, Rousseau, Hegel and Marx*, London.
—— (1977) *For Marx*, London.
—— and Balibar, E. (1975) *Reading Capital*, London.
Amin, S. (1976) *Unequal Development*, Hassocks.
Anderson, P. (1976) *Considerations on Western Marxism*, London.
—— (1977) *Passages from Antiquity to Feudalism*, London.
—— (1979) *Lineages of the Absolutist State*, London.
—— (1980) *Arguments within English Marxism*, London.
—— (1983) 'Class struggle in the ancient world', *History Workshop* 16.
—— (1992) *English Questions*, London.
Anderson, R. J., Hughes, J. A. and Sharrock, W. W. (1986) *Philosophy and the Human Sciences*, Beckenham.
Aston, T. (ed.) (1965) *Crisis in Europe, 1560–1660*, London.
Atkinson, R. F. (1989) *Knowledge and Explanation in History*, London.
Avineri, S. (ed.) (1964) *Karl Marx on Colonialism and Modernization*, New York.
Bailey, M. (1989) *A Marginal Economy?*, Cambridge.
Bak, J. M (1980) 'Serfs and serfdom: words and things', *Review* 4.
Barbalet, J. M. (1982) 'Social closure in class analysis: a critique of Parkin', *Sociology* 16.
Barg, M. (1991) 'The social structure of manorial freeholders: an analysis of the Hundred Rolls of 1279', *Agricultural History Review* 39.
Barrett, M. (1984) *Women's Oppression Today*, London.
Bellis, P. (1979) *Marxism and the U.S.S.R.*, London.
Bennett, T. (1979) *Formalism and Marxism*, London.
Benton, T. (1977) *Philosophical Foundations of the Three Sociologies*, London.
Bergesen, A. (1993) 'The rise of semiotic Marxism', *Sociological Perspectives* 36.
Bertram, C. (1990) 'International competition in historical materialism', *New Left Review* 183.
Bertrand, M. (1979) *Le Marxisme et l'histoire*, Paris.
Bettelheim, C. (1976) *The Class Struggles in the U.S.S.R., 1917–23*, Hassocks.
Blackbourn, D. and Eley, G. (1984) *The Peculiarities of German History*, Oxford.
Blackburn, R. (ed.) (1972) *Ideology in Social Science: Readings in Critical Social Theory*, London.
Blackburn, R. (1988) *The Overthrow of Colonial Slavery, 1776–1848*, London.
—— and Jones. G. S. (1972) 'Louis Althusser and the struggle for Marxism', in Howard and Klare 1972.
Blanning, T. C. W. (1987) *The French Revolution: Aristocrats versus Bourgeois?*, London.
Bloch, M. (1983) *Marxism and Anthropology*, Oxford.
Böhm-Bawerk, E. von (1975) *Karl Marx and the Close of his System*, ed. P. Sweezy, London.
Bois, G. (1976) *Crise de féodalisme*, Paris.
—— (1978) 'Against the neo-Malthusian orthodoxy', *Past and Present* 79.
—— (1992) *The Transformation of the Year One Thousand*, Manchester.
Brenner, R. (1976) 'Agrarian class structure and economic development in pre-industrial Europe', *Past and Present* 70.
—— (1977) 'The origins of capitalist development: a critique of neo-Smithian Marxism', *New Left Review* 104 (July–August).
—— (1978) 'Dobb on the transition from feudalism to capitalism', *Cambridge Journal of Economics* 2.
—— (1982) 'The agrarian roots of European capitalism', *Past and Present* 97.

—— (1989) 'Bourgeois revolution and transition to capitalism', in A. L. Beier, D. Cannadine and J. M. Rosenheim (eds) *The First Modern Society*, Cambridge.

—— (1993) *Merchants and Revolution: Commercial Change, Political Conflict and London's Overseas Traders, 1550–1653*, Cambridge.

Breuilly, J. (1987) 'The making of the German working class', *Archiv für Sozialgeschichte* 27.

Brodbeck, M. (1962) 'Explanation, prediction and "imperfect knowledge"', in H. Feigl and G. Maxwell (eds) *Minnesota Studies in the Philosophy of Science*, vol. 3, Minneapolis.

Browning, R. (1981) 'The class struggle in ancient Greece', *Past and Present* 100.

Brunt, P. A. (1982) 'A Marxist view of Roman history', *Journal of Roman History* 72.

Bukharin, N. (1969) *Historical Materialism*, New York.

Burris, V. (1987) 'The neo-Marxist synthesis of Marx and Weber on class', in N. Wiley (ed.) *The Marx–Weber Debate*, Newbury Park.

Callinicos, A. (1987) *Making History: Agency, Structure and Change in Social Theory*, Cambridge.

—— (1989) 'Bourgeois revolution and historical materialism', *International Socialism* 43.

—— (1990) 'The limits of "political Marxism"', *New Left Review* 184.

—— (1995) *Theories and Narratives: Reflections on the Philosophy of History*, Cambridge.

Campbell, S. (1988) 'Carnival, calypso and class struggle in nineteenth-century Trinidad', *History Workshop* 26.

Carling, A. (1986) 'Rational choice Marxism', *New Left Review* 160.

—— (1990) 'In defence of rational choice: a reply to Ellen Meiskins Wood', *New Left Review* 184.

—— (1991) *Social Division*, London.

Carver, T. (ed.) (1991) *The Cambridge Companion to Marx*, Cambridge.

Childe, V. G. (1941) *Man Makes Himself*, London.

—— (1947) *History*, London.

—— (1954) *What Happened in History*, Harmondsworth.

Clarke, S. (1979) 'Socialist humanism and the critique of economism', *History Workshop* 8.

—— *et al.* (1980) *One-Dimensional Marxism*, London.

Cockburn, C. (1986) 'The relations of technology: what implications for theories of sex and class', in R. Crompton and M. Mann (eds) *Gender and Stratification*, Cambridge.

Cohen, G. A. (1970) 'On some criticism of historical materialism', *Proceedings of the Aristotelian Society* 44 (Supplement).

—— (1974) 'Being, consciousness and roles: on the foundation of historical materialism', in C. Abramsky and B. J. Williams (eds) *Essays in Honour of E. H. Carr*, London.

—— (1978) *Karl Marx's Theory of History: A Defence*, Oxford.

—— (1980) 'Functional explanation: reply to Elster', *Political Studies* 28.

—— (1982a) 'Functional explanation, consequence explanation and Marxism', *Inquiry* 25.

—— (1982b) 'Reply to Elster on "Marxism, functionalism and game theory"', *Theory and Society* 11.

—— (1983) 'Forces and relations of production' in Mathews, 1983.

—— (1988) *History, Labour and Freedom*, Oxford.

Cohen, J. S. (1978) 'The achievements of economic history: the Marxist school', *Journal of Economic History* 38: 29–57.

—— (1982) Review of G. A. Cohen 1978, *Journal of Philosophy* 79.

Cohen, M., Nagel, T. and Scanlon, S. (eds) (1980) *Marx, Justice and History*, Princeton.

Coleman, D. C. (1983) 'Proto-industrialization: a concept too many', *Economic History Review*, 2nd ser., 36.

Colletti, L. (1972) *From Rousseau to Lenin*, London.

Collins, R. (1975) *Conflict Sociology*, New York.

Collinson, P. (1982) *The Religion of Protestants*, Oxford.
—— (1983) *English Puritanism*, Historical Association Pamphlet 106.
Comninel, G. (1987) *Rethinking the French Revolution*, London.
Coontz, S. and Henderson, P. (1986) *Women's Work and Men's Property*, London.
Cornforth, M. (1968) *The Open Philosophy and the Open Society*, London.
Corrigan, P. and Sayer, D. (1985) *The Great Arch: English State Formation as Cultural Revolution*, Oxford.
Coss, P. R. (1985) 'Aspects of cultural diffusion in medieval England', *Past and Present* 108.
Coveney, P. J. (ed.) (1977) *France in Crisis 1620–1675*, London.
Croce, B. (1981) *Historical Materialism and the Economics of Karl Marx*, New Brunswick.
Crossick, G. (1980) *An Artisan Elite in Victorian Society*, London.
Cunningham, H. (1981) 'The language of patriotism, 1750–1914', *History Workshop* 12.
Dalton, G. (1974) 'How exactly are peasants "exploited"?', *American Anthropologist* 76.
Davin, A. (1981) 'Feminism and labour history', in R. Samuel (ed.) *People's History and Socialist Theory*, London.
De Beauvoir, S. (1974) *The Second Sex*, Harmondsworth.
De Ste Croix, G. E. M. (1975) 'Karl Marx and the history of classical antiquity', *Arethusa* 8.
—— (1981) *The Class Struggle in the Ancient Greek World*, London.
—— (1984) 'Class in Marx's conception of history, ancient and modern', *New Left Review* 146.
Delany, S. (1990) *Medieval Literary Politics*, Manchester.
Delphy, C. (1984) *Close to Home*, London.
Deutscher, I. (1954) *The Prophet Armed, Trotsky: 1879–1921*, Oxford.
Dobb, M. (1951) 'Historical materialism and the role of the economic factor', *History* 36.
—— (1963) *Studies in the Development of Capitalism*, London.
—— (1976a) 'From feudalism to capitalism', in Hilton *et al.* 1976.
—— (1976b) 'A reply', in Hilton *et al.* 1976.
Dockès, P. (1982) *Medieval Slavery and Liberation*, London.
Dorpalen, A. (1985) *German History in Marxist Perspective: The East German Approach*, London.
Draper, H. (1977) *Karl Marx's Theory of Revolution*, New York.
Dray, W. (1957) *Laws and Explanations in History*, Oxford.
Dretske, F. (1972) 'Contrastive statements', *Philosophical Review* 81.
Dunn, S. P. (1982) *The Fall and Rise of the Asiatic Mode of Production*, London.
Dyer, C. (1981) 'A redistribution of incomes in fifteenth-century England?', in Hilton 1981.
—— (1989) *Standards of Living in the Later Middle Ages*, Cambridge.
—— (1992) 'Small-town conflict in the later Middle Ages: events at Shipston-on-Stour', *Urban History* 19.
Eagleton, T. (1991) *Ideology*, London.
Eisenstein, Z. (1979) 'Developing a theory of capitalist patriarchy and socialist feminism', in Z. Eisenstein (ed.) *Capitalist Patriarchy and the Case for Socialist Feminism*, New York.
Elliot, G. (1987) *Althusser: The Detour of Theory*, London.
Elster, J. (1979) *Ulysses and the Sirens*, Cambridge.
—— (1980) 'Cohen on Marx's theory of history', *Political Studies* 28.
—— (1983a) *Explaining Technical Change*, Cambridge.
—— (1983b) *Sour Grapes*, Cambridge.
—— (1985) *Making Sense of Marx*, Cambridge.
Engels, F. (n.d.) *Herr Eugen Dühring's Revolution in Science*, London.
—— (1964) *Dialectics of Nature*, Moscow.

—— (1965) *The Peasant War in Germany*, London.
—— (1968) *The Origin of the Family, Private Property and the State*, Moscow.
—— (1969a) *The Condition of the Working Class in England*, London.
—— (1969b) *Germany: Revolution and Counter-Revolution*, London.
—— [1892] (1978) 'Introduction', *Socialism: Utopian and Scientific*, Moscow.
Evans, M. (1981) *Lucien Goldmann: An Introduction*, Brighton.
Firestone, S. (1979) *The Dialectic of Sex*, London.
Fleischer, H. (1975) *Marxism and History*, Harmondsworth.
Forgacs, D. (1986) 'Marxist literary theories', in A. Jefferson and D. Robey (eds) *Modern Literary Theory*, London.
Foster, J. (1974) *Class Struggle and the Industrial Revolution*, London.
—— (1976) 'Some comments on "class struggle and the labour aristocracy, 1830–60"', *Social History* 1.
Fox-Genovese, E. (1982) 'Placing women's history in history', *New Left Review* 133.
Frankfort, H. G. and Poole, B. (1966–7) 'Functional analysis in biology', *British Journal for the Philosophy of Science* 17.
Fromm, E. (1975) *The Fear of Freedom*, London.
Furet, F. (1981) *Interpreting the French Revolution*, Cambridge.
—— (1988) *Marx and the French Revolution*, Chicago.
Gandy, D. R. (1979) *Marx and History*, Austin.
Gardiner, P. (1961) *The Nature of Historical Explanation*, Oxford.
Garfinkel, A. (1981) *Forms of Explanation*, New Haven, CT.
Genovese E. D. (1965) *The Political Economy of Slavery*, New York.
—— (1969) *The World the Slaveholders Made*, New York. (Repr. London, 1970.)
—— (1972) *In Red and Black*, New York.
—— (1974) *Roll, Jordan, Roll: The World the Slaves Made*, New York.
—— 1979) *From Rebellion to Revolution*, Baton Rouge.
Geras, N. (1978) 'Althusser's Marxism: an assessment', in Jones *et al.* 1978.
—— (1985) 'The controversy about Marx and justice', *New Left Review* 150.
—— (1990) 'Seven types of obloquy: travesties of Marxism', in R. Miliband, L. Pantich and J. Saville (eds) *The Socialist Register*, London.
Giddens, A. (1979a) *Central Problems in Social Theory*, London.
—— (1979b) *Studies in Social and Political Theory*, London.
—— (1981) *A Contemporary Critique of Historical Materialism*, London.
Gimenez, M. (1987) 'Marxist and non-Marxist elements in Engels' views on the oppression of women', in Sayers *et al.* 1987.
Given, J. (1984) 'The economic consequences of the English conquest of Gwynedd', *Speculum* 64.
Glennie, P. (1987) 'The transition from feudalism to capitalism as a problem for historical geography', *Journal of Historical Geography* 13: 296–302.
—— (1988) 'In search of agrarian capitalism: manorial land markets and the acquisition of land in the Lea valley, *c.*1450–1560', *Continuity and Change* 15.
Glucksmann, A. (1978) 'A ventriloquist structuralism', in Jones *et al.* 1978.
Godelier, M. (1977) *Perspectives in Marxist Anthropology*, Cambridge.
—— (1978) 'Infrastructures, society and history', *New Left Review* 112.
—— (1981) 'The Asiatic mode of production', in A. M. Bailey and J. R. Llobera (eds) *The Asiatic Mode of Production*, London.
—— (1988) *The Mental and the Material*, London.
Goldmann, L. (1972) *Racine*. Cambridge.
Gordy, N. (1983) 'Reading Althusser: time and the social whole', *History and Theory* 22.
Gorovitz, S. (1965) 'Causal judgements and causal explanations', *Journal of Philosophy* 62.

Gottlieb, R. S. (1984) 'Feudalism and historical materialism; a critique and a synthesis', *Science and Society* 48.

Gouldner, A. (1980) *The Two Marxisms*, London.

Graham, K. (1992) *Karl Marx: Our Contemporary*, Hemel Hempstead.

Gramsci, A. (1977) *Selections from the Prison Notebooks*, ed. Q. Hoare and G. N. Smith, London.

Gray, R. (1976) *The Labour Aristocracy in Victorian Edinburgh*, Oxford.

—— (1981) *The Aristocracy of Labour in Nineteenth-Century Britain, c.1850–1900*, Basingstoke.

Green, S. (1981) *Prehistorian: A Biography of V. Gordon Childe*, Bradford-on-Avon.

Grenon, M. and Robin, R. (1976) 'A propos de la polémique sur l'ancien régime et la Révolution: pour une problématique de la transition', *La Pensée* 167.

Gurevich, (1985) *Categories of Medieval Culture*, London.

Haldon, J. (1991) 'The Ottoman state and the questions of state autonomy: comparative perspectives', *Journal of Peasant Studies* 18.

Halfpenny, P. (1983) 'A refutation of historical materialism', *Social Science Information* 22.

Hall, S. (1977) 'Re-thinking the base and superstructure metaphor', in J. Bloomfield (ed.) *Class, Harmony and Party*, London.

Hart, H. L. A. and Honoré, T. (1985) *Causation in the Law*, Oxford.

Hartmann, H. (1981) 'The unhappy marriage of Marxism and feminism: towards a more progressive union', in L. Sargent (ed.) *Women and Revolution: A Discussion of the Unhappy Marriage of Marxism and Feminism*, London.

Hauser, A. (1971) 'Propaganda, art and ideology', in I. Mészaros (ed.) *Aspects of History and Class Consciousness*, London.

Hay, D. (1975) 'Property, authority and the criminal law', in D. Hay (ed.) *Albion's Fatal Tree: Crime and Society in Eighteenth-Century England*, New York.

Hearn, J. (1991) 'Gender: biology, nature and capitalism', in Carver 1991.

Heller, A. (1982) *A Theory of History*, London.

Hellman, G. (1979) 'Historical materialism', in J. Mepham and D. Hillel-Ruben (eds) *Issues in Marxist Philosophy*, vol. 2, Brighton.

Hibbert, A. B. (1978) 'The origins of the medieval town patriciate', in P. Abrams and E. A. Wrigley (eds) *Towns in Societies*, Cambridge.

Hilferding, R. (1981) 'The materialist conception of history', in T. Bottomore (ed.) *Modern Interpretations of Marx*, Oxford.

Hill, C. (1940) *The English Revolution, 1640*, London.

—— (1956) *Economic Problems of the Church*, London.

—— (1958) *Puritanism and Revolution*, London.

—— (1968) *Society and Puritanism*, London.

—— (1969) *Reformation to Industrial Revolution*, Harmondsworth.

—— (1971) *Antichrist in Seventeenth-century England*, London.

—— (1972a) *God's Englishman: Oliver Cromwell and the English Revolution*, Harmondsworth.

—— (1972b) *The Intellectual Origins of the English Revolution*, London.

—— (ed.) (1973) *Winstanley: The Law of Freedom*, Harmondsworth.

—— (1974a) *Change and Continuity in Seventeenth Century England*, London.

—— (1974b) *The Century of Revolution, 1603–1714*, London.

—— (1975) *The World Turned Upside Down*, Harmondsworth.

—— (1976) 'A comment', in Hilton *et al.* 1976.

—— (1977) *Milton and the English Revolution*, London.

—— (1980) 'A bourgeois revolution', in J. G. A. Pocock (ed.) *Three British Revolutions: 1641, 1688, 1776*, Princeton.

—— (1984) 'God and the English Revolution', *History Workshop* 17.

—— (1986) 'The bourgeois revolution in Soviet scholarship', *New Left Review* 155.

Hilton, R. H. (1967) *A Medieval Society*, London.

—— (1969) *The Decline of Serfdom in Medieval England*, London.

—— (1975) *The English Peasantry in the Later Middle Ages*, Oxford.

—— (1976a) 'A comment', in Hilton *et al.* 1976.

—— (1976b) 'Introduction', in Hilton *et al.* 1976.

—— (1977) *Bond Men Made Free*, London.

—— (1980) 'Robin des Bois', *L'Histoire* 38.

—— (1984) 'Feudalism in Europe: problems for historical materialists', *New Left Review* 147: 84–93.

—— (1985) *Class Conflict and the Crisis of Feudalism*, London.

—— (1990) 'Unjust taxation and popular resistance', *New Left Review* 180.

—— (1992) *English and French Towns in Feudal Society*, Cambridge.

—— (ed.) (1981) *Peasants, Knights and Heretics*, Cambridge and New York.

—— *et al.* (1976) *The Transition from Feudalism to Capitalism*, London.

Himmelweit, S. (1991) 'Reproduction and the materialist conception of history: a feminist critique', in Carver 1991.

Hindess, B. and Hirst, P. Q. (1975) *Pre-capitalist Modes of Production*, London.

—— (1977) *Mode of Production and Social Formation*, London.

Hirst P. Q. (1977) *Mode of Production and Social Formation*, London.

—— (1985) *Marxism and Historical Writing*, London.

Hobsbawm, E. (1962) *The Age of Revolution, 1789–1848*, New York.

—— (1964a) *Labouring Men*, London.

Hobsbawm, E. (ed.) (1964b) *Pre-capitalist Modes of Production*, London.

—— (1965) 'The crisis of the seventeenth century', in Aston 1965.

—— (1969) *Industry and Empire*, Harmondsworth.

—— (1970) 'Lenin and the "aristocracy of labour"', *Marxism Today*, July.

—— (1971) *Primitive Rebels*, Manchester.

—— (1972) 'Karl Marx's contribution to historiography', in Blackburn 1972.

—— (1982) *Bandits*, Harmondsworth.

—— (1984) 'Marx and history', *New Left Review* 143.

—— (1989) *The Age of Empire, 1875–1914*, London.

—— (1990) *Echoes of the Marseillaise: Two Centuries Look Back on the French Revolution*, London.

—— and Rudé, G. (1973) *Captain Swing*, Harmondsworth.

Holt, J. C. (1981) 'The origins and audience of the ballads of Robin Hood', in Hilton 1981.

—— (1989) *Robin Hood*, London.

Holton, R. J. (1978) 'The crowd in history: some problems of theory and method', *Social History* 3.

—— (1985) *The Transition from Feudalism to Capitalism*, Basingstoke.

Hook, S. (1934) *Towards the Understanding of Karl Marx*, London.

Hospers, J. (1973) *An Introduction to Philosophical Analysis*, London.

Howard, D. and Klare, K. E. (eds) (1972) *The Unknown Dimension: European Marxism since Lenin*, New York.

Howkins, A. (1977) 'Edwardian liberalism and industrial unrest: a class view of the decline of liberalism', *History Workshop* 4.

Hudson, P. (1981) 'Proto-industrialisation: the case of the West Riding wool textile industry in the eighteenth and early nineteenth centuries', *History Workshop* 12.

Hughes, A. L. (1991) *The Causes of the English Civil War*, Basingstoke.

Isajiw, W. W. (1968) *Causation and Functionalism in Sociology*, London.

RITICAL

Jakubowski, F. (1976) *Ideology and Superstructure in Historical Materialism*, London.

James, C. L. R. (1969) *The Black Jacobins*, New York.

Jay, M. (1984) *Marxism and Totality*, Cambridge.

John, E. (1953) 'Some questions on the materialist interpretation of history', *History* 38.

Johnson, R. (1978) 'Edward Thompson, Eugene Genovese and socialist-humanist history', *History Workshop* 6.

Johnston, L. (1986) *Marxism, Class Analysis and Socialist Pluralism*, London.

Jones, G. S. (1987) *Languages of Class: Studies in English Working Class Culture, 1832–1982*, London.

—— et al. (1978) *Western Marxism: A Critical Reader*, London.

Jordan, Z. A. (1967) *The Evolution of Dialectical Materialism*, London.

Joshua, I. (1988) *La Face cachée du Moyen Age*, Montreuil.

Kain, P. J. (1986) *Marx, Method, Epistemology and Humanism: A Study in the Development of his Thought*, Sovietica 48, Dordrecht and Lancaster.

Katz, C. J. (1989) *From Feudalism to Capitalism: Marxian Theories of Class Struggle and Social Change*, New York.

Katznelson, I. (1992) *Marxism and the City*, Oxford.

Kautsky, K. (n.d.) *Ethics and the Materialist Conception of History*, 4th edn, Chicago.

—— (1988) *The Materialist Conception of History*, New Haven, CT.

Kaye, H. J. (1979) 'Totality: its application to historical and social analysis by Wallerstein and Genovese', *Historical Reflections/Réflexions Historiques* 6.

—— (1984) *The British Marxist Historians*, Cambridge.

—— (1985) 'Acts of re-appropriation: Rodney Hilton as Robin Hood', *Peasant Studies* 12.

—— (ed.) (1988) *History, Classes and Nation States: Selected Writings of V. G. Kiernan*, Cambridge.

—— (1992) *The Education of Desire: Marxists and the Writing of History*, London.

Kiernan, V. G. (1965) 'Foreign mercenaries and absolute monarchy', in Aston 1965.

—— (1987) 'Problems of Marxist history', *New Left Review* 161.

Kirk, N. (1994) 'History, language, ideas and post-modernism: a materialist view', *Social History* 19.

Kitching, G. (1988) *Karl Marx and the Philosophy of Praxis*, London.

Klare, K. E. (1972) 'The critique of everyday life, the new left and unrecognizable Marxism', in Howard and Klare 1972.

Kolakowski, L. (1978) *Main Currents of Marxism*, Oxford.

Konstan, D. (1975) 'Marxism and Roman slavery', *Arethusa* 8.

Korsch, K. (1938) *Karl Marx*, London.

Kosminsky, E. (1955) 'Evolution of feudal rent in England from the eleventh century to the fifteenth century', *Past and Present* 7.

—— (1956) *Studies in the Agrarian History of England*, Oxford.

Krader, L. (1975) *The Asiatic Mode of Production*, Assen, The Netherlands.

Kriedte, P., Medick, H. and Schlumbohm, J. (1981) *Industrialization before Industrialization*, Cambridge.

Krieger, L. (1953) 'Marx and Engels as historians', *Journal of the History of Ideas* 14.

Kula, W. (1976) *An Economic Theory of the Feudal System*, London.

Laclau, E. (1979) *Politics and Ideology in Marxist Theory*, London.

Larrain, J. (1979) *The Concept of Ideology*, London.

—— (1986) *A Reconstruction of Historical Materialism*, London.

Laurenson, D. and Swingewood, A. (1972) *The Sociology of Literature*, London.

Lefebvre, G. (1962) *The French Revolution from its Origins to 1793*, New York.

—— (1967) *The French Revolution from 1793 to 1799*, London.

—— (1969) *The Coming of the French Revolution*, Princeton.

Leff, G. (1961) *The Tyranny of Concepts*, 2nd edn, London.

Lekas, P. (1988) *Marx on Classical Antiquity: Problems of Historical Methodology*, Brighton.

Lenin, V. I. (1966a) *Imperialism, the Highest Stage of Capitalism*, Moscow.

—— (1966b) *Imperialism and the Split in Socialism*, Moscow.

—— (1969) *The Three Sources and Component Parts of Marxism*, Moscow.

Levine, A. (1987) 'The German historical school of law and the origins of historical materialism', *Journal of the History of Ideas* 48.

Levine, A. and Wright, E. O. (1980) 'Rationality and class struggle', *New Left Review* 123.

Levine, A., Sober, E. and Wright, E. O. (1987) 'Marxism and methodological individualism', *New Left Review* 162.

Lewis, G. (1993) *The French Revolution: Rethinking the Debate*, London.

Lichtheim, G. (1964) *Marxism: An Historical and Critical Study*, 2nd rev. edn, London.

Liebman, M. (1970) *The Russian Revolution*, New York.

Lis, C. and Soly, H. (1982) *Poverty and Capitalism in Pre-Industrial Europe*, Brighton.

Littlejohn, G. M. (1972) 'An introduction to Lublinskaya', *Economy and Society* 1.

Loone, E. (1992) *Soviet Marxism and Analytical Philosophies of History*, London.

Lovell, T. (1980) *Pictures of Reality: Aesthetics, Politics and Pleasure*, London.

Lowe, C. (1985) 'Cohen and Lukes on rights and power', *Political Studies* 33.

Löwy, M. (1989) '"The poetry of the past": Marx and the French Revolution', *New Left Review* 177.

Lubasz, H. (1984) 'Marx's conception of the Asiatic mode of production', *Economy and Society* 13.

Lublinskaya, A. D. (1968) *French Absolutism: The Crucial Phase, 1620–1629*, Cambridge.

—— (1972) 'The contemporary bourgeois conception of absolute monarchy', *Economy and Society* 1.

Lukács, G. (1974) *History and Class Consciousness*, London.

Lukes, S. (1983) 'Can the base be distinguished from the superstructure?', in Miller and Siedentop 1983.

—— (1985) *Marxism and Morality*, Oxford.

McCarthy, T. (1978) *Marx and the Proletariat*, Westport, Ont.

McClelland, K. (1979) 'Some comments on Richard Johnson, "Edward Thompson, Eugene Genovese and socialist-humanist history"', *History Workshop* 7.

McCullagh, C. B. (1984) *Justifying Historical Descriptions*, Cambridge.

McDonnell, K. and Robins, K. (1980) 'Marxist cultural theory: the Althusserian smokescreen', in Clarke *et al.* 1980.

McDonough, R. and Harrison, R. (1978) 'Patriarchy and relations of production', in A. Kuhn and A. Wolpe (eds) *Feminism and Materialism*, London.

McGarr, P. (1989) 'The Great French Revolution', *International Socialism* 43.

Mackenzie, G. (1980) Review of Parkin 1979a, *British Journal of Sociology* 31.

McLellan, D. (1976) *Karl Marx: His Life and Thought*, St Albans.

McLennan, G. (1979) 'Richard Johnson and his critics: towards a constructive debate', *History Workshop* 8.

—— (1980) 'The historical materialism debate', *Radical Philosophy* 50.

—— (1981) *Marxism and the Methodologies of History*, London.

—— (1989) *Marxism, Pluralism and Beyond*, Cambridge.

McMurtry, J. (1978) *The Structure of Marx's World View*, Princeton.

Maguire, D. (1972) *Marx's Paris Writings: An Analysis*, Dublin.

Mann, M. (1986) *The Sources of Social Power*, vol. 1, Cambridge.

Manning, B. (1965) 'The nobles, the people and the constitution', in Aston 1965.

—— (1970) 'The outbreak of the English Civil War', in R. H. Parry (ed.) *The English Civil War and After*, London.

—— (ed.) (1973) *Politics, Religion and the English Civil War*, London.

Manning, B. (1976) *The English People and the English Revolution 1640–49*, London.

Martin, J. E. (1983) *Feudalism to Capitalism*, London.

Marx, K. (1968–72) *Theories of Surplus Value*, 3 vols, London.

—— (1970a) *The Civil War in France*, Peking.

—— (1970b) *Wage Labor and Capital*, Moscow.

—— (1971) *A Contribution to the Critique of Political Economy*, London.

—— (1972a) *The Class Struggles in France, 1848 to 1850*, Moscow.

—— (1972b) *The Eighteenth Brumaire of Louis Bonaparte*, Moscow.

—— (1973a) *The Poverty of Philosophy*, Moscow.

—— (1973b) *The Revolutions of 1848*, ed. D. Fernbach, Harmondsworth.

—— (1973c) *Surveys from Exile*, Harmondsworth.

—— (1974a) *The First International and After*, ed. D. Fernbach, Harmondsworth.

—— (1974b) *Grundrisse*, Harmondsworth.

—— (1976–81) *Capital*, 3 vols, Harmondsworth.

Marx, K. and Engels, F. (1949) *Selected Works*, Vol. II, Moscow.

—— (1962) *Selected Works*, Vol I, Moscow.

—— (1967) *The Communist Manifesto*, Harmondsworth.

—— (1975) *Selected Correspondence*, Moscow.

—— (1975–6) *Collected Works*, vols 1–6, London.

—— (1982) *Collected Works*, vol. 38, London.

Mason, T. (1981) 'The workers' opposition in Nazi Germany', *History Workshop* 11.

Mathews, B. (ed.) (1983) *Marx: A Hundred Years On*, London.

Meikle, S. (1985) *Essentialism in the Thought of Karl Marx*, London.

Merrington, J. (1976) 'The transition from feudalism to capitalism', in Hilton *et al.* 1976.

Merton, R. K. (1962) *Social Theory and Social Structure*, Glencoe, IL.

Middleton, C. (1974) 'Sexual inequality and stratification theory', in Parkin 1974.

—— (1979) 'The sexual division of labour in feudal England', *New Left Review* 113–14.

—— (1981) 'Peasants, patriarchy and the feudal mode of production in England', *Sociological Review* 29.

—— (1983) 'Patriarchal exploitation and the rise of English capitalism', in E. Gamarnikow, D. Morgan, J. Purvis and D. Taylorson (eds) *Gender, Class and Work*, London.

—— (1985) 'Women's labour and the transition to pre-industrial capitalism', in L. Charles and L. Duffin (eds) *Women and Work in Pre-industrial England*, London.

Miliband, R. (1972) 'Reply to N. Poulantzas', in Blackburn 1972.

—— (1973) *The State in Capitalist Society*, London.

—— (1979) *Marxism and Politics*, Oxford.

—— (1983) *Class Power and State Power*, London.

Mill, J. S. (1970) *A System of Logic*, London.

Miller, D. and Siedentop, L. (eds) (1983) *The Nature of Political Theory*, Oxford.

Miller, J. (1979) *History and Human Existence: From Marx to Merleau-Ponty*, Berkeley.

Miller, R. W. (1981) 'Productive forces and the forces of change', *The Philosophical Review* 9.

—— (1984) *Analyzing Marx*, Princeton.

—— (1991) 'Social and political theory: class, state and revolution', in Carver 1991.

Millett, K. (1985) *Sexual Politics*, London.

Milner, A. (1981) 'Considerations on English Marxism', *Labour History* 41.

Mishra, R. (1979) 'Technology and social structure in Marx's theory: an exploratory analysis', *Science and Society* 43.

Montgomery, D. (1987) *The Fall of the House of Labour*, Cambridge.

Mooers, C. (1981) *The Making of Bourgeois Europe*, London.

Moorhouse, H. F. (1978) 'The Marxist theory of the labour aristocracy', *Social History* 3.

Morton, A. L. (1938) *A People's History of England*, London.

—— (1978) 'Pilgrim's Progress, a commemoration', *History Workshop* 5.

Mumy, G. E. (1978–9) 'Town and country in Adam Smith's *The Wealth of Nations*', *Science and Society* 42.

Murphy, R. (1988) *Social Closure*, Oxford.

Musson, E. (1976) 'Class struggle and the labour aristocracy, 1830–60', *Social History* 1.

Neale, R. S. (1985) *Writing Marxist History*, Oxford.

Neuwirth, G. (1969) 'A Weberian outline of a theory of community: its application to the "Dark Ghetto"', *British Journal of Sociology* 20.

Oliva, P. (1962) *Pannonia and the Onset of Crisis in the Roman Empire*, Prague.

Ollman, B. (1972) *Alienation*, Cambridge.

Parijs, P. van (1979) 'From contradiction to catastrophe', *New Left Review* 115.

—— (1982) 'Functionalist Marxism rehabilitated', *Theory and Society* 11.

—— (1993) *Marxism Recycled*, Cambridge.

Parker, D. (1971) 'The social foundation of French absolutism, 1610–30', *Past and Present* 53.

—— (1983) *The Making of French Absolutism*, London.

—— (1990) 'French absolutism, the English state and the utility of the base-superstructure model', *Social History* 15.

Parkin, F. (ed.) (1974) *The Social Analysis of Class Structure*, London.

Parkin, F. (1979a) *Marxism and Class Theory*, London.

—— (1979b) 'Social stratification', in T. Bottomore and R. Nisbet (eds) *A History of Sociological Analysis*, London.

—— (1982) *Max Weber*, London.

Plamenatz, J. P. (1963) *Man and Society: A Critical Examination of Some Important Social and Political Theories from Machiavelli to Marx*, 2 vols, London.

Plekhanov, G. V. (1969) *Fundamental Problems of Marxism*, London.

—— (1972) *The Development of the Monist Conception of History*, Moscow.

Popper, K. R. (1966) *The Open Society and its Enemies*, London.

—— (1969) *The Poverty of Historicism*, London.

Porshnev, B. (1963) *Les Soulèvements populaires en France de 1623 à 1648*, Paris.

Poulantzas, N. (1972) 'The problem of the capitalist state', in Blackburn 1972.

Price, R. (1993) *A Concise History of France*, Cambridge.

Putnam, H. (1979) *Meaning and the Moral Sciences*, London.

—— (1983) *Philosophical Papers*, vol. 3, Cambridge.

Rader, M. (1979) *Marx's Interpretation of History*, New York.

Razi, Z. (1979) 'The Toronto school's reconstitution of medieval peasant society: a critical view', *Past and Present* 85.

—— (1983) 'The struggles between the abbots of Halesowen and their tenants in the thirteenth and fourteenth centuries', in T. H. Aston, P. R. Coss, C. Dyer and J. Thirsk (eds) *Social Relations and Ideas*, Cambridge.

Rigby, S. H. (1987) *Marxism and History: A Critical Introduction*, Manchester.

—— (1990) 'Making history', *History of European Ideas* 12.

—— (1992a) *Engels and the Formation of Marxism*, Manchester.

—— (1992b) 'Marxism and the Middle Ages', in A. Ryan *et al.* (eds) *After the End of History*, London.

—— (1993) Review of Carling 1991, *Social History* 18.

—— (1995a) *English Society in the Later Middle Ages: Class, Status and Gender*, Basingstoke.

—— (1995b) 'Historical causation: is one thing more important than another?', *History* 80.

Robinson, J. (1962) *Economic Philosophy*, London.

—— (1966) *An Essay on Marxian Economics*, London.

Rodinson, M. (1973) *Mohammed*, Harmondsworth.

Roemer, J. E. (1982) *A General Theory of Exploitation and Class*, Cambridge, MA.

—— (1989) 'What is exploitation? Reply to Jeffrey Reima', *Philosophy and Public Affairs* 18.

Rosenberg, N. (1981) 'Marx as a student of technology', in L. Levidow and B. Young (eds) *Science, Technology and the Labour Process*, London.

Rudé, G. (1959) *The Crowd in the French Revolution*, Oxford.

—— (1964a) *The Crowd in History, 1730–1848*, New York.

—— (1964b) *Revolutionary Europe, 1783–1815*, London.

—— (1965) *Wilkes and Liberty*, Oxford.

—— (1974a) *Europe in the Eighteenth Century*, London.

—— (1974b) *Paris and London in the Eighteenth Century*, London.

—— (1989) *The French Revolution*, London.

Runciman, W. G. (1969) 'The three dimensions of social inequality', in A. Béteille (ed.) *Social Inequality*, Harmondsworth.

—— (1974) 'Towards a theory of social stratification', in Parkin 1974.

—— (1983–9) *A Treatise on Social Theory*, 3 vols, Cambridge.

Ryan, A. (1974) *J. S. Mill*, London.

—— (1987) *The Philosophy of John Stuart Mill*, London.

Ryan, M. (1986) *Marxism and Deconstruction*, Baltimore.

Ryle, G. (1963) *The Concept of Mind*, London.

Samuel, R. (1977) 'The workshop of the world: steam power and hand technology in mid-Victorian Britain', *History Workshop* 3.

—— (1980) 'British Marxist historians', *New Left Review* 120.

Saville, J. (1974) *Marxism and History*, Hull.

Sawer, M. (1977) 'The concept of the Asiatic mode of production and contemporary Marxism', in S. Avineri (ed.) *Varieties of Marxism*, The Hague.

Sayer, D. (1987) *The Violence of Abstraction*, Oxford.

Sayers, J., Evans, M. and Redclift, N. (1987) *Engels Revisited*, London.

Schwarz, B. (1982) '"The people" in history: the Communist Party Historians' Group', in R. Johnson, G. McLennan, B. Schwarz and D. Sutton (eds) *Making Histories*, London.

Scriven, M. (1966) 'Causes, connections and conditions in history', in W. H. Dray (ed.) *Philosophical Analysis and History*, New York.

Seccombe, W. (1983) 'Marxism and demography', *New Left Review* 137.

—— (1992) *A Millennium of Family Change*, London.

Shaw, B. D. (1984) 'The anatomy of the vampire bat', *Economy and Society* 13.

Shaw, W. H. (1978) *Marx's Theory of History*, London.

—— (1979) '"The handmill gives you the feudal lord": Marx's technological determinism', *History and Theory* 18.

Skorupski, J. (1989) *John Stuart Mill*, London.

Smith, A. A. (1984) 'Two theories of historical materialism', *Theory and Society* 13.

Soboul, A. (1974a) *The French Revolution, 1787–1799*, London.

—— (1974b) 'L'Historiographie classique de la Révolution française', *Historical Reflections/ Réflexions Historiques* 1.

—— (1977) *A Short History of the French Revolution*, Berkeley.

—— (1978) *La Civilisation et la Révolution Française*, vol. 2, Paris.

—— (1981) *Comprendre la Révolution*, Paris.

Stalin, J. (1951) *Dialectical and Historical Materialism*, Moscow.

Steedman, I. (1975) 'Value, price and profit', *New Left Review* 90.

—— (1977) *Marx after Sraffa*, London.

—— et al. (1981) *The Value Controversy*, London.

Stinchcombe, A. L. (1975) 'Merton's theory of social structure', in L. A. Coser (ed.) *The Idea of Social Structure*, New York.
Sweezy, P. (1976) 'A critique', in Hilton *et al.* 1976.
Sztompka, P. (1964) *Systems and Function*, New York.
Tännsjö, T. (1990) 'Methodological individualism', *Inquiry* 33.
Therborn, G. (1980) *What Does the Ruling Class Do When it Rules?*, London.
Thompson, E. P. (1971) 'The moral economy of the English crowd in the eighteenth century', *Past and Present* 50.
—— (1972) [1963] *The Making of the English Working Class*, Harmondsworth.
—— (1975) *Whigs and Hunters*, London.
—— (1978) *The Poverty of Theory*, London.
Tillich, P. (1970) 'Marx's view of history: a study in the history of the philosophy of history', in S. Diamond (ed.) *Culture in History*, New York.
Torrance, J. (1985) 'Reproduction and development: a case for a "Darwinian" mechanism in Marx's theory of history', *Political Studies* 33.
Torras, J. (1980) 'Class struggle in Catalonia: a note on Brenner', *Review* 4.
Trotsky, L. (1967) *The History of the Russian Revolution*, 3 vols, London.
—— (1970) *Marxism in our Time*, New York.
—— (1971) *The Permanent Revolution and Results and Prospects*, London.
—— (1973) *1905*, Harmondsworth.
Veyne, P. (1984) *Writing History*, Manchester.
Vogel, L. (1983) *Marxism and the Oppression of Women*, London.
Walbank, F. W. (1946) *The Decline of the Roman Empire in the West*, London.
—— (1969) *The Awful Revolution*, Liverpool.
Weber, M. (1976) *The Protestant Ethic and the Spirit of Capitalism*, London.
—— (1978) *Economy and Society*, 2 vols, Berkeley.
Wetherly, P. (ed.) (1992) *Marx's Theory of History: The Contemporary Debate*, Aldershot.
Wickham, C. (1978) 'The uniqueness of the East', in J. Baechler, J. A. Hall and M. Mann (eds) *Europe and the Rise of Capitalism*, Oxford.
—— (1981) *Early Medieval Italy: Central Power and Local Society, 400–1000*, London.
—— (1984) 'The other transition: from the ancient world to feudalism', *Past and Present* 103.
—— (1988a) 'Historical materialism, historical sociology', *New Left Review* 171.
—— (1988b) 'Marx, Sherlock Holmes and late Roman commerce', *Journal of Roman Studies* 78.
—— (1988c) *The Mountains and the City: The Tuscan Apennines in the Early Middle Ages*, Oxford.
—— (1991) 'Systactic structures: social theory for historians', *Past and Present* 132.
Will, F. L. (1974) *Induction and Justification*, London.
Williams, G. (1979) 'In defence of history', *History Workshop* 7.
—— (1983) '18 Brumaire: Karl Marx and defeat', in B. Matthews (ed.) *Marx: A Hundred Years On*, London.
Williams, R. (1973) 'Base and superstructure in Marxist cultural theory', *New Left Review* 82.
Wokler, R. (1983) 'Rousseau and Marx', in Miller and Siedentop 1983.
Wood, A. W. (1981) *Karl Marx*, London.
Wood, E. M. (1981a) 'Marxism and ancient Greece', *History Workshop* 11.
—— (1981b) 'The separation of the economic and the political in capitalism', *New Left Review* 127.
—— (1982) 'E. P. Thompson and his critics', *Studies in Political Economy* 9.
—— (1984) 'Marxism and the course of history', *New Left Review* 147.

—— (1989a) *Peasant, Citizen and Slave*, London.

—— (1989b) 'Rational choice Marxism: is the game worth the candle?', *New Left Review* 177.

—— (1990) 'Explaining everything or nothing', *New Left Review* 184.

—— (1991) *The Pristine Culture of Capitalism*, London.

—— (1995) *Democracy against Capitalism: Renewing Historical Materialism*, Cambridge.

Wright, E. O. (1983) 'Giddens's critique of Marxism', *New Left Review* 138.

—— Levine, A. and Sober, E. (1992) *Reconstructing Marxism*, London.

37

WOMEN, GENDER AND THE *FIN DE SIÈCLE*

Olwen Hufton

A recent number of the French publication *Autrement* entitled 'Passés recomposés', edited by Jean Boutier and Dominique Julia, was concerned to trace changes in the writing of history and the *métier* of the historian over the past thirty years. Many of the contributors attested to the unease or disquiet they sensed in the discipline. Some spoke of the passing of the great and global vision: the emergence of micro-history concentrating on a single episode, the art of thinking small or of history in a raindrop: the concomitant shrinkage of grand history and the constrained vision of a new generation of historians who were experts on the events of a few years over a few square miles of territory or masters of a single text. Some drew contrasts between those countries where history in the hands of the commercial publishers ensured it reached a broad spectrum with the ivory-tower approach of the British, American and to a degree French academics concerned more to impress each other than to share historical experience. Others brooded upon the triumph of theory in manifold form. The emergence of the great gurus of our time, for example Foucault, who sought to distinguish the process of domination, of power relation-ships within Western society, some arising from the growth of capitalism, others from religious change, a process which manifested itself in institutions like the prison and the lunatic asylum and criminal processes attacking sexual deviance, carried history deeper into the realms of the story of social control. Another influential figure in changing historical styles was the anthropologist Clifford Geertz who in the 1970s urged the examination of ritual and the symbolism encoded in the forms it took and spoke of 'thick description', a narrative form which took account of these complexities, as a means to understanding a culture. And then there was linguistic theory, the triumph of discourse and of deconstruction of Derrida, Saussure and Barthes and the advent of the new historicism (meaning the conversion of the historical document or 'text' into a semantic exercise concerned to demonstrate the meaning of the language used within it), which caused history to take a linguistic turn (Bowana 1981). The focus of the historian (supposing such a generic personage exists) could be said to have shifted away from the recovery and interpretation of hard evidence to theories of representation, to symbolism and collective memory (itself the subject of a plethora of theories and studies about the selection of what to remember about the past) as a means to understanding culture. The search for 'identity' (national, regional, sexual), and the definition of alterity, insiders and outsiders to a culture, have, in the view of some, changed history beyond recognition. If we add to this the relative ignorance of new generations about the content of the Bible and lack of understanding about religious belief (religion is just a form of social control), the demise of Marxist analysis which, whatever one's political persuasion, produced some historical classics and some active debate, then the belief that history is not quite what it was and the question 'what is history?' takes one away from the familiar landscape of past generations. The road from Braudel's *Material Civilisation* (1981) to Thomas Laqueur's *Making Sex: Body and Gender from the Greeks to Freud* (1990) or Keith Baker's *Inventing the French Revolution* (1990) is by any reckoning quite an odyssey.

What have these changes got to do with women's history? The short answer is quite a lot. Indeed, viewed in an international context to take in American and European historiography as well as British, what has happened to the history of women has reflected the twists and turns, the bifurcations and the culs-de-sac of the entire discipline (or should one say, of the category history?). If for no other reason than that, it is worth reflecting upon its evolution; its different emphases in different national contexts; its strengths and its weaknesses; the debates waged within it and of course the questions: 'has it arrived as an acknowledged part of the discipline?' and, most speculative of all, 'where is it going?'

The concern with the history of women developed in a significant way from the late 1960s. It grew in relatively propitious circumstances in certain senses and in other senses circumstances of suspicion and some hostility. The discipline was perhaps in these years led by social history, and social history was to be the hospitable ground in which the history of women was initially nurtured. The *Annales* school had spearheaded a preoccupation with demography, and demography in turn a concern with the history of the family. The major study by Lawrence Stone *The Family, Sex and Marriage in Early Modern England* (English edition, 1976) and the work by Edward Shorter on *The Making of the Modern Family* (English edition, 1976), which argued for the birth of affection in Europe as coincident with a new sexual liberty generated by the Industrial Revolution which took the young out of traditional rural communities, were important opportunities for the first debates on where women were located in family and community. Keith Thomas had already published an essay on attitudes to women in 'The double standard' (*Journal of the History of Ideas* (1959) which for me remains one of the classics of women's history) and *Religion and the Decline of Magic* (1971) which brought out the complexities of the witch-as-woman question. Witchcraft and heresy were in fact two of the issues in which the importance of understanding relationships between, and attitudes to, the sexes first became apparent. However, the American civil rights movement, the drive for equality which lay behind the women's movement and the anti-establishment ethos of the 1960s lay behind the impulse for further enquiry.

The initial intent, whether among American women academics or young women scholars in Britain, was very modest: to give women a past, to put them in the record. Without a past, as Simone de Beauvoir said, no individual could have dignity. For those anxious to develop the field, it was, in the first instance, necessary to gather the evidence, and the first evidence to hand related to demography. It was possible to determine a life course, dependent on class and with some national specificities, and to reply to most of the questions which Virginia Woolf had asked in the 1920s about women's lives in her *A Room of One's Own*:

> What one wants, I thought – and why does not some brilliant student at Newnham or Girton supply it? – is a mass of information; at what age did she marry; how many children had she as a rule; what was her house like; had she a room to herself; did she do the cooking; would she be likely to have a servant?

Knowing age at marriage, the average number of children, the odds on dying in childbed and on being a widow, and how class, geography and period modified the picture contributed to some appreciation of an average life, but one that was rather static. It did not take women out of the home or give them roles other than that of reproductive vessel. As well as this kind of question about, as it were, the logistics of life, another set intruded designed to show women as actors. Joan Gadol Kelly's question 'Did women have a Renaissance?' (and by implication a Reformation, an Enlightenment, a special experience of a particular war or of fascism) demanded a reconsideration of events with a view to uncovering a specific female experience. Even if the answer was 'no', it demanded an explanation to justify a missing presence. If 'yes', then their slice of the action needed consideration both in respect of those events in which they participated and in respect of what this showed about their lives. A number of women historians followed Linda Kerber and talked about this kind of history as 'refocussing the vision', meaning reviewing an event from the point of view of the involvement of groups of women. To what extent were women actors, positively as opposed to passively involved or drawn into unfolding events? Natalie Zemon Davis's work on the Protestant women of Lyons in the sixteenth century in *Society and Culture in Early Modern France* (1979) is a fine early example of this kind of approach.

In some instances it was a matter of re-reading evidence accumulated for quite other purposes and discovering what had been left out. I remember quite graphically being part of this re-reading process. In the autumn of 1968 I was asked by the history society of Balliol College, Oxford to make a contribution to a series of talks on 'Revolutions' (in those days seen as necessary, desirable and arguably fun) with a piece on women in the French Revolution. The series included several big names – Christopher Hill, George Rudé and Edward Thompson – to set beside my relative obscurity as the author of a monograph on a provincial town during the Revolution, but I sensed the audience was very receptive. News that I had given such a lecture sparked off endless invitations of a similar nature. The essence of the piece was the result of reflecting upon the moments when certain groups of women (whom I did not suppose to be the same or to speak for all women) were actors in political disturbances and what caused them to be so. When the piece was published in *Past and Present*, I was inundated with letters and it was important in the formation of transatlantic contacts with Natalie Davis, Joan Scott and Louise Tilly. The first was launching with Jill Conway one of the first courses on the history of women at Toronto and was compiling a pioneer bibliography. I passed on what I had. That was how the first steps were taken: we networked with those we had never even met.

Ab initio, significant differences marked out the American situation from that of other countries. The American university is market led (although there can be a very considerable lag between demand and supply). The American degree courses are modular and the notion of a wide chronological coverage at the undergraduate level in a very specialized subject course has little or no purchase. It is possible for students majoring in a certain field to elect individual courses in other fields. Multidisciplinarity rules. To possess an island of knowledge in a sea of ignorance is of less concern than in the European universities. Boasting a broad spectrum of higher education institutions and significant numbers of faculty women prepared to give time and energy to the development not only of women's history but of women's studies (a multidisciplinary concept), action and development of the field was on the agenda. Specialist centres were developed (like the Pembroke Center at Brown), and the Schlesinger Library of Radcliffe College for the History of Women in America, which has no European parallel, expanded considerably. It is easy for Europeans to be dazzled by the achievements of American women scholars and to underestimate the intensity of some of the battles which had to be fought. However, certainly the American structure gave scope for rapid development in a multidisciplinary context in contrast to, for example, the French experience, which has generated three specialist chairs in women's history, and the English model which has no positions at all in women's history but an increasing number of MA courses in the field.

In the 1980s, it became increasingly common to talk not of 'women's history' but of 'gender history', and what this means has been the subject of much debate. One factor lying behind this development was the fairly obvious realization that one cannot talk about women without talking about men. Simone de Beauvoir in *The Second Sex* (trans. 1954) pronounced (as had, it transpired, a whole series of feminists *avant la lettre* stretching back to Christine de Pisane, and even certain male philosophers like Poulain de la Barre and John Stuart Mill) that women were made, not born. They, as well as men, were a cultural construction, but the cultural construction of women had left them weak and essentially outsiders in a society largely organized for the benefit of men. She mustered an impressive range of thinkers from the Greeks to Freud via Genesis, Saint Paul and Karl Marx in support of the thesis. What this meant was that every child was subjected to an elaborate and complex process of acculturation provided by family, church, community and tradition, as well as by institutions such as the law court or the labour market. The result was that the *tabula rasa* of the infant mind was inscribed with notions of the appropriate, and in addition to the biological difference which was the spurious justification for the process, every little girl was given a part to play, a life role as supporting actor in which her intelligence was not given free rein. The historic process of conditioning rested on a biblical foundation text (Genesis) in which woman was made subservient to man and placed in a state of obedience: her transgression (the Eve legend) meant that she must sit in silence in church. To the Bible, medical thought stretching back to the Greeks, and possibly before, added that her different physical form (weaker, colder and wetter than the male masterpiece) fitted her for the home but not for the more active life of warfare or politics: this weaker physical form and restricted period in the labour market meant that she could be paid less etc. Nature had fitted her to be a reproductive object, a second-class citizen, someone without a history, whose growth was stunted to prevent her realizing her capacities.

The development of ideas and theories about gender had a great deal of importance for burgeoning women's studies departments because these notions were a co-ordinating concept bringing together a variety of subjects to form a multidisciplinary package, since they were of relevance not just to an interpretation of history but also areas in sociology, psychology, anthropology, legal studies, and perhaps above all in literature. Literary studies in fact in the 1980s began to dominate women's studies and gender analysis became one of the tools of deconstruction, the decoding of literary and historical texts to reveal the intent and mentalities of the writer taken to represent the culture.

The notion of a gender system constructed by the Church, the law, medical thought, economic ideas and tradition and perpetuated in the family had considerable effects upon historical writing. First, this system could be worked out in detail, be it from the point of view of the good-conduct literature of the Reformation, studied for example by Kathleen Davies (1981) or Steven Ozment (1985); from the point of view of early anatomical treatises: or the law could be unravelled to show how arbitrary views on the nature or the two sexes influenced the construction of property, marriage and even criminal law (British law, for example, until the 1790s treated the murder of a wife by a husband as homicide but the other way round as treason). The sauce society deemed appropriate for the goose could thus be distinguished from that deemed appropriate for the gander. Again, of course this was retrieval, but a form of retrieval which enhanced the understanding of mentalities even if it did not tell us the degree to which people built their lives on prescription.

To look at the possibilities available to each sex at a given time provided the dynamic of a classic work in women's history of the 1980s, Natalie Zemon Davis's *The Return of Martin Guerre* (1983), which used the evidence provided by a trial of an alleged impostor, who replaced at bed, board and in the community an aberrant husband who had gone off to war and had stayed away with whatever intent, but then chose to return and claim his place. The trial was used to reveal the expectations and possibilities a a given village society made available to either sex. This was both 'thick description' and microhistory: thinking small and interpreting the evidence by reference to notions of gender so as to give the study broader import The work was a huge success even outside purely academic circles.

For some historians the concentration on the construction of both men and women promised men a slice of the action in a dynamic branch of social history. It became possible to talk of 'a crisis of masculinity' which accounted for male behaviour towards women at certain periods, such as when women threatened to intrude upon terrain deemed appropriate only for men, as they did during the suffrage movements or when they attempted to enter jobs deemed male (the 'when threatened, attack' principle). Or, the definition of rigid gender roles and sexual behaviour clearly had application to the history of sexuality and gay studies (other growth areas). Non-conformity to society's norms produced victims of both sexes. Gender was clearly a part of 'cultural studies', another collective in steady development. It certainly lent edge to Black Studies as they evolved in post-civil rights America. For the black woman clearly experienced a double oppression, first from the white establishment which converted her body into a mechanism for the replication of slaves, and second from black male partners.

For some feminist scholars the emphasis on gender was an act of appropriation which again threatened to reduce women to a subsidiary role. For others the positing of a gender system which could be unravelled like a thread in a complex web and used to interpret any given document (text) and hence be made to reflect on the culture that produced it offered considerable possibilities. History generally was taking a 'linguistic turn' and women's history should join the movement and embrace the techniques of deconstruction. Indeed, it could be argued that already women's history was a pioneer in the field. One of the most reproduced essays ever written, Carol Smith-Rosenburg's 'The Female World of Love and Ritual' (1986) examined a correspondence between friends and relatives in nineteenth-century America, and picked out forms of expression and ways of conveying affection and bonding, a female use of language no less. However, more crucial to gender history was the language men used about women. Michel Foucault had accentuated the power of language in the assertion of dominance by a particular group – though his main concern was class struggle and the definition of deviance. But surely male dominance of women was also reflected in language which could then be the key to cultural analysis?

A preoccupation with power relations was an early characteristic of American women's historiography. Starting from the assumption that the historical record is that of an ongoing (and even in some views intensifying) onslaught upon women's power, two types of women were elected for early attention in furtherance of the thesis. The first type was the witch. Certainly most witches were women, but the claim was made that they were 'strong' women, healers and midwives, figures of authority in their communities. Closer analysis revealed that few fell into the healer/midwife category, but most were frightened poor old women trying to fend for themselves in harsh agrarian societies by cursing those who refused them assistance. Why these should be singled out for persecution of course needs explanation, but it can hardly be given in terms of their power. Moreover their incidence is far from even across Europe and that too needs explanation. Furthermore, in some countries most were denounced by women. The second figure involved in early power debates was the midwife who, it was alleged, was progressively ousted from her job by the male midwife. A recent collection of essays made by Hilary Marland ranging over all the countries of western Europe has revealed how hasty such a judgement was and that what was at stake, in a very few countries and in the cities, was the upper end of the business. In Catholic Europe the Church kept the business firmly in the hands of women and for the bulk of the population, cheapness was the determinant.

These early essays on gender power struggles lacked the sophisticated theories later formulated by some American feminist historians whose work fell most under the influence of French deconstructionist theory (which has had a much longer reign in the United States than in France itself). For this group, of which Joan Scott (1988) has become the chief exponent, the business of the feminist historian is to uncover the strategies of male dominance in the past or the mechanisms whereby patriarchy replicated itself. Social history *tout court* in this view is not enough: the approach is locked in economic determinism and description so that gender is no more than one among a number of devices for describing a given society. Instead, it should be a serious analytical tool concentrating on the forms of expression (discourse) employed to secure male hegemony.

Such a view has not gone uncontested. Louise Tilly challenged the interpretation as minimizing the achievement of survival strategies adopted by women in the past which made it possible for the working class to survive. For her, Scott's view of the social constraints on women was overweighted and left little scope for initiative. Her criticism will find sympathetic resonances in Italy where women's history at the present time seems particularly concerned to recreate a qualitative appreciation of the experiences of women which evades the rhetoric of oppression. The history of the convent, for example, is being rewritten so that it emerges as the possible centre of artistic musical and literary endeavour. (Hildegard of Bingen, currently in the music charts, has many counterparts.) The conversion of all women into eternal victims is not always how they themselves interpreted their lives and is hence to distort their vision. Is it defensible to graft on to the past the anger of the present?

Perhaps more dangerously, an exercise which involves writing up an event by reference to a specific 'meta'-framework (an ideology?) without an in-depth knowledge of the socio-economic framework of reference can only give a very partial rendering, a gross reduction. It is possible that no historian can ever convey all the story, but surely the aim should be as much of it as possible?

Where has British historiography chosen to locate itself? The impetus to develop women's history in Britain in the late 1960s and 1970s came from the left-wing historical tradition (sometimes referred to as the Thompson school, although Thompson was no significant protagonist of this field of enquiry, and indeed most of this school could at the beginning fairly be called gender blind, though his inspiration has led others further). However, women's history found an important organ in the *History Workshop Journal*, which proclaimed itself the journal of socialist and feminist historians. Its overt aim was to examine the interplay between gender and class. In some respects it drew on an older legacy; from the beginning of the twentieth century a number of young historians were shaped at the London School of Economics by Professor Lilian Knowles. They included Alice Clark who, though not a professional scholar as such, had received an impeccable training in the use of archival sources. Her *Working Life of Women in the Seventeenth Century* (1919), reprinted in two new editions (1982, 1992), has subsequently formed the point of reference for an active debate on the chronology of women's history and on the effects of capitalism on women's lives. Whether or not one agrees with Clark's conclusions about these issues, her reflection on how changes in the economy could transform certain areas of women's lives promoted active questioning. But the new generation of the 1970s went much further. Barbara Taylor's *Eve and the New Jerusalem: Socialism and Feminism in the Nineteenth Century* (1983) was a highly influential and sophisticated analysis of women in Owenite socialism which constitutes now a classic study in women's historiography. It made apparent that the sexes were not one in their notions of an ideal society. Pioneering work by Sally Alexander on London women's working lives and by Anna Davin on motherhood and nationalism/imperialism, to cite merely two examples, opened up issues in which economic, social and political considerations accentuated the differing experiences of women and men. Tribute should be paid to this generation of historians, whose work came to fruition at the point when British universities were shedding staff. Most of them knew disconcerting discontinuity in their working lives and many found a home in part-time work in the Open University (which fairly early on showed a great sensitivity to women's history) or the then polytechnics, where teaching loads were heavy and research time limited. Their relationship to the formal academic establishment was therefore tenuous.

Some of the most adventurous steps in the forward movement of women's history in Britain were then taken in unpropitious circumstances and it was not until the universities in the 1980s became more market orientated – in particular in search of money from overseas students for MA courses – that the British higher-education establishment in general adopted a more genial attitude towards women, gender, culture and those forms of history which did not follow traditional paths but which attracted the American student, as well as the British student who could raise the money for the fees. The foundation of MA courses in women's history in York, in Sussex, at Royal Holloway College and elsewhere promised the training of new research students. The adoption of modularity (courses which extend over only two or three academic terms) and a more 'American' approach to the structure of higher education has also meant the introduction of greater interdisciplinarity, already conspicuous in what are now called the new universities, and with these new kinds of degree courses came less concern with chronological coverage or what some would consider mainstream history. The plus side of change is the greater propensity for more experimental and innovative courses: the downside is the lack of breadth and the reduced propensity of historians to think comparatively or to have 'flags' – that is, an overall concept of the key issues of a period. The risk then is that gender analysis floats in a sea of contextual ignorance which detracts from its significance and exposes it to criticism.

How far has British historiography reflected the 'linguistic turn', the concern with textual analysis, or with power relationships, the rejection of the socio-economic and the sovereignty of class on the grounds that economic determinism clouds the significance of gender? These are not the same questions. The first question could be answered 'quite significantly'. Some superb work in this direction has been done, for example, by Lyndal Roper (1994) on German witch trials or by Laura Gowring (1993) on slander suits in the seventeenth century in the context of an in-depth study of London courts. In this study Gowring makes a special point of underscoring the extent to which women define women: the wife attacks the adulterous partner of her aberrant husband in almost biblical terms (Eve as temptress) and not the husband himself, or at least she does not do so publicly. The abandonment of the socio-economic is not as evident in Britain. Indeed, some very remarkable socio-economic work has been done and is in progress on women in the labour market and their role in industrial expansion in the nineteenth and twentieth centuries. The examination by British scholars of property law relating to women, of their differential treatment and presence in criminal courts, of women in medical thought and practice, are examples of growth sectors. There is, however, a significant representation of the new historicism, textual analysis by reference to gender theory where multidisciplinarity prevails, but it is far from dominating British history. The strength of the discipline in England has always been its solid empirical base and in the higher branches of academic history I do not see this disturbed.

What then has been achieved? First, there is a woman's past, variously defined, there for the taking. If history gives identity, this is important. Second, in many fields of historical enquiry some consciousness of the differing experience of women and men is apparent. Who, for example would now write a history of the Industrial Revolution without a consideration of the cheapness and ubiquitous availability of women's labour? Who would approach the question of religious change over the last four centuries without taking into account the differing responses of women and men? Who would confront the development of welfare systems in Europe without considering why they were designed largely to protect women and which women legislators had in mind. Who would call into question that fascism in both Germany and Italy were underpinned by female endorsement, which was active not passive? In these areas and with this kind of enquiry it is very clear that women's history has taken a great deal by sap rather than storm.

If, however, it is obvious that the historical discipline has been stretched to comprehend a whole series of new considerations, of which gender is but one, can one claim a transformation of the entire discipline as a result? Certainly there has been much change, but a great deal of it has been to add additional courses to the curriculum, a case of adding (and stirring) women to the record to make a slightly different mixture. If gender was a more pervasive issue in analysis, its presence within the problematic of 'grand' history would be more apparent. Instead, for example of examining the history of the suffrage from 1832 to 1928 as a series of gradualistic inclusions, it would be debated in terms of ongoing exclusions. Or, to give another kind of example, instead of looking at what groups of women did during the French Revolution and making a few radicals speak for all women and the words of one deputy (Amar, to whose lot it fell to close the women's clubs) constitute the discourse of all men, we would examine how the entire fate of the Revolution depended in the last analysis on its reception in the localities and that opposition by rural women as well as by men, though in very different ways, undermined republicanism both in the privacy of the home and in more public matters where it hurt (such as the non-payment of taxes, military desertion or the resurgence of Catholicism, etc.). In other words, the differing experience of men and women would determine the approach.

Where is women's history or gender history going? One might avoid answering this impossible question by saying that there are plenty of unresolved debates. There are profound dissensions on the chronology of women's experience, such as how much continuity and how much change there was in their lives over the centuries, the dichotomies of public and private spheres and whether such hard and fast lines can effectively be drawn in the lives of women and men. There should be more debate on the historical plausibility of generalizing about women (and men) at all. However, the answer to the question where women's history is going will surely lie with the next generation of historians. The undergraduates of western Europe while interested in social and above all in cultural history and, cognisant of gendered identities, do not necessarily think in the same terms as did their mothers. The late Marie Brive, one of the three women who held a chair in history of women in France, observed very openly at a Brussels conference in 1991 that the history of feminism as such was a matter of indifference to her undergraduates at Toulouse. Michelle Perrot, at a conference in Rome two years ago, admitted that she could not explain the overwhelming success in Italy and France of the *Histoire des femmes* (5 vols, 1992), given the lack of interest in feminism among her students. 'Are they buying it for their mothers?' she asked.

I was recently struck by the observations on a book list of gender-history titles made by a group of female Oxford undergraduates, legatees of some privileges hard won by their predecessors and very confident in their ability to compete with men in whatever the free market economy may offer. As far as they were concerned, male dominance in the past goes without saying. There is no need to keep on tediously inventing the wheel. They have, in their terminology, been there and done (registered) that. However, they were far from disinterested in issues affecting women in history. They acknowledged the importance of recognizing and debating issues such as the constant recourse of fundamentalist religious movements and right-wing political movements, whether sixteenth-century Protestantism or John Major on lone mothers, to the control of women's bodies. They could see how nationalist movements exploited women's reproductive capacities and the role of mother of citizens. (Claudia Koonz's *Mothers of the Fatherland* (1986) secured quite wide approval.) They were quite conscious of the difference between themselves and earlier generations. If biology means little now, it must have done so before contraception and abortion, and so on. History came through to me not only as a foreign country but as something of a cautionary tale. They were suspicious of woman as a category, because they were conscious of considerable differences within the sex. Women should have a history, but it should also reflect their relationships with other women as well as with men and the wider community. Women are clearly bearers of tradition, shapers of the next generation and so colluders in the construction of gender roles. Many may have been victims, but not all were innocent.

At the age of 20, the future as well as the past is a foreign country. These privileged young women live in interesting times. *Fin-de-siècle* western Europe has a birth-rate that will not ensure population replacement, and unemployment, precarious employment and 'intermittent employment' threaten even the most highly qualified of both sexes. Women's history has reflected the preoccupations of its times and has always been political in the sense of drawing attention to a female predicament, variously defined. The pattern for women of high levels of education now is postponed parenthood while they find and establish a career or no parenthood at all (graphically described in France as *la grève des ventres*). If they opt out for maternity leaves, they fall behind irretrievably in the career path and some may regard this as a risk they do not want to run. In short they can compete in the market, but they do so at a certain cost. Or they can decide to run the risks of giving up. They have a 'choice'. For other women in part-time jobs lacking pension and other entitlements (the lot of 60 per cent of the British female labour force) and those in a context of marital precariousness the *fin-de-siècle* looks very gloomy. There will, in short, be plenty of issues to keep a woman or gender question alive.

Brooding on this on a cold December afternoon, I went into Blackwell's bookshop where the Christmas rush was in full swing. On a table towards the front of the shop lay Marina Warner's *From the Beast to the Blonde* (a study of the interweaving of gender roles in fairy stories and hagiography), Claire Tomalin's *Mrs Jordan's Profession* (the story of the actress who gave birth to ten sons by a future king of England and who was, when he ascended the throne, unceremoniously abandoned to obscurity – so much for the much-vaunted power of the royal mistress) and Stella Tillyard's *Aristocrats* (the story of the four daughters of the Duke of Richmond, who were certainly not victims of social restraints or slaves to convention, virtue and modesty). All were impeccably researched, highly readable and professional works intended to reach audiences beyond the bounds of academe. Certainly women's history could not, in these hands, be charged with an ivory-tower approach and certainly history was alive, well and profitable. Equally surely, I thought, if I have to be a prophetess, the increasing cohorts of women in higher education can only enlarge the market – if, as and when they command independent incomes.

Both inside and outside academe, then, and whether or not feminism has suffered the demise of the 'grand narratives' which have been part of the Western intellectual tradition, women and gender in the past will have some part in the historiography of the twenty-first century. My very modest proposal for the future is that the historical assumptions regarding the two sexes should be incorporated in some way into the school curriculum so that the emergent eighteen-year-old has as part of his or her intellectual baggage a cognizance of exclusions and arbitrary categorizations attendant upon sexual identity in the past and consequently the significance and value of some hard-won victories.

REFERENCES

Baker, K. (1990) *Inventing the French Revolution*, Cambridge.

Beauvoir, S. de (1954) *The Second Sex*, London.

Bowana, W. J. (1981) 'Intellectual history in the 1980s: from the history of ideas to the history of meaning', *Journal of Interdisciplinary History* 12.

Braudel, F. (1981) *Material Civilization*, 3 vols, London.

Clark, A. (1919) *Working Life of Women in the Seventeenth Century*, London.

Davies, K. M. (1981) 'Continuity and change in literary advice on marriage', in R. B. Outhwaite (ed.) *Marriage and Society. Studies in the Social History of Marriage*, London.

Davis, N. Z. (1979) *Society and Culture in Early Modern France*, Stanford, CT.

—— (1983) *The Return of Martin Guerre*, Cambridge, MA.

Gowring, L. (1993) 'Gender and the language of insult in early modern Europe', *History Workshop Journal* 35.

Koonz, C. (1986) *Mothers of the Fatherland*, New York.

Laqueur, T. (1990) *Making Sex: Body and Gender from the Greeks to Freud*, London.

Ozment, S. (1985) *When Fathers Ruled: Family Life in Reformation Europe*, Cambridge.

Perrot, M. and Duby, G. (eds) (1992) *Histoire des femmes en Occident*, 5 vols, Paris.

Roper, L. (1994) *Oedipus and the Devil: Witchcraft, Sexuality and Religion in Early Modern Europe*, London.

Rosenburg, C. Smith- (1986) *Disorderly Conduct: Visions of Gender in Victorian America*, New York.

Scott, J. W. (1988) *Gender and the Politics of History*, New York.

Shorter, E. (1976) *The Making of the Modern Family*, London.

Stone, L. (1976) *The Family, Sex and Marriage in Early Modern England*, London.

Taylor, B. (1983) *Eve and the New Jerusalem: Socialism and Feminism in the Nineteenth Century*, London.

Thomas, K. (1959) 'The double standard', *Journal of the History of Ideas*.

—— (1971) *Religion and the Decline of Magic*, London.

Tillyard, S. K. (1994) *Aristocrats: Caroline, Emily, Louisa and Sarah Lennox 1740–1832*, London.

Tomalin, C. (1994) *Mrs Jordan's Profession*, London.

Warner, M. (1994) *From the Beast to the Blonde*, London.

Woolf, V. (1993) *A Room of One's Own*, Harmondsworth.

38

WORLD HISTORY

R. I. Moore

In 1981 William H. McNeill delivered as the annual Prothero Lecture of the Royal Historical Society in London 'A Defence of World History' (McNeill 1982). It seems almost as unlikely that McNeill might have been the recipient of that distinguished invitation more than a few years earlier as that he would have felt it necessary to mount such a defence, even to the Royal Historical Society, more than a few years later. This was a moment at which 'world history', conceived as a distinctive mode of study, not merely as a statement of comprehensive content, was making what in retrospect has been a sudden and rapid movement from the margins to somewhere quite near the centre of historians' concerns. The volume, variety and quality of published work on world history, and the respect with which it is treated, have increased greatly since then. Courses in world history are being established, professional associations formed, journals founded,[1] graduate training inaugurated (see e.g. Vadney 1990; Curtin 1991), textbooks and readings published on an increasingly lavish scale, though at the time of writing no established academic post has been dedicated to the subject in the United Kingdom, and only a handful in the United States. In 1980 McNeill was still almost alone in the Anglo-American historical mainstream (and not everybody would have endorsed that description of him – cf. Allardyce 1990) in championing its cause both by precept and example, though in 1976 a substantial and elegant history of the world by a highly regarded Oxford historian, John Roberts, had not only achieved considerable commercial success but commanded the (sometimes reluctant) admiration of his professional colleagues. Roberts was probably the first British professional historian of standing to attempt, and certainly the first to publish, a history of the world embracing the

---

1 In particular, the *Journal of World History* (University of Hawaii Press, 1990– not to be confused with the *Cahiers d'histoire mondiale*/*Journal of World History*/*Quadernos de historia mundial* published under the auspices of UNESCO, 1953–72) provides an effective forum for discussion of current pedagogic as well as scholarly issues and developments in world history.

entire globe from the evolution of man to the present day and addressed to an adult readership.

McNeill argued that world history was no different from any other kind of history in its goals and methods. It was based on the systematic and critical examination of documents and other empirical sources, subject to the same rules of evidence and of logic, using the same procedures and judged by the same criteria. The problems of scale which arose from treating questions over much larger stretches of time and space than historians had been used to were problems of degree, not of kind, and did not differentiate world history in any fundamental way from other forms of historical enquiry. The frank positivism with which the case was argued risked introducing its own distortion to a world history founded on it,[2] but it was well calculated to appeal to the audience to which it was addressed, and gained credibility from Roberts's as well as from McNeill's own work. In retrospect it does not seem accidental or inappropriate that McNeill should have argued that case at that time. World history is history, no less and no more, he might have said, echoing the famous peroration of J. B. Bury's Cambridge inaugural lecture in 1902 (Bury [1903] 1957: 223). Bury's declaration that 'history is a science, no less and no more' has won few plaudits. It seemed to endorse the possibility and desirability of establishing laws of historical development all the more unacceptable when repudiation of the claim that history provided a scientific foundation for Marxism was high on the Western intellectual agenda for most of the twentieth century. More immediately influential was the celebrated assault by G. M. Trevelyan (1913), which had overtones of the broader conflict between French positivism and German Idealism (Barraclough 1991: 5 n. 9) but became particularly associated with an argument, trivial but persistent in the English manner, about the relationship between history and literature, and whether historians should be grey figures in lab coats, or prophets and men of letters. In a sense Trevelyan's was the more pertinent criticism, for Bury's main concern was to vindicate history's intellectual respectability and autonomy. It was, he maintained, a rational discipline in its own right, with its own justification, goals and methods, which had completed its emergence from the penumbra of other divisions of knowledge in which it had been embedded since antiquity – rhetoric and theology, law, metaphysics and literature.

At the end of the twentieth century, world history finds itself in a similar situation. Its novelty lies not in the attempt to see the human past as a whole but in the claim that scientific history provides the appropriate methodology and interpretative framework for doing so. Until modern times such projects belonged to the provinces of religion and metaphysics from which history has separated itself so slowly and precariously over the last two or three hundred years – and in many parts of the world still not at all. Indeed, much of the resistance to world history among professional historians has arisen precisely from the fear that the attempt to grapple with questions too large to be tackled by means of the critical appraisal *de*

---

2 Cf. the comments on McNeill 1963 – 'the first genuine world history ever written' – of his Chicago colleague Marshall G. S. Hodgson (1993: 93).

novo of the relevant primary sources, which they imagine to be their habitual procedure, might lead to a resurgence of the grandiose and sinister speculative structures that they associate pre-eminently with the names of Spengler and Toynbee.

The alternative of seeking to grasp the workings of human society as a whole, and therefore to relate the various aspects of social and cultural activity to each other, has been equally distrusted as belonging to the province of economics and sociology, and similarly tainted with deterministic and anti-historical overtones. Until the 1960s scholarly history – the history that was taught in the history departments of the leading universities of Europe and America and written by their professors – was firmly rooted in the achievements of the historical movement of the nineteenth century, and still dominated by its outlook as well as its methods. Its chief business was with the origins and development of the state, the distribution and exercise of power within it, including the culture and values of the governing classes ('the political nation' in Namier's widely used phrase), and the relations of states with each other. The parameters of the undergraduate curriculum, and of much the greater part of research as well, were very largely those which had been shaped by Ranke and his pupils for continental Europe, and by Stubbs and his followers for Oxford, and through Oxford the British Empire. The agreement of the two traditions on the essentials of content if not always of method was variously but effectively demonstrated in North America. Everywhere the history of the nation and what were held to be its predecessors, usually from around the end of antiquity until the end of the First or of the Second World War, formed the core of historical teaching. This was complemented by selections from the general history of Europe, or (more recently) of the European empires, and by courses which stood in their various traditions for some essential core of European intellectual culture – political thought from Aristotle to Mill or Marx in the United Kingdom, Western civilization from Plato to Einstein in the United States and so on.

By and large, historians did not regard the parts of history which fell outside these limits as, for practical purposes, part of their field. Economic and social history were left to dedicated departments or sections in faculties of social sciences, from which 'historians' generally stood aloof even when formally affiliated to them.[3] The ancient world was the province of classicists and archaeologists; Africa, the pre-Columbian Americas and the Pacific of archaeologists and anthropologists (cf. Trevor-Roper 1965: 9); and Asia of multidisciplinary departments of area studies, dominated by the necessity of mastering its classical languages, and largely exhausted by the effort of doing so. The same divisions were reflected in professional associations, journals and even library classifications. Ignorance and

---

3   'History: includes the main historical divisions, such as medieval, early modern and modern history; British, European and world history; cultural, scientific, diplomatic and local history. It does not include Economic and Social History' (Higher Education Funding Council for England circular RAE96 2/94 (June 1994)). Notice also the use of the term 'world history' in the time-honoured sense of 'neither British nor European'.

943

parochialism had their usual results. Voluminous research on the history of Europe and North America conventionally defined was conducted with high technical accomplishment and often presented with panache, but remained hidebound, sterile and incurably parochial. The rest, though occasionally illuminated by a Tawney or a Finlay, a Hodgson or a Needham, seldom rose above the conceptual limitations of positivism, or exceeded in imaginative range what could be achieved through the philological scrutiny of texts and chronological narrative based on its results.

There had always been critics of these limitations among professional historians, of course, including some of the greatest, but they were marginalized not only by academic conservatism but by the association of the approaches and techniques they advocated with political liberalism, and especially with Marxism. Only in France, where the historians connected with *Annales* and the Sixième section of the École des Hautes Etudes under the leadership of Lucien Febvre and Fernand Braudel became immensely (though by no means uncontroversially) influential after 1945, was the hegemony of the Rankean tradition effectively challenged. The *annalistes* did not identify themselves as world historians, or advocate world history as such, but they contributed variously and enormously to the developments from which it has emerged, and especially to acknowledging the arbitrariness of the chronological, regional and disciplinary boundaries which defined traditional historiography.

Calls for a 'new history' did not begin with the founders of *Annales*. They had been vigorously articulated at least since Voltaire's *Essai sur les mœurs* (1751), and as commonly ignored, especially after the canonization of the political and diplomatic agenda in the nineteenth century. That does not mean that they have been without influence, any more than political hostility and intellectual indifference to Marxism or to *annalisme* prevented either movement from having a substantial and pervasive influence. World history itself owes a great deal to both. Although the teleological character of the Marxist analysis unquestionably tended to reinforce both Eurocentrism and the stereotyping of 'Asia', its intellectual structure and political sympathies committed it from the outset not only to include non-European societies – indeed, all societies – in its scheme of things, but to do so without a culturally or racially based assumption of European superiority or centrality. Even apart from its direct concern with such issues as the transitions from feudalism to capitalism, and from capitalism to imperialism, which necessarily carried discussion beyond the traditional limits of European history, the best Marxist writing was always distinguished by a breadth of vision not approached by alternative methodologies. Similarly, the *annaliste* search for 'total history', though not for world history as such, has not only broken down disciplinary boundaries but stimulated work on a great variety of topics, including for example communications and long-distance trade, technology, social structures and mentalities, which are crucial for any coherent approach to world history. Any number of *Annales* itself, or of the many journals founded in its footsteps (among which *Past and Present* is outstanding), will illustrate the point.

With these exceptions, neither of them mainstream in the anglophone world, the emergence of world history since the 1970s has owed very little to developments within the discipline of history itself, but a great deal to developments of which history cannot, in the end, help taking account. Its principal intellectual debts are to archaeology, whose findings even the most conservative historians have found hard to ignore (though the converse has not invariably been the case), and to social anthropology. These disciplines have not only brushed aside the chronological and geographical limitations by which historians were customarily confined, but shattered the fundamental axiom of all previous historical study, that documentary evidence provides the only, or at least the best, rational basis for apprehending the past. On the contrary, social anthropology has drummed home the lesson that historical 'sources' and history itself are the products of culture, and cultures are socially constructed and reconstructed over time to serve the present needs and purposes of the groups to which they belong (Cohen 1987; Fentress and Wickham 1992). Archaeologists have repeatedly demonstrated the power and potential of the comparative method, the essential intellectual foundation not only of world history, but of all history that is not mere antiquarianism. Historians continue to treat the fruits of that method as purveyed by economists, sociologists and political scientists with deep distrust. Nevertheless, they have found it more and more difficult to despise the succession of increasingly substantial and sophisticated comparative studies of long-term political and social change which has flowed from this tradition. (Major examples include: Eisenstadt 1963; Moore 1966; Bendix 1978; Skocpol 1979; Mann 1988.)

If historians in the developed world were becoming more open-minded in the 1960s and 1970s – by no means an incontrovertible proposition – a more profound reason lay in the marked weakening of the professional consensus represented by the continuous study of national history and 'Western civilization' upon which the undergraduate teaching of the subject had been founded (Allardyce 1982 and, more broadly, Novick 1988: 311–14, 415–68). This was everywhere expressed by a fragmentation of the curriculum, which was reinforced by a growing demand for more 'professional' – meaning more specialized – teaching. Individual courses became more varied and often more imaginative, reflecting the wider interests and growing technical sophistication of those who taught them, but the curriculum as a whole became less coherent with the disappearance or dilution of compulsory elements and survey courses: professionalism was eating its children. Meanwhile, outside the classroom the urgency of establishing an adequate historical understanding both of every part of the world and of the world as a whole became increasingly obvious, as did the collapse of every previous basis for doing so. In those decades not only nationalism and religion, but positivism, Idealism, orientalism and Marxism finally lost (in the Western world, but not only in the Western world) whatever intellectual authority remained to them, though all have retained their devotees. If there is a single reason for the rapid advance of world history in the last twenty years or so it is that no alternative paradigm commands sufficient credibility to satisfy an obvious and urgent need to understand the world we live in. The dangers inherent in that fact are no less evident than the opportunities.

It has not always been obvious what world history is the history of. Every advance of the idea and every new statement of its claims has tended to enlarge the subject matter which it embraces. When history was conceived as comprising, in effect, politics, war and diplomacy, with occasional leavening by high culture, the area within which it was deemed to have taken place at any particular epoch was correspondingly bounded. As a popular and respected textbook on *World History since 1870* put it in 1953:

> It was natural and proper until recent times to regard the history of the world as consisting of separate accounts of each continent. Except for periodic eruptions of Europeans into North Africa or America the development of each continent was a separate story. These irruptions might, in themselves, have drastic and far-reaching consequences, as did the barbarian invasions of Europe, or the Moslem invasions of Spain. ... But even the total effect of these great movements was not to create a permanent and constant interaction between developments in each continent. Such an effect is the creation of only the last two centuries of modern history: only they constituted truly 'world' history.[4]

Even upon the criterion enunciated here, the existence of direct contacts leading to 'permanent and constant interaction between developments in each continent', the continents themselves being conceived as essentially self-contained – what has been called 'a world of socio-cultural billiard balls coursing on a global billiard table' (Wolf 1982: 17) – the domain of world history is enormously enlarged as soon as the 'significant' contacts and developments are deemed to extend beyond the fields of war and diplomacy. It was, indeed, upon the same principle, if somewhat less exactingly applied, that McNeill constructed his history of the human community largely upon the formation and diffusion of religions and cultures which shaped his essential building blocks, the 'civilizations'. In this he owed something to the influence of Toynbee, and much more to a habit of European thought stretching back at least to Hegel (though one might say to Orosius), which sits comfortably enough beside the traditional preoccupation of mainstream history with elites and their activities. This approach also had the merit of being able to accommodate without conceptual difficulty the enormous extension of the historical vision in time and space brought about by archaeology, which has also employed the civilization as its principal unit of account. In the process, however, the necessary (though also in some influential cases ideologically motivated) foundation of archaeology in material life has extended the definition of 'civilization' beyond the merely aesthetic or spiritual evaluation of dominant cultures, and thus not only added significantly to the current agenda, but extended it yet further in content. Exclusive preoccupation with 'the great civilizations' has been undermined and a very large and far from completed number of previously unknown societies and civilizations added to the list of those which must eventually be comprehended in our account of the human past – and not only the remote past, for archaeology's concern with the non-literate brings within our grasp great swathes of the history of societies of every kind,

---

4 Thomson 1965: 7. Thomson's argument, and perhaps his book, explains why the phrase 'world history', or more commonly 'European and world history' at least as used in the United Kingdom in the post-war period, almost invariably referred to courses which ran from 1870 or later.

including the urban, the industrial and even the post-industrial, which were formerly unperceived and unconsidered. The progress of archaeology therefore not only represents an almost unimaginable potential for new knowledge, but gives powerful reinforcement to the view that the central preoccupation of human history must be with man's struggle with his environment (cf. Barraclough 1991: 108).

Great strides have been made in the last twenty years, though much of what we describe as world history is still the history of the Eurasian continent, of which a coherent and unified, though of course incomplete, account, with a common chronology, could now be written at least for the period since about 800 BCE when the adoption of cavalry by the peoples of central Asia placed them in a dynamic relationship with the sedentary civilizations both of China and the Middle East, if not since around 2500–2000 BCE, when some would argue that the more or less simultaneous appearance of citied civilizations in China, South-east Asia, the Indus valley, Mesopotamia and the eastern Mediterranean reflected common participation in continent-wide patterns of exchange. The vicissitudes of those civilizations and their successors until around 1500 CE show, of course, enormous differences, and included long periods when, as it used to be thought, direct and indirect contacts between them more or less ceased. But we can now see, for example, not only that the decline of the classical civilizations in the early centuries CE, which seemed quite recently to herald 'an age of diverging traditions',[5] was the product of a single set of circumstances, but that the emergence in their wake of societies in which wealth and settlement were more firmly rooted in the countryside, power more localized, and religion more personal and more or less fiercely monotheistic (for all that the differences in degree were so great as to produce radically different consequences in different parts of the landmass), nevertheless also represented responses to circumstance which had a great deal in common. The appearance at this time of a new world civilization, that of Islam, whose expansion, continuing until c.1600 CE, quickly placed it in direct contact with all the other citied regions, and generated exchanges whose repercussions affected the most remote regions of the entire Afro-Eurasian land mass and the seaways which connected and surrounded it, provides a natural and appropriate vantage point from which the history of the whole may be written (cf. Hodgson 1993: 97–121), up to the time when the expansion of European commerce, the rise of the Atlantic economy and the emergence of industrial capitalism placed the north-western extremity at the centre of world events. It may be noted that one implication of all this is that a common periodization for world history is now emerging rapidly; its desirability and usefulness are, of course, no more dependent on incontrovertibility than those of any other periodization (cf. Green 1992).

It will be immediately apparent that such a history of the Eurasian continent includes that of North Africa from the outset, and that a similar integration of the history of sub-Saharan Africa lies in the not very distant future. Although current

---

5   The phrase is Roberts's (1976: Table of Contents), but the view is widely shared.

attempts to begin that process at a very early (that is, pre-Roman) date have commanded little agreement (e.g. that of Bernal 1987) we already know enough to be perfectly certain that the history (including the sub-Saharan history) of the continent is bound up with that of Eurasia from the earliest times. The lesson of the fact that the long habit of dismissing the possibility of such an integrated history rested upon an absurdly arbitrary equation of the writing of history with the availability of documentary sources for direct human contacts is that it would be quite wrong to discount the possibility of including Australia, New Zealand, the islands of the Pacific and the Americas in an integrated account of world history from very remote times. Beyond the ever more ancient and further-flung contacts between relatively developed societies which are almost daily revealed by archaeology, anthropology has demonstrated that even very 'primitive' cultures are not stable or self-contained entities. Change within them, for example in the balance between a tribe and its hunting grounds, could generate vast and far-reaching cultural, economic and eventually political transformations, while conversely such changes in that delicate equilibrium might easily be triggered by commercial or other activities at very great distances.[6] The point is no less powerfully made by the growing field of ecological history, whose observation of the dramatic and devastating transmission of cultural disturbance between peoples quite unaware of one anothers' existence transforms the entire surface of the globe into a millpond whose remotest beach will eventually register the intrusion of a single pebble – but where the manner and effect of the ripples will depend not only on the shape and mass of the intruder, and of the beach, but also on currents and eddies driven by the breezes of the moment, and steered and directed by hidden currents, depths and shallows that have accumulated across the previous centuries (Simmons 1993; Crosby 1986; McNeill 1976; 1980).

Once set upon this path, in other words, there is no resting place. World history is total history, regionally and chronologically as well as in respect of its range of subject matter. Even if we resist in practical terms – and it is hard to suggest upon what principle we might do so – the argument of David Christian (1991) that we must extend our vision from the Big Bang to the present,[7] the vast enlargement of the area which must be embraced by historical studies is clearly permanent and inescapable. World history need not, and indeed must not, aim to be encyclopedic – that can be left to encyclopedias. On the other hand, it cannot exclude anything from its purview *a priori*, as Swiss history or military history might do. It can only be defined as a perspective, one of many in which any particular event, structure or

---

6   See for example Wolf 1982; Hodges 1988. From a somewhat different aspect Barfield 1989 proposes a dramatically revised understanding of the relations between nomadic and sedentary peoples in traditional Eurasia.

7   Cf. Clark 1977: 1: If we seek to understand the process by which man has emerged to civilization through his capacity to adjust to almost every environment encountered on earth and even momentarily on the moon, we need to take some account of his evolution as an organism, and to recognise that both his biological and his social evolution have been accomplished in the context of a changing physical setting.'

process may be viewed. Thus, the cholera epidemic which killed 10,000 people in Hamburg in 1892, after other European cities had learned to prevent it (Evans 1987), may be seen as part of social history, urban history, or the history of medicine or sanitation; of the history of Hamburg, or of Germany, or of the world – and it will be treated differently according to the perspective. But world history is also a perspective – and the only perspective – in which all events, structures and processes must ultimately be capable of being viewed. It is, historically speaking, the set of all sets. The familiar argument of the classroom that sheer practicality demands some restriction of subject matter deserves no more time and patience than would be accorded a chemist or a physicist who sought to defend the arbitrary exclusion of inorganic chemistry or thermodynamics from the curriculum on the ground that doing so would make it easier to master. Of course it is always necessary to select. But a rational and sound selection for any purpose, including pedagogy, can only be made on the basis of a systematic assessment of the whole.

This objective is, in some respects, very much more attainable than it seemed even twenty or thirty years ago. There has been an immense increase, qualitatively and quantitatively, of published work on almost every part of the world, and on almost every period and aspect of history. The force of habit is not to be underestimated. National history, and after that the history of the developed world in recent times, still dominate both teaching curricula and the time and resources dedicated to research. Politicians still command far more attention from historians than peasants, and men than women. But the surrender of intellectual monopoly by the guardians of tradition (despite regular and well-publicized rearguard actions from champions of the old hat and the new right) has released non-traditional areas and approaches from their ghettos. There has been not only a great increase in the quantity of historical work on areas other than Europe and North America, and on non-traditional subjects, but a much greater increase in quality. What used to be the backwoods of historical method, seemingly abandoned to cultivation by scissors and paste, are now at the frontiers of innovation, as the historiography of the Indian subcontinent, or of the Islamic world or traditional China, will furnish striking testimony.[8]

These developments in themselves are the province of other chapters, but one of their consequences is to foster the creation of a common agenda in world history. The enormous field of peasant studies, in which central interests of both Marxist and *annaliste* historiography converge with those of anthropology, offers an exuberantly fertile example of the ways in which fundamental research of high

---

8 At the textbook level compare Kulke and Rothermund 1986 with the comparatively recent and widely used narratives of Wolpert 1977 or Spear 1966. (Vol. 1, by Romila Thapar (1966) is far superior). The volumes of *The New Cambridge History of India*, ed. Gordon Johnson, since 1988, though regrettably treating only the last 500 years, exemplify modern historical writing at its best, as do Lapidus 1988 and Hourani 1991. For a valuable survey and discussion of the current state of Islamic historiography see Humphreys 1991. Fairbank provides comprehensive references to recent work together with a brilliant synthesis of its conclusions and implications.

quality feeds and is fed upon theoretical discussion at successively general levels. Geertz's (1963) investigation of the impact of Dutch colonization on wet rice cultivation in Java, Stein's (1980) analysis of the agrarian foundations of political power in medieval south India or Smith's (1959) account of the economics of the Tokugawa village not only stimulate continuing research and controversy in their own and other regions (e.g. Ludden 1985; Scott 1976; Popkin 1979) but are taken up in general discussion at increasingly general and theoretical levels,[9] while one of its leading exponents, the anthropologist Eric Wolf, is the author of an outstanding essay in modern world history, *Europe and the People without History*. The range and variety of questions now being treated with similar vigour and sophistication obviously includes all those which have traditionally been central to social theory, such as the political identity and role of the city (Humphreys 1991: 228–38; Lapidus 1969; Hourani and Stern 1970; Blake 1991; Skinner 1977; Rowe 1984; 1989), the structure and activity of merchant communities,[10] the formation and dynamics of governmental and cultural elites[11] and a wide range of associated issues including the history of science and technology,[12] family structures and gender roles,[13] and social deviance and marginality.[14] Despite the abundance of opportunity offered by subjects like pilgrimage, temples and their functions, or guilt systems (Christian 1972; Turner and Turner 1978; Stein 1960; Elvin 1984),[15] there has been surprisingly little comparative (or comparatively inspired) work in the areas of religious history other than those stressed by Weber; perhaps religion continues to be seen as belonging to the province of civilizational and diffusionist studies in which it has always figured so prominently (cf. Bentley 1993).

The integration of much of this work into broader comparative and thematic studies has been in recent years a regular, stimulating and often dramatically fruitful process. Several examples have already been mentioned; others include the elegant and thoughtful essays of Philip Curtin (1984; 1989; 1990) on cross-cultural trade, Geoffrey Parker's (1988) lively discussion of the early modern 'military revolution', or the powerful reinterpretation by C. A. Bayly (1988; 1989) and others of the foundations of British imperialism, which also raises afresh the old but vital question of how far European capitalist imperialism halted the political and

---

9   e.g. Moore 1966, Skocpol 1979. It is hardly necessary to emphasize what an arbitrary selection from what an enormous field this is; see, e.g., Shanin 1989.

10   For a recent and exhaustive survey, with valuable critical bibliography, see Tracy 1990 and 1991.

11   The subject is far too large for systematic reference. For recent work on important aspects of these questions see, for example, Humphreys 1991: 187–208; Richards 1993; Fairbank 1992: 443–9; Powis 1984. Randomly chosen but contrasting and important studies (as in the following notes) include Waldron 1990; Huang 1981; Mottahedeh 1985; Bayly 1983.

12   Inspired by Needham 1954–, on which see Elvin *et al.* 1980: Mokyr 1990; Headrick 1981.

13   Another topic on which any attempt to list recent work would be futile, but see for examples Casey 1989; Ahmed 1992; Ebrey 1991.

14   e.g. the very fine and explicitly comparative studies of Dols 1992; Kuhn 1990.

15   Hansen 1989 raises issues which might be much more widely explored in comparative contexts.

economic progress of other advanced societies of the Old World, and where otherwise they were headed (e.g. Elvin 1973; Sivin 1980; Perlin 1983). The list might be endless. Most historical research, however brilliant and progressive, is not conceived in the context of world history, or primarily intended to contribute to it. World history cannot ignore it on that account. It is and must remain dependent for its data on work which is planned, undertaken and executed in a more limited perspective. A primary task of world historians, therefore, is continuously to integrate the conclusions of research and debate in numerous fields into a series of larger perspectives, of which some, though not all, will aspire to be total perspectives. One of their important needs and uses will be to encourage the identification of fresh problems for investigation, and the development of common methodologies and agenda across fields so distant that their cultivators are scarcely aware of one anothers' existence. One of their important educational functions will be to sustain a shared awareness among specialists of the advances and innovations which are taking place in areas distant from their own. If historians are to have a common historical culture, in other words, and if history is to be a coherent intellectual discipline, the place of world history in the formation of historians will become increasingly important.

The writing of world history *tout court* has been less obviously successful. It is not self-evident what such a history should comprise, or how it can be written. It is in the nature of historians to limit their field: they can hardly do otherwise. Yet the random accumulation of regional and topical studies, however distinguished, will not of itself sustain a synthesis which is coherently conceived, consistently grounded, and chronologically and regionally balanced. The collective solution, so congenial to the ideal of the objective and disinterested pursuit of knowledge, is a chimera. Acton and his successors as editors of *The Cambridge Modern History* and its progeny have demonstrated all too successfully that his conception of 'a Universal History which is distinct from the combined history of all countries, is not a rope of sand but a continuous development, and not a burden on the memory but an illumination of the soul'[16] is unattainable by his chosen method of collaboration. The ill-assorted though occasionally very distinguished legions of the Cambridge *Histories*, which have now colonized almost the entire globe, have performed a far more useful service for much of it than they ever did for Europe by providing an elementary narrative where there was none before, and by persuading many fine scholars to commit themselves to print in a relatively accessible form. Nobody could accuse them of constituting a consistent, coherent or even memorable view of the human past, as the publishers in effect confessed when they decided to issue the second edition of the *Cambridge Ancient History* chapter by chapter.[17] The *History of Mankind* (1963–) undertaken by UNESCO after the Second World War (largely on the initiative of a quintessential Cantabrigian, though not a

---

16   Lord Acton, 'Letter to the Contributors to the Cambridge Modern History', in Stern 1957: 249.
17   The experiment was attempted with Vol. 1 (1968), but does not appear to have been a resounding success. The *New Cambridge History of India* (above, n. 8) is, of course, an exception to these remarks.

historian, Julian Huxley) was planned on the same principle, for much the same reasons and with even less success.[18] More might be expected of series in which each volume is written by a single author. Of these the most ambitious, following the model of the splendid *Évolution de l'humanité* launched in 1920 under the editorship of Henri Berr, which gave birth to acknowledged masterpieces in several fields, provided a grand conspectus of the discoveries of history and archaeology, but made little or no attempt at a systematic overview, even in the arrangement of their volumes. On the other hand, those which have explicitly offered a 'history of the world' have usually been organized as sets of national histories. We have yet to see a real equivalent for world history of the multivolume textbook Histories of England and of Europe which began to appear regularly at the end of the last century, one of the more humdrum but none the less staple harvests of professionalization.[19]

Current attempts to produce a coherent synthesis of world history rely, for the most part,[20] on one of two approaches, describing and comparing the development either of 'civilizations' or of 'world systems'. That the decades since McNeill's *The Rise of the West* and Roberts's *History of the World* have not seen those works surpassed in either sweep or quality is in part because the approach by 'civilizations' which they embody has seemed increasingly problematical. Nevertheless, it continues to provide the unit of much comparative and synthetic discussion. There is, for such purposes, great utility in the possibility which the 'civilization' provides, not only of limiting the number of variables with which it is necessary to deal, but of associating political, social and cultural systems in, as it were, the same package – so long as there is a sufficient degree of consensus that the packages in question do in fact constitute coherent entities of the kind that the argument requires. Unfortunately, such consensus is almost by definition undermined by the relentlessly differentiating accumulation of knowledge.

'Civilizations' have offered a unit of discourse for world history not only because of their apparent unity but because they have never appeared to be self-contained. At the root of their formation, as McNeill (1982: 77–9) insisted, it is always necessary to postulate (within whatever theoretical parameters) a widening of human contacts and a meeting of cultures, whether by means of the diffusion of religious visions, military or agricultural technologies, or patterns of trade. Consequently, civilizations also provide a convenient currency for the main alternative approach to synthesis, that through the history of trading networks which it is now fashionable to speak of as 'world systems'. In its purest form, with a hyphen, the world-system is the invention of Immanuel Wallerstein (1974; 1980;

---

18 Accounts of the project are contained in appendices to each volume. The UNESCO *General History of Africa* (Berkeley, 1981–) is constructed on the same principle.
19 The plan for the *Blackwell History of the World*, which will provide a comprehensive series of this kind, includes volumes defined both by regional and by global parameters.
20 Notable recent exceptions include Gellner 1988 and Stavrianos 1990, which describe respectively successive dominant forms of cognitive and of social organization, and Hicks 1969. All three titles are unhelpful, since only the last is organized as a continuous narrative, and a singularly lucid one.

1989) under the inspiration of Fernand Braudel, and in the great tradition of jargon (and because it has been translated from German) means almost the opposite of what it says – not a trading system which extends across the world, but, on the contrary, one which being self-sufficient constitutes a world of its own. Wallerstein's argument, reduced to caricature, is that the 'capitalist world-system' which was formed in the centuries after 1500 differed from its predecessors precisely in that it did come to dominate the entire world economy, but as 'a kind of social system the world had not really known before ... an economic, but not a political entity' (Wallerstein 1974: 15–16) whose profits were ultimately devoted to supporting the institutions and exponents of international capitalism instead of a bureaucratic superstructure like those of the traditional empires. Wallerstein's conception has been immensely controversial and immensely fruitful,[21] and has been widely applied, with varying degrees of fidelity, both to particular societies and periods and as the basis of general interpretations of world history.[22] Particularly pertinent to the present discussion is the persuasive and well-documented contention of Janet Abu Lughod (1989) that the trading networks of Asia and Europe – and almost as good a case might have been made for adding sub-Saharan Africa – were sufficiently integrated in the century or so before the Black Death to be regarded as a functioning world economy, without a corresponding political hegemony. The sweep and vigour of the argument developed over many years and publications by Andre Gunder Frank and Barry Gills that neither the accumulation of capital nor the construction of world-embracing trading networks was peculiarly a European, or indeed a modern activity at all promises to stimulate considerable progress towards the construction of a new synthesis, though it is difficult not to sympathize with Wallerstein's plea that in the process the concept of the world-system has become so general as to lose much of its usefulness ('World system versus world-systems: a critique' in Gunder Frank and Gills 1993).

In its original form Wallerstein's capitalist world-system represents an especially powerful approach to one of the crucial and most intractable sets of issues in the writing of world history, those associated with the causes and consequences of the emergence of industrial capitalism in Europe and North America.[23] A fascination with Western hegemony, frankly expressed in the title of one of the most successful synthetic discussions of recent years, E. L. Jones's *The European Miracle* (1981; 2nd edn, with discussion of reviews etc., 1987)[24] is itself one of the most obvious consequences of the hegemony which is exercised over the discussion of world history by Western historians. Not in spite but because of the centrality of the

---

21 See the essays collected in Gunder Frank and Gills 1993, with extensive references. I am most grateful to Gills and Frank for copies of their work.

22 The most influential is that of Braudel 1982–5. On Wallerstein (whose second volume is dedicated to Braudel) and world-economies see ibid III, 45–91.

23 For a wide-ranging and useful set of recent discussions, see Baechler *et al.* 1988.

24 Jones takes vigorous issue with himself in the more ambitious and more original *Growth Recurring: Economic Change in World History* (1988), which seems to have attracted much less attention, perhaps because its publisher was slow to provide a paperback edition.

question to so many aspects of social and economic history and theory, we can make no attempt here to consider it from any other point of view.

Triumphalism is out of fashion, and the tendency is much stronger to lament than to admire the manifestations and consequences of the European and North American impacts on the rest of the world over the last two or three centuries.[25] Conversely, Eurocentrism is now sustained not by conviction or complacency, or even by the weight of inertia contained within the traditional hegemony of European and American historiography, so much as by the fact that it is deeply embedded in both of the main forms currently available for the writing of synthetic world history, the comparative study of civilizations and world-system theory. The classical social theory in which both are rooted is itself largely a product of industrial capitalism, and largely designed to explain it. The assumption of European exceptionalism is shared by Max Weber and Karl Marx, however differently they valued it, and by virtually every influential thinker of their own and subsequent generations. Consequently, it has made little difference whether discussion is conducted in a spirit of complacency or apology: even where 'Europe', 'Islam', 'India' and 'China' have not been employed as the units of comparison, the absence or presence of the 'European city', the 'European family', the 'European merchant', 'European rationality' in government and in science and so on have continued until very recently indeed to dominate the agenda of almost all cross-cultural comparison.[26]

The theoretically limitless scope of world history and the actual abundance of material pose in intensified form a very old dilemma – how to maintain scientific respectability without fragmentation, and achieve synthesis at an acceptable scholarly level. Conversely, nothing has done more to give world history a bad name than its malleability to the uses of the fanatic, the false prophet and the propagandist, and at the workaday level of classroom and study no practical question is more urgent or more intractable than how to make a rational and manageable selection of topics for attention from the enormous wealth of information that stretches back into the remotest times. The Eurocentric character of both the theory and the historiography which is based on it might seem to deny the possibility of a rational, humane and dispassionate world history. Happily it is the result of circumstance rather than logical necessity. Almost all the recent works referred to in the preceding paragraphs will supply examples of increasing sensitivity and sophistication in detecting the culturally conditioned models and expectations which have pervaded so much of the historian's vocabulary (for a recent example, see Inden

---

25 Nevertheless, the importance and continuing influence of Rostow 1960, as reflected for example by Landes 1969 or North and Thomas 1973, must not be underrated.

26 It is not the responsibility of this chapter to trace the origins and nature of the general changes in epistemological and historical thought which have identified the tradition referred to in this paragraph as a discourse of imperialism, but we must note the impact on historians of Edward Said, *Orientalism* (1978); it is too soon to estimate whether his *The Culture of Imperialism* (1993) will be similarly influential. For a pertinent and invigorating defence of European rationality, however, see Gellner 1992.

1990). At a more systematic and a more cerebral level W. G. Runciman has provided a comparative account of social evolution of extraordinary range and power which, when absorbed, may go far towards relieving us of our dependence on Max Weber.[27] In one of the most remarkable of recent historical works, *Asia before Europe*, K. N. Chaudhuri has presented a strikingly original solution to the dilemma presented by the selection of problems and information, based on mathematical set theory, which provides a culture-free basis for defining identities, and one which, in his hands, has supported brilliant and evocative historical reconstruction.[28]

The task of synthesis is greatly magnified by the prospect of an expansion of historical knowledge which will dwarf all its predecessors. The birth of 'scientific history' in the nineteenth century and of the forms and ways in which it was written was the product of both liberalism and nationalism, of the information explosion produced by the opening of the archives of Europe's chanceries, and of the enormous growth of record- and information-creating activity of every kind which was inseparable from the emergence of modern society itself. In the same way the questions and methods of world history in the twenty-first century, as well as its conclusions, will be heavily shaped by analogous movements of state-formation – and state-destruction – across the world, especially since 1945, on one side, and a massive potential for the creation and preservation of historical materials inherent in the extension of governmental and corporate activity, of the diffusion of literacy and the construction of complex societies, and of the information revolution, on the other. The mundane tasks of listing, cataloguing and chronicling, securing intellectual and physical access both to materials and to audiences, the spade-work of the pioneer archivists, librarians and committee-men of the nineteenth century, will continue to demand the greatest part of both the physical and the intellectual resources available to history for a long time to come. It is only necessary to compare the extent to which Essex, say, or the Auvergne, has been pillaged for monographs on each of the last ten centuries or so, and to consider that (like our nineteenth-century predecessors) we are only beginning to exploit the resources that exist for the investigation of Hunan, Awadh or Benin – and those are examples from some of the longest- and best-researched regions of the non-European world – to grasp that writing the history of the greatest part of the world has barely begun.

Indeed the conditions for writing it have barely begun to be established. In most parts of the world, history remains subordinate to the demands of political power and religious doctrine. Even where that is not the case (as in India and Japan, and parts of South-east Asia, Africa and Latin America) limitation of resources and a

---

27   W. G. Runciman, *A Treatise on Social Theory: II Substantive Social Theory* (1989). The title, which is not calculated to seduce historians, is one of the few parts of the book that they can afford to ignore.

28   Chaudhuri 1990, with further methodological discussion in Chaudhuri 1993. Braudel, whose influence on Chaudhuri was very great, occasionally uses the language of set theory, notably and effectively in the concluding chapter of *Capitalism and Civilization*, vol. II, 'Society: "A Set of Sets"' (pp. 458–599), but as far as I know he did not propose or elaborate it as a general basis for historical method. I have discussed Chaudhuri's thesis at greater length in Moore 1993.

natural preoccupation with national and regional issues tends to keep historians isolated from each other, and to slow the entry of new contributors to the discussion of world history itself, which continues to be dominated by Europeans and Americans. The collapse of the Soviet Empire seems likely for the time being to narrow rather than expand the meaning of 'European' in that context. Much as in the nineteenth century, the opening of the records has been seen as both a consequence and a condition of liberation, and establishing the historical record is regarded on all sides as an essential weapon against tyranny. Wherever in the world old regimes and old dominations are giving way to new ones through blood or ballot box, wherever legitimacy is challenged or to be established, the battle for the past will be waged as passionately and as destructively as the battle for the future of which it is part. The freeing of history from myth and rhetoric of which we have spoken is itself an essential element of the modernization of society. There is no reason to suppose that it will proceed any less tortuously, brutally or remorselessly than the broader process of which it is part. The methodology of modern history, like that of modern science, is a product of the West, and liable to all the suspicion, justified and unjustified, which that implies. It is also, like modern science, slowly establishing a common discourse for a rational and humane cosmopolis. In that sense, and to that extent, Bury's much-derided optimism remains defensible. Meanwhile, unevenness both in the depth and variety of documentation and in the quality and agenda of scholarship will remain the greatest single limitation on the development and standing of world history. The extension of its base beyond the dominant cultures of the literate civilizations will be a very slow business, and world history itself will continue to be, with the exceptions mentioned above, to far too great an extent a debate between the historians of the developed world.

REFERENCES

Abu Lughod, J. (1989) *Before European Hegemony: The World System, 1250–1350*, New York.

Acton, Lord [1903] (1957) 'Letter to the contributors to the Cambridge Modern History', in Stern 1957.

Ahmed, L. (1992) *Women and Gender in Islam*, New Haven.

Allardyce, G. (1982) 'The rise and fall of the Western Civilization Course', *American Historical Review*: 695–725.

—— (1990) 'Towards world history: American historians and the coming of the world history course', *Journal of World History* 1(1): 23–76.

Baechler, J., Hall, J. A. and Mann, M. (eds) (1988) *Europe and the Rise of Capitalism*, Oxford.

Barfield, T. (1989) *The Perilous Frontier*, Oxford.

Barraclough, J. (1991) *Main Trends in History*, 2nd edn, New York.

Bayly, C. A. (1983) *Rulers, Townsmen and Bazaars*, Cambridge.

—— (1988) *Indian Society and the Making of the British Empire*, Cambridge.

—— (1989) *Imperial Meridian: The British Empire and the World, 1780–1830*, London.

Bendix, R. (1978) *Kings or People: Power and the Mandate to Rule*, Berkeley.

Bentley, J. H. (1993) *Old World Encounters: Cross Cultural Contacts and Exchanges in Premodern Times*, Oxford.

Bernal, M. (1987) *Black Athena: The Afro-Asiatic Roots of Classical Civilization*, New Brunswick.

Blake, S. P. (1991) *Shahjahanabad: The Sovereign City in Mughal India 1639–1739*, Cambridge.

Braudel, F. (1982–5) *Civilization and Capitalism, 15th–18th Century*, tr. S. Reynolds; 1: *The Structures of Everyday Life*; 2: *The Wheels of Commerce*; 3: *The Perspective of the World*, London.

Bury, J. B. [1903] (1957) 'The science of history', in Stern 1957.

Casey, J. (1989) *The History of the Family*, Oxford.

Chaudhuri, K. N. (1990) *Asia before Europe*, Cambridge.

—— (1993) 'The unity and disunity of Indian Ocean history from the rise of Islam to 1750', *Journal of World History* 4(1): 1–21.

Christian, D. (1991) 'The case for "big history"', *Journal of World History* 2(2): 223–8.

Christian, W. A. (1972) *Person and God in a Spanish Valley*, New York.

Clark, G. (1977) *World Prehistory*, 3rd edn, Cambridge.

Cohen, B. S. (1987) *An Anthropologist among the Historians*, Delhi and New York.

Crosby, A. W. (1986) *Ecological Imperialism: The Biological Expansion of Europe, 900–1900*, Cambridge.

Curtin, P. D. (1984) *Cross-Cultural Trade in World History*, Cambridge.

—— (1989) *Death by Migration: Europe's Encounter with the Tropical World in the Nineteenth Century*, Cambridge.

—— (1990) *The Rise and Fall of the Plantation Complex*, Cambridge.

—— (1991) 'Graduate teaching in world history', *Journal of World History* 2(1): 81–9.

Dols, M. (1992) *Majnun: The Madman in Medieval Islamic Society*, Oxford.

Ebrey, P. B. (1991) *Confucianism and Family Rituals in Imperial China*, Princeton.

Eisenstadt, S. N. (1963) *The Political Systems of Empires*, London.

Elvin, M. (1973) *Patterns of the Chinese Past*, London.

—— (1984) 'Female virtue and the state in China', *Past and Present* 104: 111–52.

—— et al. (1980) 'The work of Joseph Needham', *Past and Present* 87: 15–53.

Evans, R. J. (1987) *Death in Hamburg*, Oxford.

Fairbank, J. K. (1992) *China: A New History*, Cambridge, Mass.

Fentress, J. and Wickham, C. (1992) *Social Memory*, Oxford.

Geertz, C. (1963) *Agricultural Involution: The Processes of Ecological Change in Indonesia*, Berkeley.

Gellner, E. (1988) *Plough, Sword and Book: The Structure of Human History*, London.

—— (1992) *Reason and Culture*, Oxford.

Green, W. A. (1992) 'Periodization in European and world history', *Journal of World History* 3(1): 13–53.

Gunder Frank, A. and Gills, B. K. (eds) (1993) *The World System: Five Hundred Years of Five Thousand?*, London.

Hansen, V. (1989) *Changing Gods in Medieval China*, Princeton.

Headrick, D. R. (1981) *The Tools of Empire*, Oxford.

Hicks, J. (1969) *A Theory of Economic History*, Oxford.

Hodges, R. (1988) *Primitive and Peasant Markets*, Oxford.

Hodgson, G. S. (1993) *Rethinking World History*, Cambridge.

Holt, P. M. (ed.) (1970) *Cambridge History of Islam*, Cambridge.

Hourani, A. (1991) *A History of the Arab Peoples*, London.

—— and Stern, S. M. (eds) (1970) *The Islamic City*, Oxford.

Huang, R. (1981) *1587: A Year of no Significance*, New Haven, CT.

Humphreys, R. S. (1991) *Islamic History: A Framework for Inquiry*, rev. edn, London and New York.

Inden, E. (1992) *Reason and Culture*, Oxford.

Inden, R. B. (1990) *Imagining India*.

Jones, E. L. (1987) *The European Miracle*, 2nd edn, Cambridge.

—— (1988) *Growth Recurring: Economic Change in World History*, Oxford.

Kuhn, P. A. (1990) *Soulstealers: The Chinese Sorcery Scare of 1768*, Cambridge, MA.

Kulke, H. and Rothermund, D. (1986) *A History of India*, London.

Landes, D. S. (1969) *The Unbound Prometheus*, Cambridge.

Lapidus, I. M. (ed.) (1969) *Middle Eastern Cities*, Berkeley.

Lapidus, I. M. (1988) *A History of Islamic Societies*, Cambridge.

Ludden, D. (1985) *Peasant History in South India*, Princeton.

McNeill, W. H. (1976) *Plagues and Peoples*, Oxford.

—— (1980) *The Human Condition: An Ecological and Historical View*, Princeton.

—— (1982) 'A defence of world history', *Transactions of the Royal Historical Society* 5(32): 75–89.

Mann, M. (1988) *The Sources of Social Power*, vol. 1, Cambridge.

Mokyr, J. (1990) *The Lever of Riches. Technological Creativity and Economic Progress*, Oxford.

Moore, B. (1966) *Social Origins of Dictatorships and Democracy: Lord and Peasant in the Making of the Modern World*, Boston.

Moore, R. I. (1993) 'World history: world-economy or a set of sets?', *Journal of the Royal Asiatic Society*, 3rd ser., 3(1): 99–105.

Mottahedeh, R. (1985) *The Mantle of the Prophet*, London.

Needham, J. H. (1954–) *Science and Civilisation in China*, Cambridge.

North, D. C. and Thomas, R. P. (1973) *The Rise of the Western World*, Cambridge.

Novick, P. (1988) *That Noble Dream*, Cambridge.

Parker, G. (1988) *The Military Revolution: Military Innovation and the Rise of the West, 1500–1800*, Cambridge.

Perlin, F. (1983) 'Proto-industrialisation in pre-colonial South Asia', *Past and Present* 98: 30–95.

Popkin, S. (1979) *The Rational Peasant*, Berkeley.

Powis, J. (1984) *Aristocracy*, Oxford.

Richards, J. F. (1993) *The Mughal Empire*, Cambridge.

Roberts, J. M. (1976) *The Hutchinson History of the World*, London. (Frequently reprinted with variations of title and imprint.)

Rostow, W. W. (1960) *The Stages of Economic Growth*, Cambridge.

Rowe, W. T. (1984) *Hankow: Commerce and Society in a Chinese City, 1796–1889*, Stanford.

—— (1989) *Hankow: Conflict and Community in a Chinese City, 1796–1895*, Stanford.

Runciman, W. G. (1989) *A Treatise on Social Theory, 2: Substantive Social Theory*, Cambridge.

Said, E. (1978) *Orientalism*, London.

—— (1993) *The Culture of Imperialism*, London.

Scott, J. C. (1976) *The Moral Economy of the Present*, New Haven, CT.

Shanin, T. (1989) *Peasants and Peasant Societies*, 2nd edn, Oxford.

Simmons, I. G. (1993) *Environmental History: A Concise Introduction*, Oxford.

Sivin, N. (1980) 'Imperial China: has its present past a future?', *Harvard Journal of Asiatic Studies* 38: 741–8.

Skinner, G. W. (ed.) (1977) *The City and in Late Imperial China*, Stanford.

Skocpol, T. (1979) *States and Social Revolutions*, Cambridge.

Smith, T. C. (1959) *The Agrarian Origins of Modern Japan*, Stanford.

Spear, P. (1966) *The Pelican History of India*, vol. 2, Harmondsworth.

Stavrianos, L. S. (1990) *Lifelines from our Past: A New World History*, London.

Stein, B. (1960) 'Economic functions of a medieval south Indian temple', *Journal of Asian Studies* 19(2): 163–76.

—— (1980) *Peasant, State and Society in Medieval South India*, Oxford.

Stern, F. (1957) *The Varieties of History*, London.

Thapar, R. (1966) *The Pelican History of India*, vol. 1, Harmondsworth.

Thomson, D. (1965) *World History*, 3rd edn, Oxford.

Tracy, J. D. (ed.) (1990) *The Rise of Merchant Empires: Long Distance Trade in the Early Modern World, 1350–1750*, Cambridge.

—— (1991) *The Political Economy of Merchant Empires*, Cambridge.

Trevelyan, G. M. [1913] (1957) *Clio, a Muse and Other Essays*, repr. in Stern 1957.

Trevor-Roper, H. (1965) *The Rise of Christian Europe*, London.

Turner, V. and Turner, E. (1978) *Image and Pilgrimage in Christian Culture*, New York.

Vadney, T. E. (1990) 'World history as an advanced academic field', *Journal of World History* 1(2): 201–23.

Waldron, A. (1990) *The Great Wall of China*, Cambridge.

Wallerstein, I. (1974) *The Modern World System, 1: Capitalist Agriculture and the Origins of the European World-Economy in the Sixteenth Century*, New York.

—— (1980) *The Modern World System, 2: Mercantilism and the Consolidation of the European World-Economy, 1600–1750*, New York.

—— (1989) *The Modern World System, 3: The Second Era of Great Expansion of the Capitalist World-Economy, 1730–1840s*, New York.

Wolf, E. R. (1982) *Europe and the People without History*, Berkeley.

Wolpert, S. (1977) *A New History of India*, New York.

39

ARCHIVES, THE HISTORIAN AND THE FUTURE

Michael Moss

Archivists have until recently rarely perceived the need to defend the preservation of documents for historical scholarship. The profession after all grew out of the emergence of history from its antiquarian antecedents into a scientific subject. Manuscripts were to the humanities what observable natural phenomena were to the sciences. Like natural phenomena they were open to different interpretations; but their central position in *Geschichtswissenschaft* was taken as axiomatic. Throughout Europe in the late eighteenth century the discovery and rescue of archives became an important preoccupation of scholars and later of government – a question of national prestige. Archives of nations subsumed within larger states were considered vital in the preservation or creation of distinct cultural identities, particularly where such nations had a common language. At first attention concentrated on medieval records, moving quickly to the modern period in an effort to preserve the papers of individuals and powers which had participated in the great events that had culminated in the defeat of Napoleon. Until the twentieth century the focus remained on great events, great men and government. National archives were established to preserve the bewildering mass of records produced by modern bureaucracies. Archive commissions busily investigated the contents of cathedrals, monastic houses, corporate institutions and the homes of great families. Some owners of important collections of manuscripts published elaborate catalogues, transcripts and sometimes facsimiles of their holdings. As the German concept of *Geschichte* spread in the late nineteenth century and as history became an accepted component of a revised university curriculum, it was to these manuscripts that the new profession of academic historians turned both for their own research and for that of their students engaged in advanced study. The care of manuscripts and their interpretation as objects, itself became a separate profession with its own skills in palaeography and *diplomatique* that demanded considerable scholarly expertise.

In the early twentieth century historical interests began to change reflecting a transformation in attitudes and perceptions throughout European and North American society. Liberal ideas informed by Hegelian Idealism and socialist aspirations informed by Marx shifted attention towards the function of the individual in society and by extension to the economy. Understanding of societies and economies required the collection of a more extensive and bulky range of archives, particularly records relating to individuals. In much of Europe since the early sixteenth century churches and government had collected information about individuals for whole variety of purposes – baptism, catechism, confirmation, marriage, burial, military service, censuses, admission to poorhouses or prison, and so on. At the same time as government became more formal and extensive, there was a need to raise regular and greater taxes both locally and nationally on individuals and on trade. At various times taxation demanded the accurate recording of property, income, estates at death, imports, exports, and the production and sale of certain goods (for example alcoholic drinks and salt). In addition many regimes themselves became engaged directly in trade and industry, which left behind large accumulations of paper. Apart from all these routine records, the rapid growth of modern states in the nineteenth century had caused major social and economic problems that had been addressed by governments through special inquiries that collected huge volumes of statistical observations.

The use by historians of such transactional records of government posed new problems for archivists; not simply in terms of their bulk. Their interpretation demanded new skills far removed from the training or experience of many existing custodians. What circumstances had led to the creation and modification of the records? How reliable were they? Although they clearly contained a great deal of information about people and economic activity, they would be used for purposes for which they had not been created. Correspondence about a battle, a building or a political event was written for that purpose; a customs account or an entry for a catechumen in a register were demonstrably not recorded to answer the questions of later generations about transatlantic trade or about patterns of migration in early modern Scandinavia. In seeking answers to these questions historians and archivists looked for sources that would complement and contextualize transactions. The search was extended to include the records of property and enterprises owned by great families and institutions, the papers of lesser families and 'ordinary' people, and the archives of businesses. Many of these were to be found amongst the vast collections of legal evidence preserved in local and central courts, which even today are often inaccessible. Others were held by notaries and solicitors, and by families and businesses themselves.

To accommodate the mountain of records that were turning up in Europe, North America and elsewhere in the world, archive provision became more plural as embryo repositories or manuscript departments were set up by regional and local governments, by universities, by museums, and by businesses and institutions. This led to tensions. National repositories that had made a virtue of collecting records of 'national significance' now found themselves under academic pressure to accept modern records that would under existing criteria not have been preserved and in competition for new accessions. Speaking in Paris at the first International Congress on Archives in 1950 Sir Hilary Jenkinson declared:

> De plus, on peut ajouter qu'il y a encore beaucoup à faire pour faire comprendre au public ce fait que les archives modernes doivent être aussi importantes que les archives anciennes et qu'en fait, un jour elles seront elles-mêmes anciennes. Le problème est également d'arriver à disposer de ces archives. Vous avez à ce sujet-là la question du lieu où l'on peut mettre de grands dépôts d'archives. Il faut savoir si ces archives sont considérées comme étant d'un intérêt national véritable ou si, au contraire, elles ne sont que d'un intérêt local.

This statement, redolent of the Anglo-Saxon approach to *Geschichtsforschung*, was in stark contrast to the aims and ambitions of the recently established *Annales* group in the École Pratique des Hautes Études in Paris, which knew no such distinction. They were determined to move away from the narrative history of great events towards the rigorous, often statistical, analysis of the rich sources (particularly the mass of transactional records) now available to explore the past from differing local and national perspectives. This was to be done not by the lone scholar working year in and year out in a great library, but by research teams (*équipes*) of historians often working in different parts of the country and later different countries on related themes designed to inform common questions. Inevitably such *équipes* had to be interdisciplinary to include statisticians, sociologists, economists and shortly computer programmers. Even today, with a few notable exceptions, such an approach is foreign to Anglo-Saxon scholarship and it is hard unless you have been a member of such an *équipe* to explain its intellectual excitement.

In the post-war years universities expanded rapidly, recruiting staff and encouraging research across all disciplines. Demand for staff with postgraduate qualifications led to the exploitation of archives on an unprecedented scale, financed for the most part by public funds. The establishment of new universities reinforced the development of local and specialist archives, which in turn encouraged the emergence of centres of research dedicated to specific themes, topics or methodologies. Some universities, particularly those in North America with generous benefactions, began buying manuscripts in Europe and even in India and the Far East in support of research centres. Although national archives shared in this growth, they increasingly became part – albeit as a senior partner – of a plural system. Amongst many historians the narrative tradition persisted; but a large number were influenced by the social science method if not the teamwork approach of the *annalistes*. Consequently they wished to experiment with new types of evidence: oral tradition, recorded memories and images. Some of these had been collected since the mid-nineteenth century; but often for different purposes, such as the recording of unwritten languages, folk music and dance. After the Second World War historians were able to collect such material in far greater quantities using the new technologies, and they shifted the emphasis towards contemporary events such as the experience of the Holocaust or the resistance movement in Austria to the *Anschluß*. Although archivists, most of whom, if they had been trained at all, had been trained in narrative schools and in traditional paper technology, found the new methodologies difficult to comprehend, they were willing to collect records in their support, because most such material was to be found locally and therefore helped local archive centres to develop. Little or no attempt was made to discriminate between collections – all records were worth keeping and if historians did not use them today they would tomorrow or in a hundred years' time.

There were other less direct but equally important changes in scholarly approaches to history, which stemmed in part from the *annaliste* method and in part from a growing interest in the development of science and technology. From at least the mid-nineteenth century there had been a fascination with industrial and commercial success, which produced such best-selling works as Samuel Smiles's *Lives of the Engineers*, 1861–2. In the wake of the massive industrial changes after the Second World War, the most obvious expression of these interests was in what became known as 'industrial archaeology', a concern to record and preserve the buildings and artefacts of the motors of economic change. This was accompanied by a recognition that the study of buildings and of urban and rural landscapes was critical to the interpretation of the past. Interest extended far beyond the efforts to preserve the great houses of Europe and colonial America, which had started in the late nineteenth century. Landscapes were also not to be preserved just because they were picturesque, but because they were of historical or natural interest. Architects and planners, particularly those involved in the massive reconstruction of bomb-damaged Europe, wanted to know what buildings and landscapes looked like so they could be faked. They naturally turned to archives in search of drawings and photographs. Industrial archaeologists, most of whom worked in loose teams, hunted for historic maps, photographs and technical drawings. Archaeologists, responding to concerns with trade and the 'ordinary', extended their activities into the more recent past where supporting documentary and oral evidence was more plentiful. By the 1990s with the fashion for ideas of 'sustainability' and conservation these approaches to the past had won a large following. For the archivist they presented a further range of difficulties. Collections of both architectural and technical drawings are bulky and difficult to interpret without specialist knowledge, as industrial historians discovered. From the late nineteenth century they were also often made on special materials that require expensive conservation. Likewise early photographs were mostly taken on glass negatives and few archivists or archival conservators have any specialist knowledge in this area.

The transformation of history from a cottage craft into an industry was accompanied by an equally rapid growth of 'local' and 'family' history. In its beginnings history as a scientific discipline owed much to antiquarian scholars, who rescued, transcribed and published documents, wrote learned articles, and helped teach the subject in universities when it was first introduced. As their profession became established, academic historians affected to disparage antiquarians and yet the antiquarian tradition survives everywhere in Europe and North America in a welter of local and specialist record and history publications. Until the mid-twentieth century antiquarian pursuits were on the whole the recreation of professional people with scholarly backgrounds – clergymen, doctors, lawyers and the gentry. Mass education, the availability locally of freely accessible archives and the increase in early retirement were to change this. From the 1950s 'history' was colonized by enthusiasts with well-defined interests, their parish, their family, their house, a locality, ships, postage stamps, railways, locomotives, beer, gardens and so on – all with long pedigrees in scholarly and popular literature. At their worst these enthusiasts are mere collectors of 'interesting' facts; at their best the enormous and highly specialized literature which they produce makes a vital contribution to debates and furthers research. Critically for the archivist, the enthusiast depends for sources on the records that began to be collected in such quantities to sustain developments in economic and social history. Family historians use registers of baptisms, catechumens, marriages, burials and probates very heavily. They now form the large constituency of users in national, regional, local and even most specialist repositories. University archives as far apart as Graz and Glasgow receive far more enquiries about former students than requests from scholars and students.

Local history was also exploited by teachers and archivists to make the school curriculum seem more relevant. It was argued that children could understand the First World War better if they could relate events to Great Grandpa Otto or Bill than if they simply learned the progress and outcome of events. Packs of original documents were prepared for use in the classroom and 'imaginative' projects devised drawing on a range of evidence – the local landscape, buildings, museum holdings, memories as well as documents. These initiatives, designed to illuminate general historical themes, were a prelude to much more radical changes in the curriculum with an emphasis on discovery or student-centred learning. Across the curriculum schoolchildren were encouraged to undertake projects (the bane of parents' lives) that would demonstrate both personal response and detective (research) skills. Schoolchildren have become in the 1990s research students without the necessary methodological skills or framework of historical reference. The undergraduate syllabus has been similarly transformed with greater emphasis on dissertations and the exploration of historical data. As a result archivists have found themselves having to provide advice and guidance to pupils and students in search of the novel rather than the attainable.

This explosion in the use of archives by enthusiasts and students changed completely the outlook of most record offices. The close links that had existed with the scholarly community broke, and even national record offices became driven by the needs of enthusiasts, who in the post-war liberal world expected access to be free to all documents, whether public or private. Deterioration in relation with academic historians was more pronounced in some countries than in others. In the English-speaking world and in the Nordic countries this was partly of the archivists' own doing. In an effort to differentiate themselves from historians, they evolved an ethos in which they provided the documents (often with an extensive critical apparatus covering questions of provenance, style and authenticity) for the historian to interpret within the context of wider historical debates. This distancing of the archival profession from academic history was confirmed by the development of procedures needed to manage non-current modern records before the selection of 'historically interesting' material and transfer to archive repositories. Records management has now developed in many parts of the world into a separate profession from that of archives. In German- and French-speaking countries and in most of central Europe, a different tradition of the scholar-archivist persisted. In these countries archivists are often very well qualified both as academic historians and as archivists; but even they have not been immune to the demands of the enthusiasts and the pressures of the information managers.

In all countries archivists have steadily arrogated to themselves the right to be the final arbiters of what records are deemed to be 'historically interesting' and therefore worthy of long-term preservation. Since they have to negotiate the budgets for their services this is understandable; but it leaves them very exposed to criticism from scholars that important material that will inform new debates and disciplines is being discarded. Indeed some specialist archives owe their origin to an academic conviction that records were either unnecessarily and wantonly being destroyed or simply being overlooked by existing provision. Academics are uneasy that selection criteria and cataloguing priorities reflect either current use in record-office search rooms by family historians and enthusiasts or economic expediency, rather than the long-term needs of the discipline. For their part archivists are concerned that many historians in the social science or *annaliste* tradition will combine with family historians to force the retention of huge series of personal transactional data whose very bulk precludes investigation. They can point to large collections on their shelves that they have been persuaded to accept, but are rarely used. The sheer bulk of modern records and the fact that procedures are in place to ensure that they are considered for long-term preservation demands selectivity. Neither historians nor archivists have engaged in any meaningful debate about how suitable criteria can be agreed. For personal data (with the exception of records of births, marriages and deaths) statistically sound sampling techniques must be employed. Both archivists and historians, particularly those trained in the narrative tradition, are deeply suspicious of such statistical methods, preferring the retention of records of whole populations. Other types of records pose problems of significance and relevance where decisions on retention have of necessity to be subjective. They could undoubtedly be improved if efforts were made to re-establish the dialogue between historians and archivists.

Some historians and archivists believe that decisions about selection will gradually cease as more and more records are held in machine-readable form. This is very questionable and in any case only applies to records created in the future in systems where long-term management is considered important at the outset. For example, most personal records held on computers are derived from forms; and such sets of data can only be considered to be archivally complete if they include all the information on the form. If items are excluded, then the dataset cannot by most criteria be considered to be the original record. Scrutiny of datasets often reveals that entries have been 'normalized': in other words variant spellings have been standardized and mistakes rectified. To some later historians the fact that someone could not spell or write well may be significant. Certain sets of personal data are very bulky, for example hospital case notes, criminal records and tax files. In these cases it is improbable that all the data will in the foreseeable future be held in machine-readable form. It is likely therefore that the archivist's task will be complicated rather than simplified by the existence of large datasets of personal records, which are already being kept in specialist (usually national) data archives. The archivist will have to draw statistically sound samples from the datasets to determine which of the actual files are to be preserved in the long term, while at the same time preserving the dataset to provide the overall context.

Narrative sources in machine-readable form present a far more complex problem. The IT (Information Technology) industry has stolen the terminology of the archivist and records manager – notably the 'archive' and the 'file'; but not their meanings. In the IT world 'archive' does not imply selection criteria or permanent preservation, and 'file' does not equate to the organized contents of a physical file. However, in approaching machine-readable text the archivist and historian have to forget these meanings and develop new frameworks of reference. There is no doubt that most narrative documents throughout the world are being produced on computers, and software, and that mark-up protocols are being developed to allow vast bulks of text to be searched very rapidly to locate references to specific information. This would suggest that the physical file of records as we know it may disappear. Paper filing, as all historians and archivists know, is wasteful, involving much duplication as documents inevitably relate to more than one subject or individual. In any case, filing is expensive in labour and space. Instead, marked-up documents will be held in text bases that can be searched freely and easily transported to other platforms. The danger for the archivist and historian in this new world is that a great deal will be lost unless adequate management controls are imposed. Crucially, what may be missing from the documents themselves are the drafts and redrafts, which clog paper files but show clearly how a policy or decisions evolved and who was responsible. Even where drafts are retained it may be difficult to attribute changes in thinking to individuals. In addition, where confidential documents only exist in machine readable form, destruction is all too easy. The historian will be able to explore such text bases much more easily than paper-based records and employ sophisticated content analysis techniques, but will be left with formidable problems of bulk in writing narrative history. The archivist will need to learn a further range of computational skills.

New technology may solve some of the problems of bulk and selection in the future, but it will do little to reduce existing accumulations of paper. Scanning typewritten records is both expensive and problematic, and the scanning of hand-written records is even more costly and uncertain. This is not say that scanning will not be used to create text bases, it will; but not for any significant proportion of current holdings. Computers, however, have long been recognized by both academic historians and enthusiasts as providing the means of unlocking information held in long runs of bulky observation data. Historians from the 1960s have been engaged in building datasets and more recently text bases to address specific historical questions, often employing teams of researchers to abstract and code data. There is an active methodological debate about data-entry techniques, which has much in common with earlier discussions about the relative merits of calendaring and cataloguing – should the dataset be an accurate transcription of the original, should it be normalized, should it be coded and should it include data not needed for the current project? In the early days when only numeric processing was possible these questions more or less answered themselves. With the advent of alpha-numeric processing in the 1980s and new generations of software they have to be addressed from the outset. Invariably a database, particularly a relational database where data is held in more than one table, is only an approximation of the original data, even if efforts have been made to respect the integrity of the source, for the simple reason that entries need to be enriched and normalized to permit analysis. For example, at a simple level a place name needs to be supplemented in the same or another table with the name of a parish, a locality, a region and even a country. Likewise occupations need to be coded and decisions taken about multiple job descriptions very common until recent times—do they represent two or three separate jobs or should they be counted as a half or a third, and was one job more important than another? In both data and text bases there is a temptation to combine data from other sources, just as there was in the critical apparatus that supported calendars. If the identity of an individual in a source is known, why not add the extra information? Archivists will assume that data and text bases, like transcripts, while they enhance access are no substitute for the originals. In any event the cost of their creation will prevent only but a small fraction of existing paper based holdings ever being available in machine-readable form.

Data and text bases will continue to be constructed by academics, enthusiasts and perhaps more importantly by archivists themselves as guides and catalogues to their holdings. National, local and specialist archives have been using computers for nearly as long as academics; in some cases research databases double as archive catalogues. Throughout the world the standard and depth of archive catalogues is very variable. Whatever their level, they mostly require elaborate indexing by names, places and sometimes subject or theme. As all historians and most archivists know, paper-based catalogues and indexes, especially those in large national repositories, are frustrating to use, largely because they are full of internal incon-sistencies in conventions. This is not necessarily the fault of the archivist and often reflects changes in procedures to take account of perceived developments in the historical sciences. Where funds allow, efforts are being made to convert catalogues into machine-readable format, either as databases or text bases, in order to make the information they contain much more accessible and to save the expense of elaborate indexing. Such initiatives are not without dilemmas. Existing catalogues often lack an adequate critical apparatus explaining provenance and background. To sustain thematic enquiry they need to be supported by thesauri and subject indexes. Moreover, many catalogues are old, placing emphasis on the historical concerns of the period when they were produced. None the less, making catalogues available in this way can only be welcome, providing users understand their weaknesses.

Searches using even the most sophisticated software can be guaranteed not to locate all the material that might be of interest. This is most obvious in information contained within an individual 'piece' – for instance a ledger, a letterbook or a diary – but will also be the case where individual items within a group are not separately catalogued.

The very existence of on-line catalogues, research data and text bases, and machine-readable archives, is already generating demands for access. This in turn poses problems for the archivist of validation, documentation, standardization and dissemination. Some of these are familiar, others derive from the new technology. Until recently, data and text bases were the responsibility of specialist national data archives, which set standards, compiled documentation and had the skills to move data between different platforms. Such national data archives will continue to have an important role, particularly in the maintenance of national datasets such as those containing population information. However, as compatibility between different software and machine platforms becomes less of an issue, as the Internet develops and the volume of machine-readable records explodes, so more and more data will be held locally, following rather more rapidly the development of archive services themselves. Remote access over the Internet in the immediate future will be differential, as some institutions in some countries have free connections to the Internet while others face high subscription rates. In the long term the experience of other IT developments suggests that costs will fall; but almost certainly existing free provision will be replaced with charges.

Undoubtedly, over the next century the 'superhighway' will greatly enhance access to historical records, many of which will be in machine-readable form for the contemporary period. The historian, working in St Petersburg, will be able to analyse data, text and image bases held in Washington or in Delhi with little difficulty, using powerful tools. In this scenario some argue that the archivist will become simply an information provider, just another byway on a superhighway jammed with data overload. The development of the historical and archive professions suggests that this is fanciful nonsense. It remains to be seen if global access to information will create convergence in any practices; it could just as easily lead to greater divergence as nations and regions seek to assert their identities. For all the claims made for text and image analysis using emerging mark-up tools like SGML and HTML, it is difficult to conceive what they can offer beyond content analysis that will allow documents or paintings to be ascribed with far greater certainty through the identification of images with similar characteristics. The historian will still have to interact with sources and there will be far more of them. The archivist will still have to select, organize, explain and reference; but perhaps not catalogue (in the traditional sense) machine-readable collections. It is difficult to believe that the global archive accessed down the superhighway represents anything more than a quantitative rather than a qualitative change in approaches to the past.

Historians of all complexions and interests will continue to be concerned about times before the advent of computers. There will still be vast accumulations of paper archives and it would be safe to assume that such traditional holdings will continue to grow, particularly in countries unable to afford mass access to the new technology. In the developed world all that can be hoped for is that the superhighway will continue to improve access to these collections through better on-line finding aids. New data, text and image bases will be created, but they will never represent anything more than a fraction of the totality of holdings. Although it will be possible to obtain copies of documents over the superhighway relatively cheaply, this will be no substitute for visiting archives. Experience suggests that far from reducing visits, on-line information to whatever depth of cataloguing increases both the number of visits and the volume of productions. For most, visiting an archive will continue to be straightforward, as the majority of users will remain predominantly local. However good the on-line catalogues, visitors to search rooms will still need assistance with palaeography, the meanings of words in the past, dialect spellings and so on. The archivist will also have to provide help and guidance to the historians surfing the Internet through navigational aids on the superhighway itself and by direct brokerage. Current thinking amongst archivists and rare book librarians suggests that this brokerage activity (helping readers locate other sources relevant to their research) will become more important as IT reduces the number of routine tasks.

There is nothing to suggest that historians will be less interested in using archives. In the written cultures that have dominated European, Middle Eastern and Eastern cultures for over two millennia, it would be strange if it were otherwise. The definition of what constitutes an archive will continue to change and extend to include new types of evidence, but it is already accepted that the term is simply a useful metaphor for a certain type of historical evidence which together with others contributes towards a holistic understanding of the past. As has happened already with images and oral recordings, these new types of evidence will present the archivist with new problems of description and conservation; but on past experience these will not be insurmountable. There will also be a continued blurring of the boundaries between printed literature and archives as more material is disseminated in machine-readable form. This is likely to present more of a problem to librarians than to archivists, because of the rigid nature of international bibliographical reference procedures. Already some librarians are demanding more flexible systems – akin to those used by archivists – in response to their changing role in information management. Where big developments can be expected is in the complementary use of physical objects held in museum reserve collections, which are being made much more accessible by the use of new technology. This in turn will transform museums back into repositories, making them more like archives.

The massive expansion in archive services throughout Europe and North America in the last fifty years has been largely funded by government, either local or national. In recent years cuts in government expenditure, coupled with the challenge to the liberal attitudes that characterized the post-war world, have squeezed funding at a time when demand has been growing rapidly. Costs have also been rising, partly through increased use but also through the introduction of new technology, which for all its advantages is expensive. Participating in the global archive will add even further costs. Archivists have on the whole resisted charging for access. They have used the management of the modern paper records of their employers as one means of cross-subsidizing historical services. With the growth of machine-readable data managed by information professionals this will become less possible. Many archives have generated income through the sale of copies of documents, plans and photographs to enthusiasts. Some, following the example of libraries and museums, have established associations of friends. Others now charge depositors and undertake paid research work for users, particularly for the ubiquitous family historians. Most solicit donations and many seek independent grants for specific cataloguing projects. As government funding is reduced, so pressures to raise more external income increase.

The concept of charging is not simply a response to reduced budgets, it is bound up with notions about the free market and transparency of transactions. It is argued that if an archive provides a records management service this should be properly costed and charged for. If enthusiasts have to pay for other recreations, then why should they not pay to use archives? Schools and universities buy services, why should they not also buy archive and library services? Are archives in one country to be freely available to *bona fide* scholars from another? Concepts of purchaser and provider relationships pervade democratic countries whose citizens' freedoms have in part been assured by rights of free access, to a greater or lesser degree, to records of government. Whether they are aware of it or not, this presents historians with a serious dilemma. Arguments for free access to the records of government based on democratic rights will be no more successful than arguments that in democracies the state has responsibilities for social welfare. In some countries it has for long been accepted that access to certain government records of family transactions have a price, which on the whole individuals (usually family historians) are willing to pay. The danger for academic history is that the enthusiasts, who contribute a large part of the external income, will drive the market. Already, collecting policies and cataloguing priorities are being influenced by their needs. Most enthusiasts only want access to very specific transactional information, grandfather's case-notes in a mental home, a drawing of a ship or a photograph of their house. Such information is always contained within larger collections, which would set it in its context. As a result large parts of collections appear to be little used in comparison to the very heavy usage of these transactional records. Against a background of financial stringency the archivist will have difficulty in justifying the decision to keep little-used records for the benefit of future academic research. Those historians, who argue beguilingly that archives are the tools of a dead discipline, do not help.

Professional historians have to accept that charging for services will come and find ways of securing the necessary budgets, but that in a sense is the least important aspect of the problems. They must seek to re-establish the relationship with the archive profession, if for nothing else than to claim their intellectual rights over their sources, particularly those that are little used by the enthusiast. They will have to avoid entering into an unholy alliance with enthusiasts to demand the retention of all records of personal transactions, whether in paper or machine-readable format. There is nothing to suggest that, despite the savings in space, there will be any significant reduction in costs when all records are in machine-readable form. IT equipment is expensive and records need continual maintenance. Historians will need to recognize that selection and cataloguing criteria can never be completely objective – they will always reflect contemporary interests and methodologies. They should also respect the heroic efforts that archivists have made to meet the demands of new approaches to the past by accepting huge accumulations of modern records and by widening their definitions to include information held in a variety of different formats. The historians with a social science perspective need to understand that they benefit from enthusiasts' use of transactional records and that they must help archivists (most of whom are unfamiliar with statistical technique) to explain that sampling will provide surrogate information. All historians need to remind their audience that contextualizing transactions makes for more interesting research and can contribute to wider debates about the past.

In rebuilding their bridges, both academic historians and archivists should look back at the scholarly foundations of *Geschichtswissenschaft*. Skills had to be acquired before sources could be approached let alone analysed, in exactly the same way that the scientist had to learn experimental method in the laboratory. Today, as all archivists will testify, students and even established scholars approach sources without the necessary methodological skills. There are many reasons for this – the growth in the range of sources available requires historians and archivists to acquire more skills from a variety of different disciplines, all of which themselves are becoming more specialized. To understand financial records the historian needs to master not only accounting techniques, but also the legal framework in which they were created. In using any transactional records the historian has to discover the purpose for which they were produced and know at least something about the method of collection, to avoid errors of interpretation. For example, with census records it is essential to know when boundaries were altered and when changes were made in enumerators' instructions. To interpret historical photographs it is necessary to know something about the development of the technology – for example, that in the late nineteenth and twentieth centuries it was only possible to take pictures on sunny days in the summer and only sunny or snowy days in the winter. There remain the persistent wider questions of representatives, not just of samples drawn from larger groups, but also of collections as a whole. Are the papers of one particular family, firm or institution representative of whole populations? The answer, as it has always been, will be subjective, based on intuition. With the growth of quantitative technique such intuition will require more justification in terms of whole populations. This is a problem that bedevils the study of enterprise where large archive collections come from firms with long histories, whose lifespans are demonstrably unrepresentative. Can a firm with a 100-year history be taken as representative of an industry where the life expectancy of the typical firm was less than ten years? The teaching of historical method has become unfashionable. Archivists find themselves, through

971

no fault of their own, providing such instruction. At the practical level of palaeography and traditional *diplomatique* they have up to now been well qualified; but at another level, particularly in social science methods, they themselves lack the necessary interpretative and analytical skills. As more students are encouraged to use primary evidence in project work, more attention needs to be given to method, if only to remind historians of the importance of respecting the integrity of the source.

Hand in hand with the teaching of method must go the development of *diplomatique* of modern documents, which has been much neglected. Little research has been undertaken into modern record keeping systems, for example the development of large central information clearing houses in the public and private sector from the mid-nineteenth century and the widespread introduction of the file after the First World War. There is almost no literature on the development of mechanized record-keeping systems apart from occasional references in management histories. The high-tech historian accessing the global archive will more than ever need *diplomatique* skills to understand the legal, political, social and cultural contexts in which data was collected and the meanings of categories and entries. Difference of meaning of the same words used in different languages or even of different regions within a country will not disappear, nor will differences in practice. Historians, more than ever before, will need to be reminded of the pitfalls of not comparing like with like. With the shift in emphasis away from long review courses towards a student-centred approach there are indications that more emphasis is being placed on method and technique.

All academic historians in the developed world by the beginning of the twenty-first century will, whether they like it or not, be connected to the superhighway and will increasingly be able to access from their desks information about the 'objects' or the 'objects' themselves that inform their particular discipline. They will be able to capture information held at a distance, even in archives in different countries. They may have to pay for these services, but will their approach to their sources change in any qualitative way? However much material is available on the Internet, it will only represent a narrow fraction of the sources available. Historians will still need to consult manuscripts in archive repositories, and because the finding aids will be more widely available, probably in greater quantities than ever before. In writing history, which will remain a narrative art, the historian will still have to interact with the sources and even where sophisticated analytical tools are employed to make judgements to inform a larger thesis. Statistical analysis can only indicate probability. It does not replace the working historian addressing data which, for all their apparent completeness, are never comprehensive. Undoubtedly the historian and the archivist will need to learn new techniques; but this has always been the case. German philosophers attributed such an important place to *Geschichte* because they believed it represented a culmination of the sciences. In the future the range of techniques may demand teamwork, but it is difficult to believe that the historical process will be very different. Those who argue otherwise themselves misunderstand the nature of research in the sciences. What will be different will be not only the speed with which sources can be located but also analysed and the greater range of sources that the historian can bring to bear on an issue. This will not mean that the writing of history will be any less time-consuming or intellectually rigorous; it will in all probability be more difficult to see the thesis for the data. Where there will certainly be difficulties is in defending the conservation of so many records in paper or machine-readable form to support a discipline whose centrality to the human sciences can no longer be taken for granted.

INDEX

Abdel-Malek, Anouar 629, 630
Absalom, Roger 606
Acton, Lord (John) 421, 427–8, 438; career and library 553
Adams, Henry Brooks 458
Adams, Herbert Baxter 458, 464
Adams, John 785–6
Adamson, J. S. A. 389
Adamson, Walter 596, 600
Adorno, Theodor 551
Al-Afghai, Sayyid Jamal al-Dim 624
Africa: anthropology and early man 692–5; disease 702–3; foreign 698–701; languages 693, 696; loss of Kongo archives 699; professional historians 703–5; recorded history and oral evidence 695–8; South Africa 701–3
Agesilaus II 32–3
agriculture: ancient 91–3; colonial 96–7; free workers 93–100; landowners 89, 97–100; late Roman archaeology 72, 73; tenant labour 88–93
Alberti, Leon Battista 834
Alexander, Sally 936
Alexander the Great 34–5
Algar, Hamid 627, 633
Algeria 704
Alison, Sir Archibald 438
Allen, Don Cameron 324
Allen, J. W. 308
Alperovitz, Gar 724
Altheim, F. 63

Althusser, Louis 488, 908, 912
Ambrosch, J. A. 59
Ambrose of Milan 74, 75
Anderson, Michael 486
Anderson, Perry 488, 896, 903, 907
Angola 697
Annales 464–73; archaeology 815; Braudel and later years 881–7; content and goals 880–5; history of Febvre years 875–82; influence 111, 224–5, 236, 325, 363, 873–5; world history 944, 949–50
Antal, F. 841
anthropology: African models of Frankish feuds 83; boundaries and rapprochement 784–90; cultural history 325–30; early Africa 692–5; family and marriage 162; generalization 867; Indian studies 685; interdisciplinary approach 783–4, 790–8; Latin America 747; medievalists 111; popular culture 368–9; religion 61, 227–33; ritual and carnival 372; warnings to historians 368–1; and world history 943–4, 945
Aquarone, Alberto 598
Aquinas, Thomas 296
Arabs: identity and the Europeans 623; position in scholarship 625–8
archaeology: *Annales* 815; archives 963; culture-history 181, 806–7; dating techniques 808; definitions and comparisons 805–6; economic determinism and ideology 114;

functionalism 807–8; and history 817–24; interpretation of data 816–17; medieval naval warfare 214; post-processualism 812–16; processual 809–12; Rome 65, 71–3; stages of enquiry 822–4; and world history 943–4, 945
architecture: siege warfare 212–13
archives: archivists 970–1; charging for access 969–71; computers 965–9, 971–3; differing national trends 964–5; the future 970–3; images 963, 969, 971; individuals 961; local and family 963–5; modern awareness of document preservation 960–3
Arendt, Hannah 554–5, 579
Argentina 729
Ariès, Philippe 326
Aristides 832
Aristotle 295, 296; dominant philospher 314; Greeks and non-Greeks 35; Polybius uses 37
art: antiquity and medieval art historians 830–3; current issues 842–3; definitions and contexts 828–9; nineteenth century 838–9; Renaissance and early modern 833–7; from 1880s to present 839–42; value judgements 771–2
Artaxerxes II of Persia 32
Ashley, W. J. 429
Asia 946 *see also* China; India; Japan
Aston, Margaret 343, 349, 354
asynchronism 553
Ibn al-Athir 15
Atkinson, R. F. 765
Atsutane, Hirata 660
Audisio, Gabriel 238
Auerbach, Erich 43
Augustine of Hippo 75
Augustus: Tacitus versus Dio 53
Aulard, Alphonse 510, 511
Australia 946
Aventius, Johannus 255
d'Avray, David 224, 240
Axtell, James 722
al-'Azm, Sadiq Jalal 629

Bachrach, Bernard S. 106, 109, 110, 114
Bacon, Francis 296, 300, 302, 311, 314
Baha'al-Din ibn Shaddad 140, 148
Bakhtin, Mikhail 328
Bal'ami 14
Baldwin, John 166–7

Baldwin, Marshall 145–6
Banaji, Jairus 4
Bancroft, George 416–17, 459, 553
Banti, Alberto 608
Barbagli, Marzio 609
Barbeyrac, Jean 274
Barnes, Harry Elmer xii, 461
Barnhart, M. A. 667
Baron, Hans 316–17
Barraclough, Geoffrey 481
Barthes, Roland 882
Basil of Caesarea 75
Batsford, B. T. 342
Bauer, Otto 551
Bauman, Zygmunt 797
Bautier, R. H. 125
Bayhaqi 15
Bayly, C. A. 950
Bayn, Nina 719
Bazant, Jan 96–7
Beard, Charles A. 459, 461, 462–3, 723, 771, 774
Beard, Mary 462–3
Beasley, W. G. 473, 660, 667
de Beaumanoir, Philippe 125
de Beauvoir, Simone 932
Becker, Carl 309, 459, 460–1, 462
St Bede 216
Belgium 434, 700
Bell, Donald 607
Bellori, G. P. 836
Ben Ghiat, Ruth 601
Bennett, Judith 160
Benson, Lee 711, 713
Berengar, Raymond 187
Bergad, Laird 88
Berlin, Sir Isaiah 399, 406
Berlin, University of 406, 444
Bernal, Martin: *Black Athena* 8
Bernheim, Ernst 429
Berr, Henri 464, 467, 952
Berube, Allan 721
Biagioli, Mario 301, 302
Biersack, Aletta 792
Biller, Peter 106, 108, 109–10, 111, 113
Binford, Lewis 809, 810–11, 824
Bintliff, J. 817
Biondo, Flavio 252
Bix, H. P. 666
Blanc, Louis 510
Blassingame, John 716
Bloch, Ernst 553

Bloch, Gustav 469
Bloch, Marc 111, 168, 224; and Febvre 467–8, 471–3; founding of *Annales* 464, 875–6; influences 466–7; life and career 468–72; power of nobility 182, 190
Bloch, R. Howard 167
Blok, Anton 609
Blumenberg, Hans 297
Bodin, Jean 264–5, 319
Bogdanov (A. A. Malinovsky) 537
Bolingbroke, Lord (Henry St John) 397
Bolivia 729
Book of Common Prayer 353
Boorstin, Daniel 710
Borkenau, Franz 878
Bossuet, Jacques Bénigne 396
Bossy, John 228, 231–2, 349, 371
Boswell, John 166
Boswell, James 404
Bosworth, Richard 597
Boulard, Canon F. 226
Bourdieu, Pierre 369, 652, 792, 799, 814
Bouwsma, William J. 324
Bowker, Margaret 346, 385
Boyle, Leonard 225
Boyle, Robert 302
Bozeman, Theodore Dwight 869–70
Bradbury, Ray 212
Bradford, Helen 88
Bradley, F. H. 764
Brahe, Tycho 299
Le Bras, Gabriel 226
Braudel, Fernand 93, 325, 485, 852, 874; *Annales* 472–3, 878, 881–7; failure of narrative in history 853–4; post-war research institutes 879–80
Brazil 729, 738
Brelich, A. 63
Brenner, Robert 895–6, 901, 907–8, 913–14
Brentano, Robert 242
Bristol, Michael D. 370
Britain: as Anglo-Saxon and Celtic nations 129–31; Boer War 701; Civil War 268–70, 380–1, 382–3; colonies in New World 373; defining modern 288; demography 486–7; fragility of institutions 390; history as a profession 442–3, 447–8; insularity 336; Marxist interpretation of Civil War 901–3, 907–8; Norman conquest and culture 439–40; Parliament and crown 379, 383, 386–7; post-Roman 80–1; questioning national myths 255; Reformation era historians 262–3; revisionism and the Stuart specialists 377–90; Romanticism 411–16; science in history 427–9; state and ruling class 903–5; Whig historians 436–42; women's historiography 935–40
British Academy 70
Brive, Marie 938
Bronowski, Jacob 310
Brooke, John 301
Broszat, Martin 561, 567–8
Brown, Allen 216
Brown, Judith 326
Brown, Peter 74, 241
Bruni, Leonardo 251, 277, 317
Brunner, Otto 126, 289
Buchheim, Hans 560, 561
Buckle, Henry Thomas 427–8
de Buffon, Comte (Georges Leclerc) 424
Bukharin, Nikolai 539–40
Bullock, Alan 562
Burckhardt, Jacob 309, 431–3, 435–6, 839
Burckhardt, Johannes 286, 288
Burgess, John William 458
Buridan, Jean 310
Burke, Peter 327, 362–3, 365, 788, 790–1; carnival 372; historical anthropology 368, 369, 370
Burns, John Horn 605
Burtt, Edwin A. 297, 311
Bury, J. B. 438, 942, 956
Butterfield, Sir Herbert xii, 139, 294, 437–8; origin of term 'Whig' 389
Bynum, Caroline Walker 165–6, 234
Byzantine empire: agricultural labour 94–5, 98; Constantinople and 'Istanbul' 15; fall of Constantinople 252; influence on Renaissance west 252; military education 216

Caesar, Gaius Julius 273, 864; military writings 216
Cafagna, Luciano 608
Cairnes, J.E. 428
Callisthenes of Olynthus 34–5
Cambridge Modern History 951
Cambridge University 444, 448
Camden, William 260–1
Cameron, Averil 70, 92
Cameron, Euan 238
Cammet, John 595
Camporeale, Salvatore 324

Cannistraro, Philip 601
Cantimori, Delio 314
Caplan, Jane 489, 490, 491
Capp, Bernard 322, 365–6
de Caprariis, Vittorio 323
Carbonnel, C.-O. 444, 447
Cardoza, Anthony 609
Carlyle, Thomas 413–15
Carnes, Mark C. 721
Carocci, Sandro 88
Carolingian empire: defining state 122;
    family and marriage 156, 164; floating
    kindreds 190–1; nobility and aristocracy
    180
Carr, E. H. 747, 780
Carrier, James 632
Carthage 36–7, 48–9
Cassels, Alan 603–4
Cassius Dio, Cocceianus 52, 53
Catharism 236–7, 239–40
Catholic Church see Roman Catholic
    Church
Cato the Elder, Marcus Porcius 46–7
Cattaneo, Carlo 595
Cavalcasselle, G. 838
di Cavour, Camillo, conte 593–6, 611
Celtic world 194
Chabod, Federico 597
Chadwick, Owen 414
Chandra, Bipan 684
Chang Hsin-pao 647
Chang Hsüeh-ch'eng 20
Channing, Edward 444
Charles I of England 380, 382, 403
Chartier, Roger 321, 322, 328, 493, 652, 792
Chaudhuri, K. N. 955
Chaunu, Pierre 326, 485
Childe, V. Gordon 808, 813, 816
Chile 97, 729
China: ancient historians 17–20;
    Confucianism 644–5, 651; critical
    scholarship 646–9; cultural studies
    652–4; difficulty of culture 17;
    ethnography 650–1; excluded from
    ancient history 3–4; influence of
    Fairbank school 641–2; narrative 649–50;
    periodization 642–6; women 651
Chomsky, Noam 814
Chrisman, Miriam Usher 322
Christian, David 948
Christianity see also Church of England;
    Orthdox Church; Protestantism; Roman

Catholic Church: African churches 698;
    archaeology and grave sites 820; art
    832–4; British Good News 439; canon
    law 222; changes in public buildings 72;
    chronology 266, 698; compatibility of
    faith and learning 267;
    confessionalization 287; defining
    'popular' religion of medieval era 221–2;
    desacrilized Bibles 241; ecclesiastical
    historians 222–5; encounter with classical
    world 74–6; and family 154; folklorized
    popular culture 367; godparents and
    spiritual ties 164; influence on medieval
    family institutions 161, 162, 164; and
    Islam 626; lay religion 112; Libri
    memoriales and lists of names 187–8; loses
    place as meaning of existence 396;
    missionaries 699; old Roman paganism
    and 57, 61–3, 65–6; Old Testament as
    history 268; popular medieval heresies
    235–40; regionalism 241–2; rise of the
    laity 225–7, 228; saints 227, 231, 235;
    secular historians out of sympathy with
    ideas 384; socio-economic organization of
    medieval Europe 83; textual criticism of
    scriptures 252, 254–5; vertical versus
    horizontal emphasis 232; warriors 193;
    women 165–7, 233–5, 237, 241, 935
Christianson, Paul 380–2, 389
chronology and dating see also time;
    asynchronism 553; BCE/CE notation 4;
    dating techniques 808; periodization
    281–4, 290–1; post-Renaissance
    adjustments 266–7; scientific dating 693
Chu Hsi 20
Church of England 225; Acts of
    Uniformity 337; Book of Common Prayer
    338, 340; break with Rome 352; debate
    about English Reformation 339–41;
    Dickens's view 340, 341–6; effect of
    Reformation 336–8; relation to Catholic
    Church 338; revisionism and Dickens
    341–51, 383–6
Cicero, Marcus Tullius 45, 49–50, 61
Cicognara, L. 837
Clapham, Sir John 484
Clarendon, Earl of (Edward Hyde) 269–70,
    277
Clark, Alice 936
Clark, J. G. D. (Grahame) 808, 811–12
Clark, Jonathan C. D. 386–8, 389
Clark, Martin 598

Clark, T. J. 841
Clarke, David L. 809–10, 811
class *see also* nobility and aristocracy; audience for historians 277; withdrawal of elite from popular culture 363
classical history *see* Greece; Rome
Clifford, L. 632
cliometrics 483–7, 747, 880–1
Clunas, Craig 652
Cobb, Richard 519
Cobban, Alfred 516–18
Cochin, Augustin 512–13
Cochrane, Eric 324
Cogswell, Thomas 382
Cohen, Bernard 784–5
Cohen, Jon 601
Cohen, Lizbeth 713, 714
Cohen, Paul 649
Cohen, Stephen 539–40
Cold War 482–3; ecclesiastical history from the east 223; effect on historians 114; impact on European historiography 106; views of Soviet history 526–9
Coleman, E. 157
Coleridge, Samuel Taylor 424
colligation 439
Collingwood, R. G. 309, 764, 767–8, 864–5
Collins, R. J. H. 818
Collinson, Patrick 342, 354
colonialism: agricultural labour 96–7; Latin America 736–7
Columbia 730
Columella, Lucius Junius Moderatus 90
Comaroff, John and Jean 791, 794, 799
Comber, Michael 7
comparativism 5–6
computers: analysis of medieval family 161; archives 965–9, 971–3; paying for access 969–71
Comte, Auguste 296, 424–5
Condorcet, Marquis of (Marie Jean de Caritat) 400–2
Confucius 17–18
Conrad, Lawrence 70
Constantine I the Great 38
constructionism 5–6
Contamine, Philippe 205–6
Contarini, Gasparo 317
Conze, Werner 494
Cook, Alice 670
Copenhaver, Brian 299
Copernicus, Nicholas 293, 294, 299, 300,

310–11; atypicality 313–14; as paradigm 313
Coppa, F. J. 597, 611
Corbin, Alain 465–6, 472
Corinth 34, 36
Corner, Paul 599, 603, 608
Cotroneo, Girolamo 324
Cott, Nancy 719
Cotton, Sir Robert Bruce 263
Counter-Enlightenment 405–411, 417
Coverdale, John 604
Craig, A.M. 660
Cranmer, Archbishop Thomas 340; *Book of Common Prayer* 353
Cremutius Cordus, Aulus 51
Croce, Benedetto xii, 8, 309, 429, 593
Crombie, Alistair C. 296, 313
Cromwell, Oliver 339–40
Cronon, William 722
Cross, Claire 347
Crowley, J.B. 667
Crusades 140
Cuba 729
culture 325–30, 652–3; archaeology and history 806–7; definitions 361–2; early modern popular culture 361–74; elite versus popular 287, 326, 328, 373–4; history and anthropology 791–4; postmodern cultural histories 493; ritual and carnival 369–70
Cumings, Bruce 724
Cummings, W. K. 669
Cunningham, William 429
Curtain, Philip 700, 950
Cust, Richard 382
Cusumano, M. A. 671
Cyrus the Younger 30, 32–3

Dale, P. N. 672
Danto, Arthur 770, 775
Darius of Persia 28
Dark, K. R. 816
Darnton, Robert 321, 327, 368, 493, 792; anthropology and popular culture 368–9; culture shocks 374
Darwin, Charles 324, 424
Davidson, Basil 705
Davies, Kathleen 933
Davies, R. R. 130, 133
Davila, E. C. 260
Davin, Anna 936
Davis, J. C. 388

Davis, Natalie Zemon 328; anthropology and history 786–7, 792; microhistory 794; popular religion 227–8; Protestant women of Lyons 931; *The Return of Martin Guerre* 326, 493, 650, 933–4
Dawley, Alan 714
Dawson, Raymond 19
De Felice, Renzo 598, 600, 601–2, 604, 606
De Giorgio, Michela 611
De Grand, Alexander 599, 605, 607
De Grazia, Victoria 602
De Ste Croix, Geoffrey E.M. 4, 897, 899
Deakin, F. W. 603, 605
Debus, Allen G. 299–300, 315
deconstructionism 748, 929; feminist historians 935
Delaruelle, Canon Etienne 228–9, 234, 236
Delbanco, Andrew 870
Delbrück, Hans 203, 212, 214, 482
Delumeau, Jean 227, 230
Delzell, Charles 603
D'Emilio, John 720, 721
demography 486–7
Demos, John P. 327
Demosthenes the orator 34
Descartes, René: initiates modern thought 284; matter and motion 313; scientific revolution 297, 311
D'Este, Carlo 605
Dézallier d'Argenville, A. J. 836
Di Scala, Spencer 607
Dianotti, Donato 317
Dickens, A. Geoffrey: *The English Reformation* 341–6, 384; evaluation of 347–9; growth of Protestantism 350; and revisionists 386; sees myopia in older historians 340
Dickie, John 610
Diggins, J. P. 603
Dijksterhuis, E.J. 295, 311
Dilthey, Wilhelm 429–30, 453–4, 456
Dio Cassius *see* Cassius Dio
disease 702–3
Dmitrov, G. 550, 575
Dobbs, B. J. T. 299
Domenico, Roy Palmer 606
Domesday Book: families and gender 164; military organization 210; reframing information 108
Donation of Constantine 115, 252
Dore, R. P. 669

Dower, J. W. 662
Doyle, William 518
Dray, William 858
Driscoll, S. T. 821
Du Bois, W. E. B. 458
Dublin, Thomas 720
Duby, Georges 124; royal families 162–3
Duffy, Eamon 223–4, 347, 349, 351–2
Duggan, Christopher 599–600
Dugmore, C.W. 344–5
Duhem, Pierre 296, 310, 311
Duke, B. 669
Dumézil, Georges 64–5
Dunn, John 316
Dupuy, Roger 522
Durkheim, Emile 232, 325, 327, 363, 429, 452–3
Dutt, R. Palme 682
Duus, P. 473, 667
Dvorak, Max 840
Dyer, C. 899

Easlea, Brian 298
Eberhard, Wolfram 650
Ebo, Archbishop of Reims 180–1
Eckenstein, Lina 233
economics 483–4
Ecuador 730
Edbury, Peter 150
education: American multidisciplinary approach 932, 936; buying archive access 970; didacticism 44; Fredericq's passion for teaching 434; German universities and counter-enlightenment 406–7; Japan 669; local and family history 964; professional historians at university 444, 703–4; world history 945
Egypt: agricultural labour 93–5, 98; contribution to Greece 8; French colonial involvement 622–3
Ehrenkreutz, Andrew S. 148–9
Eichmann, Adolph 564
Eisenstein, Elizabeth 286, 322
Eley, Geoff 794–5
Elias, Norbert 372
Elizabethan era: Protestantism 340, 342, 353, 384–5
Elkins, Stanley 711, 715–16
Elliot, Sir Henry 680
Ellis, George 141
Ellwood, David 605

Elton, Sir Geoffrey R. 344, 383, 475–6, 764–5; become target of revisionism himself 388; debate about cliometrics 484–5; knowing historical actors 776–7; relations of Church and state 339–40; revisionism 380

Elvin, Mark 646

Engels, Friedrich: historical materialism 889–94, 912; *Peasant War in Germany* 223; religion 229

Engerman, S.L. 484

England *see also* Britain: Anglo-Saxons 121, 194; ecclesiastical historians 224; effect of Reformation 336–8; formation of nation 129–30; medieval kingdom of conquest 193–4; military 215–16, 216–17; Norman Conquest 194, 217–18; Protestant nation 352; Roman military continuity 208

Enlightenment 400–5; Counter-Enlightenment 405–411, 417

Ennen, E. 234

Ennius, Quintus 45

Ephorus of Cyme 33–4

Epstein, Barbara 719

Erikson, Erik 328

Esherick, Joseph 648–9

ethnicity and race: American salad bowl rather than melting pot 712–15; Black Studies in US 934; ethnography in China 650–1; fascism 567–8, 578–9, 603; Indian diversity and violence 677–8; medieval formation of nations 122–3; Native Americans 275, 721–2; orientalism 622–35; postmodern issues 492

Europe: world history 944, 946, 953–4

European Science Foundation 70

Eusebius of Caesarea 75

Evans, Austin 235–6

Evans, R. J. W. 315

Evans Pritchard, E. E. 325

Everitt, Allan 379

Fabius Pictor, Quintus 5, 36

facts 854–7

Fairbank, John King 641–2, 642–5, 647, 652–3

Falke, Johannes 430

families *see also* nobility and aristocracy; godparents and spiritual ties 164; idealization of maternity 167; medieval

property management 160–4; trends and factors in historiography 153–5

Faragher, John Mack 719

Farrington, Benjamin 296

Farriss, Nancy 734

fascism: debate on Italian fascism 598–606; Japan 666–7; and Marxism 564–6; post-war scholarship in National Socialism 546–55; roots in Italy's risorgimento 592–6; West German historiography 564–7

Febvre, Lucien 309, 321, 325; *Annales* years 875–82; and Bloch 467–8, 471–3; founding of *Annales* 464; influences 466–7; life and career 467–8; and Lucie Varga 878–9, 880; personal characteristics and friendships 885–6

Feingold, Mordechai 300

Femia, Joseph 596

Ferrari, Giuseppi 595

Fest, Joachim 562

feudalism: Bloch's agrarian regimes 470–1; France 124–6; Marxist interpretation 895–8; socio-economic organization of medieval Europe 83; warfare 204–5, 209–12

Figgis, John Neville 308

Fines, John 350

Finley, Sir Moses I. 4, 95

Fiorello, J. D. 836

Firth, C. H. 438

Fischer, Fritz 547, 562

Fleming, D. F. 723–4

Fletcher, Anthony 381

Floud, Roderick 487

Fogel, R. W. 484–5

folklore *see* anthropology

Foner, Eric 718

Fontaine, Jacques 74–5

de Fontette, Micheline 234

Formisano, Ronald P. 713

Forster, E. M. 858

Forsyth, Douglas 599

Foster, John 900

Foucault, Michel 329, 490, 783, 792, 934

Fowler, W. Warde 60–2, 63

Foxe, John 337

France *see also Annales*; Africa 700, 704; Carlyle on the revolution 414–15; diversity of Revolution 523–4; ecclesiastical history 224–5, 225–6; effect of revolution on Germany 407; the Enlightenment 400–2; folkloric religion 229–31; French Revolution as beginning of modern era 288, 290; Huguenot resistance arguments 319; late antiquity 77, 79–80; Lefebvre on the Revolution 509–14; Marxism and the Revolution 510–16; Marxism and the revolution 521–2, 902, 907–8; medieval formation of state 124–6; post-war research institutes 879–80; professional historians 443–4, 446–7; Reformation era historians 259–60; revolution as chaos and relentless conflict 518–19; Romanticism and Michelet 417–19; scientific history 424–7

France, Anatole 866
Frank, Walter 557
Frankfurt School 551–2, 814
Franklin, Benjamin 862
Franklin, Julian H. 323
Franks 189–90
Frazer, Sir James G. 61, 429
Frederick the Great 414–15
Fredericq, Paul 434
Freeman, Edward A. 437, 438, 439, 440–1, 464
Freeman, Estelle 720
Freud, Sigmund 840, 864
Freudianism 328; and Marxism 551–2
Freyre, Gilberto 744, 749
Friedmann, Georges 877, 885
Friedrich, Carl 554
Friedrich, Paul 747
Fromm, Erich 551
Froude, James Anthony 415, 438, 440–1
Fry, Roger 840
Fueter, Eduard xii
Fukui, H. 671
functionalism: archaeology 807–8
Furet, François 321, 400, 485, 519–21
Fussner, F. Smith 324
Fustel de Coulanges, Numa Denis 425–6

Galilei, Galileo 310–11; heresy trial 301–2, 314; politics 302; scientific revolution 284, 295, 296, 297
Gallagher, John 488, 686
Gallie, W. B. 775
Galpern, A. N. 227
Gambetta, Diego 610
Garcia de León, Antonio 747

Gardiner, Samuel Rawson 379, 381, 438, 441–2, 869–70
Garin, Eugenio 315
Garrett, G.T. 681
Gascou, J. 92
Gatterer, Johann Christoph 406–7
Gaxotte, Pierre 512
Gay, Peter 404, 559
Geertz, Clifford 111, 228, 325, 792; current position in anthropology 788–9; thick description 326, 369, 929; world history 950
gender: postmodernism 492–3
genealogy: medieval nobility 184–9; names and naming convention 186–7
van Gennep, Arnold 369
Genovese, Eugene D. 716–17, 896, 913–14
Gentilcore, David 367
Gentile, Emilio 600, 602
Gerhard, Dietrich 289
Germany: concentration on political 494–5; controversy over responsibility for Nazism 8; the Counter-Enlightenment 405–411; ecclesiastical historians 223–4; effect of unification 545–6; end of national power 288; GDR historiography 573–8; *Historikerstreit* (historian's dispute) 571–3; historism 408, 420; Holocaust 567–9; industrialization 563–4; influence on American scholars 458–9; inheritance of historicism and National Socialism 545–8; *Kultur* 430–6; late antiquity 77–8; medieval formation of nation 126–8; *Monumenta Germaniae Historica* 108; mustering military force 215; periodization 282–3; post-war politics and scholarship 546–55; professional historians 444–5; Romano-Germanic military 207; social sciences and history 428–30; Third Reich repression of historians 474–80, 555–8; West German historiography 558–73
Gerschenkron, Alexander 596–7
Ghiberti, Lorenzo 833–4
Giannantonio, Pompeo 324
Giannone, Pietro 398
Gibb, Sir Hamilton 144–5
Gibbon, Edward 273–6, 277; death of Roman Empire 107; the Enlightenment 403–5
Gibson, Charles 88, 734

Gibson, Mary 611
Giddens, Anthony 814
Gilbert, Felix 317
Gills, Barry 953
Ginsborg, Paul 596, 605
Ginzburg, Carlo 224–5, 230, 326, 327, 493;
    problem of typicality 371
Ginzburg, Leone 225
Giolitti, Giovanni 592
Gluck, Carol 663
Godbeer, Richard 373
Godechot, Jacques 516
Godelier, M. 897, 911–12
Godinho, Vitorino Magalhaes 289
Goetz, Hans-Werner 158
Goffart, Walter 78–9, 93
Goldberg, Jeremy 235
Goldin, Claudia 720
Goldmann, Lucien 882, 905
Goldthwaite, Richard 652
Gombrich, Ernst 480, 829, 840
González, Luis 739
Gooch, George Peabody xii, 406, 418
Goodich, Michael 235
Goody, Jack 162, 163
Gordon, A. 671
Gorgias 32
Göttingen, University of 406, 417, 444
Gould, Jeffrey 745
Gowring, Laura 937
Grafton, Anthony 321
Gramsci, Antonio 593, 595–6, 597; cultural
    history 328; influence in India 698;
    religion 229
Gratian, Franciscus 222, 227
Grebing, Helga 561
Greece: art 830, 832, 837; Athenian
    Empire 29–30; Black Athena debate
    7–8; chronology 266; contrasts self with
    barbarians 24–30; historians' questions
    6–7; influence on Rome 47; Pan-
    Hellenism 32–3; Peloponnesian War
    30–2; and Rome 36–8; source material on
    religion 58; tradition as value 4–5
Greek language 70–1
Green, John Richard 438, 440
Green, Louis 324
Green, Monica 234
Greenblatt, Stephen 354
Greenfield, Kent R. 595
Gregor, A. J. 600–1
Grendler, Paul 314

Grew, Raymond 595
Grierson, P. 817
Griffen, Clyde 721
Grotius, Hugo 263, 274, 319
von Grunebaum, Gustave 140
Guenée, Bernard 325
Guérin, Daniel 515
Guicciardini, Francesco 255–7, 277, 323
Guizot, François Pierre 424–5
Gunder Frank, Andre 953
Gunn, A.W. 320
Gurevich, Aaron 225, 230–1, 368
Gutman, Herbert 711, 714, 717–18
Guy, John 385–6

Habermas, Jürgen 552, 572
Haggard, H. Rider 144
Haigh, Christopher 344, 345, 347, 389;
    process of Reformation 348; revisionist
    English Reformation 346, 350, 384–5,
    388
Haiti 729
Halbwachs, Maurice 325, 469
Hall, A. R. 293, 313
Hall, David D. 373
Hall, Marie Boas 313
Hallam, Henry 440
Hallgarten, George 557
Halperín, Tulio 737, 749
Hamilton, Bernard 150, 239–40
Hammer, Carl 157–8
Handlin, Oscar 712
Hane, M. 659, 662, 668
Hanley, S. B. 660
Haraway, Donna 797
Hardy, E. R. 95–6
Hareven, Tamara 712
Harlan, Louis 718
Harold II of England 217–18
Harper, John 605
Harrington, James 276, 317
Hartlib, Samuel 303
Hartung, J. A. 58
Harvey, William 311
Haskins, Charles Homer 459, 463
Hatt, Jean-Jacques 807
Hauser, A. 841
Havens, Thomas 667–8
Hawkes, C. F. C. 808, 813, 818
Hayashi, Hiroko 670
Hayes, Carlton 464–5
Heal, Felicity 345

Hearder, Harry 611
Heather, Peter 3
Hegel, Georg W. F. 408, 410–11; influence on Ranke 422; Roman religion 59–60
Heiber, Helmut 562
van Helmont, J. B. 300
Hempel, Carl G. 764, 858
Hendry, R. J. 672
Henry VIII: Froude defends 440–1
Hentsch, Thierry 620
Henty, G. A. 143–4
von Herder, Johann Gottfried 407, 410, 422
Herlihy, David 156, 160–4
Herodotus: ethico-tragical context 43–4; ethnographic approach 28–30; first historian 5, 6; oral evidence from Africa 695; scorns myth 25; sense of enquiry 24; Thrace 31; and Thucydides 25–6
Hessen, Boris 298
Hevia, James 653
Hexter, J. H. 381, 382, 389, 764–5, 779
Heydemann, Günther 573–4, 576
Higham, John 429
Hildebrand, Bruno 429
Hill, Christopher 382, 899; attack by Davis 388; Marxism 339, 488, 901–5, 907; revisionism 379
Hillgruber, Andreas 571
Hilton, Rodney 899–902, 903, 905–6
Himmelfarb, Gertrude 855
Hindess, B. 897
Hindley, Geoffrey 148
Hinduism 678, 685–6; approach to history 698–9; nationalism 681–3
Hintze, Otto 446, 478
Hirohito, Emperor of Japan 665–6, 668
Hirst, Derek 381–2, 383, 389
Hirst, P. Q. 897
Ibn Hisham 13
historians: beliefs and ideologies 113–15; criticism of the canon xii–xiii; and information technology 970–3; insidious objectivity 258; interaction with other disciplines 111–12, 294–5; national assumptions 112–13; origin of term 'Whig' 389; and philosophers 779–81; political circumstances 111–13; professionals 960; role as academic profession 442–9; twentieth-century repression 473–80, 555–8
historical materialism 889–94
historicism 546

historiography: agents of historical action 769; anachronism 397; and anthropology 368–71, 795–8; assumptions of students xi; audience for historians 110, 276–8; the canon of historians questioned 6–7; cliometrics 483–7, 747; comparison of different histories 252; context and relevance 8, 43–4, 318–20; as correction of past historians xi–xiv; distrust between generations of scholars 378; explanation 857–63; French atomism versus German historism 408, 420; generalizations versus narrow monographs 731; goals 780–1; interdisciplinary study 328–9; internalists and contextualists 313–14; Kuhn's paradigms 311–13, 316, 330; linear versus cyclical view 250–1, 275, 310–11, 372–3, 398–400, 678–9; literary critique 491–2; modernism and postmodernism 487–95; narrative 774–9; national points of view 282–3; philosophical history of eighteenth century 272; reasons for fascination with the past 851; research teams and analysis of archives 962; revisionism and the Stuart specialists 377–83; scholarship of 323–5; scientific revolution 293–304; secularization and scientific enquiry 424–30; structural functionalism 747; theoretical models xiii–xiv, 746–51; Thucydidean model of contemporary history 25–6; valuing old versus new 4–6; world history 481–2, 929–30
history: accuracy 52–4; breaks into smaller histories 5; etymology 3, 23–4; philosophy 763–6, 766–70
Hitler, Adolf: and Mussolini 604; psychological interpretation 553; value judgements and cause 773–4; West German historiography 560, 564, 567–70
Hobbes, Thomas 31, 302, 319
Hobsbawm, Eric 488, 742
Hodder, Ian 810, 812, 816
Hodges, Richard 812, 818, 820
Hofstadter, Richard 710
Hoggart, Richard 488
Holborn, Hajo 557, 559
Hollister, C. W. 211
von Holst, Hermann E. 459
Homer 26, 28
Honoré, A. M. 76
Hooft, P. C. 270

Hopkins, K. 90
Horace (Quintus Horatius Flaccus) 24, 46
Horkheimer, Max 551
Horton, Robin 227
Hoston, Germaine 661
Hourani, Albert 633
Huber, T. M. 660–1
Hudson, Anne 239, 344
Hufton, Olwen 492–3
Hughes, Ann 382
Hughes, D. O. 163
Hughes, H. Stuart 595, 603
Hughes, Philip 341
Hughes, Steven 610
Huizinga, Johan 432–3, 436
humanism 250–3
von Humboldt, Wilhelm 419, 499
Hume, David 272, 274, 275, 402–3, 439
Hunecke, Volker 607
Hunt, Lynn 327, 493, 523
Hunter, J. L. 473
Hunter, Michael 315
Huntington, Samuel 630, 633
Huppert, George 323
Hus, John 258
Huxley, Julian 951–2
Hyde, Edward (later Earl of Clarendon)
    269–70, 277

Ichisada, Miyazaki 646
ideologies and beliefs: effect on historians
    113–15
Iggers, Georg 420, 546, 577
Iliffe, John 692
imperialism 622–3, 736–7, 950–1; Athenian
    Empire 29–30; cultural 106; Dio on
    writing about 52; India 680, 686; New
    World colonies 373; Said and
    orientalism 628–32
Inden, Ronald 631
India 686–90; fits no obvious paradigm
    677–8; Hindu and Muslim approaches to
    history 678–9; imperialism 680, 686;
    nationalism 681–3; post-independence
    683–6
information technology see archives;
    computers
Innis, Harold 322
intellectual history: background to 1945
    307–10; cultural 325–30; focus on great
    minds 308–9, 318; internalists and
    contextualists 313–14; Kuhn's

paradigms 311–13; political thought
    316–20; printing press and
    communication 320–2
Iqbal, Maulana Muhammad 683
Iran 14
Ireland 106, 130–1
Irwin, Robert 106, 109–10, 111–12
Ibn Ishaq 13
Islam 624; ancient historians 11–16;
    calendars and dating 698; India 678–9,
    681–3, 698–9; missionaries 699
Isocrates 33, 34–5
Italy: defining modern history 289; fascism
    567, 598–606; formation of medieval
    state 128–9; modernization 596–7;
    nineteenth century 607–11; periods of
    historical shift 591–2; professional
    historians 448–9; Resistance 606;
    risorgimento and fascism 592–6;
    women's historiography 935

Jackson, D. E. P. 149
Jacob, J. R. and Margaret 315
Jacobs, Wilbur R. 722
Jahn, Otto 445
James, Daniel 745
Jameson, Anna 839
Japan: education 669; fascism 666–7;
    Marxist interpretations 660–1; Meiji
    Restoration years 659–62;
    modernization 662–3; post-war 659,
    670–3; power elites 664–7; pre-war
    667–70; women 670
Jardine, Lisa 321
Jaurès, Jean 511, 514
Jeffrey, Julie Ray 719–20
Jenkinson, Sir Hilary 962
Jennings, Francis 722
Jerusalem 193–4
Jessup, Dr Henry 634–5
Jews: African 697–8; Alexandria 35; anti-
    Semitism 553, 568; chronology 266; in
    fascist Italy 603; German guilt 570–2;
    Holocaust 551, 567–9; twentieth-century
    repression 474–80
Johansen, B. 631
John, Evan 147
John Chrysostom 75
Johnson, Chalmers 671
Johnson, Dr Samuel 396–7, 404
Joll, James 595
Jones, A. H. M. 71, 76, 90, 93–4

Jones, E. L. 953
Jones, Jacqueline 720
Jones, P. M. 523
Jordan, Winthrop 716
Joseph of Arimathea 255
Joyce, Patrick 796
Juwayni 15–16

Kaelble, Harmut 494
Kahn, H. 671
Kaltenstadler, W. 93
Kamenev, Lev 536
Kamlah, Wilhelm 283–5, 290
Kant, Immanuel 408–10
Kantorowicz, Ernst 477–8, 557
Katz, Jonathan 721
Katzman, David M. 720
Kawai, Kazuo 668
Kay, Sarah 167
Kedar, Benjamin 150
Keegan, Tim 88
Kehr, Eckart 557
Kelikian, Alice 611
Kelley, Donald R. 323
Kelley, Joan Gadol 931
Kemble, John Mitchell 439–40
Kenya 704
Keohane, Nannerl O. 320
Kepler, Johannes 298, 311, 314
Kerensky, Alexander 533, 534
Kertzer, David 609
Kessler, Eckhard 324
Kessler-Harris, Alice 720
Ibn Khaldun 15–16
Khan, Sir Syed Ahmed 683
King, Bolton 611
King, Geoffrey 70
King, John 354
Kirov, Sergei 543
Kishlansky, Mark 383, 389
Kitching, G. 914
Kleppner, Paul 713
Knape, Joachim 324
Knies, Carl 429
Knowles, Dom David 341
Knowles, Lilian 936
Knox, Magregor 604
Koch, C. 63
Koch, Gottfried 233, 237
Koenker, D. P. 532
Kolko, Joyce and Gabriel 724
Kongo 699

Koon, T. 602
Koonz, Claudia 938
Kornilov, Lavr Georgyevich 534, 535
Koselleck, Reinhart 285, 288, 296, 319
Kossak, Zofia 146–7
Kossinna, Gustav 807
Koyré, Alexandre 295, 297, 299, 310, 311, 882
Krahner, L. 58
Krausnick, Helmut 561
Kugler, Franz 838
Kuhn, Philip A. 648
Kuhn, Thomas S. 861; *The Copernican Revolution* 297, 298–9, 314; *The Structure of Scientific Revolutions* 307, 311–13, 330; use in political historiography 316
Kurd Ali, Muhammad 624–6
Kurdish people 142

Labarre, Albert 322
labour: agricultural labour 88–93, 96–9; Marxism and class struggle 899–902; medieval women working outside 160
Labrousse, Elisabeth 323
Labrousse, Ernest 514, 877
LaCapra, Dominick 330, 493
de Lamarck, Chevalier (Jean de Monet) 424
Lambert, Malcolm 239
Lamprecht, Karl 430–1, 433–4, 450, 455, 457
Lanaro, Silvio 608
Lane-Pool, Stanley (novelist) 144
Langlois, C. V. 465, 466
languages: context of political thought 319; glottochronology 693; medieval sources 109; spread of gospels and literacy 76; translations and decrease of classical languages 70–1; translations and international discourse 267–8; use in textual criticism 253; and world history 943–4
Lanzi, Luigi 837
Lapsley, Gaillard 182
Larner, Christina 327
Laroui, Abdallah 623
Larson, Brooke 735
Laslett, Peter 316, 486
Late Antiquity *see also* Byzantine era; Greece; Rome: coming together of related fields 69–70; early medieval western Europe 77–83; late Roman empire 70–7

Latin America: common people's histories 739–46; diversity 728–33; Marxism 749; regional approach 733–9; theoretical approach 746–51; women 745–6

Latin language: decreasing role in schools 70–1; loses place as international discourse 267; post-Roman Europe 81, 82

Latour, Bruno 798

Latreille, André 513

Latte, K. 63

Laufer, Otto 289

de Laveleye, Emile 434

law: early medieval Europe 83; Gratian's canon law 222; marriage and family 155; medieval ideas of justice and custom 120; nobility and aristocracy 179–80; property and women in Medieval era 160–4

Le Bon, Gustave 429

Le Goff, Jacques 224, 236, 289, 882

Le Roy Ladurie, Emmanuel 236, 325, 328, 365, 494; *Annales* 878; on the computer 485; microhistory and anthropology 791; narrative and facts 866; translation 874

Leakey, L. S. B. 692

Leavitt, Judith Walzer 721

Lebstock, Suzanne 719

Lecky, W. E. H. 438

LeFeber, Walter 724

Lefebvre, Georges 509–18; new trends 521, 523

Lefkowitz, Mary: *Not Out of Africa* 8

Leiris, Michel 627

Lemmens, Henri 625

Lenin, V. I. 532, 724; ideology 534–5; terror and state-building 537–9

Leone, Mark 815

Lepelley, Claude 72

Lerner, Gerda 719

Levack, Brian P. 327

Leverhulme Trust 70

Lévi-Strauss, Claude 325, 490, 882

Levin, N. Gordon 724

Levine, Joseph M. 324

Levine, Lawrence W. 717

Levison, Wilhelm 477

Lewis, Bernard 628, 630

Lewis, Norman 605

Licinius Macer 47

Lin Zixu 647

Linehan, Peter 448

Linnaeus, Carl 424

Lipsius, Justus 319

literacy: importance to Reformation 286; and medieval heresies 239; sources for medievalists 108; spread of gospels in different languages 76; transition from oral culture 366

literature: fairy and folk tales 141; of the French Enlightenment 401; literary critique of history 491–2; medieval distance from classical style 80; medieval military and epic poems 211; narrative and facts 865–6; popular culture 366; Renaissance beginning of textual criticism 252–5; Saladin as fictional subject 139–40; Sir Walter Scott 140–3; source of rhetoric for nobility 183; women's studies 933

Little, Lester K. 224

Livy (Titus Livius) 7, 45–6, 49–50, 251

LoRomer, David 596

local history: archives 963–5; English Reformation 340–1, 343, 350

Locke, John 319

Lockhart, James 734

Lockyer, Roger 381

Lot, Ferdinand 203, 480

Lovejoy, Arthur O.: *The Great Chain of Being* 309–10

Lovett, Clara M. 595

Lowenthal, David 863

Lubell, Samuel 712, 713

Lüdtke, Alf 795

Luebke, Frederick C. 712–13

Lughod, Janet Abu 953

Lukács, Georg 865; *The Historical Novel* 142

Luther, Martin 257–8, 261, 284, 286

Lyell, Charles 324

Lyons, Malcolm 149

Lyotard, J.-F. 491

Lysias 32

Lyttelton, Adrian 600, 609, 610

Maalouf, Amin 148

Mabillon, Jean 108, 267

Macartney, George, Earl 653

Macaulay, Thomas Babington, Lord 53, 390, 412–14, 415–16, 440

McCormack, G. 671

MacCulloch, Diarmaid 385–6

Macedon 33–5

Macfarlane, Alan 372, 388, 788

McFarlane, K. B. 177, 182
McGuire, J. E. 299
Machiavelli, Niccolo 255–7, 277; *Discourses on Livy's History of Rome* 256; gender and politics 320; Pocock's study 316–17; *The Prince* 256; Skinner's study 318, 319
Mack Smith, Denis 594–5, 600, 604, 605, 611
McLuhan, Marshall 322
MacMillan, C.J. 671
McNeill, William H. 482, 941–2, 946, 952
Maier, Charles S. 599
Maine, Sir Henry 450, 677
Mair/Major, John 255
Maitland, Frederic William 440, 441, 448
Majumdar, R. 682
Malatesta, Maria 609
Malinowski, Bronislaw 361, 364
Mallon, Florencia 741, 746
Malory, Sir Thomas 141
Mandelbaum, Maurice 774–5
van Mander, Karl 835–6
Mandrou, Robert 295, 322, 365, 882
Manilius, Marcus 46
Mannheim, Karl 314
Manning, Brian 901
Manselli, Raoul 227, 228
Manuel, Frank E. 314
Marcone, A. 92–3
Marcus, George 798
de Mariana, Juan 264, 319
Marion, Michel 322
Marks, Gary 713
Marks, Shula 702
Marland, Hilary 935
Marquardt, J. 59
Marr, Nikolai 807
marriage: dowries and payments 159–60; medieval context 155–6, 158, 166
Marrou, Henri 74
Martin, Henri-Jean 321, 322
Martin, J. E. 901
Martin, Jean-Clément 522
Martin, Julian 302
Marx, Karl 450–2, 954; *The Eighteenth Brumaire of Louis Bonaparte* 551
Marxism: analysis of feudalism 114; *Annales* has fill of its theorizing 885; archaeology 808, 814, 816–17; art 841; base and superstructure 910–12; China 644; cultural history 328; era of scientific analysis 429; externalism and scientific

revolution 297–8; family and property 168; and fascism 564–6; feudalism 107, 895–8; and French Revolution 510–15, 521–2; and Freudianism 551–2; and Hegel 411; historians 894–907; historical materialism 889–94, 911–12; historical process 450–2; ideologies and social conditions 905–7; India 681–2, 684; industrial society and class struggle 899–902; influence on revisionism 379, 381, 388; interpretative generalizations from facts 866–7; Japan 660–1; Latin America 749; leftist movement of the 1960s 488; Leninist theory of capitalist crisis 549–50; mode of production 892–4; orientalism as cultural imperialism 626; peasant studies and world history 949; and post-war German historiography 546, 549–54; power of nobility 181–2; problem of popular culture 368; Russian revolution 531, 534–43; social relations of production 894–8, 908–10, 911–12; state 903–5, 906–7; steering between reductionism and pluralism 907–15; transition from ancient to feudal state 121; world history 944
Mary I of England 340, 349, 353
Mason, Tim W. 900
Mas'udi 14–15
Mathiez, Albert 510–11, 521
Matthaei, Julie A. 720
Matthews, Glenna 719
Matthews, John 77
Mau, Hermann 561
Mauss, Marcel 325, 369, 869
Mayer, Theodor 126
Mazrui, Ali 705
Mazzini, Giuseppe 611
Meakins, Neville 144
Medieval era: art history 832–3; Bloch's agrarian regimes 470–1; building projects 216–17; chronological markers 107; comparative work on states 132–3; context of family and gender 155–60; definitions 105–10; genealogy and prosopography 184–9; periodization of Middle Ages 284; sexuality, gender and spirituality 164–9; state 117–21, 122–32; warfare of feudal lords and knights 204–5, 209–12; women and property 160–4
Meinecke, Friedrich 309, 410, 433, 446,

477, 556, 557; National Socialism as
    European 559, 560
Melos 31
Menéndez Pidal, Ramn 448
Menéndez y Pelayo, Marcelino 448
Menger, Carl 455
Merchant, Carolyn 296, 303, 315
Meriggi, M. 609
Merli, Stefano 607
Merlo, Grado 238
Mertens, Hans-Günther 88
Merton, Robert K. 301, 314
methodology: archaeology 810–12, 822–4;
    crisis and social theory 449–57;
    philosophical explanation 766–70;
    Renaissance appearance of textual
    criticism 252–5; world history 942–4,
    954–6
de Meun, Jean 167
Mexico 729, 730; agricultural labour 96,
    100; archives and sources 731; economy
    738; Revolution 738–9
Meyer, Conrad Ferdinand 866
Meyerowitz, Joanne J. 720
Meyrick, Samuel 141
Michael, Franz 644–5
Michelet, Jules 398, 402, 887; biographies
    414; dissertation 444; French
    Revolution 509, 511; life and career
    417–19; symbolic history 413
Michelis, Meir 603
microhistory 791, 794–5
Middle East: orientalism debate 622–35;
    world history context 946
Midelfort, H. C. Erik 327
Mignone, G. G. 605
military: arms and armour 213; cavalry
    211, 213; continuity between ancient and
    medieval 206–8; demography 215–16;
    feudal 204–5, 209–12; logistics 214;
    medieval nobility 191–4; naval warfare
    213–14; pay 208, 210; siege warfare
    212–13; state institutionalization 287;
    strategy and tactics 216–18
Mill, James 677, 680
Mill, John Stuart 764
Miller, Frank 665
Miller, James E. 605, 607
Miller, Perry 309
Mills, Charles 141
Milton, John 268–9
Minami, R. 671

Minear, Richard 631–2
Mink, Louis 775, 777, 779–80
Minogue, Kenneth 310
Modern era: art history 835–9; defining
    284–91; early popular culture 361–74;
    periodization 281–5
modernism 487–8, 494–5, 646–7; China
    653
Mohr, James 721
Mohring, Hannes 149
Momigliano, Arnaldo 4, 476
Mommsen, Hans 560, 567–8, 570, 571
Mommsen, Theodor 59–60, 61, 214; career
    and publications 445; and Ranke 423
Mommsen, Theodor ('Ted'), repression
    477–8
monarchy: emergence of military 205–6;
    and nobility 180–1, 183, 195; and
    Parliament 379, 383, 386–7; role in
    Anglican church 338; royals as family
    models 161–2
Mongolian Empire 15–16
Monod, Gabriel 426, 447, 465
de Montaigne, Michel 259
Monter, E. William 327
de Montesquieu, Charles Louis de
    Secondat, baron 272, 274–5, 401
Montgomery, David 714
Monumenta Germaniae Historica (MGH)
    108
Moore, Barrington 325, 750
Moore, R. I. 239–40, 482
Morazé, Charles 885
More, Sir Thomas: *Utopia* 259
Moreland, John 821
Moreland, W. H. 681
Morelli, G. 838
Morelos, Zapatista 738–9
Morgan, David 4
Morgan, John 301
Morgan, M. R. 140
Morishima, M. 671
Morrill, John 379, 382
Morris, Colin 241
Morris, Ian 817, 819
Morris, Jonathan 609
Morris, Morris D. 683
von Mosheim, J. L. 271
Mosse, George 559, 600
Motley, John Lothrop 459
Mubarak, Ali Basha 623–4
Mubarak, Zaki 625

Muchembled, Robert 327, 362, 363–4, 366; folklorized popular Christianity 367; otherness of peasants 372; state formation 367
Muhammad 11–14
Müller, C. O. 58–9
Müller, Johann 430
Mumford, Lewis 322
Munich Institut für Zeitgeschichte 561
Munz, Peter 491–2
Münzer, F. 62
Muratori, Ludovico 267, 397–8
Murray, A. C. 156
Murray, Alexander 224, 240
Mussolini, Benito 592–3, 599, 600–2, 604
Myers, R. H. 667
mythology: common triple structure 64–5; scorned by Greek historians 25

Naitō Torajirō 645–6
Nakamura, T. 670
Nakane, C. 672
Namier, Lewis Bernstein 318, 474
Napier, John 314
Napoleon Bonaparte 513
narrative 774–9; causation and series of events 851–4; China 649–50; competing generalizations 868–70; facts 854–7; generalization about cause and explanation 857–63; interpretation and empathy 863–7; maintaining objectivity 867–70; postmodernism and metanarrative 867–8
Nathan, Andrew 649
natural history 23–4
Neale, R. S. 907
Neale, Sir John 339, 379, 380, 383
Nehru, Jawaharlal 684
Nelson, Janet L. 106, 110, 111, 112, 493; changing uses for texts 108; defining state 122
Nero Claudius Caesar 38–9; Tacitus 50–1
The Netherlands: Reformation historians 260, 263
Neumann, Franz 552
New Historicism 6, 329, 650, 929, 937
New World: colonial discoveries 258–9; modern perspectives 457–64; world history context 946
New Zealand 946
Newby, Eric 605
Newby, P. H. 148

Newton, Isaac: alchemy and religion 314; atypicality 313–14; biography 299; as paradigm 313; scientific revolution 293, 294, 296; shifting perception of time 395–6
Nicaragua 729
Niebuhr, Barthold Georg 407
Nietzsche, Friedrich 411
Nish, Ian 661, 667
nobility and aristocracy: defining 178–80; family consciousness 191–2; genealogy and prosopography 184–9; late medieval crisis 195; and monarchy 180–1, 183, 195; origins 189–91; public and private power 181–4; warrior ethos 191–4
Nolte, Ernst 552, 566, 571, 600
Nora, Pierre 521
Norinaga, Motoori 660
Norman, E. H. 660
Notestein, Wallace 379, 380, 381
Novick, Peter 464, 553–4
Novus, Tiberius Claudius 38
Nugent, Daniel 747

Oakeshott, Michael 488, 764, 768, 862
Oberman, H. 227
O'Day, Rosemary 345, 346
Offner, R. 838
O'Gorman, Frank 486
Okimoto, D. I. 667
Olson, Roberta 609
Oman, Sir Charles 203
Ong, Father Walter J. 320–1
Ono, Kazuko 651
oral tradition 366, 695–8
Oresme, Nicole 310
orientalism: early scholarship 622–8; redefinining in current debate 620–2; Said's debate 628–32
Origen 75
Orthodox Church 537
Ortner, Sherry 789–90, 791
Ostrogorski, George 475
Ottoman empire: Christian world 259; source of information about Africa 698
Owen, E. R. J. 98–9
Oxford (Tractarian) Movement 337
Oxford University 444, 448
Oxyrhynchus: agricultural labour 91, 99
Ozment, Steven 326, 933
Ozouf, Jacques 321
Ozouf, Mona 521

Pagel, Walter 299–300
Palladio, Andrea 834–5
Palladius Aemilianus 93
Pallavicino, Sforza 261
Palmer, Bryan 492
Palmer, Robert 516, 521
Pan Ku 19
Panofsky, Erwin 480, 841
Pantin, William 225
Paracelsus (Theophrastus Bombastus von Hohenheim) 299–300
Paraguay 729
Paravy, Pierette 238
Paris, University of: history as a profession 444, 446–7
Parker, Geoffrey 950
Parkman, Francis 459
Parrington, Vernon 309
Parsons, Talcott 325
Partiarca, Silvana 610
Pasquier, Etienne 320
Passavant, J. D. 838
Passerini, Luisa 603
Patrick, H. 671
Paulinus of Nola 74
Pavone, Claudio 606
Peattie, M. R. 667
Pedersen, Olaf 301
Pelaja, Margherita 611
Peloponnesian War 30–2
Perdue, Theda 722
periodization 281–4, 397–8; art 829, 837; modern China 642–6; world history 946
Perrot, Michelle 938
Persia 26–30, 32
Pertusi, Agostino 324
Pertz, Carl August Friedrich 407
Petit-Dutaillis, Charles 182
Petrarch (Francesco Petrarca) 105, 250–1
Petrusewicz, Marta 610
Pettazzoni, R. 63
Philip of Macedon 33–4
Philippson, John (Sleidan) 257–8
Phillipps, John A. 486
Phillips, Mark 323, 326
Phillips, Patricia 303
Phillips-Matz, Mary Jane 609
philosophy: causation 773; critical philosophy of history 763–6; the Enlightenment 400–5; explanation 766–70, 774–6, 779, 857–63; German counter-enlightenment 405–11; historians and philosophers 779–81; influences on Christianity 75; narrative 774–9; and science 295; science as natural philosophy 300–3; Sophists 28, 32; value judgements 770–4, 779–80
Phoenicians 8; Punic Wars 36–7
Pick, Daniel 610
Pirenne, Henri 434–5
Pirenne, Jacques 482
Pitkin, Hanna F. 320
Plato: all that follows him is a footnote 308; Greek frogs at the pond 26; influence on Christianity 75; writing makes thought more superficial 321
Pliny the Elder 831–2, 833
Pliny the Younger 695
Plumb, Sir John 387
Plutarch 38, 267, 864
Pocock, J. G. A. 316–17, 320
politics 316–20
Pollard, A.F. 441
Polybius 33, 36–8, 47; didactic function 44; uses Aristotle 37
Polydore Vergil of Urbano 255
de la Popelinière, Lancelot-Voisin 259, 265–6
Popkin, Richard H. 315
Popper, Sir Karl 312, 314, 476, 858
Porter, Roy 294, 315, 324
Portugal: and Africa 698; defining modern 288–9
positivism 5
Postan, Michael 475, 489
postmodernism 115, 487–95, 748, 796; metanarratives and generalizations 867–8; narrative 649–50, 855, 857; West German historians 572–3
poststructuralism 329–30, 490
Potter, David M. 710–11
Power, Eileen 167, 233
Powicke, Maurice 340
Prakash, Gyan 634
Prawer, Joshua 149
Prescott, William H. 459
printing and publishing: audience for historians 276–8; intellectual history 320–2; translations of vernacular works 267
privatization: feudal power 124–5
Propertius, Sextus 46
prosopography 62, 77, 730; and genealogy

of medieval nobility 184–9; growth of Protestantism 350

Protestantism: capital enterprise 904; English identity 340, 343; Huguenot resistance arguments 319; Lollards 343–4; Lutheranism versus Calvinism 257–8, 259–60; Puritans and science 301; Reformation era historians 257–64; responsibility in England 352–3; revisionism 383–4

psephology 486–7

Psuedo-Clement 377

psychobiography 328

Pufendorf, Samuel 270–1, 276

Punic Wars 36, 48–9

Purvis, J. S. 343

Putnam, Robert D. 610

Quine, Maria 603

Quinet, Edgar 510

The Qur'an: *hadith criticism* 12–14

Rabb, Theodore 295

Rabinow, Paul 789

race and ethnicity: *Black Athena* project 8; Greeks and barbarians 26–30

Radek, Karl 550

Rahtz, Philip 812

Ralegh, Sir Walter 267–8

Ramus, Peter (Pierre de la Ramée) 320–1

von Ranke, Leopold xiii, xv; appointed to Berlin University 407–8; essence of history 421; influence on English 437–8; life and career 419–23; orientalism 631; positivism 296; reservations against periodization 285; on Sarpi 261–2; on states 117; truth of narrative 861

Ranum, Orest A. 324

Rashid al-Din 15–16

Rath, R. J. 595

Rathbone, Dominic 89, 91

Rattansi, P. M. 299

Ratzel, Friedrich 468

Rawick, George 717

Raychaudhuri, T. 11

Razi, Z. 899

Reading, B. 671

Reddy, William 790

Redondi, Pietro 301, 314

Redworth, Glyn 385

Reed, James 721

Reformation era *see also* Church of England;

communications 322; contemporary historians 257–64; periodization 284

Regan, Geoffrey 148

Reich, Wilhelm 551

Reichhardt, Rolf 319

Reinerman, A. J. 611

Reinhard, Wolfgang 282

religion: anthropological and social studies 227–33; common triple structure of myth and divine systems 64; conflict in India 677–8, 685, 698–9; defining 221–2, 232; Japan 672; Marxist interpretation of capitalism and 904–5; and Newton 299; paradoxes of Roman studies 57–60; polytheism 58–9; popular 351–2; and science 301–3, 314–15; sociology of 111

Renaissance era: art history 833–5; rise of humanism 250–2; textual criticism 252–5

Renan, Ernest 426, 624

Renfrew, Colin 810

repression 473–80, 558–8; historians under National Socialism 555–8; National Socialism 474–80; Russia 473–4, 528–9, 538–43

Reuter, Timothy 106, 109, 112

revisionism: English Reformation 346–51, 383–6; never achieved status as school of thought 389–90; post-revisionism 385; Stuart specialists and the Civil War 379–83; three aspects of phenomenon in 1970s 377–8

Reynolds, Susan 106, 109, 112

Rhenanus, Beatus 255

rhetoric 6; and art 830; invention 52–4; Tacitus's instrument 49–54

Richard I of England 140, 142

Richards, Alan 98

Richards, Donald 149

Richards, Sidney 370

Richet, Denis 519–21

Rickert, Heinrich 455–6

Ricoeur, Paul 493

Riegl, Alois 840

Riley-Smith, Jonathan 149

Ritter, Gerhard 559, 560–1

Ritter, Joachim 319

Roberts, David D. 599

Roberts, John M. 941–2, 952

Roberts, Michael 205

Roberts, Stephen 382

Robertson, Esmonde 603, 604

Robertson, William 397, 403

de Robespierre, Maximillien 510
Robin, Régine 908
Robinson, James Harvey 459, 460, 461–2
Robinson, Ronald 488, 686
Rodinson, Maxime 628
Rohlen, T. P. 669
Roman Catholic Church: accommodates popular beliefs 367; Council of Trent 261; dissent in England 337, 349; ecclesiastical historians 223–5; in fascist Italy 603; and French Revolution 512, 513, 514; Galileo's heresy trial 301–2; Latin America 730, 740; Reformation era historians 257–64; sovereignty and state 119–20
Romanelli, Raffaele 607, 609
Romanticism 411–19
Rome: agriculture 91–3; art history 831–2; chronology 266; early cosmopolitanism 65; ethico-tragical context 43–9; Gibbon's history 273–6; Hellenism 36–8, 47; historians' questions 6–7; kingdom 61; late empire studies 70–7; military continuity into medieval era 206–8, 212, 214; moral point of view 6; paganism and development of Christianity 57–67; post-empire western Europe 80–2; Punic Wars 36–7, 48–9; source material on religion 58; traditional as good 4–5; Walbank's Marxist interpretation 895
Romeo, Rosario 594, 596, 611
Roper, Lyndal 937
Rosaldo, Renato 791
Roscher, Wilhelm 429
Roscoe, William 839
Rosen, Ruth 720
Rosenberg, Alfred 557
Rosenberg, Arthur 557
Rosenberg, Hans 557
Rosenberg, W. G. 532
Rosenburg, Carol Smith 934
Rosenhaft, Eve 795
Rosovsky, H. 671
Rosselli, John 609
Rossi, Paolo 315, 324
Rostovtzeff, M. I. 473–4
Rothfels, Hans 478, 557, 559–560
Round, John Horace 441
Roy, M. N. 682
Rubin, Miri 241
Rudé, George 899–902

Rumohr, C. F. 838
Runciman, Sir Steven 146, 148
Runciman, W. G. 955
Rushdie, Salman 678
Russell, Conrad 380–1, 382, 383
Russell, D. A. 52–3
Russia see also Soviet Union: authoritarianism 533; post-Soviet fascination with past 529; pre-revolution conditions 529–33, 902; repression of historians 473–4; revolution and Bolshevik rule 533–8
Rustum, Mikhā'īl 634–5
Ruttman, Darrett 787–8

Sabean, David Warren 326, 365, 367
Sabine, George Holland 308
Sahlins, Marshall 325, 791, 792
Said, Edward 653; cultural imperialism 106; debate on orientalism 628–32, 634, 635; Orientalism 142–3; redefinining orientalism 620–2
saints and hagiography 227, 231, 235; medieval women 165
Saladin (Salah al-Din Yusuf ibn Ayub) 15, 112; as fictional character 139–40, 142–8; as historical character 144–50; popular appeal 110
Salamone, A. W. 592
Sallust (Gaius Sallustius Crispus) 251; morality 46, 48–9
Salvemini, Gaetano 480, 592, 598
Sansovino, Francesco 835
Sansovino, Jacopo 835
Sarkar, Sir Jadunath 682
Sarpi, Paul of 261–2
Sarti, Roland 599
de Saussure, Ferdinand 492
Savarkar, V. D. 681
Scaliger, Joseph Justus 266
Scandanavia 194
Scarisbrick, J. J. 346, 347, 348, 385
Schacht, Joseph 13
Schaffer, S. 295
Schama, Simon 366, 521
Scheid, J. 62
Schiebinger, Londa 303
Schiffer, Michael 811, 813
Schilling, Heinz 282
von Schlözer, August Ludwig 406
Schmid, Karl 190
Schmitt, Charles 300, 314

Schmitt, Jean-Claude 224, 229–30, 231, 232, 240, 368
Schmoller, Gustav 429, 454
Schneider, Peter and Jane 609–10
Schochet, Gordon J. 320
Schöttler, Peter 880
Schreiner, A. 556
Schreiner, Klaus 558
Schulze, Hagen 546
Schuster, John 296
science and technology: archives 963; associations and group discourse 303; dating techniques 693; intellectual history 310–15; Kuhn's paradigms 311–13; methodology and secularization of social sciences 424–30; occult and magical studies 299–300, 315; and philosophy 300–3; professional histories 294–5; and religion 314–15; scientific revolution 293–304, 310–11; women 303
scientism 5
Scotland: Enlightenment 402–3; medieval nation 130
Scott, Anne Firor 719
Scott, Joan 935
Scott, Sir Walter 110, 405–6; influence on narrative style 412–13; *The Talisman* 140–3, 144, 148
Scribner, Robert W. 322, 348, 366
sea power 213–14
Searle, Eleanor 159
Seaver, Paul 326
Seeley, Sir John R. 426, 438, 441–2
Segre, Claudio 604
Seignobos, C. 465, 466
Sejanus, Lucius Aelius 50–1
Selden, John 262
Selge, Kurt-Viktor 223
semiotics 842
Seroux d'Agincourt, J. B. L. G. 836
Seton-Watson, Christopher 595
Sewell, William 790
sexuality: Greece 29; homosexuality 166; spirituality and gender in Middle Ages 164–7; two-fold delight of women 166
Shaffer, S. 297
Shahar, S. 233
Shang Yue 646
Shapin, Steven 295, 297, 303
Shapiro, Barbara 303
Sharpe, Kevin 380, 382
Shelby, Graham 147

Sheldon, C. D. 666
Shillony, B.-A. 666–7
Shorter, Edward 930
Sicily 128–9, 193–4
Sidgwick, Henry 428
Siefert, Arno 324
Sievers, Sharon 670
Simms, Katharine 131
Simon, Christian 446
Simpson, L. B. 738
Sked, Alan 596
Skinner, G. William 648
Skinner, Quentin 317–20, 493
Sklar, Kathryn Kish 719
slavery 484, 699–700; agricultural labour 90; late Roman archaeology 72; Latin America 743; Marxist class struggle 899–900; medieval persistence in southern Europe 159; United States 715–19
Sleidan, John (Johannes Philippson) 257–8
Smail, R. C. 150
Smith, J. M. H. 8, 165–6
Smith, R. J. 672
Smith, T. C. 950
Smith, Vincent 681
Smith-Rosenberg, Carroll 721
Snow, C. P. 297
Snowden, Frank 88
Soboul, Albert 515, 866
Society for the History of Authorship, Reading and Publishing 322
sociology: religion and medievalists 111
Sohn-Rethel, Alfred 551
Sommerville, Johann 382
Song of Roland 211
Sophists 28, 32
Sorbonne 444
Sorel, Albert 514
sources *see also* texts: archives 960–73; British archival revolution 377–8; complexity in Latin America 731–2; early modern popular culture 367–8; images 963; local antiquarian research 340–1; loss of Kongo archives 699; new availability in Russia 543–4; oral tradition 695–8; Public Records Act (Britain) 448
South Africa 88–9, 97
Southgate, Beverly 300
Soviet Union *see also* Russia: diverse views 526–9; repression of historians 528–9; Stalinism 539–43; terror and Lenin 537

Spain: colonies in New World 373;
Counter-Reformation era 264; defining
modern 288; history as a profession 448;
late antiquity 77
Sparta 27–8, 30–2
Spelman, Sir Henry 262
Spence, Jonathan 650
Spencer, Herbert 428, 450
Spengler, Oswald 411
Spenser, Edmund 141
Spierenburg, Pieter 372
Spriano, Paolo 598
Spufford, Margaret 322, 366
Ssu-ma Ch'ien 18–19, 22
Ssu-ma Kuang 20
Ssu-ma T'an 18–19
Stafford, Pauline 162
Stalin, Joseph 527; compared to fascists
567, 570; terror and repression 538–43
Stampp, Kenneth 715, 717
Stansell, Christine 720
state: British antiquity 442; comparative
work 132–3; defining 117–22, 119;
formation of Germany 126–8;
institutionalization and
confessionalization 287; Marxism
903–5, 906–7; medieval formation of
nations 122–32; nation-states 120
Steedman, Carolyn 796
Stein, B. 950
vom Stein, Baron Heinrich 407–8
Steinberg, Jonathan 603
Steiner, George 139
Stephen of Bourbon 229–30, 232
Stern, Fritz 559
Sternhell, Zeev 600
Stewart, Larry 300
Stille, Alexander 603
Stock, Brian 239
Stockwin, J. A. A. 671
Stoics 75
Stolypin, Pyotr 530
Stone, Lawrence 339, 381, 768, 930;
narrative 776; revisionism 379
Stone, Marla 601
Storry, R. 473
Strada, Faminius 260
Strahern, Marilyn 798
Strauss, David 426
Strayer, J. R. 125
Strozier, Charles 711
structuralism: archaeology 814; China

studies 648; problem of historical
periods 290
Struever, Nancy 324
Strutt, Joseph 141
Stuard, Susan M. 159
Stubbs, William 438, 440
Stürmer, Michael 571
Suetonius (Gaius Suetonius Tranquillus)
864
Sugimoto, Y. 671
Sullivan, B. R. 601
Sun Yatsen 644
Sutherland, Donald 519
Syme, R. 53
Syria 71, 624–5
systems theory 810, 952–3

Tabari 13–14
Tabatabai, Ghulam Hussain 679
Tacitus, Publius Cornelius 251;
partisanship 7; use of rhetoric to
investigate history 49–54
Tackett, Timothy 523
Taine, Hippolyte 426–7, 512, 521, 839
Tanara, Vicenzo 90
Tannenbaum, Frank 715
Tarrow, Sidney 605
Tasca, Angelo 598
Tawney, R. H. 339
Taylor, A. J. P. 143, 488, 773–4, 780;
debate with Trevor-Roper 568; on use of
prosopography 185
Taylor, Barbara 936
Tchalenko, G. 71
Tellenbach, Gerd 177, 190
Tenbruck, Friedrich 454
Tentler, Thomas 227
texts see also sources: archaeology and
history 805, 819; contextualists 313–15;
libraries 321; medieval sources 108–10;
New Historicism 329; papyrological
evidence 70; printing and
communication 320–2; theses of
historians 444
Thalheimer, August 551
Thayer, N. B. 671
Theopompus of Chios 33–4
Thomas, Keith 327, 345–6, 788, 930
Thomas of Chobham 241–2
Thompson, Edward P. 788; class struggle
368; criticizes Althusser 912; historical
context 369; imperialism 681; law and

politics 904; Marxism 488, 741, 891, 900–1; radicalism of population 907

Thompson, L. 701

Thomson, D. 601

Thomson, J. A. F. 343

Thornton, Russell 722

Thorpe, Benjamin 440

de Thou, Jacques-Auguste (Thuanus) 259

Thrace 31

Thucydides 7, 25, 265; avoids word 'history' 24; breakdown of Pan-Hellenism 30–2; contemporary history 25; criticism of Herodotus 5; ethico-tragical context 43–4; and Herodotus 25–6

Tibawi, Abdel-Latif 626, 630

Tibble, Stephen 150

Tiberius Claudius Nero 50–1

de Tillemont, Louis Sebastian le Nain 274

Tilly, Louise 607, 935

time see also chronology and dating: the discovery of time 324; jumble versus a series of events 851–4; Newtonian shift to absolute time 395–6; world history back to the Big Bang 948

Titus, D. A. 666, 668

de Tocqueville, Alexis 513–14

Togliatti, Palmiro 592

Tolstoy, Leo 853–4

Tomaselli, Sylvana 303

Tönnies, Ferdinand 450

totalitarianism 554–5

Totman, C. 660

Toynbee, Arnold 411, 482

'Tradition of Tso' 18

von Treitschke, Heinrich 433

Trevelyan, George M. 594, 942

Trevor-Roper, Hugh (Lord Dacre) 339, 568, 774, 780

Trinkaus, C. 227

Trotsky, Leon 528, 536–7

Turner, Frederick Jackson 459, 460

Turner, Sharon 440

Turner, Terence 791

Turner, Victor 325, 369

Tutino, John 734

Tylor, Sir Edward Burnet 61, 429

Tyndale, William 353

Ulbricht, Walter 575

Ullmann, Walter 119

Underdown, David 382

United States: approach compared to Europeans' 113; Atlantic slave trade 700; consensus approach 709–14; diplomatic history 723–5; the elusive 'new history' 458–64; ethnic diversity 712–19; moral view of Soviet history 527–8; Native American Indians 721–2; professional historians 443–4; slavery 715–19; women 718–21, 932–5

Uruguay 729

Usener, Herman 60, 61

Valentin, Veit 479, 557

Valerius Antias 47

Valeton, I. M. J. 62

Valla, Lorenzo 115, 252, 324

value judgements 43–9, 770–4, 779–80

Van Young, Eric 735, 746

Varga, Lucie 878–9, 880

Vasari, Giorgio 834, 835–6, 838

Vauchez, André 222, 227, 231, 235, 241

Vegetius (Flavius Vegetius Renatus) 206, 216

Venezuela 729, 730

Venturi, Franco 475, 593–4, 881

Verbruggen, J. F. 205, 216

Vesalius, Andreas 311

Veyne, Pierre 150

Vickers, Brian 299

Vico, Giambattista 323–4, 398–400, 866

Victorian era 390

Vidal de la Blache, Paul 466

Vinogradoff, Paul 473

Vitruvius Pollio 832

Vivarelli, Roberto 598

Voegelin, Eric 396

Vogel, E. F. 671

de Volney, Comte (Constantin François Chaseboeuf) 622

Volpe, Gioachimo 449

Voltaire (François Marie Arouet) 272, 276, 400–1

Vovelle, Michel 326, 368, 522

Waagen, G. F. 838

Waardenburg, Jacques 628

Waitz, Georg 423, 445

Wakefield, Walter 230

Walbank, F. W. 895

Waldensians 237–8

Wales 129–30

Walker, D. P. 315

Wallace, Alfred Russel 424
Wallace, William 296
Wallace-Hadrill, J. M. 83
Wallerstein, Immanuel 810, 952–3
Walpole, Horace 836
Walsh, W. H. 763, 777
Walsham, Alexandra 354
Walzer, Michael 870
Wandersee, Winifred 720
Wansbrough, John 150
war: as topic of history 25–6
Warburg, Aby 479–80, 840
Ward, R. E. 669, 671
Waszynski, S. 95
Watt, Tessa 322, 354
Weber, Max 325, 954; definition of state
   118; life and influence 456–7; science
   301; sociology of knowledge 314
Webster, Charles 300, 315
Webster, Richard 597
Wehler, Hans-Ulrich 494
Weinstock, S. 64
Welch, Ronald 147
Welter, Barbara 719
Wenskus, Reinhard 78
Werner, Karl Ferdinand 214–15
Westfall, Richard 315
Westman, Robert 300
Wheeler, Sir Mortimer 807
Whewell, William 310
White, A. D. 301
White, Hayden 330, 401, 418–19, 493, 775,
   778; metahistory 868; narrative 860
White, Morton 774
Whitehead, Alfred North: on Plato 308
Whiting, Roger 385–6
Wickham, C. J. 107, 123
Wiener, Martin 493
Wilentz, Sean 714
William I the Conqueror 194, 210–11,
   217–18
Williams, C. H. 281
Williams, Raymond 319, 488
Williams, William Appleman 723–4
Wilson, M. 701
Wilson, Perry 602
Wiltenburg, Joy 366
Winckelmann, J. J. 837
Windelband, Wilhelm 455
Winn, Peter 745
Wiskemann, Elizabeth 603
Wissowa, Georg 59, 60, 61

witchcraft and magic 300; cultural study
   327; popular culture 364, 365; science
   299–300, 315
Witte, Sergei 530
Wittfogel, K. 644
Wolf, Eric 950
Wölfflin, H. 840
Wolfram, Herwig 78
women: archaeology 815–16; art history
   842–3; breaking history into smaller
   histories 5–6; China 651; Christianity
   233–5, 237, 241; context of women's
   movement 112; in fascist Italy 602;
   Herodotus respectfully avoids 28–9;
   Italy 611; Japan 670; Latin America
   745–6; medieval studies 155, 167–9;
   popular culture 362–3; postmodern
   gender issues 492–3; present
   historiography and historians 930–40;
   and property in Medieval era 160–4; in
   science 303; slavery 159; social
   organization 83; spirituality and
   sainthood 165–7; trends and factors in
   study 153–5; United States 718–21;
   widows' status 169; working outside
   home 160
Woolf, Stuart 605, 607, 610
Woolf, Virginia 931
Wooton, David 324
World Council of Christian Churches 226
world history: changing approaches 941–5;
   Eurocentrism 953–4; idea and subject
   matter 945–9; integration of themes
   949–52; methodology 954–6; synthesis of
   themes 955; systems approach 952–3
Woronoff, J. 671
Worringer, Wilhelm 840
Wright, Mary Clabaugh 642–3
Wrigley, E. A. 486
Wundt, Wilhelm 453

Xenophon: *Cyropaedia* 33; *Hellenica* 32;
   Panhellenism 32–3
Xerxes of Persia 29

Yamamura, K. 660, 671
Yans-McLaughlin, Virginia 712
Ya'qubi 14
Yasuba, Y. 671
Yates, Frances 299–300, 315
Yergin, Daniel 724
York Powell, Frederick 443

Yoshinobu, Shiba 646
Young, Arthur 276
Yugoslavian War 578–9

Zamagni, Vera 601

Zavala, Silvio 96
Zilsel, Edgar 298
Zimbabwe 695
Zinoviev, Grigorii 536
Zucotti, Susan 603

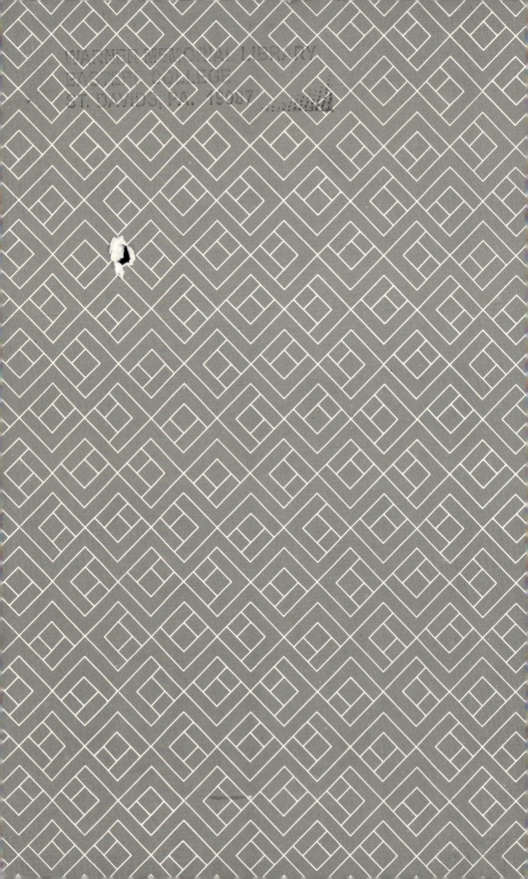